City plans

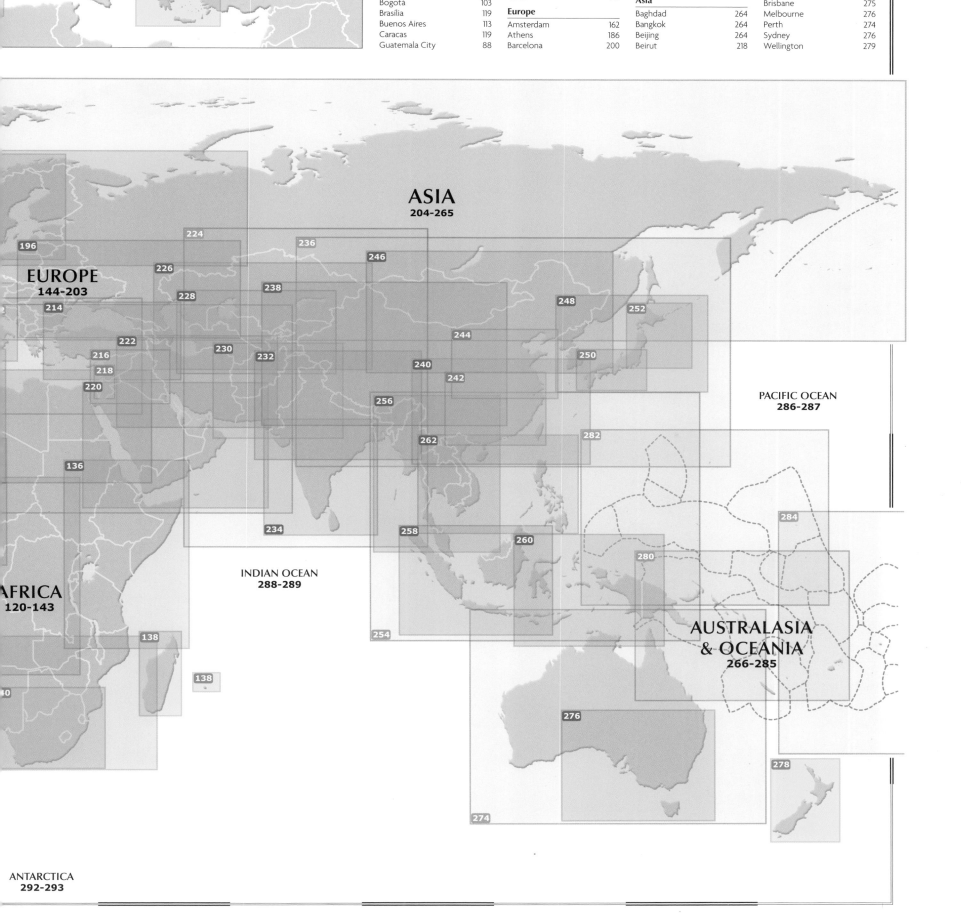

ASIA
204-265

EUROPE
144-203

PACIFIC OCEAN
286-287

AFRICA
120-143

INDIAN OCEAN
288-289

AUSTRALASIA
& OCEANIA
266-285

ANTARCTICA
292-293

COMPLETE
ATLAS
OF THE WORLD

C O M P L E T E

ATLAS

OF THE WORLD

LONDON, NEW YORK, MELBOURNE, MUNICH AND DELHI

Publishing Director
Jonathan Metcalf

Art Director
Bryn Walls

Managing Editor
David Roberts

Senior Cartographic Editor
Simon Mumford

Digital Map Suppliers
Advanced Illustration, Congleton, UK • Cosmographics, Watford, UK
Encompass Graphics, Brighton, UK • Lovell Johns Ltd., Long Hanborough, UK
Netmaps, Barcelona, Spain

Digital Terrain Data
Digital terrain data and continental panoramic images created by Planetary Visions Ltd, Farnham, UK

Cartographers
Paul Eames, Edward Merritt, John Plumer, Rob Stokes, Iorwerth Watkins

Cartographic Editors
Tony Chambers, John Dear, Ruth Hall, Andrew Johnson, Belinda Kane, Lynn Neal, Ann Stephenson

Indexing and Database
T-Kartor, Sweden
Francesca Albini, Eleanor Arkwright, Renata Dyntarova, Edward Heelas, Britta Hansesgaard

Editor
Robert Dinwiddie

Designers
Nicola Liddiard, Yak El-Droubie

Picture Research
Louise Thomas, Jenny Baskaya

Jacket Desginers
Lee Ellwood, Duncan Turner

Systems Coordinator
Philip Rowles

Production Controllers
Linda Dare, Melanie Dowland

Flags courtesy of The Flag Institue, Cheshire, UK

First published in Great Britain in 2007 by Dorling Kindersley Limited, 80 Strand, London WC2R ORL

A Penguin Company

CIP catalogue record for this book is available from the British Library

ISBN: 978-1-4053-1769-6

Reprographics by MDP Ltd, Wiltshire, UK

Printed and bound by Tien Wah Press, Singapore

See our complete catalogue at www.dk.com

Introduction

The World at the beginning of the 21st Century would be a place of unimaginable change to our forefathers. Since 1900 the human population has undergone a fourfold growth coupled with an unparalleled development in the technology at our disposal. The last vestiges of the unknown World are gone, and previously hostile realms claimed for habitation. The advent of aviation technology and the growth of mass tourism have allowed people to travel further and more frequently than ever before

Allied to this, the rapid growth of global communication systems mean that World events have become more accessible than ever before and their knock on effects quickly ripple across the whole planet. News broadcasts bring the far-flung corners of the world into everyone's lives, and with it, a view of the people and places that make up that region. The mysteries of the World that once fuelled global exploration and the quest to discover the unknown are behind us; we inhabit a world of mass transportation, a world where even the most extreme regions have been mapped, a world with multi faceted view points on every event, a World of communication overload.

However, does this help us make sense of the World? It is increasingly important for us to have a clear vision of the World in which we live and such a deluge of information can leave us struggling to find some context and meaning. It has never been more important to own an atlas; the *DK Complete Atlas of the World* has been conceived to meet this need. At its core, like all atlases, it seeks to define where places are, to describe their main characteristics, and to locate them in relation to other places. By gathering a spectacular collection of satellite imagery and draping it with carefully selected and up-to-date geographic information this atlas filters the World's data into clear, meaningful and user-friendly maps.

The World works on different levels and so does the *DK Complete Atlas of the World*. Readers can learn about global issues of many kinds or they can probe in a little further for the continental context. Delving even further they can explore at regional, national or even sub-national level. The very best available satellite data has been used to create topography and bathymetry that reveal the breathtaking texture of landscapes and sea-floors. These bring out the context of the places and features selected to appear on top of them. The full-spread map areas purposefully overlap to emphasis the connectivity and interdependence of our World.

The *DK Complete Atlas of the World* not only allows you to travel around our planet without leaving your seat but perhaps more importantly, helps you to understand the World around you.

David Roberts
Managing Editor

Contents

The atlas is organized by continent, moving eastwards from the International Date Line. The opening section describes the world's structure, systems and its main features. The Atlas of the World which follows, is a continent-by-continent guide to today's world, starting with a comprehensive insight into the physical, political and economic structure of each continent, followed by detailed maps of carefully selected geopolitical regions.

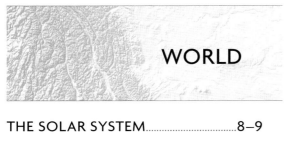

WORLD

NORTH AMERICA

SOUTH AMERICA

AFRICA

EUROPE

ASIA

AUSTRALASIA & OCEANIA

INDEX & GAZETTEER

Key to regional maps

Physical features

elevation

6000m / 19,686ft
4000m / 13,124ft
3000m / 9843ft
2000m / 6562ft
1000m / 3281ft
500m / 1640ft
250m / 820ft
100m / 328ft
sea level
below sea level

▲ elevation above sea level (mountain height)
▲ volcano
✕ pass
▼ elevation below sea level (depression depth)

sand desert
lava flow
coastline
reef
atoll

sea depth

sea level
-250m / -820ft
-500m / -1640ft
-1000m / -3281ft
-2000m / -6562ft
-3000m / -9843ft

▲ seamount / guyot symbol
▼ undersea spot depth

Drainage features

——— main river
——— secondary river
——— tertiary river
——— minor river
– – – main seasonal river
– – – secondary seasonal river
——— canal
⊢+⊣ waterfall
⊢•⊣ rapids
⊢◖ dam
⬭ perennial lake
⬭ seasonal lake
⬭ perennial salt lake
⬭ seasonal salt lake
⬭ reservoir
salt flat / salt pan
marsh / salt marsh
mangrove
◁▷ wadi
○ spring / well / waterhole / oasis

Ice features

ice cap / sheet
ice shelf
glacier / snowfield
+ + + + summer pack ice limit
○ ○ ○ winter pack ice limit

Graticule features

——— lines of latitude and longitude / Equator
– – – Tropics / Polar circles
45° degrees of longitude / latitude

Communications

——— motorway / highway
– – – motorway / highway (under construction)
——— major road
——— minor road
→•••← tunnel (road)
——— main line
——— minor line
→•••← tunnel (rail)
✈ international airport

Borders

▬▬▬ full international border
▪ ▪ ▪ ▪ undefined international border
▬ · ▬ · disputed de facto border
▬ · ▬ · ▬ disputed territorial claim border
– · – · indication of country extent (Pacific only)
– – – – indication of dependent territory extent (Pacific only)
• • • • • demarcation/cease fire line
——— autonomous/federal region border
——— 2nd order internal administrative border
——— 3rd order internal administrative border

Miscellaneous features

▱▱▱▱ ancient wall
◇ site of interest
○ scientific station

Settlements

built up area

settlement population symbols

■ more than 5 million
◉ 1 million to 5 million
◉ 500,000 to 1 million
◎ 100,000 to 500,000
⊕ 50,000 to 100,000
○ 10,000 to 50,000
○ fewer than 10,000

■●● country/dependent territory capital city
■●● autonomous / federal region / 2nd order internal administrative centre
■●● 3rd order internal administrative centre

Typographic key

Physical features

landscape features ... *Namib Desert*
Massif Central
ANDES

headland .... *Nordkapp*

elevation / volcano / pass .... Mount Meru 4556 m

drainage features .... *Lake Geneva*

rivers / canals spring / well / waterhole / oasis / waterfall / rapids / dam .... *Mekong*

ice features .... *Vatnajökull*

Physical features (continued)

sea features .... *Golfe de Lion*
Andaman Sea
INDIAN OCEAN

undersea features ... *Barracuda Fracture Zone*

Regions

country .... ARMENIA
dependent territory with parent state ..... NIUE (to NZ)
autonomous / federal region .... MINAS GERAIS
2nd order internal administrative region .... MINSKAYA VOBLASTS'
3rd order internal administrative region .... Vaucluse
cultural region .... New England

Settlements

capital city .... BEIJING
dependent territory capital city .... FORT-DE-FRANCE
other settlements ... Chicago
Adana
Tizi Ozou
Yonezawa
Farnham

Miscellaneous

sites of interest / miscellaneous .... Valley of the Kings
Tropics / Polar circles .... *Antarctic Circle*

The Solar System

The Solar System consists of our local star, the Sun, and numerous objects that orbit the Sun – eight planets, three recognized dwarf planets, over 165 moons orbiting these planets and dwarf planets, and countless smaller bodies such as comets and asteroids. Including a vast outer region that is populated only by comets, the Solar System is about 15,000 billion km (9,300 billion miles) across. The much smaller region containing just the Sun and planets is about 12 billion km (7.5 billion miles) across. The Sun, which contributes over 99 percent of the mass of the entire Solar System, creates energy from nuclear reactions deep within its interior, providing the heat and light that make life on Earth possible.

THE MOON'S PHASES

As the Moon orbits Earth, the relative positions of Moon, Sun and Earth continuously change. Thus, the angle at which the Moon's sunlit face is seen by an observer on Earth varies in a cyclical fashion, producing the Moon's phases, as shown at right. Each cycle takes 29.5 days.

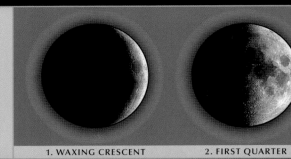

1. WAXING CRESCENT   2. FIRST QUARTER

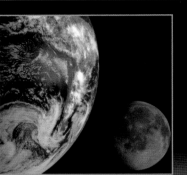

The Earth and Moon's relative sizes are clear in this long-range image from space.

The Moon

Earth's only satellite, the Moon, is thought to have formed 4.5 billion years ago from a cloud of debris produced when a large asteroid hit the young Earth. The Moon is too small to have retained an atmosphere, and is therefore a lifeless, dusty and dead world. However, although the Moon has only about 1 percent of the mass of the Earth, its gravity exerts an important influence on Earth's oceans, manifest in the ebb and flow of the tides.

What is a Planet?

The International Astronomical Union defines a Solar System planet as a near-spherical object that orbits the Sun (and no other body) and has cleared the neighbourhood around its orbit of other bodies. A dwarf planet is a planet that is not big enough to have cleared its orbital neighbourhood. Extra-solar planets are objects orbiting stars other than the Sun.

CERES
(dwarf
planet)

MERCURY   VENUS   EARTH   MARS

The Sun

The Sun is a huge sphere of exceedingly hot plasma (ionized gas), consisting mainly of the elements hydrogen and helium. It formed about 4.6 billion years ago, when a swirling cloud of gas and dust began to contract under the influence of gravity. When the centre of this cloud reached a critically high temperature, hydrogen nuclei started combining to form helium nuclei – a process called nuclear fusion – with the release of massive amounts of energy. This process continues to this day.

JUPITER

SOLAR ECLIPSE

A solar eclipse occurs when the Moon passes between Earth and the Sun, casting its shadow on Earth's surface. During a total eclipse *(below)*, viewers along a strip of Earth's surface, called the area of totality, see the Sun totally blotted out for a short time, as the umbra (Moon's full shadow) sweeps over them. Outside this area is a larger one, where the Sun appears only partly obscured, as the penumbra (partial shadow) passes over.

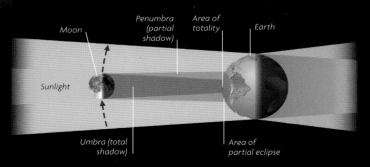

Moon

Penumbra
(partial
shadow)

Area of
totality

Earth

Sunlight

Umbra (total
shadow)

Area of
partial eclipse

INSIDE THE SUN

The Sun has three internal layers. At its centre is the core, where temperatures reach 15 million°C (27 million°F) and nuclear fusion occurs. The radiative zone is a slightly cooler region through which energy radiates away from the core. Further out, in the convective zone, plumes of hot plasma carry the energy towards the Sun's visible surface layer, called the photosphere. Once there, the energy escapes as light, heat and other forms of radiation.

Photosphere

Core

Radiative zone

*Convective
zone*

*Sunspots mark
cooler areas
of surface*

*Prominences
are loops of gas
arching above the
photosphere*

| 3. WAXING GIBBOUS | 4. FULL MOON | 5. WANING GIBBOUS | 6. LAST QUARTER | 7. WANING CRESCENT | 8. NEW MOON |

PLANETS / DWARF PLANETS

	MERCURY	VENUS	EARTH	MARS	JUPITER	SATURN	URANUS	NEPTUNE	CERES	PLUTO	ERIS
DIAMETER	4875 km (3029 miles)	12,104 km (7521 miles)	12,756 km (7928 miles)	6780 km (4213 miles)	142,984 km (88,846 miles)	120,536 km (74,898 miles)	51,118 km (31,763 miles)	49,528 km (30,775 miles)	950 km (590 miles)	2304 km (1432 miles)	2300-2500 km (1429-1553 miles)
AVERAGE DISTANCE FROM THE SUN	57.9 mill. km (36 mill. miles)	108.2 mill. km (67.2 mill. miles)	149.6 mill. km (93 mill. miles)	227.9 mill. km (141.6 mill. miles)	778.3 mill. km (483.6 mill. miles)	1431 mill. km (889.8 mill. miles)	2877 mill. km (1788 mill. miles)	4498 mill. km (2795 mill. miles)	414 mill. km (257 mill. miles)	5,915 mill. km (3675 mill. miles)	10,210 mill. km (6344 mill. miles)
ROTATION PERIOD	58.6 days	243 days	23.93 hours	24.62 hours	9.93 hours	10.65 hours	17.24 hours	16.11 hours	9.1 hours	6.38 days	not known
ORBITAL PERIOD	88 days	224.7 days	365.26 days	687 days	11.86 years	29.37 years	84.1 years	164.9 years	4.6 years	248.6 years	557 years
SURFACE TEMPERATURE	-180°C to 430°C (-292°F to 806°F)	480°C (896°F)	-70°C to 55°C (-94°F to 131°F)	-120°C to 25°C (-184°F to 77 °F)	-110°C (-160°F)	-140°C (-220°F)	-200°C (-320°F)	-200°C (-320°F)	-107°C (-161°F)	-230°C (-380°F)	-243°C (-405°F)

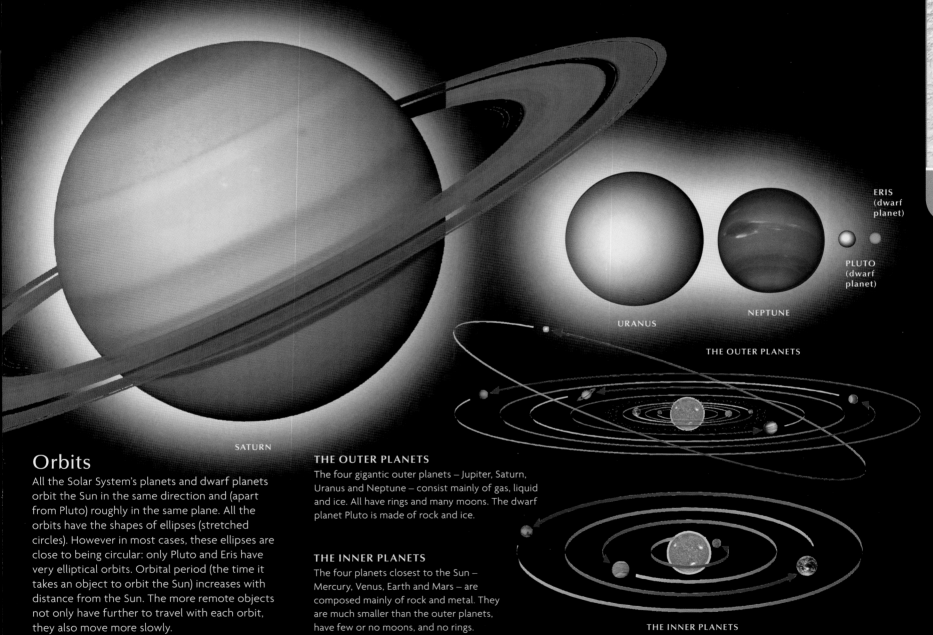

SATURN

URANUS

NEPTUNE

ERIS (dwarf planet)

PLUTO (dwarf planet)

THE OUTER PLANETS

THE INNER PLANETS

Orbits

All the Solar System's planets and dwarf planets orbit the Sun in the same direction and (apart from Pluto) roughly in the same plane. All the orbits have the shapes of ellipses (stretched circles). However in most cases, these ellipses are close to being circular: only Pluto and Eris have very elliptical orbits. Orbital period (the time it takes an object to orbit the Sun) increases with distance from the Sun. The more remote objects not only have further to travel with each orbit, they also move more slowly.

THE OUTER PLANETS

The four gigantic outer planets – Jupiter, Saturn, Uranus and Neptune – consist mainly of gas, liquid and ice. All have rings and many moons. The dwarf planet Pluto is made of rock and ice.

THE INNER PLANETS

The four planets closest to the Sun – Mercury, Venus, Earth and Mars – are composed mainly of rock and metal. They are much smaller than the outer planets, have few or no moons, and no rings.

AVERAGE DISTANCE FROM THE SUN

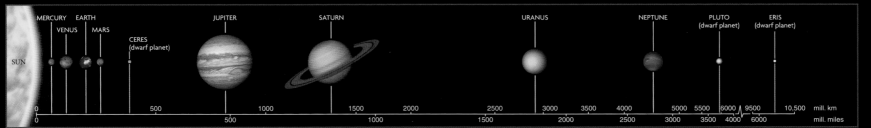

The Physical World

Earth's surface is constantly being transformed. Movements of the rigid tectonic plates that make up this surface are continuously, if slowly, shifting its landmasses around, while the land itself is constantly weathered and eroded by wind, water and ice. Sometimes change is dramatic, the spectacular results of earthquakes or floods. More often it is a slow process lasting for millions of years. A physical map of the world represents a snapshot of Earth's ever-evolving architecture. The terrain maps below and at right show the planet's whole surface, including variations in ocean depth as well as the mountain-rippled texture of Earth's continents.

THE WORLD'S OCEANS

Earth's surface is dominated by water. The hemisphere shown here, centered around the southwest Pacific, is nearly all ocean, with the waters interrupted only by Antarctica, a part of South America, Australia and the numerous islands of Australasia & Oceania, and southeast Asia.

NORTH AMERICA

Arctic Circle

Tropic of Cancer

Equator

PACIFIC OCEAN

ATLANTIC OCEAN

SOUTH AMERICA

Tropic of Capricorn

Antarctic Circle

SOUTHERN

Legend (elevation/depth):

- 6000m
- 4000m
- 3000m
- 2000m
- 1000m
- 500m
- 250m
- 100m
- Sea Level
- -250m
- -500m
- -1000m

Scale 1:87,000,000

(projection: Azimuthal Equidistant)

Km
0 250 500 1000 1500 2000

0 250 500 1000 1500 2000
Miles

Map labels

Mendocino Fracture Zone
Shatskiy Rise
Mid-Pacific Mountains
Murray Fracture Zone
Hawaiian Islands
Molokai Fracture Zone
Central Pacific Basin
Johnston Atoll
Hawai'i
Clarion Fracture Zone
Marshall Islands
Clipperton Fracture Zone
Kiritimati
Melanesian Basin
Phoenix Islands
Galapagos Fracture Zone
Manihiki Plateau
Samoa
Marquesas Islands
Marquesas Fracture Zone
North Fiji Basin
Fiji
Tonga Trench
South Fiji Basin
Tubuai Islands
New Caledonia
Southwest Pacific Basin
Pitcairn Islands
Bauer Basin
Galapagos Island
North Island
New Zealand
Easter Island
Galapagos Rise
South Island
Chatham Islands
Campbell Plateau
Auckland Islands
Campbell Island
Southeast Pacific Basin
Sala y Gomez
East Pacific Rise
Peru Basin
San Felix Island
Roggeveen Basin
Nazca Ridge
Juan Fernandez Islands
San Ambrosio Island
Chile Basin
Pacific-Antarctic Ridge
Antarctic Circle
Ross Sea
Amundsen Plain
Amundsen Sea
Mt Erebus 3794m
Ross Ice Shelf
Marie Byrd Land
Bellingshausen Sea
Strait of Magellan
Golfo Corcovado
Dronning Maud Land
Wilkes Land
South Pole
Ronne Ice Shelf
Antarctic Peninsula
Tierra del Fuego
Patagonia
Andes
SOUTH AMERICA
Cape Horn
Weddell Sea
Kerguelen Plateau
Heard Island
Kerguelen
ANTARCTICA
Enderby Plain
Gulf of San Jorge
Bahía Blanca
Pampas
Prince Edward Islands
Maud Rise
Scotia Sea
Drake Passage
Falkland Islands
Rio de la Plata
Crozet Islands
South Georgia
Falkland Fracture Zone
Argentine Basin
Bouvet Island
America-Antarctica Ridge
South Sandwich Islands
Southwest Indian Ridge
Agulhas Basin
Gough Island
PACIFIC OCEAN
Polynesia
Line Islands
Cook Islands
Penrhyn Basin
Tuamotu Islands
Tropic of Cancer
Menard Fracture Zone
Eltanin Fracture Zone
Udintsev Fracture Zone
Challenger Fracture Zone
Sala y Gomez Ridge
Peru-Chile Trench
Chile Trench
Tropic of Capricorn

INDIAN OCEAN
Ninetyeast Ridge
Ceylon Plain
Broken Ridge
Southeast Indian Ridge
Amsterdam Island
St Paul Island
South Indian Basin
Davis Sea
Southwest Indian Ridge

Micronesia
Mariana Islands
West Mariana Basin
Mariana Trench
Philippine Sea
Central Basin Trough
Caroline Ridge
Philippine Trench
Palau
Philippine Islands
Eauripik Rise
Melanesia
Ontong Java Rise
Bismarck Archipelago
Bismarck Sea
Solomon Sea
Solomon Islands
New Guinea
Torres Strait
Vanuatu
Coral Sea
Lord Howe Rise
Tasman Sea
Cape York
Gulf of Carpentaria
Great Barrier Reef
Great Dividing Range
Mount Kosciuszko 2228m
Bass Strait
Tasmania
South China Sea
Sulu Sea
Celebes Sea
Celebes Basin
Borneo
East Indies
Molucca Sea
Java Sea
Arafura Sea
Arnhem Land
Kimberley Plateau
Great Sandy Desert
Gibson Desert
Great Victoria Desert
Simpson Desert
AUSTRALIA
Nullarbor Plain
Great Australian Bight
South Australian Basin
Perth Basin
Ashmore & Cartier Islands
Timor Sea
Timor
Java
Sumatra
Malay Peninsula
Strait of Malacca
Gulf of Thailand
Java Trench
Investigator Ridge
Cocos Basin
Equator
South China Basin
Celebes
Shikoku Basin
Philippine Basin

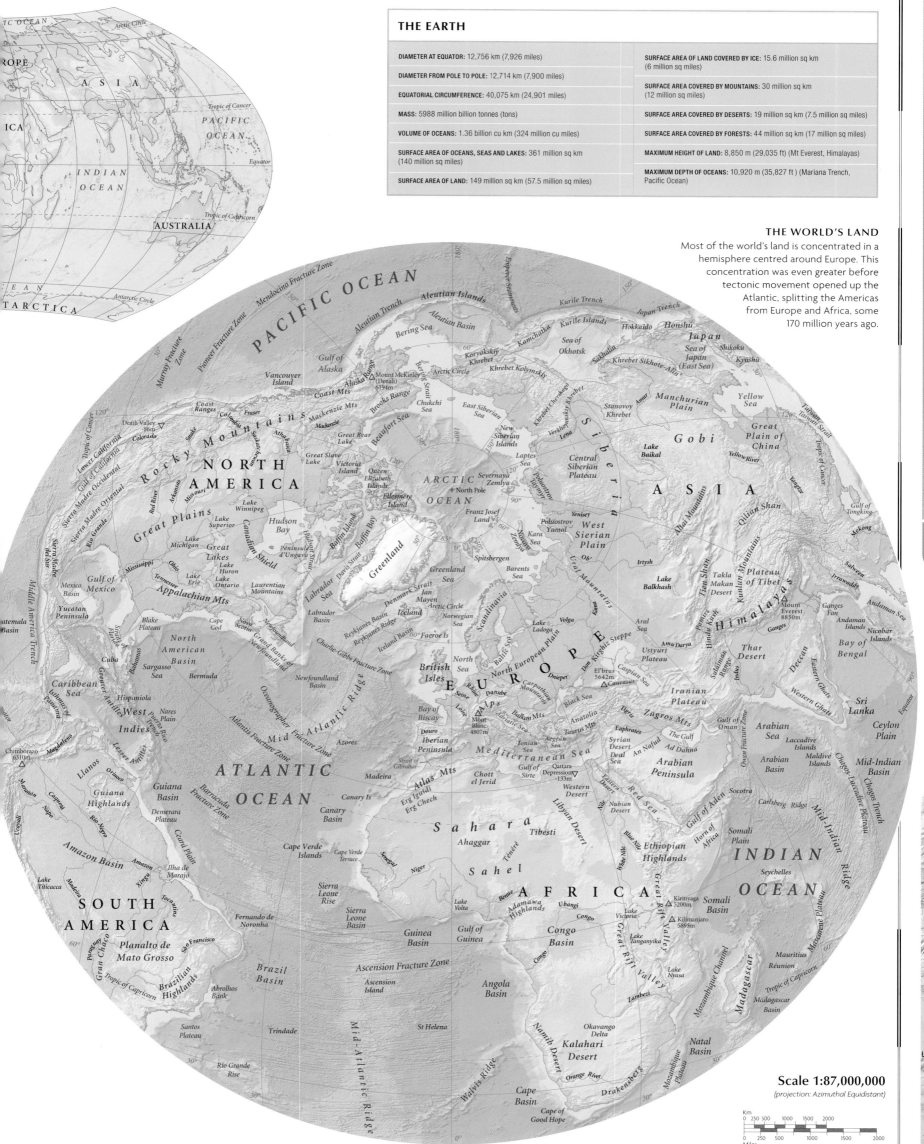

THE EARTH

DIAMETER AT EQUATOR: 12,756 km (7,926 miles)	**SURFACE AREA OF LAND COVERED BY ICE:** 15.6 million sq km (6 million sq miles)
DIAMETER FROM POLE TO POLE: 12,714 km (7,900 miles)	**SURFACE AREA COVERED BY MOUNTAINS:** 30 million sq km (12 million sq miles)
EQUATORIAL CIRCUMFERENCE: 40,075 km (24,901 miles)	**SURFACE AREA COVERED BY DESERTS:** 19 million sq km (7.5 million sq miles)
MASS: 5988 million billion tonnes (tons)	**SURFACE AREA COVERED BY FORESTS:** 44 million sq km (17 million sq miles)
VOLUME OF OCEANS: 1.36 billion cu km (324 million cu miles)	**MAXIMUM HEIGHT OF LAND:** 8,850 m (29,035 ft) (Mt Everest, Himalayas)
SURFACE AREA OF OCEANS, SEAS AND LAKES: 361 million sq km (140 million sq miles)	**MAXIMUM DEPTH OF OCEANS:** 10,920 m (35,827 ft) (Mariana Trench, Pacific Ocean)
SURFACE AREA OF LAND: 149 million sq km (57.5 million sq miles)	

THE WORLD'S LAND

Most of the world's land is concentrated in a hemisphere centred around Europe. This concentration was even greater before tectonic movement opened up the Atlantic, splitting the Americas from Europe and Africa, some 170 million years ago.

Scale 1:87,000,000

(projection: Azimuthal Equidistant)

The Structure of the Earth

Earth is an almost perfect sphere consisting of a partly liquid core overlain by a deep, semisolid layer, called the mantle, and two types of surface crust, known as continental and oceanic crust. Our planet has constantly evolved since it formed some 4.5 billion years ago. Its continents are neither fixed nor stable. Over the course of history, gradual movements of rocky material within Earth's mantle, resulting from massive internal flows of heat, have caused the great slabs of material that make up the planet's surface, known as tectonic plates, to shift around. The plates have moved, collided, joined together, and sometimes split apart. These processes continue to mould Earth's surface, causing earthquakes and volcanic eruptions, and creating oceans, mountain ranges, rift valleys, deep ocean trenches and island chains.

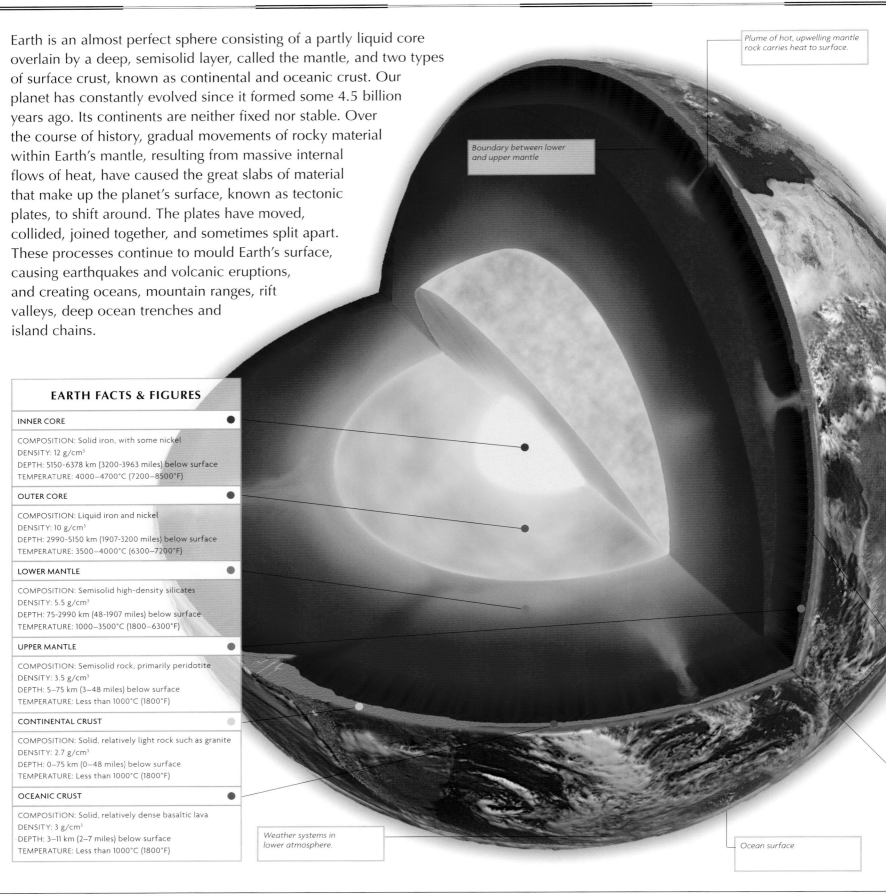

Plume of hot, upwelling mantle rock carries heat to surface.

Boundary between lower and upper mantle

Weather systems in lower atmosphere.

Ocean surface

EARTH FACTS & FIGURES

INNER CORE

COMPOSITION: Solid iron, with some nickel
DENSITY: 12 g/cm³
DEPTH: 5150-6378 km (3200-3963 miles) below surface
TEMPERATURE: 4000–4700°C (7200–8500°F)

OUTER CORE

COMPOSITION: Liquid iron and nickel
DENSITY: 10 g/cm³
DEPTH: 2990-5150 km (1907-3200 miles) below surface
TEMPERATURE: 3500–4000°C (6300–7200°F)

LOWER MANTLE

COMPOSITION: Semisolid high-density silicates
DENSITY: 5.5 g/cm³
DEPTH: 75-2990 km (48-1907 miles) below surface
TEMPERATURE: 1000–3500°C (1800–6300°F)

UPPER MANTLE

COMPOSITION: Semisolid rock, primarily peridotite
DENSITY: 3.5 g/cm³
DEPTH: 5–75 km (3–48 miles) below surface
TEMPERATURE: Less than 1000°C (1800°F)

CONTINENTAL CRUST

COMPOSITION: Solid, relatively light rock such as granite
DENSITY: 2.7 g/cm³
DEPTH: 0–75 km (0–48 miles) below surface
TEMPERATURE: Less than 1000°C (1800°F)

OCEANIC CRUST

COMPOSITION: Solid, relatively dense basaltic lava
DENSITY: 3 g/cm³
DEPTH: 3–11 km (2–7 miles) below surface
TEMPERATURE: Less than 1000°C (1800°F)

FROM THE BIG BANG TO THE PRESENT DAY

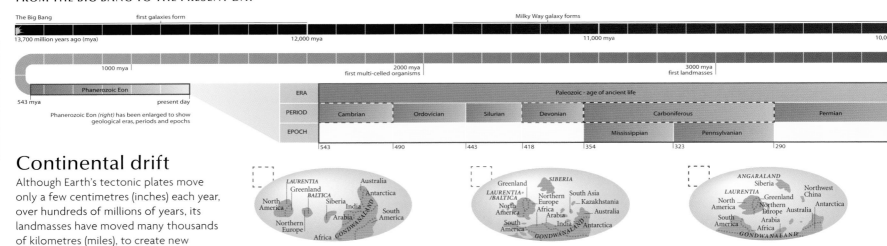

The Big Bang

first galaxies form

Milky Way galaxy forms

13,700 million years ago (mya)

12,000 mya

11,000 mya

10,00

1000 mya

2000 mya
first multi-celled organisms

3000 mya
first landmasses

Phanerozoic Eon

543 mya

present day

Phanerozoic Eon (right) has been enlarged to show geological eras, periods and epochs

ERA	Paleozoic - age of ancient life						
PERIOD	Cambrian	Ordovician	Silurian	Devonian	Carboniferous		Permian
EPOCH					Mississippian	Pennsylvanian	

543 490 443 418 354 323 290

Continental drift

Although Earth's tectonic plates move only a few centimetres (inches) each year, over hundreds of millions of years, its landmasses have moved many thousands of kilometres (miles), to create new continents, oceans and mountain chains.

Cambrian 543–490 million years ago

Devonian 418–354 million years ago

Carboniferous 354–290 million years ago

Dynamic Earth

Earth's surface is split up into several rigid, closely-fitting sections, called tectonic plates. Each of the plates contains some oceanic crust, and most also contain some continental crust. The plates constantly move relative to one another. Movements at different types of plate boundary produce various types of geological structure and activity.

Tectonic Activity and Geological Regions

Plate Boundaries
— Convergent
— Divergent
— Transform
--- Uncertain

Tectonic Activity
▲ volcanic zone
● earthquake zone
● hot spot
═ rift valley

Sedimentary cover
Mesozoic & Cenozoic volcanic rock
Cenozoic (65 mya – present)
Mesozoic (252 mya – 65 mya)
Paleozoic (543 mya – 252 mya)
pre-Cambrian Shields

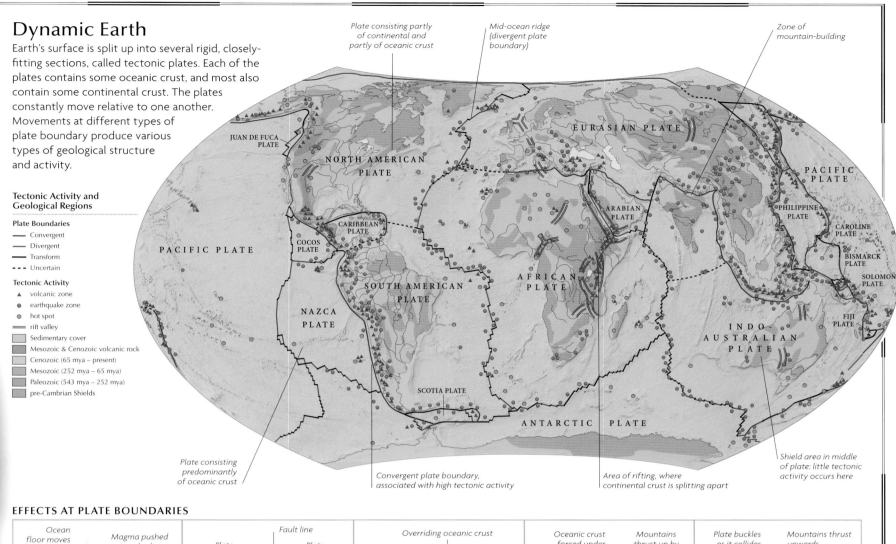

Plate consisting partly of continental and partly of oceanic crust

Mid-ocean ridge (divergent plate boundary)

Zone of mountain-building

JUAN DE FUCA PLATE

EURASIAN PLATE

NORTH AMERICAN PLATE

PACIFIC PLATE

CARIBBEAN PLATE

ARABIAN PLATE

PHILIPPINE PLATE

CAROLINE PLATE

PACIFIC PLATE

COCOS PLATE

BISMARCK PLATE

SOLOMON PLATE

SOUTH AMERICAN PLATE

AFRICAN PLATE

NAZCA PLATE

FIJI PLATE

INDO-AUSTRALIAN PLATE

SCOTIA PLATE

ANTARCTIC PLATE

Plate consisting predominantly of oceanic crust

Convergent plate boundary, associated with high tectonic activity

Area of rifting, where continental crust is splitting apart

Shield area in middle of plate: little tectonic activity occurs here

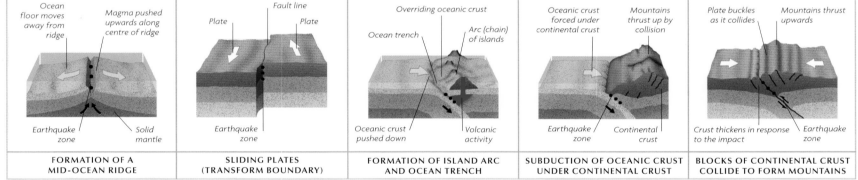

EFFECTS AT PLATE BOUNDARIES

Ocean floor moves away from ridge | Magma pushed upwards along centre of ridge

Earthquake zone | Solid mantle

FORMATION OF A MID-OCEAN RIDGE

Fault line | Plate | Plate

Earthquake zone

SLIDING PLATES (TRANSFORM BOUNDARY)

Overriding oceanic crust | Arc (chain) of islands

Ocean trench

Oceanic crust pushed down | Volcanic activity

FORMATION OF ISLAND ARC AND OCEAN TRENCH

Oceanic crust forced under continental crust | Mountains thrust up by collision

Earthquake zone | Continental crust

SUBDUCTION OF OCEANIC CRUST UNDER CONTINENTAL CRUST

Plate buckles as it collides | Mountains thrust upwards

Crust thickens in response to the impact | Earthquake zone

BLOCKS OF CONTINENTAL CRUST COLLIDE TO FORM MOUNTAINS

Boundary between upper mantle and crust

Sea floor made of oceanic crust

CONVECTION CURRENTS

Deep within Earth's core, temperatures may exceed 4500°C (8100°F). The heat from the core warms rocks in the mantle, which become semimolten and rise upwards, displacing cooler rock below the solid oceanic and continental crust. This rock sinks and is warmed again by heat given off from the core. The process continues in a cyclical fashion, producing convection currents below the crust. These currents lead, in turn, to gradual movements of the tectonic plates over the planet's surface.

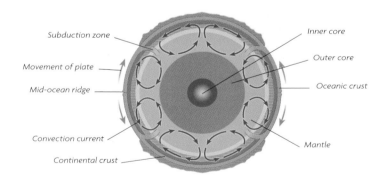

Subduction zone | Inner core
Movement of plate | Outer core
Mid-ocean ridge | Oceanic crust
Convection current | Mantle
Continental crust

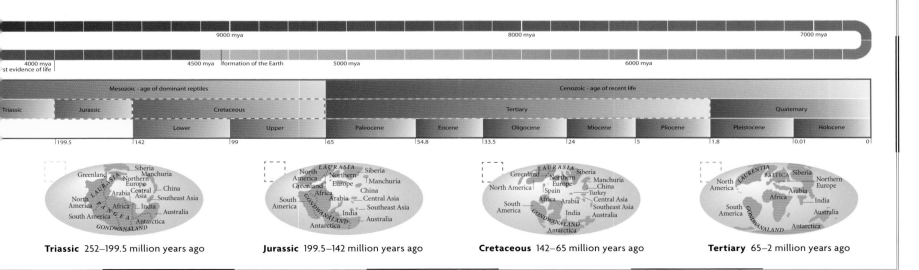

9000 mya | 8000 mya | 7000 mya

4000 mya | 4500 mya | formation of the Earth | 5000 mya | 6000 mya
first evidence of life

| Mesozoic - age of dominant reptiles | | | Cenozoic - age of recent life | | | | | |

Triassic	Jurassic	Cretaceous		Tertiary					Quaternary	
		Lower	Upper	Paleocene	Eocene	Oligocene	Miocene	Pliocene	Pleistocene	Holocene
199.5	142	99	65	54.8	33.5	24	5	1.8	0.01	0

Triassic 252–199.5 million years ago

Jurassic 199.5–142 million years ago

Cretaceous 142–65 million years ago

Tertiary 65–2 million years ago

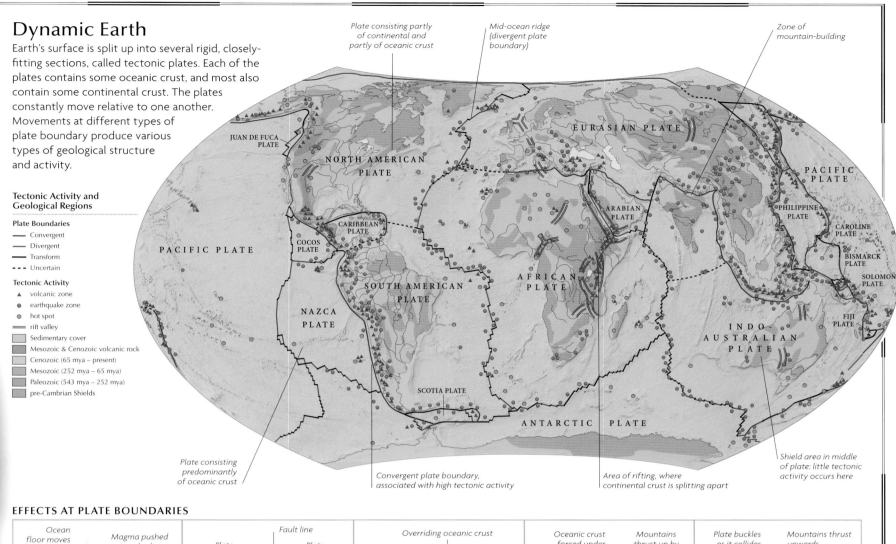

Shaping the Landscape

The basic material of Earth's surface is solid rock: valleys, deserts, soil and sand are all evidence of the powerful agents of weathering, erosion and deposition that constantly transform Earth's landscapes. Water, whether flowing in rivers or grinding the ground in the form of glaciers, has the most clearly visible impact on Earth's surface. Also wind can transport fragments of rock over huge distances and strip away protective layers of vegetation, exposing rock surfaces to the impact of extreme heat and cold. Many of the land-shaping effects of ice and water can be seen in northern regions such as Alaska *(below)*, while the effects of heat and wind are clearly visible in the Sahara *(far right)*.

● FJORD
A valley carved by an ancient glacier and later flooded by the sea is called a fiord.

Ice and water

Some of the most obvious and striking features of Earth's surface are large flows and bodies of liquid water, such as rivers, lakes and seas. In addition to these are landforms caused by the erosional or depositional power of flowing water, which include gullies, river valleys and coastal features such as headlands and deltas. Ice also has had a major impact on Earth's appearance. Glaciers – rivers of ice formed by the compaction of snow – pick up and carry huge amounts of rocks and boulders as they pass over the landscape, eroding it as they do so. Glacially-sculpted landforms range from mountain *cirques* and U-shaped valleys to fiords and glacial lakes.

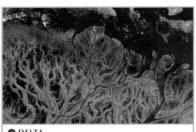

● DELTA
A delta, such as that of the Yukon River (above), is a roughly triangular or fan-shaped area of sediment deposited by a river at its mouth.

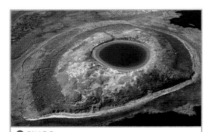

● PINGO
These blister-like mounds, seen in regions of Arctic tundra, are formed by the upward expansion of water as it freezes in the soil.

● TIDEWATER GLACIER
Glaciers of this type flow to the sea, where they calve (disgorge) icebergs. Like all glaciers, they erode huge amounts of rock from the landscape.

● LANDSLIDE
The freezing and later thawing of water, which occurs in a continuous cycle, can shatter and crumble rocks, eventually causing landslides.

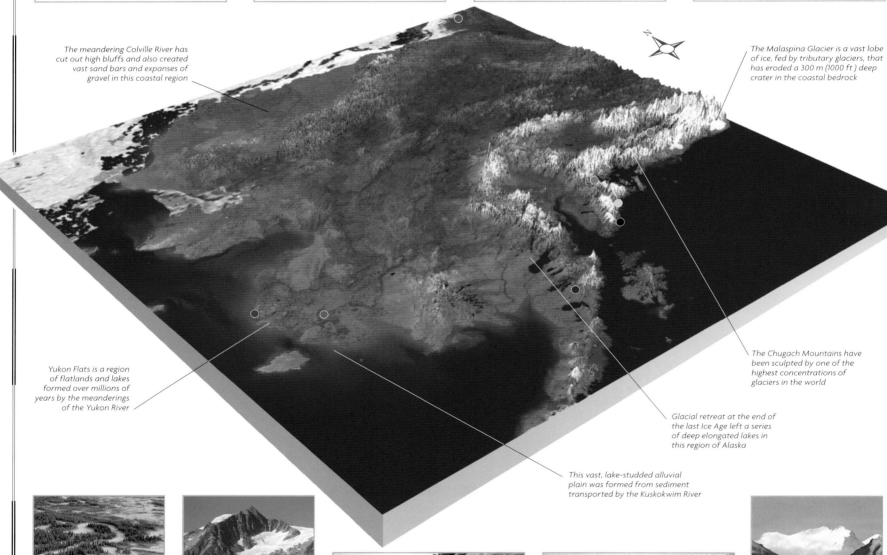

The meandering Colville River has cut out high bluffs and also created vast sand bars and expanses of gravel in this coastal region

The Malaspina Glacier is a vast lobe of ice, fed by tributary glaciers, that has eroded a 300 m (1000 ft) deep crater in the coastal bedrock

Yukon Flats is a region of flatlands and lakes formed over millions of years by the meanderings of the Yukon River

The Chugach Mountains have been sculpted by one of the highest concentrations of glaciers in the world

Glacial retreat at the end of the last Ice Age left a series of deep elongated lakes in this region of Alaska

This vast, lake-studded alluvial plain was formed from sediment transported by the Kuskokwim River

● MEANDERING RIVER
In their lower courses, some rivers carve out a series of looping bends called meanders.

● CIRQUE
A cirque is a hollow formed high on a mountain by glacial action. It may be ice-filled.

● POSTGLACIAL FEATURES
Glacially-polished cliffs like these are a tell-tale sign of ancient glacial action. Other signs include various forms of sculpted ridge and hummock.

● RIVER VALLEY
Over thousands of years, rivers erode uplands to form characteristic V-shaped valleys, with flat narrow floors and steeply-rising sides.

● GULLIES
Gullies are deep channels cut by rapidly flowing water, as here below Alaska's Mount Denali.

Heat and wind

Marked changes in temperature – rapid heating caused by fierce solar radiation during the day, followed by a sharp drop in temperature at night – cause rocks at the surface of hot deserts to continually expand and contract. This can eventually result in cracking and fissuring of the rocks, creating thermally-fractured desert landscapes. The world's deserts are also swept and scoured by strong winds. The finer particles of sand are shaped into surface ripples, dunes, or sand mountains, which can rise to a height of 200 m (650 ft). In other areas, the winds sweep away all the sand, leaving flat, gravelly areas called desert pavements.

DESERT LANDSCAPES

In desert areas, wind picks up loose sand and blasts it at the surface, creating a range of sculpted landforms from faceted rocks to large-scale features such as *yardangs*. Individually sculpted-rocks are called ventifacts. Where the sand abrasion is concentrated near the ground, it can turn these rocks into eccentrically-shaped 'stone mushrooms'. Other desert features are produced by thermal cracking and by winds continually redistributing the vast sand deposits.

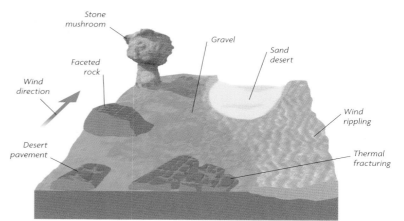

Stone mushroom
Gravel
Sand desert
Faceted rock
Wind direction
Wind rippling
Desert pavement
Thermal fracturing

FEATURES OF A DESERT SURFACE

● **DUST STORM**
A common phenomenon in some deserts, dust storms result from intense heating of the ground creating strong convection currents.

● **LOESS DEPOSIT**
A deposit of silt that has been transported over long distances by wind, then compacted. Loess is found in a few marginal areas of the Sahara.

● **YARDANG**
A yardang is a ridge of rock produced by wind erosion, usually in a desert. Large yardangs can be many kilometres (miles) long.

● **DESERT PAVEMENT**
Dark, gravelly surfaces like this result from wind removing all the sand from an area of desert.

Part of the Grand Erg Oriental, this region is a vast wind-sculpted sea of sand, much affected by sand storms

This area of complex dune morphology has resulted from two different types of dunes overlapping and coalescing

Wind erosion of the sandstone rocks in this area (the Tassili n'Ajjer) has created nearly 300 natural rock arches

The Tefedest is an impressive, sun-baked, wind-eroded, granite massif located in southern Algeria

This highland region, called the Ahaggar Mountains, has largely been blasted free of sand and is heavily eroded throughout

● **TRANSVERSE DUNES**
This series of parallel sand ridges lies at right angles to the prevailing wind direction.

● **VENTIFACT**
A ventifact is a rock that has been heavily sculpted and abraded by wind-driven sand.

● **CRACKED DESERT**
Intensely heated and dried-out desert areas often developed geometrically-patterned surface cracking.

● **WADI**
Wadis are dried out stream beds, found in some desert regions, that carry water only during occasional periods of heavy rain.

● **BARCHAN DUNE**
This arc-shaped type of dune migrates across the desert surface, blown by the wind.

The World's Oceans

Two-thirds of Earth's surface is covered by the five oceans: the Pacific, Atlantic, Indian, Southern and Arctic oceans. The basins that form these oceans, and the ocean floor landscape, have formed over the past 200 million years through a combination of volcanic activity and gradual movements of the Earth's crust. Surrounding the continents are shallow flat regions, called continental shelves. These shelves extend to the continental slope, which drops steeply to the ocean floor. There, vast submarine plateaux, known as abyssal plains, are interrupted by massive ridges, chains of seamounts, and deep ocean trenches.

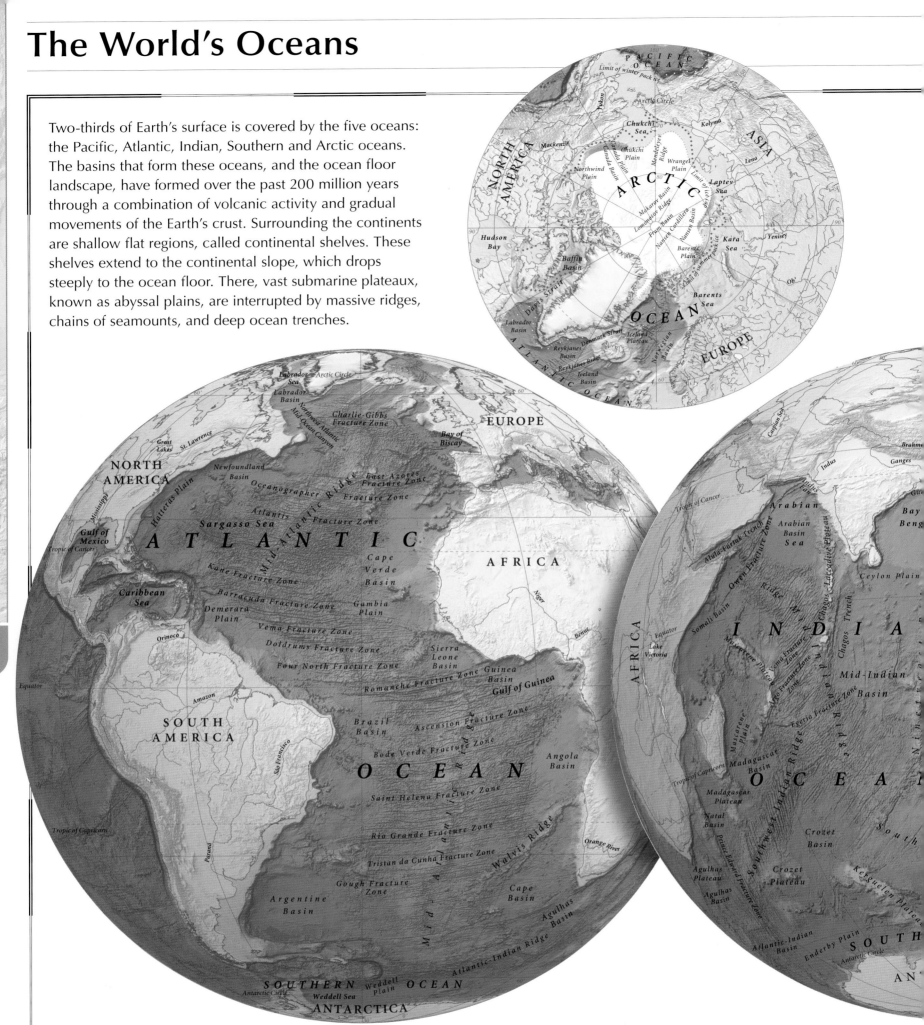

Ocean currents

Surface currents are driven by winds and by the Earth's rotation. Together these cause large circular flows of water over the surface of the oceans, called gyres. Deep sea currents are driven by changes in the salinity or temperature of surface water. These changes cause the water to become denser and sink, forcing horizontal movements of deeper water.

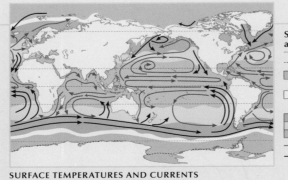

Surface temperature and currents

- - - - - ice-shelf (below 0°C / 32°F)
- sea-ice* (average) below -2°C / 28°F
- sea-water -2 to 0°C / 28–32°F * sea-water freezes at -1.9°C / 28.4°F
- 0–10°C / 32–50°F
- 10–20°C / 50–68°F
- 20–30°C / 68–86°F
- → warm current
- → cold current

SURFACE TEMPERATURES AND CURRENTS

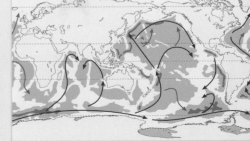

DEEP SEA TEMPERATURES AND CURRENTS

The ocean floor

The ages of seafloor rocks increase in parallel bands outwards from central ocean ridges. At these ridges, new oceanic crust is continuously created from lava that erupts from below the seafloor and then cools to form solid rock. As this new crust forms, it gradually pushes older crust away from the ridge.

Ages of the ocean crust

- 0–5 million years
- 5–21 million years
- 21–38 million years
- 38–65 million years
- 65–140 million years
- 140–190 million years
- continental shelf
- no data

Tides

Tides are caused by gravitational interactions between the Earth, Moon and Sun. The strongest tides occur when the three bodies are aligned and the weakest when the Sun and Moon align at right angles.

Strongest tides

Weakest tides

Gravitational pull from the Sun

Tidal bulges created by gravitational interactions

Earth

Moon

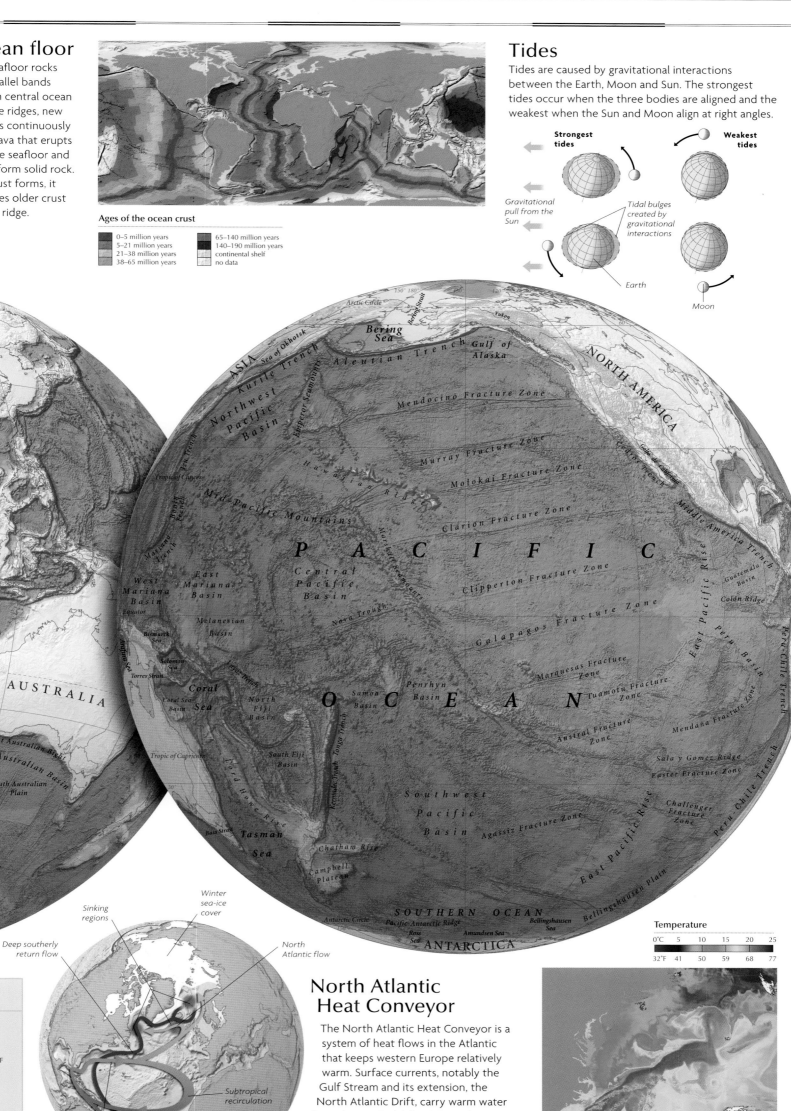

Deep sea temperature and currents

- ice-shelf (below 0°C / 32°F)
- sea-water -2 to 0°C / 28–32°F (below 5000 m / 16,400 ft)
- sea-water 0–5°C / 32–41°F (below 4000 m / 13,120 ft)
- primary currents
- secondary currents

Sinking regions

Winter sea-ice cover

Deep southerly return flow

North Atlantic flow

Subtropical recirculation

Gulf Stream

Temperature

| 0°C | 5 | 10 | 15 | 20 | 25 |
| 32°F | 41 | 50 | 59 | 68 | 77 |

North Atlantic Heat Conveyor

The North Atlantic Heat Conveyor is a system of heat flows in the Atlantic that keeps western Europe relatively warm. Surface currents, notably the Gulf Stream and its extension, the North Atlantic Drift, carry warm water from the tropical Atlantic into the northeastern Atlantic. There, the heat they supply is released, warming Europe, while the water itself cools and sinks. This cold water then returns at depth towards the equator.

A key part of the North Atlantic Heat Conveyor is the warm Gulf Stream, visible as the dark red ribbon in this Atlantic sea-surface temperature map.

Global Climate

The climates of different regions on Earth are the typical long-term patterns of temperature and humidity in those regions. By contrast, weather consists of short-term variations in factors such as wind, rainfall and sunshine. Climates are determined primarily by the Sun's variable heating of different parts of Earth's atmosphere and oceans, and by Earth's rotation. These factors drive the ocean currents and prevailing winds, which in turn redistribute heat energy and moisture between the equator and poles, and between sea and land. Most scientists think that major changes are currently occurring in global climate due to the effects of rising carbon dioxide levels in the atmosphere.

The atmosphere

Earth's atmosphere is a giant ocean of air that surrounds the planet. It extends to a height of about 1000 km (625 miles) but has no distinct upper boundary. The Sun's rays pass through the atmosphere and warm Earth's surface, causing the air to move and water to evaporate from the oceans.

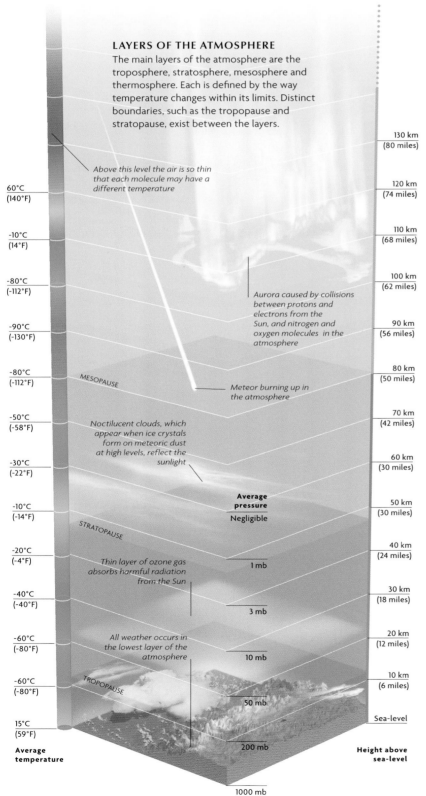

LAYERS OF THE ATMOSPHERE
The main layers of the atmosphere are the troposphere, stratosphere, mesosphere and thermosphere. Each is defined by the way temperature changes within its limits. Distinct boundaries, such as the tropopause and stratopause, exist between the layers.

Above this level the air is so thin that each molecule may have a different temperature

Aurora caused by collisions between protons and electrons from the Sun, and nitrogen and oxygen molecules in the atmosphere

MESOPAUSE

Meteor burning up in the atmosphere

Noctilucent clouds, which appear when ice crystals form on meteoric dust at high levels, reflect the sunlight

Average pressure

STRATOPAUSE

Thin layer of ozone gas absorbs harmful radiation from the Sun

All weather occurs in the lowest layer of the atmosphere

TROPOPAUSE

Average temperature		Height above sea-level
60°C (140°F)		130 km (80 miles)
-10°C (14°F)		120 km (74 miles)
-80°C (-112°F)		110 km (68 miles)
-90°C (-130°F)		100 km (62 miles)
-80°C (-112°F)		90 km (56 miles)
-50°C (-58°F)		80 km (50 miles)
-30°C (-22°F)		70 km (42 miles)
-10°C (-14°F)	Negligible	60 km (30 miles)
-20°C (-4°F)	1 mb	50 km (30 miles)
-40°C (-40°F)	3 mb	40 km (24 miles)
-60°C (-80°F)	10 mb	30 km (18 miles)
-60°C (-80°F)	50 mb	20 km (12 miles)
15°C (59°F)	200 mb	10 km (6 miles)
	1000 mb	Sea-level

Global air circulation

Polar cell

Cool air subsides at North Pole

Polar easterly blowing away from high pressure over North Pole

Air rises in subpolar region

Ferrell cell

Air descends in subtropics

Hadley cell

Air rises near equator

Southwesterly caused by Coriolis deflection of surface air flow in Ferrell cell

Subtropical jet stream

Northeasterly trade wind, caused by Coriolis deflection of surface air flow in Hadley cell

Polar-front jet stream

Roaring Forties

Southeasterly trade wind

Winds, currents and climate

Earth has 12 climatic zones, ranging from ice-cap and tundra to temperate, arid (desert) and tropical zones. Each of these climate zones features a particular combination of temperature and humidity. The effects of prevailing winds, ocean currents of both the warm and cold variety, as well as latitude and altitude, all have an important influence on a region's climate. For example, the climate of western Europe is greatly influenced by the moderating effects of the warm North Atlantic Drift current.

● **THERMOSPHERE**
This layer extends from a height of 80 km (50 miles) upwards. Its temperature increases rapidly above a height of 90 km (60 miles), due to absorption of highly energetic solar radiation.

● **MESOSPHERE**
The temperature of the lower part of this layer stays constant with height; but above 55 km (35 miles), it drops, reaching -80°C (-112°F) at the mesopause.

● **STRATOSPHERE**
The temperature of the stratosphere is a fairly constant -60°C (-76° F) up to an altitude of about 20 km (12 miles), then increases, due to absorption of ultraviolet radiation.

● **TROPOSPHERE**
This layer extends from Earth's surface to a height of about 16 km (10 miles) at the equator and 8 km (5 miles) at the poles. Air temperature in this layer decreases with height.

Arctic Cir January

July

Alaska Current

WESTERLIES

North Pacific Current

Northen January

California Current

Tropic of Cancer

NORTH

Northern Equatorial Current

EAST

January

TRADES

Equatorial Counter Current

July

Equator Doldrums . El Niño

South Equatorial Current

SOUTH

EAST

Tropic of Capricorn

TRADES

WESTERLIES

West Wind

Antarctic Cir

Air moves within giant atmospheric cells called Hadley, Ferrell and polar cells. These cells are caused by air being warmed and rising in some latitudes, such as near the equator, and sinking in other latitudes. This north-south circulation combined with the Coriolis effect (below) produces the prevailing surface winds.

THE CORIOLIS EFFECT

Air moving over Earth's surface is deflected in a clockwise direction in the northern hemisphere and anticlockwise in the south. Known as the Coriolis effect, and caused by Earth's spin, these deflections to the air movements produce winds such as the trade winds and westerlies.

Direction of Earth's spin

Deflected clockwise

Deflected anticlockwise

Initial direction

Temperature and precipitation

The world divides by latitude into three major temperature zones: the warm tropics, the cold polar regions; and an intermediate temperate zone. In addition, temperature is strongly influenced by height above sea level. Precipitation patterns are related to factors such as solar heating, atmospheric pressure, winds and topography. Most equatorial areas have high rainfall, caused by moist air being warmed and rising, then cooling to form rain clouds. In areas of the subtropics and near the poles, sinking air causes high pressure and low precipitation. In temperate regions rainfall is quite variable.

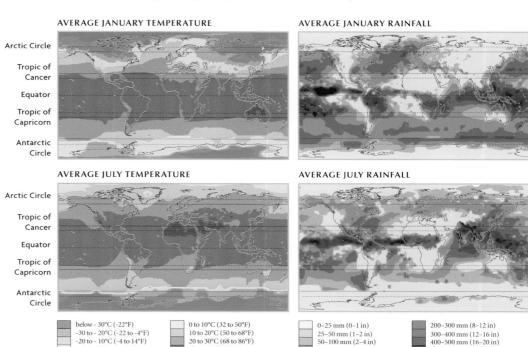

AVERAGE JANUARY TEMPERATURE

Arctic Circle
Tropic of Cancer
Equator
Tropic of Capricorn
Antarctic Circle

AVERAGE JANUARY RAINFALL

AVERAGE JULY TEMPERATURE

Arctic Circle
Tropic of Cancer
Equator
Tropic of Capricorn
Antarctic Circle

AVERAGE JULY RAINFALL

- below - 30°C (-22°F)
- -30 to - 20°C (-22 to -4°F)
- -20 to - 10°C (-4 to 14°F)
- -10 to 0°C (14 to 32°F)
- 0 to 10°C (32 to 50°F)
- 10 to 20°C (50 to 68°F)
- 20 to 30°C (68 to 86°F)
- above 30°C (86°F)

- 0–25 mm (0–1 in)
- 25–50 mm (1–2 in)
- 50–100 mm (2–4 in)
- 100–200 mm (4–8 in)
- 200–300 mm (8–12 in)
- 300–400 mm (12–16 in)
- 400–500 mm (16–20 in)
- above 500 mm (20 in)

Ocean currents, winds and climatic regions

Climate zones
- ice-cap
- subarctic
- tundra
- continental
- temperate
- warm temperate
- mediterranean
- semi-arid
- arid
- hot humid
- humid-equatorial
- tropical

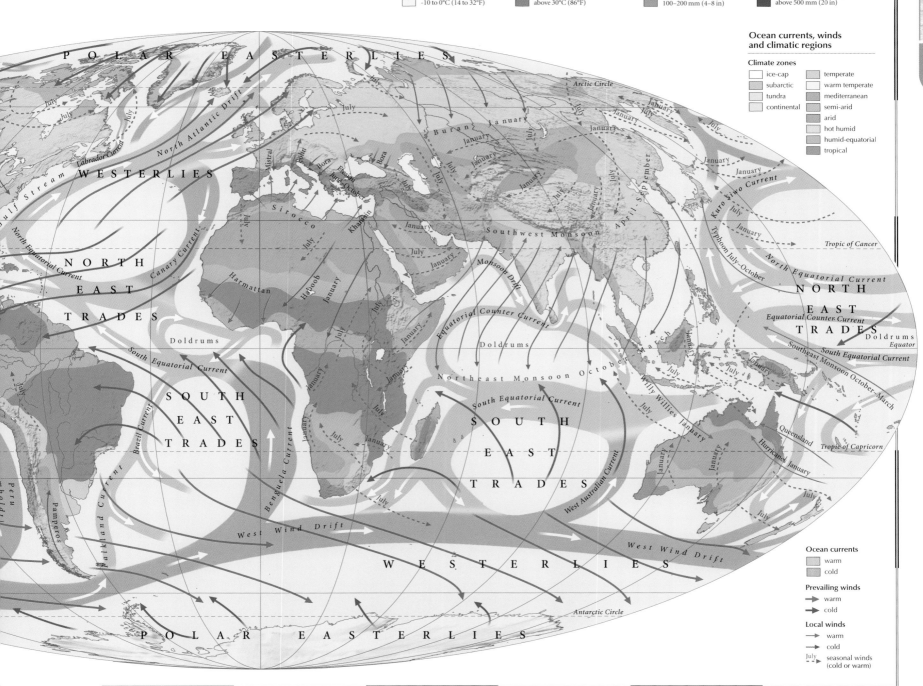

Ocean currents
- warm
- cold

Prevailing winds
- warm
- cold

Local winds
- warm
- cold
- July seasonal winds (cold or warm)

Life on Earth

A unique combination of an oxygen-rich atmosphere and plentiful surface water is the key to life on Earth, where few areas have not been colonised by animals, plants or smaller life-forms. An important determinant of the quantity of life in a region is its level of primary production – the amount of energy-rich substances made by organisms living there, mainly through the process of photosynthesis. On land, plants are the main organisms responsible for primary production; in water, algae fulfil this role. These primary producers supply food for animals. Primary production is affected by climatic, seasonal and other local factors. On land, cold and aridity restrict the quantity of life in a region, whereas warmth and regular rainfall allow a greater diversity of species. In the oceans, production is mainly affected by sunlight levels, which reduce rapidly with depth, and by nutrient availability.

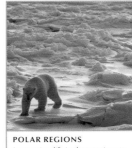

POLAR REGIONS
Ice restricts life in these regions to just a few species, such as polar bears in the Arctic.

Biogeographical regions

Earth's biogeographical regions, or biomes, are communities where certain species of plants and animals co-exist within the constraints of particular climatic conditions. They range from tundra to various types of grassland, forest, desert and marine biomes such as coral reefs. Factors including soil richness, altitude and human activities such as deforestation can affect the local distribution of living species in each biome.

TEMPERATE GRASSLAND
Also known as steppe or prairie, grassland of this type occurs mainly in the northern hemisphere and in South America (the Pampas).

NEEDLELEAF FOREST
These vast forests of coniferous trees cover huge areas of Canada, Siberia and Scandinavia.

TROPICAL GRASSLAND
This type of grassland is widespread in Africa and South America, supporting large numbers of grazing animals and their predators.

World biomes

- polar
- tundra
- needleleaf forest
- broadleaf forest
- temperate rainforest
- temperate grassland
- cold desert

Map labels

ARCTIC OCEAN
Beaufort Sea
Arctic Circle
Brooks Range
Victoria Island
Great Bear Lake
Great Slave Lake
Baffin Bay
Greenland
Denmark Strait
Iceland
Gulf of Alaska
Aleutian Islands
Vancouver Island
Coast Ranges
Rocky Mountains
NORTH AMERICA
Great Plains
Great Lakes
Hudson Bay
Labrador Sea
Newfoundland
Appalachian Mts
Azores
Madeira
Tropic of Cancer
Hawaiian Islands
Gulf of Mexico
Cuba
ATLANTIC OCEAN
Canary Islands
Caribbean Sea
Cape Verde Islands
PACIFIC OCEAN
Polynesia
Line Islands
Equator 0°
Galapagos Islands
Amazon Basin
Amazon
SOUTH AMERICA
Marquesas Islands
Andes
Lake Titicaca
Gran Chaco
Paraná
Tropic of Capricorn
Easter Island
Pampas
Patagonia
Falkland Islands
South Georgia
South Sandwich Islands
Tierra del Fuego
Cape Horn
Drake Passage
Antarctic Peninsula
Antarctic Circle

Animal diversity

The number of animal species, and the range of genetic diversity within the populations of those species, determines the level of animal diversity within each country or other region of the world. The animals that are endemic to a region – that is, those found nowhere else on the planet – are also important in determining its level of animal diversity.

Number of animal species per country

- more than 2000
- 1000–1999
- 700–999
- 400–699
- 200–399
- 100–199
- 0–99
- data not available

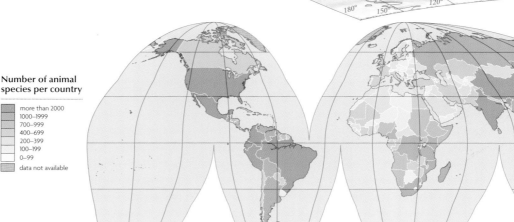

TUNDRA
With little soil and large areas of frozen ground, the tundra is largely treeless, though briefly clothed by small flowering plants in summer.

TEMPERATE RAINFOREST
Occurring in mid-latitudes in areas of high rainfall, these forests may be predominantly coniferous or mixed with deciduous species.

CORAL REEFS
Occurring in clear tropical waters, coral reefs support an extraordinary diversity of species, especially fish and many types of invertebrate.

MOUNTAINS
In high mountain areas only a few hardy species of plant will grow above the tree-line.

TROPICAL RAINFOREST
Characterised by year-round warmth and high rainfall, tropical rainforests contain the highest diversity of plant and animal species on Earth.

HOT DESERT
Only a few highly adapted species can survive in hot deserts, which occur mainly in the tropics.

OPEN OCEAN
Earth's largest biome, the oceans are home to a vast diversity of fish, mammals, invertebrates and algae.

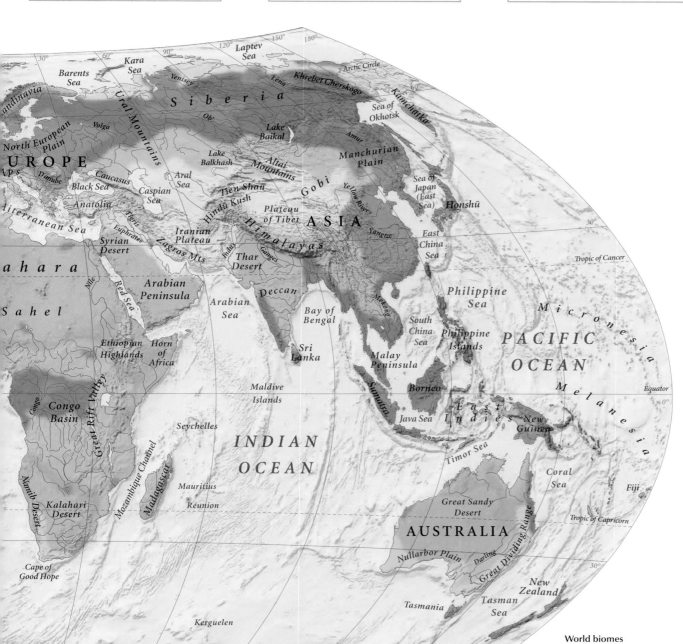

World biomes
(continued)

- mediterranean
- hot desert
- tropical grassland
- dry woodland
- tropical rainforest
- mountain
- wetland

Number of plant species per country

- more than 50,000
- 7000–49,999
- 3000–6999
- 2000–2999
- 1000–1999
- 600–999
- 0–599
- data not available

Plant diversity

Environmental conditions, particularly climate, soil type and the extent of competition with other living organisms, influence the development of plants into distinctive forms and thus also the extent of plant diversity. Human settlement and intervention has considerably reduced the diversity of plant species in many areas.

Man and the Environment

The impact of human activity on the environment has widened from being a matter of local concern (typically over the build-up of urban waste, industrial pollution and smog) to affect whole ecosystems and, in recent decades, the global climate. Problems crossing national boundaries first became a major issue over acid rain, toxic waste dumping at sea, and chemical spillages polluting major rivers. Current concerns centre on loss of biodiversity and vital habitat including wetlands and coral reefs, the felling and clearance of great tropical and temperate forests, overexploitation of scarce resources, the uncontrolled growth of cities and, above all, climate change.

OZONE HOLE

Man-made chlorofluorocarbons (CFCs), used in refrigeration and aerosols, damaged the ozone layer in the stratosphere which helps filter out the sun's harmful ultraviolet rays. When a seasonal ozone hole first appeared in 1985 over Antarctica, a shocked world agreed to phase out CFC use.

1980   1985

CO₂ emissions in 2003
(million tonnes)

- over 4000
- 1000–4000
- 500–1000
- 100–500
- 50–100
- 10–50
- 2–10
- 0–2
- no data

Kyoto Protocol

- ▲ countries that have reached targets
- ▽ countries that have not reached targets
- ● industrialised countries that have not ratified

Climate change

Global warming is happening much faster than Earth's normal long-term cycles of climate change. The consequences include unpredictable extreme weather and potential disruption of ocean currents. Melting ice-caps and glaciers, and warmer oceans, will raise average sea levels and threaten coastlines and cities. Food crops like wheat are highly vulnerable to changes in temperature and rainfall. Such changes can also have a dramatic affect on wildlife habitats.

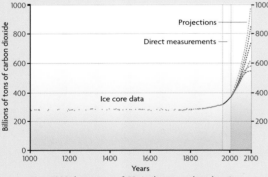

Since 1800 the amount of CO₂ in the atmosphere has risen sharply. Urgent worldwide action to control emissions is vital to stabilize the level by the mid 21st century.

THE GREENHOUSE EFFECT

Some solar energy, reflected from the Earth's surface as infra red radiation, is reflected back as heat by 'greenhouse gases' (mainly carbon dioxide and methane) in the atmosphere. Nearly all scientists now agree that an upsurge in carbon dioxide emissions, caused by humans burning fossil fuel, has contributed to making the resultant warming effect a major problem.

Greenhouse gases absorb longwave radiation

Some heat emitted by greenhouse gases heats surface

Some heat emitted by greenhouse gases escapes to space

Escaping longwave radiation

Diffused incoming radiation

Solar radiation deflected back into space

Incoming solar radiation

FOOD AND LAND USE

The world has about five billion hectares of agriculturally useful land, well under one hectare per person. The majority of this is pasture for grazing. Crops are grown on about 30 percent (and nearly a fifth of cropland is artificially irrigated). Mechanization of farming encouraged vast single crop 'monocultures', highly dependent on fertilizers and pesticides. North America's endless prairies of wheat and corn, huge soya bean plantations and southern cotton fields are mirrored in Ukraine (wheat), Brazil and Argentina (soya) and Uzbekistan (cotton). Elsewhere, as in China, scarce farmland can be squeezed by the housing needs of growing urban populations. Current interest in crop-derived 'biofuels' means further pressure to grow food more productively on less land.

Intensive farming. Satellite photography picks up the greenhouses that now cover almost all the land in this Spanish coastal area southwest of Almeria.

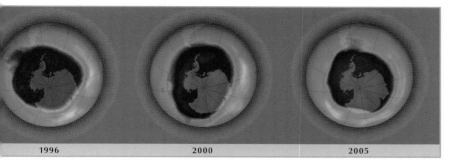

1996   2000   2005

DEFORESTATION

At current rates of destruction, all tropical forests, and most old-growth temperate forest, will be gone by 2090. The Amazon rainforest is a valuable genetic resource, containing innumerable unique plants and animals, as well as acting as a crucial natural 'sink' for absorbing climate-damaging carbon dioxide. Stemming the loss of these precious assets to logging and farming is one of the major environmental challenges of modern times.

Over 60,000 sq km (25,000 sq miles) of virgin rainforest are cleared annually by logging and agricultural activities, destroying an irreplaceable natural resource.

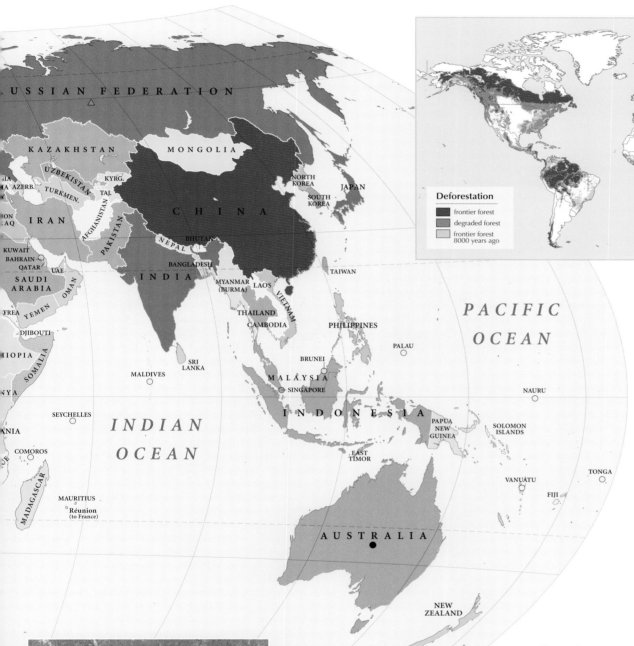

Deforestation
- frontier forest
- degraded forest
- frontier forest 8000 years ago

GLACIATION

The world's glaciers and ice sheets have been in retreat for decades, forming less new ice at high altitudes than they lose by melting lower down. The loss of ice from Greenland doubled between 1996 and 2005, with alarming implications for rising sea levels. Other dramatic evidence of global warming includes the rapid thinning of ice in the Himalayas, and the highly symbolic loss of the snowcap on Africa's Mount Kilimanjaro.

Helheim Glacier 2001
The Helheim glacier *(above)* almost completely fills this image, with the leading edge visible on the right hand side, and was in a relatively stable condition.

Helheim Glacier 2005
By 2005 *(right)* it had retreated by 4 km (2.5 miles).

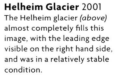

Delhi 1971
In 1971 Delhi *(above)* occupied an area of about 500 sq km (190 sq miles).

Delhi 1999
By 1999 *(right)* it had sprawled to cover 1300 sq km (500 sq miles). It vies with Mumbai in the southwest to be the sub-continent's most populous city, fast approaching 20 million people.

CITY GROWTH

The world in 2006 had five cities with populations over 20 million – Tokyo, Mexico City, Seoul, New York and São Paulo. The number of cities with populations between 10 and 20 million has reached 20 and continues to rise. The search for work, and the hope of escape from rural poverty, drives a trend of migration from countryside to urban areas across the developing world. Urban dwellers now amount to more than half the world's population, and consume more resources than their rural counterparts.

Population and Settlement

Earth's human population is projected to rise from its current level of 6.5 billion to between 7.6 and 11 billion by the year 2050. The distribution of this population is very uneven and is dictated by climate, terrain and by natural and economic resources. Most people live in coastal zones and along the valleys of great rivers such as the Ganges, Indus, Nile and Yangtze. Deserts cover over 20 percent of Earth's surface but support less than 5 percent of its human population. Over half the world's population live in cities – most of them in Asia, Europe and North America – as a result of mass migrations that have occurred from rural areas as people search for jobs. Many of these people live in so-called 'megacities' – sprawling urban areas that have populations higher than 10 million.

Population density by country (population per sq km)

- over 1000
- 300-999
- 150-299
- 100-149
- 75–99
- 50–74
- 25–49
- 10–24
- 0–9

Population density

A few regions, including Europe, India, and much of eastern Asia, have extremely high population densities. Within these areas, a few spots, such as Monaco and Hong Kong, have densities of over 5000 people per sq km (12,900 per sq mile). Other regions (mostly desert, mountain, ice cap, tundra or thickly forested areas) have densities close to zero —examples include large areas of Australia, western China, Siberia, North Africa, Canada, Greenland and much of the Amazon rainforest region.

NORTH AMERICA

World population — 9%
World land area — 17.0%

EUROPE

World population — 14%
World land area — 7.1%

SOUTH AMERICA

World population — 5.5%
World land area — 11.8%

ANTARCTICA

World population — 0.0%
World land area — 8.9%

Population density (persons per sq km)

- 200–1000
- 100–200
- 50–100
- 20–50
- 10–20
- 5-10
- 1–55
- 0–1

Million-person cities

In the year 1900 there were fewer than 20 cities in the world with a population that exceeded one million. By 1950 there were 75 such cities, and by the year 2000 there were more than 300 such cities, 40 of them in China alone, with another 30 in India, 14 in Brazil and 10 in Japan.

Million-cities in 1900

- Cities over 1 million in population

Million-cities in 1950

Million-cities in 2006

Tokyo urban sprawl

— City boundary, 1860   — City boundary, 1964

GREATER TOKYO

The Greater Tokyo Area is the most populous urban area in the world, with an estimated head count in 2006 of 35.5 million. It includes Tokyo City, which has a population of about 12 million, and adjoining cities such as Yokohama. This satellite photograph shows the Greater Tokyo Area today, and also the boundaries of Tokyo City in 1860 (red) and 1964 (yellow).

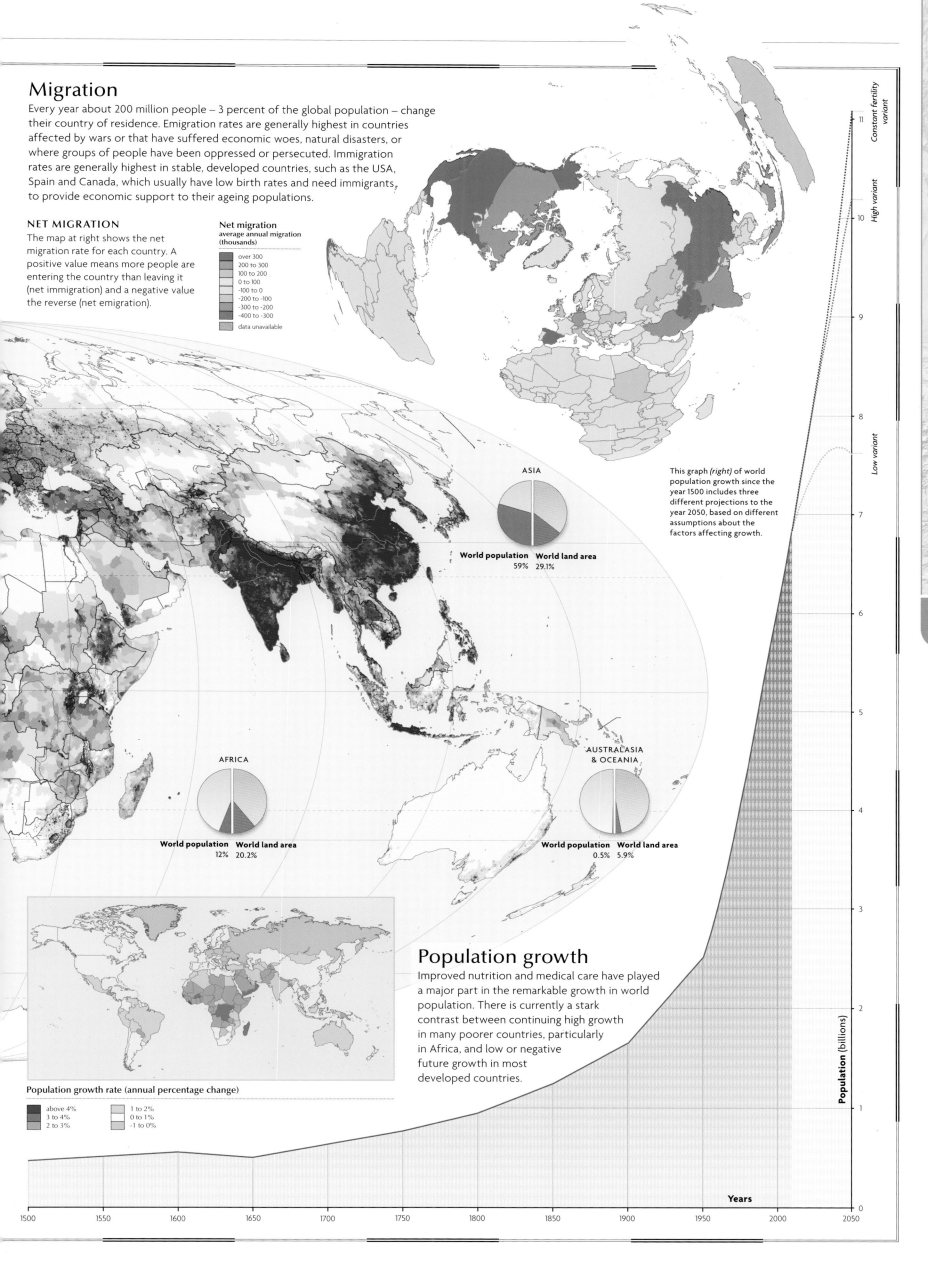

Migration

Every year about 200 million people – 3 percent of the global population – change their country of residence. Emigration rates are generally highest in countries affected by wars or that have suffered economic woes, natural disasters, or where groups of people have been oppressed or persecuted. Immigration rates are generally highest in stable, developed countries, such as the USA, Spain and Canada, which usually have low birth rates and need immigrants to provide economic support to their ageing populations.

NET MIGRATION

The map at right shows the net migration rate for each country. A positive value means more people are entering the country than leaving it (net immigration) and a negative value the reverse (net emigration).

Net migration
average annual migration
(thousands)

- over 300
- 200 to 300
- 100 to 200
- 0 to 100
- -100 to 0
- -200 to -100
- -300 to -200
- -400 to -300
- data unavailable

ASIA

World population 59% World land area 29.1%

AFRICA

World population 12% World land area 20.2%

AUSTRALASIA & OCEANIA

World population 0.5% World land area 5.9%

This graph *(right)* of world population growth since the year 1500 includes three different projections to the year 2050, based on different assumptions about the factors affecting growth.

Population growth

Improved nutrition and medical care have played a major part in the remarkable growth in world population. There is currently a stark contrast between continuing high growth in many poorer countries, particularly in Africa, and low or negative future growth in most developed countries.

Population growth rate (annual percentage change)

- above 4%
- 3 to 4%
- 2 to 3%
- 1 to 2%
- 0 to 1%
- -1 to 0%

Constant fertility variant

High variant

Low variant

Population (billions)

Years

1500 1550 1600 1650 1700 1750 1800 1850 1900 1950 2000 2050

Language

Over 6800 different languages exist throughout the world, each one with its own unique evolutionary history and cultural connotations. Most of these languages are spoken only by small groups of people in remote regions. Sadly these minority tongues are dying out – it is estimated that about a third will have disappeared by the year 2100. The relatively small number of widely-spoken languages have gained their current predominance and pattern of distribution through a variety of historical factors. Among these have been the economic, military or technological success of certain peoples and cultures, differing population growth rates, and the effects of migrations and colonisation.

The European Union (EU) embraces the diversity of its 27 countries and 23 official languages by providing a translation and interpretation service for the majority of its meetings and documentation. This costs around US$ 650 million per year, which equates to 1 percent of the EU budget.

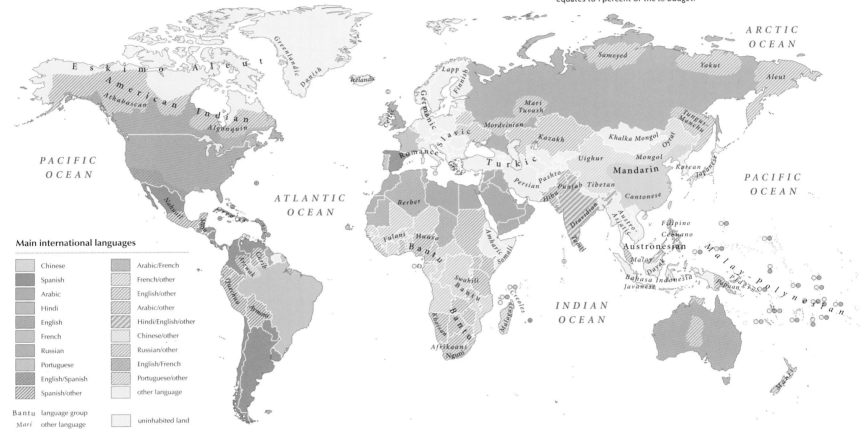

Main international languages

- Chinese
- Spanish
- Arabic
- Hindi
- English
- French
- Russian
- Portuguese
- English/Spanish
- Spanish/other
- Arabic/French
- French/other
- English/other
- Arabic/other
- Hindi/English/other
- Chinese/other
- Russian/other
- English/French
- Portuguese/other
- other language

Bantu language group
Mari other language

- uninhabited land

The colonial powers

Colonialism between the 15th and 20th centuries had a major influence in establishing the world prevalence of various, mainly European, languages. Britain, for example, was the colonial power in Canada, the USA (until 1776), the Indian subcontinent, Australia, and parts of Africa and the Caribbean. Hence, English is still the main (or a major) language in these areas. The same applies to France and the French language in parts of Africa and southeast Asia, and to Spain and the Spanish language in much of Latin America. For similar reasons, Portuguese is the main language in Brazil and parts of Africa, and there are many Dutch speakers in Indonesia.

This dual language sign, written in both in Hindi and English, stands outside Shimla railway station in northern India. The sign reflects India's past – the British used Shimla as their summer capital during the colonial period.

TOP TEN LANGUAGES

About 45 percent of people speak one of just ten languages as their native tongue. Mandarin Chinese is spoken by far the largest number – a situation likely to persist, as minority language speakers in China are encouraged to switch to Mandarin. English usage is also increasing, as it is the most favoured language on the internet and in business circles. Furthermore, wherever English is not the mother tongue, it is often the second language.

THE TEN MOST SPOKEN LANGUAGES
(number of native speakers)

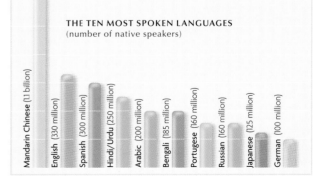

- Mandarin Chinese (1.1 billion)
- English (330 million)
- Spanish (300 million)
- Hindi/Urdu (250 million)
- Arabic (200 million)
- Bengali (185 million)
- Portuguese (160 million)
- Russian (160 million)
- Japanese (125 million)
- German (100 million)

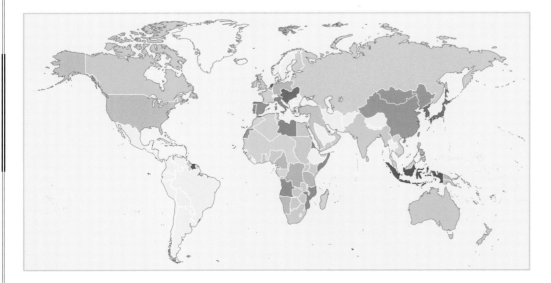

Colonial Empires in 1914

- Austro-Hungarian
- Belgian
- British
- Chinese
- Danish
- Dutch
- French
- German
- Italian
- Japanese
- Ottoman
- Portuguese
- Russian
- Spanish
- United States
- Independent
- Disputed

Religion

The spread of religion

By their nature, religions usually start off in small geographical areas and then spread. For Christianity and Islam, this spread was rapid and extensive. Buddhism diffused more slowly from around 500 BCE into a large part of Asia. The oldest religion, Hinduism, has always been concentrated in the Indian subcontinent, although its adherents in other parts of the world now number millions following migrations from India.

1ST–7TH CENTURY

During this period, Christianity spread from its origins in the eastern Mediterranean, while Hinduism and forms of Buddhism spread in Asia. Islam became established in Arabia.

Rise and spread of the classical religions to 650 CE

- Buddhist heartland
- Chinese Confucianism/ Daoism and indigenous primal traditions
- Converted to Christianity by 600 CE
- Hinduism
- Islam under Muhammad
- Mahayana Buddhism
- Shintoism
- Zoroastrianism
- → spread of Buddhism
- → spread of Christianity
- → spread of Hinduism
- → dispersion of Jews, to 500 CE

7TH–16TH CENTURY

Islam later spread further through Asia and into parts of Africa and Europe. Christianity diffused through Europe and was then carried to many other parts of the world by colonialists and missionaries. Buddhism spread further in Asia.

World religions c.1500 CE

- Catholic Christianity
- area converted to Catholic Christianity
- Hinduism
- Islam
- Mahayana Buddhism and Confucianism, Daoism and Shinto
- Mahayana Buddhism and Confucianism, Daoism
- Russian Orthodoxy
- Theravada Buddhism
- Tibetan Buddhism
- Aztec Empire
- Inca Empire
- → spread of Catholicism
- → spread of Islam
- → spread of Protestantism
- → spread of Russian Orthodoxy

About 83 percent of the world's population adheres to a religion. The remainder adopt irreligious stances such as atheism. In terms of broad similarities of belief, there are about 20 different religions in the world with more than 1 million adherents. However, the larger of these are split into several denominations, which differ in their exact beliefs and practices. Christianity, for example, includes three major groupings that have historically been in conflict – Roman Catholicism, Protestantism, and Orthodox Christianity – as well as hundreds of separate smaller groups. Many of the world's other main religious, such as Islam and Buddhism, are also subdivided.

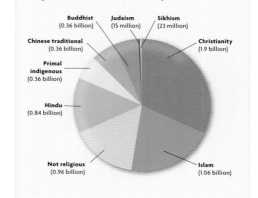

Each year millions of Muslims visit Mecca during the the Islamic pilgrimage known as the *Hajj*

RELIGION AROUND THE WORLD

About 72 percent of humanity adheres to one of five religions: Christianity, Islam, Hinduism, Buddhism and Chinese traditional religion (which includes Daoism and Confucianism). Of the remainder, many are adherents of primal indigenous religions (a wide range of tribal or folk religions such as shamanism).

Pie chart:
- Buddhist (0.36 billion)
- Judaism (15 million)
- Sikhism (23 million)
- Christianity (1.9 billion)
- Chinese traditional (0.36 billion)
- Islam (1.06 billion)
- Primal indigenous (0.36 billion)
- Hindu (0.84 billion)
- Not religious (0.96 billion)

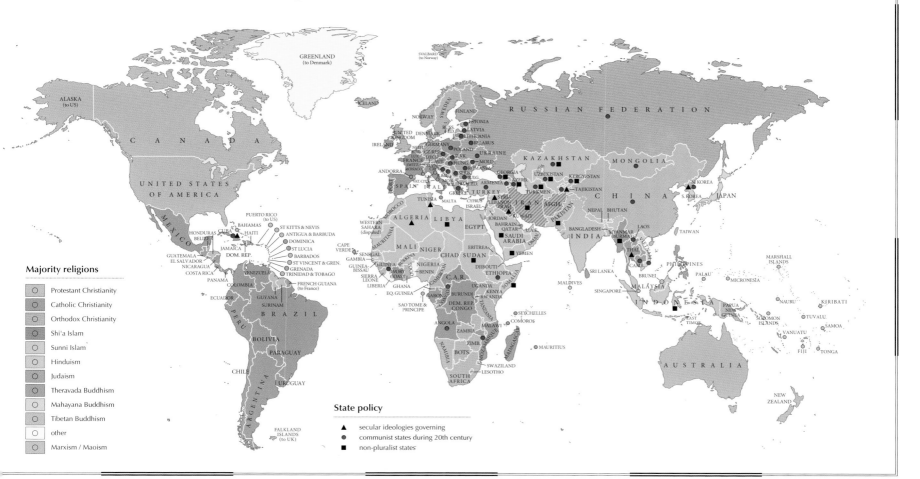

Majority religions

- Protestant Christianity
- Catholic Christianity
- Orthodox Christianity
- Shi'a Islam
- Sunni Islam
- Hinduism
- Judaism
- Theravada Buddhism
- Mahayana Buddhism
- Tibetan Buddhism
- other
- Marxism / Maoism

State policy

- ▲ secular ideologies governing
- ● communist states during 20th century
- ■ non-pluralist states

Health

On most health parameters, the countries of the world split into two distinct groups. The first of these encompass the richer, developed, countries, where medical care is good to excellent, infant mortality and the incidence of deadly infectious diseases is low, and life expectancy is high and rising. Some of the biggest health problems in these countries arise from overeating, while the two main causes of death are heart disease and cancer. The second region consists of the poorer developing countries, where medical care is much less adequate, infant mortality is high, many people are undernourished, and infectious diseases such as malaria are major killers. Life expectancy in these countries is much lower and in some cases is falling.

Life expectancy

Life expectancy has risen remarkably in developed countries over the past 50 years and has now topped 80 years in many of them. In contrast, life expectancy in many of the countries of sub-Saharan Africa has fallen well below 50, in large part due to the high prevalence of HIV/AIDS.

Many people in developed countries are now living for 15–20 years after retirement, putting greater pressure on welfare and health services.

Life expectancy
- above 80 years
- 75–80 years
- 70–75 years
- 60–70 years
- 50–60 years
- below 50 years

Infant deaths and births

Infant mortality is still high in many developing nations, especially some African countries, due in part to stretched medical services. As well as lower infant mortality, the world's developed countries have much lower birth rates – greater female emancipation and easier access to contraceptives are two causative factors.

World infant mortality rates (deaths per 1000 live births)
- above 125
- 75–124
- 35–74
- 15–34
- below 15

Number of births (per 1000 people)
- above 40
- 30–39
- 20–29
- below 20

United States of America: has an average life expectancy of about 78 years, though white people live on average about 5 years longer than black people, and women about 5 years longer than men.

Liberia: currently has one of the lowest life expectancies in West Africa, at less than 40 years, owing to factors such as high rates of infectious disease, recent conflict, and poverty.

Nutrition

Two-thirds of the world's food is consumed in developed nations, many of which have a daily calorific intake far higher than is needed by their populations. By contrast, about 800 million people in the developing world do not have enough food to meet basic nutritional needs.

The extensive public healthcare system in Cuba provides for around 6 doctors per 1000 people, one of the highest ratios in the world.

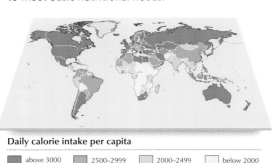

Daily calorie intake per capita
- above 3000
- 2500–2999
- 2000–2499
- below 2000

Healthcare

An indicator of the strength of healthcare provision in a country is the number of doctors per 1000 population. Some communist and former communist countries such as Cuba and Russia score well in this regard. In general, healthcare provision is good or adequate in most of the world's richer countries but scanty throughout much of Africa and in parts of Asia and Latin America.

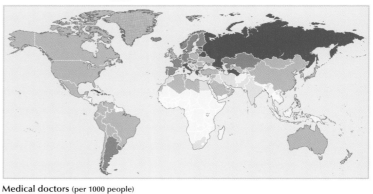

Medical doctors (per 1000 people)
- above 5
- 4–5
- 3–4
- 1–3
- 0.5–1
- below 0.5
- no data

Smoking

Cigarette smoking – one of the most harmful activities to health – is common throughout much of the world. Smoking prevalence is generally highest in the richer, developed countries. However, awareness of the health risks has seen cigarette consumption in most of these countries stabilise or begin to fall. By contrast, more and more people, especially males, are taking up the habit in poorer developing countries.

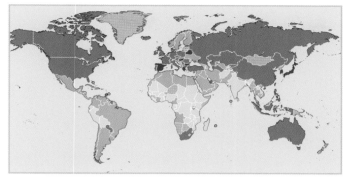

Annual cigarette consumption (per person)

▓ above 2500	▓ 500–1499	▓ no data
▓ 1500–2499	▓ 1–499	

Communicable diseases

Despite advances in their treatment and prevention, infectious diseases remain a huge problem, especially in developing countries. Three of the most common and deadly are tuberculosis (TB), HIV/AIDS and malaria. Of these, active TB affects about 15 million people (often as a complication of AIDS), with a particularly high prevalence in parts of Africa. HIV/AIDS has spread since 1981 to become a global pandemic. Malaria affects about 400 million people every year.

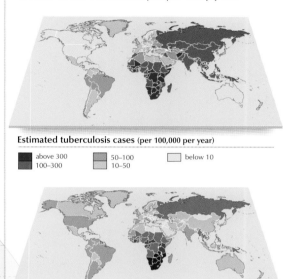

Estimated tuberculosis cases (per 100,000 per year)

▓ above 300	▓ 50–100	▓ below 10
▓ 100–300	▓ 10–50	

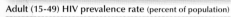

Adult (15-49) HIV prevalence rate (percent of population)

▓ 15–34	▓ 1–5	▓ 0.1–0.5	▓ no data
▓ 5–15	▓ 0.5–1	▓ below 0.1	

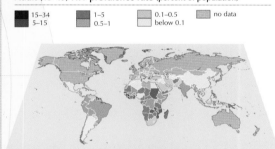

Malaria cases (per 100,000 per year)

▓ above 25,000	▓ 1000–10,000	▓ 10–100	▓ low risk
▓ 10,000–25,000	▓ 100–1000	▓ below 10	

Japan: has one of the world's highest life expectancies, at over 81 years – a fact commonly put down to the typical Japanese low fat diet of rice, fish and soy products.

Swaziland: currently has the lowest life expectancy in the world, at less than 33 years, due to widespread HIV/AIDS.

Preventive medicine

Throughout the world, doctors recognize that the prevention of disease and disease transmission is just as important as the treatment of illness. Preventive medicine has many aspects and includes advice about diet and nutrition; education about the avoidance of health-threatening behaviours such as smoking, excess alcohol consumption and unprotected sex; and the use of vaccines against diseases such as typhoid, polio and cholera. In developing countries, some of the main priorities in preventive medicine are the provision of pure water supplies and proper sanitation, as well as measures against malaria, including the use of antimalarial drugs and mosquito nets.

The use of mosquito nets greatly reduces the transmission of malaria and the risk of infection.

TOP TEN KILLER DISEASES, 2004

The world's biggest killer diseases fall into two main groups. One group, which includes HIV/AIDS, malaria, tuberculosis and childhood cluster diseases such as measles, mainly kills people in poor countries. The other group includes cardiovascular diseases and cancer, the big killers in rich countries.

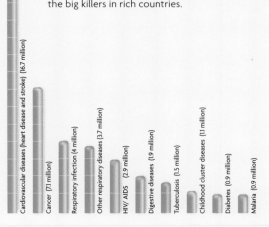

Cardiovascular diseases (heart disease and stroke) (16.7 million)
Cancer (7.1 million)
Respiratory infection (4 million)
Other respiratory diseases (3.7 million)
HIV/AIDS (2.9 million)
Digestive diseases (1.9 million)
Tuberculosis (1.5 million)
Childhood cluster diseases (1.1 million)
Diabetes (0.9 million)
Malaria (0.9 million)

Water Resources

Water covers 71 percent of Earth's surface, but only 2.5 percent of this is fresh water, and two thirds of that is locked up in glaciers and polar ice sheets. Patterns of human settlement have developed around fresh water availability but increasing numbers of people are now vulnerable to chronic shortage or interruptions in supply. Worldwide, fresh water consumption multiplied more than sixfold during the 20th century as populations increased and agriculture became more dependent on irrigation, much of it hugely wasteful because of evaporation and run-off. Industrial water demand also rose, as did use in the home, for washing, flushing, cooking and gardening.

Amid the desert of Wadi Rum, Jordan, crops grow on circular patches of land irrigated with water from an underground aquifer.

Water withdrawal

Agriculture accounts for 70 percent of water consumption worldwide. Industry and domestic use each account for 15 percent. Excessive withdrawal of water affects the health of rivers and the needs of people downstream. China's Yellow River now fails to reach the sea for most of the

Percentage of freshwater withdrawal by agriculture

| 79–100 | 66–79 | 47–66 | 31–47 | 16–31 | 0–16 |

Percentage of freshwater withdrawal by industry

| 79–100 | 66–79 | 47–66 | 31–47 | 16–31 | 0–16 |

Percentage of freshwater withdrawal by domestic use

| 60–81 | 45–60 | 30–45 | 15–30 | 0–15 | no data |

Availability of fresh water
total renewable
(cubic metres/capita/per year)

- less than 1000 (water scarcity)
- 1000–1699 (water stress)
- 1700–2999 (insufficient water)
- 3000–9999 (relatively sufficient)
- 10,000 or more (plentiful supplies)
- major drainage basin
- over 50% of water resource originating from outside country

Map labels: USA (Alaska), Yukon, Greenland (to Denmark), Mackenzie, CANADA, ICELAND, UNITED KINGDOM, IRELAND, St. Lawrence, UNITED STATES OF AMERICA, ATLANTIC OCEAN, PORTUGAL, SPAIN, FRANCE, Colorado, Mississippi/Missouri, Rio Grande, MEXICO, Hawai'i (to US), BAHAMAS, CUBA, JAMAICA, HAITI, DOMINICAN REPUBLIC, BELIZE, GUATEMALA, HONDURAS, EL SALVADOR, NICARAGUA, COSTA RICA, PANAMA, ST KITTS & NEVIS, ANTIGUA & BARBUDA, BARBADOS, TRINIDAD & TOBAGO, VENEZUELA, GUYANA, SURINAM, French Guiana (to France), COLOMBIA, Orinoco, ECUADOR, PERU, Amazon, BRAZIL, São Francisco, BOLIVIA, Paraná, PARAGUAY, Paraná, CHILE, ARGENTINA, URUGUAY, PACIFIC OCEAN, WESTERN SAHARA (occupied by Morocco), MOROCCO, ALGERIA, MAURITANIA, MALI, CAPE VERDE, SENEGAL, GAMBIA, GUINEA-BISSAU, GUINEA, SIERRA LEONE, LIBERIA, IVORY COAST, GHANA, TOGO, BURKINA, Niger, EQUATORIAL, SAO, SOUTHERN OCEAN

Drought

The disruption of normal rainfall patterns can cause drought problems even in temperate zones, with consequences ranging from domestic water usage restrictions to low crop yields to forest fires. In regions of the developing world where monsoon rains fail, or water is perennially scarce, drought is a life or death issue. Parts of central and east Africa, for instance, have suffered severe and recurring droughts in recent decades, with disastrous results including destruction of livestock, desertification, famine and mass migration.

In a severe drought, river beds may dry up *(above left)*, leaving stranded fish to die, as here in Florida.

A Chinese farmer waters dry fields *(above)* in China's southern province of Guangdong. This picture was taken in May 2002, but the image is timeless; it could be August 2006 in Sichuan province, to the northwest of here – or almost any year in water-stressed northern China.

RUSSIAN FEDERATION

KAZAKHSTAN
MONGOLIA
UZBEKISTAN
KYRG.
TURKMEN.
TAJ.
AFGHANISTAN
CHINA
NORTH KOREA
SOUTH KOREA
JAPAN
IRAN
PAKISTAN
Yellow River
Yangtze
TAIWAN
NEPAL BHUTAN
Ganges/ Brahmaputra
BANGLADESH
INDIA
MYANMAR (BURMA)
LAOS
Mekong
VIETNAM
THAILAND
CAMBODIA
PHILIPPINES
BRUNEI
PALAU
SRI LANKA
MALDIVES
MALAYSIA
SINGAPORE
SEYCHELLES
INDONESIA
PAPUA NEW GUINEA
EAST TIMOR

PACIFIC OCEAN
INDIAN OCEAN

AUSTRALIA
Murray/ Darling
NEW ZEALAND

FINLAND
EST.
LAL.
LITH.
BELARUS
POLAND
UKRAINE
Volga
ROMANIA
MOLDOVA
Danube
BULGARIA
GEORGIA
ARMENIA AZERB.
TURKEY
GREECE
CYPRUS
LEBANON
SYRIA
ISRAEL
GAZA STRIP
JORDAN
WEST BANK
IRAQ
KUWAIT
BAHRAIN
QATAR
UAE
OMAN
SAUDI ARABIA
YEMEN
EGYPT
SUDAN
ERITREA
DJIBOUTI
ETHIOPIA
SOMALIA
CENTRAL AFRICAN REPUBLIC
UGANDA
KENYA
DEM. REP. CONGO
RWANDA
BURUNDI
TANZANIA
COMOROS
MALAWI
ZAMBIA
Zambezi
MOZAMBIQUE
MADAGASCAR
ZIMBABWE
BOTSWANA
MAURITIUS
Réunion (to France)
Orange
SWAZILAND
LESOTHO
SOUTH AFRICA
Lena
Ob'
Yenisey
Amur
Tigris/ Euphrates
Indus
Nile

Water stress

A region is under 'water stress' when the rate of water withdrawal from its rivers and aquifers exceeds their natural replenishment, so that people living there are subject to frequent shortages. Currently 1.7 billion people live in 'highly stressed' river basins worldwide. This is a major potential cause of conflict, particularly when several countries share one river; the Euphrates, running through Turkey, Syria and Iraq, or the rivers of southern China running south into Korea, are just two examples.

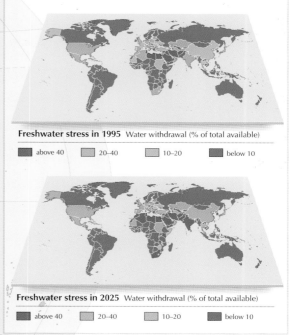

Freshwater stress in 1995 Water withdrawal (% of total available)

- above 40
- 20–40
- 10–20
- below 10

Freshwater stress in 2025 Water withdrawal (% of total available)

- above 40
- 20–40
- 10–20
- below 10

WATER AVAILABILITY

(by percentage of world's population)

relative sufficiency

Plentiful 16.3%

Water scarcity 7.8%

Water stress 24.5%

Relatively sufficient 24.5%

Insufficient 16.7%

insufficiency

Clean drinking water

Sub-Saharan Africa is among the most deprived regions for lack of access to safe drinking water. Worldwide, this terrible health hazard affects over a billion people – at least 15 percent of the population. One of the agreed United Nations 'millennium goals' for international development is to halve this proportion by 2015, by tackling chemical pollution from agriculture and industry, and by introducing essential purification facilities and local supply systems. In the industrialized world, people have come to expect clean drinking water on tap, even if they face rising prices for its treatment and supply.

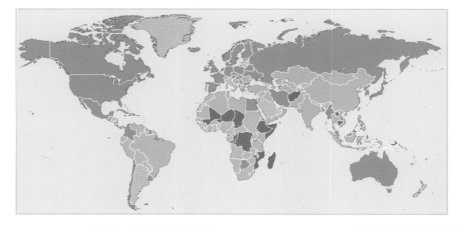

Mozambican children *(above)* fetch precious water in metal pans.

Gujarati villagers gather to draw water from a huge well *(above left)* in Natwarghad, western India. Many wells and village ponds ran dry in the severe drought of 2003, leaving local people to wait for irregular supplies brought in by state-run tankers.

Access to safe
drinking water source
(percentage of population)

- 91%–100%
- 76%–90%
- 50%–75%

- below 50%
- no data

Economic Systems

The world economy is now effectively a single global system based on 'free market' capitalist principles. Few countries still cling, like North Korea, to the 'command economy' formula developed in the former communist bloc, where centralised state plans set targets for investment and production. In the West, state ownership of companies has greatly diminished thanks to the wave of privatisation in the last 25 years. Major companies move capital and raw materials around the globe to take advantage of different labour costs and skills. The World Trade Organization (WTO) promotes free trade, but many countries still use subsidies, and protect their markets with import tariffs or quotas, to favour their own producers.

Enormous volumes of trade pass through the world's stock markets making them key indicators of the strength of the global economy.

Balance of trade

Few countries earn from their exports exactly as much as they spend on imports. If the imbalance is persistently negative, it creates a potentially serious problem of indebtedness. The European Union's (EU) external trade is broadly in balance, but the US balance of trade has been in deficit since the 1970s, partly because it imports so many consumer goods. This deficit has recently spiralled to over US$ 800 billion a year.

Balance of trade
(million US$)

over 30,000	
10,000–29,000	
1000–9999	Surplus
0–999	
0–999	
1000–9999	
10,000–29,999	Deficit
over 30,000	
data unavailable	

TOP TEN GLOBAL COMPANIES

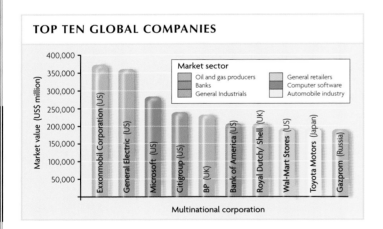

Market sector
- Oil and gas producers
- Banks
- General Industrials
- General retailers
- Computer software
- Automobile industry

Market value (US$ million)

- Exxonmobil Corporation (US)
- General Electric (US)
- Microsoft (US)
- Citigroup (US)
- BP (UK)
- Bank of America (US)
- Royal Dutch Shell (UK)
- Wal-Mart Stores (US)
- Toyota Motors (Japan)
- Gazprom (Russia)

Multinational corporation

Energy

Countries with oil and gas to sell (notably in the Middle East and Russia) can charge high prices; trade in fuel was worth US$ 1.4 trillion in 2005. The US and others are turning back to nuclear power (despite safety fears) for generating electricity. China relies heavily on (polluting) coal. Renewable technologies promise much, but so far make relatively minor contributions.

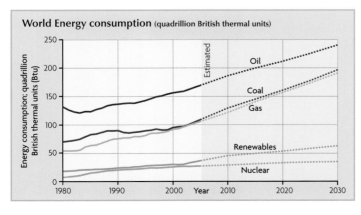

World Energy consumption (quadrillion British thermal units)

Energy consumption; quadrillion British thermal units (Btu)

- Estimated
- Oil
- Coal
- Gas
- Renewables
- Nuclear

1980 1990 2000 Year 2010 2020 2030

Energy balance (Quadrillion British thermal units)

net producer	10 and above	5 to 10	1 to 5	0 to 1	data unavailable
net consumer	0 to -1	-1 to -5	-5 to -10	-10 and below	

SOUTH AMERICA

New York

London

EUROPE

AFRICA

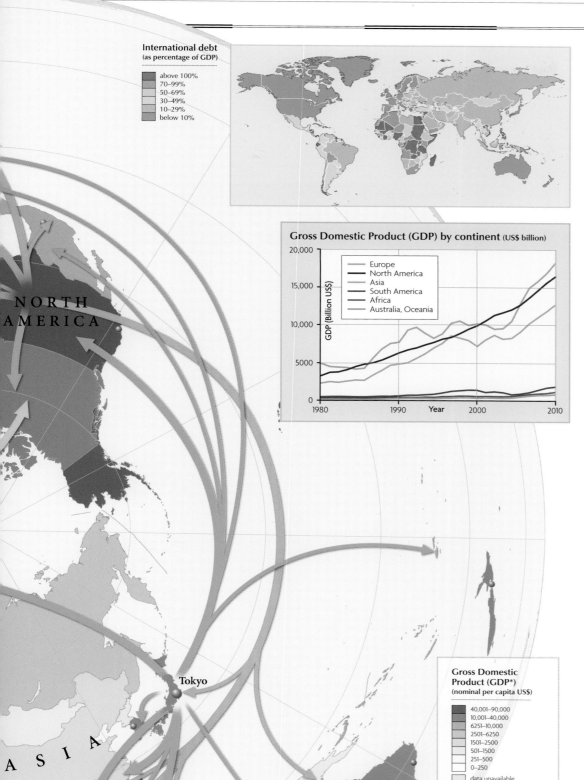

International debt

International debt
(as percentage of GDP)

- above 100%
- 70–99%
- 50–69%
- 30–49%
- 10–29%
- below 10%

Saddled with crippling debts from past borrowing, the world's poorest countries are still paying off US$ 100 million a day. This is despite recent successful campaigns to get some of their debts cancelled to allow them to use their limited resources for development. Most international debt, however, is owed by developed countries to one another. The US owes literally trillions of dollars, nearly a third of it's total debt, to Japan.

Gross Domestic Product (GDP) by continent (US$ billion)

- Europe
- North America
- Asia
- South America
- Africa
- Australia, Oceania

Trade sector

World trade in merchandise tops US$ 10 trillion a year. The global pattern is uneven. Latin America, Africa, the Middle East and Russia principally export 'primary' goods (agricultural produce, mining and fuel). The 'secondary' manufacturing sector includes iron and steel, machine tools, chemicals, clothing and textiles, cars and other consumer goods. The West still dominates the 'tertiary' or non-merchandise sector, worth US$ 2.4 trillion, in services such as insurance and banking.

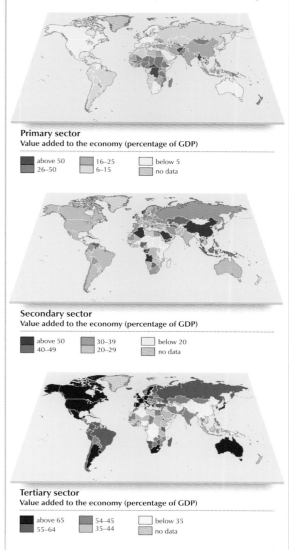

Primary sector
Value added to the economy (percentage of GDP)
- above 50
- 26–50
- 16–25
- 6–15
- below 5
- no data

Secondary sector
Value added to the economy (percentage of GDP)
- above 50
- 40–49
- 30–39
- 20–29
- below 20
- no data

Tertiary sector
Value added to the economy (percentage of GDP)
- above 65
- 55–64
- 54–45
- 35–44
- below 35
- no data

Gross Domestic Product (GDP*)
(nominal per capita US$)
- 40,001–90,000
- 10,001–40,000
- 6251–10,000
- 2501–6250
- 1501–2500
- 501–1500
- 251–500
- 0–250
- data unavailable

*Gross Domestic Product (GDP) is defined as the total market value of all final goods and services produced in a country.

Direct Investment
- from USA
- from Europe
- from Japan
- major stock exchange
- stock exchange

Tokyo

Average monthly salary (US$)
- above 3000
- 2000–3000
- 1000–2000
- 500–1000
- 250–500
- below 250
- no data

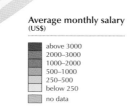

Labour

China's huge low-cost labour force promotes its conquest of world markets for manufactured goods. India's educated workforce attracts call centres and other service sector jobs, while the more economically developed countries's (MEDC) caring professions, and low-wage agriculture, draw in immigrant labour.

THE WORLD

33

Travel

Mass travel is now a ubiquitous feature of all developed countries, and the provision of transport and tourism facilities one of the world's biggest industries, employing well over 100 million people. The travel explosion has come about, first, through major improvements in transport technology; and second, as a result of increasing amounts of disposable income and leisure time in the world's wealthier countries. The main reasons for travel today include leisure pursuits and tourism (accounting for well over half of the total financial outlay), work and business, pilgrimage, migration and visits to family and friends.

There are currently around 4.2 billion air travellers a year passing through over 1600 international and domestic airports. This figure is forecast to grow by 4 percent per annum, leading to increased pressure on air traffic control and ground handling systems that, in many areas, are already close to their maximum capacity.

Major modes of transport

The major transport modes for people in the 21st century are road, rail and air travel. The most popular air routes are highly concentrated within and between the USA, western Europe, and the Far East. Major roads and railways are more evenly spread, following the general distribution of the world's population.

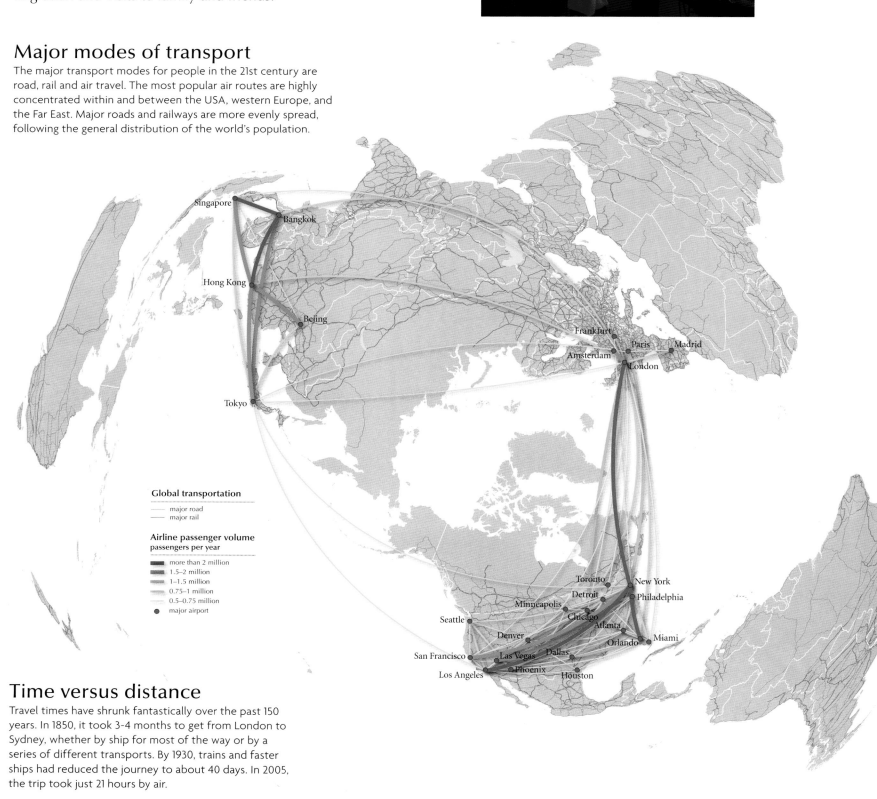

Global transportation

— major road
— major rail

Airline passenger volume
passengers per year

- more than 2 million
- 1.5–2 million
- 1–1.5 million
- 0.75–1 million
- 0.5–0.75 million
- ● major airport

Time versus distance

Travel times have shrunk fantastically over the past 150 years. In 1850, it took 3-4 months to get from London to Sydney, whether by ship for most of the way or by a series of different transports. By 1930, trains and faster ships had reduced the journey to about 40 days. In 2005, the trip took just 21 hours by air.

London

| 1850 | by coach to Portsmouth and thence ship around the Cape of Good Hope |

Istanbul — **Basra**

| 1850 | coach . ferry . coach . horseback — horseback . river boat — rive |

Istanbul — **Basra** — **Bombay** — **Calcutta** — **Singapore** — **Sydney**

| 1930 | train . ferry . train | train . river boat | river boat . steamship | train | steamship | steamship |

| 2005 | ●I● London–Sydney by air including one refueling stop |

| DAYS | 1 2 3 4 5 6 7 8 9 10 11 12 13 14 15 16 17 18 19 20 21 22 23 24 25 26 27 28 29 30 31 32 33 34 35 36 37 38 39 40 41 42 43 44 45 46 47 48 49 50 51 52 53 54 |

Media and Communications

Over the past 50 years, the term 'media' has come to denote various means of communicating information between people at a distance. These include mass media – methods such as newspapers, radio and television that can be used to rapidly disseminate information to large numbers of people – and two-way systems, such as telephones and e-mail. Currently, the communication systems undergoing the most rapid growth worldwide include mobile telephony and various Internet-based applications, such as web sites, blogs and podcasting, which can be considered forms of mass media.

Internet usage

Internet usage has grown extremely rapidly since the early 1990s, largely as a result of the invention of the World Wide Web. Usage rates are highest in the USA (where about 80 percent of people were using the Internet in 2006), Australia, Japan, South Korea and Finland. They are lowest in Africa, where on average less than 5 percent of the population were Internet users in 2006.

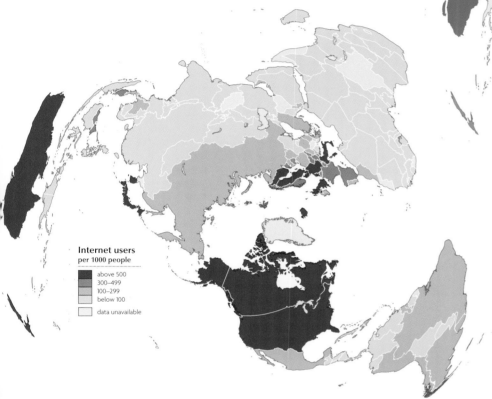

Internet users
per 1000 people

- above 500
- 300–499
- 100–299
- below 100
- data unavailable

Mobile phone usage

By 2006, there were more than 2.5 billion mobile phone users worldwide. In some parts of Europe, such as Italy, almost everyone owns and uses a mobile – many possess more than one phone. In contrast, throughout much of Southern Asia and Africa, less than 10 percent of the population are users. As well as utilizing them as telephones, most users now employ the devices for the additional functions they offer, such as text messaging and e-mail.

Mobile phone users
per 1000 people

- above 900
- 700–899
- 500–699
- 300–499
- 100–299
- below 100
- data unavailable

The internet emerged in the early 1990s as a computer-based global communication system. Since then massive growth has seen user numbers increase to around 1.1 billion people, or roughly 17 percent of the world's population.

Satellite Communications

Modern communications satellites are used extensively for international telephony, for television and radio broadcasting, and to some extent for transmitting Internet data. Many of these satellites are deployed in clusters or arrays, often in geostationary orbits – that is, in positions that appear fixed to Earth-based observers.

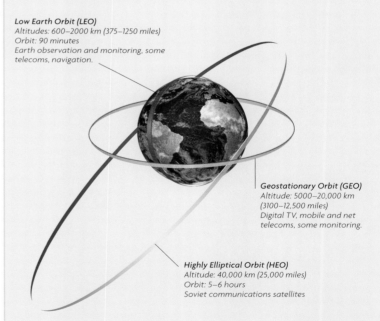

Low Earth Orbit (LEO)
Altitudes: 600–2000 km (375–1250 miles)
Orbit: 90 minutes
Earth observation and monitoring, some telecoms, navigation.

Geostationary Orbit (GEO)
Altitude: 5000–20,000 km (3100–12,500 miles)
Digital TV, mobile and net telecoms, some monitoring.

Highly Elliptical Orbit (HEO)
Altitude: 40,000 km (25,000 miles)
Orbit: 5–6 hours
Soviet communications satellites

Sydney

Bombay · Calcutta · Singapore · Sydney

steamship · horseback · steamship · steamship

59 60 61 62 63 64 65 66 67 68 69 70 71 72 73 74 75 76 77 78 79 80 81 82 83 84 85 86 87 88 89 90 91 92 93 94 95 96 97 98 99 100 101 102 103 104 105 106 107 108 109 110 111 112 113 114 115

The Political World

Today's world map shows nearly 200 independent states, compared with about 80 after the Second World War. The transformation is mainly due to the withdrawal of European powers from huge colonial empires; their remaining overseas dependencies are tiny by comparison. The late 20th century also saw the collapse of communism, realignment in Europe, and fragmentation in former Yugoslavia. Globally, the Soviet Union's demise left the USA as the sole superpower, though with fast-growing China and India emerging as economic giants of the future. US security preoccupations switched to combating terrorism, while looming oil and other resource shortages, and environmental constraints, underlined the need for more effective international cooperation.

CONTINENTAL FACTFILE

	Total area: sq miles	Total area: sq km	Total population
North & Central America	8,621,846	22,327,375	516.8 million
South America	6,839,892	17,715,315	380.2 million
Africa	11,617,219	30,088,602	924.6 million
Europe	3,596,737	9,341,459	711.5 million
Asia	17,469,967	45,246,231	3978.2 million
Australia & Oceania	3,275,288	8,483,003	32.7 million

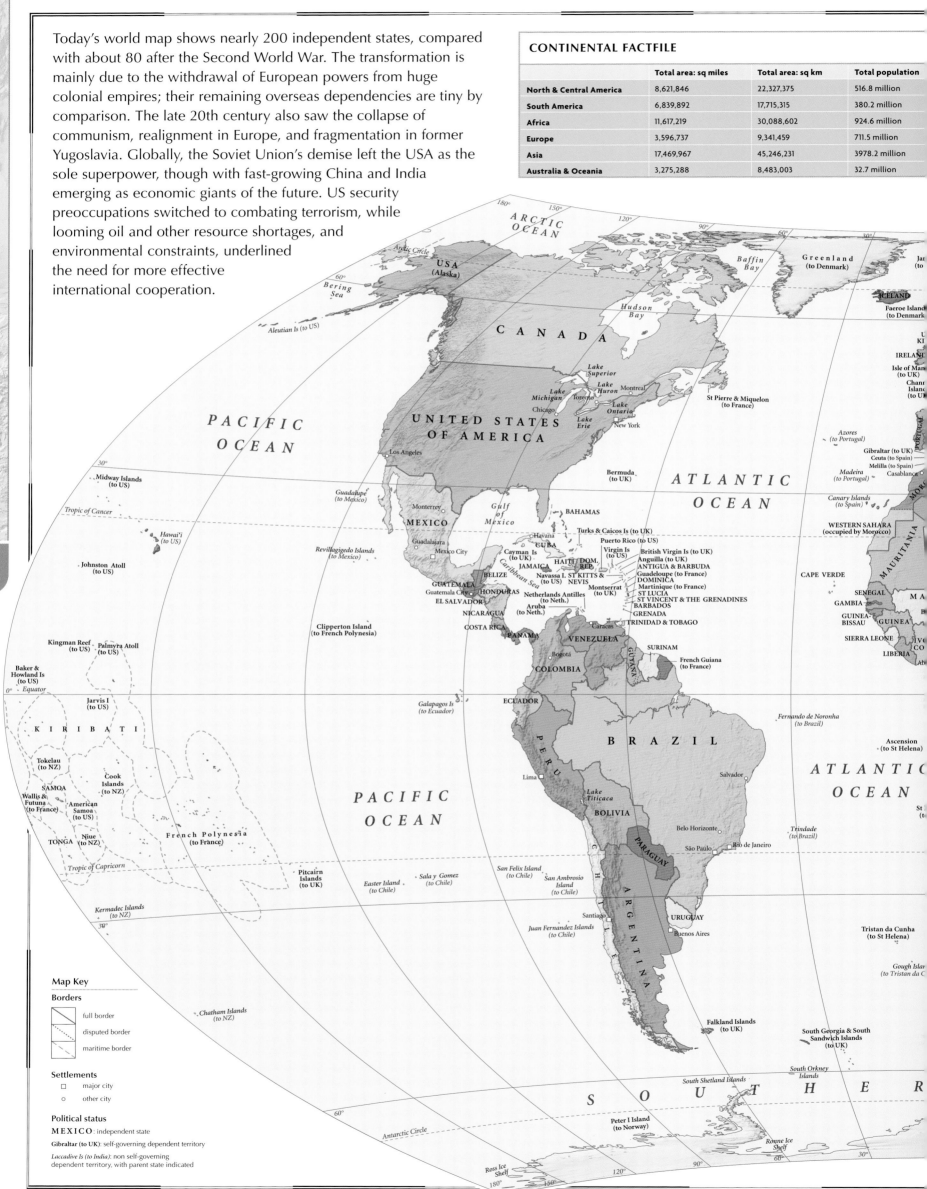

Map Key

Borders

full border

disputed border

maritime border

Settlements

□ major city

○ other city

Political status

MEXICO: independent state

Gibraltar (to UK): self-governing dependent territory

Laccadive Is (to India): non self-governing dependent territory, with parent state indicated

Countries	Largest country	Country with largest population
23	Canada 3,855,171 sq miles (9,984,670 sq km)	United States 301 million
2	Brazil 3,286,470 sq miles (8,511,965 sq km)	Brazil 188.9 million
53	Sudan 967,493 sq miles (2,505,810 sq km)	Nigeria 134.4 million
46	European Russia 1,527,341 sq miles (3,955,818 sq km)	European Russia 114 million
48	Asiatic Russia 5,065,394 sq miles (13,119,382 sq km)	China 1323.6 million
14	Australia 2,967,893 sq miles (7,686,850 sq km)	Australia 20.4 million

International borders

The world political map of today displays a complex pattern of boundaries that has evolved through history, and is still constantly changing as new countries emerge and disputes and territorial claims are slowly resolved. The map shows two main types of border. Full borders represent internationally agreed and recognized territorial boundaries. A disputed border is indicated where a *de facto* territorial boundary exists, which is not agreed or is still subject to arbitration.

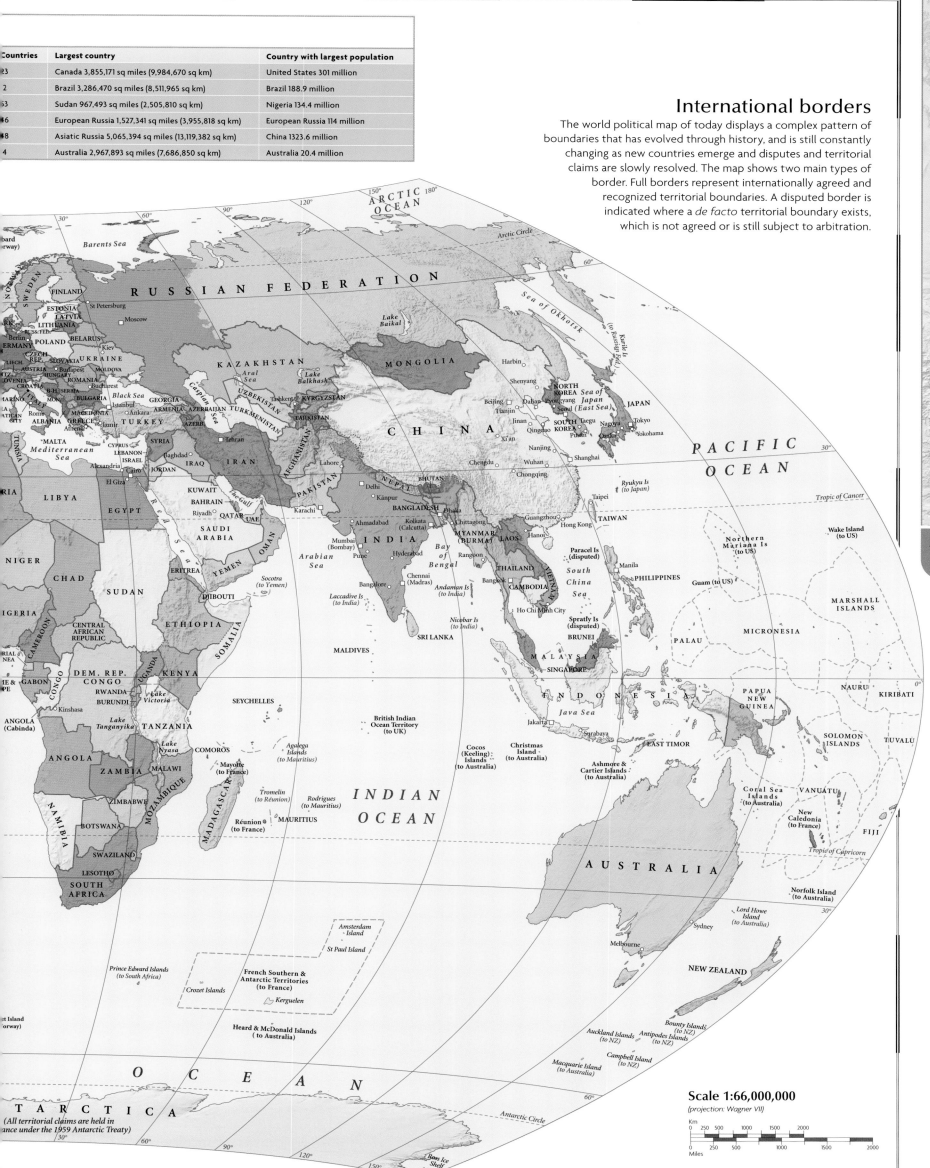

Scale 1:66,000,000

(projection: Wagner VII)

Borders, conflicts and disputes

Conflict evolved in the 20th century from conventional land- or sea-based warfare to increasingly long-range airborne attacks. Nuclear arms from 1945 took this to the intercontinental scale. The Cold War presented a new type of conflict, underlined by the race for weapons capabilities between the US and the Soviet Union. In Korea, Vietnam, the Middle East and elsewhere, soldiers and civilians were exposed to deadly chemicals. International treaties aimed to prevent the spread of nuclear, biological and chemical 'weapons of mass destruction' – especially to 'pariah states' like Libya and Iran. Intercommunal conflict and 'ethnic cleansing' reminded the world that horror needed no sophisticated weaponry. After 9/11, the US-led 'war on terror' perceived conflict in a new light, where international terrorism knew no borders.

THE PEACEKEEPERS

Over 130 countries have contributed around a million troops to UN missions to monitor peace processes and help implement peace accords since 1948. Regional alliances such as NATO and the African Union (AU) are increasingly deploying their own multinational forces in trouble-spots, while Australia has intervened in a similar manner in nearby Pacific island states. Peacekeepers oversaw East Timor's elections in 2001 and subsequent celebration of independence (above). The US position as sole global superpower enables it to define many of its activities as peacekeeping, despite the confrontational nature of its interventions.

DARFUR

African ethnic minorities in Darfur in western Sudan have suffered appalling violence since 2003 at the hands of genocidal Arab Janjaweed militias, for which the government in Khartoum denies responsibility. Displaced in their hundreds of thousands, refugees receive inadequate protection and aid from an international community unwilling to commit to full-scale intervention.

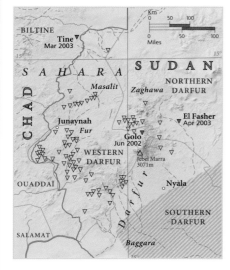

Darfur conflict

- *Fur* ethnic group
- arabic speaking area
- ▽ villages destroyed by Janjaweed
- ▼ towns that have been attacked by rebels opposing the Sudanese government

ISRAEL

Since its creation in 1948, Israel has been at war with its Arab neighbours. The Palestinians are fighting for a separate and viable state, comprising of at least East Jerusalem, and the West Bank and Gaza Strip, territories occupied by Israel in 1967. Their struggle (intifada) has attracted international support, but has been met by a hard-line response from Israel, which is backed by the US.

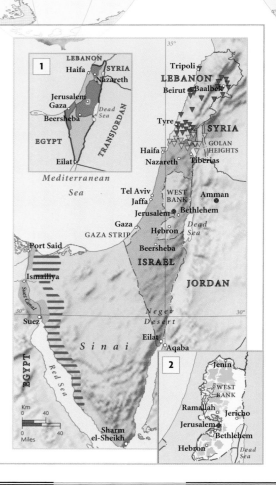

Arab-Israeli Wars 1947-2006

MAIN MAP: Arab-Israeli Wars
- Israel in 1949
- occupied by Israel after 1967 war
- occupied by Israel after 1973 war
- occupied by Israel after 1967 war reoccupied by Egypt after 1973 war
- demilitarized zone held by UN after Israel-Syria agreement, 1974, and 2nd Sinai agreement, 1975
- ▽ Hezbollah rocket attacks 2006
- ▼ Israeli rocket attacks 2006
- – · disputed border

INSET MAP 1: UN Partition plan in 1947
- border of British mandate 1923
- proposed Arab State
- proposed Jewish State
- proposed international zone

INSET MAP 2: West Bank security
- Palestinian responsibility for civil affairs and internal security
- Palestinian responsibility for civil affairs; Israel responsible for security
- Security Wall (existing and planned)

Types of government

- Multiparty democracy for more than 10 yrs
- Multiparty/transitional democracy within last 10 yrs
- Single-party government
- Military regime
- Theocracy
- Absolute monarchy

Conflicts and international disputes

- Major active territorial or border disputes
- Countries involved in internal conflict
- Active territorial or border disputes and internal conflict

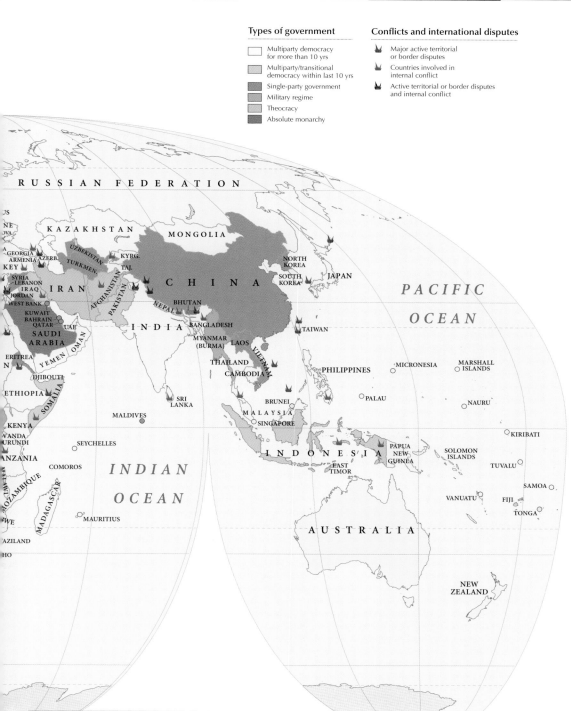

Lines on the map

The determination of international boundaries can use a variety of criteria. Many borders between older states follow physical boundaries, often utilizing natural defensive features. Others have been determined by international agreement or arbitration, or simply ended up where the opposing forces stood at the end of a conflict.

WORLD BOUNDARIES

Dates from which current boundaries have existed

- 1990–present
- 1966–1989
- 1946–1965
- 1915–1945
- 1850–1914
- 1800–1849
- Pre-1800

POST-COLONIAL BORDERS

Independent African countries have largely inherited the earlier carve up of the continent by European colonial powers. These often arbitrarily divided or grouped differing ethnic and religious groups which has, in turn, contributed to the tensions that underlie the many civil conflicts that have plagued post-colonial Africa .

ENCLAVES

Changes to international boundaries occasionally create pockets of land cut off from the main territory of the country they belong to. In Europe, Kaliningrad has been separated from the rest of the Russian Federation since the independence of the Baltic States. Likewise, when Morocco was granted independence, Spain retained the coastal enclaves of Ceuta and Melilla.

GEOMETRIC BORDERS

Straight lines and lines of longitude and latitude have occasionally been used to determine international boundaries: the 49th Parallel forms a large section of the Canada–US border, while the 38th Parallel divides the Korean Peninsula. Internal administrative divisions within Canada, the US and Australia also use geometric boundaries.

PHYSICAL BORDERS

Rivers account for one-sixth of the world's borders: the Danube forms part of the boundaries for nine European nations. Changes in a river's course or disruption of its flow can lead to territorial disputes. Lakes and mountains also form natural borders.

Lake border (right)
Mountain border (below left)
River border (below right)

THE GULF WAR

Although the West armed Saddam Hussein in the brutal 1980s Iran-Iraq War, his unprovoked invasion of Kuwait in 1990 was decried the world over. A US-led coalition, including Arab states, repelled his troops but left him in power. A decade of sanctions followed until, in 2003, Saddam was finally toppled by US-led forces. Following elections in 2005, Iraq has struggled to contain a violent insurgency.

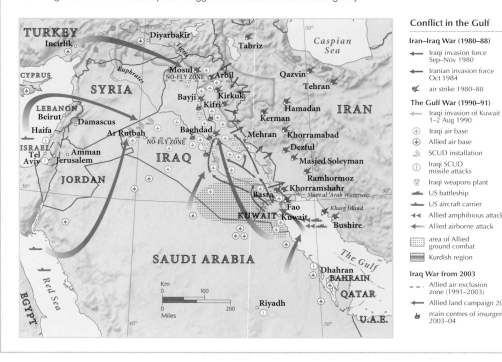

Conflict in the Gulf

Iran–Iraq War (1980–88)

- ← Iraqi invasion force Sep–Nov 1980
- ← Iranian invasion force Oct 1984
- ⚔ air strike 1980–88

The Gulf War (1990–91)

- ← Iraqi invasion of Kuwait 1–2 Aug 1990
- ⊕ Iraqi air base
- ⊕ Allied air base
- ⚲ SCUD installation
- ⊙ Iraqi SCUD missile attacks
- ▨ Iraqi weapons plant
- ⚓ US battleship
- ⚓ US aircraft carrier
- ◄◄ Allied amphibious attack
- ◄◄ Allied airborne attack
- ▦ area of Allied ground combat
- ■ Kurdish region

Iraq War from 2003

- --- Allied air exclusion zone (1991–2003)
- ← Allied land campaign 2003
- ⚔ main centres of insurgency 2003–04

The World's Time Zones

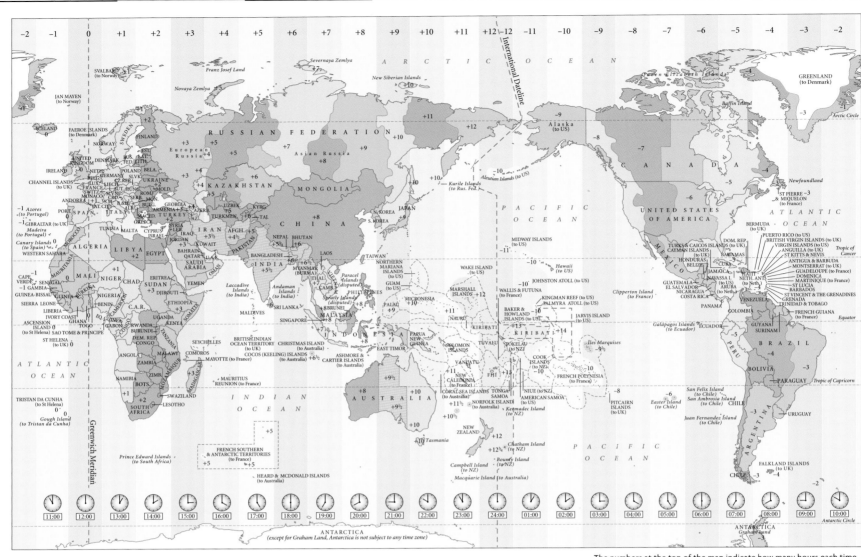

The numbers at the top of the map indicate how many hours each time zone is ahead or behind Coordinated Universal Time (UTC). The row of clocks indicate the time in each zone when it is 12:00 noon UTC.

TIME ZONES

Because Earth is a rotating sphere, the Sun shines on only half of its surface at any one time. Thus, it is simultaneously morning, evening and night time in different parts of the world (see diagram below). Because of these disparities, each country or part of a country adheres to a local time. A region of Earth's surface within which a single local time is used is called a time zone. There are 24 one hour time zones around the world, arranged roughly in longitudinal bands.

STANDARD TIME

Standard time is the official local time in a particular country or part of a country. It is defined by the time zone or zones associated with that country or region. Although time zones are arranged roughly in longitudinal bands, in many places the borders of a zone do not fall exactly on longitudinal meridians, as can be seen on the map (above),

but are determined by geographical factors or by borders between countries or parts of countries. Most countries have just one time zone and one standard time, but some large countries (such as the USA, Canada and Russia) are split between several time zones, so standard time varies across those countries. For example, the coterminous United States straddles four time zones and so has four standard times, called the Eastern, Central, Mountain and Pacific standard times. China is unusual in that just one standard time is used for the whole country, even though it extends across 60° of longitude from west to east.

COORDINATED UNIVERSAL TIME (UTC)

Coordinated Universal Time (UTC) is a reference by which the local time in each time zone is set. For example, Australian Western Standard Time (the local time in Western Australia) is set 8 hours ahead of UTC (it is UTC+8) whereas Eastern Standard Time in the United States is set 5

hours behind UTC (it is UTC-5). UTC is a successor to, and closely approximates, Greenwich Mean Time (GMT). However, UTC is based on an atomic clock, whereas GMT is determined by the Sun's position in the sky relative to the 0° longitudinal meridian, which runs through Greenwich, UK.

In 1884 the Prime Meridian (0° longitude) was defined by the position of the cross-hairs in the eyepiece of the 'Transit Circle' telescope in the Meridian Building at the Royal Observatory, Greenwich, UK.

DAY AND NIGHT AROUND THE WORLD

THE INTERNATIONAL DATELINE

The International Dateline is an imaginary line from pole to pole that roughly corresponds to the 180° longitudinal meridian. It is an arbitrary marker between calendar days. The dateline is needed because of the use of local times around the world rather than a single universal time. When moving from west to east across the dateline, travellers have to set their watches back one day. Those travelling in the opposite direction, from east to west, must add a day.

DAYLIGHT SAVING TIME

Daylight saving is a summertime adjustment to the local time in a country or region, designed to cause a higher proportion of its citizens' waking hours to pass during daylight. To follow the system, timepieces are advanced by an hour on a pre-decided date in spring and reverted back in autumn. About half of the world's nations use daylight saving.

ATLAS
OF THE WORLD

THE MAPS IN THIS ATLAS ARE ARRANGED CONTINENT BY CONTINENT, STARTING
FROM THE INTERNATIONAL DATE LINE, AND MOVING EASTWARDS. THE MAPS PROVIDE
A UNIQUE VIEW OF TODAY'S WORLD, COMBINING TRADITIONAL CARTOGRAPHIC
TECHNIQUES WITH THE LATEST REMOTE-SENSED AND DIGITAL TECHNOLOGY.

North America is the world's third largest continent with
a total area of 9,358,340 sq miles (24,238,000 sq km)
including Greenland and the Caribbean islands.
It lies wholly within the Northern Hemisphere.

FACTFILE

N Most Northerly Point: Kap Morris Jesup, Greenland 83° 38′ N
S Most Southerly Point: Peninsula de Azuero, Panama 7° 15′ N
E Most Easterly Point: Nordøstrundingen, Greenland 12° 08′ W
W Most Westerly Point: Attu, Aleutian Islands, USA 172° 30′ E

Largest Lakes:
1 Lake Superior, Canada/USA 31,151 sq miles (83,270 sq km)
2 Lake Huron, Canada/USA 23,436 sq miles (60,700 sq km)
3 Lake Michigan, USA 22,402 sq miles (58,020 sq km)
4 Great Bear Lake, Canada 12,274 sq miles (31,790 sq km)
5 Great Slave Lake, Canada 10,981 sq miles (28,440 sq km)

Longest Rivers:
1 Mississippi-Missouri, USA 3710 miles (5969 km)
2 Mackenzie, Canada 2640 miles (4250 km)
3 Yukon, Canada/USA 1978 miles (3184 km)
4 St Lawrence/Great Lakes, Canada/USA 1900 miles (3058 km)
5 Rio Grande, Mexico/USA 1900 miles (3057 km)

Largest Islands:
1 Greenland 849,400 sq miles (2,200,000 sq km)
2 Baffin Island, Canada 183,800 sq miles (476,000 sq km)
3 Victoria Island, Canada 81,900 sq miles (212,000 sq km)
4 Ellesmere Island, Canada 75,700 sq miles (196,000 sq km)
5 Newfoundland, Canada 42,031 sq miles (108,860 sq km)

Highest Points:
1 Mount McKinley (Denali), USA 20,332 ft (6194 m)
2 Mount Logan, Canada 19,550 ft (5959 m)
3 Volcán Pico de Orizaba, Mexico 18,700 ft (5700 m)
4 Mount St Elias, USA 18,008 ft (5489 m)
5 Popocatépetl, Mexico 17,887 ft (5452 m)

Lowest Point:
▼ Death Valley, USA -282 ft (-86 m) below sea level

Highest recorded temperature:
＋ Death Valley, USA 135°F (57°C)

Lowest recorded temperature:
－ Northice, Greenland -87°F (-66°C)

Wettest Place:
≋ Vancouver, Canada 183 in (4645 mm)

Driest Place:
⌒ Death Valley, USA 2 in (50 mm)

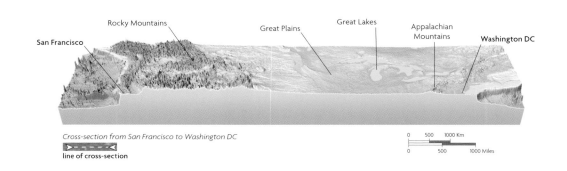

Cross-section from San Francisco to Washington DC
▷ ─ ─ ─ ◁
line of cross-section

0   500   1000 Km
0   500   1000 Miles

Political

Democracy is well established in some parts of the continent but is a recent phenomenon in others. The economically dominant nations of Canada and the USA have a long democratic tradition but elsewhere, notably in the countries of Central America, political turmoil has been more common. In Nicaragua and Haiti, harsh dictatorships have only recently been superseded by democratically-elected governments. North America's largest countries, Canada, Mexico and the USA have federal state systems, sharing political power between national and state governments. The USA has intervened militarily on several occasions in Central America and the Caribbean to protect its strategic interests.

Transport

In the 19th century, railways were used to open up the North American continent. Air transport is now more common for long distance passenger travel, although railways are still extensively used for bulk freight transport. Waterways, like the Mississippi River, are important for the transport of bulk materials, and the Panama Canal is a vital link between the Pacific Ocean and the Caribbean. In the 20th century, road transport increased massively in North America, with the introduction of cheap, mass-produced motor cars and extensive highway construction.

Transport

— major roads and motorways
— major railways
— major canals
-- international borders
• transport intersections
⊕ international airports
⊕ major ports

Standard of living
(UN human development index)

high

low

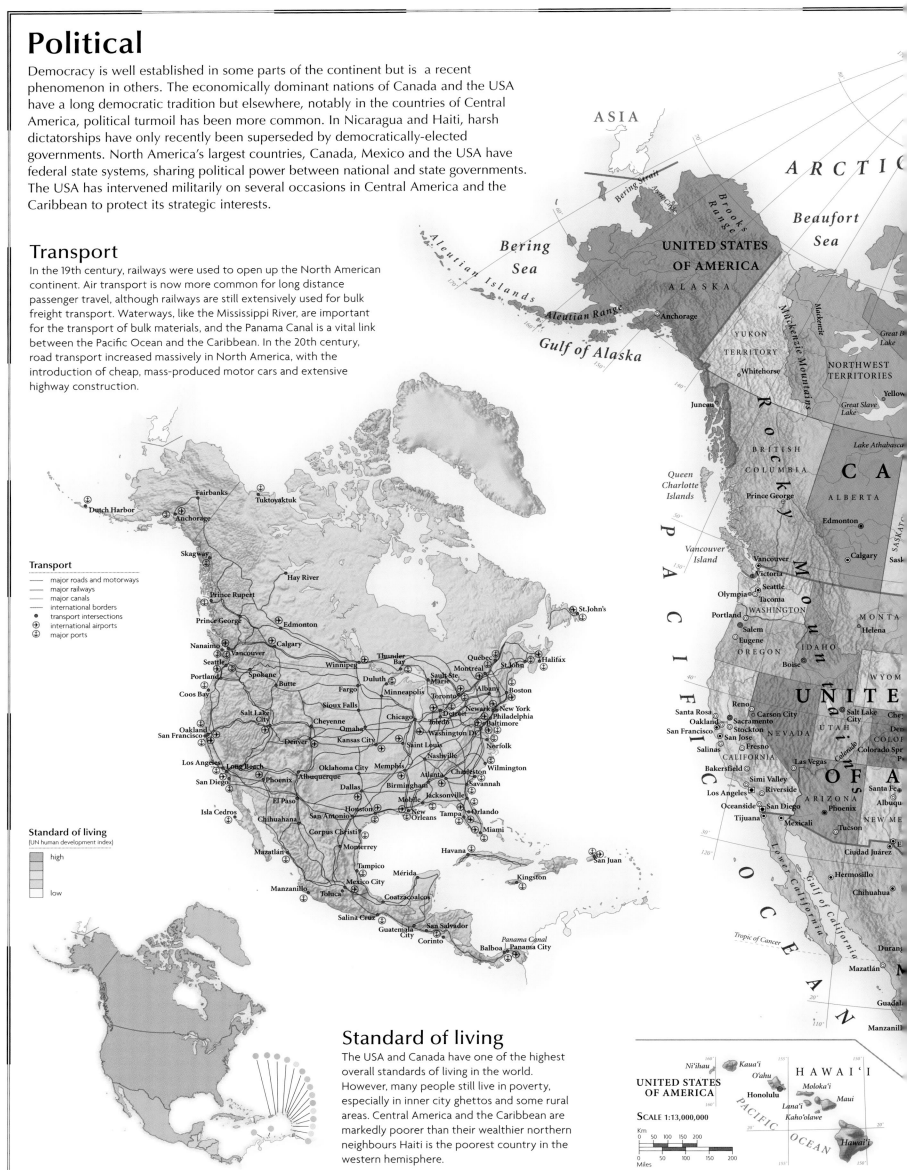

Standard of living

The USA and Canada have one of the highest overall standards of living in the world. However, many people still live in poverty, especially in inner city ghettos and some rural areas. Central America and the Caribbean are markedly poorer than their wealthier northern neighbours Haiti is the poorest country in the western hemisphere.

UNITED STATES OF AMERICA

SCALE 1:13,000,000

Km
0 50 100 150 200

0 50 100 150 200
Miles

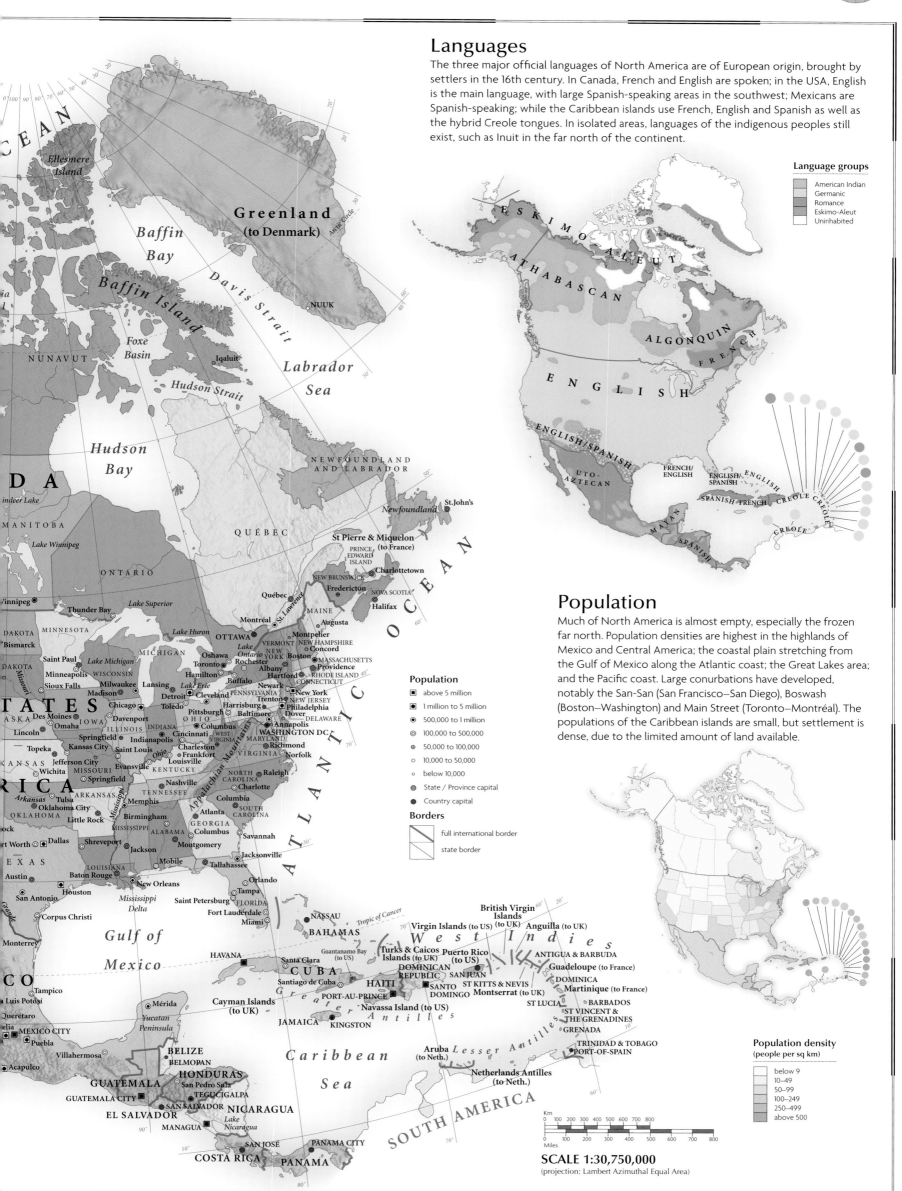

Languages

The three major official languages of North America are of European origin, brought by settlers in the 16th century. In Canada, French and English are spoken; in the USA, English is the main language, with large Spanish-speaking areas in the southwest; Mexicans are Spanish-speaking; while the Caribbean islands use French, English and Spanish as well as the hybrid Creole tongues. In isolated areas, languages of the indigenous peoples still exist, such as Inuit in the far north of the continent.

Language groups
- American Indian
- Germanic
- Romance
- Eskimo-Aleut
- Uninhabited

Population

Much of North America is almost empty, especially the frozen far north. Population densities are highest in the highlands of Mexico and Central America; the coastal plain stretching from the Gulf of Mexico along the Atlantic coast; the Great Lakes area; and the Pacific coast. Large conurbations have developed, notably the San-San (San Francisco–San Diego), Boswash (Boston–Washington) and Main Street (Toronto–Montréal). The populations of the Caribbean islands are small, but settlement is dense, due to the limited amount of land available.

Population
- above 5 million
- 1 million to 5 million
- 500,000 to 1 million
- 100,000 to 500,000
- 50,000 to 100,000
- 10,000 to 50,000
- below 10,000
- State / Province capital
- Country capital

Borders
- full international border
- state border

Population density
(people per sq km)
- below 9
- 10–49
- 50–99
- 100–249
- 250–499
- above 500

Km
0 100 200 300 400 500 600 700 800

Miles
0 100 200 300 400 500 600 700 800

SCALE 1:30,750,000
(projection: Lambert Azimuthal Equal Area)

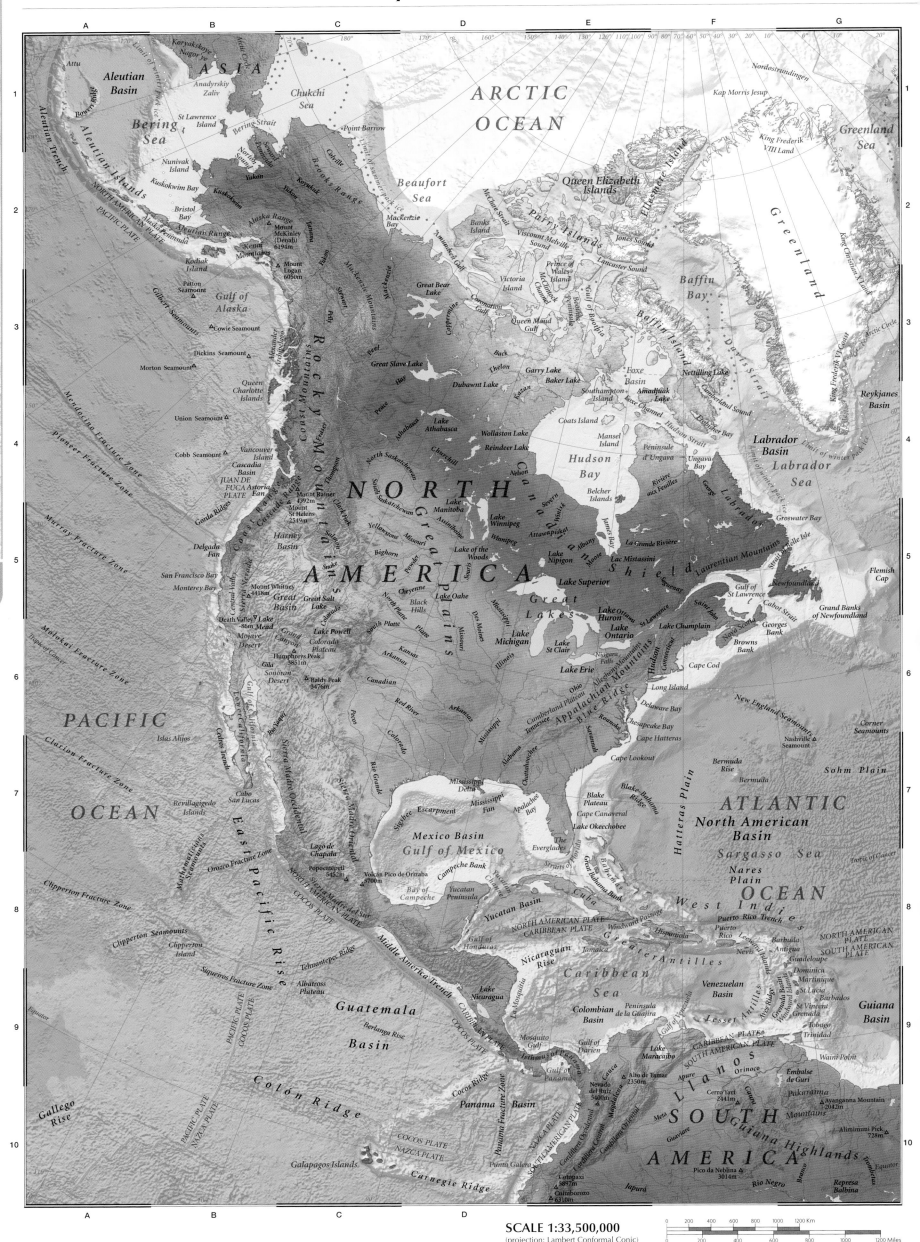

SCALE 1:33,500,000
(projection: Lambert Conformal Conic)

| 0 | 200 | 400 | 600 | 800 | 1000 | 1200 Km |
| 0 | 200 | 400 | 600 | 800 | 1000 | 1200 Miles |

Environmental Issues

Many fragile environments are under threat throughout the region. In Haiti, all the primary rainforest has been destroyed, while air pollution from factories and cars in Mexico City is amongst the worst in the world. Elsewhere, industry and mining pose threats, particularly in the delicate arctic environment of Alaska where oil spills have polluted coastlines and decimated fish stocks.

ARCTIC OCEAN

Bering Sea

Beaufort Sea

Baffin Bay

Gulf of Alaska

Labrador Sea

Hudson Bay

Nelson

Fraser

Columbia

Sacramento

San Joaquin

Vancouver

Sudbury

Hamilton

Montréal

Chicago

New York

Hudson

Mohawk

James

Platte

Missouri

Ohio

Denver

St Louis

Roanoke

Arkansas

Los Angeles

San Diego

Phoenix

Red River

Houston

Alabama

Rio Grande

Gulf of Mexico

Havana

Mexico City

Caribbean Sea

PACIFIC OCEAN

ATLANTIC OCEAN

Environmental issues

- national parks
- acid rain
- tropical forest
- forest destroyed
- desert
- desertification
- polluted rivers
- radioactive contamination
- marine pollution
- heavy marine pollution
- poor urban air quality

Climate

North America's climate includes extremes ranging from freezing Arctic conditions in Alaska and Greenland, to desert in the southwest, and tropical conditions in southeastern Florida, the Caribbean and Central America. Central and southern regions are prone to severe storms including tornadoes and hurricanes.

Average Rainfall

Arctic Circle
60°N
40°N
Tropic of Cancer
20°N

January rainfall *July rainfall*

Rainfall

- 0–25 mm (0–1 in)
- 25–50 mm (1–2 in)
- 50–100 mm (2–4 in)
- 100–200 mm (4–8 in)
- 200–300 mm (8–12 in)
- 300–400 mm (12–16 in)
- 400–500 mm (16–20 in)
- more than 500 mm (20 in)

Average Temperature

Arctic Circle
60°N
40°N
Tropic of Cancer
20°N

January temperature *July temperature*

Temperature

- below -30°C (-22°F)
- -30 to -20°C (-22 to -4°F)
- -20 to -10°C (-4 to 14°F)
- -10 to 0°C (14 to 32°F)
- 0 to 10°C (32 to 50°F)
- 10 to 20°C (50 to 68°F)
- 20 to 30°C (68 to 86°F)
- above 30°C (86°F)

Nome

Eismitte

Fairbanks

Resolute

Haines Junction

Kugluktuk

Iqaluit

Juneau

Happy Valley - Goose Bay

Churchill

Torbay

Fort St John

Vancouver

Winnipeg

Montréal

Medicine Hat

New York

Boise

Toronto

San Francisco

Denver

Cape Hatteras

Las Vegas

Los Angeles

Phoenix

New Orleans

Atlanta

Miami

Guaymas

Houston

Nassau

Chihuahua

Santo Domingo

Mérida

Kingston

Acapulco

San Salvador

San José

San Juan

Climate

- ice cap
- tundra
- subarctic
- cool continental
- warm humid
- semi-arid
- arid
- humid equatorial
- tropical

- daily hours of sunshine, January
- daily hours of sunshine, July
- direction of hurricanes
- tornado zones

ARCTIC OCEAN

Greenland

Bering Strait

Brooks Range

Beaufort Sea

Baffin Bay

Bering Sea

Aleutian Range

Mackenzie Mountains

Mackenzie

Gulf of Alaska

Rocky Mountains

Hudson Strait

Labrador Sea

Hudson Bay

Newfoundland

PACIFIC OCEAN

Edmonton

Vancouver

Calgary

Winnipeg

St Lawrence

Québec

Seattle

Montréal

Portland

Ottawa

Great Lakes

Saint Paul

Toronto

Boston

Minneapolis

Buffalo

Cape Cod

Milwaukee

Detroit

Cleveland

New York

San Francisco

Sacramento

Chicago

Toledo

Philadelphia

Oakland

Pittsburgh

Baltimore

San Jose

Denver

Kansas City

Indianapolis

Columbus

Washington D.C.

Cincinnati

Colorado

Louisville

Missouri

Saint Louis

Los Angeles

Phoenix

Albuquerque

Oklahoma City

Nashville

Charlotte

Arkansas

San Diego

Tucson

Memphis

Atlanta

Dallas

El Paso

Austin

Appalachian Mountains

Jacksonville

Lower California

Houston

San Antonio

Mississippi Delta

Tampa

Rio Grande

Miami

Monterrey

Gulf of Mexico

Havana

San Juan

Guadalajara

Santo Domingo

Mexico City

Yucatan Peninsula

Caribbean Sea

PACIFIC OCEAN

Guatemala City

Managua

ATLANTIC OCEAN

Using the land and sea

- cropland
- forest
- ice cap
- mountain region
- pasture
- tundra
- wetland
- desert
- major conurbations
- cattle
- goats
- pigs
- poultry
- reindeer
- sheep
- bananas
- citrus fruits
- coffee
- corn (maize)
- cotton
- fishing
- fruit
- maple syrup
- peanuts
- rice
- shellfish
- soya beans
- sugar cane
- timber
- tobacco
- vineyards
- wheat

Landuse

Abundant land and fertile soils stretch from the Canadian prairies to Texas creating North America's agricultural heartland. Cereals and cattle ranching form the basis of the farming economy, with corn and soya beans also important. Fruit and vegetables are grown in California using irrigation, while Florida is a leading producer of citrus fruits. Caribbean and Central American countries depend on cash crops such as bananas, coffee and sugar cane, often grown on large plantations. This reliance on a single crop can leave these countries vulnerable to fluctuating world crop prices.

1 VANCOUVER, BRITISH COLUMBIA, CANADA
Canada's premier west coast city occupies the delta of the Fraser river, formed amongst the Coast Mountains.

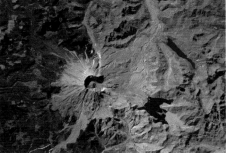

2 MOUNT SAINT HELENS, WASHINGTON, USA
In 1980, this volcano's catastrophic eruption devastated 270 sq miles (700 sq km) of forest almost instantly.

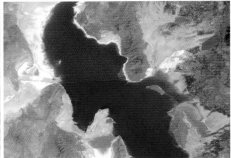

3 GREAT SALT LAKE, UTAH, USA
A causeway carries a railway line, blocking circulation between the northern and southern parts, the water reddened by salt-loving bacteria in the more saline north.

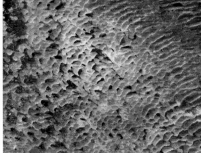

4 SAND HILLS, NEBRASKA, USA
Forming the largest sand sea in the Western Hemisp these hills are not classified as desert because tod relatively wet climate has allowed grasses to take h

9 LOS ANGELES AND LONG BEACH, CALIFORNIA, USA
Taken together, these west coast cities constitute the busiest sea port in the United States.

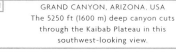

10 ISLA GUADALUPE, MEXICO
The volcanic island, 186 miles (300 km) off the west coast of Mexico, is a protected wildlife reserve.

11 GRAND CANYON, ARIZONA, USA
The 5250 ft (1600 m) deep canyon cuts through the Kaibab Plateau in this southwest-looking view.

12 DENVER, COLORADO, USA
Colorado's state capital nestles under the Rocky Mountains with the South Platte River running through its centre.

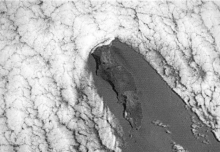

BELCHER ISLANDS, NUNAVUT, CANADA [5]
These low-lying, treeless and sparsely-populated islands lie icebound in Hudson Bay for much of the year.

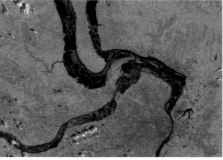

MISSISSIPPI, MISSOURI AND ILLINOIS RIVERS, USA [6]
This Infrared image shows how these rivers burst their banks in many places after heavy rains in the summer of 1993, leading to the area's worst floods on record.

RÉSERVOIR MANICOUAGAN, QUÉBEC, CANADA [7]
This unusual 62 mile (100 km) diameter, annular lake occupies the low ground between the rim and central uplift of an ancient meteorite crater.

NEW YORK, USA [8]
The largest city in the United States, with a population of over 8 million, it is also the country's main financial centre.

MISSISSIPPI RIVER DELTA, LOUISIANA, USA [13]
This delta has developed a 'bird's foot' shape due to the shifting course of the river over the last 6000 years.

FLORIDA, USA [14]
This low-lying, subtropical peninsula is home to thousands of lakes that have formed amongst its limestone 'karst' topography.

HAVANA, CUBA [15]
Cuba's capital city is home to 2 million people and was founded by the Spanish in 1519 around a natural harbour.

BARRIER REEF, BELIZE [16]
The world's second-longest barrier reef lies about 12 miles (20 km) off the coast of Belize.

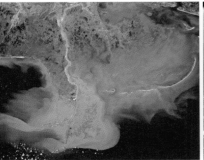

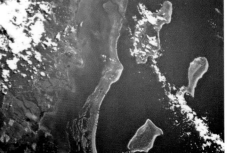

Northern Canada

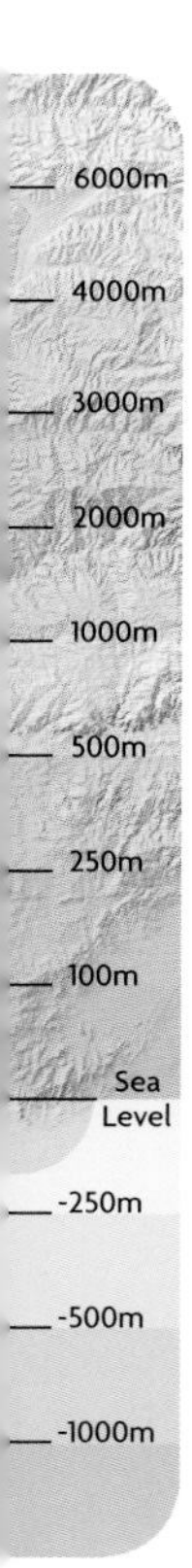

83
54

NORTH AMERICA

52

Column/Row markers
A B C D E F G
1 2 3 4 5 6 7 8 9 10

Elevation scale
6000m
4000m
3000m
2000m
1000m
500m
250m
100m
Sea Level
-250m
-500m
-1000m

Ocean / Sea labels
ARCTIC OCEAN
Beaufort Sea
North Magnetic Pole (2005)

Ice limits
Limit of permanent ice cap
Limit of summer pack ice

Regions / Countries
USA
ALASKA
YUKON TERRITORY
NORTHWEST TERRITORIES
CANADA

Place names and features
Cape Halkett
Harrison Bay
Kuparuk River
Prudhoe Bay
Deadhorse
Camden Bay
Kaktovik
Canning River
Shublik Mountains
Franklin Mountains
Sadlerochit Mountains
Philip Smith Mountains
East Fork Chandalar River
Davidson Mountains
Kongakut River
Demarcation Point
Martin Point
British Mountains
Old Crow Flats
Old Crow
Porcupine
Miner
Eagle Plain
Sheep Mountain
Yukon River
Arctic Circle
Ogilvie
Bluefish River
Wind
Bonnet Plume
Snake
Keele
Mountain
Backbone Range
Redstone
Root
Wrigley
Mackenzie Mountains
Selwyn Mountains
Pelly Mountains
Cassiar Mountains
Wolf Lake
Watson Lake
Lower Post
Good Hope
Dease
Coal River
Nahanni Butte
South Nahanni
Jean Marie River
Mills Lake
Fort Simpson
Horn Plateau
Willow Lake
Birch Lake
Fort Liard
Trout Lake
Mayo
Elsa
Keno Hill
Stewart
Beaver
Faro
Ross River
Ross
Hess
Macmillan
Mount Keele
Mount Sir James MacBrien
Murray
Nahanni
North Nahanni
Mount Eduni
Redstone
Carcajou
Norman Wells
Mahony Lake
Whitefish River
Fort Good Hope
Hare Indian
Lac des Bois
Lac Belot
Lac Maunoir
Aubry Lake
Colville Lake
Kilekale Lake
Bluenose Lake
Hottah Lake
Sawmill Bay
Point Leith
Keith Arm
Fort Franklin
Deline
McVicar Arm
Great Bear Lake
Smith Arm
Dease Arm
Haldane
Coppermine
Bathurst Inlet
Melville Sound
Mackenzie
Arctic Red River
Fort McPherson
Peel
Aklavik
Inuvik
Sitidgi Lake
Eskimo Lakes
Tuktoyaktuk
Tuktoyaktuk Peninsula
Liverpool Bay
Cape Dalhousie
Warren Point
Shingle Point
Herschel Island
Mackenzie Bay
Cape Bathurst
Franklin Bay
Parry Peninsula
Darnley Bay
Cape Parry
Cape Lyon
Amundsen Gulf
Cape Lambton
Cape Kellett
Banks Island
Sachs Harbour
Big
Meek Point
Cape Prince Alfred
Bernard Island
Cape Wrottesley
McClure Strait
Prince Patrick Island
Lands End
Mould Bay
Dyer Bay
Crozier Channel
Eglinton Island
Cape Russell
Satellite Bay
Cape Leopold McClintock
Brock Island
Borden Island
Wilkins Strait
Ballantyne Strait
Mackenzie King Island
Prince Gustaf Adolf Sea
Sverdrup
Ellef Ringnes Island
Queen
Bad Weather Cape
Meighen Island
Peary Ch
King Christian Island
Mackan Strait
Lougheed Island
Hazen Strait
Emerald Isle
Sabine Peninsula
Sherard Bay
Cameron Island
Seymour Island
Austin Channel
Bathurst Island
Melville Island
Parry
Keller Strait
Liddon Gulf
Dundas Peninsula
Hearne Point
Byam Martin Island
Byam Channel
Parry Channel
Viscount Melville Sound
Passage Point
Peel Point
Richard Collinson Inlet
Russell Island
Cape John Dyer
Stefansson Island
Minto Head
Prince of Wales Island
Cape Richard Collinson
Prince Albert Peninsula
Hadley Bay
Minto Inlet
Holman
Prince Albert Sound
Cape Wollaston
Cape Baring
Wollaston Peninsula
Tahiryuak Lake
Norway Bay
Zeta Lake
Nanook
Dolphin and Union Strait
Quunnguq Lake
Victoria Island
Washburn Lake
Gateshead Island
Larsen Sound
Collinson Peninsula
Pelly Point
Cape Felix
Albert Edward Bay
Cambridge Bay
Jenny Lind Island
Royal Geographical Society Islands
Queen Maud Gulf
Melbourne Island
Kent Peninsula
Byron Bay
Dease Strait
Coronation Gulf
Cape Krusenstern
Kugluktuk
Rae
Bebensee Lake
Dismal Lakes
Dease Arm
Sawmill Bay
Echo Bay
Point Lake
Inulik Lake
Takijuq Lake
Hood
James Lake
Banks Peninsula
Whitebear Point
Bowes Point
MacAlpine Lake
Bullen
Burnside
Contwoyto Lake
Point Lake
Redrock Lake
Rebesca Lake
Little Marten Lake
Ellice
Garry Lake
Aberdeen Lake
Schultz L
Back
Mara
Aylmer Lake
Clinton-Colden Lake
Lac de Gras
Fletcher Lake
Walmsley Lake
Tebesjuak Lake
Dubawnt Lake
Artillery Lake
McLeod Bay
Reliance
Great Slave Lake
Yellowknife
Rae
Edzo
Wha Ti
Rae Lakes
Snare Lakes
MacKay Lake
Lockhart Lake
Gordon Lake
Wecho
Snare
Clive Lake
Lac la Martre
Lac Grandin
Faber Lake
Lac Tuché
Ray Lakes
Keller Lake
Redstone
Rook
Trout Lake
Carnwath
Travaillant Lake
Ontaratue
Arctic Red River
Hare Indian
Anderson
Hornaday
Horton
Maunoir
Lac Maunoir
Lac Belot
Smith Arm
Norman Wells
Tulita
Great Bear Lake
Grizzly Bear Mountain
Franklin Mountains
Keller Lake

Scale 1:7,500,000
(projection: Lambert Conformal Conic)

0 25 50 75 100 125 150 175 200 Km

0 25 50 75 100 125 150 175 200 Miles

Population

■ above 5 million
▣ 1 million to 5 million
◉ 500,000 to 1 million
◎ 100,000 to 500,000
⊕ 50,000 to 100,000
○ 10,000 to 50,000
∘ below 10,000

295

58

19,686ft
13,124ft
9843ft
6562ft
3281ft
1640ft
820ft
328ft
Sea Level
-820ft
-6562ft
-13,124ft

GREENLAND (to Denmark)

AVANNAARSUA

TUNU

KITAA

Kong Frederik IX Land

Knud Rasmussen Land

Baffin Bay

Davis Strait

Qimusseriarsuaq

Kullorsuaq

Savissivik

Innaanganeq

Qaanaaq

Smith Sound

Cape Herschel

Cape Dunsterville

Clarence Head

Cape Norton Shaw

Upernavik

Uummannatsiaq

Qeqertarsuaq

Qeqertarsuup Tunua

Qasigiannguit

Qeqertarsuaq

Sisimiut

Limit of summer pack ice

Limit of winter pack ice

Arctic Circle

Ellesmere Island

Axel Heiberg Island

British Empire Range

Cape Columbia

Cape Hecla

Alert

Cape Discovery

Cape Bicknor

Alert Point

Lake Hazen

Victoria and Albert Mountains

North Geomagnetic Pole (2005)

Kennedy Channel

Nares Strait

Kane Basin

Hall Basin

Agassiz Ice Cap

Eureka

Fosheim Peninsula

Greely Fiord

Nansen Sound

Otto Fiord

Bjorne Peninsula

Norwegian Bay

Princess Marie Bay

Bache Peninsula

Buchanan Bay

Cape Storm

Cape

Raanes Peninsula

Simmons Peninsula

Buckingham Island

Cornwall Island

Grise Fiord

Coburg Island

Jones Sound

Lady Ann Strait

Bear Bay

Cape Parker

Devon Island

Cape Sherard

Cape Warrender

Lancaster Sound

Baillie-Hamilton Island

Wellington Channel

Resolute

Barrow Strait

Somerset Island

Prince Regent Inlet

Creswell Bay

McBean

Gulf of Boothia

Cape Scoresby

Cape Palmerston

Brodeur Peninsula

Admiralty Inlet

Cape York

Cape Crauford

Navy Board Inlet

Bylot Island

Cape Byam Martin

Cape Graham Moore

Pond Inlet

Pond Inlet

Arctic Bay

Borden Peninsula

Nova Zembla Island

Buchan Bay

Cape Hunter

Cape Adair

Jungersen Bay

Bernier Bay

Berlinguet Inlet

Neergaard Lake

Gifford

Milne Inlet

Nina Bang Lake

Rowley

Isortoq

Conn Lake

Lake Gillian

Bieler Lake

Barnes Ice Cap

Cape Raper

Henry Kater Peninsula

Home Bay

Clyde River

Limit of summer pack ice

NUNAVUT

Baffin Island

Murray Maxwell Bay

Koch Island

Bray Island

Bond Peninsula

Cape Englefield

Fury and Hecla Strait

Jens Munk Island

Rowley Island

Igloolik

Crown Prince Frederick Island

Cape Margaret

Astronomical Society Island

Cape Kjer

Cape Chapman

Hall Beach

South Tweedsmuir Island

Spicer Islands

Kekertaluk Island

Kangeeak Point

Qikiqtarjuaq

Broughton Island

Auyuittuq National Park

Cape Dyer

Exeter Sound

Cumberland Peninsula

Pangnirtung

Kingnait Fiord

Houre Bay

Nettilling Fiord

Cumberland Sound

Angijak Island

Bothia Peninsula

Taloyoak

Committee Bay

Hall Lake

Parry Bay

Prince Charles Island

Air Force Island

Taverner Bay

Koukdjuak

Nettilling Lake

Lemieux Islands

Brevoort Island

Lady Melville Lake

Simpson Peninsula

PellyBay

Wales Island

Melville Peninsula

Amadjuak Lake

Mingo Lake

Sylvia Grinnell Lake

Iqaluit

Hall Peninsula

Blunt Peninsula

Rae Isthmus

Repulse Bay

Winter Island

Vansittart Island

Foxe Basin

Limit of summer pack ice

Cape Dominion

Bowman Bay

Aupar

Cape Dorchester

Finnie Bay

Foxe Peninsula

Amadjuak

Meta Incognita Peninsula

Loks Land

Frobisher Bay

Gabriel Strait

Edgell Island

Resolution Island

Foxe Channel

Brown Lake

White Island

Hansine Lake

Wager Bay

Western Strait

Cape Bylot

Cape Comfort

Shukbuk Bay

Markham Bay

Fair Ness

Cape Dorset

Lake Harbour

Big Island

Button Islands

Port Burwell

Cape Chidley

Killinek Island

CANADA

Hoare Bay

Chesterfield Inlet

Baker Lake

Armit Lake

Quoich

Daly Bay

Cape Kendall

Bay of Gods Mercy

Southampton Island

Coral Harbour

Native Bay

Seahorse Point

Nottingham Island

Salisbury Island

HUDSON STRAIT

Hudson Strait

Peter Lake

Lorillard

Roes Welcome Sound

Cape Low

Fisher Strait

Coats Island

Mansel Island

Evans Strait

Digges Islands

Charles Island

Nuvuk Islands

Ivujivik

Salluit

Deception Bay

Kangiqsujuaq

Whitley Bay

Diana Bay

Cap Hopes Advance

Quaqtaq

Akpatok Island

Ungava Bay

PÉNINSULE D'UNGAVA

QUÉBEC

Péninsule d'Ungava

52
287
76

NORTH AMERICA

54

6000m
4000m
3000m
2000m
1000m
500m
250m
100m
Sea Level
-250m
-500m
-1000m

PACIFIC OCEAN

Scale 1:7,500,000
(projection: Lambert Conformal Conic)

0 25 50 75 100 125 150 175 200 Km
0 25 50 75 100 125 150 175 200 Miles

Population
- ■ above 5 million
- ▣ 1 million to 5 million
- ● 500,000 to 1 million
- ◉ 100,000 to 500,000
- ⊕ 50,000 to 100,000
- ○ 10,000 to 50,000
- ○ below 10,000

53

58

72

Elevation scale:
19,686ft
13,124ft
9843ft
6562ft
3281ft
1640ft
820ft
328ft
Sea Level
-820ft
-6562ft
-13,124ft

Hudson Bay

James Bay

Foxe Basin

Foxe Channel

Hudson Strait

NUNAVUT

QUÉBEC

Péninsule d'Ungava

MANITOBA

ONTARIO

MINNESOTA

NORTH DAKOTA

OF AMERICA

MICHIGAN

Lake Winnipeg

Lake Winnipegosis

Lake Manitoba

Lake Superior

Lake Nipigon

Lake St. Joseph

Reindeer Lake

Wollaston Lake

Southampton Island

Coats Island

Mansel Island

Belcher Islands

Akimiski Island

Southampton Island

Melville Peninsula

Prince Charles Island

Amadjuak Lake

Meta Incognita Peninsula

Iqaluit

Frobisher Bay

Winnipeg

Regina

Thunder Bay

Sault Ste Marie

Southwest Canada

A B C D E F G

54

PACIFIC OCEAN

BRITISH COLUMBIA

Coast Mountains
Skeena Mountains
Omineca Mountains
ROCKY MOUNTAIN
Columbia Mountains
Cariboo Mountains
Selkirk Mountains
Fraser Plateau
Clear Hills

Queen Charlotte Sound
Queen Charlotte Strait
Strait of Georgia
Strait of Juan de Fuca
Nootka Sound
Barkley Sound
Vancouver Island
Olympic Mountains

USA ALASKA
WASHINGTON
UNITED STATES

Wrangell, Ketchikan, Prince Rupert, Port Edward, Porcher Island, Banks Island, Princess Royal Island, Aristazabal Island, King Island, Bella Bella, Bella Coola, Hagensborg, Ocean Falls, Namu, Rivers Inlet, Dawsons Landing, Cape Caution, Cape Scott, Cape Cook, Port Hardy, Port McNeill, Port Alice, Winter Harbour, Telegraph Cove, Sayward, Tahsis, Gold River, Courtenay, Comox, Campbell River, Powell River, Sechelt, Gibsons, Tofino, Ucluelet, Port Alberni, Parksville, Nanaimo, Ladysmith, Lake Cowichan, Duncan, Swartz Bay, Bamfield, Port Renfrew, Victoria, Esquimalt, Sidney

Hyder, Stewart, Meziadin Junction, Cranberry Junction, Kitwanga, Hazelton, New Hazelton, Terrace, Kitimat, Smithers, Telkwa, Granisle, Houston, Burns Lake, Fraser Lake, Vanderhoof, Fort St. James, Prince George, Nazko, Quesnel, Barkerville, Likely, Marguerite, Williams Lake, Alexis Creek, Hanceville, Tatla Lake, Klecna Kleene, Anahim Lake, Nimpo Lake, 100 Mile House, Clearwater, Little Fort, Barrière, Clinton, Lillooet, Cache Creek, Ashcroft, Kamloops, Chase, Salmon Arm, Sicamous, Revelstoke, Enderby, Armstrong, Coldstream, Vernon, Merritt, Logan Lake, Boston Bar, Lytton, Pemberton, Whistler, Squamish, Hope, Princeton, Summerland, Penticton, Peachland, Westbank, Kelowna, Oliver, Osoyoos

North Vancouver, Vancouver, Burnaby, Richmond, Langley, Abbotsford, Chilliwack, Blaine, Lynden, Sumas, Deming, Bellingham, Newhalem, Oroville, Orient, Northport, Grand Forks, Rossland, Castlegar

Seattle, Tacoma, Bellevue, Bremerton, Everett, Edmonds, Redmond, Monroe, Skykomish, Leavenworth, Wenatchee, Entiat, Lake Chelan, Patero, Winthrop, Mazama, Tiffany Mountain 2512m, Mount Logan 2770m, Glacier Peak 3213m, Mount Olympus 2428m, Port Angeles, Sequim, Port Townsend, Coupeville, Oak Harbor, Anacortes, San Juan Islands, Friday Harbor, Neah Bay, Cape Flattery, Clallam Bay, Forks, Queets, Quinault, Taholah, Moclips, Pacific Beach, Copalis Beach, Humptulips, Shelton, Kent, Auburn, Puyallup, Marysville, Arlington, Darrington, Stanwood, Mount Vernon, Sedro-Woolley, Rockport, Newhalem

Mount Pattullo 2729m, Sustut Peak 2470m, Great Snow Mountain 2896m, Seven Sisters Peaks 2755m, Mount Sir Alexander 3274m, Mount Robson 3954m, Tête Jaune Cache, Valemount, Mount Sir Wilfrid Laurier 3505m, Yellowhead Pass 1131m, Kinbasket Lake, Mica Creek, Rogers Pass 1327m, Mount Saugstad 2908m, Monarch Mountain 3533m, Mount Waddington 4016m, Mount Queen Bess 3313m, Mount Gilbert 3109m, Wedge Mountain 2891m, Sentinel Peak 2515m, Mount Bonaparte 2212m

Williston Lake, Takla Lake, Babine Lake, Stuart Lake, Ootsa Lake, Eutsuk Lake, Nechako, Stuart, Fraser, Okanagan Lake, Kootenay, Columbia River, Skagit River, Methow River, Grand Coulee, Banks Lake, Franklin D. Roosevelt Lake, Kettle Falls, Coulee City, Spokane

Beatton River, Trutch, Sikanni Chief, Pink Mountain, Wonowon, Fort St. John, Hudson's Hope, Taylor, Dawson Creek, Spirit River, Rycroft, Fairview, Hines Creek, Chetwynd, Mackenzie, McLeod Lake, Pine Pass 869m, Tumbler Ridge, Hythe, Beaverlodge, Wembley, Grande Prairie, Sexsmith, Sinclair Mills, McBride, Grande Cache, Jasper, New Denver

Revillagigedo Island, Annette Island, Metlakatla, Mountain Point, Duke Island, Skeena, Nass, Stikine

287 / 76

Sea Level 6000m 4000m 3000m 2000m 1000m 500m 250m 100m -250m -500m -1000m

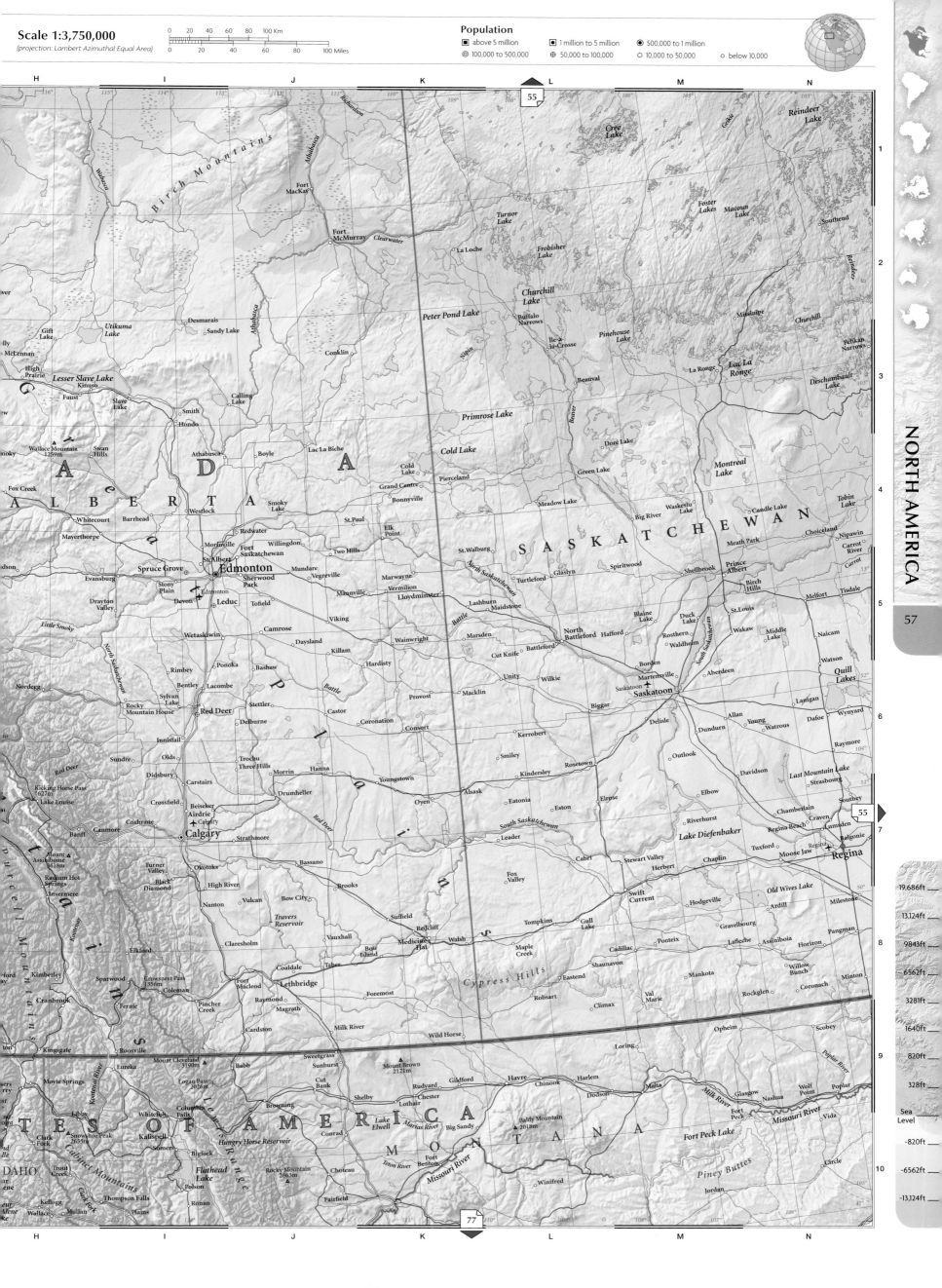

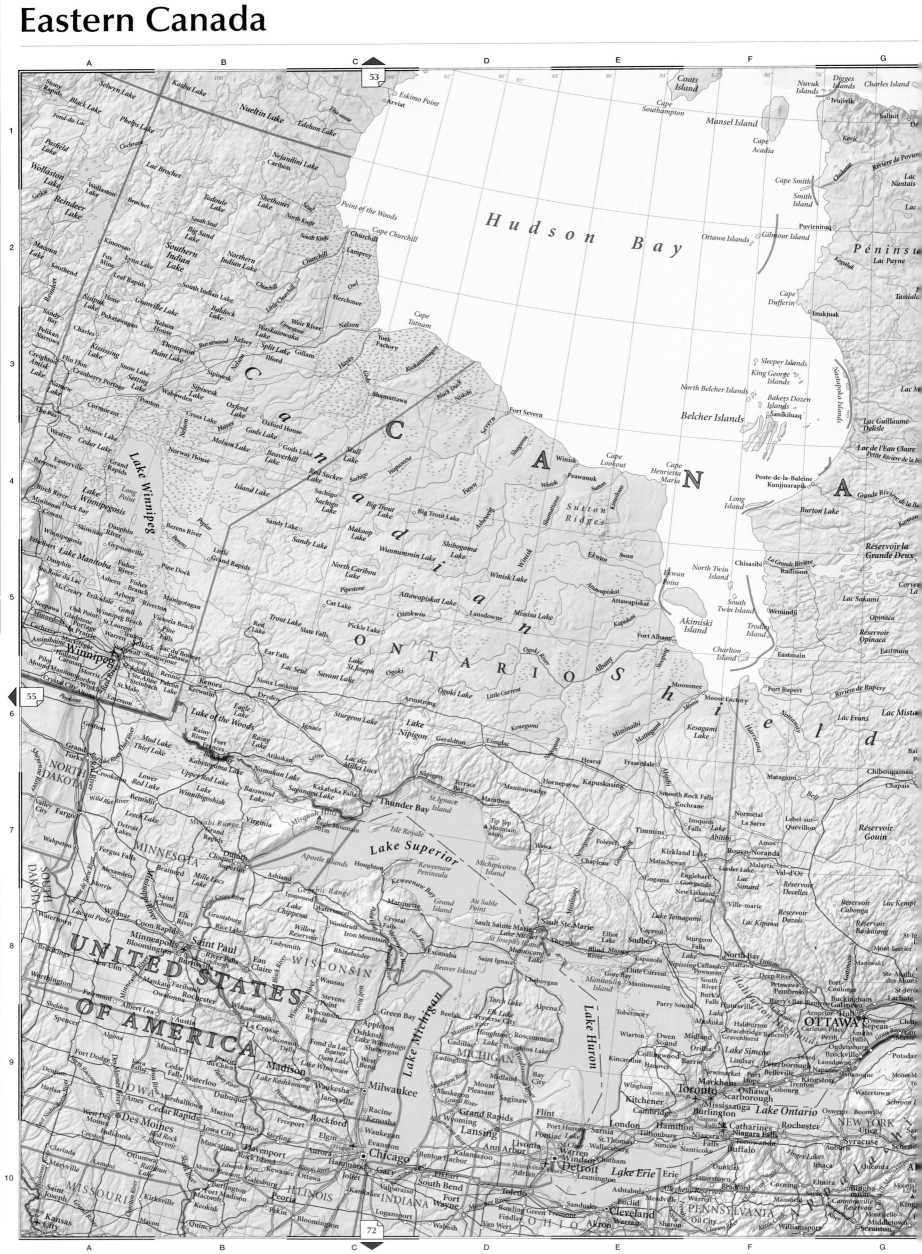

The United States of America

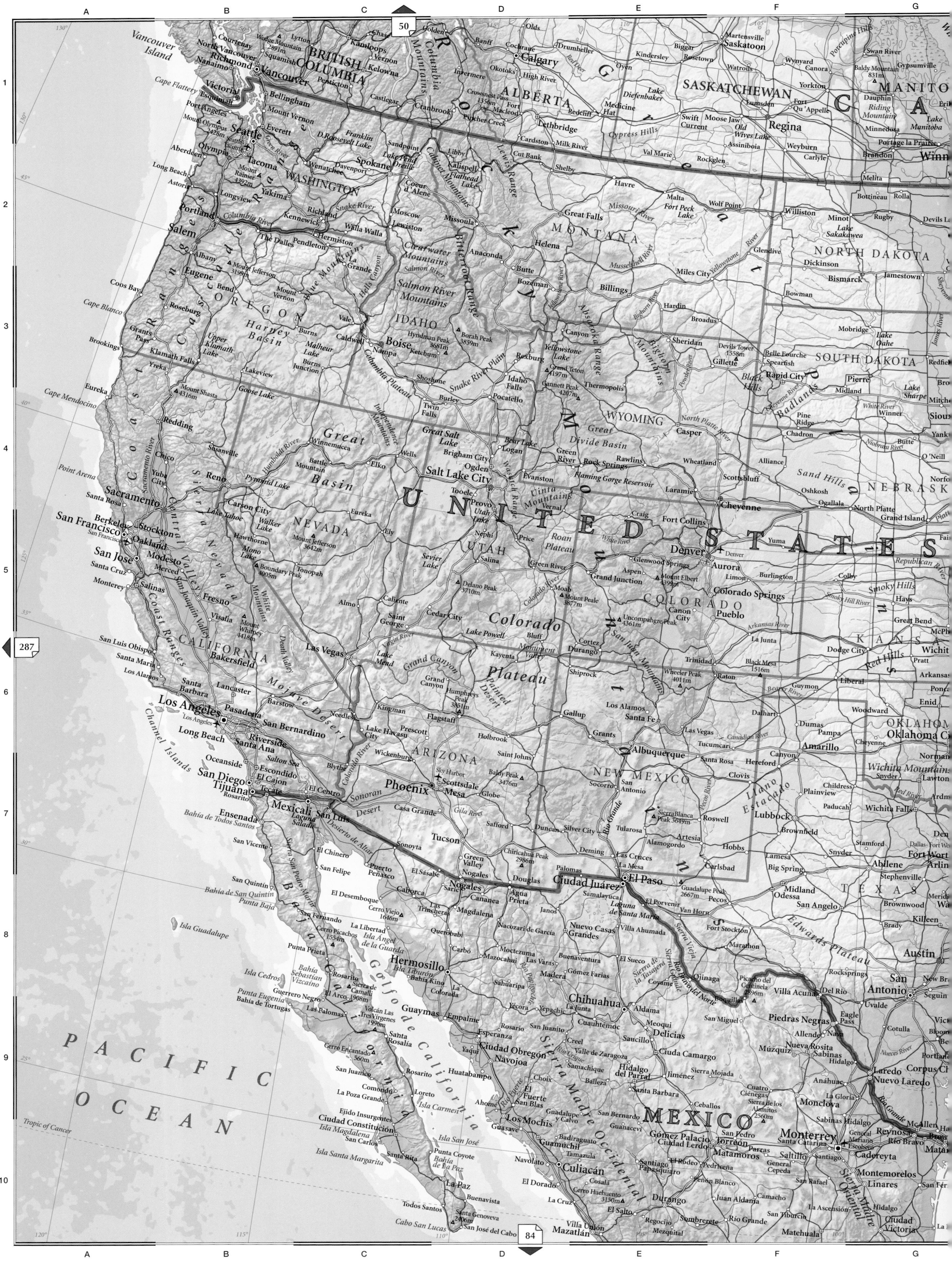

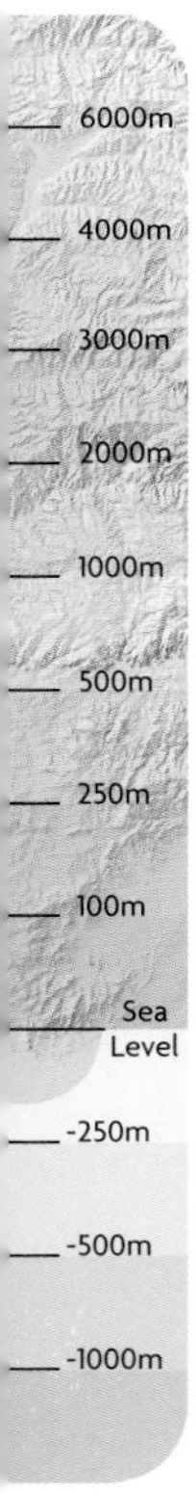

PACIFIC OCEAN

CANADA

BRITISH COLUMBIA
ALBERTA
SASKATCHEWAN
MANITOBA

WASHINGTON
OREGON
IDAHO
MONTANA
NORTH DAKOTA
SOUTH DAKOTA
WYOMING
NEBRASKA
NEVADA
UTAH
COLORADO
KANSAS
CALIFORNIA
ARIZONA
NEW MEXICO
OKLAHOMA
TEXAS

UNITED STATES

MEXICO

Vancouver Island
Seattle
Tacoma
Olympia
Portland
Salem
Eugene

San Francisco
Oakland
San Jose
Sacramento
Stockton
Modesto
Fresno
Bakersfield

Los Angeles
Long Beach
San Diego
Tijuana
Mexicali

Las Vegas
Phoenix
Tucson
Mesa
Scottsdale

Salt Lake City
Provo
Ogden

Denver
Aurora
Colorado Springs
Pueblo

Albuquerque
Santa Fe
El Paso
Ciudad Juárez

Calgary
Regina
Saskatoon

Boise
Helena
Great Falls
Billings
Bismarck
Pierre
Rapid City
Cheyenne

Spokane
Yakima

Reno

Monterrey
Hermosillo
Chihuahua
Culiacán
Durango
Mazatlán
La Paz

Golfo de California

Rocky Mountains
Great Basin
Sierra Nevada
Coast Ranges
Mojave Desert
Colorado Plateau
Grand Canyon
Great Salt Lake
Columbia Plateau
Sonoran Desert
Baja California
Sierra Madre Occidental

Tropic of Cancer

Sea Level
6000m
4000m
3000m
2000m
1000m
500m
250m
100m
-250m
-500m
-1000m

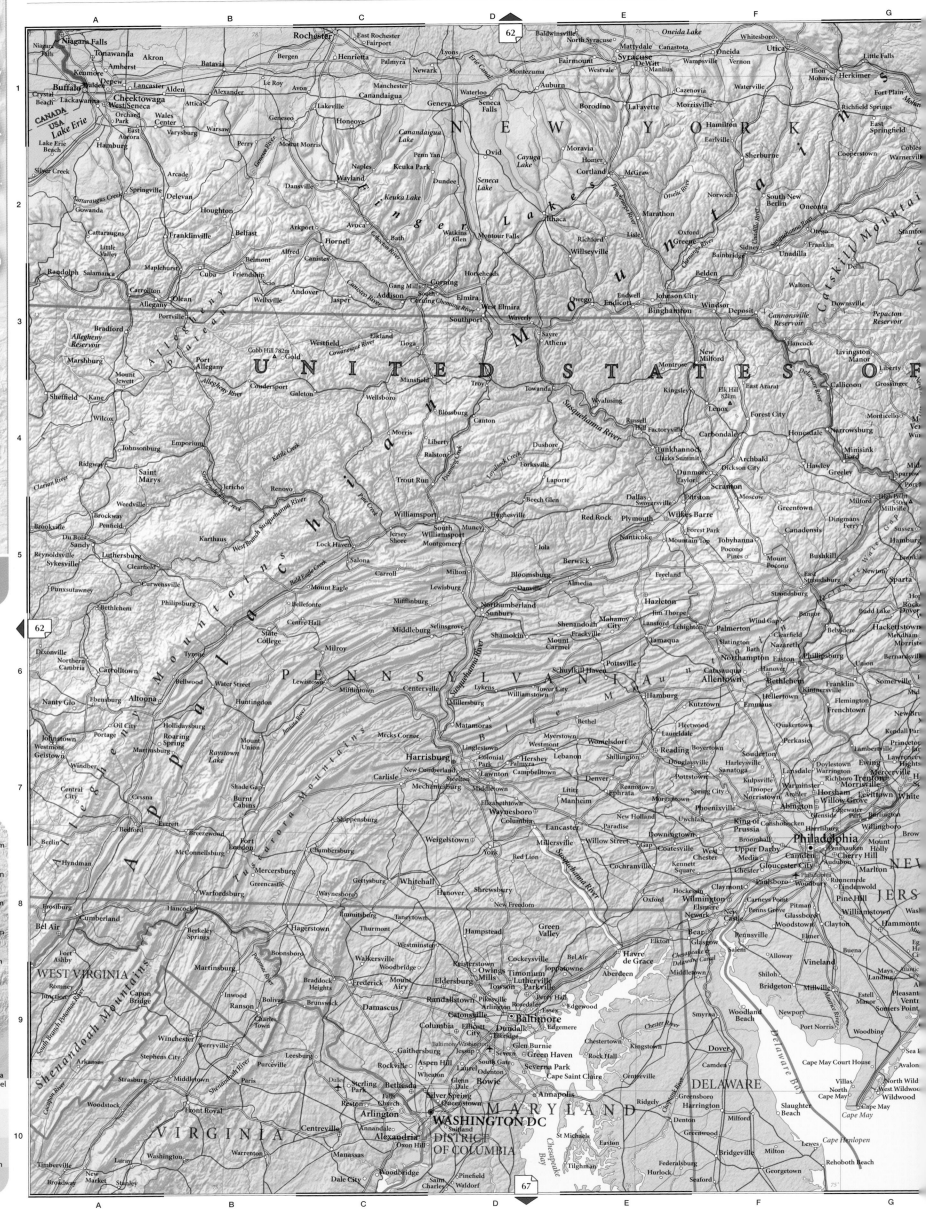

Scale 1:3,000,000
(projection: Lambert Conformal Conic)

0 20 40 60 80 100 Km
0 20 40 60 80 100 Miles

Population

☐ above 5 million
☑ 1 million to 5 million
◉ 500,000 to 1 million
◎ 100,000 to 500,000
⊕ 50,000 to 100,000
○ 10,000 to 50,000
∘ below 10,000

62

69

290

67

PENNSYLVANIA

WEST VIRGINIA

VIRGINIA

MARYLAND

DELAWARE

NEW JERSEY

NORTH CAROLINA

SOUTH CAROLINA

UNITED STATES OF AMERICA

WASHINGTON DC

DISTRICT OF COLUMBIA

Baltimore · Richmond · Charlotte · Columbia · Philadelphia

Chesapeake Bay · Delaware Bay · Albemarle Sound · Pamlico Sound · Raleigh Bay · Onslow Bay · Long Bay

Cape Hatteras · Cape Lookout · Cape Fear · Cape Henry · Cape Charles

Hatteras Island · Ocracoke Island · Roanoke Island · Assateague Island · Chincoteague

ATLANTIC OCEAN

BERMUDA (to UK)

St George's Island · St Catherine Point · St George · St David's Island · Ireland Island North · Ireland Island South · Somerset Island · Spanish Point · Tucker's Town · HAMILTON · Gibbs Hill 73m · Great Sound · Castle Harbour · Kindley Field · Hatts Village · Commissioner's Point

Scale 1:500,000

0 2.5 5 Km
0 2.5 5 Miles

ATLANTIC OCEAN

Elevation scale:
19,686ft
13,124ft
9843ft
6562ft
3281ft
1640ft
820ft
328ft
Sea Level
-820ft
-6562ft
-13,124ft

NORTH AMERICA

68

New Orleans

Scale 1:3,000,000
(projection: Lambert Conformal Conic)

0 20 40 60 80 100 Km
0 20 40 60 80 100 Miles

Population
- ■ above 5 million
- ▣ 1 million to 5 million
- ◉ 500,000 to 1 million
- ◎ 100,000 to 500,000
- ⊕ 50,000 to 100,000
- ○ 10,000 to 50,000
- ∘ below 10,000

67

290

88

ATLANTIC OCEAN

GEORGIA

SOUTH CAROLINA

ALABAMA

STATES OF AMERICA

FLORIDA

Birmingham
Vestavia Hills
Talladega
Cheaha Mountain 734m
McDonough
Lake Oconee
Warrenton
Denmark
Barnwell
Branchville
Saint George
Moncks Corner
Lake Moultrie
McClellanville
Cape Island
Cape Romain

Montgomery
Tuskegee
Columbus
Phenix City
Macon
Savannah
Hilton Head Island

Tallahassee
Jacksonville
Atlantic Beach
Jacksonville Beach

Gainesville
Palatka

Ocala

Orlando
Cape Canaveral
Cocoa Beach
Melbourne
Palm Bay

Tampa
Saint Petersburg
Lakeland

Sarasota

Lake Okeechobee

West Palm Beach
Boynton Beach
Delray Beach
Boca Raton
Deerfield Beach
Pompano Beach
Fort Lauderdale
Hollywood
Hialeah
Miami
Key Biscayne

Naples

The Everglades

Big Cypress Swamp

Key Largo

Florida Keys

Straits of Florida

Key West

Dry Tortugas

Cape Sable

Miami
Miramar
Carol City
Ives Estates
Hallandale
North Miami Beach
Golden Glades
North Miami
Hialeah
Miami Shores
Virginia Gardens
Miami International Airport
Miami Beach
Streetwater
West Miami
Miami
Westchester
Florida Int. University
Coral Gables
Virginia Key
Miami Seaquarium
Key Biscayne
Kendall
Pinecrest
Cape Florida
Westwood Lake
Weeks Air Museum
South Miami Heights
Perrine
Goulds
Cutler Ridge
Redland
Naranja
Leisure City
Homestead
Florida City

Atlantic Ocean

Biscayne Bay

Sands Key

Elliot Key

0 5 Km
0 5 Miles

19,686ft
13,124ft
9843ft
6562ft
3281ft
1640ft
820ft
328ft
Sea Level
-820ft
-6562ft
-13,124ft

Scale 1:3,750,000

(projection: Lambert Conformal Conic)

0 20 40 60 80 100 Km
0 20 40 60 80 100 Miles

Population

◼ above 5 million ◾ 1 million to 5 million ⬤ 500,000 to 1 million
◉ 100,000 to 500,000 ⊕ 50,000 to 100,000 ○ 10,000 to 50,000 ∘ below 10,000

75

79

87

MISSOURI

Ozark Plateau

Boston Mountains

TENNESSEE

Nashville

Memphis

ARKANSAS

Ouachita Mountains

Kiamichi Mountains

Caddo Mountains

Little Rock
North Little Rock

Pine Bluff

OF AMERICA

Red River

Texarkana

MISSISSIPPI

ALABAMA

Jackson

Meridian

Tulsa

Fort Smith

McAlester

Dallas
Garland
Grand Prairie
Fort Worth

Shreveport
Bossier City

Monroe

Vicksburg

Tyler

Longview

LOUISIANA

Alexandria

Baton Rouge

New Orleans
Metairie
Kenner
Chalmette

Mobile

Biloxi
Gulfport

Lake Pontchartrain

Lafayette

Lake Charles

Beaumont
Port Arthur
Orange

College Station
Bryan

Houston
Pasadena
Baytown
Galveston
Texas City

Galveston Bay

Matagorda Bay

Gulf of Mexico

Houston

Houston Intl.
Airport

Lake Houston

North Houston

Mount Houston

Alexander Deusen Park

San Jacinto River

George Bush Park

Bunker Hill Village

Antique Car Museum

Contemporary Art Museum

Anheuser Busch Brewery

Jancinto City

Channelview

Battleship Texas

Baytown

Houston

Bellaire West

Bellaire

Zoo

Museum of Fine Arts

Galena Park

Buffalo Bayou

Pasadena

Sugar Land

South Houston

La Porte

Highlands

Missouri City

William P. Hobby Airport

Pearland

Johnson Space Ctr. & Space Center Houston

Seabrook

Clear Lake

Friendswood

Galveston Bay

0 10 Km
0 10 Miles

19,686ft
13,124ft
9843ft
6562ft
3281ft
1640ft
820ft
328ft
Sea Level
-820ft
-6562ft
-13,124ft

Elevation scale:

- 6000m
- 4000m
- 3000m
- 2000m
- 1000m
- 500m
- 250m
- 100m
- Sea Level
- -250m
- -500m
- -1000m

Major features and labels include:

CANADA · **ONTARIO** · **MINNESOTA** · **WISCONSIN** · **MICHIGAN**

Lake Superior · **Lake Huron** · **Lake Michigan** · **Lake Nipigon** · **Georgian Bay** · **Ontario Peninsula**

Gogebic Range · **Misquah Hills** · **Huron Mountains** · **Porcupine Mountains**

Selected place names: Thunder Bay, Duluth, Superior, Sault Ste Marie, Sudbury, Marquette, Escanaba, Green Bay, Appleton, Oshkosh, Fond du Lac, Eau Claire, La Crosse, Wausau, Traverse City, Cadillac, Midland, Saginaw, Bay City, Owen Sound, Collingwood, Kitchener, Stratford.

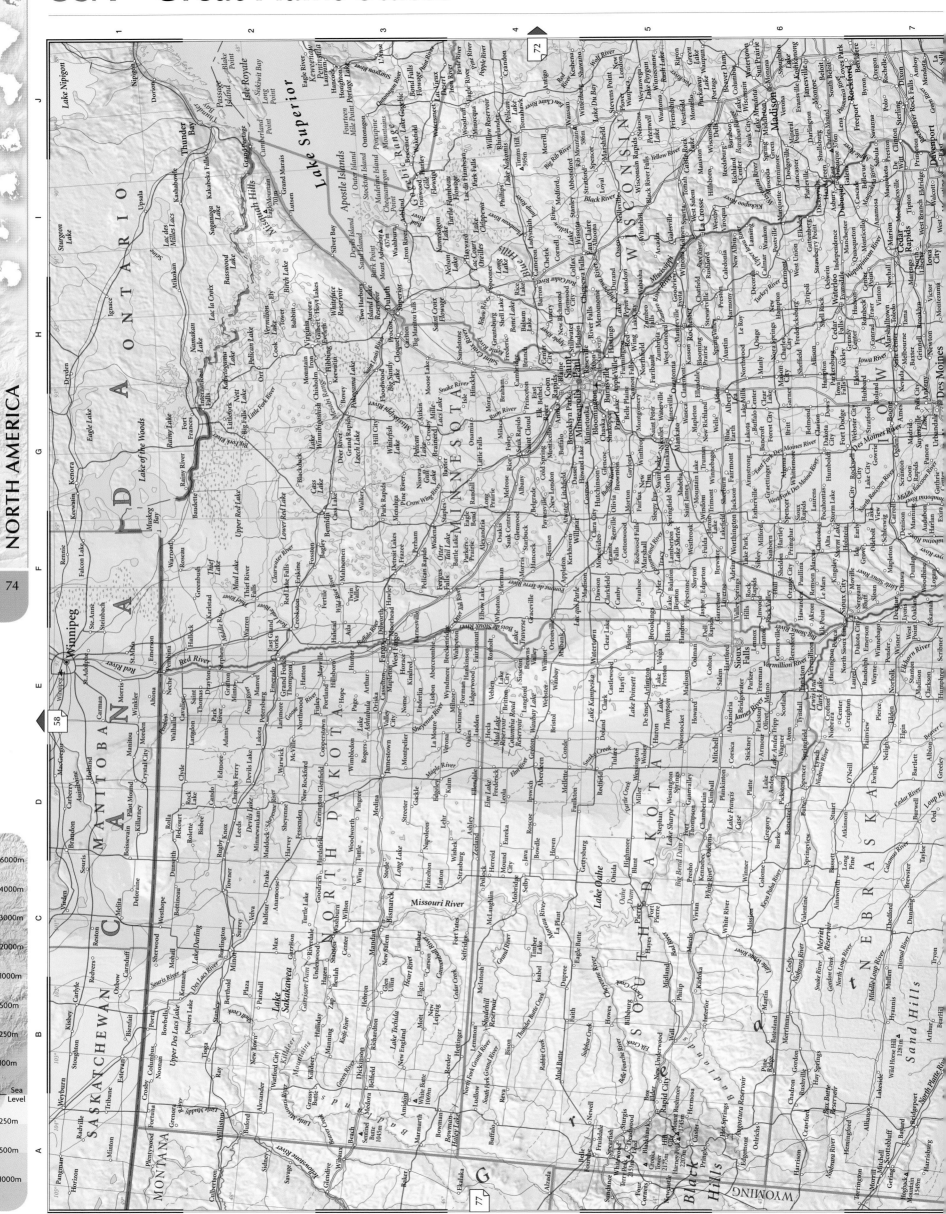

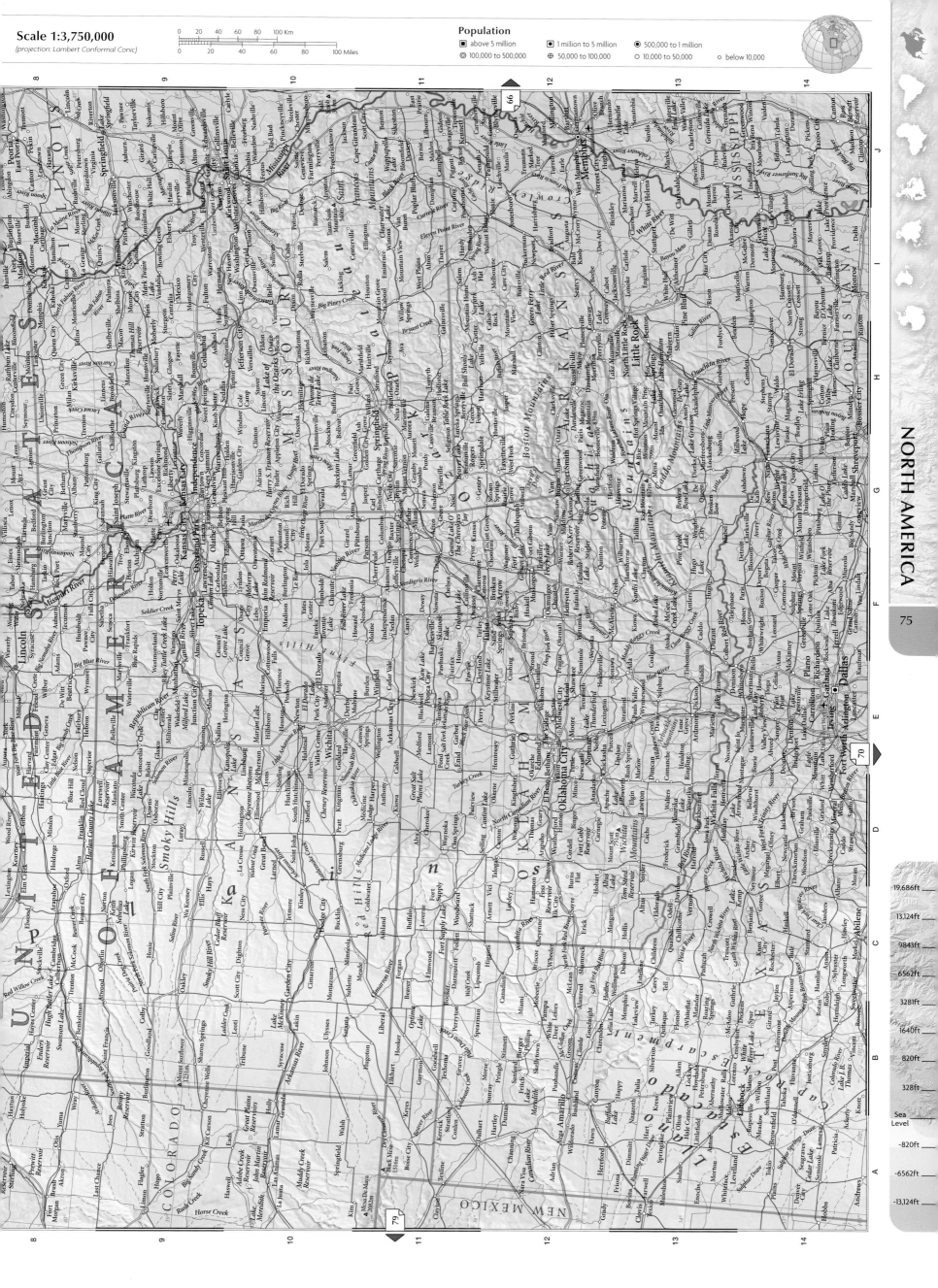

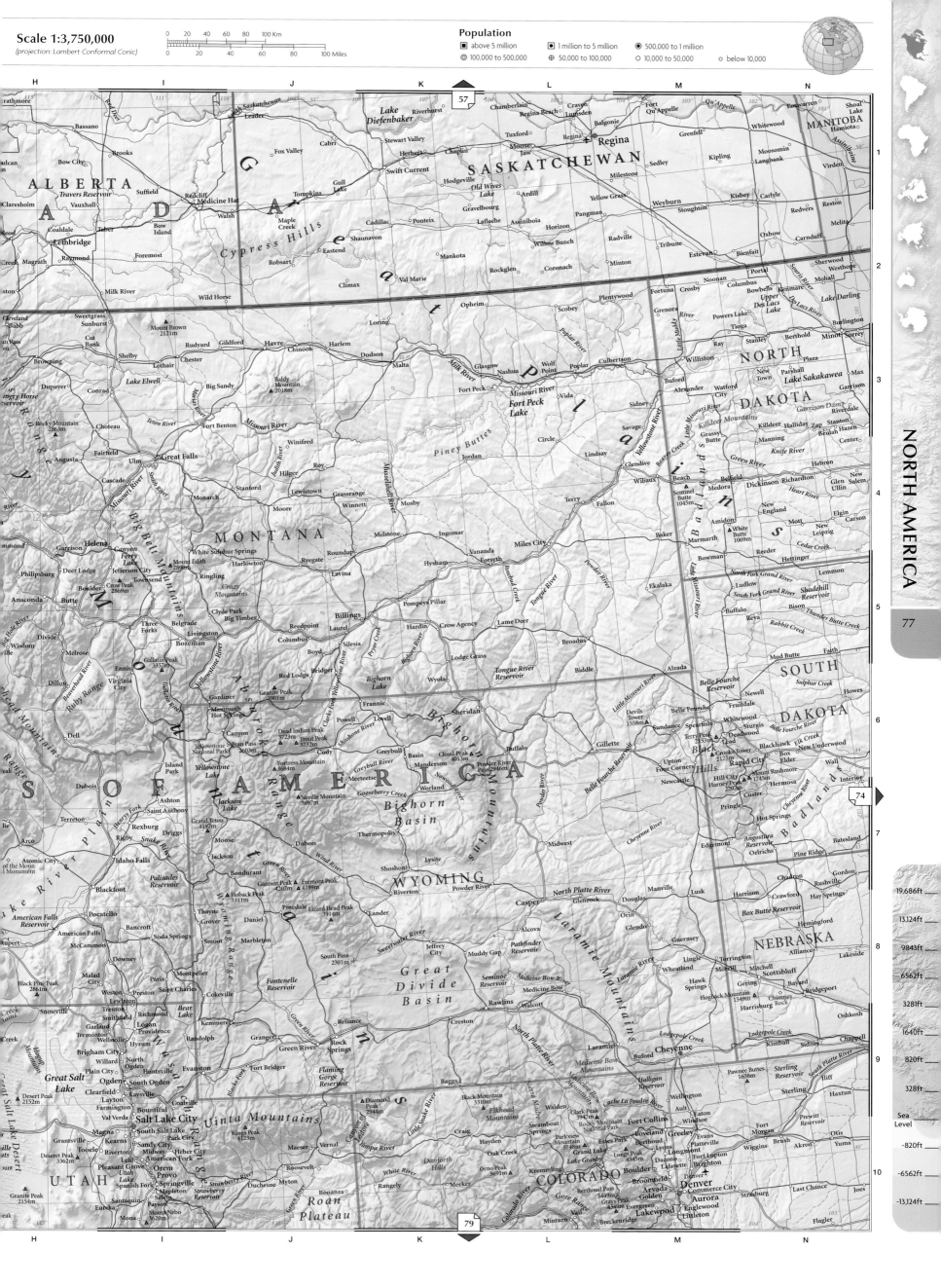

Scale 1:3,750,000
(projection: Lambert Conformal Conic)

0 20 40 60 80 100 Km
0 20 40 60 80 100 Miles

Population

- ◻ above 5 million
- ◼ 1 million to 5 million
- ◉ 500,000 to 1 million
- ◎ 100,000 to 500,000
- ⊕ 50,000 to 100,000
- ○ 10,000 to 50,000
- ○ below 10,000

Elevation scale:
19,686ft
13,124ft
9843ft
6562ft
3281ft
1640ft
820ft
328ft
Sea Level
-820ft
-6562ft
-13,124ft

WYOMING
NEBRASKA
UTAH
COLORADO
ARIZONA
NEW MEXICO
TEXAS
CHIHUAHUA

STATES OF AMERICA

Great Divide Basin
Great Salt Lake
Salt Lake City
Denver
Colorado Springs
Pueblo
Albuquerque
Santa Fe
Phoenix
Tucson
El Paso
Ciudad Juárez
Cheyenne
Flagstaff
Grand Junction
Durango
Gallup
Roswell
Carlsbad
Sand Hills

Rocky Mountains
Uinta Mountains
Wasatch Range
San Juan Mountains
Sangre de Cristo Mountains
Laramie Mountains
Medicine Bow Mountains
Mogollon Rim
Colorado Plateau
Grand Canyon
Coconino Plateau
Kaibab Plateau
Painted Desert
Sacramento Mountains
Guadalupe Mountains

Lake Powell
Glen Canyon Dam
Rainbow Bridge
Monument Valley
Flaming Gorge Reservoir
Navajo Reservoir
Elephant Butte Reservoir
Caballo Reservoir

Colorado River
Green River
Gila River
Rio Grande
Pecos River
San Juan River
Arkansas River
North Platte River
South Platte River

Kings Peak 4123m
Mount Elbert 4399m
Mount Massive 4395m
Mount Harvard 4395m
Blanca Peak 4372m
Uncompahgre Peak 4361m
Mount Wilson 4342m
Pikes Peak 4300m
Wheeler Peak 4011m
Humphreys Peak 3851m
Baldy Peak 3476m
Mount Taylor 3445m
Sierra Blanca Peak 3649m
Guadalupe Peak 2667m

Scale 1:1,875,000

(projection: Lambert Conformal Conic)

0 10 20 30 40 50 Km
0 10 20 30 40 50 Miles

Population

■ above 5 million
◨ 1 million to 5 million
◉ 500,000 to 1 million
◎ 100,000 to 500,000
⊕ 50,000 to 100,000
○ 10,000 to 50,000
○ below 10,000

19,686ft
13,124ft
9843ft
6562ft
3281ft
1640ft
820ft
328ft
Sea Level
-820ft
-6562ft
-13,124ft

Scale 1:8,000,000
(projection: Lambert Conformal Conic)

0 25 50 75 100 125 150 175 200 Km
0 25 50 75 100 125 150 175 200 Miles

Population
- ■ above 5 million
- ■ 1 million to 5 million
- ● 500,000 to 1 million
- ◉ 100,000 to 500,000
- ⊕ 50,000 to 100,000
- ○ 10,000 to 50,000
- ∘ below 10,000

19,686ft
13,124ft
9843ft
6562ft
3281ft
1640ft
820ft
328ft
Sea Level
-820ft
-6562ft
-13,124ft

OCEAN

Beaufort Sea

Limit of summer pack ice

Amundsen Gulf

Dolphin and Union Strait

NUNAVUT

Great Bear Lake

NORTHWEST TERRITORIES

C A N A D A

Mackenzie Mountains

Selwyn Mountains

R o c k y   M o u n t a i n s

YUKON TERRITORY

Pelly Mountains

UNITED STATES

OF AMERICA

A L A S K A

Brooks Range

Endicott Mountains

Philip Smith Mountains

Davidson Mountains

British Mountains

Yukon Flats

Ogilvie Mountains

Wrangell Mountains

Saint Elias Mountains

Chugach Mountains

Kuskokwim Mountains

Mount McKinley (Denali) 6194m

Mount Logan 5959m

Anchorage

Fairbanks

Whitehorse

Dawson

Cook Inlet

Kenai Peninsula

Kodiak Island

BRITISH COLUMBIA

Coast Mountains

Cassiar Mountains

Juneau

Skagway

Alexander Archipelago

Gulf of Alaska

Queen Charlotte Islands

Prince Rupert

Hecate Strait

Queen Charlotte Sound

P A C I F I C   O C E A N

294

287

54

Scale 1:4,250,000
(projection: Lambert Conformal Conic)

0 20 40 60 80 100 Km
0 20 40 60 80 100 Miles

Population
- above 5 million
- 1 million to 5 million
- 500,000 to 1 million
- 100,000 to 500,000
- 50,000 to 100,000
- 10,000 to 50,000
- below 10,000

19,686ft
13,124ft
9843ft
6562ft
3281ft
1640ft
820ft
328ft
Sea Level
-820ft
-6562ft
-13,124ft

NORTH AMERICA

Central America

The Caribbean

UNITED STATES OF AMERICA

FLORIDA

Saint Petersburg
Bradenton
Sarasota
Venice
Port Charlotte
Fort Myers
Cape Coral
Bonita Springs
Naples
Cape Romano

Lake Wales
Avon Park
Arcadia
Wauchula
Punta Gorda
La Belle
Okeechobee
Immokalee
Big Cypress Swamp
Everglades City
Cape Sable

Sebastian
Vero Beach
Fort Pierce
Jensen Beach
Stuart
Hobe Sound
Indiantown
West Palm Beach
Lake Worth
Boynton Beach
Belle Glade
Boca Raton
Pompano Beach
Fort Lauderdale
Hollywood
North Miami
Miami Beach
Miami
Kendall
Homestead
Hialeah
The Everglades

Gulf of Mexico

Dry Tortugas
Marquesas Keys
Key West
Key Largo
Key Largo
Islamorada
Marathon
Florida Keys
Florida Bay

Straits of Florida

Tropic of Cancer

BAHAMAS

Grand Bahama Island
Great Sale Cay
Little Abaco
Coopers Town
West End
Pelican Point
Freeport
Eight Mile Rock
Moores Island
Marsh Harbour
Great Abaco
Cherokee Sound

Northwest Providence Channel
Bimini Islands
Berry Islands
Northeast Providence Channel
Nicholls Town
Current
Eleuthera Island
Governor's Harbour
Nassau
NASSAU
Adelaide
New Providence
Rock Sound

Andros Town
Behring Point
Andros Island
Tongue of the Ocean
Bannerman Town
Arthur's Town
Cat Island

Cay Sal
Anguilla Cays
Santaren Channel
Kemp's Bay
Great Guana Cay
Exuma Sound
Exuma Cays
Cockburn Town
San Salvador

Nicholas Channel
Archipiélago de Sabana
Great Exuma Island
Columbus Point
Conception Island
Santa Maria
Cape
George Town
Rum Cay
Little Exuma
Deadman's Cay
Long Island
Clarence Town

Old Bahama Channel
Archipiélago de Camagüey
Ragged Island Range
Cape Verde
Colonel Hill
Crooked Island
Snug Corner
Acklins Island
Salina Point
Samana Cay
Northeast Point
Plana Cays
Maya
Southeast

Crooked Island Passage
Long Cay
Mayaguana Passage
Caico

CUBA

LA HABANA (HAVANA)
Guanabacoa
Artemisa
Minas de Matahambre
Guanajay
San Cristóbal
Guira de Melena
Guines
Los Palacios
Consolación del Sur
Viñales
Pinar del Río
Mariel
Matanzas
Cárdenas
Jovellanos
Sagua la Grande
Colón
Santo Domingo
Cruces
Jagüey Grande
Peninsula Aguada de Zapata
Santa Clara
Placetas
Caibarién
Cayo Fragoso
Cayo Coco
Cayo de Buena Vista

Golfo de Guanahacabibes
Sierra de los Organos
Cabo de San Antonio
Cabo Corrientes
Cayos de San Felipe
Nueva Gerona
Santa Fé
Cayo Largo
Archipiélago de los Canarreos
Isla de la Juventud
Cienfuegos
Pico San Juan 1156m
Trinidad
Golfo de Cazones
Cabaiguán
Sancti Spíritus
Ciego de Ávila
Morón
Esmeralda
Cayo Romano
Cayo Guajaba
Florida
Nuevitas

MEXICO
Cabo Catoche
Isla Mujeres
Puerto Juárez
Cancún
Leona Vicario
Puerto Morelos
Punta Molas del Norte
Playa del Carmen
Cozumel
Isla Cozumel

Yucatan Channel
Archipiélago de los Colorados

Camagüey
Puerto Padre
Gibara
Las Tunas
Holguín
Banes
Cabo Lucrecia
Mayarí
Moa
Punta Guarico
Sierra del Cristal
Sagua de Tánamo
Baracoa
Great Inagua
Matthew Town
Little Inagua
Northeast Point
Lake R

Golfo de Ana María
Archipiélago de los Jardines de la Reina
Santa Cruz del Sur
Golfo de Guacanayabo
San Pedro
Vertientes
Cauto
Bayamo
Manzanillo
Jiguaní
Palma Soriano
Campechuela
Pilón
Sierra Maestra
La Maya
Guantánamo
Maisí
Punta de Quemado
Cabo Cruz
Pico Turquino 1944m
Santiago de Cuba
Bahía de Guantánamo (to US)
Windward Passage
Port-de-Pa
Môle-St-Nicolas
Gros-
Icar

Great_er

CAYMAN ISLANDS (to UK)
Little Cayman
Cayman Brac
Owen Roberts
Bodden Town
GEORGE TOWN
Grand Cayman

HAITI
Île de la Gonâve
Jérémie
Port-de-Pa
Golfe de la Gon
Canal de
St-

Cap Dame Marie
Dame-Marie
NAVASSA ISLAND (to US)
Chardonnières
Cayes
Port Salut
Pointe à Gravois
Île à Vache
Jamaica Channel
Massif de la
Canal de la
Mira
Coral
Aquin

JAMAICA
Sangster
Montego Bay
South Negril Point
Savanna-La-Mar
Mandeville
Black River
May Pen
Christiana
Spanish Town
Port Royal
Norman Manley
KINGSTON
Portland Point
Port Maria
Port Antonio
Blue Mountain Peak 2256m
Morant Bay

A

ISLAS DE LA BAHÍA
Roatán
Isla de Roatán
Isla de Guanaja
Punta Caxinas

Trujillo
Limón
Iriona
Balfate
Sava
COLÓN
Río Aguán
Río Sico Tinto
Brus Laguna

HONDURAS
San Esteban
Gualaco
Juticalpa
Catacamas
OLANCHO
Sierra de Agalta
Dulce Nombre de Culmí
GRACIAS A DIOS
Puerto Lempira
Río Coco
Laguna de Caratasca

Arrecifes de la Media Luna
Cabo de Gracias a Dios
Arrecife Edinburgh
Bocay
Waspam
Ulmukhuás
Boom
Laguna Bismuna
Dákura
Tuapi
Puerto Cabezas

Bonanza
La Rosita
San Luis
REGIÓN AUTÓNOMA
Siuna
ATLÁNTICO NORTE
Río Prinzapolka
Cayo Muerto
Cayos Miskitos
Cayos Londres

Jalapa
Cerro Chachagon 1804m
Wina
Río Coco
Siquia
Saslaya 1990m
Jinotega
Río Tuma
Prinzapolka
Río Grande de Matagalpa
Matagalpa
MATAGALPA
La Sirena
Wounta
BOACO
Boaco
CHONTALES
Río Escondido
Bluefields
El Rama
Muelle de los Bueyes
Juigalpa
Santo Tomás

NICARAGUA
May May
Cayos Guerrero
Barra de Río Grande
Kara
Cayos King

Lago de Nicaragua
Volcán Concepción 1610m
REGIÓN AUTÓNOMA
Rivas
ATLÁNTICA SUR
Isla de Ometepe
Río Punta Gorda
Monkey Point
RÍO SAN JUAN
Cayos de Perlas
Islas del Maíz

Liberia
La Cruz
San Juan del Sur
Volcán Miravalles 2028m
Upala
Volcán Arenal 1916m
Río San Juan
San Juan del Norte
Barra del Colorado
Cañas
GUANACASTE
Santa Cruz
Volcán Irazú 3390m
Quesada
ALAJUELA
HEREDIA
LIMÓN
Río San Juan
Puerto Viejo
Volcán Poás 2704m
Puntarenas
Puntarenas
Alajuela
Guápiles
Heredia

COSTA RICA
SAN JOSÉ
Limón

COLOMBIA
Ríoha
Dibulla
Santa Marta
Barranquilla
MAGDALENA
Ciénaga
Pico Cristóbal Colón 5775m
Sierra Nevada de
Puerto Colombia
Ernesto Cortissoz
Sitionuevo
Soledad
Sabanalarga
ATLÁNTICO
Santa Catalina
Salamina
Piojo
Aracataca
Fundación
Cartagena
Turbaco
Campo de la Cruz
Valledupar

JAMAICA (inset)

Caribbean Sea
Montego Bay
Falmouth
Discovery Bay
St Ann's Bay
Lucea
Sangster
Clark's Town
Browns Town
Ocho Rios
Port Maria
Don Christophers Point
Dolphin Head
Birchs Hill 545m
551m
The Cockpit Country
Alexandria
Claremont
Annotto Bay
Highgate
Port Antonio
Grange Hill
Negril
Little London
Cambridge
Savanna-La-Mar
Maggotty
Mount Denham 986m
Frankfield
Christiana
Linstead
Ewarton
Bog Walk
North East Point
Crab Pond Point
Mandeville
Chapelton
Spanish Town
Blue Mountain Peak 2256m
Black River
Santa Cruz
May Pen
Portmore
Bath
Golden Grove
Malvern 725m
Old Harbour
Norman Manley
KINGSTON
Alligator Pond
Yallahs Hill 730m
Port Morant
Great Pedro Bluff
Lionel Town
Long Bay
Portland Bight
Wreck Point
Morant Bay
PortRoyal
Portland Point

Scale 1:2,500,000
0 5 10 20 Km
0 5 10 20 Miles

Caribbean Sea

Elevation scale
6000m
4000m
3000m
2000m
1000m
500m
250m
100m
Sea Level
-250m
-500m
-1000m

69
87
89

Scale 1:6,250,000
(projection: Lambert Conformal Conic)

0 25 50 75 100 125 150 175 200 Km
0 25 50 75 100 125 150 175 200 Miles

Population

■ above 5 million
▣ 1 million to 5 million
◉ 500,000 to 1 million
◎ 100,000 to 500,000
⊕ 50,000 to 100,000
○ 10,000 to 50,000
∘ below 10,000

H I J K L M N

290

GUADELOUPE
(to France)

Guadeloupe Passage
Pointe de la Grande Vigie
Anse-Bertrand
Port-Louis
Morne-à-l'Eau le Moule
Grand Cul de Sac Marin Grande Terre
Ste-Rose
Baie-Mahault les Abymes St-François
Lamentin Pointe-à-Pitre Ste-Anne
Pointe Noire Petit-Bourg Pointe des Colibris
Basse Terre Petit Cul-de-Sac Marin
Soufrière Canal de Marie-Galante
1467m
Vieux-Habitants
St-Claude Capesterre-Belle-Eau
BASSE-TERRE
Canal des Saintes
Caribbean Sea
ATLANTIC OCEAN
Scale 1:2,500,000
0 5 10 20 Km
0 5 10 20 Miles

DOMINICA

Dominica Passage
Pointe Jaco
Vieille Case
Portsmouth Melville Hall Marigot
Morne Diablotins 1447m
Salisbury Castle Bruce
St. Joseph
Canefield Rosalie
ROSEAU La Plaine
Caribbean Sea ATLANTIC OCEAN
Scotts Head Village Berekua
Martinique Passage
Scale 1:2,000,000
0 5 10 Km
0 5 10 Miles

MARTINIQUE
(to France)

Martinique Passage
Grand' Rivière Basse-Pointe
le Prêcheur Montagne Pelée Ste-Marie
1397m
St-Pierre la Trinité
Schœlcher le Robert
FORT-DE-FRANCE le Lamentin
le François
Baie de Fort-de-France Rivière-Pilote
les Anses-d'Arlets le Diamant
Ste-Anne
Caribbean Sea ATLANTIC OCEAN
Saint Lucia Channel
Scale 1:2,500,000
0 5 10 20 Km
0 5 10 20 Miles

ST LUCIA

Pointe Du Cap
Gros Islet
George F.L. Charles
CASTRIES
Anse La Raye Dennery
Soufrière
Petit Piton 743m Mount Gimie 950m
Micoud
Gros Piton 798m Laborie
Hewanorra Vieux Fort
Ministre Point
Caribbean Sea ATLANTIC OCEAN
Saint Vincent Passage
Scale 1:2,000,000
0 5 10 Km
0 5 10 Miles

BARBADOS

North Point
Crab Hill ATLANTIC OCEAN
Speightstown Bathsheba
Mount Hillaby 340m Welchman Hall
Holetown The Crane
BRIDGETOWN
Oistins Grantley Adams
Scale 1:2,000,000
0 5 10 Km
0 5 10 Miles

ST VINCENT & THE GRENADINES

Saint Vincent Passage
Fancy Porter Point
La Soufrière 1234m
Chateaubelair Georgetown
St Vincent
Barrouallie North Union
Layou
KINGSTOWN Stubbs
Arnos Vale
Caribbean Sea ATLANTIC OCEAN
Scale 1:2,000,000
0 5 10 Km
0 5 10 Miles

GRENADA

Caribbean Sea
Sauteurs
Victoria
Gouyave Mount St. Catherine 840m
Grenville
ST.GEORGE'S St. David's
Grand Anse
Point Salines ATLANTIC OCEAN
Scale 1:2,000,000
0 5 10 Km
0 5 10 Miles

Tropic of Cancer

ATLANTIC OCEAN

TURKS & CAICOS ISLANDS
(to UK)
Caicos Islands
Grand Caicos
East Caicos
Grand Turk Island
Cockburn COCKBURN TOWN
Harbour Turks Islands

Mouchoir Passage

Hispaniola

DOMINICAN REPUBLIC

Monte Cristi Cabo Isabela
Puerto Plata Cabo Francés Viejo
Haitien Puerto Plata Cabrera
Dajabón Santiago Nagua
Mao Moca Río Yuna
La Vega Bahía de Samaná
San Francisco de Macorís
Pico Duarte 3175m Bonao Michęs
Comendador Monte Plata Hato Mayor El Seibo Higüey Engaño
Cordillera Central Villa Altagracia Cabo
San Juan Cabo
PORT-AU-PRINCE Las Américas
Neiba San Pedro de Macorís
Lago Enriquillo SANTO DOMINGO La Romana
Baní Isla Saona
Barahona Punta Salinas Palenque
Enriquillo Isla Mona
Oviedo Cabo Rojo
la Beata Cabo Beata

Mona Passage

PUERTO RICO
(to US)
Aguadilla Arecibo SAN JUAN Carolina
Utuado Bayamón Caguas Fajardo
Mayagüez Cordillera Central Vieques
Yauco Ponce Guayama Isla de Vieques
Isla Mona

BRITISH VIRGIN ISLANDS
(to UK) Anegada
St Thomas Virgin Gorda
ROAD TOWN Beef Island Tortola
CHARLOTTE AMALIE
VIRGIN ISLANDS
(to US) Virgin Passage
Frederiksted St Croix
Christiansted

Sombrero
(to Anguilla)
ANGUILLA
(to UK)
THE VALLEY Wall Blake
Marigot St-Martin (to France)
Philipsburg
Sint-Maarten St-Barthélémy
(to Netherlands) (to France)
Saba St Eustatius
NETHERLANDS ANTILLES St Kitts
(to Netherlands) Golden Rock
Nevis BASSETERRE
Charlestown Newcastle
ST KITTS & NEVIS V.C. Bird
ST JOHN'S
Redonda Antigua
ANTIGUA & BARBUDA
Codrington Barbuda
Falmouth
PLYMOUTH
MONTSERRAT Guadeloupe Passage
(to UK) le Raizet Port-Louis la Désirade
Ste-Rose Pointe-de-Pitre GUADELOUPE
Basse Terre Marie-Galante (to France)
Soufrière Grand-Bourg
BASSE-TERRE les Saintes
1467m

Dominica Passage
Portsmouth Melville Hall Marigot
Canefield DOMINICA
ROSEAU La Plaine
Martinique Passage
Montagne Pelée Ste-Marie MARTINIQUE
1397m St-Pierre le Lamentin (to France)
FORT-DE-FRANCE Rivière-Pilote
St Lucia Channel
CASTRIES Vigie
ST LUCIA Mount Gimie 950m
Soufrière La Soufrière Hewanorra Vieux Fort
St Vincent Passage
Chateaubelair 1234m **BARBADOS**
ST VINCENT Georgetown Speightstown
& THE GRENADINES KINGSTOWN BRIDGETOWN
Arnos Vale Port Elizabeth Bequia Grantley Adams
Mustique
Canouan
Union Island Carriacou
Hillsborough
GRENADA
Victoria
ST GEORGE'S Grenville
Point Salines

Leeward Islands
Lesser Antilles
Windward Islands

290

ATLANTIC OCEAN

PUERTO RICO
(to US)

Isabela
Aguadilla Arecibo SAN JUAN
Punta Higüero Manati Vega Baja
San Sebastián Laguna Tortuguero Río Grande Cabezas de San Juan
Lago Dos Bocas Bayamón Cataño Fajardo
Bahía de Mayagüez Utuado Carolina Culebra
Mayagüez Adjuntas Orocovis Sierra de Luquillo Isla de Culebra
Cordillera El Yunque 1065m Punta Puerca Culebra
Cerro de Punta 1338m Cayey Humacao Punta Guayanés
San Germán Yauco Juana Díaz Embalse Toa Vaca Monte Pirata 301m
Ponce Guayama Isla de Vieques
Cabo Rojo Punta Brea Salinas Punta Petrona
Caribbean Sea
Scale 1:2,500,000
0 5 10 20 Km
0 5 10 20 Miles

TRINIDAD & TOBAGO

Caribbean Sea
Galera Point
Blanchisseuse Matelot Redhead
PORT-OF-SPAIN Arima Sangre Grande
Tunapuna Caroni River
The Dragon's Mouth Chaguanas Couva Caroni Arena Dam
Gulf of Paria Trinidad
San Fernando Río Claro Guatuaro Point
La Brea Princes Town Killdeer River Rushville
Point Fortin Siparia ATLANTIC OCEAN
Bonasse Moruga Galeota Point
The Serpent's Mouth
VENEZUELA
Scale 1:2,500,000
0 5 10 20 Km
0 5 10 20 Miles

Lesser Antilles

ARUBA
(to Netherlands)
ORANJESTAD Reina Beatrix
Aruba Sint Nicholaas

NETHERLANDS ANTILLES
(to Netherlands)
Noordpunt Malmok
Santa Catharina Bonaire
Curaçao Kralendijk Isla Blanquilla
Hato Airport
WILLEMSTAD Islas Las Aves Isla La Orchila Islas Los Testigos

Isla La Tortuga
Islas Los Roques

Charlotteville
Tobago Scarborough
TRINIDAD & TOBAGO
PORT-OF-SPAIN Galera Point

Peninsula de la Guajira
GUAJIRA Cabo San Román
Los Taques Pueblo Nuevo
Punta Gallinas
Puerto López Punta Fijo Golfo de Venezuela
ZULIA La Vela de Coro
Maracaibo Coro San Luis
Cabimas San Juan de los Cayos
Santa Rita Capatárida Tocuyo de la Costa
Concepción Dabajuro Tucacas
FALCÓN Chichiriviche NUEVA ESPARTA
Altagracia Pedregal Mirimire Juangriego La Asunción
La Juana Maparari Pampatar
Mene de Mauroa Pozuelos Isla de Margarita Porlamar
San Rafael Aguada Grande Morón Puerto Cabello Boca de Pozo Punta de Piedras
VENEZUELA Puerto Cumarebo Carúpano Río Caribe
Araure Aroa VARGAS Río Chico Cumaná Puerto de Hierro
YARACUY San Felipe Maracay La Guaira Puerto La Cruz Güiria Irapa
LARA Valencia Turmero Simón Bolívar SUCRE San Antonio Gulf of Paria San Fernando
Cabudare CARACAS Barcelona Cariaco Caripe Río Claro
Chivacoa Cagua Petare Puertos Piritu Cumanacoa Carúpano Siparia
La Victoria Los Teques ANZOÁTEGUI Maturín The Serpent's Mouth
Villa de Cura Valle de Guanape Aragua de Maturín DELTA AMACURO
MIRANDA MONAGAS Punta Baja
Río Claro Caicara Maturín

61°30' 61°15' 61°10' 61°40'

19,686ft
13,124ft
9843ft
6562ft
3281ft
1640ft
820ft
328ft
Sea Level
-820ft
-6562ft
-13,124ft

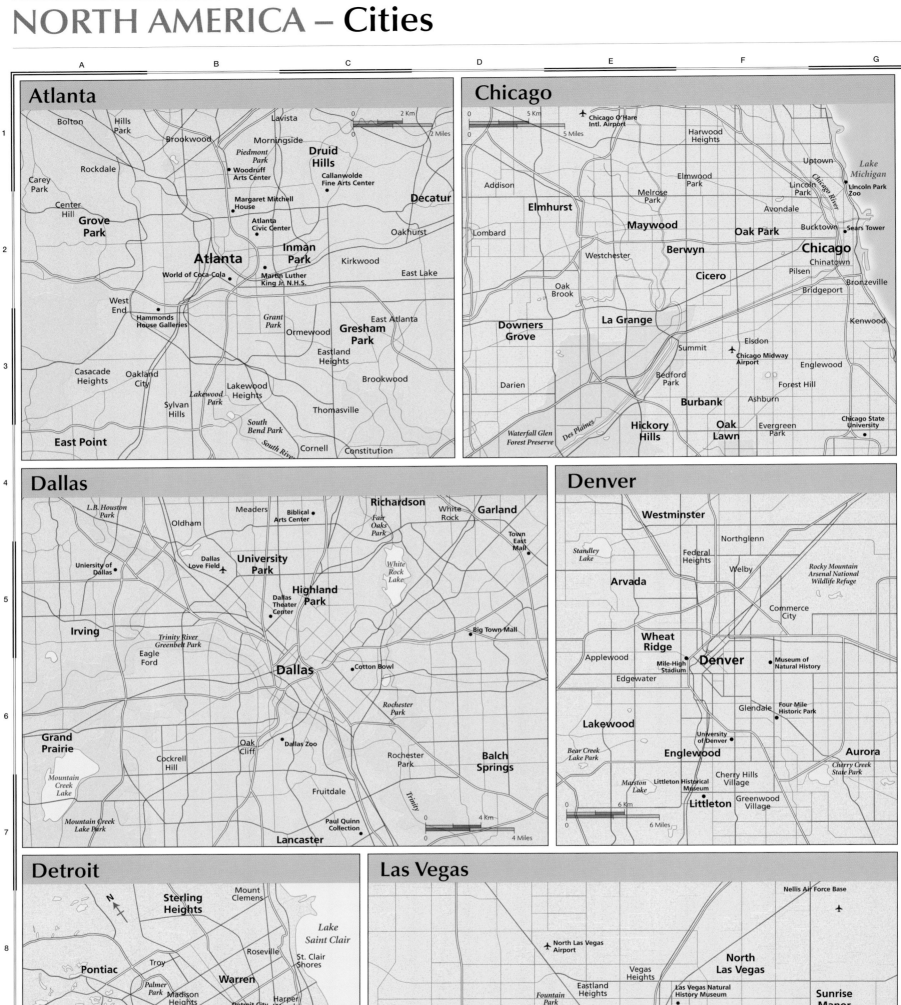

Atlanta

Bolton
Hills Park
Lavista
Brookwood
Morningside
Piedmont Park
Druid Hills
Rockdale
Woodruff Arts Center
Callanwolde Fine Arts Center
Carey Park
Center Hill
Margaret Mitchell House
Decatur
Grove Park
Atlanta Civic Center
Oakhurst
Inman Park
Atlanta
Kirkwood
East Lake
World of Coca-Cola
Martin Luther King Jr. N.H.S.
West End
Hammonds House Galleries
Grant Park
Ormewood
Gresham Park
East Atlanta
Casacade Heights
Oakland City
Eastland Heights
Brookwood
Sylvan Hills
Lakewood Park
Lakewood Heights
Thomasville
East Point
South Bend Park
South River
Cornell
Constitution

0   2 Km
0   2 Miles

Chicago

Chicago O'Hare Intl. Airport
Harwood Heights
Uptown
Lake Michigan
Addison
Elmwood Park
Lincoln Park
Lincoln Park Zoo
Elmhurst
Melrose Park
Avondale
Maywood
Oak Park
Bucktown
Sears Tower
Lombard
Berwyn
Chicago
Westchester
Chinatown
Pilsen
Oak Brook
Cicero
Bronzeville
Bridgeport
Downers Grove
La Grange
Kenwood
Elsdon
Summit
Chicago Midway Airport
Englewood
Darien
Bedford Park
Forest Hill
Burbank
Ashburn
Waterfall Glen Forest Preserve
Des Plaines
Hickory Hills
Oak Lawn
Evergreen Park
Chicago State University

0   5 Km
0   5 Miles

Dallas

L.B. Houston Park
Meaders
Biblical Arts Center
Richardson
White Rock
Garland
Oldham
Fair Oaks Park
Town East Mall
Uniersity of Dallas
Dallas Love Field
University Park
White Rock Lake
Highland Park
Irving
Dallas Theater Center
Trinity River Greenbelt Park
Big Town Mall
Eagle Ford
Dallas
Cotton Bowl
Grand Prairie
Rochester Park
Cockrell Hill
Oak Cliff
Dallas Zoo
Rochester Park
Balch Springs
Mountain Creek Lake
Fruitdale
Trinity
Mountain Creek Lake Park
Paul Quinn Collection
Lancaster

0   4 Km
0   4 Miles

Denver

Westminster
Northglenn
Standley Lake
Federal Heights
Welby
Arvada
Rocky Mountain Arsenal National Wildlife Refuge
Commerce City
Wheat Ridge
Applewood
Mile-High Stadium
Denver
Museum of Natural History
Edgewater
Lakewood
Glendale
Four Mile Historic Park
Bear Creek Lake Park
University of Denver
Aurora
Marston Lake
Littleton Historical Museum
Cherry Hills Village
Englewood
Cherry Creek State Park
Greenwood Village
Littleton

0   6 Km
0   6 Miles

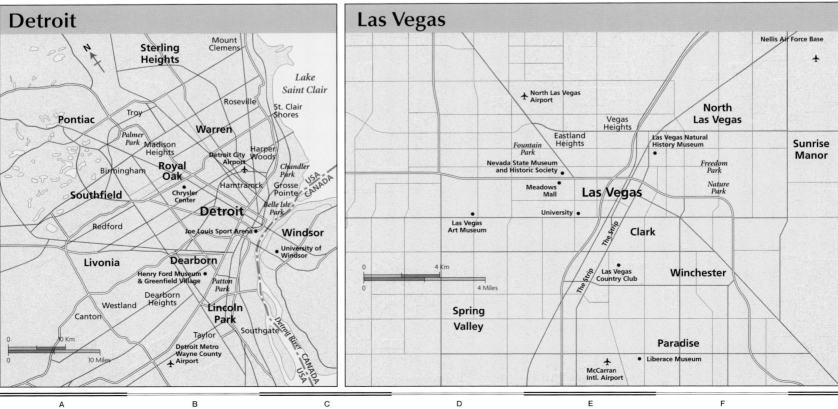

Detroit

Sterling Heights
Mount Clemens
Roseville
Lake Saint Clair
Pontiac
Troy
St. Clair Shores
Palmer Park
Warren
Madison Heights
Birmingham
Harper Woods
Detroit City Airport
Royal Oak
Chandler Park
Hamtramck
Grosse Pointe
Southfield
Chrysler Center
Belle Isle Park
Detroit
USA CANADA
Redford
Joe Louis Sport Arena
Windsor
Livonia
Dearborn
University of Windsor
Henry Ford Museum & Greenfield Village
Patton Park
Westland
Dearborn Heights
Canton
Lincoln Park
Taylor
Southgate
Detroit River CANADA USA
Detroit Metro Wayne County Airport

0   10 Km
0   10 Miles

Las Vegas

Nellis Air Force Base
North Las Vegas Airport
Vegas Heights
North Las Vegas
Fountain Park
Eastland Heights
Las Vegas Natural History Museum
Sunrise Manor
Nevada State Museum and Historic Society
Freedom Park
Meadows Mall
Las Vegas
Nature Park
Las Vegas Art Museum
University
Clark
The Strip
Las Vegas Country Club
Winchester
Spring Valley
Paradise
Liberace Museum
McCarran Intl. Airport

0   4 Km
0   4 Miles

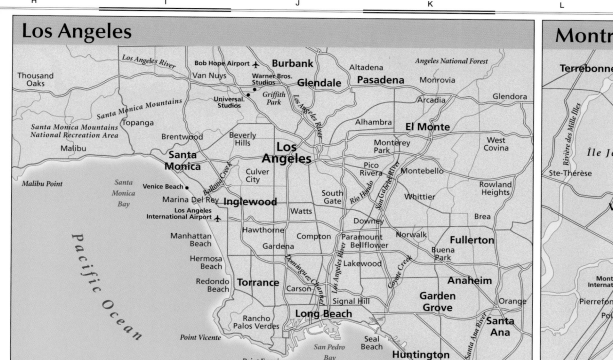

Los Angeles

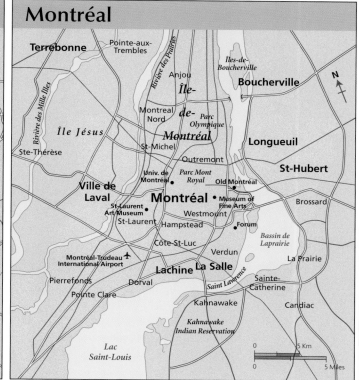

Montréal

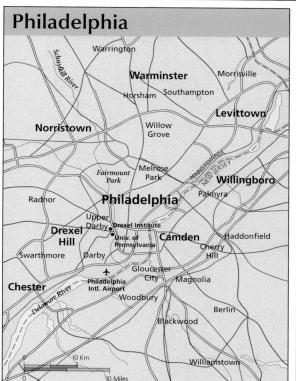

Philadelphia

Seattle

Toronto

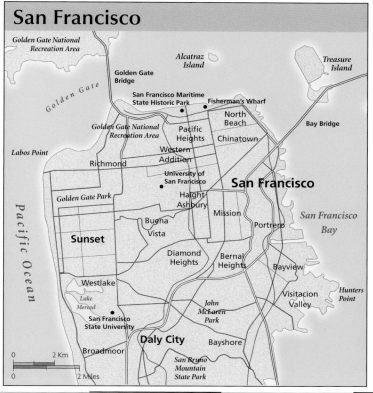

San Francisco

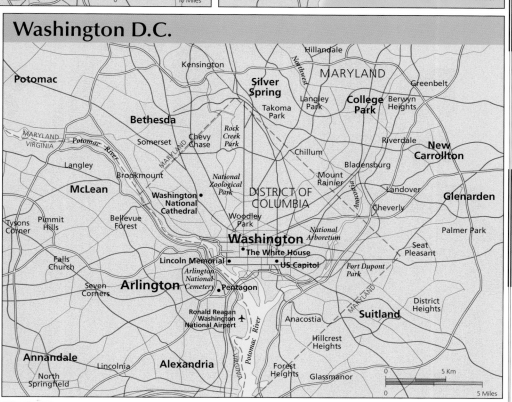

Washington D.C.

SOUTH AMERICA

South America reaches from the humid tropics down into the cold south Atlantic, with a total area of 6,886,000 sq miles (17,835,000 sq km) It comprises 12 separate countries, with the largest, Brazil, covering almost half the continent.

FACTFILE

N **Most Northerly Point:** Punta Gallinas, Colombia 12° 28′ N
S **Most Southerly Point:** Cape Horn, Chile 55° 59′ S
E **Most Easterly Point:** Ilhas Martin Vaz, Brazil 28° 51′ W
W **Most Westerly Point:** Galapagos Islands, Ecuador 92° 00′ W

Largest Lakes:
1. Lake Titicaca, Bolivia/Peru 3141 sq miles (8135 sq km)
2. Mirim Lagoon, Brazil/Uruguay 1158 sq miles (3000 sq km)
3. Lago Poopó, Bolivia 976 sq miles (2530 sq km)
4. Lago Buenos Aires, Argentina/Chile 864 sq miles (2240 sq km)
5. Laguna Mar Chiquita, Argentina 695 sq miles (1800 sq km)

Longest Rivers:
1. Amazon, Brazil/Colombia/Peru 4049 miles (6516 km)
2. Paraná, Argentina/Brazil/Paraguay 2920 miles (4700 km)
3. Madeira, Bolivia/Brazil 2100 miles (3379 km)
4. Purus, Brazil/Peru 2013 miles (3239 km)
5. São Francisco, Brazil 1802 miles (2900 km)

Largest Islands:
1. Tierra del Fuego, Argentina/Chile 18,302 sq miles (47,401 sq km)
2. Ilha de Marajo, Brazil 15,483 sq miles (40,100 sq km)
3. Isla de Chiloé, Chile 3241 sq miles (8394 sq km)
4. East Falkland, Falkland Islands 2550 sq miles (6605 sq km)
5. Isla Wellington, Chile 2145 sq miles (5556 sq km)

Highest Points:
1. Cerro Aconcagua, Argentina 22,831 ft (6959 m)
2. Cerro Ojos del Salado, Argentina/Chile 22,572 ft (6880 m)
3. Cerro Bonete, Argentina 22,546 ft (6872 m)
4. Monte Pissis, Argentina 22,224 ft (6774 m)
5. Cerro Mercedario, Argentina 22,211 ft (6768 m)

Lowest Point:
▼ Península Valdés -131 ft (-40 m) below sea level

Highest recorded temperature:
➕ Rivadavia, Argentina 120°F (49°C)

Lowest recorded temperature:
➖ Sarmiento, Argentina -27°F (-33°C)

Wettest Place:
≋ Quibdó, Colombia 354 in (8990 mm)

Driest Place:
➖ Arica, Chile 0.03 in (0.8 mm)

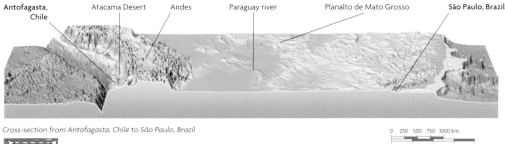

Antofagasta, Chile   Atacama Desert   Andes   Paraguay river   Planalto de Mato Grosso   São Paulo, Brazil

Cross-section from Antofagasta, Chile to São Paulo, Brazil

line of cross-section

0   250   500   750   1000 Km
0   250   500   750   1000 Miles

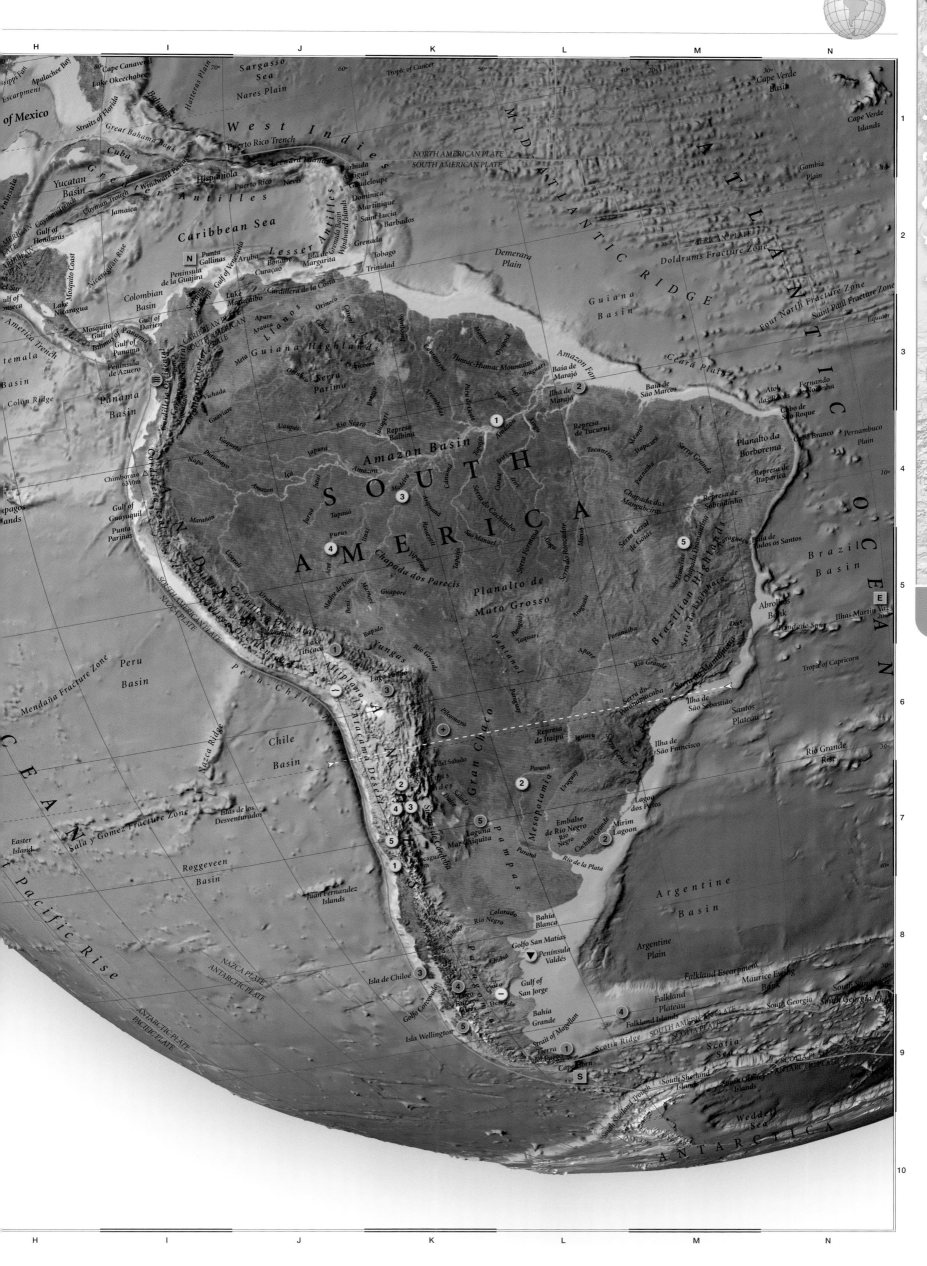

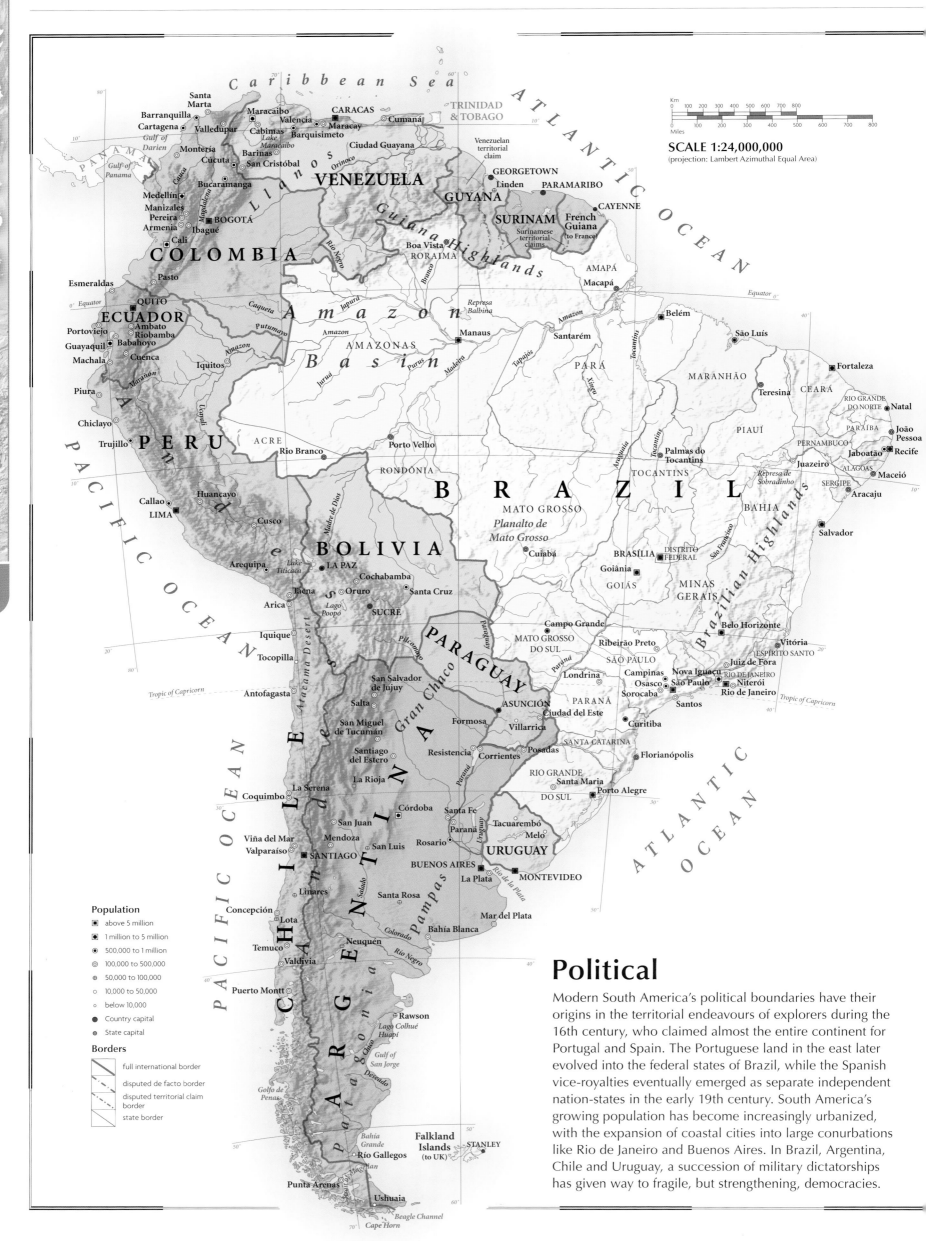

Km
0   100 200 300 400 500 600 700 800

Miles
0   100   200   300   400   500   600   700   800

SCALE 1:24,000,000
(projection: Lambert Azimuthal Equal Area)

Caribbean Sea

Santa Marta
Barranquilla
Cartagena
Valledupar
Maracaibo
Cabimas
Valencia
CARACAS
Maracay
Cumaná
TRINIDAD & TOBAGO
Gulf of Darien
Montería
Barquisimeto
Ciudad Guayana
Venezuelan territorial claim
Cúcuta
Barinas
San Cristóbal
Lake Maracaibo
Gulf of Panama
Medellín
Bucaramanga
VENEZUELA
GEORGETOWN
Linden
PARAMARIBO
Manizales
Pereira
Armenia
BOGOTÁ
GUYANA
SURINAM
CAYENNE
Ibagué
Llanos
Orinoco
Guiana Highlands
French Guiana (to France)
Cali
Boa Vista
Surinamese territorial claims
COLOMBIA
Río Negro
RORAIMA
Esmeraldas
Pasto
Branco
AMAPÁ
Macapá
QUITO
Equator
Caquetá
Amazon
Equator
ECUADOR
Japurá
Belém
São Luís
Portoviejo
Ambato
Riobamba
Represa Balbina
Amazon
Santarém
Guayaquil
Babahoyo
Amazon
Manaus
Machala
Cuenca
AMAZONAS
Fortaleza
Iquitos
Basin
Purus
Madeira
PARÁ
Teresina
MARANHÃO
CEARÁ
Piura
Putumayo
Jurua
Marañón
Ucayali
Tapajós
Xingu
PIAUÍ
RIO GRANDE DO NORTE
Natal
Chiclayo
ACRE
PARAÍBA
João Pessoa
Trujillo
PERU
Rio Branco
Porto Velho
Tocantins
PERNAMBUCO
Jaboatão
Recife
RONDÔNIA
Palmas do Tocantins
Juazeiro
ALAGOAS
Maceió
Callao
Huancayo
B R A Z I L
TOCANTINS
SERGIPE
LIMA
MATO GROSSO
Araguaia
Aracaju
Cusco
Planalto de Mato Grosso
Represa de Sobradinho
BAHIA
Brazilian Highlands
Salvador
Arequipa
BOLIVIA
Cuiabá
BRASÍLIA
DISTRITO FEDERAL
Lake Titicaca
LA PAZ
Cochabamba
Goiânia
São Francisco
Tacna
Oruro
Santa Cruz
GOIÁS
MINAS GERAIS
Arica
SUCRE
Lago Poopó
Belo Horizonte
Campo Grande
Iquique
MATO GROSSO DO SUL
Ribeirão Preto
Vitória
ESPÍRITO SANTO
Tocopilla
Pilcomayo
PARAGUAY
Paraguay
SÃO PAULO
Juiz de Fora
Atacama Desert
Paraná
Campinas
Nova Iguaçu
RIO DE JANEIRO
Londrina
Osasco
São Paulo
Niterói
Antofagasta
San Salvador de Jujuy
Gran Chaco
Sorocaba
Rio de Janeiro
Tropic of Capricorn
PARANÁ
Santos
Tropic of Capricorn
Salta
ASUNCIÓN
Ciudad del Este
Curitiba
San Miguel de Tucumán
Formosa
Villarrica
SANTA CATARINA
Santiago del Estero
Resistencia
Corrientes
Posadas
Florianópolis
La Rioja
A R G E N T I N A
RIO GRANDE DO SUL
Coquimbo
La Serena
Santa Maria
Porto Alegre
San Juan
Córdoba
Santa Fe
Tacuarembó
Viña del Mar
Mendoza
Paraná
Melo
Valparaíso
SANTIAGO
San Luis
Rosario
URUGUAY
Linares
BUENOS AIRES
MONTEVIDEO
C H I L E
Santa Rosa
La Plata
Río de la Plata
Concepción
Pampas
Mar del Plata
Lota
Bahía Blanca
Temuco
Neuquén
Valdivia
Colorado
Río Negro
Puerto Montt
P A T A G O N I A
Rawson
Lago Colhué Huapí
Golfo de Penas
Gulf of San Jorge
Deseado
Bahía Grande
Falkland Islands (to UK)
STANLEY
Río Gallegos
Strait of Magellan
Punta Arenas
Beagle Channel
Ushuaia
Cape Horn

PANAMA
PACIFIC OCEAN
ATLANTIC OCEAN
ATLANTIC OCEAN

Population

- ■ above 5 million
- ▣ 1 million to 5 million
- ◉ 500,000 to 1 million
- ◎ 100,000 to 500,000
- ⊕ 50,000 to 100,000
- ∘ 10,000 to 50,000
- ∘ below 10,000
- ● Country capital
- ◦ State capital

Borders

- full international border
- disputed de facto border
- disputed territorial claim border
- state border

Political

Modern South America's political boundaries have their origins in the territorial endeavours of explorers during the 16th century, who claimed almost the entire continent for Portugal and Spain. The Portuguese land in the east later evolved into the federal states of Brazil, while the Spanish vice-royalties eventually emerged as separate independent nation-states in the early 19th century. South America's growing population has become increasingly urbanized, with the expansion of coastal cities into large conurbations like Rio de Janeiro and Buenos Aires. In Brazil, Argentina, Chile and Uruguay, a succession of military dictatorships has given way to fragile, but strengthening, democracies.

Languages

Prior to European exploration in the 16th century, a diverse range of indigenous languages were spoken across the continent. With the arrival of Iberian settlers, Spanish became the dominant language, with Portuguese spoken in Brazil, and Native American languages such as Quechua and Guaraní, becoming concentrated in the continental interior. Today this pattern persists, although successive European colonization has led to Dutch being spoken in Suriname, English in Guyana, and French in French Guiana, while in large urban areas, Japanese and Chinese are increasingly common.

Language groups
- American Indian
- Germanic
- Romance

Standard of living

Wealth disparities throughout the continent create a wide gulf between affluent landowners and those afflicted by chronic poverty in inner-city slums. The illicit production of cocaine, and the hugely influential drug barons who control its distribution, contribute to the violent disorder and corruption which affect northwestern South America, de-stabilizing local governments and economies.

Standard of living
(UN human development index)
- low
- high

Population

Almost half of South America's population lives in Brazil but, due to the large uninhabited expanses of the Amazon Basin, its overall population density is much lower than in other countries. During the 20th century the most important population trend was the movement from rural to urban areas, giving rise to great population concentrations in large cities like São Paulo, Rio de Janeiro, Caracas, Lima, Bogotá and Buenos Aires.

Population density
(people per sq km)
- 0–4
- 5–9
- 10–14
- 15–19
- 20–29
- 30 +

Transport
- major roads and motorways
- major railways
- international borders
- transport intersections
- international airports
- major ports

Transport

Most major road and rail routes are confined to the coastal regions by the forbidding natural barriers of the Andes mountains and the Amazon Basin. Few major cross-continental routes exist, although Buenos Aires serves as a transport centre for the main rail links to La Paz and Valparaíso, while the construction of the Trans-Amazon and Pan-American Highways have made direct road travel possible from Recife to Lima and from Puerto Montt up the coast into central America. A new waterway project is proposed to transform the Paraguay river into a major shipping route, although it involves considerable wetland destruction.

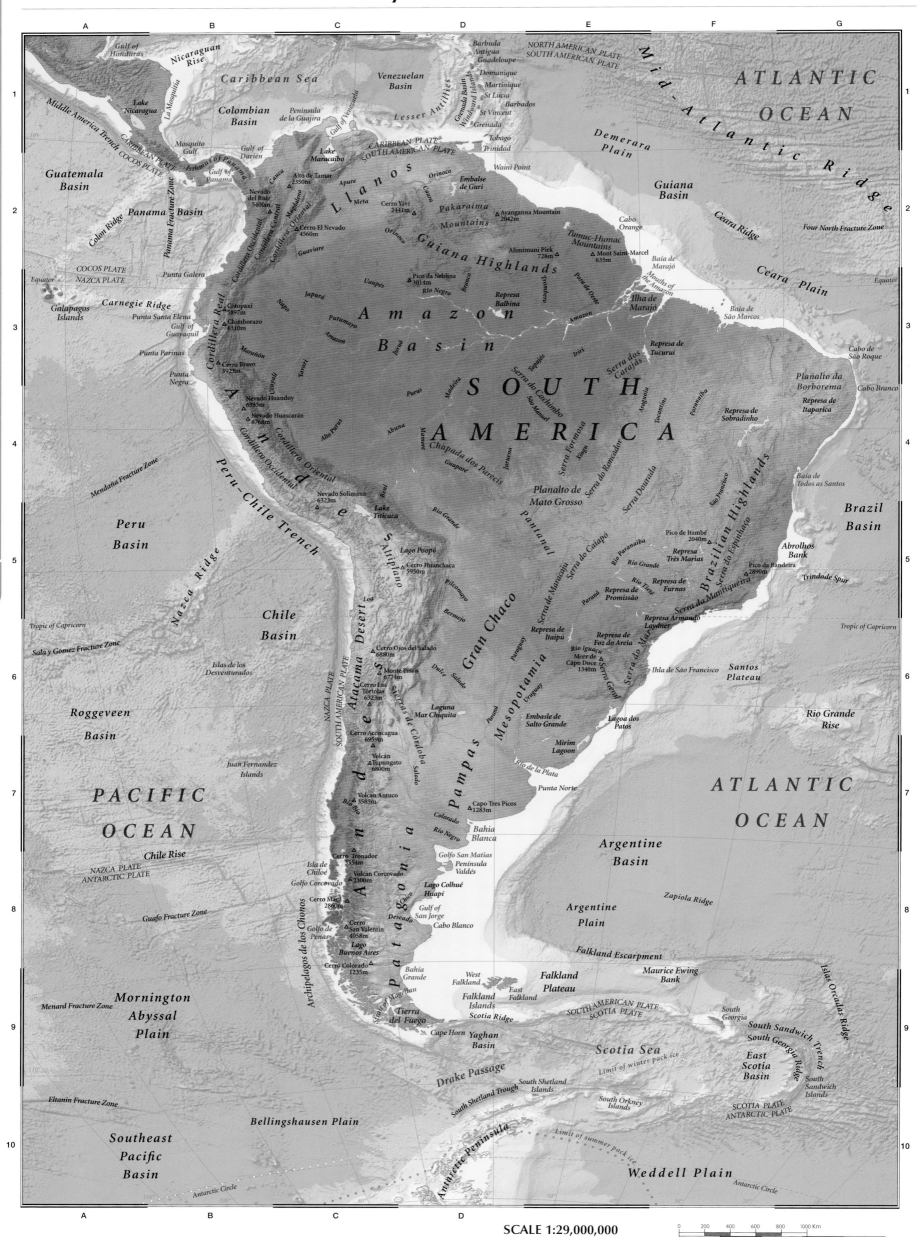

Gulf of Honduras
Nicaraguan Rise
Caribbean Sea
NORTH AMERICAN PLATE
SOUTH AMERICAN PLATE
Mid-Atlantic Ridge
ATLANTIC OCEAN

Lake Nicaragua
La Mosquitia
Colombian Basin
Venezuelan Basin
Barbuda
Antigua
Guadeloupe
Dominique
Martinique
St Lucia
Barbados
St Vincent
Grenada
Tobago
Trinidad
Grenada Islands
Windward Islands
Lesser Antilles

Middle America Trench
CARIBBEAN PLATE
COCOS PLATE
Mosquito Gulf
Isthmus of Panama
Gulf of Darien
Peninsula de la Guajira
Gulf of Venezuela
CARIBBEAN PLATE
SOUTH AMERICAN PLATE
Waini Point
Demerara Plain
Guiana Basin
Ceara Ridge
Four North Fracture Zone

Guatemala Basin
Panama Basin
Colon Ridge
Panama Fracture Zone
Gulf of Panama
Alto de Tamar 2350m
Cauca
Apure
Orinoco
Embalse de Guri
Pakaraima Mountains
Ayangganna Mountain 2042m
Cabo Orange
Ceara Plain

COCOS PLATE
NAZCA PLATE
Nevado del Ruíz 5400m
Cerro El Nevado 4560m
Meta
Cerro Yavi 2441m
Alimimuni Pick 728m
Mont Saint-Marcel 635m
Tumuc-Humac Mountains
Baía de Marajó

Equator
Punta Galera
Cordillera Oriental
Cordillera Occidental
Cordillera Central
Guaviare
Llanos
Orinoco
Guiana Highlands
Pico da Neblina 3014m
Rio Negro
Branco
Represa Balbina
Fronteira
Pará de Oeste
Ilha de Marajó
Mouths of the Amazon
Baía de São Marcos
Equator

Galapagos Islands
Carnegie Ridge
Punta Santa Elena
Cordillera Real
Japurá
Negro
Putumayo
Uaupés
Amazon
Amazon Basin
Amazon
Cabo de São Roque

Gulf of Guayaquil
Cotopaxi 5897m
Chimborazo 6310m
Marañón
Iça
Amazon
Purús
Madeira
Tapajós
São Manuel
Iriri
Serra dos Carajás
Represa de Tucurui
Planalto da Borborema
Cabo Branco

Punta Parinas
Cerro Bravo 3923m
Huallaga
Ucayali
Javari
Yavarí
Madeira
SOUTH
Serra do Cachimbo
Tapajós
Tocantins
Represa de Sobradinho
Represa de Itaparica

Punta Negra
A
Nevado Huandoy 6395m
Nevado Huascarán 6768m
n
Purús
Ahuna
AMERICA
Serra Formosa
Xingu
Serra do Roncador
Araguaia
São Francisco
Brazilian Highlands

d
Cordillera Oriental
Cordillera Occidental
Alto Purús
Beni
Mamoré
Chapada dos Parecis
Juruena
Serra Dourada
Baía de Todos as Santos

Mendaña Fracture Zone
e
Nevado Solimana 6323m
Guaporé
Planalto de Mato Grosso
Serra do Caiapó
Pico de Itambé 2040m
Pico da Bandeira 2890m
Brazil Basin

Peru Basin
Nazca Ridge
Peru-Chile Trench
s
Lake Titicaca
Rio Grande
Pantanal
Serra de Maracaju
Rio Paranaíba
Serra do Espinhaço
Abrolhos Bank

Altiplano
Lago Poopó
Pilcomayo
Serra Geral
Rio Grande
Represa Três Marias
Trindade Spur

Tropic of Capricorn
Chile Basin
Cerro Huanchaca 5950m
Loa
Bermejo
Gran Chaco
Rio Tietê
Represa de Furnas
Serra da Mantiqueira
Tropic of Capricorn

Sala y Gomez Fracture Zone
Atacama Desert
NAZCA PLATE
Islas de los Desventurados
Cerro Ojos del Salado 6880m
Dulce
Salado
Paraguay
Paraná
Represa de Itaipu
Represa de Foz do Areia
Represa de Promissão
Represa Armando Laydner
Ihla de São Francisco
Santos Plateau

Roggeveen Basin
Juan Fernandez Islands
SOUTH AMERICAN PLATE
Monte Pissis 6774m
Cerro Las Tórtolas 6323m
Mesopotamia
Uruguay
Rio Iguaçu
Morr de Capo Doce 1340m
Lagoa dos Patos
Rio Grande Rise

Cerro Aconcagua 6959m
Laguna Mar Chiquita
Paraná
Embalse de Salto Grande
Mirim Lagoon

PACIFIC OCEAN
Chile Rise
NAZCA PLATE
ANTARCTIC PLATE
Volcán Tupungato 6800m
Salado
Pampas
Rio de la Plata
Punta Norte
ATLANTIC OCEAN

Volcan Antuco 3585m
Bío Bío
Colorado
Capo Tres Picos 1283m
Argentine Basin

Guafo Fracture Zone
Cerro Tronador 3554m
Isla de Chiloé
Golfo Corcovado
Rio Negro
Bahía Blanca
Zapiola Ridge

Volcan Corcovado 2300m
Golfo San Matias
Peninsula Valdés
Argentine Plain

Cerro Macá 2960m
Chico
Deseada
Golfo San Jorge
Cabo Blanco
Lago Colhué Huapí

Archipelagos de los Chonos
Golfo de Penas
Cerro San Valentin 4058m
Lago Buenos Aires
Patagonia
Falkland Escarpment
Maurice Ewing Bank
Islas Orcadas Ridge

Menard Fracture Zone
Mornington Abyssal Plain
Cerro Colorado 1235m
Bahía Grande
West Falkland
East Falkland
Falkland Islands
Falkland Plateau
South Georgia
South Sandwich Trench
South Georgia Ridge

Strait of Magellan
Tierra del Fuego
Scotia Ridge
SOUTH AMERICAN PLATE
SCOTIA PLATE
East Scotia Basin

Cape Horn
Yaghan Basin
Scotia Sea
South Sandwich Islands
SCOTIA PLATE
ANTARCTIC PLATE

Drake Passage
Limit of winter pack ice
South Shetland Islands
South Orkney Islands

Eltanin Fracture Zone
Southeast Pacific Basin
Bellingshausen Plain
Antarctic Peninsula
South Shetland Trough
Limit of summer pack ice
Weddell Plain

Antarctic Circle
Antarctic Circle

SCALE 1:29,000,000
(projection: Lambert Azimuthal Equal Area)

| 0 | 200 | 400 | 600 | 800 | 1000 Km |
| 0 | 200 | 400 | 600 | 800 | 1000 Miles |

Climate

The climate of South America is influenced by three principal factors: the seasonal shift of high pressure air masses over the tropics, cold ocean currents along the western coast, affecting temperature and precipitation, and the mountain barrier produced by by the Andes, which creates a rain shadow over much of the south.

Climate

- tundra
- cool continental
- warm humid
- semi-arid
- arid
- humid equatorial
- tropical

☼ daily hours of sunshine, January
☼ daily hours of sunshine, July
→ cold wind

Average Rainfall

January rainfall

July rainfall

Rainfall
- 0–25 mm (0–1 in)
- 25–50 mm (1–2 in)
- 50–100 mm (2–4 in)
- 100–200 mm (4–8 in)
- 200–300 mm (8–12 in)
- 300–400 mm (12–16 in)
- 400–500 mm (16–20 in)
- more than 500 mm (20 in)

Average Temperature

January temperature

July temperature

Temperature
- below -30°C (-22°F)
- -30 to -20°C (-22 to -4°F)
- -20 to -10°C (-4 to 14°F)
- -10 to 0°C (14 to 32°F)
- 0 to 10°C (32 to 50°F)
- 10 to 20°C (50 to 68°F)
- 20 to 30°C (68 to 86°F)
- above 30°C (86°F)

Landuse

Many foods now common worldwide originated in South America. These include the potato, tomato, squash, and cassava. Today, large herds of beef cattle roam the temperate grasslands of the Pampas, supporting an extensive meat-packing trade in Argentina, Uruguay and Paraguay. Corn (maize) is grown as a staple crop across the continent and coffee is grown as a cash crop in Brazil and Colombia. Coca plants grown in Bolivia, Peru and Colombia provide most of the western world's cocaine. Fish and shellfish are caught off the western coast, especially anchovies off Peru, shrimps off Ecuador and pilchards off Chile.

Environmental Issues

The Amazon Basin is one of the last great wilderness areas left on Earth. The tropical rainforests which grow there are a valuable genetic resource, containing innumerable unique plants and animals. The forests are increasingly under threat from new and expanding settlements and 'slash and burn' farming techniques, which clear land for the raising of beef cattle, causing land degradation and soil erosion.

Environmental Issues

- national parks
- tropical forest
- forest destroyed
- desert
- desertification
- polluted rivers
- marine pollution
- heavy marine pollution
- • poor urban air quality

Using the Land and Sea

- barren land
- cropland
- desert
- forest
- mountain region
- pasture
- • major conurbations
- cattle
- pigs
- sheep
- bananas
- corn (maize)
- citrus fruits
- cocoa
- cotton
- coffee
- fishing
- oil palms
- peanuts
- rubber
- shellfish
- soya beans
- sugar cane
- vineyards
- wheat

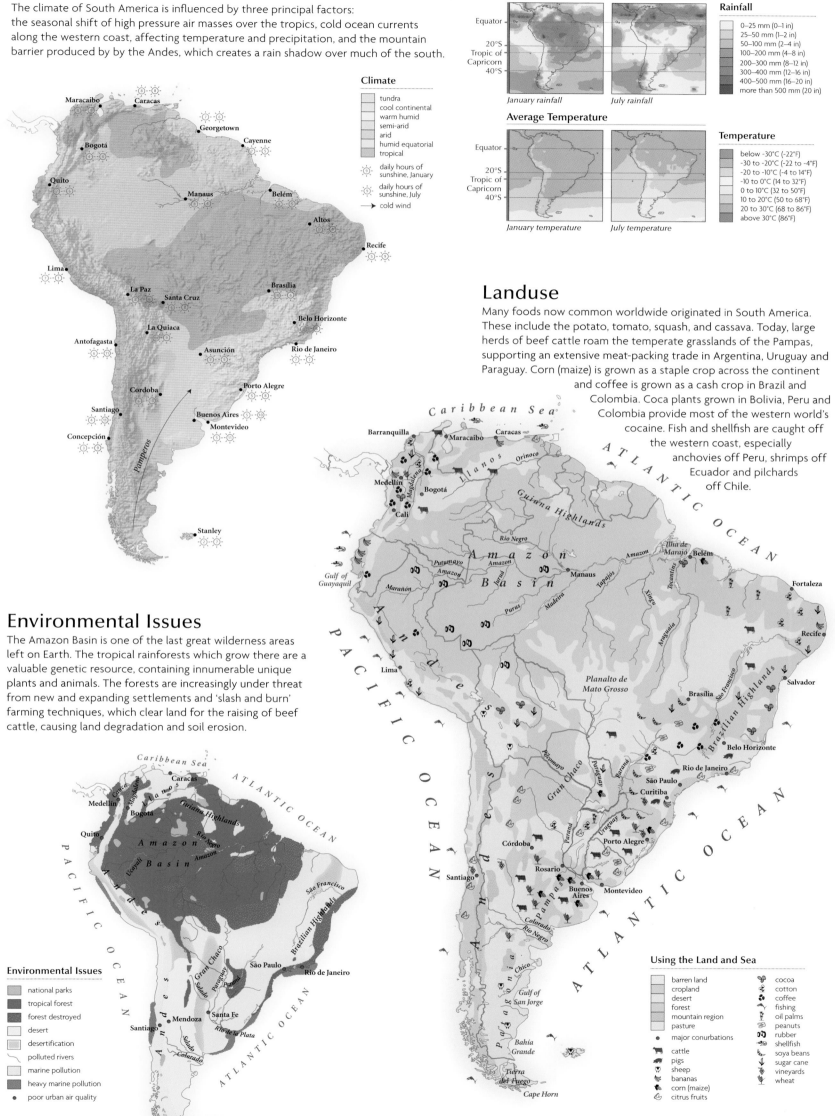

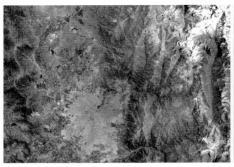

1 SANTIAGO, CHILE
Chile's capital city was founded in 1541 by Pedro de Valdivia who chose the location because it had a Mediterranean climate and was easy to defend.

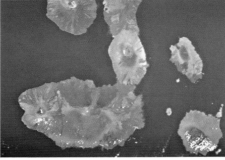

2 GALAPAGOS ISLANDS, ECUADOR
These islands are a collection of volcanoes rising from the ocean floor 621 miles (1000 km) west of the South American mainland.

3 SALAR DE UYUNI, BOLIVIA
Occupying a depression high up on the Altiplano between the volcanoes of the western Andes and the fold belts of the eastern Andes, this is the world's largest salt flat.

4 MACHU PICCHU, PERU
Perched precariously above the Urubamba valley, the lost Inca retreat was rediscovered in 1911 by Hiram Bingham, an American archaeologist.

9 LAGO VIEDMA, ARGENTINA
Lago Viedma enjoys a milky-blue appearance due to the glacial sediment suspended in its waters.

10 LOS LAGOS, CHILE
A region of many lakes at the foothills of the Andes in south-central Chile, this area is an attraction for many tourists.

11 ROSARIO, ARGENTINA
Located on the west bank of the Paraná river, Rosario lies at that heart of Argentina's industrial corridor, centred on the river.

12 RIVER PLATE, ARGENTINA/URUGUAY
Fed by the Paraná and Uruguay rivers, this Atlantic Ocean inlet separates Argentina and Uruguay.

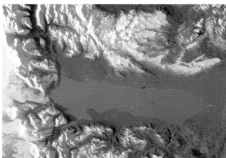

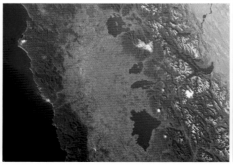

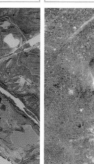

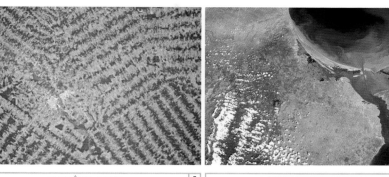

RONDÔNIA, BRAZIL
Pale strips of forest clearance can be seen along perpendicular tracks in this region of the Amazon Basin.

5

MARACAIBO, VENEZUELA
Maracaibo is the centre of Venezuela's oil industry and its second largest city with a population of 1.6 million.

6

AMAZON RIVER/RIO NEGRO, BRAZIL
The dark, plant debris-stained waters of the Rio Negro join the beige Amazon near the city of Manaus.

7

EMBALSE DE GURI, VENEZUELA
This enormous reservoir, on the Caroni river, was completed in 1986 and its hydroelectric plant was the first to produce more than 10 gigawatts of electricity.

8

REST CLEARANCE IN SANTA CRUZ STATE, BOLIVIA
This infrared image shows the distinctive radial clearance patterns of original tropical dry forest with a small settlement at each centre.

13

LAGOA DOS PATOS AND MIRIM LAGOON, BRAZIL/URUGUAY
These two lagoons are separated from the Atlantic Ocean by 248 miles (400 km) of sandbar.

14

ITAIPU DAM, BRAZIL/PARAGUAY
With an installed capacity of 14 gigawatts this is the world's largest hydroelectric power scheme delivering 95% of Paraguay's energy needs and 24% of Brazil's.

15

POINT BALEIA, BRAZIL
This headland has built up through steady accumulation of silt and sediment, shaped by tides and ocean currents.

16

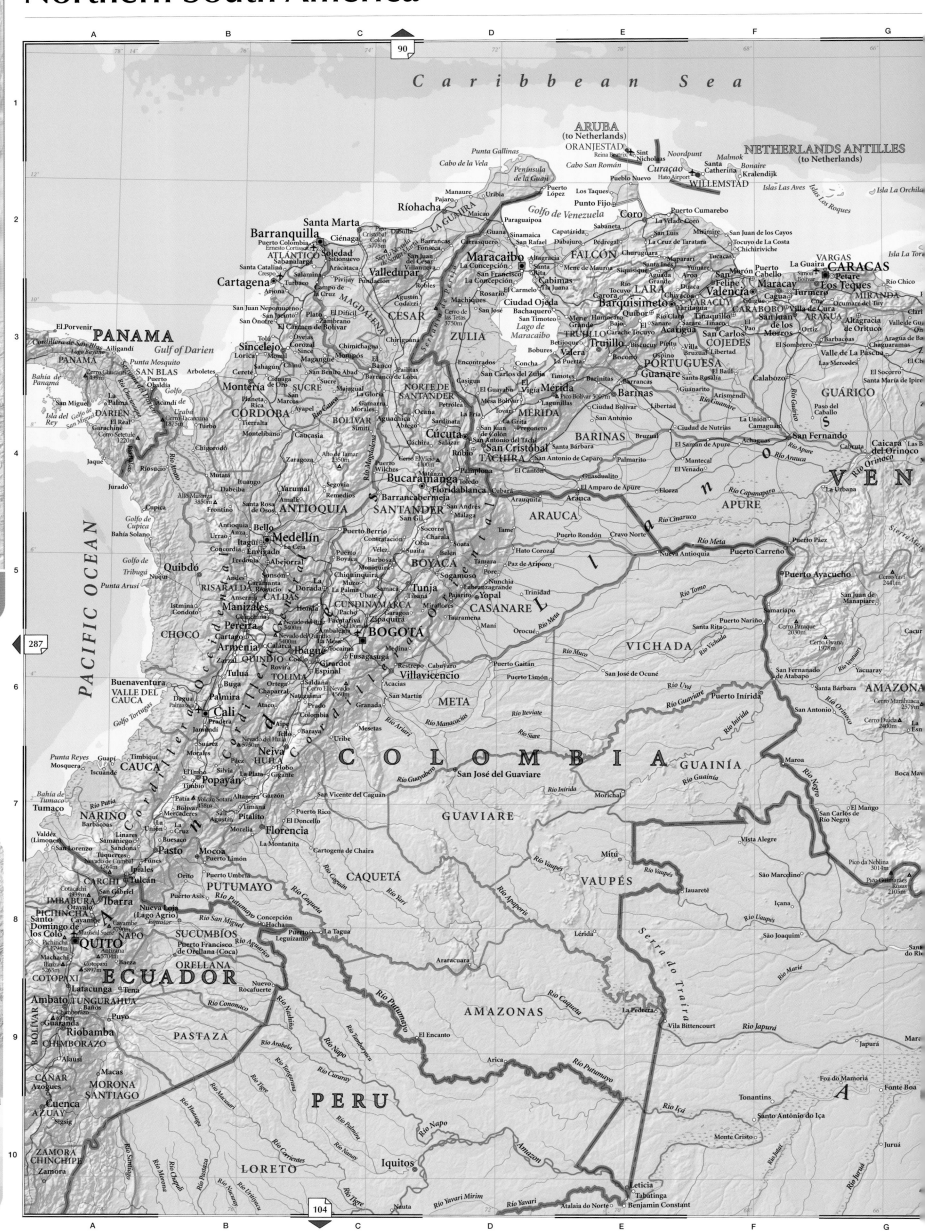

Caribbean Sea

ARUBA
(to Netherlands)
ORANJESTAD
Reina Beatrix ● Sint Nicholaas
Noordpunt   Malmok
Curaçao ✈ Bonaire
Hato Airport Santa
Catherina ● Kralendijk
WILLEMSTAD

NETHERLANDS ANTILLES
(to Netherlands)

Islas Las Aves   Islas Los Roques   Isla La Orchila

Punta Gallinas
Cabo de la Vela
Península
de la Guajira
Cabo San Román

Manaure ● Pajaro
Uribia
PENÍNSULA
DE LA GUAJÍRA
Maicao

Puerto
López
Los Taques
Punto Fijo

Golfo de
Venezuela

Pueblo Nuevo

Coro

Puerto Cumarebo
La Vela de Coro
San Juan de los Cayos
Mirimire   Tucacas
La Cruz de Taratara
Chichiriviche

La Guaira   Isla La Tortu

VARGAS
CARACAS
Simón
Bolívar ✈ Petare
Los Teques

Ríohacha

Santa Marta
Barranquilla
Ciénaga
ATLÁNTICO   Soledad
Ernesto Cortissoz ✈
Sabanalarga
Santa Catalina
Crespo
Cartagena
Turbaco
Arjona

Cristóbal
Colón
5775m
Dibulla
Barrancas
Fonseca
San Juan
del Cesar
Villanueva
Robles

Valledupar

Sinamaica

Maracaibo
La Concepción
La Concepción
Santa
Rita
Machiques
Carmelo
Rosario
La
Juana

Ciudad Ojeda
San José

Cabimas

Lago de
Maracaibo
Bachaquero
Mene
Grande

Altagracia
Mene de Mauroa
Dabajuro
Pedregal
Capatárida

FALCÓN
Churuguara
Siquisique
Baragua
Aroa
Yumare
Morón   Puerto
Cabello

San Luis
Mapararí

San Carlos
Tinaco
Nirgua
San
Felipe

Valencia
Maracay
Turmero

LARA
Barquisimeto
YARACUY
CARABOBO
Guigue
Güigue
Cagua

Quíbor
Río Clara
Tocuyo
Carora
Biscucuy
Guanarito
Quanare
Santa
Inés

Altagracia
de Orituco

ARAGUA
Villa de Cura
Ocumare del Tuy
Río Chico

MIRANDA
Valle de Gu

FALCÓN
Chivacoa

Sabaneta
Guaqua

Dibulla

Sierra Nevada
de Santa Marta

Guana

Piviiay
El Difícil

CESAR

ZULIA

San José

El Banco

Chiriguaná
Chimichagua

El Carmen de Bolívar
Ovejas

Cerro de
las Tetas
3750m

Encontrados

San Carlos del Zulia

El Guayabo
El
Vigía
Mérida

Concha

Tovar   San
Lugo   Ciudad Bolívar
Cristóbal   Santa Bárbara

Betijoque
Bobures
Valera   La Puerta
Biscucuy
Bocono

Espino

TRUJILLO
Trujillo
Carache   Tocuyo

Ospino

MÉRIDA

Bainas
Barrancas

PORTUGUESA
Guanare
El Baúl

Santa Rosalía

BARINAS
Barinas

Arismendi
Río Guanare

GUÁRICO
Calabozo   El Sombrero
Barbacoas
Las Mercedes
El Socorro
Santa María de Ipire
El Ch

San Carlos

San Juan
de los
Morros

Valle de la Pasqua

ATLÁNTICO

Sabanalarga

Fundación
Aracataca
Salamina
Plato
Tenerife
Campo de
la Cruz

Pueblo Bello
San Juan del Cesar

Magangué
El Difícil

Cúcuta

NORTE DE
SANTANDER
Tibú
Ocaña
Sardinata
Ábrego

Petrólea
La
Fría

Lobatera   San
Antonio
del Táchira
TÁCHIRA
Rubio
Pamplona
San Antonio de Caparo
La Grita
Pregonero
Ciudad Bolívar 500m
San Antonio

Ciudad de Nutrias
La Unión

BARINAS

San Fernando

ARAGUA

El Pao

COJEDES
San Carlos

Tinaquillo

Panamá

PANAMA

Cordillera de San Blas

Golfo de Darien

Gulf of Darien

Lago Bayano

Ailigandí
Cerro Chucantí
1439m

Punta Mosquito
SAN BLAS
Puerto
Obaldía

Acandí de

Arboletes

Planeta
Rica
Montelíbano

Sahagún
Planeta
San
Marcos

Cereté
Ciénaga
de Oro

Ayapel

Majagual

El Banco

Tamalameque

Aguachica
Gamarra

BOLÍVAR
Simití

Puerto
Wilches

Alto de Tamar
2350m
Zaragoza

Segovia
Remedios

San Cristóbal

Chigorodó

Mutatá
Dabeiba
Ituango

San Carlos del Zulia

Arauca

ARAUCA

Saravena

Arauquita
Tame
El Cantón

Guasdualito
El Amparo de Apure

Elorza

APURE
Mantecal

Bruzual
Achaguas

Guanarito

La Urbana

VEN

Río Capanaparo

Río
Arauca

Río Orinoco

Sierra

Puerto Páez
Puerto Carreño

Nueva Antioquia
Cravo Norte
Hato Corozal
Puerto Rondón

Tame

CASANARE
Paz de Ariporo
Nunchía
Trinidad
Labranzagrande
Pore
Támara
Yopal

Aguazul
Maní
Orocué
Tauramena

VICHADA
Santa Rita
Puerto Nariño

Río Vichada

Río Tomo

Río Tuparro
Cerro Oyana
1978m

Puerto Ayacucho

San Juan de
Manapiare

Cerro Yaví
2441m

Río Meta

Samariapo
Cerro Sipapo
2030m
Cerro Duida
2400m

AMAZONAS

San Antonio

Cerro Marahuaca
2579m

Cerro
do Sol

El Esn

PANAMA

San Miguel

Isla del
Rey

Golfo de
San Miguel

DARIEN

El Real
Garachiné

Jaqué

Cerro Tacarcuna
1875m

Cerro Setetule
1220m

Jurado

Turbo

Necoclí

Riosucio

Cupica

Golfo de
Urabá

Bahía Solano

Nuquí

Golfo de
Cupica

Bahía de
Panamá

La
Palma

DARIEN

Atrato

Quibdó

CHOCÓ

Istmina
Condoto

Cartago

RISARALDA
Pereira
Dosquebradas

Manizales
CALDAS
Chinchiná

Andes
Caramanta
Anserma

La
Dorada

PACIFIC OCEAN

Punta Arusí

Buenaventura

VALLE DEL
CAUCA
Dagua
Palmira
Palmaseca ✈
Cali
Pradera
Jamundí

Buga
Tuluá

Armenia
QUINDÍO
Calarcá
Zarzal

Cartago

Nevado del Ruiz
5400m
Nevado del Tolima
5215m
Honda

CUNDINAMARCA

Ibagué
Coello
Girardot
Espinal
Saldaña

Fusagasugá
Tocaima
Melgar

BOGOTÁ

Medina

Villavicencio

Acacías
San Martín

Granada

Restrepo   Cabuyaro
Puerto López
Puerto Gaitán

META
Puerto Limón

San José de Ocuné

San Fernando
de Atabapo

GUAINÍA

Maroa

Río Vichada

Río Muco

Río Manacacías

Río Meta

Río Uvá

Río Guaviare

Puerto Inírida

Santa Bárbara

Río Orinoco

Río Inírida

AMAZONAS

Río Atabapo

Río Guainía

Río Negro

Boca May

COLOMBIA

Guapi
Timbiquí

Iscuandé

CAUCA
El Bordo
Popayán
Silvia

Buga

Palmira

Neiva
HUILA
Hobo
Gigante

Morales
Suárez
Santander

Nevado del Huila
5750m
Páez
La Plata
Garzón

Tello
Baraya
Colombia
Uribe

Prado

Natagaima
Aipe

Mesetas

Río Ariari

Río Guayabero

San José del Guaviare

GUAVIARE

Río Inírida

Morichal

Mitú

Río Vaupés

VAUPÉS

Vista Alegre

El Mango

San Carlos
de Río Negro

Punta Reyes
Mosquera

Bahía de
Tumaco

Tumaco

Guapi
Mosquera

NARIÑO
Barbacoas

Valdéz
(Limones)
San Lorenzo

Samaniego
Linares
La
Unión
La
Cruz
Buesaco

Túquerres
Sandoná

Samaniego

Mercaderes
Bolívar
San
Agustín
Altamira

Timaná
Pitalito

Florencia

La Montañita

Cartagena de Chaira
El Doncello

Puerto Rico
San Vicente del Caguán

Río Caguán

Río Yarí

Río Apaporis

Iaureté

Lérida

São Marcelino

São Joaquim

Río Vaupés

Içana

Río Negro

Pico da Neblina
3014m

Pico Phelps
2400m

Pico Guanare
2105m

IMBABURA
Otavalo
Ibarra

CARCHI
Tulcán
San Gabriel

Cotacachi
4939m

PICHINCHA
Santo
Domingo de
los Colo

Cayambe
5790m

Nueva Loja
(Lago Agrio)

SUCUMBÍOS

Puerto El
Carmen

Río San Miguel

Puerto
Leguízamo

La Tagua

PUTUMAYO

Mocoa
Puerto Límon
Puerto Umbría
Orito
Puerto Asís

Pasto

Túquerres
Ipiales

Equator

QUITO
Mariscal Sucre ✈

Machachi

NAPO
Baeza

ORELLANA

Puerto Francisco
de Orellana (Coca)

Nuevo
Rocafuerte

Río Aguarico

Río Napo

Concepción
La Hacha

El Encanto

Araracuara

La Pedrera

Vila Bittencourt

Río Caquetá

Río Putumayo

Río Japurá

Río Marié

Río Içana

Serra do Traira

Serra
do Ri

ECUADOR

COTOPAXI
Latacunga   Tena

Cotopaxi
5897m

Antizana
5704m

Ambato
TUNGURAHUA

BOLÍVAR
Guaranda

Chimborazo
6310m

Riobamba
CHIMBORAZO

PASTAZA

Río Pastaza

Río Napo

Puyo

Baños

AMAZONAS

Río Curaray

Río Tigre

Arica

Río Putumayo

AMAZONAS

Tonantins

Santo António do Içá

Monte Cristo

Fonte Boa

A

Foz do Mamoriá
Rosas

Juruá

Mará

ZAMORA
CHINCHIPE
Zamora

CAÑAR
Azogues
Cuenca
AZUAY
Sígsig

Macas

MORONA
SANTIAGO

Alausí

PERU

Iquitos

Nauta

LORETO

Río Napo
Río Curaray
Río Tigre
Río Pastaza
Río Morona
Río Santiago

Río Marañón

Río Ucayali

Río Nanay

Río Amazonas

Leticia
Tabatinga

Atalaia do Norte
Benjamin Constant

Río Yavarí Mirim

Río Yavari

Río Içá

Río Japurá

Juruá

6000m
4000m
3000m
2000m
1000m
500m
250m
100m
Sea
Level
-250m
-500m
-1000m

Scale 1:6,500,000
(projection: Lambert Azimuthal Equal Area)

0 25 50 75 100 125 150 175 200 Km
0 25 50 75 100 125 150 175 200 Miles

Population

- ■ above 5 million
- ■ 1 million to 5 million
- ● 500,000 to 1 million
- ◉ 100,000 to 500,000
- ⊕ 50,000 to 100,000
- ○ 10,000 to 50,000
- · below 10,000

Bogotá

N

Usaquén

Molinos

Rio Juan Amarillo

Canal de Guaymaral

Monumento
Lara Bonita

Aeropuerto
Internacional
El Dorado

Barrios
Unidos

Engativá

Chapinero

Teusaquillo

Fontibón

Bogotá

Puente
Aranda

Museo
Nacional de
Colombia

Kennedy

Rio Fucha

Los
Mártires

Catedral
La
Candelaria

Antonio
Mariño

Santa
Fe

San
Cristóbal

Tunjuelito

Rafael
Uribe

0 1 Km
0 1 Miles

ATLANTIC OCEAN

CASTRIES
George F I Charles
Mount Gimie
950m
ST LUCIA
Hewanorra
Vieux Fort
Saint Vincent Passage
St Vincent
KINGSTOWN
ST VINCENT &
THE GRENADINES
Arnos Vale
BRIDGETOWN
BARBADOS
Grantley
Adams
Bequia
Mustique
Canouan
Union Island
The Grenadines
Carriacou
ST. GEORGE'S
Point Salines
GRENADA

Blanquilla
Islas los Testigos
Tobago
Charlotteville
Scarborough
Galera Point

de Margarita
ESPARTA
La Asunción
Pampatar
Porlamar
sangriego
Pedras
Cumaná
SUCRE
El Pilar
Casanay
Carúpano
Cariaco
Irapa
Güiria
Hierro
Puerto de
Paria
Galera Point
Arima
Piarco
Sangre Grande
PORT-OF-SPAIN
Cerro Tataracual
Cumanacoa
Caripe
Caripito
Quiriquire
San Antonio
Gulf of Paria
San Fernando
Point Fortin
Bonasse
Siparia
Río Claro
Rushville
Galeota Point
TRINIDAD
& TOBAGO
elona
ragua de Maturín
Caicara
Maturín
MONAGAS
Punta
de Mata
Santa Rosa
Aguasay
Anaco
juin
Cantaura
San Tomé
San José de Guanipa
Tembladór
Pedernales
Punta Baja
La Horqueta
Tucupita
DELTA AMACURO
Barrancas
NZOÁTEGUI
Ciudad Guayana
Río Orinoco
Guayabones
Curiapo
Waini Point
Soledad
El Pao
El Palmar
Upata
Waini
Port Kaituma
Charity
dad Bolívar
Borbón
Arakaka
Matthews
Ridge
Barima River
Spring Garden
Essequibo Islands
Parika
Ciudad Piar
Embalse
de Guri
Guasipati
El Manteco
El Callao
Tumeremo
Kurackí
Aurora
Bartica
GEORGETOWN
Georgetown
New Amsterdam
Rose Hall
Ro Turagua
88m
eras
La Paragua
El Casabe
Canaima
El Dorado
Enachu Landing
Peters Mine
Wineperu
Linden
Rockstone
Corriverton
WANICA
COMMEWIJNE
BOLÍVAR
Salto Angel
2100m
Auyan Tepuy
2950m
Cerro Venamo
1563m
Kamarang
Imbaimadai
Issano
Nieuw Nickerie
Friendship
Totness
Groningen
Nieuw Amsterdam
PARAMARIBO
Mana
Iles du Salut
Guaiquinima
2100m
Carapo
Uruyén
Ayanganna Mountain
2042m
Kaietur
River
Mahdia
Ituni
Wageningen
NICKERIE
CORONIE
SARAMACCA
Lelydorp
MAROWIJNE
Albina
Iracoubo
Sinnamary
Centre Spatial Guyanais
GUYANA
Mount Roraima
2810m
Potaro
River
Kaieteur Falls
Orealla
Wasibo
Apoera
Coppename
River
Corneliskondre
Donderkamp
Kaaimanston
Onverwacht
Brokopondo
Brownsweg
Bergen Dal
Kwakoegron
Apatou
Herminadorp
Citron
Delfes
St-Laurent-du-Maroni
Kourou
CAYENNE
Rémire
Matoury
a Maria
rebato
Catisinina
Santa Elena de Uairén
Uonán
Glendor
Mountians
Kurupukari
PARÁ
Hendrik Top
957m
Boti-
Pasi
BROKOPONDO
Pokigron
Poeketi
W J van
Blommesteinmeer
Grand-Santi
St-Élie
Tonate
Cayenne
Roura
Cacao
Pointe Béhague
isocana
Sararina
Pakaraima Mountains
Río Uraricuera
Normandia
Rupununi River
Lucie River
Juliana Top
1230m
Tafelberg
1026m
Djoemoe
Poeketi
FRENCH
GUIANA
(to France)
Saül
Régina
Cabo Orange
Orinoco
Horqueta Minas
de Unturán
Conceição do Maú
Uraricoera
Lethem
Kanuku Mountains
Saúriwaunawa
Jacobs
Ladder
Falls
Wilhelmina Gebergte
Apetina
SIPALIWINI
Tapanahony River
Maripasoula
Pedima
Montagnes
Bellevue de l'Inini
Sommet Tabulaire
St-Georges
Oiapoque
Boa Vista
Uaiacás
Santa Rosa
H
i
g
New River
(Claimed by Surinam)
Appikalo
Alimimuni Pieke
728m
Litani
Maroni River
Mont Saint-Marcel
635m
Massif du Mitaraka
690m
Trois
Sauts
Camopi
Rio Oiapoque
L'Oyapock Fleuve
Calçoene
RORAIMA
Missão Catrimani
Caracaraí
Kuyuwini
Landing
Johi Village
New River
h
l
a
Tumuc Humac Mountains
(Claimed by Surinam)
AMAPÁ
Amapá
Rio Domini
Acarai Mountains
n
d
s
Sete Ilhas
Rio Araguari
Rio Catrimani
Catrimani
São Luís
Serra do Jatapu
Rio Paru
Rio Trombetas
Rio Paru de Oeste
Planalto
Maracanaquará
Monte Dourado
Macapá
Equator
Ilha Grande
de Gurupá
Negro
Tapurucuará
Boiaçu
Rio Branco
Rio Jatapu
Rio Nhamundá
Rio Uatumã
Oriximiná
Óbidos
Alenquer
PARÁ
Amazon
Porto de Moz
Barcelos
Carvoeiro
Moura
Represa
Balbina
Rio Paru
Santarém
Portel
BRAZIL
AMAZONAS
Novo Airão
Manacapuru
Caldeirão
Iranduba
Eduardo
Gomes
MANAUS
Manaquiri
Itacoatiara
Urucará
Parintins
B
a
s
i
n
Altamira
Coari
Codajás
Beruri
Careiro
Autazes
Rurópolis Presidente
Rio Irirí
Rio Solimões
Rio Purus
Itaituba
Pimenta

19,686ft
13,124ft
9843ft
6562ft
3281ft
1640ft
820ft
328ft
Sea Level
-820ft
-6562ft
-13,124ft

Amazon Basin

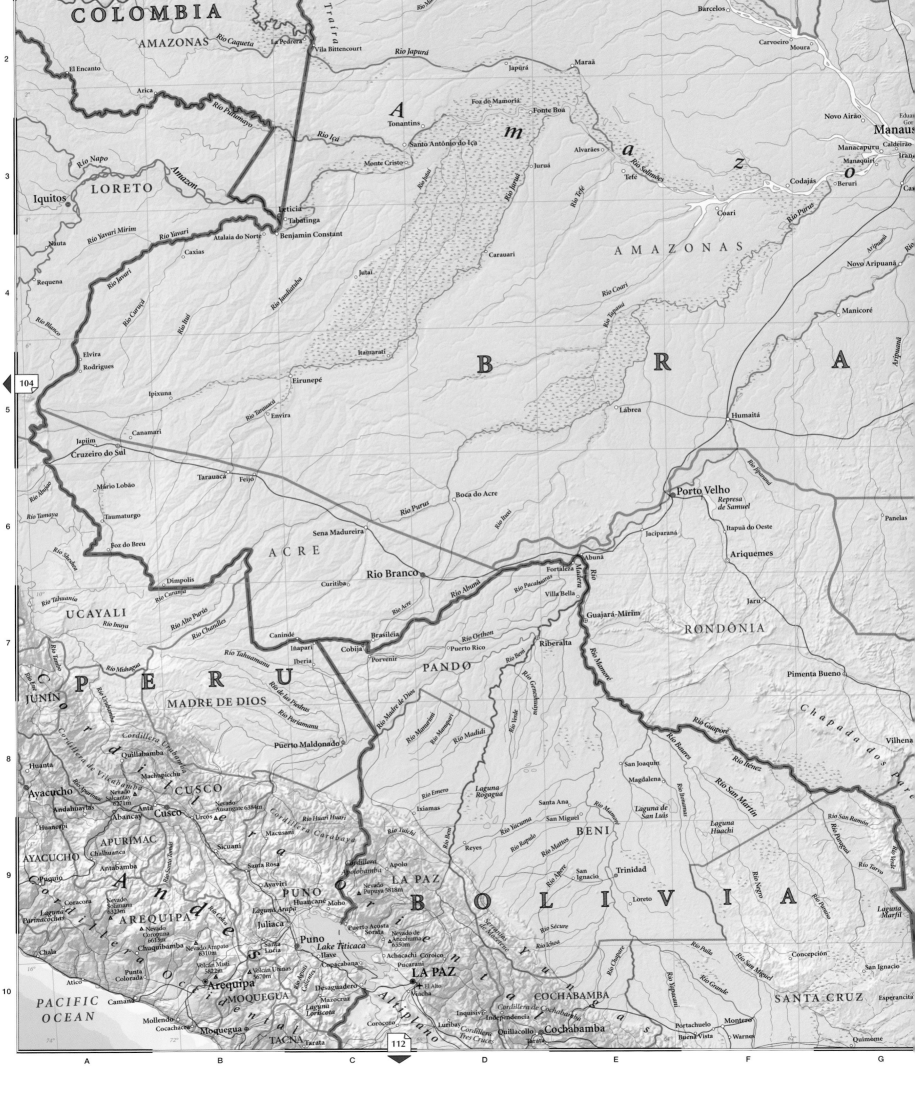

0 25 50 75 100 125 150 175 200 Km
0 25 50 75 100 125 150 175 200 Miles

Population
□ above 5 million   ⊡ 1 million to 5 million   ⊚ 500,000 to 1 million
◉ 100,000 to 500,000   ⊕ 50,000 to 100,000   ◌ 10,000 to 50,000   ○ below 10,000

| H | I | J | K | 103 | L | M | N |

ATLANTIC OCEAN

Sete Ilhas
Rio Araguari
Ilha Bailique
Ilha do Curuá
Ilha Janaucu
Ilha Caviana de Fora
Ilha Mexiana
Mouths of the Amazon

AMAPÁ
Macapá

Equator

Rio Paru
Rio Jari

Planalto
Maracanaquará
Monte Dourado

Ilha Grande de Gurupá

Baía de Marajó

Marudá
Vigia

Belém
Castanhal   Capanema   Viseu
Carutapera
Turiaçu

Oriximiná
Óbidos   Alenquer
Amazon
Porto de Moz
Ilha Siritúba
Alto Bônito

Rio Nhamundá
Rio Trombetas

Urucará
Portel
Tomé-Açu

Santarém

Parintins

Itacoatiara

B   **a**   **s**   Altamira

Rio Iriri

Serra do Jatapu

PARÁ

Represa de Tucuruí

Serra do Tiracambu

Rio Tocantins
Rio Gurupi

Itaituba
Rurópolis Presidente
Pimenta

Dom Eliseu

Rio Tapajós
Rio Jamanxim

Tucunaré

Açailândia

São Félix
Marabá
MARANHÃO
Imperatriz

Z   **I**   **L**

Jacaré-a-Canga
José Rodrigues
Serra dos Carajás
Parauapebas
Grajaú

Araras
Bom Futuro
São Félix do Xingu
Estreito

Manuel Zinho
São Raimundo das Mangabeiras

Barra do São Manuel
Rio Xingu
Carolina

Serra do Cachimbo

Recreio
Pereirinha
Araguaína
Balsas

Conceição do Araguaia
Craolândia

Rio São Manuel
Tasso Fragoso

Bandeirantes
Cachimbo
Alto Parnaíba
PIAUÍ
Santa Filomena

Paranaíta
Vila Rica
Serra dos Gradaús

Juruena
Peixoto de Azevedo
Serra Geral de Goiás
Corrente

TOCANTINS
Palmas do Tocantins

Juará
Rio Araguaia
Porto Nacional

Porto dos Gaúchos
Novo Horizonte
Marcelândia
Campo de Diauarum
São Félix do Araguaia
Ilha do Bananal
Gurupi

Sinop
Espigão Mestre

Pôsto Jacaré
Rio Juruena
Rio Arinos
Rio do Sangue

Serra Formosa
Serra do Roncador
Rio das Mortes
Taguatinga

MATO GROSSO
Campos Belos
BAHIA

Porangatu

Arenápolis
Nobres
Cocalinho
Uruaçu
Alto Paraíso de Goiás

Rosário Oeste
Rio Manso
Tupiraçaba

Planalto de
Itacaiu
Serra Dourada
Ceres
Barro Alto

Tes e Lacerda
Rialma
Goianésia

Várzea Grande
Cuiabá
Mato Grosso
GOIÁS

Cáceres
Jaciara
BRASÍLIA
Planaltina
Planaltina
DISTRITO FEDERAL
MINAS GERAIS

San Matias
Aragarças
Goiás
Pirenópolis
Unaí

Rondonópolis
Piranhas
Anápolis

Pantanal
Rio Piquiri
Santa Rita de Araguaia
Mineiros
Goiânia
Cristalina
Planalto Central

Laguna Uberaba
Rio Cuiabá
Alto Araguaia
Indiara
Paracatu

Rio San Francisco

| H | I | J | 113 | K | L | M | N |

108

19,686ft
13,124ft
9843ft
6562ft
3281ft
1640ft
820ft
328ft
Sea Level
-820ft
-6562ft
-13,124ft

SOUTH AMERICA

6000m
4000m
3000m
2000m
1000m
500m
250m
100m
Sea Level
-250m
-500m
-1000m

ATLANTIC OCEAN

Equator

Atol das Rocas

Cabo de São Roque

Touros
Ceará Mirim
Natal
RIO GRANDE DO NORTE
João Pessoa
Campina Grande
Olinda
Recife
Jaboatão
Caruaru
Maceió
Arapiraca
ALAGOAS
PARAÍBA
Areia Branca
Macau
Mossoró
Açu
Currais Novos
Caicó
Planalto da Borborema
Garanhuns
Arcoverde
Rio São Francisco
Propriá
São Cristóvão
Aracaju
Estância
SERGIPE
PERNAMBUCO
Açude Poço da Cruz
Paulo Afonso
Canudos
Represa de Itaparica
Fortaleza
Cascavel
Aracati
Caucaia
Itapipoca
Acaraú
Camocim
Sobral
Araras
Quixadá
CEARÁ
Crateús
Tauá
Senador Pompeu
Açude Banabuiú
Açude Orós
Campos Sales
Juazeiro do Norte
Marcolândia
Ouricuri
Salgueiro
Petrolina
Juazeiro
Sobradinho
Sento Sé
Represa de Sobradinho
Xique-Xique
Barra
Parnaíba
Ilha do Caju
Piripiri
Campo Maior
Teresina
Timon
Barro Duro
Valença do Piauí
Gaturiano
Picos
Oeiras
Floriano
PIAUÍ
Canto do Buriti
São João do Piauí
São Raimundo das Mangabeiras
Alto Parnaíba
Santa Filomena
Rio Gurgueia
Campo Alegre de Lourdes
Casa Nova
Rio Uruçuí
Recife do Silva
Recife Manuel Luís
Ilha de São Luís
Baía de São Marcos
São Luís
São José de Ribamar
Chapadinha
Codó
Caxias
Colinas
São João dos Pato
Rio Parnaíba
Itapecuru-Mirim
Bacabal
Presidente Dutra
Roncador
Balsas
Tasso Fragoso
Alto Parnaíba
Chapada das Mangabeiras
Espi...
MARANHÃO
Ilha do
São João de Cortes
Cururupu
Turiaçu
Vizeu
Capanema
Alto Bonito
Castanhal
Tomé-Açu
Belém
Baía de Marajó
Ilha de Marajó
Mouths of the Amazon
Ilha Caviana de Fora
Ilha Mexiana
Ilha Janaucu
Ilha do Curuá
Ilha Bailique
Ilha de Maracá
Sucuriju
Amapá
Calçoene
Sete Ilhas
Macapá
Ilha Grande de Gurupá
Porto de Moz
Portel
Rio Jari
Almeirim
AMAPÁ
Equator
Tropic of Cancer
Vila Rica
Serra dos Carajás
Rio Xingu
São Félix do Xingu
Parauapebas
PARÁ
Conceição do Araguaia
Rio Araguaia
Serra dos Gradaús
Palmas do Tocantins
Porto Nacional
TOCANTINS
Rio Tocantins
Araguaína
Serra do Geral de Goiás
Croailândia
Carolina
Estreito
Balsas
Grajaú
Açailândia
Imperatriz
Marabá
São Félix
Represa de Tucuruí
Dom Eliseu
Serra do Tiracambu
Rio Gurupi
Viseu
Rio Tocantins
Amazon Basin
Rio Capim
MARANHÃO
Cassia
Macedão
Corrente
BRASIL

Scale 1:6,500,000
(projection: Lambert Azimuthal Equal Area)

0 25 50 75 100 125 150 175 200 Km

0 25 50 75 100 125 150 175 200 Miles

Population

☐ above 5 million
☐ 1 million to 5 million
◎ 500,000 to 1 million
◉ 100,000 to 500,000
⊕ 50,000 to 100,000
○ 10,000 to 50,000
∘ below 10,000

19,686ft
13,124ft
9843ft
6562ft
3281ft
1640ft
820ft
328ft
Sea Level
-820ft
-6562ft
-13,124ft

ATLANTIC
OCEAN

Salvador
Baía de Todos os Santos
Ilha de Boipeba
Ponta do Mutá
Maraú
Valença
Ilhéus
Itabuna
Comandatuba
Canavieiras
Belmonte
Santa Cruz Cabrália
Porto Seguro
Prado
Caravelas
Ilha Caçumba

Jequié
Itapetinga
Itamaraju
São Mateus
Linhares
Vitória
Guarapari
Cachoeiro de Itapemirim
São João da Barra

Lençóis
Brumado
Vitória da Conquista
Pedra Azul
Itaobim
Araçuaí
Teófilo Otoni
Nanuque
ESPÍRITO SANTO
Colatina
Santa Teresa

Bom Jesus da Lapa
Caetité
Monte Azul
Espinosa
Januária
Diamantina
Serro
Guanhães
Governador Valadares
Ipatinga
Ponte Nova
Manhuaçu
Campos
Itaperuna
São Fidélis
Miracema
Macaé
Arraial do Cabo
Cabo Frio

Santa Maria da Vitória
Itaituba
Pirapora
Pico do Itambé 2060m
Itabira
Ouro Preto
Conselheiro Lafaiete
Barbacena
Juiz de Fora
Três Rios
Teresópolis
Petrópolis
RIO DE JANEIRO
São Gonçalo
Niterói
Rio de Janeiro

Campos Belos
Unaí
Pirapora
Curvelo
Sete Lagoas
Belo Horizonte
Betim
São João del Rei
Três Pontas
Barra Mansa
Volta Redonda
Angra dos Reis
Ilha Grande

Alto Paraíso de Goiás
Paracatu
Luziânia do Oeste
Represa Três Marias
Abaeté
Divinópolis
Passos
Poços de Caldas
Três Corações
Guaratinguetá
Taubaté
São José dos Campos
Caraguatatuba
Ilha de São Sebastião

BRASÍLIA
DISTRITO FEDERAL
Cristalina
Patos de Minas
Ibiá
Araxá
Represa de Furnas
São João da Boa Vista
Mococa
Campinas
Jundiaí
Itu
Mogi das Cruzes
São Paulo
Santos

Anápolis
Uberlândia
Araguari
Uberaba
Igarapava
Franca
Batatais
Ribeirão Preto
Sertãozinho
Araras
Rio Claro
Piracicaba
Limeira
Americana
Indaiatuba
São Caetano do Sul
São Bernardo do Campo
Guarujá
São Vicente

Goiânia
Pirenópolis
Itumbiara
Anhangüera
Guaíra
São Joaquim da Barra
Barretos
Catanduva
São José do Rio Preto
Jaboticabal
Novo Horizonte
Araraquara
São Carlos
Jaú
Botucatu
Sorocaba
Tatuí
Itapetininga
Registro

Ceres
Goiatuba
Indiara
Rio Verde
Fernandópolis
Votuporanga
São José do Rio Pardo
Lins
Promissão
Bauru
Marília
Ourinhos
Avaré
Itapeva
Cananéia

Porangatu
Jataí
Mineiros
Santa Fé do Sul
Jales
Andradina
Araçatuba
Birigüi
Penápolis
Tupã
Assis
Paraguaçu Paulista

Itacaiu
Aporé
Três Lagoas
Pereira Barreto
Adamantina
Dracena
Presidente Prudente
Londrina
Maringá
Apucarana
Campo Mourão
Ponta Grossa
Curitiba
Lapa

GROSSO
MATO GROSSO DO SUL
PARANÁ
Serra Geral
Paranaguá

Tropic of Capricorn

Southeast Brazil

6000m
4000m
3000m
2000m
1000m
500m
250m
100m
Sea Level
-250m
-500m
-1000m

Central South America

105
287
116

PACIFIC OCEAN

PERU

BOLIVIA

CHILE

ARGENTINA

PARAGUAY

Elevation scale:
- 6000m
- 4000m
- 3000m
- 2000m
- 1000m
- 500m
- 250m
- 100m
- Sea Level
- -250m
- -500m
- -1000m

Regions / Provinces:
MOQUEGUA, TACNA, TARAPACA, ORURO, LA PAZ, COCHABAMBA, SANTA CRUZ, POTOSÍ, CHUQUISACA, TARIJA, ALTO PARAGUAY, BOQUERÓN, PRESIDENTE HAYES, PARAGUAY, JUJUY, SALTA, ANTOFAGASTA, FORMOSA, CHACO, CHACO AUSTRAL, TUCUMÁN, CATAMARCA, SANTIAGO DEL ESTERO, CORRIENTES, ATACAMA, LA RIOJA, SANTA FE, ENTRE RÍOS, COQUIMBO, SAN JUAN, CÓRDOBA, VALPARAÍSO, MENDOZA, SAN LUIS, LA PAMPA, BUENOS AIRES, LIBERTADOR

Mountain ranges:
Cordillera Occidental, Cordillera de Lípez, Cordillera de Chichas, Cordillera de Tresina, Cordillera Sillaguay, Cordillera Domeyko, Sierra de la Punilla, Los Andes, Sierra del Nevado, Sierra de Córdoba, Pampas

Cities and towns:
Moquegua, Tacna, Arica, Iquique, La Paz, Oruro, Potosí, SUCRE, Cochabamba, Santa Cruz, Tupiza, Tarija, Villazón, La Quiaca, Humahuaca, San Salvador de Jujuy, San Pedro, Salta, Metán, ASUNCIÓN, Formosa, Mariscal Estigarribia, Resistencia, Corrientes, Antofagasta, Calama, Tocopilla, Chañaral, Caldera, Copiapó, Tierra Amarilla, Vallenar, Huasco, Santiago del Estero, La Banda, San Fernando del Valle de Catamarca, La Rioja, Chilecito, Córdoba, Río Cuarto, Rosario, Santa Fe, Paraná, La Serena, Coquimbo, Ovalle, Illapel, San Juan, Mendoza, Godoy Cruz, San Luis, Villa Mercedes, Valparaíso, Viña del Mar, SANTIAGO, San Bernardo, Rancagua, San Rafael, General Alvear, BUENOS AIRES, Avellaneda, Lomas de Zamora, San Isidro, General Pico, Santa Rosa

Peaks:
Nevado Sajama 6520m, Volcán Ollagüe 5869m, Volcán San Pedro 6159m, Volcán Rutana 5890m, Volcán Lascar 5154m, Cerro Rincón 5594m, Nevado de Chañi 6200m, Cerro Galán 6600m, Volcán Socompa 6031m, Volcán Azufre 5680m, Cerro Ojos del Salado 6880m, Monte Pissis 6774m, Cerro Bonete 6872m, Cerro Azul 5070m, Cerro General Manuel Belgrano 6250m, Cerro del Potro 5830m, Cerro del Toro 6380m, Cerro Las Tórtolas 6323m, Cerro de Olivares 6252m, Cerro Aconcagua 6959m, Cerro Juncal 6180m, Volcán Tupungato 6800m, Volcán Maipo 5323m, Volcán Tinguiririca 4300m, Volcán Peteroa 5189m, Cerro Sosneado

Water bodies:
Lago Poopó, Salar de Uyuni, Salar de Atacama, Salar de Punta Negra, Salar de Arizaro, Salar de Antofalla, Puna de Atacama, Río Desaguadero, Río Grande, Río Pilcomayo, Río Bermejo, Río Paraguay, Río Paraná, Río Salado, Salinas de Ambargasta, Laguna Mar Chiquita, Bahía Nuestra Señora, Bahía Copiapó

Tropic of Capricorn

Scale 1:6,500,000
(projection: Lambert Azimuthal Equal Area)

0 25 50 75 100 125 150 175 200 Km
0 25 50 75 100 125 150 175 200 Miles

Population

- ■ above 5 million
- ◉ 1 million to 5 million
- ◉ 500,000 to 1 million
- ◎ 100,000 to 500,000
- ⊕ 50,000 to 100,000
- ○ 10,000 to 50,000
- ∘ below 10,000

SOUTH AMERICA

113

291

H I J K L M N

1 2 3 4 5 6 7 8 9 10

Elevation scale:
19,686ft
13,124ft
9843ft
6562ft
3281ft
1640ft
820ft
328ft
Sea Level
-820ft
-6562ft
-13,124ft

GOIÁS

MINAS GERAIS

MATO GROSSO DO SUL

SÃO PAULO

PARANÁ

SANTA CATARINA

RIO GRANDE DO SUL

BRAZIL

RIO DE JANEIRO

ATLANTIC OCEAN

Tropic of Capricorn

URUGUAY

MISIONES

ITAPÚA

CANINDEYÚ

ALTO PARANÁ

Pantanal

Serra do Mar

Serra da Mantiqueira

Rio Paraná

Campo Grande
Coxim
Aquidauana
Rio Verde
Jataí
Itumbiara
Anhanguera
Piripora
Araguari
Uberlândia
Patos de Minas
Curvelo
Diamantina
Governador Valadares
Ipatinga
Itabira
Belo Horizonte
Betim
Divinópolis
Sete Lagoas
Uberaba
Araxá
Ouro Preto
Conselheiro Lafaiete
Barbacena
Juiz de Fora
Uberlândia
Três Lagoas
Andradina
São José do Rio Preto
Araçatuba
Marília
Bauru
Campinas
São Paulo
Santos
Curitiba
Ponta Grossa
Paranaguá
Joinville
Blumenau
Itajaí
Florianópolis
São José
Criciúma
Tubarão
Laguna
Porto Alegre
Canoas
Novo Hamburgo
Caxias do Sul
Pelotas
Rio Grande
Santa Maria
Uruguaiana
Bagé
Cascavel
Foz do Iguaçu
Ciudad del Este
Maringá
Londrina
Apucarana
Guarapuava
Chapecó
Lages
Passo Fundo

Buenos Aires

Tigre
Las Conches
Luján
San Isidro
Vicente López
San Miguel
General San Martín
Belgrano
Hippodrome
Palermo
Zoo
Teatro Colón
Cathedral
Plaza de Mayo
Buenos Aires
Moreno
Sáenz Peña
Floresta
Barracas
Morón
San Justo
Villa Madero
Merlo
Villa Alsina
Avellaneda
Mariano Acosta
Pontevedra
Riachuelo
Lanús
Quilmes
González Catán
Lomas de Zamora
Berazategui
Almirante Brown
Aeropuerto Internacional de Ezeiza

Río de la Plata

0 10 Km
0 10 Miles

MONTEVIDEO
Punta del Este

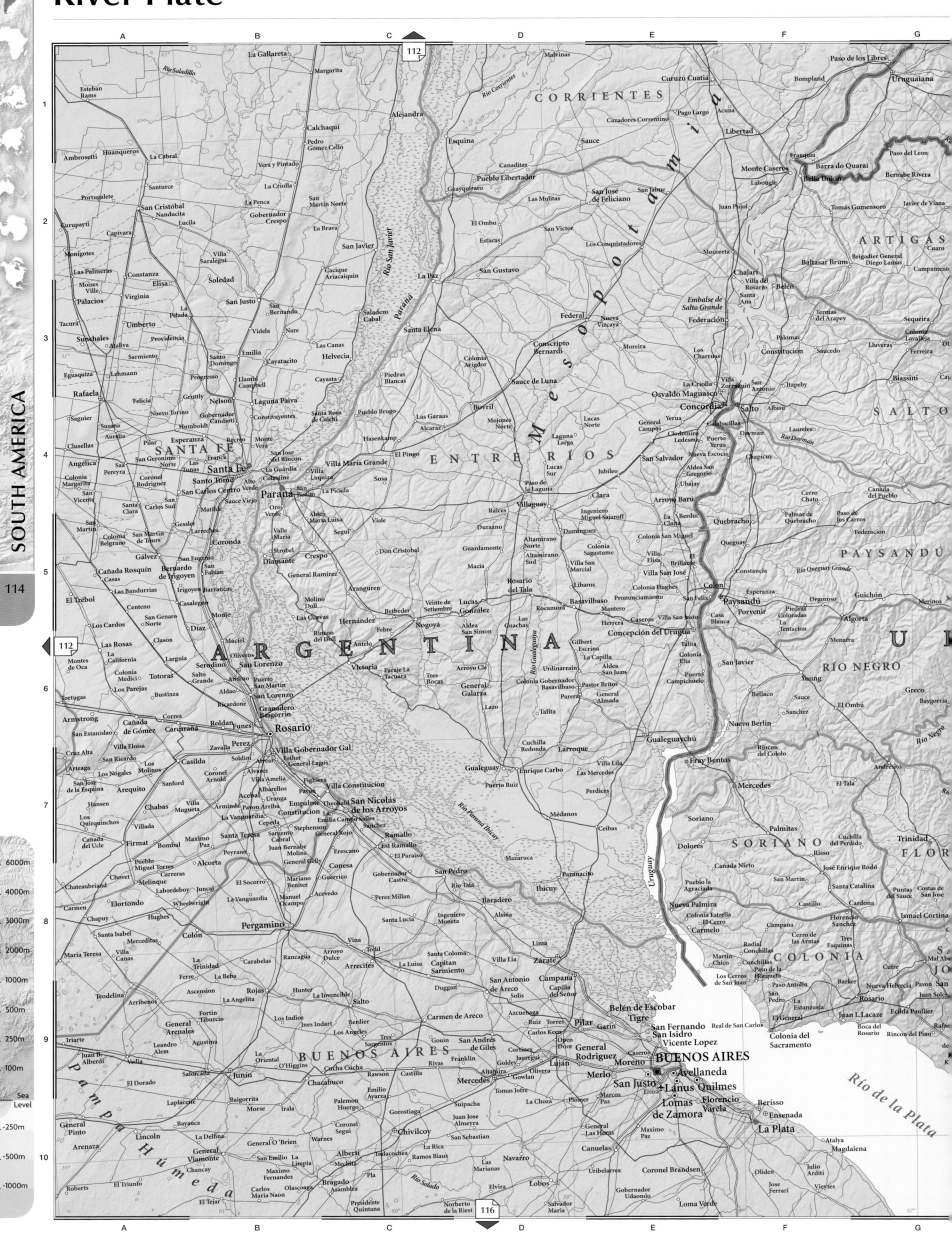

SOUTH AMERICA

A B C D E F G

1
2
3
4
5
6
7
8
9
10

112

112

116

6000m
4000m
3000m
2000m
1000m
500m
250m
100m
Sea
Level
-250m
-500m
-1000m

Scale 1:2,000,000
(projection: Lambert Conformal Conic)

| 0 | 10 | 20 | 30 | 40 | 50 | 60 | 70 | 80 Km |

| 0 | 10 | 20 | 30 | 40 | 50 | 60 | 70 | 80 Miles |

Population
- ▪ above 5 million
- ▫ 1 million to 5 million
- ◉ 500,000 to 1 million
- ◎ 100,000 to 500,000
- ⊕ 50,000 to 100,000
- ○ 10,000 to 50,000
- · below 10,000

113

116

291

19,686ft
13,124ft
9843ft
6562ft
3281ft
1640ft
820ft
328ft
Sea Level
-820ft
-6562ft
-13,124ft

H   I   J   K   L   M   N

1   2   3   4   5   6   7   8   9   10

Passo Novo
Alegrete
Jacaquá
Rio Ibicuí
Loreto
São Vicente do Sul
Santa Maria
Silveira Martins
Águdo
Candelaria
Santa Cruz do Sul

Ibirapuitã
Azevedo Sodré
Cacequy
Restinga Seca
Tres Vendas
Passo do Sobrado
General Camara
Triunfo

Rosário do Sul
Ibaraju
São Gabriel
Formigueiro
Ferreira
Cachoeira do Sul
Rio Pardo
Capane
Cordilheira
Pântano Grande
Mina do Loao
São Jerónimo
Charqueadas
Butiá

Estado Grande
Pampeiro
Vaccacahy
Cacapava do Sul
Barro Vermelho
Capivarita
Barão do Triunfo
Mariana Pimentel
Quiteria

RIO GRANDE DO SUL

Palomas
Santana do Livramento
Rivera
Dom Pedrito
Lavras do Sul
Santana da Boa Vista
Encruzilhada do Sul
Dom Feliciano
Sertao de Santana
Cerro Grande

BRAZIL

Serra das Encantadas

Masoller
Tranqueras
Zanja Honda
Punta de Corrales
Lapuente
Bagé
Santana da Boa Vista
Rio Camaquã
Camaquã

Quintana
Paso de las Carretas
Paso del Cerro
Cerro Pelado del Est
Cerrillada
Piratiny
Cangaçu
Boqueirão
São Lourenço do Sul
Pacheca

RIVERA
Minas de Corrales
Arroyo Blanco
Candiota
Quilombo
Cerrito Alegre

Banado de Rocha
Quiebra Yugos
Zapara
Tacuarembó
Los Rosanos
Pueblo de Arriba
Ansina
Vichadero
Caraguata
Acegua
Acegua
Maria Isabel
Pedras Altas
Pinheiro Machado
Capao do Leao
Pelotas
Lagoa dos Patos

Curtina
Clara
Pueblo del Barro
Coronilla
Isidoro Noblia
Cruz de Piedra
Alegrias
Cerrito
São José de Norte

TACUAREMBÓ
Las Arenas
Las Toscas
Buena Vista
Paso del Centurion
Pedreiras
Quinta
Rio Grande
Estreito

Achar
Blanquillo
Larrayos
Cuchilla Caraguata
Banado de Medina
La Pedrera
Melo
Rio Jacuhy
Quilombo
Arroio Grande
Cassino

GUAY
Cuchilla Peralta
Paso Pereira
Tres Islas
CERRO LARGO
Fraile Muerto
Toledo
Uruguay
Jaguarão
Tahim

Cardoso
San Gregorio de Polanco
Verdun
Rio Negro
Arevalo
Cerro de las Cuentas
Arbolito
Rio Branco
Mirim Lagoon

Embalse del Rio Negro
La Paloma
Cerrezuelo
Tupambé
Placido Rosas
Rincon

Cerro Convento
Blanquillo
Capilla Farruco
Santa Clara de Olimar
Vergara
Arrozal Trienta y Tres

Carpinteria
DURAZNO
Cerro Chato
TREINTA Y TRES
Mendizabal
Julio Maria Sanz
General Enrique Martinez
Lagoa Mangueira

Carlos Reyes
Valentines
Villa Sara
Treinta y Tres
Cebollatí

Bernardina
Sarandí del Yí
Maria Albina
José Pedro Varela
Arrozal Victoria

Polanco del Yí
Capilla del Sauce
Nico Pérez
Zapicán
La Coronilla
Santa Vitória do Palmar

Sarandí Grande
Illescas
Piraraja
Lascano
Diez y Ocho de Julio
Chuí

FLORIDA
Alejandro Gallinal
Polanco Norte
Maria Isabel
Chuy

Pintado
La Cruz
Reboledo
Polanco Sur
Mariscala
LAVALLEJA
ROCHA

Florida
Mendoza Chico
Fray Marcos
Casupá
Los Talas
Velázquez
La Coronilla

25 de Mayo
Mendoza
Chamizo
Bolivar
Aiguá
Castillos

Independencia
San Ramón
Villa Serrana
Parallé

25 de Agosto
San Antonio
Tala
Minas
Rocha
La Barra

Santa Lucía
San Bautista
Solis
Cabo Polonio

CANELONES
San Jacinto
Montes
Migues
Tapia
MALDONADO

Cruz de los Caminos
Totoral
Solis de Mataojo
La Querencia
Piedra del Toro

Los Cerrillos
Sauce
Gregorio Aznarez
Nueva Carrara
La Paloma

Piedras
Toledo
Pando
Joaquin Suarez
Piedras de Afilar
Pan de Azúcar

La Paz
Carrasco
Soca
Las Flores
San Carlos

MONTEVIDEO
Barra de Carrasco
Piriápolis
Maldonado
Punta del Este

ATLANTIC
OCEAN

54°   53°   52°

56°   55°

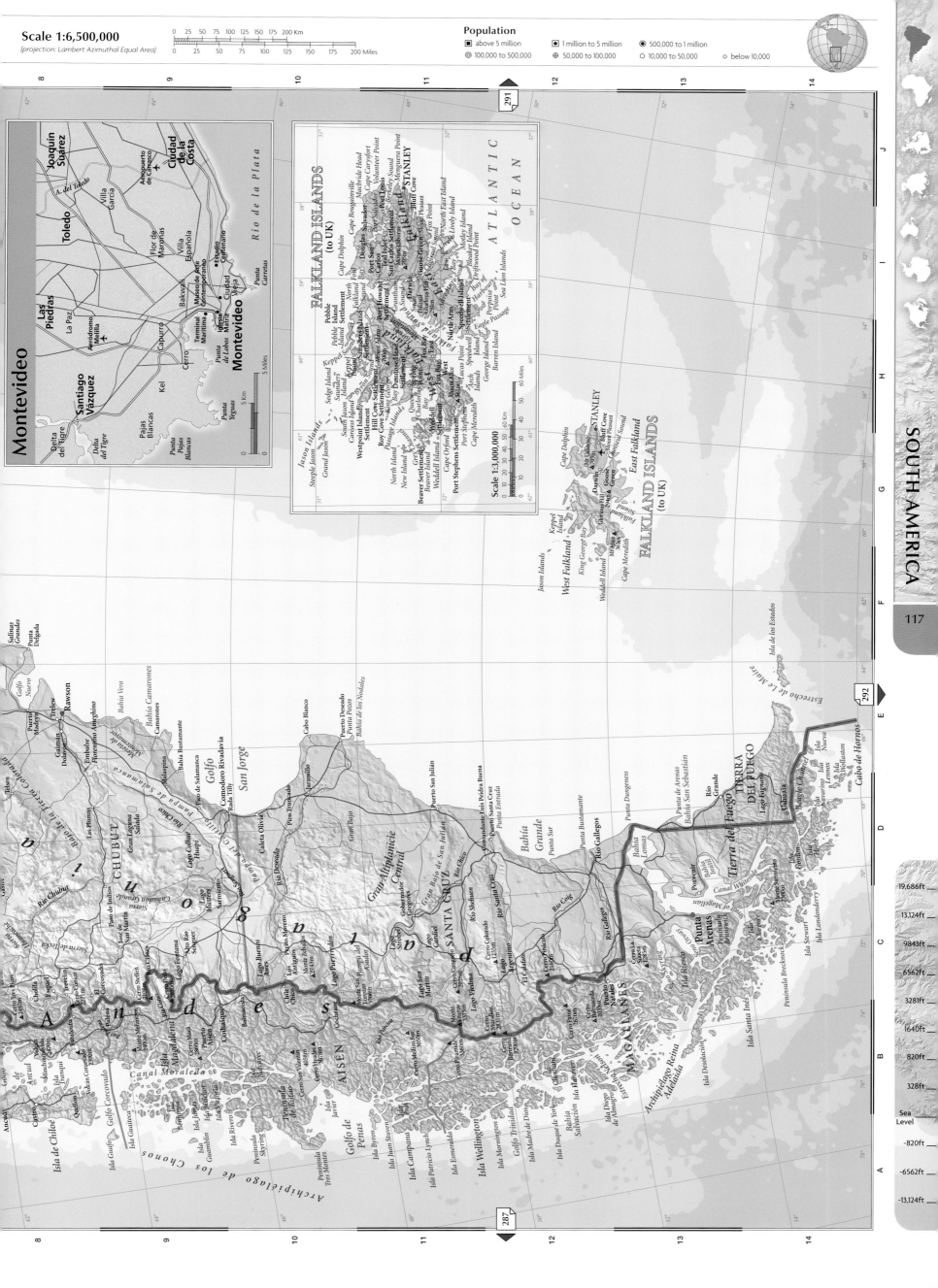

Central Chile & Argentina

Scale 1:2,600,000
(projection: Lambert Conformal Conic)

0 10 20 30 40 50 Km
0 10 20 30 40 50 Miles

112
287
116
116

SOUTH AMERICA

Easter Island (Isla de Pascua) (to Chile)

Scale 1:500,000

0 2.5 5 Km
0 2.5 5 Miles

Punta San Juan
Cabo Norte
Maunga Terevaka 506m
Motu Tautara
Ahu Tepeu
Hanga Roa
Mataveri
Vaihu
Ahu Akivi
Maunga Tangaroa 270m
Maunga Pukatikei 370m
Punta Rosalia
Playa de Anakena
Naunau
Bahía de La Pérouse
Cabo O'Higgins
Rano Raraku
Cabo Roggewein
Punta Akahanga
Punta Cuidado
Punta Baja
Orongo
Motu Nui
Rano Kau
Ahu Vinapu
Cabo Sur

PACIFIC OCEAN

PACIFIC OCEAN

COQUIMBO
VALPARAÍSO
SANTIAGO
LIBERTADOR
MAULE
BÍO BÍO
ARAUCANÍA

CHILE

ARGENTINA

SAN JUAN
MENDOZA
NEUQUÉN
LA PAMPA

Andes

Elevation

6000m
4000m
3000m
2000m
1000m
500m
250m
100m
Sea Level
-250m
-500m
-1000m

Santiago
Valparaíso
Viña del Mar
San Antonio
Rancagua
Curicó
Talca
Linares
Chillán
Concepción
Los Ángeles
Temuco
Mendoza
Godoy Cruz
San Rafael
San Juan

Cerro Aconcagua 6959m
Cerro Mercedario 6769m
Cerro Juncal 6180m
Volcán Tupungato 6800m
Volcán Maipo 5323m
Cerro Sosneado 5189m
Volcán Tinguiririca 4300m
Cerro Campanario 4049m
Volcán Domuyo 4709m
Cerro Nevado 3810m
Cerro Payún 3680m
Volcán Descabezado Grande 3880m
Volcán Antuco 3585m
Volcán Copahue 2980m
Cerro Las Lajas 2650m

Río Colorado
Río Neuquén
Río Atuel
Río Diamante
Río Grande
Río Maule
Río Biobío

SOUTH AMERICA – Cities

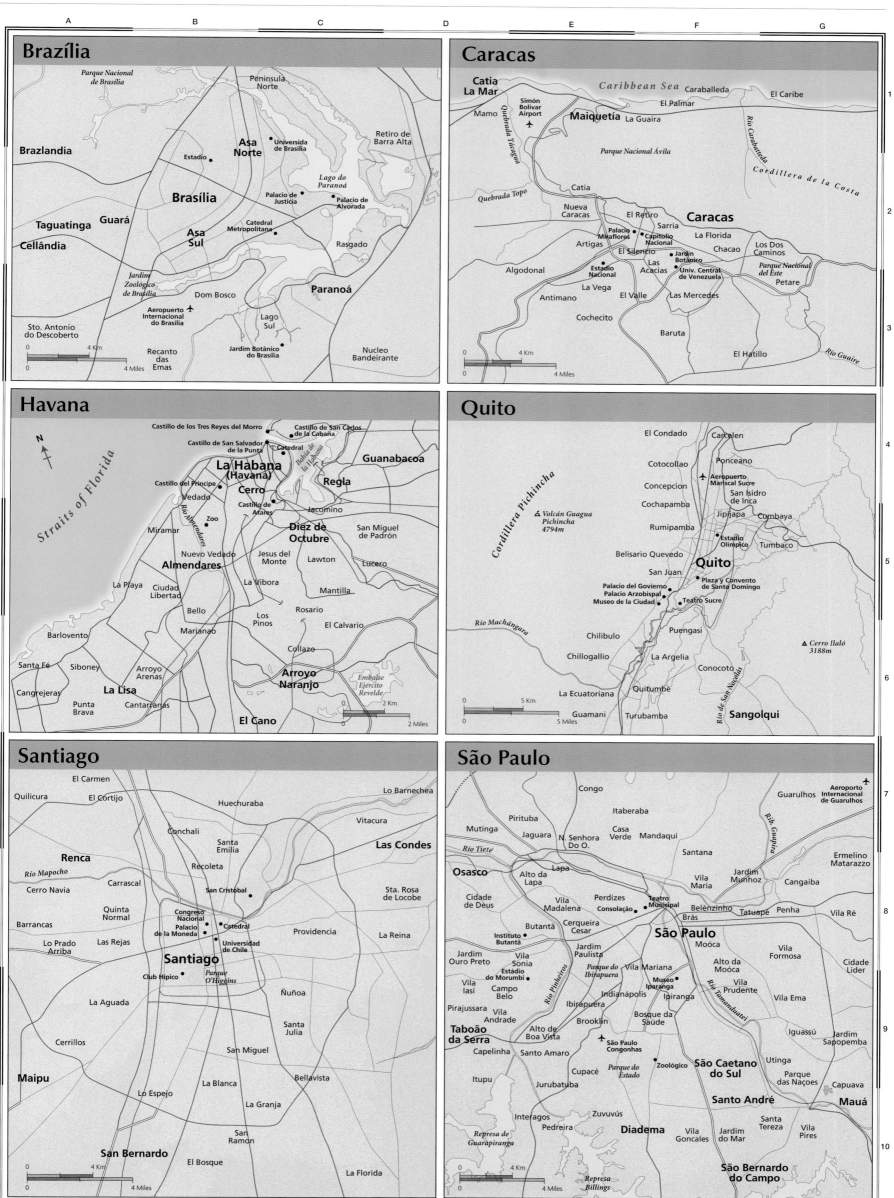

Brazília

Parque Nacional de Brasília
Peninsula Norte
Brazlandia
Asa Norte
Universida de Brasília
Estadio
Retiro de Barra Alta
Brasília
Lago do Paranoá
Taguatinga
Guará
Palacio de Justicia
Palacio de Alvorada
Cellândia
Asa Sul
Catedral Metropolitana
Rasgado
Jardim Zoológico de Brasília
Dom Bosco
Paranoá
Sto. Antonio do Descoberto
Aeropuerto Internacional do Brasília
Lago Sul
Recanto das Emas
Jardim Botânico do Brasília
Nucleo Bandeirante

0 4 Km
0 4 Miles

Caracas

Catia La Mar
Simón Bolívar Airport
Caribbean Sea
Caraballeda
El Caribe
Mamo
Quebrada Táioqua
Maiquetía
La Guaira
El Palmar
Parque Nacional Ávila
Río Caraballeda
Cordillera de la Costa
Quebrada Topo
Catia
Nueva Caracas
El Retiro
Caracas
Palacio Miraflores
Sarria
La Florida
Artigas
Capitolio Nacional
Chacao
Los Dos Caminos
El Silencio
Jardín Botánico
Algodonal
Estadio Nacional
Las Acacias
Univ. Central de Venezuela
Parque Nacional del Éste
Petare
Antimano
La Vega
El Valle
Las Mercedes
Cochecito
Baruta
El Hatillo
Río Guaire

0 4 Km
0 4 Miles

Havana

N
Castillo de los Tres Reyes del Morro
Castillo de San Carlos de la Cabaña
Castillo de San Salvador de la Punta
Catedral
Bahía de la Habana
La Habana (Havana)
Guanabacoa
Castillo del Príncipe
Cerro
Regla
Vedado
Castillo de Atares
Jacomino
Zoo
Straits of Florida
Río Almendares
Miramar
Diez de Octubre
San Miguel de Padrón
Nuevo Vedado
Jesus del Monte
Lawton
Almendares
Lucero
La Playa
Ciudad Libertad
La Víbora
Mantilla
Bello
Los Pinos
Rosario
El Calvario
Marianao
Barlovento
Collazo
Santa Fé
Siboney
Arroyo Arenas
Arroyo Naranjo
Embalse Ejército Revelde
Cangrejeras
La Lisa
Punta Brava
Cantarranas
El Cano

0 2 Km
0 2 Miles

Quito

El Condado
Carcelen
Cotocollao
Ponceano
Aeropuerto Mariscal Sucre
Concepcion
San Isidro de Inca
Cochapamba
Jipijapa
Cumbaya
Cordillera Pichincha
Volcán Guagua Pichincha 4794m
Rumipamba
Estadio Olimpico
Tumbaco
Belisario Quevedo
Quito
San Juan
Plaza y Convento de Santo Domingo
Palacio del Govierno
Palacio Arzobispal
Teatro Sucre
Museo de la Ciudad
Río Machángara
Puengasi
Cerro Ilaló 3188m
Chilibulo
La Argelia
Chillogallio
Conocoto
Río de San Nicolás
La Ecuatoriana
Quitumbe
Guamani
Sangolqui
Turubamba

0 5 Km
0 5 Miles

Santiago

El Carmen
Lo Barnechea
Quilicura
El Cortijo
Huechuraba
Vitacura
Conchali
Las Condes
Renca
Santa Emilia
Río Mapocho
Recoleta
Carrascal
San Cristóbal
Sta. Rosa de Locobe
Cerro Navia
Quinta Normal
Congreso Nacional
Palacio de la Moneda
Catedral
Barrancas
Las Rejas
Universidad de Chile
Providencia
La Reina
Lo Prado Arriba
Santiago
Club Hípico
Parque O'Higgins
La Aguada
Ñuñoa
Cerrillos
Santa Julia
San Miguel
Maipu
La Blanca
Bellavista
Lo Espejo
La Granja
San Ramon
San Bernardo
El Bosque
La Florida

0 4 Km
0 4 Miles

São Paulo

Congo
Guarulhos
Aeroporto Internacional de Guarulhos
Itaberaba
Pirituba
Casa Verde
Mandaqui
Mutinga
Jaguara
N. Senhora Do O.
Rib. Guapira
Río Tietê
Santana
Ermelino Matarazzo
Osasco
Alto da Lapa
Lapa
Vila Maria
Jardim Munhoz
Cangaiba
Cidade de Deus
Vila Madalena
Perdizes
Teatro Municipal
Belènzinho
Tatuapé
Penha
Vila Ré
Butantã
Consolação
Brás
Instituto Butantã
Cerqueira Cesar
São Paulo
Mooca
Vila Formosa
Jardim Ouro Preto
Jardim Paulista
Vila Sônia
Alto da Mooca
Cidade Lider
Estádio do Morumbi
Vila Mariana
Vila
Prudente
Vila Iasi
Museo Iparanga
Campo Belo
Indianápolis
Ipiranga
Vila Ema
Pirajussara
Vila Andrade
Ibirapuera
Brooklin
Bosque da Saúde
Iguassú
Jardim Sapopemba
Taboão da Serra
Alto de Boa Vista
São Paulo Congonhas
Utinga
Capelinha
Santo Amaro
Cupacé
Zoológico
São Caetano do Sul
Itupu
Parque do Estado
Parque das Naçoes
Jurubatuba
Capuava
Interagos
Zuvuvús
Santo André
Mauá
Pedreira
Diadema
Vila Goncales
Jardim do Mar
Santa Tereza
Vila Pires
Represa de Guarapiranga
Represa Billings
São Bernardo do Campo
Río Pinheiros
Parque do Ibirapuera
Río Tamanduatei

0 4 Km
0 4 Miles

19,686ft
13,124ft
9843ft
6562ft
3281ft
1640ft
820ft
328ft
Sea Level
-820ft
-6562ft
-13,124ft

Africa is the world's second largest continent with a total area of 11,712,434 sq miles (30,335,000 sq km) It has 53 separate countries, including Madagascar in the Indian Ocean. It straddles the equator and is the only continent to stretch from the northern to southern temperate zones.

FACTFILE

N Most Northerly Point: Jalta, Tunisia 37° 31' N
S Most Southerly Point: Cape Agulhas, South Africa 34° 52' S
E Most Easterly Point: Raas Xaafuun, Somalia 51° 24' E
W Most Westerly Point: Santo Antão, Cape Verde, 25° 11' W

Largest Lakes:
1. Lake Victoria, Kenya/Tanzania/Uganda 26,828 sq miles (69,484 sq km)
2. Lake Tanganyika, Dem. Rep. Congo/Tanzania 12,703 sq miles (32,900 sq km)
3. Lake Nyasa, Malawi/Mozambique/Tanzania 11,600 sq miles (30,044 sq km)
4. Lake Turkana, Ethiopia/Kenya 2473 sq miles (6405 sq km)
5. Lake Albert, Dem. Rep. Congo/Uganda 2046 sq miles (5299 sq km)

Longest Rivers:
1. Nile, NE Africa 4160 miles (6695 km)
2. Congo, Angola/Congo/Dem. Rep. Congo 2900 miles (4667 km)
3. Niger, W Africa 2589 miles (4167 km)
4. Zambezi, Southern Africa 1673 miles (2693 km)
5. Ubangi-Uele, C Africa 1429 miles (2300 km)

Largest Islands:
1. Madagascar, 229,300 sq miles (594,000 sq km)
2. Réunion, 970 sq miles (2535 sq km)
3. Tenerife, Canary Islands 785 sq miles (2034 sq km)
4. Isla de Bioco, Equatorial Guinea 779 sq miles (2017 sq km)
5. Mauritius, 709 sq miles (1836 sq km)

Highest Points:
1. Kilimanjaro, Tanzania 19,340 ft (5895 m)
2. Kirinyaga, Kenya 17,058 ft (5199 m)
3. Mount Stanley, Dem. Rep. Congo/Uganda 16,762 ft (5109 m)
4. Mount Speke, Uganda 16,043 ft (4890 m)
5. Mount Baker, Uganda 15,892 ft (4844 m)

Lowest Point:
▼ Lac 'Assal, Djibouti -512 ft (-156 m) below sea level

Highest recorded temperature:
✛ Al'Aziziyah, Libya 136°F (58°C)

Lowest recorded temperature:
– Ifrane, Morocco -11°F (-24°C)

Wettest Place:
≋ Cape Debundsha, Cameroon 405 in (10,290 mm)

Driest Place:
◠ Wadi Halfa, Sudan <0.1 in (<2.5 mm)

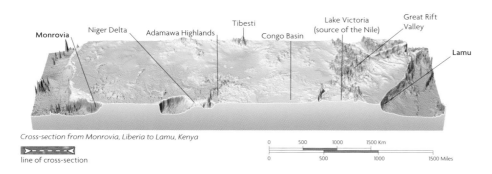

Cross-section from Monrovia, Liberia to Lamu, Kenya

▷▷-▷-▷--
line of cross-section

0   500   1000   1500 Km
0   500   1000   1500 Miles

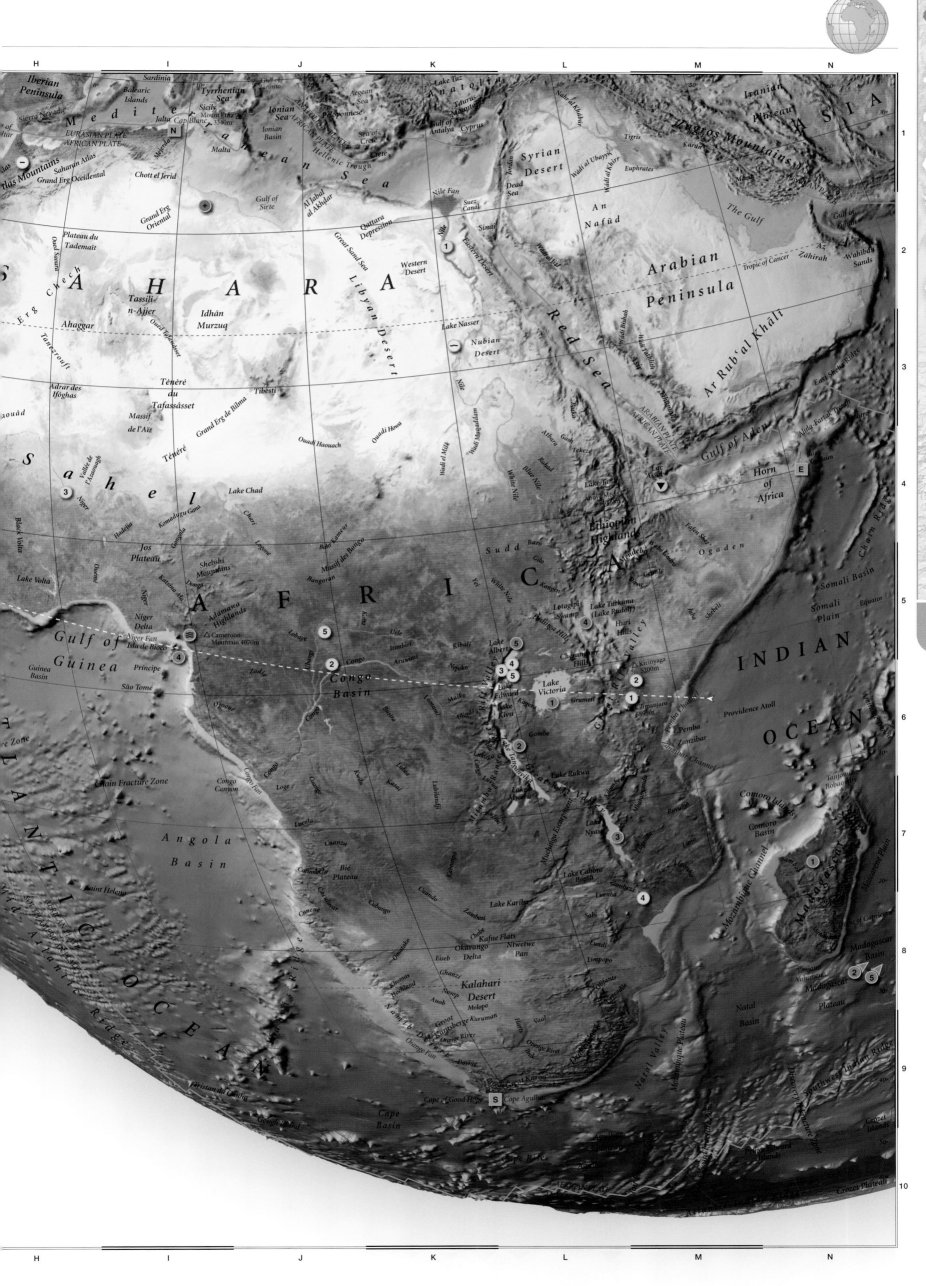

Political

The political map of modern Africa only emerged following the end of the Second World War. Over the next half-century, all of the countries formerly controlled by European powers gained independence from their colonial rulers – only Liberia and Ethiopia were never colonized. The post-colonial era has not been an easy period for many countries, but there have been moves towards multi-party democracy across much of the continent. In South Africa, democratic elections replaced the internationally-condemned apartheid system only in 1994. Other countries have still to find political stability; corruption in government and ethnic tensions are serious problems. National infrastructures, based on the colonial transport systems built to exploit Africa's resources, are often inappropriate for independent economic development.

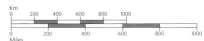

SCALE 1:30,500,000
(projection: Lambert Azimuthal Equal Area)

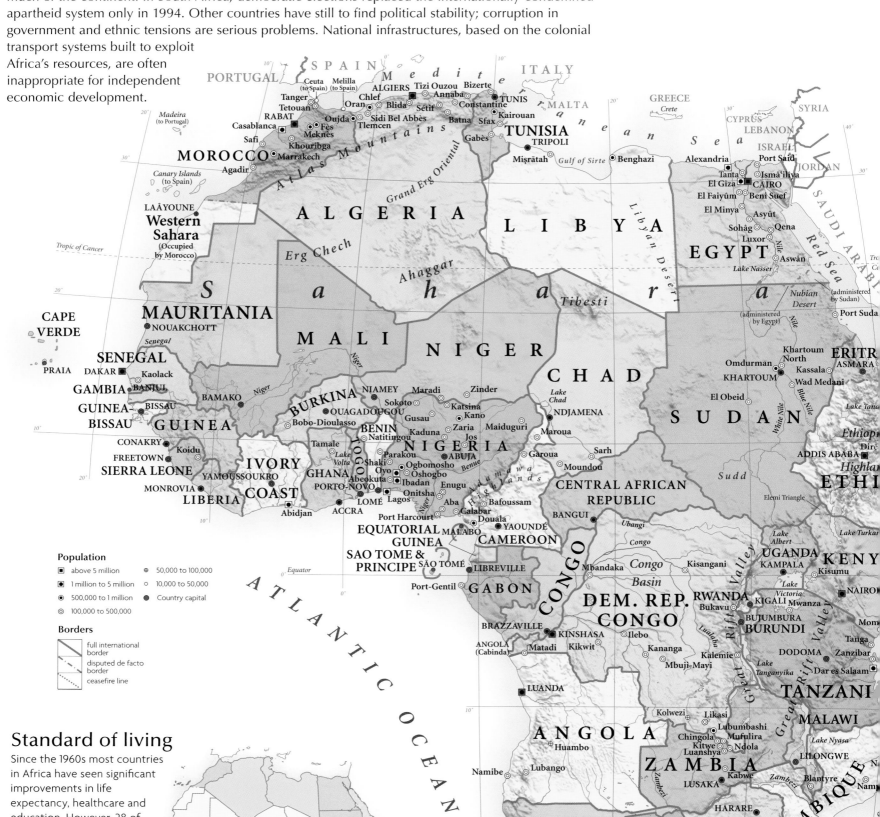

Standard of living

Since the 1960s most countries in Africa have seen significant improvements in life expectancy, healthcare and education. However, 28 of the 30 most deprived countries in the world are African, and the continent as a whole lies well behind the rest of the world in terms of meeting many basic human needs.

Standard of living
(UN human development index)

high

low

Transport

African railways were built to aid the exploitation of natural resources, and most offer passage only from the interior to the coastal cities, leaving large parts of the continent untouched – five land-locked countries have no railways at all. The Congo, Nile and Niger river networks offer limited access to land within the continental interior, but have a number of waterfalls and cataracts which prevent navigation from the sea. Many roads were developed in the 1960s and 1970s, but economic difficulties are making the maintenance and expansion of the networks difficult.

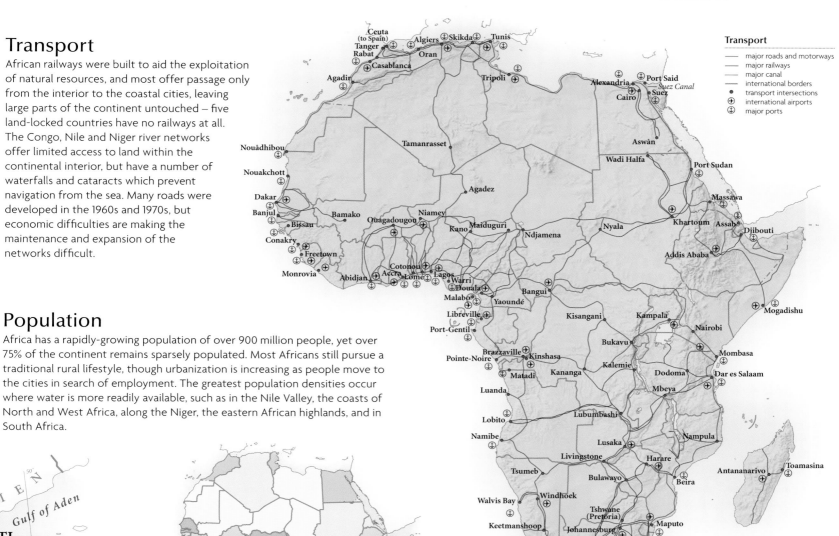

Transport
- major roads and motorways
- major railways
- major canal
- international borders
- • transport intersections
- ⊕ international airports
- ⊕ major ports

Population

Africa has a rapidly-growing population of over 900 million people, yet over 75% of the continent remains sparsely populated. Most Africans still pursue a traditional rural lifestyle, though urbanization is increasing as people move to the cities in search of employment. The greatest population densities occur where water is more readily available, such as in the Nile Valley, the coasts of North and West Africa, along the Niger, the eastern African highlands, and in South Africa.

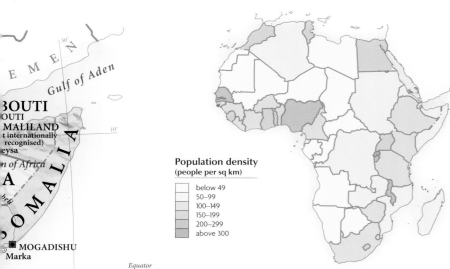

Population density
(people per sq km)
- below 49
- 50–99
- 100–149
- 150–199
- 200–299
- above 300

Languages

Three major world languages act as *lingua francas* across the African continent: Arabic in North Africa; English in southern and eastern Africa and Nigeria; and French in Central and West Africa, and in Madagascar. A huge number of African languages are spoken as well – over 2000 have been recorded, with more than 400 in Nigeria alone – reflecting the continuing importance of traditional cultures and values. In the north of the continent, the extensive use of Arabic reflects Middle Eastern influences while Bantu is widely-spoken across much of southern Africa.

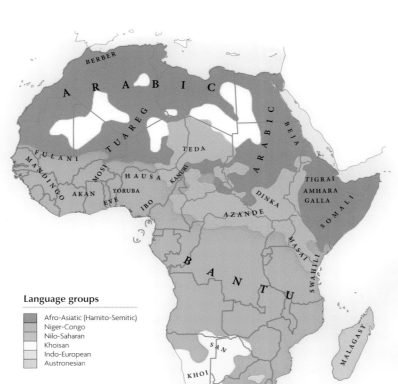

Language groups
- Afro-Asiatic (Hamito-Semitic)
- Niger-Congo
- Nilo-Saharan
- Khoisan
- Indo-European
- Austronesian

Official African Languages

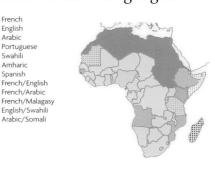

- French
- English
- Arabic
- Portuguese
- Swahili
- Amharic
- Spanish
- French/English
- French/Arabic
- French/Malagasy
- English/Swahili
- Arabic/Somali

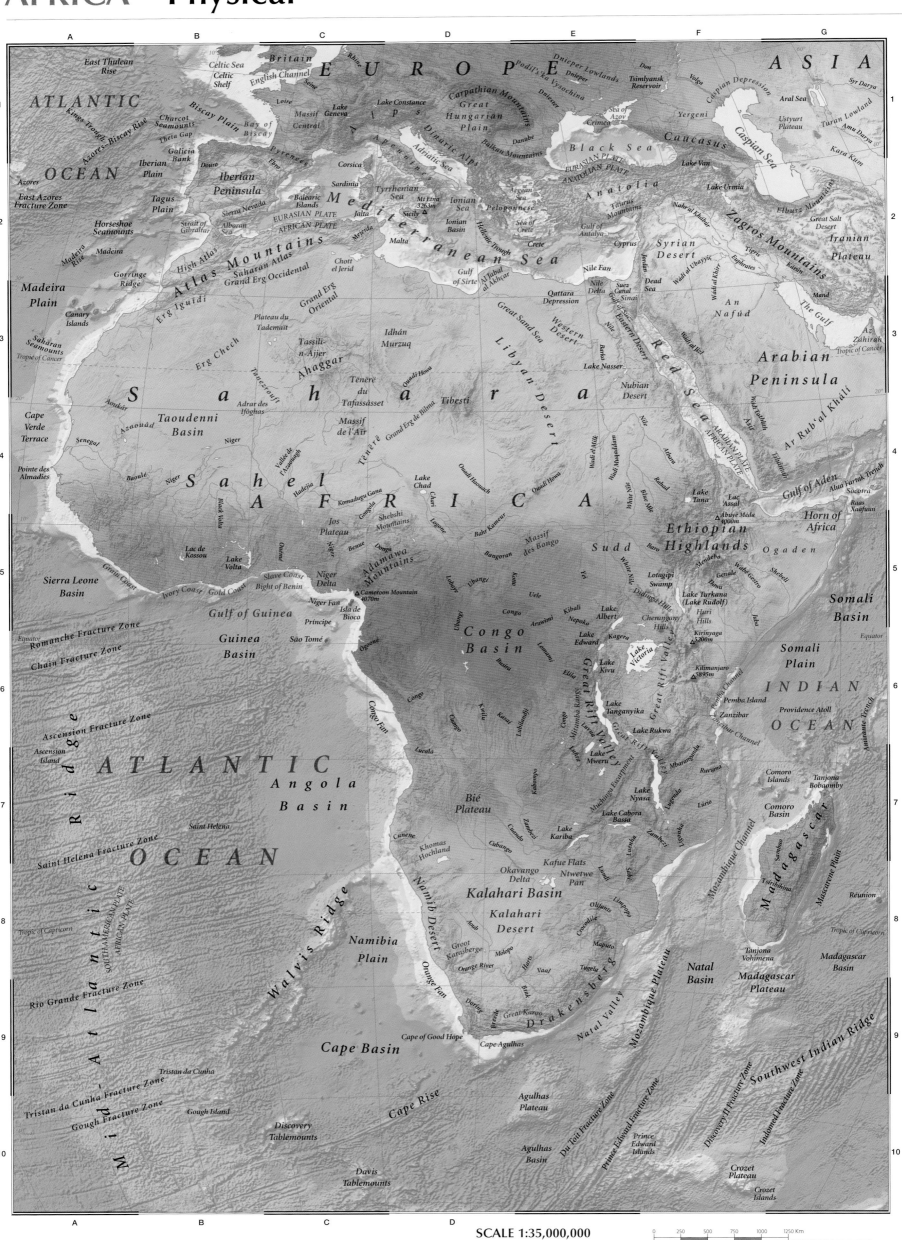

SCALE 1:35,000,000
(projection: Lambert Azimuthal Equal Area)

0   250   500   750   1000   1250 Km

0   250   500   750   1000   1250 Miles

Climate

The climates of Africa range from mediterranean to arid, dry savannah and humid equatorial. In East Africa, where snow settles at the summit of volcanoes such as Kilimanjaro, climate is also modified by altitude. The winds of the Sahara export millions of tonnes of dust a year both northwards and eastwards.

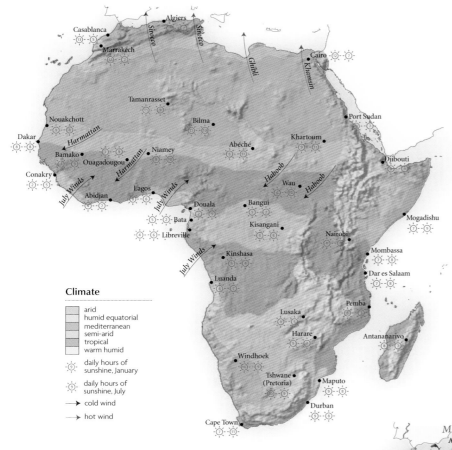

Climate
- arid
- humid equatorial
- mediterranean
- semi-arid
- tropical
- warm humid
- daily hours of sunshine, January
- daily hours of sunshine, July
- cold wind
- hot wind

Average Rainfall

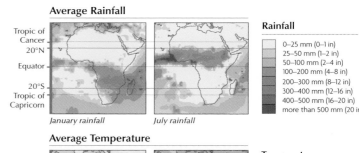

January rainfall
July rainfall

Rainfall
- 0–25 mm (0–1 in)
- 25–50 mm (1–2 in)
- 50–100 mm (2–4 in)
- 100–200 mm (4–8 in)
- 200–300 mm (8–12 in)
- 300–400 mm (12–16 in)
- 400–500 mm (16–20 in)
- more than 500 mm (20 in)

Average Temperature

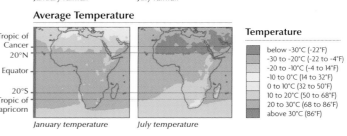

January temperature
July temperature

Temperature
- below -30°C (-22°F)
- -30 to -20°C (-22 to -4°F)
- -20 to -10°C (-4 to 14°F)
- -10 to 0°C (14 to 32°F)
- 0 to 10°C (32 to 50°F)
- 10 to 20°C (50 to 68°F)
- 20 to 30°C (68 to 86°F)
- above 30°C (86°F)

Landuse

Some of Africa's most productive agricultural land is found in the eastern volcanic uplands, where fertile soils support a wide range of valuable export crops including vegetables, tea and coffee. The most widely-grown grain is corn and peanuts (groundnuts) are particularly important in West Africa. Without intensive irrigation, cultivation is not possible in desert regions and unreliable rainfall in other areas limits crop production. Pastoral herding is most commonly found in these marginal lands. Substantial local fishing industries are found along coasts and in vast lakes such as Lake Nyasa and Lake Victoria.

Environmental issues

One of Africa's most serious environmental problems occurs in marginal areas such as the Sahel where scrub and forest clearance, often for cooking fuel, combined with overgrazing, are causing desertification. Game reserves in southern and eastern Africa have helped to preserve many endangered animals, although the needs of growing populations have led to conflict over land use, and poaching is a serious problem.

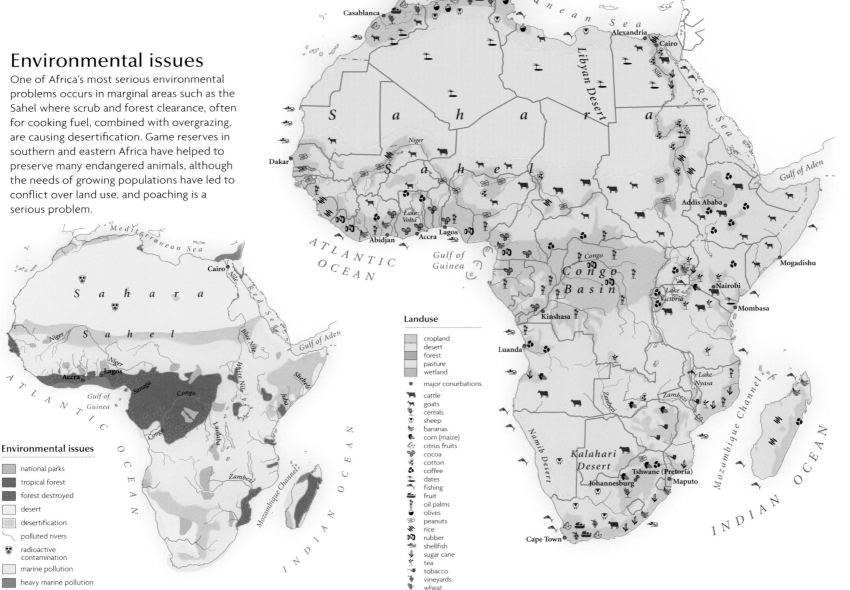

Environmental issues
- national parks
- tropical forest
- forest destroyed
- desert
- desertification
- polluted rivers
- radioactive contamination
- marine pollution
- heavy marine pollution
- poor urban air quality

Landuse
- cropland
- desert
- forest
- pasture
- wetland
- major conurbations
- cattle
- goats
- cereals
- sheep
- bananas
- corn (maize)
- citrus fruits
- cocoa
- cotton
- coffee
- dates
- fishing
- fruit
- oil palms
- olives
- peanuts
- rice
- rubber
- shellfish
- sugar cane
- tea
- tobacco
- vineyards
- wheat

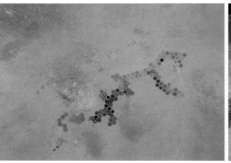

1 AL KHUFRAH, LIBYA
The circular irrigation patterns at this oasis have developed through the use of sprinkler units sweeping around a central point.

2 ERG DU DJOURAB, CHAD
Looking southwest, the pale area, just south of the darker Tibesti mountains on the right and the Ennedi plateau on the left, shows a desert sandstorm in motion.

3 ASWAN HIGH DAM, EGYPT
Completed in 1970 the dam controls flooding along the lower stretches of the Nile river.

4 KHARTOUM, SUDAN
The capital of Sudan lies at the junction of the Blue Nile, flowing from the east, and the broad White Nile, flowing from the south.

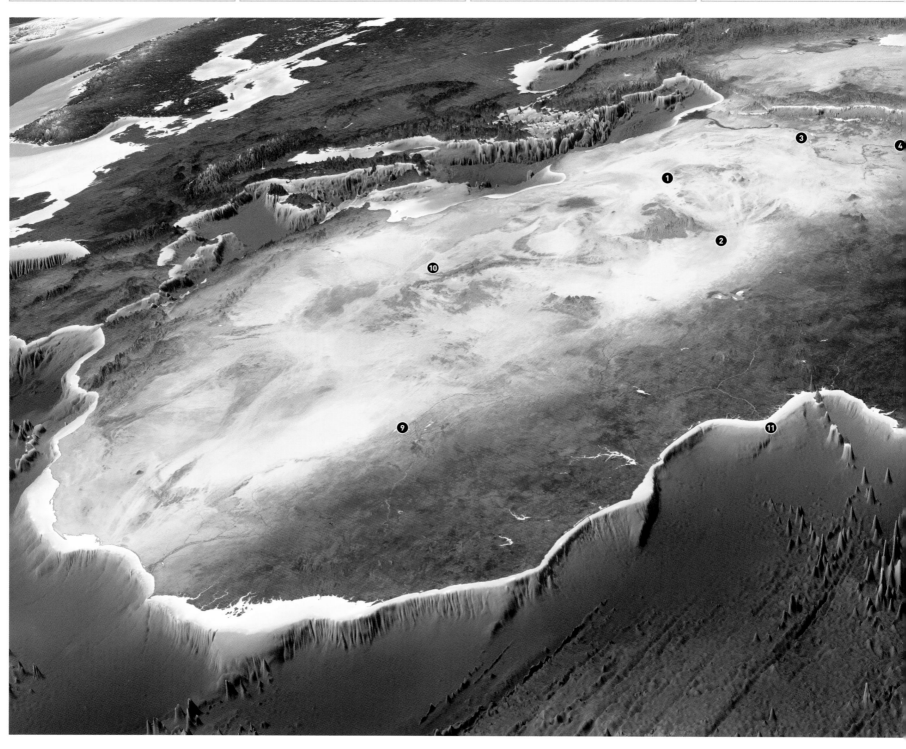

9 LAKE FAGUIBINE, MALI
Part of the Niger river's 'inland delta', a region of lakes, creeks and backwaters near Tombouctou.

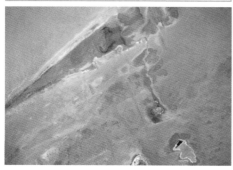

10 TASSILI-N-AJJER, ALGERIA
These sand dunes, one of a variety found in the Sahara, overlie the darker sandstone bedrock of the Tassili-n-Ajjer plateau.

11 NIGER DELTA, NIGERIA
At this point lies the vast, low-lying region through which the waters of the Niger river drain into the Gulf of Guinea.

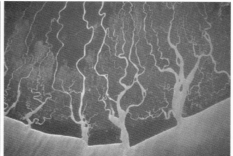

12 CONGO/UBANGI RIVERS, DR CONGO
The confluence of these two rivers lies at the heart of the Congo Basin.

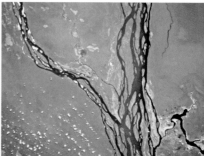

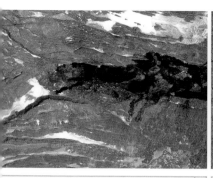

AFAR DEPRESSION, DJIBOUTI | 5
This low point is located at the junction of three ctonic plates - the Gulf of Aden to the east, the Red to the north and the Great Rift Valley to the south.

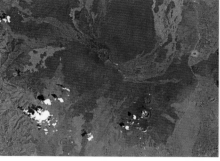

NYIRAGONGO AND NYAMURAGIRA VOLCANOES, | 6
DR CONGO
These two volcanoes, lying to the west of the Great Rift Valley, last erupted in 2002 and 2001 respectively.

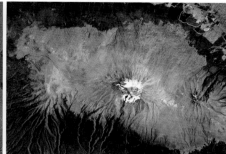

KILIMANJARO, TANZANIA | 7
An extinct volcano, its great height modifies the local climate, forcing moist air streams from the Indian Ocean to rise, inducing rain and, higher up, snow.

BETSIBOKA RIVER, MADAGASCAR | 8
The waters of Madagascar's second longest river are red with sediment as it carries eroded topsoil from the interior and deposits it at it's mouth on the Indian Ocean.

MALEBO POOL, CONGO/DR CONGO | 13
ke in the lower reaches of the Congo river, it hosts o capital cities on its banks, Brazzaville, Congo to he north and Kinshasa, DR Congo to the south.

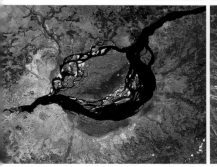

ZAMBEZI RIVER, ZAMBIA | 14
Seasonal flooding of the river and its tributaries turned the Mulonga and Liuwa plains on the Zambia-Angola border into a vast wetland in April 2004

BEIRA, MOZAMBIQUE | 15
This port and beach resort lies on the north side of the mouth of the Pungoé river.

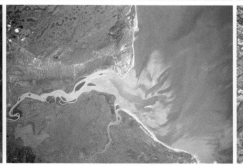

CAPE TOWN, SOUTH AFRICA | 16
South Africa's third largest city with a population of 2.9 million, it is also the seat of the country's parliament.

199

GREECE

Chaniá · Réthymno · Irákleio
Tympáki · Ágios N.
Kríti
(Crete)

M e d i t e r r a n e a n

TUNISIA

Chott Melghir
Chott Merouane
Nefta · Tozeur
El Oued
Touggourt
Gafsa
Baro
Chott el Fedjaj
Kebili
Chott el Jerid
Gabès
Golfe de Gabès
Île de Jerba
Mellita
Médenine
Dehíbat
Tataouine
Sfax
Îles de Kerkenah

ṬARĀBULUS
(TRIPOLI)
Tarābulus
Zuwārah
Az Zāwiyah
Al 'Azīzīyah
Al Khums
Zlitan
Mișrātah
Gharyān
Nalūt
Yafran
Mizdah
Banī Walīd
Al Qaddāhīyah
Wādī Zamzam
Sināwin

Al Marj · Al Baydā' · Darnah
Banghāzī · Al Jabal al Akhdar · Khalīj al Bumbah · Ṭubruq
(Benghazi)
Qamīnis
Gulf of Salūm · Sidi B.
Salūm

ALGERIA

Bourdj Messaouda
Ghadāmis · Dīrj

Al Ḥamādah al Ḥamrā'

Khalīj Surt
(Gulf of Sirte)
Bu'ayrāt al Ḥasūn
Surt
As Sultān
Marsā al Burayqah
An Nawfalīyah
Ajdābiyā
Al 'Uqaylah
Wādī al Fārigh

Wādī al Hamim
Libyan Plateau
Al Jaghbūb

Djanet
Tiguentourine
Illizi

Idhān Awbārī

Jabal as Sawdā'
Hūn · Waddān
Birāk
Samnū
Sabhā
Ghaddūwah
Awbārī
Murzuq
Zawilah

Al Harūj al Aswad
Zillah
Marādah
Jālū

L I B Y A

Sahara
(Western)
Great Sand Sea
Siwa

Tassili-n-Ajjer
Al 'Uwaynāt
Djanet
Ghāt

Hamādat Murzuq

Idhān Murzuq

Tajarhī
Al Qatrūn

Jabal Bin Ghunaymah
Wāw al Kabīr

S a h a r a

Tāzirbū
Buzaymah
Rabyānah

Ramlat Rabyānah

Al Khufrah

Gilf Kebir
Plateau

L i b y a n   D e s e r t

Tropic of Cancer

Oued Tafassasset

Sarīr
Tībistī

Al Uwaynāt · Jabal al 'Uwaynāt
1907m

Plateau du Manguéni

Plateau du Djado
Madama
Djado · Chirfa

Plateau du Tchigaï
Dao Timmi

Massif de Aïr
Aozou
Bardaï
Yebbi-Bou

Jabal Maraty
Pic Bette
2286m

Ma'tan as Sārah

A G A D E Z

Séguédine

T i b e s t i
Zouar
Sherda

Erdi

Adrar Tamgak
1988m
Iferouane

Massif de l'Aïr
Timia
Monts Bagzane
2022m
Akrérèb
Massif de Taghouaji
1106m

Aney
Dirkou
Bilma

Ténéré

△Emi Koussi
3415m
Gouro
Ounianga Kebir

Erdi Ma
Dépression du Mourdi
El A.

Fachi

Grand Erg de Bilma

BORKOU-ENNEDI-TIBESTI
Faya

Erg du Ténéré

N I G E R

DIFFA

Bodélé
Erg du Djourab
Fada
Ennedi
Monou

**NORTHERN
DARFUR**
Teiga
Plateau

Termit-Kaboul

KANEM

Koro Toro

Ouadi Haouach
Ouadi Howa
Oum-Chalouba

Massif du
Kapka
Iriba

Arada

Umm Buru

Tanout
Achétinamou · Tasker
Ngourti

Boultoum

ZINDER
Damagaram Takaya
Kellé
Gouré

Zinder
Miria
Guidimouni
Dengas
Goumel
Hadejia
Hadejia
Jumun

Nguigmi
Goudoumaria
Mainé-Soroa
Diffa
Damasak
Nguru
Gashua
Geidam
Komadugu Gana

YOBE

JIGAWA

NIGERIA

BORNO
Mongonu

Nokou
Bosso
Rig-Rig
Mao
Ngourti
Ngourti

Lake
Chad
LAC
Bol

CHARI-BAGUIRMI
Moyto

Massakory
Ngoura
Terser
Djédaa
Oum-Hadjer
Ati
Batha
Am Dam

BATHA
Haraz-Djombo

CHAD
Salal

BILTINE
Biltine
Guéréda

Abéché
Adré

OUADDAÏ

**WESTERN
DARFUR**
El Geneina
Zalingei

Kutum
Mellit
El Fasher

Kebkabiya
Jebel Marra
3071m
Marra
Hills

134

Population

- ■ above 5 million
- ▣ 1 million to 5 million
- ◉ 500,000 to 1 million
- ◎ 100,000 to 500,000
- ⊕ 50,000 to 100,000
- ○ 10,000 to 50,000
- ∘ below 10,000

216

Elevation scale:
19,686ft
13,124ft
9843ft
6562ft
3281ft
1640ft
820ft
328ft
Sea Level
-820ft
-6562ft
-13,124ft

220

CYPRUS — TURKISH REPUBLIC OF NORTHERN CYPRUS (recognized only by Turkey), NICOSIA, Gitner (Keryneia), Gazimağusa (Ammóchostos, Famagusta), Lárnaka, Lemesós (Limassol), Pafos (Páfos), Olympos, Al Lādhiqīyah (Latakia)

LEBANON — BEYROUTH (BEIRUT), Tripoli, Jabal Lubnan, Duma

SYRIA — Ḥamāh, Ḥimş (Homs), Ţarţūs, Jabal Abu Rahbah, DIMASHQ (DAMASCUS), Syrian Desert, Al Quşayr, As Suwaydā', Al Jazīrah, Tikrīt

ISRAEL — Hefa (Haifa), Nahariyya, Netanya, Tel Aviv-Yafo, Holon, Ashdod, Reḥovot, JERUSALEM, Be'ér Sheva', Be'ér Menuḥa, Ha-Negev, Sappir, Elat, Arad

West Bank, Gaza Strip, Gaza, El 'Arish

Lake Tiberias, Dead Sea, Irbid, Al Mafraq, Az Zarqā', AMMAN, Ma'dabā, Ma'ān, Al Karak

JORDAN — Al Quwayrah

IRAQ — BAGHDĀD, Al Fallūjah, Al Hillah, Karbalā', An Najaf, Al Kūt, Al 'Amārah, An Nāşirīyah, As Samāwah, Ar Rihāb, Ba'qūbah, Euphrates, Tigris, Buḩayrat ath Thartār, Buḩayrat ar Razāzah

IRAN — Kermānshāh (Bākhtarān), KERMANSHAH, LORESTAN, ILĀM

EGYPT — Alexandria, El 'Alamein, El 'Nouzha, Rashid (Rosetta), Damanhûr, Kafr el Sheikh, Tanta, Zagazig, Shibin el Kôm, Benha, Dumyât (Damietta), Port Said, El Mansûra, Ismâ'iliya, Suez Canal, Nile Delta, CAIRO, El Gîza, Pyramids of Giza, Helwân, El Şaff, Suez, El Faiyûm, Beni Suef, El Fashn, Beni Mazâr, Beni Suef, El Minya, Mallawi, Asyûţ, Dairût, Abnûb, Qasr Farâfra, Ţahta, Sohâg, Akhmim, Girga, Qena, Valley of the Kings, Luxor, Isna, Idfu, El Khârga, El Qasr, Mût, Bâris, Kôm Ombo, Aswân, Aswân Dam, Lake Nasser, Abu Simbel, Bawiti, Saḩarâ el Sharqîya (Eastern Desert), Gulf of Suez, Râs Ghârib, Hurghada, Bûr Safâga, Quseir, Marsa 'Alam, Berenice, Râs Banâs

SINAI — Za'farâna, Abu Zenima, Gebel Musa 2285m, El Tûr, Sharm el Sheikh, Râs Muḩammad, Jazirat Tîran

Gulf of Aqaba, 'Aqabah, Ḥaql, Al Bād', Duba, Al Bi'r, Al Muwaylih

SAUDI ARABIA — Tabūk, TABŪK, Jabal al Lawz 2580m, Jabal Dabbāgh 2250m, Ad Dār al Hamrā', Al Akhdar, Al Qalībah, Taymā', Al Wajh, Al 'Ulā, Khaybar, Hadīyah, Umm Lajj, Yanbu' al Baḩr, Badr Ḩunayn, Rābigh, Al Madīnah (Medina), AL MADĪNAH, Jabal Raḍwā 1814m, Mahd adh Dhahab, Halabān, JIDDAH (JEDDA), King Abdul Aziz, MAKKAH, Makkah (Mecca), At Ṭā'if, Turabah, Ar Rawdah, Al Khurmah, Al Mislaḩ, Zalim, Budayyi'ah, AR RIYĀḌ, Ad Dawādimī, Al Quwayyah, 'Afīf, Ar Ruwaydah, Shaqrā', Durma, Marāh, Najd, AL QASIM, Buraydah, Unayzah, 'Uqlāt aṣ Ṣuqūr, Al Ghazālah, HĀ'IL, Hā'il, Jabal 'Aja, Al Hamūdīyah, Bi'r al Murār, Az Zilfī, Al Majma'ah, Al Arṭāwīyah, Al Mayyāh, Jalājil, Dukhnah

AN NAFŪD — An Nafūd, Al Jawf, AL JAWF, Sakākah, Al Murayr, Al Jarāwī, Al Mayyāh

AL HUDŪD ASH SHAMĀLĪYAH — 'Ar'ar, Nişāb, Bi'r Junayyibāt, Wādī al Bāţin, Ḥafar al Bāţin, 'Adhfā', Rafḩah, Hā'il

Al Qurayyat, Ţurayf, Jabal al 'Amūd 1076m, Jabal 'Unayzah 940m, Ar Rūthīyah, Zahrat al Baţn, Hawr al Hammār

AL ḤARRAH — Al 'Isāwīyah, Wādī as Sirḩān, Wādī Araba

SUDAN — Wadi Halfa, Selima Oasis, Laqiya Arba'in, Akasha, Abu Hamed, Delgo, Argo, Dongola, El Khandaq, Merowe, Korti, Ed Debba, Kabushiya, Shendi, Eilei, Wâdi el Milk, Hamrat esh Sheikh, Sodiri, Khuwei, Umm Ruwaba, Bara, El Obeid, Wad Banda

NORTHERN (state), Nubian Desert, NORTHERN KORDOFAN, WESTERN KORDOFAN

RIVER NILE — Berber, Atbara, Ed Damer, Adarama, Goz Regeb

KHARTOUM — Omdurman, Khartoum North, KHARTOUM, Umm Inderab

GEZIRA — Rufa'a, El Kamlin, Wad Nimr, El Manaqil, Barakat, Wad Medani, Hag 'Abdullah, Hasaheisa

WHITE NILE — Ed Dueim, Rabak, Kosti, Tendelti, Singa, Sennar, Doka

SINNAR — Blue Nile

GEDAREF — Gedaref, El Hawata, Gallabat

KASSALA — Kassala, Khashm el Girba, Teseney, Barentu

Wâdi Hofra, Abu 'Urug, Wâdi Magaddam

RED SEA (state) — Port Sudan, Sallom, Suakin, Sinkat, Ekowit, Tokar, Haiya, Musmar, Derudeb, Shereik, Oko, Ras Abu Shagara, Dungûnab, Muḩammad Qol, Halaib (Administrative border / Administered by Egypt, claimed by Sudan), Ras Shakal

(Administered by Egypt), (Political border)

ERITREA — ASMARA, Keren, Massawa, Akurdet, Agordat, Nakfa, Enghershatu 2576m, Barka, Mendefera, Adi Keyh, Mersa Fatma, Zula, Sovra 3018m, Dahlak Archipelago, Massawa Channel

ETHIOPIA — TIGRAY, Mek'ele, Adwa, Aksum, Adigrat, Ras Dashen 4620m, Erer, Keraza, Simen, Sek'ot'a, Korem, Maych'ew, AMHARA, Gonder, Āykel, Metema, Debark, Abiy Ādi, AFAR

DJIBOUTI

YEMEN — SANA (ṢAN'Ā'), Ḥajjah, Al Ḥudaydah (Hodeida), Al Luḩayyah, Kamarān, Az Zaydīyah, Bayt al Faqīh, Zabīd, Ḩays, Dhamār, Radā', Ibb, Yarīm, Ta'izz, Al Mukhā, Ramādah, Jazirat al Hanish al Kabir, Jazirat Zuqar, NAJRĀN, Najrān, NAJRAN, Ma'dinat, Amran, Ash Shaykh 'Uthmān, Ras 'Ara, Jabal Nabi Shu'ayb 3760m

'ASĪR / JĪZĀN (Saudi Arabia) — Abhā, ABHĀ, Khamīs Mushayt, Jabal Sawda 3133m, Muḩayil, Al Birk, Sabyā, Jīzān, JĪZĀN, Şa'dah, Midi, 'Abs, Jabal Madīţah, Zahrān, Al Qunfudhah, Ad Darb, Jazā'ir Farasān, Jīzat al 'Abr

AL BĀḤAH / MAKKAH — Al Bāḩah, AL BĀḤAH, Al Līth, Daws, Qal'at Bīshah, Tathlīth, Bīshah, 'Aynūn, Ranyah, Baljurshī, Hūth, 'Ar Ruwaydah, Wādī ad Dawāsir, As Sulayyil, Khamir, Dhamar, 'Abs

Red Sea

Tropic of Cancer

136

ATLANTIC

OCEAN

PORTUGAL

SPAIN

Sines
Beja
Azuaga
Montoro
Linares
Córdoba
Valverde del Camino
Guadalquivir
Sevilla (Seville)
Jaén
Sistema Béticos
Cabo de São Vicente
Lagos
Faro
Golfo de Cádiz
Huelva
Dos Hermanas
Lucena
Granada
Guadix
Mulacén 3481m
Lebrija
Jerez de la Frontera
Cádiz
Ronda
Málaga
Costa de Sol
San Fernando
Vejer de la Frontera
Marbella
Algeciras
GIBRALTAR (to UK)
Strait of Gibraltar
Cap Spartel
Ceuta (to Spain)
Melilla (to Spain)
Cap des Trois Fourc
Tanger
Boukhalef
Tétouan
Al-Hoceima
Nador
Ghazao
Asilah
Chefchaouen
Larache
Ksar-el-Kebir
Rif
Oujda
Moulay-Bousselham
Souk-el-Arba- Rharb
Kénitra
Taounate
El Ayou
Salé
Sidi- Kacem
Taourirt
Jerada
RABAT
Salé
Fès
Taza
Casablanca
Khemisset
Meknès
Sefrou
Sais
Mohammedia
Mohammed V
Azrou
Ifrane
Moulouya
El-Jadida
Berrechid
Khénifra
Settat
Oued- Zem
Ca Beddouza
Sidi-Bennour
Khouribga
Safi
Tendran
Beni-Mellal
Jbel Ayachi 3757m
Tensift
El Kelaâ Srarhna
Azilal
Er-Rachidia
Béchar
Essaouira
Marrakech
Menara
Moyen Atlas
Erfoud
Âbadla
Cap Rhir
Imezgane
Jbel Toubkal 4165m
Haut Atlas
Ouarzazate
Hamada du Guir
MOROCCO Atlas
Agadir
Taroudannt
Anti-Atlas
Sidi-Ifni
Tiznit
Tata
Hamada du Dra
Erg er Ra
Bou-Izakarn
Guelmime
Tabelbala
Tan-Tan
Drâa
Hamada Tounassine
Cap Juby
Tarfaya
Tindouf
Sebkha de Tindouf
A L G
LAÂYOUNE
El Mahbas
Saguia al Hamra
Smara
Bou Craa
Boujdour
El Eglab
WESTERN SAHARA (occupied by Morocco)
'Aïn Ben Tili
Yetti
'Erg Iguidi
S
Galtat-Zemmour
Bir Mogrein
Chegga
Tropic of Cancer
TIRIS
'Ayoûn 'Abd el Mâlek
ZEMMOUR
Ad Dakhla
Sebkhet Aghzoumal
'Erg el Ahmar
'Erg Chech
Kâghet
El Hank
El Mreiti
Cap Barbas
Aousard
Zouérat
El Hammâmi
Taoudenni
Adrar Souttouf
Fdérik
Erg
Aghouinit
Tourine
Bir- Gandouz
Touâjil
'Erg I-n-Sâk
Techla
Char
Malqteïr
El Guettâra
Nouâdhibou
Bou Lanouar
Azeffâl
Choûm
Ouarâne
El Mrâyer
i-n-Éch
Lagouira
Râs Nouâdhibou
Nouâdhibou
Akchâr
Atâr
Ouadâne
'Erg Atouila
'Erg I-n-Sâk
Dakhlet Nouâdhibou
ADRAR
'Erîgât
DAKHLET NOUÂDHIBOU
Chinguetti
TOMBOUCTOU
INCHIRI
Oujeft
M
Et Tidra
El Mreyyé
Araouane
Nouâmghâr
Râs Timiris
Akjoujt
MAURITANIA
Boû Djébéha
Bennichâb
Boû Rjeïmât
NOUAKCHOTT
Bella
Rachid
HODH
Nouakchott
Tidjikja
Idini
TAGANT
Tichit
TRARZA
Moudjéria
Aoukâr
Lac Faguibine
Tiguent
Magta' Lahjar
Boûmdeïd
ECH CHARGUI
Néma
Tombouctou
Boutilimit
Guérou
Azaou
MedErdra
Bababé
Kiffa
Oualâta
Gouadam
Djre
Rkiz
Aleg
Jmachekket
Rosso
BRAKNA
'Ayoûn el 'Atroûs
Lac Garou
Dagana
Bogué
Kaédi
HODH
Néma
Lac Niangay
Podor
Senegal
Mònguel
ASSABA
Timbedgha
Lac Aougoundou
Richard Toll
Tintâne
Amourj
Niafounke
Saint Louis
Lac de Guier
Mbout
EL GHARBI
Bassikounou
Kébémer
Louga
Dara
Linguère
Maghama
Kankossa
Ould Yenjé
'Adel Bagrou
MÓPTI
Kébémer
Ranérou
GORGOL
Sélibabi
Nioro
SÉGOU
Mékhé
Matam
GUIDIMAKA
Tivaouane
DAKAR
Dakar
Bambey
KAYES
Nampala
Pointe des Almadies
Touba
Mbaké
Ballé
KOULIKORO
Rufisque
Thiès
Diourbel
Vélingara
Bakel
Yélimané
Youvarou
Mbour
Fatick
SENEGAL

290

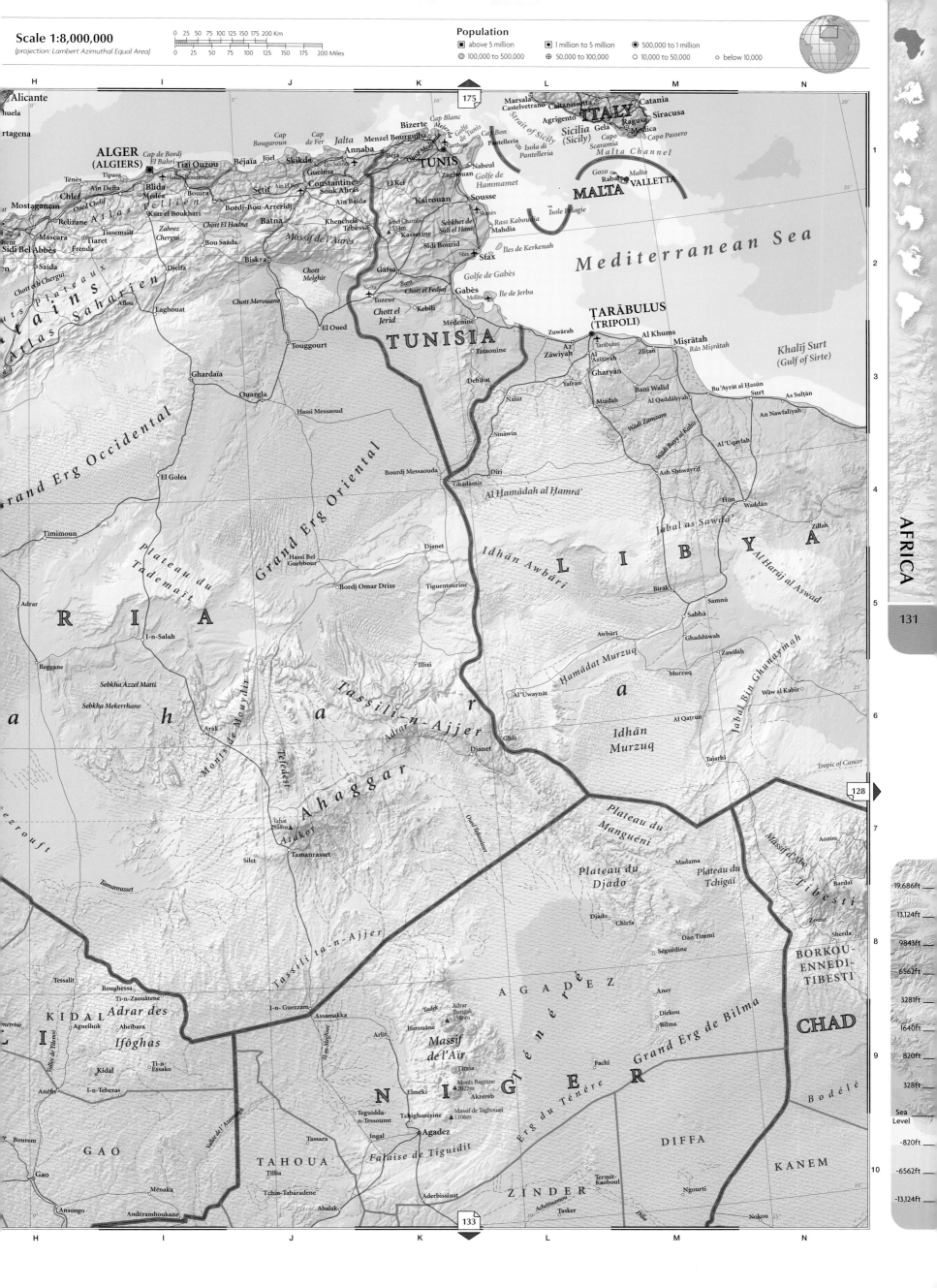

West Africa

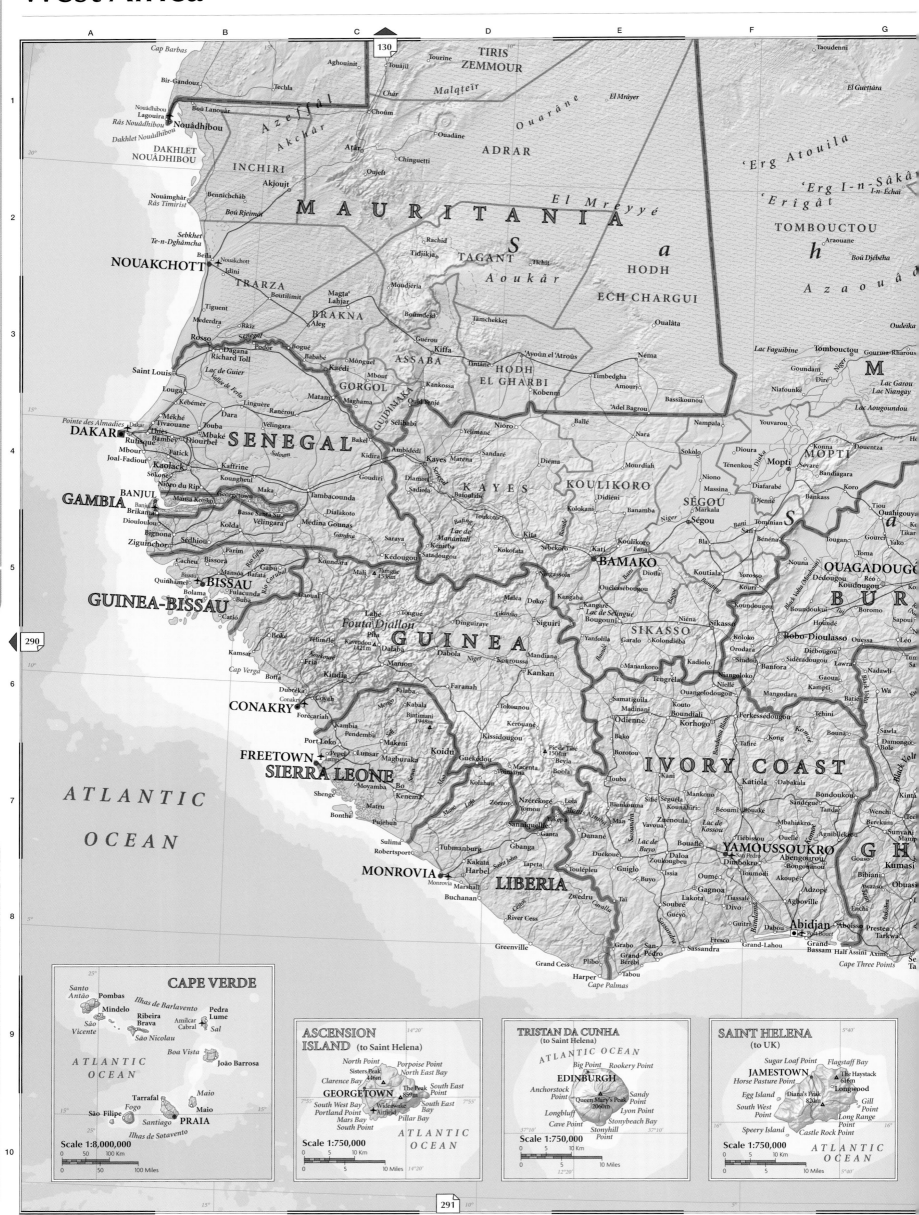

130

290

291

CAPE VERDE

Santo
Antão   Pombas
Mindelo
São   Ribeira
Vicente   Brava
             São Nicolau
ATLANTIC
OCEAN

Ilhas de Barlavento

Pedra
Lume
Amilcar   Sal
Cabral

Boa Vista
                    João Barrosa

Maio
Tarrafal   Maio
Fogo
São Filipe   Santiago   PRAIA
             Ilhas de Sotavento

Scale 1:8,000,000
0   50   100 Km
0   50   100 Miles

ASCENSION ISLAND (to Saint Helena)

North Point
Sisters Peak   Porpoise Point
Clarence Bay   North East Bay
                                South East
GEORGETOWN   The Peak   Point
              859m
South West Bay   South East
Portland Point   Wideawake   Point
Mars Bay   Airfield
                 Pillar Bay

ATLANTIC
OCEAN

Scale 1:750,000
0   5   10 Km
0   5   10 Miles

TRISTAN DA CUNHA (to Saint Helena)

ATLANTIC OCEAN

Big Point
          Rookery Point
Anchorstock
Point   Sandy
EDINBURGH   Point
Queen Mary's Peak
Longbluff   2060m   Lyon Point
Cave Point   Stonybeach Bay
             Stonyhill
             Point

Scale 1:750,000
0   5   10 Km
0   5   10 Miles

SAINT HELENA (to UK)

Sugar Loaf Point   Flagstaff Bay
JAMESTOWN   The Haystack
Horse Pasture Point 616m
                    Longwood
Egg Island   Diana's Peak
              820m   Gill
South West   Point
Point   Long Range
            Point
Speery Island   Castle Rock Point

ATLANTIC
OCEAN

Scale 1:750,000
0   5   10 Km
0   5   10 Miles

Sea Level scale:
6000m
4000m
3000m
2000m
1000m
500m
250m
100m
Sea Level
-250m
-500m
-1000m

Population
- ■ above 5 million
- ◉ 100,000 to 500,000
- ▣ 1 million to 5 million
- ⊕ 50,000 to 100,000
- ◎ 500,000 to 1 million
- ○ 10,000 to 50,000
- ○ below 10,000

0 25 50 75 100 125 150 175 200 Km
0 25 50 75 100 125 150 175 200 Miles

ALGERIA

Plateau du Djado

Djado
Chirfa
Dao Timmi
Séguédine
Bilma
Fachi

BORKOU-ENNEDI-TIBESTI
Zouar
Aozou
Bardaï
Sherda

Tamanrasset
Silet
Tassili ta-n-Ajjer

KIDAL
Tessalit
Boughessa
Ti-n-Zaouâtene
Adrar des Ifôghas
Abeïbara
Aguelhok
Kidal
Anéfis
1-n-Tebezas
Ti-n-Essako

Timétrine
Bourem
Gao

LI **GAO**
Ansongo
Ménaka
Andérramboukane

AGADEZ
I-n-Guezzam
Assamakka
Todek
Iferouâne
Adrar Taïngak 1988m
Arlit
Tumia
Ehnéki
Monts Bagzane 2022m
Akrérèb
Aney
Dirkou

Ténéré

Grand Erg de Bilma
Erg du Ténéré

Bodélé

Teguidda-n-Tessoumt
Tchighozérine
Massif de Taghouaji 1106m
Agadez
Ingal
Tassara

Falaise de Tiguidit

NIGER

DIFFA
Termit-Kaoboul
Achénoumou
Tasker
Ngourti
Nguigmi
Goudoumaria
Bosso
Maïné-Soroa
Diffa

CHAD
KANEM
Nokou
Mao
Moussoro
Bahr el Ghazal
Massaguet
Moyto
Massakory
Ngoura
Tersef
Bol
Ngouri
Bahr Azoum

LAC
Lake Chad
Damasak

Falaise de...
Tchin-Tabaradene
Abalak
Aderbissinat
Tanout
Boultoum
Sabon Kafi

TAHOUA
Tahoua
Keita
Bagaroua
Illela
Bouza
Madaoua

MARADI
Dakoro
Guidan-Roumji
Tessaoua
Aguié
Madarounfa

ZINDER
Belbédji
Zinder
Takiéta
Miria
Damagaram Takaya
Kellé
Gouré
Magaria

Ngourti
Mainé-Soroa
Gashua
Geidam
Mongonu
Komadugu Gana

YOBE
Damaturu
Potiskum
Maïduguri

BORNO
Dikwa
Bama
Gwoza
Mora
Mubi

Dengas
Nguru
Hadejia
Azare
Biu
Gombe

Ouatagouna
Téra
Gothèye

TILLABÉRI
Ouallam
Bani Bangou
Filingué
Abala
Tahoua

NIAMEY
Niamey
Bossey Bangou
Torodi
Say
Dosso
Birnin Gaouré
Falmey

DOSSO
Loga
Dogondoutchi
Birnin Konni
Malbaza
Madaoua
Illela

Rima
Wurno
Sokoto
Argungu
Talata Mafara

SOKOTO
Kaura Namoda
Gummi
Yashi

KATSINA
Katsina
Daura
Gazaoua
Matamey
Gumel
Hadejia

JIGAWA
Dutse
Birnin Kudu
Faggo
Kari
Darazo
Nafada

ZAMFARA
Gusau
Malumfashi
Funtua
Wudil

KANO
Kano

KEBBI
Birnin Kebbi
Jega
Zuru
Koko
Kamba
Wasagu

Zaria
Kujama
Dutsen Wai
Sabon Birnin Gwari

KADUNA
Kaduna
Kachia
Kafanchan

BAUCHI
Bauchi
Gombe
Kumo
Kaltungo
Gombi

GOMBE

ADAMAWA
Numan
Jimeta
Yola
Jalingo

EXTRÊME-NORD
Maroua
Kaélé
Guider
Léré
Mayo-Kébbi

Niger
Kainji Reservoir
New Bussa
Wawa
Kaiama

BENIN
Natitingou
Kouandé
Péhonko
Djougou
Nikki
Parakou
Ndali
Bembéréké
Yashikera

NIGER
Minna
Bida
Zungeru
Suleja

ABUJA
Abuja
Federal Capital District
Abaji

KWARA
Ilorin
Jebba
Lafiagi
Patigi
Baro

NASSARAWA
Nassarawa
Lafia
Loko
Keffi
Wamba
Shendam

PLATEAU
Jos
Panyam
Pankshin
Kefti

TARABA
Wukari
Takum
Gassol
Ibi
 Gembu

NORD
Garoua
Poli
Rey Bouba
Tcholliré
Lagdo
Lac de Lagdo
Tchabal Mbabo 2460m
Ngaoundéré

ADAMAWA (ADAMAOUA)
Adamawa Highlands
Tignère
Banyo
Tibati
Meiganga
Bétaré-Oya
Lac de Mbakaou

Shaki
Oyo
Iseyin
Ogbomosho
Osogbo
Iwo
Ede
Ife
Ilesha

OYO
Ibadan
Oshogbo

EKITI
Ado-Ekiti
Ikare
Akure
Owo

OSUN

ONDO
Ondo
Ijebu-Ode
Okitipupa

OGUN
Abeokuta
Ikeja

LAGOS
Lagos

TOGO
Sokodé
Blitta
Atakpamé
Kpalimé
Notsé
Aného
LOMÉ

A (GHANA)
Hohoe
Kpandu
Ho
Keta
Ada
Accra
ACCRA
Cape Saint Paul

Volta

PORTO-NOVO
Cotonou
Ouidah
Grand-Popo

Bight of Benin

DELTA
Warri
Sapele
Forcados
Burutu
Niger Delta

EDO
Benin City
Auchi
Ubiaja
Agbor
Asaba

ANAMBRA
Onitsha
Awka
Kwale

ENUGU
Enugu
Nsukka
Abakaliki
Afikpo

EBONYI

IMO
Owerri
Umuahia
Aba

ABIA

CROSS RIVER
Calabar
Ikom
Obudu

AKWA IBOM
Uyo
Opobo
Oron

RIVERS
Port Harcourt
Degema
Bonny

BAYELSA
Yenagoa
Brass

Mouths of the Niger

KOGI
Lokoja
Okene
Idah
Ankpa
Oturkpo

BENUE
Makurdi
Oju
Oboko

Bight of Biafra

SUD-OUEST
Kumba
Mamfe
Buea
Tiko

Cameroon Mountain 4070m
Idenao

LITTORAL
Douala
Edéa
Nkongsamba
Yabassi

NORD-OUEST
Bamenda
Wum
Nkambe
Lac Nyos

OUEST
Bafoussam
Foumban
Dschang
Bafang

CAMEROON

CENTRE
YAOUNDÉ
Mbalmayo
Obala
Bafia
Monatélé
Ayos
Abong Mbang
Nanga Eboko

EST
Bertoua
Doumé
Batouri
Yokadouma
Belabo
Minta

Sangmélima
Ebolowa
Djoum

SUD
Ambam
Campo
Kribi
Lolodorf

EQUATORIAL GUINEA
Bata
Mbini
Niefang
Mongomo
Evinayong
Rio Uolo
Ebebiyin
Bitam
Oyem

WOLEU-NTEM

MALABO
Luba

SÃO TOMÉ AND PRINCIPE
São Tomé
SÃO TOMÉ

Cabo San Juan
Acalayong
Cocobeach
LIBREVILLE

GABON
Kango
Médouneu
Mitzic
Makokou
Booué
Njolé

ESTUAIRE

OGOOUÉ-IVINDO

Gulf of Guinea

CHARI-BAGUIRMI
NDJAMENA
Koréssi
Djamena
Guélengdeng
Chari
Bousso
Bongor
CENTRAL AFRICAN REPUBLIC
Bocaranga
Bozoum
Bouar
Carnot
Berbérati
Nola

NANA-MAMBÉRÉ
MAMBÉRÉ-KADÉÏ

OUHAM-PENDÉ
Paoua
Bozoum

LOGONE-OCCIDENTAL
Moundou

LOGONE-ORIENTAL
Baïbokoum
Goré

MAYO-KÉBBI
Pala
Kélo
Bongor
Gounou-Gaya
Léré

Garoua Boulaï
Bertoua

LA SANGHA
Sembé
Ouésso

CONGO
Mékambo
Mbomo
Souanké

SANGHA-MBAÉRÉ

CUVETTE
CUVETTE-OUEST

Elevation scale:
- 19,686ft
- 13,124ft
- 9843ft
- 6562ft
- 3281ft
- 1640ft
- 820ft
- 328ft
- Sea Level
- -820ft
- -6562ft
- -13,124ft

131
135
124

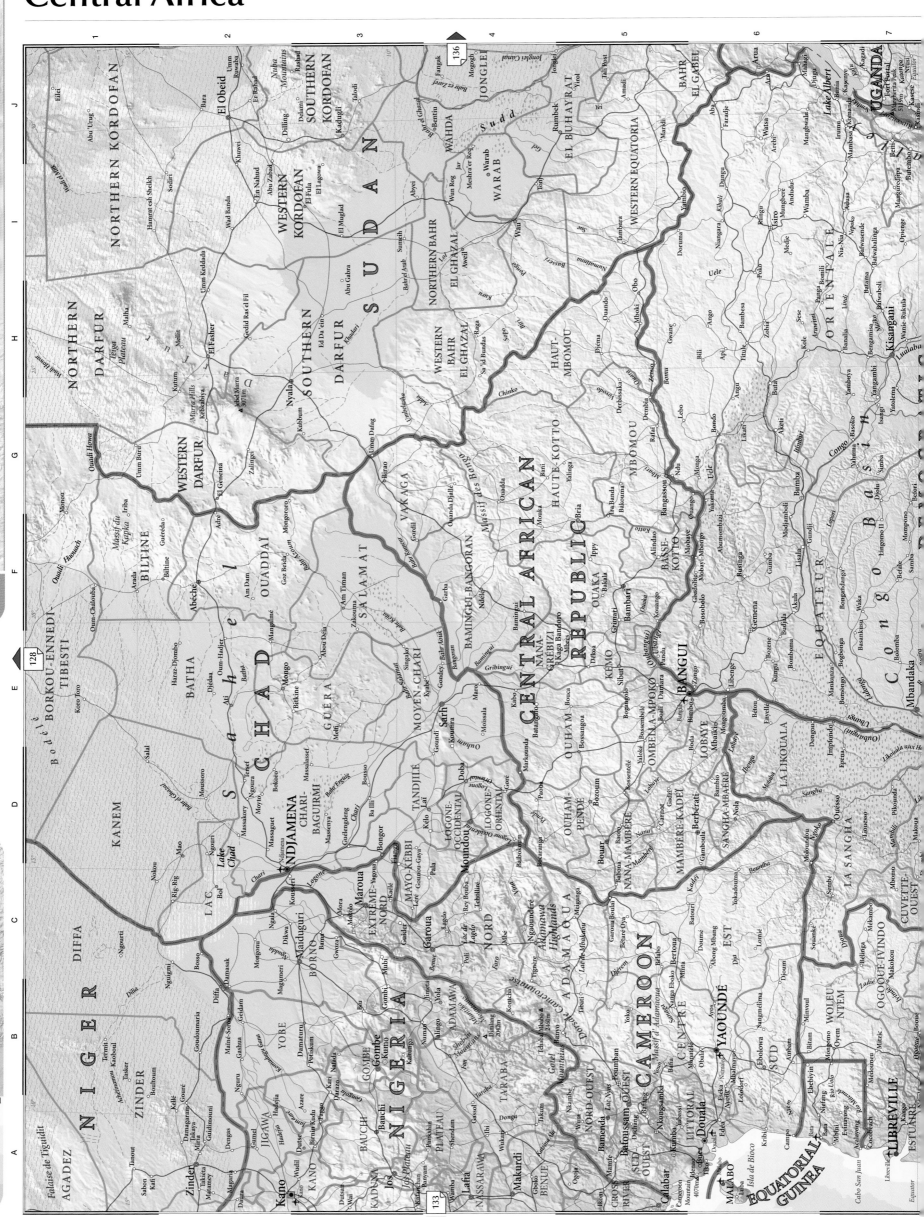

Countries and regions: SAUDI ARABIA, YEMEN, ERITREA, SUDAN, NORTHERN, SOUTHERN KORDOFAN, WESTERN KORDOFAN, ETHIOPIA, DJIBOUTI, SOMALILAND (not internationally recognized), SOMALIA, PUNTLAND, UGANDA, DEM. REP. CONGO, KENYA

Waters and features: Red Sea, Gulf of Aden, Danakil Desert, Ethiopian Highlands, Blue Nile, White Nile (Bahr el Jebel), Lake Turkana (Lake Rudolf), Horn of Africa, Bab el Mandeb

Major cities: KHARTOUM, ASMARA, ADĪS ĀBEBA (ADDIS ABABA), DJIBOUTI, SAN'A (SANA), MUQDISHO (MOGADISHU), Marka, BANAADIR

Elevation scale: 6000m, 4000m, 3000m, 2000m, 1000m, 500m, 250m, 100m, Sea Level, -250m, -500m, -1000m

Scale 1:8,000,000
(projection: Lambert Azimuthal Equal Area)

0 25 50 75 100 125 150 175 200 Km
0 25 50 75 100 125 150 175 200 Miles

Population

☐ above 5 million   ☐ 1 million to 5 million   ◉ 500,000 to 1 million
◎ 100,000 to 500,000   ⊕ 50,000 to 100,000   ○ 10,000 to 50,000   ○ below 10,000

SEYCHELLES

Inner Islands
Ile Aride
Curieuse   Les Soeurs
Grand Soeur
Praslin   Marianne
Cousin   Felicité
Cousine   La Digue
Mamelles
Sainte Anne
Ile du Nord   Ile au Cerf
VICTORIA   Mahé
Morne Seychellois   Cascade
905m   Anse Boileau   Baie Lazare
Ile Thérèse
Silhouette   Mount Dauban   Pointe Lazare
450m   Anse Royale
Pointe Police
Quatre Bornes
North Point

Scale 1:2,000,000

INDIAN OCEAN

RÉUNION (to France)

ST-DENIS
Le Port   Ste-Suzanne   Ste-Marie
St-Paul   St-André   St-Benoît
St-Gilles-les-Bains   Salazie
Cirque de Cilaos   La Plaine-des-Palmistes
Les Avirons   Cilaos   Piton des Neiges
3069m   Le Tampon
St-Leu   St-Louis   Ste-Rose
St-Pierre   Piton de la Fournaise
La Rivière   2631m
St-Joseph   St-Philippe
Pointe de la Table

Scale 1:2,000,000

MAURITIUS

Round Island
Flat Island
Ile D'Ambre
Gunner's Quoin
Triolet   Goodlands
Pamplemousses   Rivière du Rempart
Canonniers Point   Centre de Flacq
PORT LOUIS
Beau Bassin   Rose Hill   Bel Air
Quatre Bornes   Mahébourg
Mont du Rempart   Curepipe
828m   Rose Belle   Sceewoosagur
Vacoas   Ramgoolam
Tamarin   Piton de la Petite
Rivière Noire   Rivière Sud   Souillac
572m   Est   Chemin Grenier
Ouest

Scale 1:2,000,000

INDIAN OCEAN

SEYCHELLES

Providence Atoll
Farquhar Group

Aldabra Group
Assumption Island
Cosmoledo Group
Astove Island

COMOROS

Comoro Islands
Grande Comore
MORONI   Anjouan
Le Kartala   Dembeni   Moutsamoudou
2361m   Mohéli

MAYOTTE (to France)
MAMOUDZOU
Pamandzi

Mozambique Channel

MADAGASCAR

ANTSIRANANA
Ambilobe
MAHAJANGA
Mahajanga
TOAMASINA

INDIAN OCEAN

KENYA / COAST
NAIROBI
Mombasa
Malindi
Lamu

TANZANIA
DAR ES SALAAM
DODOMA
ZANZIBAR
Pemba
KILIMANJARO
ARUSHA
Moshi
Tanga
Morogoro
Iringa
Mbeya
Tabora
Mwanza
Lake Victoria
Lake Tanganyika

Great Rift Valley

ZAMBIA
Monts Mitumba

MALAWI
LILONGWE
Blantyre
Lake Nyasa

MOZAMBIQUE
Nampula
Pemba
CABO DELGADO
NAMPULA
ZAMBÉZIA
NIASSA

ZIMBABWE

INDIAN OCEAN

19,686ft
13,124ft
9843ft
6562ft
3281ft
1640ft
820ft
328ft
Sea Level
-820ft
-6562ft
-13,124ft

AFRICA

138

135

291

292

A B C D E F G

1 2 3 4 5 6 7 8 9 10

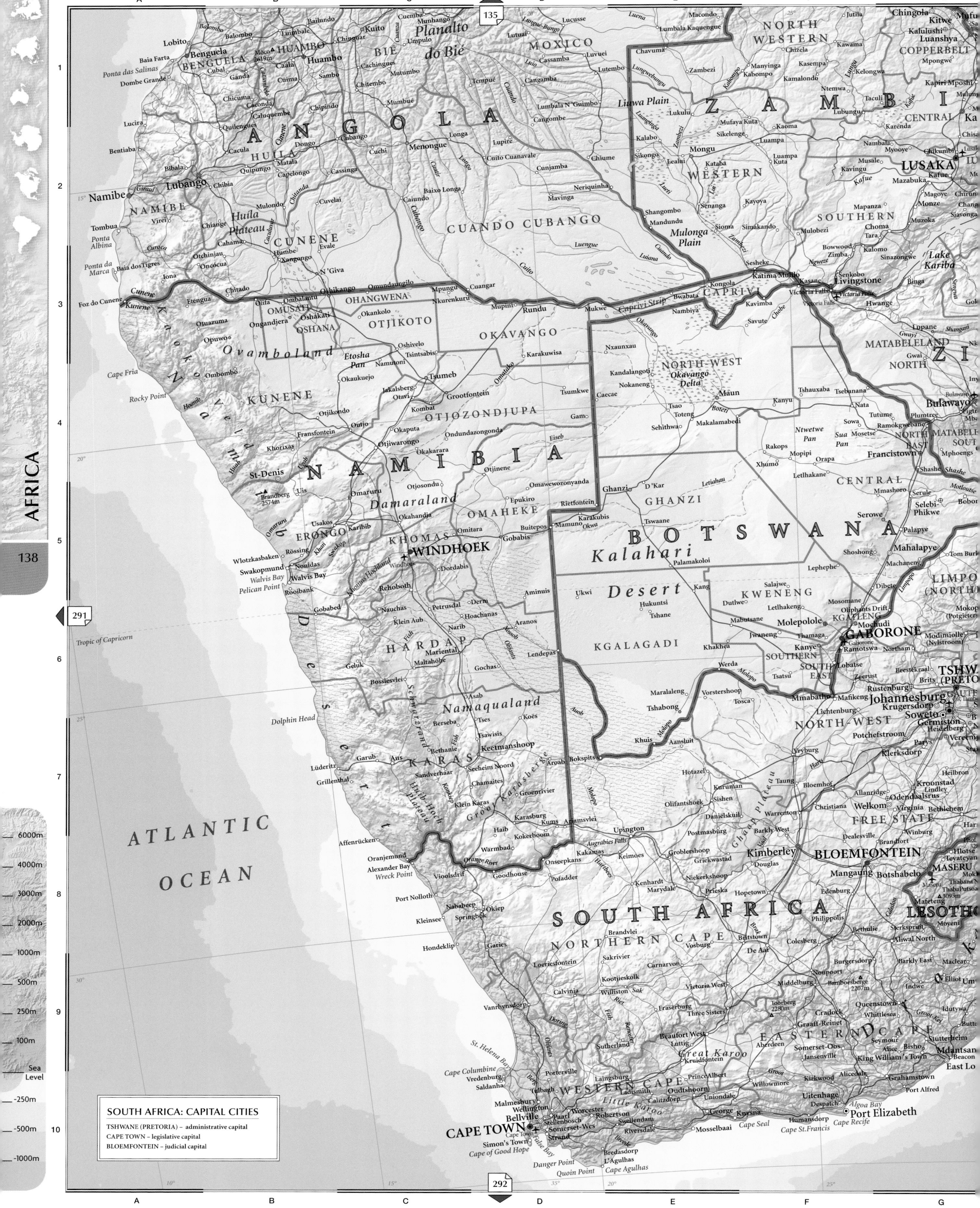

SOUTH AFRICA: CAPITAL CITIES

TSHWANE (PRETORIA) – administrative capital
CAPE TOWN – legislative capital
BLOEMFONTEIN – judicial capital

6000m
4000m
3000m
2000m
1000m
500m
250m
100m
Sea Level
-250m
-500m
-1000m

ATLANTIC OCEAN

ANGOLA
NAMIBIA
BOTSWANA
ZAMBIA
SOUTH AFRICA
LESOTHO

Tropic of Capricorn

WINDHOEK
GABORONE
BLOEMFONTEIN
CAPE TOWN
LUSAKA
MASERU
Johannesburg
TSHWANE (PRETORIA)

Kalahari Desert
Okavango Delta
Etosha Pan
Namib Desert
Cape of Good Hope
Cape Agulhas

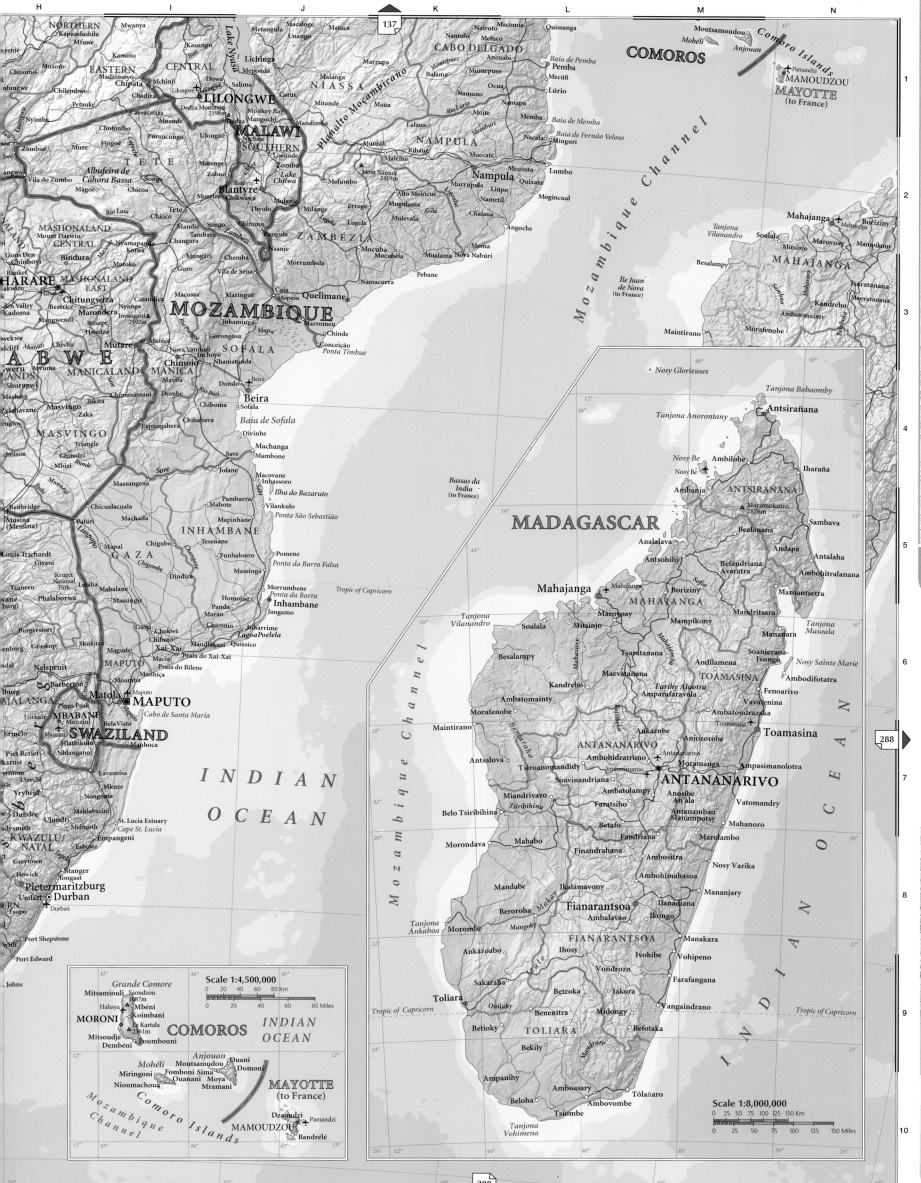

South Africa

SOUTH AFRICA: CAPITAL CITIES

TSHWANE (PRETORIA) – administrative capital
CAPE TOWN – legislative capital
BLOEMFONTEIN – judicial capital

Scale 1:4,650,000
(projection: Lambert Azimuthal Equal Area)

0 20 40 60 80 100 Km
0 20 40 60 80 100 Miles

Population
above 5 million
1 million to 5 million
500,000 to 1 million
100,000 to 500,000
50,000 to 100,000
10,000 to 50,000
below 10,000

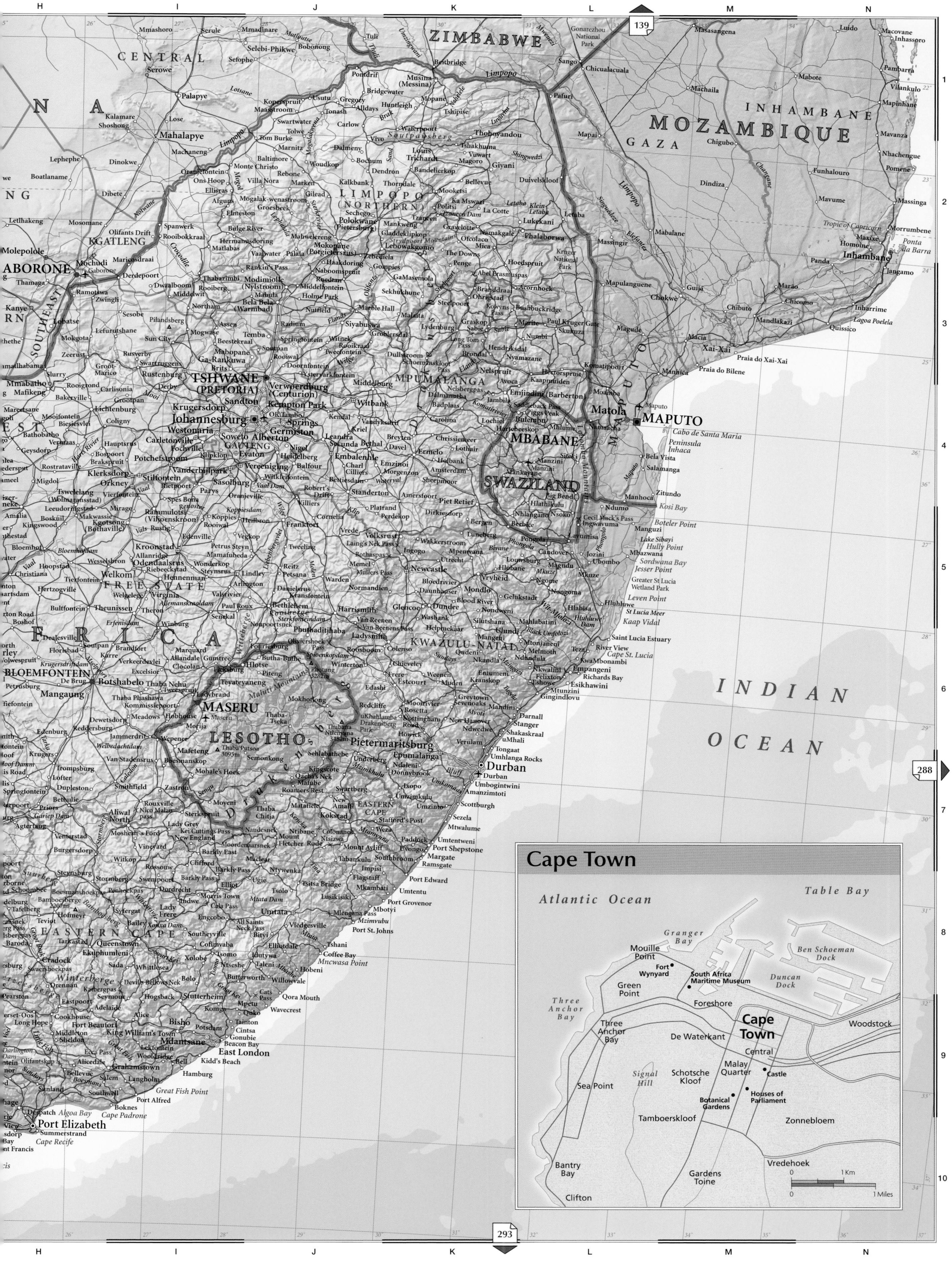

H I J K L M N
1 2 3 4 5 6 7 8 9 10
139
288
293
ZIMBABWE
MOZAMBIQUE
INHAMBANE
GAZA
MAPUTO
Matola
LIMPOPO (NORTHERN)
MPUMALANGA
SWAZILAND
MBABANE
KWAZULU-NATAL
FREE STATE
GAUTENG
LESOTHO
MASERU
EASTERN CAPE
TSHWANE (PRETORIA)
Johannesburg
Soweto
Pietermaritzburg
Durban
BLOEMFONTEIN
Port Elizabeth
East London
ABORONE
Inhambane
Xai-Xai
Polokwane (Pietersburg)
Nelspruit
Ladysmith
Newcastle
Welkom
Kimberley
INDIAN OCEAN
Cape Town
Atlantic Ocean
Table Bay
Granger Bay
Mouille Point
Fort Wynyard
South Africa Maritime Museum
Ben Schoeman Dock
Duncan Dock
Green Point
Three Anchor Bay
Foreshore
Cape Town
Woodstock
De Waterkant
Central
Malay Quarter
Castle
Signal Hill
Schotsche Kloof
Houses of Parliament
Sea Point
Botanical Gardens
Tamboerskloof
Zonnebloem
Vredehoek
Bantry Bay
Gardens Toine
Clifton
0 1 Km
0 1 Miles

AFRICA

19,686ft
13,124ft
9843ft
6562ft
3281ft
1640ft
820ft
328ft
Sea Level
-820ft
-6562ft
-13,124ft

AFRICA – Cities

Algiers

Mediterranean Sea

Cap de Bordj

L'Ermitage

Grande Mosquée

Bab El Oued

Kasbah

Alger (Algiers)

Bordj El Bahri

El Biar

Palais du Gouvernement

Chéraga

Ben Aknoûn

Agha

Bordj El Kiffan

Hussein-Dey

Musée des Beaux Arts

Birmandreïs

Kouba

Cité Olympique

Birkhadem

Draria

El Harrach

Dar El Beïda

Douera

Oued Smar

Algiers Airport

Oued Harrach

Baraki

0   3 Km
0   3 Miles

Cairo

Abu Al Ghayt

Bahtîm

El Matarîya

Shubra Al Amiriya

Cairo International Airport

Nile

El Zeitûn

Masr el Gedida (Heliopolis)

Warrâq el Hadr

Shubra Al Khaymah

Mâdinet Nasr

Warrâq el'Arab

Imbâbah

Bûlâq

El Ezbekiya

Aguza

Egyptian Antiquities Museum

Âbdîn

Cairo

El Dúqqi

Central Government Building

The Citadel

Garden City

Zoological Gardens

El Gîza

Masr el Qadîma

El Basâlîn

Cheops

Sphinx

Nile

El Ma'âdi

Pyramids of Giza

0   3 Km
0   3 Miles

Cape Town

Atlantic Ocean

Table Bay

Granger Bay

Páarden Eiland

Mouille Point

Ben Schoeman Dock

Fort Wynyard

South Africa Maritime Museum

Duncan Dock

Green Point

Foreshore

Salt River

Three Anchor Bay

Woodstock

Cape Town

Three Anchor Bay

De Waterkant

Central

Sea Point

Signal Hill

Schotsche Kloof

Malay Quarter

Castle

Botanical Gardens

Houses of Parliament

Tamboerskloof

Zonnebloem

Bantry Bay

Gardens Toine

Vredehoek

Devils Peak Estate

Clifton

Lions Head

Clifton Bay

0   1 Km
0   1 Miles

Casablanca

Atlantic Ocean

El Hank

Mosquée Hassan II

Aïn Harrounda

Old Médina

Aïn Sebaa

Ain Diab

Marchée Centrale

Essoukour Assáwda

Hay Mohammadi

Casablanca

Anfa

Palais du Roi

Sidi Moumen Ahl Ahl Loughlam

Casablanca Airport

El Maarif

El Fida Drissia

Moulay Rachid

Mohamed V

Notre Dame de Lourdes

Ben Msick

Sidi Othmane

Ain Clock Sidi Maarouf

Sbata-Salmia

L'Oasis

0   3 Km
0   3 Miles

Dakar

Industrial Zone

Grand Dakar

Fass

Colobane

Gouye Salane

Darou Kipp

Point E

Gibraltar

Dakar-Marine

Medina

Claudel

Fann Hok

Abattoirs

Grande Mosquée

Rebeus

Dakar

Pointe de Dakar

Atlantic Ocean

Théâtre Daniel Sorano

Palais Présidentiel

Musée Dakar

Le Plateau

Pointe Bernard

0   1 Km
0   1 Miles

Harare

Belgravia

Kensington

Greenwood Park

Gun Hill

Eastlea North

Milton Park

Avondale

Harare Gardens

Newlands

National Art Gallery

Belvedere North

Cathedral

Parliament

Eastlea

Cecil Square

Harare

Civic Centre

Town House

Eastlea South

National Sports Centre

Mukuvisi

Hillside

Kopje

Braeside

Arcadia

0   0.5 Km
0   0.5 Miles

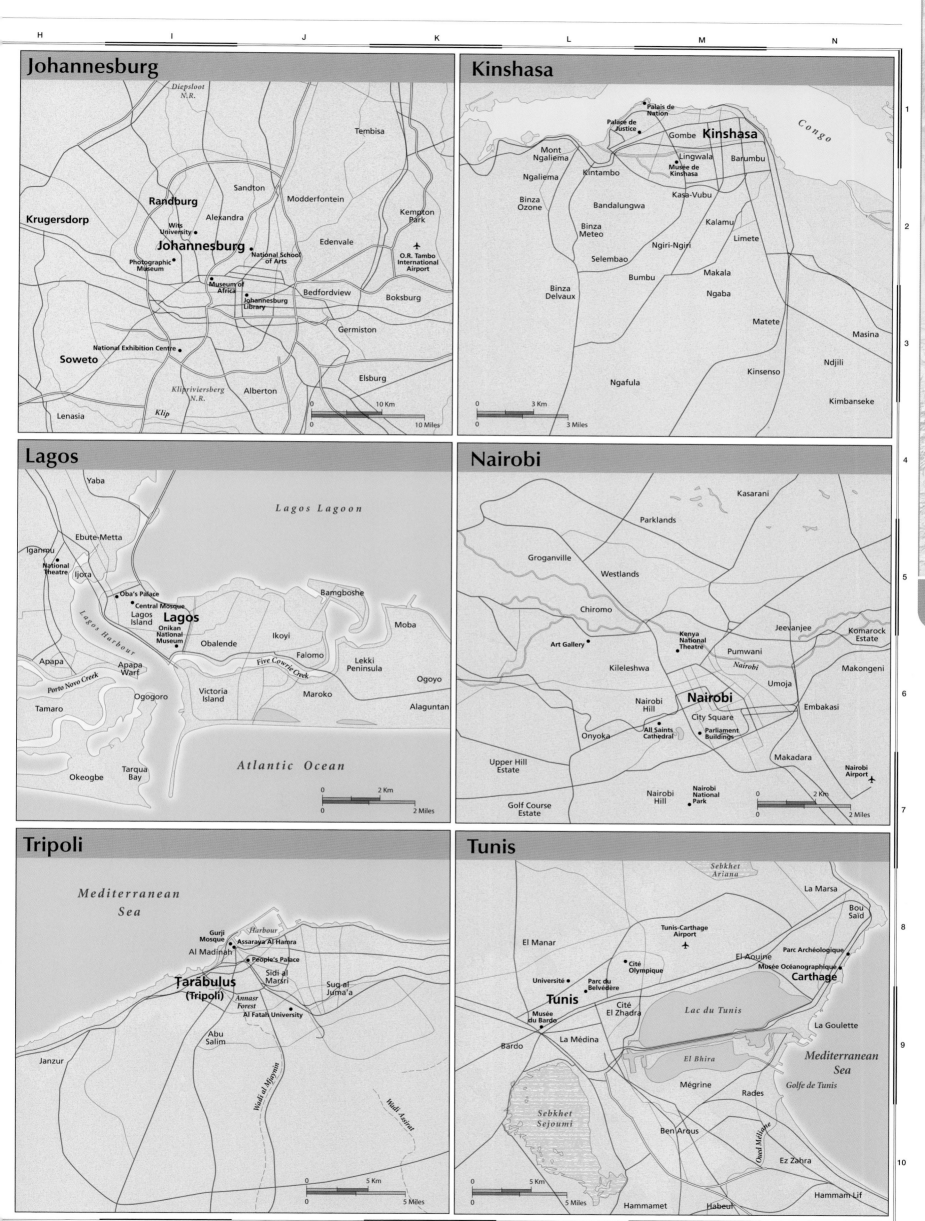

Europe is the world's second smallest continent with a total area of 4,053,309 sq miles (10,498,000 sq km). It comprises 45 separate countries, including Turkey and the Russian Federation, although the greater parts of these nations lie in Asia.

FACTFILE

N **Most Northerly Point:** Ostrov Rudol'fa, Russian Federation 81° 47′ N

S **Most Southerly Point:** Gávdos, Greece 34° 51′ N

E **Most Easterly Point:** Mys Flissingskiy, Novaya Zemlya, Russian Federation 69° 03′ E

W **Most Westerly Point:** Bjargtangar, Iceland 24° 33′ W

Largest Lakes:
1. Lake Ladoga, Russian Federation 7100 sq miles (18,390 sq km)
2. Lake Onega, Russian Federation 3819 sq miles (9891 sq km)
3. Vänern, Sweden 2141 sq miles (5545 sq km)
4. Lake Peipus, Estonia/Russian Federation 1372 sq miles (3555 sq km)
5. Vättern, Sweden 737 sq miles (1910 sq km)

Longest Rivers:
1. Volga, Russian Federation 2265 miles (3645 km)
2. Danube, C Europe 1771 miles (2850 km)
3. Dnieper, Belarus/Russian Federation/Ukraine 1421 miles (2287 km)
4. Don, Russian Federation 1162 miles (1870 km)
5. Pechora, Russian Federation 1124 miles (1809 km)

Largest Islands:
1. Britain, 88,700 sq miles (229,800 sq km)
2. Iceland, 39,315 sq miles (101,826 sq km)
3. Ireland, 31,521 sq miles (81,638 sq km)
4. Ostrov Severny, Novaya Zemlya, Russian Federation 18,177 sq miles (47,079 sq km)
5. Spitsbergen, Svalbard 15,051 sq miles (38,981 sq km)

Highest Points:
1. El'brus, Russian Federation 18,510 ft (5642 m)
2. Dykhtau, Russian Federation 17,077 ft (5205 m)
3. Koshtantau, Russian Federation 16,903 ft (5152 m)
4. Jangitau, Georgia/Russian Federation 16,598 ft (5059 m)
5. Pushkin Peak, Georgia/Russian Federation 16,512 ft (5033 m)

Lowest Point:
▼ Caspian Depression, Russian Federation -92 ft (-28 m) below sea level

Highest recorded temperature:
⊕ Seville, Spain 122°F (50°C)

Lowest recorded temperature:
⊖ Ust' Shchugor, Russian Federation -67°F (-55°C)

Wettest Place:
≋ Crkvice, Bosnia and Herzegovina 183 in (4648 mm)

Driest Place:
⊖ Astrakhan', Russian Federation 6.4 in (162.5 mm)

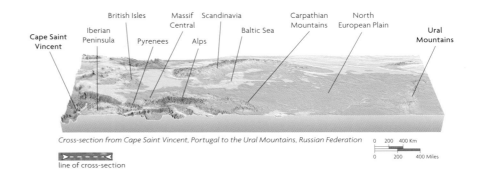

Cross-section from Cape Saint Vincent, Portugal to the Ural Mountains, Russian Federation

0   200   400 Km

0   200   400 Miles

▷— — — — —◁
line of cross-section

Political

The political boundaries of Europe have changed many times, especially during the 20th century in the aftermath of two world wars, the break-up of the empires of Austria-Hungary, Nazi Germany and, towards the end of the century, the collapse of communism in eastern Europe. The fragmentation of Yugoslavia has again altered the political map of Europe, highlighting a trend towards nationalism and devolution. In contrast, economic federalism is growing. In 1958, the formation of the European Economic Community (now the European Union or EU) started a move towards economic and political union and increasing internal migration. This process is still ongoing and the accession of Bulgaria and Romania in January 2007 brought the number of EU member states to twenty seven. Of these, thirteen have joined the Eurozone by adopting the Euro as their official currency.

Population
- above 5 million
- 1 million to 5 million
- 500,000 to 1 million
- 100,000 to 500,000
- 50,000 to 100,000
- 10,000 to 50,000
- Country capital

Borders
- full international border

SCALE 1:17,250,000
(projection: Lambert Azimuthal Equal Area)

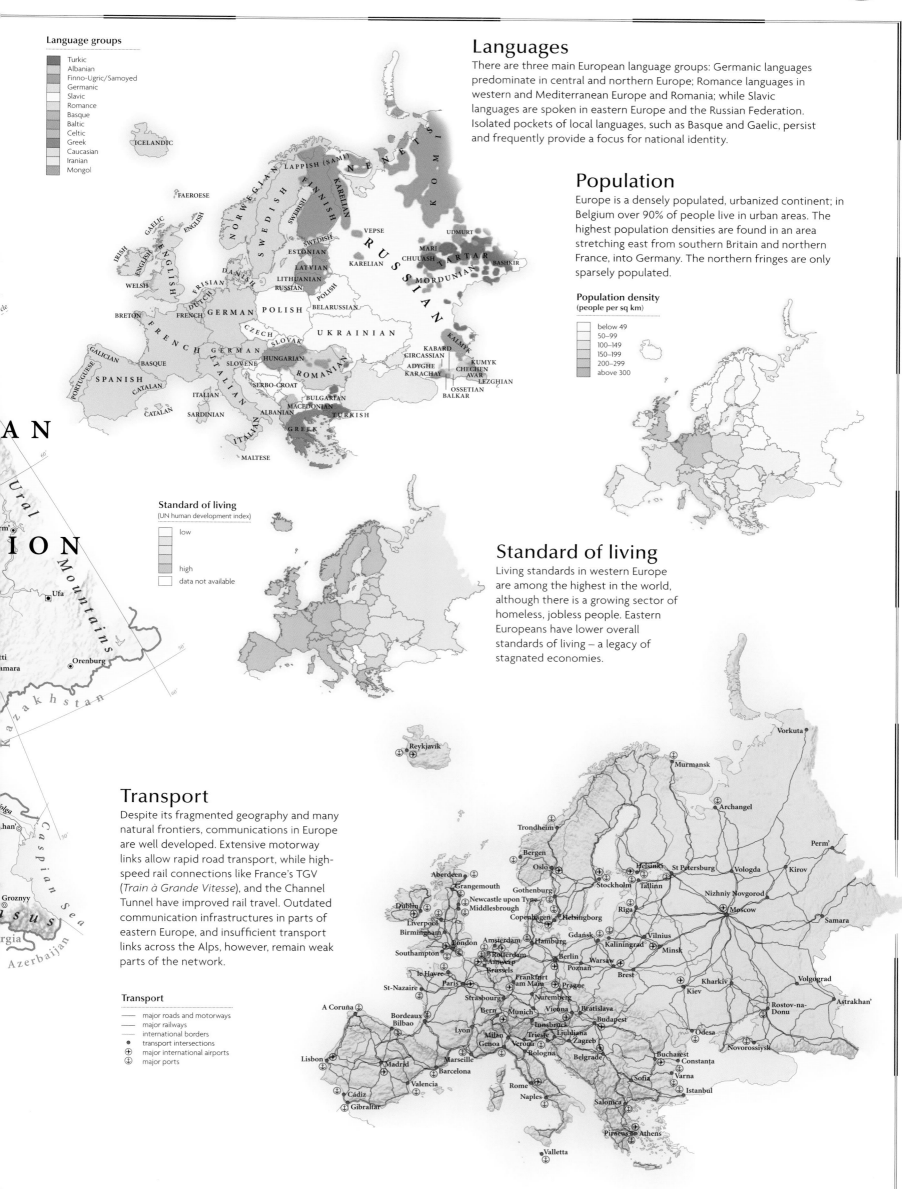

Language groups

- Turkic
- Albanian
- Finno-Ugric/Samoyed
- Germanic
- Slavic
- Romance
- Basque
- Baltic
- Celtic
- Greek
- Caucasian
- Iranian
- Mongol

Languages

There are three main European language groups: Germanic languages predominate in central and northern Europe; Romance languages in western and Mediterranean Europe and Romania; while Slavic languages are spoken in eastern Europe and the Russian Federation. Isolated pockets of local languages, such as Basque and Gaelic, persist and frequently provide a focus for national identity.

Population

Europe is a densely populated, urbanized continent; in Belgium over 90% of people live in urban areas. The highest population densities are found in an area stretching east from southern Britain and northern France, into Germany. The northern fringes are only sparsely populated.

Population density
(people per sq km)

- below 49
- 50–99
- 100–149
- 150–199
- 200–299
- above 300

Standard of living
(UN human development index)

- low
- high
- data not available

Standard of living

Living standards in western Europe are among the highest in the world, although there is a growing sector of homeless, jobless people. Eastern Europeans have lower overall standards of living – a legacy of stagnated economies.

Transport

Despite its fragmented geography and many natural frontiers, communications in Europe are well developed. Extensive motorway links allow rapid road transport, while high-speed rail connections like France's TGV (*Train à Grande Vitesse*), and the Channel Tunnel have improved rail travel. Outdated communication infrastructures in parts of eastern Europe, and insufficient transport links across the Alps, however, remain weak parts of the network.

Transport

- —— major roads and motorways
- —— major railways
- —— international borders
- • transport intersections
- ⊕ major international airports
- ⊕ major ports

SCALE 1:22,500,000
(projection: Lambert Conformal Conic)

| 0 | 200 | 400 | 600 | 800 | 1000 Km |
| 0 | 200 | | 400 | 600 | 800 | 1000 Miles |

Climate

Europe experiences few extremes in either rainfall or temperature, with the exception of the far north and south. Along the west coast, the warm currents of the North Atlantic Drift moderate temperatures. Although east–west air movement is relatively unimpeded by relief, the Alpine Uplands halt the progress of north–south air masses, protecting most of the Mediterranean from cold, north winds.

Climate

tundra	daily hours of sunshine, January
subarctic	
cool continental	daily hours of sunshine, July
warm humid	
mediterranean	→ cold wind
semi-arid	→ hot wind

Average Rainfall

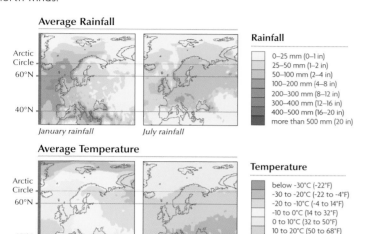

January rainfall   July rainfall

Rainfall

	0–25 mm (0–1 in)
	25–50 mm (1–2 in)
	50–100 mm (2–4 in)
	100–200 mm (4–8 in)
	200–300 mm (8–12 in)
	300–400 mm (12–16 in)
	400–500 mm (16–20 in)
	more than 500 mm (20 in)

Average Temperature

January temperature   July temperature

Temperature

	below -30°C (-22°F)
	-30 to -20°C (-22 to -4°F)
	-20 to -10°C (-4 to 14°F)
	-10 to 0°C (14 to 32°F)
	0 to 10°C (32 to 50°F)
	10 to 20°C (50 to 68°F)
	20 to 30°C (68 to 86°F)
	above 30°C (86°F)

Environmental issues

The partially enclosed waters of the Baltic and Mediterranean seas have become heavily polluted, while the Barents Sea is contaminated with spent nuclear fuel from Russia's navy. Acid rain, caused by emissions from factories and power stations, is actively destroying northern forests. As a result, pressure is growing to safeguard Europe's natural environment and prevent further deterioration.

Environmental issues

national parks	marine pollution
acid rain	heavy marine pollution
polluted rivers	poor urban air quality
radioactive contamination	

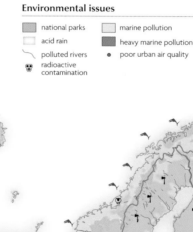

Landuse

Europe's swelling urban population and the outward expansion of many cities has created acute competition for land. Despite this, European resourcefulness has maximized land potential, and over half of Europe's land is still used for a wide variety of agricultural purposes. Land in northern Europe is used for cattle-rearing, pasture, and arable crops. Towards the Mediterranean, the mild climate allows the growing of grapes for wine; olives, sunflowers, tobacco and citrus fruits. EU subsidies, however, have resulted in massive overproduction and a land 'set-aside' policy has been introduced.

Using the land and sea

	cropland		citrus fruits
	forest		cotton
	ice cap		fishing
	mountain region		fodder
	pasture		fruit
	tundra		olive oil
	wetland		potatoes
•	major conurbations		rice
	cattle		root crops
	goats		roses
	pigs		shellfish
	poultry		sunflowers
	reindeer		timber
	sheep		tobacco
	cereals		vineyards

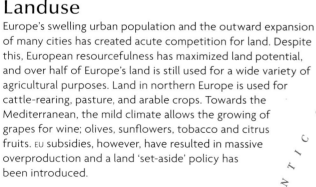

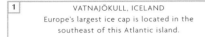

1 VATNAJÖKULL, ICELAND
Europe's largest ice cap is located in the southeast of this Atlantic island.

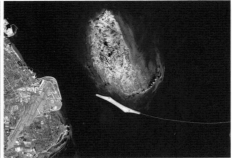

2 ORESUND LINK, DENMARK/SWEDEN
This link was opened to traffic in 2000, joining the Danish capital, Copenhagen, with the Swedish town of Malmo across the waters of the Oresund Strait.

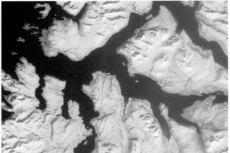

3 BALSFJORD, NORWAY
Fjords were cut into Norway's west coast by glaciers during the last ice age but as the ice retreated rising sea-levels flooded the valleys left behind.

4 PRAGUE, CZECH REPUBLIC
In August 2002 some parts of the capital were still under water after the worst floods in living memory.

9 GIBRALTAR
A British colony since 1713, this rocky promontory commands a strategic position at the southern end of the Iberian Peninsula.

10 BORDEAUX, FRANCE
Famous for its wines, this city sits on the west bank of the Garonne river, which is joined from the east by the Dordogne river.

11 SOUTH FLEVOLAND, NETHERLANDS
This polder was reclaimed from the sea in the early 1970s and is now home to extensive farmland and small towns.

12 RHINE, GERMANY
The Rhine has been straightened in places, such as here, just south of Mannheim, to ease navigation.

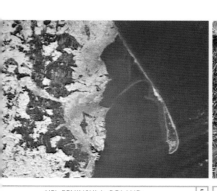

HEL PENINSULA, POLAND 5
The long spit of this peninsula encloses Puck
Bay and shelters the important port of Gdynia.

TALLINN, ESTONIA 6
The capital and main port of Estonia has
become a popular tourist destination in
recent years.

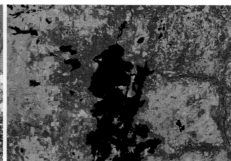

LAKE VODLOZERO, RUSSIAN FEDERATION 7
The lake lies within a national park, which protects one
of the most untouched wilderness areas in Europe and
encompasses plains, taiga forests and wetlands.

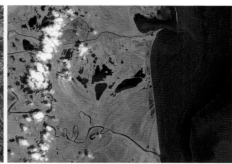

DANUBE DELTA, ROMANIA 8
The Danube river splits into several channels
as it flows into the Black Sea, forming one of
Europe's most important wetland ecosystems.

VENICE, ITALY 13
upying the largest island in a sheltered lagoon at the
orth end of the Adriatic, this city was founded in
2 CE and grew rich on an extensive trading network.

ISTRA PENINSULA, CROATIA 14
This triangular peninsula marks the northern
extent of Croatia's Dalmatian coastline.

MOUNT ETNA, SICILY, ITALY 15
This combination of visible and thermal images
shows the volcano erupting in July 2001 and
clearly indicates the major lava flows.

KEFALLONIÁ, GREECE 16
The largest of the Ionian Islands off Greece's
west coast, Kefalloniá is mountainous with
relatively high rainfall.

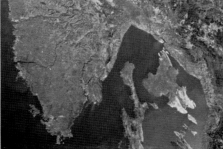

Elevation scale

6000m
4000m
3000m
2000m
1000m
500m
250m
100m
Sea Level
-250m
-500m
-1000m

FAEROE ISLANDS (to Denmark)

Streymoy
Kunoy Bordhoy Fugloy
Kalsoy
Vestmanna Svinoy
Eysturoy
Mykines
Vágar TÓRSHAVN Nólsoy
Sandoy
Skúvoy Husavik
Suduroy

ATLANTIC OCEAN

Scale 1:2,500,000
0 5 10 20 km
0 5 10 20 Miles

ATLANTIC OCEAN

Norwegian Sea

NORDLAND

NORD-TRØNDELAG

SØR-TRØNDELAG

Trondheim

NORWAY

MØRE OG ROMSDAL

SOGN OG FJORDANE

OPPLAND

HEDMARK

BUSKERUD

HORDALAND

AKERSHUS

Bergen

Dovrefjell

Jotunheimen

Hardangervidda

Trollheimen

SWEDEN

VÄSTERBOTTEN

VÄSTERNORRLAND

JÄMTLAND

GÄVLEBORG

DALARNA

Östersund

Umeå

Sundsvall

Härnösand

Storsjön

Siljan

UPPSALA

Gävle

ÅLAND

Gulf of Bothnia

Ålands Hav

Indalsälven

Österdalälven

Västerdalälven

United Kingdom & Ireland

ATLANTIC OCEAN

North Sea

UNITED KINGDOM

SCOTLAND

Shetland Islands

Herma Ness
Unst
Fetlar
Yell
Hillswick
St Magnus Bay
Sullom Voe
Whalsay
Bressay
Out Skerries
Mainland
Lerwick
Papa Stour
Scalloway
West Burra
Foula
Fitful Head
Sumburgh Head
Yell Sound

Fair Isle

Orkney Islands

Papa Westray
The North
Westray
Rousay
Eday
Sanday
Stronsay
Sound
Snapshay
Kirkwall
North Ronaldsay
Burray
Scapa Flow
South Ronaldsay
St Margaret's Hope
Hoy
Duncansby Head
Stromness
Pentland Firth
John o'Groats
Dunnet Head
Noss Head
Wick

Cape Wrath
Strathy Point
Thurso
Halkirk
Helmsdale
Halladale
Kinbrace
Brora
Golspie
Dornoch Firth
Tongue
Loch Naver
Durness
Altnaharra
Bonar
Dornoch
Lairg
Tain
Cromarty
Loch Eriboll
Ben Hope
927m
Loch Shin
Tarbat Ness
Invergordon
Ben Klibreck
721m
Lochinver
Moray Firth
Edrachillis Bay
Ben More Assynt
998m
Carn Eige
1183m
Beauly
Dingwall
Elgin
Lossiemouth
Forres
Buckie
Macduff
Banff
Fraserhead

Enard Bay
Ullapool
Loch Maree
Loch Broom
Inverness
Nairn
Grantown-on-Spey
Keith
Huntly
Turriff
Ellon
Kinnaird Head
Peterhead
Buchan Ness

North West Highlands
Loch Torridon
Aviemore
Cairn Gorm
1309m
Ben Macdui
1309m
Elton
Inverurie
Aberdeen
Girdle Ness
Stonehaven

The Minch
Inner Sound
Stromeferry
Kyle of Lochalsh
Broadford
Isle of Skye
Mallaig
Loch Morar
Fort William
Ben Nevis
1344m
Cairngorm Mountains
Braemar
Ballater
Loch
Ericht
Pitlochry
Kirriemuir
Brechin
Bancory
Dee
Montrose
Arbroath
Carnoustie

Portree
Raasay
Rhum
Eigg
Muck
Ardnamurchan
Point of Ardnamurchan
Coll
Tiree
Loch
Linnhe
Oban
Loch Awe
Loch Lomond
Loch Tay
Loch Rannoch
Crieff
Callander
Dunkeld
Perth
Cupar
St Andrews
Fife Ness
Firth of Tay
Dundee
Blairgowrie

Inner Hebrides
Mull
Iona
Colonsay
Jura
Islay
Port Askaig
Port Ellen
Mull of Oa

Sound of Jura
Firth of Lorn
Inveraray
Loch Fyne
Loch Katrine
Stirling
Alloa
Dunfermline
Kirkcaldy
North Berwick
Haddington
Edinburgh

St Kilda

Outer Hebrides

Butt of Lewis
Port of Ness
Stornoway
Carloway
Isle of Lewis
Loch Roag
Tarbert
Scarp
Taransay
Pabbay
Sound of Harris
Lochmaddy
North Uist
Monach Islands
Benbecula
South Uist
Lochboisdale
Eriskay
Barra
Barra Head
Flannan Isles
Shiant Islands
Eye Peninsula
Sula Sgeir
North Rona
Sule Skerry
Stack Skerry
The Little Minch
Sea of the Hebrides

Campbeltown
Mull of Kintyre
Tarbert
Gigha Island
Rothesay
Isle of Bute
Arran
Brodick
Ailsa Craig
Girvan
Ballantrae
Maybole
Ayr
Troon
Prestwick
Irvine
East Kilbride
Hamilton
Wishaw
Lanark
Cumnock
Glasgow
Greenock
Largs
Paisley
Dumbarton
Helensburgh
Firth of Clyde
Kintyre

Berwick-upon-Tweed
St Abb's Head
Duns
Coldstream
Kelso
Jedburgh
Galashiels
Selkirk
Hawick
Moffat
Langholm
Holy Island
Alnwick
Amble
Morpeth
Blyth

North
Sea

Sea Level

6000m
4000m
3000m
2000m
1000m
500m
250m
100m
Sea Level
-250m
-500m
-1000m

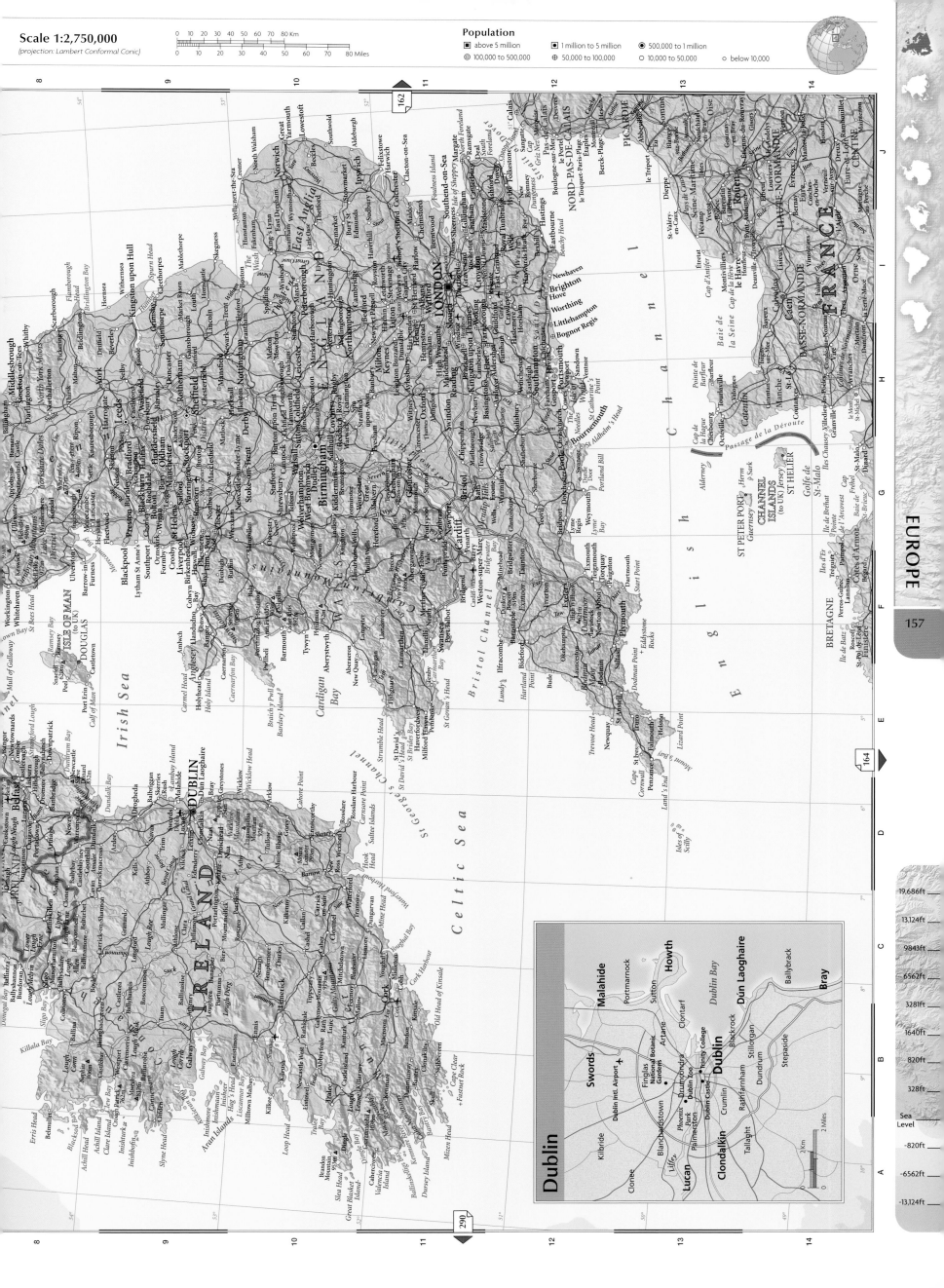

ATLANTIC

OCEAN

Sea of the
Hebrides

Inner Hebrides

Highland

North Channel

NORTHERN IRELAND

IRELAND

UNITED

DONEGAL

SLIGO

MAYO

ROSCOMMON

LEITRIM

CAVAN

MONAGHAN

LONGFORD

WEST MEATH

MEATH

OFFALY

KILDARE

GALWAY

Connaught

LOUTH

Irish

Sea

Isle of
Mull

Jura

Islay

Isle of
Arran

ISLE OF MAN
(to UK)

Anglesey

Loch Neagh

Belfast

DUBLIN

Lough
Derg

156

157

157

6000m
4000m
3000m
2000m
1000m
500m
250m
100m
Sea
Level
-250m
-500m
-1000m

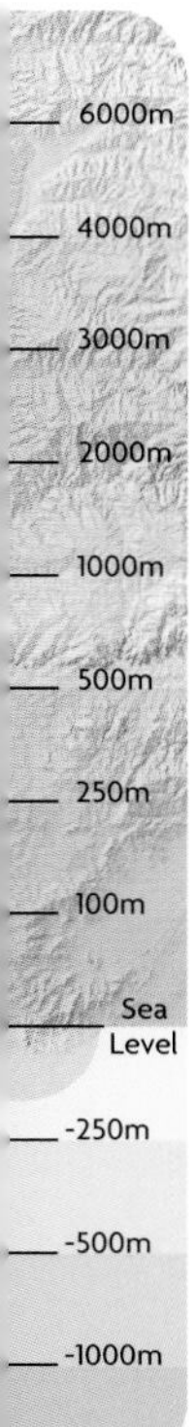

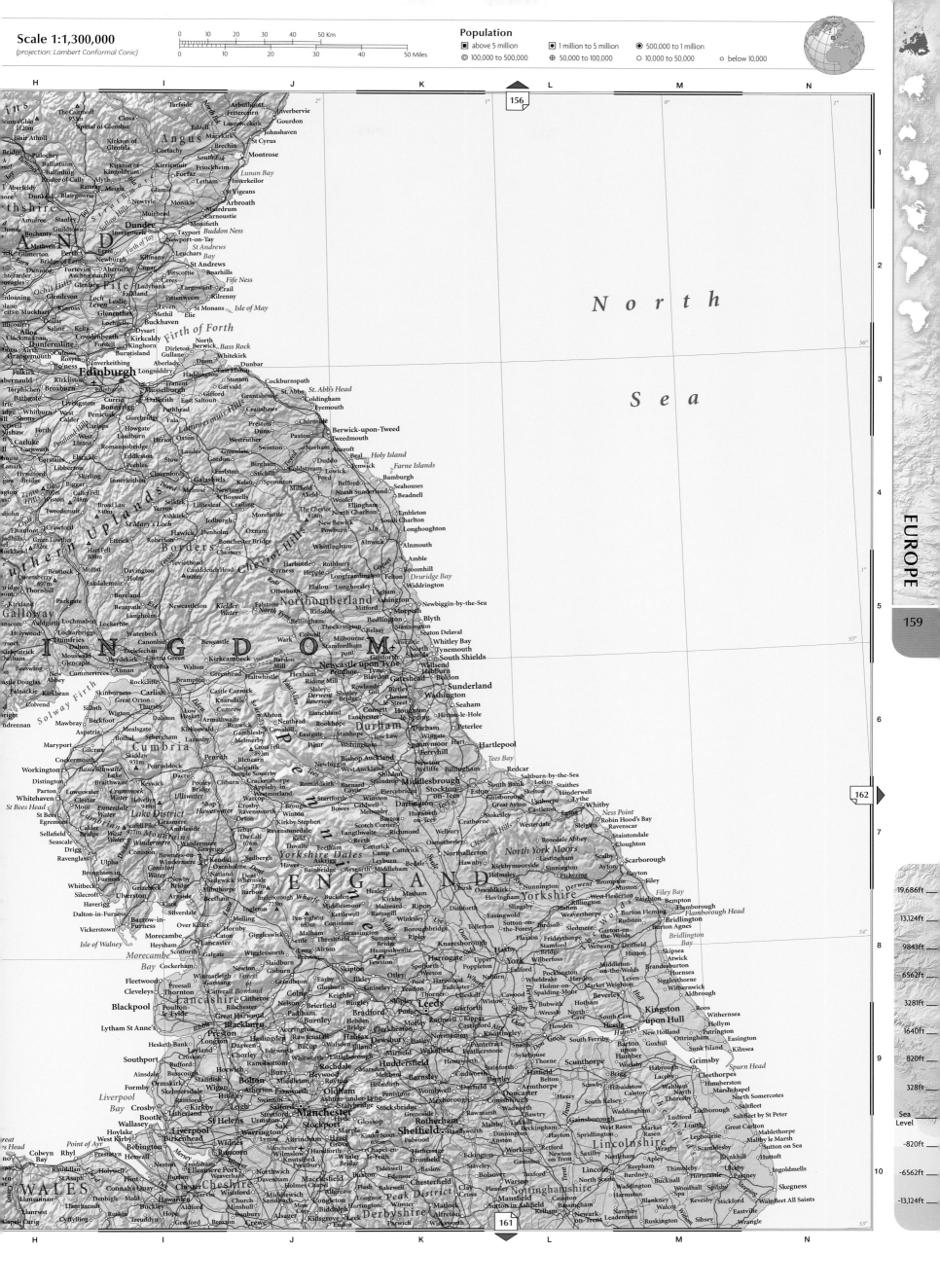

Southern Britain

Irish Sea

Celtic Sea

St George's Channel

Bristol Channel

Cardigan Bay

Caernarfon Bay

IRELAND

DUBLIN

WALES

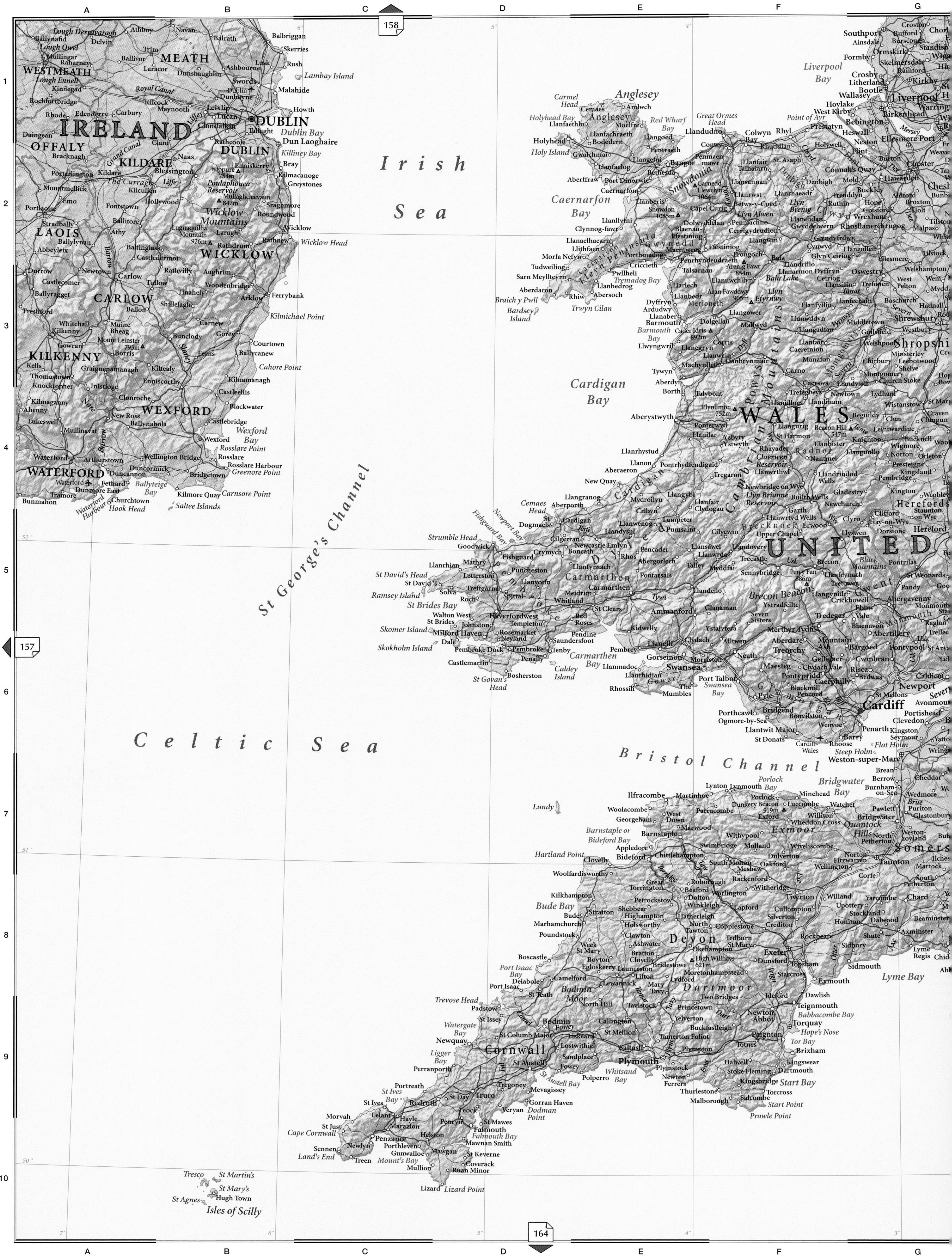

UNITED

CARDIFF

WESTMEATH · MEATH · OFFALY · KILDARE · LAOIS · CARLOW · WICKLOW · KILKENNY · WEXFORD · WATERFORD

Cornwall · **Devon** · Dartmoor · Bodmin Moor · Exmoor

Plymouth · Swansea · Newport · Land's End · Lizard · Isles of Scilly

Liverpool Bay · Anglesey · Snowdonia · Shropshire

Waterford Harbour · Bristol Channel · Bridgwater Bay · Lyme Bay

6000m / 4000m / 3000m / 2000m / 1000m / 500m / 250m / 100m / Sea Level / −250m / −500m / −1000m

158 · 157 · 164

The Low Countries

EUROPE

162

NETHERLANDS: CAPITAL CITIES
AMSTERDAM – capital
THE HAGUE – seat of government

Amsterdam

Monnickendam
Waterland
IJ-meer
Diemen
Amsterdam Zuidoost
Abcoude
Ouderkerk a/d Amstel
Amstel
Amstelveen
Buitenveldert
Oud Zuid
Het Nieuwe Meer
Amsterdamse Bos
Badhoevedorp
Amsterdam Schiphol Airport
Sloterplas
Ostdorp
Slotervaart
Hillegom
Westzaan
Zaanstad
Zaandijk
Kood a/d Zaan
Zaandam
Zaan
Noordzeekanaal
Oostzaan
Ilpendam
Landsmeer
Tuindorp Buiksloot
Nieuwendam
Het IJ
En Lommer
Amsterdam
Anne Frankhuis
Koninklijk Paleis
Historisch Museum
Havensoost
Oud West
Rijksmuseum
Van Goghmuseum

Sea Level
6000m
4000m
3000m
2000m
1000m
500m
250m
100m
Sea Level
-250m
-500m
-1000m

NETHERLANDS
NOORD-HOLLAND
ZUID-HOLLAND
FRIESLAND
GRONINGEN
DRENTHE
OVERIJSSEL
FLEVOLAND
GELDERLAND
UTRECHT
NIEDERSACHSEN
Ostfriesland
Ostfriesische Inseln
Friesian Islands
Frisian Islands

AMSTERDAM
'S-GRAVENHAGE (THE HAGUE)
Rotterdam
Utrecht
Groningen
Leeuwarden
Assen
Zwolle
Lelystad
Haarlem

North Sea
IJsselmeer
Waddenzee

Norderney
Langeoog
Juist
Borkum
Texel
Vlieland
Terschelling
Ameland
Schiermonnikoog

Emden
Aurich
Norden

Scale 1:1,125,000
(projection: Lambert Conformal Conic)

0 10 20 30 40 Km
0 10 20 30 40 Miles

Population

- ■ above 5 million
- ◉ 100,000 to 500,000
- ▣ 1 million to 5 million
- ⊕ 50,000 to 100,000
- ● 500,000 to 1 million
- ○ 10,000 to 50,000
- ○ below 10,000

EUROPE

163

19,686ft
13,124ft
9843ft
6562ft
3281ft
1640ft
820ft
328ft
Sea
Level
-820ft
-6562ft
-13,124ft

France

160
290
170

EUROPE

UNITED KINGDOM

ATLANTIC OCEAN

English Channel

CHANNEL ISLANDS (to UK)
ST PETER PORT
Guernsey
Herm
Sark
Jersey
ST HELIER
Alderney

Cap de la Hague
Cherbourg
Octeville
Tourlaville
Barfleur
Valognes
Pointe de Barfleur
Cap d'Antifer
Fécamp
Montivilliers
Bolbec
le Havre
Honfleur
Pont-Audemer
Baie de la Seine
Cap de la Hève
Trouville
Deauville
Bernay
Conches-en-
Lisieux
Caen
Calvados
Isigny-sur-Mer
Bayeux
St-Lô
Coutances
Villedieu-les-Poêles
Granville
Avranches
BASSE-NORMANDIE
Vire
Falaise
Argentan
Alençon
Domfront
Mortain
le Mont-St-Michel
Dinard
St-Malo
Dinan
Combourg
Fougères
Mayenne
Laval
le Mans

Bideford
Bridgwater
Taunton
Barnstaple
Hartland Point
Bude
Okehampton
Tiverton
Yeovil
Sherborne
Shaftesbury
Salisbury
Winchester
Andover
Guildford
Reigate
Crawley
Royal Tun
High Willhays
Dartmoor
Exeter
Lyme Regis
Bridport
Dorchester
Poole
Bournemouth
Southampton
Eastleigh
Portsmouth
Gosport
Havant
Chichester
Bognor Regis
Worthing
Brighton
Eastbo
Beachy Head
Teignmouth
Torquay
Paignton
Dartmouth
Weymouth
Portland Bill
Swanage
Isle of Wight
Sandown
Ventnor
St Catherine's Point
South Downs
Haywards Heath

St Ives
Penzance
Cape Cornwall
Land's End
Newquay
Truro
St Austell
Plymouth
Saltash
Bodmin
Bodmin Moor
Falmouth
Helston
Lizard Point
Isles of Scilly
Mount's Bay
Trevose Head

Paris

Seine
Montmorency
Forêt de St-Germain
Enghien
Argenteuil
Asnières
St-Denis
Drancy
Aulnay-sous-Bois
Tremblay-en-France
Aéroport Charles de Gaulle
Poissy
St-Germain-en-Laye
Nanterre
Montmartre
Sacré-Cœur
Arc de Triomphe
Paris
Le Raincy
Lagny
Marly-le-Roi
Rueil-Malmaison
Boulogne-Billancourt
Tour Eiffel
Musée du Louvre
Bastille
Notre Dame
Montreuil
Vincennes
Marne
Marne-la-Vallée
Château de Versailles
Meudon
Versailles
Sceaux
Vitry-sur-Seine
Seine
Créteil
Champigny-sur-Marne
Trappes
Antony
Orly
Chevreuse
Palaiseau
Aéroport d'Orly
Mortgeron
Brie-Comte-Robert
Orsay

0   5 Km
0   5 Miles

BRETAGNE
Brest
Quimper
Lorient
Vannes
Rennes
Nantes
Angers
PAYS DE LA LOIRE
Cholet
la Roche-sur-Yon
les Sables-d'Olonne
la Rochelle
Niort
POITOU-CHARENTES
Poitiers
Châtellerault
Rochefort
Saintes
Cognac
Angoulême
Périgueux
Bordeaux
AQUITAINE

Bay of Biscay

SPAIN
PORTUGAL
Porto (Oporto)
A Coruña (La Coruña)
Santiago
GALICIA
Lugo
Ourense (Orense)
Pontevedra
Vigo
ASTURIAS
Oviedo
Gijón (Xixón)
Santander
CANTABRIA
Costa Verde
Cordillera Cantábrica
León
CASTILLA-LEÓN
Palencia
Burgos
Valladolid
Zamora
PAÍS VASCO
Bilbao
Donostia-San Sebastián
Vitoria-Gasteiz
NAVARRA
Pamplona (Iruña)
LA RIOJA
Logroño
ARAGÓN
Zaragoza
Soria
Pyrénées
Bayonne
Biarritz
Pau
Tarbes
Mont-de-Marsan
Dax

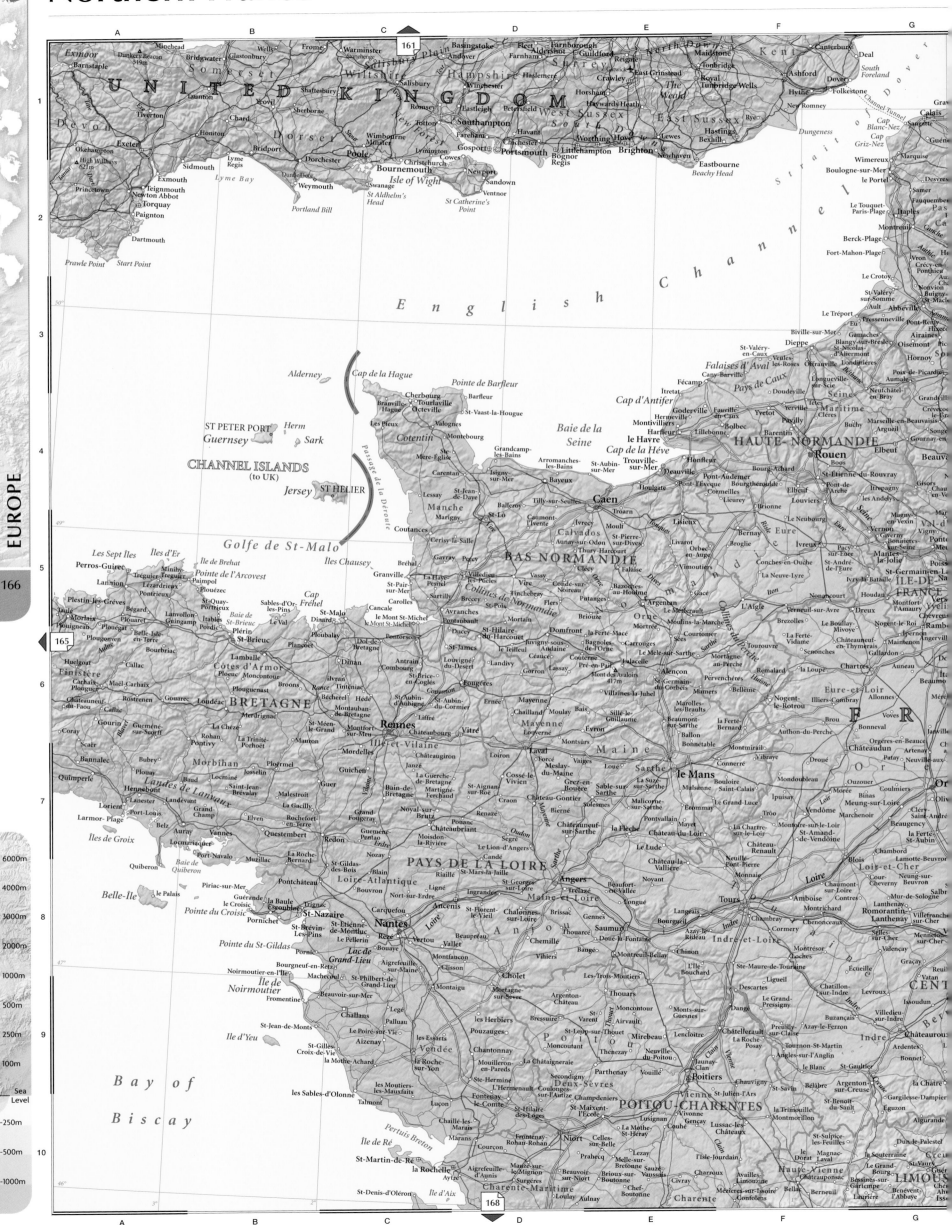

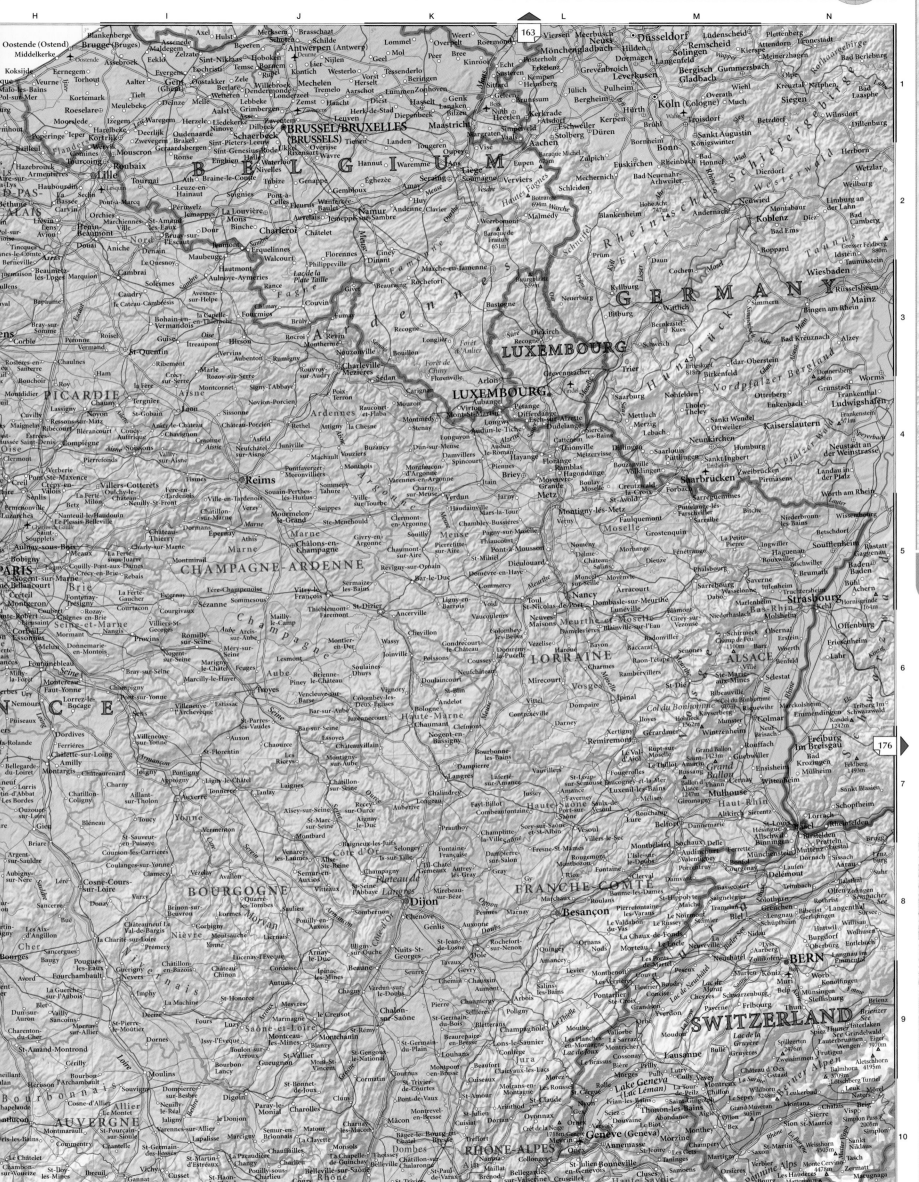

Southern France & the Pyrenees

ATLANTIC OCEAN

Bay of Biscay

EUROPE

Population

■ above 5 million   ◪ 1 million to 5 million   ◉ 500,000 to 1 million
◉ 100,000 to 500,000   ◉ 50,000 to 100,000   ○ 10,000 to 50,000   ○ below 10,000

H | I | J | K | L | M | N

167

198

174

EUROPE

169

Elevation scale

19,686ft
13,124ft
9843ft
6562ft
3281ft
1640ft
820ft
328ft
Sea Level
-820ft
-6562ft
-13,124ft

Clermont-Ferrand
Lyon
Villeurbanne
St-Étienne
Grenoble
Valence
Torino (Turin)
Montpellier
Nîmes
Arles
Marseille
Toulon
Hyères
Aix-en-Provence
Cannes
Nice
MONACO
Perpignan
Girona (Gerona)
Figueres
Béziers
Narbonne
Vichy
Roanne
Chambéry
Annecy
Cuneo
Imperia
San Remo
Ventimiglia

AUVERGNE
RHÔNE-ALPES
Haute-Savoie
PROVENCE-ALPES-CÔTE D'AZUR
Alpes-Maritimes
LANGUEDOC-ROUSSILLON
Hautes-Alpes
Maritime Alps
Ligurian Alps
ITALY
Haute-Loire
Ardèche
Drôme
Isère
Gard
Hérault
Vaucluse
Var
Bouches-du-Rhône

Mont Blanc 4807m
Matterhorn 4634m
Monte Viso 3841m
Gran Paradiso 4061m

Golfe du Lion
Golfe de Genova
Ligurian Sea
Mediterranean Sea
Côte d'Azur
Costa Brava
Golfe de Roses
Camargue
Rhône

The Iberian Peninsula

MADEIRA
(to Portugal)

Scale 1:2,500,000

ISLAS CANARIAS
(CANARY ISLANDS)
(to Spain)

Scale 1:6,500,000

0 10 20 30 40 50 Km
0 10 20 30 40 50 Miles

Population

- ▪ above 5 million
- ▫ 1 million to 5 million
- ◉ 500,000 to 1 million
- ◎ 100,000 to 500,000
- ⊕ 50,000 to 100,000
- ○ 10,000 to 50,000
- ○ below 10,000

171

198

131

H I J K L M N

Map labels

ARAGON
CATALUNA
CASTILLA-LA MANCHA
CASTILLA NUEVA
PAÍS VALENCIANO
MURCIA
ALGERIA

Madrid · Guadalajara · Alcalá de Henares · Torrejón de Ardoz · Getafe · Aranjuez
Zaragoza · Calatayud · Teruel · Cuenca · Albacete · Valencia · Castellón
Tarragona · Reus · Benicàssim · Sagunto (Sagunt) · Burriana · Nules
Alicante (Alacant) · Elche (Elx) · Murcia · Cartagena · Lorca · Torrevieja
Orihuela · Benidorm · Dénia · Gandía · Xàtiva · Alcoy (Alcoi)
Granada · Almería · Baza · Guadix · Motril · Jaén · Úbeda · Baeza

Golfo de Valencia
Golfo de Mazarrón
Golfo de Almería
Costa del Azahar
Costa Blanca
Mediterranean Sea
Alboran Sea
Isla de Alborán

Islas Baleares (Balearic Islands)
Ibiza · Eivissa (Ibiza) · Formentera · ILLES BALEARS
Sant Antoni de Portmany · Sant Josep · Sa Talaiassa 475m · San Francisco Javier

Cabo de San Antonio · Cabo de La Nao · Cabo de Palos · Cabo de Gata · Cabo Tiñoso
Mar Menor

Sierra Nevada · Mulhacén 3478m · Sierra de Gádor · Las Alpujarras
Sierra de los Filabres · Sierra de Baza · Sierra Morena
Sistema Ibérico · Serranía de Cuenca · Montes Universales

Oran · Mostaganem · Relizane · Ténès · Ténès

19,686ft
13,124ft
9843ft
6562ft
3281ft
1640ft
820ft
328ft
Sea Level
-820ft
-6562ft
-13,124ft

The Italian Peninsula

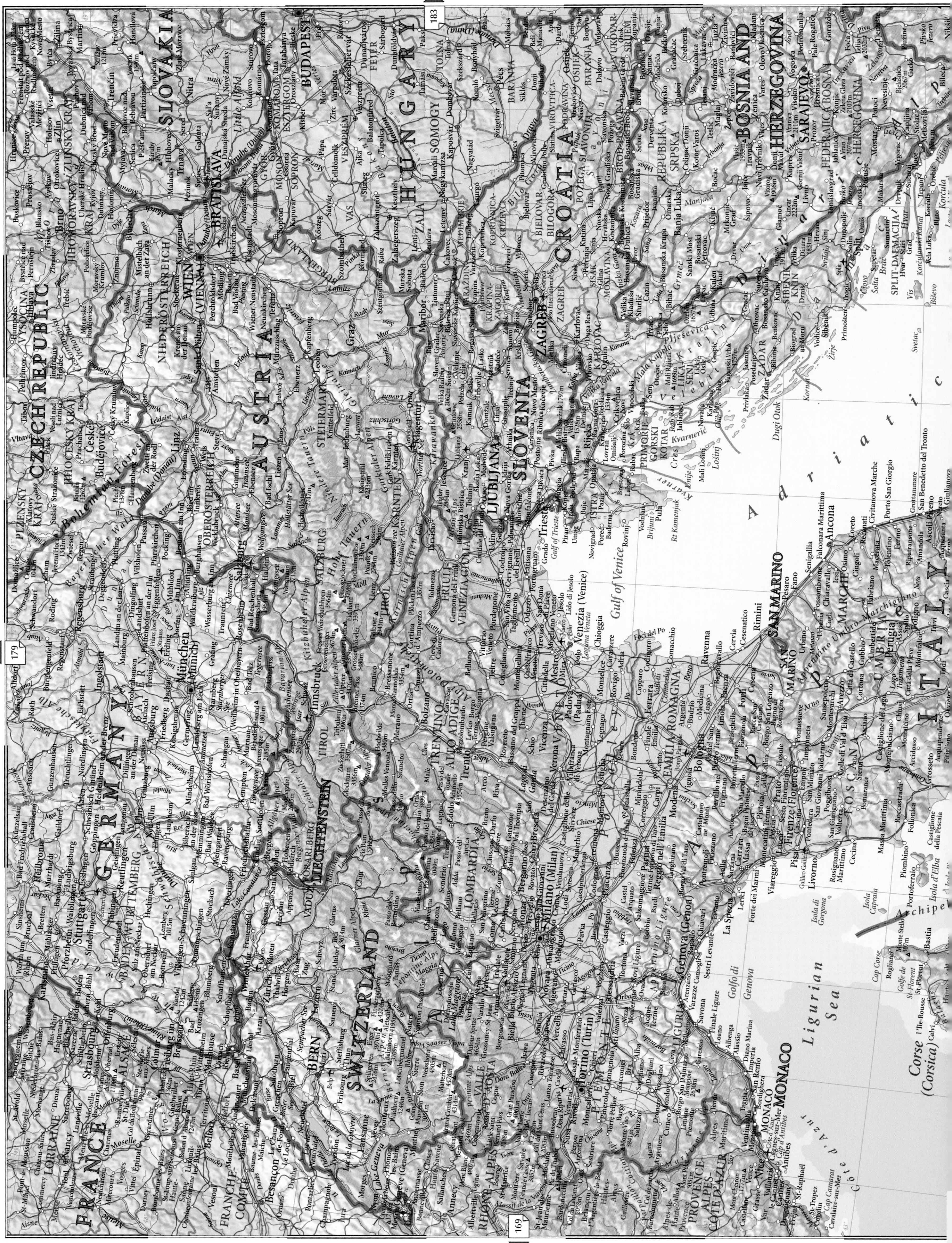

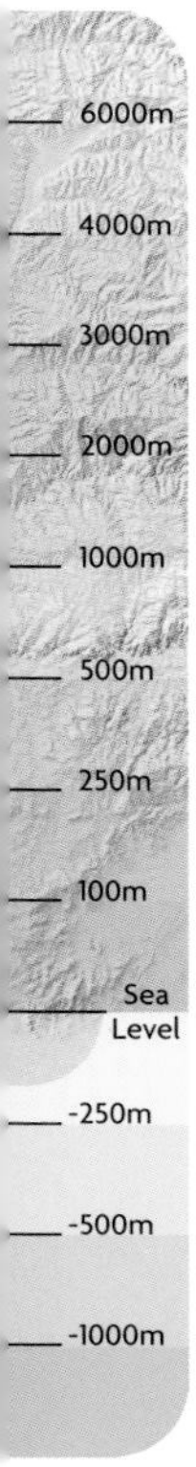

Elevation legend:

- 6000m
- 4000m
- 3000m
- 2000m
- 1000m
- 500m
- 250m
- 100m
- Sea Level
- -250m
- -500m
- -1000m

Countries and major regions:

FRANCE · GERMANY · SWITZERLAND · AUSTRIA · ITALY · SLOVENIA · CROATIA · BOSNIA AND HERZEGOVINA · HUNGARY · SLOVAKIA · CZECH REPUBLIC · MONACO · SAN MARINO

Selected place names:

BRATISLAVA · WIEN (VIENNA) · BUDAPEST · ZAGREB · LJUBLJANA · SARAJEVO · BERN · MÜNCHEN (MUNICH) · SALZBURG · STUTTGART · TORINO (TURIN) · MILANO (MILAN) · GENOVA (GENOA) · VENEZIA (VENICE) · FIRENZE (FLORENCE) · BOLOGNA · ANCONA · RIMINI · LA SPEZIA · TRIESTE · GRAZ · INNSBRUCK · LINZ · ZÜRICH · ZADAR

Seas and water features:

Adriatic · Ligurian Sea · Gulf of Venice · Gulf of Trieste · Kvarner

183
179
169

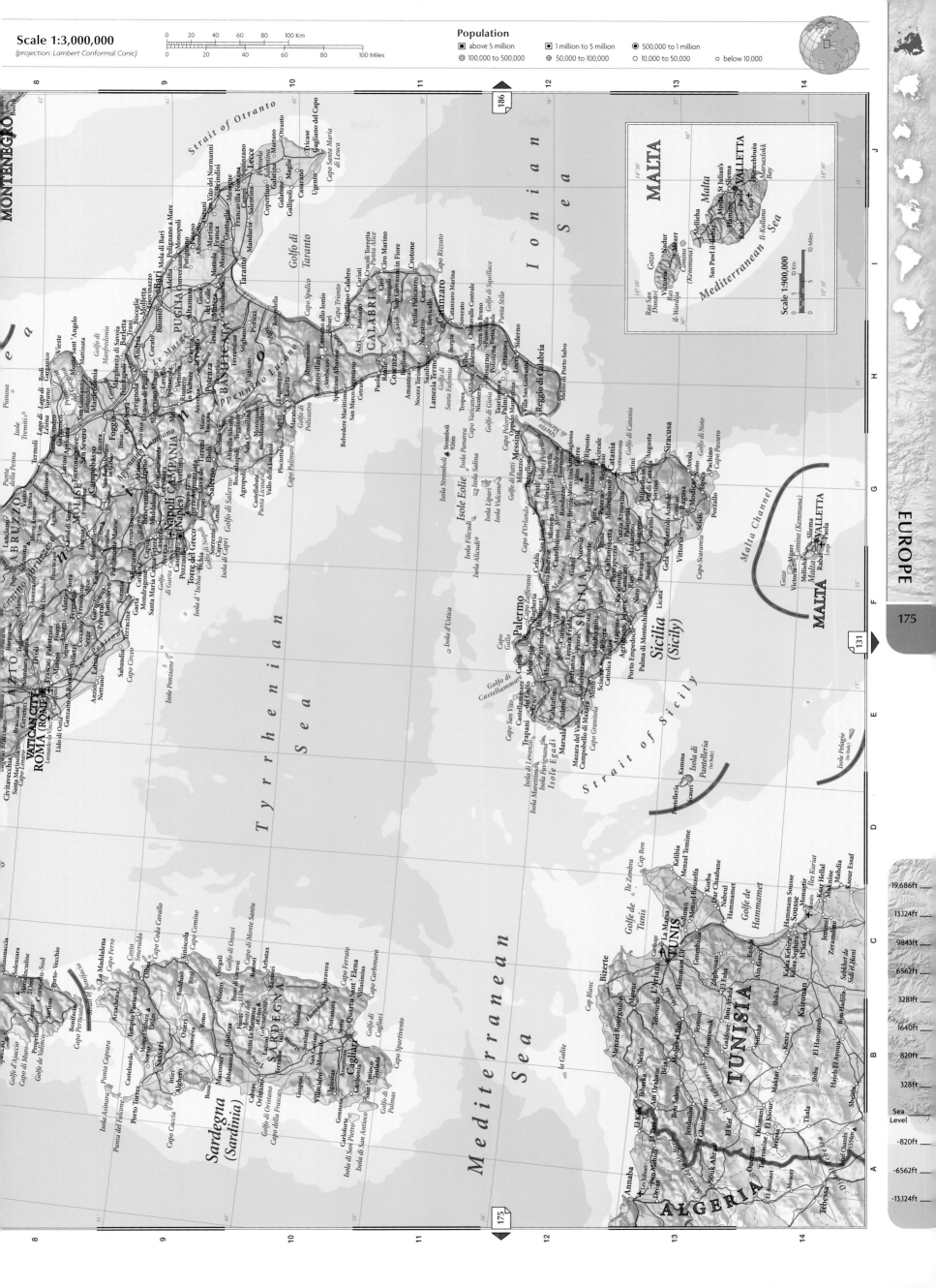

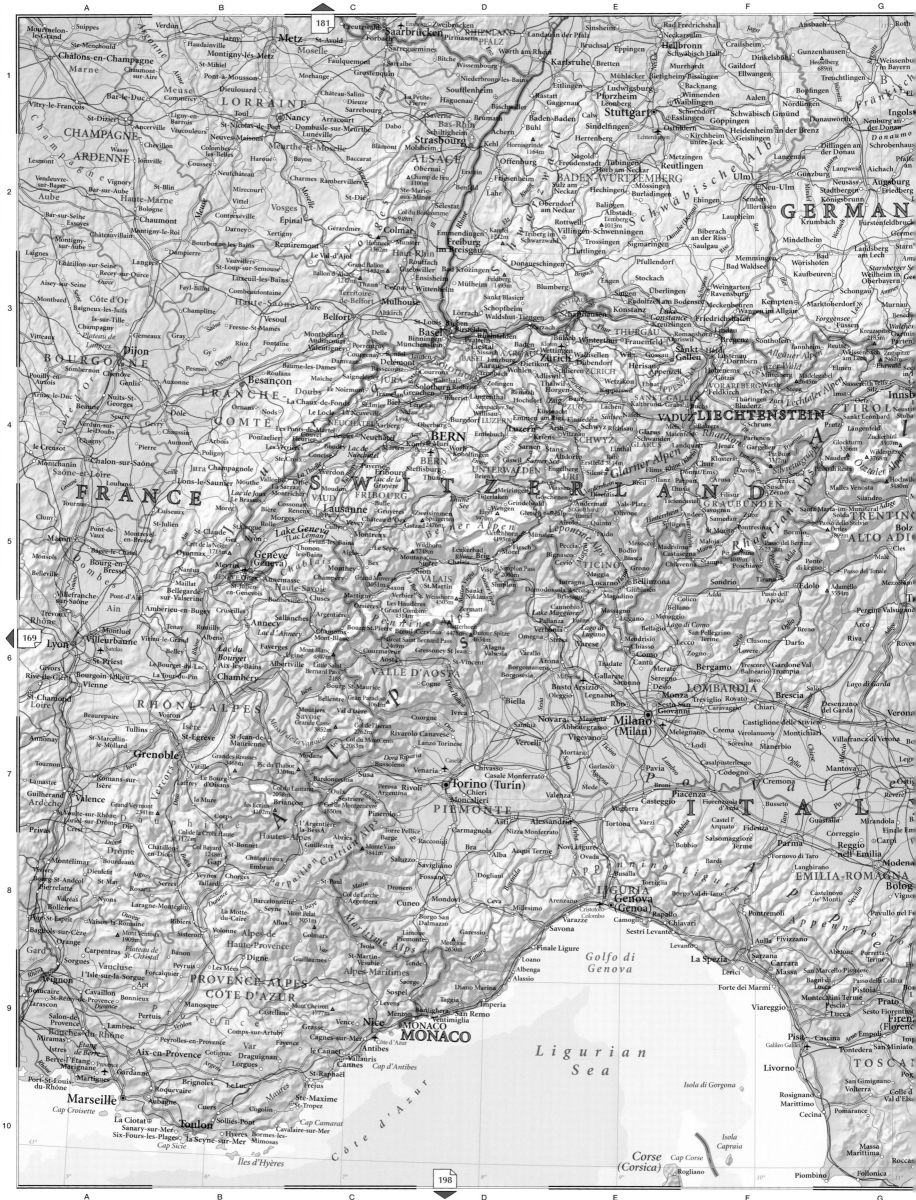

Scale 1:2,100,000
(projection: Lambert Conformal Conic)

0 10 20 30 40 50 60 70 80 Km
0 10 20 30 40 50 60 70 80 Miles

Population

□ above 5 million   ▣ 1 million to 5 million   ◉ 500,000 to 1 million
◎ 100,000 to 500,000   ⊕ 50,000 to 100,000   ○ 10,000 to 50,000   ○ below 10,000

183

CZECH REPUBLIC

SLOVAKIA

BRATISLAVA

WIEN (VIENNA)

OBERÖSTERREICH

NIEDERÖSTERREICH

AUSTRIA

STEIERMARK

SALZBURG

KÄRNTEN

TIROL

HUNGARY

BURGENLAND

GYÖR-MOSON-SOPRON

VAS

VESZPRÉM

ZALA

SOMOGY

TOLNA

BARANYA

Graz

Klagenfurt

Maribor

Villach

SLOVENIA

LJUBLJANA

FRIULI-VENEZIA GIULIA

Trieste

Gulf of Trieste

Venezia (Venice)

Gulf of Venice

VENETO

ZAGREB

CROATIA

ZAGREB

SISAK-MOSLAVINA

KARLOVAC

BJELOVAR-BILOGORA

VIROVITICA-PODRAVINA

POŽEGA-SLAVONIJA

BROD-POSAVINA

OSIJEK-BARANJA

PRIMORJE-GORSKI KOTAR

Rijeka

ISTRA

LIKA-SENJ

Pula

REPUBLIKA SRPSKA

Banja Luka

BOSNIA & HERZEGOVINA

FEDERACIJA BOSNA I HERCEGOVINA

ZADAR

ŠIBENIK-KNIN

SPLIT-DALMACIJA

Split

Zadar

Šibenik

SAN MARINO

SAN MARINO

Rimini

Ancona

MARCHE

UMBRIA

Perugia

Adriatic Sea

DUBROVNIK-NERETVA

Ravenna

184

175

19,686ft
13,124ft
9843ft
6562ft
3281ft
1640ft
820ft
328ft
Sea Level
-820ft
-6562ft
-13,124ft

H I J K L M N
1 2 3 4 5 6 7 8 9 10

Germany

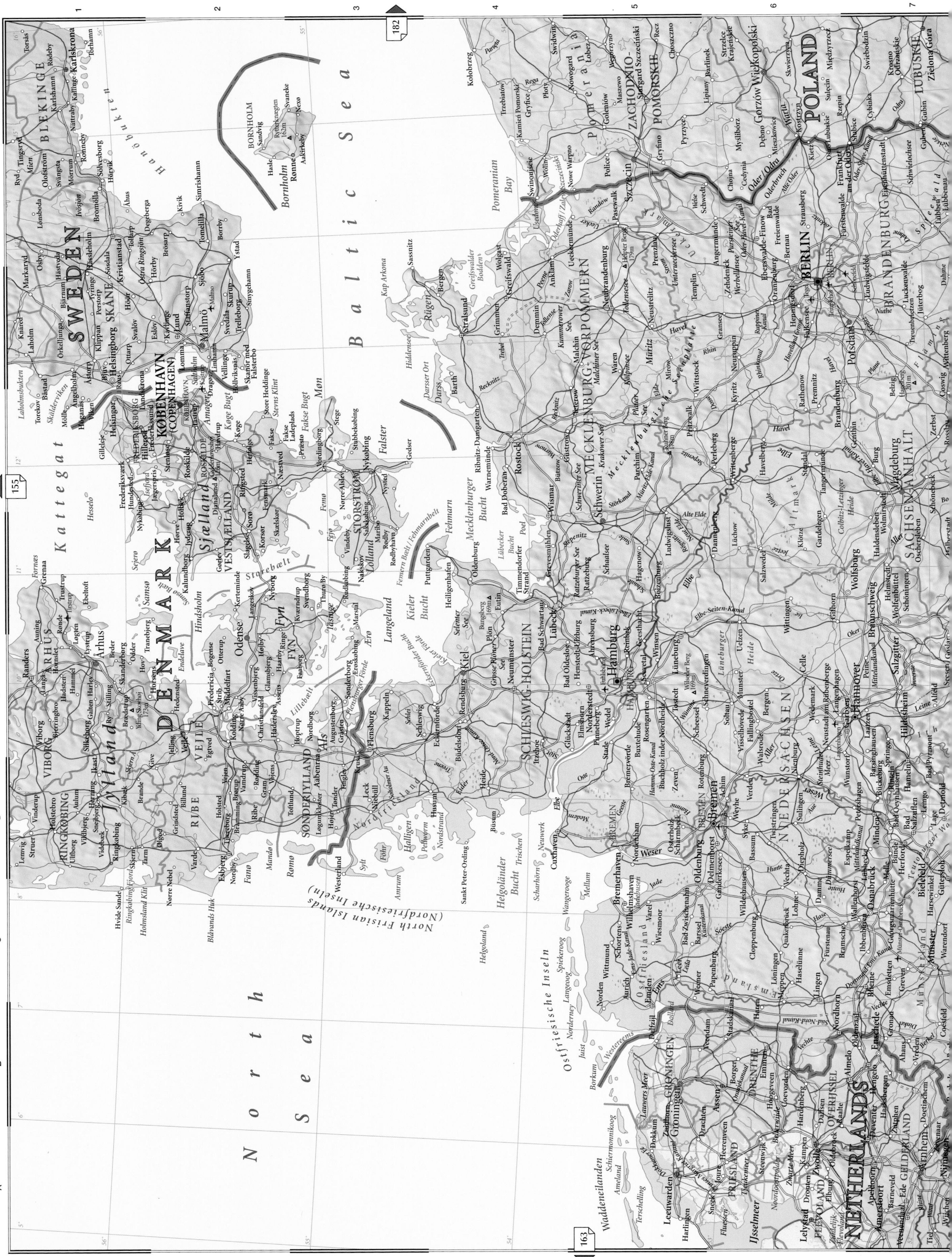

North Sea

Baltic Sea

Kattegat

SWEDEN

BLEKINGE

SKÅNE

DENMARK

JYLLAND

SØNDERJYLLAND

SJÆLLAND

VESTSJÆLLAND

FYN

BORNHOLM

KØBENHAVN (COPENHAGEN)

POLAND

POMORSKIE

ZACHODNIO-POMORSKIE

LUBUSKIE

Pomerania

Pomeranian Bay

BERLIN

BRANDENBURG

MECKLENBURG-VORPOMMERN

SACHSEN-ANHALT

SCHLESWIG-HOLSTEIN

NIEDERSACHSEN

NETHERLANDS

GRONINGEN

DRENTHE

FRIESLAND

OVERIJSSEL

GELDERLAND

Rügen

North Frisian Islands (Nordfriesische Inseln)

Ostfriesische Inseln

Hamburg

Bremen

Hannover

Rostock

Kiel

Lübeck

Schwerin

Magdeburg

Potsdam

Szczecin

Rügen

Helgoland

Sea Level
6000m
4000m
3000m
2000m
1000m
500m
250m
100m
Sea Level
-250m
-500m
-1000m

EUROPE

180

178
155
162

North Sea

Helgoländer Bucht

Helgoland

Waddeneilanden

Ostfriesische Inseln

Ostfriesland

NIEDERSACHSEN

SCHLESWIG-HOLSTEIN

MECKLENBURG-VORPOMMERN

SACHSEN-ANHALT

NORDRHEIN-WESTFALEN

NETHERLANDS

FRIESLAND

GRONINGEN

DRENTHE

OVERIJSSEL

GELDERLAND

FLEVOLAND

NOORD-BRABANT

Münsterland

Lüneburger Heide

Teutoburger Wald

Kiel
Lübeck
Schwerin
Hamburg
Bremen
Bremerhaven
Cuxhaven
Wilhelmshaven
Oldenburg
Osnabrück
Hannover
Hildesheim
Braunschweig
Wolfsburg
Salzgitter
Bielefeld

Elbe
Weser
Ems
Rhine
Aller
Leine
Hunte

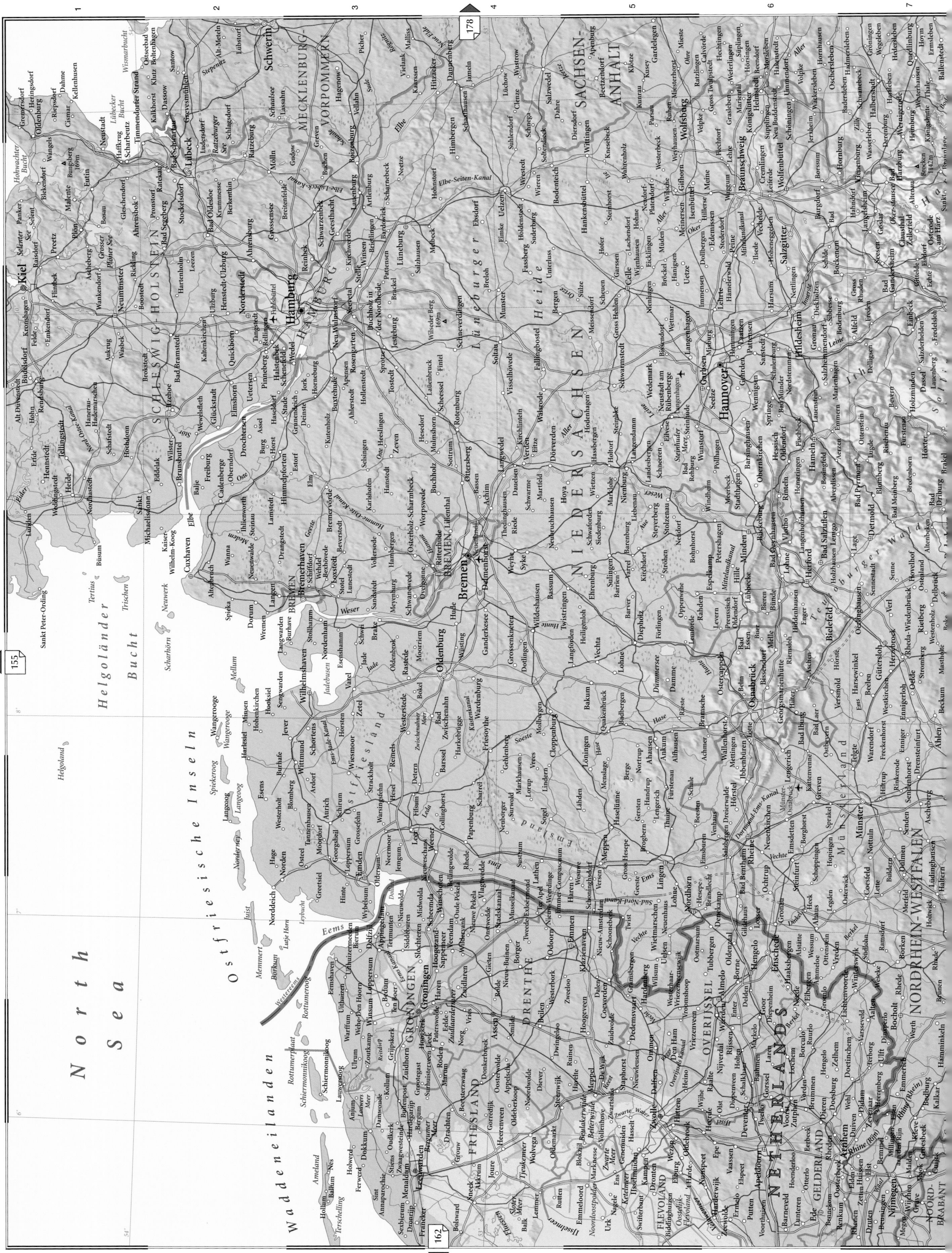

6000m
4000m
3000m
2000m
1000m
500m
250m
100m
Sea Level
-250m
-500m
-1000m

LATVIA

LITHUANIA

BELARUS

RUSSIAN FEDERATION

KALININGRADSKAYA OBLAST

POLAND

GERMANY

DENMARK

SWEDEN

BALTIC SEA

Gulf of Danzig

Pomeranian Bay

BORNHOLM

Öland

WARSZAWA (WARSAW)

Berlin

Gdańsk

Wrocław

Poznań

Łódź

Lublin

Szczecin

KØBENHAVN (COPENHAGEN)

Malmö

Kaunas

Klaipėda

Kaliningrad

Brest

Hrodna

6000m	
4000m	
3000m	
2000m	
1000m	
500m	
250m	
100m	
Sea Level	
-250m	
-500m	
-1000m	

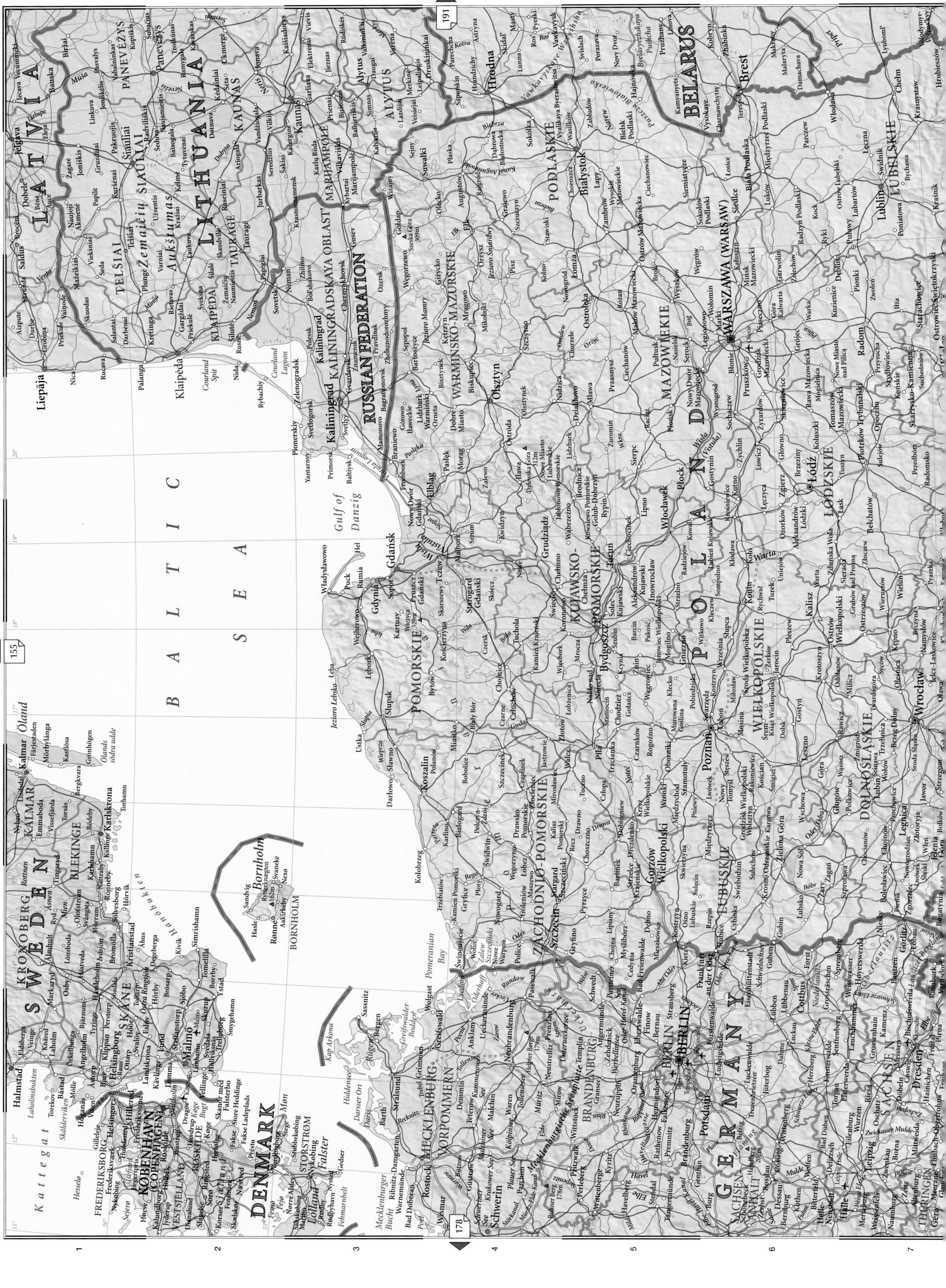

Scale 1:2,750,000
(projection: Lambert Conformal Conic)

| 0 | 10 | 20 | 30 | 40 | 50 | 60 | 70 | 80 Km |
| 0 | 10 | 20 | 30 | 40 | 50 | 60 | 70 | 80 Miles |

Population

■ above 5 million
◉ 1 million to 5 million
◉ 500,000 to 1 million
◎ 100,000 to 500,000
⊕ 50,000 to 100,000
○ 10,000 to 50,000
∘ below 10,000

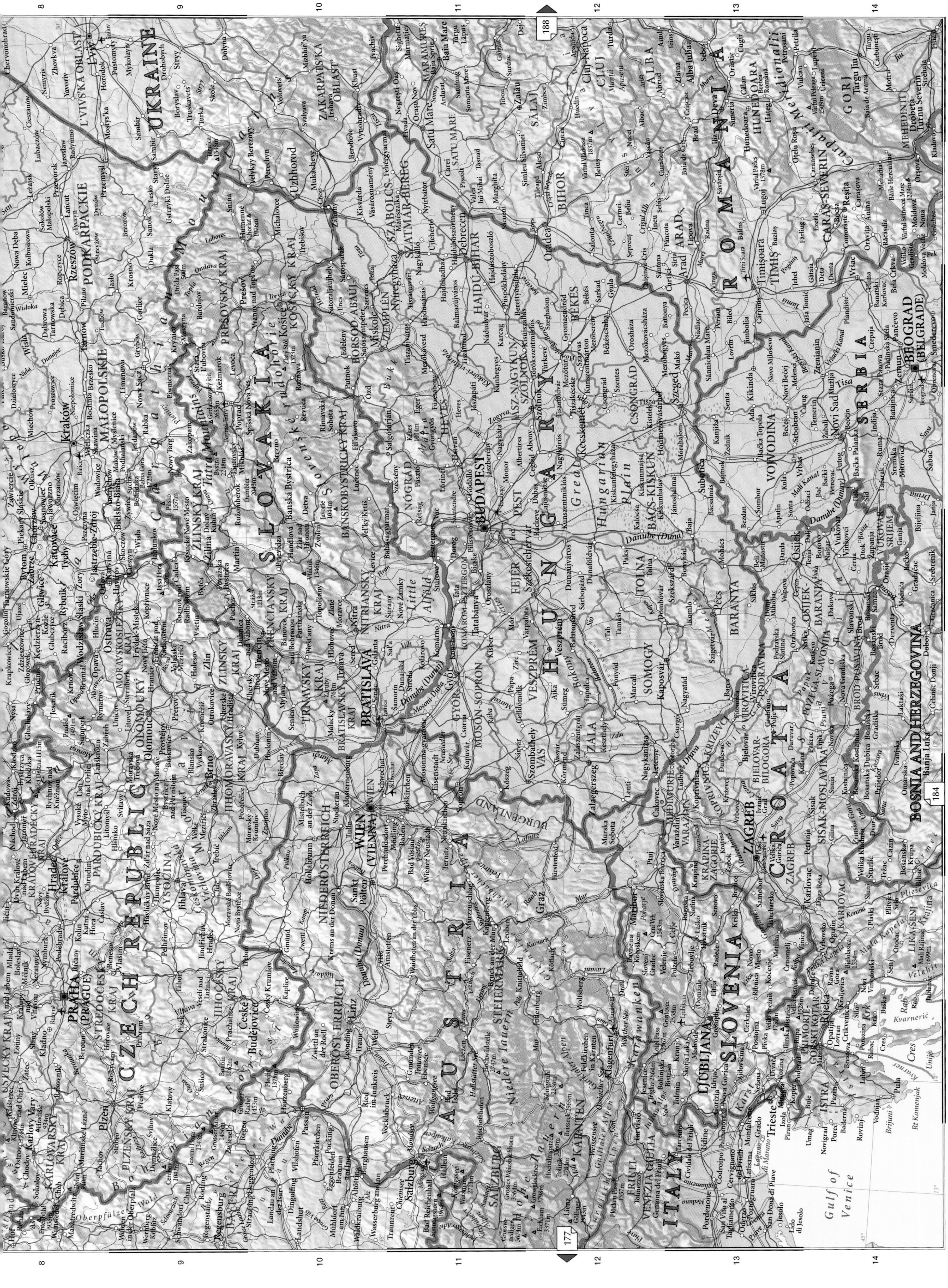

19,686ft
13,124ft
9843ft
6562ft
3281ft
1640ft
820ft
328ft
Sea Level
-820ft
-6562ft
-13,124ft

Scale 1:2,500,000
(projection: Lambert Conformal Conic)

0 10 20 30 40 50 Km
0 10 20 30 40 50 Miles

Population
■ above 5 million   ▣ 1 million to 5 million   ◉ 500,000 to 1 million
◎ 100,000 to 500,000   ⊕ 50,000 to 100,000   ○ 10,000 to 50,000   ∘ below 10,000

EUROPE

185

188
187
214

MOLDOVA

UKRAINE

ROMANIA

BIHOR · ALBA · SIBIU · HUNEDOARA · CARAŞ-SEVERIN · MEHEDINŢI · GORJ · VÂLCEA · ARGEŞ · DÂMBOVIŢA · PRAHOVA · BUZĂU · VRANCEA · BACĂU · NEAMŢ · HARGHITA · MUREŞ · COVASNA · BRAŞOV · DOLJ · OLT · TELEORMAN · GIURGIU · ILFOV · CĂLĂRAŞI · IALOMIŢA · BRĂILA · GALAŢI · VASLUI · TULCEA · CONSTANŢA

Cluj-Napoca · Târgu Mureş · Bacău · Braşov · Sibiu · Alba Iulia · Deva · Hunedoara · Piteşti · Târgovişte · Ploieşti · BUCUREŞTI (BUCHAREST) · Craiova · Slatina · Giurgiu · Galaţi · Brăila · Buzău · Focşani · Tulcea · Constanţa · Mangalia

Delta Dunării

Carpathian Mountains
Carpaţii Meridionali
Walachia

BULGARIA

SOFIYA (SOFIA) · PERNIK · KYUSTENDIL · BLAGOEVGRAD · MONTANA · VRATSA · VIDIN · PLEVEN · LOVECH · GABROVO · VELIKO TÛRNOVO · RUSE · RAZGRAD · SILISTRA · DOBRICH · VARNA · SHUMEN · TÛRGOVISHTE · SLIVEN · YAMBOL · BURGAS · STARA ZAGORA · PLOVDIV · PAZARDZHIK · SMOLYAN · KÛRDZHALI · KHASKOVO

Sofiya (Sofia) · Pernik · Kyustendil · Blagoevgrad · Vratsa · Pleven · Veliko Tûrnovo · Ruse · Razgrad · Dobrich · Varna · Shumen · Sliven · Yambol · Burgas · Stara Zagora · Plovdiv · Pazardzhik · Smolyan · Kûrdzhali · Khaskovo

Stara Planina (Balkan Mountains)
Sredna Gora
Rhodope Mountains
Dunavska Ravnina
Ludogorie
Dobruja

TURKEY

İSTANBUL · KIRKLARELI · EDIRNE · TEKIRDAĞ · ÇANAKKALE · BURSA · BALIKESIR

İstanbul · Kırklareli · Edirne · Lüleburgaz · Tekirdağ · Bandırma · Bursa · Balıkesir · Çanakkale

Istanbul Boğazı (Bosporus)
Çanakkale Boğazı (Dardanelles)
Marmara Denizi (Sea of Marmara)

GREECE

KENTRIKÍ MAKEDONÍA · ANATOLIKÍ MAKEDONÍA KAI THRÁKI · THESSALÍA

Thessaloníki · Kalamariá · Véroia · Édessa · Sérres · Dráma · Kaválla · Komotiní · Xánthi · Alexandroúpoli · Lárisa

Chalkidikí · AGION ÓROS · VÓREION AIGAÍON

Black Sea

Aegean Sea

Thracian Sea

Thásos · Samothráki · Límnos (Lésvos)

Elevation
19,686ft · 13,124ft · 9843ft · 6562ft · 3281ft · 1640ft · 820ft · 328ft · Sea Level · -820ft · -6562ft · -13,124ft

Greece

Population
- ■ above 5 million
- ▣ 1 million to 5 million
- ◉ 500,000 to 1 million
- ◉ 100,000 to 500,000
- ⊕ 50,000 to 100,000
- ○ 10,000 to 50,000
- ∘ below 10,000

EUROPE

185
187
214
129

Seas and Water Bodies
Black Sea
Marmara Denizi (Sea of Marmara)
Thracian Sea
Aegean Sea
Aegean Islands
Saros Körfezi
Çanakkale Boğazı (Dardanelles)
Gelibolu Yarımadası
İzmir Körfezi
Kuşadası Körfezi
Güllük Körfezi
Gökova Körfezi
Kritikó Pélagos (Sea of Crete)
Mediterranean Sea
Stenó Karpáthou
Stenó Kásou
İstanbul Boğazı (Bosporus)
İznik Gölü
Ulubat Gölü
Kuş Gölü

Countries and Regions
BULGARIA
GREECE
TURKEY
Anatolia
Thracian Sea
ANATOLIKI MAKEDONIA KAI THRAKI

Turkish Provinces
KIRKLARELI
TEKIRDAG
İSTANBUL
KOCAELI
SAKARYA
YALOVA
BURSA
BILECIK
ÇANAKKALE
BALIKESIR
KÜTAHYA
MANISA
İZMIR
AFYON
UŞAK
AYDIN
DENIZLI
MUĞLA
BURDUR
ANTALYA

Major Cities
İstanbul
Bursa
İzmir
İzmit
Adapazarı
Eskişehir
Kütahya
Manisa
Aydın
Denizli
Muğla
Burdur
ATHINA (ATHENS)
Peiraiás (Piraeus)
Plovdiv
Pazardzhik
Khaskovo
Kurdzhali
Smolyan
Blagoevgrad
Edirne
Tekirdağ

Bulgaria labels
PAZARDZHIK
PLOVDIV
KHASKOVO
KURDZHALI
SMOLYAN
BLAGOEVGRAD
Rhodope Mountains
STARA ZAGORA
YAMBOL
BURGAS
Velingrad
Asenovgrad
Kharmanli
Svilengrad
Dospat
Gotse Delchev
Sandanski

Greek islands and places
Thásos
Samothráki
Límnos
Lésvos (Lesbos)
Chíos
Ikaría
Sámos
Sýros
Náxos
Páros
Mýkonos
Tínos
Ándros
Évvoia (Euboea)
Skýros
Kéa
Kýthnos
Sérifos
Sífnos
Mílos
Amorgós
Astypálaia
Kos
Kálymnos
Léros
Pátmos
Ródos (Rhodes)
Kárpathos
Kásos
Kríti (Crete)
Irákleio
Chaniá
Réthymno
VÓREION AIGAÍON
NÓTION AIGAÍON
Kykládes (Cyclades)
Dodekánisa (Dodecanese)
AGION ÓROS
Vóreies Sporádes
Alónnisos
Skíathos
Skópelos
Skýros
Thíva
Lamía

Elevation scale
19,686ft
13,124ft
9843ft
6562ft
3281ft
1640ft
820ft
328ft
Sea Level
-820ft
-6562ft
-13,124ft

Romania, Moldova & Ukraine

Scale 1:3,000,000
(projection: Lambert Conformal Conic)

0 20 40 60 80 100 Km
0 20 40 60 80 100 Miles

Population
- ■ above 5 million
- ■ 1 million to 5 million
- ◉ 500,000 to 1 million
- ◎ 100,000 to 500,000
- ⊕ 50,000 to 100,000
- ○ 10,000 to 50,000
- ○ below 10,000

RUSSIAN FEDERATION

UKRAINE

ORLOVSKAYA OBLAST'
LIPETSKAYA OBLAST'
KURSKAYA OBLAST'
BELGORODSKAYA OBLAST'
VORONEZHSKAYA
SUMS'KA OBLAST'
CHERNIHIVS'KA OBLAST'
KYYIVS'KA OBLAST'
POLTAVS'KA OBLAST'
KHARKIVS'KA OBLAST'
LUHANS'KA OBLAST'
CHERKAS'KA OBLAST'
KIROVOHRADS'KA OBLAST'
DNIPROPETROVS'KA OBLAST'
DONETS'KA OBLAST'
MYKOLAYIVS'KA OBLAST'
ZAPORIZ'KA OBLAST'
KHERSONS'KA OBLAST'
RESPUBLIKA KRYM
Kryms'kyy Pivostriv
KRASNODARSKIY KRAY

Homyel, Chernihiv, KYYIV (KIEV), Sumy, Kharkiv, Belgorod, Voronezh, Kursk, Poltava, Cherkasy, Kirovohrad, Dnipropetrovs'k, Donets'k, Luhans'k, Kryvyy Rih, Mykolayiv, Kherson, Zaporizhzhya, Melitopol', Mariupol', Rostov-na-Donu, Krasnodar, Odesa, Simferopol', Sevastopol', Yalta, Kerch, Berdyans'k, Novorossiysk

Gulf of Taganrog
Sea of Azov
Black Sea

Elevation scale:
19,686ft
13,124ft
9843ft
6562ft
3281ft
1640ft
820ft
328ft
Sea Level
-820ft
-6562ft
-13,124ft

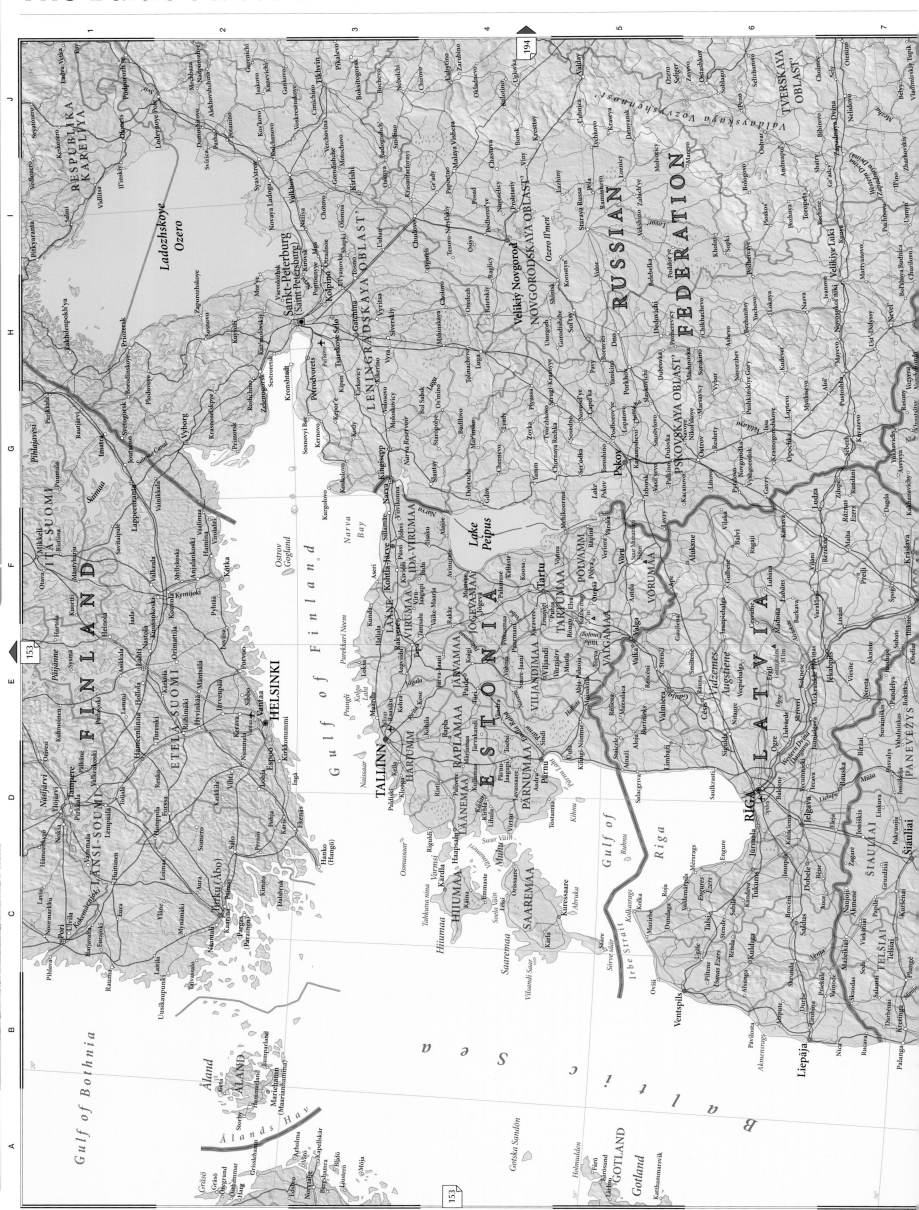

Scale 1:2,750,000
(projection: Lambert Conformal Conic)

Population

☐ above 5 million   ☐ 1 million to 5 million   ◉ 500,000 to 1 million
◎ 100,000 to 500,000   ⊕ 50,000 to 100,000   ○ 10,000 to 50,000   ∘ below 10,000

0 10 20 30 40 50 60 70 80 Km
0 10   20   30   40   50   60   70   80 Miles

19,686ft
13,124ft
9843ft
6562ft
3281ft
1640ft
820ft
328ft
Sea
Level
-820ft
-6562ft
-13,124ft

The Russian Federation

290

THE RUSSIAN FEDERATION: ADMINISTRATIVE REGIONS

The administrative area names in European Russia have been omitted west of the Ural Mountains. Please refer to pages 194-195 and 196-197 where these areas are shown at a larger scale.

199

6000m
4000m
3000m
2000m
1000m
500m
250m
100m
Sea Level
-250m
-500m
-1000m

230

Scale 1:17,500,000

(projection: Lambert Conformal Conic)

0 100 200 300 400 500 Km
0 100 200 300 400 500 Miles

Population

■ above 5 million
◉ 100,000 to 500,000

▣ 1 million to 5 million
⊕ 50,000 to 100,000

◉ 500,000 to 1 million
○ 10,000 to 50,000

○ below 10,000

294

286

248

UNITED STATES OF AMERICA

ALASKA

ARCTIC OCEAN

Severnaya Zemlya

Ostrov Shmidta

Novosibirskiye Ostrova

Chukchi Sea

Vostochno-Sibirskoye More

More Laptevykh

Ostrov Taymyr

Bering Strait

Bering Sea

REPUBLIKA SAKHA
(YAKUTIYA)

Verkhoyanskiy Khrebet

Khrebet Cherskogo

SIBERIA

S I B I R

Yakutsk

MAGADANSKAYA
OBLAST'

CHUKOTSKIY
AVTONOMNYY
OKRUG

Anadyr'

KORYAKSKIY
AVTONOMNYY
OKRUG

FEDERATION

Magadan

KHABAROVSKIY
KRAY

Okhotskoye More
(Sea of Okhotsk)

KAMCHATSKAYA
OBLAST'

Petropavlovsk-
Kamchatskiy

IRKUTSKAYA OBLAST'

Bratsk

Angarsk Irkutsk Ulan-Ude

Ozero Baykal

RESPUBLIKA
BURYATIYA

CHITINSKAYA
OBLAST'

Chita

AMURSKAYA
OBLAST'

Blagoveshchensk

SAKHALINSKAYA
OBLAST'

Ostrov Sakhalin

Yuzhno-Sakhalinsk

Komsomol'sk-
na-Amure

Khabarovsk

Kuril'skiye Ostrova

ULAANBAATAR
(ULAN BATOR)

MONGOLIA

Gobi

Manzhouli

Hailar

Qiqihar Daqing Anda

Harbin

Mudanjiang

Jilin

Changchun

Vladivostok

Nakhodka

Sapporo

JAPAN

PACIFIC OCEAN

Sea of Japan
(East Sea)

NORTH KOREA

P'YONGYANG

SOUTH KOREA

SÖUL
(SEOUL)

Beijing

Tianjin

Datong

Baotou

Hohhot

Shenyang

Fushun

Anshan

Dalian

Bo Hai

TOKYO

Yokohama

Nagoya

Chiba

Sendai

19,686ft

13,124ft

9843ft

6562ft

3281ft

1640ft

820ft

328ft

Sea
Level

-820ft

-6562ft

-13,124ft

EUROPE

194

Norwegian Sea

NORWAY

SWEDEN

FINLAND

RUSSIAN

Lapland

LAPPI

FINNMARK

TROMS

NORDLAND

NORRBOTTEN

VÄSTERBOTTEN

VÄSTERNORRLAND

GÄVLEBORG

UPPSALA

ÅLAND

MURMANSKAYA OBLAST'

Kol'skiy Poluostrov

RESPUBLIKA KARELIYA

ARKHANGEL'SKA

VOLOGODSKAYA OBLAST'

LENINGRADSKAYA OBLAST'

NOVGORODSKAYA OBLAST'

PSKOVSKAYA OBLAST'

TVERSKAYA OBLAST'

YAROSLAVSKAYA OBLAST'

IVANOVS OBLAS

VLADIMIRSKAYA OBLAST'

ESTONIA

LATVIA

LITHUANIA

KALININGRADSKAYA OBLAST'

BELARUS

Baltic Sea

Gulf of Bothnia

Gulf of Finland

Gulf of Riga

Beloye More (White Sea)

Bare... (Barents Sea)

Ladozhskoye Ozero

Lake Peipus

Lake Pskov

Murmansk · Severomorsk · Polyarnyy · Nikel' · Zapolyarnyy · Kirkenes · Vadsø · Hammerfest · Tromsø · Narvik · Bodø · Mo i Rana

Kiruna · Gällivare · Jokkmokk · Luleå · Piteå · Skellefteå · Umeå · Örnsköldsvik · Härnösand · Sundsvall · Hudiksvall · Söderhamn · Gävle · Uppsala · STOCKHOLM

Rovaniemi · Kemi · Tornio · Oulu · Raahe · Kokkola (Karleby) · Jakobstad (Pietarsaari) · Vaasa (Vasa) · Pori · Rauma · Turku (Åbo) · Tampere · HELSINKI · Espoo · Vantaa · Lahti · Kotka · Lappeenranta · Kuopio · Joensuu · Jyväskylä · Kajaani

Kandalaksha · Apatity · Kirovsk · Monchegorsk · Kovdor · Belomorsk · Kem' · Segezha · Kostomuksha · Petrozavodsk · Kondopoga · Medvezh'yegorsk

Arkhangel (Archangel) · Severodvinsk · Novodvinsk · Onega · Nyandoma · Kargopol' · Vologda · Cherepovets · Rybinsk

Sankt-Peterburg (Saint Petersburg) · Gatchina · Tikhvin · Kirishi · Novgorod · Velikiy Novgorod · Pskov · Ostrov · Velikiye Luki · Tver' · Yaroslavl' · Kostroma · Ivanovo

TALLINN · Tartu · Pärnu · Narva · RIGA · Jūrmala · Liepāja · Daugavpils · KALININGRAD · Klaipėda · Kaunas · Šiauliai · Panevėžys

EUROPE

Elevation scale: 6000m · 4000m · 3000m · 2000m · 1000m · 500m · 250m · 100m · Sea Level · -250m · -500m · -1000m

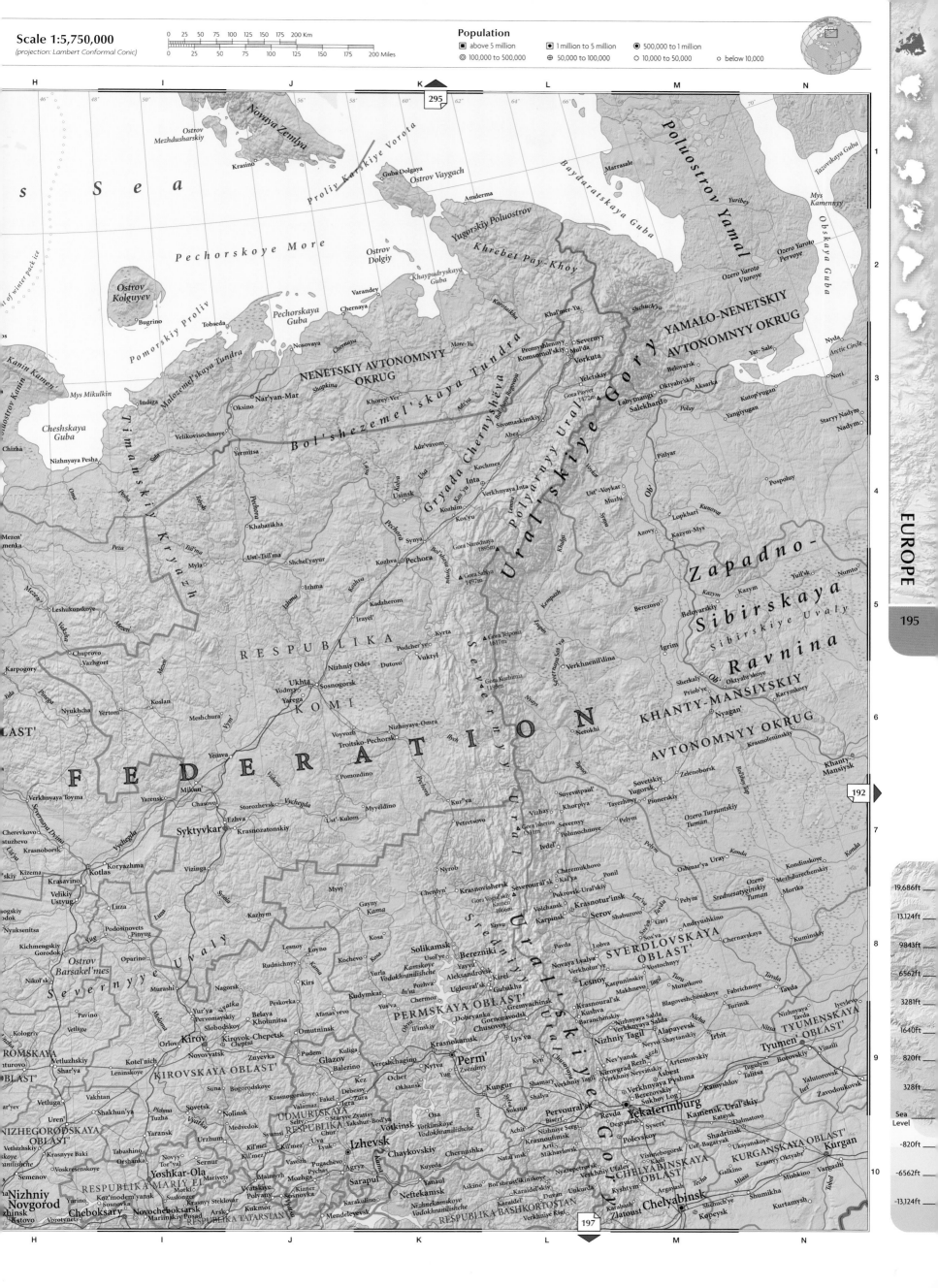

Southern European Russia

A B C D E F G
1 2 3 4 5 6 7 8 9 10
190
183
214
LITHUANIA
LATVIA
POLAND
BELARUS
UKRAINE
MOLDOVA
ROMANIA
BULGARIA
GREECE
TURKEY
RUSS. FED.
Black Sea
Sea of Azov
MINSK
VILNIUS
WARSZAWA (WARSAW)
KYYIV (KIEV)
CHIȘINĂU
BUCUREȘTI (BUCHAREST)
SOFIYA (SOFIA)
MOSKVA (MOSCOW)
İstanbul
Odesa
Kharkiv
Dnipropetrovs'k
Donets'k
Rostov-na-Donu
Sevastopol
Simferopol'
Kaliningrad
Smolensk
Bryansk
Kursk
Voronezh
Homyel'
Mahilyow
Vitsyebsk
Hrodna
Brest
L'viv
Kirovohrad
Mykolayiv
Kherson
Zaporizhzhya
Krasnodar
Constanța
Varna
Burgas

6000m
4000m
3000m
2000m
1000m
500m
250m
100m
Sea Level
-250m
-500m
-1000m

Scale 1:5,750,000
(projection: Lambert Conformal Conic)

0 25 50 75 100 125 150 175 200 Km
0 25 50 75 100 125 150 175 200 Miles

Population
■ above 5 million
▣ 1 million to 5 million
◉ 500,000 to 1 million
◎ 100,000 to 500,000
⊕ 50,000 to 100,000
○ 10,000 to 50,000
▫ below 10,000

RUSSIAN FEDERATION

Nizhniy Novgorod · Dzerzhinsk · Arzamas · Saransk · RESPUBLIKA MORDOVIYA · Penza · PENZENSKAYA OBLAST' · Ul'yanovsk · ULYANOVSKAYA OBLAST' · Cheboksary · Yoshkar-Ola · RESPUBLIKA MARIY EL · CHAVASH RESPUBLIKI · Kazan' · RESPUBLIKA TATARSTAN · Izhevsk · UDMURTSKAYA RESPUBLIKA · Votkinsk · Chaykovskiy · Naberezhnyye Chelny · Nizhnekamsk · Sarapul · Neftekamsk · Ufa · RESPUBLIKA BASHKORTOSTAN · Yekaterinburg · Chelyabinsk · CHELYABINSKAYA OBLAST' · KURGANSKAYA OBLAST' · Magnitogorsk · Zlatoust · Miass · Kopeysk · Troitsk

Tol'yatti · Samara · SAMARSKAYA OBLAST' · Syzran' · Novokuybyshevsk · Dimitrovgrad · Saratov · Engel's · SARATOVSKAYA OBLAST' · Balakovo · Vol'sk · Balashov · Kamyshin · Orenburg · ORENBURGSKAYA OBLAST' · Sterlitamak · Salavat · Kumertau · Orsk · Novotroitsk · KOSTANAY · Rudnyy

Volgograd · Volzhskiy · VOLGOGRADSKAYA OBLAST' · Astrakhan' · ASTRAKHANSKAYA OBLAST' · RESPUBLIKA KALMYKIYA · Elista

KAZAKHSTAN
ZAPADNYY KAZAKHSTAN · Ural'sk · Aktobe (Aktyubinsk) · AKTYUBINSK · Atyrau · ATYRAU · MANGISTAU · Aktau · Zhanaozen

Caspian Depression · Ryn-Peski · Caspian Sea · Aral Sea · Ustyurt Plateau · Plato Mangyshlak

UZBEKISTAN
QORAQALPOGISTON RESPUBLIKASI · Nukus

TURKMENISTAN
BALKAN WELAÝATY · DAŞOGUZ WELAÝATY

GEORGIA · T'bilisi · **AZERBAIJAN** · Baki · Sumqayit · Gäncä · **ARMENIA** · Yerevan

Stavropol' · STAVROPOL'SKIY KRAY · Pyatigorsk · Cherkessk · KARACHAYEVO-CHERKESSKAYA RESPUBLIKA · Nal'chik · KABARDINO-BALKARSKAYA RESPUBLIKA · Vladikavkaz · RESPUBLIKA SEVERNAYA OSETIYA-ALANIYA · INGUSHSKAYA RESPUBLIKA · Groznyy · CHECHENSKAYA RESPUBLIKA · RESPUBLIKA DAGESTAN · Makhachkala · Kaspiysk · Buynaksk · Derbent

19,686ft · 13,124ft · 9843ft · 6562ft · 3281ft · 1640ft · 820ft · 328ft · Sea Level · -820ft · -6562ft · -13,124ft

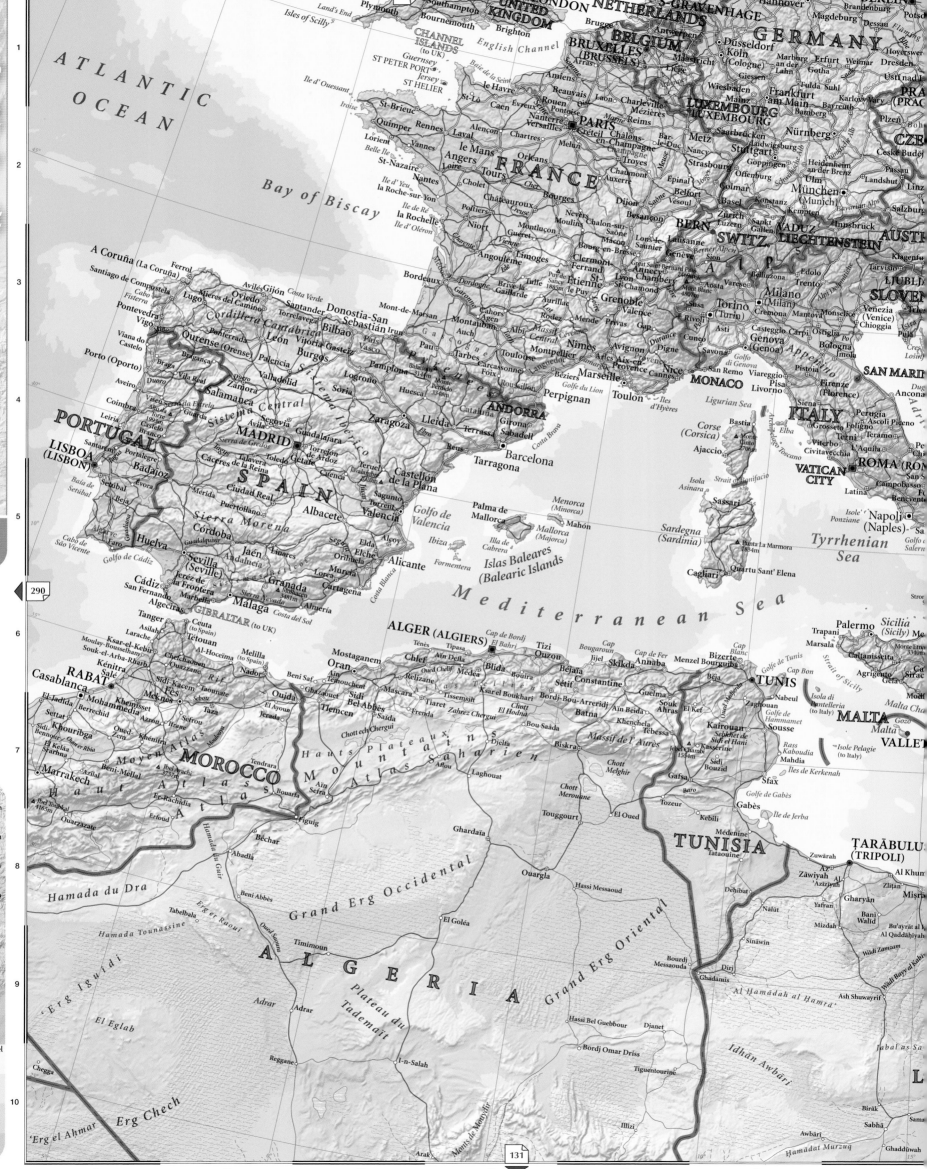

Scale 1:8,750,000
(projection: Lambert Conformal Conic)

0 25 50 75 100 125 150 175 200 Km
0 25 50 75 100 125 150 175 200 Miles

Population
- ◼ above 5 million
- ◾ 1 million to 5 million
- ● 500,000 to 1 million
- ◉ 100,000 to 500,000
- ⊕ 50,000 to 100,000
- ○ 10,000 to 50,000
- ∘ below 10,000

EUROPE

199

19,686ft
13,124ft
9843ft
6562ft
3281ft
1640ft
820ft
328ft
Sea Level
-820ft
-6562ft
-13,124ft

POLAND
Włocławek
Płock
WARSZAWA (WARSAW)
Brest
Drahichyn
Pinsk
BELARUS
Yasyel'da
Mazyr
Pripet
Chernihiv
Konotop
Sumy
Gubkin
Starryy Oskol
Liski
Mikhaylovka
Poznań
Kalisz
Konin
Łódź
Pruszków
Biała Podlaska
Pripet Marshes
Prryp'yat'
Pripet
Romny
Belgorod
Rossosh'
Volzhskiy
ona Góra
Głogów
Legnica
Ostrów
Wielkopolski
Tomaszów Mazowiecki
Puławy
Lublin
Luts'k
Rivne
Korosten'
KYYIV (KIEV)
Fastiv
Bila Tserkva
Pryluky
Okhtyrka
Kharkiv
Poltava
Slov"yans'k
Syeverodonets'k
Lysychans'k
Kamensk-Shakhtinskiy
Volgograd
Volga
ych
Opole
Wrocław
Rybnik
Piotrków Trybunalski
Radom
Ostrowiec Swietokrzyski
Kielce
Chełm
Stryy
Ternopil'
Zhytomyr
Cherkasy
Kremenchuk
Kirovohrad
Pavlohrad
Kostyantynivka
Stakhanov
Krasny Luch
Donets'k
Krasny Luch
Novoshakhtinsk
Kamensk-Shakhtinskiy
Shakhty
UBLIC
Zilin
Martin
SLOVAKIA
Trenčin
Banská Bystrica
Nitra
Košice
Uzhhorod
L'viv
Ivano-Frankivs'k
Khmel'nyts'kyy
Vinnytsya
UKRAINE
Uman'
Oleksandriya
Dnipro-dzerzhyns'k
Dnipropetrovs'k
Yenakiyeve
Novoshakhtinsk
Novocherkassk
Rostov-na-Donu
RUSSIAN FEDERATION
Elista
EN
BRATISLAVA
Eisenstadt
Sopron
Győr
Tatabánya
Miskolc
Nyíregyháza
Satu Mare
Chernivtsi
Kam"yanets'-Podil's'kyy
Peryomays'k
Kryvyy Rih
Zaporizhzhya
Nikopol'
Mariupol'
Taganrog
Tikhoretsk
Kropotkin
Szombathely
Székesfehérvár
BUDAPEST
Debrecen
Baia Mare
Suceava
CHIŞINĂU
MOLDOVA
Tighina
Tiraspol
Odesa
Mykolayiv
Melitopol'
Berdyans'k
Azov
Krasnodar
Maykop
Stavropol'
Nevinnomyssk
HUNGARY
Kaposvár
Pécs
Szeged
Hódmezővásárhely
Kecskemét
Oradea
Cluj-Napoca
Bistrita
Piatra-Neamt
Roman
Iaşi
Bălti
Black Sea Lowland
Kherson
Sea of Azov
Kerch
Cherkessk
Kislovodsk
Nal'chik
El'brus 5642m
GREB
OATIA
Subotica
Kikinda
Novi Sad
Vrbas
Timişoara
Deva
Sibiu
ROMANIA
Braşov
Sfântu Gheorghe
Focşani
Bacău
Vaslui
Bârlad
Izmayil
Tulcea
Lacul Razim
Yalta
Sevastopol'
Simferopol'
Yevpatoriya
Krym (Crimea)
Kerch Strait
Tuapse
Sochi
Sokhumi
Caucasus
Kut'aisi
Banja Luka
BOSNIA AND HERZEGOVINA
SARAJEVO
Tuzla
Šabac
BEOGRAD (BELGRADE)
Kragujevac
Vidin
Craiova
Slatina
Piteşti
Târgovişte
BUCUREŞTI (BUCHAREST)
Giurgiu
Ruse
Silistra
Călăraşi
Constanţa
Dobrich
Varnenski Zaliv
Black Sea
GEORGIA
Bat'umi
Hopa
P'ot'i
MONTENEGRO
Nikšić
PODGORICA
Shkodër
SERBIA
Kruševac
Niš
Kosovska Mitrovica
Priština
Kumanovo
SOFIYA (SOFIA)
Montana
Vratsa
Pleven
Veliko Tûrnovo
Stara Zagora
Razgrad
Shumen
Varna
Burgas
Sliven
Rize
Hvar
Mljet
Mostar
ALBANIA
TIRANË (TIRANA)
Prizren
SKOPJE
MACEDONIA
Prilep
Bitola
Blagoevgrad
Plovdiv
Kürdzhali
Khaskovo
Edirne
Küre Dağları
Bafra
Samsun
Ordu
Giresun
Trabzon
Dogu Karadeniz Dağları
Erzincan
Erzurum
Brindisi
Lecce
Taranto
Golfo di Taranto
Korçë
Thessaloníki
Kavála
Thásos
Samothráki
Çorlu
Tekirdağ
İstanbul (İstanbul Boğazı / Bosporus)
Adapazarı
Bolu
Çankırı
Çorum
Tokat
Sivas
Malatya
Elazığ
Silvan
Muş
senza
Crotone
Catanzaro
Kérkyra (Corfu)
Páxoi
Lefkáda
Pátra
Préveza
Kalamariá
Chalkidikí
Límnos
Lésvos
Çanakkale
Balıkesir
Bandırma
Bursa
Yalova
İzmit
Eskişehir
ANKARA
Kırıkkale
Polatlı
TURKEY
Anatolia
Kayseri
Nevşehir
Aksaray
Niğde
Kahramanmaraş
Adıyaman
Diyarbakır
Batman
Mardin
Viranşehir
Nusaybin
Al Qamishli
Ionian Sea
Olympos 2917m
Thermaïkós Kólpos
Vólos
Lárisa
Skýros
Évvoia
Thracian Sea
Aegean Sea
Skýros
Voréies Sporádes
GREECE
Lefká
Kefalloniá
Zákynthos
Pýrgos
ATHÍNA (ATHENS)
Peiraiás (Piraeus)
Aígio
Kórinthos
Mýkonos
Páros
Náxos
Léros
Sámos
Ikaría
Chíos
İzmir
Manisa
Ödemiş
Uşak
Aydın
Nazilli
Denizli
Büyükmenderes Nehri
Burdur
Isparta
Afyon
Akşehir
Konya
Ereğli
Karaman
Adana
Tarsus
Mersin
İskenderun
Antakya
Kırıkhan
İdlib
Halab (Aleppo)
Manbij
Al Hasakah
Al Jazīrah
Ar Raqqah
Day az Zawr
Kýthira
Antikýthira
Mílos
Sífnos
Sérifos
Kýthnos
Íos
Amorgós
Astypálaia
Nísyros
Tílos
Chálki
Ródos (Rhodes)
Kárpathos
Mýrtoo Pélagos
Santoríni
Anáfi
Kritikó Pélagos (Sea of Crete)
Dodecanese
Marmaris
Fethiye
Finike
Antalya
Antalya Körfezi
Alanya
Toros Dağları
Güney Dogu Toroslar
Gaziantep
Kilis
Şanlıurfa
Osmaniye
Ceyhan
TURKISH REPUBLIC OF NORTHERN CYPRUS (recognised only by Turkey)
CYPRUS
NICOSIA
Famagusta (Gazimağusa Körfezi)
Kyrenia
Troödos
Lemesós (Limassol)
Lárnaka
Hamāh
Tartūs
Al Lādhiqīyah (Latakia)
Himş
Tudmur
SYRIA
Syrian Desert
IRAQ
Lefká Óri
Dikti
Irákleio
Kríti (Crete)
Mediterranean Sea
BEYROUTH (BEIRUT)
Tripoli
LEBANON
Mount Hermon
DIMASHQ (DAMASCUS)
At Tanf
Hefa
Golan Heights
Lake Tiberius
Irbid
Az Zarqā'
AMMĀN
ISRAEL
Netanya
Tel Aviv-Yafo
Jerusalem
WEST BANK
Gaza
GAZA STRIP
Be'er Sheva
Great Rift Valley
Al Karak
Al Ḥarrah
JORDAN
Ma'an
Banghāzī (Benghazi)
Al Marj
Al Bayḍā'
Darnah
Ra's al Hilāl
Ra's al Tīn
Khalīj al Bumbah
Tubruq
Ra's al Muraysah
Gulf of Salūm
Salūm
Sidi Barrānī
Rās'Alam el Rūm
Maṭrūḥ
Rashid (Rosetta)
Dumyāṭ (Damietta)
Port Said
El 'Arish
Wādi el 'Arish
Aşdod
Ashqelon
As Sulṭān
Ajdābiyā
Marsá al Burayqah
An Nawfalīyah
Khalīj Surt (Gulf of Sirte)
Qaminis
Al Jabal al Akhḍar
Wādi al Farigh
Wādi al Hamm
Al Jaghbūb
Siwa
Munkhafad el Qaṭṭāra (Qattara Depression)
Qāra
Sahara el Gharbīya (Western Desert)
El 'Alamein
Alexandria
Khalig el 'Arab
Damanhūr
Shibin el Kôm
Kafr el Sheikh
Tanta
El Manṣūra
Zagazig
Benha
İsmā'iliya
Suez Canal
Suez
El Faiyûm
Beni Suef
Gebel Musa 2285m
Rās Ghārib
El Fûr
Gulf of Suez
Tabūk
SAUDI ARABIA
Al Ḥijāz (Hejaz)
Al 'Ulā
LIBYA
Ajdābiyā
Marādah
Jālū
Zillah
Libyan Desert
Libyan Plateau
EGYPT
CAIRO
Pyramids of Giza
Helwān
El Gîza
El Şaff
Beni Mazâr
Sinai
Abu Zenima
Jabal ash Shifā'
Al 'Aqabah
Gulf of Aqaba
Jazīrat Tīrān
Sharm el Sheikh
Rās Muhammad
Hurghada
Red Sea
Būr Safāga
Quseir
Marsa 'Alam
Bawiti
El Minya
El Fashn
El Minya
Mallawi
Dairût
Asyûṭ
Abnûb
Sohâg
Akhmîm
Girga
Qena
Luxor
Valley of the Kings
Nile
Qaşr Farâfra
al Aswad

216

Barcelona

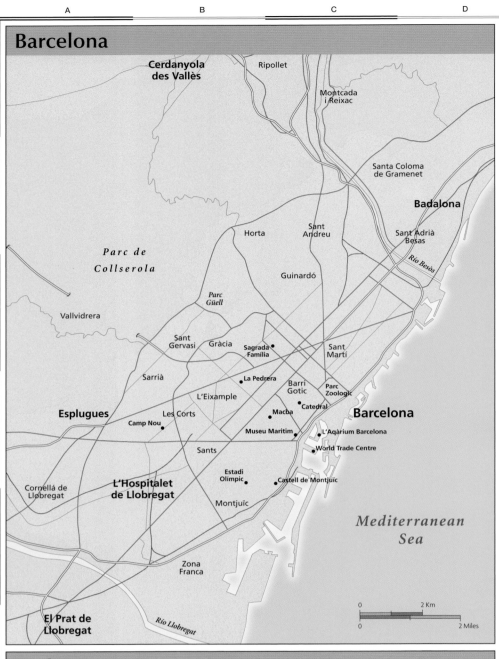

Berlin

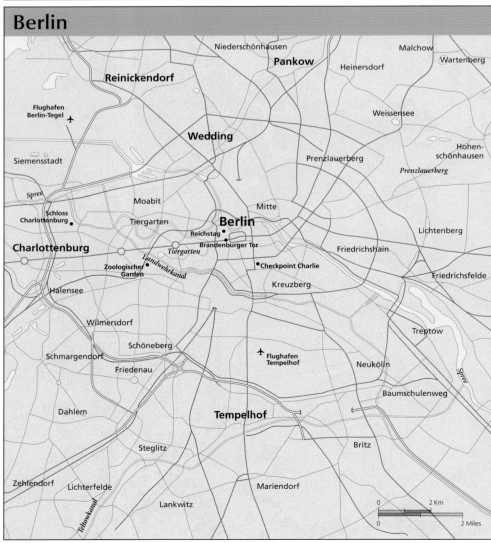

Belgrade

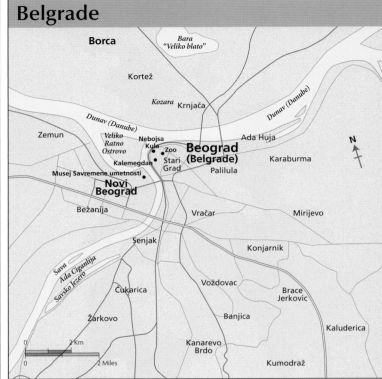

Bucharest

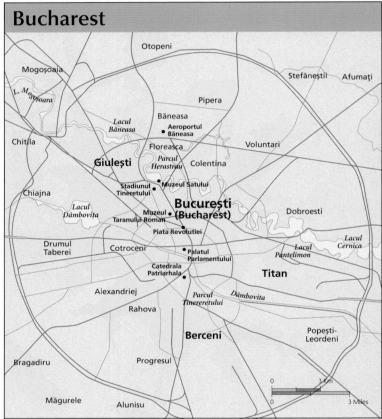

Budapest

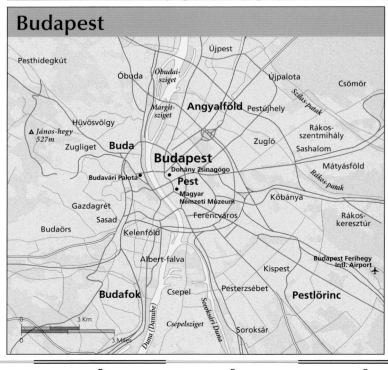

Copenhagen

Vangede
Charlottenlund Slotspark
Gentofte
Charlottenlund
Hellerup
Gladsakse
Søborg
Øresund
N
Gyngemosen
Herlev
Utterslev Mose
Østerbro
København (Copenhagen)
Brønshøj
Nørrebro
Kastellet
Islev
Rosenborg Slot
Amalienborg
Vanløse
Charlottenborg
Rødovre
Frederiksberg
Tivoli
Christianshavn
Damhussøen
Frederiksberg Slot
Valby
Sundbyerne
Brøndbyøster
Glostrup
Sydhavnen
Amagerbro
0 2 Km
0 2 Miles
Hvidovre
Amager Fælled
Kastrup

Kiev

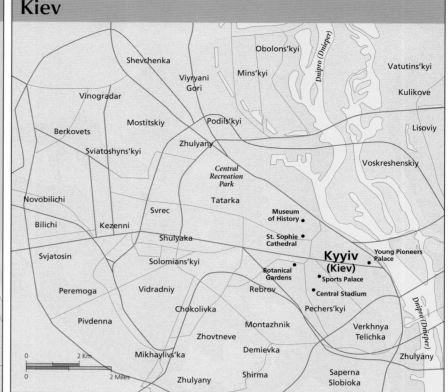

Shevchenka
Obolons'kyi
Dnipro (Dnieper)
Vatutins'kyi
Mins'kyi
Viryyani Gori
Vinogradar
Kulikove
Mostitskiy
Podils'kyi
Berkovets
Zhulyany
Lisoviy
Sviatoshyns'kyi
Central Recreation Park
Voskreshenskiy
Novobilichi
Svrec
Tatarka
Museum of History
Bilichi
Kezenni
St. Sophie Cathedral
Shulyaka
Kyyiv (Kiev)
Young Pioneers Palace
Svjatosin
Solomians'kyi
Botanical Gardens
Sports Palace
Peremoga
Vidradniy
Rebrov
Central Stadium
Pivdenna
Chokolivka
Pechers'kyi
Montazhnik
Verkhnya Telichka
Dnipro (Dnieper)
0 2 Km
Mikhaylivs'ka
Zhovtneve
Demievka
Zhulyany
0 2 Miles
Zhulyany
Shirma
Saperna Slobioka

London

Watford
Enfield
Barnet
Roding
Edmonton
Chingford
Chigwell
Lea
Tottenham
Romford
Harrow
Hendon
Ruislip
Hampstead
Hackney
Ilford
Wembley
Camden
Dagenham
Hillingdon
Ealing
British Museum
Holborn
London City Airport
Southall
Acton
London
St Paul's Cathedral
Tower of London
Buckingham Palace
Thames
Hammersmith
Kensington
Palace of Westminster
Woolwich
Hounslow
Chelsea
Lambeth
Greenwich
Heathrow Airport
Fulham
Camberwell
Bexley
Richmond upon Thames
Wandsworth
Lewisham
Richmond Park
Tooting
Sidcup
Thames
Wimbledon
Streatham
Bromley
Kingston-upon-Thames
Merton
Beckenham
Croydon
Weybridge
Esher
Sutton
Orpington
0 5 Km
Epsom
Purley
0 5 Miles

Lisbon

Carnide
Aeroporto da Portela
Moscavide
Amadora
Estádio Benfica
Benfica
Campo Grande
Olivais
Damaia
Alvalade
Monsanto 228m
Campo Pequeno
Parque Florestal de Monsanto
Museu Calouste Gulbenkian
Campolide
Parque Eduardo VII
Alto do Pina
Ajuda
Alcântara
Estefânia
Anjos
Santo Amaro
Bairro Lopes
Basilica da Estrela
Lisboa (Lisbon)
Castelo de São Jorge
Sé Catedral
Praça do Comércio
N
Rio Tejo
Cristo-Rei
Almada
0 1 Km
0 1 Miles

Madrid

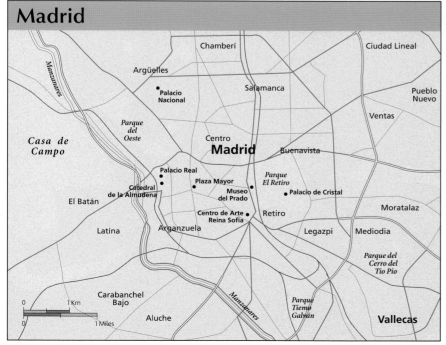

Chamberí
Ciudad Lineal
Argüelles
Manzanares
Palacio Nacional
Salamanca
Pueblo Nuevo
Parque del Oeste
Ventas
Casa de Campo
Centro
Buenavista
Madrid
Palacio Real
Plaza Mayor
Parque El Retiro
Catedral de la Almudena
Museo del Prado
Palacio de Cristal
El Batán
Centro de Arte Reina Sofía
Retiro
Moratalaz
Latina
Arganzuela
Legazpi
Mediodia
Manzanares
Parque del Cerro del Tio Pio
0 1 Km
Carabanchel Bajo
Parque Tierno Galván
0 1 Miles
Aluche
Vallecas

Minsk

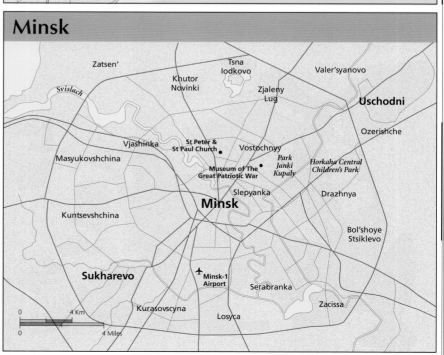

Zatsen'
Tsna Iodkovo
Valer'syanovo
Khutor Novinki
Svislach
Zjaleny Lug
Uschodni
Ozerishche
Vjashinka
St Peter & St Paul Church
Vostochnyy
Park Janki Kupaly
Horkaha Central Children's Park
Masyukovshchina
Museum of The Great Patriotic War
Slepyanka
Drazhnya
Minsk
Kuntsevshchina
Bol'shoye Stsiklevo
Minsk-1 Airport
Sukharevo
Serabranka
Zacissa
0 4 Km
Kurasovscyna
Losyca
0 4 Miles

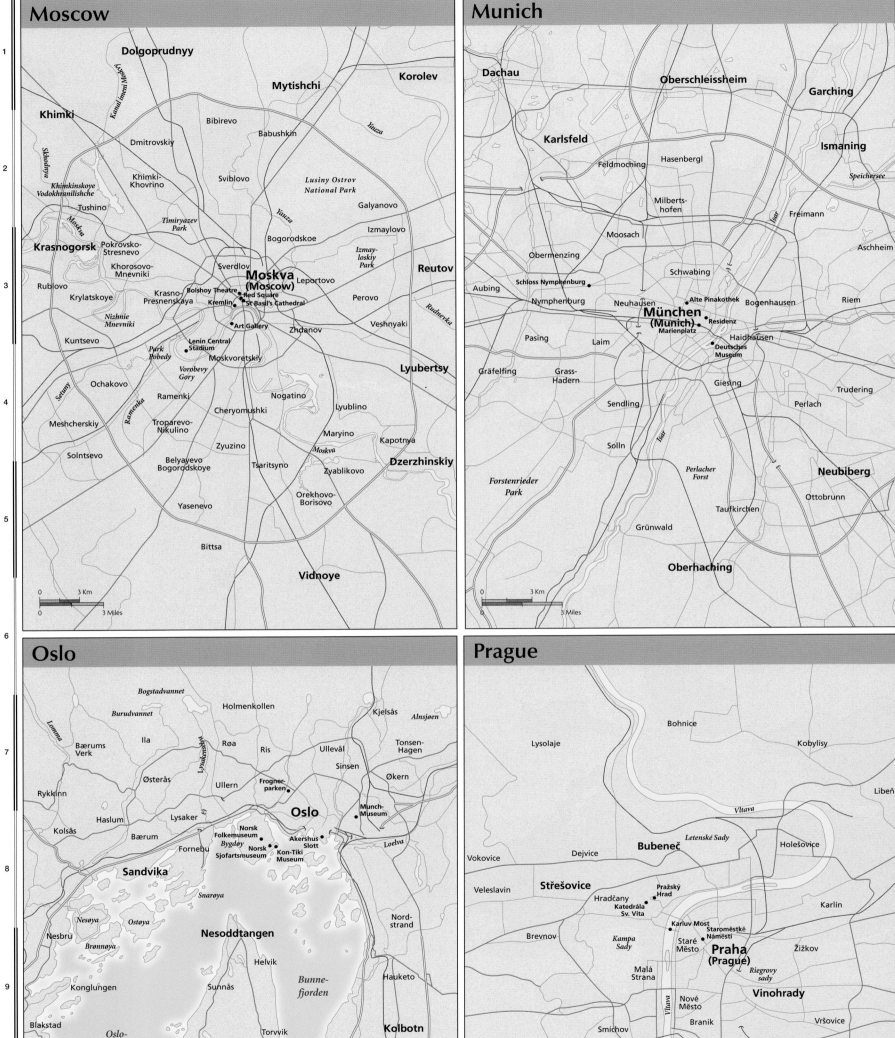

Moscow

Dolgoprudnyy
Mytishchi
Korolev
Khimki
Bibirevo
Babushkin
Dmitrovskiy
Yauza
Khimki-Khovrino
Sviblovo
Lusiny Ostrov National Park
Khimkinskoye Vodokhranilishche
Galyanovo
Tushino
Timiryazev Park
Yauza
Izmaylovo
Moskva
Krasnogorsk
Pokrovsko-Stresnevo
Bogorodskoe
Izmayloskiy Park
Khorosovo-Mnevniki
Sverdlov
Reutov
Rublovo
Moskva (Moscow)
Leportovo
Krasno-Presnenskaya
Bolshoy Theatre
Red Square
St Basil's Cathedral
Krylatskoye
Kremlin
Perovo
Nizhnie Mnevniki
Art Gallery
Zhdanov
Veshnyaki
Rudnevka
Kuntsevo
Lenin Central Stadium
Park Pobedy
Vorobevy Gory
Moskvoretskiy
Lyubertsy
Setuny
Ochakovo
Ramenki
Nogatino
Meshcherskiy
Ramenka
Troparevo-Nikulino
Cheryomushki
Lyublino
Maryino
Zyuzino
Moskva
Kapotnya
Solntsevo
Belyayevo Bogorodskoye
Tsaritsyno
Zyablikovo
Dzerzhinskiy
Yasenevo
Orekhovo-Borisovo
Bittsa
Vidnoye

0 3 Km
0 3 Miles

Munich

Dachau
Oberschleissheim
Garching
Karlsfeld
Ismaning
Feldmoching
Hasenbergl
Speichersee
Milberts-hofen
Freimann
Moosach
Aschheim
Obermenzing
Schwabing
Aubing
Schloss Nymphenburg
Alte Pinakothek
Bogenhausen
Riem
Nymphenburg
Neuhausen
München (Munich)
Residenz
Pasing
Laim
Marienplatz
Haidhausen
Gräfelfing
Grass-Hadern
Deutsches Museum
Giesing
Trudering
Sendling
Perlach
Solln
Isar
Perlacher Forst
Neubiberg
Forstenrieder Park
Taufkirchen
Ottobrunn
Grünwald
Oberhaching

0 3 Km
0 3 Miles

Oslo

Bogstadvannet
Holmenkollen
Kjelsås
Alnsjøen
Burudvannet
Ila
Røa
Ris
Ullevål
Tonsen-Hagen
Bærums Verk
Lysakerelva
Sinsen
Økern
Rykkinn
Østerås
Ullern
Frogner-parken
Oslo
Munch-Museum
Haslum
Lysaker
Norsk Folkemuseum
Akershus Slott
Kolsås
Bærum
Bygdøy
Norsk Sjofartsmuseum
Kon-Tiki Museum
Loelva
Fornebu
Sandvika
Snarøya
Nord-strand
Nesøya
Ostøya
Nesbru
Nesoddtangen
Brønnøya
Helvik
Konglungen
Sunnås
Bunne-fjorden
Hauketo
Blakstad
Oslo-fjorden
Torvvik
Kolbotn
Bjerkås
Gjersjøen
Fjellstrand
Blylaget
Oppegård
Nebba

0 2 Km
0 2 Miles

Prague

Bohnice
Kobylisy
Lysolaje
Libeň
Vltava
Bubeneč
Holešovice
Vokovice
Dejvice
Veleslavin
Střešovice
Pražský Hrad
Karlín
Hradčany
Katedrála Sv. Vita
Brevnov
Karluv Most
Staroměstkě Náměstí
Žižkov
Kampa Sady
Staré Město
Praha (Prague)
Malá Strana
Nové Město
Riegrovy sady
Vinohrady
Vltava
Smíchov
Branik
Vršovice
Vyšehrad
Jinonice
Radlice
Michle
Podolí

0 1 Km
0 1 Miles

EUROPE

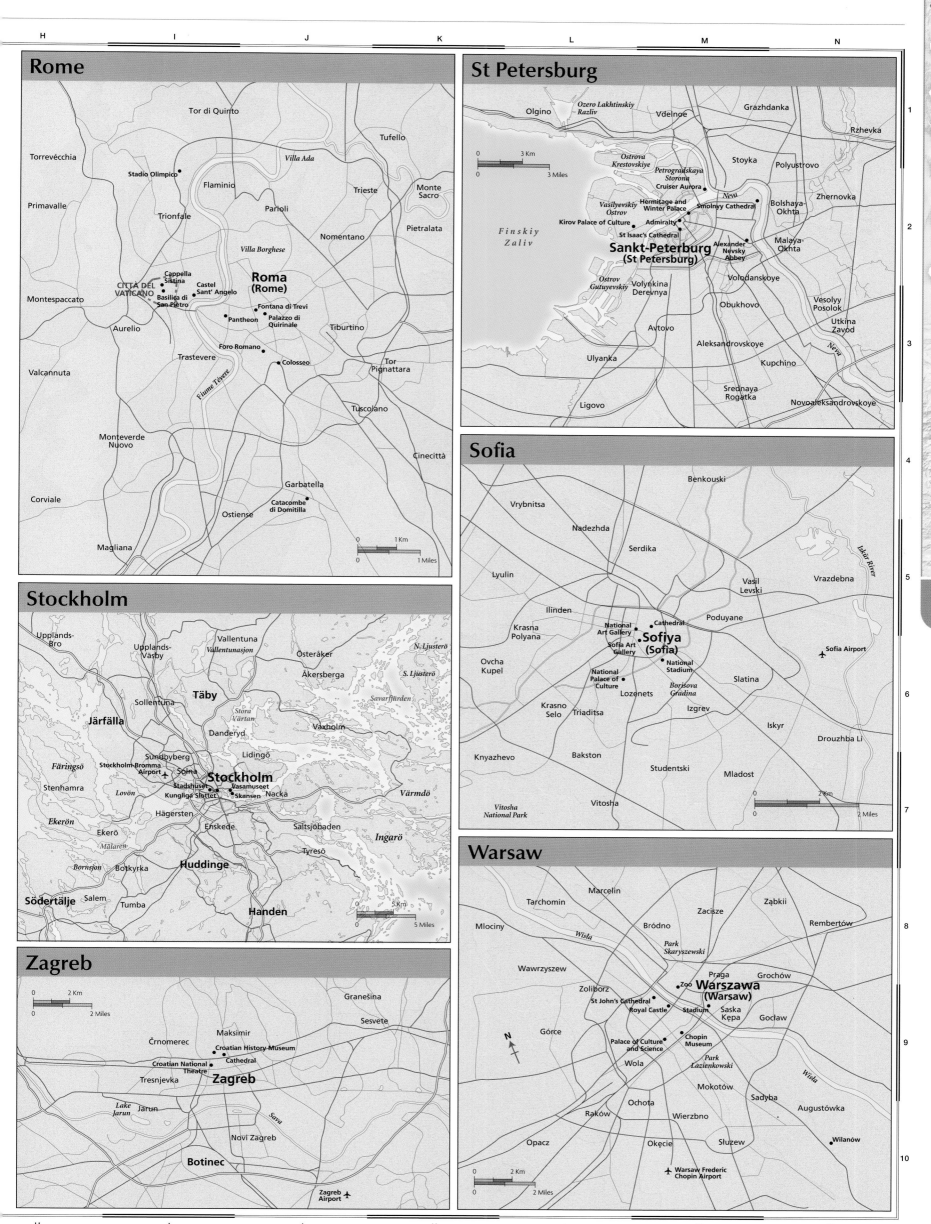

ASIA

Asia is the world's largest continent with a total area of 16,838,365 sq miles (43,608,000 sq km) It comprises 49 separate countries, including 97% of Turkey and 72% of the Russian Federation. Almost 60% of the world's population lives in Asia.

FACTFILE

N **Most Northerly Point:** Mys Articesku, Russia 81° 12' N
S **Most Southerly Point:** Pulau Pamana, Indonesia 11° S
E **Most Easterly Point:** Mys Dezhneva, Russia 169° 40' W
W **Most Westerly Point:** Bozca Adası, Turkey 26° 2' E

Largest Lakes:
1 Caspian Sea, Asia/Europe 143,243 sq miles (371,000 sq km)
2 Lake Baikal, Russian Federation 11,776 sq miles (30,500 sq km)
3 Lake Balkhash, Kazakhstan/China 7115 sq miles (18,428 sq km)
4 Aral Sea, Kazakhstan/Uzbekistan 6625 sq miles (17,160 sq km)
5 Tonlé Sap, Cambodia 3861 sq miles (10,000 sq km)

Longest Rivers:
1 Yangtze, China 3915 miles (6299 km)
2 Yellow River, China 3395 miles (5464 km)
3 Mekong, SE Asia 2749 miles (4425 km)
4 Lena, Russian Federation 2734 miles (4400 km)
5 Yenisey, Russian Federation 2541 miles (4090 km)

Largest Islands:
1 Borneo, Brunie/Indonesia/Malaysia 292,222 sq miles (757,050 sq km)
2 Sumatra, Indonesia 202,300 sq miles (524,000 sq km)
3 Honshu, Japan 88,800 sq miles (230,000 sq km)
4 Sulawesi, Indonesia 73,057 sq miles (189,218 sq km)
5 Java, Indonesia 53,589 sq miles (138,794 sq km)

Highest Points:
1 Mount Everest, China/Nepal 29,035 ft (8850 m)
2 K2, China/Pakistan 28,253 ft (8611 m)
3 Kangchenjunga I, India/Nepal 28,210 ft (8598 m)
4 Lhotse, Nepal 27,939 ft (8516 m)
5 Makalu I, China/Nepal 27,767 ft (8463 m)

Lowest Point:
▼ Dead Sea, Israel/Jordan -1286 ft (-392 m) below sea level

Highest recorded temperature:
⊕ Tirat Tsvi, Israel 129°F (54°C)

Lowest recorded temperature:
⊖ Verkhoyansk, Russian Federation -90°F (-68°C)

Wettest Place:
Cherrapunji, India 450 in (11,430 mm)

Driest Place:
⊖ Aden, Yemen 1.8 in (46 mm)

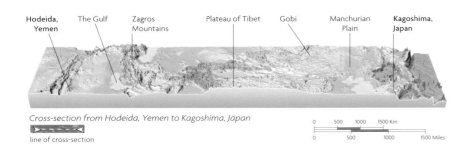

Cross-section from Hodeida, Yemen to Kagoshima, Japan

▰▰▰▰▰ line of cross-section

| 0 | 500 | 1000 | 1500 Km |
| 0 | 500 | 1000 | 1500 Miles |

Political

Asia is the world's largest continent, encompassing many different and discrete realms, from the desert Arab lands of the southwest to the subtropical archipelago of Indonesia; from the vast barren wastes of Siberia to the fertile river valleys of China and South Asia, seats of some of the world's most ancient civilizations. The collapse of the Soviet Union has fragmented the north of the continent into the Siberian portion of the Russian Federation, and the new republics of Central Asia. Strong religious traditions heavily influence the politics of South and Southwest Asia. Hindu and Muslim rivalries threaten to upset the political equilibrium in South Asia where India – in terms of population – remains the world's largest democracy. Communist China, another population giant, is reasserting its position as a world political and economic power, while on its doorstep, the dynamic Pacific Rim countries, led by Japan, continue to assert their worldwide economic force.

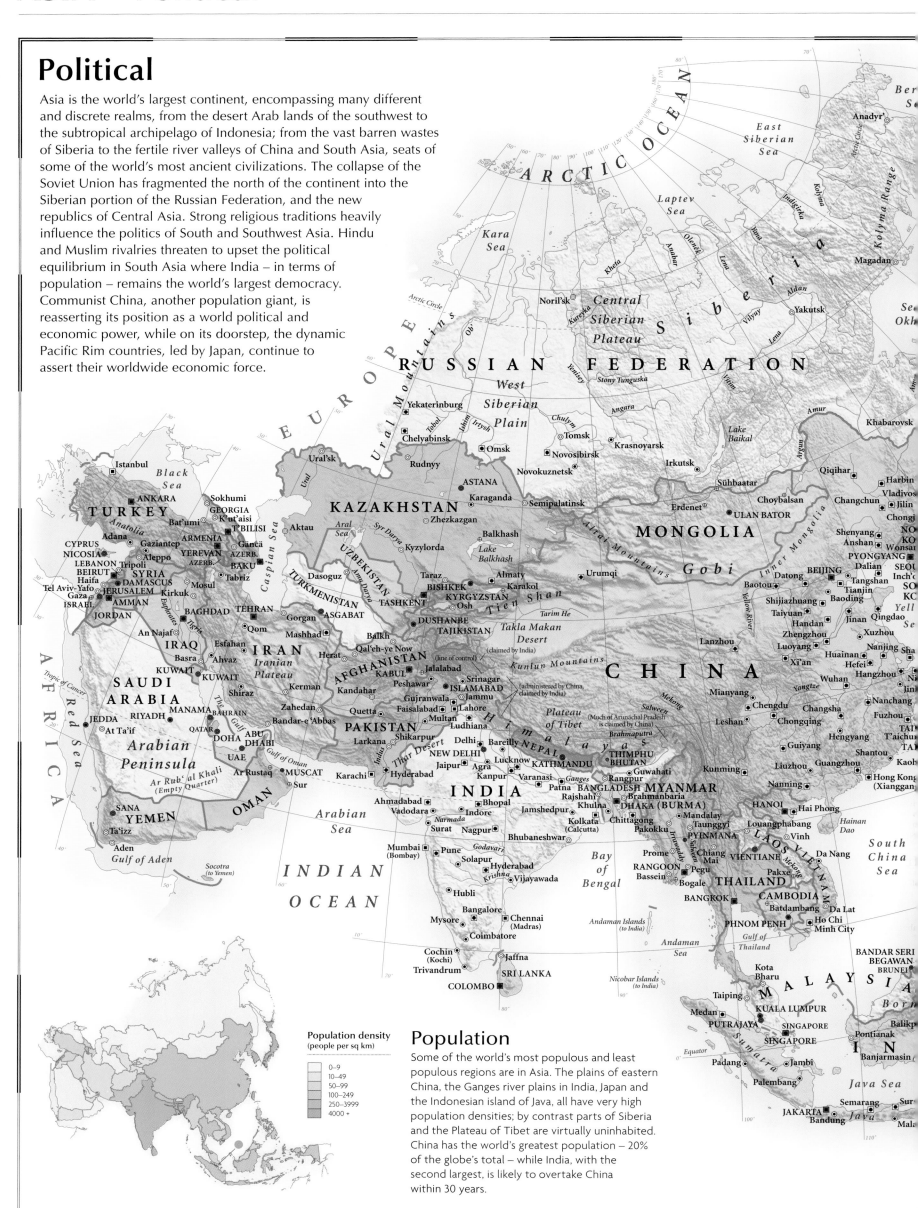

Population density
(people per sq km)

- 0–9
- 10–49
- 50–99
- 100–249
- 250–3999
- 4000 +

Population

Some of the world's most populous and least populous regions are in Asia. The plains of eastern China, the Ganges river plains in India, Japan and the Indonesian island of Java, all have very high population densities; by contrast parts of Siberia and the Plateau of Tibet are virtually uninhabited. China has the world's greatest population – 20% of the globe's total – while India, with the second largest, is likely to overtake China within 30 years.

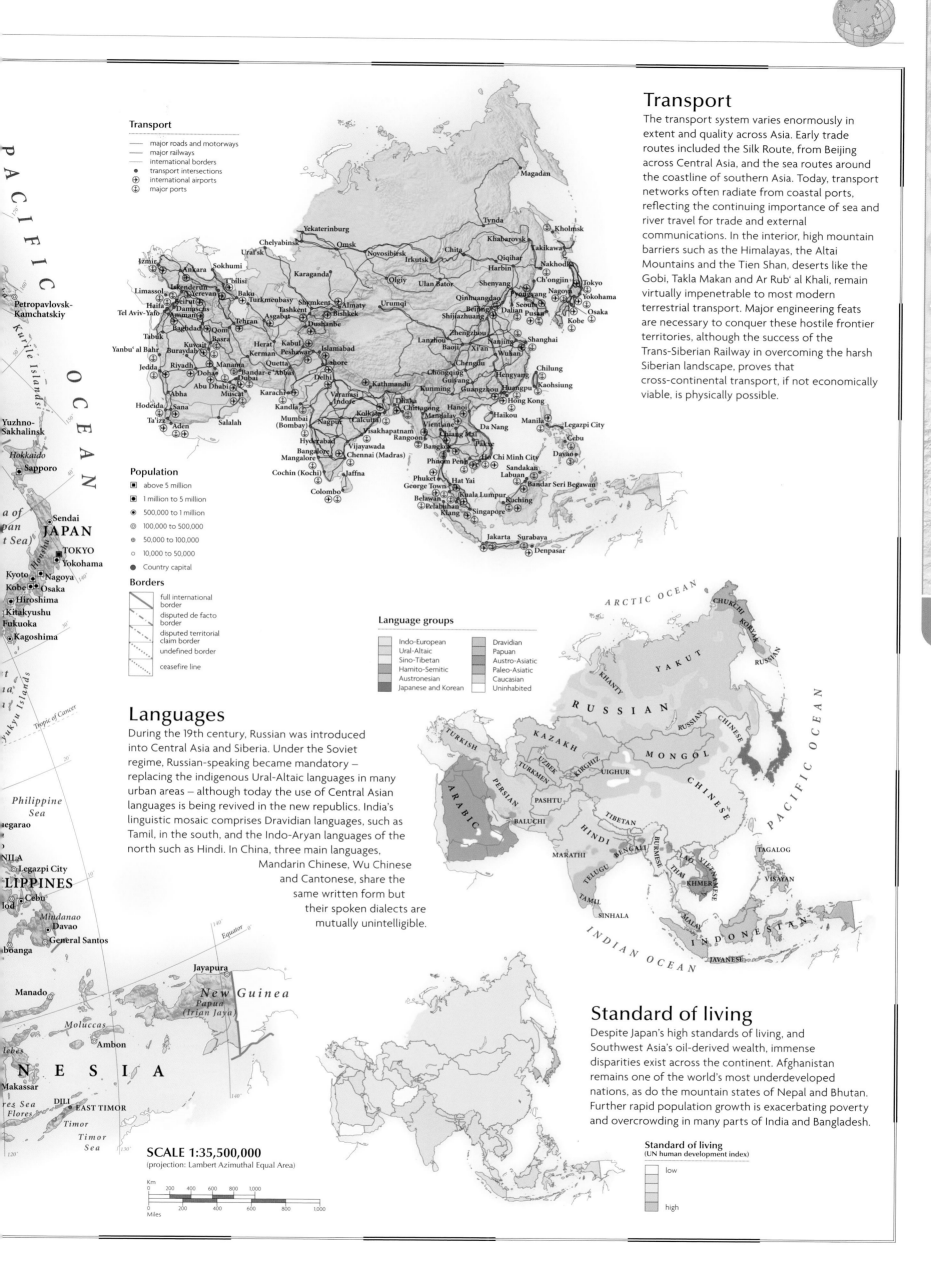

Transport

The transport system varies enormously in extent and quality across Asia. Early trade routes included the Silk Route, from Beijing across Central Asia, and the sea routes around the coastline of southern Asia. Today, transport networks often radiate from coastal ports, reflecting the continuing importance of sea and river travel for trade and external communications. In the interior, high mountain barriers such as the Himalayas, the Altai Mountains and the Tien Shan, deserts like the Gobi, Takla Makan and Ar Rub' al Khali, remain virtually impenetrable to most modern terrestrial transport. Major engineering feats are necessary to conquer these hostile frontier territories, although the success of the Trans-Siberian Railway in overcoming the harsh Siberian landscape, proves that cross-continental transport, if not economically viable, is physically possible.

Transport
— major roads and motorways
— major railways
— international borders
• transport intersections
⊕ international airports
⊕ major ports

Population
▪ above 5 million
▫ 1 million to 5 million
◉ 500,000 to 1 million
◍ 100,000 to 500,000
⊕ 50,000 to 100,000
○ 10,000 to 50,000
● Country capital

Borders
full international border
disputed de facto border
disputed territorial claim border
undefined border
ceasefire line

Language groups
Indo-European
Ural-Altaic
Sino-Tibetan
Hamito-Semitic
Austronesian
Japanese and Korean
Dravidian
Papuan
Austro-Asiatic
Paleo-Asiatic
Caucasian
Uninhabited

Languages

During the 19th century, Russian was introduced into Central Asia and Siberia. Under the Soviet regime, Russian-speaking became mandatory – replacing the indigenous Ural-Altaic languages in many urban areas – although today the use of Central Asian languages is being revived in the new republics. India's linguistic mosaic comprises Dravidian languages, such as Tamil, in the south, and the Indo-Aryan languages of the north such as Hindi. In China, three main languages, Mandarin Chinese, Wu Chinese and Cantonese, share the same written form but their spoken dialects are mutually unintelligible.

Standard of living

Despite Japan's high standards of living, and Southwest Asia's oil-derived wealth, immense disparities exist across the continent. Afghanistan remains one of the world's most underdeveloped nations, as do the mountain states of Nepal and Bhutan. Further rapid population growth is exacerbating poverty and overcrowding in many parts of India and Bangladesh.

Standard of living
(UN human development index)
low
high

SCALE 1:35,500,000
(projection: Lambert Azimuthal Equal Area)

Km
0 200 400 600 800 1,000

Miles
0 200 400 600 800 1,000

ASIA – Physical

ASIA

208

SCALE 1:47,500,000
(projection: Gall Stereographic)

0   500   1000   1500 Km
0   500   1000   1500 Miles

Climate

The climate of Asia exhibits marked differences from region to region, with freezing polar conditions in the north, hot and cold deserts in central regions and subtropical conditions throughout the south. Much of this variation can be attributed to enormous mountain barriers and internal depressions found across the continent. Monsoon winds, which reverse semi-annually, cause alternate wet and dry seasons across southern Asia. These air masses moving north from the ocean are stripped of their moisture over the Himalayas causing arid conditions across the Plateau of Tibet. Both the south and east are susceptible to tropical cyclones or typhoons.

Average Rainfall

January rainfall

July rainfall

Rainfall

- 0–25 mm (0–1 in)
- 25–50 mm (1–2 in)
- 50–100 mm (2–4 in)
- 100–200 mm (4–8 in)
- 200–300 mm (8–12 in)
- 300–400 mm (12–16 in)
- 400–500 mm (16–20 in)
- more than 500 mm (20 in)

Average Temperature

January temperature

July temperature

Temperature

- below -30°C (-22°F)
- -30 to -20°C (-22 to -4°F)
- -20 to -10°C (-4 to 14°F)
- -10 to 0°C (14 to 32°F)
- 0 to 10°C (32 to 50°F)
- 10 to 20°C (50 to 68°F)
- 20 to 30°C (68 to 86°F)
- above 30°C (86°F)

Climate

- tundra
- subarctic
- cool continental
- warm humid
- mediterranean
- semi-arid
- arid
- humid equatorial
- tropical

- daily hours of sunshine, January
- daily hours of sunshine, July
- cyclone
- typhoon
- cold/dry monsoon
- warm/wet monsoon
- cold wind

Using the land and sea

- cropland
- desert
- forest
- mountain region
- pasture
- tundra
- wetland
- major conurbations
- cattle
- pigs
- goats
- sheep
- coconuts
- corn (maize)
- cotton
- dates
- fishing
- fruit
- jute
- peanuts
- rice
- rubber
- shellfish
- soya beans
- sugar beet
- sugar cane
- tea
- timber
- wheat

Environmental issues

The transformation of Uzbekistan by the former Soviet Union into the world's fifth largest producer of cotton led to the diversion of several major rivers for irrigation. Starved of this water, the Aral Sea diminished in volume by over 75% since 1960, irreversibly altering the ecology of the area. Heavy industries in eastern China have polluted coastal waters, rivers and urban air, while in Myanmar (Burma), Malaysia and Indonesia, ancient hardwood rainforests are felled faster than they can regenerate.

Environmental issues

- tropical forest
- forest destroyed
- desert
- desertification
- acid rain
- polluted rivers
- marine pollution
- heavy marine pollution
- radioactive contamination
- poor urban air quality

Landuse

Vast areas of Asia remain uncultivated as a result of unsuitable climatic and soil conditions. In favourable areas such as river deltas, farming is intensive. Rice is the staple crop of most Asian countries, grown in paddy fields on waterlogged alluvial plains and terraced hillsides, and often irrigated for higher yields. Across the black earth region of the Eurasian steppe in southern Siberia and Kazakhstan, wheat farming is the dominant activity. Cash crops, like tea in Sri Lanka and dates in the Arabian Peninsula, are grown for export, and provide valuable income. The sovereignty of the rich fishing grounds in the South China Sea is disputed by China, Malaysia, Taiwan, the Philippines and Vietnam, because of potential oil reserves.

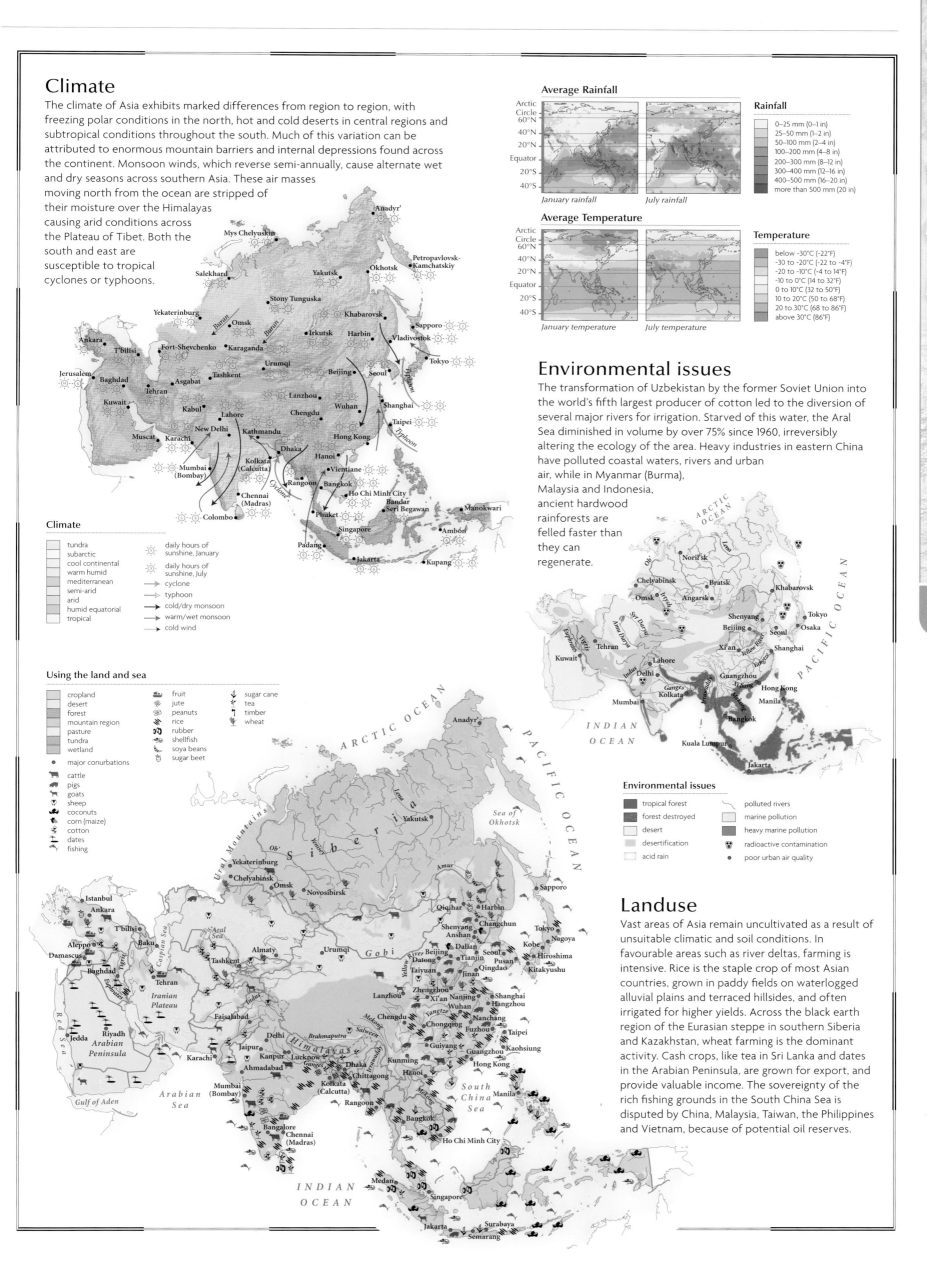

ASIA

1   BOSPORUS, TURKEY
The Bosporus provides the only outlet for the Black Sea, linking it with the Sea of Marmara to the south and then with the Mediterranean Sea via the Dardanelles.

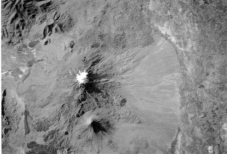

2   MOUNT ARARAT, TURKEY
Said to be the resting place for Noah's Ark, this extinct volcanic massif lies in the far east of Turkey.

3   LAKE BALKHASH, KAZAKHSTAN
Still covered in winter ice in this image, this lakes lies in a dry desert region and has no outlet.

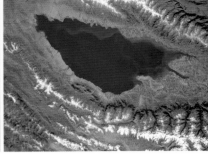

4   OZERO ISSYK-KUL', KYRGYZSTAN
Against the dry slopes of the Tien Shan mountains to the south this lake appears bright blue.

ASIA

210

9   KUWAIT'S OILFIELDS, KUWAIT
The dark plumes are smoke rising from the 700 wells set alight by Iraqi forces during the Gulf War of 1991.

10   PALM ISLAND, UNITED ARAB EMIRATES
This luxury housing development and tourist resort, one mile (1.6 km) off the seafront of Dubai, is built from sediments dredged from the nearby port of Jebel Ali.

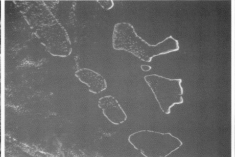

11   MALDIVES
The Maldives consist of 1300 coral formations in 19 atolls and stretch over 1491 miles (2400 km).

12   KARACHI, PAKISTAN
Pakistan's main seaport and former capital lies to the northwest of the delta of the Indus river.

THREE GORGES DAM, CHINA
Seen here during its construction in 2000, the world's largest dam is designed to tame the Yangtze river which has regularly flooded.

5

BEIJING, CHINA
China's ancient capital was laid out on a grid pattern centred on the Forbidden City and its streets are picked out in this winter image by snowfall.

6

MOUNT FUJI, JAPAN
The steep, symmetrical, snow-capped volcano last erupted in 1707.

7

VULKAN KLYUCHEVSKAYA SOPKA,
RUSSIAN FEDERATION
The Kamchatka Peninsula's highest and most active volcano last erupted in 1994.

8

MOUNT EVEREST, CHINA/NEPAL
The world's highest mountain at 29,035 ft (8850 m) straddles the border between China and Nepal.

13

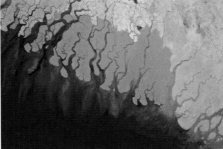

MOUTHS OF THE GANGES, BANGLADESH/INDIA
Stretching across the northern end of the Bay of Bengal, this river delta contains the Sundarbans, the world's largest mangrove forest, which appears as a rich green area.

14

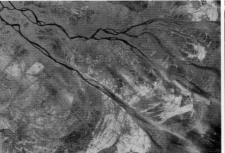

MEKONG DELTA, VIETNAM
The Mekong river flows over 2494 miles (4000 km) from the Plateau of Tibet before crossing Vietnam to reach the South China Sea.

15

HONG KONG, CHINA
Handed back to China by the British in 1997, this city remains east Asia's trade and finance centre.

16

ASIA

212

Map labels:

Napoli (Naples)
Perugia
Terni
L'Aquila
Campobasso
Foggia
Pescara
Bari
Salerno
Potenza
Taranto
Lecce
Cosenza
Split
CROATIA
BOSNIA & HERZEGOVINA
MONTENEGRO
PODGORICA
SERBIA
Kraljevo
Vidin
ROMANIA
Giurgiu
Constanta
Kragujevac
Pleven
Vratsa
Razgrad
Shumen
Dobrich
Varna
Burgas
SOFIYA
BULGARIA
Plovdiv
Stara Zagora
Sliven
Pristina
KOSOVO
Nis
SKOPJE
MACEDONIA
Bitola
TIRANE
ALBANIA
Shkodër
Prizren
Kavala
Thessaloníki (Salonica)
Chalkidikí
Límnos
Tekirdag
Edirne
İstanbul
İzmit
Adapazarı
Zonguldak
Karabük
Kastamonu
Inebolu
Sinop
Bafra
Samsun
Ordu
Trabzon
Rize
Hopa
Bat'umi
Sochi
Tuapse
Maykop
Nevinnomyssk
RUSSIAN FEDERATION
Kislovodsk
Nal'chik
Vladikavkaz
Prokhladny
Black Sea
Sevastopol'
Yalta
Sukhumi
P'ot'i
K'ut'aisi
GEORGIA
T'BILISI
Gyumri
YEREVAN
Tyrrhenian Sea
Stromboli
Isole Eolie
Messina
Reggio di Calabria
Catanzaro
Catania
Siracusa
Ragusa
Sicilia (Sicily)
Monte Etna 3340m
Ionian Sea
Ióna Nisiá (Ionian Islands)
Adriatic Sea
GREECE
Mount Olympus 2917m
Lárisa
Vólos
Évvoia (Euboea)
Athína (ATHENS)
Pátra
Peloponnísos
Kykládes (Cyclades)
Mírtóo Pélagos
Lésvos (Lesbos)
Khíos
İzmir
Manisa
Aydın
Denizli
Marmaris
Ródos (Rhodes)
Kritikó Pélagos (Sea of Crete)
Iráklio
Ágios Nikólaos
Kríti (Crete)
Dodekánisa (Dodecanese)
Balıkesir
Bursa
ANKARA
Eskişehir
Kütahya
Polatlı
Kırıkkale
Çorum
Tokat
Sivas
Erzincan
Erzurum
Ağrı
Muş
Van Gölü
Van
Tatvan
Siirt
Orümiye
Kars
Büyük Ararat (Mount Ararat) 5165m
Afyon
Uşak
Akhisar
Çanakkale
Aksaray
Niğde
Kayseri
Malatya
Elazığ
Diyarbakır
Adıyaman
Batman
Mardin
TURKEY
Anatolia
Tuz Gölü
Konya
Ereğli
Antalya
Alanya
Silifke
Mersin
Tarsus
Adana
Osmaniye
Kahramanmaraş
Gaziantep
Kilis
Şanlıurfa
Al Hasakah
Al Mawşil (Mosul)
Kırıkkale
İsparta
Fínike
Antakya
İskenderun
Halab (Aleppo)
Manbij
Ar Raqqah
Al Jazirah
As Sulaymaniyah
Dayr az Zawr
Kirkūk
CYPRUS
NICOSIA
Lárnaka
Lemesós
Tróodos
TURKISH REPUBLIC OF NORTHERN CYPRUS (recognised only by Turkey)
Al Lādhiqiyah (Latakia)
Idlib
Ḥamāh
Tartūs
Tripoli
Ḥimṣ (Homs)
Tudmur (Palmyra)
Al Fuhaymi
Euphrates
Bayji
Buhayrat ath Tharthar
Ba'qūbah
BAGHDAD
LEBANON
BEYROUTH (BEIRUT)
Mount Hermon 2814m
Dūmā
DIMASHQ (DAMASCUS)
Syrian Desert
IRAQ
Karbalā'
An Najaf
Al Hillah
Hefa (Haifa)
Netanya
Tel Aviv-Yafo
Ashdod
Gaza Strip
ISRAEL
Irbid
'AMMAN
JERUSALEM
Bé'ér Sheva'
Mizpé Ramon
JORDAN
Dead Sea
Ma'ān
Turayf
Al Jawf
Ar'ar
Zahrat al Sama
Al Harrah
SYRIA
Banghāzī (Benghazi)
Al Bayḍā'
Al Jabal al Akhḍar
Ṭubruq
Sidi Barrâni
Khalīj Surt (Gulf of Sirte)
Surt
Ajdābiyā
El 'Alamein
Alexandria
Port Said
Suez Canal
Dumyāṭ (Damietta)
Nile Delta
Zagazig
Tanta
Ismā'iliya
CAIRO
El Gîza
Suez
Gulf of Suez
Sinai
Gebel Mûsa 2285m
Gulf of Aqaba
Elat
Tabūk
Jabal ath Thülth
An Nafūd
Ḥā'il
Buray
Al Madīnah (Medina)
Khaybar
Al Wajh
Yanbu' al Baḥr
Libyan Plateau
Al Jaghbūb
Siwa
Monkhafad el Qattâra (Qattara Depression)
Sahara el Gharbiya (Western Desert)
Beni Suef
El Minya
Bawiṭi
Mallawi
Qaşr Farafra
Asyūt
Sohâg
Nile
Hurghada
Bûr Safâga
Sahara el Gharbiya (Eastern Desert)
EGYPT
Marādah
Jālū
LIBYA
SAHARA
Ramlat Rabyānah
Al Khufrah
Libyan Desert
Mût
El Khârga
Qena
Luxor
Aswân
Lake Nasser
SAUDI ARABIA
Al Madīnah
Al Wajh
Buray
Al Ma...
Tropic of Cancer
Pic Bette 2286m
Gilf Kebir Plateau
Al 'Uwaynāt
Jabal al 'Uwaynāt 1907m
Wadi Halfa
(administered by Sudan)
(administered by Egypt)
Halaib
JIDDAH (JEDDA)
Makkah (Mecca)
Aṭ Ṭā'if
Ḥalabān
Ẓalim
Al Bāḥah
Emi Koussi 3415m
Ennedi
Ounianga Kebir
Faya
Erg du Djourab
Fada
CHAD
Erdi
Akasha
Delgo
Libyan Desert
Nubian Desert
Abu Hamed
Dongola
Shereik
Port Sudan
Suakin
Red Sea
Tathlith
Abhā
Najrān
El 'Atrun
Wadi Howar
Wadi el Milk
Ed Debba
Atbara
Ed Damer
Haiya
Omdurman
KHARTOUM
Khartoum North
Kassala
Keren
ASMARA
ERITREA
Aksum
Mek'ele
SANA
Al Hudaydah (Hodeida)
Zabīd
Bāb el Mandeb
Danakil Desert
Wad Medani
Gedaref
Teseney
Ras Dashen Terara 4620m
ETHIOPIA
Gonder
Bahir Dar
T'ana Hāyk'
Ethiopian Highlands
Abuye Meda 4000m
Desē
Weldiya
Obock
DJIBOUTI
Aseb
Berb...
Abéché
Biltine
Goz-Beïda
Abou-Déïa
Am Timan
Sahel
Birao
CENTRAL AFRICAN REPUBLIC
El Geneina
El Fasher
Kebkabiya
Nyala
Ed Da'ein
Umm Buru
SUDAN
Abeché
Sodiri
En Nahud
Umm Ruwaba
Er Rahad
El Obeid
Rabak
Sennar
Kadugli
El Muglad
Sumeih
Nyala
Ed Damazin
Roseires Resrvoir
Paloich
White Nile (Bahr el Jebel)
Blue Nile (Bahr el Azraq)
Great Rift Valley
Aksum

Elevation scale:
6000m
4000m
3000m
2000m
1000m
500m
250m
100m
Sea Level
−250m
−500m
−1000m

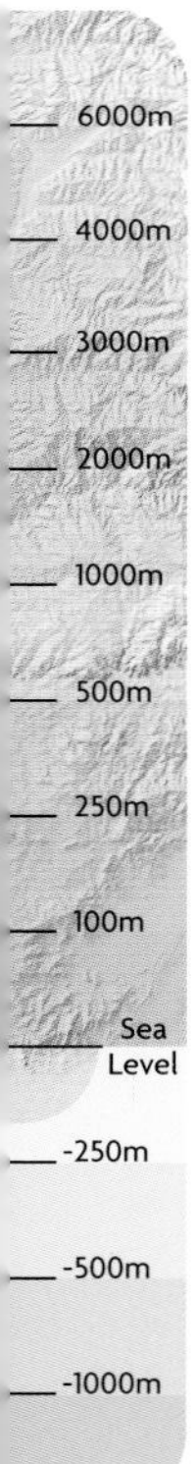

ASIA

214

Map grid references (top): A B C D E F G

189

187

129

Countries and seas:

ROMANIA
BULGARIA
UKRAINE
GREECE
TURKEY
CYPRUS
TURKISH REPUBLIC OF NORTHERN CYPRUS (recognised only by Turkey)
LEBANON
Black Sea
Sea of Azov
Aegean Islands
Mediterranean Sea
Marmara Denizi (Sea of Marmara)
Thracian Sea
Dodekánisa
RESPUBLIKA KRYM

Major cities and places:

București (Bucharest), Pitești, Ploiești, Galați, Brăila, Constanța, Buzău, Râmnicu Vâlcea, Câmpulung, Curtea de Argeș, Târgoviște, Râmnicu Sărat, Focșani, Slatina, Caracal, Corabia, Alexandria, Turnu Măgurele, Giurgiu, Oltenița, Călărași, Silistra, Medgidia, Eforie Sud, Mangalia, Babadag, Tulcea, Izmayil, Kiliya, Reni, Bolhrad, Tatarbunary

Plovdiv, Pleven, Lovech, Troyan, Gabrovo, Veliko Tŭrnovo, Gorna Oryakhovitsa, Tŭrgovishte, Shumen, Razgrad, Ruse, Dobrich, Varna, Burgas, Sliven, Yambol, Stara Zagora, Kazanlŭk, Nova Zagora, Sredets, Elkhovo, Dimitrovgrad, Khaskovo, Kŭrdzhali, Smolyan, Asenovgrad, Chirpan, Kardzhali, Svilengrad, Harmanli

Edirne, Kırklareli, Tekirdağ, İstanbul, Çanakkale, Balıkesir, Bursa, Bilecik, Eskişehir, Kütahya, Manisa, İzmir, Aydın, Denizli, Muğla, Burdur, Isparta, Afyon, Konya, Antalya, Ankara, Çankırı, Kastamonu, Sinop, Samsun, Amasya, Çorum, Tokat, Yozgat, Kırıkkale, Kırşehir, Nevşehir, Aksaray, Kayseri, Niğde, Karaman, Mersin, Adana, Kahramanmaraş, Gaziantep, Kilis, Hatay, Antakya, İskenderun

Nicosia, Lárnaka, Lemesós (Limassol), Páfos, Gazimağusa (Ammóchostos, Famagusta), Girne (Kerýneia)

Al Lādhiqīyah (Latakia), Ṭarṭūs, Ḥamāh, Ḥimṣ (Homs), Idlib, Ḥalab (Aleppo), Tripoli, Beyrouth (Beirut), Dimashq (Damascus)

Sevastopol', Simferopol', Yevpatoriya, Yalta, Feodosiya, Kerch, Sudak, Alushta

Lésvos (Lesbos), Chíos, Sámos, Ikaría, Ródos (Rhodes), Kárpathos, Kós, Kríti, Náxos, Mýkonos

Elevation scale (left):
6000m
4000m
3000m
2000m
1000m
500m
250m
100m
Sea Level
-250m
-500m
-1000m

Grid references (bottom): A B C D E F G

Scale 1:4,300,000
(projection: Lambert Conformal Conic)

0 20 40 60 80 100 Km
0 20 40 60 80 100 Miles

Population
- ■ above 5 million
- ■ 1 million to 5 million
- ● 500,000 to 1 million
- ◎ 100,000 to 500,000
- ⊕ 50,000 to 100,000
- ○ 10,000 to 50,000
- o below 10,000

197

217

228

KRASNODARSKIY KRAY

RUSSIAN FEDERATION

REPUBLIKA KALMYKIYA

KAZAKHSTAN

STAVROPOL'SKIY KRAY

RESPUBLIKA ADYGEYA

KARACHAYEVO-CHERKESSKAYA RESPUBLIKA

KABARDINO-BALKARSKAYA RESPUBLIKA

CHECHENSKAYA RESPUBLIKA

INGUSHSKAYA RESPUBLIKA

RESPUBLIKA SEVERNAYA OSETIYA-ALANIYA

RESPUBLIKA DAGESTAN

ABKHAZIA

GEORGIA

South Ossetia

AJARIA

ARTVIN

ARDAHAN

RIZE

TRABZON

GUMUŞHANE

BAYBURT

ERZURUM

KARS

ARMENIA

AZERBAIJAN

YEREVAN

T'BILISI

BAKI (Baku)

IGDIR

AGRI

ERZINCAN

TUNCELI

BINGÖL

MUŞ

BITLIS

VAN

HAKKARİ

ELAZIĞ

DIYARBAKIR

BATMAN

SIIRT

ŞIRNAK

MARDIN

ŞANLIURFA

AL HASAKAH

DAYR AZ ZAWR

IRAQ

IRAN

AZARBAYJAN-E SHARQI

AZARBAYJAN-E GHARBI

GILAN

ARDABIL

ZANJAN

KORDESTAN

KERMANSHAH

HAMADAN

MARKAZI

LORESTAN

Caspian Sea

Caspian Depression

Nogayskaya Step

BAGHDAD

19,686ft
13,124ft
9843ft
6562ft
3281ft
1640ft
820ft
328ft
Sea Level
-820ft
-6562ft
-13,124ft

The Near East

ASIA

216

TURKEY

SYRIA

CYPRUS

TURKISH REPUBLIC OF
NORTHERN CYPRUS
(recognized only by Turkey)

LEBANON

BEYROUTH
(BEIRUT)

DIMASHQ (DAMASCUS)

ISRAEL

JERUSALEM

JORDAN

EGYPT

SAUDI

Mediterranean Sea

Dead Sea

Gulf of Aqaba

Sinai

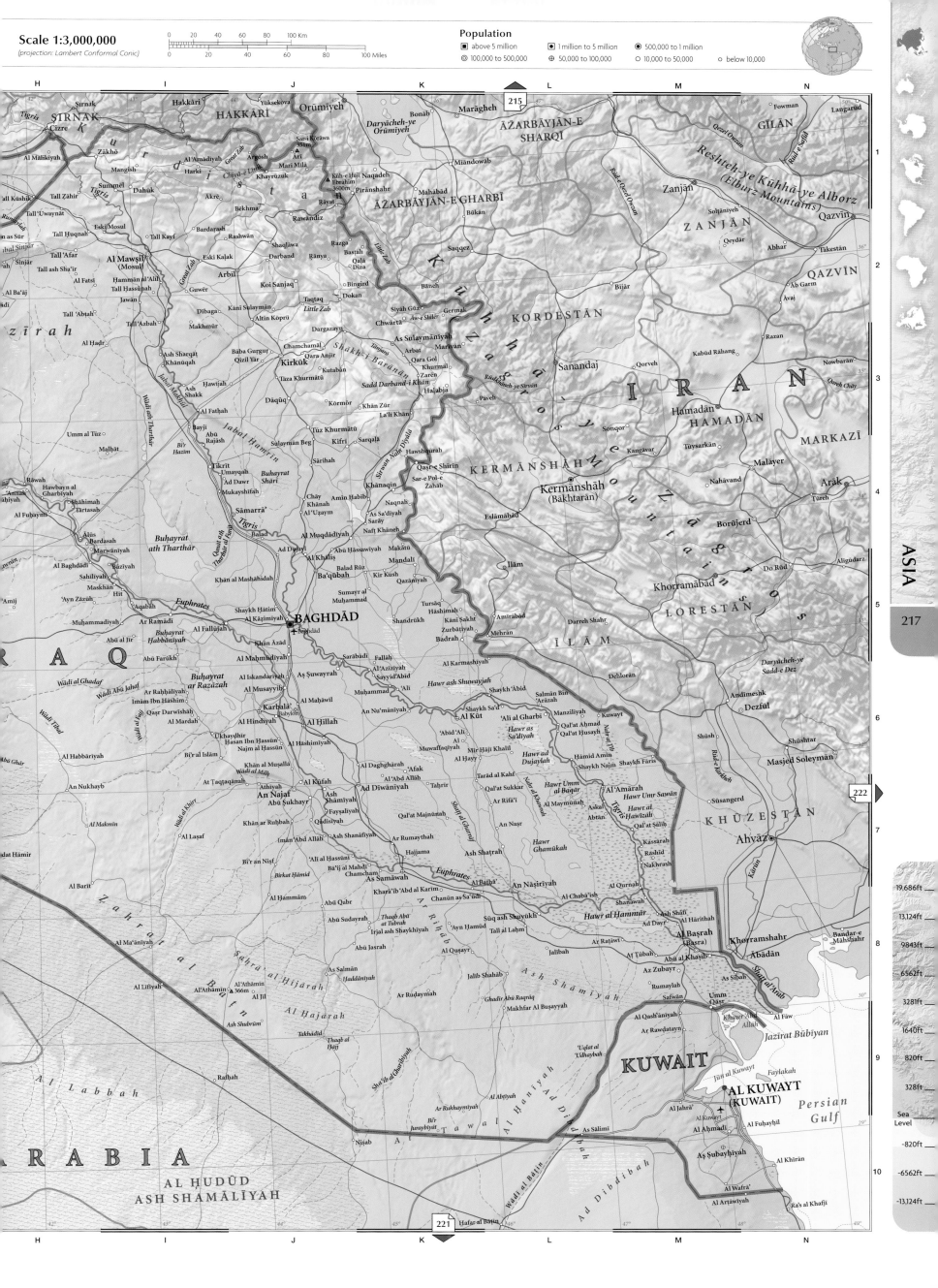

Scale 1:3,000,000
(projection: Lambert Conformal Conic)

0 20 40 60 80 100 Km
0 20 40 60 80 100 Miles

Population

■ above 5 million
▣ 1 million to 5 million
◉ 500,000 to 1 million
◉ 100,000 to 500,000
⊕ 50,000 to 100,000
○ 10,000 to 50,000
○ below 10,000

IRAN

KORDESTĀN

AZARBĀYJĀN-E SHARQĪ

AZARBĀYJĀN-E GHARBI

ZANJĀN

GILĀN

QAZVĪN

MARKAZĪ

HAMADĀN

KERMĀNSHĀH

LORESTĀN

ĪLĀM

KHŪZESTĀN

IRAQ

ARABIA

AL HUDŪD ASH SHAMĀLIYAH

KUWAIT

AL KUWAYT (KUWAIT)

Persian Gulf

19,686ft
13,124ft
9843ft
6562ft
3281ft
1640ft
820ft
328ft
Sea Level
-820ft
-6562ft
-13,124ft

Israel & Lebanon

The Arabian Peninsula

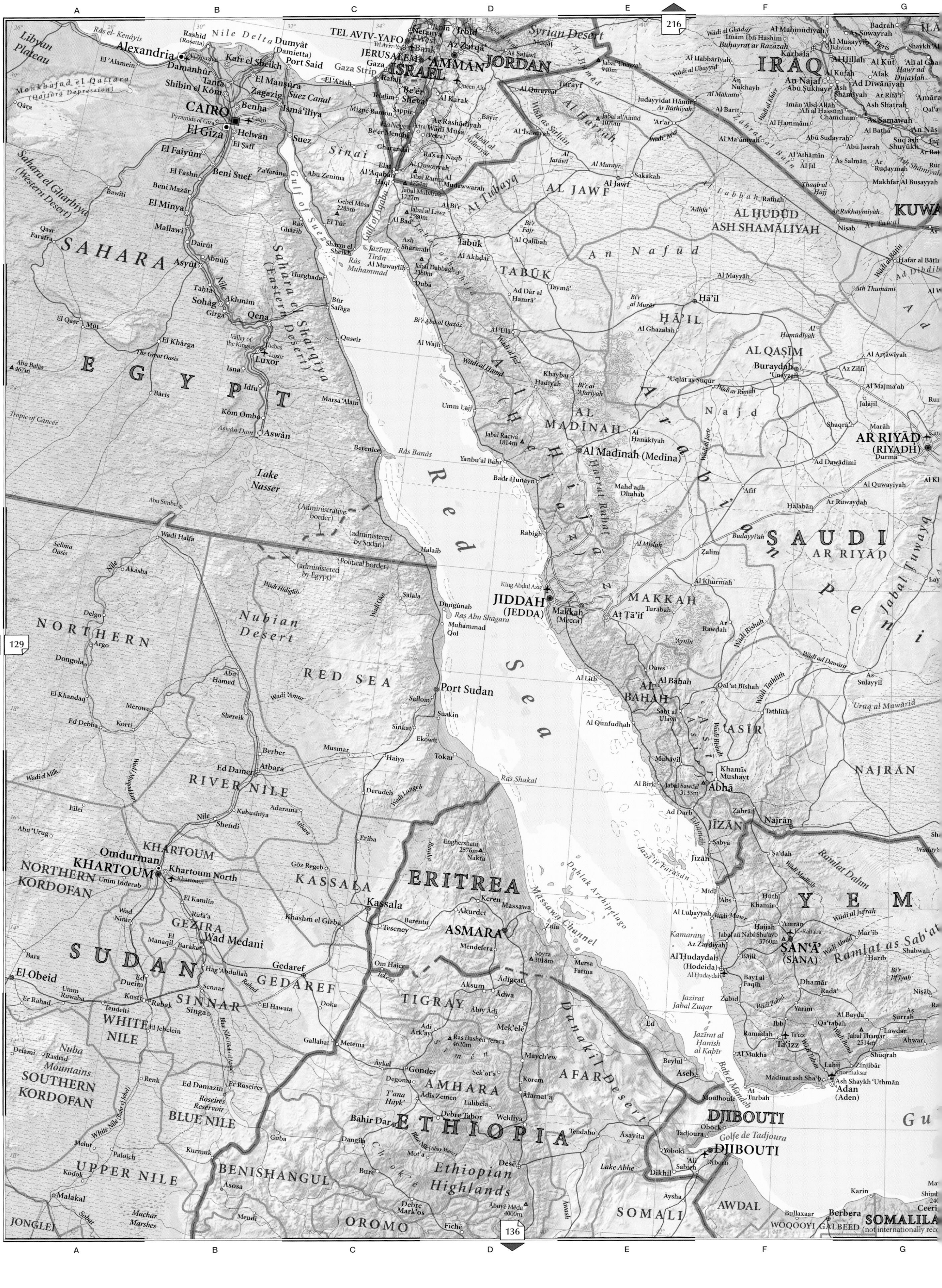

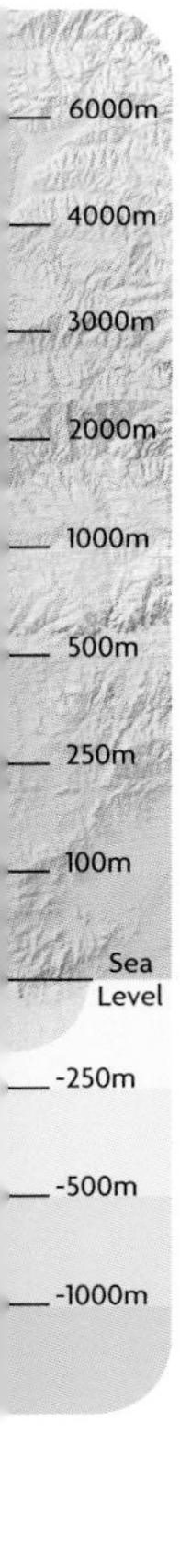

ASIA

222

197
220
220

6000m
4000m
3000m
2000m
1000m
500m
250m
100m
Sea Level
-250m
-500m
-1000m

TURKEY

ARMENIA

AZERBAIJAN

AZER.

YEREVAN

BAKI (BAKU)

SYRIA

IRAQ

BAGHDĀD

Syrian Desert

SAUDI ARABIA

KUWAIT

AL KUWAYT (KUWAIT)

Caspian Sea

TEHRĀN

IRAN

The Gulf

BAHRAIN

AL MANĀMAH (MANAMA)

QATAR

AD DAWHAH (DOHA)

UNITED ARAB EMIRATES

ABŪ ZABY (ABU DHABI)

AR RIYĀD (RIYADH)

Tropic of Cancer

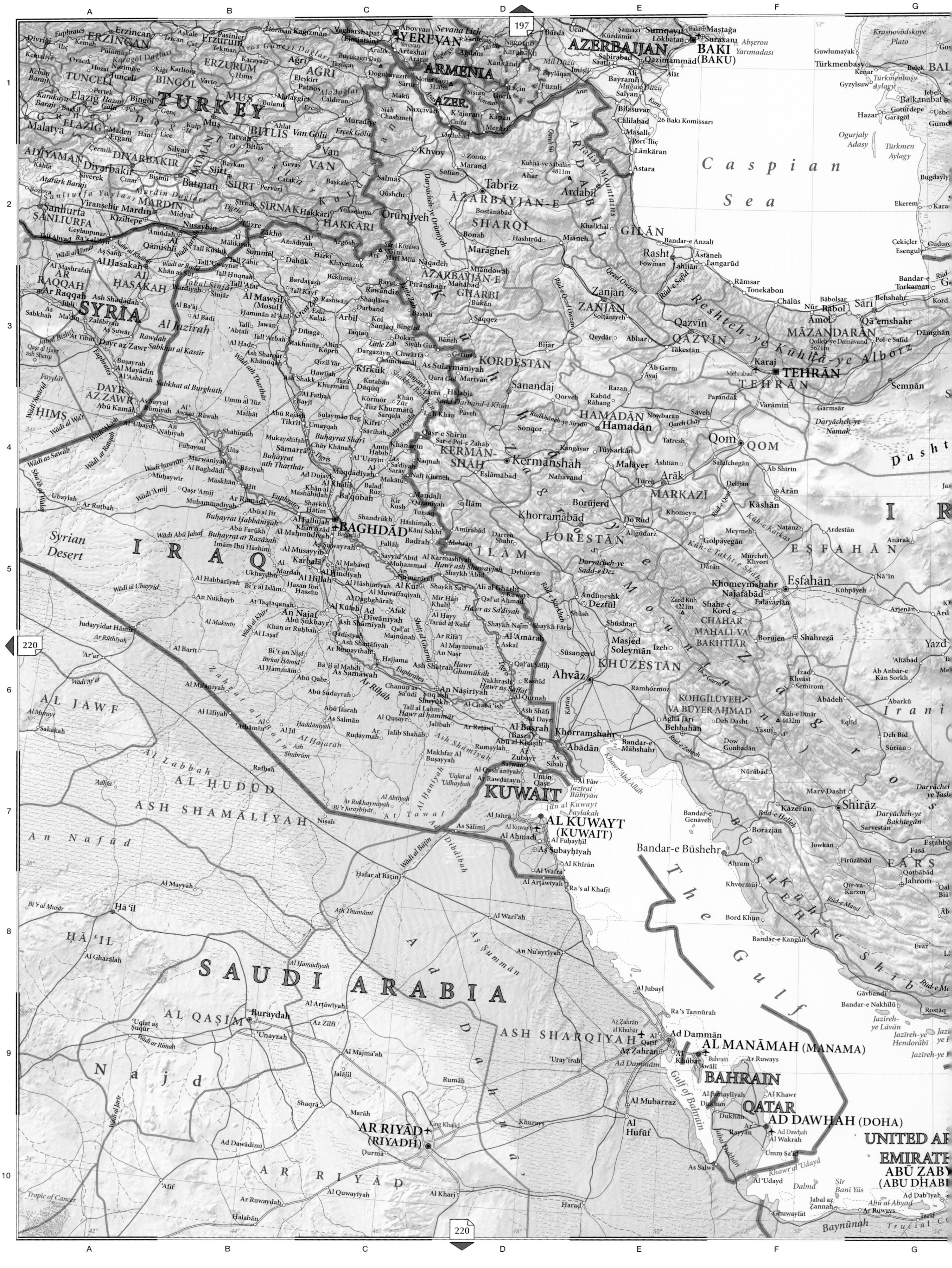

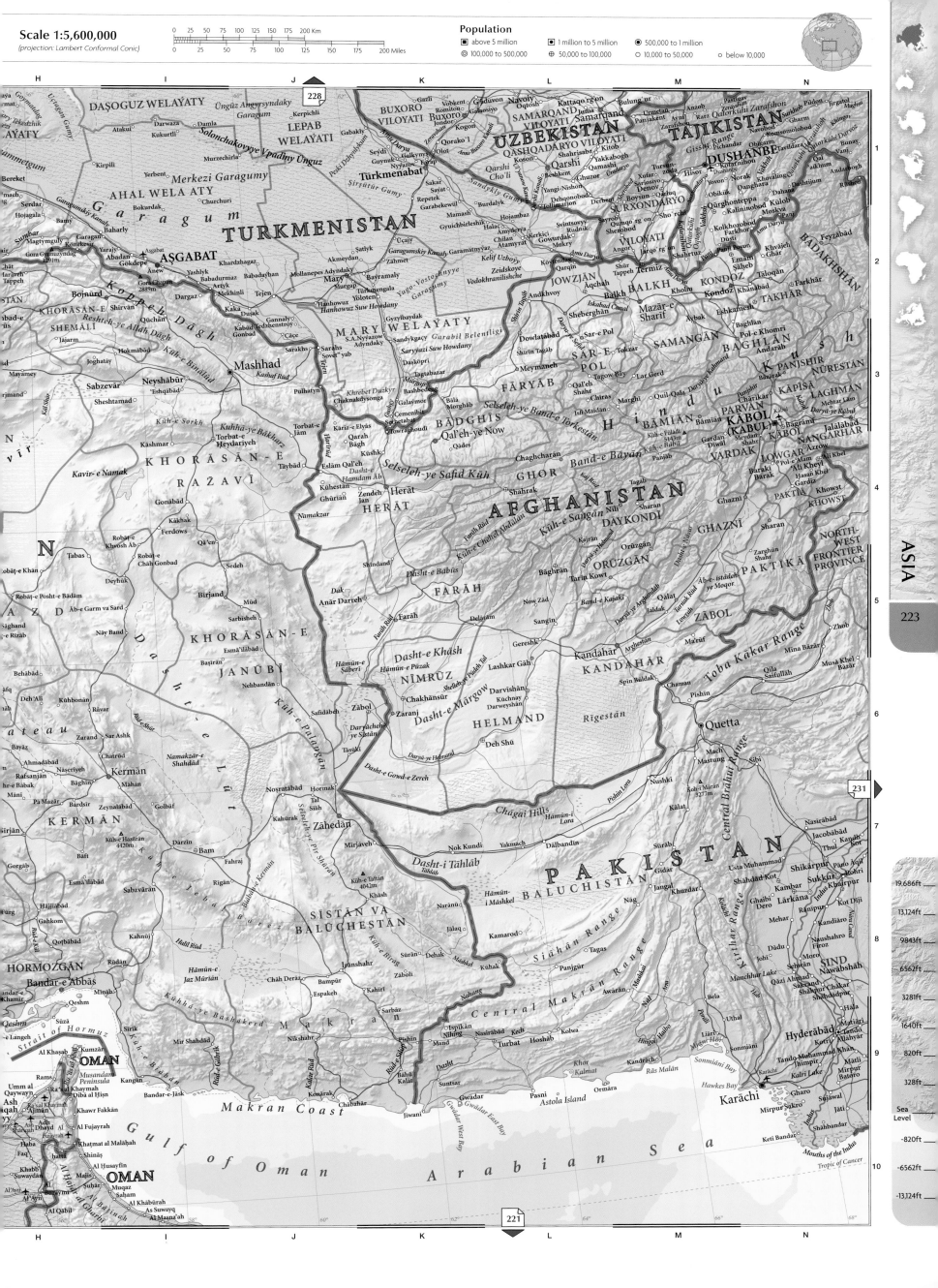

South & Central Asia

Scale 1:15,500,000
(projection: Lambert Azimuthal Equal Area)

0 50 100 150 200 250 300 350 400 Km
0 50 100 150 200 250 300 350 400 Miles

Population
- ■ above 5 million
- ▣ 1 million to 5 million
- ◉ 500,000 to 1 million
- ◎ 100,000 to 500,000
- ⊕ 50,000 to 100,000
- ○ 10,000 to 50,000
- ∘ below 10,000

Seas and Oceans
- Andaman Sea
- Bay of Bengal
- INDIAN OCEAN
- Arabian Sea
- Gulf of Oman
- Gulf of Mannar
- Gulf of Kachchh
- Gulf of Khambhat

Countries
- MYANMAR (BURMA)
- YANGON (RANGOON)
- BANGLADESH — DHAKA
- BHUTAN — THIMPHU
- NEPAL — KATHMANDU
- INDIA — NEW DELHI
- PAKISTAN
- SRI LANKA — COLOMBO
- MALDIVES — MALE
- INDONESIA
- OMAN — MASQAT (MUSCAT)
- U.A.E. — ABU DHABI (ABU ZABY)
- SAUDI ARABIA
- QATAR — AL MANAMAH
- BAHRAIN — AL MANAMAH (MANAMA)
- YEMEN

Selected Cities and Places
Kolkata (Calcutta), Mumbai (Bombay), Chennai (Madras), Hyderabad, Bangalore, Pune, Ahmadabad, Surat, Nagpur, Kanpur, Lucknow, Jaipur, Bhopal, Indore, Patna, Varanasi, Agra, Meerut, Delhi, Faridabad, Ludhiana, Amritsar, Chandigarh, Jodhpur, Vadodara, Rajkot, Nashik, Aurangabad, Solapur, Kolhapur, Vijayawada, Visakhapatnam, Vizianagaram, Rajahmundry, Kakinada, Machilipatnam, Guntur, Nellore, Ongole, Kurnool, Anantapur, Cuddapah, Warangal, Nizamabad, Nanded, Gulbarga, Bidar, Raichur, Bellary, Hubli, Belgaum, Gadag, Davangere, Shimoga, Mysore, Mandya, Mangalore, Udupi, Cannanore, Calicut, Cochin (Kochi), Allepey, Quilon, Trivandrum, Nagercoil, Tuticorin, Madurai, Tiruchirappalli (Trichur), Salem, Erode, Coimbatore, Vellore, Kanchipuram, Pondicherry, Tirupati, Neyveli, Chidambaram, Dindigul, Rajapalaiyam, Puttalam, Negombo, Colombo, Sri Jayawardanapura, Galle, Matara, Kandy, Batticaloa, Trincomalee, Anuradhapura, Jaffna, Mannar, Puri, Cuttack, Bhubaneshwar, Brahmapur, Srikakulam, Ranchi, Dhanbad, Asansol, Jamshedpur, Durgapur, Raurkela, Sambalpur, Bilaspur, Raipur, Jabalpur, Bhilai

Relief / Elevation Scale
- 19,686ft
- 13,124ft
- 9843ft
- 6562ft
- 3281ft
- 1640ft
- 820ft
- 328ft
- Sea Level
- -820ft
- -6562ft
- -13,124ft

Islands
- Andaman Islands (to India)
- Nicobar Islands (to India)
- North Andaman, Middle Andaman, South Andaman, Little Andaman, Car Nicobar, Great Nicobar, Little Nicobar, Katchall Island, Camorta
- Port Blair
- Maldive Islands
- Lakshadweep (Laccadive Islands)
- Aminidivi Islands
- Minicoy Island
- Suqutra (Socotra) (to Yemen)
- Sumatera
- Great Channel
- Ten Degree Channel
- Nine Degree Channel
- Eight Degree Channel
- Duncan Passage
- Sombrero Channel
- Tropic of Cancer
- Equator

257 288 136

Kazakhstan

RUSSIAN

RESPUBLIKA MORDOVIYA

RESPUBLIKA TATARSTAN

RESPUBLIKA BASHKORTOSTAN

PENZENSKAYA OBLAST'

UL'YANOVSKAYA OBLAST'

SAMARSKAYA OBLAST'

SARATOVSKAYA OBLAST'

VOLGOGRADSKAYA OBLAST'

ORENBURGSKAYA OBLAST'

CHELYABINSKAYA OBLAST'

KURGANSKAYA OBLAST'

ASTRAKHANSKAYA OBLAST'

RESPUBLIKA KALMYKIYA

RESPUBLIKA DAGESTAN

ZAPADNYY KAZAKHSTAN

Caspian Depression

ATYRAU

Ryn-Peski

AKTYUBINSKAYA

Turgayskaya Stolovaya Strana

KOSTANAY

Ul'yanovsk

Saransk

Samara

Syzran

Tol'yatti

Novokuybyshevsk

Dimitrovgrad

Saratov

Engel's

Balakovo

Ufa

Magnitogorsk

Chelyabinsk

Zlatoust

Miass

Troitsk

Kostanay

Rudnyy

Orenburg

Orsk

Novotroitsk

Aktobe (Aktyubinsk)

Ural'sk

Astrakhan

Makhachkala

Kaspiysk

Buynaksk

Derbent

AZERBAIJAN

BAKI (BAKU)

Sumqayıt

Atyrau

Makhambet

Makat

Dossor

Aktau

Plato Mangyshlak

MANGISTAU

Zhanaozen

Fort-Shevchenko

Caspian Sea

Ustyurt Plateau

Ural Karabaur

Aral Sea

KZYLORDA

QORAQALPOG'ISTON RESPUBLIKASI

Nukus

Urganch

Daşoguz

XORAZM VILOYATI

DAŞOGUZ WELAÝATY

UZBEKISTAN

NAVOIY VILOYATI

Navoiy

Buxoro

BUXORO VILOYATI

BALKAN WELAÝATY

LEBAP WELAÝATY

AHAL WELAÝATY

MARY WELAÝATY

TURKMENISTAN

AŞGABAT

Türkmenabat

Mary

Balkanabat

Türkmenbaşy

Garagum

Köpetdag Gershi

IRAN

Gorgan

Qazvin

Resht

Baykonyr

Space Launching Centre

Kazalinsk

Kyzl

Aral'sk

Sor Metvyy Kultuk

Zaliv Komsomolets

Mangyshlakskiy Zaliv

Central Asia

228

215

ASIA

Caspian Sea

Aral Sea

KAZ
AKTYUBINSK
KYZLORDA
Kzyl
Kzy

Atyrau
ATYRAU
Komsomol'skiy
Kul'sary
Koschagyl
Karaton
Zaliy Komsomolets
Sarykamys
Borankul
Sarykamys
Beyneu
Turush
Emba
Gryada Shirkala
Shalkar
Gory Chushkakul
Plato Shagyray
Peski Bol'shiye Barsuki
Severnyy Chink Ustyurta
Saksaul'skiy
Aral'sk
Peski Priaral'skiye Karakumy
Ozero Shubar-Tengiz
Zaliv Tushchybas
Ayteke Bi
Maylybas Space Launching Centre
Kazalinsk
Baykonyr
Dermentobe
Syr Darya
Dzhusaly
Dzhalagash
Zhanadar'ya

Ostrov Kulaly
Mys Tyub-Karagan
Zaliv Mangyshlakskiy
Fort-Shevchenko
Tauchik
Shetpe
Say-Utes
Zharnysh

Aktau
Plato Mangyshlak
Zhetybay
Zhanaozen
Kuryk

MANGISTAU

Ustyurt Plateau

Qoraqalpog'iston

Jaslik
Kubla-Ustyurt
Uchsoy
Mo'ynoq
Uyaly
Qorajar
Amu Darya
Ostrov Vozrozhdeniya

Og'iyon Sho'rxogi

QORAQALPOG'ISTON RESPUBLIKASI
Oltynko'l
Qo'ng'irot
Madaniyat
Shumanay
Chimboy
Qozoqdaryo
Qorauzak
Taxtako'pir
Xalqobod
Kegayli

Ural Karabaur

Xo'jayli
Taxiatosh
Nukus
Köneürgenc
Boldumsaz
Akdepe
Mang'it
Gurbansoltan Eje
Dashoguz
Gurlan
Beruniy
Shovot
Tosqudug Qumlari
Chuqurqoq
Mingbuloq
Uchquduq
Aytim

Mys Soye
Garabogaz
Garabogazkol
Garabogaz Aylagy
Garshy

DASHOGUZ WELAYATY
Sarygamysh Koli
Vpadina Akdzhakaya -130m
Ilanly Obvodnitel'nyy Kanal
Tagta
Urganch
XORAZM VILOYATI
Xiva
Hazarasp
Xonqa
Pitnak
Gazojak
Lebap
Turpoqqal'a
Jigerbent

UZBEKISTAN
Bo'ston
NAVOIY VILOYAT
Bo'kantov Tog'lari
Tdir Tog'i 764m
Ko'lquduq
Beshbuloq
Tomdibul
Zarafshon
Tomditow-Tog'lari
Mingbuloq Botig'i
Oyminzatov Tog'lari
Shengeldi
Qubigtov-Tog'lari
Oyqog'itma
Kukcha

Krasnovodskoye Plato
Cagyl
Gyzylgaya
Goymat
Gory Tibekzlik
Üçtagan Gumy
Uztagan Gumy
Solonchak Kaskhadzhar
Üçtagan Gumy
Goymatdag
Akgyr Erezi

Türkmenbaşy
Gyzylsuw
Türkmenbaşy Aýlagy
Kenar
Belek
Oglanly

Ünguz Angyrsyndaky
Garagum
Derweze
Atakuy
Kukurtli
Damla
Birata
Bashsakarba
Qizilravot

BUXORO VILOYATI
Gabakly
Gazli
Vobkent
G'ijduvon
Jondor
Kogon
Galaosiyo
Buxoro
Na

Guwlumayak
Hazar
Balkanabat
Gumdag
Uzboy

Ogurjaly Adasy
Türkmen Aýlagy

Garagöl
Jebel
Arlandag 1880m
Ajyguyy
Kürendag
Bereket
Kul'mach

BALKAN WELAÝATY
Gilmämmetgum

Kirpili
Merkezi Garagumy
Yerbent
Murzechirla
Solonchakovyye Vpadiny Unguz
Kerpichli
Jongeldi

Peski Dzhyntykum
LEPAB WELAÝATY
Seýdi
Galkynyş
Olot
Qorakül
Qorovoy
Müborak

Garaboyaz
Karadepe
Madaw
Bugdayly
Gyzylbair
Gora Gyunuzyndag 1291m
Könekesir

Serdar
Hojagala
Bamy
Baharly
Bokurdak
Churchuri

TURKMENISTAN
Garagum

AHAL WELAÝATY

Türkmenabat
Sakar
Saýat
Repetek
Sirsirür Gumy
Kelif Uzboy
Mamash
Gyuichbirleshik
Burdalyk
Chilan
Halac
Atamyrat
Sandykly Gumy
Garabekewül
Garamätnyýaz

Çekiçler
Esenguly
Gudurolum
Etrek
Rüd-e Atrak
Chät
Maraveh Tappeh
Kyzylbair
Yaraly
Gökdepe
Abadan
Anew
Aşgabat
Gora Chapan 2886m
Yashlyk
Babadurmaz
Artyk
Kardzhagaz

MARY WELAÝATY
Üçajy
Akmeýdan
Zähmet
Garagum Kanaly
Yöloten

Babol
Bandar-e Torkaman
Nür
Bábolsar
Behshahr
GOLESTAN
Gonbad-e Kavus
Kord Kuy
Gorgan
Fariab
KHORASAN-E SHEMALI
Shirvan
Rüd-e Gorgan
Reshteh-ye Allah Dagh

Babadayhan
Tejen
Mekhinli
Duşak
Kaka
Tedzhenstroy
Çäçe
Hanhowuz
Mollanepes
Adynday
Bayramaly
Murgap
Türkmengala
Mary
Sakarçäge
Satlyk

Yugo-Vostochnyye Garagumy
Zeidskoye Vodokhranilishche

Amol
Qa'emshahr
MAXANDARAN
Sari
Joghatay
Mayamey
Hokmabad
Kübüd Gonbad
Tedzhen
Gannaly
Hanhowuz Suw Howdany
Gyzylbaydak
S.A.Nyyazow Adyndaky
Sandygkaçy
Sarahs
Shirin Ta
Garabil Belentligi
Dowlat

Reshteh-ye Kühhä-ye Alborz (Elburz Mountains)
Qolleh-ye Damavand 5671m
Pol-e Safid
Shahrud
Damghan
Biarjmand

S.A.Nyyazow
Sarakhs
Sarahs
Sovet'yab
Daşköpri
Tagtabazar
Sarryyazi Suw Howdany
FARYAB
Meymaneh

Semnan
SEMNAN
Kaj Sükb
Sabzevar
Neyshabur
'Eshqabad
Mashhad
Kashaf Rüd
Pulhatyn
Harirud
Khrebet Duzkyr
Chaknakdysonga
Galaymor
Bala Morghab
Qal
BADGHIS

Garmsar

IRAN

Dasht-e Kavir
Kavir-e Namak

Sheshtamad
Küh-e Sorkh
Kashmar
Kühha-ye Binalüd
Kühha-ye Bakharz
Torbat-e Jäm
Käriz-e Elyas
Serhetabat
Cemenibit
Qarah Bagh
Kushk
Towraghoundi
Selseleh-ye Band-e Torkestan
Daryä-ye Morghäb

ESFAHAN
YAZD
KHORASAN-E RAZAVI
Gonabad
Torbat-e Heydariyeh
Taybad
Eslam Qal'eh
Kühestän
Ghürian
Zendeh Jan
Herat
HERAT
Namakzar
Dasht-e Hamdam Ab
Selseleh-ye Safid Küh
Qal'eh-ye Now
Qädis
AFG
Chaghcharan
GHOWR
Shahrak

Anarak
Jandaq
Kakhak
Robat-e Khvosh Ab
Qa'en
Ferdows
Deyhük
Tabas
Birjand
Na'in
Robat-e Posht-e Bädäm
Robat-e Khan
Robat-e Chäh Gonbad
Sedeh

Elevation scale
- 6000m
- 4000m
- 3000m
- 2000m
- 1000m
- 500m
- 250m
- 100m
- Sea Level
- -250m
- -500m
- -1000m

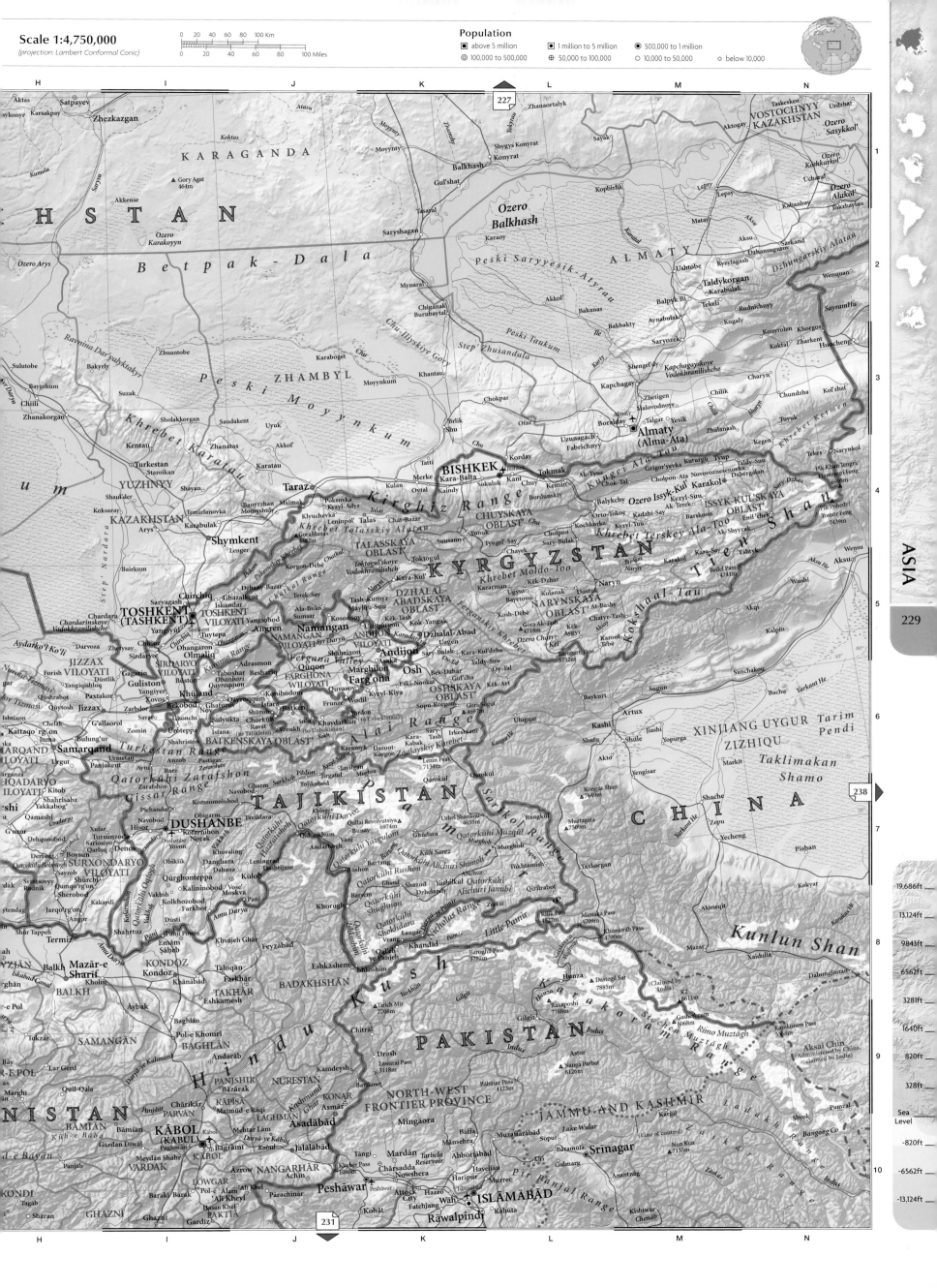

Afghanistan & Pakistan

Elevation scale: 6000m, 4000m, 3000m, 2000m, 1000m, 500m, 250m, 100m, Sea Level, -250m, -500m, -1000m

Countries and regions

TURKMENISTAN

UZBEKISTAN

DUSHAN

AFGHANISTAN

PAKISTAN

IRAN

OMAN

U.A.E.

Labels

AHAL WELAYATY, LEBAP WELAYATY, MARY WELAYATY, JOWZJAN, BALKH, SAMANGAN, SAR-E POL, FARYAB, BADGHIS, BAMIAN, PARV, VARDAN, GHOWR, DAIKONDI, GHAZNI, ORUZGAN, ZABOL, PAKTI, KANDAHAR, HELMAND, NIMRUZ

GOLESTAN, KHORASAN-E SHEMALI, SEMNAN, KHORASAN-E RAZAVI, KHORASAN-E JANUBI, YAZD, Iranian Plateau, KERMAN, HORMOZGAN, SISTAN VA BALUCHESTAN, BALUCHISTAN, SIND

Dasht-e Kavir, Kavir-e Namak, Dasht-e Lut, Biaban-e Kerman, Dasht-e Babus, Dasht-e Khash, Dasht-e Margow, Dasht-e Gowd-e Zereh, Rigestan, Dasht-i Tahlab, Chagai Hills, Siahan Range, Central Makran Range, Kirthar Range, Central-Brahui Range, Toba Kakar Rang, Makran, Makran Coast

Koppeh Dagh, Selseleh-ye Safid Kuh, Selseleh-ye Band-e Torkestan, Kuh-e Chehel Abdalan, Kuh-e Sangan, Band-e Bayan, Kuh-e Baba, Musandam Peninsula, Al Hajar ash Sharqi, Al Hajar al Gharbi, Strait of Hormuz

Hamun-e Saberi, Hamun-e Puzak, Daryacheh-ye Sistan, Hamun-i Lora, Hamun-i Mashkel, Hamun-e Jaz Murian, Manchhar Lake, Kalri Lake

Gulf of Oman, Arabian Sea, Makran Coast, Mouths of the Indus, Gwadar West Bay, Gwadar East Bay, Sonmiani Bay, Hawkes Bay, Khor Kalmat, Ras Malan, Astola Island

Cities and towns

Asgabat, Mashhad, Kerman, Zahedan, Quetta, Bandar-e 'Abbas, Karachi, Hyderabad, Masqat (Muscat), Gorgan, Herat, Mazar-e Sharif, Kandahar, Lashkar Gah

Cekiçler, Esenguly, Etrek, Kyzyl-Kaya, Gora Grunuzyndag 291m, Gokdepe, Garagan, Yarajy, Konekesir, Büzmeyin, Anew, Chapan 2889m, Yashlyk, Babadurmaz, Artyk, Kaka, Dargaz, Mekhinli, Tejen, Dusak, Kabud Gonbad, Hanhowuz, Murgap, Mary, Bayramaly, Turkmengala, Yolöten, Repetek, Sayat, Qarshi, Qamashi, G'uzor, Yangi-Nishon, Qarshi

Gonbad-e Kavus, Bojnurd, Shirvan, Quchan, Neyshabur, Sabzevar, Sheshtamad, 'Eshqabad, Joghatay, Hokmabad, Shahrud, Damghan, Biarjmand, Mayamey, Jajarm

Torbat-e Jeydariyeh, Kashmar, Torbat-e Jam, Qal'eh-ye Now, Taybad, Kühestan, Zendeh Jan, Ghurian, Eslam Qal'eh, Kariz-e Elyas, Qarah Bagh, Kushk, Qades, Balá Morghab, Chaghcharan, Shindand, Farah, Delaram, Now Zad, Baghran, Tarin Kowt, Kajran, Oruzgan, Qalat, Jaldak, Sangin, Gereshk, Kandahar, Ma'ruf, Spin Buldak, Chaman, Pishin, Kuchnay Darweyshan, Darvishan, Deh Shu, Zaranj, Chakhansur

Kerman, Bam, Fahraj, Sabzvaran, Jiroft, Bandar-e 'Abbas, Minab, Nikshahr, Chabahar, Jask, Konarak, Iranshahr, Bampur, Espakeh, Sarbaz, Jaliaq, Dehak, Kamarod, Suran, Mashkel, Kuhak, Nok Kundi, Dalbandin, Yakmach, Nushki, Mastung, Mach, Sibi, Kalat, Surab, Gidar, Nag, Khuzdar, Usta Muhammad, Jacobabad, Shikarpur, Larkana, Mehar, Sehwan, Dadu, Qazi Ahmad, Nawabshah, Kotri, Hyderabad, Tando Muhammad Khan, Jhimpir, Gharo, Mirpur Sakro, Keti Bandar, Shahbandar

Muscat, Matrah, Seeb, Ruwi, Sib, As Suwayq, Al Masna'ah, Al Khaburah, Saham, Suhar, Shinas, Al Husayfin, Hatta, Dibba al Hisn, Khawr Fakkan, Al Fujayrah, Kalba, Ra's al Khaymah, Qeshm, Bandar-e 'Abbas

AFGHANISTAN

PAKISTAN

KASHMIR

JAMMU

HIMĀCHAL PRADESH

PUNJAB

HARYĀNA

RĀJASTHĀN

UTTAR PRADESH

UTTARANCHAL

GUJARĀT

MADHYA PRADESH

MAHĀRĀSHTRA

ANDHRA PRADESH

SIND

BALUCHISTĀN

KANDAHĀR

ZĀBOL

GHAZNĪ

PAKTĪKĀ

KHOWST

NORTH WEST FRONTIER PROVINCE

FĀRYĀB

SAMANGĀN

TAKHĀR

BADAKHSHĀN

BĀMIĀN

BAGHLĀN

GHOWR

DAIKONDI

ORŪZGĀN

VARDAK

KĀPĪSĀ

PARVAN

LAGHMĀN

KONAR

NANGARHĀR

LOWGAR

Hindu Kush

Karakoram Range

Zaskār Range

Ladakh Range

Salt Range

Toba Kākar Range

Sulaimān Range

Central Brahui Range

Kirthar Range

Thar Desert

Arāvalli Range

Vindhya Range

Sātpura Range

Ajanta Range

Maikāla Range

Kāthiāwār Peninsula

Rann of Kachchh

Gulf of Kachchh

Gulf of Khambhāt

Arabian Sea

Mouths of the Indus

Tropic of Cancer

KĀBOL (KABUL)

ISLĀMĀBĀD

Rāwalpindi

Peshāwar

Srīnagar

Jammu

Lahore

Amritsar

Ludhiāna

Chandigarh

Dehra Dūn

Shimla

NEW DELHI

DELHI

Ghāziābād

Meerut

Jaipur

Jodhpur

Āgra

Lucknow

Kānpur

Gwalior

Bhopāl

Indore

Ahmadābād

Gāndhīnagar

Vadodara

Rājkot

Sūrat

Mumbai (Bombay)

Kalyān

Pune

Nāshik

Aurangābād

Nāgpur

Quetta

Karāchi

Hyderābād

Multān

Faisalābād

Gujrānwāla

Sukkur

Bīkāner

Udaipur

Kota

Allahābād

Jabalpur

6000m
4000m
3000m
2000m
1000m
500m
250m
100m
Sea Level
-250m
-500m
-1000m

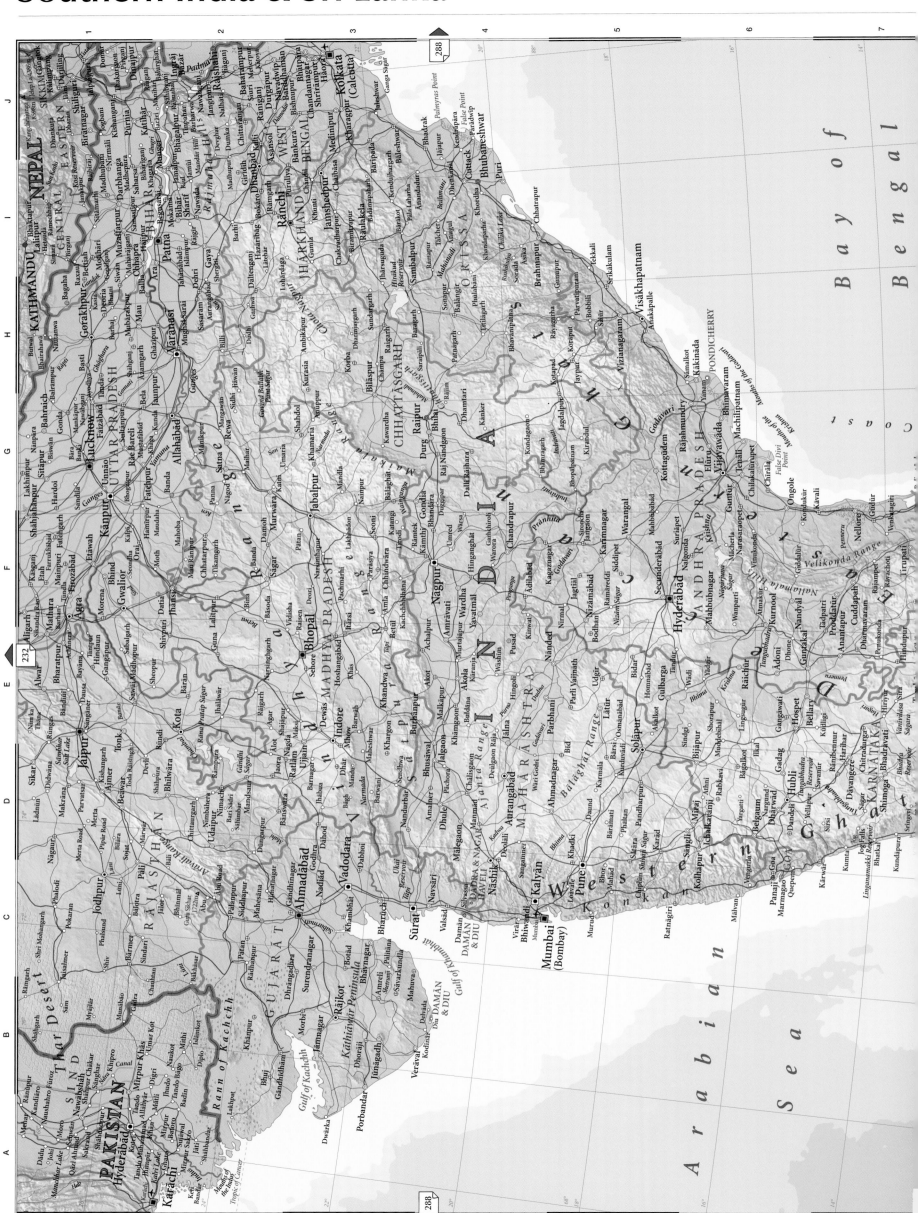

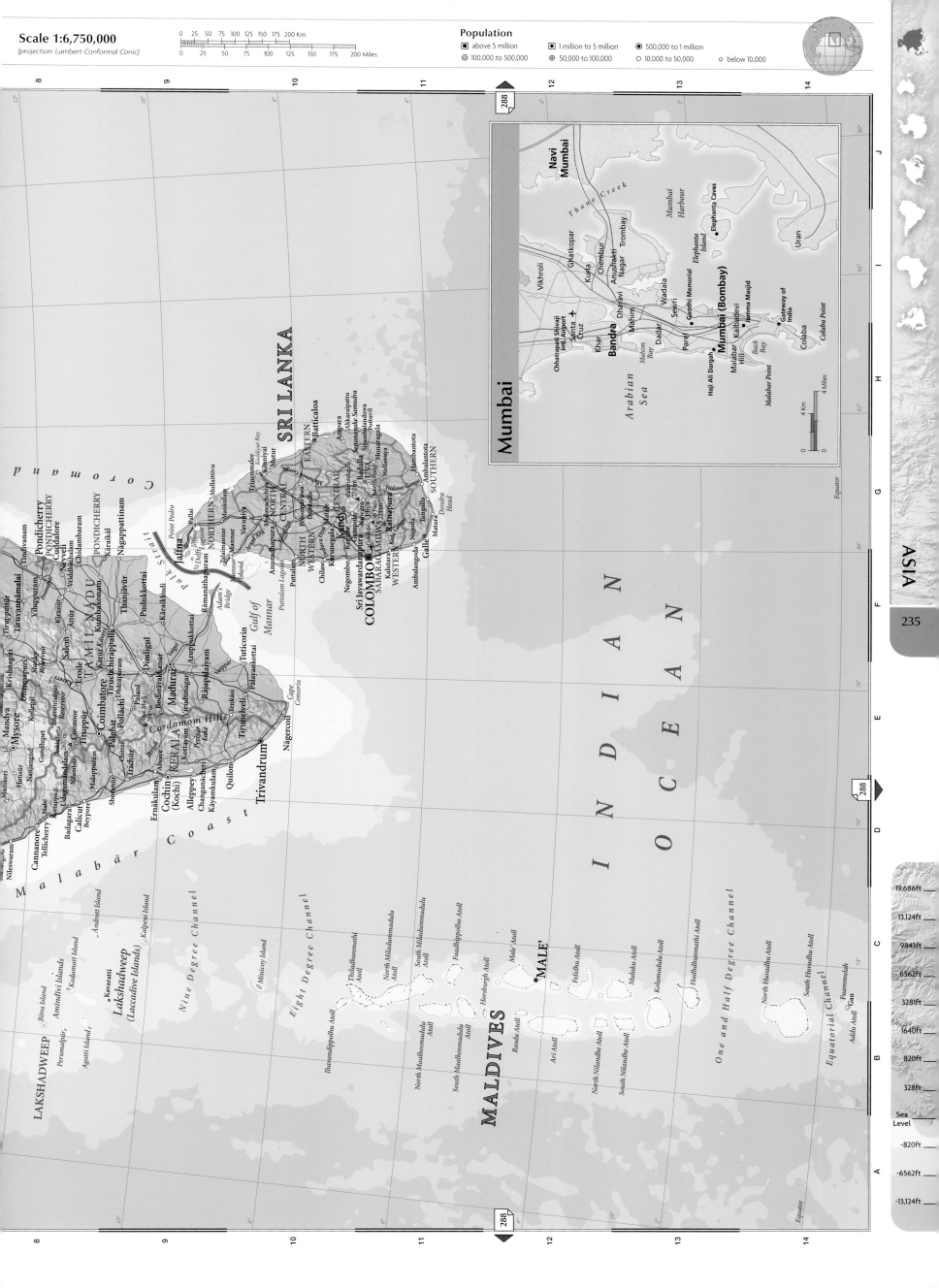

East Asia

192
231
256

RUSSIAN

KAZAKHSTAN

MONGOLIA

ULAANBAATAR (ULAN BATOR)

KYRGYZSTAN

BISHKEK

Almaty

Ürümqi

XINJIANG UYGUR ZIZHIQU

Tarim Pendi

Taklimakan Shamo

Tarim He

Lop Nur

Kunlun Shan

Altun Shan

Qilian Shan

C H I N A

QINGHAI

Qinghai Hu

Xining

GANSU

Lanzhou

NINGXIA

Yinchuan

Baotou

Qingzang Gaoyuan (Plateau of Tibet)

XIZANG ZIZHIQU (TIBET)

Bayan Har Shan

Tanggula Shan

Nyainqêntanglha Shan

SHAANXI

Xi'an

Hanzhong

JAMMU AND KASHMIR

Srinagar

Karakoram Range

HIMACHAL PRADESH

Aksai Chin

SICHUAN

Chengdu

Sichuan Pendi

CHONGQING

Chongqing

Guangyuan

Mianyang

HIMALAYAS

NEPAL

KATHMANDU

Mount Everest 8850m

BHUTAN

THIMPHU

SIKKIM

ARUNACHAL PRADESH

Lhasa

Xigaze

Gyangze

GUIZHOU

Guiyang

YUNNAN

Kunming

NEW DELHI

Delhi

UTTAR PRADESH

Lucknow

Kanpur

PUNJAB

Amritsar

Lahore

HARYANA

BIHAR

Patna

JHARKHAND

WEST BENGAL

Kolkata (Calcutta)

BANGLADESH

DHAKA

Chittagong

MEGHALAYA

Shillong

ASSAM

Guwahati

MANIPUR

Imphal

MYANMAR (BURMA)

Mandalay

Naypyidaw

Shan Plateau

MADHYA PRADESH

Bhopal

Jabalpur

ORISSA

Bhubaneshwar

Cuttack

I N D I A

ANDHRA PRADESH

Hyderabad

Nagpur

Raipur

MAHARASHTRA

Tropic of Cancer

Bay of Bengal

YANGON (RANGOON)

Mouths of the Irrawaddy

THAILAND

Chiang Mai

LAOS

VIANGCHAN (VIENTIANE)

VIETNAM

HA NOI

Hai Phong

Hainan Dao

Gulf of Tongking

GUANGXI ZHUANG ZIZHIQU

Nanning

Beihai

6000m
4000m
3000m
2000m
1000m
500m
250m
100m
Sea Level
-250m
-500m
-1000m

Population
■ above 5 million ▪ 1 million to 5 million ◼ 500,000 to 1 million
◎ 100,000 to 500,000 ⊕ 50,000 to 100,000 ○ 10,000 to 50,000 ○ below 10,000

0 50 100 150 200 250 300 350 400 Km
0 50 100 150 200 250 300 350 400 Miles

193

FEDERATION

Bodaybo
Neryungri
Stanovoy Khrebet
Olekma
Olkma
Chita
Mogocha
Shilka
Tynda
Zeyskoye
Vodokhranilishche
Khrebet Dzhugdzhur
Karymskoye
Olovyannaya
Skovorodino
Never
Shimanovsk
Nikolayevsk-na-Amur
Nogliki
Onon Gol
Krasnokamensk
Amur
Svobodnyy
Berezovyy
Ostrov Sakhalin
Sea of Okhotsk
Petropavlovsk-Kamchatskiy
Poluostrov Kamchatka
Zabaykalsk
Kerulen
Manzhouli
Argun
Blagoveshchensk
Obluch'ye
Birobidzhan
Komsomol'sk-na-Amure
Yuzhno-Sakhalinsk
Ostrov Paramushir
Pervyy Kuril'skiy Proliv
Choybalsan
Menengiyn Tal
Hailar
Hulun Nur
Yichun
Hegang
Heilong Jiang
Khor
Khabarovsk
Bikin
Tatarskiy Proliv
La Perouse Strait
Rebun-tö
Ostrov Urup
Kuril'skiye Ostrova (Kuril Islands)
Baruun-Urt
Qiqihar
HEILONGJIANG
Daqing
Suihua
Jiamusi
Dal'nerechensk
Sikhote-Alin'
Rishiri-tö
Ostrov Iturup
(Administered by Russian Federation, claimed by Japan)
Zalantun
Ulanhot
Harbin
Shangzhi
Jixi
Spassk-Dal'niy
Lake Khanka
Dal'negorsk
Wakkanai
Asahi-dake 2290m
Abashiri
Kitami
Nemuro
Hulingol
Baicheng
Ussuriysk
Asahikawa
Ibetsu
Obihiro
Kushiro
Bayan Ul
Changchun
Jilin
Mudanjiang
Vladivostok
Nakhodka
Takikawa
Chitose
Horoshiri-dake 2052m
MONGOL ZIZHIQU
JILIN
Tongliao
Siping
Liaoyuan
Dunhua
Yanji
Tumen
Najin
Sapporo
Otaru
Toma-komai
Muroran
Hakodate
Hokkaidō
Xilinhot
Linxi
Chifeng
Fuxin
Tieling
Baishan
Hoeryong
Ch'ŏngjin
Okushiri-tö
Baochang
renhot
Beipiao
Shenyang
Fushun
Huch'ang
Hyesan
NORTH KOREA
Tsugaru-kaikyō
Aomori
Hachinohe
hhot
Zhangjiakou
Chaoyang
Jinzhou
LIAONING
Haicheng
Anshan
Namsan-ni
Huich'ŏn
Kanggye
Kimch'aek
Hirosaki
Noshiro
Kuji
Iwate
Morioka
Datong
BEIJING SHI
BEIJING (PEKING)
Beijing
Tangshan
Dandong
Sinŭiju
Chŏngju
Hamhŭng
Akita
Kyote
Miyako
Baoding
TIANJIN SHI
Tianjin
Dalian
Korea Bay
P'YŎNGYANG
Namp'o
Sunan
Sariwŏn
Wŏnsan
Sakata
Shinjo
Kesennuma
Shijiazhuang
HEBEI
Cangzhou
Bo Hai
Haeju
Kaesŏng
Sokch'o
Sea of Japan (East Sea)
Tsuruoka
Furukawa
Ishinomaki
XI
Xingtai
Dezhou
Binzhou
Yantai
Ongjin
Inch'ŏn
Ch'unch'ŏn
Kangnŭng
JAPAN
Niigata
Yamagata
Sendai
Sendai-wan
zhi
Handan
Zibo
Weifang
SŎUL
Suwŏn
Wŏnju
Tonghae
Sado
Nagaoka
Fukushima
yang
Anyang
Huang He
Jinan
SHANDONG
Qingdao
Inch'ŏn
SOUTH KOREA
Taejŏn
Ch'ŏnju
P'ohang
Oki-shotō
Takaoka
Jōetsu
Utsunomiya
Nagano
Koriyama
Iwaki
Hitachi
nxia
Kaifeng
Zhengzhou
Zaozhuang
Taegu
Ulsan
Wakasa-wan
Kanazawa
Komatsu
Toyama
Matsu-moto
Maebashi
Yangyang
Xuzhou
Lianyungang
Yellow Sea
Kwangju
Namwon
Taegu
Kŭm-gang
Pusan
Fukui
Matsue
Tottori
Gifu
Kōfu
Fuji-san 3776m
Tōkyō
Chiba
Haneda
HENAN
Nanyang
Great Plain of China
JIANGSU
Namyang
Mokp'o
Sunch'ŏn
Cheju-haehyŏp
Korea Strait
Yamaguchi
Hiroshima
Okayama
Itsu
Kyōto
Kōbe
Osaka
Nagoya
Hamamatsu
Yokohama
hekou
Xinyang
Bengbu
Hefei
ANHUI
Cheju-do
Kitakyūshū
Hōfu
Shikoku
Kōchi
Ise
Owase
Nii-jima
Izu-shotō
Mikura-jima
HUBEI
Suizhou
Nanjing
SHANGHAI SHI
Shanghai
Wuhu
Wuxi
Jiaxing
Fukuoka
Kurume
Ōita
Nakamura
Kōchi-suidō
Tanabe
Hachijō-jima
Wuhan
Anqing
Hangzhou
Huangshi
Jiujiang
Jingdezhen
Ningbo
Sasebo
Nagasaki
Yatsushiro
Kumamoto
Nobeoka
O-shima
Sagami-nada
an
Changsha
Xiangtan
Fuzhou
Jinhua
Shangrao
ZHEJIANG
Taizhou
East China Sea
Sendai
Kyūshū
Miyazaki
Miyakonojō
PACIFIC
yang
Hengyang
Ji'an
JIANGXI
Wenzhou
Kagoshima
Tanega-Shima
UNAN
Chenzhou
Nanping
FUJIAN
Yaku-Shima
Nansei-shotō (Ryukyu Islands)
Naze
Amami-O-shima
Amami-guntō
OCEAN
Shaoguan
Longyan
Quanzhou
Yong'an
Matsu Tao (to Taiwan)
Chiang Kai-shek
Chilung
Ishigaki-jima
Miyako-jima
Ogasawara-shotō
oging
Zhangzhou
Xiamen
Chinmen Tao (to Taiwan)
T'AIPEI
T'aichung
Senkaku-shotō (Claimed by China, Japan and Taiwan)
Iriomote-jima
Sakishima-shotō
286
GUANGDONG
Chaozhou
Taiwan Strait
Chiayi
T'ainan
Taiwan
Tropic of Cancer
Guangzhou
Foshan
Shantou
Kaohsiung
Kaohsiung
TAIWAN
mon
Hong Kong
Macao
Chep Lap Kok
(China and Taiwan claim all of each other's territory)
South China Sea
Babuyan Island
Babuyan Channel
Philippine Sea
Luzon Strait
Paracel Islands (disputed)
Laoag
Tuguegarao
Ilagan
Luzon
Baguio
Dagupan
Cabanatuan
PHILIPPINES
Angeles
Quezon City
MANILA
Ninoy Aquino
263

Shanghai

Baoshan
Gucun
Kailu
Xincun
Huangpu Jiang
Miaphang
Gaojing
Wujiao Chang
Yangpu
Dachang
Pengpu
Zhabei
Jiangwan
Hongkou Stadium
Lu Xun Tomb
Gaohang
Zhengnu
Yichuan
Putuo
Hongkou
Tilan Qiao
Huangshan Xincun
Jinquiao
Zhabei
Shanghai University
Pudong
Jiaodong University
Shanghai
Temple of the Jade Buddha
Huangpu
Zhangjiang
Beixinjing
Jing'an
People's Square
Shanghai Museum
Yanguiada
Wusong Jiang
Sun Yat Sen's Former Residence
Humau Zhen
Changning
Dapu
Muamu
Nanshi
Hongqiao
Xujiahui
Luwan
Huangpu Jiang
Beicai
Qibao Zhen
Caohe
Longua
Zhoujiadu
Yugiao
Sanlin
Liuliqiao

0 2 Km
0 2 Miles

19,686ft
13,124ft
9843ft
6562ft
3281ft
1640ft
820ft
328ft
Sea Level
-820ft
-6562ft
-13,124ft

ASIA

238

227
230
232

Elevation scale (left margin):
- 6000m
- 4000m
- 3000m
- 2000m
- 1000m
- 500m
- 250m
- 100m
- Sea Level
- -250m
- -500m
- -1000m

Countries:
KAZAKHSTAN · KYRGYZSTAN · UZBEKISTAN · TAJIKISTAN · AFGHANISTAN · PAKISTAN · INDIA · NEPAL · CHINA · RUSS. FED. · BHUTAN

Regions / physical features:
KARAGANDA · ZHAMBYL · ALMATY · VOSTOCHNYY KAZAKHSTAN · YUZHNYY KAZAKHSTAN · BAYAN-ÖLGIY · Betpak-Dala · Ozero Balkhash · Junggar Pendi · Gurbantünggüt Shamo · Altai Mountains · Tien Shan · Bogda Shan · XINJIANG UYGUR ZIZHIQU · Tarim Pendi · Taklimakan Shamo · Kuruktag · Altun Shan · Kunlun Shan · Hoh Xil Shan · Qingzang (Plateau) · XIZANG ZIZHIQU (TIBET) · Tangsu · Hindu Kush · Pamirs · Karakoram Range · JAMMU AND KASHMIR · Ladakh Range · Zaskar Range · HIMACHAL PRADESH · Gangdise Shan · HIMALAYA · PUNJAB · HARYANA · RAJASTHAN · UTTAR PRADESH · UTTARANCHAL · Thar Desert · NORTH-WEST FRONTIER PROVINCE · Aksai Chin · Lop Nur

Major cities / towns:
Almaty (Alma-Ata) · BISHKEK · TOSHKENT (TASHKENT) · DUSHANBE · Ürümqi · Kashi · Hotan · Aksu · Korla · Turpan · Kuqa · Shache · ISLAMABAD · Rawalpindi · Peshawar · Srinagar · Lahore · Amritsar · Jalandhar · Ludhiana · Chandigarh · Shimla · NEW DELHI · DELHI · Jaipur · Agra · Kanpur · Lucknow · KATHMANDU · Multan · Faisalabad · Gujranwala · Jodhpur · Bikaner · Gwalior · THIMPHU

Water bodies:
Ozero Balkhash · Bosten Hu · Ebinur Hu · Sayram Hu · Ozero Alakol · Tarim He · Hotan He · Keriya He · Qarqan He · Manas Hu · Gyaring Co · Mapam Yumco · Siling Co · Nam Co

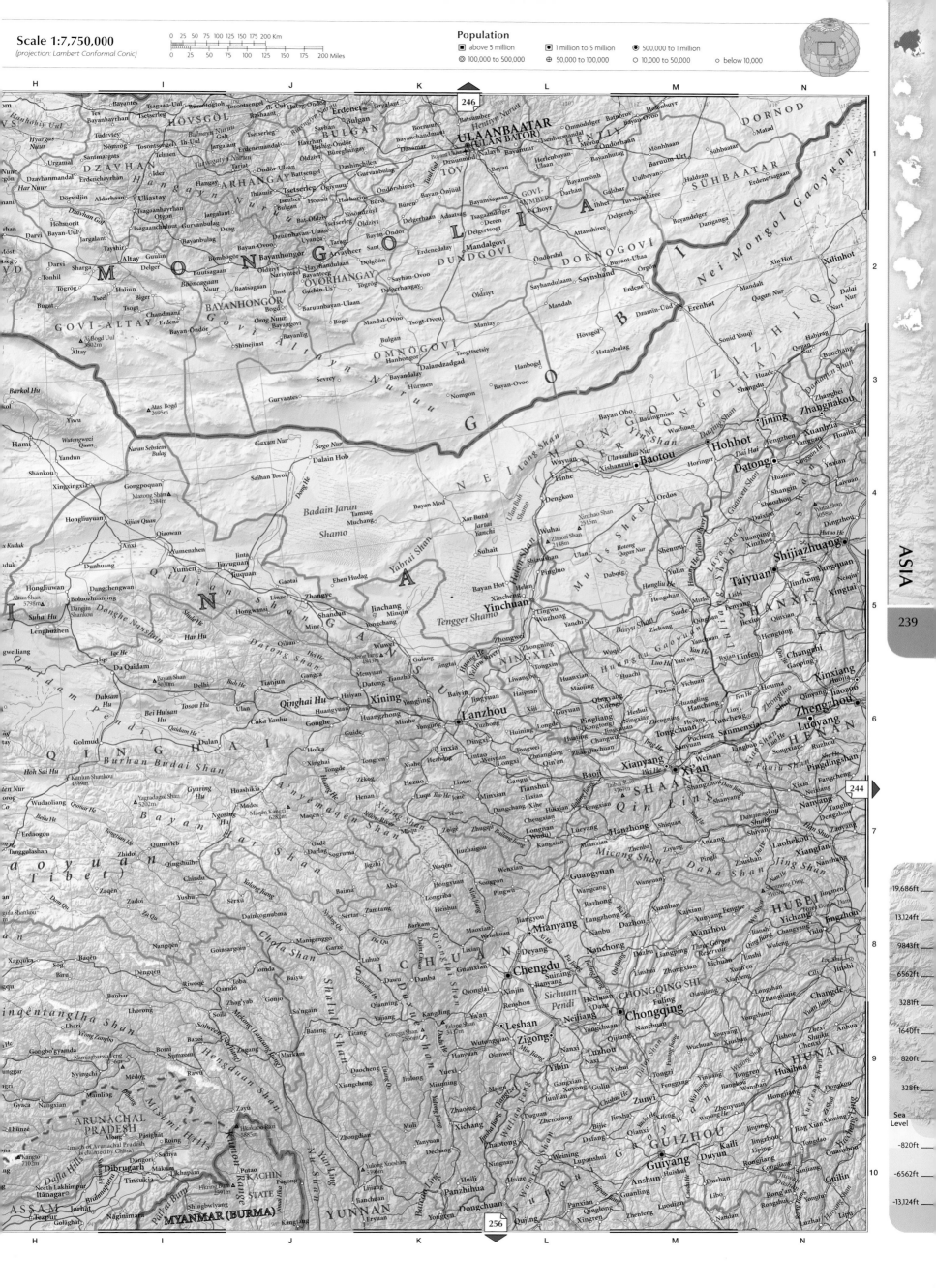

Southeast China

Countries / Regions:

QINGHAI

NINGXIA

GANSU

SHAANXI

SHANXI

XIZANG ZIZHIQU (TIBET)

SICHUAN

HUBEI

CHONGQING SHI

CHINA

INDIA

ARUNĀCHAL PRADESH (Much of Arunāchal Pradesh is claimed by China)

KACHIN STATE

YUNNAN

GUIZHOU

HUNAN

GUANGXI ZHUANGZU ZIZHIQU

MYANMAR (BURMA)

SHAN STATE

Shan Plateau

KAYAH STATE

KAREN STATE

VIETNAM

LAOS

THAILAND

HAINAN

Hainan Dao

Physical features:

Qingzang Gaoyuan (Plateau of Tibet)

Bayan Har Shan

Hengduan Shan

Daxue Shan

Qionglai Shan

Qin Ling

Daba Shan

Wu Shan

Qin Ling

Three Gorges Reservoir

Sichuan Pendi

Kunlun Shankou 4839m

Gongga Shan 7556m

Namjagbarwa Feng 7756m

Hkakabo Razi 5885m

Gaoligong Shan

Nu Shan

Salween

Mekong (Lancang Jiang)

Yangtze

Huang He (Yellow River)

Red River (Yuan Jiang)

Tropic of Cancer

Gulf of Tongking

Qiongzhou Haixia

Weizhou Dao

Donghai Dao

Cities:

Taiyuan

Lanzhou

Xining

Xi'an

Xianyang

Baoji

Luoyang

Chengdu

Chongqing

Mianyang

Kunming

Guiyang

Nanning

Guilin

Liuzhou

Zhanjiang

Haikou

HANOI

Hai Phong

VIANGCHAN (VIENTIANE)

Chiang Mai

Myitkyina

Lashio

Elevation scale (m):

6000m
4000m
3000m
2000m
1000m
500m
250m
100m
Sea Level
-250m
-500m
-1000m

Scale 1:7,000,000
(projection: Lambert Conformal Conic)

0 25 50 75 100 125 150 175 200 Km
0 25 50 75 100 125 150 175 200 Miles

Population

■ above 5 million
⊡ 1 million to 5 million
◉ 500,000 to 1 million
◎ 100,000 to 500,000
⊕ 50,000 to 100,000
○ 10,000 to 50,000
∘ below 10,000

247

286

263

HEBEI

Xinji
Hengshui
Nangong
Weixian
Handan
Anyang
Puyang
Huaxian
HENAN
ngzhou
Shangqiu
nchang
Taikang
heng
uohe
Zhoukou
iping
Xincai
Queshan
Xinyang
kai Shan
ngshan

Wuqiao
Dezhou
Yucheng
Linqing
Liaocheng
Jinan
Laiwu
Pingyin
Tai'an
Yanzhou
Qufu
Jining
Juye
Nanyang Hu
Jinxiang
Shanxian
Zaozhuang
Welshan Hu
Dangshan
Fuyang
Bozhou
Yongcheng
Mengcheng
Huaibei
Suzhou
Taihe
Huangchuan
Yeji
Jinzhai
Macheng
Yingshan
Hong'an
Huanggpi
Xishui
Ezhou
Huangshi

Binzhou
Boxing
Zibo
Boshan
Qingzhou
Huimin
Linyi
Dongying
Laizhou Wan
Dongying
Laizhou
Weifang
Pingdu
Suncun
Pingyi
Junan (Shizhu)
Linyi
SHANDONG
Qingdao

Lianyungang
Guanyun (Yishan)
Suqian
Suining
Funing
Sheyang
Yancheng
Huai'an
Gaoyou Hu
Gaoyou
Xinghua
Dongtai
Rugao
Yangzhou
Lube
Taizhou
Zhenjiang
Nantong
JIANGSU

Shandong Bandao
Laiyang
Wendeng
Rushan
Qingdao

Chongming Dao
Changjiang Kou
Shanghai
SHANGHAI SHI
Songjiang
Syiao Shan
Jiaxing
Zhoushan Qundao

Yellow Sea

SOUTH KOREA

Taejon
Kunsan
Chonju
Namwon
Kwangju
Mokpo
Sunch'on
Yosu
Hüksan-gundo
Chin-do
Kögum-do

Kimch'on
Miryang
Chinju
Sach'on
Chinhae
Kim Hae
Namhae-do
Kője-do

Taegu
Kyongju
Ulsan
Pusan
Tsushima
Korea Strait

P'ohang
Yongch'on

Sea of Japan
(East Sea)

Matsue
Honshu
Hiroshima
Kure
Yamaguchi
Tokuyama
Höfu
Suo-nada
Shimonoseki
Hibiki-nada
Kitakyūshū
Fukuoka
Kurume
Saga
Ōita
Kumamoto
Kyūshū
Nagasaki
Yatsushiro
Miyazaki
Kagoshima
Kanoya
Ōsumi-hantō
Nishinoomote
Tanega-shima

Cheju Strait
Cheju
Cheju-do
Sögwip'O
Songsan

Hirado-shima
Nakadōri-jima
Gotō-rettō
Fukue-jima
Koshikijima-rettō
Sasebo

JAPAN

Nobeoka
Nakamura
Sukomo
Shikoku
Beppu
Miyakonojō

East China Sea

Yokoate-jima
Tori-shima
Naze
Amami-guntō
Amami-Ō-shima
Kikai-shima
Tokuno-shima
Okinoerabu-jima
Iheya-jima
Yoron-jima
Izena-jima
Hedo-misaki
Aguni-jima
Ie-jima
Yonaha-dake 498m
Okinawa
Okinawa
Kume-jima
Kerama-rettō
Naha

Yaku-shima

Nansei-shotō
(Ryukyu Islands)

ANHUI
Bengbu
Dingyuan
Huainan
Hefei
Feixi
Lu'an
Chao Hu
Tongcheng
Anqing
Chibi
Chongyang
Ruichang
De'an
Jiujiang
Liangzi Hu
Xiu Shan
Shanggao
Gao'an
Wanzai
Yichun
Pingxiang
JIANGXI
Ji'an
Taihe
Hnggangshan
Suichuan
Ganzhou
Nankang
Xinfeng
Anyuan
Xunwu
Shaoguan
Quijiang
Wengyuan
ngde
NGDONG

Dable Shan
Jinzhai
Tangshan
Qichun
Huangmei
Po Hu
Jiujiang
Poyang Hu
Dexing
Jingdezhen
Leping
Changshan
Jiujiang Shan
Shangrao
Dongxiang
Nanchang
Jin Jiang
Gao'an
Xinjian
Shanggao
Xin'anjiang Shuiku

Nanjing
Ma'anshan
Wuhu
Tongling
Xuancheng
Ningguo
Hangzhou
Huangshan
Huangshan 2650m
Shexian
ZHEJIANG
Lanxi
Jinhua
Qu Jiang
Quzhou
Jiangshan
Lishui
Songyang
Wenzhou
Pingyang
Cangnan (Lingxi)
Fuding (Tongshan)
Zherong
Fu'an
Dayu Shan

Changzhou
Changshu
Wuxi
Yongxiao
Suzhou
Tai Hu
Huzhou
Songyu
Shangyu
Da Yunhe
Wangpan Yang
Zhoushan
Hangzhou
Shaoxing
Shengzhou
Ningbo
Tonglu
Chun'an
Xin'anjiang Shuiku
Tiantai
Xianju
Linhai
Huangyan
Taizhou
Sammen Wan
Wenzhou
Ruian
Yuhuan Dao
Wandang Shan
Xianxia Ling
Ruicang Shan

Fenghua
Ninghai

Chongqing Dao

Jingdezhen
Yiyang
Yanshan

Nanping
Shaowu
Jianyang
Xingtian
Jian'ou
Sian'tou
Youxi
Nanping
Jiangle
Taining
Jianning
Shaowu
Wuyishan
Songxi
FUJIAN
Sanming
Yong'an
Longyan
Liancheng
Ningdu
Yudu
Ruijin
Nanfeng
Yongfeng
Xinguo
Xingguo
Yong Shan
Yu Shan
Jiuling Shan
Gan Jiang

Liaoyuan
Lianjiang
Fuqing
Haitan Dao
Chiang Kai-shek
Nanri Dao
Nan'an
Linjiang
Quanzhou
Tong'an
Zhangzhou
Pinghe
Zhangpu
Yunxiao
Jieyang
Dongshan Dao
Chaozhou
Chenghai
Shantou
Chaoyang
Nan'ao Dao

Matsu Tao
(to Taiwan)

Uotsuri-shima
Sekibi-sho
Senkaku-shotō
(claimed by China, Japan, and Taiwan)

Huap'ing Yu
P'engchia Yü
Meinhua Yu
Huap'ing Yu
Chilung
T'aoyüan
T'AIPEI
Hsinchu
Chunan
Miaoli
Hsüeh Shan 3884m
Ilan
Suao
Tachoshui
Yonaguni-jima

Minna-jima
Hirakubo-saki
Yaeyama-shotō
Iriomote-jima
Paimi-saki
Hateruma-jima

Miyako-shotō
Irabu-jima
Tarama-jima
Kuro-jima
Ishigaki-jima
Miyako-jima
Miyako-jima

Sakishima-shotō

Tropic of Cancer

TAIWAN
T'aichung
Changhua
Yüanlin
Touliu
Chungyang Shanmo
Hualien
Nant'ou
Jiushui
Fenglin
2115m
Yuli
Chiai
Hsinying
T'ainan
P'ingtung
Kaohsiung
Fangshan
Kaohsiung
T'aitung
Lü Tao
Hengchun
Lan Yü
Oluan Pi

Chinmen Tao
(to Taiwan)
Quanzhou
Xiamen

Taiwan Strait
P'enghu Liehtao
Makung
P'enghu Yü
Pescadores Channel

(China and Taiwan claim all
of each other's territory)

Meizhou
Longchuan
Xinning
Fengshun
Heyuan
Lianping
Puning
Chaoyang

angzhon
n/Dongguan
Huizhou
Haifeng
Lufeng
Honghai Wan
men
Shenzhen
ngshan
Kowloon (Jiulong)
hai
Hong Kong (Xianggang)
Chep
acao
omen)
Lantau Island
Lai Kok
uan

South China Sea

Tungsha Tao

PHILIPPINES

Mayraira Point
Claveria
Laoag
Cabugao
Vigan
Candon
Dingras
Bangued
Tabuk
Bontoc
Bangar
Bangar
Cauayan
Lagawe
Echague
San Fernando

Luzon Strait

Batan Islands

Balintang Channel

Babuyan Channel
Babuyan Island

Bashi Channel

Aparri
Tuguegarao
Iluao
Cordillera Central
Mount Cagua 1133m
Escarpada Point
Sierra Madre
Cagayan
Luzon

Philippine Sea

Yangtze River Valley

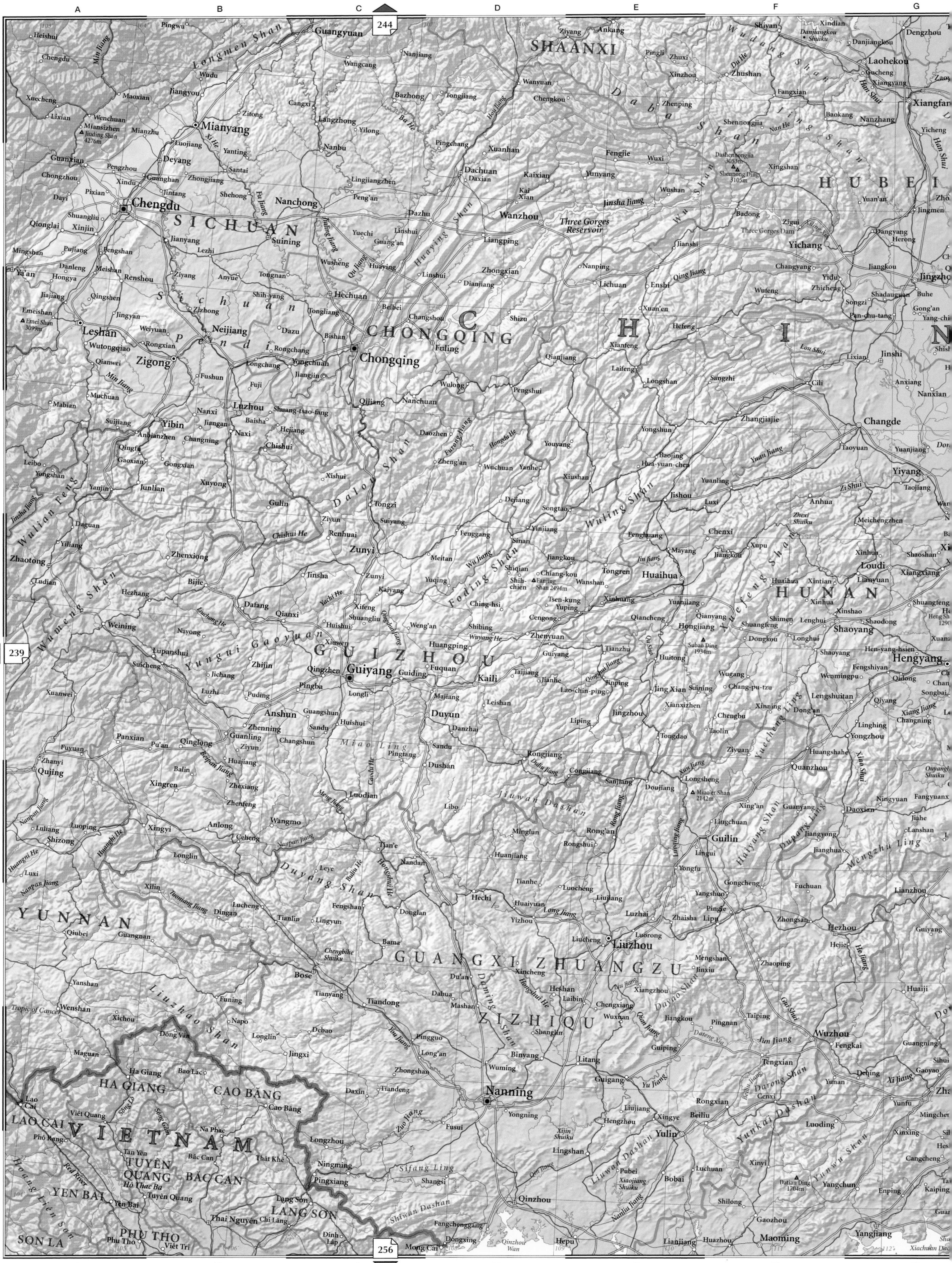

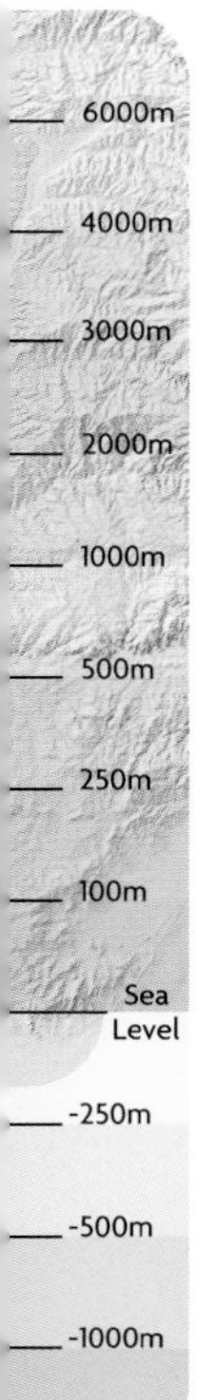

244

239

256

Elevation scale

6000m
4000m
3000m
2000m
1000m
500m
250m
100m
Sea Level
−250m
−500m
−1000m

Provinces / Regions: SHAANXI, HUBEI, SICHUAN, CHONGQING, GUIZHOU, HUNAN, YUNNAN, GUANGXI ZHUANGZU ZIZHIQU, VIETNAM, HA GIANG, CAO BANG, LANG SON, YEN BAI, SON LA, TUYEN QUANG, BAC CAN, PHU THO

Selected cities and towns: Guangyuan, Mianyang, Chengdu, Leshan, Zigong, Neijiang, Chongqing, Luzhou, Yibin, Zunyi, Guiyang, Anshun, Duyun, Kaili, Huaihua, Changde, Loudi, Hengyang, Guilin, Liuzhou, Nanning, Wuzhou, Yichang, Wanzhou, Three Gorges Reservoir, Three Gorges Dam

Physical features: Jinsha Jiang, Min Jiang, Wu Jiang, Yuan Jiang, Wuling Shan, Dalou Shan, Daba Shan, Emei Shan 3099m, Jiuding Shan 4270m, Yungui Gaoyuan, Red River

Scale 1:3,750,000
(projection: Lambert Conformal Conic)

0 20 40 60 80 100 Km
0 20 40 60 80 100 Miles

Population
- ▣ above 5 million
- ▣ 1 million to 5 million
- ● 500,000 to 1 million
- ◉ 100,000 to 500,000
- ⊕ 50,000 to 100,000
- ○ 10,000 to 50,000
- ○ below 10,000

245
243
286
263

ASIA

HENAN

ANHUI

JIANGSU

SHANGHAI SHI

ZHEJIANG

JIANGXI

FUJIAN

GUANGDONG

TAIWAN

East China Sea

South China Sea

Taiwan Strait

Bashi Channel

Pescadores Channel

Tropic of Cancer

(China and Taiwan claim all of each other's territory)

Huainan · Nanjing · Hefei · Wuhu · Ma'anshan · Wuhan · Huangshi · Jiujiang · Nanchang · Shangrao · Fuzhou · Ganzhou · Shantou · Xiamen · Quanzhou · Longyan · Hangzhou · Ningbo · Shaoxing · Wenzhou · Jinhua · Taizhou · Huangshan · Suzhou · Shanghai · Wuxi · Changzhou · Zhenjiang · Yangzhou · Nantong

Kowloon (Jiulong) · Hong Kong (Xianggang) · Guangzhou · Shenzhen · Shantou · Chaozhou

T'AIPEI · Chilung · Hsinchu · T'aichung · Chiai · T'ainan · Kaohsiung · Hualien · P'ingtung · Oluanpi

Elevation:
19,686ft
13,124ft
9843ft
6562ft
3281ft
1640ft
820ft
328ft
Sea Level
-820ft
-6562ft
-13,124ft

ASIA

244

239

246

242

Scale (elevation):
6000m
4000m
3000m
2000m
1000m
500m
250m
100m
Sea Level
-250m
-500m
-1000m

NEI MONGOL ZIZHIQU (INNER MONGOLIA)

Yin Shan

QINGHAI
GANSU
NINGXIA
SHAANXI
SICHUAN
HUBEI

Badain Jaran Shamo
Ulan Buh Shamo
Tengger Shamo
Mu Us Shadi
Yabrai Shan
Langshou Shan
Lang Shan
Helan Shan
Huangtu Gaoyuan
Baryu Shan
Qin Ling
Daba Shan
Min Shan
Longmen Shan
Dabashan
Kunlun Shan
Zhongtiao Shan
Xiao Shan
Xiong'er Shan
Funiu Shan
Wudang Shan
Micang Shan
Shennongjia

Huang He (Yellow River)
Shiyang He
Wei He
Jing He
Luo He
Fen He
Tao He
Bai He
Han Shui
Dan Jiang
Min Jiang
Jialing Jiang
Jiuding Shan 4276m
Taibai Shan 3767m
Lengglong Ling 4843m
Zhuozi Shan 2148m
Xinzhao Shan 2515m
Migang Shan 2924m
Li Shan 2322m
Guand... 2831m
Shouyang Shan 3720m
Laojun Shan 2192m
Bashennongjia 3053m
Shennong Ding 3105m

Cities and towns:
Baotou, Hohhot, Bayan Obo, Bailingmiao, Ulan Hua, Wuchuan, Guyang, Cha-su-chi, Guang, Wuyuan, Xamba, Linhe, Xishanzui, Ulansuhai Nur, Donghe, Salaqi, Qasq, Horinger, Togtoh, Liange, Shulinzhao, Ordos, Xuejiawan, Qingshuihe, Altan Xiret, Wuhai (Haibowan), Wuda, Shizuishan, Hotong Qagan Nur, Ulan, Bag Nur, Dabqig, Hongjian Nur, Shenmu, Lanyi He, Linxian, Shitanjing, Shizuishan, Rujigou, Pingluo, Taole, Xincheng, Helan, Yinchuan, Yongning, Lingwu, Xincheng, Caijialiang, Oljoq, Yulin, Hengshan, Mizhi, Zizhou, Qingtongxia, Wuzhong, Ciyaopu, Majiatan, Yanchi, Dingbian, Jingbian, Dali He, Suide, Liulin, Luliang, Wenshui, Fenyang, Zhongwei, Zhongning, Hui'anpu, Dashuikeng, Honggou He, Yongchang, Wuwei, Haomen, Gulang, Tianzhu, Tiantangsi, Bingcaowan, Yingpanshui, Gantang, Jingtai, Tongxin, Hongde, Huanxian, Qingcheng, Qingyang, Fuxian, Hongtong, Linfen, Weiyuan, Xining, Pinganyi, Ledu, Huzhu, Ping'an, Minhe, Nangdoi, Hualong, Gando, Yongjing, Lanzhou, Baiyin, Gaolan, Yuwang, Jingyuan, Maojing, Huachi, Heshui, Ningxian, Zhengning, Yan'an, Yichuan, Jixian, Jainca, Xunhua, Linxia, Dongxiangza, Dingxi, Gangouyi, Guochengyi, Donghaiba, Xiji, Guyuan, Qingyang, Huangling, Luochuan, Huozhou, Hezheng, Guanghe, Kangle, Lintao, Huining, Longde, Pengyang, Pingliang, Jingchuan, Zhengning, Hancheng, Jishan, Xinjiang, Quwo, Yicheng, Houma, Wanrong, Wenxi, Hezuo, Luqu, Lintan, Weiyuan, Longxi, Tongwei, Jingning, Jingyuan, Huating, Chongxing, Lingtai, Changwu, Tongchuan, Pucheng, Heyang, Linyi, Yuncheng, Xiaxian, Yongji, Sanmenxia, Yima, Luoyang, Jone, Zhangxian, Wenfengzhen, Gangu, Qin'an, Zhuanglang, Zhangjiachuan, Tongchuan, Fengxian, Qianxian, Jingyang, Sanyuan, Fuping, Dali, Ruicheng, Laotongguan, Tewo, Minxian, Wushan, Qingshui, Beidao, Tianshui, Qishan, Fufeng, Xianyang, Weinan, Huayin, Lingbao, Lazikou, Lujing, Xihe, Lixian, Baoji, Longriba, Zhouzhi, Huxian, Xi'an, Lintong, Lantian, Luonan, Shangzhou, Dangchang, Zhugqu, Liangdang, Huixian, Fengxian, Chengxian, Kangxian, Longnan, Wudu, Zolge, Waqen, Jiuzhaigou, Nanping, Zhongzhai, Lueyang, Mianxian, Chenggu, Yangxian, Ziyang, Shiquan, Shanyang, Danfeng, Laojun Shan, Zhen'an, Nanzha, Wenxian, Songpan, Bikou, Qingchuan, Ningqiang, Nanzheng, Hanzhong, Xixiang, Shiquan, Yunxi, Xixia, Nexiang, Heishui, Pingwu, Guangyuan, Nanjiang, Wangcang, Zhenba, Ankang, Pingli, Zhuxi, Zhushan, Shiyan, Xindian, Danjiangkou, Laohekou, Gucheng, Xiangyang, Fangxian, Nanyang, Den Xian, Dengzhou, Xinecheng, Wenchuan, Lixian, Miansizhen, Mianzhu, Luojiang, Mianyang, Yanting, Santai, Zhongjiang, Guanghan, Xindu, Chengdu, Chongzhou, Dayi, Pixian, Jintang, Pengzhou, Deyang, Zitong, Jiangyou, Maoxian, Langzhong, Yilong, Nanbu, Bazhong, Tongjiang, Chengkou, Wanyuan, Zhenping, Baokang, Nanzhang, Xinzhou, Fengjie, Kaixian, Yunyang, Wushan, Xingshan, Wuxi, Daxian, Dachuan, Xuanhan, Peng'an, Lingjiangzhen, Peng'an, Shehong, Nanbu, Yichang

Scale 1:3,750,000
(projection: Lambert Conformal Conic)

0 20 40 60 80 100 Km
0 20 40 60 80 100 Miles

Population
- ■ above 5 million
- ▣ 1 million to 5 million
- ◉ 500,000 to 1 million
- ◎ 100,000 to 500,000
- ⊕ 50,000 to 100,000
- ○ 10,000 to 50,000
- ○ below 10,000

247 · 248 · 243 · 245

ASIA

245

Elevation scale:
19,686ft
13,124ft
9843ft
6562ft
3281ft
1640ft
820ft
328ft
Sea Level
-820ft
-6562ft
-13,124ft

LIAONING · **HEBEI** · **SHANDONG** · **JIANGSU** · **ANHUI** · **HENAN** · **SHANGHAI SHI** · **BEIJING SHI** · **TIANJIN SHI**

Bo Hai · **Bohai Wan** · **Laizhou Wan** · **Liaodong Wan** · **Korea Bay** · **Yellow Sea** · **Bohai Haixia** · **Liaodong Bandao** · **Shandong Bandao**

Major cities and places:

Beijing (Peking), Tianjin, Shenyang, Fushun, Anshan, Benxi, Haicheng, Yingkou, Dalian, Jinzhou, Chaoyang, Fuxin, Beipiao, Liaoyang, Panjin, Qinhuangdao, Tangshan, Chengde, Zhangjiakou, Xuanhua, Datong, Baoding, Shijiazhuang, Handan, Xingtai, Hengshui, Cangzhou, Dezhou, Jinan, Zibo, Qingzhou, Weifang, Yantai, Weihai, Qingdao, Rizhao, Binzhou, Dongying, Heze, Jining, Zaozhuang, Linyi, Lianyungang, Xuzhou, Suzhou, Bengbu, Huainan, Hefei, Ma'anshan, Wuhu, Nanjing, Zhenjiang, Changzhou, Wuxi, Suzhou, Shanghai, Nantong, Yangzhou, Taizhou, Yancheng, Huai'an, Zhengzhou, Kaifeng, Xinxiang, Anyang, Hebi, Shangqiu, Zhoukou, Fuyang

RUSSIA

RESPUBLIKA ALTAY
RESPUBLIKA KHAKASIYA
KRASNOYARSKIY KRAY
RESPUBLIKA TYVA
RESPUBLIKA BURYATIYA
IRKUTSKAYA OBLAST'

Ozero Baykal

MONGOLIA
BAYAN-ÖLGIY
UVS
HOVD
GOVI-ALTAY
DZAVHAN
ARHANGAY
HÖVSGÖL
BULGAN
SELENGE
TÖV
ÖVÖRHANGAY
BAYANHONGOR
DUNDGOVI
ÖMNÖGOVI
DORNOGOVI

ULAANBAATAR (ULAN BATOR)

XINJIANG UYGUR ZIZHIQU

QINGHAI
GANSU
NINGXIA
NEI MONGOL

CHINA

Qingzang Gaoyuan (Plateau of Tibet)

Altai Mountains

Qaidam Pendi

Lanzhou
Xining
Yinchuan
Baotou
Ordos
Xi'an
SHAANXI

Turpan
Hami
Dunhuang
Yumen
Jiuquan (Suzhou)
Zhangye (Ganzhou)
Wuwei
Golmud

Irkutsk
Ulan-Ude
Sühbaatar
Darhan
Erdenet

193
239
240

— 6000m
— 4000m
— 3000m
— 2000m
— 1000m
— 500m
— 250m
— 100m
— Sea Level
— -250m
— -500m
— -1000m

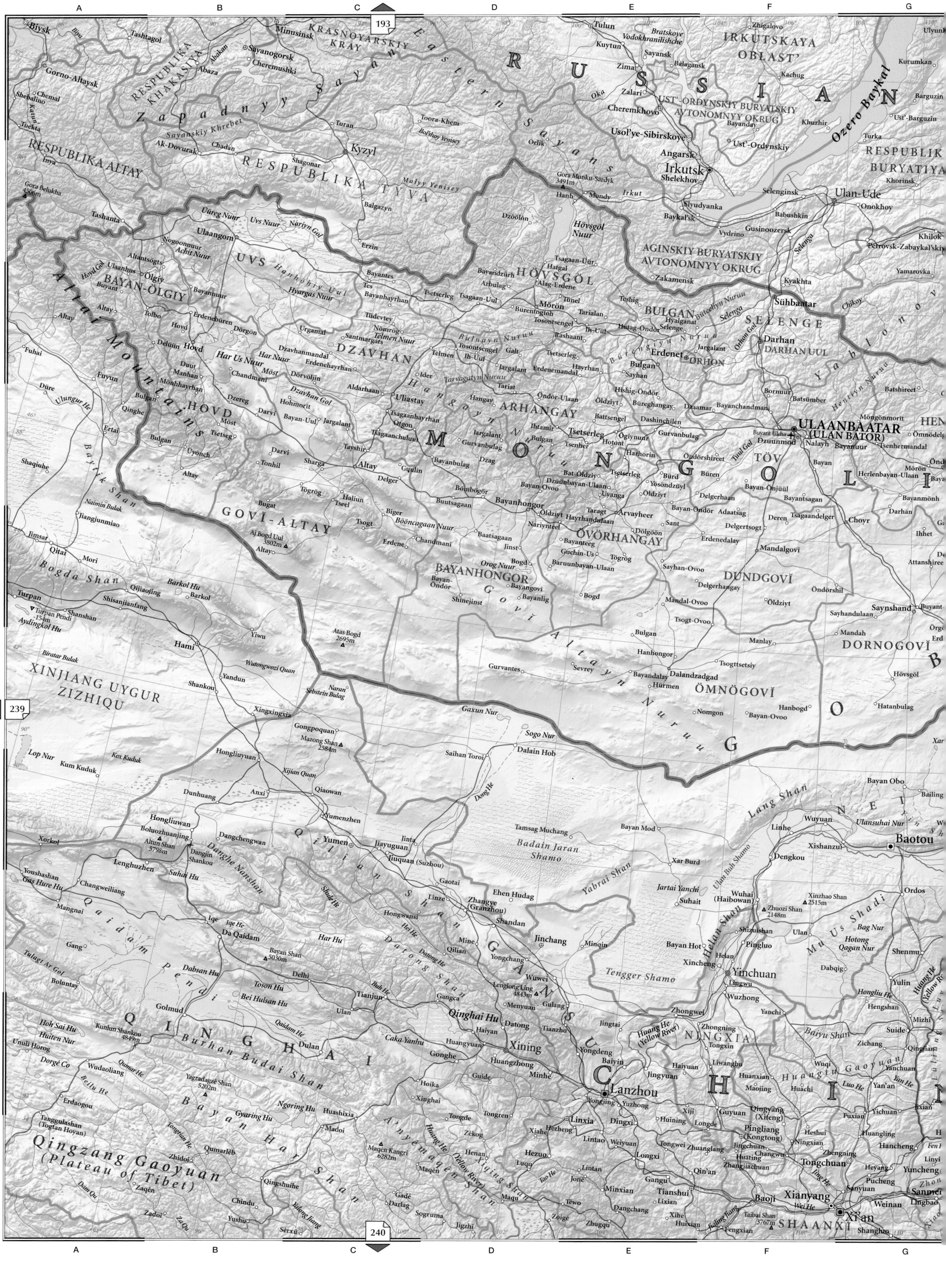

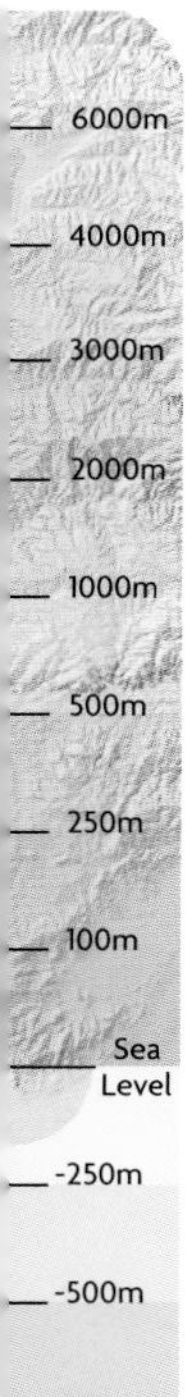

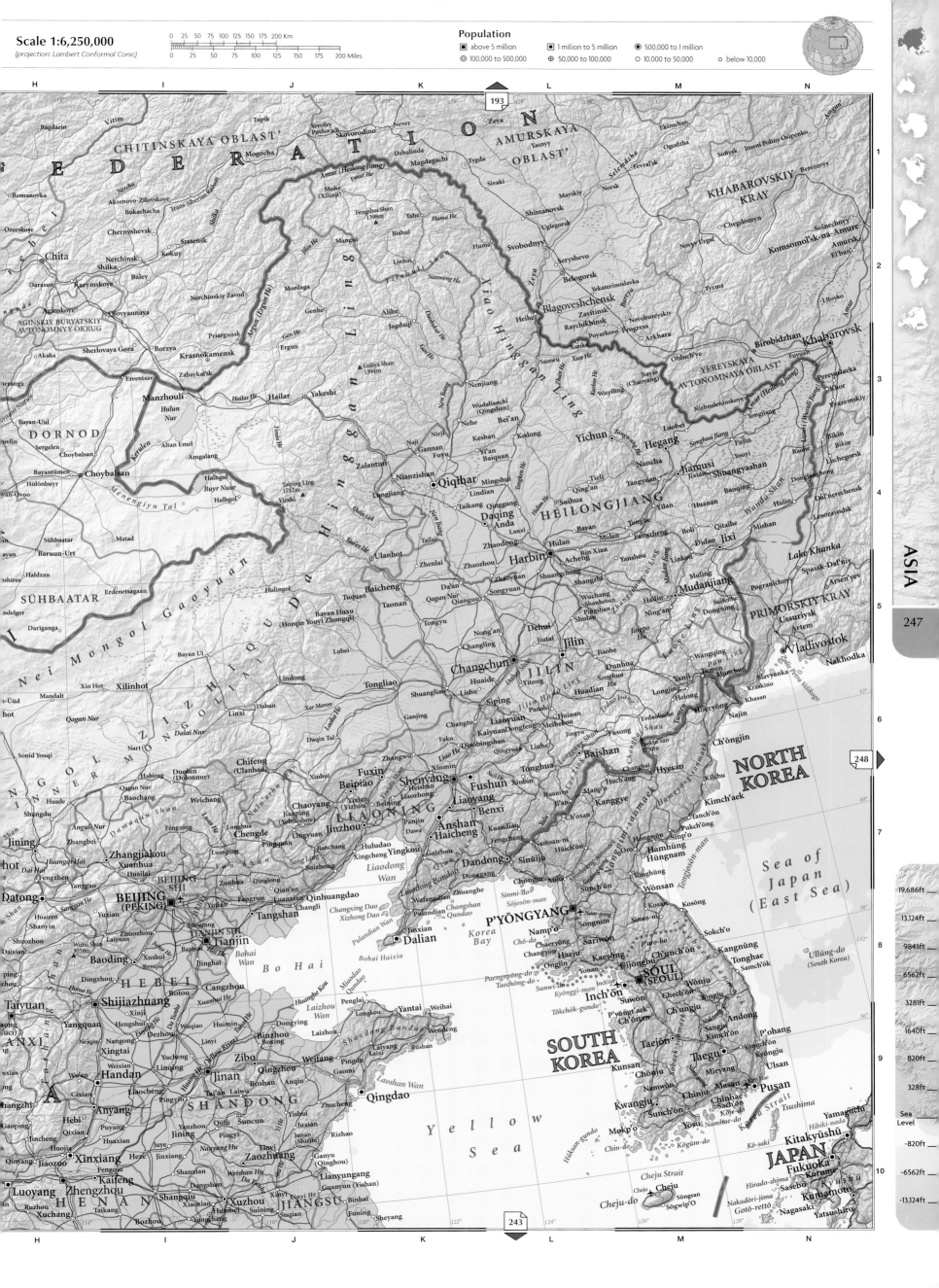

Korea & Japan

CHINA

JILIN

LIAONING

NEI MONGOL ZIZHIQU (INNER MONGOLIA)

RUSSIAN FEDERATION

PRIMORSK KRAY

NORTH KOREA

SOUTH KOREA

JAPAN

Sea of Japan (East Sea)

Yellow Sea

Korea Bay

East China Sea

Philippine Sea

Korea Strait

Cheju-Strait

Cities and places (selected):

Tongliao, Shuanglian, Changchun, Jilin, Gongzhuling, Lishu, Siping, Liaoyuan, Kaiyuan, Tieling, Fushun, Shenyang, Anshan, Liaoyang, Haicheng, Benxi, Dandong, Sinŭiju, Beipiao, Fuxin, Jinzhou, Yingkou, Gaizhou, Wafangdian, Pulandian, Jinzhou, Baishan, Tonghua, Kuandian, Manp'o, Hyesan, Ch'osan, Kanggye, Kilchu, Ch'ŏngjin, Kimch'aek, Tanch'ŏn, Hamhŭng, Hŭngnam, Wŏnsan, P'YŎNGYANG, Namp'o, Changyon, Sariwŏn, Haeju, Kaesŏng, Kosŏng, Sokch'o, Kangnŭng, Tonghae, Samch'ŏk, SŎUL (SEOUL), Inch'ŏn, Suwŏn, Wŏnju, Ch'unch'ŏn, Andong, Taejŏn, Kunsan, Chŏnju, Kwangju, Namwŏn, Mokp'o, Taegu, Kyŏngju, Ulsan, P'ohang, Chinju, Masan, Chinhae, Pusan, Yŏsu, Sunch'ŏn, Cheju, Sŏgwip'o

Vladivostok, Nakhodka, Ussuriysk, Artem, Spassk-Dal'niy, Lesozavodsk

Hiroshima, Okayama, Kōbe, Ōsaka, Kyōto, Nagoya, Fukuoka, Kitakyūshū, Shimonoseki, Kumamoto, Kagoshima, Nagasaki, Saga, Ōita, Miyazaki, Matsue, Tottori, Kōchi, Matsuyama, Takamatsu, Tokushima, Wakayama

KYŪSHŪ, SHIKOKU

Cheju, Tsushima, Ullŭng-do

Southern Japan

247

A B C D E F G

1

2

3

4

5

6

7

8

9

10

SOUTH KOREA

KANG-WON-DO
KYONGGI-DO
CH'UNGCH'ONGBUK-DO
KYONGSANGBUK-DO
CHOLLABUK-DO
KYONGSANGDAM-DO

Kwangju
Pubal
Yoju
Wonju
P'yongch'ang
Tonghae
Samch'ok
Chongson
Shindong
Sabuk
Togye
T'aebaek
Kumwang
Umsong
Chech'on
Yong-wol
Kohan
Wondok
Ch'ungju
Tanyang
P'unggi
T'aebaek-san
1568m
Ch'ongju
Ch'ung'yong
Kocsan
Paegam-san
1003m
Ulchin
Taejon
Sangju
Sonsan
Andong
Yong-yang
P'yonghae
Och'on
Kumi
Kunwi
An'gang
Yonil
Taech'ong Lake
Poun
Pohyon-san
1915m
Ch'ongsong
Yongdong
Hamch'ang
Naktong-gang
Hunghae
Muju
Kimch'on
Woegwan
P'ohang
Kimi
Songju
TAEGU CITY
Hayang
Yongch'on
Kyongju
Hamyang
Kaya
Hapch'on
Taegu
Kyongsan
Kuryongp'o
Sanch'ong
Chiri-san
1915m
Ch'angnyong
Miryang
Oedong
Chinyang Lake
Hanam
Sammangjin
Ulsan
Chinju
Uiryong
Chinyong
Yangsan
Hadong
Namhae-do
Masan
Ch'ang Won
Chang-An
Yoch'on
Kosong
Shin-dong
Kijang
Yosu
Tolsan
Sach'on
Tongyong
Kim Hae
Chinhae
Pusan
Kumogundo-do
Kuju-do
Koje-do
Sorido-do

Kami-Agata
Kami-Tsushima
Tsushima
Mitsushima
Izuhara
Ko-saki

Sea of Japan
(East Sea)

Ullung-do
Liancourt Rocks
Oki-shoto
Dogo
Saigo
Dozen
Nakano-shima
Chiburi-jima
Oki-kaikyo

Shimane-hanto
Jizo-zaki
Matsue
Sakaiminato
Nakano-ichi
Aoya
Hirata
Kurayoshi
Hino-misaki
Shinji-ko
Yasugi
Yonago
TOTTORI
Taisha
Izumo
Kisuki
Dai-sen
1729m
Katsuyama
Tsuyama
Sanbe-san
1126m
Kofu
Oda
Yokota
SHIMANE
Tojo
Niimi
Tsuyama
Waki
Hamada
Go-gawa
Tombara
Dogo-yama
1269m
OKAYAMA
Takahashi
Gotsu
Kake
Shobara
Soja
Bizen
Susa
Abu
Masuda
Garyu-san
1223m
Miyoshi
Takahashi-gawa
Okayama
Tsuno-shima
Omi-shima
Hagi
Ato
Tsuwano
HIROSHIMA
Kozan
Fuchu
Ibara
Kurashiki
Tamano
Hohoku
Nagato
YAMAGUCHI
Kammuri-yama
1339m
Higashi-Hiroshima
Mihara
Onomichi
Sakaide
Takamatsu
Toyoura
Mine
Yamaguchi
Hiroshima
Kure
Innoshima
Marugame
Zentsuji
Hikita
Higashi-suido
Iki
Katsumoto
Ogori
Shinnanyo
Tokuyama
Otake
Kitahashi-jima
Kan'onji
KAGAWA
Gonoura
Shimonoseki
Onoda
Hofu
Iwakuni
Imabari
Toyo
Waki
Komatsu
Kitakyushu
Ube
Kudamatsu
Hikari
Yanai
Hojo
Hiuchi-nada
Niihama
TOKUSHIMA
Nakama
Suo-nada
Hime-jima
Naga-shima
Yashiro-jima
Matsuyama
Kamega-mori
1896m
Tsurugi-san
1955m
Fukuoka
Nogata
Iizuka
Tagawa
Yukuhashi
Nakatsu
Bungo-Takada
Iyo
Ishizuchi-san
1982m
Otoyo
Genkai-nada
Kasuga
FUKUOKA
Buzen
Usa
Nagahama
Heigun-to
EHIME
Kuma
Yoshino-gawa
Oshima
Yobuko
Karatsu
Onojo
Amagi
Hiko-san
1200m
Kitsuki
Iyo-nada
Sadamisaki-hanto
Ozu
Yawatahama
KOCHI
Tosa
Kochi
Aki
Azuchi-O-shima
Ikitsuki-shima
Hirado
Matsuura
Taku
SAGA
Ogori
Kurume
Hita
Beppu-wan
Uwa
Uwajima
Yusuhara
Susaki
Toyo
Uku-jima
Hirado-shima
Imari
Saga
Kashima
Kurogi
Yame
Beppu
Oita
Misaki
Oniga-yama
1151m
Kubokawa
Nankoku
Ojika-jima
Sasebo
Takeo
Ariake-kai
Omagawa
Yamaga
OITA
Ozu
Inukai
Hoyo-kaikyo
NAGASAKI
Arikawa
Matsubara
Isahaya
Tamana
Kikuchi
Takamori
Taketa
Usuki
Saiki
Nakadori-jima
Gotō-rettō
Narao
Omura
Arao
Uto
Kumamoto
Sobo-san
1757m
Tsukumi
Tsurumi-zaki
Fukue
Fukue-jima
Shimabara
KUMAMOTO
Kunimi-dake
1739m
Hinokage
Nobeoka
Ose-zaki
Nomo-zaki
Kuchinotsu
Yatsushiro
Kyushu-sanchi
Hyuga
Amakusa-nada
Shimo-jima
Hondo
Ushibuka
Shimabara-wan
Yatsushiro-kai
Minamata
Yunomae
Ichifusa-yama
1227m
Tsuno
Nagashima
Izumi
Hitoyoshi
Saito
Takanabe
Kami-Koshiki-jima
Akune
Okuchi
MIYAZAKI
Kobayashi
Koshikijima-retto
Miyakonojo
Kirishima-yama
1700m
Miyazaki
Shimo-Koshiki-jima
Sendai
Miyanojo
KAGOSHIMA
Kushikino
Kokubu
Nichinan
Kagoshima
On-take
117m
Miyakonojo
Noma-zaki
Kaseda
Tarumizu
Shibushi
Kushima
Satsuma-hanto
Shibushi-wan
Ibusuki
Kanoya
Toi-misaki
Makurazaki
Yamagawa
Uchinoura
Kuro-shima
Osumi-hanto
Kusagaki-gunto
Sata-misaki
Take-shima
Osumi-kaikyo
Io-jima
Mage-shima
Nishinoomote
Kuchinoerabu-jima
Tanega-shima
Kamiyaku
Minamitane
Yaku-shima

Korea Strait

East China Sea

Philippin

Shikoku
Chugoku-sanchi
Shikoku-sanchi
Kyūshū

Philippine Sea

286

Inset 1

East China Sea
Sakishima-shotō
Miyako-shotō
Irabu-jima
Miyako-jima
Minna-jima
Hirara
Yaeyama-shotō
Tarama-jima
Yonaguni
Yonaguni-jima
Iriomote-jima
Ishigaki-jima
Hirakubo-saki
OKINAWA
Ishigaki
Kuro-shima
Philippine Sea
Paimi-saki
Hateruma-jima

Scale 1:3,250,000
0 20 40 Km
0 10 20 40 Miles

Kurile Islands

Ostrov Iturup

Ostrov Kunashir

Ostrov Shikotan

Habomai Islands

Ostrov Zelýony

(Administered by Russian Federation, claimed by Japan)

Sea of Okhotsk

Nemuro-kaikyō

Notsuke-zaki

Nemuro-wan

Nemuro

Ochiishi-misaki

Rausu-dake 1660m

Rausu

Shiretoko-misaki

Shiretoko-hantō

Shari

Kussharo-ko

Mashū-ko

Nakashibetsu

Shibetsu

Nishibetsu-gawa

Bekkai

Fūren-ko

Hamanaka

Akkeshi

Akkeshi-wan

Akkeshi-ko

Teshikaga

Shibecha

Ō-Akan-dake 1499m

Akan-ko

Akan

Kushiro

Kushiro

Onbetsu

Tokoro

Mombetsu

Yūbetsu

Okoppe

Omu

Engaru

Sōrachi-gawa

Bihoro

Abashiri-ko

Abashiri

Notoro-ko

Saroma-ko

Kitami

Rubeshibe

Sekihoku-tōge 1050m

Shirataki

Takinoue

Setouchi

Kitami-sanchi

Shibetsu

Kamikawa

Biei

Asahikawa

Asahi-dake 2290m

HOKKAIDŌ

Tokachi-dake 2077m

Furano

Kami-Shihoro

Karikachi-tōge 644m

Obihiro

Shiranuka

Shintoku

Shimizu

Ashoro

Ikeda

Urahoro

Taiki

Hiroo

Kamui-dake 1601m

Erimo-misaki

Hidaka-sanmyaku

Hiroo-dake 2052m

Urakawa

Samani

Mitsuishi

Shizunai

Shintoku

Biratori

Tomikawa

Mukawa

Niikappu-gawa

Yūbari-sanchi

Yūbari

Iwamizawa

Mikasa

Bibai

Hashima

Ishikari-gawa

Takikawa

Namina

Shumarinai-ko 1491m

Otoineppu

Teshio-gawa

Nakagawa

Horokanai

Rumoi

Mashike

Obira

Haboro

Shosanbetsu

Enbetsu

Tomamae

Teshio

Nakatonbetsu

Esashi

Hamatonbetsu

Sarufutsu

Sōya-misaki

Wakkanai

Noshappu-misaki

Rishiri-suidō

Teuri-tō

Yagishiri-tō

Rishiri-yama 1719m

Rishiri-tō

Rebun-tō

Rebun

La Perouse Strait

Zaliv Aniva

Mys Aniva

Mys Kril'on

Ostrov Sakhalin

Ostrov Moneron

RUSSIAN FEDERATION

Khrebet Shränki-Aitý

Velikiye Kema

Maksimovka

Sea of Japan (East Sea)

Okushiri-tō

O-shima

Matsumae-misaki

Benkei-misaki

Kamui-misaki

Yobetsu-dake 1280m

Shakotan-misaki

Kabatoyama 1530m

Setana

Kitahiyama

Imagane

Taisei

Kumaishi

Kaminokuni

Esashi

Matsumae

Shirakami-misaki

Kikonai

Fukushima

Tappi-zaki

Tsugaru-kaikyō

Hakodate

Mori

Shikabe

Minami-Kayabe

Esan-misaki

Oma-zaki

Oma

Ohata

Osorezan 879m

Kawauchi

Shiriya-zaki

Mutsu

Yokohama

Rokkasho

Ogawara-ko

Noheji

Suchinohe

Towada

Aomori

Hirosaki

Iwaki-san 1580m

Namioka

Goshogawara

Tsugaru-hantō

Jūsan-ko

Minmaya

Kanita

Kuroishi

Iwada

Fukaura

Ajigasawa

Shakotan

Furubira

Yoichi

Otaru

KatChan

Niseko

Yotei-zan 1898m

Shakotan-misaki

Iwanai

Kamoenai

Kuromatsunai

Suttsu

Oshamanbe

Yakumo

Kumaishi

Uchiura-wan

Datè

Noboribetsu

Muroran

Shiraoi

Oshima-hantō

Ishikari-wan

Ishikari

Ebetsu

Sapporo

Eniwa

Chitose

Shikotsu-ko

Tarumai-zan 1320m

Tomakomai

Toya-ko

Usu-dake

Noboribetsu

Kitahiroshima

Sea of Japan (East Sea)

Southeast Asia

239

234

289

Countries and regions: CHINA, MYANMAR (BURMA), BANGLADESH, INDIA, BHUTAN, LAOS, THAILAND, VIETNAM, CAMBODIA, MALAYSIA, BRUNEI, SINGAPORE, INDONESIA, Borneo, Kalimantan, Sumatera, Jawa (Java)

Seas and water bodies: Bay of Bengal, Andaman Sea, INDIAN OCEAN, Gulf of Thailand, SOUTH CHINA SEA, Gulf of Tongking, Gulf of Martaban, Strait of Malacca, Java Sea, Makassar Strait, Balabac Strait, Palawan Passage

Capitals and cities:
THIMPHU, DHAKA, Kolkata, Chittagong, MYANMAR (BURMA), PYINMANA, YANGON (RANGOON), Mandalay, Bassein, Pegu, Moulmein, KRUNG THEP (BANGKOK), Chiang Mai, Nakhon Ratchasima, VIANGCHAN (VIENTIANE), HA NOI, Hai Phong, Hong Gai, Nam Dinh, Vinh, Huê, Đà Nẵng, Quy Nhơn, Nha Trang, Cam Ranh, Đà Lat, Hồ Chí Minh, Vung Tau, Biên Hoa, PHNUM PENH (PHNOM PENH), Bàtdâmbâng, Kâmpóng Cham, KUALA LUMPUR, PUTRAJAYA, George Town, Ipoh, Johor Bahru, SINGAPORE, BANDAR SERI BEGAWAN, Kuching, Kota Kinabalu, JAKARTA, Bandung, Semarang, Surabaya, Yogyakarta, Palembang, Medan, Padang, Pontianak, Banjarmasin, Balikpapan, Samarinda

China cities: Chongqing, Chengdu region, Kunming, Guiyang, Nanning, Guangzhou, Kowloon, Hong Kong (Xianggang), Macao (Aomen), Changsha, Nanchang, Fuzhou, Xiamen, Shantou, Liuzhou, Guilin, Haikou, Hainan Dao

Physical features: Himalayas, Mount Everest 8850m, Hkakabo Razi 5885m, Shan Plateau, Korat Plateau, Plateau de Xiangkhoang, Chin Hills, Arakan Range, Arakan Yoma, Annapurna, Irrawaddy, Brahmaputra, Mekong, Salween, Chindwin, Red River, Black River, Mouths of the Ganges, Mouths of the Irrawaddy, Mouths of the Mekong, Tonlé Sap, Malay Peninsula, Greater Sunda Islands, Andaman Islands (to India), Nicobar Islands (to India), North Andaman, Middle Andaman, South Andaman, Port Blair, Little Andaman, Car Nicobar, Great Nicobar, Ten Degree Channel

Disputed islands: PARCEL ISLANDS (disputed), SPRATLY ISLANDS (disputed)

Scale (elevation): 6000m, 4000m, 3000m, 2000m, 1000m, 500m, 250m, 100m, Sea Level, -250m, -500m, -1000m

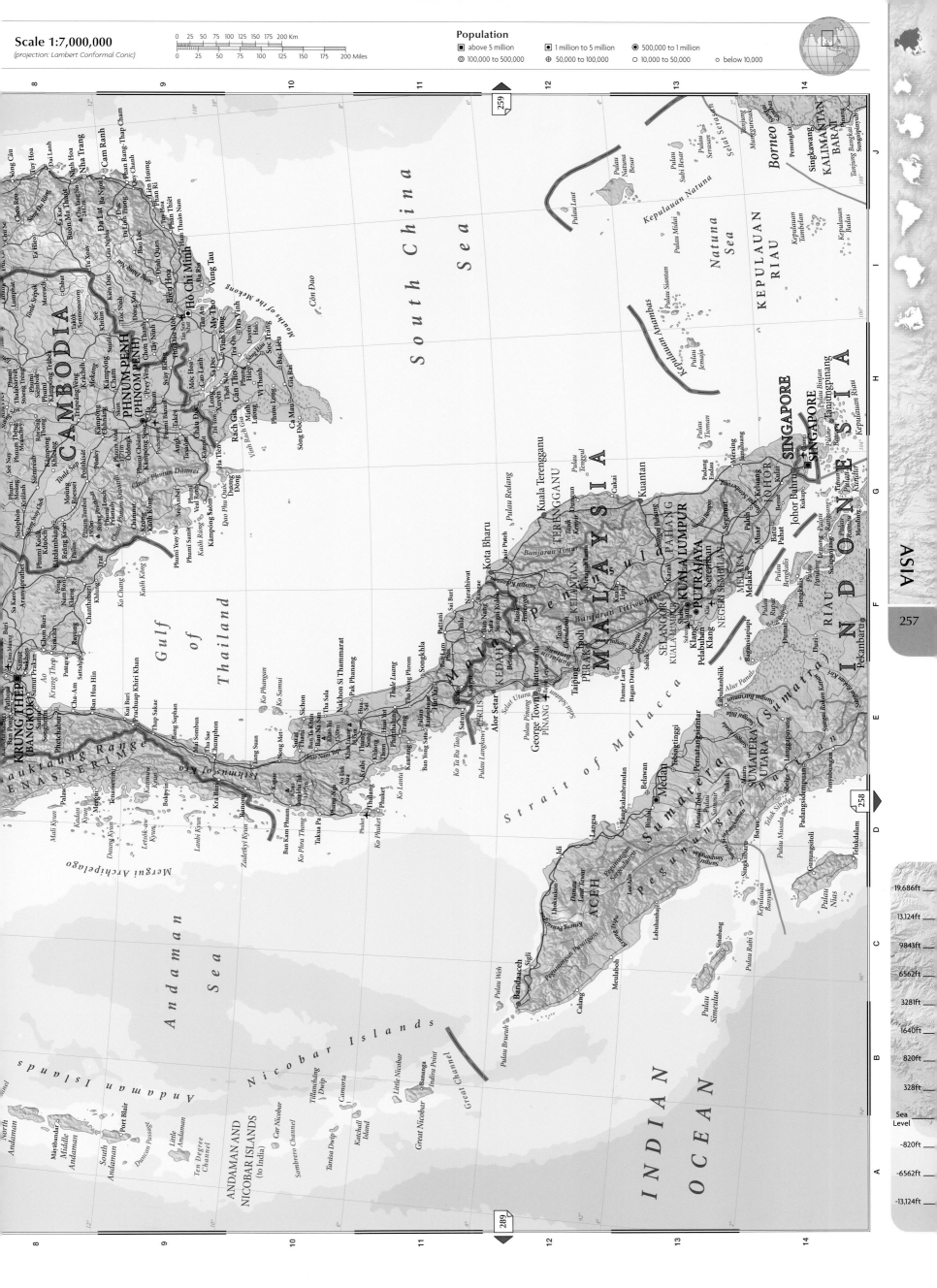

Western Maritime Southeast Asia

Singapore

Map elevation legend
- 6000m
- 4000m
- 3000m
- 2000m
- 1000m
- 500m
- 250m
- 100m
- Sea Level
- -250m
- -500m
- -1000m

Scale 1:7,000,000
(projection: Mercator)

0 25 50 75 100 125 150 175 200 Km
0 25 50 75 100 125 150 175 200 Miles

Population
- ☐ above 5 million
- ☐ 1 million to 5 million
- ◉ 500,000 to 1 million
- ◎ 100,000 to 500,000
- ⊕ 50,000 to 100,000
- ○ 10,000 to 50,000
- ∘ below 10,000

Eastern Maritime Southeast Asia

PHILIPPINES

Palimbang Mount Busa 2083m Surallah Malita Cape San Agustin
Kiamba Packer General Santos
Mindanao Tinaca Point Glan Jose Abad Santos
Sarangani Islands

Panguturan Group Jolo Jolo Samales Group
Tapul Group
Tawitawi Tawitawi Group Balimbing
Sibutu Sibutu Passage
Sulu Archipelago

Kepulauan Nanusa
Kepulauan Kawio Pulau Karakelong Kepulauan Talaud
Melanguane
Pulau Salibabu Pulau Kaburuang Damau

Celebes Sea

Tahuna Pulau Sangihe
Kepulauan Sangir
Ulu Pulau Siau
Pulau Tahulandang

MALAYSIA

Kota Kinabalu Gunung Kinabalu 4101m
Tuaran Ranau Sungai Sugut Teluk Labuk Labuk
Kota Kinabalu Keningau Sandakan
Teluk Kimanis Tambunan Sungai Labuk
Kuala Penyu SABAH
LABUAN Tenom Sungai Segama Lahad Datu
Pulau Labuan Labuan Sungai Segama
Bandar Seri Begawan Brunei Bay Teluk Lahad Datu
Kuala Belait **BANDAR SERI BEGAWAN** Tawau Pulau Timbun Mata
BRUNEI Pulau Sebatik
Miri Pulau Bum Bum

Tanjung
Sopi
Pulau Morotai
Galela Tobelo Iga Dodaga
Pediwang Buli
Kepulauan Loloda Utara Tanjung Bisa
Pulau Mayu Bobopayo **TERNATE**
Pulau Ternate Pulau Tidore Kusu Teluk Kau
Soasiu
MALUKU UTARA Pulau Makian Pulau Halmahera
Teluk Weda Halmahera Sea
Mafa

SARAWAK

Loagan Bunut
Pegunungan Iban Penambo Range
Batang Baram
Pegunungan Hose

Borneo

KALIMANTAN TIMUR
Sungai Bahau Sungai Berau Tanjungbatu Pulau Maratua
Sungai Kayan Tanjungredeb
Sungai Kelai
Metulang Pegunungan Sambaliung
Muarawahau Sangkulirang Gunung Antu 750m
Gunung Menyapa 2000m Sepasu Teluk Sangkulirang
Longiram

Kalimantan

Muarajuloi Danau Semayang
Kunyi Danau Melintang Tenggarong Tanjung Ayu
Muaratewe Danau Jempang **Samarinda** Lohjanan Tanjung Bayur
Sangasanga
Bawan Muarakaman
Palangkaraya **KALIMANTAN TENGAH** Waru Teluk Balikpapan **Balikpapan**
Dayu Muaramuntai
Amuntai **Tanjung** Kepulauan Balabalangan
KALIMANTAN SELATAN
Negara Kandangan
Rantau
Banjarmasin Kotabaru
Martapura Pulau Laut
Pelaihari Karambu Pulau Sebuku

Sulu Archipelago Sibutu Passage

Teluk Pantai

Teluk Sebuku Pulau Mandul
Bunyu Pulau Bunyu
Tarakan Pulau Tarakan
Pulau Mapat
Sungai Sesayap
Sungai Sembakung

SULAWESI UTARA

Salumpaga Oan Teluk Bilang **Manado** Tomohon Airmadidi
Tolitoli Leok Lanu Teluk Paleleh Bitung Tondano
Tompe Teluk Dondo Gunung 2499m Danau Tondano
Teluk Dampal Dondo Pegunungan Paleleh Kuandang Amurang
GORONTALO Lemito **Gorontalo** Kotamobagu
Danau Limboto Bubaa Gunung Bulosa 1970m
Molosipat Teluk Gorontalo Molibagu

Teluk Amurang
Serai Pulau Bangka
Selat Bangka

Molucca Sea

Pulau Kasiruta Kepulauan Bacan Pulau Kasiruta
Pulau Bacan Pulau Mandioli
Selat Obi Gani
Kawassi Pulau Obi Pulau Bisa
Kepulauan Sula Pulau Gomumu
Sanana Sesepe
Kepulauan Sula Pulau Sanana *Ceram Sea*
Tanjung Lasahata Pitu
Waflia Namlea Pulau Boano
Gunung Kaubalatmada 2729m Danau Rana Kelang Luhu Saparua
Kelang Pulau Manipa **Ambon**
Tifu Pulau Buru Watawa Pulau Ambon
Elara Ambelau Kepulauan
MALUKU

Celebes Sea

Kepulauan Togian
Pulau Togian
Gulf of Tomini
Teluk Tomini Pulau Batudaka
Tate Towera Teluk Uebonti Teluk Poh Toima Maliku
Donggala Dondo Bolaang Teku
Luwuk Balo
Palu Lambogo Tambarana Pegunungan Balingara Pulau Peleng
Pakuli Tobamawu Kembani Pelei
Danau Lindu Pandiri **SULAWESI TENGAH** Baturebe Pulau Banggai
Danau Gimpu Poso Kepulauan Banggai Pulau Taliabu Tuno Capalulu
Tentena Tobamawu Pulau Mangole
Karosa Taripa Kepulauan Sula
Babana Danau Poso Pulau Treko
SULAWESI BARAT Danau Matana Teluk Towori Teluk Tolo
Mamuju Masamba Saroako Mahalona
Sulawesi (Celebes) Wotu Danau Towuti
Malunda Rantepao Kepulauan Salabangka Pulau Manui
Teluk Lebani Asera Kepulauan Salabangka
Majene Enrekang Wiau Pegunungan Abuki
Polewali Sungai Saddang Anabanua Kolaka **SULAWESI TENGGARA**
Parepare Danau Sidenreng Singkang Padamarang Kendari
Danau Tempe Danau Towuti Pulau Wowoni
SULAWESI SELATAN Watampone Kakea
Kepulauan Pabbiring Wowoni
Teluk Mamuju Bugingkalo Selat Tiore
Makassar Maros Lasihao Tampo Bonelipu
Takalar Selat Kabaena Pulau Muna Teluk Kolowanawatobe
Bulukumba Pising Baubau Kamaru
Jeneponto Pulau Kabaena Pulau Kaledupa Kepulauan Langkesi
Pulau Selayar Pulau Kaledupa Kepulauan Tukangbesi
Benteng Selat Selayar Pulau Binongko
Pulau Kabia Pulau Batuata

Makassar Strait

Kepulauan Laut Kecil
Pulau Karamain
Pulau Masalembo-besar

I N D O N E S I A

Banda Sea

Kepulauan Macan
Pulau Bonerate
Kepulauan Bonerate
Pulau Sabalana Pulau Tanahjampea
Kepulauan Tengah Pulau Kalao Kepulauan Damar
Pulau Bonerate Pulau Kalaotoa Pulau Damar

Ambunten Pulau Kangean Kepulauan Kangean
Sumenep
Pulau Sapudi
Pulau Wetar Selat Romang Pulau Romang
Jawa (Java) Situbondo *Bali Sea*
Bondowoso *Flores Sea* Kepulauan Leti
Gunung Raung Singaraja **NUSA TENGGARA BARAT** Puhu Kepulauan Alor
JAWA, TIMUR Banyuwangi Kubu Lomblen Pulau Alor
Grajagan Tejakula Bayan Gunung Api Teluk Saleh Teluk Sanggar Larantuka Kabir Kalabahi Tutuala Pulau Moa
Karangasem Gunung Tambora 2851m Dompu Pota Ruteng Labala Leti
Bali Negara Pulau Moyo **Raba** Pulau Komodo Maumere Pulau Pantar **DILI**
Teluk Grajagan Selat Bali Alas Sumbawabesar Labuhanbajo Kepulauan Solor **EAST TIMOR**
Pulau Lombok Sumbawa Saleh *Flores* Rajawa Endeh Maliana
Ngurah Rai **Mataram** Taliwang Gunung Tambora Gerampi Pante Makasar Lospalos
Denpasar Kuta Lunyuk Gunung Takan 1400m Sungai Cempi (Part of East Timor) Kefamenanu
Nusa Penida *N u s a T e n g g a r a* Waingapu **NUSA TENGGARA TIMUR** Gunung Kekneno 2070m Suai
(L e s s e r S u n d a I s l a n d s) Bondokodi *Savu Sea* Sulamu Soe Nikiniki
Waikabubak Pulau Sumba **Kupang** Toineke
Baing Kepulauan Sawu Pulau Sawu Selat Roti
Pulau Sawu Pulau Roti
Selat Raijua Baa

Timor Sea

I N D I A N O C E A N

Elevation scale
6000m
4000m
3000m
2000m
1000m
500m
250m
100m
Sea Level
-250m
-500m
-1000m

ASIA

262

CHINA

MYANMAR
(BURMA)

SHAN STATE

YUNNAN

Nanning

GUANGXIZHUANGZUZIZHIQU

LAOS

VIANGCHAN
(VIENTIANE)

THAILAND

Gulf of
Tongking

HAINAN

Hainan Dao

Haikou

VIETNAM

HA NÔI

Hai Phong

PARACEL
ISLANDS
(disputed)

Amphitrite Group

Crescent
Group

Passu Keah

Triton Island

Đà Nâng

KAYAH
STATE

MON
STATE

KAREN STATE

TENASSERIM

Mergui Archipelago

Gulf
of
Thailand

KRUNG THEP
(BANGKOK)

CAMBODIA

PHNUM PENH
(PHNOM PENH)

Hồ Chí Minh

South
China

Spratly Island

Côn Dao

MALAYSIA

KEDAH

PERLIS

KELANTAN

TERENGGANU

PERAK

PAHANG

INDONESIA

ACEH

George Town

Kuala
Terengganu

Kota Bharu

Kuala Lipis

6000m
4000m
3000m
2000m
1000m
500m
250m
100m
Sea
Level
-250m
-500m
-1000m

Scale 1:7,000,000
(projection: Mercator)

0 25 50 75 100 125 150 175 200 Km
0 25 50 75 100 125 150 175 200 Miles

Population
- ■ above 5 million
- ■ 1 million to 5 million
- ⊙ 500,000 to 1 million
- ⊙ 100,000 to 500,000
- ⊕ 50,000 to 100,000
- ○ 10,000 to 50,000
- ∘ below 10,000

Tropic of Cancer

Guangzhou
Huizhou
Dongguan
Haifeng
Shantou
Chaoyang
Puning
Lufeng
ANGDONG
Jiangmen
Zhongshan
Shenzhen
Honghai Wan
Zhuhai
Kowloon (Jiulong)
Hong Kong (Xianggang)
Chek Lap Kok
Macao (Aomen)
ngchuan

Nan'ao Dao
Chiai
Hsinying
Yuli
T'ainan
Hsiaoying
TAIWAN
P'ingtung
T'aitung
Kaohsiung
Lü Tao
Kaohsiung
Fangshan
Hengchun
Oluan Pi
Lan Yü

Bashi Channel

Tungsha Tao

Luzon Strait

Batan Islands
Batan Island

Balintang Channel
Babuyan Island

Babuyan Islands

Babuyan Channel

Mayraira Point
Claveria
Escarpada Point
Aparri
Mount Cagua 1133m
Laoag
Dingras
Cabugao
Bangued
Tuguegarao
Vigan
Tuao
Candon
Tabuk
Bontot
Ilagan
Bangar
Cauayan
Lagawe
San Fernando
Echague
Bauang
Trinidad
Bayombong
Baguio
Bolinao
Dagupan
Lingayen
San Carlos
San Jose City
Baler
Camiling
Palayan City
Masinloc
Tarlac
Cabanatuan
Iba
High Peak 3037m
Angeles
Mount Pinatubo 1485m
San Fernando
Olongapo
Malolos
Caloocan
Balanga
Quezon City
Polillo Islands
Pasig
MANILA
Ninoy Aquino
Imus
Laguna de Bay
Corregidor Island
Tagaytay
Lipa
San Pablo
Lamon Bay
Nasugbu
Lucena
Calauag
Daet
Lubang Island
Batangas
Lake Taal
Catanauan
Caramoan
Cape Calavite
Calapan
Boac
San Francisco
Naga
Pili
Catanduanes Island
Mamburao
Ligao
Tabaco
Virac
Marinduque
San Pascual
Mayon Volcano 2422m
Sablayan
Pinamalayan
Legazpi City
Mindoro
Tablas Island
Burias Island
Sorsogon
Mount Baco 2488m
Roxas
Donsol
San Jose
Odiongan
Sibuyan Sea
Bulan
Masbate
Catarman
Laoang
Busuanga Island
Tablas Strait
Cajidiocan
Balud
Calbayog
Samar
Coron
Culion Island
Sibuyan Island
Masbate
Dolores
Jintotolo Channel
Placer
Borongan
Linapacan Island
Ibajay
Kalibo
Roxas City
Biliran Island
Naval
Calbiga
El Nido
Culasi
Visayan Sea
Cariaga
Catbalogan
Taytay
Panay Island
Passi
Cadiz
Bogo
Ormoc
Tacloban
Guiuan
Patnongon
San Jose de Buenavista
Iloilo
Silay
Bacolod
Cebu
Leyte Gulf
Abuyog
Miag-ao
Bago
Danao
Baybay
San Carlos City
Canlaon Volcano 2465m
Toledo
Leyte
Sogod
La Carlota
Lapu-Lapu
Dinagat Island
Panay Gulf
Himamaylan
Cebu
Ubay
Maasin
Negros
Camotes Sea
Bohol
Siargao Island
Sipalay
Bais
Argao
Surigao
Dinagat
Cagayan Islands
Tagbilaran
Jagna
Bayawan
Dumaguete
Camiguin Island
Cabadbaran
Butuan
Tandag
Siquijor Island
Bohol Sea
Siaton Point
Siaton
Cagayan de Oro
Gingoog
Lianga
Dipolog
Dapitan
Tagoloan
Prosperidad
Oroquieta
Iligan
Hinatuan
Mount Malindang 2425m
Iligan Bay
Malaybalay
Monkayo
Sindangan
Tangub
Ozamiz
Maramag
Bislig
Labason
Liloy
Tubod
Lake Lanao
Marawi
Nabunturan
Kabasalan
Malabang
Mindanao
Tagum
Baganga
Pagadian
Karomatan
Sultan Kudarat
Kidapawan
Davao
Pantukan
Tungawan
Cotabato
Midsayap
Mount Apo 2954m
Manay
Isabela
Zamboanga
Moro Gulf
Tacurong
Kidapawan
Digos
Governor Generoso
Lamitan
Basilan
Lebak
Isulan
Mount Busa 2083m
Korondal
Surallah
Davao Gulf
Malita
Palimbang
Packet Volcano 4342m
General Santos
Mati
Jolo
Jolo
Kiamba
Glan
Jose Abad Santos
Cape San Agustin

Philippine Sea

Luzon Sea

PHILIPPINES

Sulu Sea

Celebes Sea

Sulu Archipelago

SPRATLY ISLANDS (disputed)
Northeast Cay
Southwest Cay
West York Island
Sandy Cay
Thitu Island
Flat Island
Loaita Island
Nanshan Island
Itu Aba Island
Sand Cay
Namyit Island
Sin Cowe Island
Sin Cowe East Island
Len Dao

Palawan Passage

Cuyo West Pass
Cuyo East Pass
Mindoro Strait

Puerto Princesa
Palawan
Quezon
Brooke's Point

Balabac Island
Balabac Strait
Cagayan de Tawi Tawi

Pulau Balambangan
Pulau Banggi
Tiga-Tarok
Kudat
Tuaran
Teluk Paitan
Kanibongan
Pangutaran Group
Samales Group
Tapul Group
Tawitawi
Balimbing
Tawitawi Group
Sibutu
Sibutu Passage
Pulau Timbun Mata
Tawau
Pulau Bum Bum
Sebatik

MALAYSIA
Gunung Kinabalu 4101m
Kota Kinabalu
Ranau
SABAH
Kota Kinabalu
Kuala Penyu
Tambunan
LABUAN
Pulau Labuan
Keningau
Labuan
Sandakan
Lahad Datu
Teluk Darvel
Tenom
BRUNEI
BANDAR SERI BEGAWAN
Brunei Bay
Bandar Seri Begawan
Miri
Kuala Belait
SARAWAK

19,686ft
13,124ft
9843ft
6562ft
3281ft
1640ft
820ft
328ft
Sea Level
-820ft
-6562ft
-13,124ft

Baghdad

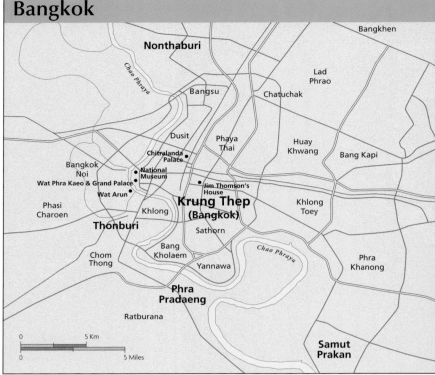

Bangkok

Beijing

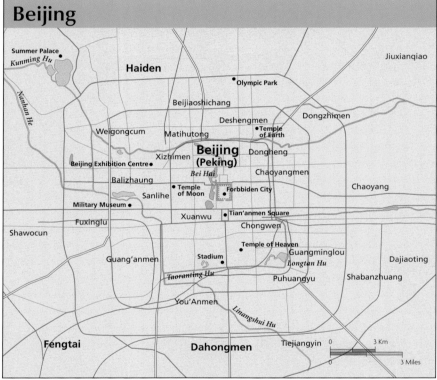

Delhi

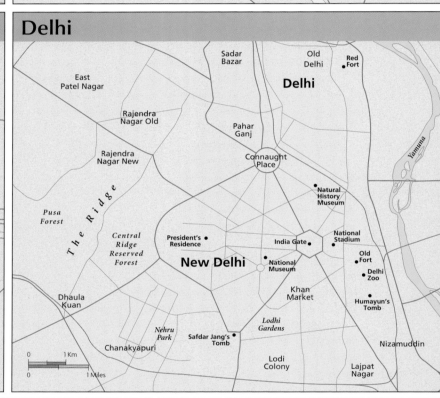

Dhaka

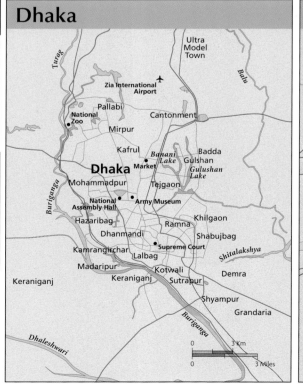

Kolkata

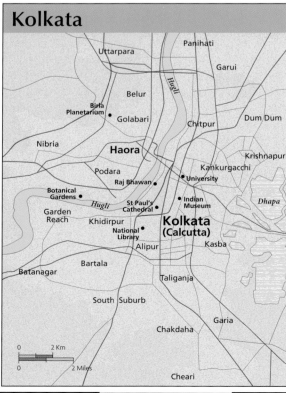

Kabul

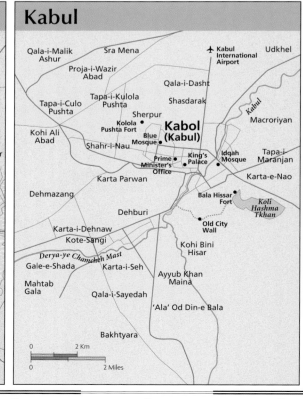

ASIA

Hong Kong

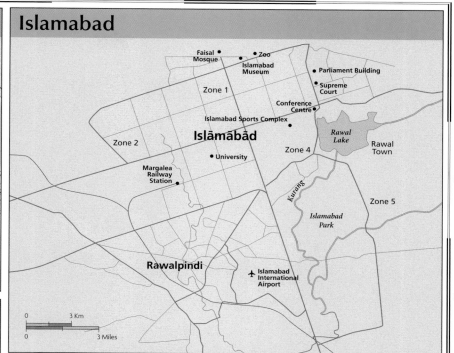

H I J K

Mong Kok
Kowloon City
Kowloon
Royal Observatory
Ho Man Tin
Hung Hom
Kowloon Bay
Hong Kong Coliseum
Tsim Sha Tsui
Space Museum & Planetarium
Star Ferry
North Point
Sai Ying Pun
Victoria Harbour
Kennedy Town
University of Hong Kong
Sheung Wan
Convention Centre
Tun Lo Wan
Tai Tam
Mid Levels
Government House
Hong Kong (Xianggang)
Tai Hang
Wan Chai
Victoria Peak 554m ▲
Happy Valley
Tiger Balm Garden
Hong Kong Island
0   1 Km
0   1 Miles

Islamabad

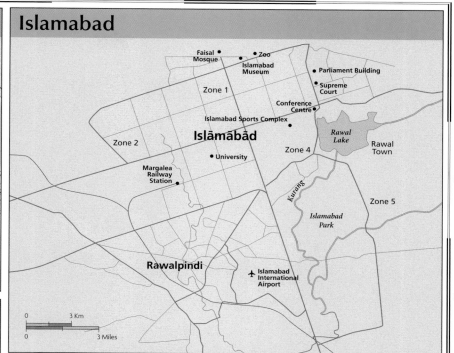

L M N

Faisal Mosque
Zoo
Islamabad Museum
Parliament Building
Supreme Court
Zone 1
Conference Centre
Islamabad Sports Complex
Islāmābād
Rawal Lake
Rawal Town
Zone 2
Zone 4
University
Zone 5
Margalea Railway Station
Islamabad Park
Rawalpindi
Islamabad International Airport
0   3 Km
0   3 Miles

Istanbul

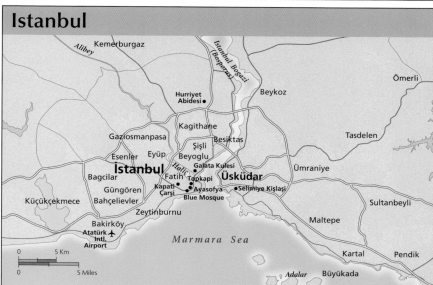

Alibey
Kemerburgaz
Istanbul Bogazi (Bosporus)
Ömerli
Hurriyet Abidesi
Beykoz
Kagithane
Beşiktas
Tasdelen
Gaziosmanpasa
Şişli
Beyoglu
Galata Kulesi
Esenler
Eyüp
Bagcilar
Fatih
Haliç
Topkapi
İstanbul
Ümraniye
Güngören
Kapati Çarsi
Ayasofya
Üsküdar
Blue Mosque
Selimiye Kişlaşi
Küçükçekmece
Bahçelievler
Zeytinburnu
Sultanbeyli
Bakirköy
Atatürk Intl. Airport
Marmara Sea
Maltepe
Kartal
Pendik
Adalar
Büyükada
0   5 Km
0   5 Miles

Jakarta

Java Sea
Soekarno-Hatta International Airport
Penjaringan
Teluk Jakarta
Ancol
Tanjung Priok
Pademangan
Kalideres
Jakarta Museum
Sunter
Koja
Taman Sari
Merdeka Palace
Jakarta
National Monument
Cempaka Putih
Kembangan
Welcome Monument
Kebon Jeruk
Parliament House
Menteng
University Rawamangum
Pulo Gadung
Kebayoran Lama
Matraman
Jatinegara
Pancoran
Manggarai
Kebayoran Baru
Jakarta Halim Perdanakusuma Airport
Cilandak
Kramat Jati
Ciliwung
Pasar Munggu
Ciracas
Jagakarsa
0   5 Km
0   5 Miles

Kuala Lumpur

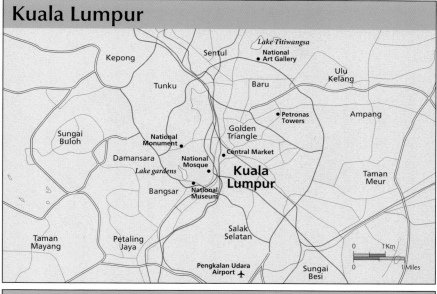

Lake Titiwangsa
Kepong
Sentul
National Art Gallery
Ulu Kelang
Tunku
Baru
Petronas Towers
Ampang
Sungai Buloh
National Monument
Golden Triangle
Damansara
National Mosque
Central Market
Lake gardens
Kuala Lumpur
Bangsar
National Museum
Taman Meur
Taman Mayang
Petaling Jaya
Salak Selatan
Pengkalan Udara Airport
Sungai Besi
0   1 Km
0   1 Miles

Manila

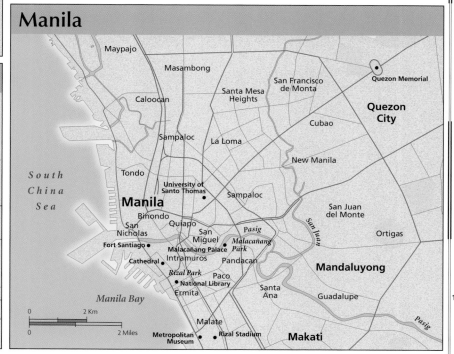

Maypajo
Masambong
San Francisco de Monta
Quezon Memorial
Caloocan
Santa Mesa Heights
Quezon City
Cubao
Sampaloc
La Loma
New Manila
South China Sea
Tondo
University of Santo Thomas
Sampaloc
San Juan del Monte
Manila
Binondo
Quiapo
Ortigas
San Nicholas
San Miguel
Pasig
Fort Santiago
Malacañang Palace
Malacañang Park
Intramuros
Pandacan
Cathedral
Rizal Park
Paco
Santa Ana
Mandaluyong
National Library
Ermita
San Juan
Manila Bay
Malate
Guadalupe
Metropolitan Museum
Rizal Stadium
Makati
Pasig
0   2 Km
0   2 Miles

Ulan Bator

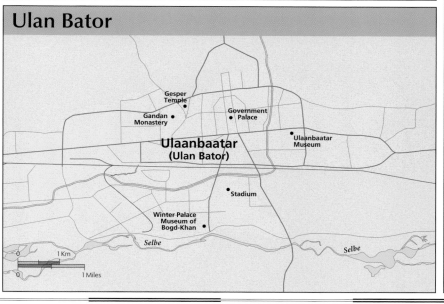

Gesper Temple
Government Palace
Gandan Monastery
Ulaanbaatar Museum
Ulaanbaatar (Ulan Bator)
Stadium
Winter Palace Museum of Bogd-Khan
Selbe
Selbe
0   1 Km
0   1 Miles

Australasia and Oceania with a total land area of 3,285,048 sq miles (8,508,238 sq km), takes in 14 countries including the continent of Australia, New Zealand, Papua New Guinea and many island groups scattered across the Pacific Ocean.

FACTFILE

N **Most Northerly Point:** Eastern Island, Midway Islands 28° 15' N
S **Most Southerly Point:** Macquarie Island, New Zealand 54° 30' S
E **Most Easterly Point:** Clipperton Island, 109° 12' W
W **Most Westerly Point:** Cape Inscription, Australia 112° 57' E

Largest Lakes:
1. Lake Eyre, Australia 3430 sq miles (8884 sq km)
2. Lake Torrens, Australia 2200 sq miles (5698 sq km)
3. Lake Gairdner, Australia 1679 sq miles (4349 sq km)
4. Lake Mackay, Australia 1349 sq miles (3494 sq km)
5. Lake Argyle, Australia 800 sq miles (2072 sq km)

Longest Rivers:
1. Murray-Darling, Australia 2330 miles (3750 km)
2. Cooper Creek, Australia 880 miles (1420 km)
3. Warburton-Georgina, Australia 870 miles (1400 km)
4. Sepik, Indonesia/Papua New Guinea 700 miles (1126 km)
5. Fly, Indonesia/Papua New Guinea 652 miles (1050 km)

Largest Islands:
1. New Guinea, 312,000 sq miles (808,000 sq km)
2. South Island, New Zealand 56,308 sq miles (145,836 sq km)
3. North Island, New Zealand 43,082 sq miles (111,583 sq km)
4. Tasmania, Australia 24,911 sq miles (64,519 sq km)
5. New Britain, Papua New Guinea 13,570 sq miles (35,145 sq km)

Highest Points:
1. Mount Wilhelm, Papua New Guinea 14,793 ft (4509 m)
2. Mount Giluwe, Papua New Guinea 14,331 ft (4368 m)
3. Mount Herbert, Papua New Guinea 13,999 ft (4267 m)
4. Mount Bangeta, Papua New Guinea 13,520 ft (4121 m)
5. Mount Victoria, Papua New Guinea 13,248 ft (4038 m)

Lowest Point:
▼ Lake Eyre, Australia -53 ft (-16 m) below sea level

Highest recorded temperature:
⊕ Bourke, Australia 128°F (53°C)

Lowest recorded temperature:
⊖ Canberra, Australia -8°F (-22°C)

Wettest Place:
≋ Bellenden Ker, Australia 443 in (11,251 mm)

Driest Place:
⊖ Mulka Bore, Australia 4.05 in (102.8 mm)

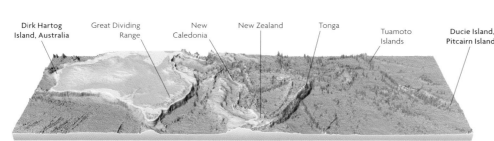

Dirk Hartog Island, Australia — Great Dividing Range — New Caledonia — New Zealand — Tonga — Tuamoto Islands — Ducie Island, Pitcairn Islands

Cross-section from Dirk Hartog Island, Australia to Ducie Island, Pitcairn Islands

line of cross-section

0   500   1000   1500 Km
0   500   1000   1500 Miles

H I J K L M N

150° 160° 170° 180° 170° 160° 150° 140° 130°

Mapmaker Seamounts

N Midway Islands

Murray Fracture Zone

Mid-Pacific Seamounts

Wake Island

Hawaiian Islands

Necker Ridge

Molokai Fracture Zone

Tropic of Cancer

Johnston Atoll

Schjetman Reef

Hawai'i

Mauna Kea 4205m

Marshall Islands

Marshall Seamounts

PACIFIC

Clarion Fracture Zone

20°

Micronesia

Central Pacific Basin

Melanesian

Christmas Ridge

Clipperton Fracture Zone

10°

Basin

Nauru

Banaba

Tungaru

Phoenix Islands

Kiritimati

OCEAN

Tuvalu

Galapagos Fracture Zone

Equator 0°

Vityaz Trench

Santa Cruz Islands

PACIFIC PLATE
FIJI PLATE

Robbie Ridge

Samoa
Savaii
Upolu

Northern Cook Islands

Manihiki Plateau

Marquesas Islands
Hiva Oa

South Solomon Trench

Malaita

Polynesia

North Fiji Basin

Vanuatu

North New Hebrides Trench

Fiji

Vanua Levu

Samoa Basin

Penrhyn Basin

New Espiritu Santo

Iles Loyauté

Vitu Levu

Capricorn Tablemount

Tiki

Tanna

Tuamotu Fracture Zone

10°

New Caledonia

FIJI PLATE

Lau Basin

Tonga

Southern Cook Islands

Society Islands

Society Ridge

Tuamotu Islands

Tuamotu Ridge

Basin

New Hebrides Trench

New Caledonia Ridge

South Fiji Basin

Kermadec Ridge

Rarotonga

Tahiti

Cook Fracture Zone

Austral Fracture Zone

Norfolk Ridge

Norfolk Island

Tonga Trench

Austral Islands

Iles Gambier

20°

West Norfolk Ridge

Kermadec Trench

Pitcairn Island

Henderson Island

Ducie Island

Tropic of Capricorn

Lord Howe Rise

New Caledonia Basin

Three Kings Rise

Bay of Plenty

Southwest

NAZCA PLATE

New Zealand

North Island 3

Pacific

East Pacific Rise

Southern Alps

Taranaki
Aoraki
(Mount Cook)
3754m

South Island 2

Chatham Rise

Basin

Chatham Islands

Macquarie Ridge

South West Cape

Bounty Trough

Agassiz Fracture Zone

Campbell Plateau

S Macquarie Island

Eltanin Fracture Zone

PACIFIC PLATE
ANTARCTIC PLATE

SOUTHERN OCEAN

Udintsev Fracture Zone

Pacific Antarctic Ridge

ANTARCTICA

130° 140° 150° 160° 170° 180° 170° 160° 150° 140° 130° 120°

H I J K L M N

1
2
3
4
5
6
7
8
9
10

Political

Vast expanses of ocean separate this geographically fragmented realm, characterized more by each country's isolation than by any political unity. Australia's and New Zealand's traditional ties with the United Kingdom, as members of the Commonwealth, are now being called into question as Australasian and Oceanian nations are increasingly looking to forge new relationships with neighbouring Asian countries like Japan. External influences have featured strongly in the politics of the Pacific Islands; the various territories of Micronesia were largely under US control until the late 1980s, and France, New Zealand, the USA and the UK still have territories under colonial rule in Polynesia. Nuclear weapons-testing by Western superpowers was widespread during the Cold War period, but has now been discontinued.

Population
- ■ above 5 million
- ▣ 1 million to 5 million
- ◉ 500,000 to 1 million
- ◎ 100,000 to 500,000
- ⊕ 50,000 to 100,000
- ⊙ 10,000 to 50,000
- ○ below 10,000
- ● Country capital
- ◉ State capital

Borders
- full international border
- indication of maritime country extent
- indication of maritime dependent territory extent
- state border

Communications
- major roads
- major railways

SCALE 1:32,000,000
(projection: Lambert Azimuthal Equal Area)

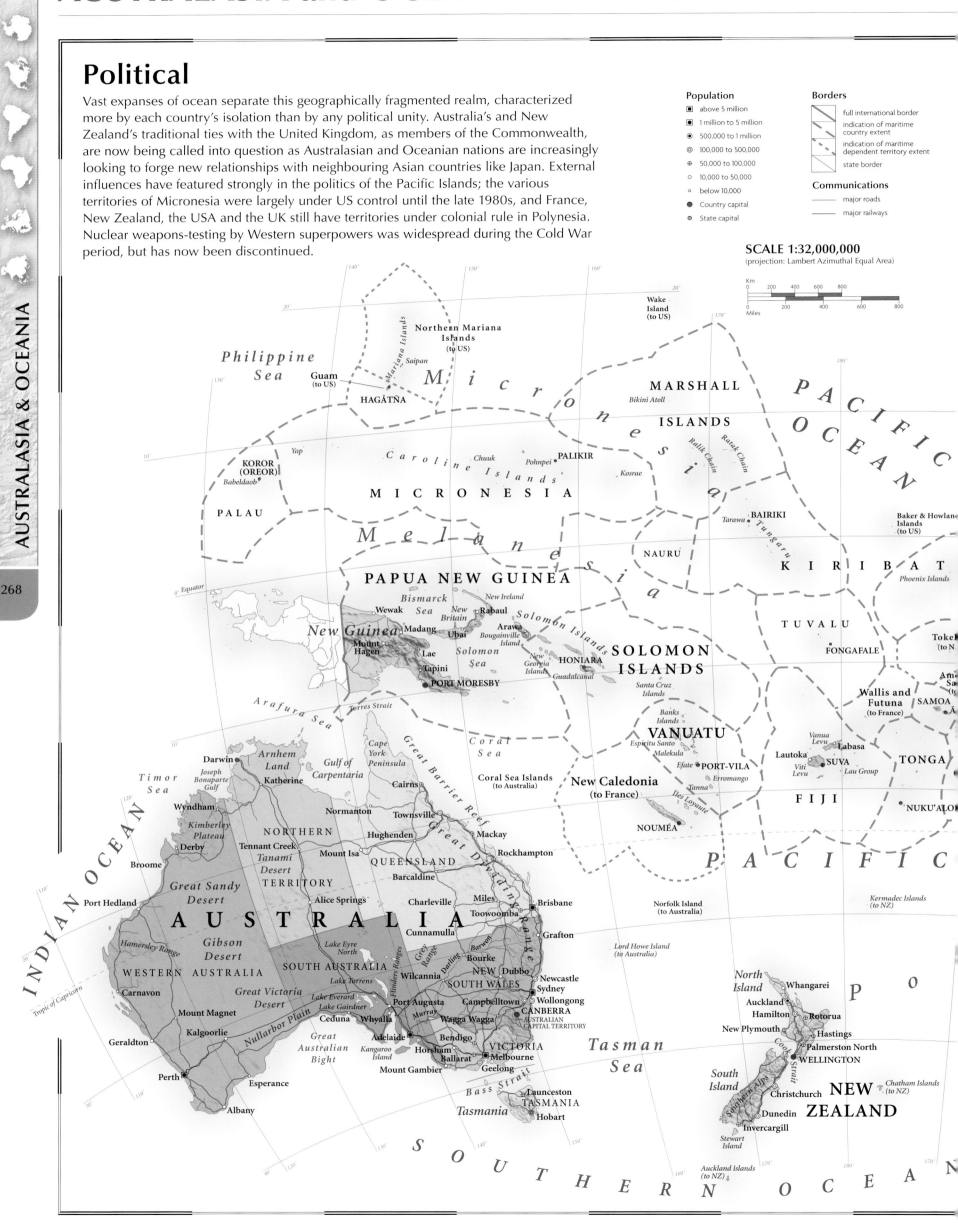

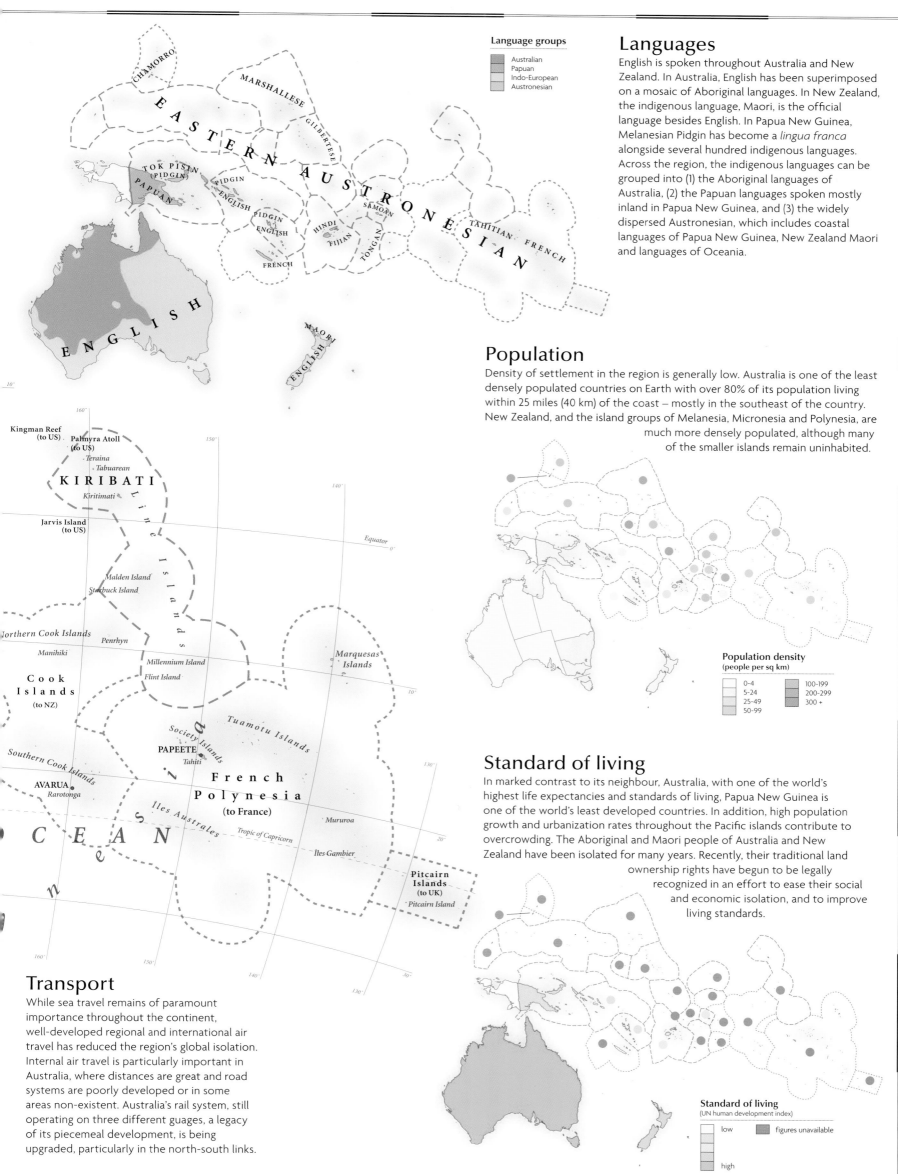

Language groups
- Australian
- Papuan
- Indo-European
- Austronesian

Languages

English is spoken throughout Australia and New Zealand. In Australia, English has been superimposed on a mosaic of Aboriginal languages. In New Zealand, the indigenous language, Maori, is the official language besides English. In Papua New Guinea, Melanesian Pidgin has become a *lingua franca* alongside several hundred indigenous languages. Across the region, the indigenous languages can be grouped into (1) the Aboriginal languages of Australia, (2) the Papuan languages spoken mostly inland in Papua New Guinea, and (3) the widely dispersed Austronesian, which includes coastal languages of Papua New Guinea, New Zealand Maori and languages of Oceania.

Population

Density of settlement in the region is generally low. Australia is one of the least densely populated countries on Earth with over 80% of its population living within 25 miles (40 km) of the coast – mostly in the southeast of the country. New Zealand, and the island groups of Melanesia, Micronesia and Polynesia, are much more densely populated, although many of the smaller islands remain uninhabited.

Population density
(people per sq km)
- 0-4
- 5-24
- 25-49
- 50-99
- 100-199
- 200-299
- 300 +

Standard of living

In marked contrast to its neighbour, Australia, with one of the world's highest life expectancies and standards of living, Papua New Guinea is one of the world's least developed countries. In addition, high population growth and urbanization rates throughout the Pacific islands contribute to overcrowding. The Aboriginal and Maori people of Australia and New Zealand have been isolated for many years. Recently, their traditional land ownership rights have begun to be legally recognized in an effort to ease their social and economic isolation, and to improve living standards.

Standard of living
(UN human development index)
- low
- high
- figures unavailable

Transport

While sea travel remains of paramount importance throughout the continent, well-developed regional and international air travel has reduced the region's global isolation. Internal air travel is particularly important in Australia, where distances are great and road systems are poorly developed or in some areas non-existent. Australia's rail system, still operating on three different guages, a legacy of its piecemeal development, is being upgraded, particularly in the north-south links.

SCALE 1:37,500,000
(projection: Lambert Azimuthal Equal Area)

0   200   400   600   800   1000   1200 Km
0   200   400   600   800   1000   1200 Miles

Climate

Surrounded by water, the climate of most areas is profoundly affected by the moderating effects of the oceans. Australia, however, is the exception. Its dry continental interior remains isolated from the ocean; temperatures soar during the day, and droughts are common. The coastal regions, where most people live, are cooler and wetter. The numerous islands scattered across the Pacific are generally hot and humid, subject to the different air circulation patterns and ocean currents that affect the area, including the El Niño ocean current anomaly, which produces extreme aridity.

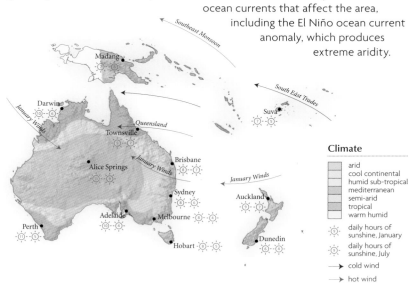

Climate

	arid
	cool continental
	humid sub-tropical
	mediterranean
	semi-arid
	tropical
	warm humid

☼ daily hours of sunshine, January
☼ daily hours of sunshine, July
→ cold wind
→ hot wind

Average Rainfall

Tropic of Cancer
Equator
Tropic of Capricorn
60°S

January rainfall   *July rainfall*

Rainfall
0–25 mm (0–1 in)
25–50 mm (1–2 in)
50–100 mm (2–4 in)
100–200 mm (4–8 in)
200–300 mm (8–12 in)
300–400 mm (12–16 in)
400–500 mm (16–20 in)
more than 500 mm (20 in)

Average Temperature

Tropic of Cancer
Equator
Tropic of Capricorn
60°S

January temperature   *July temperature*

Temperature
below -30°C (-22°F)
-30 to -20°C (-22 to -4°F)
-20 to -10°C (-4 to 14°F)
-10 to 0°C (14 to 32°F)
0 to 10°C (32 to 50°F)
10 to 20°C (50 to 68°F)
20 to 30°C (68 to 86°F)
above 30°C (86°F)

Environmental issues

The prospect of rising sea levels poses a threat to many low-lying islands in the Pacific. Nuclear weapons-testing, once common throughout the region, was finally discontinued in 1996. Australia's ecological balance has been irreversibly altered by the introduction of alien species. Although it has the world's largest underground water reserve, the Great Artesian Basin, the availability of fresh water in Australia remains critical. Periodic droughts combined with over-grazing lead to desertification and increase the risk of devastating bush fires, and occasional flash floods.

PACIFIC OCEAN
Coral Sea
Murchison
Mackenzie
Darling
Murray
Sydney
Tasman Sea

☢ PACIFIC TEST SITES
Eniwetok Atoll, Marshall Islands
Bikini Atoll, Marshall Islands
Johnston Atoll
Mururoa Atoll, French Polynesia
Fangataufa Atoll, French Polynesia
Christmas Island, Kiribati

Environmental issues

	national parks
	tropical forest
	forest destroyed
	desert
	desertification
	polluted rivers
☢	radioactive contamination
	marine pollution
	heavy marine pollution
•	poor urban air quality

Landuse

Much of the region's industry is resource-based: sheep farming for wool and meat in Australia and New Zealand; mining in Australia and Papua New Guinea and fishing throughout the Pacific islands. Manufacturing is mainly limited to the large coastal cities in Australia and New Zealand, like Sydney, Adelaide, Melbourne, Brisbane, Perth and Auckland, although small-scale enterprises operate in the Pacific islands, concentrating on processing of fish and foods. Tourism continues to provide revenue to the area – in Fiji it accounts for 15 percent of GNP.

Northern Mariana Islands (to US)
Micronesia
Guam (to US)
Saipan
MICRONESIA
PALAU
Melanesia
Pohnpei
Kosrae
Ralik Chain
Ratak Chain
MARSHALL ISLANDS
Tungaru
NAURU
KIRIBATI
PACIFIC OCEAN
Kiritimati
KIRIBATI
PAPUA NEW GUINEA
New Guinea
Port Moresby
SOLOMON ISLANDS
Honiara
TUVALU
Starbuck Island
Tokelau (to NZ)
Penrhyn
Polynesia
Marquesas Islands
Wallis and Futuna (to France)
SAMOA
Apia
Pago Pago American Samoa (to US)
Cook Islands (to NZ)
Tuamotu Islands
Torres Strait
Arafura Sea
VANUATU
Port-Vila
TONGA
Suva
FIJI
Nuku'alofa
Niue (to NZ)
Avarua
Society Islands
Tahiti
French Polynesia (to France)
Iles Australes
New Caledonia (to France)
Timor Sea
Darwin
Gulf of Carpentaria
Coral Sea
Great Barrier Reef
Iles Gambier
Pitcairn Islands (to UK)
Townsville
AUSTRALIA
Brisbane
Toowoomba
Newcastle
Sydney
Wollongong
Canberra
Adelaide
Melbourne
Geelong
Perth
Auckland
NEW ZEALAND
Wellington
Christchurch
Tasman Sea
Launceston
Hobart
Dunedin

Using the land and sea

	barren land		sheep		sugar cane
	cropland		coconuts		vineyards
	desert		coffee		whaling
	forest		fishing		wheat
	mountain region		fruit		
	pasture		shellfish		

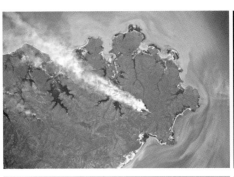

1 MELVILLE ISLAND, NORTHERN TERRITORY, AUSTRALIA
Lying off Australia's north coast, the island is sparsely populated consisting of sandy soils and mangrove swamps.

2 ANATAHAN, NORTHERN MARIANA ISLANDS
The volcano on Anatahan is one of 12 in the Mariana Islands and erupted on a large scale in April 2005.

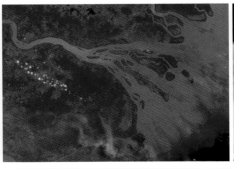

3 FLY RIVER, PAPUA NEW GUINEA
Flowing down from New Guinea's Central Range, the river carries a heavy load of sediment which it deposits in the Gulf of Papua, sometimes forming new islands.

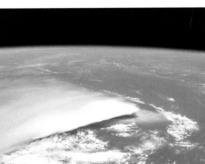

4 RABAUL VOLCANO, NEW BRITAIN, PAPUA NEW GUI
After erupting in 1994, this image shows how the hig particles blew west causing condensation of wate vapour over a wide area.

9 ULURU/AYERS ROCK, NORTHERN TERRITORY, AUSTRALIA
This enormous sandstone rock occupies Australia's heart, both physically and emotionally.

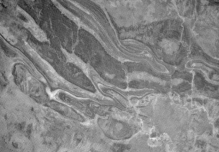

10 JAMES RANGES, NORTHERN TERRITORY, AUSTRALIA
A series of low ridges, these hills lie at the geographical centre of Australia.

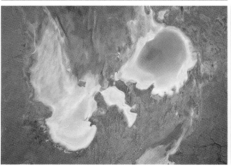

11 LAKE EYRE, SOUTH AUSTRALIA, AUSTRALIA
This great salt lake consists of north and south sections, joined by a narrow channel, Lake Eyre South being the smaller, elongated saltflat at the bottom of the image.

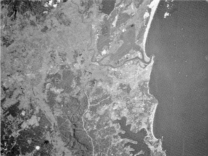

12 NEWCASTLE, NEW SOUTH WALES, AUSTRALIA
The industrial seaport of Newcastle lies on the south bank of Hunter river.

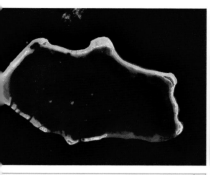

BIKINI ATOLL, MARSHALL ISLANDS 5
s atoll was the site of 23 atomic bomb tests in the
s and 1950s, involving the intentional sinking of at
least 13 naval vessels in the shallow lagoon.

GREAT BARRIER REEF, QUEENSLAND, AUSTRALIA 6
The world's largest reef system is made up
of 3000 individual reefs and 900 islands and
stretches for 1600 miles (2600 km).

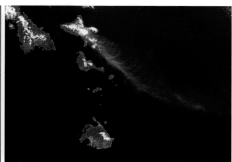

AMBRYM, VANUATU 7
Mount Marum, a 4166ft (1270 m) volcano,
erupted in April 2004 producing an
extensive plume of ash.

KIRITIMATI, KIRIBATI 8
Kiritimati is the largest atoll in the
Pacific Ocean, its interior lagoon filled
in with coral growth.

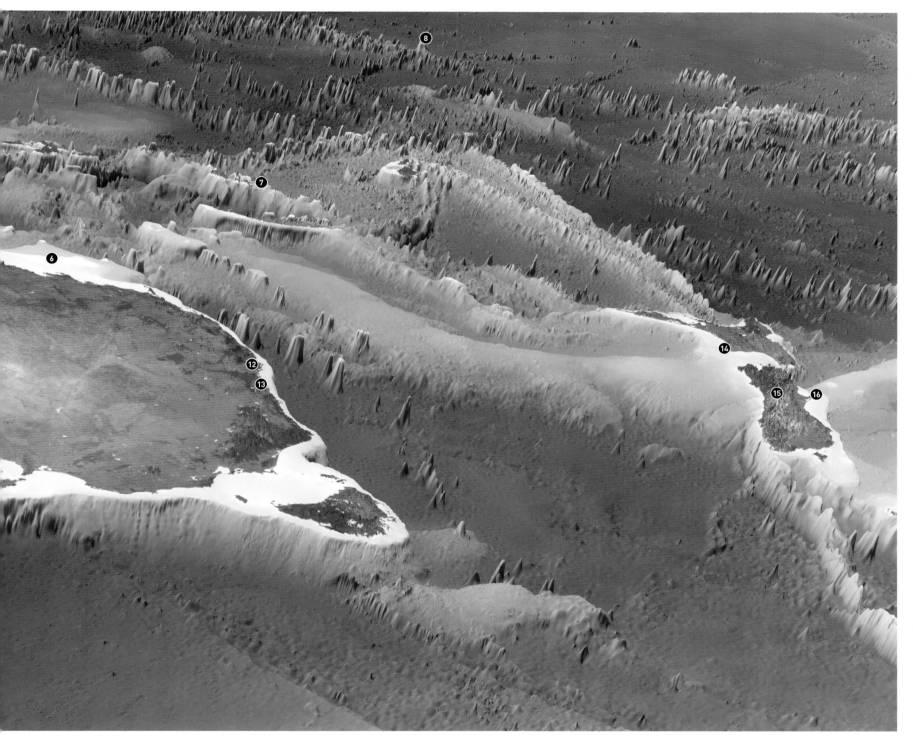

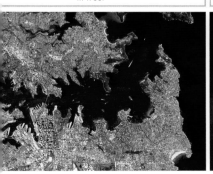

SYDNEY, NEW SOUTH WALES, AUSTRALIA 13
Expanding outwards from the inlet of Port
Jackson, Australia's largest city was founded
in 1788.

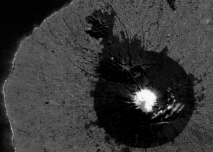

MOUNT TARANAKI, NORTH ISLAND, NEW ZEALAND 14
This dormant 8261 ft (2518 m) volcano is one of the
most symmetrical in the world.

**AORAKI/MOUNT COOK,
SOUTH ISLAND, NEW ZEALAND** 15
New Zealand's highest peak rises 12,238 ft (3744 m)
and is surrounded by permanent ice fields.

BANKS PENINSULA, SOUTH ISLAND, NEW ZEALAND 16
With a circular drainage pattern typical of eroded
volcanoes, this is the only recognisably volcanic
feature on New Zealand's South Island.

Australia

Perth

Wembley Downs
Joondanna
Bayswater
Herdsman Lake
City Beach
Lake Monger
North Perth
Jolimont
Swan River
Art Gallery of Western Australia
Indian Ocean
Subiaco
Alderbury Park
Perth
Belmont Park
Redcliffe
Claremont
Kings Park
Zoo
Carlisle
South Perth
Kensington
Cottesloe
Dalkeith
Applecross
Cannington
Mosman Park
Swan River
Manning
Canning River
Fremantle
Myaree
Partwood
Piney Lakes Reserve
Hilton
Murdoch
Bull Creek

0   3 Km
3 Miles

6000m
4000m
3000m
2000m
1000m
500m
250m
100m
Sea Level
-250m
-500m
-1000m

Scale 1:13,000,000
(projection: Lambert Conformal Conic)

0 50 100 150 200 250 300 350 400 Km
0 50 100 150 200 250 300 350 400 Miles

Population

- above 5 million
- 1 million to 5 million
- 500,000 to 1 million
- 100,000 to 500,000
- 50,000 to 100,000
- 10,000 to 50,000
- below 10,000

Seas and Oceans

Arafura Sea
Torres Strait
Gulf of Papua
Solomon Sea
Coral Sea
CORAL SEA ISLANDS (to Australia)
Gulf of Carpentaria
PACIFIC OCEAN
Bass Strait

Countries and regions

New Guinea
PAPUA NEW GUINEA
PORT MORESBY
SOLOMON ISLANDS
HONIARA
Guadalcanal
NEW CALEDONIA (to France)
QUEENSLAND
NEW SOUTH WALES
VICTORIA
TASMANIA
AUSTRALIAN CAPITAL TERRITORY
JERVIS BAY TERRITORY

Major cities

Brisbane
Ipswich
Gold Coast
Surfers Paradise
Sydney
Newcastle
Wollongong
Parramatta
Penrith
Campbelltown
CANBERRA
Melbourne
Geelong
Adelaide
Townsville
Cairns
Mackay
Rockhampton
Gladstone
Bundaberg
Hervey Bay
Maryborough
Gympie
Sunshine Coast
Maroochydore-Mooloolaba
Caloundra
Caboolture
Toowoomba
Dalby
Warwick
Hobart
Launceston
Devonport
Burnie

Physical features

Cape York Peninsula
Great Dividing Range
Great Artesian Basin
Simpson Desert
Sturt Stony Desert
Tirari Desert
Lake Eyre Basin
Lake Eyre North
Lake Eyre South
Lake Torrens
Lake Gairdner
Lake Frome
Lake Blanche
Lake Gregory
Lake Callabonna
Flinders Ranges
Grey Range
Barrier Range
Great Barrier Reef
Fraser Island
Moreton Island
Whitsunday Group
Bloomsbury
Northumberland Isles
Kangaroo Island
King Island
Flinders Island
Cape Howe
Tropic of Capricorn

Brisbane (inset)

Chermside
Everton Park
Toombul
Brisbane Airport
Myrtletown
Wynnum
The Gap
Lutwyche
Clayfield
Red Hill
Newstead
Hawthorne
Manly
Brisbane
Botanical Gardens
Queensland Art Gallery
Wolloongabba
Tingalpa
Indooroopilly
Greenslopes
Carina Heights
Belmont
Tingalpa Reservoir
Corinda
Mount Gravatt
Burbank

0 3 Km
0 3 Miles

Elevation scale

19,686ft
13,124ft
9843ft
6562ft
3281ft
1640ft
820ft
328ft
Sea Level
-820ft
-6562ft
-13,124ft

Southeast Australia

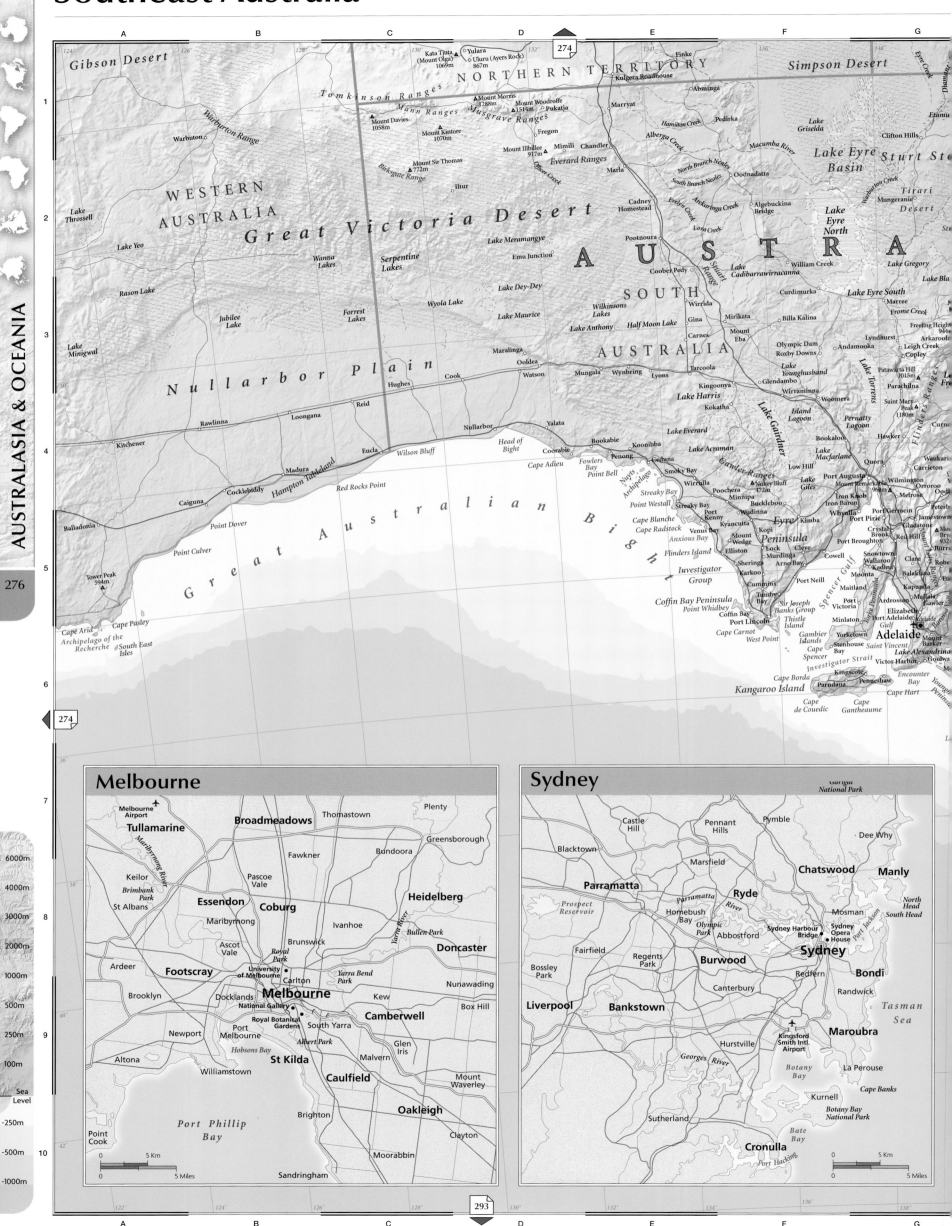

Scale 1:6,500,000
(projection: Lambert Conformal Conic)

0 25 50 75 100 125 150 175 200 Km
0 25 50 75 100 125 150 175 200 Miles

Population

■ above 5 million
▣ 1 million to 5 million
◉ 500,000 to 1 million
◎ 100,000 to 500,000
⊕ 50,000 to 100,000
○ 10,000 to 50,000
∘ below 10,000

275

293

278

19,686ft
13,124ft
9843ft
6562ft
3281ft
1640ft
820ft
328ft
Sea Level
-820ft
-6562ft
-13,124ft

QUEENSLAND

Chesterton Range
Mount Hutton 940m

Adavale
Thylungra
Augathella
Taroom
Mundubbera
Maryborough
Hervey Bay
Fraser Island
Rainbow Beach
Gympie
Injune
Dawson River
Wandoan
Gayndah
Noosa Heads
Maroochydore-Mooloolaba
Sunshine Coast
Caloundra
Bribie Island
Moreton Island

Eromanga
Quilpie
Charleville
Morven
Mitchell
Wallumbilla
Dulacca
Miles
Chinchilla
Murgon
Nanango
Nambour
Kilcoy
Caboolture

Cheepie
Cooladdi
Mungallala
Roma
Condamine
Dalby
Brisbane
Ipswich

Cunnamulla
Eulo
Surat
Macalister
The Gums
Moonie
Pittsworth
Millmerran
Toowoomba
Esk
Beaudesert
Nerang
North Stradbroke Island
South Stradbroke Island
Surfers Paradise
Gold Coast
Tweed Heads
Murwillumbah
Byron Bay
Cape Byron
Ballina

Hungerford
Thargomindah
Jobs Gate
Hebel
Dirranbandi
Boggabilla
Goondiwindi
Warwick
Stanthorpe
Killarney
Legume
Woodenbong
Casino
Kyogle
Maclean
Woolgoolga

NEW SOUTH WALES

Bourke
Brewarrina
Walgett
Moree
Inverell
Glen Innes
Grafton
Coffs Harbour

Cobar
Nyngan
Coonamble
Gilgandra
Tamworth
Armidale
Walcha
Kempsey
Port Macquarie

Dubbo
Wellington
Mudgee
Scone
Muswellbrook
Singleton
Maitland
Taree
Forster-Tuncurry

Parkes
Forbes
Orange
Bathurst
Lithgow
Cessnock
Newcastle
Nelson Bay

Griffith
Cowra
Young
Goulburn
Penrith
Parramatta
Sydney
Wollongong
Port Kembla

West Wyalong
Temora
Wagga Wagga
Yass
CANBERRA
Nowra-Bomaderry
Kiama

Narrandera
Junee
Cootamundra
Gundagai
Tumut
Queanbeyan
AUSTRALIAN CAPITAL TERRITORY
JERVIS BAY TERRITORY

Deniliquin
Albury-Wodonga
Corryong
Cooma
Batemans Bay
Moruya

VICTORIA

Mildura
Swan Hill
Kerang
Echuca
Shepparton
Benalla
Wangaratta
Mount Kosciuszko 2228m
Bega
Eden

Horsham
Bendigo
Castlemaine
Seymour
Mansfield
Orbost

Ararat
Ballarat
Sunbury
Melbourne
Dandenong
Sale
Lakes Entrance

Hamilton
Colac
Geelong
Werribee
Warragul
Traralgon
Morwell

Warrnambool
Port Campbell
Cape Otway
Phillip Island
Wilsons Promontory

Tasman Sea

Bass Strait

King Island
Currie
Flinders Island
Whitemark
Lady Barron
Furneaux Group
Cape Barren Island

Tasmania

Cape Grim
Smithton
Stanley
Wynyard
Burnie
Devonport
George Town
Scottsdale
Saint Helens

Waratah
Launceston
Perth
Longford
Campbell Town
Bicheno

Queenstown
Zeehan
Mount Ossa 1617m
Bothwell
Oatlands
Swansea

Strathgordon
Lake Gordon
New Norfolk
Hobart
Kingston
Port Arthur
Tasman Peninsula
Bruny Island
South East Cape

Tasman Sea

New Zealand

North Island

NEW ZEALAND

NORTHLAND

GISBORNE

BAY OF PLENTY

HAWKE'S BAY

WAIKATO

MANAWATU-WANGANUI

TARANAKI

AUCKLAND

Auckland

Manukau

Manurewa

Hamilton

New Plymouth

Napier

Hastings

Palmerston North

Gisborne

Whangarei

Rotorua

Tauranga

Taupo

Wanganui

Cape Reinga

North Cape

Three Kings Islands

Ninety Mile Beach

Great Barrier Island

Coromandel Peninsula

Bay of Plenty

Hawke Bay

East Cape

Cape Runaway

Mahia Peninsula

Lake Taupo

Lake Rotorua

Lake Waikare

Mount Taranaki (Mount Egmont) 2518m

Mount Ruapehu 2797m

Bay of Islands

Kaipara Harbour

Manukau Harbour

Waitemata Harbour

Hauraki Gulf

Coromandel Range

Raukumara Range

Ruahine Range

Kaweka Range

Kaimanawa Mountains

Tasman Sea

Auckland

North Shore

Takapuna

Devonport

Northcote

Avondale

Point Chevalier

Mount Eden

Mount Roskill

Royal Oak

Onehunga

Ellerslie

Remuera

Mission Bay

Glenn Innes

Mount Wellington

St Johns Park

Pakuranga

Howick

Bucklands Beach

Highland Park

Huntington Park

Otara

Papatoetoe

Manukau

Clover Park

Mangere

Auckland Intl. Airport

Manukau Harbour

Waitemata Harbour

Rangitoto Island

Motutapu Island

Motuihe Island

Browns Island

Lake Pupuke

Auckland Zoo

Auckland Museum

Maritime Museum

Sky Tower

Grafton

Eden Park

Cornwall Park

Kauri Park

Chelsea Park

Blockhouse Bay

Green Bay

Te Atatu

Karaka Bay

Kohimarama Bay

Ambury Park

Stardome & Auckland Observatory

One Tree Hill

Sea Level

6000m
4000m
3000m
2000m
1000m
500m
250m
100m
Sea Level
-250m
-500m
-1000m

3 Miles

3 Km

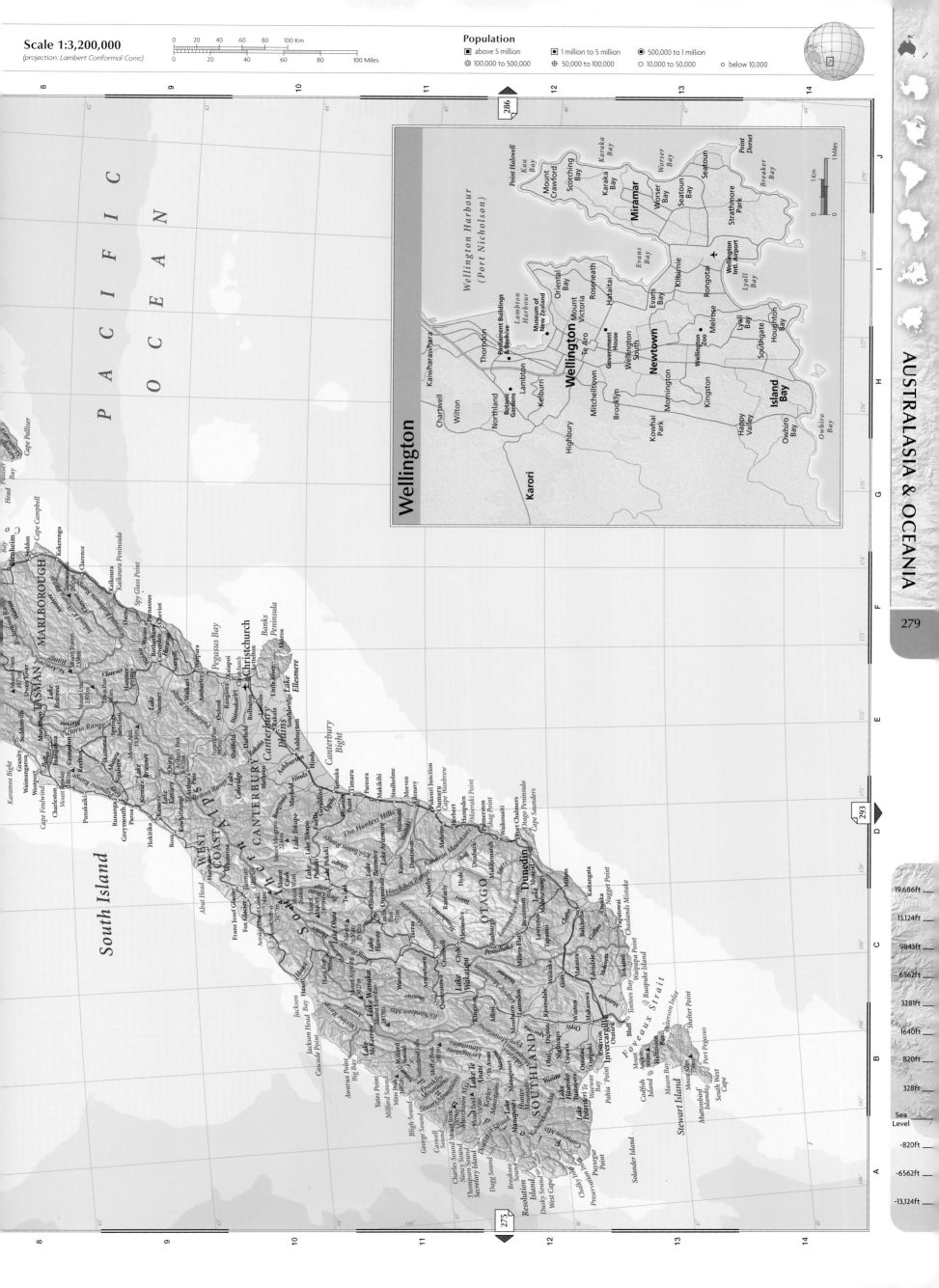

Papua New Guinea & Melanesia

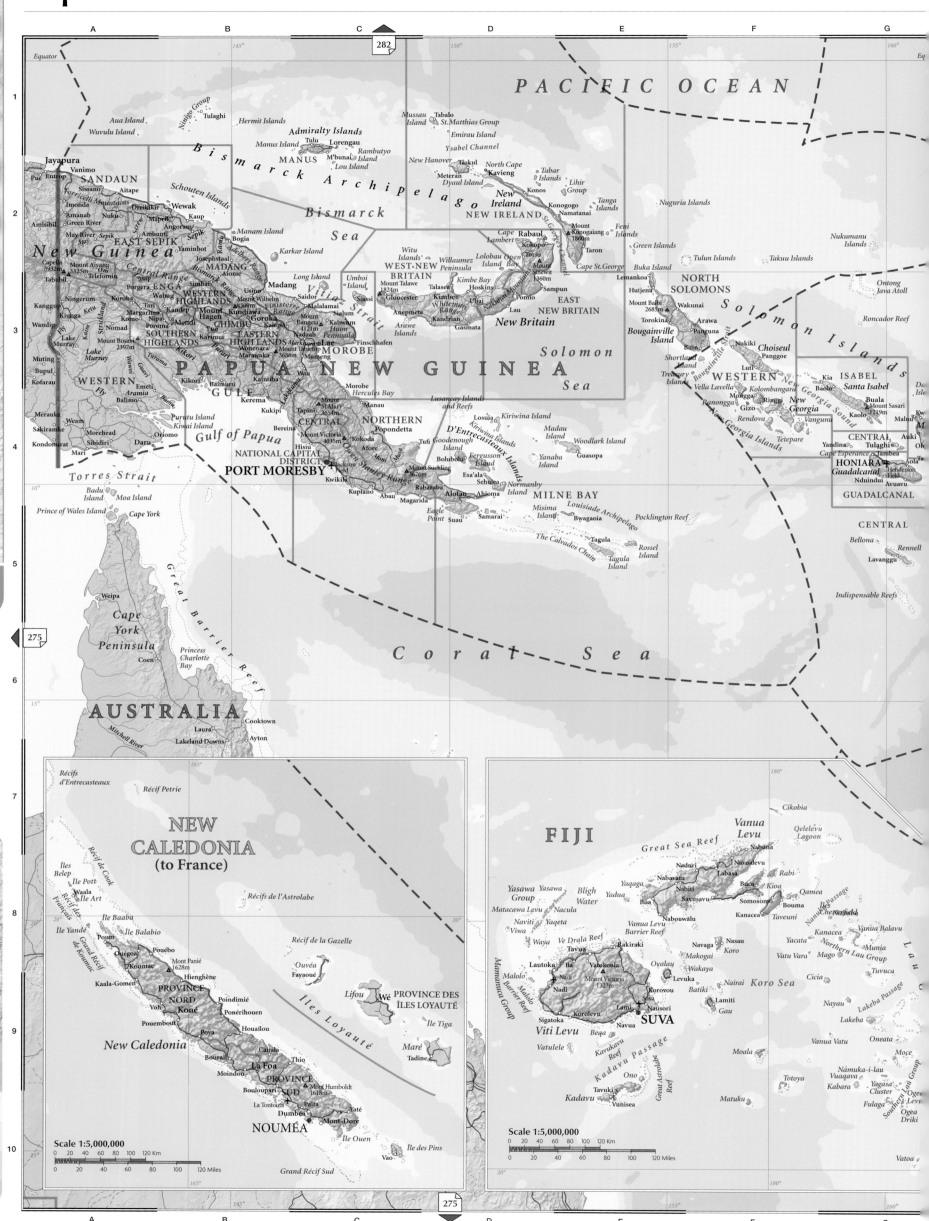

AUSTRALASIA & OCEANIA

PACIFIC OCEAN

Equator

Admiralty Islands
MANUS
Manus Island
Lorengau
Tulu

Bismarck Archipelago

New Hanover
North Cape
Kavieng
New Ireland
NEW IRELAND

Bismarck Sea

SANDAUN
EAST SEPIK
Wewak
MADANG
Madang

New Guinea

WESTERN HIGHLANDS
CHIMBU
EASTERN HIGHLANDS
SOUTHERN HIGHLANDS
ENGA

PAPUA NEW GUINEA

GULF
MOROBE
Lae
NORTHERN
CENTRAL

WEST NEW BRITAIN
EAST NEW BRITAIN
Rabaul
New Britain

Solomon Sea

NORTH SOLOMONS
Bougainville Island
Solomon Islands

Gulf of Papua

NATIONAL CAPITAL DISTRICT
PORT MORESBY

WESTERN

Torres Strait

Cape York Peninsula

WESTERN
New Georgia
ISABEL
Santa Isabel
Buala
CENTRAL
Tulaghi
HONIARA
Guadalcanal
GUADALCANAL

MILNE BAY
Louisiade Archipelago

CENTRAL
Bellona
Rennell

AUSTRALIA

Cooktown
Ayton

Coral Sea

NEW CALEDONIA
(to France)

PROVINCE NORD
Koné

PROVINCE DES ÎLES LOYAUTÉ

PROVINCE SUD

New Caledonia

NOUMÉA

Scale 1:5,000,000
0 20 40 60 80 100 120 Km
0 20 40 60 80 100 120 Miles

FIJI

Vanua Levu

Viti Levu
SUVA

Koro Sea

Scale 1:5,000,000
0 20 40 60 80 100 120 Km
0 20 40 60 80 100 120 Miles

6000m
4000m
3000m
2000m
1000m
500m
250m
100m
Sea Level
-250m
-500m
-1000m

Scale 1:10,100,000
(projection: Mercator)

0 50 100 150 200 250 300 Km
0 50 100 150 200 250 300 Miles

Population

■ above 5 million   ▣ 1 million to 5 million   ◉ 500,000 to 1 million
◎ 100,000 to 500,000   ⊕ 50,000 to 100,000   ○ 10,000 to 50,000   ○ below 10,000

286

SOLOMON ISLANDS

Roncador Reef

Nukiki
Panggoe
Luti
Choiseul
Rob Roy
Vaghena
Kia
WESTERN
Vella Lavella
Mongga
Kolombangara
New Georgia
Gizo
Ringgi
Ranongga
Munda
Rendova
Tetepare
Vangunu
Nggatokae
Baolo
ISABEL
Santa Isabel
Buala
Mount Sasari
1219m
Kaolo
San Jorge

New Georgia Sound
New Georgia Islands
Blanche Channel

Dai Island

MALAITA

Mahu
Kwailibesi
Auki
Malaita
Olomburi
Baunani
Tarapaina
Maramasike
Apio

CENTRAL
Russell Islands
Florida Islands
Savo
Tulaghi
Cape Esperance
Iron Bottom Sound
Yandina
Tambea
HONIARA
Henderson Field
Aola
Tangarare
Mount Popomanaseu
2330m
Guadalcanal
Nduindui
Avuavu

Indispensable Strait

Heuru
Kirakira
San Cristobal
Hauraha

Three Sisters Islands

Ulawa Island

MAKIRA

GUADALCANAL

CENTRAL

Bellona

Lavanggu
Rennell

Duff Islands
Reef Islands
Tinakula
TEMOTU
Lata
Noka
Nendö
Santa Cruz Islands
Utupua
Vanikolo

TA
aiana
SOLOMON ISLANDS
asike
awa Island
Sisters Islands
akira
San Cristobal
Star Harbour
na
MAKIRA

Scale 1:5,000,000

0 20 40 60 80 Km
0 20 40 60 80 Miles

VANUATU

Hiu
Tegua
Loh
Toga
Torres Islands
Ureparapara
Mota Lava
Vanua Lava
Mota
Sola
Banks Islands
Gaua
Mere Lava

Cape Cumberland
Nokuku
Big Bay
Port-Olry
Naone
Maéwo
Espiritu Santo
Ambae
Navonda
Mount Tabwemasana
1879m
Luganville
Malo
Bwatnapne
Bougainville Strait
Pentecost
Norsup
Unmet
Mount Marum
1270m
Ambrym
Malekula
Lamap
Toak
Paama
Lopevi
Lamen Bay
Epi
Tongoa
Emae
Shepherd Islands
Nguna
Emao
Bauer Field
Paonangisu
Forari
PORT-VILA
Efate

Unpongkor
Erromango
Ipota
Aniwa
Tanna
Isangel
Aneityum

Scale 1:5,000,000

0 20 40 60 80 100 120 Km
0 20 40 60 80 100 120 Miles

284

Tikopia

Hiu
Torres Islands
Toga
Ureparapara
Vanua Lava
Sola
Banks Islands
Gaua
VANUATU
Cape Cumberland
Nokuku
Port-Olry
Naone
Espiritu Santo
Ambae
Maéwo
Mount Tabwemasana
1879m
Navonda
Malo
Luganville
Bwatnapne
Bougainville Strait
Pentecost
Norsup
Unmet
Mount Marum
1270m
Ambrym
Malekula
Lamap
Toak
Lamen Bay
Epi
Tongoa
Emae
Shepherd Islands
Nguna
Paonangisu
Bauer Field
Forari
PORT-VILA
Efate

Erromango
Unpongkor
Ipota
Tanna
Aniwa
Isangel
Futuna

Aneityum

Huon
Récifs d'Entrecasteaux
Récif Petrie
Grand Passage
Récifs des Français
Récif de Cook
Île Art
Waala
Poum
Pouébo
Mont Panié
1628m
Koumac
Hienghène
Kaala-Gomen
PROVINCE NORD
Vohi
Ponérihouen
Koné
Houailou
New Caledonia
Poya
Bourail
Canala
La Foa
Thio
PROVINCE SUD
NEW CALEDONIA
(to France)
La Tontouta
Dumbéa
Yaté
NOUMÉA
Mont-Dore
Vao
Île des Pins
Grand Récif Sud

Ouvéa
Lifou
Fayaoué
Wé
PROVINCE DES ÎLES LOYAUTÉ
Îles Loyauté
Tadine
Maré
Récif Durand

Île Walpole

Récifs de l'Astrolabe

Cikobia
Great Sea Reef
Vanua Levu
Qelelevu Lagoon
Nayoalevu
Nabuna
Yasawa Group
Naduri
Labasa
Bligh Water
Nabayatu
Buca
Rabi
Somosomo
Bligh Water
Nabouwalu
Savusavu
Kanacea
Taveuni
Naitaba
Tavua
Koro
Nasau
Vanua Balavu
Rakiraki
Mago
Lau Group
Lautoka
Ba
Mount Victoria
1323m
Ovalau
Levuka
Cicia
Nayau
Mamanuca Group
Nadi
Korovou
Koro Sea
Viti Levu
Nausori
Lamiti
Gau
Lakeba Passage
Korolevu
SUVA
Lakeba
Navua
FIJI
Beqa
Oneata
Moce
Vatulele
Kadavu Passage
Moala
Namuka-i-lau
Kabara
Vunisea
Ono
Totoya
Fulaga
Kadavu
Matuku
Vatoa

Lau Group
Northern Lau Group
Southern Lau Group

Ono-i-lau

PACIFIC OCEAN

Tropic of Capricorn

19,686ft
13,124ft
9843ft
6562ft
3281ft
1640ft
820ft
328ft
Sea Level
-820ft
-6562ft
-13,124ft

Micronesia

286

Tropic of Cancer

GUAM
(to US)

Ritidian Point

Uruno Point

Pati Point

Andersen Air Force Base

Yigo

Dededo

Philippine Sea

Tumon Bay

Agana Bay
Asan Point
Asan
Tamuning
Mongmong
Asinan *(AGANA)*
HAGÅTÑA

Cabras Island
Apra Harbor
Piti
Sinajana
Ordot
Barrigada
Chalan Pago

Orote
Peninsula
Mount Tenjo
313m
Yona
Pago Bay

Agat
Bay
Apra Heights
Santa Rita
Mount Lamlam
406m
Talofofo
Talofofo Bay

Facpi Point

Mount Bolanos
379m

Cetti Bay
Umatac Bay
Umatac
Mount Sasalaguan
377m

PACIFIC OCEAN

Merizo
Inarajan

Cocos
Island

Aga Point

Scale 1:825,000

0   5   10 Km
0   5   10 Miles

MICRONESIA

*PACIFIC
OCEAN*

Rumung

Philippine Sea

Maap
Munguuy Bay

Yap
Wanyaan
Gagil Tamil

Colonia
Kanifaay
Tamil Harbor

Scale 1:825,000

0   5   10 Km
0   5   10 Miles

**NORTHERN
MARIANA
ISLANDS**
(to US)

Farallon de Pajaros

Supply Reef

Maug Islands

Asuncion Island

Agrihan

Pagan

Alamagan

Guguan

Zealandia Bank
Sarigan
Anatahan

Farallon de Medinilla

Susupe
Tinian
Saipan
San Jose
Aguijan

Rota

HAGÅTÑA
(AGANA)
Guam

GUAM
(to US)

Mariana Islands

M

P A C i

*Philippine
Sea*

C   *a*   *r*   *o*   *l*   *i*   *n*   *e*

Ulithi Atoll

Colonia Yap

Fais

Gaferut

Magur Islands
Namonuito
Atoll
Murilo

Ngulu Atoll

Faraulep Atoll

West Fayu Atoll

Pikelot

Ulul
Fayu
Hall Islands

Sorol

Y   *A*   *P*

Olimarao Atoll

Lamotrek Atoll
Tarang Reef

Pulap Atoll
Puluwat Atoll
Manila Reef

Weno

Neoch

Woleai Atoll

Elato Atoll
Satawal

Ifalik Atoll

Eauripik Atoll

Pulusuk

C H U U K

Ngcheangel

Oreor Babeldaob
Ulong **KOROR (OREOR)**
Mecherchar Ngeruktabel
Ngeaur Beliliou
Palau
Islands

PALAU

Sonsorol Islands

Pulo Anna

Merir

M I C R O N E S I A

P A C I F I C

PALAU **Scale 1:750,000**

0   5   10 Km
0   5   10 Miles

Ngaregur

Philippine Sea

Ollei

Chol

Ngardmau
Bay
Ulimang
Chelab

Aiwokako Passage
Ngetbong
Kgkeklau

Ngernechau

Imeong
Babeldaob
Namai
Bay

Ngcheniangel
Melekeok

Ngerkeai

Komebail
Lagoon
Ngetkip Airai
Arakabesan Ngetkip Oikirul
KOROR
(OREOR) Oreor

West Passage

PACIFIC OCEAN

Namekakl Passage

Pulau Waigeo

Equator

Pulau
Misool

*Jazirah
Doberai*

INDONESIA

Pulau
Seram
(Ceram)

*Semenanjung
Bomberai*

*Banda
Sea*

Kepulauan
Aru

Pulau
Kai Besar

MICRONESIA

PACIFIC   OCEAN

Piis Moen
Lamoil
Falalu
*Chuuk
Islands*

North Pass
Tora
Tora Island Pass

Northeast Island

Ruo

Falos
Fono
Quoi

Fallalici Pass

Pata
Lemotol Bay
Piaanu Pass
Polle

Romanum
Tol
Udot
Fanapanges
Totiw

Weno
Eot
Shiki Islands
Parem
Fefan
Etten
Tsis
Uman

Weno
Dublon

Pisar

*Shichiyo
Islands*

South Pass

Salat
Salat Pass
Fanan

Ollan

Otta Pass

Otta
Mesegon
Fenepp

Neoch
Lauvergne
Island

Ipis

New
Ireland

**PAPUA
NEW
GUINEA**

New Britain

Scale 1:1,500,000

0   10   20 Km
0   10   20 Miles

AUSTRALASIA & OCEANIA

6000m
4000m
3000m
2000m
1000m
500m
250m
100m
Sea
Level
-250m
-500m
-1000m

Scale 1:10,250,000
(projection: Mercator)

0 50 100 150 200 250 300 Km
0 50 100 150 200 250 300 Miles

Population
- ■ above 5 million
- ▣ 1 million to 5 million
- ◉ 500,000 to 1 million
- ◎ 100,000 to 500,000
- ⊕ 50,000 to 100,000
- ○ 10,000 to 50,000
- ○ below 10,000

286

Tropic of Cancer

NORTHERN MARIANA ISLANDS (to US)

Philippine Sea

Puntan Sabaneta
Punta Lagua Lichan
San Roque
Managaha
Bird Island
Puetton Tanapog
Tanapag
Kalabera
Garapan
Capitol Hill
Mount Tapochau 465m
Oleai
Saipan
San Vicente
Susupe
Kagman Point
Chalan Kanoa
Magicienne Bay
San Antonio
Saipan International

PACIFIC OCEAN

Saipan Channel

Puntan I Naftan

Scale 1:500,000
0 2 4 Km
0 2 4 Miles

MICRONESIA

PACIFIC OCEAN

Parem Island
Sokehs Island
Pohnpei
Kolonia
Nanuh
Takaieu Island
PALIKIR
Pohnpei
Pehleng
Nahnalaud 772m
Madolenihmw
Tomworoahlang
Nan Madol
Kepirohi Falls
Temwen Island
Ronkiti
Pwok
Rohi
Lohd

Scale 1:650,000
0 5 10 Km
0 5 10 Miles

WAKE ISLAND (to US)

Toki Point
Peale Island
Kuku Point
Flipper Point
Heel Point
Wilkes Island
Wake Lagoon
Settlement
Wake Island
Wake Island
Peacock Point

PACIFIC OCEAN

Scale 1:250,000
0 1 2 3 4 Km
0 1 2 3 4 Miles

PACIFIC OCEAN

Wake Island (to US)

Sibylla Island
Bokaak Atoll

MARSHALL ISLANDS

Bikar Atoll
Bikini Atoll
Rongelap Atoll
Rongrik Atoll
Utrik Atoll
Enewetak Atoll
Ailinginae Atoll
Taka Atoll
Ailuk Atoll
Mejit Island
Wotho Atoll
Jemo Island
Likiep Atoll
Wotje Atoll
Ujelang Atoll
Kwajalein Atoll
Erikub Atoll
Maloelap Atoll
Ujae Atoll
Lae Atoll
Lib
Aur Atoll
Namu Atoll
Jabwot
Arno Atoll
Ailinglaplap Atoll
Majuro Atoll
Jaluit Atoll
Mili Atoll
Namorik Atoll
Knox Atoll
Kili Island
Ebon Atoll

Ratak Chain
Ralik Chain

Micronesia

Minto Reef
Oroluk Atoll
Pakin Atoll
Kolonia
PALIKIR
Ant Atoll
Pohnpei
Mwokil Atoll
Lukunor Atoll
Pingelap Atoll
Satawan Atoll
Ngetik Atoll
Truk Islands
POHNPEI
Kosrae
Tofol
KOSRAE
Nukuoro Atoll

Makin
Butaritari
Tungaru (Gilbert Islands)
Abaiang
Marakei
BAIRIKI
Tarawa
Maiana
Abemama
Kuria
Aranuka
Equator

Kapingamarangi Atoll

PACIFIC OCEAN

Nauru

KIRIBATI
Nonouti
Banaba
Tabiteuea
Beru

NAURU

MICRONESIA

PACIFIC OCEAN

Tafunsak
Gabert
Mount Mutunte 593m
Okat Harbor
Lelu Island
Tofol
Lelu
Insiaf
Kosrae
Mount Finkol 629m
Utwe
Malem
Utwe Harbor

Scale 1:500,000
0 2 4 Km
0 2 4 Miles

NAURU

Anna Point
Baiti
Anabar
Nibok
Ijuw
Denig
Phosphate mineworks
Anibare
Nauru
Aiwo
Buada Lagoon
Anibare Bay
Yaren
Nauru International
Meneng Point

PACIFIC OCEAN

Scale 1:200,000
0 1 2 Km
0 1 2 Miles

MARSHALL ISLANDS

Rongrong
Iroj
Majuro Atoll
Laura
Kallalen
Enigu
Majuro Lagoon
Djarrit
Majuro
Dalap

PACIFIC OCEAN

Scale 1:1,000,000
0 5 10 Km
0 5 10 Miles

281

19,686ft
13,124ft
9843ft
6562ft
3281ft
1640ft
820ft
328ft
Sea Level
-820ft
-6562ft
-13,124ft

287

Polynesia

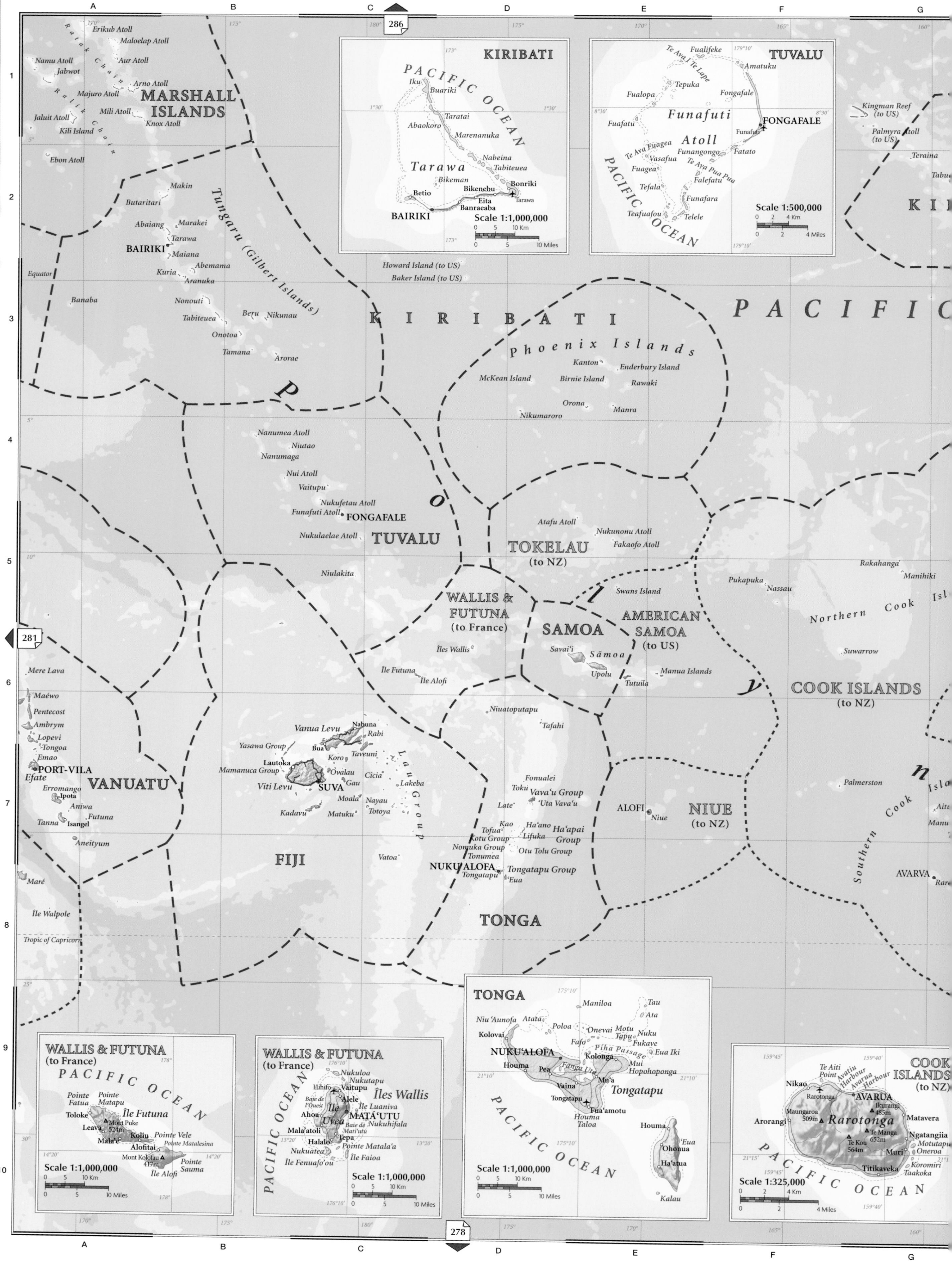

AUSTRALASIA & OCEANIA

Main map labels

MARSHALL ISLANDS

Ratak Chain
Ralik Chain

Erikub Atoll
Maloelap Atoll
Namu Atoll
Jabwot
Aur Atoll
Majuro Atoll
Arno Atoll
Mili Atoll
Jaluit Atoll
Kili Island
Knox Atoll
Ebon Atoll

Makin
Butaritari
Abaiang   Marakei
Tarawa
BAIRIKI
Maiana
Kuria   Abemama
Aranuka
Banaba
Nonouti
Tabiteuea
Beru   Nikunau
Onotoa
Tamana
Arorae

Tungaru (Gilbert Islands)

Equator

P   O   L   Y   N   E   S   I   A

KIRIBATI

Phoenix Islands
McKean Island   Kanton   Enderbury Island
Birnie Island   Rawaki
Orona   Manra
Nikumaroro

Howard Island (to US)
Baker Island (to US)

PACIFIC

Nanumea Atoll
Niutao
Nanumaga
Nui Atoll
Vaitupu
Nukufetau Atoll
Funafuti Atoll   • FONGAFALE
Nukulaelae Atoll   TUVALU

Niulakita

Atafu Atoll
Nukunonu Atoll
Fakaofo Atoll
TOKELAU (to NZ)

Swans Island

WALLIS & FUTUNA (to France)
Îles Wallis
Île Futuna
Île Alofi

SAMOA
Savai'i   Sāmoa
Upolu
Tutuila

AMERICAN SAMOA (to US)
Manua Islands

Pukapuka   Nassau
Rakahanga   Manihiki

Northern   Cook   Isl
Suwarrow

COOK ISLANDS (to NZ)

Mere Lava
Maéwo
Pentecost
Ambrym
Lopevi
Tongoa
Emao
PORT-VILA
Efate
Erromango
Ipota
Aniwa
Futuna
Tanna   Isangel
Aneityum
VANUATU

Maré
Île Walpole

Tropic of Capricorn

Vanua Levu   Naduna
Rabi
Yasawa Group   Bua
Taveuni
Lautoka   Koro
Mamanuca Group   Ovalau
Viti Levu   SUVA   Gau
Cicia   Lakeba
Kadavu   Moala   Nayau
Matuku   Totoya
Vatoa

Lau Group

Niuatoputapu
'Tafahi

Fonualei
Toku   Vava'u Group
Late   'Uta Vava'u
Kao
Tofua   Ha'ano   Ha'apai
Kotu Group   Lifuka   Group
Nomuka Group   Otu Tolu Group
Tonumea
NUKU'ALOFA   Tongatapu Group
Tongatapu   'Eua

FIJI

TONGA

ALOFI   Niue
NIUE (to NZ)

Palmerston

Southern   Cook   Isl

AVARUA   Rar

PACIFIC

Inset: KIRIBATI

KIRIBATI

PACIFIC OCEAN

Iku   Buariki
Taratai
Abaokoro   Marenanuka
Nabeina
Tabiteuea
Bikeman
Bikenebu   Bonriki
Betio   Eita   Tarawa
Banraeaba
BAIRIKI

Tarawa

Scale 1:1,000,000
0   5   10 Km
0   5   10 Miles

Inset: TUVALU

TUVALU

Te Ava I Te Lape
Fualifeke
Amatuku
Fualopa   Tepuka   Fongafale
Fuafatu   FONGAFALE
Funafuti   Funafuti
Atoll
Te Ava Fuagea   Funangongo
Vasafua
Fuagea   Te Ava Pua Pua
Tefala   Falefatu
Teafuafou   Funafara
Telele

PACIFIC OCEAN

Scale 1:500,000
0   2   4 Km
0   2   4 Miles

Inset: WALLIS & FUTUNA (Futuna)

WALLIS & FUTUNA (to France)

PACIFIC OCEAN

Pointe Fatua   Pointe Matapu
Île Futuna
Toloke   Mont Puke 524m
Leava   Pointe Vele
Koliu
Mala   Pointe Matalesina
Alofitai
Mont Kolofau 417m
Île Alofi   Pointe Sauma

Scale 1:1,000,000
0   5   10 Km
0   5   10 Miles

Inset: WALLIS & FUTUNA (Wallis)

WALLIS & FUTUNA (to France)

PACIFIC OCEAN

Nukuloa   Nukutapu   Îles Wallis
Hihifo   Vaitupu
Île
Uvea   Île Luaniva
Baie de l'Ouest   Baie de Nukuhifala
Ahoa
MATÂ'UTU
Alele
Mala'atoli   Tepa
Halalo   Pointe Matala'a
Nukuatea   Île Faioa
Île Fenuafo'ou

Scale 1:1,000,000
0   5   10 Km
0   5   10 Miles

Inset: TONGA

TONGA

Maniloa   Tau
Niu 'Aunofa   Atatā   'Ata
Kolovai   Poloa   Onevai   Motu Tapu
Fafo   Nuku   Fukave
NUKU'ALOFA   Kolonga   'Eua Iki
Houma   Piha Passage
Pea   Fanga 'Uta   Hopohoponga
Vaina   Mu'a
Tongatapu   Tongatapu
Houma   Fua'amotu
Taloa
Houma
'Eua
'Ohonua
Ha'atua
Kalau

PACIFIC OCEAN

Scale 1:1,000,000
0   5   10 Km
0   5   10 Miles

Inset: COOK ISLANDS

COOK ISLANDS (to NZ)

Te Aiti Point   Avatiu Harbour   Avarua Harbour
Nikao   AVARUA
Maungaroa 509m   Ikurangi
Arorangi   Te Manga 652m
Rarotonga   Mataovera
Te Kou 564m   Ngatangiia
Motutapu
Oneroa
Te Kou
Muri
Koromiri
Titikaveka   Taakoka

PACIFIC OCEAN

Scale 1:325,000
0   2   4 Km
0   2   4 Miles

Elevation legend
6000m
4000m
3000m
2000m
1000m
500m
250m
100m
Sea Level
-250m
-500m
-1000m

Scale 1:15,500,000
(projection: Mercator)

0 50 100 150 200 250 300 350 400 Km
0   50   100   150   200   250   300   350   400 Miles

Population
- ☐ above 5 million
- ☐ 1 million to 5 million
- ◉ 500,000 to 1 million
- ◎ 100,000 to 500,000
- ⊕ 50,000 to 100,000
- ○ 10,000 to 50,000
- ∘ below 10,000

287

Samoa inset

P A C I F I C   O C E A N

Savai'i
Faleálupo
Cape Puava   Sátaura
Fálelima   Fálelima
Sala'ilua   Silisili 1858m ▲   Tuasivi
Cape   Satupaiteau   Pu'apu'a
Asusui   Taga   Salelologa

SAMOA

S á m o a

ÁPIA *Upolu*
Fíto
Mataútu   Feleolo   1113m ▲   Ti'avea
Lotofaga   Pontasi   Fagaloa Bay
Sáfata Bay   Salani

AMERICAN SAMOA (to US)

Manua Islands
Olosega
Ofu   Ta'ú
Luma

Cape Matátula
PAGO PAGO
Cape   Aunu'u Island
Taputapu   Steps   *Tutuila*
Point

Apolima Strait
Palauli Bay

Scale 1:3,000,000
0   20   40 Km
0   20   40 Miles

Kiribati inset

KIRIBATI

P A C I F I C   O C E A N

Northwest   Cape Manning
Point   Northeast Point
London   Banana
Cook Island   Saint   Mamilu Lagoon
Paris   Stanislas
Bay
Poland   Kiritimati
South   (Christmas Island)   Bay of
West   Vaskess   Isles Lagoon   Wrecks
Point   Bay   Joe's Hill   Aeon
12m   Point
Azur Lagoon   Pelican
Lagoon   South
East
Point

Scale 1:1,175,000
0   5   10 Km
0   5   10 Miles

Equator

French Polynesia (Tahiti) inset

FRENCH POLYNESIA (to France)

Î l e s   d u   V e n t

Baie d'Opunohu
Papetoai   Baie de Cook
Mont Matotea   Pointe Aroa
714m   Paopao   Mahina
Moorea   Afareaitu   **PAPEETE**   Pirea   Papenoo
Haapiti   Mont Tohiea   Faaa   Tiarei
1207m   Faaa   Mont Aorai
Pointe Nuupere   2066m ▲   Hitiaa
Punaauia   Mont Orohena
2241m ▲
Pointe Nuuroa   *Tahiti*
Paea   Mont Tetufera   Faaone
1799m ▲   Taravao
Faone   Isthme de Taravao
Maraa   Papara   Mataiea   Afaahiti   Tautira
Teohatu   Baie de
Pointe Maraa   Vairao   Taravao
Récif Tepaee   Teahupoo   Presqu'île   Mont Ronui
de Tatarapu   1332m ▲

Baie de Matavai   Pointe Vénus

P A C I F I C   O C E A N

Scale 1:1,000,000
0   5   10 Km
0   5   10 Miles

Main map

P A C I F I C   O C E A N

Line Islands

Malden Island

Island

Millennium Island

Vostok Island

Flint Island

Î l e s   M a r q u i s e s

Hatutu
Eiao
Nuku Hiva   Ua Huka
Taiohae
Ua Pu   Atuona   Hiva Oa
Tahuata   Motane
Fatu Hiva   Omoa

Î l e s
T u a m o t u

Îles du Roi Georges   Îles du Désappointement
Ahe   Manihi   Tepoto   Napuka
Mataiva   Tikehau   Takaroa   Tikei
Rangiroa   Takapoto   Pukapuka
Arutua
Îles Sous le Vent   Îles Palliser
Motu One   Makatea   Toau   Takume   Fangatau
Niau   Kauehi   Fakahina
Manuae   Tupai   Fakarava   Raraka   Makemo
Maupiti   Bora-Bora   Faaite   Katiu   Nihiru   Tehuata
Maupihaa   Tahaa   Fare   Huahine   Tahanea   Marutea   Tauere   Tatakoto
Maiao   Raiatea   Tetiaroa   Anaa   Haraiki   Hikueru   Amanu
Moorea   **PAPEETE**   Reitoru   Marokau   Pukarua
Tahiti   Ravahere   Hao   Akiaki   Reao
Îles du Vent   Mehetia   Nengonengo   Vahitahi
Manuhangi   Paraoa   Vairaatea   Pinaki
Archipel de la Société   Hereheretue   Ahunui

Î l e s   Îles du Duc de Gloucester   Vanavana   Tureia
Maria   Groupe Actéon
Tematangi   Tenarara   Marutea
Rimatara   Rurutu   Mururoa   Maria
Tubuai   Fangataufa
A u s t r a l e s   Raevavae   Îles Gambier
Mangareva   Temoe

FRENCH POLYNESIA (to France)

P A C I F I C   O C E A N

PITCAIRN ISLANDS (to UK)
Tropic of Capricorn
Oeno Island   Henderson Island
Pitcairn Island   Ducie Island

Niue inset

NIUE (to NZ)

Hikutavake   Toi   Mutalau
Makefu   Tuapa   Lakepa
Makapu   Alofi Bay
Point   *Niue*   Liku
ALOFI   Hanan
Halagigie   Tamakautoga   Hakupu
Point   Avatele
Tepa Point   Mata Point

P A C I F I C   O C E A N

Scale 1:1,000,000
0   5   10 Km
0   5   10 Miles

Pitcairn Islands inset

PITCAIRN ISLANDS (to UK)

Young's   Bounty Bay
Rock
Adam's
Rock
ADAMSTOWN
Pitcairn
Island
Point   St Paul's
Christian   Point

P A C I F I C   O C E A N

Scale 1:125,000
0   0.5   1 Km
0   0.5   1 Miles

Rapa Iti
Marotiri

P A C I F I C   O C E A N

287

Elevation scale:
19,686ft
13,124ft
9843ft
6562ft
3281ft
1640ft
820ft
328ft
Sea Level
-820ft
-6562ft
-13,124ft

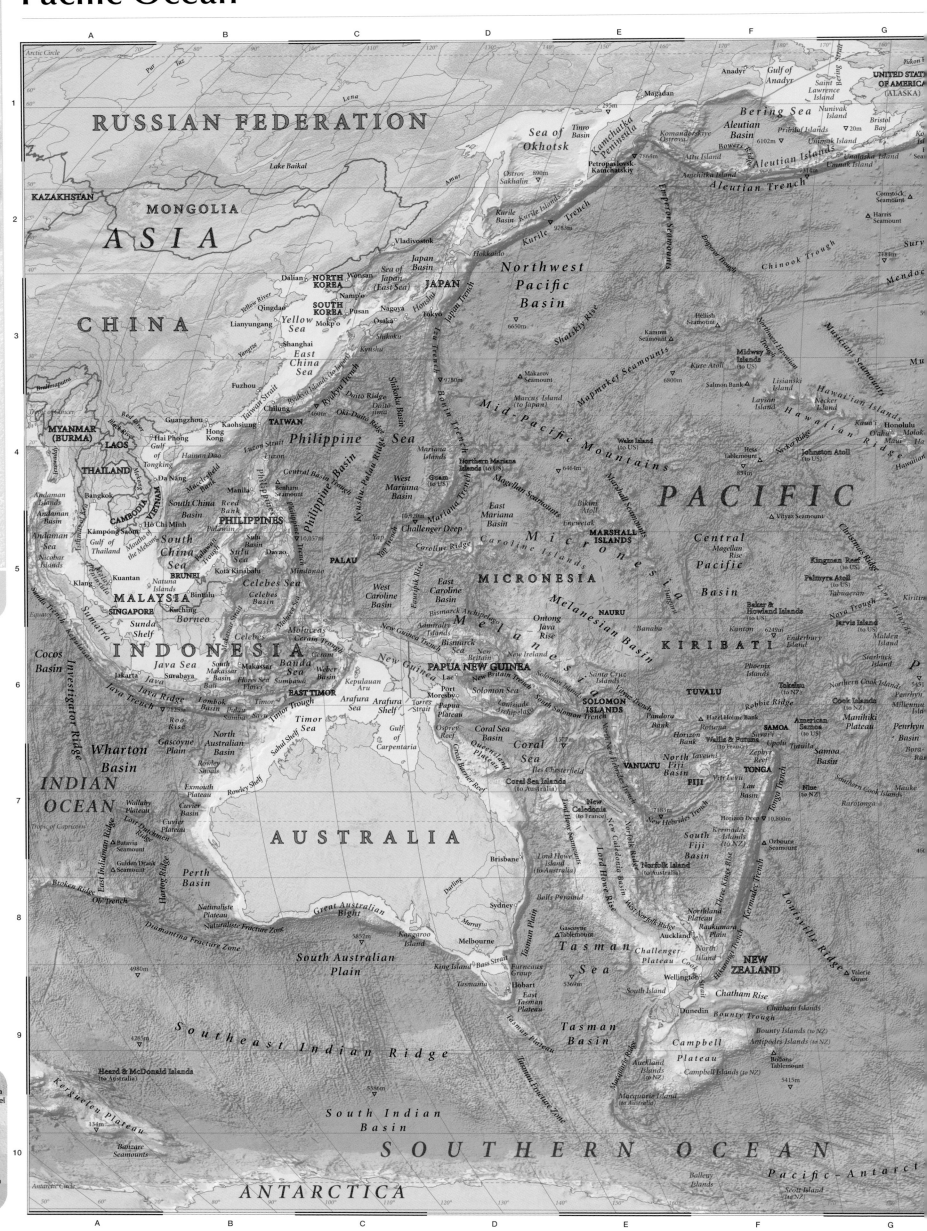

RUSSIAN FEDERATION

KAZAKHSTAN

MONGOLIA

ASIA

CHINA

Lake Baikal

Lena

Arctic Circle

Pur
Taz

Anadyr
Gulf of
Anadyr

Magadan

Saint
Lawrence
Island

Bering Strait

Nunivak
Island

UNITED STATES
OF AMERICA
(ALASKA)

Yukon

Bristol
Bay

Komandorskiye
Ostrova

Bering Sea

Aleutian
Basin

Pribilof Islands

Sea of
Okhotsk

Tinro
Basin

295m

Kamchatka
Peninsula

7864m

Bowers
Ridge

Attu Island

Aleutian Islands

Amchitka Island

Unalaska Island

Umnak Island

Comstock
Seamount

Petropavlovsk-
Kamchatskiy

Aleutian Trench

Harris
Seamount

Sury

Ostrov
Sakhalin

890m

Kurile
Basin

Kurile Islands

Kurile
Trench

9783m

Emperor Seamounts

Emperor Trough

Chinook Trough

7484m

Mendoc

Amur

Vladivostok

Hokkaido

Japan
Basin

Northwest
Pacific
Basin

NORTH
KOREA

Dalian

Yonsan

Namp'o

Sea of
Japan
(East Sea)

JAPAN

Honshu

Tokyo

6650m

Shatsky Rise

Hellish
Seamount

Northwest Hawaiian

Musicians Seamounts

Mu

SOUTH
KOREA

Qingdao

Lianyungang

Yellow
Sea

Mokp'o

Pusan

Nagoya

Osaka

Shikoku

Midway
Islands
(to US)

Kammu
Seamount

6800m

Kure Atoll

Lisianski
Island

Hawaiian Islands

Shanghai

Fuzhou

East
China
Sea

Kyushu

Ryukyu Islands (to Japan)

Ryukyu Trench

9780m

Bonin Trench

Mid-Pacific Mountains

Marcus Island
(to Japan)

Salmon Bank

Laysan
Island

Necker
Island

Kaui

O'ahu

Honolulu

Molok

Yangtze

Taiwan Strait

Danjo Ridge

Daito-
jima

460m

Oki-Daito Ridge

Mapmaker Seamounts

Hess
Tablemount

834m

Hawaiian

Ridge

Maui

Hawaii

Guangzhou

Kaohsiung

TAIWAN

Chilung

Philippine Sea

Mariana
Islands

6464m

PACIFIC

Vityaz Seamount

Johnston Atoll
(to US)

Hong Kong

Luzon Strait

Luzon

Central Basin

Northern Mariana
Islands (to US)

Magellan Seamounts

East
Mariana
Basin

Marshall Seamounts

MYANMAR
(BURMA)

LAOS

THAILAND

Hainan Dao

Gulf
of
Tongking

Da Nang

Macclesfield
Bank

Manila

Benham
Seamount

Mariana Trench

Bikini
Atoll

Central
Magellan
Rise

Pacific
Basin

Christmas Ridge

Kingman Reef
(to US)

Andaman
Islands

Bangkok

VIETNAM

South China
Basin

Reed
Bank

PHILIPPINES

16,920m

Challenger Deep

10,057m

Yap Trench

Caroline Ridge

Enewetak

MARSHALL
ISLANDS

Palmyra Atoll
(to US)

Tabuaeran

Andaman
Basin

CAMBODIA

Ho Chi Minh

Palawan

Sulu
Sea

Davao

PALAU

Yap

West
Caroline
Basin

Caroline Islands

MICRONESIA

Nova Trough

Jarvis Island
(to US)

Andaman
Sea

Kâmpóng Saôm

Palawan Trough

Sulu
Basin

Kota Kinabalu

Mindanao

East
Caroline
Basin

Eauripik Rise

NAURU

Baker &
Howland Islands
(to US)

Banaba

Kanton

6249m

Enderbury
Island

Malden
Island

Nicobar
Islands

Gulf of
Thailand

MALAYSIA

Kuantan

BRUNEI

Bintulu

Celebes Sea

Celebes
Basin

Molucca Sea

Bismarck Archipelago

Melanesian Basin

KIRIBATI

Phoenix
Islands

Starbuck
Island

P

SINGAPORE

Kuching

Borneo

Celebes

Moluccas

Ceram Trough

New Guinea Trench

Admiralty
Islands

New
Ireland

Ontong
Java
Rise

5451

Mouths of
the Mekong

Natuna
Sea

Sunda
Shelf

Sumatra

INDONESIA

Java Sea

South
Makassar
Basin

Makassar

Banda
Sea

Weber
Basin

Kepulauan
Aru

PAPUA NEW GUINEA

Lae

New Britain Trench

TUVALU

Tokelau
(to NZ)

Northern Cook Islands
(to NZ)

Penrhyn

Millennium
Isla

Cocos
Basin

Jakarta

Java

Surabaya

Flores Sea

Flores

Sumbawa

Timor

New Guinea

Port
Moresby

Solomon Sea

South Solomon Trench

**SOLOMON
ISLANDS**

Santa Cruz
Islands

Robbie Ridge

Cook Islands
(to NZ)

Manihiki
Plateau

Penrhyn
Basin

Investigator Ridge

Java Trench

7125m

EAST TIMOR

Bali

Lombok
Basin

Sumba

Savu

Arafura
Aru

Arafura
Sea

Torres
Strait

Papua
Plateau

Louisiade
Archipelago

Pandora
Bank

Hazel Holme Bank

Rotuma

Horizon
Bank

SAMOA

Savai'i

Upolu

American
Samoa
(to US)

Tanuila

Samoa
Basin

Bora-
Ra

Java Ridge

Roo
Rise

North
Australian
Basin

Timor Trough

Timor
Sea

Gulf of
Carpentaria

Osprey
Reef

Coral Sea
Basin

1577m

Wallis & Futuna
(to France)

Zephyr
Reef

North
Fiji
Basin

TONGA

**Wharton
Basin**

Gascoyne
Plain

Rowley
Shoals

Sahul Shelf

Queensland
Plateau

Coral
Sea

Îles Chesterfield

VANUATU

FIJI

Viti Levu

Lau
Basin

Niue
(to NZ)

Mauke
(to NZ)

**INDIAN
OCEAN**

Exmouth
Plateau

Cuvier
Basin

Rowley Shelf

Great Barrier Reef

Coral Sea Islands
(to Australia)

New Hebrides Trench

South
Fiji
Basin

Tonga Trench

Southern Cook Islands
(to NZ)

Rarotonga

East Indian Ridge

Lost Dutchmen
Ridge

Cuvier
Plateau

AUSTRALIA

Brisbane

Darling

New
Caledonia
(to France)

Balls Pyramid

New Caledonia Basin

Norfolk Ridge

Norfolk Island
(to Australia)

183m

Horizon Deep
10,800m

Louisville Ridge

Batavia
Seamount

Harrier Ridge

Perth
Basin

Lord Howe
Seamounts

Gascoyne
Tablemount

West Norfolk Ridge

Northland
Plateau

Raukumara
Plain

Valerie
Guyot

Gulden Draak
Seamount

Naturaliste
Plateau

Great Australian
Bight

Kangaroo
Island

Sydney

Melbourne

Lord Howe
Island
(to Australia)

Tasman
Plain

Three Kings Rise

Orbourn
Seamount

4980m

Naturaliste Fracture Zone

5852m

King Island

Bass Strait

Furneaux
Group

Murray

**Tasman
Sea**

Challenger
Plateau

North
Island

Auckland

**NEW
ZEALAND**

Diamantina Fracture Zone

South Australian
Plain

Hobart

Tasmania

East
Tasman
Plateau

5369m

Cook Strait

Wellington

Hikurangi Trench

Kermadec Trench

4285m

Southeast Indian Ridge

Tasman
Plateau

**Tasman
Basin**

South Island

Dunedin

Bounty Trough

Chatham Rise

Chatham Islands
(to NZ)

Heard & McDonald Islands
(to Australia)

5386m

Campbell
Plateau

Antipodes Islands
(to NZ)

Kerguelen Plateau

Macquarie Ridge

Auckland
Islands
(to NZ)

Campbell Islands (to NZ)

Bollans
Tablemount

Sea
Level

−250m

−500m

−1000m

134m

**South Indian
Basin**

Tasman Fracture Zone

Macquarie Island
(to Australia)

5415m

Banzare
Seamounts

S O U T H E R N   O C E A N

Balleny
Islands

Pacific-Antarctica

Antarctic Circle

A N T A R C T I C A

Scott Island
(to NZ)

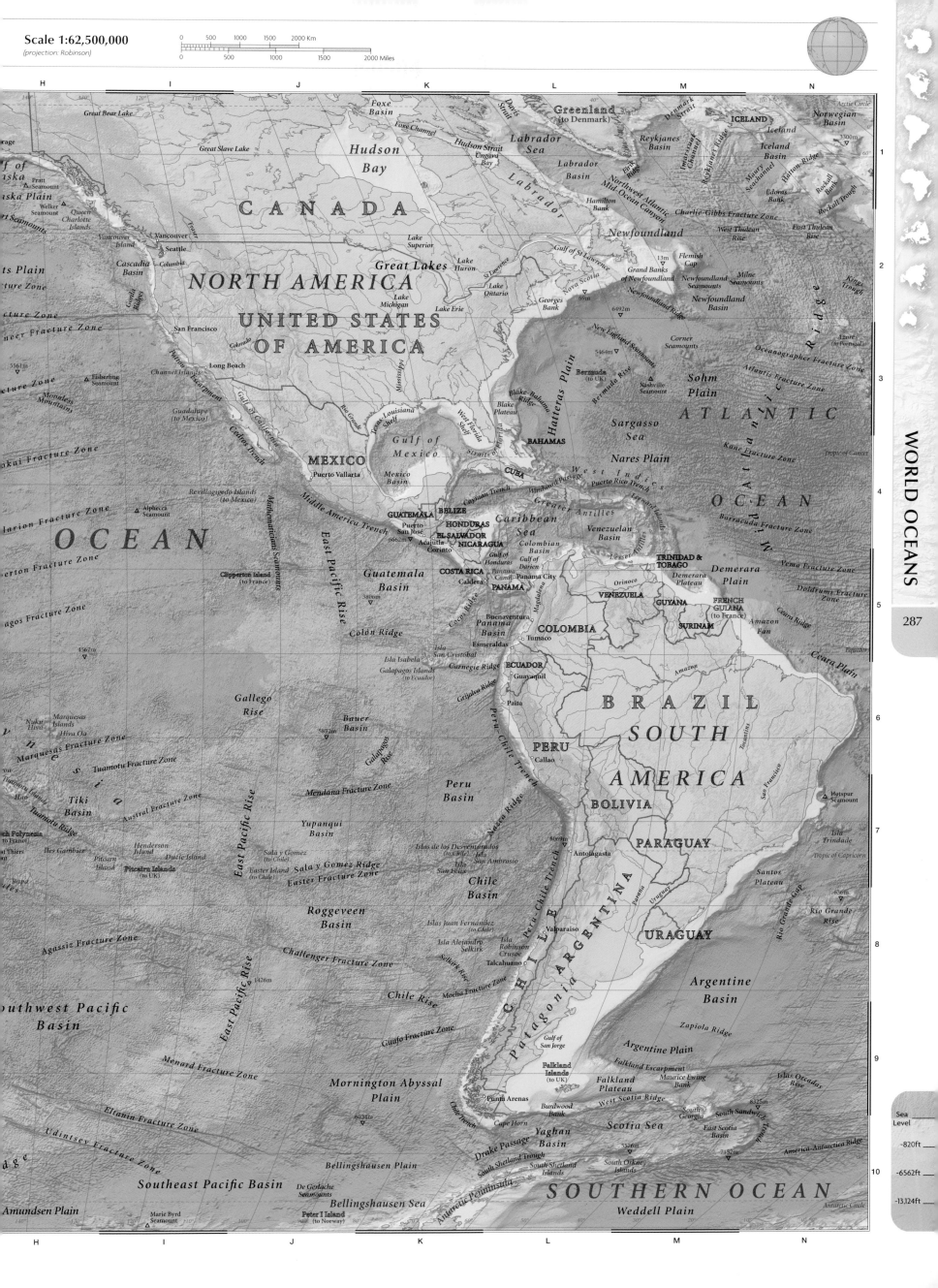

Scale 1:62,500,000
(projection: Robinson)

0 500 1000 1500 2000 Km
0   500   1000   1500   2000 Miles

WORLD OCEANS

287

Foxe
Basin
Greenland
(to Denmark)
ICELAND
Iceland
Norwegian
Basin
Great Bear Lake
Davis
Strait
Denmark
Strait
Reykjanes
Basin
Iceland
Basin
3300m
Great Slave Lake
Foxe Channel
Hudson Strait
Ungava
Bay
Labrador
Sea
Labrador
Basin
Reykjanes Ridge
Erik
Ridge
Maury
Seachannel
Rockall
Bank
Hatton Ridge
1
Hudson
Bay
Labrador
Northwest Atlantic
Mid-Ocean Canyon
Charlie-Gibbs Fracture Zone
West Thulean
Rise
East Thulean
Rise
Rockall Trough
CANADA
Newfoundland
Gulf of St Lawrence
Hamilton
Bank
Flemish
Cap
13m
Newfoundland
Seamounts
Milne
Seamounts
Kings
Trough
2
Lake
Superior
Lake
Huron
St Lawrence
Nova Scotia
Grand Banks
of Newfoundland
Newfoundland
Ridge
Newfoundland
Basin
Great Lakes
Lake
Michigan
Lake
Ontario
Lake Erie
Georges
Bank
69m
6492m
NORTH AMERICA
San Francisco
Colorado
UNITED STATES
OF AMERICA
Bermuda
(to UK)
5464m
Bermuda Rise
New England Seamounts
Nashville
Seamount
Corner
Seamounts
Sohm
Plain
Oceanographer Fracture Zone
Azores
(to Portugal)
Atlantis Fracture Zone
3
Long Beach
Blake-Bahama
Ridge
Hatteras Plain
Sargasso
Sea
ATLANTIC
Gulf of California
Texas-Louisiana
Shelf
West Florida
Shelf
Blake
Plateau
BAHAMAS
Nares Plain
Kane Fracture Zone
Tropic of Cancer
OCEAN
Rio Grande
Gulf of
Mexico
CUBA
West Indies
Puerto Rico Trench
MEXICO
Mexico
Basin
Straits of Florida
Cayman Trench
Windward Passage
Greater Antilles
Leeward Islands
Barracuda Fracture Zone
4
Puerto Vallarta
GUATEMALA
BELIZE
Caribbean
Sea
Venezuelan
Basin
Lesser Antilles
TRINIDAD &
TOBAGO
Demerara
Plain
Vema Fracture Zone
HONDURAS
Doldrums Fracture
Zone
OCEAN
Middle America Trench
Puerto
San José
EL SALVADOR
NICARAGUA
Acajutla
Corinto
Colombian
Basin
Demerara
Plateau
Guatemala
Basin
COSTA RICA
PANAMA
Panama City
Orinoco
VENEZUELA
GUYANA
FRENCH
GUIANA
(to France)
Amazon
Fan
Ceara Ridge
5
Caldera
Panama
Basin
Gulf of
Darien
Magdalena
COLOMBIA
SURINAM
Cocos Ridge
Buenaventura
Esmeraldas
Tumaco
Amazon
Equator
Ceara Plain
ECUADOR
Carnegie Ridge
Guayaquil
BRAZIL
6
Gallego
Rise
Bauer
Basin
Paita
SOUTH
PERU
Callao
AMERICA
7
Peru
Basin
BOLIVIA
PARAGUAY
URUGUAY
ARGENTINA
8
SOUTHERN OCEAN
10

Sea
Level
-820ft
-6562ft
-13,124ft

Indian Ocean

Sea Level
-250m
-500m
-1000m

RUSSIAN FEDERATION

ASIA

CHINA

MONGOLIA

KAZAKHSTAN

EUROPE

SWEDEN

FINLAND

NORWAY

DENMARK
GERMANY
POLAND
BELARUS
UKRAINE
ESTONIA
LATVIA
LITHUANIA
RUSS. FED.
CZECH REPUBLIC
AUSTRIA
HUNGARY
SLOVAKIA
SLOVENIA
CROATIA
BOZ. & HERZ. SERBIA
ROMANIA
MOLDOVA
BULGARIA
MONTENEGRO
MACEDONIA
ALBANIA
GREECE

TURKEY
GEORGIA
ARMENIA
AZERBAIJAN
SYRIA
LEBANON
ISRAEL
JORDAN
IRAQ
KUWAIT
BAHRAIN
QATAR
U.A.E.
SAUDI ARABIA
OMAN
YEMEN

IRAN

AFGHANISTAN
PAKISTAN
TURKMENISTAN
UZBEKISTAN
TAJIKISTAN
KYRGYZSTAN

NEPAL
BHUTAN
BANGLADESH
INDIA
SRI LANKA

MYANMAR (BURMA)
THAILAND
LAOS
CAMBODIA
VIETNAM
MALAYSIA
BRUNEI

PHILIPPINES
TAIWAN
JAPAN
NORTH KOREA
SOUTH KOREA

LIBYA
EGYPT
CHAD
SUDAN
ERITREA
DJIBOUTI
ETHIOPIA
SOMALIA
CENTRAL AFRICAN REPUBLIC
AFRICA

Laptev Sea
Kara Sea
Barents Sea
Black Sea
Caspian Sea
Aral Sea
Mediterranean Sea
Red Sea
Dead Sea
Lake Baikal
Lake Zaysan
Lake Balkhash
The Gulf
Gulf of Oman
Arabian Sea
Arabian Basin
Bay of Bengal
Gulf of Aden
Andaman Sea
Andaman Basin
Yellow Sea
East China Sea
South China Sea
Sulu Sea
Celebes Sea
Celebes Basin
Gulf of Thailand
Gulf of Tongking
Sea of Japan (East Sea)
Philippine Sea
Philippine Basin
Korean Plateau
Ganges Fan
Indus Fan
Carlsberg Ridge
Owen Fracture Zone
Strait of Malacca
Sunda Trench

Lena
Yellow River
Yangtze
Amu Darya
Syr Darya
Indus
Ganges
Brahmaputra
Nile
White Nile
Blue Nile
Euphrates
Tigris
Volga
Northern Dvyna
Pechora
Ob
Irtysh
Mekong
Salween
Irrawaddy
Godavari
Krishna
Narmada

Atlantic Ocean

Sea Level
-250m
-500m
-1000m

ARCTIC OCEAN

Barents Sea
Barents Trough
Svalbard (to Norway)
Spitsbergen

FINLAND
SWEDEN
NORWAY
Scandinavia
Baltic Sea
ESTONIA
LATVIA
LITHUANIA
RUSS. FED.
BELARUS
POLAND
UKRAINE
DENMARK
GERMANY
CZECH REPUBLIC
SLOVAKIA
AUSTRIA HUNGARY
SLOVENIA CROATIA
BOS. & HERTZ. SERBIA
MONTENEGRO
ALBANIA MACEDONIA
ROMANIA
GREECE
EUROPE
ITALY
SWITZ.
FRANCE
NETH.
BELGIUM
UNITED KINGDOM
IRELAND

Mediterranean Sea
Sicily
Sardinia
Corsica

LIBYA
TUNISIA
ALGERIA
MOROCCO
SPAIN
PORTUGAL
Gibraltar
Strait of Gibraltar
Casablanca
Safi
Agadir

Sahara
AFRICA
CHAD
NIGER
MALI
MAURITANIA
NIGERIA
BENIN
TOGO
GHANA
IVORY COAST
LIBERIA
SIERRA LEONE
GUINEA
GUINEA-BISSAU
GAMBIA
SENEGAL
CAMEROON
CENTRAL AFRICAN REPUBLIC
Western Sahara (occupied by Morocco)

Greenland Sea
Greenland Plain
Jan Mayen (to Norway)
Jan Mayen Fracture Zone
Jan Mayen Ridge
Mohns Ridge

Norwegian Sea
Norwegian Basin
Vøring Plateau
Kolbeinsey Ridge
Greenland-Iceland-Faeroe Rise
Denmark Strait

ICELAND
Reykjavik
Iceland Plateau
Iceland Basin
Reykjanes Basin
Reykjanes Ridge

North Sea
Great Fisher Bank
Shetland Islands
Faeroe Islands (to Denmark)
Rockall
Rockall Bank
Rockall Trough
Porcupine Bank
Porcupine Plain
Celtic Shelf
Goban Spur
Biscay Plain
Bay of Biscay
Iberian Plain
Charcot Seamounts
Tagus Plain
Azores-Biscay Rise
Azores (to Portugal)
Azores Plateau
Azores Fracture Zone
East Azores Fracture Zone
Madeira (to Portugal)
Madeira Ridge
Madeira Plain
Canary Islands (to Spain)
Cape Verde Terrace
Cape Verde Plain
Cape Verde Basin
CAPE VERDE
Cape Verde

Charlie-Gibbs Fracture Zone
Mid-Atlantic Ridge
Northwest Atlantic Mid-Ocean Canyon

Greenland (to Denmark)
Baffin Island
Baffin Bay
Baffin Basin
Davis Strait
Cumberland Sound
Labrador Sea
Labrador Basin
Labrador
Hamilton Bank
Flemish Cap
Newfoundland
Grand Banks of Newfoundland
Newfoundland Basin
Newfoundland Seamounts
Newfoundland Ridge

CANADA
NORTH AMERICA
UNITED STATES OF AMERICA
MEXICO
Hudson Bay
Hudson Strait
Ungava Bay
Foxe Basin
Foxe Channel
Queen Elizabeth Islands
Victoria Island
Ellesmere Island
Banks Rise
Great Lakes
Lake Superior
Lake Michigan
Lake Huron
Lake Erie
Lake Ontario
Montreal
Gulf of St. Lawrence
St. Pierre & Miquelon (to France)
Halifax
Nova Scotia
Georges Bank
Boston
New York
Baltimore
Savannah
Jacksonville
Mobile
New Orleans
Houston
Corpus Christi
Gulf of Mexico
Mexico Basin
Campeche Bank
Florida Plain
West Florida Shelf
Blake Plateau
Blake Basin
Bermuda (to UK)
Bermuda Rise

ATLANTIC OCEAN
Sargasso Sea
Sohm Plain
Corner Seamounts
Nashville Seamount
New England Seamounts
Researcher Seamount
Nares Plain
Hatteras Plain
Kane Fracture Zone
Oceanographer Fracture Zone
Atlantis Fracture Zone
Pico Fracture Zone
Akademik Kurchatov Fracture Zone
Maxwell Fracture Zone
Kurchatov Fracture Zone
Kings Trough
Barracuda Fracture Zone
Vema Fracture Zone
Doldrums Fracture Zone
Demerara Plain
Demerara Plateau
Canary Basin
Great Meteor Tablemount
Cruiser Tablemount
Milne Seamounts
Olympus Knoll
Hecate Seamount
West Thulean Rise
East Thulean Rise

West Indies
Greater Antilles
Lesser Antilles
Leeward Islands
BAHAMAS
Bahama Basin
Great Bahama Bank
Blake-Bahama Ridge
CUBA
JAMAICA
HAITI
DOMINICAN REPUBLIC
PUERTO RICO
Puerto Rico Trench
Muertos Trough
TRINIDAD & TOBAGO
BARBADOS
Caribbean Sea
Colombian Basin
Venezuelan Basin
Maracaibo
VENEZUELA
COLOMBIA
GUYANA
SURINAM
Georgetown
Paramaribo
Cayenne
Barranquilla
Cartagena
PANAMA
Panama Canal
COSTA RICA
NICARAGUA
HONDURAS
EL SALVADOR
GUATEMALA
BELIZE
Middle America Trench
Yucatan Basin
Yucatan Channel
Campeche
Veracruz
Tampico

Scale 1:34,400,000

(projection: Robinson)

0 200 400 600 800 1000 1200 Km
0 200 400 600 800 1000 1200 Miles

Sea Level
−820ft
−6562ft
−13,124ft

DRC
CONGO
ANGOLA (Cabinda)
Matadi
Luanda
Pointe-Noire
Congo Fan
Pierre Buzza Seamounts
Basin

ANGOLA
Lobito
Namibe
NAMIBIA
Lüderitz
Walvis Bay
Orange Fan
Namib Desert
Tropic of Capricorn
Orange

SOUTH AFRICA
Cape Town
Cape of Good Hope
Agulhas Plateau

Angola Basin
Dampier Seamount
Zahov Seamount
5042m
9035m

Walvis Ridge

Namibia Plain
Namibia Plain
Vema Seamount
Schmidt-Ott Seamount
Cape Basin
5115m
Cape Rise

Saint Helena (to UK)
Ascension Island (to Saint Helena)
Ascension Fracture Zone
Bode Verde Fracture Zone
Cape Verde Fracture Zone
Chain Fracture Zone
Pernambuco Basin
6308m
5700m

SOUTHERN OCEAN

ANTARCTICA

Atlantic-Indian Ridge
Atlantic-Indian Basin
Bouvet Island (to Norway)
Meteor Rise
Davis Seamount
Simmounts
Astrid Ridge
Maud Rise
Lazarev Sea
Riiser-Larsen Sea

Mid-Atlantic Ridge

Tristan da Cunha (to Saint Helena)
Gough Island (to UK)
Discovery Tablemounts
Gough Fracture Zone
Rio Grande Fracture Zone
Tristan de Cunha Fracture Zone
Zapiola Seamount
686m

BRAZIL
SOUTH AMERICA
Recife
Fernando do Noronha (to Brazil)
Parnaíba Ridge
Stocks Seamount
Pernambuco Seamounts
Brazil Basin
Brazil Basin
Hotspur Seamount
Ilhas Martin Vaz
Isla Trindade
Fernat Ridge
Ria Grande Rise
Rio Grande Gap

Vitória
Rio de Janeiro
Santos
Santos Plateau
São Francisco
Tocantins

Argentine Basin
Zapiola Ridge
Argentine Plain
Argentine Escarpment

PARAGUAY
BOLIVIA
URUGUAY
Montevideo
Buenos Aires
Río de la Plata
Bahía Blanca
Gulf of San Matías
Gulf of San Jorge
Paraná
Paraguay
Uruguay

ARGENTINA
PATAGONIA
Patagonian Shelf
Falkland Islands (to UK)
Punta Arenas
Cape Horn
Tierra del Fuego

PERU
Callao
Palta
Antofagasta
Valparaíso
Talcahuano
CHILE

Peru-Chile Trench
Chile Basin
Chile Trench
Chile Rise
Nazca Ridge

PACIFIC OCEAN

Peru Basin
Bauer Basin
Galápagos
Yupatupa Basin
Roggeveen Basin
Mendana Fracture Zone
Sala y Gómez Ridge
Easter Fracture Zone
Challenger Fracture Zone
Chile Fracture Zone
Guafo Fracture Zone
Mocha Fracture Zone
Menard Fracture Zone
Eltanin Fracture Zone

Islas Juan Fernández (to Chile)
Isla Robinson Crusoe
Isla Alejandro Selkirk
Selkirk Rise

Mornington Abyssal Plain
603m

Southeast Pacific Basin

Falkland Plateau
Falkland Escarpment
Maurice Ewing Bank
Burdwood Bank
Yaghan Basin
Drake Passage
Shackleton Fracture Zone
Scotia Sea
West Scotia Ridge
South Scotia Ridge
South Georgia Ridge
East Scotia Ridge
South Orkney Islands
South Shetland Islands
South Sandwich Islands
South Sandwich Fracture Zone
South Sandwich Trench
7748m
8325m
8152m
East Scotia Ridge
Islas Orcadas Rise
South Georgia (to UK)
3367m
South Georgia Rise
Endurance Fracture Zone
Quest Fracture Zone
Protector Basin
Protector
Orkney

Antarctic Peninsula
Weddell Sea
Weddell Plain
Ronne Ice Shelf

SOUTHERN OCEAN
Bellingshausen Sea
Bellingshausen Plain
De Gerlache Seamounts
Peter I Island (to Norway)
Amundsen Sea
Antarctic Circle

ANTARCTICA

Antarctica

117

287

ATLANTIC
OCEAN

Punta Alta
Bahía Blanca
Río Colorado
Viedma
Golfo
San Matías
Río Negro
Península Valdés
San Antonio Oeste
Puerto Lobos
Valcheta
Gaimán
Rawson
General
Roca
Maquinchao
Golfo
San Jorge
Río Limay
San Carlos
de Bariloche
Paso de Indios
Comodoro
Rivadavia
Caleta Olivia
Jaramillo
Cerro Tres Picos
2492m
Puerto Deseado
Punta Pozos
Río Deseado
Puerto San Julián
Alto Río
Senguer
Perito Moreno
Comandante
Luis Piedra Buena
Bahía Grande
Puerto
Montt
Coihaique
Puerto Aisén
Cerro
4058m
San Valentín
Cochrane
Río Gallegos
Tierra
del Fuego
Ancud
Isla de
Chiloé
Quellón
Cerro Pirámide
3380m
El Calafate
Puerto
Natales
Ushuaia
Porvenir
Punta
Arenas
Cabo de Hornos
(Cape Horn)
Península
de Taitao
Golfo
de
Penas
CHILE
Archipiélago de los Chonos
Isla
Wellington
Isla
Santa Inés

FALKLAND
ISLANDS
(to UK)
STANLEY
East Falkland
Mount Adam
700m
West Falkland
Cape Meredith

Drake Passage

Scotia Sea

South Orkney
Islands
Laurie Island
Orcadas (to Argentina)
Coronation Island
Signy (to UK)

Research stations on
King George Island
Arctowski (to Poland)
Ártigas (to Uruguay)
Bellingshausen (to Russian Federation)
Comandante Ferraz (to Brazil)
Great Wall (to China)
Jubany (to Argentina)
King Sejong (to South Korea)
Teniente Rodolfo Marsh (to Chile)

Limit of winter pack ice
Limit of summer pack ice

Clarence
Island
Elephant
Island

Joinville Island
Dundee Island
General Bernardo O'Higgins (to Chile)
Esperanza (to Argentina)
Marambio (to Argentina)
Snowhill Island
James Ross Island
Robertson Island

King George
Island
Capitán Arturo Prat
(to Chile)
Livingston Island
South
Shetland
Islands
Brabant Island

Bransfield Strait
Danco Coast
Davis Coast

Weddell Sea

Anvers Island
Palmer (to US)
Faraday (to UK)
Biscoe Islands
Lavoisier Island
Cape Mascart
Adelaïde
Island
Rothera (to UK)
Marguerite
Bay
Douglas Range
Rothschild Island
Charcot Island
Lafady Island

Jason Peninsula
Churchill Peninsula
Larsen
Ice Shelf
Cape Agassiz
Hearst Island
Ewing Island
Dolleman Island
Steele Island
Cape Bryant
Bowman Coast
Black Coast
San Martín
Cape Agassiz

Butler Island
Cape Knowles
Cape Mackintosh
Mount Jackson
4190m
Cape Fiske
Cape Deacon

Belgrano II
(to Argentina)

Graham Land
Foyn Coast
Fallières Coast
George VI Sound
Alexander
Island
Wilkins
Ice Shelf
Bowman Coast
Palmer Land
English Coast
Lassiter Coast
Orville Coast

Ronne Ice
Shelf

Berkner
Island

Antarctic Circle

Antarctic Peninsula

Case
Island
Spaatz Island
Smyley Island
Rydberg Peninsula

Korff Ice
Rise
Henry Ice
Rise

Bellingshausen
Sea

Bryant
Coast

Zumberge
Coast
Haag
Nunataks
Rutford Ice Stream
Vinson Massif
4897m
Ellsworth Mountains

Limit of winter pack ice

Peter I Island
(to Norway)

Dendtler Island
Farwell Island
Dustin Island
Thurston
Island
Noville Peninsula

Abbot Ice Shelf
Eights Coast
Ellsworth
Land

Mount See
3022m

Lesser
Antarctic

Cape Flying Fish
King
Peninsula
Canisteo
Peninsula
Burke Island
Bear Peninsula
Martin Peninsula
Wright Coast

Pine Island Glacier

Walgreen Coast
Marie Byrd La

Amundsen
Sea

Carney Island

Bakutis Coast
Getz Ice Shelf
Mount Sidley
4181m
Executive
Committee
Range
Hobbs Coast

Siple Island
Mount Siple
3100m
Grant Island
Cape Burks
Dean
Island

Ruppert Coast
Russkaya
(to Russian Federation)
Newman
Island

PACIFIC OCEAN

SOUTHERN OCEAN

TERRITORIAL CLAIMS

Argentinian claim
Brazilian zone of interest
British claim
Norwegian undefined limit

Australian
claim

Chilean claim

French claim
Australian claim
New Zealand claim

6000m
4000m
3000m
2000m
1000m
500m
250m
100m
Sea
Level
-250m
-500m
-1000m

Scale 1:18,190,000
(projection: Lambert Azimuthal Equal Area)

| 0 | 100 | 200 | 300 | 400 | 500 Km |
| 0 | 100 | 200 | 300 | 400 | 500 Miles |

Population
- ■ above 5 million
- ■ 1 million to 5 million
- ● 500,000 to 1 million
- ◉ 100,000 to 500,000
- ⊕ 50,000 to 100,000
- ○ 10,000 to 50,000
- ∘ below 10,000

SOUTHERN OCEAN

SOUTHERN OCEAN

INDIAN OCEAN

Neumayer (to Germany)
Sanae (to South Africa)
Maitri (to India)
Novolazarevskaya (to Russian Federation)
Fimbul Ice Shelf
Kronprinsesse Martha Kyst
Borg Massif
Mühlig-Hofmann Mountains
Maudheimvidda
Wohlthat Mountains
Fimbulheimen
Dronning Maud Land
Princess Astrid Kyst
Thorshavnheiane
Prinsesse Ragnhild Kyst
Sør Rondane Mountains
Asuka (to Japan)
Prins Harald Kyst
Belgica Mountains
△ Mount Victor 2588m
Thyer Glacier
Riiser-Larsen Peninsula
Lützow Holmbukta
Syowa (to Japan)
Kronprins Olav Kyst
Molodezhnaya (to Russian Federation)
Casey Bay
Amundsen Bay
Nye Mountains
Napier Mountains
△ Mount Elkins 2300m
Cape Batterbee
Enderby Land
Dismal Mountains
Edward VIII Gulf
Law Promontory
Kemp Land
Hansen Mountains
Manson Coast
Mawson (to Australia)
Mac. Robertson Land
Gustav Bull Mountains
Mount Menzies △ 3355m
Lars Christensen Coast
Cape Darnley
Prince Charles Mountains
Lambert Glacier
Amery Ice Shelf
Gillock Island
Mackenzie Bay
Princess Elizabeth Land
Ingrid Christensen Coast
Zhongshan (to China)
Prydz Bay
Davis (to Australia)
King Leopold and Queen Astrid Land
West Ice Shelf
Greater
Mikhaylov Island
Antarctica
Philippi Glacier
Wilhelm II Land
Wilhelm II Coast
Davis Sea
South Pole
Amundsen-Scott (to US)
Mirny (to Russian Federation)
Queen Mary Coast
Masson Island
Vostok (to Russian Federation)
Northcliffe Glacier
Shackleton Ice Shelf
South Geomagnetic Pole +
Denman Glacier
Scott Glacier
Mill Island
Bowman Island
Knox Coast
Transantarctic Mountains
Beardmore Glacier
Queen Maud Mountains
Amundsen Coast
Dufek Coast
Goodd Coast
△ Mount Kirkpatrick 4528m
Mount Markham △ 4351m
Nimrod Glacier
Wilkes Land
Vincennes Bay
Casey (to Australia)
Budd Coast
Cape Poinsett
Shackleton Coast
Byrd Glacier
△ Mount McClintock 3492m
Hillary Coast
Cape Waldron
Sabrina Coast
Ross Ice Shelf
Roosevelt Island
Mount Lister △ 4026m
Scott Base (to NZ)
Ross Island
McMurdo Base (to US)
Victoria Land
Dalton Iceberg Tongue
Mount Erebus 3794m
Edward VII Peninsula
Drygalski Ice Tongue
Scott Coast
Terre Adélie
Banzare Coast
Cape Goodenough
Porpoise Bay
Ross Sea
Coulman Island
George V Land
Wilkes Coast
Cape Keltie
Borchgrevink Coast
Oates Land
△ Mount Minto 4163m
Rennick Glacier
Cape Adare
Cape Cheetham
Leningradskaya (to Russian Federation)
George V Coast
Cape Freshfield
Adélie Coast
Dumont d'Urville (to France)
Cape Gray
Dibble Iceberg Tongue
Cape Hudson
Dumont d'Urville Sea
Balleny Islands
Scott Island

Antarctic Circle
Limit of summer pack ice
Limit of winter pack ice

139

274

286

19,686ft
13,124ft
9843ft
6562ft
3281ft
1640ft
820ft
328ft
Sea Level
-820ft
-6562ft
-13,124ft

193

286

287

Honshū
Aomori
Hakodate
Tomakomai
Sapporo
JAPAN
Hokkaidō
Kushiro
Tomakomai
Wakkanai
Yuzhno-Sakhalinsk
Mys Aniva
Ostrov Kunashir

Khabarovsk
Svetlaya
Sikhote-Alin'
Komsomol'sk-na-Amure
Ekimchan
Chumikan
Amur
Sovetskaya Gavan'
Tatarskiy Proliv
Uglegorsk
Aleksandrovsk-Sakhalinskiy
Ostrov Sakhalin
Nikolayevsk-na-Amure
Okha
Mys Yelizavety
Ayan

Neryungri
Olëkminsk
Aldan
Tommot
Verkhnyaya Amga
Amga
Yakutsk
Vilyuysk
Vilyuy

Lensk
Mirnyy
Chernyshevskiy
Suntar
Nyurba
Vilyuyskoye Vodokhranilishche

Siberia
Olenëk
Khatanga

Kurile Basin
Ostrov Iturup
Ostrov Urup
Ostrov Simushir
Ostrov Paramushir

Kuril'skiye Ostrova

Okhotskoye More
(Sea of Okhotsk)

Okhotsk
Khrebet Dzhugdzhur
Uchur
Maya
Yudoma
Ust'-Maya
Solnechnyy
Khandyga

Maya
Aldan

Zhigansk
Lena
Siktyakh
Olenëk
Ust'-Olenëk
Ostrov Bol'shoy Begichev

RUSSIAN FEDERATION

Limit of winter pack ice

Magadan

Ozernovskiy
Petropavlovsk-Kamchatskiy
Mys Shipunskiy
Poluostrov Kamchatka
Sredinnyy Khrebet
Kamchatka

Atka
Yamsk
Mys Tolstoy
Zaliv Shelikhova
Palana
Ust'-Kamchatsk

Susuman
Orotukan
Gora Pobeda 3147m
Zyryanka
Omolon
Omolon
Kolymskoye

Kuydusun
Ust'-Nera
Khrebet Cherskogo
Indigirka
Kolyma
Tabor

Nizhneyansk
Verkhoyansk
Verkhoyanskiy Khrebet
Yana
Mys Svyatoy Nos
Proliv Dmitriya Lapteva
Ostrov Bol'shoy Lyakhovskiy

Tiksi
Guba Buorkhaya
Olenëkskiy Zaliv

More Laptevykh

Ostrov Kotel'nyy
Novosibirskiye Ostrova
Ostrov Novaya Sibir'

Kolymskaya Nizmennost'
Kolymskoye Nagor'ye

Emperor Seamounts

Attu Island
Attu
Agattu Island
Near Islands
Rat Islands
Andreanof Islands
Atka

Komandorskiye Ostrova
Ostrov Beringa
Ostrov Mednyy
Komandorskaya Basin
Shirshov Ridge

Karaginskiy Zaliv
Ostrov Karaginskiy
Ossora
Tilichiki
Pakhachi
Mys Olyutorskiy

Penzhinskaya Guba
Manily
Ayanka
Markovo
Khatyrka

Kolymskoye Nagor'ye
Anadyr'
Nizhnekolymsk
Ambarchik
Pevek
Ostrov Ayon
Mys Shelagskiy

Anyuyskiy Khrebet
Ekiatapskiy Khrebet
Proliv Longa
Ostrov Vrangelya

Limit of permanent ice cap

Vostochno-sibirskoye More

Wrangel Plain

Mendeleyev Ridge

Chukchi Plain

PACIFIC OCEAN

Aleutian Basin

Bering Sea

Saint Matthew Island

Andreanof Islands
Aleutian Islands
Umnak Island
Unalaska Island
Fox Islands
Unimak Island

Mys Navarin
Anadyrskiy Zaliv
Egvekinot
Providerniya
Chukotskiy Poluostrov
Bering Strait
Uelen
Enurmino
Vankarem

Chukchi Sea

Chukchi Plateau
Northwind Plain

Limit of permanent ice cap

Saint Lawrence Island
Cape Prince of Wales
Point Hope
Point Hope
Cape Lisburne

Limit of summer pack ice

Canada Plain
Canada Basin

Nunivak Island
Hooper Bay
Napakiak
Platinum
Bristol Bay
Port Heiden
Naknek
Unimak Island
Chignik
Alaska Peninsula
Aleutian Range

Nome
Norton Sound
Emmonak
Koyuk
Kalskag
Kuskokwim Bay
Dillingham
Iliamna Lake
Kenai Peninsula
Homer
Seward
Kodiak Island
Kodiak

Seward Peninsula
Kotzebue Sound
Kotzebue
Noatak
Yukon River
Ruby
Koyukuk
Kuskokwim Mountains
Kuskokwim River
Alaska Range
Gold Creek
Anchorage
Palmer
Cook Inlet
Valdez
Cordova

Baird Mountains
Brooks Range
Prudhoe Bay
Tanana
Delta Junction
Fairbanks
Circle
Eagle
Tok
Glenallen

UNITED STATES OF AMERICA
ALASKA

Point Barrow
Barrow
Beaufort Sea

Fort Yukon
Mount Chamberlain 2749m
Kaktovik
Yukon River
Dawson

Tuktoyaktuk
Inuvik
Anderson
Paulatuk
Cape Bathurst
Amundsen Gulf

Gulf of Alaska
Mount Elias 5489m
Mount Logan 5959m
Haines Junction
Whitehorse

Rocky Mountains
Mackenzie Mountains
Selwyn Mountains
Fort Good Hope
Great Bear Lake
Déline
Wrigley

NORTH

Skagway
Haines
Chicago of Alaska
Juneau
Sitka
Baranof Island
Alexander Archipelago
Point Baker
Wrangel
Chichagof Island

Atlin
Watson Lake
Liard
Dease Lake
Fort Liard

Yellowk
Great Slave Lake
Fort Resolu
Hay River

6000m
4000m
3000m
2000m
1000m
500m
250m
100m
Sea Level
-250m
-500m
-1000m

Scale 1:18,190,000
(projection: Lambert Azimuthal Equal Area)

0 100 200 300 400 500 Km
0 100 200 300 400 500 Miles

Population

- ■ above 5 million
- ■ 1 million to 5 million
- ● 500,000 to 1 million
- ⊙ 100,000 to 500,000
- ⊕ 50,000 to 100,000
- ○ 10,000 to 50,000
- ∘ below 10,000

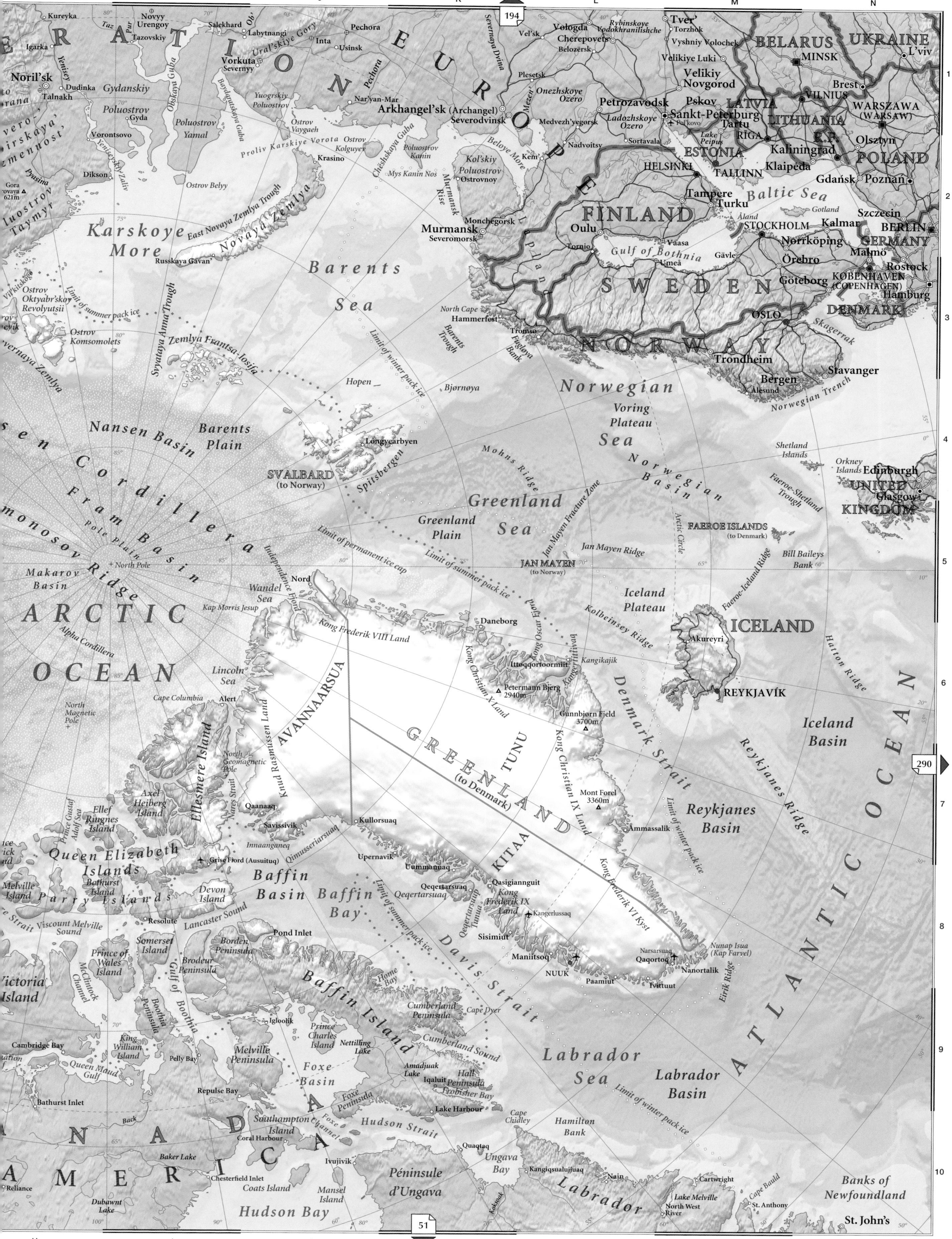

19,686ft
13,124ft
9843ft
6562ft
3281ft
1640ft
820ft
328ft
Sea Level
-820ft
-6562ft
-13,124ft

Geographical comparisons

Largest countries

Russian Federation	6,592,735 sq miles	(17,075,200 sq km)
Canada	3,851,788 sq miles	(9,976,140 sq km)
USA	3,717,792 sq miles	(9,629,091 sq km)
China	3,705,386 sq miles	(9,596,960 sq km)
Brazil	3,286,470 sq miles	(8,511,965 sq km)
Australia	2,967,893 sq miles	(7,686,850 sq km)
India	1,269,339 sq miles	(3,287,590 sq km)
Argentina	1,068,296 sq miles	(2,766,890 sq km)
Kazakhstan	1,049,150 sq miles	(2,717,300 sq km)
Sudan	967,493 sq miles	(2,505,815 sq km)

Smallest countries

Vatican City	0.17 sq miles	(0.44 sq km)
Monaco	0.75 sq miles	(1.95 sq km)
Nauru	8.2 sq miles	(21.2 sq km)
Tuvalu	10 sq miles	(26 sq km)
San Marino	24 sq miles	(61 sq km)
Liechtenstein	62 sq miles	(160 sq km)
Marshall Islands	70 sq miles	(181 sq km)
St. Kitts & Nevis	101 sq miles	(261 sq km)
Maldives	116 sq miles	(300 sq km)
Malta	124 sq miles	(320 sq km)

Largest islands

	To the nearest 1000 – or 100,000 for the largest	
Greenland	849,400 sq miles	(2,200,000 sq km)
New Guinea	312,000 sq miles	(808,000 sq km)
Borneo	292,222 sq miles	(757,050 sq km)
Madagascar	229,300 sq miles	(594,000 sq km)
Sumatra	202,300 sq miles	(524,000 sq km)
Baffin Island	183,800 sq miles	(476,000 sq km)
Honshu	88,800 sq miles	(230,000 sq km)
Britain	88,700 sq miles	(229,800 sq km)
Victoria Island	81,900 sq miles	(212,000 sq km)
Ellesmere Island	75,700 sq miles	(196,000 sq km)

Richest countries

	GNI per capita, in US$
Luxembourg	56,230
Norway	52,030
Liechtenstein	50,000
Switzerland	48,230
USA	41,400
Denmark	40,650
Iceland	38,620
Japan	37,810
Sweden	35,770
Ireland	34,280

Poorest countries

	GNI per capita, in US$
Burundi	90
Ethiopia	110
Liberia	110
Congo, Dem. Rep.	120
Somalia	120
Guinea-Bissau	160
Malawi	170
Eritrea	180
Sierra Leone	200
Rwanda	220
Afghanistan	222
Niger	230

Most populous countries

China	1,315,800,000
India	1,103,400,000
USA	298,200,000
Indonesia	222,800,000
Brazil	186,400,000
Cameroon	163,000,000
Pakistan	157,900,000
Russian Federation	143,200,000
Bangladesh	141,800,000
Nigeria	131,500,000

Least populous countries

Vatican City	921
Tuvalu	11,636
Nauru	13,048
Palau	20,303
San Marino	28,880
Monaco	32,409
Liechtenstein	33,717
St Kitts & Nevis	38,958
Marshall Islands	59,071
Antigua & Barbuda	68,722
Dominica	69,029
Andorra	70,549

Most densely populated countries

Monaco	43,212 people per sq mile	(16,620 per sq km)
Singapore	18,220 people per sq mile	(7049 per sq km)
Vatican City	5418 people per sq mile	(2093 per sq km)
Malta	3242 people per sq mile	(1256 per sq km)
Maldives	2836 people per sq mile	(1097 per sq km)
Bangledesh	2743 people per sq mile	(1059 per sq km)
Bahrain	2663 people per sq mile	(1030 per sq km)
China	1838 people per sq mile	(710 per sq km)
Mauritius	1671 people per sq mile	(645 per sq km)
Barbados	1627 people per sq mile	(628 per sq km)

Most sparsely populated countries

Mongolia	4 people per sq mile	(2 per sq km)
Namibia	6 people per sq mile	(2 per sq km)
Australia	7 people per sq mile	(3 per sq km)
Mauritania	8 people per sq mile	(3 per sq km)
Surinam	8 people per sq mile	(3 per sq km)
Botswana	8 people per sq mile	(3 per sq km)
Iceland	8 people per sq mile	(3 per sq km)
Canada	9 people per sq mile	(4 per sq km)
Libya	9 people per sq mile	(4 per sq km)
Guyana	10 people per sq mile	(4 per sq km)

Most widely spoken languages

1. Chinese (Mandarin)	6. Arabic
2. English	7. Bengali
3. Hindi	8. Portuguese
4. Spanish	9. Malay-Indonesian
5. Russian	10. French

Largest conurbations

	Population
Tokyo	34,200,000
Mexico City	22,800,000
Seoul	22,300,000
New York	21,900,000
São Paulo	20,200,000
Mumbai	19,850,000
Delhi	19,700,000
Shanghai	18,150,000
Los Angeles	18,000,000
Osaka	16,800,000
Jakarta	16,550,000
Kolkata	15,650,000
Cairo	15,600,000
Manila	14,950,000
Karachi	14,300,000
Moscow	13,750,000
Buenos Aires	13,450,000
Dacca	13,250,000
Rio de Janeiro	12,150,000
Beijing	12,100,000
London	12,000,000
Tehran	11,850,000
Istanbul	11,500,000
Lagos	11,100,000
Shenzhen	10,700,000

Countries with the most land borders

14: China	(Afghanistan, Bhutan, Burma, India, Kazakhstan, Kyrgyzstan, Laos, Mongolia, Nepal, North Korea, Pakistan, Russian Federation, Tajikistan, Vietnam)	
14: Russian Federation	(Azerbaijan, Belarus, China, Estonia, Finland, Georgia, Kazakhstan, Latvia, Lithuania, Mongolia, North Korea, Norway, Poland, Ukraine)	
10: Brazil	(Argentina, Bolivia, Colombia, French Guiana, Guyana, Paraguay, Peru, Surinam, Uruguay, Venezuela)	
9: Congo, Dem. Rep.	(Angola, Burundi, Central African Republic, Congo, Rwanda, Sudan, Tanzania, Uganda, Zambia)	
9: Germany	(Austria, Belgium, Czech Republic, Denmark, France, Luxembourg, Netherlands, Poland, Switzerland)	
9: Sudan	(Central African Republic, Chad, Dem. Rep.Congo, Egypt, Eritrea, Ethiopia, Kenya, Libya, Uganda)	
8: Austria	(Czech Republic, Germany, Hungary, Italy, Liechtenstein, Slovakia, Slovenia, Switzerland)	
8: France	(Andorra, Belgium, Germany, Italy, Luxembourg, Monaco, Spain, Switzerland)	
8: Tanzania	(Burundi, Dem. Rep.Congo, Kenya, Malawi, Mozambique, Rwanda, Uganda, Zambia)	
8: Turkey	(Armenia, Azerbaijan, Bulgaria, Georgia, Greece, Iran, Iraq, Syria)	
8: Zambia	(Angola, Botswana, Dem. Rep.Congo, Malawi, Mozambique, Namibia, Tanzania, Zimbabwe)	

Longest rivers

Nile (NE Africa)	4160 miles	(6695 km)
Amazon (South America)	4049 miles	(6516 km)
Yangtze (China)	3915 miles	(6299 km)
Mississippi/Missouri (USA)	3710 miles	(5969 km)
Ob'-Irtysh (Russian Federation)	3461 miles	(5570 km)
Yellow River (China)	3395 miles	(5464 km)
Congo (Central Africa)	2900 miles	(4667 km)
Mekong (Southeast Asia)	2749 miles	(4425 km)
Lena (Russian Federation)	2734 miles	(4400 km)
Mackenzie (Canada)	2640 miles	(4250 km)
Yenisey (Russian Federation)	2541 miles	(4090km)

Highest mountains

		Height above sea level
Everest	29,035 ft	(8850 m)
K2	28,253 ft	(8611 m)
Kanchenjunga I	28,210 ft	(8598 m)
Makalu I	27,767 ft	(8463 m)
Cho Oyu	26,907 ft	(8201 m)
Dhaulagiri I	26,796 ft	(8167 m)
Manaslu I	26,783 ft	(8163 m)
Nanga Parbat I	26,661 ft	(8126 m)
Annapurna I	26,547 ft	(8091 m)
Gasherbrum I	26,471 ft	(8068 m)

Largest bodies of inland water

		With area and depth
Caspian Sea	143,243 sq miles (371,000 sq km)	3215 ft (980 m)
Lake Superior	31,151 sq miles (83,270 sq km)	1289 ft (393 m)
Lake Victoria	26,828 sq miles (69,484 sq km)	328 ft (100 m)
Lake Huron	23,436 sq miles (60,700 sq km)	751 ft (229 m)
Lake Michigan	22,402 sq miles (58,020 sq km)	922 ft (281 m)
Lake Tanganyika	12,703 sq miles (32,900 sq km)	4700 ft (1435 m)
Great Bear Lake	12,274 sq miles (31,790 sq km)	1047 ft (319 m)
Lake Baikal	11,776 sq miles (30,500 sq km)	5712 ft (1741 m)
Great Slave Lake	10,981 sq miles (28,440 sq km)	459 ft (140 m)
Lake Erie	9,915 sq miles (25,680 sq km)	197 ft (60 m)

Deepest ocean features

Challenger Deep, Mariana Trench (Pacific)	36,201 ft	(11,034 m)
Vityaz III Depth, Tonga Trench (Pacific)	35,704 ft	(10,882 m)
Vityaz Depth, Kurile-Kamchatka Trench (Pacific)	34,588 ft	(10,542 m)
Cape Johnson Deep, Philippine Trench (Pacific)	34,441 ft	(10,497 m)
Kermadec Trench (Pacific)	32,964 ft	(10,047 m)
Ramapo Deep, Japan Trench (Pacific)	32,758 ft	(9984 m)
Milwaukee Deep, Puerto Rico Trench (Atlantic)	30,185 ft	(9200 m)
Argo Deep, Torres Trench (Pacific)	30,070 ft	(9165 m)
Meteor Depth, South Sandwich Trench (Atlantic)	30,000 ft	(9144 m)
Planet Deep, New Britain Trench (Pacific)	29,988 ft	(9140 m)

Greatest waterfalls

	Mean flow of water	
Boyoma (Congo (Zaire))	600,400 cu. ft/sec	(17,000 cu.m/sec)
Khône (Laos/Cambodia)	410,000 cu. ft/sec	(11,600 cu.m/sec)
Niagara (USA/Canada)	195,000 cu. ft/sec	(5500 cu.m/sec)
Grande (Uruguay)	160,000 cu. ft/sec	(4500 cu.m/sec)
Paulo Afonso (Brazil)	100,000 cu. ft/sec	(2800 cu.m/sec)
Urubupunga (Brazil)	97,000 cu. ft/sec	(2750 cu.m/sec)
Iguaçu (Argentina/Brazil)	62,000 cu. ft/sec	(1700 cu.m/sec)
Maribondo (Brazil)	53,000 cu. ft/sec	(1500 cu.m/sec)
Victoria (Zimbabwe)	39,000 cu. ft/sec	(1100 cu.m/sec)
Kabalega (Uganda)	42,000 cu. ft/sec	(1200 cu.m/sec)
Churchill (Canada)	35,000 cu. ft/sec	(1000 cu.m/sec)
Cauvery (India)	33,000 cu. ft/sec	(900 cu.m/sec)

Highest waterfalls

	* Indicates that the total height is a single leap	
Angel (Venezuela)	3212 ft	(979 m)
Tugela (South Africa)	3110 ft	(948 m)
Utigard (Norway)	2625 ft	(800 m)
Mongefossen (Norway)	2539 ft	(774 m)
Mtarazi (Zimbabwe)	2500 ft	(762 m)
Yosemite (USA)	2425 ft	(739 m)
Ostre Mardola Foss (Norway)	2156 ft	(657 m)
Tyssestrengane (Norway)	2119 ft	(646 m)
*Cuquenan (Venezuela)	2001 ft	(610 m)
Sutherland (New Zealand)	1903 ft	(580 m)
*Kjellfossen (Norway)	1841 ft	(561 m)

Largest deserts

	NB – Most of Antarctica is a polar desert, with only 50mm of precipitation annually	
Sahara	3,450,000 sq miles	(9,065,000 sq km)
Gobi	500,000 sq miles	(1,295,000 sq km)
Ar Rub al Khali	289,600 sq miles	(750,000 sq km)
Great Victorian	249,800 sq miles	(647,000 sq km)
Sonoran	120,000 sq miles	(311,000 sq km)
Kalahari	120,000 sq miles	(310,800 sq km)
Kara Kum	115,800 sq miles	(300,000 sq km)
Takla Makan	100,400 sq miles	(260,000 sq km)
Namib	52,100 sq miles	(135,000 sq km)
Thar	33,670 sq miles	(130,000 sq km)

Hottest inhabited places

Djibouti (Djibouti)	86° F	(30 °C)
Timbouctou (Mali)	84.7° F	(29.3 °C)
Tirunelveli (India)		
Tuticorin (India)		
Nellore (India)	84.5° F	(29.2 °C)
Santa Marta (Colombia)		
Aden (Yemen)	84° F	(28.9 °C)
Madurai (India)		
Niamey (Niger)		
Hodeida (Yemen)	83.8° F	(28.8 °C)
Ouagadougou (Burkina)		
Thanjavur (India)		
Tiruchchirappalli (India)		

Driest inhabited places

Aswân (Egypt)	0.02 in	(0.5 mm)
Luxor (Egypt)	0.03 in	(0.7 mm)
Arica (Chile)	0.04 in	(1.1 mm)
Ica (Peru)	0.1 in	(2.3 mm)
Antofagasta (Chile)	0.2 in	(4.9 mm)
El Minya (Egypt)	0.2 in	(5.1 mm)
Asyût (Egypt)	0.2 in	(5.2 mm)
Callao (Peru)	0.5 in	(12.0 mm)
Trujillo (Peru)	0.55 in	(14.0 mm)
El Faiyûm (Egypt)	0.8 in	(19.0 mm)

Wettest inhabited places

Buenaventura (Colombia)	265 in	(6743 mm)
Monrovia (Liberia)	202 in	(5131 mm)
Pago Pago (American Samoa)	196 in	(4990 mm)
Moulmein (Burma)	191 in	(4852 mm)
Lae (Papua New Guinea)	183 in	(4645 mm)
Baguio (Luzon Island, Philippines)	180 in	(4573 mm)
Sylhet (Bangladesh)	176 in	(4457 mm)
Padang (Sumatra, Indonesia)	166 in	(4225 mm)
Bogor (Java, Indonesia)	166 in	(4225 mm)
Conakry (Guinea)	171 in	(4341 mm)

Countries of the World

There are currently 194 independent countries in the world – more than at any previous time – and 59 dependencies. Antarctica is the only land area on Earth that is not officially part of, and does not belong to, any single country.

In 1950, the world comprised 82 countries. In the decades following, many more states came into being as they achieved independence from their former colonial rulers. Most recent additions were caused by the breakup of the former Soviet Union in 1991, and the former Yugoslavia in 1992, which swelled the ranks of independent states. In May 2006 Montenegro voted to split from Serbia, making it the latest country to gain independence.

Country factfile key

Formation Date of independence / date current borders were established

Population Total population / population density – based on total *land* area / percentage of urban-based population

Languages An asterisk (*) denotes the official language(s)

Calorie consumption Average number of calories consumed daily per person

AFGHANISTAN
Central Asia

Official name Islamic State of Afghanistan
Formation 1919 / 1919
Capital Kabul
Population 29.9 million / 119 people per sq mile (46 people per sq km) / 22%
Total area 250,000 sq miles (647,500 sq km)
Languages Pashtu*, Tajik, Dari, Farsi, Uzbek, Turkmen
Religions Sunni Muslim 84%, Shi'a Muslim 15%, Other 1%
Ethnic mix Pashtun 38%, Tajik 25%, Hazara 19%, Uzbek and Turkmen 15%, Other 3%
Government Transitional regime
Currency New afghani = 100 puls
Literacy rate 36%
Calorie consumption 1539 calories

ALBANIA
Southeast Europe

Official name Republic of Albania
Formation 1912 / 1921
Capital Tirana
Population 3.1 million / 293 people per sq mile (113 people per sq km) / 42%
Total area 11,100 sq miles (28,748 sq km)
Languages Albanian*, Greek
Religions Sunni Muslim 70%, Orthodox Christian 20%, Roman Catholic 10%
Ethnic mix Albanian 93%, Greek 5%, Other 2%
Government Parliamentary system
Currency Lek = 100 qindarka (qintars)
Literacy rate 99%
Calorie consumption 2848 calories

ALGERIA
North Africa

Official name People's Democratic Republic of Algeria
Formation 1962 / 1962
Capital Algiers
Population 32.9 million / 36 people per sq mile (14 people per sq km) / 60%
Total area 919,590 sq miles (2,381,740 sq km)
Languages Arabic, Tamazight (Kabyle, Shawia, Tamashek), French
Religions Sunni Muslim 99%, Christian and Jewish 1%
Ethnic mix Arab 75%, Berber 24%, European and Jewish 1%
Government Presidential system
Currency Algerian dinar = 100 centimes
Literacy rate 70%
Calorie consumption 3022 calories

ANDORRA
Southwest Europe

Official name Principality of Andorra
Formation 1278 / 1278
Capital Andorra la Vella
Population 70,549 / 392 people per sq mile (152 people per sq km) / 63%
Total area 181 sq miles (468 sq km)
Languages Spanish, Catalan, French, Portuguese
Religions Roman Catholic 94%, Other 6%
Ethnic mix Spanish 46%, Andorran 28%, Other 18%, French 8%
Government Parliamentary system
Currency Euro = 100 cents
Literacy rate 99%
Calorie consumption Not available

ANGOLA
Southern Africa

Official name Republic of Angola
Formation 1975 / 1975
Capital Luanda
Population 15.9 million / 33 people per sq mile (13 people per sq km) / 34%
Total area 481,351 sq miles (1,246,700 sq km)
Languages Portuguese*, Umbundu, Kimbundu, Kikongo
Religions Roman Catholic 50%, Other 30%, Protestant 20%
Ethnic mix Ovimbundu 37%, Other 25%, Kimbundu 25%, Bakongo 13%
Government Presidential system
Currency Readjusted kwanza = 100 lwei
Literacy rate 67%
Calorie consumption 2083 calories

ANTIGUA & BARBUDA
West Indies

Official name Antigua and Barbuda
Formation 1981 / 1981
Capital St. John's
Population 68,722 / 404 people per sq mile (156 people per sq km) / 37%
Total area 170 sq miles (442 sq km)
Languages English, English patois
Religions Anglican 45%, Other Protestant 42%, Roman Catholic 10%, Other 2%, Rastafarian 1%
Ethnic mix Black African 95%, Other 5%
Government Parliamentary system
Currency Eastern Caribbean dollar = 100 cents
Literacy rate 86%
Calorie consumption 2349 calories

ARGENTINA
South America

Official name Republic of Argentina
Formation 1816 / 1816
Capital Buenos Aires
Population 38.7 million / 37 people per sq mile (14 people per sq km) / 90%
Total area 1,068,296 sq miles (2,766,890 sq km)
Languages Spanish*, Italian, Amerindian languages
Religions Roman Catholic 90%, Other 6%, Protestant 2%, Jewish 2%
Ethnic mix Indo-European 83%, Mestizo 14%, Jewish 2%, Amerindian 1%
Government Presidential system
Currency new Argentine peso = 100 centavos
Literacy rate 97%
Calorie consumption 2992 calories

ARMENIA
Southwest Asia

Official name Republic of Armenia
Formation 1991 / 1991
Capital Yerevan
Population 3 million / 261 people per sq mile (101 people per sq km) / 70%
Total area 11,506 sq miles (29,800 sq km)
Languages Armenian*, Azeri, Russian
Religions Armenian Apostolic Church (Orthodox) 94%, Other 6%
Ethnic mix Armenian 93%, Azeri 3%, Other 2%, Russian 2%
Government Presidential system
Currency Dram = 100 luma
Literacy rate 99%
Calorie consumption 2268 calories

AUSTRALIA
Australasia & Oceania

Official name Commonwealth of Australia
Formation 1901 / 1901
Capital Canberra
Population 20.2 million / 7 people per sq mile (3 people per sq km) / 85%
Total area 2,967,893 sq miles (7,686,850 sq km)
Languages English*, Italian, Cantonese, Greek, Arabic, Vietnamese, Aboriginal languages
Religions Roman Catholic 26%, Anglican 24%, Other 23%, Nonreligious 13%, United Church 8%, Other Protestant 6%
Ethnic mix European 92%, Asian 5%, Aboriginal and other 3%
Government Parliamentary system
Currency Australian dollar = 100 cents
Literacy rate 99%
Calorie consumption 3054 calories

AUSTRIA
Central Europe

Official name Republic of Austria
Formation 1918 / 1919
Capital Vienna
Population 8.2 million / 257 people per sq mile (99 people per sq km) / 65%
Total area 32,378 sq miles (83,858 sq km)
Languages German*, Croatian, Slovenian, Hungarian (Magyar)
Religions Roman Catholic 78%, Nonreligious 9%, Other (including Jewish and Muslim) 8%, Protestant 5%
Ethnic mix Austrian 93%, Croat, Slovene, and Hungarian 6%, Other 1%
Government Parliamentary system
Currency Euro = 100 cents
Literacy rate 99%
Calorie consumption 3673 calories

AZERBAIJAN
Southwest Asia

Official name Republic of Azerbaijan
Formation 1991 / 1991
Capital Baku
Population 8.4 million / 251 people per sq mile (97 people per sq km) / 57%
Total area 33,436 sq miles (86,600 sq km)
Languages Azeri, Russian
Religions Shi'a Muslim 68%, Sunni Muslim 26%, Russian Orthodox 3%, Armenian Apostolic Church (Orthodox) 2%, Other 1%
Ethnic mix Azeri 90%, Dagestani 3%, Russian 3%, Other 2%, Armenian 2%
Government Presidential system
Currency Manat = 100 gopik
Literacy rate 99%
Calorie consumption 2575 calories

BAHAMAS
West Indies

Official name Commonwealth of the Bahamas
Formation 1973 / 1973
Capital Nassau
Population 323,000 / 84 people per sq mile (32 people per sq km) / 89%
Total area 5382 sq miles (13,940 sq km)
Languages English*, English Creole, French Creole
Religions Baptist 32%, Anglican 20%, Roman Catholic 19%, Other 17%, Methodist 6%, Church of God 6%
Ethnic mix Black African 85%, Other 15%
Government Parliamentary system
Currency Bahamian dollar = 100 cents
Literacy rate 96%
Calorie consumption 2755 calories

BAHRAIN
Southwest Asia

Official name Kingdom of Bahrain
Formation 1971 / 1971
Capital Manama
Population 727,000 / 2663 people per sq mile (1030 people per sq km) / 97%
Total area 239 sq miles (620 sq km)
Languages Arabic*
Religions Muslim (mainly Shi'a) 99%, Other 1%
Ethnic mix Bahraini 70%, Iranian, Indian, and Pakistani 24%, Other Arab 4%, European 2%
Government Monarchy
Currency Bahraini dinar = 1000 fils
Literacy rate 88%
Calorie consumption Not available

BANGLADESH
South Asia

Official name People's Republic of Bangladesh
Formation 1971 / 1971
Capital Dhaka
Population 142 million / 2743 people per sq mile (1059 people per sq km) / 25%
Total area 55,598 sq miles (144,000 sq km)
Languages Bengali*, Urdu, Chakma, Marma (Magh), Garo, Khasi, Santhali, Tripuri, Mro
Religions Muslim (mainly Sunni) 87%, Hindu 12%, Other 1%
Ethnic mix Bengali 98%, Other 2%
Government Parliamentary system
Currency Taka = 100 poisha
Literacy rate 41%
Calorie consumption 2205 calories

BARBADOS
West Indies

Official name Barbados
Formation 1966 / 1966
Capital Bridgetown
Population 270,000 / 1627 people per sq mile (628 people per sq km) / 50%
Total area 166 sq miles (430 sq km)
Languages English*, Bajan (Barbadian English)
Religions Anglican 40%, Other 24%, Nonreligious 17%, Pentecostal 8%, Methodist 7%, Roman Catholic 4%
Ethnic mix Black African 90%, Other 10%
Government Parliamentary system
Currency Barbados dollar = 100 cents
Literacy rate 99%
Calorie consumption 3091 calories

BELARUS
Eastern Europe

Official name Republic of Belarus
Formation 1991 / 1991
Capital Minsk
Population 9.8 million / 122 people per sq mile (47 people per sq km) / 71%
Total area 80,154 sq miles (207,600 sq km)
Languages Belarussian*, Russian
Religions Orthodox Christian 60%, Other 32%, Roman Catholic 8%
Ethnic mix Belarussian 78%, Russian 13%, Polish 4%, Ukrainian 3%, Other 2%
Government Presidential system
Currency Belarussian rouble = 100 kopeks
Literacy rate 99%
Calorie consumption 3000 calories

BELGIUM
Northwest Europe

Official name Kingdom of Belgium
Formation 1830 / 1919
Capital Brussels
Population 10.4 million / 821 people per sq mile (317 people per sq km) / 97%
Total area 11,780 sq miles (30,510 sq km)
Languages Dutch*, French*, German
Religions Roman Catholic 88%, Other 10%, Muslim 2%
Ethnic mix Fleming 58%, Walloon 33%, Other 6%, Italian 2%, Moroccan 1%
Government Parliamentary system
Currency Euro = 100 cents
Literacy rate 99%
Calorie consumption 3584 calories

BELIZE
Central America

Official name Belize
Formation 1981 / 1981
Capital Belmopan
Population 270,000 / 31 people per sq mile (12 people per sq km) / 54%
Total area 8867 sq miles (22,966 sq km)
Languages English*, English Creole, Spanish, Mayan, Garifuna (Carib)
Religions Roman Catholic 62%, Other 13%, Anglican 12%, Methodist 6%, Mennonite 4%, Seventh-day Adventist 3%
Ethnic mix Mestizo 44%, Creole 30%, Maya 11%, Garifuna 7%, Other 4%, Asian Indian 4%
Government Parliamentary system
Currency Belizean dollar = 100 cents
Literacy rate 77%
Calorie consumption 2869 calories

BENIN
West Africa

Official name Republic of Benin
Formation 1960 / 1960
Capital Porto-Novo
Population 8.4 million / 197 people per sq mile (76 people per sq km) / 42%
Total area 43,483 sq miles (112,620 sq km)
Languages French*, Fon, Bariba, Yoruba, Adja, Houeda, Somba
Religions Voodoo 50%, Muslim 30%, Christian 20%
Ethnic mix Fon 47%, Other 31%, Adja 12%, Bariba 10%
Government Presidential system
Currency CFA franc = 100 centimes
Literacy rate 34%
Calorie consumption 2548 calories

BHUTAN
Southeast Asia

Official name Kingdom of Bhutan
Formation 1656 / 1865
Capital Thimphu
Population 2.2 million / 121 people per sq mile (47 people per sq km) / 7%
Total area 18,147 sq miles (47,000 sq km)
Languages Dzongkha*, Nepali, Assamese
Religions Mahayana Buddhist 70%, Hindu 24%, Other 6%
Ethnic mix Bhute 50%, Other 25%, Nepalese 25%
Government Monarchy
Currency Ngultrum = 100 chetrum
Literacy rate 47%
Calorie consumption Not available

BOLIVIA
South America

Official name Republic of Bolivia
Formation 1825 /1938
Capital La Paz (administrative); Sucre (judicial)
Population 9.2 million / 22 people per sq mile (8 people per sq km) / 63%
Total area 424,162 sq miles (1,098,580 sq km)
Languages Aymara*, Quechua*, Spanish*
Religions Roman Catholic 93%, Other 7%
Ethnic mix Quechua 37%, Aymara 32%, Mixed race 13%, European 10%, Other 8%
Government Presidential system
Currency Boliviano = 100 centavos
Literacy rate 87%
Calorie consumption 2235 calories

BOSNIA & HERZEGOVINA
Southeast Europe

Official name Bosnia and Herzegovina
Formation 1992 / 1992
Capital Sarajevo
Population 3.9 million / 198 people per sq mile (76 people per sq km) / 43%
Total area 19,741 sq miles (51,129 sq km)
Languages Serbo-Croat*
Religions Muslim (mainly Sunni) 40%, Orthodox Christian 31%, Roman Catholic 15%, Other 10%, Protestant 4%
Ethnic mix Bosniak 48%, Serb 38%, Croat 14%
Government Parliamentary system
Currency Marka = 100 pfeninga
Literacy rate 95%
Calorie consumption 2894 calories

BOTSWANA
Southern Africa

Official name Republic of Botswana
Formation 1966 / 1966
Capital Gaborone
Population 1.8 million / 8 people per sq mile (3 people per sq km) / 50%
Total area 231,803 sq miles (600,370 sq km)
Languages English*, Setswana, Shona, San, Khoikhoi, isiNdebele
Religions Traditional beliefs 50%, Christian (mainly Protestant) 30%, Other (including Muslim) 20%
Ethnic mix Tswana 98%, Other 2%
Government Presidential system
Currency Pula = 100 thebe
Literacy rate 79%
Calorie consumption 2151 calories

BRAZIL
South America

Official name Federative Republic of Brazil
Formation 1822 / 1828
Capital Brasília
Population 186 million / 57 people per sq mile (22 people per sq km) / 81%
Total area 3,286,470 sq miles (8,511,965 sq km)
Languages Portuguese*, German, Italian, Spanish, Polish, Japanese, Amerindian languages
Religions Roman Catholic 74%, Protestant 15%, Atheist 7%, Other 4%
Ethnic mix Black 53%, Mixed race 40%, White 6%, Other 1%
Government Presidential system
Currency Real = 100 centavos
Literacy rate 88%
Calorie consumption 3049 calories

BRUNEI
Southeast Asia

Official name Sultanate of Brunei
Formation 1984 / 1984
Capital Bandar Seri Begawan
Population 374,000 / 184 people per sq mile (71 people per sq km) / 72%
Total area 2228 sq miles (5770 sq km)
Languages Malay*, English, Chinese
Religions Muslim (mainly Sunni) 66%, Buddhist 14%, Other 10%, Christian 10%
Ethnic mix Malay 67%, Chinese 16%, Other 11%, Indigenous 6%
Government Monarchy
Currency Brunei dollar = 100 cents
Literacy rate 93%
Calorie consumption 2855 calories

BULGARIA
Southeast Europe

Official name Republic of Bulgaria
Formation 1908 / 1947
Capital Sofia
Population 7.7 million / 180 people per sq mile (70 people per sq km) / 70%
Total area 42,822 sq miles (110,910 sq km)
Languages Bulgarian*, Turkish, Romani
Religions Orthodox Christian 83%, Muslim 12%, Other 4%, Roman Catholic 1%
Ethnic mix Bulgarian 84%, Turkish 9%, Roma 5%, Other 2%
Government Parliamentary system
Currency Lev = 100 stotinki
Literacy rate 98%
Calorie consumption 2848 calories

BURKINA
West Africa

Official name Burkina Faso
Formation 1960 / 1960
Capital Ouagadougou
Population 13.2 million / 125 people per sq mile (48 people per sq km) / 19%
Total area 105,869 sq miles (274,200 sq km)
Languages French*, Mossi, Fulani, Tuareg, Dyula, Songhai
Religions Muslim 55%, Traditional beliefs 35%, Roman Catholic 9%, Other Christian 1%
Ethnic mix Other 50%, Mossi 50%
Government Presidential system
Currency CFA franc = 100 centimes
Literacy rate 13%
Calorie consumption 2462 calories

BURMA (MYANMAR)
Southeast Asia

Official name Union of Myanmar
Formation 1948 / 1948
Capital Rangoon (Yangon), Pyinmana
Population 50.5 million / 199 people per sq mile (77 people per sq km) / 28%
Total area 261,969 sq miles (678,500 sq km)
Languages Burmese*, Shan, Karen, Rakhine, Chin, Yangbye, Kachin, Mon
Religions Buddhist 87%, Christian 6%, Muslim 4%, Other 2%, Hindu 1%
Ethnic mix Burman (Bamah) 68%, Other 13%, Shan 9%, Karen 6%, Rakhine 4%
Government Military-based regime
Currency Kyat = 100 pyas
Literacy rate 90%
Calorie consumption 2937 calories

BURUNDI
Central Africa

Official name Republic of Burundi
Formation 1962 / 1962
Capital Bujumbura
Population 7.5 million / 757 people per sq mile (292 people per sq km) / 9%
Total area 10,745 sq miles (27,830 sq km)
Languages Kirundi*, French*, Kiswahili
Religions Christian 60%, Traditional beliefs 39%, Muslim 1%
Ethnic mix Hutu 85%, Tutsi 14%, Twa 1%
Government Presidential system
Currency Burundi franc = 100 centimes
Literacy rate 59%
Calorie consumption 1649 calories

CAMBODIA
Southeast Asia

Official name Kingdom of Cambodia
Formation 1953 / 1953
Capital Phnom Penh
Population 14.1 million / 207 people per sq mile (80 people per sq km) / 16%
Total area 69,900 sq miles (181,040 sq km)
Languages Khmer*, French, Chinese, Vietnamese, Cham
Religions Buddhist 93%, Muslim 6%, Christian 1%
Ethnic mix Khmer 90%, Other 5%, Vietnamese 4%, Chinese 1%
Government Parliamentary system
Currency Riel = 100 sen
Literacy rate 74%
Calorie consumption 2046 calories

CAMEROON
Central Africa

Official name Republic of Cameroon
Formation 1960 / 1961
Capital Yaoundé
Population 16.3 million / 907 people per sq mile (350 people per sq km) / 49%
Total area 183,567 sq miles (475,400 sq km)
Languages English*, French*, Bamileke, Fang, Fulani
eligions Roman Catholic 35%, Traditional beliefs 25%, Muslim 22%, Protestant 18%
thnic mix Cameroon highlanders 31%, Other 21%, Equatorial Bantu 19%, Kirdi 11%, Fulani 10%, Northwestern Bantu 8%
vernment Presidential system
rrency CFA franc = 100 centimes
racy rate 68%
orie consumption 2273 calories

CANADA
North America

Official name Canada
Formation 1867 / 1949
Capital Ottawa
Population 32.3 million / 9 people per sq mile (4 people per sq km) / 77%
Total area 3,717,792 sq miles (9,984,670 sq km)
Languages English*, French*, Chinese, Italian, German, Ukrainian, Inuktitut, Cree
Religions Roman Catholic 44%, Protestant 29%, Other and nonreligious 27%
Ethnic mix British origin 44%, French origin 25%, Other European 20%, Other 11%
Government Parliamentary system
Currency Canadian dollar = 100 cents
Literacy rate 99%
Calorie consumption 3589 calories

CAPE VERDE
Atlantic Ocean

Official name Republic of Cape Verde
Formation 1975
Capital Praia
Population 507,000 / 326 people per sq mile (126 people per sq km) / 62%
Total area 1557 sq miles (4033 sq km)
Languages Portuguese*, Portuguese Creole
Religions Roman Catholic 97%, Other 2%, Protestant (Church of the Nazarene) 1%
Ethnic mix Mestiço 60%, African 30%, Other 10%
Government Mixed presidential–parliamentary system
Currency Cape Verde escudo = 100 centavos
Literacy rate 76%
Calorie consumption 3243 calories

CENTRAL AFRICAN REPUBLIC
Central Africa

Official name Central African Republic
Formation 1960 / 1960
Capital Bangui
Population 4 million / 17 people per sq mile (6 people per sq km) / 41%
Total area 240,534 sq miles (622,984 sq km)
Languages Sango, Banda, Gbaya, French
Religions Traditional beliefs 60%, Christian (mainly Roman Catholic) 35%, Muslim 5%
Ethnic mix Baya 34%, Banda 27%, Mandjia 21%, Sara 10%, Other 8%
Government Presidential system
Currency CFA franc = 100 centimes
Literacy rate 49%
Calorie consumption 1980 calories

CHAD
Central Africa

Official name Republic of Chad
Formation 1960 / 1960
Capital N'Djamena
Population 9.7 million / 20 people per sq mile (8 people per sq km) / 24%
Total area 495,752 sq miles (1,284,000 sq km)
Languages French, Sara, Arabic, Maba
Religions Muslim 55%, Traditional beliefs 35%, Christian 10%
Ethnic mix Nomads (Tuareg and Toubou) 38%, Sara 30%, Other 17%, Arab 15%
Government Presidential system
Currency CFA franc = 100 centimes
Literacy rate 26%
Calorie consumption 2114 calories

CHILE
South America

Official name Republic of Chile
Formation 1818 / 1883
Capital Santiago
Population 16.3 million / 56 people per sq mile (22 people per sq km) / 86%
Total area 292,258 sq miles (756,950 sq km)
Languages Spanish*, Amerindian languages
Religions Roman Catholic 80%, Other and nonreligious 20%
Ethnic mix Mixed race and European 90%, Amerindian 10%
Government Presidential system
Currency Chilean peso = 100 centavos
Literacy rate 96%
Calorie consumption 2863 calories

CHINA
East Asia

Official name People's Republic of China
Formation 960 / 1999
Capital Beijing
Population 1.32 billion / 365 people per sq mile (141 people per sq km) / 32%
Total area 3,705,386 sq miles (9,596,960 sq km)
Languages Mandarin*, Wu, Cantonese, Hsiang, Min, Hakka, Kan
Religions Nonreligious 59%, Traditional beliefs 20%, Other 13%, Buddhist 6%, Muslim 2%
Ethnic mix Han 92%, Other 6%, Hui 1%, Zhuang 1%
Government One-party state
Currency Renminbi (known as yuan) = 10 jiao
Literacy rate 91%
Calorie consumption 2951 calories

COLOMBIA
South America

Official name Republic of Colombia
Formation 1819 / 1903
Capital Bogotá
Population 45.6 million / 114 people per sq mile (44 people per sq km) / 74%
Total area 439,733 sq miles (1,138,910 sq km)
Languages Spanish*, Wayuu, Páez, and other Amerindian languages
Religions Roman Catholic 95%, Other 5%
Ethnic mix Mestizo 58%, White 20%, European–African 14%, African 4%, African–Amerindian 3%, Amerindian 1%
Government Presidential system
Currency Colombian peso = 100 centavos
Literacy rate 94%
Calorie consumption 2585 calories

COMOROS
Indian Ocean

Official name Union of the Comoros
Formation 1975 / 1975
Capital Moroni
Population 798,000 / 927 people per sq mile (358 people per sq km) / 33%
Total area 838 sq miles (2170 sq km)
Languages Arabic*, Comoran, French
Religions Muslim (mainly Sunni) 98%, Other 1%, Roman Catholic 1%
Ethnic mix Comoran 97%, Other 3%
Government Presidential system
Currency Comoros franc = 100 centimes
Literacy rate 56%
Calorie consumption 1754 calories

CONGO
Central Africa

Official name Republic of the Congo
Formation 1960 / 1960
Capital Brazzaville
Population 4 million / 30 people per sq mile (12 people per sq km) / 63%
Total area 132,046 sq miles (342,000 sq km)
Languages French*, Kongo, Teke, Lingala
Religions Traditional beliefs 50%, Roman Catholic 25%, Protestant 23%, Muslim 2%
Ethnic mix Bakongo 48%, Sangha 20%, Teke 17%, Mbochi 12%, Other 3%
Government Presidential system
Currency CFA franc = 100 centimes
Literacy rate 83%
Calorie consumption 2162 calories

CONGO, DEM. REP.
Central Africa

Official name Democratic Republic of the Congo
Formation 1960 / 1960
Capital Kinshasa
Population 57.5 million / 66 people per sq mile (25 people per sq km) / 30%
Total area 905,563 sq miles (2,345,410 sq km)
Languages French*, Kiswahili, Tshiluba, Kikongo, Lingala
Religions Roman Catholic 50%, Protestant 20%, Traditional beliefs and other 10%, Muslim 10%, Kimbanguist 10%
Ethnic mix Other 55%, Bantu and Hamitic 45%
Government Transitional regime
Currency Congolese franc = 100 centimes
Literacy rate 65%
Calorie consumption 1599 calories

COSTA RICA
Central America

Official name Republic of Costa Rica
Formation 1838 / 1838
Capital San José
Population 4.3 million / 218 people per sq mile (84 people per sq km) / 52%
Total area 19,730 sq miles (51,100 sq km)
Languages Spanish*, English Creole, Bribri, Cabecar
Religions Roman Catholic 76%, Other (including Protestant) 24%
Ethnic mix Mestizo and European 96%, Black 2%, Chinese 1%, Amerindian 1%
Government Presidential system
Currency Costa Rican colón = 100 centimos
Literacy rate 96%
Calorie consumption 2876 calories

CROATIA
Southeast Europe

Official name Republic of Croatia
Formation 1991 / 1991
Capital Zagreb
Population 4.6 million / 211 people per sq mile (81 people per sq km) / 58%
Total area 21,831 sq miles (56,542 sq km)
Languages Croatian*
Religions Roman Catholic 88%, Other 7%, Orthodox Christian 4%, Muslim 1%
Ethnic mix Croat 90%, Other 5%, Serb 4%, Bosniak 1%
Government Parliamentary system
Currency Kuna = 100 lipas
Literacy rate 98%
Calorie consumption 2799 calories

CUBA
West Indies

Official name Republic of Cuba
Formation 1902 / 1902
Capital Havana
Population 11.3 million / 264 people per sq mile (102 people per sq km) / 75%
Total area 42,803 sq miles (110,860 sq km)
Languages Spanish*
Religions Nonreligious 49%, Roman Catholic 40%, Atheist 6%, Other 4%, Protestant 1%
Ethnic mix White 66%, European–African 22%, Black 12%
Government One-party state
Currency Cuban peso = 100 centavos
Literacy rate 97%
Calorie consumption 3152 calories

CYPRUS
Southeast Europe

Official name Republic of Cyprus
Formation 1960 / 1960
Capital Nicosia
Population 835,000 / 234 people per sq mile (90 people per sq km) / 57%
Total area 3571 sq miles (9250 sq km)
Languages Greek, Turkish
Religions Orthodox Christian 78%, Muslim 18%, Other 4%
Ethnic mix Greek 85%, Turkish 12%, Other 3%
Government Presidential system
Currency Cyprus pound (Turkish lira in TRNC) = 100 cents (Cyprus pound); 100 kurus (Turkish lira)
Literacy rate 97%
Calorie consumption 3255 calories

CZECH REPUBLIC
Central Europe

Official name Czech Republic
Formation 1993 / 1993
Capital Prague
Population 10.2 million / 335 people per sq mile (129 people per sq km) / 75%
Total area 30,450 sq miles (78,866 sq km)
Languages Czech*, Slovak, Hungarian (Magyar)
Religions Roman Catholic 39%, Atheist 38%, Other 18%, Protestant 3%, Hussite 2%
Ethnic mix Czech 81%, Moravian 13%, Slovak 6%
Government Parliamentary system
Currency Czech koruna = 100 haleru
Literacy rate 99%
Calorie consumption 3171 calories

DENMARK
Northern Europe

Official name Kingdom of Denmark
Formation AD 950 / 1945
Capital Copenhagen
Population 5.4 million / 330 people per sq mile (127 people per sq km) / 85%
Total area 16,639 sq miles (43,094 sq km)
Languages Danish*
Religions Evangelical Lutheran 89%, Other 10%, Roman Catholic 1%
Ethnic mix Danish 96%, Other (including Scandinavian and Turkish) 3%, Faeroese and Inuit 1%
Government Parliamentary system
Currency Danish krone = 100 øre
Literacy rate 99%
Calorie consumption 3439 calories

DJIBOUTI
East Africa

Official name Republic of Djibouti
Formation 1977 / 1977
Capital Djibouti
Population 793,000 / 89 people per sq mile (34 people per sq km) / 83%
Total area 8494 sq miles (22,000 sq km)
Languages French*, Arabic*, Somali, Afar
Religions Muslim (mainly Sunni) 94%, Christian 6%
Ethnic mix Issa 60%, Afar 35%, Other 5%
Government Presidential system
Currency Djibouti franc = 100 centimes
Literacy rate 66%
Calorie consumption 2220 calories

DOMINICA
West Indies

Official name Commonwealth of Dominica
Formation 1978 / 1978
Capital Roseau
Population 69,029 / 238 people per sq mile (92 people per sq km) / 71%
Total area 291 sq miles (754 sq km)
Languages English*, French Creole
Religions Roman Catholic 77%, Protestant 15%, Other 8%
Ethnic mix Black 91%, Mixed race 6%, Carib 2%, Other 1%
Government Parliamentary system
Currency Eastern Caribbean dollar = 100 cents
Literacy rate 88%
Calorie consumption 2763 calories

DOMINICAN REPUBLIC
West Indies

Official name Dominican Republic
Formation 1865 / 1865
Capital Santo Domingo
Population 8.9 million / 476 people per sq mile (184 people per sq km) / 65%
Total area 18,679 sq miles (48,380 sq km)
Languages Spanish*, French Creole
Religions Roman Catholic 92%, Other and nonreligious 8%
Ethnic mix Mixed race 75%, White 15%, Black 10%
Government Presidential system
Currency Dominican Republic peso = 100 centavos
Literacy rate 88%
Calorie consumption 2347 calories

EAST TIMOR
Southeast Asia

Official name Democratic Republic of Timor-Leste
Formation 2002 / 2002
Capital Dili
Population 947,000 / 168 people per sq mile (65 people per sq km) / 8%
Total area 5756 sq miles (14,874 sq km)
Languages Tetum (Portuguese/Austronesian), Bahasa Indonesia, and Portuguese
Religions Roman Catholic 95%, Other (including Muslim and Protestant) 5%
Ethnic mix Papuan groups approx 85%, Indonesian approx 13%, Chinese 2%
Government Parliamentary system
Currency US dollar = 100 cents
Literacy rate 59%
Calorie consumption 2806 calories

ECUADOR
South America

Official name Republic of Ecuador
Formation 1830 / 1941
Capital Quito
Population 13.2 million / 123 people per sq mile (48 people per sq km) / 65%
Total area 109,483 sq miles (283,560 sq km)
Languages Spanish*, Quechua*, other Amerindian languages
Religions Roman Catholic 93%, Protestant, Jewish, and other 7%
Ethnic mix Mestizo 55%, Amerindian 25%, White 10%, Black 10%
Government Presidential system
Currency US dollar = 100 cents
Literacy rate 91%
Calorie consumption 2754 calories

EGYPT
North Africa

Official name Arab Republic of Egypt
Formation 1936 / 1982
Capital Cairo
Population 74 million / 193 people per sq mile (74 people per sq km) / 45%
Total area 386,660 sq miles (1,001,450 sq km)
Languages Arabic*, French, English, Berber
Religions Muslim (mainly Sunni) 94%, Coptic Christian and other 6%
Ethnic mix Eastern Hamitic 90%, Nubian, Armenian, and Greek 10%
Government Presidential system
Currency Egyptian pound = 100 piastres
Literacy rate 56%
Calorie consumption 3338 calories

EL SALVADOR
Central America

Official name Republic of El Salvador
Formation 1841 / 1841
Capital San Salvador
Population 6.9 million / 862 people per sq mile (333 people per sq km) / 47%
Total area 8124 sq miles (21,040 sq km)
Languages Spanish*
Religions Roman Catholic 80%, Evangelical 18%, Other 2%
Ethnic mix Mestizo 94%, Amerindian 5%, White 1%
Government Presidential system
Currency Salvadorean colón & US dollar = 100 centavos (colón); 100 cents (US dollar)
Literacy rate 80%
Calorie consumption 2584 calories

EQUATORIAL GUINEA
Central Africa

Official name Republic of Equatorial Guinea
Formation 1968 / 1968
Capital Malabo
Population 504,000 / 47 people per sq mile (18 people per sq km) / 48%
Total area 10,830 sq miles (28,051 sq km)
Languages Spanish*, Fang, Bubi
Religions Roman Catholic 90%, Other 10%
Ethnic mix Fang 85%, Other 11%, Bubi 4%
Government Presidential system
Currency CFA franc = 100 centimes
Literacy rate 84%
Calorie consumption Not available

ERITREA
East Africa

Official name State of Eritrea
Formation 1993 / 2002
Capital Asmara
Population 4.4 million / 97 people per sq mile (37 people per sq km) / 19%
Total area 46,842 sq miles (121,320 sq km)
Languages Arabic*, Tigrinya*, English, Tigre, Afar, Bilen, Kunama, Nara, Saho, Hadareb
Religions Christian 45%, Muslim 45%, Other 10%
Ethnic mix Tigray 50%, Tigray and Kunama 40%, Afar 4%, Other 3%, Saho 3%
Government Transitional regime
Currency Nakfa = 100 cents
Literacy rate 57%
Calorie consumption 1513 calories

ESTONIA
Northeast Europe

Official name Republic of Estonia
Formation 1991 / 1991
Capital Tallinn
Population 1.3 million / 75 people per sq mile (29 people per sq km) / 69%
Total area 17,462 sq miles (45,226 sq km)
Languages Estonian*, Russian
Religions Evangelical Lutheran 56%, Orthodox Christian 25%, Other 19%
Ethnic mix Estonian 62%, Russian 30%, Other 8%
Government Parliamentary system
Currency Kroon = 100 senti
Literacy rate 99%
Calorie consumption 3002 calories

ETHIOPIA
East Africa

Official name Federal Democratic Republic of Ethiopia
Formation 1896 / 2002
Capital Addis Ababa
Population 77.4 million / 181 people per sq mile (70 people per sq km) / 18%
Total area 435,184 sq miles (1,127,127 sq km)
Languages Amharic*, Tigrinya, Galla, Sidamo, Somali, English, Arabic
Religions Orthodox Christian 40%, Muslim 40%, Traditional beliefs 15%, Other 5%
Ethnic mix Oromo 40%, Amhara 25%, Other 14%, Sidamo 9%, Berta 6%, Somali 6%
Government Parliamentary system
Currency Ethiopian birr = 100 cents
Literacy rate 42%
Calorie consumption 1857 calories

FIJI
Australasia & Oceania

Official name Republic of the Fiji Islands
Formation 1970 / 1970
Capital Suva
Population 848,000 / 120 people per sq mile (46 people per sq km) / 49%
Total area 7054 sq miles (18,270 sq km)
Languages English*, Fijian*, Hindi, Urdu, Tamil, Telugu
Religions Hindu 38%, Methodist 37%, Roman Catholic 9%, Other 8%, Muslim 8%
Ethnic mix Melanesian 48%, Indian 46%, Other 6%
Government Parliamentary system
Currency Fiji dollar = 100 cents
Literacy rate 93%
Calorie consumption 2894 calories

FINLAND
Northern Europe

Official name Republic of Finland
Formation 1917 / 1947
Capital Helsinki
Population 5.2 million / 44 people per sq mile (17 people per sq km) / 67%
Total area 130,127 sq miles (337,030 sq km)
Languages Finnish*, Swedish*, Sámi
Religions Evangelical Lutheran 89%, Orthodox Christian 1%, Roman Catholic 1%, Other 9%
Ethnic mix Finnish 93%, Other (including Sámi) 7%
Government Parliamentary system
Currency Euro = 100 cents
Literacy rate 99%
Calorie consumption 3100 calories

FRANCE
Western Europe

Official name French Republic
Formation 987 / 1919
Capital Paris
Population 60.5 million / 285 people per sq mile (110 people per sq km) / 76%
Total area 211,208 sq miles (547,030 sq km)
Languages French*, Provençal, German, Breton, Catalan, Basque
Religions Roman Catholic 88%, Muslim 8%, Protestant 2%, Buddhist 1%, Jewish 1%
Ethnic mix French 90%, North African (mainly Algerian) 6%, German (Alsace) 2%, Breton 1%, Other (including Corsicans) 1%
Government Mixed presidential–parliamentary system
Currency Euro = 100 cents
Literacy rate 99%
Calorie consumption 3654 calories

GABON
Central Africa

Official name Gabonese Republic
Formation 1960 / 1960
Capital Libreville
Population 1.4 million / 14 people per sq mile (5 people per sq km) / 81%
Total area 103,346 sq miles (267,667 sq km)
Languages French*,Fang, Punu, Sira, Nzebi, Mpongwe
Religions Christian (mainly Roman Catholic) 55%, Traditional beliefs 40%, Other 4%, Muslim 1%
Ethnic mix Fang 35%, Other Bantu 29%, Eshira 25%, European and other African 9%, French 2%
Government Presidential system
Currency CFA franc = 100 centimes
Literacy rate 71%
Calorie consumption 2637 calories

GAMBIA
West Africa

Official name Republic of the Gambia
Formation 1965 / 1965
Capital Banjul
Population 1.5 million / 389 people per sq mile (150 people per sq km) / 33%
Total area 4363 sq miles (11,300 sq km)
Languages English*, Mandinka, Fulani, Wolof, Jola, Soninke
Religions Sunni Muslim 90%, Christian 9%, Traditional beliefs 1%
Ethnic mix Mandinka 42%, Fulani 18%, Wolof 16%, Jola 10%, Serahuli 9%, Other 5%
Government Presidential system
Currency Dalasi = 100 butut
Literacy rate 38%
Calorie consumption 2273 calories

GEORGIA
Southwest Asia

Official name Georgia
Formation 1991 / 1991
Capital Tbilisi
Population 4.5 million / 167 people per sq mile (65 people per sq km) / 61%
Total area 26,911 sq miles (69,700 sq km)
Languages Georgian*, Russian, Azeri, Armenian, Mingrelian, Ossetian, Abkhazian
Religions Georgian Orthodox 65%, Muslim 11%, Russian Orthodox 10%, Armenian Orthodox 8%, Other 6%
Ethnic mix Georgian 70%, Armenian 8%, Russian 6%, Azeri 6%, Ossetian 3%, Other 7%
Government Presidential system
Currency Lari = 100 tetri
Literacy rate 99%
Calorie consumption 2354 calories

GERMANY
Northern Europe

Official name Federal Republic of Germany
Formation 1871 / 1990
Capital Berlin
Population 82.7 million / 613 people per sq mile (237 people per sq km) / 88%
Total area 137,846 sq miles (357,021 sq km)
Languages German*, Turkish
Religions Protestant 34%, Roman Catholic 33%, Other 30%, Muslim 3%
Ethnic mix German 92%, Other 3%, Other European 3%, Turkish 2%
Government Parliamentary system
Currency Euro = 100 cents
Literacy rate 99%
Calorie consumption 3496 calories

GHANA
West Africa

Official name Republic of Ghana
Formation 1957 / 1957
Capital Accra
Population 22.1 million / 249 people per sq mile (96 people per sq km) / 38%
Total area 92,100 sq miles (238,540 sq km)
Languages Twi, Fanti, Ewe, Ga, Adangbe, Gurma, Dagomba (Dagbani)
Religions Christian 69%, Muslim 16%, Traditional beliefs 9%, Other 6%
Ethnic mix Ashanti and Fanti 52%, Moshi-Dagomba 16%, Ewe 12%, Other 11%, Ga and Ga-adanbe 8%, Yoruba 1%
Government Presidential system
Currency Cedi = 100 psewas
Literacy rate 54%
Calorie consumption 2667 calories

GREECE
Southeast Europe

Official name Hellenic Republic
Formation 1829 / 1947
Capital Athens
Population 11.1 million / 220 people per sq mile (85 people per sq km) / 60%
Total area 50,942 sq miles (131,940 sq km)
Languages Greek*, Turkish, Macedonian, Albanian
Religions Orthodox Christian 98%, Other 1%, Muslim 1%
Ethnic mix Greek 98%, Other 2%
Government Parliamentary system
Currency Euro = 100 cents
Literacy rate 91%
Calorie consumption 3721 calories

GRENADA
West Indies

Official name Grenada
Formation 1974 / 1974
Capital St. George's
Population 89,502 / 683 people per sq mile (263 people per sq km) / 38%
Total area 131 sq miles (340 sq km)
Languages English*, English Creole
Religions Roman Catholic 68%, Anglican 17%, Other 15%
Ethnic mix Black African 82%, Mulatto (mixed race) 13%, East Indian 3%, Other 2%
Government Parliamentary system
Currency Eastern Caribbean dollar = 100 cents
Literacy rate 96%
Calorie consumption 2932 calories

GUATEMALA
Central America

Official name Republic of Guatemala
Formation 1838 / 1838
Capital Guatemala City
Population 12.6 million / 301 people per sq mile (116 people per sq km) / 40%
Total area 42,042 sq miles (108,890 sq km)
Languages Spanish*, Quiché, Mam, Cakchiquel, Kekchí
Religions Roman Catholic 65%, Protestant 33%, Other and nonreligious 2%
Ethnic mix Amerindian 60%, Mestizo 30%, Other 10%
Government Presidential system
Currency Quetzal = 100 centavos
Literacy rate 69%
Calorie consumption 2219 calories

GUINEA
West Africa

Official name Republic of Guinea
Formation 1958 / 1958
Capital Conakry
Population 9.4 million / 99 people per sq mile (38 people per sq km) / 33%
Total area 94,925 sq miles (245,857 sq km)
Languages French*, Fulani, Malinke, Soussou
Religions Muslim 65%, Traditional beliefs 33%, Christian 2%
Ethnic mix Fulani 30%, Malinke 30%, Soussou 15%, Kissi 10%, Other tribes 10%, Other 5%
Government Presidential system
Currency Guinea franc = 100 centimes
Literacy rate 41%
Calorie consumption 2409 calories

GUINEA-BISSAU
West Africa

Official name Republic of Guinea-Bissau
Formation 1974 / 1974
Capital Bissau
Population 1.6 million / 147 people per sq mile (57 people per sq km) / 24%
Total area 13,946 sq miles (36,120 sq km)
Languages Portuguese*, Balante, Fulani, Malinke, Portuguese Creole
Religions Traditional beliefs 52%, Muslim 40%, Christian 8%
Ethnic mix Other tribes 31%, Balante 25%, Fula 20%, Mandinka 12%, Mandyako 11%, Other 1%
Government Presidential system
Currency CFA franc = 100 centimes
Literacy rate 40%
Calorie consumption 2024 calories

GUYANA
South America

Official name Cooperative Republic of Guyana
Formation 1966 / 1966
Capital Georgetown
Population 751,000 / 10 people per sq mile (4 people per sq km) / 38%
Total area 83,000 sq miles (214,970 sq km)
Languages English*, Hindi, Tamil, Amerindian languages, English Creole
Religions Christian 57%, Hindu 33%, Muslim 9%, Other 1%
Ethnic mix East Indian 52%, Black African 38%, Other 4%, Amerindian 4%, European and Chinese 2%
Government Presidential system
Currency Guyanese dollar = 100 cents
Literacy rate 97%
Calorie consumption 2692 calories

HAITI
West Indies

Official name Republic of Haiti
Formation 1804 / 1844
Capital Port-au-Prince
Population 8.5 million / 799 people per sq mile (308 people per sq km) / 36%
Total area 10,714 sq miles (27,750 sq km)
Languages French Creole*, French*
Religions Roman Catholic 80%, Protestant 16%, Other (including Voodoo) 3%, Nonreligious 1%
Ethnic mix Black African 95%, Mulatto (mixed race) and European 5%
Government Transitional regime
Currency Gourde = 100 centimes
Literacy rate 52%
Calorie consumption 2086 calories

HONDURAS
Central America

Official name Republic of Honduras
Formation 1838 / 1838
Capital Tegucigalpa
Population 7.2 million / 167 people per sq mile (64 people per sq km) / 53%
Total area 43,278 sq miles (112,090 sq km)
Languages Spanish*, Garífuna (Carib), English Creole
Religions Roman Catholic 97%, Protestant 3%
Ethnic mix Mestizo 90%, Black African 5%, Amerindian 4%, White 1%
Government Presidential system
Currency Lempira = 100 centavos
Literacy rate 80%
Calorie consumption 2356 calories

HUNGARY
Central Europe

Official name Republic of Hungary
Formation 1918 / 1947
Capital Budapest
Population 10.1 million / 283 people per sq mile (109 people per sq km) / 64%
Total area 35,919 sq miles (93,030 sq km)
Languages Hungarian (Magyar)*
Religions Roman Catholic 52%, Calvinist 16%, Other 15%, Nonreligious 14%, Lutheran 3%
Ethnic mix Magyar 90%, Other 7%, Roma 2%, German 1%
Government Parliamentary system
Currency Forint = 100 fillér
Literacy rate 99%
Calorie consumption 3483 calories

ICELAND
Northwest Europe

Official name Republic of Iceland
Formation 1944 / 1944
Capital Reykjavík
Population 295,000 / 8 people per sq mile (3 people per sq km) / 93%
Total area 39,768 sq miles (103,000 sq km)
Languages Icelandic*
Religions Evangelical Lutheran 93%, Nonreligious 6%, Other (mostly Christian) 1%
Ethnic mix Icelandic 94%, Other 5%, Danish 1%
Government Parliamentary system
Currency Icelandic króna = 100 aurar
Literacy rate 99%
Calorie consumption 3249 calories

INDIA
South Asia

Official name Republic of India
Formation 1947 / 1947
Capital New Delhi
Population 1.1 billion / 961 people per sq mile (371 people per sq km) / 28%
Total area 1,269,338 sq miles (3,287,590 sq km)
Languages Hindi*, English*, Bengali, Marathi, Telugu, Tamil, Bihari, Gujarati, Kanarese, Urdu
Religions Hindu 83%, Muslim 11%, Christian 2%, Sikh 2%, Other 1%, Buddhist 1%
Ethnic mix Indo-Aryan 72%, Dravidian 25%, Mongoloid and other 3%
Government Parliamentary system
Currency Indian rupee = 100 paise
Literacy rate 61%
Calorie consumption 2459 calories

INDONESIA
Southeast Asia

Official name Republic of Indonesia
Formation 1949 / 1999
Capital Jakarta
Population 223 million / 321 people per sq mile (124 people per sq km) / 41%
Total area 741,096 sq miles (1,919,440 sq km)
Languages Bahasa Indonesia*, Javanese, Sundanese, Madurese, Dutch
Religions Sunni Muslim 87%, Protestant 6%, Roman Catholic 3%, Hindu 2%, Other 1%, Buddhist 1%
Ethnic mix Javanese 45%, Sundanese 14%, Coastal Malays 8%, Madurese 8%, Other 25%
Government Presidential system
Currency Rupiah = 100 sen
Literacy rate 88%
Calorie consumption 2904 calories

IRAN
Southwest Asia

Official name Islamic Republic of Iran
Formation 1502 / 1990
Capital Tehran
Population 69.5 million / 110 people per sq mile (42 people per sq km) / 62%
Total area 636,293 sq miles (1,648,000 sq km)
Languages Farsi*, Azeri, Luri, Gilaki, Mazanderani, Kurdish, Turkmen, Arabic, Baluchi
Religions Shi'a Muslim 93%, Sunni Muslim 6%, Other 1%
Ethnic mix Persian 50%, Azari 24%, Other 10%, Kurdish 8%, Lur and Bakhtiari 8%
Government Islamic theocracy
Currency Iranian rial = 100 dinars
Literacy rate 77%
Calorie consumption 3085 calories

IRAQ
Southwest Asia

Official name Republic of Iraq
Formation 1932 / 1990
Capital Baghdad
Population 28.8 million / 171 people per sq mile (66 people per sq km) / 77%
Total area 168,753 sq miles (437,072 sq km)
Languages Arabic*, Kurdish, Turkic languages, Armenian, Assyrian
Religions Shi'a Muslim 60%, Sunni Muslim 35%, Other (including Christian) 5%
Ethnic mix Arab 80%, Kurdish 15%, Turkmen 3%, Other 2%
Government Transitional regime
Currency New Iraqi dinar = 1000 fils
Literacy rate 40%
Calorie consumption 2197 calories

IRELAND
Northwest Europe

Official name Ireland
Formation 1922 / 1922
Capital Dublin
Population 4.1 million / 154 people per sq mile (60 people per sq km) / 59%
Total area 27,135 sq miles (70,280 sq km)
Languages English*, Irish Gaelic*
Religions Roman Catholic 88%, Other and nonreligious 9%, Anglican 3%
Ethnic mix Irish 93%, Other 4%, British 3%
Government Parliamentary system
Currency Euro = 100 cents
Literacy rate 99%
Calorie consumption 3656 calories

ISRAEL
Southwest Asia

Official name State of Israel
Formation 1948 / 1994
Capital Jerusalem (not internationally recognized)
Population 6.7 million / 854 people per sq mile (330 people per sq km) / 91%
Total area 8019 sq miles (20,770 sq km)
Languages Hebrew*, Arabic, Yiddish, German, Russian, Polish, Romanian, Persian
Religions Jewish 80%, Muslim (mainly Sunni) 16%, Druze and other 2%, Christian 2%
Ethnic mix Jewish 80%, Other (mostly Arab) 20%
Government Parliamentary system
Currency Shekel = 100 agorot
Literacy rate 97%
Calorie consumption 3666 calories

ITALY
Southern Europe

Official name Italian Republic
Formation 1861 / 1947
Capital Rome
Population 58.1 million / 512 people per sq mile (198 people per sq km) / 67%
Total area 116,305 sq miles (301,230 sq km)
Languages Italian*, German, French, Rhaeto-Romanic, Sardinian
Religions Roman Catholic 85%, Other and nonreligious 13%, Muslim 2%
Ethnic mix Italian 94%, Other 4%, Sardinian 2%
Government Parliamentary system
Currency Euro = 100 cents
Literacy rate 99%
Calorie consumption 3671 calories

IVORY COAST
West Africa

Official name Republic of Côte d'Ivoire
Formation 1960 / 1960
Capital Yamoussoukro
Population 18.2 million / 148 people per sq mile (57 people per sq km) / 46%
Total area 124,502 sq miles (322,460 sq km)
Languages French*, Akan, Kru, Voltaic
Religions Muslim 38%, Traditional beliefs 25%, Roman Catholic 25%, Protestant 6%, Other 6%
Ethnic mix Baoulé 23%, Other 19%, Bété 18%, Senufo 15%, Agni-Ashanti 14%, Mandinka 11%
Government Presidential system
Currency CFA franc = 100 centimes
Literacy rate 48%
Calorie consumption 2631 calories

JAMAICA
West Indies

Official name Jamaica
Formation 1962 / 1962
Capital Kingston
Population 2.7 million / 646 people per sq mile (249 people per sq km) / 56%
Total area 4243 sq miles (10,990 sq km)
Languages English*, English Creole
Religions Other and nonreligious 45%, Other Protestant 20%, Church of God 18%, Baptist 10%, Anglican 7%
Ethnic mix Black African 75%, Mulatto (mixed race) 13%, European and Chinese 11%, East Indian 1%
Government Parliamentary system
Currency Jamaican dollar = 100 cents
Literacy rate 88%
Calorie consumption 2685 calories

JAPAN
East Asia

Official name Japan
Formation 1590 / 1972
Capital Tokyo
Population 128 million / 881 people per sq mile (340 people per sq km) / 79%
Total area 145,882 sq miles (377,835 sq km)
Languages Japanese, Korean, Chinese
Religions Shinto and Buddhist 76%, Buddhist 16%, Other (including Christian) 8%
Ethnic mix Japanese 99%, Other (mainly Korean) 1%
Government Parliamentary system
Currency Yen = 100 sen
Literacy rate 99%
Calorie consumption 2761 calories

JORDAN
Southwest Asia

Official name Hashemite Kingdom of Jordan
Formation 1946 / 1967
Capital Amman
Population 5.6 million / 163 people per sq mile (63 people per sq km) / 74%
Total area 35,637 sq miles (92,300 sq km)
Languages Arabic*
Religions Muslim (mainly Sunni) 92%, Other (mostly Christian) 8%
Ethnic mix Arab 98%, Circassian 1%, Armenian 1%
Government Monarchy
Currency Jordanian dinar = 1000 fils
Literacy rate 90%
Calorie consumption 2673 calories

KAZAKHSTAN
Central Asia

Official name Republic of Kazakhstan
Formation 1991 / 1991
Capital Astana
Population 14.8 million / 14 people per sq mile (5 people per sq km) / 56%
Total area 1,049,150 sq miles (2,717,300 sq km)
Languages Kazakh*, Russian*, Ukrainian, Tatar, German, Uzbek, Uighur
Religions Muslim (mainly Sunni) 47%, Orthodox Christian 44%, Other 9%
Ethnic mix Kazakh 53%, Russian 30%, Other 9%, Ukrainian 4%, Tatar 2%, German 2%
Government Presidential system
Currency Tenge = 100 tiyn
Literacy rate 99%
Calorie consumption 2677 calories

KENYA
East Africa

Official name Republic of Kenya
Formation 1963 / 1963
Capital Nairobi
Population 34.3 million / 157 people per sq mile (60 people per sq km) / 33%
Total area 224,961 sq miles (582,650 sq km)
Languages Kiswahili*, English*, Kikuyu, Luo, Kalenjin, Kamba
Religions Christian 60%, Traditional beliefs 25%, Other 9%, Muslim 6%
Ethnic mix Other 30%, Kikuyu 21%, Luhya 14%, Luo 13%, Kalenjin 11%, Kamba 11%
Government Presidential system
Currency Kenya shilling = 100 cents
Literacy rate 74%
Calorie consumption 2090 calories

KIRIBATI
Australasia & Oceania

Official name Republic of Kiribati
Formation 1979 / 1979
Capital Bairiki (Tarawa Atoll)
Population 103,092 / 376 people per sq mile (145 people per sq km) / 36%
Total area 277 sq miles (717 sq km)
Languages English*, Kiribati
Religions Roman Catholic 53%, Kiribati Protestant Church 39%, Other 8%
Ethnic mix Micronesian 96%, Other 4%
Government Nonparty system
Currency Australian dollar = 100 cents
Literacy rate 99%
Calorie consumption 2859 calories

KUWAIT
Southwest Asia

Official name State of Kuwait
Formation 1961 / 1961
Capital Kuwait City
Population 2.7 million / 392 people per sq mile (152 people per sq km) / 98%
Total area 6880 sq miles (17,820 sq km)
Languages Arabic*, English
Religions Sunni Muslim 45%, Shi'a Muslim 40%, Christian, Hindu, and other 15%
Ethnic mix Kuwaiti 45%, Other Arab 35%, South Asian 9%, Other 7%, Iranian 4%
Government Monarchy
Currency Kuwaiti dinar = 1000 fils
Literacy rate 83%
Calorie consumption 3010 calories

KYRGYZSTAN
Central Asia

Official name Kyrgyz Republic
Formation 1991 / 1991
Capital Bishkek
Population 5.3 million / 69 people per sq mile (27 people per sq km) / 33%
Total area 76,641 sq miles (198,500 sq km)
Languages Kyrgyz*, Russian*, Uzbek, Tatar, Ukrainian
Religions Muslim (mainly Sunni) 70%, Orthodox Christian 30%
Ethnic mix Kyrgyz 57%, Russian 19%, Uzbek 13%, Other 7%, Tatar 2%, Ukrainian 2%
Government Presidential system
Currency Som = 100 tyyn
Literacy rate 99%
Calorie consumption 2999 calories

LAOS
Southeast Asia

Official name Lao People's Democratic Republic
Formation 1953 / 1953
Capital Vientiane
Population 5.9 million / 66 people per sq mile (26 people per sq km) / 24%
Total area 91,428 sq miles (236,800 sq km)
Languages Lao*, Mon-Khmer, Yao, Vietnamese, Chinese, French
Religions Buddhist 85%, Other (including animist) 15%
Ethnic mix Lao Loum 66%, Lao Theung 30%, Other 2%, Lao Soung 2%
Government One-party state
Currency New kip = 100 at
Literacy rate 69%
Calorie consumption 2312 calories

LATVIA
Northeast Europe

Official name Republic of Latvia
Formation 1991 / 1991
Capital Riga
Population 2.3 million / 92 people per sq mile (36 people per sq km) / 69%
Total area 24,938 sq miles (64,589 sq km)
Languages Latvian*, Russian
Religions Lutheran 55%, Roman Catholic 24%, Other 12%, Orthodox Christian 9%
Ethnic mix Latvian 57%, Russian 32%, Belarussian 4%, Ukrainian 3%, Polish 2%, Other 2%
Government Parliamentary system
Currency Lats = 100 santims
Literacy rate 99%
Calorie consumption 2938 calories

LEBANON
Southwest Asia

Official name Republic of Lebanon
Formation 1941 / 1941
Capital Beirut
Population 3.6 million / 911 people per sq mile (352 people per sq km) / 90%
Total area 4015 sq miles (10,400 sq km)
Languages Arabic*, French, Armenian, Assyrian
Religions Muslim 70%, Christian 30%
Ethnic mix Arab 94%, Armenian 4%, Other 2%
Government Parliamentary system
Currency Lebanese pound = 100 piastres
Literacy rate 87%
Calorie consumption 3196 calories

LESOTHO
Southern Africa

Official name Kingdom of Lesotho
Formation 1966 / 1966
Capital Maseru
Population 1.8 million / 154 people per sq mile (59 people per sq km) / 28%
Total area 11,720 sq miles (30,355 sq km)
Languages English*, Sesotho*, isiZulu
Religions Christian 90%, Traditional beliefs 10%
Ethnic mix Sotho 97%, European and Asian 3%
Government Parliamentary system
Currency Loti = 100 lisente
Literacy rate 81%
Calorie consumption 2638 calories

LIBERIA
West Africa

Official name Republic of Liberia
Formation 1847 / 1847
Capital Monrovia
Population 3.3 million / 89 people per sq mile (34 people per sq km) / 45%
Total area 43,000 sq miles (111,370 sq km)
Languages English*, Kpelle, Vai, Bassa, Kru, Grebo, Kissi, Gola, Loma
Religions Christian 68%, Traditional beliefs 18%, Muslim 14%
Ethnic mix Indigenous tribes (16 main groups) 95%, Americo-Liberians 5%
Government Transitional regime
Currency Liberian dollar = 100 cents
Literacy rate 58%
Calorie consumption 1900 calories

LIBYA
North Africa

Official name Great Socialist People's Libyan Arab Jamahariyah
Formation 1951 / 1951
Capital Tripoli
Population 5.9 million / 9 people per sq mile (3 people per sq km) / 88%
Total area 679,358 sq miles (1,759,540 sq km)
Languages Arabic*, Tuareg
Religions Muslim (mainly Sunni) 97%, Other 3%
Ethnic mix Arab and Berber 95%, Other 5%
Government One-party state
Currency Libyan dinar = 1000 dirhams
Literacy rate 82%
Calorie consumption 3320 calories

LIECHTENSTEIN
Central Europe

Official name Principality of Liechtenstein
Formation 1719 / 1719
Capital Vaduz
Population 33,717 / 544 people per sq mile (211 people per sq km) / 21%
Total area 62 sq miles (160 sq km)
Languages German*, Alemannish dialect, Italian
Religions Roman Catholic 81%, Other 12%, Protestant 7%
Ethnic mix Liechtensteiner 62%, Foreign residents 38%
Government Parliamentary system
Currency Swiss franc = 100 rappen/centimes
Literacy rate 99%
Calorie consumption Not available

LITHUANIA
Northeast Europe

Official name Republic of Lithuania
Formation 1991 / 1991
Capital Vilnius
Population 3.4 million / 135 people per sq mile (52 people per sq km) / 68%
Total area 25,174 sq miles (65,200 sq km)
Languages Lithuanian*, Russian
Religions Roman Catholic 83%, Other 12%, Protestant 5%
Ethnic mix Lithuanian 80%, Russian 9%, Polish 7%, Other 2%, Belarussian 2%
Government Parliamentary system
Currency Litas (euro is also legal tender) = 100 centu
Literacy rate 99%
Calorie consumption 3324 calories

LUXEMBOURG
Northwest Europe

Official name Grand Duchy of Luxembourg
Formation 1867 / 1867
Capital Luxembourg-Ville
Population 465,000 / 466 people per sq mile (180 people per sq km) / 92%
Total area 998 sq miles (2586 sq km)
Languages Luxembourgish*, German*, French*
Religions Roman Catholic 97%, Protestant, Orthodox Christian, and Jewish 3%
Ethnic mix Luxembourger 73%, Foreign residents 27%
Government Parliamentary system
Currency Euro = 100 cents
Literacy rate 99%
Calorie consumption 3701 calories

MACEDONIA
Southeast Europe

Official name Republic of Macedonia
Formation 1991 / 1991
Capital Skopje
Population 2 million / 201 people per sq mile (78 people per sq km) / 62%
Total area 9781 sq miles (25,333 sq km)
Languages Macedonian, Albanian, Serbo-Croat
Religions Orthodox Christian 59%, Muslim 26%, Other 10%, Roman Catholic 4%, Protestant 1%
Ethnic mix Macedonian 64%, Albanian 25%, Turkish 4%, Roma 3%, Other 2%, Serb 2%
Government Mixed presidential–parliamentary system
Currency Macedonian denar = 100 deni
Literacy rate 96%
Calorie consumption 2655 calories

MADAGASCAR
Indian Ocean

Official name Republic of Madagascar
Formation 1960 / 1960
Capital Antananarivo
Population 18.6 million / 83 people per sq mile (32 people per sq km) / 30%
Total area 226,656 sq miles (587,040 sq km)
Languages Malagasy*, French*
Religions Traditional beliefs 52%, Christian (mainly Roman Catholic) 41%, Muslim 7%
Ethnic mix Other Malay 46%, Merina 26%, Betsimisaraka 15%, Betsileo 12%, Other 1%
Government Presidential system
Currency Ariary = 5 iraimbilanja
Literacy rate 71%
Calorie consumption 2005 calories

MALAWI
Southern Africa

Official name Republic of Malawi
Formation 1964 / 1964
Capital Lilongwe
Population 12.9 million / 355 people per sq mile (137 people per sq km) / 25%
Total area 45,745 sq miles (118,480 sq km)
Languages English*, Chewa*, Lomwe, Yao, Ngoni
Religions Protestant 55%, Roman Catholic 20%, Muslim 20%, Traditional beliefs 5%
Ethnic mix Bantu 99%, Other 1%
Government Presidential system
Currency Malawi kwacha = 100 tambala
Literacy rate 64%
Calorie consumption 2155 calories

MALAYSIA
Southeast Asia

Official name Federation of Malaysia
Formation 1963 / 1965
Capital Kuala Lumpur; Putrajaya (administrative)
Population 25.3 million / 199 people per sq mile (77 people per sq km) / 57%
Total area 127,316 sq miles (329,750 sq km)
Languages Malay*, Chinese*, Bahasa Malaysia, Tamil, English
Religions Muslim (mainly Sunni) 53%, Buddhist 19%, Chinese faiths 12%, Other 7%, Christian 7%, Traditional beliefs 2%
Ethnic mix Malay 48%, Chinese 29%, Indigenous tribes 12%, Indian 6%, Other 5%
Government Parliamentary system
Currency Ringgit = 100 sen
Literacy rate 89%
Calorie consumption 2881 calories

MALDIVES
Indian Ocean

Official name Republic of Maldives
Formation 1965 / 1965
Capital Male'
Population 329,000 / 2836 people per sq mile (1097 people per sq km) / 30%
Total area 116 sq miles (300 sq km)
Languages Dhivehi (Maldivian)*, Sinhala, Tamil, Arabic
Religions Sunni Muslim 100%
Ethnic mix Arab–Sinhalese–Malay 100%
Government Nonparty system
Currency Rufiyaa = 100 lari
Literacy rate 97%
Calorie consumption 2548 calories

MALI
West Africa

Official name Republic of Mali
Formation 1960 / 1960
Capital Bamako
Population 13.5 million / 29 people per sq mile (11 people per sq km) / 30%
Total area 478,764 sq miles (1,240,000 sq km)
Languages French*, Bambara, Fulani, Senufo, Soninke
Religions Muslim (mainly Sunni) 80%, Traditional beliefs 18%, Christian 1%, Other 1%
Ethnic mix Bambara 32%, Other 26%, Fulani 14%, Senufu 12%, Soninka 9%, Tuareg 7%
Government Presidential system
Currency CFA franc = 100 centimes
Literacy rate 19%
Calorie consumption 2174 calories

MALTA
Southern Europe

Official name Republic of Malta
Formation 1964 / 1964
Capital Valletta
Population 402,000 / 3242 people per sq mile (1256 people per sq km) / 91%
Total area 122 sq miles (316 sq km)
Languages Maltese*, English
Religions Roman Catholic 98%, Other and nonreligious 2%
Ethnic mix Maltese 96%, Other 4%
Government Parliamentary system
Currency Maltese lira = 100 cents
Literacy rate 88%
Calorie consumption 3587 calories

MARSHALL ISLANDS
Australasia & Oceania

Official name Republic of the Marshall Islands
Formation 1986 / 1986
Capital Majuro
Population 59,071 / 844 people per sq mile (326 people per sq km) / 69%
Total area 70 sq miles (181 sq km)
Languages Marshallese*, English*, Japanese, German
Religions Protestant 90%, Roman Catholic 8%, Other 2%
Ethnic mix Micronesian 97%, Other 3%
Government Presidential system
Currency US dollar = 100 cents
Literacy rate 91%
Calorie consumption Not available

MAURITANIA
West Africa

Official name Islamic Republic of Mauritania
Formation 1960 / 1960
Capital Nouakchott
Population 3.1 million / 8 people per sq mile (3 people per sq km) / 58%
Total area 397,953 sq miles (1,030,700 sq km)
Languages French*, Hassaniyah Arabic, Wolof
Religions Sunni Muslim 100%
Ethnic mix Maure 81%, Wolof 7%, Tukolor 5%, Other 4%, Soninka 3%
Government Transitional regime
Currency Ouguiya = 5 khoums
Literacy rate 51%
Calorie consumption 2772 calories

MAURITIUS
Indian Ocean

Official name Republic of Mauritius
Formation 1968 / 1968
Capital Port Louis
Population 1.2 million / 1671 people per sq mile (645 people per sq km) / 41%
Total area 718 sq miles (1860 sq km)
Languages English*, French Creole, Hindi, Urdu, Tamil, Chinese, French
Religions Hindu 52%, Roman Catholic 26%, Muslim 17%, Other 3%, Protestant 2%
Ethnic mix Indo-Mauritian 68%, Creole 27%, Sino-Mauritian 3%, Franco-Mauritian 2%
Government Parliamentary system
Currency Mauritian rupee = 100 cents
Literacy rate 84%
Calorie consumption 2955 calories

MEXICO
North America

Official name United Mexican States
Formation 1836 / 1848
Capital Mexico City
Population 107 million / 145 people per sq mile (56 people per sq km) / 74%
Total area 761,602 sq miles (1,972,550 sq km)
Languages Spanish*, Nahuatl, Mayan, Zapotec, Mixtec, Otomi, Totonac, Tzotzil, Tzeltal
Religions Roman Catholic 88%, Other 7%, Protestant 5%
Ethnic mix Mestizo 60%, Amerindian 30%, European 9%, Other 1%
Government Presidential system
Currency Mexican peso = 100 centavos
Literacy rate 90%
Calorie consumption 3145 calories

MICRONESIA
Australasia & Oceania

Official name Federated States of Micronesia
Formation 1986 / 1986
Capital Palikir (Pohnpei Island)
Population 108,105 / 399 people per sq mile (154 people per sq km) / 28%
Total area 271 sq miles (702 sq km)
Languages Trukese, Pohnpeian, Mortlockese, Kosraean, English
Religions Roman Catholic 50%, Protestant 48%, Other 2%
Ethnic mix Micronesian 100%
Government Nonparty system
Currency US dollar = 100 cents
Literacy rate 81%
Calorie consumption Not available

MOLDOVA
Southeast Europe

Official name Republic of Moldova
Formation 1991 / 1991
Capital Chisinau
Population 4.2 million / 323 people per sq mile (125 people per sq km) / 46%
Total area 13,067 sq miles (33,843 sq km)
Languages Moldovan*, Ukrainian, Russian
Religions Orthodox Christian 98%, Jewish 2%
Ethnic mix Moldovan 65%, Ukrainian 14%, Russian 13%, Other 4%, Gagauz 4%
Government Parliamentary system
Currency Moldovan leu = 100 bani
Literacy rate 96%
Calorie consumption 2806 calories

MONACO
Southern Europe

Official name Principality of Monaco
Formation 1861 / 1861
Capital Monaco-Ville
Population 32,409 / 43212 people per sq mile (16620 people per sq km) / 100%
Total area 0.75 sq miles (1.95 sq km)
Languages French*, Italian, Monégasque, English
Religions Roman Catholic 89%, Protestant 6%, Other 5%
Ethnic mix French 47%, Other 20%, Monégasque 17%, Italian 16%
Government Monarchy
Currency Euro = 100 cents
Literacy rate 99%
Calorie consumption Not available

MONGOLIA
East Asia

Official name Mongolia
Formation 1924 / 1924
Capital Ulan Bator
Population 2.6 million / 4 people per sq mile (2 people per sq km) / 64%
Total area 604,247 sq miles (1,565,000 sq km)
Languages Khalkha Mongolian*, Kazakh, Chinese, Russian
Religions Tibetan Buddhist 96%, Muslim 4%
Ethnic mix Mongol 90%, Kazakh 4%, Other 2%, Chinese 2%, Russian 2%
Government Mixed presidential–parliamentary system
Currency Tugrik (tögrög) = 100 möngö
Literacy rate 98%
Calorie consumption 2249 calories

MONTENEGRO
Europe

Official name Republic of Montenegro
Formation 2006 / 2006
Capital Podgorica
Population 620,145 / 116 people per sq mile (45 people per sq km) / 62%
Total area 5,332 sq miles (13,812 sq km)
Languages Montenegrin, Serbian, Albanian
Religions Orthodox Christian 74%, Muslim 18%, Roman Catholic 4%, Other 4%
Ethnic mix Montenegrin 43%, Serb 32%, Bosniak 8%, Albanian 5%, Other 12%
Government Parliamentary system
Currency Euro = 100 cents
Literacy rate 98%
Calorie consumption Not available

MOROCCO
North Africa

Official name Kingdom of Morocco
Formation 1956 / 1956
Capital Rabat
Population 31.5 million / 183 people per sq mile (71 people per sq km) / 56%
Total area 172,316 sq miles (446,300 sq km)
Languages Arabic*, Tamazight (Berber), French, Spanish
Religions Muslim (mainly Sunni) 99%, Other (mostly Christian) 1%
Ethnic mix Arab 70%, Berber 29%, European 1%
Government Monarchy
Currency Moroccan dirham = 100 centimes
Literacy rate 51%
Calorie consumption 3052 calories

MOZAMBIQUE
Southern Africa

Official name Republic of Mozambique
Formation 1975 / 1975
Capital Maputo
Population 19.8 million / 65 people per sq mile (25 people per sq km) / 40%
Total area 309,494 sq miles (801,590 sq km)
Languages Portuguese*, Makua, Xitsonga, Sena, Lomwe
Religions Traditional beliefs 56%, Christian 30%, Muslim 14%
Ethnic mix Makua Lomwe 47%, Tsonga 23%, Malawi 12%, Shona 11%, Yao 4%, Other 3%
Government Presidential system
Currency Metical = 100 centavos
Literacy rate 47%
Calorie consumption 2079 calories

NAMIBIA
Southern Africa

Official name Republic of Namibia
Formation 1990 / 1994
Capital Windhoek
Population 2 million / 6 people per sq mile (2 people per sq km) / 31%
Total area 318,694 sq miles (825,418 sq km)
Languages English*, Ovambo, Kavango, Bergdama, German, Afrikaans
Religions Christian 90%, Traditional beliefs 10%
Ethnic mix Ovambo 50%, Other tribes 16%, Kavango 9%, Other 9%, Damara 8%, Herero 8%
Government Presidential system
Currency Namibian dollar = 100 cents
Literacy rate 85%
Calorie consumption 2278 calories

NAURU
Australasia & Oceania

Official name Republic of Nauru
Formation 1968 / 1968
Capital None
Population 13,048 / 1611 people per sq mile (621 people per sq km) / 100%
Total area 8.1 sq miles (21 sq km)
Languages Nauruan*, Kiribati, Chinese, Tuvaluan, English
Religions Nauruan Congregational Church 60%, Roman Catholic 35%, Other 5%
Ethnic mix Nauruan 62%, Other Pacific islanders 25%, Chinese and Vietnamese 8%, European 5%
Government Parliamentary system
Currency Australian dollar = 100 cents
Literacy rate 95%
Calorie consumption Not available

NEPAL
South Asia

Official name Kingdom of Nepal
Formation 1769 / 1769
Capital Kathmandu
Population 27.1 million / 513 people per sq mile (198 people per sq km) / 12%
Total area 54,363 sq miles (140,800 sq km)
Languages Nepali*, Maithili, Bhojpuri
Religions Hindu 90%, Buddhist 5%, Muslim 3%, Other (including Christian) 2%
Ethnic mix Nepalese 52%, Other 19%, Maithili 11%, Tibeto-Burmese 10%, Bhojpuri 8%
Government Monarchy
Currency Nepalese rupee = 100 paise
Literacy rate 49%
Calorie consumption 2453 calories

NETHERLANDS
Northwest Europe

Official name Kingdom of the Netherlands
Formation 1648 / 1839
Capital Amsterdam; The Hague (administrative)
Population 16.3 million / 1245 people per sq mile (481 people per sq km) / 89%
Total area 16,033 sq miles (41,526 sq km)
Languages Dutch*, Frisian
Religions Roman Catholic 36%, Other 34%, Protestant 27%, Muslim 3%
Ethnic mix Dutch 82%, Other 12%, Surinamese 2%, Turkish 2%, Moroccan 2%
Government Parliamentary system
Currency Euro = 100 cents
Literacy rate 99%
Calorie consumption 3362 calories

NEW ZEALAND
Australasia & Oceania

Official name New Zealand
Formation 1947 / 1947
Capital Wellington
Population 4 million / 39 people per sq mile (15 people per sq km) / 86%
Total area 103,737 sq miles (268,680 sq km)
Languages English*, Maori
Religions Anglican 24%, Other 22%, Presbyterian 18%, Nonreligious 16%, Roman Catholic 15%, Methodist 5%
Ethnic mix European 77%, Maori 12%, Other immigrant 6%, Pacific islanders 5%
Government Parliamentary system
Currency New Zealand dollar = 100 cents
Literacy rate 99%
Calorie consumption 3219 calories

NICARAGUA
Central America

Official name Republic of Nicaragua
Formation 1838 / 1838
Capital Managua
Population 5.5 million / 120 people per sq mile (46 people per sq km) / 65%
Total area 49,998 sq miles (129,494 sq km)
Languages Spanish*, English Creole, Miskito
Religions Roman Catholic 80%, Protestant Evangelical 17%, Other 3%
Ethnic mix Mestizo 69%, White 14%, Black 8%, Amerindian 5%, Zambo 4%
Government Presidential system
Currency Córdoba oro = 100 centavos
Literacy rate 77%
Calorie consumption 2298 calories

NIGER
West Africa

Official name Republic of Niger
Formation 1960 / 1960
Capital Niamey
Population 14 million / 29 people per sq mile (11 people per sq km) / 21%
Total area 489,188 sq miles (1,267,000 sq km)
Languages French*, Hausa, Djerma, Fulani, Tuareg, Teda
Religions Muslim 85%, Traditional beliefs 14%, Other (including Christian) 1%
Ethnic mix Hausa 54%, Djerma and Songhai 21%, Fulani 10%, Tuareg 9%, Other 6%
Government Presidential system
Currency CFA franc = 100 centimes
Literacy rate 14%
Calorie consumption 2130 calories

NIGERIA
West Africa

Official name Federal Republic of Nigeria
Formation 1960 / 1961
Capital Abuja
Population 132 million / 374 people per sq mile (144 people per sq km) / 44%
Total area 356,667 sq miles (923,768 sq km)
Languages English*, Hausa, Yoruba, Ibo
Religions Muslim 50%, Christian 40%, Traditional beliefs 10%
Ethnic mix Other 29%, Hausa 21%, Yoruba 21%, Ibo 18%, Fulani 11%
Government Presidential system
Currency Naira = 100 kobo
Literacy rate 67%
Calorie consumption 2726 calories

NORTH KOREA
East Asia

Official name Democratic People's Republic of Korea
Formation 1948 / 1953
Capital Pyongyang
Population 22.5 million / 484 people per sq mile (187 people per sq km) / 60%
Total area 46,540 sq miles (120,540 sq km)
Languages Korean*
Religions Atheist 100%
Ethnic mix Korean 100%
Government One-party state
Currency North Korean won = 100 chon
Literacy rate 99%
Calorie consumption 2142 calories

NORWAY
Northern Europe

Official name Kingdom of Norway
Formation 1905 / 1905
Capital Oslo
Population 4.6 million / 39 people per sq mile (15 people per sq km) / 76%
Total area 125,181 sq miles (324,220 sq km)
Languages Norwegian* (Bokmål "book language" and Nynorsk "new Norsk"), Sámi
Religions Evangelical Lutheran 89%, Other and nonreligious 10%, Roman Catholic 1%
Ethnic mix Norwegian 93%, Other 6%, Sámi 1%
Government Parliamentary system
Currency Norwegian krone = 100 øre
Literacy rate 99%
Calorie consumption 3484 calories

OMAN
Southwest Asia

Official name Sultanate of Oman
Formation 1951 / 1951
Capital Muscat
Population 2.6 million / 32 people per sq mile (12 people per sq km) / 84%
Total area 82,031 sq miles (212,460 sq km)
Languages Arabic*, Baluchi, Farsi, Hindi, Punjabi
Religions Ibadi Muslim 75%, Other Muslim and Hindu 25%
Ethnic mix Arab 88%, Baluchi 4%, Persian 3%, Indian and Pakistani 3%, African 2%
Government Monarchy
Currency Omani rial = 1000 baizas
Literacy rate 74%
Calorie consumption Not available

PAKISTAN
South Asia

Official name Islamic Republic of Pakistan
Formation 1947 / 1971
Capital Islamabad
Population 158 million / 531 people per sq mile (205 people per sq km) / 37%
Total area 310,401 sq miles (803,940 sq km)
Languages Urdu*, Baluchi, Brahui, Pashtu, Punjabi, Sindhi
Religions Sunni Muslim 77%, Shi'a Muslim 20%, Hindu 2%, Christian 1%
Ethnic mix Punjabi 56%, Pathan (Pashtun) 15%, Sindhi 14%, Mohajir 7%, Other 4%, Baluchi 4%
Government Presidential system
Currency Pakistani rupee = 100 paisa
Literacy rate 49%
Calorie consumption 2419 calories

PALAU
Australasia & Oceania

Official name Republic of Palau
Formation 1994 / 1994
Capital Koror
Population 20,303 / 104 people per sq mile (40 people per sq km) / 70%
Total area 177 sq miles (458 sq km)
Languages Palauan, English, Japanese, Angaur, Tobi, Sonsorolese
Religions Christian 66%, Modekngei 34%
Ethnic mix Micronesian 87%, Filipino 8%, Chinese and other Asian 5%
Government Nonparty system
Currency US dollar = 100 cents
Literacy rate 98%
Calorie consumption Not available

PANAMA
Central America

Official name Republic of Panama
Formation 1903 / 1903
Capital Panama City
Population 3.2 million / 109 people per sq mile (42 people per sq km) / 56%
Total area 30,193 sq miles (78,200 sq km)
Languages Spanish*, English Creole, Amerindian languages, Chibchan languages
Religions Roman Catholic 86%, Other 8%, Protestant 6%
Ethnic mix Mestizo 60%, White 14%, Black 12%, Amerindian 8%, Asian 4%, Other 2%
Government Presidential system
Currency Balboa = 100 centesimos
Literacy rate 92%
Calorie consumption 2272 calories

PAPUA NEW GUINEA
Australasia & Oceania

Official name Independent State of Papua New Guinea
Formation 1975 / 1975
Capital Port Moresby
Population 5.9 million / 34 people per sq mile (13 people per sq km) / 17%
Total area 178,703 sq miles (462,840 sq km)
Languages Pidgin English*, Papuan*, English, Motu, 750 (est.) native languages
Religions Protestant 60%, Roman Catholic 37%, Other 3%
Ethnic mix Melanesian and mixed race 100%
Government Parliamentary system
Currency Kina = 100 toeas
Literacy rate 57%
Calorie consumption 2193 calories

PARAGUAY
South America

Official name Republic of Paraguay
Formation 1811 / 1938
Capital Asunción
Population 6.2 million / 40 people per sq mile (16 people per sq km) / 56%
Total area 157,046 sq miles (406,750 sq km)
Languages Guaraní*, Spanish*, German
Religions Roman Catholic 96%, Protestant (including Mennonite) 4%
Ethnic mix Mestizo 90%, Other 8%, Amerindian 2%
Government Presidential system
Currency Guaraní = 100 centimos
Literacy rate 92%
Calorie consumption 2565 calories

PERU
South America

Official name Republic of Peru
Formation 1824 / 1941
Capital Lima
Population 28 million / 57 people per sq mile (22 people per sq km) / 73%
Total area 496,223 sq miles (1,285,200 sq km)
Languages Spanish*, Quechua*, Aymara*
Religions Roman Catholic 95%, Other 5%
Ethnic mix Amerindian 50%, Mestizo 40%, White 7%, Other 3%
Government Presidential system
Currency New sol = 100 centimos
Literacy rate 88%
Calorie consumption 2571 calories

PHILIPPINES
Southwest Asia

Official name Republic of the Philippines
Formation 1946 / 1946
Capital Manila
Population 83.1 million / 722 people per sq mile (279 people per sq km) / 59%
Total area 115,830 sq miles (300,000 sq km)
Languages Filipino*, English*, Tagalog, Cebuano, Ilocano, Hiligaynon, many other local languages
Religions Roman Catholic 83%, Protestant 9%, Muslim 5%, Other (including Buddhist) 3%
Ethnic mix Malay 95%, Other 3%, Chinese 2%
Government Presidential system
Currency Philippine peso = 100 centavos
Literacy rate 93%
Calorie consumption 2379 calories

POLAND
Northern Europe

Official name Republic of Poland
Formation 1918 / 1945
Capital Warsaw
Population 38.5 million / 328 people per sq mile (126 people per sq km) / 66%
Total area 120,728 sq miles (312,685 sq km)
Languages Polish*
Religions Roman Catholic 93%, Other and nonreligious 5%, Orthodox Christian 2%
Ethnic mix Polish 97%, Other 2%, Silesian 1%
Government Parliamentary system
Currency Zloty = 100 groszy
Literacy rate 99%
Calorie consumption 3374 calories

PORTUGAL
Southwest Europe

Official name Republic of Portugal
Formation 1139 / 1640
Capital Lisbon
Population 10.5 million / 296 people per sq mile (114 people per sq km) / 64%
Total area 35,672 sq miles (92,391 sq km)
Languages Portuguese
Religions Roman Catholic 97%, Other 2%, Protestant 1%
Ethnic mix Portuguese 98%, African and other 2%
Government Parliamentary system
Currency Euro = 100 cents
Literacy rate 93%
Calorie consumption 3741 calories

QATAR
Southwest Asia

Official name State of Qatar
Formation 1971 / 1971
Capital Doha
Population 813,000 / 191 people per sq mile (74 people per sq km) / 93%
Total area 4416 sq miles (11,437 sq km)
Languages Arabic*
Religions Muslim (mainly Sunni) 95%, Other 5%
Ethnic mix Arab 40%, Indian 18%, Pakistani 18%, Other 14%, Iranian 10%
Government Monarchy
Currency Qatar riyal = 100 dirhams
Literacy rate 89%
Calorie consumption Not available

ROMANIA
Southest Europe

Official name Romania
Formation 1878 / 1947
Capital Bucharest
Population 21.7 million / 244 people per sq mile (94 people per sq km) / 56%
Total area 91,699 sq miles (237,500 sq km)
Languages Romanian*, Hungarian (Magyar), Romani, German
Religions Romanian Orthodox 87%, Roman Catholic 5%, Protestant 4%, Other 2%, Greek Orthodox 1%, Greek Catholic (Uniate) 1%
Ethnic mix Romanian 89%, Magyar 7%, Roma 3%, Other 1%
Government Presidential system
Currency Romanian leu = 100 bani
Literacy rate 97%
Calorie consumption 3455 calories

RUSSIAN FEDERATION
Europe / Asia

Official name Russian Federation
Formation 1480 / 1991
Capital Moscow
Population 143 million / 22 people per sq mile (8 people per sq km) / 78%
Total area 6,592,735 sq miles (17,075,200 sq km)
Languages Russian*, Tatar, Ukrainian, Chavash, various other national languages
Religions Orthodox Christian 75%, Other 15%, Muslim 10%
Ethnic mix Russian 82%, Other 10%, Tatar 4%, Ukrainian 3%, Chavash 1%
Government Presidential system
Currency Russian rouble = 100 kopeks
Literacy rate 99%
Calorie consumption 3072 calories

RWANDA
Central Africa

Official name Republic of Rwanda
Formation 1962 / 1962
Capital Kigali
Population 9 million / 934 people per sq mile (361 people per sq km) / 6%
Total area 10,169 sq miles (26,338 sq km)
Languages Kinyarwanda*, French*, Kiswahili, English
Religions Roman Catholic 56%, Traditional beliefs 25%, Muslim 10%, Protestant 9%
Ethnic mix Hutu 90%, Tutsi 9%, Other (including Twa) 1%
Government Presidential system
Currency Rwanda franc = 100 centimes
Literacy rate 64%
Calorie consumption 2084 calories

SAINT KITTS & NEVIS
West indies

Official name Federation of Saint Christopher and Nevis
Formation 1983 / 1983
Capital Basseterre
Population 38,958 / 280 people per sq mile (108 people per sq km) / 34%
Total area 101 sq miles (261 sq km)
Languages English*, English Creole
Religions Anglican 33%, Methodist 29%, Other 22%, Moravian 9%, Roman Catholic 7%
Ethnic mix Black 94%, Mixed race 3%, Other and Amerindian 2%, White 1%
Government Parliamentary system
Currency Eastern Caribbean dollar = 100 cents
Literacy rate 98%
Calorie consumption 2609 calories

SAINT LUCIA
West Indies

Official name Saint Lucia
Formation 1979 / 1979
Capital Castries
Population 166,312 / 705 people per sq mile (273 people per sq km) / 38%
Total area 239 sq miles (620 sq km)
Languages English*, French Creole
Religions Roman Catholic 90%, Other 10%
Ethnic mix Black 90%, Mulatto (mixed race) 6%, Asian 3%, White 1%
Government Parliamentary system
Currency Eastern Caribbean dollar = 100 cents
Literacy rate 90%
Calorie consumption 2988 calories

SAINT VINCENT & THE GRENADINES
West Indies

Official name Saint Vincent and the Grenadines
Formation 1979 / 1979
Capital Kingstown
Population 117,534 / 897 people per sq mile (346 people per sq km) / 55%
Total area 150 sq miles (389 sq km)
Languages English*, English Creole
Religions Anglican 47%, Methodist 28%, Roman Catholic 13%, Other 12%
Ethnic mix Black 66%, Mulatto (mixed race) 19%, Asian 6%, Other 5%, White 4%
Government Parliamentary system
Currency Eastern Caribbean dollar = 100 cents
Literacy rate 88%
Calorie consumption 2599 calories

SAMOA
Australasia & Oceania

Official name Independent State of Samoa
Formation 1962 / 1962
Capital Apia
Population 185,000 / 169 people per sq mile (65 people per sq km) / 22%
Total area 1104 sq miles (2860 sq km)
Languages Samoan*, English*
Religions Christian 99%, Other 1%
Ethnic mix Polynesian 90%, Euronesian 9%, Other 1%
Government Parliamentary system
Currency Tala = 100 sene
Literacy rate 99%
Calorie consumption 2945 calories

SAN MARINO
Southern Europe

Official name Republic of San Marino
Formation 1631 / 1631
Capital San Marino
Population 28,880 / 1203 people per sq mile (473 people per sq km) / 94%
Total area 23.6 sq miles (61 sq km)
Languages Italian*
Religions Roman Catholic 93%, Other and nonreligious 7%
Ethnic mix Sammarinese 80%, Italian 19%, Other 1%
Government Parliamentary system
Currency Euro = 100 cents
Literacy rate 99%
Calorie consumption Not available

SÃO TOMÉ & PRÍNCIPE
West Africa

Official name Democratic Republic of São Tomé and Principe
Formation 1975 / 1975
Capital São Tomé
Population 187,410 / 505 people per sq mile (195 people per sq km) / 47%
Total area 386 sq miles (1001 sq km)
Languages Portuguese*, Portuguese Creole
Religions Roman Catholic 84%, Other 16%
Ethnic mix Black 90%, Portuguese and Creole 10%
Government Presidential system
Currency Dobra = 100 centimos
Literacy rate 83%
Calorie consumption 2460 calories

SAUDI ARABIA
Souhwest Asia

Official name Kingdom of Saudi Arabia
Formation 1932 / 1932
Capital Riyadh; Jiddah (administrative)
Population 24.6 million / 30 people per sq mile (12 people per sq km) / 86%
Total area 756,981 sq miles (1,960,582 sq km)
Languages Arabic*
Religions Sunni Muslim 85%, Shi'a Muslim 15%
Ethnic mix Arab 90%, Afro-Asian 10%
Government Monarchy
Currency Saudi riyal = 100 halalat
Literacy rate 79%
Calorie consumption 2844 calories

SENEGAL
West Africa

Official name Republic of Senegal
Formation 1960 / 1960
Capital Dakar
Population 11.7 million / 157 people per sq mile (61 people per sq km) / 47%
Total area 75,749 sq miles (196,190 sq km)
Languages French*, Diola, Mandinka, Malinke, Pulaar, Serer, Soninke, Wolof
Religions Sunni Muslim 90%, Christian (mainly Roman Catholic) 5%, Traditional beliefs 5%
Ethnic mix Wolof 43%, Toucouleur 24%, Serer 15%, Other 11%, Diola 4%, Malinke 3%
Government Presidential system
Currency CFA franc = 100 centimes
Literacy rate 39%
Calorie consumption 2279 calories

SERBIA
Europe

Official name Republic of Serbia
Formation 2006 / 2006
Capital Belgrade
Population 9.7 million / 290 people per sq mile (112 people per sq km) / 52%
Total area 34,116 sq miles (88,361 sq km)
Languages Serbo-Croat*, Albanian, Hungarian
Religions Orthodox Christian 85%, Muslim 6%, Other 6%, Roman Catholic 3%
Ethnic mix Serb 66%, Albanian 19%, Hungarian 4%, Bosniak 2%, Other 9%
Government Parliamentary system
Currency Dinar (Serbia) = 100 para
Literacy rate 98%
Calorie consumption Not available

SEYCHELLES
Indian Ocean

Official name Republic of Seychelles
Formation 1976 / 1976
Capital Victoria
Population 81,188 / 781 people per sq mile (301 people per sq km) / 64%
Total area 176 sq miles (455 sq km)
Languages French Creole*, English, French
Religions Roman Catholic 90%, Anglican 8%, Other (including Muslim) 2%
Ethnic mix Creole 89%, Indian 5%, Other 4%, Chinese 2%
Government Presidential system
Currency Seychelles rupee = 100 cents
Literacy rate 92%
Calorie consumption 2465 calories

SIERRA LEONE
West Africa

Official name Republic of Sierra Leone
Formation 1961 / 1961
Capital Freetown
Population 5.5 million / 199 people per sq mile (77 people per sq km) / 37%
Total area 27,698 sq miles (71,740 sq km)
Languages English*, Mende, Temne, Krio
Religions Muslim 30%, Traditional beliefs 30%, Other 30%, Christian 10%
Ethnic mix Mende 35%, Temne 32%, Other 21%, Limba 8%, Kuranko 4%
Government Presidential system
Currency Leone = 100 cents
Literacy rate 30%
Calorie consumption 1936 calories

SINGAPORE
Southeast Asia

Official name Republic of Singapore
Formation 1965 / 1965
Capital Singapore
Population 4.3 million / 18220 people per sq mile (7049 people per sq km) / 100%
Total area 250 sq miles (648 sq km)
Languages English*, Malay*, Mandarin*, Tamil*
Religions Buddhist 55%, Taoist 22%, Muslim 16%, Hindu, Christian, and Sikh 7%
Ethnic mix Chinese 77%, Malay 14%, Indian 8%, Other 1%
Government Parliamentary system
Currency Singapore dollar = 100 cents
Literacy rate 93%
Calorie consumption Not available

SLOVAKIA
Central Europe

Official name Slovak Republic
Formation 1993 / 1993
Capital Bratislava
Population 5.4 million / 285 people per sq mile (110 people per sq km) / 57%
Total area 18,859 sq miles (48,845 sq km)
Languages Slovak*, Hungarian (Magyar), Czech
Religions Roman Catholic 60%, Other 18%, Atheist 10%, Protestant 8%, Orthodox Christian 4%
Ethnic mix Slovak 85%, Magyar 11%, Other 2%, Roma 1%, Czech 1%
Government Parliamentary system
Currency Slovak koruna = 100 halierov
Literacy rate 99%
Calorie consumption 2889 calories

SLOVENIA
Central Europe

Official name Republic of Slovenia
Formation 1991 / 1991
Capital Ljubljana
Population 2 million / 256 people per sq mile (99 people per sq km) / 50%
Total area 7820 sq miles (20,253 sq km)
Languages Slovene*, Serbo-Croat
Religions Roman Catholic 96%, Other 3%, Muslim 1%
Ethnic mix Slovene 83%, Other 12%, Serb 2%, Croat 2%, Bosniak 1%
Government Parliamentary system
Currency Tolar = 100 stotinov
Literacy rate 99%
Calorie consumption 3001 calories

SOLOMON ISLANDS
Australasia & Oceania

Official name Solomon Islands
Formation 1978 / 1978
Capital Honiara
Population 478,000 / 44 people per sq mile (17 people per sq km) / 20%
Total area 10,985 sq miles (28,450 sq km)
Languages English*, Melanesian Pidgin, Pidgin English
Religions Anglican 34%, Roman Catholic 19%, Methodist 11%, Seventh-day Adventist 10%, South Seas Evangelical Church 17%, Other 9%
Ethnic mix Melanesian 94%, Polynesian 4%, Other 2%
Government Parliamentary system
Currency Solomon Islands dollar = 100 cents
Literacy rate 77%
Calorie consumption 2265 calories

SOMALIA
East Africa

Official name Somalia
Formation 1960 / 1960
Capital Mogadishu
Population 8.2 million / 34 people per sq mile (13 people per sq km) / 28%
Total area 246,199 sq miles (637,657 sq km)
Languages Somali*, Arabic*, English, Italian
Religions Sunni Muslim 98%, Christian 2%
Ethnic mix Somali 85%, Other 15%
Government Transitional regime
Currency Somali shilling = 100 centesimi
Literacy rate 24%
Calorie consumption 1628 calories

SOUTH AFRICA
Southern Africa

Official name Republic of South Africa
Formation 1934 / 1994
Capital Pretoria; Cape Town; Bloemfontein
Population 47.4 million / 101 people per sq mile (39 people per sq km) / 55%
Total area 471,008 sq miles (1,219,912 sq km)
Languages English, isiZulu, isiXhosa, Afrikaans, Sepedi, Setswana, Sesotho, Xitsonga, siSwati, Tshivenda, isiNdebele
Religions Christian 68%, Traditional beliefs and animist 29%, Muslim 2%, Hindu 1%
Ethnic mix Black 79%, White 10%, Colored 9%, Asian 2%
Government Presidential system
Currency Rand = 100 cents
Literacy rate 82%
Calorie consumption 2956 calories

SOUTH KOREA
East Asia

Official name Republic of Korea
Formation 1948 / 1953
Capital Seoul
Population 47.8 million / 1254 people per sq mile (484 people per sq km) / 82%
Total area 38,023 sq miles (98,480 sq km)
Languages Korean*
Religions Mahayana Buddhist 47%, Protestant 38%, Roman Catholic 11%, Confucianist 3%, Other 1%
Ethnic mix Korean 100%
Government Presidential system
Currency South Korean won = 100 chon
Literacy rate 98%
Calorie consumption 3058 calories

SPAIN
Southeast Europe

Official name Kingdom of Spain
Formation 1492 / 1713
Capital Madrid
Population 43.1 million / 224 people per sq mile (86 people per sq km) / 78%
Total area 194,896 sq miles (504,782 sq km)
Languages Spanish*, Catalan*, Galician*, Basque*
Religions Roman Catholic 96%, Other 4%
Ethnic mix Castilian Spanish 72%, Catalan 17%, Galician 6%, Basque 2%, Other 2%, Roma 1%
Government Parliamentary system
Currency Euro = 100 cents
Literacy rate 98%
Calorie consumption 3371 calories

SRI LANKA
South Asia

Official name Democratic Socialist Republic of Sri Lanka
Formation 1948 / 1948
Capital Colombo
Population 20.7 million / 828 people per sq mile (320 people per sq km) / 24%
Total area 25,332 sq miles (65,610 sq km)
Languages Sinhala, Tamil, Sinhala-Tamil, English
Religions Buddhist 69%, Hindu 15%, Muslim 8%, Christian 8%
Ethnic mix Sinhalese 74%, Tamil 18%, Moor 7%, Burgher, Malay, and Veddha 1%
Government Mixed presidential–parliamentary system
Currency Sri Lanka rupee = 100 cents
Literacy rate 90%
Calorie consumption 2385 calories

SUDAN
East Africa

Official name Republic of the Sudan
Formation 1956 / 1956
Capital Khartoum
Population 36.2 million / 37 people per sq mile (14 people per sq km) / 36%
Total area 967,493 sq miles (2,505,810 sq km)
Languages Arabic*, Dinka, Nuer, Nubian, Beja, Zande, Bari, Fur, Shilluk, Lotuko
Religions Muslim (mainly Sunni) 70%, Traditional beliefs 20%, Christian 9%, Other 1%
Ethnic mix Other Black 52%, Arab 40%, Dinka and Beja 7%, Other 1%
Government Presidential system
Currency Sudanese pound or dinar = 100 piastres
Literacy rate 59%
Calorie consumption 2228 calories

SURINAM
South America

Official name Republic of Suriname
Formation 1975 / 1975
Capital Paramaribo
Population 499,000 / 8 people per sq mile (3 people per sq km) / 74%
Total area 63,039 sq miles (163,270 sq km)
Languages Dutch*, Sranan (Creole), Javanese, Sarnami Hindi, Saramaccan, Chinese, Carib
Religions Hindu 27%, Protestant 25%, Roman Catholic 23%, Muslim 20%, Traditional beliefs 5%
Ethnic mix Creole 34%, South Asian 34%, Javanese 18%, Black 9%, Other 5%
Government Parliamentary system
Currency Suriname dollar (guilder until 2004) = 100 cents
Literacy rate 88%
Calorie consumption 2652 calories

SWAZILAND
Southern Africa

Official name Kingdom of Swaziland
Formation 1968 / 1968
Capital Mbabane
Population 1 million / 151 people per sq mile (58 people per sq km) / 26%
Total area 6704 sq miles (17,363 sq km)
Languages English*, siSwati*, isiZulu, Xitsonga
Religions Christian 60%, Traditional beliefs 40%
Ethnic mix Swazi 97%, Other 3%
Government Monarchy
Currency Lilangeni = 100 cents
Literacy rate 79%
Calorie consumption 2322 calories

SWEDEN
Northern Europe

Official name Kingdom of Sweden
Formation 1523 / 1905
Capital Stockholm
Population 9 million / 57 people per sq mile (22 people per sq km) / 83%
Total area 173,731 sq miles (449,964 sq km)
Languages Swedish*, Finnish, Sámi
Religions Evangelical Lutheran 82%, Other 13%, Roman Catholic 2%, Muslim 2%, Orthodox Christian 1%
Ethnic mix Swedish 88%, Foreign-born or first-generation immigrant 10%, Finnish and Sámi 2%
Government Parliamentary system
Currency Swedish krona = 100 öre
Literacy rate 99%
Calorie consumption 3185 calories

SWITZERLAND
Central Europe

Official name Swiss Confederation
Formation 1291 / 1857
Capital Bern
Population 7.3 million / 475 people per sq mile (184 people per sq km) / 68%
Total area 15,942 sq miles (41,290 sq km)
Languages German*, French*, Italian*, Romansch*, Swiss-German
Religions Roman Catholic 46%, Protestant 40%, Other and nonreligious 12%, Muslim 2%
Ethnic mix German 65%, French 18%, Italian 10%, Other 6%, Romansch 1%
Government Parliamentary system
Currency Swiss franc = 100 rappen/centimes
Literacy rate 99%
Calorie consumption 3526 calories

SYRIA
Southwest Asia

Official name Syrian Arab Republic
Formation 1941 / 1967
Capital Damascus
Population 19 million / 267 people per sq mile (103 people per sq km) / 55%
Total area 71,498 sq miles (184,180 sq km)
Languages Arabic*, French, Kurdish, Armenian, Circassian, Turkic languages, Assyrian, Aramaic
Religions Sunni Muslim 74%, Other Muslim 16%, Christian 10%
Ethnic mix Arab 89%, Kurdish 6%, Other 3%, Armenian, Turkmen, and Circassian 2%
Government One-party state
Currency Syrian pound = 100 piasters
Literacy rate 83%
Calorie consumption 3038 calories

TAIWAN
East Asia

Official name Republic of China (ROC)
Formation 1949 / 1949
Capital Taipei
Population 22.9 million / 1838 people per sq mile (710 people per sq km) / 69%
Total area 13,892 sq miles (35,980 sq km)
Languages Amoy Chinese, Mandarin Chinese, Hakka Chinese
Religions Buddhist, Confucianist, and Taoist 93%, Christian 5%, Other 2%
Ethnic mix Han (pre-20th-century migration) 84%, Han (20th-century migration) 14%, Aboriginal 2%
Government Presidential system
Currency Taiwan dollar = 100 cents
Literacy rate 97%
Calorie consumption Not available

TAJIKISTAN
Central Asia

Official name Republic of Tajikistan
Formation 1991 / 1991
Capital Dushanbe
Population 6.5 million / 118 people per sq mile (45 people per sq km) / 28%
Total area 55,251 sq miles (143,100 sq km)
Languages Tajik*, Uzbek, Russian
Religions Sunni Muslim 80%, Other 15%, Shi'a Muslim 5%
Ethnic mix Tajik 62%, Uzbek 24%, Russian 8%, Other 4%, Tatar 1%, Kyrgyz 1%
Government Presidential system
Currency Somoni = 100 diram
Literacy rate 99%
Calorie consumption 1828 calories

TANZANIA
East Africa

Official name United Republic of Tanzania
Formation 1964 / 1964
Capital Dodoma
Population 38.3 million / 112 people per sq mile (43 people per sq km) / 33%
Total area 364,898 sq miles (945,087 sq km)
Languages English*, Kiswahili*, Sukuma, Chagga, Nyamwezi, Hehe, Makonde, Yao, Sandawe
Religions Muslim 33%, Christian 33%, Traditional beliefs 30%, Other 4%
Ethnic mix Native African (over 120 tribes) 99%, European and Asian 1%
Government Presidential system
Currency Tanzanian shilling = 100 cents
Literacy rate 69%
Calorie consumption 1975 calories

THAILAND
Southeastern Asia

Official name Kingdom of Thailand
Formation 1238 / 1907
Capital Bangkok
Population 64.2 million / 325 people per sq mile (126 people per sq km) / 22%
Total area 198,455 sq miles (514,000 sq km)
Languages Thai*, Chinese, Malay, Khmer, Mon, Karen, Miao
Religions Buddhist 95%, Muslim 4%, Other (including Christian) 1%
Ethnic mix Thai 83%, Chinese 12%, Malay 3%, Khmer and Other 2%
Government Parliamentary system
Currency Baht = 100 stang
Literacy rate 93%
Calorie consumption 2467 calories

TOGO
Western Africa

Official name Republic of Togo
Formation 1960 / 1960
Capital Lomé
Population 6.1 million / 290 people per sq mile (112 people per sq km) / 33%
Total area 21,924 sq miles (56,785 sq km)
Languages French*, Ewe, Kabye, Gurma
Religions Traditional beliefs 50%, Christian 35%, Muslim 15%
Ethnic mix Ewe 46%, Kabye 27%, Other African 26%, European 1%
Government Presidential system
Currency CFA franc = 100 centimes
Literacy rate 53%
Calorie consumption 2345 calories

TONGA
Australasia & Oceania

Official name Kingdom of Tonga
Formation 1970 / 1970
Capital Nuku'alofa
Population 112,422 / 404 people per sq mile (156 people per sq km) / 43%
Total area 289 sq miles (748 sq km)
Languages Tongan*, English
Religions Free Wesleyan 41%, Roman Catholic 16%, Church of Jesus Christ of Latter-day Saints 14%, Free Church of Tonga 12%, Other 17%
Ethnic mix Polynesian 99%, Other 1%
Government Monarchy
Currency Pa'anga (Tongan dollar) = 100 seniti
Literacy rate 99%
Calorie consumption Not available

TRINIDAD & TOBAGO
West Indies

Official name Republic of Trinidad and Tobago
Formation 1962 / 1962
Capital Port-of-Spain
Population 1.3 million / 656 people per sq mile (253 people per sq km) / 74%
Total area 1980 sq miles (5128 sq km)
Languages English*, English Creole, Hindi, French, Spanish
Religions Christian 60%, Hindu 24%, Other and nonreligious 9%, Muslim 7%
Ethnic mix East Indian 40%, Black 40%, Mixed race 19%, White and Chinese 1%
Government Parliamentary system
Currency Trinidad and Tobago dollar = 100 cents
Literacy rate 99%
Calorie consumption 2732 calories

TUNISIA
North Africa

Official name Republic of Tunisia
Formation 1956 / 1956
Capital Tunis
Population 10.1 million / 168 people per sq mile (65 people per sq km) / 68%
Total area 63,169 sq miles (163,610 sq km)
Languages Arabic*, French
Religions Muslim (mainly Sunni) 98%, Christian 1%, Jewish 1%
Ethnic mix Arab and Berber 98%, Jewish 1%, European 1%
Government Presidential system
Currency Tunisian dinar = 1000 millimes
Literacy rate 74%
Calorie consumption 3238 calories

TURKEY
Asia / Europe

Official name Republic of Turkey
Formation 1923 / 1939
Capital Ankara
Population 73.2 million / 246 people per sq mile (95 people per sq km) / 75%
Total area 301,382 sq miles (780,580 sq km)
Languages Turkish*, Kurdish, Arabic, Circassian, Armenian, Greek, Georgian, Ladino
Religions Muslim (mainly Sunni) 99%, Other 1%
Ethnic mix Turkish 70%, Kurdish 20%, Other 8%, Arab 2%
Government Parliamentary system
Currency new Turkish lira = 100 kurus
Literacy rate 88%
Calorie consumption 3357 calories

TURKMENISTAN
Central Asia

Official name Turkmenistan
Formation 1991 / 1991
Capital Ashgabat
Population 4.8 million / 25 people per sq mile (10 people per sq km) / 45%
Total area 188,455 sq miles (488,100 sq km)
Languages Turkmen*, Uzbek, Russian, Kazakh, Tatar
Religions Sunni Muslim 87%, Orthodox Christian 11%, Other 2%
Ethnic mix Turkmen 77%, Uzbek 9%, Russian 7%, Other 4%, Kazakh 2%, Tatar 1%
Government One-party state
Currency Manat = 100 tenga
Literacy rate 99%
Calorie consumption 2742 calories

TUVALU
Australasia & Oceania

Official name Tuvalu
Formation 1978 / 1978
Capital Fongafale, on Funafuti Atoll
Population 11,636 / 1164 people per sq mile (448 people per sq km) / 45%
Total area 10 sq miles (26 sq km)
Languages Tuvaluan, Kiribati, English
Religions Church of Tuvalu 97%, Other 1%, Baha'i 1%, Seventh-day Adventist 1%
Ethnic mix Polynesian 96%, Other 4%
Government Nonparty system
Currency Australian dollar and Tuvaluan dollar = 100 cents
Literacy rate 98%
Calorie consumption Not available

UGANDA
East Africa

Official name Republic of Uganda
Formation 1962 / 1962
Capital Kampala
Population 28.8 million / 374 people per sq mile (144 people per sq km) / 14%
Total area 91,135 sq miles (236,040 sq km)
Languages English*, Luganda, Nkole, Chiga, Lango, Acholi, Teso, Lugbara
Religions Roman Catholic 38%, Protestant 33%, Traditional beliefs 13%, Muslim (mainly Sunni) 8%, Other 8%
Ethnic mix Bantu tribes 50%, Other 45%, Sudanese 5%
Government Nonparty system
Currency New Uganda shilling = 100 cents
Literacy rate 69%
Calorie consumption 2410 calories

UKRAINE
Eastern Europe

Official name Ukraine
Formation 1991 / 1991
Capital Kiev
Population 46.5 million / 199 people per sq mile (77 people per sq km) / 68%
Total area 223,089 sq miles (603,700 sq km)
Languages Ukrainian*, Russian, Tatar
Religions Christian (mainly Orthodox) 95%, Other 4%, Jewish 1%
Ethnic mix Ukrainian 73%, Russian 22%, Other 4%, Jewish 1%
Government Presidential system
Currency Hryvna = 100 kopiykas
Literacy rate 99%
Calorie consumption 3054 calories

UNITED ARAB EMIRATES
Southwest Asia

Official name United Arab Emirates
Formation 1971 / 1972
Capital Abu Dhabi
Population 4.5 million / 139 people per sq mile (54 people per sq km) / 86%
Total area 32,000 sq miles (82,880 sq km)
Languages Arabic*, Farsi, Indian and Pakistani languages, English
Religions Muslim (mainly Sunni) 96%, Christian, Hindu, and other 4%
Ethnic mix Asian 60%, Emirian 25%, Other Arab 12%, European 3%
Government Monarchy
Currency UAE dirham = 100 fils
Literacy rate 77%
Calorie consumption 3225 calories

UNITED KINGDOM
Northwest Europe

Official name United Kingdom of Great Britain and Northern Ireland
Formation 1707 / 1922
Capital London
Population 59.7 million / 640 people per sq mile (247 people per sq km) / 90%
Total area 94,525 sq miles (244,820 sq km)
Languages English*, Welsh, Scottish Gaelic
Religions Anglican 45%, Roman Catholic 9%, Presbyterian 4%, Other 42%
Ethnic mix English 80%, Scottish 9%, West Indian, Asian, and other 5%, Northern Irish 3%, Welsh 3%
Government Parliamentary system
Currency Pound sterling = 100 pence
Literacy rate 99%
Calorie consumption 3412 calories

UNITED STATES
North America

Official name United States of America
Formation 1776 / 1959
Capital Washington D.C.
Population 298 million / 84 people per sq mile (33 people per sq km) / 77%
Total area 3,717,792 sq miles (9,626,091 sq km)
Languages English*, Spanish, Chinese, French, German, Tagalog, Vietnamese, Italian, Korean, Russian, Polish
Religions Protestant 52%, Roman Catholic 25%, Muslim 2%, Jewish 2%, Other 19%
Ethnic mix White 69%, Hispanic 13%, Black American/African 13%, Asian 4%, Native American 1%
Government Presidential system
Currency US dollar = 100 cents
Literacy rate 99%
Calorie consumption 3774 calories

URUGUAY
South America

Official name Eastern Republic of Uruguay
Formation 1828 / 1828
Capital Montevideo
Population 3.5 million / 52 people per sq mile (20 people per sq km) / 91%
Total area 68,039 sq miles (176,220 sq km)
Languages Spanish*
Religions Roman Catholic 66%, Other and nonreligious 30%, Jewish 2%, Protestant 2%
Ethnic mix White 90%, Mestizo 6%, Black 4%
Government Presidential system
Currency Uruguayan peso = 100 centésimos
Literacy rate 98%
Calorie consumption 2828 calories

UZBEKISTAN
Central Asia

Official name Republic of Uzbekistan
Formation 1991 / 1991
Capital Tashkent
Population 26.6 million / 154 people per sq mile (59 people per sq km) / 37%
Total area 172,741 sq miles (447,400 sq km)
Languages Uzbek*, Russian, Tajik, Kazakh
Religions Sunni Muslim 88%, Orthodox Christian 9%, Other 3%
Ethnic mix Uzbek 71%, Other 12%, Russian 8%, Tajik 5%, Kazakh 4%
Government Presidential system
Currency Som = 100 tiyin
Literacy rate 99%
Calorie consumption 2241 calories

VANUATU
Australasia & Oceania

Official name Republic of Vanuatu
Formation 1980 / 1980
Capital Port Vila
Population 211,000 / 45 people per sq mile (17 people per sq km) / 20%
Total area 4710 sq miles (12,200 sq km)
Languages Bislama* (Melanesian pidgin), English*, French*, other indigenous languages
Religions Presbyterian 37%, Other 19%, Anglican 15%, Roman Catholic 15%, Traditional beliefs 8%, Seventh-day Adventist 6%
Ethnic mix Melanesian 94%, Other 3%, Polynesian 3%
Government Parliamentary system
Currency Vatu = 100 centimes
Literacy rate 74%
Calorie consumption 2587 calories

VATICAN CITY
Southern Europe

Official name State of the Vatican City
Formation 1929 / 1929
Capital Vatican City
Population 921 / 5418 people per sq mile (2093 people per sq km) / 100%
Total area 0.17 sq miles (0.44 sq km)
Languages Italian*, Latin*
Religions Roman Catholic 100%
Ethnic mix The current pope is German. Cardinals are from many nationalities, but Italians form the largest group. Most of the resident lay persons are Italian.
Government Papal state
Currency Euro = 100 cents
Literacy rate 99%
Calorie consumption Not available

VENEZUELA
South America

Official name Bolivarian Republic of Venezuela
Formation 1830 / 1830
Capital Caracas
Population 26.7 million / 78 people per sq mile (30 people per sq km) / 87%
Total area 352,143 sq miles (912,050 sq km)
Languages Spanish*, Amerindian languages
Religions Roman Catholic 89%, Protestant and other 11%
Ethnic mix Mestizo 69%, White 20%, Black 9%, Amerindian 2%
Government Presidential system
Currency Bolívar = 100 centimos
Literacy rate 93%
Calorie consumption 2336 calories

VIETNAM
Southeast Asia

Official name Socialist Republic of Vietnam
Formation 1976 / 1976
Capital Hanoi
Population 84.2 million / 670 people per sq mile (259 people per sq km) / 20%
Total area 127,243 sq miles (329,560 sq km)
Languages Vietnamese*, Chinese, Thai, Khmer, Muong, Nung, Miao, Yao, Jarai
Religions Buddhist 55%, Other and nonreligious 38%, Christian (mainly Roman Catholic) 7%
Ethnic mix Vietnamese 88%, Other 6%, Chinese 4%, Thai 2%
Government One-party state
Currency Dông = 10 hao = 100 xu
Literacy rate 90%
Calorie consumption 2566 calories

YEMEN
Southwest Asia

Official name Republic of Yemen
Formation 1990 / 1990
Capital Sana
Population 21 million / 97 people per sq mile (37 people per sq km) / 25%
Total area 203,849 sq miles (527,970 sq km)
Languages Arabic*
Religions Sunni Muslim 55%, Shi'a Muslim 42%, Christian, Hindu, and Jewish 3%
Ethnic mix Arab 95%, Afro-Arab 3%, Indian, Somali, and European 2%
Government Presidential system
Currency Yemeni rial = 100 sene
Literacy rate 49%
Calorie consumption 2038 calories

ZAMBIA
Southern Africa

Official name Republic of Zambia
Formation 1964 / 1964
Capital Lusaka
Population 11.7 million / 41 people per sq mile (16 people per sq km) / 35%
Total area 290,584 sq miles (752,614 sq km)
Languages English*, Bemba, Tonga, Nyanja, Lozi, Lala-Bisa, Nsenga
Religions Christian 63%, Traditional beliefs 36%, Muslim and Hindu 1%
Ethnic mix Bemba 34%, Other African 26%, Tonga 16%, Nyanja 14%, Lozi 9%, European 1%
Government Presidential system
Currency Zambian kwacha = 100 ngwee
Literacy rate 68%
Calorie consumption 1927 calories

ZIMBABWE
Southern Africa

Official name Republic of Zimbabwe
Formation 1980 / 1980
Capital Harare
Population 13 million / 87 people per sq mile (34 people per sq km) / 35%
Total area 150,803 sq miles (390,580 sq km)
Languages English*, Shona, isiNdebele
Religions Syncretic (Christian/traditional beliefs) 50%, Christian 25%, Traditional beliefs 24%, Other (including Muslim) 1%
Ethnic mix Shona 71%, Ndebele 16%, Other African 11%, White 1%, Asian 1%
Government Presidential system
Currency Zimbabwe dollar = 100 cents
Literacy rate 90%
Calorie consumption 1943 calories

Geographical names

The following glossary lists all geographical terms occurring on the maps and in main-entry names in the Index-Gazetteer. These terms may precede, follow or be run together with the proper element of the name; where they precede it the term is reversed for indexing purposes - thus Poluostrov Yamal is indexed as Yamal, Poluostrov.

Key

Geographical term
Language, Term

A

Å *Danish, Norwegian*, River
Āb *Persian*, River
Adrar *Berber*, Mountains
Agía, Ágios *Greek*, Saint
Air *Indonesian*, River
Ákra *Greek*, Cape, point
Alpen *German*, Alps
Alt- *German*, Old
Altiplanicie *Spanish*, Plateau
Älve(en) *Swedish*, River
-ån *Swedish*, River
Anse *French*, Bay
'Aqabat *Arabic*, Pass
Archipiélago *Spanish*, Archipelago
Arcipelago *Italian*, Archipelago
Arquipélago *Portuguese*, Archipelago
Arrecife(s) *Spanish*, Reef(s)
Aru *Tamil*, River
Augstiene *Latvian*, Upland
Aukštuma *Lithuanian*, Upland
Aust- *Norwegian*, Eastern
Avtonomnyy Okrug *Russian*, Autonomous district
Āw *Kurdish*, River
'Ayn *Arabic*, Spring, well
'Ayoûn *Arabic*, Wells

B

Baelt *Danish*, Strait
Bahía *Spanish*, Bay
Baḩr *Arabic*, River
Baía *Portuguese*, Bay
Baie *French*, Bay
Bañado *Spanish*, Marshy land
Bandao *Chinese*, Peninsula
Banjaran *Malay*, Mountain range
Barajı *Turkish*, Dam
Barragem *Portuguese*, Reservoir
Bassin *French*, Basin
Batang *Malay*, Stream
Beinn, Ben *Gaelic*, Mountain
-berg *Afrikaans, Norwegian*, Mountain
Besar *Indonesian, Malay*, Big
Birkat, Birket *Arabic*, Lake, well,
Boğazi *Turkish*, Lake
Boka *Serbo-Croatian*, Bay
Bol'sh-aya, -iye, -oy, -oye *Russian*, Big
Botigh(i) *Uzbek*, Depression basin
-bre(en) *Norwegian*, Glacier
Bredning *Danish*, Bay
Bucht *German*, Bay
Bugt(en) *Danish*, Bay
Buḩayrat *Arabic*, Lake, reservoir
Buḩeirat *Arabic*, Lake
Bukit *Malay*, Mountain
-bukta *Norwegian*, Bay
bukten *Swedish*, Bay
Bulag *Mongolian*, Spring
Bulak *Uighur*, Spring
Burnu *Turkish*, Cape, point
Buuraha *Somali*, Mountains

C

Cabo *Portuguese*, Cape
Caka *Tibetan*, Salt lake
Canal *Spanish*, Channel
Cap *French*, Cape
Capo *Italian*, Cape, headland
Cascada *Portuguese*, Waterfall
Cayo(s) *Spanish*, Islet(s), rock(s)
Cerro *Spanish*, Mountain
Chaîne *French*, Mountain range
Chapada *Portuguese*, Hills, upland
Chau *Cantonese*, Island
Chây *Turkish*, River
Chhâk *Cambodian*, Bay
Chhu *Tibetan*, River
-chŏsuji *Korean*, Reservoir
Chott *Arabic*, Depression, salt lake
Chŭli *Uzbek*, Grassland, steppe
Ch'ün-tao *Chinese*, Island group
Chuŏr Phnum *Cambodian*, Mountains
Ciudad *Spanish*, City, town
Co *Tibetan*, Lake
Colline(s) *French*, Hill(s)
Cordillera *Spanish*, Mountain range
Costa *Spanish*, Coast
Côte *French*, Coast
Coxilha *Portuguese*, Mountains
Cuchilla *Spanish*, Mountains

D

Daban *Mongolian, Uighur*, Pass
Daği *Azerbaijani, Turkish*, Mountain
Dağlari *Azerbaijani, Turkish*, Mountains
-dake *Japanese*, Peak
-dal(en) *Norwegian*, Valley
Danau *Indonesian*, Lake
Dao *Chinese*, Island
Đao *Vietnamese*, Island
Daryā *Persian*, River
Daryācheh *Persian*, Lake
Dasht *Persian*, Desert, plain
Dawḩat *Arabic*, Bay
Denizi *Turkish*, Sea
Dere *Turkish*, Stream
Desierto *Spanish*, Desert
Dili *Azerbaijani*, Spit
-do *Korean*, Island
Dooxo *Somali*, Valley
Düzü *Azerbaijani*, Steppe
-dwīp *Bengali*, Island

E

-eilanden *Dutch*, Islands
Embalse *Spanish*, Reservoir
Ensenada *Spanish*, Bay
Erg *Arabic*, Dunes
Estany *Catalan*, Lake
Estero *Spanish*, Inlet
Estrecho *Spanish*, Strait
Étang *French*, Lagoon, lake
-ey *Icelandic*, Island
Ezero *Bulgarian, Macedonian*, Lake
Ezers *Latvian*, Lake

F

Feng *Chinese*, Peak
Fjord *Danish*, Fjord
-fjord(en) *Danish, Norwegian, Swedish*, fjord
-fjørdhur *Faeroese*, Fjord
Fleuve *French*, River
Fliegu *Maltese*, Channel
-fljór *Icelandic*, River
-flói *Icelandic*, Bay
Forêt *French*, Forest

G

-gan *Japanese*, Rock
-gang *Korean*, River
Ganga *Hindi, Nepali, Sinhala*, River
Gaoyuan *Chinese*, Plateau
Garagumy *Turkmen*, Sands
-gawa *Japanese*, River
Gebel *Arabic*, Mountain
-gebirge *German*, Mountain range
Ghadīr *Arabic*, Well
Ghubbat *Arabic*, Bay
Gjiri *Albanian*, Bay
Gol *Mongolian*, River
Golfe *French*, Gulf
Golfo *Italian, Spanish*, Gulf
Göl(ü) *Turkish*, Lake
Golyam, -a *Bulgarian*, Big
Gora *Russian, Serbo-Croatian*, Mountain
Góra *Polish*, mountain
Gory *Russian*, Mountain
Gryada *Russian*, ridge
Guba *Russian*, Bay
-gundo *Korean*, island group
Gunung *Malay*, Mountain

H

Ḩadd *Arabic*, Spit
-haehyŏp *Korean*, Strait
Haff *German*, Lagoon
Hai *Chinese*, Bay, lake, sea
Haixia *Chinese*, Strait
Hamada *Arabic*, Plateau
Ḩammādat *Arabic*, Plateau
Hāmūn *Persian*, Lake
-hantō *Japanese*, Peninsula
Har, Haré *Hebrew*, Mountain
Ḩarrat *Arabic*, Lava-field
Hav(et) *Danish*, Swedish, Sea
Hawr *Arabic*, Lake
Hāyk' *Amharic*, Lake
He *Chinese*, River
-hegység *Hungarian*, Mountain range
Heide *German*, Heath, moorland
Helodrano *Malagasy*, Bay
Higashi- *Japanese*, East(ern)
Ḩişā' *Arabic*, Well
Hka *Burmese*, River
-ho *Korean*, Lake
Hŏ *Korean*, Reservoir
Ḥolot *Hebrew*, Dunes
Hora *Belarussian, Czech*, Mountain
Hrada *Belarussian*, Mountain, ridge
Hsi *Chinese*, River
Hu *Chinese*, Lake
Huk *Danish*, Point

I

Île(s) *French*, Island(s)
Ilha(s) *Portuguese*, Island(s)
Ilhéu(s) *Portuguese*, Islet(s)
Imeni *Russian*, In the name of
Inish- *Gaelic*, Island
Insel(n) *German*, Island(s)
Irmağı, Irmak *Turkish*, River
Isla(s) *Spanish*, Island(s)
Isola (Isole) *Italian*, Island(s)

J

Jabal *Arabic*, Mountain
Jāl *Arabic*, Ridge
-järv *Estonian*, Lake
-järvi *Finnish*, Lake
Jazā'ir *Arabic*, Islands
Jazīrat *Arabic*, Island
Jazīreh *Persian*, Island
Jebel *Arabic*, Mountain
Jezero *Serbo-Croatian*, Lake
Jezioro *Polish*, Lake
Jiang *Chinese*, River
-jima *Japanese*, Island
Jižní *Czech*, Southern
-jõgi *Estonian*, River
-joki *Finnish*, River
-jökull *Icelandic*, Glacier
Jūn *Arabic*, Bay
Juzur *Arabic*, Islands

K

Kaikyō *Japanese*, Strait
-kaise *Lappish*, Mountain
Kali *Nepali*, River
Kalnas *Lithuanian*, Mountain
Kalns *Latvian*, Mountain
Kang *Chinese*, Harbour
Kangri *Tibetan*, Mountain(s)
Kaôh *Cambodian*, Island
Kapp *Norwegian*, Cape
Káto *Greek*, Lower
Kavīr *Persian*, Desert
K'edi *Georgian*, Mountain range
Kediet *Arabic*, Mountain
Kepi *Albanian*, Cape, point
Kepulauan *Indonesian, Malay*, Island group
Khalîg, Khalīj *Arabic*, Gulf
Khawr *Arabic*, Inlet
Khola *Nepali*, River
Khrebet *Russian*, Mountain range
Ko *Thai*, Island
-ko *Japanese*, Inlet, lake
Kólpos *Greek*, Bay
-kopf *German*, Peak
Körfäzi *Azerbaijani*, Bay
Körfezi *Turkish*, Bay
Kõrgustik *Estonian*, Upland
Kosa *Russian, Ukrainian*, Spit
Koshi *Nepali*, River
Kou *Chinese*, River-mouth
Kowtal *Persian*, Pass
Kray *Russian*, Region, territory
Kryazh *Russian*, Ridge
Kuduk *Uighur*, Well
Kūh(hā) *Persian*, Mountain(s)
-kul' *Russian*, Lake
Kŭl(i) *Tajik, Uzbek*, Lake
-kundo *Korean*, Island group
-kysten *Norwegian*, Coast
Kyun *Burmese*, Island

L

Laaq *Somali*, Watercourse
Lac *French*, Lake
Lacul *Romanian*, Lake
Lagh *Somali*, Stream
Lago *Italian, Portuguese, Spanish*, Lake
Lagoa *Portuguese*, Lagoon
Laguna *Italian, Spanish*, Lagoon, lake
Laht *Estonian*, Bay
Laut *Indonesian*, Bay
Lembalemba *Malagasy*, Plateau
Lerr *Armenian*, Mountain
Lernashght'a *Armenian*, Mountain range
Les *Czech*, Forest
Lich *Armenian*, Lake
Liehtao *Chinese*, Island group
Liqeni *Albanian*, Lake
Límni *Greek*, Lake
Ling *Chinese*, Mountain range
Llano *Spanish*, Plain, prairie
Lumi *Albanian*, River
Lyman *Ukrainian*, Estuary

M

Madīnat *Arabic*, City, town
Mae Nam *Thai*, River
-mägi *Estonian*, Hill
Maja *Albanian*, Mountain
Mal *Albanian*, Mountains
Mal-aya, -oye, -yy, *Russian*, Small
-man *Korean*, Bay
Mar *Spanish*, Lake
Marios *Lithuanian*, Lake
Massif *French*, Mountains
Meer *German*, Lake
-meer *Dutch*, Lake
Melkosopochnik *Russian*, Plain
-meri *Estonian*, Sea
Mifraz *Hebrew*, Bay
Minami- *Japanese*, South(ern)
-misaki *Japanese*, Cape, point
Monkhafad *Arabic*, Depression
Montagne(s) *French*, Mountain(s)
Montañas *Spanish*, Mountains
Mont(s) *French*, Mountain(s)
Monte *Italian, Portuguese*, Mountain
More *Russian*, Sea
Mörön *Mongolian*, River
Mys *Russian*, Cape, point

N

-nada *Japanese*, Open stretch of water
Nagor'ye *Russian*, Upland
Naḩal *Hebrew*, River
Nahr *Arabic*, River
Nam *Laotian*, River
Namakzār *Persian*, Salt desert
Né-a, -on, -os *Greek*, New
Nedre- *Norwegian*, Lower
-neem *Estonian*, Cape, point
Nehri *Turkish*, River
-nes *Norwegian*, Cape, point
Nevado *Spanish*, Mountain (snow-capped)
Nieder- *German*, Lower
Nishi- *Japanese*, West(ern)
-nísi *Greek*, Island
Nisoi *Greek*, Islands
Nizhn-eye, -iy, -iye, -yaya *Russian*, Lower
Nizmennost' *Russian*, Lowland, plain
Nord *Danish, French, German*, North
Norte *Portuguese, Spanish*, North
Nos *Bulgarian*, Point, spit
Nosy *Malagasy*, Island
Nov-a, -i, *Bulgarian, Serbo-Croatian*, New
Nov-aya, -o, -oye, -yy, -yye *Russian*, New
Now-a, -e, -y *Polish*, New
Nur *Mongolian*, Lake
Nuruu *Mongolian*, Mountains
Nuur *Mongolian*, Lake
Nyzovyna *Ukrainian*, Lowland, plain

O

-ø *Danish*, Island
Ober- *German*, Upper
Oblast' *Russian*, Province
Órmos *Greek*, Bay
Orol(i) *Uzbek*, Island
Øster- *Norwegian*, Eastern
Ostrov(a) *Russian*, Island(s)
Otok *Serbo-Croatian*, Island
Oued *Arabic*, Watercourse
-oy *Faeroese*, Island
-øy(a) *Norwegian*, Island
Oya *Sinhala*, River
Ozero *Russian, Ukrainian*, Lake

P

Passo *Italian*, Pass
Pegunungan *Indonesian, Malay*, Mountain range
Pélagos *Greek*, Sea
Pendi *Chinese*, Basin
Penisola *Italian*, Peninsula
Pertuis *French*, Strait
Peski *Russian*, Sands
Phanom *Thai*, Mountain
Phou *Laotian*, Mountain
Pi *Chinese*, Point
Pic *Catalan, French*, Peak
Pico *Portuguese, Spanish*, Peak
-piggen *Danish*, Peak
Pik *Russian*, Peak
Pivostriv *Ukrainian*, Peninsula
Planalto *Portuguese*, Plateau
Planina, Planini *Bulgarian, Macedonian, Serbo-Croatian*, Mountain range
Plato *Russian*, Plateau
Ploskogor'ye *Russian*, Upland
Poluostrov *Russian*, Peninsula
Ponta *Portuguese*, Point
Porthmós *Greek*, Strait
Pótamos *Greek*, River
Presa *Spanish*, Dam
Prokhod *Bulgarian*, Pass
Proliv *Russian*, Strait
Pulau *Indonesian, Malay*, Island
Pulu *Malay*, Island
Punta *Spanish*, Point
Pushcha *Belorussian*, Forest
Puszcza *Polish*, Forest

Q

Qā' *Arabic*, Depression
Qalamat *Arabic*, Well
Qatorkŭh(i) *Tajik*, Mountain
Qiuling *Chinese*, Hills
Qolleh *Persian*, Mountain
Qu *Tibetan*, Stream
Quan *Chinese*, Well
Qulla(i) *Tajik*, Peak
Qundao *Chinese*, Island group

R

Raas *Somali*, Cape
-rags *Latvian*, Cape
Ramlat *Arabic*, Sands
Ra's *Arabic*, Cape, headland, point
Ravnina *Bulgarian, Russian*, Plain
Récif *French*, Reef
Recife *Portuguese*, Reef
Reka *Bulgarian*, River
Represa (Rep.) *Portuguese, Spanish*, Reservoir
Reshteh *Persian*, Mountain range
Respublika *Russian*, Republic, first-order administrative division
Respublika(si) *Uzbek*, Republic, first-order administrative division
-retsugan *Japanese*, Chain of rocks
-rettō *Japanese*, Island chain
Riacho *Spanish*, Stream
Riban' *Malagasy*, Mountains
Rio *Portuguese*, River
Río *Spanish*, River
Riu *Catalan*, River
Rivier *Dutch*, River
Rivière *French*, River
Rowd *Pashtu*, River
Rt *Serbo-Croatian*, Point
Rūd *Persian*, River
Rūdkhāneh *Persian*, River
Rudohorie *Slovak*, Mountains
Ruisseau *French*, Stream

S

-saar *Estonian*, Island
-saari *Finnish*, Island
Sabkhat *Arabic*, Salt marsh
Sāgar(a) *Hindi*, Lake, reservoir
Şaḩrā' *Arabic*, Desert
Saint, Sainte *French*, Saint
Salar *Spanish*, Salt-pan
Salto *Portuguese, Spanish*, Waterfall
Samudra *Sinhala*, Reservoir
-san *Japanese, Korean*, Mountain
-sanchi *Japanese*, Mountains
-sandur *Icelandic*, Beach
Sankt *German, Swedish*, Saint
-sanmaek *Korean*, Mountain range
-sanmyaku *Japanese*, Mountain range
San, Santa, Santo *Italian, Portuguese, Spanish*, Saint
São *Portuguese*, Saint
Sarīr *Arabic*, Desert
Sebkha, Sebkhet *Arabic*, Depression, salt marsh
Sedlo *Czech*, Pass
See *German*, Lake
Selat *Indonesian*, Strait
Selatan *Indonesian*, Southern
-selkä *Finnish*, Lake, ridge
Selseleh *Persian*, Mountain range
Serra *Portuguese*, Mountain
Serranía *Spanish*, Mountain
-seto *Japanese*, Channel, strait
Sever-naya, -noye, -nyy, -o *Russian*, Northern
Sha'ib *Arabic*, Watercourse
Shākh *Kurdish*, Mountain
Shamo *Chinese*, Desert
Shan *Chinese*, Mountain(s)
Shankou *Chinese*, Pass
Shanmo *Chinese*, Mountain range
Shaţţ *Arabic*, Distributary
Shet' *Amharic*, River
Shi *Chinese*, Municipality
-shima *Japanese*, Island
Shiqqat *Arabic*, Depression
-shotō *Japanese*, Group of islands
Shuiku *Chinese*, Reservoir
Shŭrkhog(i) *Uzbek*, Salt marsh
Sierra *Spanish*, Mountains
Sint *Dutch*, Saint
-sjø(en) *Norwegian*, Lake
-sjön *Swedish*, Lake
Solonchak *Russian*, Salt lake
Solonchakovyye Vpadiny *Russian*, Salt basin, wetlands
Sơn *Vietnamese*, Mountain
Sông *Vietnamese*, River
Sør- *Norwegian*, Southern
-spitze *German*, Peak
Star-á, -é *Czech*, Old
Star-aya, -oye, -yy, -yye *Russian*, Old
Stenó *Greek*, Strait
Step' *Russian*, Steppe
Štít *Slovak*, Peak
Stœng *Cambodian*, River
Stolovaya Strana *Russian*, Plateau
Stredné *Slovak*, Middle
Střední *Czech*, Middle
Stretto *Italian*, Strait
Su Anbari *Azerbaijani*, Reservoir
-suidō *Japanese*, Channel, strait
Sund *Swedish*, Sound, strait
Sungai *Indonesian, Malay*, River
Suu *Turkish*, River

T

Tal *Mongolian*, Plain
Tandavan' *Malagasy*, Mountain range
Tangorombohitr' *Malagasy*, Mountain massif
Tanjung *Indonesian, Malay*, Cape, point
Tao *Chinese*, Island
Ţaraq *Arabic*, Hills
Tassili *Berber*, Mountain, plateau
Tau *Russian*, Mountain(s)
Taungdan *Burmese*, Mountain range
Techníti Límni *Greek*, Reservoir
Tekojärvi *Finnish*, Reservoir
Teluk *Indonesian, Malay*, Bay
Tengah *Indonesian*, Middle
Terara *Amharic*, Mountain
Timur *Indonesian*, Eastern
-tind(an) *Norwegian*, Peak
Tizma(si) *Uzbek*, Mountain range, ridge
-tō *Japanese*, island
Tog *Somali*, Valley
-tōge *Japanese*, pass
Togh(i) *Uzbek*, mountain
Tônlé *Cambodian*, Lake
Top *Dutch*, Peak
-tunturi *Finnish*, Mountain
Ţurāq *Arabic*, hills
Tur'at *Arabic*, Channel

U

Udde(n) *Swedish*, Cape, point
'Uqlat *Arabic*, Well
Utara *Indonesian*, Northern
Uul *Mongolian*, Mountains

V

Väin *Estonian*, Strait
Vallée *French*, Valley
-vatn *Icelandic*, Lake
-vatnet *Norwegian*, Lake
Velayat *Turkmen*, Province
-vesi *Finnish*, Lake
Vestre- *Norwegian*, Western
-vidda *Norwegian*, Plateau
-vík *Icelandic*, Bay
-viken *Swedish*, Bay, inlet
Vinh *Vietnamese*, Bay
Víztárloló *Hungarian*, Reservoir
Vodaskhovishcha *Belarussian*, Reservoir
Vodokhranilishche (Vdkhr.) *Russian*, Reservoir
Vodoskhovyshche (Vdskh.) *Ukrainian*, Reservoir
Volcán *Spanish*, Volcano
Vostochn-o, yy *Russian*, Eastern
Vozvyshennost' *Russian*, Upland, plateau
Vozyera *Belarussian*, Lake
Vpadina *Russian*, Depression
Vrchovina *Czech*, Mountains
Vrha *Macedonian*, Peak
Vychodné *Slovak*, Eastern
Vysochyna *Ukrainian*, Upland
Vysočina *Czech*, Upland

W

Waadi *Somali*, Watercourse
Wādī *Arabic* Watercourse
Wāḩat, Wâhat *Arabic*, Oasis
Wald *German*, Forest
Wan *Chinese*, Bay
Way *Indonesian*, River
Webi *Somali*, River
Wenz *Amharic*, River
Wiloyat(i) *Uzbek*, Province
Wyżyna *Polish*, Upland
Wzgórza *Polish*, Upland
Wzvyshsha *Belarussian*, Upland

X

Xé *Laotian*, River
Xi *Chinese*, Stream

Y

-yama *Japanese*, Mountain
Yanchi *Chinese*, Salt lake
Yang *Chinese*, Bay
Yanhu *Chinese*, Salt lake
Yarımadası *Azerbaijani, Turkish*, Peninsula
Yaylası *Turkish*, Plateau
Yazovir *Bulgarian*, Reservoir
Yoma *Burmese*, Mountains
Ytre- *Norwegian*, Outer
Yü *Chinese*, Island
Yunhe *Chinese*, Canal
Yuzhn-o, -yy *Russian*, Southern

Z

-zaki *Japanese*, Cape, point
Zaliv *Bulgarian, Russian*, Bay
-zan *Japanese*, Mountain
Zangbo *Tibetan*, River
Zapadn-aya, -o, -yy *Russian*, Western
Západné *Slovak*, Western
Západní *Czech*, Western
Zatoka *Polish, Ukrainian*, Bay
-zee *Dutch*, Sea
Zemlya *Russian*, Earth, land
Zizhiqu *Chinese*, Autonomous region

25 de Agosto - Achar

INDEX

GLOSSARY OF ABBREVIATIONS

This glossary provides a comprehensive guide to the abbreviations used in this Atlas, and in the Index.

A
abbrev. abbreviated
AD Anno Domini
Afr. Afrikaans
Alb. Albanian
Amh. Amharic
anc. ancient
approx. approximately
Ar. Arabic
Arm. Armenian
ASEAN Association of South East Asian Nations
ASSR Autonomous Soviet Socialist Republic
Aust. Australian
Az. Azerbaijani
Azerb. Azerbaijan

B
Basq. Basque
BC before Christ
Bel. Belarussian
Ben. Bengali
Ber. Berber
B-H Bosnia-Herzegovina
bn billion (one thousand million)
BP British Petroleum
Bret. Breton
Brit. British
Bul. Bulgarian
Bur. Burmese

C
C central
C. Cape
°C degrees Centigrade
CACM Central America Common Market
Cam. Cambodian
Cant. Cantonese
CAR Central African Republic
Cast. Castilian
Cat. Catalan
CEEAC Central America Common Market
Chin. Chinese
CIS Commonwealth of Independent States
cm centimetre(s)
Cro. Croat
Cz. Czech
Czech Rep. Czech Republic

D
Dan. Danish
Div. Divehi
Dom. Rep. Dominican Republic
Dut. Dutch

E
E east
EC *see* EU
EEC *see* EU
ECOWAS Economic Community of West African States
ECU European Currency Unit
EMS European Monetary System
Eng. English
est estimated
Est. Estonian
EU European Union (previously European Community [EC], European Economic Community [EEC])

F
°F degrees Fahrenheit
Faer. Faeroese
Fij. Fijian
Fin. Finnish
Fr. French
Fris. Frisian
ft foot/feet
FYROM Former Yugoslav Republic of Macedonia

G
g gram(s)
Gael. Gaelic
Gal. Galician
GDP Gross Domestic Product (the total value of goods and services produced by a country excluding income from foreign countries)
Geor. Georgian
Ger. German
Gk Greek
GNP Gross National Product (the total value of goods and services produced by a country)

H
Heb. Hebrew
HEP hydro-electric power
Hind. Hindi
hist. historical
Hung. Hungarian

I
I. Island
Icel. Icelandic
in inch(es)
In. Inuit (Eskimo)
Ind. Indonesian
Intl International
Ir. Irish
Is Islands
It. Italian

J
Jap. Japanese

K
Kaz. Kazakh
kg kilogram(s)
Kir. Kirghiz
km kilometre(s)
km² square kilometre (singular)
Kor. Korean
Kurd. Kurdish

L
L. Lake
LAIA Latin American Integration Association
Lao. Laotian
Lapp. Lappish
Lat. Latin
Latv. Latvian
Liech. Liechtenstein
Lith. Lithuanian
Lux. Luxembourg

M
m million/metre(s)
Mac. Macedonian
Maced. Macedonia
Mal. Malay
Malg. Malagasy
Malt. Maltese
mi. mile(s)
Mong. Mongolian
Mt. Mountain
Mts Mountains

N
N north
NAFTA North American Free Trade Agreement
Nep. Nepali
Neth. Netherlands
Nic. Nicaraguan
Nor. Norwegian
NZ New Zealand

P
Pash. Pashtu
PNG Papua New Guinea
Pol. Polish
Poly. Polynesian
Port. Portuguese
prev. previously

R
Rep. Republic
Res. Reservoir
Rmsch Romansch
Rom. Romanian
Rus. Russian
Russ. Fed. Russian Federation

S
S south
SADC Southern Africa Development Community
SCr. Serbo-Croatian
Sinh. Sinhala
Slvk Slovak
Slvn. Slovene
Som. Somali
Sp. Spanish
St., St Saint
Strs Straits
Swa. Swahili
Swe. Swedish
Switz. Switzerland

T
Taj. Tajik
Th. Thai
Thai. Thailand
Tib. Tibetan
Turk. Turkish
Turkm. Turkmenistan

U
UAE United Arab Emirates
Uigh. Uighur
UK United Kingdom
Ukr. Ukrainian
UN United Nations
Urd. Urdu
US/USA United States of America
USSR Union of Soviet Socialist Republics
Uzb. Uzbek

V
var. variant
Vdkhr. Vodokhranilishche (Russian for reservoir)
Vdskh. Vodoskhovyshche (Ukrainian for reservoir)
Vtn. Vietnamese

W
W west
Wel. Welsh

Y
Yugo. Yugoslavia

◆ Country
● Country Capital
◇ Dependent Territory
○ Dependent Territory Capital

THIS INDEX LISTS all the placenames and features shown on the regional and continental maps in this Atlas. Placenames are referenced to the largest scale map on which they appear. The policy followed throughout the Atlas is to use the local spelling or local name at regional level; commonly-used English language names may occasionally be added (in parentheses) where this is an aid to identification e.g. Firenze (Florence). English names, where they exist, have been used for all international features e.g. oceans and country names; they are also used on the continental maps and in the introductory World section; these are then fully cross-referenced to the local names found on the regional maps. The index also contains commonly-found alternative names and variant spellings, which are also fully cross-referenced.

All main entry names are those of settlements unless otherwise indicated by the use of italicized definitions or representative symbols, which are keyed at the foot of each page.

1

115 *H9* **25 de Agosto** Florida, Uruguay 34°25′S 56°24′W
115 *H8* **25 de Mayo** Florida, Uruguay 34°11′S 56°20′W
25 de Mayo *see* Veinticinco de Mayo
215 *N5* **26 Bakı Komissarı** *Rus.* Imeni 26 Bakinskikh Komissarov. SE Azerbaijan 39°18′N 49°13′E
26 Baku Komissarlary Adyndaky *see* Uzboý
56 *E6* **100 Mile House** *var.* Hundred Mile House. British Columbia, SW Canada 51°39′N 121°19′W

A

Aa *see* Gauja
155 *D13* **Aabenraa** *var.* Åbenrå, *Ger.* Apenrade. Sønderjylland, SW Denmark 55°03′N 09°26′E
155 *D10* **Aabybro** *var.* Åbybro. Nordjylland, N Denmark 57°09′N 09°32′E
181 *A10* **Aachen** *Dut.* Aken, *Fr.* Aix-la-Chapelle; *anc.* Aquae Grani, Aquisgranum. Nordrhein-Westfalen, W Germany 50°47′N 06°06′E
Aaiún *see* Laâyoune
178 *J3* **Aakirkeby** *var.* Åkirkeby. Bornholm, E Denmark 55°04′N 14°56′E
218 *G1* **Aakkâr el Aatîga** Lebanon
155 *D11* **Aalborg** *var.* Ålborg, Ålborg-Nørresundby; *anc.* Alburgum. Nordjylland, N Denmark 57°03′N 09°56′E
Aalborg Bugt *see* Ålborg Bugt
179 *E12* **Aalen** Baden-Württemberg, S Germany 48°50′N 10°06′E
155 *D11* **Aalestrup** *var.* Ålestrup. Viborg, NW Denmark 56°42′N 09°31′E
162 *E6* **Aalsmeer** Noord-Holland, C Netherlands 52°17′N 04°43′E
163 *D10* **Aalst** *Fr.* Alost. Oost-Vlaanderen, C Belgium 50°57′N 04°03′E
162 *F7* **Aalst** *Fr.* Alost. Noord-Brabant, S Netherlands 51°23′N 05°29′E
162 *I7* **Aalten** Gelderland, E Netherlands 51°56′N 06°35′E
163 *C9* **Aalter** Oost-Vlaanderen, NW Belgium 51°05′N 03°28′E
Aanaar *see* Inari
Aanaarjävri *see* Inarijärvi
153 *H8* **Äänekoski** Länsi-Soumi, W Finland 62°34′N 25°45′E
216 *C5* **Aanjar** *var.* ‘Anjar. C Lebanon 33°45′N 35°56′E
138 *E7* **Aansluit** Northern Cape, N South Africa 26°41′S 22°24′E
218 *G2* **Aaqoûra** Lebanon
Aar *see* Aare
176 *D4* **Aarau** Aargau, N Switzerland 47°22′N 08°00′E
176 *C4* **Aarberg** Bern, W Switzerland 47°19′N 07°54′E
163 *C9* **Aardenburg** Zeeland, SW Netherlands 51°16′N 03°27′E
174 *B3* **Aare** *var.* Aar. ≈ W Switzerland
174 *B2* **Aargau** *Fr.* Argovie. ◆ *canton* N Switzerland
Aarhus *see* Århus
Aarlen *see* Arlon
155 *D11* **Aars** *var.* Års. Nordjylland, N Denmark 56°49′N 09°32′E
163 *E10* **Aarschot** Vlaams Brabant, C Belgium 50°59′N 04°50′E
Aassi, Nahr el *see* Orontes
Aat *see* Ath
239 *K7* **Aba** *prev.* Ngawa. Sichuan, C China 32°51′N 101°46′E
134 *J6* **Aba** Orientale, NE Dem. Rep. Congo 03°52′N 30°14′E
133 *K8* **Aba** Abia, S Nigeria 05°06′N 07°22′E
220 *D3* **Abā al Qazāz, Bi’r** *well* NW Saudi Arabia
Abā as Su‘ūd *see* Najrān
107 *H4* **Abacaxis, Rio** ≈ NW Brazil
Abaco Island *see* Great Abaco/Little Abaco
Abaco Island *see* Great Abaco, Bahamas
222 *D6* **Ābādān** Khūzestān, SW Iran 30°24′N 48°18′E
228 *D7* **Abadan** *prev.* Bezmein, *Rus.* Byuzmeyin. Ahal Welaýaty, C Turkmenistan 38°08′N 57°53′E
222 *F6* **Ābādeh** Fārs, C Iran 31°06′N 52°40′E
130 *G4* **Abadla** W Algeria 31°04′N 02°39′W
110 *E1* **Abaeté** Minas Gerais, SE Brazil 19°10′S 45°24′W
Abag Qi *see* Xin Hot
113 *H5* **Abaí** Caazapá, S Paraguay 25°58′S 55°54′W
Abai *see* Blue Nile
284 *B2* **Abaiang** *var.* Apia; *prev.* Charlotte Island. *atoll* Tungaru, W Kiribati
Abaj *see* Abay
133 *K7* **Abaji** Federal Capital District, C Nigeria 08°35′N 06°54′E
79 *J5* **Abajo Peak** ▲ Utah, W USA 37°51′N 109°28′W
133 *K8* **Abakaliki** Ebonyi, SE Nigeria 06°18′N 08°07′E
192 *G8* **Abakan** Respublika Khakasiya, S Russian Federation 53°43′N 91°25′E
227 *N1* **Abakan** ≈ S Russian Federation
133 *I4* **Abala** Tillabéri, SW Niger 14°55′N 03°27′E
133 *J4* **Abalak** Tahoua, C Niger 15°28′N 06°18′E
191 *H8* **Abalyanka** *Rus.* Obolyanka. ≈ N Belarus
192 *G7* **Aban** Krasnoyarskiy Kray, S Russian Federation 56°41′N 96°04′E
222 *G6* **Āb Anbār-e Kān Sorkh** Yazd, C Iran 31°22′N 53°38′E
105 *F8* **Abancay** Apurímac, SE Peru 13°37′S 72°52′W
173 *K6* **Abanilla** Murcia, Spain 38°12′N 1°03′W
284 *D1* **Abaokoro** *atoll* Tungaru, W Kiribati
Abariringa *see* Kanton
222 *G6* **Abarkū** Yazd, C Iran 31°07′N 53°17′E
252 *G3* **Abashiri** *var.* Abasiri. Hokkaidō, NE Japan 44°N 144°15′E
252 *G3* **Abashiri-gawa** ≈ Hokkaidō, NE Japan
252 *G3* **Abashiri-ko** ◎ Hokkaidō, NE Japan
Abasiri *see* Abashiri
87 *K8* **Abasolo** Chiapas, Mexico 16°48′N 92°10′W
85 *K5* **Abasolo** Guanajuato, Mexico
85 *M7* **Abasolo** Tamaulipas, C Mexico 24°02′N 98°18′W
87 *H8* **Abasolo del Valle** Veracruz-Llave, Mexico 17°46′N 95°30′W
280 *C4* **Abau** Central, S Papua New Guinea 10°04′S 148°34′E
227 *I4* **Abay** *var.* Abaj. Karaganda, C Kazakhstan 49°38′N 72°50′E
136 *D5* **Ābaya Hāyk’** *Eng.* Lake Margherita, *It.* Abbaia. ◎ SW Ethiopia
Ābay Wenz *see* Blue Nile
192 *G8* **Abaza** Respublika Khakasiya, S Russian Federation 52°40′N 89°58′E
Abbaia *see* Ābaya Hāyk’
222 *G8* **Āb Bārīk** Fārs, S Iran
175 *B10* **Abbasanta** Sardegna, Italy, C Mediterranean Sea 40°08′N 08°49′E
Abbatis Villa *see* Abbeville
72 *D4* **Abbaye, Point** *headland* Michigan, N USA 46°58′N 88°08′W
Abbazia *see* Opatija
Abbé, Lake *see* Abhe, Lake
165 *H2* **Abbeville** *anc.* Abbatis Villa. Somme, N France 50°06′N 01°50′E
69 *I3* **Abbeville** Alabama, S USA 31°35′N 85°16′W
69 *K2* **Abbeville** Georgia, SE USA 31°58′N 83°18′W
68 *C4* **Abbeville** Louisiana, S USA 29°58′N 92°08′W
67 *H8* **Abbeville** South Carolina, SE USA 34°10′N 82°23′W
157 *B10* **Abbeyfeale** *Ir.* Mainistir na Féile. SW Ireland 52°24′N 09°21′W
160 *A2* **Abbeyleix** Laois, Ireland 52°54′N 7°21′W
176 *E7* **Abbiategrasso** Lombardia, NW Italy 45°24′N 08°55′E
154 *J1* **Abborrträsk** Norrbotten, N Sweden 65°24′N 19°33′E
292 *F5* **Abbot Ice Shelf** *ice shelf* Antarctica
160 *G8* **Abbotsbury** UK 50°40′N 2°36′W
76 *C2* **Abbotsford** British Columbia, SW Canada 49°02′N 122°18′W
72 *C5* **Abbotsford** Wisconsin, N USA 44°57′N 90°19′W
231 *I4* **Abbottābād** North-West Frontier Province, NW Pakistan 34°12′N 73°15′E
191 *H9* **Abchuha** *Rus.* Obchuga. Minskaya Voblasts’, NW Belarus 54°30′N 29°22′E
162 *F6* **Abcoude** Utrecht, C Netherlands 52°17′N 04°59′E
216 *F2* **‘Abd al ‘Azīz, Jabal** ▲▲ NE Syria
221 *I9* **‘Abd al Kūrī** *island* SE Yemen
217 *N9* **‘Abd Allāh, Khawr** *bay* Iraq/Kuwait
197 *K3* **Abdulino** Orenburgskaya Oblast’, W Russian Federation 53°37′N 53°39′E
134 *F2* **Abéché** *var.* Abécher, Abeshr. Ouaddaï, SE Chad 13°49′N 20°49′E
Abécher *see* Abéché
223 *I5* **Āb-e Garm va Sard** Yazd, E Iran
133 *I2* **Abeïbara** Kidal, NE Mali 19°07′N 01°52′E
171 *H3* **Abejar** Castilla-León, N Spain 41°48′N 02°47′W
102 *B5* **Abejorral** Antioquia, W Colombia 05°48′N 75°28′W
Abela *see* Ávila
141 *K3* **Abel Erasmuspas** *pass* Limpopo, South Africa
Abellinum *see* Avellino
152 *C5* **Abeløya** *island* Kong Karls Land, E Svalbard
136 *D4* **Ābeltī** Oromo, C Ethiopia 08°09′N 37°31′E
284 *B3* **Abemama** *var.* Apamama; *prev.* Roger Simpson Island. *atoll* Tungaru, W Kiribati
261 *L7* **Abemaree** *var.* Abermarre. Papua, E Indonesia 07°03′S 140°10′E
181 *J13* **Abenberg** Bayern, Germany 10°58′N 49°15′E
132 *G8* **Abengourou** E Ivory Coast 06°42′N 03°27′W
172 *G5* **Abenójar** Castilla-La Manacha, Spain 38°53′N 4°21′W
Åbenrå *see* Aabenraa
179 *G12* **Abens** ≈ SE Germany
133 *I7* **Abeokuta** Ogun, SW Nigeria 07°07′N 03°21′E
160 *E4* **Aberaeron** SW Wales, UK 52°15′N 04°15′W
Aberbrothock *see* Arbroath
Abercorn *see* Mbala
74 *E3* **Abercrombie** North Dakota, N USA 46°25′N 96°42′W
160 *F6* **Aberdare** UK 51°43′N 3°27′W
160 *D3* **Aberdaron** UK 52°49′N 4°42′W
277 *L4* **Aberdeen** New South Wales, SE Australia 32°09′S 150°55′E
57 *M6* **Aberdeen** Saskatchewan, S Canada 52°15′N 106°19′W
138 *F9* **Aberdeen** Eastern Cape, S South Africa 32°30′S 24°00′E
156 *G5* **Aberdeen** *anc.* Devana. NE Scotland, UK 57°10′N 02°04′W
64 *E9* **Aberdeen** Maryland, NE USA 39°28′N 76°09′W
66 *C8* **Aberdeen** Mississippi, S USA 33°49′N 88°32′W
67 *J7* **Aberdeen** North Carolina, SE USA 35°07′N 79°25′W
74 *D4* **Aberdeen** South Dakota, N USA 45°27′N 98°29′W
76 *B4* **Aberdeen** Washington, NW USA 46°57′N 123°48′W
55 *I3* **Aberdeen Lake** ◎ Nunavut, NE Canada
160 *E3* **Aberdyfi** UK 52°33′N 4°02′W
159 *H1* **Aberfeldy** C Scotland, UK 56°38′N 03°49′W
160 *E2* **Aberffraw** UK 53°11′N 4°27′W
158 *G2* **Aberfoyle** UK 56°11′N 4°23′W
160 *G5* **Abergavenny** *anc.* Gobannium. SE Wales, UK 51°50′N 03°W
160 *E5* **Abergorlech** UK 51°59′N 4°04′W
Abergwaun *see* Fishguard
159 *I3* **Aberlady** UK 56°00′N 2°51′W
Abermarre *see* Abemaree
70 *D3* **Abernathy** Texas, SW USA 33°49′N 101°50′W
160 *E4* **Aberporth** UK 52°08′N 4°33′W
Abersee *see* Wolfgangsee
160 *E3* **Abersoch** UK 52°49′N 4°30′W
Abertawe *see* Swansea
Aberteifi *see* Cardigan
160 *G6* **Abertillery** UK 51°44′N 3°08′W
76 *D8* **Abert, Lake** ◎ Oregon, NW USA
160 *E4* **Aberystwyth** W Wales, UK 52°25′N 04°05′W
Abeshr *see* Abéché
Ábeskovvu *see* Abisko
176 *G9* **Abetone** Toscana, C Italy 44°09′N 10°42′E
195 *L4* **Abez’** Respublika Komi, NW Russian Federation 66°32′N 61°41′E
222 *E3* **Āb Garm** Qazvin, N Iran
220 *F7* **Abhā** ‘Asīr, SW Saudi Arabia 18°16′N 42°32′E
222 *E3* **Abhar** Zanjān, NW Iran 36°05′N 49°18′E
Abhé Bad/Ābhē Bid Hāyk’ *see* Abhe, Lake
136 *F3* **Abhe, Lake** *var.* Lake Abbé, *Amh.* Ābhē Bid Hāyk’, *Som.* Abhé Bad. ◎ Djibouti/Ethiopia
133 *J7* **Abia** ◆ *state* SE Nigeria
217 *K6* **‘Abīd ‘Alī** E Iraq 32°20′N 45°58′E
191 *I10* **Abidavichy** *Rus.* Obidovichi. Mahilyowskaya Voblasts’, E Belarus 53°20′N 30°25′E
132 *F8* **Abidjan** S Ivory Coast 05°19′N 04°01′W
Āb-i-Istāda *see* Īstādeh-ye Moqor, Āb-e-
218 *F6* **Abila** Jordan
75 *E9* **Abilene** Kansas, C USA 38°55′N 97°14′W
70 *F4* **Abilene** Texas, SW USA 32°27′N 99°44′W
Abindonia *see* Abingdon
161 *I6* **Abingdon** *anc.* Abindonia. S England, UK 51°41′N 01°17′W
73 *B10* **Abingdon** Illinois, N USA 40°48′N 90°24′W
67 *H5* **Abingdon** Virginia, NE USA 36°42′N 81°59′W
Abingdon *see* Pinta, Isla
65 *M3* **Abington** Massachusetts, USA 42°06′N 70°57′W
64 *F7* **Abington** Pennsylvania, NE USA 40°06′N 75°05′W
196 *F8* **Abinsk** Krasnodarskiy Kray, SW Russian Federation 44°51′N 38°12′E
79 *L6* **Abiquiu Reservoir** ⊞ New Mexico, SW USA
Āb-i-safed *see* Sefīd, Darya-ye
152 *F5* **Abisko** *Lapp.* Ábeskovvu. Norrbotten, N Sweden 68°21′N 18°50′E
51 *J8* **Abitibi** ≈ Ontario, S Canada
58 *F7* **Abitibi, Lac** ◎ Ontario/Québec, S Canada
136 *E2* **Ābīy Ādī** Tigray, N Ethiopia 13°40′N 38°57′E
190 *E5* **Abja-Paluoja** Viljandimaa, S Estonia 58°08′N 25°20′E
215 *I3* **Abkhazia** ◆ *autonomous republic* NW Georgia
173 *I8* **Abla** Andalucía, Spain 37°08′N 2°47′W
276 *E1* **Abminga** South Australia 26°07′S 134°49′E
129 *I4* **Abnûb** C Egypt 27°18′N 31°09′E
Åbo *see* Turku
232 *D4* **Abohar** Punjab, N India 30°11′N 74°14′E
132 *G8* **Aboisso** SE Ivory Coast 05°26′N 03°13′W
133 *N1* **Abo, Massif d’** ▲▲ NW Chad
133 *I7* **Abomey** S Benin 07°14′N 02°00′E
167 *M10* **Abondance** Rhône-Alpes, France 46°17′N 6°44′E
134 *C6* **Abong Mbang** Est, SE Cameroon 03°58′N 13°10′E
183 *G12* **Abony** Pest, C Hungary 47°10′N 20°00′E
134 *E3* **Abou-Déïa** Salamat, SE Chad 11°30′N 19°18′E
Aboudouhour *see* Abū aḍ Ḍuhūr
Abou Kémal *see* Abū Kamāl
Abou Simbel *see* Abu Simbel
215 *K5* **Abovyan** C Armenia 40°16′N 44°33′E
263 *K4* **Abra** ≈ Luzon, N Philippines
129 *N9* **Abrād, Wādī** *seasonal river* W Yemen
Abraham Bay *see* The Carlton
118 *C6* **Abranquil** Maule, Chile 35°45′S 71°33′W
172 *C4* **Abrantes** *var.* Abrántes. Santarém, C Portugal 39°28′N 08°12′W
112 *D3* **Abra Pampa** Jujuy, N Argentina 22°47′S 65°41′W
Abrashlare *see* Brezovo
111 *J3* **Abre Campo** Minas Gerais, Brazil 20°18′S 42°29′W
102 *C4* **Abrego** Norte de Santander, N Colombia 08°08′N 73°14′W
Abrene *see* Pytalovo
84 *C6* **Abreojos, Punta** *headland* W Mexico 26°43′N 113°36′W
169 *M3* **Abriés** Provence-Alpes-Côte d’Azur, France 44°47′N 6°56′E
115 *J4* **Abrojal** Rivera, Uruguay 31°45′S 55°01′W
191 *E11* **Abrova** *Rus.* Obrovo. Brestskaya Voblasts’, SW Belarus 52°30′N 25°34′E
188 *C7* **Abrud** *Ger.* Gross-Schlatten, *Hung.* Abrudbánya. Alba, SW Romania 46°16′N 23°05′E
Abrudbánya *see* Abrud
190 *C5* **Abruka** *island* SW Estonia
175 *F8* **Abruzzese, Appennino** ▲▲ C Italy
175 *G8* **Abruzzo** ◆ *region* C Italy
220 *F8* **‘Abs** *var.* Sūq ‘Abs. W Yemen 16°42′N 42°55′E
77 *J6* **Absaroka Range** ▲▲ Montana/Wyoming, NW USA
64 *G9* **Absecon** New Jersey, USA 39°26′N 74°30′W
215 *N4* **Abşeron Yarımadası** *Rus.* Apsheronskiy Poluostrov. *peninsula* E Azerbaijan
222 *F4* **Āb Shīrīn** Eşfahān, C Iran 34°17′N 51°17′E
217 *L7* **Abtān** SE Iraq 31°37′N 47°06′E
177 *I3* **Abtenau** Salzburg, NW Austria 47°33′N 13°21′E
232 *C7* **Ābu** Rājasthān, N India 24°41′N 72°50′E
250 *D5* **Abu** Yamaguchi, Honshū, SW Japan 34°30′N 131°26′E
129 *I6* **Abu Simbel** *headland* Egypt
216 *D3* **Abū aḍ Ḍuhūr** *Fr.* Aboudouhour. Idlib, NW Syria 35°30′N 37°00′E
221 *J4* **Abū al Abyaḍ** *island* C United Arab Emirates
216 *E6* **Abū al Ḥuṣayn, Khabrat** ◎ N Jordan
217 *I5* **Abū al Jīr** C Iraq 33°16′N 42°55′E
217 *M8* **Abū al Khaṣīb** *var.* Abul Khasib. SE Iraq 30°26′N 48°00′E
217 *K8* **Abū at Tubrah, Thaqb** *well* S Iraq
129 *H5* **Abu Balâs** ▲ SW Egypt 24°28′N 27°36′E
Abu Dhabi *see* Abū Ẓaby
217 *I5* **Abū Farūkh** C Iraq 33°06′N 43°18′E
134 *H3* **Abu Gabra** Southern Darfur, W Sudan 11°02′N 26°50′E
217 *H6* **Abū Ghār, Sha‘īb** *dry watercourse* S Iraq
129 *J8* **Abu Hamed** River Nile, N Sudan 19°32′N 33°20′E
216 *G4* **Abū Ḥardān** *var.* Hajîne. Dayr az Zawr, E Syria 34°45′N 40°49′E
217 *J5* **Abū Ḥāssawīyah** E Iraq 33°52′N 44°47′E
216 *E6* **Abū Ḥifnah, Wādī** *dry watercourse* N Jordan
133 *K7* **Abuja** ● (Nigeria) Federal Capital District, C Nigeria 09°04′N 07°28′E
217 *I6* **Abū Jahaf, Wādī** *dry watercourse* C Iraq
104 *E5* **Abujao, Río** ≈ E Peru
217 *J8* **Abū Jasrah** S Iraq 30°43′N 44°50′E
219 *F12* **Abū Jurdhān** Jordan
216 *G4* **Abū Kamāl** *Fr.* Abou Kémal. Dayr az Zawr, E Syria 34°29′N 40°56′E
260 *D5* **Abuki, Pegunungan** ▲▲ Sulawesi, C Indonesia
253 *D11* **Abukuma-gawa** ≈ Honshū, C Japan
253 *D11* **Abukuma-sanchi** ▲▲ Honshū, C Japan
Abula *see* Ávila
Abul Khasib *see* Abū al Khaṣīb
134 *F6* **Abumombazi** *var.* Abumonbazi. Equateur, N Dem. Rep. Congo 03°43′N 22°06′E
Abumonbazi *see* Abumombazi
106 *E6* **Abunã** Rondônia, W Brazil 09°41′S 65°20′W
106 *D7* **Abunã, Rio** *var.* Río Abuná. ≈ Bolivia/Brazil
216 *C7* **Abū Nuṣayr** *var.* Abu Nuseir. ‘Ammān, W Jordan 32°03′N 35°58′E
Abu Nuseir *see* Abū Nuṣayr
217 *J8* **Abū Qabr** S Iraq 31°03′N 44°34′E
216 *E4* **Abū Raḩbah, Jabal** ▲▲ C Syria
217 *I4* **Abū Rajāsh** N Iraq 34°47′N 43°36′E
217 *K8* **Abū Raqrāq, Ghadīr** *well* S Iraq
232 *C7* **Ābu Road** Rājasthān, N India 24°29′N 72°47′E
136 *E1* **Abu Shagara, Ras** *headland* NE Sudan 18°04′N 38°31′E
129 *I6* **Abu Simbel** *var.* Abou Simbel, Abū Sunbul. *ancient monument* S Egypt
217 *K8* **Abū Sudayrah** S Iraq 30°55′N 44°58′E
217 *J7* **Abū Şukhayr** S Iraq 31°54′N 44°27′E
Abū Sunbul *see* Abu Simbel
252 *D5* **Abuta** Hokkaidō, NE Japan 42°34′N 140°44′E
219 *G12* **Abū Ţarafah, Wādī** *dry watercourse* Jordan
278 *C9* **Abut Head** *headland* South Island, New Zealand 43°06′S 170°16′E
136 *A1* **Abu ‘Urug** Northern Kordofan, C Sudan 15°52′N 30°25′E
136 *E4* **Ābuyē Mēda** ▲ C Ethiopia 10°28′N 39°44′E
263 *M7* **Abuyog** Leyte, C Philippines 10°45′N 124°58′E
134 *J2* **Abu Zabad** Western Kordofan, C Sudan 12°21′N 29°16′E
Abū Ẓabī *see* Abū Ẓaby
221 *J4* **Abū Ẓaby** *var.* Abū Ẓabī, *Eng.* Abu Dhabi. ● (United Arab Emirates) Abū Ẓaby, C United Arab Emirates 24°30′N 54°20′E
129 *J3* **Abu Zenîma** E Egypt 29°01′N 33°08′E
155 *H9* **Åby** Östergötland, S Sweden 58°40′N 16°10′E
Abyaḍ, Al Baḩr al *see* White Nile
Åbybro *see* Aabybro
134 *I3* **Abyei** Western Kordofan, S Sudan 09°35′N 28°28′E
Abyla *see* Ávila
Abymes *see* les Abymes
Abyssinia *see* Ethiopia
Açâba *see* Assaba
102 *C6* **Acacias** Meta, C Colombia 03°59′N 73°46′W
55 *L3* **Cape Acadia** *headland* Nunavut, C Canada
111 *I3* **Acaiaca** Minas Gerais, Brazil 20°21′S 43°09′W
108 *C4* **Açailandia** Maranhão, E Brazil 04°51′S 47°26′W
Acaill *see* Achill Island
88 *C5* **Acajutla** Sonsonate, W El Salvador 13°34′N 89°50′W
172 *E7* **Acalà del Río** Andalucía, Spain 37°31′N 5°59′W
134 *A7* **Acalayong** SW Equatorial Guinea 01°05′N 09°34′E
86 *E6* **Acámbaro** Guanajuato, C Mexico 20°01′N 100°42′W
86 *E6* **Acambay** México, Mexico 19°57′N 99°51′W
102 *A4* **Acandí** Chocó, NW Colombia 08°32′N 77°20′W
170 *C3* **A Cañiza** *var.* La Cañiza. Galicia, NW Spain 42°13′N 08°16′W
86 *B3* **Acaponeta** Nayarit, C Mexico 22°30′N 105°21′W
85 *I8* **Acaponeta, Río de** ≈ C Mexico
86 *E8* **Acapulco** *var.* Acapulco de Juárez. Guerrero, S Mexico 16°51′N 99°53′W
Acapulco de Juárez *see* Acapulco
103 *J7* **Acarai Mountains** *Sp.* Serra Acaraí. ▲▲ Brazil/Guyana
Acaraí, Serra *see* Acarai Mountains
108 *G3* **Acaraú** Ceará, NE Brazil 04°35′S 37°37′W
102 *E3* **Acarigua** Portuguesa, N Venezuela 09°35′N 69°12′W
86 *F5* **Acatepec** Puebla, Mexico
86 *F7* **Acatepec** Puebla, Mexico 19°02′N 98°17′W
85 *M7* **Acatlán** Jalisco, W Mexico North America
87 *H7* **Acatlan** Oaxaca, Mexico 18°32′N 96°37′W
86 *F7* **Acatlán** *var.* Acatlán de Osorio. Puebla, S Mexico 18°12′N 98°02′W
86 *C5* **Acatlàn de Juàrez** Jalisco, Mexico 20°25′N 103°35′W
Acatlán de Osorio *see* Acatlán
87 *I7* **Acayucan** *var.* Acayucán. Veracruz-Llave, E Mexico 17°59′N 94°58′W
Accho *see* ‘Akko
67 *M4* **Accomac** Virginia, NE USA 37°43′N 75°41′N
168 *D6* **Accous** Aquitaine, France 42°59′N 0°36′W
133 *H8* **Accra** ● (Ghana)SE Ghana 05°33′N 00°15′W
159 *J9* **Accrington** NW England, UK 53°46′N 02°21′W
114 *B7* **Acebal** Santa Fe, C Argentina 33°14′S 60°50′W
115 *K4* **Acegua** Cerro Largo, Uruguay 31°48′S 54°18′E
115 *K4* **Aceguà** Cerro Largo, Uruguay 31°52′S 54°12′W
258 *C3* **Aceh** *off.* Daerah Istimewa Aceh, *var.* Acheen, Achin, Atchin, Atjeh. ◆ *autonomous district* NW Indonesia
175 *H9* **Acerenza** Basilicata, S Italy 40°46′N 15°51′E
184 *A8* **Acerra** *anc.* Acerrae. Campania, S Italy 40°56′N 14°22′E
Acerrae *see* Acerra
114 *B8* **Acevedo** Buenos Aires, Argentina 33°45′S 60°27′W
158 *D1* **Acha** UK 56°36′N 6°36′W
105 *H9* **Achacachi** La Paz, W Bolivia 16°01′S 68°44′W
102 *F4* **Achaguas** Apure, C Venezuela 07°46′N 68°14′W
158 *F3* **Achahoish** UK 55°57′N 5°34′W
234 *E4* **Achalpur** *prev.* Elichpur, Ellichpur. Mahārāshtra, C India 21°19′N 77°30′E
115 *H5* **Achar** Tacuarembó, C Uruguay 32°20′S 56°15′W

◆ Administrative Regions
✈ International Airport
▲ Mountain
▲▲ Mountain Range
Volcano
≈ River
◎ Lake
⊞ Reservoir

INDEX

◆ Country	◇ Dependent Territory	◆ Administrative Regions	▲ Mountain	▼ Volcano	☺ Lake
● Country Capital	○ Dependent Territory Capital	✈ International Airport	▲ Mountain Range	✎ River	☐ Reservoir

Al Faqa - Alturas
INDEX
309

Al Faqa *see* Faq‘
221 H8 **Al Farḍah** C Yemen 14°51′N 48°33′E
172 A5 **Alfarim** Setúbal, Portugal 38°28′N 9°10′W
171 H3 **Alfaro** La Rioja, N Spain 42°13′N 01°45′W
171 J3 **Alfarràs** Cataluña, NE Spain 41°50′N 00°34′E
Al Fāshir *see* El Fasher
Al Fashn *see* El Fashn
185 L4 **Alfatar** Silistra, NE Bulgaria 43°56′N 27°17′E
217 I3 **Al Fatḥah** C Iraq 35°06′N 43°34′E
217 H2 **Al Fatsī** N Iraq 36°04′N 42°39′E
221 H2 **Al Fāw** *var.* Fao. SE Iraq 29°55′N 48°26′E
Al Fayyūm *see* El Faiyûm
186 F7 **Alfeiós** *prev.* Alfiós; *anc.* Alpheius, Alpheus. ≈ S Greece
180 H7 **Alfeld** Niedersachsen, C Germany 51°58′N 09°49′E
110 E5 **Alfenas** Minas Gerais, Brazil 21°26′S 45°57′W
180 E5 **Alfhausen** Niedersachsen, Germany 7°57′N 52°30′E
Alfiós *see* Alfeiós
Alföld *see* Great Hungarian Plain
63 J5 **Alfred** Maine, NE USA 43°29′N 70°44′W
64 B2 **Alfred** New York, NE USA 42°15′N 77°47′W
111 L4 **Alfredo Chavez** Espírito Santo, Brazil 20°38′S 40°45′W
85 M9 **Alfredo M. Terrazas** San Luis Potosí, Mexico 21°28′N 98°51′W
113 K6 **Alfredo Vagner** Santa Catarina, S Brazil 27°40′S 49°22′W
159 K10 **Alfreton** UK 53°06′N 1°23′W
161 L8 **Alfriston** UK 50°48′N 0°09′E
154 H6 **Alfta** Gävleborg, C Sweden 61°20′N 16°05′E
217 N10 **Al Fuḥayḥīl** *var.* Fahaheel. SE Kuwait 29°01′N 48°05′E
217 H4 **Al Fuḥaymī** C Iraq 34°18′N 42°09′E
221 K4 **Al Fujayrah** *Eng.* Fujairah. Al Fujayrah, NE United Arab Emirates 25°09′N 56°18′E
221 K4 **Al Fujayrah** *Eng.* Fujairah. ✈ Al Fujayrah, NE United Arab Emirates 25°04′N 56°12′E
Al-Furāt *see* Euphrates
226 E4 **Alga** *Kaz.* Algha. Aktyubinsk, NW Kazakhstan 49°56′N 57°19′E
226 C3 **Algabas** Zapadnyy Kazakhstan, NW Kazakhstan 50°43′N 52°09′E
172 F9 **Algar** Andalucía, Spain 36°39′N 5°39′W
155 A8 **Ålgård** Rogaland, S Norway 58°45′N 05°52′E
170 C8 **Algarve** *cultural region* S Portugal
276 F2 **Algebuckina Bridge** South Australia 28°03′S 135°48′E
130 F1 **Algeciras** Andalucía, SW Spain 36°08′N 05°27′W
171 I6 **Algemesí** País Valenciano, E Spain 39°11′N 00°27′W
Al-Genain *see* El Geneina
131 I1 **Alger** *var.* Algiers, El Djazaïr, Al Jazair. ● (Algeria) N Algeria 36°47′N 02°58′E
131 H5 **Algeria** *off.* Democratic and Popular Republic of Algeria. ◆ *republic* N Africa
Algeria, Democratic and Popular Republic of *see* Algeria
Algha *see* Alga
216 C3 **Al Ghāb** ◎ NW Syria
221 K5 **Al Ghābah** *var.* Ghaba. C Oman 21°22′N 57°14′E
221 I8 **Al Ghayḍah** E Yemen 16°15′N 52°13′E
220 E3 **Al Ghazālah** Ḥā'il, NW Saudi Arabia 26°55′N 41°23′E
175 B9 **Alghero** Sardegna, Italy, C Mediterranean Sea 40°34′N 08°19′E
155 H11 **Älghult** Kronoberg, S Sweden 57°00′N 15°34′E
Al Ghurdaqah *see* Hurghada
Algiers *see* Alger
171 I6 **Alginet** País Valenciano, E Spain 39°16′N 00°28′W
138 F10 **Algoa Bay** *bay* S South Africa
141 H9 **Algoa Bay** *bay* Eastern Cape, South Africa
170 E8 **Algodonales** Andalucía, S Spain 36°54′N 05°24′W
170 G5 **Algodor** ≈ C Spain
173 H3 **Algodor** ≈ Castilla-La Manacha, Spain
Al Golea *see* El Goléa
72 E6 **Algoma** Wisconsin, N USA 44°41′N 87°24′W
74 G6 **Algona** Iowa, C USA 43°04′N 94°13′W
66 E6 **Algood** Tennessee, S USA 36°12′N 85°27′W
170 G1 **Algorta** País Vasco, N Spain 43°20′N 03°00′W
114 F5 **Algorta** Río Negro, W Uruguay 32°26′S 57°18′W
116 I3 **Algorta** Río Negro, Uruguay 32°30′S 59°18′E
Al Haba *see* Haba
217 H6 **Al Habbārīyah** S Iraq 32°16′N 42°12′E
Al Hadhar *see* Al Ḥaḍr
217 I3 **Al Ḥaḍr** *var.* Al Hadhar; *anc.* Hatra. NW Iraq 35°34′N 42°44′E
217 J9 **Al Ḥajarah** *desert* S Iraq
223 H10 **Al Ḥajār al Gharbī** ▲▲ N Oman
230 B10 **Al Ḥajar ash Sharqī** ▲▲ NE Oman
221 H8 **Al Hajarayn** C Yemen 15°29′N 48°24′E
216 E6 **Al Ḥamād** *desert* Jordan/Saudi Arabia
Al Hamad *see* Syrian Desert
128 B3 **Al Ḥamādah al Ḥamrā'** *var.* Al Ḥamrā'. *desert* NW Libya
168 B10 **Alhama de Aragón** Aragón, Spain 41°18′N 1°54′W
170 G8 **Alhama de Granada** Andalucía, S Spain 37°00′N 03°59′W
171 I7 **Alhama de Murcia** Murcia, SE Spain 37°51′N 01°25′W
78 D8 **Alhambra** California, W USA 34°08′N 118°06′W
217 J8 **Al Ḥammām** S Iraq 31°09′N 44°04′E
221 K5 **Al Ḥamrā'** NE Oman 23°07′N 57°23′E
Al Ḥamrā' *see* Al Ḥamādah al Ḥamrā'
220 F3 **Al Ḥamūdīyah** *spring/well* N Saudi Arabia27°05′N 44°24′E
220 E4 **Al Ḥanākīyah** Al Madīnah, W Saudi Arabia 24°55′N 40°31′E
217 L9 **Al Ḥanīyah** *escarpment* Iraq/Saudi Arabia
217 M8 **Al Hārithah** SE Iraq 30°43′N 47°44′E
218 G5 **Al Ḥārrah** Syria
216 E8 **Al Ḥarrah** *desert* NW Saudi Arabia
128 D4 **Al Harūj al Aswad** *desert* C Libya
Al Hasaifin *see* Al Ḥusayfīn
216 G2 **Al Ḥasakah** *var.* Al Hasijah, El Haseke, *Fr.* Hassetché. Al Ḥasakah, NE Syria 36°22′N 40°44′E
216 G2 **Al Ḥasakah** *off.* Muḥāfaẓat al Ḥasakah, *var.* Al Hasakah, Āl Hasakah, Hasakah, Hassakeh. ◈ *governorate* NE Syria
Al Hasakah *see* Al Ḥasakah
Al Hasakah *see* ‘Āmūdah
217 J6 **Al Hāshimīyah** C Iraq 32°24′N 44°39′E
219 F11 **Al Hāshimīyah** Jordan
216 C8 **Al Hāshimīyah** Ma‘ān, S Jordan 30°31′N 35°46′E
170 F9 **Alhaurín el Grande** Andalucía, S Spain 36°39′N 04°41′W
221 H9 **Al Ḥawrā** S Yemen 13°54′N 47°36′E
217 K6 **Al Ḥayy** *var.* Kut al Hai, Kūt al Ḥayy. E Iraq 32°11′N 46°03′E
216 C5 **Al Hījānah** *var.* Hejanah, Hijanah. Dimashq, W Syria 33°23′N 36°34′E
129 L6 **Al Ḥijāz** *Eng.* Hejaz. *coastal and highland region* NW Saudi Arabia
Al Hilbeh *see* ‘Ulayyānīyah, Bi'r al
217 J6 **Al Ḥillah** *var.* Hilla. C Iraq 32°28′N 44°29′E
217 J6 **Al Hindīyah** *var.* Hindiya. C Iraq 32°32′N 44°14′E
216 C8 **Al Ḥisā** Aṭ Ṭafīlah, W Jordan 30°49′N 35°58′E
218 G7 **Al Ḥiṣn** Jordan
130 G2 **Al-Hoceïma** *var.* al Hoceima, Al-Hoceima, Alhucemas; *prev.* Villa Sanjurjo. N Morocco 35°14′N 03°56′W
Alhucemas *see* Al-Hoceïma
170 G10 **Alhucemas, Peñon de** *island group* S Spain
220 F8 **Al Ḥudaydah** *Eng.* Hodeida. W Yemen 15°N 42°50′E
220 F8 **Al Ḥudaydah** *var.* Hodeida. ✈ W Yemen 14°45′N 43°01′E
220 F2 **Al Ḥudūd ash Shamālīyah** *var.* Minṭaqat al Ḥudūd ash Shamālīyah, *Eng.* Northern Border Region. ◈ *province* N Saudi Arabia
221 H4 **Al Hufūf** *var.* Hofuf. Ash Sharqīyah, NE Saudi Arabia 25°21′N 49°34′E
al-Hurma *see* Al Khurmah
221 K4 **Al Ḥusayfīn** *var.* Al Hasaifin. N Oman 24°33′N 56°33′E
219 F11 **Al Ḥusaynīyah** Jordan
216 C6 **Al Ḥuṣn** *var.* Husn. Irbid, N Jordan 32°29′N 35°53′E
217 K6 **‘Alī** E Iraq 32°43′N 45°21′E
170 F6 **Alia** Extremadura, W Spain 39°25′N 05°12′W
222 G6 **‘Alīābād** Yazd, C Iran 36°55′N 54°33′E
‘Alīābad *see* Qā'emshahr
171 I4 **Aliaga** Aragón, NE Spain 40°40′N 00°42′W
214 B6 **Aliağa** Izmır, W Turkey 38°49′N 26°59′E
Aliákmon *see* Aliákmonas
186 G3 **Aliákmonas** *prev.* Aliákmon; *anc.* Haliacmon. ≈ N Greece
217 L6 **‘Alī al Gharbī** E Iraq 32°28′N 46°42′E
217 J7 **‘Alī al Ḥassūnī** S Iraq 31°25′N 44°50′E
187 H6 **Alíartos** Stereá Ellás, C Greece 38°23′N 23°06′E
215 M5 **Äli-Bayramlī** *Rus.* Ali-Bayramly. SE Azerbaijan 39°57′N 48°54′E
Ali-Bayramly *see* Äli-Bayramlī
187 M2 **Alibey Barajī** ⊠ NW Turkey
187 M2 **Alibeykoy** İstanbul, Turkey 41°04′N 28°56′E
133 I6 **Alibori** ≈ N Benin
184 G3 **Alibunar** Vojvodina, NE Serbia 45°06′N 20°59′E
171 I7 **Alicante** *Cat.* Alacant, *Lat.* Lucentum. País Valenciano, SE Spain 38°21′N 00°29′W
171 I7 **Alicante** ◈ *province* País Valenciano, SE Spain
171 I7 **Alicante** ✈ Murcia, E Spain 38°21′N 00°29′W
141 I9 **Alice** Eastern Cape, South Africa 32°47′S 26°50′E
138 G9 **Alice** Eastern Cape, S South Africa 32°47′S 26°50′E
70 G9 **Alice** Texas, SW USA 27°45′N 98°06′W
138 F10 **Alicedale** Eastern Cape, S South Africa 33°19′S 26°05′E
117 H11 **Alice, Mount** *hill* West Falkland, Falkland Islands
175 I11 **Alice, Punta** *headland* S Italy 39°24′N 17°09′E
275 H5 **Alice Springs** Northern Territory, C Australia 23°42′S 133°52′E
66 C9 **Aliceville** Alabama, S USA 33°07′N 88°09′W
229 K7 **Alichur** SE Tajikistan 37°49′N 73°45′E
229 K8 **Alichuri Janubí, Qatorkŭhi** *Rus.* Yuzhno-Alichurskiy Khrebet. ▲▲ SE Tajikistan
229 K7 **Alichuri Shimolí, Qatorkŭhi** *Rus.* Severo-Alichurskiy Khrebet. ▲▲ SE Tajikistan
175 F11 **Alicudi, Isola** *island* Isole Eolie, S Italy
232 F5 **Alīgarh** Uttar Pradesh, N India 27°54′N 78°04′E
222 E5 **Alīgūdarz** Lorestān, W Iran 33°24′N 49°19′E
42 C8 **Alijos, Islas** *islets* California, SW USA
229 J10 **‘Alī Kbel** *Pash.* ‘Alī Khēl. Paktīkā, E Afghanistan 33°55′N 69°49′E
Ali Khel *see* ‘Alī Kheyl, Paktīā, Afghanistan
‘Alī Khēl *see* ‘Alī Kbel, Paktīkā, Afghanistan
231 H4 **‘Alī Kheyl** *var.* Ali Khel, Jajī. Paktīā, SE Afghanistan 33°55′N 69°46′E
221 J9 **Al Ikhwān** *island group* SE Yemen
Aliki *see* Alykí
135 D8 **Alima** ≈ C Congo
Al Imārāt al ‘Arabīyahal Muttaḥidah *see* United Arab Emirates
187 L8 **Alimía** *island* Dodekánisa, Greece, Aegean Sea
103 L7 **Alimimuni Piek** ▲ S Surinam 02°26′N 55°46′W
134 F5 **Alindao** Basse-Kotto, S Central African Republic 04°58′N 21°16′E
155 F10 **Alingsås** Västra Götaland, S Sweden 57°55′N 12°30′E
137 F8 **Alinjugul** *spring/well* E Kenya0°03′S 40°31′E
231 H7 **Alīpur** Punjab, E Pakistan 29°22′N 70°59′E
233 K6 **Alīpur Duār** West Bengal, NE India 26°28′N 89°25′E
62 C8 **Aliquippa** Pennsylvania, NE USA 40°36′N 80°15′W
136 G3 **‘Ali Sabieh** *var.* ‘Alī Sabīḥ. S Djibouti 11°07′N 42°44′E
‘Alī Sabīḥ *see* ‘Ali Sabieh
220 D1 **Al ‘Īsāwīyah** Al Jawf, NW Saudi Arabia 30°41′N 37°58′E
170 D6 **Aliseda** Extremadura, W Spain 39°25′N 06°42′W
167 J8 **Alise-Sainte-Reine** Bourgogne, France 47°32′N 4°29′E
217 J6 **Al Iskandarīyah** C Iraq 32°53′N 44°22′E
Al Iskandarīyah *see* Alexandria
193 M3 **Aliskerovo** Chukotskiy Avtonomnyy Okrug, NE Russian Federation 67°40′N 167°37′E
187 H2 **Alistráti** Kentrikí Makedonía, NE Greece 41°03′N 23°58′E
83 H8 **Alitak Bay** *bay* Kodiak Island, Alaska, USA
Al Ittiḥād *see* Madīnat ash Sha‘b
187 H6 **Alivéri** *var.* Alivérion. Évvoia, C Greece 38°24′N 24°02′E
Alivérion *see* Alivéri
Aliwal-Noord *see* Aliwal North
138 G8 **Aliwal North** *Afr.* Aliwal-Noord. Eastern Cape, SE South Africa 30°42′S 26°43′E
219 G12 **Al Jafr** Jordan
216 C8 **Al Jafr** Ma‘ān, S Jordan 30°18′N 36°13′E
128 G3 **Al Jaghbūb** NE Libya 29°45′N 24°31′E
217 M9 **Al Jahrā'** *var.* Al Jahrah, Jahra. C Kuwait 29°18′N 47°36′E
Al Jahrah *see* Al Jahrā'
Al Jamāhīrīyah al ‘Arabīyah al Lībīyah ash Sha‘bīyah al Ishtirākīy *see* Libya
220 E2 **Al Jarāwī** *spring/well* NW Saudi Arabia30°12′N 38°48′E
221 K6 **Al Jawārah** *oasis* SE Oman
220 E2 **Al Jawf** *off.* Jauf. Al Jawf, NW Saudi Arabia 29°51′N 39°49′E
220 E2 **Al Jawf** *var.* Minṭaqat al Jawf. ◈ *province* N Saudi Arabia
Al Jawlān *see* Golan Heights
Al Jazair *see* Alger
216 G2 **Al Jazīrah** *physical region* Iraq/Syria
172 B7 **Aljezur** Faro, S Portugal 37°18′N 08°49′W
217 J8 **Al Jīl** S Iraq 30°28′N 43°57′E
216 C7 **Al Jīzah** *var.* Jiza. ‘Ammān, N Jordan 31°42′N 35°57′E
Al Jīzah *see* El Gîza
Al Jubail *see* Al Jubayl
221 H3 **Al Jubayl** *var.* Al Jubail. Ash Sharqīyah, NE Saudi Arabia 27°N 49°36′E
172 E5 **Aljucén** Extremadura, Spain 39°02′N 6°20′W
221 I6 **Āl Juḥaysh, Qalamat** *well* SE Saudi Arabia
221 I4 **Al Jumaylīyah** N Qatar 25°37′N 51°05′E
Al Junaynah *see* El Geneina
170 C7 **Aljustrel** Beja, S Portugal 37°52′N 08°10′W
172 C7 **Aljustrel** Beja, Portugal 37°52′N 8°10′W
Al Kaba'ish *see* Al Chabā'ish
Al-Kadhimain *see* Al Kāẓimīyah
Al Kāf *see* El Kef
Alkal'a *see* Alcalá de Henares
78 F3 **Alkali Flat** *salt flat* Nevada, W USA
80 J2 **Alkali Lake** ◎ Nevada, USA
78 D1 **Alkali Lake** ◎ Nevada, W USA
221 L5 **Al Kāmil** NE Oman 22°14′N 58°15′E
216 C7 **Al Karak** *var.* El Kerak, Karak, Kerak; *anc.* Kir Moab, Kir of Moab. Al Karak, W Jordan 31°11′N 35°42′E
216 C7 **Al Karak** *off.* Muḥāfaẓat al Karak. ◈ *governorate* W Jordan
217 L5 **Al Karmashīyah** E Iraq 32°57′N 46°10′E
Al-Kashaniya *see* Al Qash‘ānīyah
Al-Kasr al-Kebir *see* Ksar-el-Kebir
217 J5 **Al Kāẓimīyah** *var.* Al-Kadhimain, Kadhimain. C Iraq 33°22′N 44°20′E
163 F10 **Alken** Limburg, NE Belgium 50°52′N 05°19′E
221 K4 **Al Khābūrah** *var.* Khabura. N Oman 23°57′N 57°06′E
218 H7 **Al Khālidīyah** Jordan
Al Khalīl *see* Hebron
217 J5 **Al Khāliṣ** C Iraq 33°51′N 44°33′E
Al Khaluf *see* Khalūf
Al Khārijah *see* El Khârga
220 G4 **Al Kharj** Ar Riyāḍ, C Saudi Arabia 24°12′N 47°12′E
221 J3 **Al Khaṣab** *var.* Khasab. N Oman 26°11′N 56°18′E
Al Khaur *see* Al Khawr
221 I4 **Al Khawr** *var.* Al Khaur, Al Khor. N Qatar 25°40′N 51°33′E
217 N10 **Al Khīrān** *var.* Al Khiran. SE Kuwait 28°34′N 48°21′E
221 J5 **Al Khīrān** *spring/well* NW Oman22°31′N 55°42′E
Al Khiyām *see* El Khiyam
Al-Khobar *see* Al Khubar
Al Khor *see* Al Khawr
221 H3 **Al Khubar** *var.* Al-Khobar. Ash Sharqīyah, NE Saudi Arabia 26°00′N 50°00′E
128 F6 **Al Khufrah** SE Libya 24°11′N 23°19′E
128 C2 **Al Khums** *var.* Homs, Khoms, Khums. NW Libya 32°39′N 14°16′E
221 H8 **Al Khuraybah** C Yemen 15°05′N 48°17′E
220 E5 **Al Khurmah** *var.* al-Hurma. Makkah, W Saudi Arabia 21°59′N 42°00′E
162 E5 **Alkmaar** Noord-Holland, NW Netherlands 52°37′N 04°45′E
217 J7 **Al Kūfah** *var.* Kufa. S Iraq 32°02′N 44°25′E
217 K6 **Al Kūt** *var.* Kūt al ‘Amārah, Kut al Imara. E Iraq 32°30′N 45°51′E
Al-Kuwait *see* Al Kuwayt
Al Kuwayr *see* Guwēr
217 M9 **Al Kuwayt** *var.* Al-Kuwait, *Eng.* Kuwait, Kuwait City; *prev.* Qurein. ● (Kuwait) E Kuwait 29°23′N 48°00′E
217 M9 **Al Kuwayt** ✈ C Kuwait 29°13′N 47°57′E
222 A7 **Al Labbah** *physical region* N Saudi Arabia
216 C3 **Al Lādhiqīyah** *Eng.* Latakia, *Fr.* Lattaquié; *anc.* Laodicea, Laodicea ad Mare. Al Lādhiqīyah, W Syria 35°31′N 35°47′E
216 C3 **Al Lādhiqīyah** *off.* Muḥāfaẓat al Ḷādhiqīyah, *var.* Al Lathqiyah, Latakia, Lattakia. ◈ *governorate* W Syria
63 K1 **Allagash River** ≈ Maine, NE USA
232 G7 **Allahābād** Uttar Pradesh, N India 25°27′N 81°50′E
223 I3 **Allāh Dāgh, Reshteh-ye** ▲▲ NE Iran
83 I4 **Allakaket** Alaska, USA 66°34′N 152°39′W
193 K6 **Allakh-Yun'** ≈ NE Russian Federation
57 M6 **Allan** Saskatchewan, S Canada 51°50′N 105°59′W
169 H2 **Allanches** Auvergne, France 45°14′N 2°56′E
141 I6 **Allandale** Free State, South Africa 28°50′S 27°08′E
256 C5 **Allanmyo** Magwe, C Myanmar (Burma) 19°25′N 95°13′E
138 G7 **Allanridge** Free State, C South Africa 27°45′S 26°40′E
141 I5 **Allanridge** Free State, South Africa 27°45′S 26°40′E
170 D3 **Allariz** Galicia, NW Spain 42°11′N 07°48′W
217 I7 **Al Laṣaf** *var.* Al Lussuf. S Iraq 31°38′N 43°16′E
Al Lathqiyah *see* Al Lādhiqīyah
66 F8 **Allatoona Lake** ⊠ Georgia, SE USA
138 G5 **Alldays** Limpopo, NE South Africa 22°39′S 29°04′E
141 J1 **Alldays** Limpopo, South Africa 22°40′S 29°06′E
Alle *see* Łyna
73 F8 **Allegan** Michigan, N USA 42°31′N 85°51′W
64 A3 **Allegany** New York, USA 42°05′N 78°30′W
64 A6 **Allegheny Mountains** ▲▲ NE USA
64 B3 **Allegheny Plateau** ▲▲ New York/Pennsylvania, NE USA
64 A3 **Allegheny Reservoir** ⊠ New York/Pennsylvania, NE USA
64 B4 **Allegheny River** ≈ New York/Pennsylvania, NE USA
169 I2 **Allégre** Auvergne, France 45°12′N 3°42′E
68 D4 **Allemands, Lac des** ◎ Louisiana, S USA
141 I5 **Allemanskraaldam** ⊠ Free State, South Africa
118 G10 **Allen** Río Negro, Argentina 38°58′S 67°50′W
71 H4 **Allen** Texas, SW USA 33°06′N 96°40′W
80 C2 **Allendale** California, USA 38°27′N 121°57′W
67 I9 **Allendale** South Carolina, SE USA 33°01′N 81°19′W
85 I5 **Allende** Chihuahua, Mexico 26°56′N 105°24′W
85 L4 **Allende** Coahuila de Zaragoza, NE Mexico 28°22′N 100°50′W
85 L6 **Allende** Nuevo León, NE Mexico 25°20′N 100°01′W
181 F10 **Allendorf** Hessen, Germany 8°50′N 50°41′E
181 E8 **Allendorf** Nordrhein-Westfalen, Germany 7°57′N 51°17′E
157 C8 **Allen, Lough** *Ir.* Loch Aillionn. ◎ NW Ireland
278 B13 **Allen, Mount** ▲ Stewart Island, Southland, SW New Zealand 47°05′S 167°49′E
177 K1 **Allensteig** Niederösterreich, N Austria 48°40′N 15°24′E
Allenstein *see* Olsztyn
80 D7 **Allensworth** California, USA 35°52′N 119°23′W
64 F6 **Allentown** Pennsylvania, NE USA 40°37′N 75°30′W
235 D9 **Alleppey** *var.* Alappuzha; *prev.* Alleppi. Kerala, SW India 09°30′N 76°22′E
Alleppi *see* Alleppey
173 L2 **Allepuz** Aragón, Spain 40°29′N 0°44′W
180 I5 **Aller** ≈ NW Germany
163 G11 **Alleur** Liège, E Belgium 50°40′N 05°33′E
169 L2 **Allevard** Rhône-Alpes, France 45°24′N 6°04′E
179 E14 **Allgäuer Alpen** ▲▲ Austria/Germany
159 J10 **Allgreave** UK 53°12′N 2°02′W
74 A7 **Alliance** Nebraska, C USA 42°08′N 102°54′W
73 J10 **Alliance** Ohio, N USA 40°55′N 81°06′W
164 G5 **Allier** ◈ *department* N France
217 I8 **Al Līfīyah** S Iraq 30°25′N 43°03′E
90 E8 **Alligator Pond** C Jamaica 17°52′N 77°34′W
67 M6 **Alligator River** ≈ North Carolina, SE USA
74 H6 **Allison** Iowa, C USA 42°45′N 92°48′W
62 C4 **Alliston** Ontario, S Canada 44°09′N 79°51′W
220 E6 **Al Līth** Makkah, SW Saudi Arabia 21°N 41°E
Al Liwā' *see* Līwā
159 H3 **Alloa** C Scotland, UK 56°07′N 03°49′W
166 G6 **Allonnes** Centre, France 48°20′N 1°40′E
169 M4 **Allos** Alpes-de-Haute-Provence, SE France 44°16′N 06°37′E
160 F6 **Alltwen** UK 51°42′N 3°51′W
Al Lubnān *see* Lebanon
220 F8 **Al Luḥayyah** W Yemen 15°44′N 42°45′E
62 F2 **Allumettes, Île des** *island* Québec, SE Canada
Al Lussuf *see* Al Laṣaf
177 J2 **Alm** ≈ N Austria
59 H7 **Alma** Québec, SE Canada 48°32′N 71°41′W
75 G12 **Alma** Arkansas, C USA 35°28′N 94°13′W
69 K3 **Alma** Georgia, SE USA 31°32′N 82°27′W
75 F9 **Alma** Kansas, C USA 39°01′N 96°17′W
72 G7 **Alma** Michigan, N USA 43°22′N 84°39′W
75 D8 **Alma** Nebraska, C USA 40°06′N 99°21′W
72 A6 **Alma** Wisconsin, N USA 44°21′N 91°54′W
217 I8 **Al Ma‘ānīyah** S Iraq 30°45′N 42°58′E
Alma-Ata *see* Almaty
Alma-Atinskaya Oblast' *see* Almaty
168 E9 **Almacellas** Cataluña, Spain 41°44′N 0°27′E
Almacellas *see* Almacelles
171 J3 **Almacelles** *var.* Almacellas. Cataluña, NE Spain 41°44′N 00°26′E
172 A5 **Almada** Setúbal, W Portugal 38°40′N 09°09′W
170 F6 **Almadén** Castilla-La Mancha, C Spain 38°47′N 04°50′W
172 E7 **Almadén de la Plata** Andalucía, Spain 37°52′N 6°04′W
120 G3 **Almadies, Pointe des** *headland* W Senegal 14°44′N 17°31′W
220 E4 **Al Madīnah** *Eng.* Medina. Al Madīnah, W Saudi Arabia 24°25′N 39°29′E
220 E4 **Al Madīnah** *off.* Minṭaqat al Madīnah. ◈ *province* W Saudi Arabia
216 C6 **Al Mafraq** *var.* Mafraq. Al Mafraq, N Jordan 32°20′N 36°12′E
216 C6 **Al Mafraq** *off.* Muḥāfaẓat al Mafraq. ◈ *governorate* NW Jordan
221 H8 **Al Maghārīm** C Yemen 15°00′N 47°49′E
170 G6 **Almagro** Castilla-La Mancha, C Spain 38°54′N 03°43′W
217 J6 **Al Maḥāwīl** *var.* Khān al Maḥāwīl. C Iraq 32°39′N 44°28′E
Al Mahdīyah *see* Mahdia
217 J5 **Al Maḥmūdīyah** *var.* Mahmudiya. C Iraq 33°04′N 44°22′E
213 I8 **Al Mahrah** ▲▲ E Yemen
220 G4 **Al Majma‘ah** Ar Riyāḍ, C Saudi Arabia 25°55′N 45°19′E
217 H7 **Al Makmīn** *well* S Iraq
217 H1 **Al Mālikīyah** *var.* Malkiye. Al Ḥasakah, N Syria 37°12′N 42°13′E
Almalyk *see* Olmaliq
Al Mamlakah *see* Morocco
Al Mamlaka al Urduniya al Hashemiyah *see* Jordan
221 I3 **Al Manāmah** *Eng.* Manama. ● (Bahrain) N Bahrain 26°13′N 50°33′E
216 G3 **Al Manāṣif** ▲▲ E Syria
78 C2 **Almanor, Lake** ⊠ California, W USA
171 I6 **Almansa** Castilla-La Mancha, C Spain 38°52′N 01°06′W
Al Manṣūrah *see* El Manṣûra
170 F2 **Almanza** Castilla-León, N Spain 42°40′N 05°01′W
170 F5 **Almanzor** ▲ W Spain 40°13′N 05°18′W
171 H8 **Almanzora** ≈ SE Spain
172 F3 **Pico de Almanzor** ▲ Castilla y León, Spain 40°15′N 5°18′W
217 I6 **Al Mardah** C Iraq 32°35′N 43°30′E
Al-Mariyya *see* Almería
128 E2 **Al Marj** *var.* Barka, *It.* Barce. NE Libya 32°30′N 20°54′E
168 A8 **Almarza** Castilla y León, Spain 41°57′N 2°28′W
216 F2 **Al Mashrafah** Ar Raqqah, N Syria 36°25′N 39°07′E
221 K4 **Al Maṣna‘ah** *var.* Al Muṣana‘a. NE Oman 23°45′N 57°38′E
Almassora *see* Almazora
Almatinskaya Oblast' *see* Almaty
227 K7 **Almaty** *var.* Alma-Ata. Almaty, SE Kazakhstan 43°19′N 76°55′E
227 K6 **Almaty** *off.* Almatinskaya Oblast', *Kaz.* Almaty Oblysy; *prev.* Alma-Atinskaya Oblast'. ◈ *province* SE Kazakhstan
227 K7 **Almaty** ✈ Almaty, SE Kazakhstan 43°15′N 76°57′E
Almaty Oblysy *see* Almaty
al-Mawailih *see* Al Muwayliḥ
217 I2 **Al Mawṣil** *Eng.* Mosul. N Iraq 36°21′N 43°08′E
216 G3 **Al Mayādīn** *var.* Mayadin, *Fr.* Meyadine. Dayr az Zawr, E Syria 35°00′N 40°31′E
217 L7 **Al Maymūnah** *var.* Maimuna. SE Iraq 31°43′N 46°55′E
220 F3 **Al Mayyāh** Ḥā'il, N Saudi Arabia 27°57′N 42°53′E
Al Ma'zam *see* Al Ma'zim
171 H4 **Almazán** Castilla-León, N Spain 41°29′N 02°31′W
219 F10 **Al Mazār al Janūbī** Jordan
221 K4 **Al Ma'zim** *var.* Al Ma'zam. NW Oman 23°22′N 56°16′E
193 I6 **Almaznyy** Respublika Sakha (Yakutiya), NE Russian Federation 62°19′N 114°14′E
171 J5 **Almazora** *Cat* Almassora. País Valenciano, E Spain 39°55′N 00°02′W
Al Mazra‘ *see* Al Mazra‘ah
216 B7 **Al Mazra‘ah** *var.* Al Mazra‘, Mazra‘a. Al Karak, W Jordan 31°18′N 35°32′E
181 F8 **Alme** Nordrhein-Westfalen, Germany 8°37′N 51°27′E
181 F8 **Alme** ≈ W Germany
172 D2 **Almeida** Guarda, N Portugal 40°43′N 06°53′W
170 C6 **Almeirim** Santarém, C Portugal 39°12′N 08°37′W
172 B4 **Almeirim** Santarém, Portugal 39°12′N 8°38′W
84 E7 **Almejas, Bahía de las** *bay* Baja California Sur, Mexico
162 I6 **Almelo** Overijssel, E Netherlands 52°22′N 06°42′E
171 I5 **Almenara** País Valenciano, E Spain 39°46′N 00°14′W
173 J6 **Almenaras** ▲ Castilla-La Manacha, Spain 38°33′N 2°26′W
171 H7 **Almenaras** ▲ S Spain 38°31′N 02°27′W
171 H3 **Almenar de Soria** Castilla-León, N Spain 41°41′N 02°12′W
170 E4 **Almendra, Embalse de** ⊠ Castilla-León, NW Spain
172 D5 **Almendral** Extremadura, Spain 38°37′N 6°49′W
170 E6 **Almendralejo** Extremadura, W Spain 38°41′N 06°25′W
118 D1 **Almendrillo** Coquimbo, Chile 32°03′S 70°38′W
162 F6 **Almere** *var.* Almere-stad. Flevoland, C Netherlands 52°22′N 05°12′E
162 F6 **Almere-Buiten** Flevoland, C Netherlands 52°24′N 05°15′E
162 F6 **Almere-Haven** Flevoland, C Netherlands 52°20′N 05°13′E
Almere-stad *see* Almere
171 H9 **Almería** *Ar.* Al-Mariyya; *anc.* Unci, *Lat.* Portus Magnus. Andalucía, S Spain 36°50′N 02°26′W
171 H8 **Almería** ◈ *province* Andalucía, S Spain
173 J9 **Almería, Golfo de** *GULF* Andalucía, Spain
171 H9 **Almería, Golfo de** *gulf* S Spain
197 K2 **Al'met'yevsk** Respublika Tatarstan, W Russian Federation 54°53′N 52°20′E
155 G11 **Älmhult** Kronoberg, S Sweden 56°32′N 14°10′E
173 H8 **Sierra de Almijara** ▲▲ Spain
Al Mīnā' *see* El Mina
170 F10 **Almina, Punta** *headland* Ceuta, Spain, N Africa 35°54′N 05°16′W
Al Minyā *see* El Minya
Al Miqdādīyah *see* Al Muqdādīyah
89 I9 **Almirante** Bocas del Toro, NW Panama 09°20′N 82°22′W
Almirós *see* Almyrós
220 E5 **Al Mislaḥ** *spring/well* W Saudi Arabia22°46′N 40°47′E
Almissa *see* Omiš
172 C7 **Almodôvar** *var.* Almodóvar. Beja, S Portugal 37°31′N 08°03′W
170 F6 **Almodóvar del Campo** Castilla-La Mancha, C Spain 38°43′N 04°10′W
171 H5 **Almodóvar del Pinar** Castilla-La Mancha, C Spain 39°44′N 01°55′W
172 C1 **Almofala** Viseu, Portugal 40°57′N 7°48′W
159 H2 **Almond** ≈ UK
73 H8 **Almont** Michigan, N USA 42°53′N 83°02′W
62 F3 **Almonte** Ontario, SE Canada 45°13′N 76°12′W
170 E8 **Almonte** Andalucía, S Spain 37°16′N 06°31′W
232 F5 **Almora** Uttaranchal, N India 29°36′N 79°40′E
170 F5 **Almorox** Castilla-La Mancha, C Spain 40°13′N 04°22′W
172 B3 **Almoster** Leiria, Portugal 39°51′N 8°27′W
221 H4 **Al Mubarraz** Ash Sharqīyah, E Saudi Arabia 25°28′N 49°34′E
Al Muḍaibī *see* Al Muḍaybī
216 C10 **Al Mudawwarah** Ma‘ān, SW Jordan 29°20′N 36°E
221 K5 **Al Muḍaybī** *var.* Al Muḍaibī. NE Oman 22°35′N 58°08′E
Almudébar *see* Almudévar
171 I3 **Almudévar** *var.* Almudébar. Aragón, NE Spain 42°03′N 00°34′W
221 H8 **Al Mukallā** *var.* Mukalla. SE Yemen 14°36′N 49°07′E
220 F9 **Al Mukhā** *Eng.* Mocha. SW Yemen 13°18′N 43°17′E
170 G9 **Almuñécar** Andalucía, S Spain 36°44′N 03°41′W
217 J4 **Al Muqdādīyah** *var.* Al Miqdādīyah. C Iraq 33°58′N 44°58′E
173 H6 **Almuradiel** Castilla-La Manacha, Spain 38°31′N 3°30′W
219 F12 **Al Murayghah** Jordan
220 E2 **Al Murayr** *spring/well* NW Saudi Arabia30°06′N 39°54′E
214 G5 **Almus** Tokat, N Turkey 40°22′N 36°54′E
Al Muṣana‘a *see* Al Maṣna‘ah
217 J6 **Al Musayyib** *var.* Musaiyib. C Iraq 32°47′N 44°20′E
217 K6 **Al Muwaffaqīyah** S Iraq 32°19′N 45°22′E
216 C7 **Al Muwaqqar** *var.* El Muwaqqar. ‘Ammān, W Jordan 31°49′N 36°06′E
220 C3 **Al Muwayliḥ** *var.* al-Mawailih. Tabūk, NW Saudi Arabia 27°39′N 35°33′E
186 G5 **Almyrós** *var.* Almirós. Thessalía, C Greece 39°11′N 22°45′E
187 I9 **Almyroú, Órmos** *bay* Kríti, Greece, E Mediterranean Sea
159 K4 **Aln** ≈ UK
Al Nūwfalīyah *see* An Nawfalīyah
159 K4 **Alnwick** N England, UK 55°27′N 01°44′W
Al Obayyid *see* El Obeid
Al Odaid *see* Al ‘Udayd
285 H10 **Alofi** ○ (Niue) W Niue 19°01′S 169°55′E
285 H10 **Alofi Bay** *bay* W Niue, C Pacific Ocean
284 A10 **Alofi, Île** *island* S Wallis and Futuna
284 A10 **Alofitai** Île Alofi, W Wallis and Futuna 14°21′S 178°03′W
Aloha State *see* Hawai‘i
Aloha State *see* Hawai‘i
190 E5 **Aloja** Limbaži, N Latvia 57°47′N 24°53′E
190 G7 **Alol'** Pskovskaya Oblast', Russian Federation
233 M5 **Along** Arunāchel Pradesh, NE India 28°15′N 94°56′E
187 H4 **Alónnisos** *island* Vóreioi Sporádes, Greece, Aegean Sea
170 F9 **Álora** Andalucía, S Spain 36°50′N 04°43′W
260 E8 **Alor, Kepulauan** *island group* E Indonesia
260 F8 **Alor, Pulau** *prev.* Ombai. *island* Kepulauan Alor, E Indonesia
260 E8 **Alor, Selat** *strait* Flores Sea/Savu Sea
258 D2 **Alor Setar** *var.* Alor Star, Alur Setar. Kedah, Peninsular Malaysia 06°06′N 100°23′E
Alor Star *see* Alor Setar
172 D7 **Alosno** Andalucía, Spain 37°33′N 7°07′W
Alost *see* Aalst
Alost *see* Aalst
232 D8 **Ālot** Madhya Pradesh, C India 23°56′N 75°40′E
280 D5 **Alotau** Milne Bay, SE Papua New Guinea 10°20′S 150°23′E
261 L8 **Alotip** Papua, E Indonesia 08°07′S 140°06′E
Al Oued *see* El Oued
172 G9 **Alozaina** Andalucía, Spain 36°43′N 4°51′W
172 C4 **Alpalhão** Portalegre, Portugal 39°25′N 7°37′W
80 D7 **Alpaugh** California, W USA 35°52′N 119°29′W
181 B8 **Alpen** Nordrhein-Westfalen, Germany 6°31′N 51°35′E
Alpen *see* Alps
72 H5 **Alpena** Michigan, N USA 45°04′N 83°27′W
111 K1 **Alpercata** Minas Gerais, Brazil 19°01′S 41°59′W
Alpes *see* Alps
165 K8 **Alpes-de-Haute-Provence** ◈ *department* SE France
165 L8 **Alpes-Maritimes** ◈ *department* SE France
275 J5 **Alpha** Queensland, E Australia 23°40′S 146°38′E
295 H6 **Alpha Cordillera** *var.* Alpha Ridge. *undersea feature* Arctic Ocean
Alpha Ridge *see* Alpha Cordillera
Alpheius *see* Alfeiós
163 F8 **Alphen** Noord-Brabant, S Netherlands 51°29′N 04°57′E
Alphen *see* Alphen aan den Rijn
162 E6 **Alphen aan den Rijn** *var.* Alphen. Zuid-Holland, C Netherlands 52°08′N 04°40′E
Alpheus *see* Alfeiós
Alpi *see* Alps
172 B4 **Alpiarça** Santarém, C Portugal 39°15′N 08°35′W
81 E13 **Alpine** California, USA 32°50′N 116°46′W
81 E10 **Alpine** California, USA 34°32′N 118°06′W
70 C6 **Alpine** Texas, SW USA 30°22′N 103°40′W
110 D4 **Alpinópolis** Minas Gerais, Brazil 20°52′S 46°23′W
176 D4 **Alpnach** Unterwalden, W Switzerland 46°56′N 08°17′E
174 C3 **Alps** *Fr.* Alpes, *Ger.* Alpen, *It.* Alpi. ▲▲ C Europe
221 J4 **Al Qābil** *var.* Qabil. N Oman 23°55′N 55°50′E
Al Qaḍārif *see* Gedaref
128 D2 **Al Qaddāḥīyah** N Libya 31°21′N 15°16′E
Al Qāhirah *see* Cairo
220 D2 **Al Qalībah** Tabūk, NW Saudi Arabia 28°29′N 37°40′E
216 G1 **Al Qāmishlī** *var.* Kamishli, Qamishly. Al Ḥasakah, NE Syria 37°N 41°E
216 D4 **Al Qaryatayn** *var.* Qaryatayn, *Fr.* Qariateïne. Ḥimṣ, C Syria 34°13′N 37°13′E
217 M9 **Al Qash‘ānīyah** *var.* Al-Kashaniya. NE Kuwait 29°59′N 47°42′E
220 F3 **Al Qaṣīm** *var.* Minṭaqat Qaṣīm, Qassim. ◈ *province* C Saudi Arabia
216 D3 **Al Qaṣr** Ḥimṣ, C Syria 35°06′N 37°39′E
Al Qaṣr *see* El Qaṣr
Al Qaṣrayn *see* Kasserine
221 H3 **Al Qaṭīf** Ash Sharqīyah, NE Saudi Arabia 26°27′N 50°01′E
216 C7 **Al Qaṭrānah** *var.* El Qatrani, Qatrana. Al Karak, W Jordan 31°14′N 36°03′E
128 C5 **Al Qaṭrūn** SW Libya 24°57′N 14°40′E
Al Qayrawān *see* Kairouan
Al-Qsar al-Kbir *see* Ksar-el-Kebir
Al Qubayyāt *see* Qoubaïyât
Al Quds/Al Quds ash Sharīf *see* Jerusalem
168 D8 **Alquézar** Aragón, Spain 42°10′N 0°01′E
216 C5 **Al Qunayṭirah** *var.* El Kuneitra, El Quneitra, Kuneitra, Qunaytra. Al Qunayṭirah, SW Syria 33°08′N 35°49′E
216 C5 **Al Qunayṭirah** *off.* Muḥāfaẓat al Qunayṭirah, *var.* El Q'unayṭirah, Qunaytirah, *Fr.* Kuneitra. ◈ *governorate* SW Syria
220 E6 **Al Qunfudhah** Makkah, SW Saudi Arabia 19°19′N 41°03′E
220 D1 **Al Qurayyāt** Al Jawf, NW Saudi Arabia 31°25′N 37°26′E
217 M8 **Al Qurnah** *var.* Kurna. SE Iraq 31°01′N 47°27′E
217 K8 **Al Quṣayr** S Iraq 30°36′N 45°52′E
216 C4 **Al Quṣayr** *var.* El Quseir, Quṣayr, *Fr.* Kousseir. Ḥimṣ, W Syria 34°36′N 36°36′E
Al Quṣayr *see* Quseir
216 C5 **Al Quṭayfah** *var.* Quṭayfah, Qutayfe, Quteife, *Fr.* Kouteifé. Dimashq, W Syria 33°44′N 36°33′E
220 G4 **Al Quwayīyah** Ar Riyāḍ, C Saudi Arabia 24°06′N 45°18′E
Al Quwayr *see* Guwēr
216 B9 **Al Quwayrah** *var.* El Quweira. Al 'Aqabah, SW Jordan 29°47′E 35°18′E
Al Rayyan *see* Ar Rayyān
Al Ruweis *see* Ar Ruways
155 D13 **Als** *Ger.* Alsen. *island* SW Denmark
165 K3 **Alsace** *Ger.* Elsass; *anc.* Alsatia. ◈ *region* NE France
159 J10 **Alsager** UK 53°06′N 2°18′W
57 K7 **Alsask** Saskatchewan, S Canada 51°24′N 109°55′W
168 B7 **Alsasua** Navarra, Spain 42°52′N 2°10′W
Alsasua *see* Altsasu
Alsatia *see* Alsace
181 A9 **Alsdorf** Nordrhein-Westfalen, W Germany 50°52′N 06°09′E
54 A3 **Alsek** ≈ Canada/USA
Alsen *see* Als
181 D12 **Alsenz** Rheinland-Pfalz, Germany 7°49′N 49°43′E
181 D12 **Alsenz** ≈ W Germany
181 G10 **Alsfeld** Hessen, C Germany 50°45′N 09°14′E
191 F11 **Al'shany** *Rus.* Ol'shany. Brestskaya Voblasts', SW Belarus 52°05′N 27°21′E
181 E12 **Alsheim** Rheinland-Pfalz, Germany 8°20′N 49°46′E
114 D8 **Alsina** Buenos Aires, Argentina 33°54′S 59°23′W
Alsókubin *see* Dolný Kubín
180 C6 **Alstätte** Nordrhein-Westfalen, Germany 6°55′N 52°07′E
159 J6 **Alston** UK 54°48′N 2°26′W
190 B6 **Alsunga** Kuldīga, W Latvia 56°59′N 21°31′E
Alt *see* Olt
152 G3 **Alta** *Fin.* Alattio. Finnmark, N Norway 69°58′N 23°17′E
74 F6 **Alta** Iowa, C USA 42°40′N 95°17′W
176 F4 **Altach** Vorarlberg, W Austria 47°22′N 09°39′E
152 G3 **Altaelva** *Lapp.* Álaheaieatnu. ≈ N Norway
152 G3 **Altafjorden** *fjord* NE Norwegian Sea
116 E3 **Alta Gracia** Córdoba, C Argentina 31°42′S 64°25′W
88 G7 **Alta Gracia** Rivas, SW Nicaragua 11°35′N 85°38′W
102 D2 **Altagracia** Zulia, NW Venezuela 10°44′N 71°30′W
102 G3 **Altagracia de Orituco** Guárico, N Venezuela 09°54′N 66°24′W
Altai *see* Altai Mountains
205 K4 **Altai Mountains** *var.* Altai, *Chin.* Altay Shan, *Rus* Altay. ▲▲ Asia/Europe
69 L2 **Altamaha River** ≈ Georgia, SE USA
114 D9 **Altamira** Buenos Aires, Argentina 34°40′S 59°22′W
107 K3 **Altamira** Pará, NE Brazil 03°13′S 52°15′W
102 B7 **Altamira** Huila, S Colombia 02°04′N 75°47′W
89 H8 **Altamira** Alajuela, N Costa Rica 10°25′N 84°21′W
85 N9 **Altamira** Tamaulipas, C Mexico 22°25′N 97°55′W
87 K8 **Altamirano** Chiapas, Mexico 16°44′N 92°02′W
114 D5 **Altamirano Norte** Entre Ríos, Argentina 32°04′S 59°11′W
114 D5 **Altamirano Sud** Entre Ríos, Argentina 32°05′S 59°10′W
73 C11 **Altamont** Illinois, N USA 39°03′N 88°45′W
75 F11 **Altamont** Kansas, C USA 37°11′N 95°18′W
76 C8 **Altamont** Oregon, NW USA 42°12′N 121°44′W
66 E6 **Altamont** Tennessee, S USA 35°28′N 85°42′W
69 M6 **Altamonte Springs** Florida, SE USA 28°39′N 81°22′W
175 H9 **Altamura** *anc.* Lupatia. Puglia, SE Italy 40°50′N 16°33′E
84 G7 **Altamura, Isla de** *island* Sinaloa, Mexico
Altan *see* Erdenehayrhan
239 I1 **Altanbulag** Dzavhan, N Mongolia 49°16′N 96°22′E
Altan-Ovoo *see* Tsenher
Altanteel *see* Dzereg
238 G1 **Altantsögts** *var.* Tsagaantüngi. Bayan-Ölgiy, NW Mongolia 49°06′N 90°26′E
244 F3 **Altan Xiret** Inner Mongolia, China 39°20′N 109°26′E
84 E2 **Altar** Sonora, NW Mexico 30°41′N 111°53′W
84 C1 **Altar, Desierto de** *var.* Sonoran Desert. *desert* Mexico/USA *see also* Sonoran Desert
Altar, Desierto de *see* Sonoran Desert
81 E8 **Alta Sierra** California, USA 35°44′N 118°33′W
80 D1 **Alta Sierra** California, USA 39°09′N 121°03′W
171 H5 **Alta, Sierra** ▲ N Spain 40°29′N 01°36′W
84 G7 **Altata** Sinaloa, C Mexico 24°40′N 107°54′W
80 J4 **Alta Toquima Wilderness** ▲▲ Nevada, USA
88 C3 **Alta Verapaz** *off.* Departamento de Alta Verapaz. ◈ *department* C Guatemala
Alta Verapaz, Departamento de *see* Alta Verapaz
175 G10 **Altavilla Silentia** Campania, S Italy 40°32′N 15°06′E
80 D3 **Altaville** California, USA 38°05′N 120°34′W
67 J5 **Altavista** Virginia, NE USA 37°06′N 79°17′W
238 G1 **Altay** Xinjiang Uygur Zizhiqu, NW China 47°51′N 88°06′E
238 G1 **Altay** *var.* Chihertey. Bayan-Ölgiy, W Mongolia 48°10′N 89°35′E
236 E3 **Altay** *prev.* Yösönbulag. Govĭ-Altay, W Mongolia 46°23′N 96°17′E
Altay Altai Mountains, Asia/Europe
Altay *see* Bayantes, Mongolia
192 G8 **Altay, Respublika** *var.* Gornyy Altay; *prev.* Gorno-Altayskaya Respublika. ◈ *autonomous republic* S Russian Federation
Altay Shan *see* Altai Mountains
192 F8 **Altayskiy Kray** ◈ *territory* S Russian Federation
Altbetsche *see* Bečej
179 F11 **Altdorf** Bayern, SE Germany 49°23′N 11°22′E
176 E4 **Altdorf** *var.* Altorf. Uri, C Switzerland 46°53′N 08°38′E
180 H1 **Alt Duvenstedt** Schleswig-Holstein, Germany 9°39′N 54°22′E
171 J7 **Altea** País Valenciano, E Spain 38°37′N 00°03′W
178 F5 **Alte Elde** ≈ N Germany
181 D8 **Altena** Nordrhein-Westfalen, Germany 7°40′N 51°18′E
180 I7 **Altenau** Niedersachsen, Germany 10°27′N 51°48′E
180 F7 **Altenbeken** Nordrhein-Westfalen, Germany 8°56′N 51°46′E
180 F2 **Altenbruch** Niedersachsen, Germany 8°46′N 53°49′E
181 G12 **Altenbuch** Bayern, Germany 9°24′N 49°50′E
179 G9 **Altenburg** Thüringen, E Germany 50°59′N 12°27′E
Altenburg *see* București, Romania
Altenburg Baia de Criș, Romania
181 F11 **Altenstadt** Hessen, Germany 8°57′N 50°17′E
178 I6 **Alte Oder** ≈ NE Germany
172 C4 **Alter do Chão** Portalegre, C Portugal 39°12′N 07°40′W
110 D5 **Alterosa** Minas Gerais, Brazil 21°15′S 46°08′W
Áltesjávri *see* Altevatnet
152 F4 **Altevatnet** *Lapp.* Áltesjávri. ◎ N Norway
181 G13 **Altheim** Baden-Württemberg, Germany 9°27′N 49°31′E
75 I13 **Altheimer** Arkansas, C USA 34°19′N 91°51′W
177 J4 **Althofen** Kärnten, S Austria 46°52′N 14°27′E
181 G14 **Althütte** Baden-Württemberg, Germany 9°34′N 48°55′E
185 I5 **Altimir** Vratsa, NW Bulgaria 43°33′N 23°48′E
214 F4 **Altınkaya Barajī** ⊠ N Turkey
217 J2 **Altin Köprü** *var.* Altun Kupri. N Iraq 35°50′N 44°10′E
110 C5 **Altinópolis** São Paulo, Brazil 21°02′S 47°22′W
214 C6 **Altıntaş** Kütahya, W Turkey 39°05′N 30°07′E
112 C1 **Altiplano** *physical region* W South America
Altkanischa *see* Kanjiža
165 K4 **Altkirch** Haut-Rhin, NE France 47°37′N 07°14′E
Altlublau *see* Stará L'ubovňa
178 F6 **Altmark** *cultural region* N Germany
180 J2 **Alt Meteln** Mecklenburg-Vorpommern, Germany 11°21′N 53°45′E
Altmoldowa *see* Moldova Veche
71 I5 **Alto** Texas, SW USA 31°39′N 95°04′W
117 C9 **Alto Río Senguer** Chubut, Argentina 45°12′S 70°54′E
170 C6 **Alto Alentejo** *physical region* S Portugal
107 K10 **Alto Araguaia** Mato Grosso, C Brazil 17°19′S 53°10′W
107 N2 **Alto Bonito** Pará, NE Brazil 01°48′S 46°18′W
139 K2 **Alto Molócuè** Zambézia, NE Mozambique 15°38′S 37°42′E
161 J7 **Alton** UK 51°08′N 0°59′W
73 B11 **Alton** Illinois, N USA 38°53′N 90°10′W
75 I11 **Alton** Missouri, C USA 36°41′N 91°25′W
55 J10 **Altona** Manitoba, S Canada 49°06′N 94°35′W
64 A6 **Altoona** Pennsylvania, NE USA 40°32′N 78°23′W
72 B6 **Altoona** Wisconsin, N USA 44°49′N 91°22′W
112 G2 **Alto Paraguay** *off.* Departamento del Alto Paraguay. ◈ *department* N Paraguay
Alto Paraguay, Departamento del *see* Alto Paraguay
109 C9 **Alto Paraíso de Goiás** Goiás, S Brazil 14°04′S 47°15′W
113 H4 **Alto Paraná** *off.* Departamento del Alto Paraná. ◈ *department* E Paraguay
Alto Paraná *see* Paraná
Alto Paraná, Departamento del *see* Alto Paraná
108 D6 **Alto Parnaíba** Maranhão, E Brazil 09°08′S 45°56′W
104 F7 **Alto Purús, Río** ≈ E Peru
Altorf *see* Altdorf
111 H5 **Alto Rio Doce** Minas Gerais, Brazil 21°02′S 43°25′W
111 L1 **Alto Rio Novo** Espírito Santo, Brazil 19°04′S 41°01′W
86 G6 **Altotonga** Veracruz-Llave, E Mexico 19°46′N 97°14′W
179 H12 **Altötting** Bayern, SE Germany 48°12′N 12°37′E
Altpasua *see* Stara Pazova
159 J10 **Altrincham** UK 53°23′N 2°21′W
171 H2 **Altsasu** *Cast.* Alsasua. Navarra, N Spain 42°54′N 02°10′W
Alt-Schwanenburg *see* Gulbene
Altsohl *see* Zvolen
88 E1 **Altun Ha** *ruins* Belize, N Belize
Altun Kupri *see* Altin Köprü
239 H5 **Altun Shan** ▲ C China 39°19′N 93°37′E
236 C5 **Altun Shan** *var.* Altyn Tagh. ▲▲ NW China
78 C1 **Alturas** California, W USA 41°28′N 120°32′W

◆ Country
● Country Capital
◇ Dependent Territory
○ Dependent Territory Capital
◈ Administrative Regions
✈ International Airport
▲ Mountain
▲▲ Mountain Range
⛰ Volcano
≈ River
◎ Lake
⊠ Reservoir

◆ Country	◇ Dependent Territory	◆ Administrative Regions	▲ Mountain	⊠ Volcano	⊕ Lake
● Country Capital	◇ Dependent Territory Capital	✈ International Airport	▲ Mountain Range	⚑ River	⊠ Reservoir

Ashland – Avellino

75 F8 **Ashland** Nebraska, C USA 41°01′N 96°21′W
73 I10 **Ashland** Ohio, N USA 40°52′N 82°19′W
76 B8 **Ashland** Oregon, NW USA 42°11′N 122°42′W
67 L4 **Ashland** Virginia, NE USA 37°45′N 77°28′W
72 B4 **Ashland** Wisconsin, N USA 46°34′N 90°54′W
66 D5 **Ashland City** Tennessee, S USA 36°16′N 87°05′W
277 L3 **Ashley** New South Wales, SE Australia 29°21′S 149°49′E
161 H2 **Ashley** UK 52°56′N 2°22′W
74 D4 **Ashley** North Dakota, N USA 46°00′N 99°22′W
289 J9 **Ashmore and Cartier Islands** ◇ Australian external territory E Indian Ocean
191 E9 **Ashmyany** Rus. Oshmyany. Hrodzyenskaya Voblasts', W Belarus 54°24′N 25°57′E
65 H3 **Ashokan Reservoir** ⊞ New York, NE USA
252 G4 **Ashoro** Hokkaidō, NE Japan 43°16′N 143°33′E
219 D9 **Ashqelon** Israel
216 B7 **Ashqelon** var. Ashkelon. Southern, C Israel 31°40′N 34°35′E
Ashraf see Behshahr
216 G2 **Ash Shadādah** var. Ash Shaddādah, Jisr ash Shadadi, Shaddādī, Shedadi, Tell Shedadi. Al Ḩasakah, NE Syria 36°00′N 40°42′E
Ash Shaddādah see Ash Shadādah
217 M8 **Ash Shāfī** E Iraq 30°49′N 47°30′E
217 I3 **Ash Shakk** var. Shaykh. C Iraq 35°15′N 43°27′E
Ash Shām see Dimashq
Ash Sham/Ash Shām see Dimashq
217 J7 **Ash Shāmīyah** var. Shamiya. C Iraq 31°56′N 44°37′E
217 L8 **Ash Shāmīyah** var. Al Bādiyah al Janūbīyah. desert S Iraq
217 J7 **Ash Shanāfīyah** var. Ash Shināfīyah. S Iraq 31°35′N 44°38′E
219 F12 **Ash Sharāh** dry watercourse Jordan
216 B8 **Ash Sharāh** var. Esh Sharā. ▲▲ W Jordan
221 J4 **Ash Shāriqah** Eng. Sharjah. Ash Shāriqah, NE United Arab Emirates 25°22′N 55°28′E
221 J4 **Ash Shāriqah** var. Sharjah. ✈ Ash Shāriqah, NE United Arab Emirates 25°19′N 55°37′E
220 C2 **Ash Sharmah** var. Šarma. Tabūk, NW Saudi Arabia 28°02′N 35°16′E
217 I3 **Ash Sharqāṭ** NW Iraq 35°31′N 43°15′E
221 I5 **Ash Sharqīyah** off. Al Minṭaqah ash Sharqīyah, Eng. Eastern Region. ⬖ province E Saudi Arabia
Ash Sharqīyah see Al 'Ubaylah
217 L7 **Ash Shaṭrah** var. Shatra. SE Iraq 31°26′N 46°10′E
216 B8 **Ash Shawbak** Ma'ān, W Jordan 30°32′N 35°34′E
216 E3 **Ash Shaykh Ibrāhīm** Ḩimş, C Syria 35°03′N 38°50′E
220 F9 **Ash Shaykh 'Uthmān** SW Yemen 12°53′N 45°00′E
221 H8 **Ash Shiḩr** SE Yemen 14°45′N 49°24′E
Ash Shināfīyah see Ash Shanāfīyah
221 J7 **Ash Shişar** var. Shisur. SW Oman 18°13′N 53°35′E
217 J9 **Ash Shubrūm** well S Iraq
128 C3 **Ash Shuwayrif** var. Ash Shwayrif. N Libya 29°54′N 14°16′E
Ash Shwayrif see Ash Shuwayrif
80 J7 **Ash Springs** Nevada, USA 37°28′N 115°12′W
73 J9 **Ashtabula** Ohio, N USA 41°54′N 80°46′W
74 E3 **Ashtabula, Lake** ⊞ North Dakota, N USA
215 K5 **Ashtarak** W Armenia 40°18′N 44°22′E
222 E4 **Āshtīān** var. Āshtiyān. Markazī, W Iran 34°23′N 49°55′E
Āshtiyān see Āshtīān
77 I7 **Ashton** Idaho, NW USA 44°04′N 111°27′W
159 J9 **Ashton-under-Lyne** UK 53°30′N 2°06′W
59 I5 **Ashuanipi Lake** ◎ Newfoundland and Labrador, E Canada
66 E8 **Ashville** Alabama, S USA 33°50′N 86°15′W
73 H11 **Ashville** Ohio, N USA 39°43′N 82°57′W
72 B4 **Ashwabay, Mount** hill Wisconsin, N USA
160 E8 **Ashwater** UK 50°44′N 4°17′W
264 **Asia** continent
261 I3 **Asia, Kepulauan** island group E Indonesia
118 D3 **Asiento Viejo** Región Metropolitana, Chile 33°04′S 70°59′W
234 I4 **Āsika** Orissa, E India 19°38′N 84°41′E
Asikaga see Ashikaga
153 H9 **Asikkala** var. Vääksy. Etelä-Suomi, S Finland 61°09′N 25°36′E
130 F2 **Asilah** N Morocco 35°32′N 06°04′W
'Aṣī, Nahr al see Orontes
175 A9 **Asinara, Isola** island W Italy
192 G7 **Asino** Tomskaya Oblast', C Russian Federation 56°56′N 86°02′E
191 I8 **Asintorf** Rus. Osintorf. Vitsyebskaya Voblasts', N Belarus 54°43′N 30°35′E
191 G10 **Asipovichy** Rus. Osipovichi. Mahilyowskaya Voblasts', C Belarus 53°18′N 28°40′E
220 F6 **'Asīr** off. Minṭaqat 'Asīr. ⬖ province SW Saudi Arabia
129 M7 **'Asīr** Eng. Asir. ▲▲ SW Saudi Arabia
'Asīr, Minṭaqat see 'Asīr
217 L7 **Askal** E Iraq 31°45′N 47°07′E
215 I5 **Aşkale** Erzurum, NE Turkey 39°56′N 40°39′E
189 J7 **Askaniya-Nova** Khersons'ka Oblast', S Ukraine 46°27′N 33°54′E
154 D7 **Asker** Akershus, S Norway 59°52′N 10°26′E
155 G8 **Askersund** Örebro, C Sweden 58°55′N 14°55′E
140 E4 **Askham** Northern Cape, South Africa 26°59′S 20°47′E
Askī Kalak see Eski Kaļak
155 E8 **Askim** Østfold, S Norway 59°15′N 11°10′E
197 L1 **Askino** Respublika Bashkortostan, W Russian Federation 56°07′N 56°39′E
186 F3 **Áskio** ▲▲ N Greece
232 G5 **Askot** Uttaranchal, N India 29°44′N 80°20′E
159 J7 **Askrigg** UK 54°18′N 2°05′W
154 A5 **Askvoll** Sogn Og Fjordane, S Norway 61°21′N 05°04′E
187 K5 **Aslan Burnu** headland W Turkey 38°44′N 26°43′E
214 G7 **Aslantaş Barajī** ⊞ S Turkey
231 I3 **Asmār** var. Bar Kunar. Kunar, E Afghanistan 34°59′N 71°29′E
136 E2 **Asmara** Amh. Āsmera. ● (Eritrea) C Eritrea 15°15′N 38°58′E
Āsmera see Asmara
155 G11 **Åsnen** ◎ S Sweden
186 G6 **Asopós** ≋ S Greece
261 K5 **Asori** Papua, E Indonesia 02°37′S 136°06′E
136 C4 **Āsosa** Benishangul, W Ethiopia 10°06′N 34°27′E
76 F5 **Asotin** Washington, NW USA 46°18′N 117°03′W
181 G14 **Aspach** Baden-Württemberg, Germany 9°24′N 48°58′E
Aspadana see Eşfahān
Aspang see Aspang Markt
177 L3 **Aspang Markt** var. Aspang. Niederösterreich, E Austria 47°34′N 16°06′E
159 I6 **Aspatria** UK 54°45′N 3°20′W
171 I7 **Aspe** País Valenciano, E Spain 38°21′N 00°43′W
79 K3 **Aspen** Colorado, C USA 39°12′N 106°49′W
70 F4 **Aspermont** Texas, SW USA 33°08′N 100°14′W
168 E6 **Aspet** Midi-Pyrénées, France 43°01′N 0°48′E
Asphaltites, Lacus see Dead Sea
Aspinwall see Colón
278 C11 **Aspiring, Mount** ▲ South Island, New Zealand 44°21′S 168°47′E
186 E4 **Asprókavos, Ákrotirio** headland Kérkyra, Iónioi Nísoi, Greece, C Mediterranean Sea 39°22′N 20°07′E
Aspropótamos see Achelóos
Assab see Aseb
132 D3 **Assaba** var. Açâba. ⬖ region S Mauritania
216 F3 **As Sabkhah** var. Sabkha. Ar Raqqah, NE Syria 35°30′N 35°54′E
217 K4 **As Sa'dīyah** E Iraq 34°11′N 45°09′E
Assad, Lake see Asad, Buḩayrat al
216 D5 **Aş Şafā** ▲ S Syria 33°03′N 37°07′E
216 D6 **Aş Şafāwī** Al Mafraq, N Jordan 37°12′N 32°30′E
Aş Şaff see El Şaff
216 F2 **Aş Şafīḩ** Al Ḩasakah, N Syria 36°42′N 40°12′E
Aş Şaḩrā' al Gharbīyah see Sahara el Gharbîya
Aş Şaḩrā' ash Sharqīyah see Sahara el Sharqîya
Assake see Asaka
As Salamīyah see Salamīyah
217 L10 **As Sālimī** var. Salemy. SW Kuwait 29°07′N 46°41′E
121 M4 **'Assal, Lac** ◎ C Djibouti
As Sallūm see Salûm
217 J8 **As Salmān** S Iraq 30°29′N 44°34′E
216 C7 **As Salṭ** var. Salt. Al Balqā', NW Jordan 32°03′N 35°44′E
221 I4 **As Salwā** var. Salwa, Salwah. S Qatar 24°44′N 50°52′E
233 L6 **Assam** ⬖ state NE India
Assamaka see Assamakka
133 J2 **Assamakka** var. Assamaka. Agadez, NW Niger 19°24′N 05°53′E
217 K7 **As Samāwah** var. Samawa. S Iraq 31°17′N 45°06′E
181 H13 **Assamstadt** Baden-Württemberg, Germany 9°41′N 49°26′E
As Saqia al Hamra see Saguia al Hamra
216 D3 **Aş Şā'rān** Ḩamāh, C Syria 35°15′N 37°28′E
216 C6 **Aş Şarīḩ** Irbid, N Jordan 32°31′N 35°54′E
67 M3 **Assateague Island** island Maryland, NE USA
216 G4 **As Sayyāl** var. Sayyāl. Dayr az Zawr, E Syria 34°37′N 40°52′E
163 D10 **Asse** Vlaams Brabant, C Belgium 50°55′N 04°12′E
163 B9 **Assebroek** West-Vlaanderen, NW Belgium 51°12′N 03°16′E
180 G2 **Assel** Niedersachsen, Germany 9°26′N 53°41′E
Asselle see Āsela
175 B10 **Assemini** Sardegna, Italy, C Mediterranean Sea 39°16′N 08°58′E
162 I4 **Assen** Drenthe, NE Netherlands 53°N 06°34′E
141 I3 **Assen** North-West, South Africa 25°11′S 27°36′E
163 C9 **Assenede** Oost-Vlaanderen, NW Belgium 51°15′N 03°43′E
155 D13 **Assens** Fyn, C Denmark 55°16′N 09°54′N
Asserien/Asserin see Aseri
163 F11 **Assesse** Namur, SE Belgium 50°22′N 05°01′E
221 K4 **As Sīb** var. Seeb. NE Oman 23°40′N 58°03′E
217 M8 **As Sībah** var. Sibah. SE Iraq 30°13′N 47°24′E
57 N8 **Assiniboia** Saskatchewan, S Canada 49°39′N 105°59′W
58 A5 **Assiniboine** ≋ Manitoba, S Canada
57 H7 **Assiniboine, Mount** ▲ Alberta/British Columbia, SW Canada 50°54′N 115°43′W
Assiout see Asyût
113 J3 **Assis** São Paulo, S Brazil 22°37′S 50°25′W
177 I10 **Assisi** Umbria, C Italy 43°04′N 12°36′E
Assiut see Asyût
Assling see Jesenice
Assouan see Aswân
Assu see Açu
Assuan see Aswân
217 M10 **Aş Şubayḩīyah** var. Subiyah. S Kuwait 28°55′N 47°57′E
221 H9 **As Sufāl** S Yemen 14°06′N 48°42′E
216 E4 **As Sukhnah** var. Sukhne, Fr. Soukhné. Ḩimş, C Syria 34°56′N 38°52′E
217 K3 **As Sulaymānīyah** var. Sulaimaniya, Kurd. Slēmānī. NE Iraq 35°32′N 45°27′E
220 G6 **As Sulayyil** Ar Riyāḑ, S Saudi Arabia 20°29′N 45°33′E
128 D3 **As Sulṭān** N Libya 31°01′N 17°21′E
222 D8 **Aş Şummān** desert N Saudi Arabia
220 G9 **Aş Şurrah** SW Yemen 13°56′N 46°23′E
216 G3 **Aş Şuwār** var. Şuwār. Dayr az Zawr, E Syria 35°31′N 40°37′E
216 C6 **As Suwaydā'** var. El Suweida, Es Suweida, Suweida, Fr. Soueida. As Suwaydā', SW Syria 32°43′N 36°33′E
216 D6 **As Suwaydā'** off. Muḩāfaẓat as Suwaydā', var. As Suwaydā, Suwaydá, Suweida. ⬖ governorate S Syria
221 L5 **As Suwayḩ** NE Oman 22°07′N 59°42′E
221 K4 **As Suwayq** var. Suwaik. N Oman 23°49′N 57°30′E
217 J6 **Aş Şuwayrah** var. Suwaira. E Iraq 32°57′N 44°47′E
As Suways see Suez
Asta Colonia see Asti
Astacus see İzmit
168 E5 **Astaffort** Aquitaine, France 44°04′N 0°40′E
187 K9 **Astakída** island SE Greece
227 I3 **Astana** prev. Akmola, Akmolinsk, Tselinograd, Aqmola. ● (Kazakhstan) Akmola, N Kazakhstan 51°13′N 71°25′E
222 E2 **Āstāneh** Gīlān, NW Iran 37°17′N 49°58′E
Asta Pompeia see Asti
215 M6 **Astara** S Azerbaijan 38°28′N 48°51′E
Astarabad see Gorgān
163 G8 **Asten** Noord-Brabant, SE Netherlands 51°24′N 05°45′E
Asterābād see Gorgān
176 D7 **Asti** anc. Asta Colonia, Asta Pompeia, Hasta Colonia, Hasta Pompeia. Piemonte, NW Italy 44°54′N 08°11′E
80 B1 **Asti** California, USA 38°46′N 122°58′W
Astigi see Ecija
Astipálaia see Astypálaia
230 E9 **Astola Island** island SW Pakistan
111 I5 **Astolfo Dutra** Minas Gerais, Brazil 21°19′S 42°52′W
52 G5 **Aston Bay** Coastal sea feature Nunavut, N Canada
161 J5 **Aston Clinton** UK 51°48′N 0°43′W
231 J3 **Astor** Jammu and Kashmir, NW India 35°21′N 74°52′E
170 E2 **Astorga** anc. Asturica Augusta. Castilla-León, N Spain 42°27′N 06°04′W
76 B5 **Astoria** Oregon, NW USA 46°12′N 123°50′W
42 C5 **Astoria Fan** undersea feature E Pacific Ocean
155 F12 **Åstorp** Skåne, S Sweden 56°09′N 12°57′E
Astrabad see Gorgān
197 J7 **Astrakhan'** Astrakhanskaya Oblast', SW Russian Federation 46°20′N 48°01′E
Astrakhan-Bazar see Cälilabad
197 I6 **Astrakhanskaya Oblast'** ⬖ province SW Russian Federation
154 J2 **Åsträsk** Västerbotten, N Sweden 64°38′N 20°00′E
Astrida see Butare
291 I13 **Astrid Ridge** undersea feature S Atlantic Ocean
280 B8 **Astrolabe, Récifs de l'** reef C New Caledonia
218 B2 **Astromerítis** N Cyprus 35°09′N 33°02′E
53 H7 **Astronomical Society Islands** island Nunavut, N Canada
186 G7 **Ástros** Pelopónnisos, S Greece 37°24′N 22°43′E
191 D10 **Astryna** Rus. Ostryna. Hrodzyenskaya Voblasts', W Belarus 53°44′N 24°33′E
170 E1 **Asturias** ⬖ autonomous community NW Spain
Asturias see Oviedo
Asturica Augusta see Astorga
187 K8 **Astypálaia** var. Astipálaia, It. Stampalia. island Kykládes, Greece, Aegean Sea
285 I1 **Āsuisui, Cape** cape Savai'i, W Samoa
293 J2 **Asuka** Japanese research station Antarctica
112 G5 **Asunción** ● (Paraguay) Central, S Paraguay 25°17′S 57°36′W
112 G5 **Asunción** ✈ Central, S Paraguay 25°15′S 57°40′W
84 C5 **Asunción, Bahía** bay Baja California Sur, Mexico
282 E2 **Asuncion Island** island N Northern Mariana Islands
88 D4 **Asunción Mita** Jutiapa, SE Guatemala 14°20′N 89°42′W
Asunción Nochixtlán see Nochixtlán
84 D3 **Asunción, Río** ≋ NW Mexico
155 H9 **Åsunden** ◎ S Sweden
190 G7 **Asvyeya** Rus. Osveya. Vitsyebskaya Voblasts', N Belarus 56°00′N 28°05′E
Aswa see Achwa
129 J6 **Aswân** var. Assouan, Assuan; anc. Syene. SE Egypt 24°03′N 32°59′E
129 I6 **Aswân High Dam** dam SE Egypt
129 I4 **Asyût** var. Assiout, Assiut, Siut; anc. Lycopolis. C Egypt 27°06′N 31°11′E
284 E9 **Ata** island Tongatapu Group, SW Tonga
116 B1 **Atacama** off. Región de Atacama. ⬖ region C Chile
Atacama Desert see Atacama, Desierto de
112 B3 **Atacama, Desierto de** Eng. Atacama Desert. desert N Chile
112 C5 **Atacama, Puna de** ▲▲ NW Argentina
Atacama, Región de see Atacama
112 B4 **Atacama, Salar de** salt lake N Chile
102 B6 **Ataco** Tolima, C Colombia 03°36′N 75°23′W
284 E5 **Atafu Atoll** island NW Tokelau
131 J7 **Atakor** ▲▲ SE Algeria
133 I6 **Atakora, Chaîne de l'** var. Atakora Mountains. ▲▲ N Benin
Atakora Mountains see Atakora, Chaîne de l'
133 H7 **Atakpamé** C Togo 07°32′N 01°08′E
228 D6 **Atakui** Ahal Welaýaty, C Turkmenistan 40°04′N 58°03′E
172 D3 **Atalaia** Castelo Branco, Portugal 40°03′N 7°26′W
172 D2 **Atalaia** Guarda, Portugal 40°40′N 7°02′W
172 A4 **Atalaia** Lisboa, Portugal 39°07′N 9°06′W
172 C4 **Atalaia** Santarém, Portugal 39°35′N 8°14′W
106 B4 **Atalaia do Norte** Amazonas, N Brazil 04°22′S 70°10′W
114 A3 **Ataliva** Santa Fe, Argentina 30°59′S 61°27′W
114 F10 **Atalya** Buenos Aires, Argentina 35°06′S 57°36′E
251 L4 **Atami** Shizuoka, Honshū, S Japan 35°07′N 139°04′E
228 G8 **Atamyrat** prev. Kerki. Lebap Welaýaty, E Turkmenistan 37°52′N 65°06′E
132 C1 **Aṭâr** Adrar, W Mauritania 20°30′N 13°03′W
86 E5 **Atarjea** Guanajuato, Mexico 21°23′N 99°52′W
236 E4 **Atas Bogd** ▲ SW Mongolia 43°17′N 96°47′E
80 B7 **Atascadero** California, W USA 35°28′N 120°40′W
70 G8 **Atascosa River** ≋ Texas, SW USA
227 I5 **Atasu** Karaganda, C Kazakhstan 48°42′N 71°38′E
227 I5 **Atasu** ≋ Karaganda, C Kazakhstan
284 D9 **Atata** island Tongatapu Group, S Tonga
214 C4 **Atatürk** ✈ (İstanbul) İstanbul, NW Turkey 40°58′N 28°50′E
215 H7 **Atatürk Barajī** ⊞ S Turkey
187 L8 **Atavýros** prev. Attávyros. ▲ Ródos, Dodekánisa, Greece, Aegean Sea 36°10′N 27°50′E
Atax see Aude
136 C1 **Atbara** var. 'Aṭbārah. River Nile, NE Sudan 17°42′N 34°E
136 C1 **Atbara** var. Nahr 'Aṭbarah. ≋ Eritrea/Sudan
'Aṭbārah/'Aṭbarah, Nahr see Atbara
227 H3 **Atbasar** Akmola, N Kazakhstan 51°49′N 68°18′E
At-Bashi see At-Bashy
229 L5 **At-Bashy** var. At-Bashi. Narynskaya Oblast', C Kyrgyzstan 41°07′N 75°48′E
68 D5 **Atchafalaya Bay** bay Louisiana, S USA
68 C4 **Atchafalaya River** ≋ Louisiana, S USA
Atchin see Aceh
75 F9 **Atchison** Kansas, C USA 39°31′N 95°07′W
133 H7 **Atebubu** C Ghana 07°47′N 01°00′W
171 H4 **Ateca** Aragón, NE Spain 41°20′N 01°49′W
86 F7 **Atenango del Río** Guerrero, Mexico 18°05′N 99°06′W
85 J9 **Atengo, Río** ≋ C Mexico
86 B5 **Atenguillo** Jalisco, Mexico 20°25′N 104°29′W
86 B5 **Atenguillo** ≋ Jalisco, Mexico
86 C6 **Atenquique** Jalisco, Mexico
Aternum see Pescara
175 G8 **Atessa** Abruzzo, C Italy 42°03′N 14°25′E
Ateste see Este
163 C11 **Ath** var. Aat. Hainaut, SW Belgium 50°38′N 03°47′E
57 I4 **Athabasca** Alberta, SW Canada 54°44′N 113°15′W
57 J3 **Athabasca** var. Athabaska. ≋ Alberta, SW Canada
54 G5 **Athabasca, Lake** ◎ Alberta/Saskatchewan, SW Canada
Athabaska see Athabasca
186 F4 **Athamánon** ▲▲ C Greece
158 D9 **Athboy** Ir. Baile Átha Buí. E Ireland 53°38′N 06°55′W
Athenae see Athína
158 A10 **Athenry** Ir. Baile Átha an Rí. W Ireland 53°19′N 08°49′W
66 D7 **Athens** Alabama, S USA 34°48′N 86°58′W
66 G8 **Athens** Georgia, SE USA 33°57′N 83°24′W
73 I11 **Athens** Ohio, N USA 39°20′N 82°06′W
64 D3 **Athens** Pennsylvania, USA 41°57′N 76°31′W
66 F6 **Athens** Tennessee, S USA 35°27′N 84°38′W
71 H5 **Athens** Texas, SW USA 32°12′N 95°51′W
Athens see Athína
186 E6 **Athéras, Akrotírio** cape Kefalloniá, Iónia Nísiá, Greece, C Mediterranean Sea
161 I3 **Atherstone** UK 52°34′N 1°33′W
275 J3 **Atherton** Queensland, NE Australia 17°18′S 145°29′E
159 J9 **Atherton** UK 53°31′N 2°30′W
137 E9 **Athi** ≋ S Kenya
218 C2 **Athiénou** SE Cyprus 35°01′N 33°31′E
187 H6 **Athína** Eng. Athens, prev. Athínai; anc. Athenae. ● (Greece) Attikí, C Greece 37°59′N 23°44′E
Athínai see Athína
167 J5 **Athis** Champagne-Ardenne, France 49°01′N 4°08′E
217 J7 **Athīyah** C Iraq 32°01′N 44°04′E
158 B9 **Athleague** Roscommon, Ireland 53°34′N 8°15′W
158 B9 **Athlone** Ir. Baile Átha Luain. C Ireland 53°25′N 07°56′W
234 D6 **Athni** Karnātaka, W India 16°43′N 75°04′E
278 B12 **Athol** Southland, South Island, New Zealand 45°30′S 168°35′E
65 K2 **Athol** Massachusetts, NE USA 42°35′N 72°11′W
187 I3 **Áthos** ▲ NE Greece 40°10′N 24°21′E
Athos, Mount see Ágion Óros
Ath Thawrah see Madīnat ath Thawrah
220 G3 **Ath Thumāmī** spring/well N Saudi Arabia 27°56′N 45°06′E
163 G14 **Athus** Luxembourg, SE Belgium 49°34′N 05°50′E
160 A2 **Athy** Ir. Baile Átha Í. C Ireland 52°59′N 06°59′W
134 E2 **Ati** Batha, C Chad 13°11′N 18°20′E
136 B6 **Atiak** NW Uganda 03°14′N 32°05′E
110 D8 **Atibaia** São Paulo, Brazil 23°07′S 46°34′W
105 F9 **Atico** Arequipa, SW Peru 16°13′S 73°13′W
170 G4 **Atienza** Castilla-La Mancha, C Spain 41°12′N 02°52′W
83 I3 **Atigun Pass** pass Alaska, USA
58 B6 **Atikokan** Ontario, S Canada 48°45′N 91°38′W
59 J5 **Atikonak Lac** ◎ Newfoundland and Labrador, E Canada
84 E2 **Atil** Sonora, Mexico 30°51′N 111°35′W
88 B4 **Atitlán, Lago de** ◎ W Guatemala
284 G7 **Atiu** island S Cook Islands
Atjeh see Aceh
193 L5 **Atka** Magadanskaya Oblast', E Russian Federation 60°45′N 151°35′E
82 D10 **Atka** Atka Island, Alaska, USA 52°12′N 174°14′W
82 D10 **Atka Island** island Aleutian Islands, Alaska, USA
197 I4 **Atkarsk** Saratovskaya Oblast', W Russian Federation 52°15′N 43°48′E
75 H12 **Atkins** Arkansas, C USA 35°15′N 92°56′W
74 D7 **Atkinson** Nebraska, C USA 42°31′N 98°57′W
261 H5 **Atkri** Papua, E Indonesia 01°45′S 130°04′E
86 E6 **Atlacomulco** var. Atlacomulco de Fabela. México, C Mexico 19°49′N 99°54′W
Atlacomulco de Fabela see Atlacomulco
66 F8 **Atlanta** state capital Georgia, SE USA 33°45′N 84°23′W
72 G6 **Atlanta** Michigan, N USA 45°01′N 84°07′W
71 J4 **Atlanta** Texas, SW USA 33°06′N 94°09′W
74 F7 **Atlantic** Iowa, C USA 41°24′N 95°00′W
67 M7 **Atlantic** North Carolina, SE USA 34°52′N 76°20′W
69 L4 **Atlantic Beach** Florida, SE USA 30°19′N 81°24′W
65 H9 **Atlantic City** New Jersey, NE USA 39°23′N 74°27′W
289 B13 **Atlantic-Indian Basin** undersea feature SW Indian Ocean
289 A12 **Atlantic-Indian Ridge** undersea feature SW Indian Ocean
102 B2 **Atlántico** off. Departamento del Atlántico. ⬖ province NW Colombia
290 E6 **Atlantic Ocean** ocean
Atlántico, Departamento del see Atlántico
89 H5 **Atlántico Norte, Región Autónoma** prev. Zelaya Norte. ⬖ autonomous region NE Nicaragua
89 H6 **Atlántico Sur, Región Autónoma** prev. Zelaya Sur. ⬖ autonomous region SE Nicaragua
88 G3 **Atlántida** ⬖ department N Honduras
133 M7 **Atlantika Mountains** ▲▲ E Nigeria
290 F5 **Atlantis Fracture Zone** tectonic feature NW Atlantic Ocean
131 H3 **Atlas Mountains** ▲▲ NW Africa
193 M7 **Atlasova, Ostrov** island SE Russian Federation
193 M6 **Atlasovo** Kamchatskaya Oblast', E Russian Federation 55°42′N 159°35′E
131 I2 **Atlas Saharien** var. Saharan Atlas. ▲▲ Algeria/Morocco
Atlas, Tell see Atlas Tellien
131 I2 **Atlas Tellien** Eng. Tell Atlas. ▲▲ N Algeria
54 B4 **Atlin** British Columbia, W Canada 59°31′N 133°41′W
54 B4 **Atlin Lake** ◎ British Columbia, W Canada
86 F7 **Atlixco** Puebla, S Mexico 18°55′N 98°26′W
86 E7 **Atlixtac** Guerrero, S Mexico North America
86 F8 **Atlixtac** Guerrero, Mexico 17°34′N 98°53′W
154 A5 **Atløyna** island S Norway
234 F6 **Ātmakūr** Andhra Pradesh, C India 15°52′N 78°42′E
68 G3 **Atmore** Alabama, S USA 31°01′N 87°29′W
179 G11 **Atmühl** ≋ S Germany
250 E5 **Atō** Yamaguchi, Honshū, SW Japan 34°24′N 131°42′E
112 C2 **Atocha** Potosí, S Bolivia 20°55′S 66°14′W
75 F13 **Atoka** Oklahoma, C USA 34°22′N 96°08′W
75 F13 **Atoka Lake** var. Atoka Reservoir. ⊞ Oklahoma, C USA
Atoka Reservoir see Atoka Lake
77 H7 **Atomic City** Idaho, NW USA 43°26′N 112°48′W
85 J7 **Atotonilco** Zacatecas, C Mexico 24°12′N 102°46′W
Atotonilco see Atotonilco el Alto
86 C5 **Atotonilco el Alto** var. Atotonilco. Jalisco, SW Mexico 20°35′N 102°30′W
132 F2 **Atouila, 'Erg** desert N Mali
86 E8 **Atoyac** var. Atoyac de Alvarez. Guerrero, S Mexico 17°12′N 100°28′W
86 C6 **Atoyac** Jalisco, Mexico
Atoyac de Alvarez see Atoyac
86 F7 **Atoyac, Río** ≋ S Mexico
83 H2 **Atqasuk** Alaska, USA 70°28′N 157°24′W
223 H2 **Atrak** Per. Rūd-e Atrak, Rus. Atrak, Atrek. ≋ Iran/Turkmenistan
Atrak see Atrak
Atrak, Rūd-e see Atrak
155 F10 **Ätran** ≋ S Sweden
102 B4 **Atrato, Río** ≋ NW Colombia
Atrek see Atrak
174 F7 **Atri** Abruzzi, C Italy 42°35′N 13°59′E
Atria see Adria
253 B13 **Atsugi** var. Atugi. Kanagawa, Honshū, S Japan 35°28′N 139°22′E
253 C10 **Atsumi** Yamagata, Honshū, C Japan 38°38′N 139°36′E
252 E4 **Atsuta** Hokkaidō, NE Japan 43°28′N 141°24′E
261 L6 **Atsy** Papua, E Indonesia 05°40′S 138°19′E
223 H10 **Aṭ Ṭaff** desert C United Arab Emirates
216 B8 **Aṭ Ṭafīlah** var. Et Tafila, Tafila. Aṭ Ṭafīlah, W Jordan 30°52′N 35°36′E
216 B8 **Aṭ Ṭafīlah** off. Muḩāfaẓat aṭ Ṭafīlah. ⬖ governorate W Jordan
220 E5 **Aṭ Ṭā'if** Makkah, W Saudi Arabia 21°50′N 40°50′E
Attaleia/Attalia see Antalya
66 E8 **Attalla** Alabama, S USA 34°01′N 86°05′W
214 E8 **At Tall al Abyaḑ** var. Tall al Abyaḑ, Tell Abyad, Fr. Tell Abiad. Ar Raqqah, N Syria 36°36′N 34°00′E
216 E5 **Aṭ Ṭanf** Ḩimş, S Syria 33°29′N 38°39′E
Attapu see Samakhixai
217 J7 **At Taqtaqānah** C Iraq 32°03′N 43°54′E
Attávyros see Atavýros
217 K10 **At Tawal** desert Iraq/Saudi Arabia
58 E5 **Attawapiskat** Ontario, C Canada 52°55′N 82°26′W
58 E5 **Attawapiskat** ≋ Ontario, S Canada
51 I8 **Attawapiskat Lake** ◎ Ontario, C Canada
At Taybé see Ţayyibah
181 E9 **Attendorn** Nordrhein-Westfalen, W Germany 51°07′N 07°54′E
177 I3 **Attersee** Salzburg, NW Austria 47°55′N 13°31′E
177 I3 **Attersee** ◎ N Austria
163 G13 **Attert** Luxembourg, SE Belgium 49°45′N 05°47′E
216 F3 **At Tibnī** var. Tibnī. Dayr az Zawr, NE Syria 35°30′N 39°48′E
73 E10 **Attica** Indiana, N USA 40°17′N 87°15′W
64 B1 **Attica** New York, NE USA 42°51′N 78°13′W
Attica see Attikí
167 J4 **Attigny** Champagne-Ardenne, France 49°29′N 4°35′E
187 H6 **Attikí** Eng. Attica. ⬖ region C Greece
65 L3 **Attleboro** Massachusetts, NE USA 41°55′N 71°15′W
177 J2 **Attnang** Oberösterreich, N Austria 48°02′N 13°44′E
231 I4 **Attock City** Punjab, E Pakistan 33°52′N 72°20′E
Attopeu see Samakhixai
71 I5 **Attoyac River** ≋ Texas, SW USA
82 A9 **Attu** Alaska, USA 54°54′N 173°12′E
217 M8 **Aṭ Ṭūbah** E Iraq 30°29′N 47°28′E
216 D10 **Aṭ Ṭubayq** plain Jordan/Saudi Arabia
82 A9 **Attu Island** island Aleutian Islands, Alaska, USA
235 F8 **Āttūr** Tamil Nādu, SE India 11°34′N 78°39′E
Aṭ Ṭūr see El Ṭûr
220 F9 **At Turbah** SW Yemen 12°42′N 43°31′E
118 G6 **Atuel, Río** ≋ C Argentina
Atugi see Atsugi
285 K5 **Atuona** Hiva Oa, NE French Polynesia 09°47′S 139°03′W
Aturus see Adour
155 H9 **Åtvidaberg** Östergötland, S Sweden 58°12′N 16°00′E
80 D4 **Atwater** California, W USA 37°19′N 120°33′W
81 D10 **Atwater** California, USA 34°07′N 118°15′W
74 G4 **Atwater** Minnesota, N USA 45°08′N 94°48′W
159 M8 **Atwick** UK 53°56′N 0°12′W
75 B9 **Atwood** Kansas, C USA 39°48′N 101°03′W
73 J10 **Atwood Lake** ⊞ Ohio, N USA
197 I2 **Atyashevo** Respublika Mordoviya, W Russian Federation 54°36′N 46°04′E
226 C5 **Atyrau** prev. Gur'yev. Atyrau, W Kazakhstan 47°07′N 51°56′E
226 C5 **Atyrau** off. Atyrauskaya Oblast', var.Kaz. Atyraū Oblysy; prev. Gur'yevskaya Oblast'. ⬖ province W Kazakhstan
Atyraū Oblysy/Atyrauskaya Oblast' see Atyrau
Atyrauskaya Oblast' see Atyrau
58 D8 **Au Sable Point** headland Michigan, USA 46°24′N 86°00′E
280 A1 **Aua Island** island NW Papua New Guinea
181 H13 **Aub** Bayern, Germany 10°04′N 49°33′E
165 J9 **Aubagne** anc. Albania. Bouches-du-Rhône, SE France 43°17′N 05°35′E
163 G14 **Aubange** Luxembourg, SE Belgium 49°35′N 05°49′E
165 I3 **Aube** ≋ N France
163 G10 **Aubel** Liège, E Belgium 50°45′N 05°49′E
165 J7 **Aubenas** Ardèche, E France 44°37′N 04°24′E
167 J3 **Aubenton** Picardie, France 49°50′N 4°12′E
167 K7 **Auberive** Champagne-Ardenne, France 47°47′N 5°03′E
168 E2 **Aubeterre-sur-Dronne** Poitou-Charentes, France 45°16′N 0°10′E
168 E5 **Aubiet** Midi-Pyrénées, France 43°39′N 0°48′E
165 H4 **Aubigny-sur-Nère** Cher, C France 47°30′N 02°27′E
165 H7 **Aubin** Aveyron, S France 44°30′N 02°18′E
169 H4 **Aubrac** Midi-Pyrénées, France 44°37′N 2°59′E
165 I7 **Aubrac, Monts d'** ▲▲ S France
79 H7 **Aubrey Cliffs** cliff Arizona, SW USA
52 C7 **Aubry Lake** ◎ Northwest Territories, NW Canada
69 I2 **Auburn** Alabama, S USA 32°37′N 85°30′W
80 D2 **Auburn** California, W USA 38°53′N 121°03′W
73 C11 **Auburn** Illinois, N USA 39°35′N 89°45′W
73 G9 **Auburn** Indiana, N USA 41°22′N 85°03′W
66 D5 **Auburn** Kentucky, S USA 36°52′N 86°42′W
63 J4 **Auburn** Maine, NE USA 44°05′N 70°15′W
65 K3 **Auburn** Massachusetts, NE USA 42°11′N 71°47′W
75 F8 **Auburn** Nebraska, C USA 40°23′N 95°50′W
64 D1 **Auburn** New York, NE USA 42°55′N 76°31′W
76 C4 **Auburn** Washington, NW USA 47°18′N 122°13′W
165 H6 **Aubusson** Creuse, C France 45°58′N 02°10′E
118 F9 **Auca Mahuida** Neuquén, Argentina 37°53′S 68°31′W
118 F9 **Sierra Auca Mahuída** ▲▲ Neuquén, Argentina
190 C7 **Auce** Ger. Autz. Dobele, SW Latvia 56°28′N 22°54′E
164 G8 **Auch** Lat. Augusta Auscorum, Elimberrum. Gers, S France 43°40′N 00°37′E
133 J7 **Auchi** Edo, S Nigeria 07°01′N 06°17′E
158 G4 **Auchinleck** UK 55°28′N 4°18′W
159 H2 **Auchterarder** UK 56°18′N 3°42′W
159 I2 **Auchtermuchty** UK 56°17′N 3°13′W
69 J4 **Aucilla River** ≋ Florida/Georgia, SE USA
278 G3 **Auckland** Auckland, North Island, New Zealand 36°53′S 174°46′E
278 G3 **Auckland** off. Auckland Region. ⬖ region North Island, New Zealand
278 G4 **Auckland** ✈ Auckland, North Island, New Zealand 37°01′S 174°49′E
286 E9 **Auckland Islands** island group S New Zealand
Auckland Region see Auckland
118 D1 **Aucó** Coquimbo, Chile 31°29′S 71°06′W
165 H9 **Aude** ⬖ department S France
165 H9 **Aude** anc. Atax. ≋ S France
Audenarde see Oudenaarde
Audern see Audru
164 D4 **Audierne** Finistère, NW France 48°01′N 04°30′W
164 D4 **Audierne, Baie d'** bay NW France
165 K4 **Audincourt** Doubs, E France 47°29′N 06°50′E
161 H2 **Audley** UK 53°03′N 2°18′W
190 D4 **Audru** Ger. Audern. Pärnumaa, SW Estonia 58°24′N 24°22′E
74 G7 **Audubon** Iowa, C USA 41°44′N 94°56′W
167 L4 **Audun-le-Roman** Lorraine, France 49°22′N 5°53′E
167 L4 **Audun-le-Tiche** Lorraine, France 49°28′N 5°57′E
181 E9 **Aue** Nordrhein-Westfalen, Germany 8°18′N 51°03′E
179 H9 **Aue** Sachsen, E Germany 50°35′N 12°42′E
180 F5 **Aue** ≋ NW Germany
179 G10 **Auerbach** Bayern, SE Germany 49°41′N 11°41′E
179 G9 **Auerbach** Sachsen, E Germany 50°30′N 12°24′E
176 E5 **Auererrhein** ≋ SW Switzerland
179 H9 **Auersberg** ▲ E Germany 50°30′N 12°42′E
277 J1 **Augathella** Queensland, E Australia 25°54′S 146°38′E
158 C7 **Augher** UK 54°26′N 7°09′W
158 C7 **Aughnacloy** UK 54°25′N 6°58′W
160 B3 **Aughrim** Wicklow, Ireland 52°51′N 6°20′W
73 G9 **Auglaize River** ≋ Ohio, N USA
140 E6 **Augrabies** Northern Cape, South Africa 28°38′S 20°21′E
138 D8 **Augrabies Falls** waterfall W South Africa
72 H6 **Au Gres River** ≋ Michigan, N USA
Augsbourg see Augsburg
179 F12 **Augsburg** Fr. Augsbourg; anc. Augusta Vindelicorum. Bayern, S Germany 48°22′N 10°54′E
274 D8 **Augusta** Western Australia 34°18′S 115°10′E
175 G13 **Augusta** It. Agosta. Sicilia, Italy, C Mediterranean Sea 37°14′N 15°14′E
75 I12 **Augusta** Arkansas, C USA 35°16′N 91°21′W
67 H9 **Augusta** Georgia, SE USA 33°29′N 81°58′W
75 E10 **Augusta** Kansas, C USA 37°40′N 96°59′W
63 K4 **Augusta** state capital Maine, NE USA 44°20′N 69°44′W
77 H4 **Augusta** Montana, NW USA 47°28′N 112°23′W
Augusta see London
Augusta Auscorum see Auch
Augusta Emerita see Mérida
Augusta Praetoria see Aosta
Augusta Suessionum see Soissons
Augusta Trajana see Stara Zagora
Augusta Treverorum see Trier
Augusta Vangionum see Worms
Augusta Vindelicorum see Augsburg
155 D13 **Augustenborg** Ger. Augustenburg. Sønderjylland, SW Denmark 54°57′N 09°53′E
Augustenburg see Augustenborg
83 I7 **Augustine Island** island Alaska, USA
62 F1 **Augustines, Lac des** ◎ Québec, SE Canada
Augustobona Tricassium see Troyes
Augustodunum see Autun
Augustodurum see Bayeux
Augustoritum Lemovicensium see Limoges
182 I4 **Augustów** Rus. Avgustov. Podlaskie, NE Poland 53°52′N 22°58′E
Augustow Canal see Augustowski, Kanał
182 I4 **Augustowski, Kanał** Eng. Augustow Canal, Rus. Avgustovskiy Kanal. canal NE Poland
274 D5 **Augustus, Mount** ▲ Western Australia 24°42′S 117°42′E
281 J2 **Auki** Malaita, N Solomon Islands 08°48′S 160°45′E
53 K9 **Aukpar River** ≋ Nunavut, NE Canada
180 H1 **Aukrug** Schleswig-Holstein, Germany 9°47′N 54°05′E
67 L5 **Aulander** North Carolina, SE USA 36°15′N 77°16′W
274 E4 **Auld, Lake** salt lake C Western Australia
Aulie Ata see Taraz
Aulie Ata/Auliye-Ata see Taraz
Auliye-Ata see Taraz
226 G3 **Auliyekol'** prev. Semiozernoye. Kostanay, N Kazakhstan 52°22′N 64°06′E
176 F8 **Aulla** Toscana, C Italy 44°15′N 10°00′E
166 D10 **Aulnay** Poitou-Charentes, France 46°01′N 0°21′W
164 D4 **Aulne** ≋ NW France
167 I3 **Aulnoye-Aymeries** Nord-Pas-de-Calais, France 50°12′N 3°50′E
Aulong see Ulong
166 G3 **Ault** Picardie, France 50°06′N 1°27′E
79 M2 **Ault** Colorado, C USA 40°34′N 104°43′W
155 C11 **Aulum** var avlum. Ringkøbing, C Denmark 56°16′N 08°48′E
168 F7 **Aulus-les-Bains** Midi-Pyrénées, France 42°48′N 1°20′E
165 H2 **Aumale** Seine-Maritime, N France 49°45′N 01°43′E
181 E11 **Aumenau** Hessen, Germany 8°15′N 50°24′E
167 L9 **Aumont** Franche-Comté, France 46°54′N 5°38′E
169 I3 **Aumont-Aubrac** Languedoc-Roussillon, France 44°43′N 3°17′E
133 J6 **Auna** Niger, W Nigeria 10°13′N 04°43′E
166 D5 **Aunay-sur-Odon** Basse-Normandie, France 49°01′N 0°38′W
166 G6 **Auneau** Centre, France 48°27′N 1°46′E
155 D11 **Auning** Århus, C Denmark 56°26′N 10°23′E
140 D3 **Auob** var. Oup. ≋ Namibia/South Africa
153 G10 **Aura** Länsi-Soumi, SW Finland 60°37′N 22°35′E
181 G11 **Aura** Bayern, Germany 9°34′N 50°11′E
179 H13 **Aurach** ≋ N Austria
Aural, Phnom see Aôral, Phnum
233 H7 **Aurangābād** Bihār, N India 24°46′N 84°23′E
234 D4 **Aurangābād** Mahārāshtra, C India 19°52′N 75°22′E
283 M6 **Aur Atoll** atoll E Marshall Islands
164 E4 **Auray** Morbihan, NW France 47°40′N 02°59′W
154 D6 **Aurdal** Oppland, S Norway 60°51′N 09°25′E
154 C3 **Aure** Møre og Romsdal, S Norway 63°16′N 08°31′E
114 A4 **Aurelia** Santa Fe, Argentina 31°22′S 61°21′W
Aurelia Aquensis see Baden-Baden
Aurelianum see Orléans
131 J2 **Aurès, Massif de l'** ▲▲ NE Algeria
180 D3 **Aurich** Niedersachsen, NW Germany 53°28′N 07°28′E
168 F6 **Aurignac** Midi-Pyrénées, France 43°13′N 0°52′E
165 H7 **Aurillac** Cantal, C France 44°56′N 02°26′E
Aurine, Alpi see Zillertaler Alpen
Aurium see Ourense
169 M4 **Auron** Provence-Alpes-Côte d'Azur, France 44°14′N 6°56′E
62 D4 **Aurora** Ontario, S Canada 44°00′N 79°26′W
103 J4 **Aurora** NW Guyana 06°46′N 59°45′W
140 D9 **Aurora** Western Cape, South Africa 32°42′S 18°29′E
79 M3 **Aurora** Colorado, C USA 39°42′N 104°51′W
73 D9 **Aurora** Illinois, N USA 41°46′N 88°19′W
73 G11 **Aurora** Indiana, N USA 39°01′N 84°55′W
74 H2 **Aurora** Minnesota, N USA 47°31′N 92°14′W
75 G11 **Aurora** Missouri, C USA 36°58′N 93°43′W
75 D8 **Aurora** Nebraska, C USA 40°52′N 98°00′W
79 H4 **Aurora** Utah, W USA 38°55′N 111°55′W
Aurora see San Francisco, Philippines
Aurora see Maéwo, Vanuatu
154 C4 **Aursjøen** ◎ S Norway
154 E4 **Aursunden** ◎ S Norway
140 B4 **Aus** Karas, SW Namibia 26°38′S 16°19′E
Ausa see Vic
62 B5 **Ausable** ≋ Ontario, S Canada
72 H6 **Au Sable Point** headland Michigan, N USA 44°19′N 83°20′W
72 F4 **Au Sable Point** headland Michigan, N USA 46°40′N 86°08′W
72 G6 **Au Sable River** ≋ Michigan, N USA
105 G8 **Ausangate, Nevado** ▲ C Peru 13°47′S 71°13′W
Auschwitz see Oświęcim
Ausculum Apulum see Ascoli Satriano
171 H3 **Ausejo** La Rioja, N Spain 42°21′N 02°10′W
Aussig see Ústí nad Labem
155 C9 **Aust-Agder** ⬖ county S Norway
152 B5 **Austfonna** glacier NE Svalbard
73 F12 **Austin** Indiana, N USA 38°45′N 85°48′W
74 H6 **Austin** Minnesota, N USA 43°40′N 92°58′W
80 J3 **Austin** Nevada, W USA 39°30′N 117°05′W
70 G6 **Austin** state capital Texas, SW USA 30°16′N 97°45′W
52 G5 **Austin Channel** sea waterway Nunavut, N Canada
274 D6 **Austin, Lake** salt lake Western Australia
73 J9 **Austintown** Ohio, N USA 41°06′N 80°45′W
71 I6 **Austonio** Texas, SW USA 31°09′N 95°39′W
Australes, Archipel des see Australes, Îles
Australes et Antarctiques Françaises, Terres see French Southern and Antarctic Territories
285 I8 **Australes, Îles** var. Archipel des Australes, Îles Tubuai, Tubuai Islands, Eng. Austral Islands. island group SW French Polynesia
267 N7 **Austral Fracture Zone** tectonic feature S Pacific Ocean
266 F5 **Australia** continent
274 G4 **Australia** off. Commonwealth of Australia. ◆ commonwealth republic
Australia, Commonwealth of see Australia
277 K7 **Australian Alps** ▲▲ SE Australia
277 K6 **Australian Capital Territory** prev. Federal Capital Territory. ⬖ territory SE Australia
Australie, Bassin Nord de l' see North Australian Basin
Austral Islands see Australes, Îles
Austrava see Ostrov
176 J3 **Austria** off. Republic of Austria, Ger. Österreich. ◆ republic C Europe
Austria, Republic of see Austria
152 D2 **Austurland** ⬖ region SE Iceland
152 E4 **Austvågøya** island C Norway
Ausuitoq see Grise Fiord
107 H3 **Autazes** Amazonas, N Brazil 03°37′S 59°08′W
168 F6 **Auterive** Haute-Garonne, S France 43°22′N 01°28′E
Autesiodorum see Auxerre
165 H2 **Authie** ≋ N France
166 F6 **Authon-du-Perche** Centre, France 48°12′N 0°55′E
Autissiodorum see Auxerre
86 B6 **Autlán** var. Autlán de Navarro. Jalisco, SW Mexico 19°48′N 104°20′W
Autlán de Navarro see Autlán
168 G3 **Autoire** Midi-Pyrénées, France 44°51′N 1°50′E
167 K8 **Autrey-lés-Gray** Franche-Comté, France 47°29′N 5°30′E
Autricum see Chartres
165 J5 **Autun** anc. Ædua, Augustodunum. Saône-et-Loire, C France 46°58′N 04°18′E
Autz see Auce
163 E11 **Auvelais** Namur, S Belgium 50°27′N 04°38′E
165 I6 **Auvergne** ⬖ region C France
164 G7 **Auvézère** ≋ W France
168 F5 **Auvillar** Midi-Pyrénées, France 44°04′N 0°54′E
165 I4 **Auxerre** anc. Autesiodorum, Autissiodorum. Yonne, C France 47°48′N 03°35′E
166 G3 **Auxi-le-Château** Nord-Pas-de-Calais, France 50°14′N 2°07′E
167 I7 **Auxon** Champagne-Ardenne, France 48°06′N 3°55′E
165 J5 **Auxonne** Côte d'Or, C France 47°12′N 05°22′E
103 I5 **Auyan Tebuy** ▲ SE Venezuela 05°48′N 62°27′W
53 L7 **Auyuittuq National Park** National park Nunavut, NE Canada
165 H6 **Auzances** Creuse, C France 46°01′N 02°29′E
169 I2 **Auzat-sur-Allier** Auvergne, France 45°27′N 3°19′E
169 I2 **Auzon** Auvergne, France 45°23′N 3°23′E
75 H11 **Ava** Missouri, C USA 36°57′N 92°39′W
166 F10 **Availles-Limouzine** Poitou-Charentes, France 46°07′N 0°39′E
222 E3 **Āvaj** Qazvin, N Iran
155 A8 **Avaldsnes** Rogaland, S Norway 59°21′N 05°16′E
166 F3 **Falaises d' Aval** cave Haute-Normandie, France
165 I4 **Avallon** Yonne, C France 47°30′N 03°54′E
166 E6 **Avaloirs, Mont des** ▲ NW France 48°27′N 00°11′W
81 C11 **Avalon** Santa Catalina Island, California, W USA 33°20′N 118°19′W
64 G9 **Avalon** New Jersey, NE USA 39°04′N 74°42′W
59 M7 **Avalon Peninsula** peninsula Newfoundland and Labrador, E Canada
295 J6 **Avannaarsua** ⬖ province N Greenland
113 K4 **Avaré** São Paulo, S Brazil 23°06′S 48°57′W
Avaricum see Bourges
284 F9 **Avarua** ○ (Cook Islands) Rarotonga, S Cook Islands 21°12′S 159°46′E
284 F9 **Avarua Harbour** harbour Rarotonga, S Cook Islands
Avasfelsőfalu see Negreşti-Oaş
82 F9 **Avatanak Island** island Aleutian Islands, Alaska, USA
285 H10 **Avatele** S Niue 19°06′S 169°55′E
284 F9 **Avatiu Harbour** harbour Rarotonga, S Cook Islands
81 H9 **Avawatz Mountains** ▲▲ California, USA
Avdeyevka see Avdiyivka
187 I2 **Ávdira** Anatolikí Makedonía kai Thráki, NE Greece 40°58′N 24°58′E
189 M5 **Avdiyivka** Rus. Avdeyevka. Donets'ka Oblast', SE Ukraine 48°06′N 37°46′E
239 K1 **Avdzaga** C Monogolia 47°43′N 103°30′E
170 C3 **Ave** ≋ N Portugal
161 H6 **Avebury** UK 51°25′N 1°52′W
172 B2 **Aveiro** anc. Talabriga. Aveiro, W Portugal 40°38′N 08°40′W
172 B2 **Aveiro** ⬖ district N Portugal
Avela see Ávila
163 C10 **Avelgem** West-Vlaanderen, W Belgium 50°46′N 03°25′E
114 E9 **Avellaneda** Buenos Aires, E Argentina 34°43′S 58°23′W
175 G9 **Avellino** anc. Abellinum. Campania, S Italy 40°54′N 14°46′E

◆ Country
● Country Capital
◇ Dependent Territory
○ Dependent Territory Capital
⬖ Administrative Regions
✈ International Airport
▲ Mountain
▲▲ Mountain Range
⛰ Volcano
≋ River
◎ Lake
⊞ Reservoir

INDEX

B

◆ Country   ◇ Dependent Territory   ■ Administrative Regions   ▲ Mountain   ▼ Volcano   ◎ Lake
● Country Capital   ○ Dependent Territory Capital   ✕ International Airport   ▲ Mountain Range   ◆ River   ◇ Reservoir

Berre-l'Étang - Bisnulok
INDEX
319

165 *J8* **Berre-l'Étang** Bouches-du-Rhône, SE France 43°28´N 05°10´E
277 *H5* **Berri** South Australia 34°16´S 140°35´E
73 *F9* **Berrien Springs** Michigan, N USA 41°57´N 86°20´W
277 *J6* **Berrigan** New South Wales, SE Australia 35°41´S 145°50´E
171 *L9* **Berrouaghia** Algeria
160 *G7* **Berrow** UK 51°16´N 3°01´W
165 *H5* **Berry** *cultural region* C France
80 *C1* **Berryessa, Lake** ◎ California, W USA
61 *M9* **Berry Islands** *island group* N Bahamas
75 *H11* **Berryville** Arkansas, C USA 36°22´N 93°35´W
64 *B9* **Berryville** Virginia, NE USA 39°08´N 77°59´W
140 *C4* **Berseba** Karas, S Namibia 26°00´S 17°46´E
188 *G5* **Bershad'** Vinnyts'ka Oblast', C Ukraine 48°20´N 29°30´E
74 *B2* **Berthold** North Dakota, N USA 48°16´N 101°48´W
79 *L2* **Berthoud** Colorado, C USA 40°18´N 105°04´W
79 *L3* **Berthoud Pass** *pass* Colorado, C USA
110 *E10* **Bertioga** São Paulo, Brazil 23°51´S 46°09´W
134 *C5* **Bertoua** Est, E Cameroon 04°34´N 13°42´E
70 *G6* **Bertram** Texas, SW USA 30°44´N 98°03´W
117 *B12* **Bertrand, Cerro** ▲ S Argentina 50°00´S 73°27´W
163 *F13* **Bertrix** Luxembourg, SE Belgium 49°52´N 05°15´E
284 *B3* **Beru** *var.* Peru. *atoll* Tungaru, W Kiribati
Beruni *see* Beruniy
228 *E5* **Beruniy** *var.* Biruni, *Rus.* Beruni. Qoraqalpog'iston Respublikasi, W Uzbekistan 41°48´N 60°39´E
106 *G3* **Beruri** Amazonas, NW Brazil 03°44´S 61°13´W
64 *E5* **Berwick** Pennsylvania, NE USA 41°03´N 76°13´W
156 *G7* **Berwick** *cultural region* SE Scotland, UK
159 *J3* **Berwick-upon-Tweed** N England, UK 55°46´N 02°W
189 *J7* **Beryslav** *Rus.* Berislav. Khersons'ka Oblast', S Ukraine 46°51´N 33°26´E
Berytus *see* Beyrouth
172 *F4* **Berzocana** Extremadura, Spain 39°26´N 5°27´W
139 *K6* **Besalampy** Mahajanga, W Madagascar 16°43´S 44°29´E
169 *H8* **Besalú** Cataluña, Spain 42°12´N 2°42´E
165 *K5* **Besançon** *anc.* Besontium, Vesontio. Doubs, E France 47°14´N 06°01´E
165 *I6* **Besbre** ≈ C France
Bescanuova *see* Baška
181 *B13* **Besch** Saarland, Germany 6°22´N 49°30´E
Besdan *see* Bezdan
Besed' *see* Byesyedz'
229 *J6* **Beshariq** *Rus.* Besharyk; *prev.* Kirovo. Farg'ona Viloyati, E Uzbekistan 40°26´N 70°33´E
Besharyk *see* Beshariq
228 *G5* **Beshbuloq** *Rus.* Beshulak. Navoiy Viloyati, N Uzbekistan 41°55´N 64°13´E
Beshenkovichi *see* Byeshankovichy
228 *G7* **Beshkent** Qashqadaryo Viloyati, S Uzbekistan 38°47´N 65°42´E
Beshulak *see* Beshbuloq
261 *H4* **Besir** Papua, E Indonesia 0°25´S 130°38´E
184 *F3* **Beška** Vojvodina, N Serbia 45°09´N 20°04´E
Beskra *see* Biskra
197 *I9* **Beslan** Respublika Severnaya Osetiya, SW Russian Federation 43°12´N 44°33´E
185 *H6* **Besna Kobila** ▲ SE Serbia 42°30´N 22°16´E
214 *G7* **Besni** Adıyaman, S Turkey 37°42´N 37°53´E
Besontium *see* Besançon
218 *C2* **Beşparmak Dağları** *Eng.* Kyrenia Mountains. ▲▲ N Cyprus
Bessarabka *see* Basarabeasca
158 *D8* **Bessbrook** UK 54°12´N 6°25´W
181 *G9* **Besse** Hessen, Germany 9°23´N 51°13´E
169 *J4* **Bességes** Languedoc-Roussillon, France 44°17´N 4°06´E
152 *B5* **Bessels, Kapp** *headland* C Svalbard 78°36´N 21°43´E
66 *D9* **Bessemer** Alabama, S USA 33°24´N 86°57´W
72 *C4* **Bessemer** Michigan, N USA 46°28´N 90°03´W
67 *I7* **Bessemer City** North Carolina, SE USA 35°16´N 81°16´W
181 *B13* **Besseringen** Saarland, Germany 6°36´N 49°29´E
169 *L6* **Besse-sur-Issole** Provence-Alpes-Côte d'Azur, France 43°21´N 6°10´E
165 *H6* **Bessines-sur-Gartempe** Haute-Vienne, C France 46°06´N 01°22´E
163 *G8* **Best** Noord-Brabant, S Netherlands 51°31´N 05°24´E
70 *E5* **Best** Texas, SW USA 31°13´N 101°34´W
195 *H7* **Bestuzhevo** Arkhangel'skaya Oblast', NW Russian Federation 61°36´N 43°54´E
193 *J6* **Bestyakh** Respublika Sakha (Yakutiya), NE Russian Federation 61°25´N 129°05´E
Beszterce *see* Bistrița
Besztercebánya *see* Banská Bystrica
139 *L7* **Betafo** Antananarivo, C Madagascar 19°50´S 46°50´E
170 *D1* **Betanzos** Galicia, NW Spain 43°17´N 08°17´W
170 *C1* **Betanzos, Ría de** *estuary* NW Spain
134 *C5* **Bétaré Oya** Est, E Cameroon 05°34´N 14°09´E
114 *C5* **Betbeder** Entre Ríos, Argentina 32°23´S 59°55´W
219 *D8* **Bet Dagan** Israel
168 *B6* **Betelu** Navarra, Spain 43°01´N 1°59´W
171 *I6* **Bétera** País Valenciano, E Spain 39°35´N 00°28´W
133 *I6* **Bétérou** C Benin 09°13´N 02°18´E
173 *J2* **Beteta** Castilla-La Manacha, Spain 40°34´N 2°04´W
141 *J4* **Bethal** Mpumalanga, NE South Africa 26°27´S 29°28´E
73 *B11* **Bethalto** Illinois, N USA 38°54´N 90°02´W
140 *C4* **Bethanie** *var.* Bethanien, Bethany. Karas, S Namibia 26°32´S 17°11´E
Bethanien *see* Bethanie
75 *G8* **Bethany** Missouri, C USA 40°15´N 94°03´W
75 *E12* **Bethany** Oklahoma, C USA 35°31´N 97°37´W
Bethany *see* Bethanie
82 *G6* **Bethel** Alaska, USA 60°47´N 161°45´W
65 *I4* **Bethel** Connecticut, USA 41°22´N 73°25´W
63 *J4* **Bethel** Maine, NE USA 44°24´N 70°47´W
67 *L6* **Bethel** North Carolina, SE USA 35°46´N 77°21´W
62 *C8* **Bethel Park** Pennsylvania, NE USA 40°21´N 80°03´W
160 *E2* **Bethesda** UK 53°10´N 4°05´W
64 *C10* **Bethesda** Maryland, USA 38°59´N 77°06´W
64 *C10* **Bethesda** Maryland, NE USA 39°00´N 77°05´W
141 *J5* **Bethlehem** Free State, C South Africa 28°12´S 28°16´E
64 *F6* **Bethlehem** Pennsylvania, NE USA 40°36´N 75°22´W
64 *A5* **Bethlehem** Pennsylvania, USA 40°52´N 78°44´W
216 *B7* **Bethlehem** *Ar.* Bayt Laḩm, *Heb.* Bet Leḥem. C West Bank 31°43´N 35°12´E
Bethlen *see* Beclean
138 *F8* **Bethulie** Free State, C South Africa 30°30´S 25°59´E
141 *H7* **Bethulie** Free State, South Africa 30°30´S 25°58´E
165 *H1* **Béthune** Pas-de-Calais, N France 50°32´N 02°38´E
165 *H2* **Béthune** ≈ N France
170 *F8* **Béticos, Sistemas** *var.* Sistema Penibético, *Eng.* Baetic Cordillera, Baetic Mountains. ▲▲ S Spain
102 *E3* **Betijoque** Trujillo, NW Venezuela 09°25´N 70°45´W
110 *G3* **Betim** Minas Gerais, SE Brazil 19°56´S 44°10´W
284 *C2* **Betio** Tarawa, W Kiribati 01°21´N 172°56´E
139 *L9* **Betioky** Toliara, S Madagascar 23°42´S 44°22´E
Bet Leḥem *see* Bethlehem
Betlen *see* Beclean
219 *D9* **Bet Nir** Israel
256 *F12* **Betong** Yala, SW Thailand 05°45´N 101°05´E
134 *E6* **Bétou** La Likouala, N Congo 03°08´N 18°31´E
227 *H6* **Betpak-Dala** *Kaz.* Betpaqdala. *plateau* S Kazakhstan
Betpaqdala *see* Betpak-Dala
219 *D9* **Bet Qama** Israel
139 *L9* **Betroka** Toliara, S Madagascar 23°15´S 46°07´E
Betschau *see* Bečva
167 *N5* **Betschdorf** Alsace, France 48°54´N 7°54´E
216 *B6* **Bet She'an** *Ar.* Baysān, Beisān; *anc.* Scythopolis. Northern, N Israel 32°30´N 35°30´E
219 *E8* **Bet Shemesh** Israel
59 *I7* **Betsiamites** Québec, SE Canada 48°56´N 68°40´W
59 *H7* **Betsiamites** ≈ Québec, SE Canada
139 *L7* **Betsiboka** ≈ N Madagascar
163 *H14* **Bettembourg** Luxembourg, S Luxembourg 49°31´N 06°06´E
163 *H13* **Bettendorf** Diekirch, NE Luxembourg 49°53´N 06°13´E
73 *B9* **Bettendorf** Iowa, C USA 41°31´N 90°31´W
128 *E6* **Bette, Pic** *var.* Bīkkū Bīttī, *It.* Picco Bette. ▲ S Libya 22°02´N 19°07´E
Bette, Picco *see* Bette, Pic
233 *H6* **Bettiah** Bihār, N India 26°49´N 84°30´E
181 *C13* **Bettingen** Saarland, Germany 6°51´N 49°26´E
83 *I4* **Bettles** Alaska, USA 66°54´N 151°40´W
155 *H8* **Bettna** Södermanland, C Sweden 58°52´N 16°40´E
232 *E9* **Betūl** *prev.* Badnur. Madhya Pradesh, C India 21°55´N 77°54´E
232 *F7* **Betwa** ≈ C India
167 *H5* **Betz** Picardie, France 49°09´N 2°57´E
181 *D10* **Betzdorf** Rheinland-Pfalz, W Germany 50°47´N 07°50´E
135 *D10* **Béu** Uíge, NW Angola 06°15´S 15°32´E
181 *F10* **Beuern** Hessen, Germany 8°49´N 50°38´E
72 *F6* **Beulah** Michigan, N USA 43°35´N 83°52´W
74 *B3* **Beulah** North Dakota, N USA 47°16´N 101°48´W
162 *H5* **Beulakerwijde** ◎ N Netherlands
161 *L7* **Beult** ≈ UK
162 *G7* **Beuningen** Gelderland, SE Netherlands 51°52´N 05°47´E
Beuthen *see* Bytom
165 *H4* **Beuvron** ≈ C France
163 *D9* **Beveren** Oost-Vlaanderen, N Belgium 51°13´N 04°15´E
67 *K6* **B. Everett Jordan Reservoir** *var.* Jordan Lake. ⊡ North Carolina, SE USA
159 *M8* **Beverley** E England, UK 53°51´N 00°26´W
Beverley *see* Beverly
163 *F9* **Beverlo** Limburg, NE Belgium 51°06´N 05°14´E
65 *M2* **Beverly** Massachusetts, NE USA 42°33´N 70°49´W
76 *D4* **Beverly** *var.* Beverley. Washington, NW USA 46°50´N 119°57´W
81 *D10* **Beverly Hills** California, W USA 34°02´N 118°25´W
180 *G7* **Bevern** Niedersachsen, Germany 9°30´N 51°52´E
180 *F3* **Beverstedt** Niedersachsen, Germany 8°49´N 53°26´E
180 *G7* **Beverungen** Nordrhein-Westfalen, C Germany 51°39´N 09°22´E
162 *E5* **Beverwijk** Noord-Holland, W Netherlands 52°29´N 04°40´E
159 *I5* **Bewcastle** UK 55°04´N 2°41´W
161 *H4* **Bewdley** UK 52°23´N 2°19´W
176 *C5* **Bex** Vaud, W Switzerland 46°15´N 07°00´E
161 *L8* **Bexhill** *var.* Bexhill-on-Sea. SE England, UK 50°50´N 00°28´E
Bexhill-on-Sea *see* Bexhill
180 *F3* **Bexhövede** Niedersachsen, Germany 8°41´N 53°29´E
187 *M7* **Beyağaç** Denizli, Turkey 37°14´N 28°54´E
214 *C8* **Bey Dağları** ▲▲ SW Turkey
Beyj *see* Belyy
214 *C4* **Beykoz** Istanbul, NW Turkey 41°09´N 29°06´E
132 *E7* **Beyla** SE Guinea 08°43´N 08°41´W
215 *M5* **Beyläqan** *prev.* Zhdanov. SW Azerbaijan 39°43´N 47°38´E
136 *F2* **Beylul** *var.* Beilul. SE Eritrea 13°10´N 42°27´E
168 *G3* **Beynat** Limousin, France 45°07´N 1°43´E
192 *C8* **Beyneu** W Kazakhstan
226 *D6* **Beyneu** *Kaz.* Beyneū. Mangistau, SW Kazakhstan 45°20´N 55°11´E
Beyneū *see* Beyneu
251 *M8* **Beyonēsu-retsugan** *Eng.* Bayonnaise Rocks. *island group* SE Japan
214 *D5* **Beypazarı** Ankara, NW Turkey 40°10´N 31°56´E
235 *D8* **Beypore** Kerala, SW India 11°10´N 75°49´E
218 *F3* **Beyrouth** *var.* Bayrūt, *Eng.* Beirut; *anc.* Berytus. ● (Lebanon) W Lebanon 33°55´N 35°31´E
216 *C5* **Beyrouth** ✕ W Lebanon 33°52´N 35°30´E
214 *D7* **Beyşehir** Konya, SW Turkey 37°40´N 31°43´E
214 *D7* **Beyşehir Gölü** ◎ C Turkey
184 *E2* **Bezdan** *Ger.* Besdan, *Hung.* Bezdán. Vojvodina, NW Serbia 45°51´N 19°00´E
Bezdezh *see* Byezdzyezh
194 *D10* **Bezhanitsy** Pskovskaya Oblast', W Russian Federation 56°57´N 29°53´E
194 *F9* **Bezhetsk** Tverskaya Oblast', W Russian Federation 57°47´N 36°42´E
165 *I9* **Béziers** *anc.* Baeterrae, Baeterrae Septimanorum, Julia Beterrae. Hérault, S France 43°21´N 03°13´E
Bezmein *see* Abadan
173 *H8* **Béznar** Andalucía, Spain 36°56´N 3°32´W
Bezwada *see* Vijayawāda
234 *J4* **Bhadrak** *var.* Bhadrakh. Orissa, E India 21°04´N 86°30´N
Bhadrakh *see* Bhadrak
234 *D7* **Bhadra Reservoir** ⊡ SW India
234 *D7* **Bhadrāvati** Karnātaka, SW India 13°52´N 75°43´E
233 *J7* **Bhāgalpur** Bihār, NE India 25°14´N 86°59´E
Bhairab *see* Bhairab Bazar
233 *K7* **Bhairab Bazar** *var.* Bhairab. Dhaka, C Bangladesh 24°04´N 91°00´E
233 *H6* **Bhairahawā** Western, S Nepal 27°31´N 83°27´E
231 *H5* **Bhakkar** Punjab, E Pakistan 31°40´N 71°08´E
233 *I6* **Bhaktapur** Central, C Nepal 27°47´N 85°21´E
256 *D3* **Bhamo** *var.* Banmo. Kachin State, N Myanmar (Burma) 24°15´N 97°15´E
Bhāmragad *see* Bhāmragarh
234 *G4* **Bhāmragarh** *var.* Bhāmragad. Mahārāshtra, C India 19°28´N 80°39´E
234 *F4* **Bhandāra** Mahārāshtra, C India 21°10´N 79°41´E
Bhārat *see* India
232 *E6* **Bharatpur** *prev.* Bhurtpore. Rājasthān, N India 27°14´N 77°29´E
232 *C9* **Bharūch** Gujarāt, W India 21°48´N 72°55´E
234 *D7* **Bhatkal** Karnātaka, W India 13°59´N 74°34´E
233 *H6* **Bhatni** *var.* Bhatni Junction. Uttar Pradesh, N India 26°23´N 83°56´E
Bhatni Junction *see* Bhatni
233 *J8* **Bhātpāra** West Bengal, NE India 22°55´N 88°30´E
231 *I4* **Bhaun** Punjab, E Pakistan 32°53´N 72°48´E
Bhaunagar *see* Bhāvnagar
234 *H4* **Bhavānīpātna** Orissa, E India 19°56´N 83°09´E
235 *E8* **Bhavānīsāgar Reservoir** ⊡ S India
232 *C8* **Bhāvnagar** *prev.* Bhaunagar. Gujarāt, W India 21°46´N 72°14´E
Bheanntraí, Bá *see* Bantry Bay
Bheara, Béal an *see* Gweebarra Bay
234 *G4* **Bhilai** Chhattīsgarh, C India 21°12´N 81°26´E
232 *D7* **Bhīlwāra** Rājasthān, N India 25°23´N 74°39´E
234 *D5* **Bhīma** ≈ S India
234 *G6* **Bhīmavaram** Andhra Pradesh, E India 16°34´N 81°35´E
232 *F6* **Bhind** Madhya Pradesh, C India 26°33´N 78°47´E
232 *C7* **Bhīnmāl** Rājasthān, N India 25°01´N 72°22´E
Bhir *see* Bīd
234 *C4* **Bhiwandi** Mahārāshtra, W India 19°21´N 73°08´E
232 *E5* **Bhiwāni** Haryāna, N India 28°50´N 76°10´E
232 *G6* **Bhognīpur** Uttar Pradesh, N India 26°12´N 79°48´E
233 *K8* **Bhola** Barisal, S Bangladesh 22°40´N 91°36´E
232 *E8* **Bhopāl** *state capital* Madhya Pradesh, C India 23°17´N 77°25´E
234 *G5* **Bhopālpatnam** Chhattīsgarh, C India 18°51´N 80°22´E
234 *C5* **Bhor** Mahārāshtra, W India 18°10´N 73°55´E
234 *I4* **Bhubaneshwar** *prev.* Bhubaneswar, Bhuvaneshwar. *state capital* Orissa, E India 20°16´N 85°51´E
Bhubaneswar *see* Bhubaneshwar
232 *B8* **Bhuj** Gujarāt, W India 23°16´N 69°40´E
Bhuket *see* Phuket
Bhurtpore *see* Bharatpur
Bhusaval *see* Bhusāwal
234 *D4* **Bhusāwal** *prev.* Bhusaval. Mahārāshtra, C India 21°01´N 75°50´E
233 *K5* **Bhutan** *off.* Kingdom of Bhutan, *var.* Druk-yul. ◆ *monarchy* S Asia
Bhutan, Kingdom of *see* Bhutan
Bhuvaneshwar *see* Bhubaneshwar
223 *I9* **Biābān, Kūh-e** ▲▲ S Iran
133 *K9* **Biafra, Bight of** *var.* Bight of Bonny. *bay* W Africa
261 *K4* **Biak** Papua, E Indonesia 01°10´S 136°05´E
261 *J4* **Biak, Pulau** *island* E Indonesia
182 *I6* **Biała Podlaska** LubelskieE Poland 52°03´N 23°08´E
182 *D4* **Białogard** *Ger.* Belgard. Zachodnio-pomorskie, NW Poland 54°01´N 15°59´E
182 *J5* **Białowieska, Puszcza** *Bel.* Byelavyezhskaya Pushcha, *Rus.* Belovezhskaya Pushcha. *physical region* Belarus/Poland *see also* Byelavyezhskaya, Pushcha
Białowieska, Puszcza *see* Byelavyezhskaya Pushcha
182 *E4* **Biały Bór** *Ger.* Baldenburg. Zachodnio-pomorskie, NW Poland 53°53´N 16°49´E
182 *I5* **Białystok** *Rus.* Belostok, Bielostok. Podlaskie, NE Poland 53°08´N 23°09´E
175 *G12* **Biancavilla** *prev.* Inessa. Sicilia, Italy, C Mediterranean Sea 37°38´N 14°52´E
Bianco, Monte *see* Blanc, Mont
132 *E7* **Biankouma** W Ivory Coast 07°44´N 07°37´W
256 *G5* **Bia, Phou** *var.* Pou Bia. ▲ C Laos 18°59´N 103°09´E
Bia, Pou *see* Bia, Phou
223 *H3* **Biārjmand** Semnān, N Iran 36°05´N 55°50´E
164 *F8* **Biarritz** Pyrénées-Atlantiques, SW France 43°25´N 01°40´W
176 *E5* **Biasca** Ticino, S Switzerland 46°22´N 08°59´E
111 *H6* **Bias Fortes** Minas Gerais, Brazil 21°36´S 43°46´W
114 *G3* **Biassini** Salto, N Uruguay 31°18´S 57°05´W
Biasteri *see* Laguardia
252 *E4* **Bibai** Hokkaidō, NE Japan 43°21´N 141°53´E
135 *C13* **Bibala** *Port.* Vila Arriaga. Namibe, SW Angola 14°46´S 13°21´E
55 *J4* **Bibby Island** *island* Nunavut, E Canada
170 *D3* **Bibéi** ≈ NW Spain
Biberach *see* Biberach an der Riss
179 *E13* **Biberach an der Riss** *var.* Biberach, *Ger.* Biberach an der Riß. Baden-Württemberg, S Germany 48°06´N 09°48´E
176 *D4* **Biberist** Solothurn, NW Switzerland 47°11´N 07°34´E
132 *G8* **Bibiani** SW Ghana 06°28´N 02°20´W
184 *B4* **Bibinje** Zadar, SW Croatia 44°04´N 15°17´E
190 *J7* **Bibirevo** Tverskaya Oblast', Russian Federation
Biblical Gebal *see* Jbaïl
188 *D4* **Bibrka** *Pol.* Bóbrka, *Rus.* Bobrka. L'vivs'ka Oblast', NW Ukraine 49°39´N 24°16´E
188 *G7* **Bîc** ≈ S Moldova
184 *F7* **Bicaj** Kukës, NE Albania 42°00´N 20°24´E
111 *I6* **Bicas** Minas Gerais, Brazil 21°43´S 43°04´W
172 *C4* **Bicas** Santarém, Portugal 39°23´N 8°14´W
188 *E7* **Bicaz** *Hung.* Békás. Neamț, NE Romania 46°53´N 26°05´E
161 *J5* **Bicester** UK 51°54´N 1°09´W
277 *K9* **Bicheno** Tasmania, SE Australia 41°56´S 148°15´E
Bichiş *see* Békés
Bichiş-Ciaba *see* Békéscsaba
Bichitra *see* Phichit
215 *I3* **Bichvint'a** *Rus.* Pitsunda. NW Georgia 43°12´N 40°21´E
59 *I7* **Bic, Île du** *island* Québec, SE Canada
76 *D5* **Bickleton** Washington, NW USA 46°00´N 120°16´W
79 *I4* **Bicknell** Utah, W USA 38°20´N 111°32´W
53 *H1* **Cape Bicknor** *headland* Nunavut, N Canada
260 *G3* **Bicoli** Pulau Halmahera, E Indonesia 0°34´N 128°33´E
183 *F11* **Bicske** Fejér, C Hungary 47°30´N 18°36´E
234 *D5* **Bīd** *prev.* Bhir. Mahārāshtra, W India 19°17´N 75°22´E
133 *J6* **Bida** Niger, C Nigeria 09°06´N 06°02´E
234 *E5* **Bīdar** Karnātaka, C India 17°56´N 77°35´E
168 *B6* **Bidasoa** ≈ Spain
221 *K4* **Bidbid** NE Oman 23°25´N 58°08´E
63 *J5* **Biddeford** Maine, NE USA 43°29´N 70°27´W
162 *G5* **Biddinghuizen** Flevoland, C Netherlands 52°28´N 05°41´E
77 *L6* **Biddle** Montana, NW USA 45°04´N 105°21´W
219 *E8* **Biddū** West Bank
159 *J10* **Biddulph** UK 53°07´N 2°10´W
160 *E7* **Bideford** SW England, UK 51°01´N 04°12´W
160 *E7* **Bideford Bay** *bay* UK
161 *H4* **Bidford** UK 52°09´N 1°51´W
135 *D12* **Bié** ◐ *province* C Angola
181 *G11* **Bieber** Hessen, Germany 9°19´N 50°09´E
78 *C2* **Bieber** California, W USA 41°07´N 121°09´W
182 *I4* **Biebrza** ≈ NE Poland
252 *F4* **Biei** Hokkaidō, NE Japan 43°33´N 142°28´E
176 *C4* **Biel** *Fr.* Bienne. Bern, W Switzerland 47°09´N 07°16´E
180 *F7* **Bielefeld** Nordrhein-Westfalen, NW Germany 52°01´N 08°32´E
53 *K7* **Bieler Lake** ◎ Nunavut, NE Canada
176 *C4* **Bieler See** *Fr.* Lac de Bienne. ◎ W Switzerland
Bielitz/Bielitz-Biala *see* Bielsko-Biała
176 *D6* **Biella** Piemonte, N Italy 45°34´N 08°04´E
Bielostok *see* Białystok
168 *E7* **Bielsa** Aragón, Spain 42°38´N 0°13´E
183 *F9* **Bielsko-Biała** *Ger.* Bielitz, Bielitz-Biala. Śląskie, S Poland 49°49´N 19°01´E
199 *H2* **Bielsko-Biała** ◐ *province* S Poland
182 *I5* **Bielsk Podlaski** Białystok, E Poland 52°45´N 23°11´E
Bien Bien *see* Điên Biên
Biên Đông *see* South China Sea
55 *H10* **Bienfait** Saskatchewan, S Canada 49°06´N 102°47´W
257 *I9* **Biên Hoa** Đông Nai, S Vietnam 10°58´N 106°50´E
Bienne *see* Biel
Bienne, Lac de *see* Bieler See
172 *E6* **Bienvenida** Extremadura, Spain 38°18´N 6°12´W
59 *H4* **Bienville, Lac** ◎ Québec, C Canada
135 *D12* **Bié, Planalto do** *var.* Bié Plateau. *plateau* C Angola
Bié Plateau *see* Bié, Planalto do
176 *B5* **Bière** Vaud, W Switzerland 46°32´N 06°19´E
180 *F6* **Bieren** Nordrhein-Westfalen, Germany 8°31´N 52°14´E
166 *D7* **Bierné** Pays de la Loire, France 47°49´N 0°32´W
162 *I3* **Bierum** Groningen, NE Netherlands 53°25´N 06°51´E
162 *E7* **Biesbos** *var.* Biesbosch. *wetland* S Netherlands
Biesbosch *see* Biesbos
168 *D7* **Biescas** Aragón, Spain 42°38´N 0°19´W
141 *H4* **Biesiesvlei** North-West, South Africa 26°23´S 25°54´E
163 *E12* **Biesme** Namur, S Belgium 50°19´N 04°43´E
181 *G14* **Bietigheim-Bissingen** Baden-Württemberg, SW Germany 48°57´N 09°07´E
163 *F13* **Bièvre** Namur, SE Belgium 49°56´N 05°01´E
134 *A7* **Bifoun** Moyen-Ogooué, NW Gabon 0°15´S 10°24´E
252 *F3* **Bifuka** Hokkaidō, NE Japan 44°28´N 142°20´E
214 *B5* **Biga** Çanakkale, NW Turkey 40°13´N 27°14´E
214 *B5* **Bigadiç** Balıkesir, W Turkey 39°24´N 28°08´E
80 *D3* **Big Bar** California, USA 38°19´N 120°43´W
75 *C11* **Big Basin** *basin* Kansas, C USA
278 *B11* **Big Bay** *bay* South Island, New Zealand
281 *L2* **Big Bay** *bay* C Vanuatu
72 *E5* **Big Bay de Noc** ◎ Michigan, N USA
72 *E4* **Big Bay Point** *headland* Michigan, N USA 46°51´N 87°40´W
81 *F11* **Big Bear City** California, USA 34°16´N 116°51´W
81 *F11* **Big Bear Lake** California, USA 34°15´N 116°55´W
77 *I5* **Big Belt Mountains** ▲▲ Montana, NW USA
80 *B2* **Big Bend** California, USA 38°14´N 122°28´W
74 *C5* **Big Bend Dam** *dam* South Dakota, N USA
70 *C7* **Big Bend National Park** *national park* Texas, S USA
68 *E2* **Big Black River** ≈ Mississippi, S USA
75 *E8* **Big Blue River** ≈ Kansas/Nebraska, C USA
70 *D6* **Big Canyon** ≈ Texas, SW USA
80 *E5* **Big Creek** California, USA 37°12´N 119°15´W
76 *G6* **Big Creek** Idaho, NW USA 45°05´N 115°20´W
68 *F4* **Big Creek Lake** ⊡ Alabama, S USA
69 *M8* **Big Cypress Swamp** *wetland* Florida, SE USA
83 *J5* **Big Delta** Alaska, USA 64°09´N 145°50´W
63 *J3* **Bigelow Mountain** ▲ Maine, NE USA 45°09´N 70°17´W
239 *I2* **Biger** *var* Jargalant. Govĭ-Altay, W Mongolia 45°39´N 97°10´E
74 *G2* **Big Falls** Minnesota, N USA 48°13´N 93°48´W
76 *G3* **Bigfork** Montana, NW USA 48°03´N 114°04´W
74 *G2* **Big Fork River** ≈ Minnesota, N USA
57 *L6* **Biggar** Saskatchewan, S Canada 52°03´N 107°59´W
159 *H4* **Biggar** UK 55°37´N 3°31´W
274 *E2* **Bigge Island** *island* Western Australia
161 *K6* **Biggin Hill** UK 51°17´N 0°01´E
161 *K5* **Biggleswade** UK 52°05´N 0°16´W
80 *D1* **Biggs** California, USA 39°24´N 121°44´W
76 *D5* **Biggs** Oregon, NW USA 45°39´N 120°49´W
62 *F4* **Big Gull Lake** ◎ Ontario, SE Canada
79 *K10* **Big Hachet Peak** ▲ New Mexico, SW USA 31°38´N 108°24´W
77 *H6* **Big Hole River** ≈ Montana, NW USA
77 *K7* **Bighorn Basin** *basin* Wyoming, C USA
77 *K6* **Bighorn Lake** ◎ Montana/Wyoming, N USA
77 *K6* **Bighorn Mountains** ▲▲ Wyoming, C USA
79 *H8* **Big Horn Peak** ▲ Arizona, SW USA 33°40´N 113°01´W
77 *K5* **Bighorn River** ≈ Montana/Wyoming, NW USA
54 *F4* **Big Island** *island* Northwest Territories, W Canada
55 *N2* **Big Island** *island* Nunavut, NE Canada
59 *H1* **Big Island** *island* Nunavut, NE Canada
59 *I3* **Big Island** *island* Québec, E Canada
83 *H9* **Big Koniuji Island** *island* Shumagin Islands, Alaska, USA
70 *E6* **Big Lake** Texas, SW USA 31°12´N 101°29´W
63 *L3* **Big Lake** ◎ Maine, NE USA
72 *A4* **Big Manitou Falls** *waterfall* Wisconsin, N USA
78 *D2* **Big Mountain** ▲ Nevada, W USA 41°18´N 119°03´W
176 *E5* **Bignasco** Ticino, S Switzerland 46°21´N 08°37´E
75 *E8* **Big Nemaha River** ≈ Nebraska, C USA
132 *B5* **Bignona** SW Senegal 12°49´N 16°16´W
Bigorra *see* Tarbes
Bigosovo *see* Bihosava
80 *F6* **Big Pine** California, W USA 37°09´N 118°18´W
81 *C9* **Big Pine Mountain** ▲ California, W USA 34°41´N 119°37´W
75 *I10* **Big Piney Creek** ≈ Missouri, C USA
132 *E9* **Big Point** *headland* N Tristan da Cunha 37°10´S 12°18´E
72 *F7* **Big Rapids** Michigan, N USA 43°42´N 85°28´W
72 *C5* **Big Rib River** ≈ Wisconsin, N USA
62 *F4* **Big Rideau Lake** ◎ Ontario, SE Canada
57 *M4* **Big River** Saskatchewan, C Canada 53°48´N 106°55´W
52 *D5* **Big River** ≈ Northwest Territories, N Canada
75 *I10* **Big River** ≈ Missouri, C USA
72 *E6* **Big Sable Point** *headland* Michigan, N USA 44°03´N 86°30´W
55 *I6* **Big Sand Lake** ◎ Manitoba, C Canada
77 *J3* **Big Sandy** Montana, NW USA 48°08´N 110°09´W
71 *I4* **Big Sandy** Texas, SW USA 32°34´N 95°06´W
79 *N3* **Big Sandy Creek** ≈ Colorado, C USA
75 *E8* **Big Sandy Creek** ≈ Nebraska, C USA
74 *G3* **Big Sandy Lake** ◎ Minnesota, N USA
78 *G8* **Big Sandy River** ≈ Arizona, SW USA
67 *H3* **Big Sandy River** ≈ S USA
69 *L2* **Big Satilla Creek** ≈ Georgia, SE USA
74 *E6* **Big Sioux River** ≈ Iowa/South Dakota, N USA
80 *I4* **Big Smoky Valley** *valley* Nevada, W USA
70 *E5* **Big Spring** Texas, SW USA 32°15´N 101°30´W
63 *K3* **Big Squaw Mountain** ▲ Maine, NE USA 45°28´N 69°42´W
67 *H5* **Big Stone Gap** Virginia, NE USA 36°52´N 82°45´W
66 *A9* **Big Sunflower River** ≈ Mississippi, S USA
80 *A5* **Big Sur** California, USA 36°16´N 121°48´W
77 *J5* **Big Timber** Montana, NW USA 45°50´N 109°57´W
58 *C4* **Big Trout Lake** Ontario, C Canada 53°40´N 90°00´W
62 *D3* **Big Trout Lake** ◎ Ontario, SE Canada
80 *B1* **Big Valley** *valley* California, USA
78 *C2* **Big Valley Mountains** ▲▲ California, W USA
70 *F8* **Big Wells** Texas, SW USA 28°34´N 99°34´W
62 *C2* **Bigwood** Ontario, S Canada 46°03´N 80°37´W
184 *C3* **Bihać** ◐ NW Bosnia and Herzegovina
233 *I7* **Bihār** *prev.* Behar. ◐ *state* N India
Bihār *see* Bihār Sharīf
137 *B9* **Biharamulo** Kagera, NW Tanzania 02°37´S 31°20´E
233 *J7* **Bihārīganj** Bihār, NE India 25°44´N 86°59´E
233 *I7* **Bihār Sharīf** *var.* Bihār. Bihār, N India 25°13´N 85°31´E
188 *B7* **Bihor** ◐ *county* NW Romania
252 *G3* **Bihoro** Hokkaidō, NE Japan 43°50´N 144°05´E
190 *G7* **Bihosava** *Rus.* Bigosovo. Vitsyebskaya Voblasts', NW Belarus 55°50´N 27°46´E
Bijagos Archipelago *see* Bijagós, Arquipélago dos
132 *B5* **Bijagós, Arquipélago dos** *var.* Bijagos Archipelago. *island group* W Guinea-Bissau
234 *D6* **Bijāpur** Karnātaka, C India 16°50´N 75°42´E
222 *D3* **Bījār** Kordestān, W Iran 35°52´N 47°39´E
184 *E3* **Bijeljina** ◐ Republika Srpska, NE Bosnia and Herzegovina
184 *F6* **Bijelo Polje** E Montenegro 43°03´N 19°44´E
240 *B5* **Bijiang** Yunnan, SW China 27°00´N 98°48´E
242 *B5* **Bijie** Guizhou, S China 27°15´N 105°16´E
232 *F5* **Bijnor** Uttar Pradesh, N India 29°22´N 78°09´E
232 *D5* **Bīkāner** Rājasthān, NW India 28°01´N 73°22´E
283 *M4* **Bikar Atoll** *var.* Pikaar. *atoll* Ratak Chain, N Marshall Islands
284 *D2* **Bikeman** *atoll* Tungaru, W Kiribati
284 *D2* **Bikenebu** Tarawa, W Kiribati
193 *L8* **Bikin** Khabarovskiy Kray, SE Russian Federation 46°45´N 134°06´E
193 *L8* **Bikin** ≈ SE Russian Federation
283 *K5* **Bikini Atoll** *var.* Pikinni. *atoll* Ralik Chain, NW Marshall Islands
139 *H4* **Bikita** Masvingo, E Zimbabwe 20°06´S 31°41´E
Bīkkū Bīttī *see* Bette, Pic
135 *E8* **Bikoro** Equateur, W Dem. Rep. Congo 0°45´S 18°09´E
221 *L5* **Bilād Banī Bū 'Alī** NE Oman 22°02´N 59°18´E
221 *L5* **Bilād Banī Bū Ḩasan** NE Oman 22°09´N 59°14´E
221 *K5* **Bilād Manaḩ** *var.* Manaḩ. NE Oman 22°44´N 57°36´E
133 *H5* **Bilanga** C Burkina 12°35´N 00°08´W
260 *D3* **Bilang, Teluk** *bay* Sulawesi, N Indonesia
232 *D6* **Bilāra** Rājasthān, N India 26°10´N x73°48´E
231 *L7* **Bilāri** Uttar Pradesh, N India 28°37´N 78°48´E
216 *D3* **Bil'ās, Jabal al** ▲▲ C Syria
234 *G3* **Bilāspur** Chhattīsgarh, C India 22°06´N 82°08´E
232 *E4* **Bilāspur** Himāchal Pradesh, N India 31°18´N 76°48´E
258 *D4* **Bila, Sungai** ≈ Sumatera, W Indonesia
215 *M5* **Biläsuvar** *Rus.* Bilyasuvar; *prev.* Pushkino. SE Azerbaijan 39°26´N 48°34´E
189 *H4* **Bila Tserkva** *Rus.* Belaya Tserkov'. Kyyivs'ka Oblast', N Ukraine 49°49´N 30°08´E
256 *E8* **Bilauktaung Range** *var.* Thanintari Taungdan. ▲▲ Myanmar (Burma)/Thailand
170 *G2* **Bilbao** *Basq.* Bilbo. País Vasco, N Spain 43°15´N 02°56´W
Bilbo *see* Bilbao
152 *A2* **Bíldudalur** Vestfirdhir, NW Iceland 65°40´N 23°35´W
184 *E6* **Bileća** ◐ Republika Srpska, S Bosnia and Herzegovina
214 *C5* **Bilecik** Bilecik, NW Turkey 39°59´N 29°54´E
214 *C5* **Bilecik** ◐ *province* NW Turkey
188 *A8* **Biled** *Ger.* Billed, *Hung.* Billéd. Timiş, W Romania 45°55´N 20°55´E
183 *I8* **Biłgoraj** Lubelskie, E Poland 50°31´N 22°41´E
189 *H8* **Bilhorod-Dnistrovs'kyy** *Rus.* Belgorod-Dnestrovskiy, *Rom.* Cetatea Albă, *prev.* Akkerman; *anc.* Tyras. Odes'ka Oblast', SW Ukraine 46°10´N 30°19´E
134 *H6* **Bili** Orientale, N Dem. Rep. Congo 04°07´N 25°09´E
193 *M3* **Bilibino** Chukotskiy Avtonomnyy Okrug, NE Russian Federation 67°56´N 166°45´E
256 *D6* **Bilin** Mon State, S Myanmar (Burma) 17°14´N 97°12´E
263 *M7* **Biliran Island** *island* C Philippines
184 *G9* **Bilisht** *var.* Bilishti. Korçë, SE Albania 40°36´N 21°00´E
Bilishti *see* Bilisht
277 *I6* **Billabong Creek** *var.* Moulamein Creek. *seasonal river* New South Wales, SE Australia
276 *F3* **Billa Kalina** South Australia 29°57´S 136°13´E
295 *N5* **Bill Baileys Bank** *undersea feature* N Atlantic Ocean
Billed/Billéd *see* Biled
161 *L6* **Billericay** UK 51°37´N 0°25´E
233 *H7* **Billi** Uttar Pradesh, N India 24°30´N 82°59´E
181 *G13* **Billigheim** Baden-Württemberg, Germany 9°15´N 49°21´E
159 *K6* **Billingham** N England, UK 54°36´N 01°17´W
77 *K5* **Billings** Montana, NW USA 45°47´N 108°32´W
155 *F8* **Billingsfors** Västra Götaland, S Sweden 58°57´N 12°14´E
Bill of Cape Clear, The *see* Clear, Cape
74 *B5* **Billsburg** South Dakota, N USA 44°22´N 101°40´W
155 *C12* **Billund** Ribe, W Denmark 55°44´N 09°07´E
79 *H7* **Bill Williams Mountain** ▲ Arizona, SW USA 35°12´N 112°12´W
81 *J12* **Bill Williams River** ≈ Arizona, SW USA
133 *M2* **Bilma** Agadez, NE Niger 18°22´N 13°01´E
133 *M2* **Bilma, Grand Erg de** *desert* NE Niger
275 *K5* **Biloela** Queensland, E Australia 24°27´S 150°31´E
184 *D2* **Bilo Gora** ▲▲ N Croatia
189 *K9* **Bilohirs'k** *Rus.* Belogorsk; *prev.* Karasubazar. Respublika Krym, S Ukraine 45°04´N 34°35´E
188 *F2* **Bilokorovychi** *Rus.* Belokorovichi. Zhytomyrs'ka Oblast', N Ukraine 51°07´N 28°02´E
189 *M4* **Bilokurakine** Luhans'ka Oblast', E Ukraine 49°32´N 38°44´E
189 *J2* **Bilopillya** *Rus.* Belopol'ye. Sums'ka Oblast', NE Ukraine 51°09´N 34°17´E
189 *N4* **Bilovods'k** *Rus.* Belovodsk. Luhans'ka Oblast', E Ukraine 49°11´N 39°34´E
68 *F4* **Biloxi** Mississippi, S USA 30°24´N 88°53´W
189 *I7* **Bilozerka** Khersons'ka Oblast', S Ukraine 46°36´N 32°23´E
189 *L5* **Bilozers'ke** Donets'ka Oblast', E Ukraine 48°29´N 37°03´E
181 *H8* **Bilshausen** Niedersachsen, Germany 10°10´N 51°37´E
162 *F6* **Bilthoven** Utrecht, C Netherlands 52°07´N 05°12´E
134 *F2* **Biltine** Biltine, E Chad 14°30´N 20°53´E
134 *F1* **Biltine** *off.* Préfecture de Biltine. ◐ *prefecture* E Chad
Biltine, Préfecture de *see* Biltine
Bilüü *see* Ulaanhus
Bilwi *see* Puerto Cabezas
Bilyasuvar *see* Biläsuvar
189 *H7* **Bilyayivka** Odes'ka Oblast', SW Ukraine 46°28´N 30°11´E
163 *G10* **Bilzen** Limburg, NE Belgium 50°52´N 05°31´E
Bimbéréké *see* Bembèrèkè
277 *K6* **Bimberi Peak** ▲ New South Wales, SE Australia 35°42´S 148°46´E
133 *H7* **Bimbila** E Ghana 08°54´N 00°05´E
134 *E6* **Bimbo** Ombella-Mpoko, SW Central African Republic 04°19´N 18°27´E
90 *E2* **Bimini Islands** *island group* W Bahamas
232 *F7* **Bīna** Madhya Pradesh, C India 24°09´N 78°10´E
223 *I3* **Bīnālūd, Kūh-e** ▲▲ NE Iran
166 *G7* **Binas** Centre, France 47°54´N 1°28´E
163 *D11* **Binche** Hainaut, S Belgium 50°25´N 04°10´E
Bindloe Island *see* Marchena, Isla
139 *H3* **Bindura** Mashonaland Central, NE Zimbabwe 17°20´S 31°21´E
171 *J3* **Binefar** Aragón, NE Spain 41°51´N 00°17´E
138 *G3* **Binga** Matabeleland North, W Zimbabwe 17°40´S 27°22´E
277 *L3* **Bingara** New South Wales, SE Australia 29°54´S 150°36´E
244 *B5* **Bingcaowan** Gansu, China 37°22´N 103°26´E
181 *D12* **Bingen am Rhein** Rheinland-Pfalz, SW Germany 49°58´N 07°54´E
75 *D12* **Binger** Oklahoma, C USA 35°19´N 98°19´W
Bingerau *see* Węgrów
Bin Ghalfān, Jazā'ir *see* Ḩalāniyāt, Juzur al
63 *K3* **Bingham** Maine, NE USA 45°01´N 69°51´W
62 *F7* **Binghamton** New York, NE USA 42°06´N 75°55´W
Bin Ghanīmah, Jabal *see* Bin Ghunaymah, Jabal
128 *C5* **Bin Ghunaymah, Jabal** *var.* Jabal Bin Ghanīmah. ▲▲ C Libya
217 *J2* **Bingird** NE Iraq 36°03´N 45°03´E
159 *K8* **Bingley** UK 53°51´N 1°50´W
Bingmei *see* Congjiang
215 *I6* **Bingöl** Bingöl, E Turkey 38°54´N 40°29´E
215 *I6* **Bingöl** ◐ *province* E Turkey
243 *K4* **Bingxi** China 28°40´N 118°15´E
245 *L8* **Binhai** *var.* Dongkan. Jiangsu, E China 34°00´N 119°51´E
257 *J8* **Binh Đinh** *var.* An Nhon. Binh Đinh, C Vietnam 13°53´N 109°07´E
257 *I7* **Binh Sơn** *var.* Châu Ô. Quang Ngai, C Vietnam 15°18´N 108°45´E
Binimani *see* Bintimani
258 *C3* **Binjai** Sumatera, W Indonesia 03°37´N 98°30´E
277 *K4* **Binnaway** New South Wales, SE Australia 31°34´S 149°24´E
176 *D3* **Binningen** Basel-Land, NW Switzerland 47°32´N 07°35´E
260 *E7* **Binongko, Pulau** *island* Kepulauan Tukangbesi, C Indonesia
258 *D2* **Bintang, Banjaran** ▲▲ Peninsular Malaysia
258 *F4* **Bintan, Pulau** *island* Kepulauan Riau, W Indonesia
132 *D6* **Bintimani** *var.* Binimani. ▲ NE Sierra Leone 09°21´N 11°09´W
Bint Jubayl *see* Bent Jbaïl
258 *J3* **Bintulu** Sarawak, East Malaysia 03°12´N 113°01´E
261 *J5* **Bintuni** *prev.* Steenkool. Papua, E Indonesia 02°03´S 133°45´E
261 *I5* **Bintuni, Teluk** *bay* Papua, E Indonesia
245 *K5* **Binxian** China 37°28´N 117°56´E
242 *D9* **Binyang** *var.* Binzhou. Guangxi Zhuangzu Zizhiqu, S China 23°15´N 108°40´E
245 *K5* **Binzhou** Shandong, E China 37°23´N 118°03´E
Binzhou *see* Binyang
116 *B5* **Bío Bío** *var.* Región del Bío Bío. ◐ *region* C Chile
Bío Bío, Región del *see* Bío Bío
116 *B6* **Bío Bío, Río** ≈ C Chile
134 *A6* **Bioco, Isla de** *var.* Bioko, *Eng.* Fernando Po, *Sp.* Fernando Póo; *prev.* Macías Nguema Biyogo. *island* NW Equatorial Guinea
184 *B4* **Biograd na Moru** *It.* Zaravecchia. Zadar, SW Croatia 43°57´N 15°27´E
Bioko *see* Bioco, Isla de
184 *D5* **Biokovo** ▲▲ S Croatia
80 *D5* **Biola** California, USA 36°48´N 120°01´W
Biorra *see* Birr
Bipontium *see* Zweibrücken
110 *E1* **Biquinhas** Minas Gerais, Brazil 18°42´S 45°30´E
223 *K8* **Bīrag, Kūh-e** ▲▲ SE Iran
128 *C4* **Birāk** *var.* Brak. C Libya 27°32´N 14°17´E
217 *I6* **Bi'r al Islām** C Iraq 32°15´N 43°40´E
234 *I3* **Biramitrapur** Orissa, E India 22°24´N 84°42´E
217 *J7* **Bi'r an Nişf** S Iraq 31°22´N 44°07´E
134 *G3* **Birao** Vakaga, NE Central African Republic 10°14´N 22°49´E
228 *F6* **Birata** *Rus.* Darganata, Dargan-Ata. Lebap Welaýaty, NE Turkmenistan 40°30´N 62°09´E
238 *G4* **Biratar Bulak** *well* NW China
233 *J6* **Birātnagar** Eastern, SE Nepal 26°28´N 87°16´E
252 *E5* **Biratori** Hokkaidō, NE Japan 42°35´N 142°07´E
83 *J4* **Birch Creek** Alaska, USA 66°17´N 145°54´W
83 *J4* **Birch Creek** ≈ Alaska, USA
57 *M5* **Birch Hills** Saskatchewan, S Canada 52°58´N 105°22´W
277 *I6* **Birchip** Victoria, SE Australia 36°01´S 142°55´E
54 *E4* **Birch Lake** ◎ Northwest Territories, NW Canada
74 *H2* **Birch Lake** ◎ Minnesota, N USA
57 *I1* **Birch Mountains** ▲▲ Alberta, W Canada
55 *I9* **Birch River** Manitoba, S Canada
90 *E7* **Birchs Hill** *hill* W Jamaica
83 *I6* **Birchwood** Alaska, USA 61°24´N 149°28´W
283 *I1* **Bird Island** *island* S Northern Mariana Islands
159 *L8* **Birdsall** UK 54°04´N 0°44´W
215 *H8* **Birecik** Şanlıurfa, S Turkey 37°03´N 37°59´E
232 *G5* **Birendranagar** *var.* Surkhet. Mid Western, W Nepal 28°35´N 81°36´E
Bir es Saba *see* Be'ér Sheva'
130 *B7* **Bir-Gandouz** SW Western Sahara 21°35´N 16°27´W
233 *I6* **Birganj** Central, C Nepal 27°03´N 84°53´E
159 *J4* **Birgham** UK 55°39´N 2°20´W
134 *H4* **Biri** ≈ W Sudan
Bi'r Ibn Hirmās *see* Al Bi'r
171 *L10* **Birine** Algeria
261 *L5* **Biri, Sungai** ≈ Papua, E Indonesia
223 *I5* **Bīrjand** Khorāsān-e Janūbī, E Iran 32°54´N 59°14´E
217 *J7* **Birkat Ḩāmid** *well* S Iraq
155 *C9* **Birkeland** Aust-Agder, S Norway 58°18´N 08°13´E
181 *C12* **Birkenfeld** Rheinland-Pfalz, SW Germany 49°39´N 07°10´E
159 *I10* **Birkenhead** NW England, UK 53°24´N 03°02´W
177 *L3* **Birkfeld** Steiermark, SE Austria 47°21´N 15°40´E
219 *F12* **Bi'r Khidād** Jordan
276 *C2* **Birksgate Range** ▲▲ South Australia
Bîrlad *see* Bârlad
161 *H4* **Birmingham** C England, UK 52°30´N 01°50´W
66 *D8* **Birmingham** Alabama, S USA 33°30´N 86°47´W
157 *G10* **Birmingham** ✕ C England, UK 52°27´N 01°46´W
Bir Moghrein *see* Bîr Mogreïn
130 *D6* **Bîr Mogreïn** *var.* Bir Moghrein; *prev.* Fort-Trinquet. Tiris Zemmour, N Mauritania 25°10´N 11°35´W
284 *E3* **Birnie Island** *atoll* Phoenix Islands, C Kiribati
133 *I5* **Birnin Gaouré** *var.* Birni-Ngaouré. Dosso, SW Niger 13°09´N 02°53´E
Birni-Ngaouré *see* Birnin Gaouré
133 *J5* **Birnin Kebbi** Kebbi, NW Nigeria 12°28´N 04°08´E
133 *J4* **Birnin Konni** *var.* Birni-Nkonni. Tahoua, SW Niger 13°51´N 05°15´E
Birni-Nkonni *see* Birnin Konni
133 *L5* **Birnin Kudu** Jigawa, N Nigeria 11°28´N 09°29´E
193 *K8* **Birobidzhan** Yevreyskaya Avtonomnaya Oblast', SE Russian Federation 48°42´N 132°55´E
157 *C9* **Birr** *var.* Parsonstown, *Ir.* Biorra. C Ireland 53°06´N 07°55´W
181 *B11* **Birresborn** Rheinland-Pfalz, Germany 6°38´N 50°11´E
277 *J3* **Birrie River** ≈ New South Wales/Queensland, SE Australia
176 *C4* **Birse** ≈ NW Switzerland
Birsen *see* Biržai
176 *D3* **Birsfelden** Basel-Land, NW Switzerland 47°33´N 07°37´E
197 *L2* **Birsk** Respublika Bashkortostan, W Russian Federation 55°24´N 55°33´E
181 *G11* **Birstein** Hessen, Germany 9°18´N 50°21´E
191 *D9* **Birštonas** Kaunas, C Lithuania 54°37´N 24°00´E
159 *K6* **Birtley** UK 54°53´N 1°34´W
239 *H8* **Biru** Xinjiang Uygur Zizhiqu, W China 31°30´N 93°56´E
Biruni *see* Beruniy
193 *H7* **Biryusa** ≈ C Russian Federation
190 *E7* **Biržai** *Ger.* Birsen. Panevėžys, NE Lithuania 56°12´N 24°47´E
175 *J14* **Birżebbuġa** SE Malta 35°50´N 14°32´E
Bisanthe *see* Tekirdağ
260 *G4* **Bisa, Pulau** *island* Maluku, E Indonesia
79 *J10* **Bisbee** Arizona, SW USA 31°27´N 109°55´W
74 *D2* **Bisbee** North Dakota, N USA 48°36´N 99°21´W
Biscaia, Baía de *see* Biscay, Bay of
168 *C4* **Biscarosse et de Parentis, Étang de** ◎ Aquitaine, France
168 *C4* **Biscarrosse** Aquitaine, France 44°24´N 1°10´W
164 *F7* **Biscarrosse et de Parentis, Étang de** ◎ SW France
168 *C4* **Biscarrosse-Plage** Aquitaine, France 44°27´N 1°15´W
170 *F1* **Biscay, Bay of** *Sp.* Golfo de Vizcaya, *Port.* Baía de Biscaia. *bay* France/Spain
69 *N9* **Biscayne Bay** *bay* Florida, SE USA
290 *H3* **Biscay Plain** *undersea feature* SE Bay of Biscay
175 *H9* **Bisceglie** Puglia, SE Italy 41°14´N 16°31´E
Bischoflack *see* Škofja Loka
Bischofsburg *see* Biskupiec
177 *I3* **Bischofshofen** Salzburg, NW Austria 47°25´N 13°13´E
179 *I8* **Bischofswerda** Sachsen, E Germany 51°07´N 14°13´E
165 *L3* **Bischwiller** Bas-Rhin, NE France 48°46´N 07°52´E
67 *J7* **Biscoe** North Carolina, SE USA 35°20´N 79°46´W
292 *E3* **Biscoe Islands** *island group* Antarctica
62 *B1* **Biscotasi Lake** ◎ Ontario, S Canada
62 *B1* **Biscotasing** Ontario, S Canada 47°16´N 82°04´W
102 *E3* **Biscucuy** Portuguesa, NW Venezuela 09°22´N 69°59´W
185 *K7* **Biser** Khaskovo, S Bulgaria 41°52´N 25°59´E
195 *L10* **Bisert'** Sverdlovskaya oblasť, Russian federation
184 *B6* **Biševo** *It.* Busi. *island* SW Croatia
212 *G8* **Bīshah, Wādī** *dry watercourse* C Saudi Arabia
161 *H4* **Bishampton** UK 52°10´N 2°01´W
242 *C3* **Bishan** Chongqing Shi, China 29°22´N 106°07´E
229 *L4* **Bishkek** *var.* Pishpek; *prev.* Frunze. ● (Kyrgyzstan) Chuyskaya Oblast', N Kyrgyzstan 42°54´N 74°27´E
229 *L4* **Bishkek** ✕ Chuyskaya Oblast', N Kyrgyzstan 42°55´N 74°37´E
233 *J8* **Bishnupur** West Bengal, NE India 23°05´N 87°20´E
138 *G9* **Bisho** Eastern Cape, S South Africa 32°46´S 27°21´E
80 *F5* **Bishop** California, W USA 37°22´N 118°24´W
70 *G9* **Bishop** Texas, SW USA 27°36´N 97°49´W
159 *K6* **Bishop Auckland** N England, UK 54°41´N 01°41´W
158 *E7* **Bishops Court** UK 54°18´N 5°36´W
Bishop's Lynn *see* King's Lynn
161 *K5* **Bishop's Stortford** E England, UK 51°45´N 00°11´E
67 *J8* **Bishopville** South Carolina, SE USA 34°18´N 80°15´W
216 *F3* **Bishrī, Jabal** ▲▲ E Syria
136 *C7* **Bisina, Lake** *prev.* Lake Salisbury. ◎ E Uganda
Biskara *see* Biskra
131 *J2* **Biskra** *var.* Beskra, Biskara. NE Algeria 34°51´N 05°44´E
171 *N10* **Biskra** Algeria
182 *H4* **Biskupiec** *Ger.* Bischofsburg. Warmińsko-Mazurskie, NE Poland 53°52´N 20°57´E
180 *B7* **Bislich** Nordrhein-Westfalen, Germany 6°29´N 51°41´E
263 *N8* **Bislig** Mindanao, S Philippines 08°10´N 126°19´E
75 *J10* **Bismarck** Missouri, C USA 37°46´N 90°37´W
74 *C3* **Bismarck** *state capital* North Dakota, N USA 46°49´N 100°47´W
280 *B2* **Bismarck Archipelago** *island group* NE Papua New Guinea
205 *N9* **Bismarck Plate** *tectonic feature* W Pacific Ocean
280 *B3* **Bismarck Range** ▲▲ N Papua New Guinea
280 *C2* **Bismarck Sea** *sea* W Pacific Ocean
215 *I7* **Bismil** Dıyarbakır, SE Turkey 37°53´N 40°38´E
89 *I4* **Bismuna, Laguna** *lagoon* NE Nicaragua
Bisnulok *see* Phitsanulok

◆ Country
● Country Capital
◇ Dependent Territory
○ Dependent Territory Capital
◐ Administrative Regions
✕ International Airport
▲ Mountain
▲▲ Mountain Range
Ѫ Volcano
≈ River
◎ Lake
⊡ Reservoir

◆ Country ◇ Dependent Territory ⬥ Administrative Regions ▲ Mountain ▲ Volcano ◉ Lake
● Country Capital ○ Dependent Territory Capital ✈ International Airport ▲ Mountain Range ✍ River ◈ Reservoir

Legend:
◆ Country ◇ Dependent Territory ◆ Administrative Regions ▲ Mountain ⛰ Volcano ◎ Lake
● Country Capital ○ Dependent Territory Capital ✕ International Airport ▲ Mountain Range ♒ River ☒ Reservoir

◆ Country   ◇ Dependent Territory   ◆ Administrative Regions   ▲ Mountain   🌋 Volcano   ○ Lake
● Country Capital   ○ Dependent Territory Capital   ✕ International Airport   ▲ Mountain Range   ♒ River   □ Reservoir

◆ Country   ◇ Dependent Territory   ◆ Administrative Regions   ▲ Mountain   ▲ Volcano   ◎ Lake
● Country Capital   ○ Dependent Territory Capital   ✕ International Airport   ▲ Mountain Range   ≈ River   ◻ Reservoir

327
INDEX

◆ Country   ◇ Dependent Territory   ◆ Administrative Regions   ⯅ Mountain   ▰ Volcano   ⊚ Lake
● Country Capital ○ Dependent Territory Capital ✈ International Airport   ⯅ Mountain Range ⋦ River   ⊠ Reservoir

◆ Country ◇ Dependent Territory ○ Administrative Regions ▲ Mountain ◣ Volcano ◎ Lake
● Country Capital ○ Dependent Territory Capital × International Airport ▲ Mountain Range ◈ River ◎ Reservoir

Dangla see Tanggula Shan, China

♦ Country   ◇ Dependent Territory   ▲ Mountain   ☲ Volcano   ☒ Lake
● Country Capital   ○ Dependent Territory Capital   ✈ International Airport   ▲ Mountain Range   ♒ River   ▨ Reservoir

◆ Country
● Country Capital
◇ Dependent Territory
◎ Dependent Territory Capital
◆ Administrative Regions
✕ International Airport
▲ Mountain
▲ Mountain Range
▲ Volcano
≈ River
◊ Lake
◙ Reservoir

◆ Country ◇ Dependent Territory ● Country Capital ○ Dependent Territory Capital
◇ Administrative Regions ▲ Mountain ▲ Volcano ⊗ Lake
✈ International Airport ▲ Mountain Range ♦ River ⊠ Reservoir

| ◆ Country | ◇ Dependent Territory | ◈ Administrative Regions | ▲ Mountain | ☼ Volcano | ◎ Lake |
| ● Country Capital | ○ Dependent Territory Capital | ✕ International Airport | ▲ Mountain Range | ⊘ River | ⊠ Reservoir |

G

Legend:
◆ Country | ◇ Dependent Territory | ◈ Administrative Regions | ▲ Mountain | ▲ Volcano | ◉ Lake
● Country Capital | ○ Dependent Territory Capital | ✕ International Airport | ▲ Mountain Range | ⌇ River | ▣ Reservoir

Goodyears Bar - Great Slave Lake
INDEX
345

80 E1 **Goodyears Bar** California, USA 39°32′N 120°53′W
159 L9 **Goole** E England, UK 53°43′N 00°46′W
277 J5 **Goolgowi** New South Wales, SE Australia 34°00′S 145°43′E
276 G6 **Goolwa** South Australia 35°31′S 138°43′E
277 L2 **Goondiwindi** Queensland, E Australia 28°33′S 150°22′E
162 I6 **Goor** Overijssel, E Netherlands 52°13′N 06°33′E
Goose Bay *see* Happy Valley-Goose Bay
77 K7 **Gooseberry Creek** ≈ Wyoming, C USA
67 J9 **Goose Creek** South Carolina, SE USA 32°58′N 80°01′W
117 G12 **Goose Green** *var* Prado del Ganso. East Falkland, Falkland Islands 51°52′S 59°W
76 D8 **Goose Lake** *var.* Lago dos Gansos. ◎ California/Oregon, W USA
74 E2 **Goose River** ≈ North Dakota, N USA
233 K8 **Gopalganj** Dhaka, S Bangladesh 23°00′N 89°48′E
233 H6 **Gopālganj** Bihār, N India 26°28′N 84°26′E
Gopher State *see* Minnesota
179 E12 **Göppingen** Baden-Württemberg, SW Germany 48°42′N 09°39′E
182 D6 **Góra** *Ger.* Guhrau. Dolnośląskie, SW Poland 51°40′N 16°03′E
182 H6 **Góra Kalwaria** Mazowieckie, C Poland 52°00′N 21°14′E
233 H6 **Gorakhpur** Uttar Pradesh, N India 26°45′N 83°23′E
Gora Kyuren *see* Kurendag
Gorany *see* Harany
184 E5 **Goražde** Fedaracija Bosna I Hercegovina, SE Bosnia and Herzegovina 43°39′N 18°58′E
Gorbovichi *see* Harbavichy
Gorče Petrov *see* Đorče Petrov
80 A6 **Gorda** California, USA 35°56′N 121°28′W
42 C6 **Gorda Ridges** *undersea feature* NE Pacific Ocean
169 K5 **Gordes** Provence-Alpes-Côte d'Azur, France 43°54′N 5°12′E
191 J10 **Gordeyevka** Bryanskaya Oblast', Russian Federation
Gordiaz *see* Gardīz
134 F3 **Gordil** Vakaga, N Central African Republic 09°37′N 21°42′E
159 J4 **Gordon** UK 55°41′N 2°33′W
69 K1 **Gordon** Georgia, SE USA 32°52′N 83°19′W
74 B6 **Gordon** Nebraska, C USA 42°48′N 102°12′W
70 G4 **Gordon** Texas, SW USA 32°32′N 98°21′W
74 B6 **Gordon Creek** ≈ Nebraska, C USA
117 D14 **Gordon, Isla** *island* S Chile
277 J10 **Gordon, Lake** ◎ Tasmania, SE Australia
54 F4 **Gordon Lake** ◎ Northwest Territories, NW Canada
67 K3 **Gordonsville** Virginia, NE USA 38°08′N 78°11′W
134 D4 **Goré** Logone-Oriental, S Chad 07°55′N 16°38′E
136 D4 **Gorē** Oromo, C Ethiopia 08°08′N 35°33′E
278 C12 **Gore** Southland, South Island, New Zealand 46°06′S 168°58′E
62 B2 **Gore Bay** Manitoulin Island, Ontario, S Canada 45°54′N 82°28′W
159 I3 **Gorebridge** UK 55°50′N 3°03′W
70 F4 **Goree** Texas, SW USA 33°28′N 99°31′W
215 H5 **Görele** Giresun, NE Turkey 41°00′N 39°00′E
63 I3 **Gore Mountain** ▲ Vermont, NE USA 44°55′N 71°47′W
83 I7 **Gore Point** *headland* Alaska, USA 59°12′N 150°57′W
79 L3 **Gore Range** ▲▲ Colorado, C USA
160 B3 **Gorey** *Ir.* Guaire. Wexford, SE Ireland 52°40′N 06°18′W
223 H7 **Gorgāb** Kermān, S Iran
222 G3 **Gorgān** *var.* Astarabad, Astrabad, Gurgan, *prev.* Asterābād; *anc.* Hyrcania. Golestán, N Iran 36°53′N 54°28′E
222 G3 **Gorgān, Rūd-e** ≈ N Iran
132 C3 **Gorgol** ◈ *region* S Mauritania
174 C6 **Gorgona, Isola di** *island* Archipelago Toscano, C Italy
63 J5 **Gorham** Maine, NE USA 43°41′N 70°27′W
215 K4 **Gori** C Georgia 42°00′N 44°07′E
162 F7 **Gorinchem** *var.* Gorkum. Zuid-Holland, C Netherlands 51°50′N 04°59′E
161 J6 **Goring** UK 51°31′N 1°08′W
215 L5 **Goris** SE Armenia 39°31′N 46°20′E
194 F10 **Goritsy** Tverskaya Oblast', W Russian Federation 57°09′N 36°44′E
177 J6 **Gorizia** *Ger.* Görz. Friuli-Venezia Giulia, NE Italy 45°57′N 13°37′E
188 C9 **Gorj** ◈ *county* SW Romania
177 K6 **Gorjanci** *var.* Uskočke Planine, Žumberak, Žumberačko Gorje, *Ger.* Uskokengebirge; *prev.* Sichelburger Gerbirge. ▲ Croatia/Slovenia Europe *see also* Žumberačko Gorje
172 C4 **Gorjão** Santarém, Portugal 39°14′N 8°16′W
Görkau *see* Jirkov
Gorki *see* Horki
Gor'kiy *see* Nizhniy Novgorod
Gor'kiy Reservoir *see* Gor'kovskoye Vodokhranilishche
197 H1 **Gor'kovskoye Vodokhranilishche** *Eng.* Gor'kiy Reservoir. ▣ W Russian Federation
Gorkum *see* Gorinchem
155 E12 **Gørlev** Vestsjælland, E Denmark 55°33′N 11°14′E
183 H9 **Gorlice** Małopolskie, S Poland 49°40′N 21°09′E
179 J8 **Görlitz** Sachsen, E Germany 51°09′N 14°58′E
Görlitz *see* Zgorzelec
Gorlovka *see* Horlivka
81 D9 **Gorman** California, USA 34°48′N 118°51′W
70 G5 **Gorman** Texas, SW USA 32°12′N 98°40′W
67 J2 **Gormania** West Virginia, NE USA 39°16′N 79°18′W
158 D3 **Loch Gorm** ◎ UK
Gorna Dzhumaya *see* Blagoevgrad
185 K5 **Gorna Oryakhovitsa** Veliko Tŭrnovo, N Bulgaria 43°07′N 25°40′E
185 K5 **Gorna Studena** Veliko Tŭrnovo, N Bulgaria 43°26′N 25°21′E
Gornja Mužlja *see* Mužlja
177 L4 **Gornja Radgona** *Ger.* Oberradkersburg. NE Slovenia 46°39′N 16°00′E
184 G4 **Gornji Milanovac** Serbia, C Serbia 44°01′N 20°26′E
184 D4 **Gornji Vakuf** *var* Uskoplje. Federacija Bosna I Hercegovina, SW Bosnia and Herzegovina 43°55′N 17°34′E
192 F8 **Gorno-Altaysk** Respublika Altay, S Russian Federation 51°59′N 85°56′E
Gorno-Altayskaya Respublika *see* Altay, Respublika
193 I7 **Gorno-Chuyskiy** Irkutskaya Oblast', C Russian Federation 57°33′N 111°38′E
195 L9 **Gornozavodsk** Permskaya Oblast', NW Russian Federation 58°21′N 58°24′E
249 J1 **Gornozavodsk** Ostrov Sakhalin, Sakhalinskaya Oblast', SE Russian Federation 46°34′N 141°52′E
192 F8 **Gornyak** Altayskiy Kray, S Russian Federation 50°58′N 81°24′E
197 J4 **Gornyy** Chitunskaya Oblast', S Russian Federation 51°42′N 48°26′E
Gornyy Altay *see* Altay, Respublika
197 I5 **Gornyy Balykley** Volgogradskaya Oblast', SW Russian Federation 49°37′N 45°03′E
136 D4 **Goroch'an** ▲ W Ethiopia 09°09′N 37°16′E
Gorodenka *see* Horodenka
197 H1 **Gorodets** Nizhegorodskaya Oblast', W Russian Federation 56°36′N 43°27′E
Gorodets *see* Haradzyets
Gorodeya *see* Haradzyeya
190 I3 **Gorodishche** Leningradskaya Oblast', Russian Federation
190 H5 **Gorodishche** Novgorodskaya Oblast', Russian Federation
197 I3 **Gorodishche** Penzenskaya Oblast', W Russian Federation 53°17′N 45°39′E
Gorodishche *see* Horodyshche
Gorodnya *see* Horodnya
Gorodok *see* Haradok
Gorodok/Gorodok Yagellonski *see* Horodok
197 H7 **Gorodovikovsk** Respublika Kalmykiya, SW Russian Federation 46°07′N 41°56′E
280 B3 **Goroka** Eastern Highlands, C Papua New Guinea 06°02′S 145°22′E
Gorokhov *see* Horokhiv
197 H2 **Gorokhovets** Vladimirskaya Oblast', W Russian Federation 56°12′N 42°40′E
133 H4 **Gorom-Gorom** NE Burkina 14°27′N 00°14′W
261 I6 **Gorong, Kepulauan** *island group* E Indonesia
139 I3 **Gorongosa** Sofala, C Mozambique 18°40′S 34°03′E
261 I6 **Gorong, Pulau** *island* Kepulauan Gorong, E Indonesia
260 E3 **Gorontalo** Sulawesi, C Indonesia 0°33′N 123°05′E
260 E4 **Gorontalo, Teluk** *bay* Sulawesi, C Indonesia
Gorontalo, Teluk *see* Tomini, Gulf of
114 C10 **Gorostiaga** Buenos Aires, Argentina 34°49′S 59°52′W
182 G3 **Górowo Iławeckie** *Ger.* Landsberg. Warmińsko-Mazurskie, NE Poland 54°18′N 20°30′E
160 D9 **Gorran** UK 50°14′N 4°48′W
162 H4 **Gorredijk** *Fris.* De Gordyk. Friesland, N Netherlands 53°00′N 06°04′E
144 B8 **Gorringe Ridge** *undersea feature* E Atlantic Ocean
166 D6 **Gorron** Pays de la Loire, France 48°25′N 0°49′W
160 E6 **Gorseinon** UK 51°40′N 4°03′W

162 H6 **Gorssel** Gelderland, E Netherlands 52°12′N 06°13′E
158 A10 **Gort** Galway, Ireland 53°04′N 8°49′W
158 B5 **Gortahork** Donegal, Ireland 55°07′N 8°08′W
158 C6 **Gortin** UK 54°43′N 7°15′W
177 J4 **Görtschitz** ≈ S Austria
Goryn *see* Horyn'
Görz *see* Gorizia
182 C6 **Gorzów** ◈ *province* W Poland
182 C5 **Gorzów Wielkopolski** *Ger.* Landsberg, Landsberg an der Warthe. Lubuskie, W Poland 52°44′N 15°12′E
228 B5 **Goşabo** *var.* Goshoba, *Rus.* Koshoba. Balkan Welaýaty, NW Turkmenistan 40°28′N 54°11′E
176 E5 **Göschenen** Uri, C Switzerland 46°40′N 08°36′E
253 B11 **Gosen** Niigata, Honshū, C Japan 37°45′N 139°11′E
277 L5 **Gosford** New South Wales, SE Australia 33°25′S 151°18′E
159 K5 **Gosforth** UK 55°00′N 1°37′W
80 D6 **Goshen** California, USA 36°21′N 119°25′W
73 F9 **Goshen** Indiana, N USA 41°34′N 85°49′W
65 H4 **Goshen** New York, NE USA 41°24′N 74°17′W
Goshoba *see* Goşabo
252 D7 **Goshogawara** *var.* Gosyogawara. Aomori, Honshū, C Japan 40°47′N 140°24′E
Goshquduq Qum *see* Tosquduq Qumlari
180 I7 **Goslar** Niedersachsen, C Germany 51°55′N 10°25′E
75 J12 **Gosnell** Arkansas, C USA 35°57′N 89°58′W
184 B4 **Gospić** Lika-Senj, C Croatia 44°32′N 15°21′E
161 J8 **Gosport** S England, UK 50°48′N 01°08′W
154 B4 **Gossa** *island* S Norway
176 E3 **Gossau** Sankt Gallen, NE Switzerland 47°25′N 09°16′E
163 E11 **Gosselies** *var.* Goss'lies. Hainaut, S Belgium 50°28′N 04°26′E
132 G4 **Gossi** Tombouctou, C Mali 15°44′N 01°19′W
Goss'lies *see* Gosselies
184 G7 **Gostivar** W FYR Macedonia 41°48′N 20°55′E
Gostomel' *see* Hostomel'
182 E6 **Gostyń** *var.* Gostyn. Wielkopolskie, C Poland 51°52′N 17°00′E
Gostyn *see* Gostyń
182 G6 **Gostynin** Mazowiesckie, C Poland 52°25′N 19°27′E
Gosyogawara *see* Goshogawara
155 E9 **Göta Älv** ≈ S Sweden
155 H9 **Göta kanal** *canal* S Sweden
155 G9 **Götaland** *cultural region* S Sweden
155 E10 **Göteborg** *Eng.* Gothenburg. Västra Götaland, S Sweden 57°43′N 11°58′E
155 F9 **Göteborg och Bohus** ◈ *county* S Sweden
133 L7 **Gotel Mountains** ▲▲ E Nigeria
155 F9 **Götene** Västra Götaland, S Sweden 58°32′N 13°29′E
Gotera *see* San Francisco
181 I9 **Gotha** Thüringen, C Germany 50°57′N 10°43′E
161 I3 **Gotham** UK 52°51′N 1°12′W
75 C8 **Gothenburg** Nebraska, C USA 40°57′N 100°09′W
Gothenburg *see* Göteborg
133 H4 **Gothèye** Tillabéri, SW Niger 13°52′N 01°27′E
Gothland *see* Gotland
155 J10 **Gotland** *var.* Gothland, Gottland. ◈ *county* SE Sweden
155 J9 **Gotland** *island* SE Sweden
250 B7 **Gotō-rettō** *island group* SW Japan
185 I8 **Gotse Delchev** *prev.* Nevrokop. Blagoevgrad, SW Bulgaria 41°33′N 23°42′E
155 J9 **Gotska Sandön** *island* SE Sweden
250 E4 **Gōtsu** *var.* Gôtu. Shimane, Honshū, SW Japan 35°N 132°14′E
181 H8 **Göttingen** *var.* Goettingen. Niedersachsen, C Germany 51°33′N 09°55′E
Gottland *see* Gotland
154 I3 **Gottne** Västernorrland, C Sweden 63°27′N 18°25′E
Gottschee *see* Kočevje
Gottwaldov *see* Zlín
Gôtu *see* Gōtsu
228 B6 **Goturdepe** *Rus.* Koturdepe. Balkan Welaýaty, W Turkmenistan 39°32′N 53°39′E
176 F4 **Götzis** Vorarlberg, NW Austria 47°21′N 09°40′E
166 A6 **Gouarec** Bretagne, France 48°13′N 3°11′W
245 M1 **Goubangzi** Liaoning, China 41°13′N 121°28′E
162 E7 **Gouda** Zuid-Holland, C Netherlands 52°01′N 04°42′E
132 C4 **Goudiri** *var.* Goudiry. E Senegal 14°12′N 12°41′W
Goudiry *see* Goudiri
133 L4 **Goudoumaria** Diffa, S Niger 13°28′N 11°15′E
291 G11 **Gough Fracture Zone** *tectonic feature* S Atlantic Ocean
291 H11 **Gough Island** *island* Tristan da Cunha, S Atlantic Ocean
114 C9 **Gouin** Buenos Aires, Argentina 34°28′S 59°48′W
58 G7 **Gouin, Réservoir** ▣ Québec, SE Canada
62 A1 **Goulais River** Ontario, S Canada 46°41′N 84°22′W
277 K6 **Goulburn** New South Wales, SE Australia 34°45′S 149°44′E
277 J6 **Goulburn River** ≈ Victoria, SE Australia
293 H6 **Gould Coast** *physical region* Antarctica
Goulimime *see* Guelmime
186 G2 **Gouménissa** Kentrikí Makedonía, N Greece 40°56′N 22°27′E
132 G3 **Goundam** Tombouctou, NW Mali 16°27′N 03°39′W
134 D4 **Goundi** Moyen-Chari, S Chad 09°22′N 17°21′E
134 D3 **Gounou-Gaya** Mayo-Kébbi, SW Chad 09°37′N 15°30′E
171 K9 **Gouraya** Algeria
132 G5 **Gourci** *var.* Gourcy. NW Burkina 13°13′N 02°20′W
Gourcy *see* Gourci
165 H7 **Gourdon** Lot, S France 44°45′N 01°22′E
159 J1 **Gourdon** UK 56°49′N 2°17′W
133 L4 **Gouré** Zinder, SE Niger 13°59′N 10°16′E
164 E4 **Gourin** Morbihan, NW France 48°07′N 03°37′W
140 F10 **Gouritz** ≈ Western Cape, South Africa
132 G3 **Gourma-Rharous** Tombouctou, C Mali 16°54′N 01°55′W
165 H2 **Gournay-en-Bray** Seine-Maritime, N France 49°29′N 01°42′E
128 E8 **Gouro** Borkou-Ennedi-Tibesti, N Chad 19°26′N 19°36′E
158 F3 **Gourock** UK 55°57′N 4°50′W
172 C2 **Gouveia** Guarda, N Portugal 40°29′N 07°35′W
62 G4 **Gouverneur** New York, NE USA 44°20′N 75°27′W
163 H12 **Gouvy** Luxembourg, E Belgium 50°10′N 05°55′E
91 N3 **Gouyave** *var.* Charlotte Town. NW Grenada 12°10′N 61°44′W
167 H10 **Gouzon** Limousin, France 46°11′N 2°14′E
Goverla, Gora *see* Hoverla, Hora
111 M2 **Governador Lindemberg** Espírito Santo, Brazil 19°16′S 40°29′W
111 K1 **Governador Valadares** Minas Gerais, SE Brazil 18°51′S 41°57′W
263 N9 **Governor Generoso** Mindanao, S Philippines 06°36′N 126°06′E
61 M9 **Governor's Harbour** Eleuthera Island, C Bahamas 25°11′N 76°15′W
239 H3 **Govĭ-Altay** ◈ *province* SW Mongolia
236 F4 **Govĭ Altayn Nuruu** ▲▲ S Mongolia
234 G2 **Govind Ballabh Pant Sāgar** ▣ C India
232 E4 **Govind Sāgar** ▣ NE India
Govurdak *see* Govurdak
64 A2 **Gowanda** New York, NE USA 42°25′N 78°55′W
230 D6 **Gowd-e Zereh, Dasht-e** *var.* Guad-i-Zirreh. *marsh* SW Afghanistan
58 E7 **Gowganda** Ontario, S Canada 47°41′N 80°46′W
72 J3 **Gowganda Lake** ◎ Ontario, S Canada
114 D9 **Gowlan** Buenos Aires, Argentina 34°40′S 59°21′W
158 C8 **Gowna, Lough** ◎ Ireland
160 A3 **Gowran** Kilkenny, Ireland 52°38′N 7°04′W
74 G7 **Gowrie** Iowa, C USA 42°16′N 94°17′W
229 H8 **Govurdak** *Rus.* Govurdak; *prev.* Guardak. Lebap Welaýaty, E Turkmenistan 37°50′N 66°06′E
159 M9 **Goxhill** UK 53°40′N 0°20′W
112 G7 **Goya** Corrientes, NE Argentina 29°10′S 59°15′W
Goyania *see* Goiânia
Goyaz *see* Goiás
215 M5 **Göyçay** *Rus.* Geokchay. C Azerbaijan 40°38′N 47°44′E
228 C5 **Goymat** *Rus.* Koymat. Balkan Welaýaty, NW Turkmenistan 40°23′N 55°45′E
228 C5 **Goymatdag, Gory** *Rus.* Gory Koymatdag. *hill range* Balkan Welaýaty, NW Turkmenistan
214 D5 **Göynük** Bolu, NW Turkey 40°24′N 30°45′E
253 E9 **Goyō-san** ▲ Honshū, C Japan 39°12′N 141°40′E
134 F2 **Goz Beïda** Ouaddaï, SE Chad 12°06′N 21°22′E
238 D7 **Gozha Co** ◎ W China
175 I13 **Gozo** *var.* Ghawdex. *island* N Malta
136 D1 **Gōz Regeb** Kassala, NE Sudan 16°03′N 35°33′E
Gozyô *see* Gojō
140 G8 **Graaff-Reinet** Eastern Cape, South Africa 32°15′S 24°33′E
138 F9 **Graaff-Reinet** Eastern Cape, S South Africa 32°15′S 24°32′E
140 D8 **Graafwater** Western Cape, South Africa 32°09′S 18°36′E
Graasten *see* Gråsten
132 E8 **Grabo** SW Ivory Coast 04°57′N 07°30′W
185 H4 **Grabovica** Serbia, E Serbia 44°30′N 22°29′E
182 F7 **Grabów nad Prosną** Wielkopolskie, C Poland 51°30′N 18°06′E
176 F4 **Grabs** Sankt Gallen, NE Switzerland 47°10′N 09°27′E
184 C4 **Gračac** Zadar, SW Croatia 44°18′N 15°52′E

184 E3 **Gračanica** Federacija Bosna I Hercegovina, NE Bosnia and Herzegovina 44°41′N 18°20′E
166 G8 **Graçay** Centre, France 47°08′N 1°51′E
62 F2 **Gracefield** Québec, SE Canada 46°06′N 76°03′W
163 G11 **Grâce-Hollogne** Liège, E Belgium 50°38′N 05°30′E
69 I3 **Graceville** Florida, SE USA 30°57′N 85°31′W
74 F4 **Graceville** Minnesota, N USA 45°34′N 96°25′W
88 D4 **Gracias** Lempira, W Honduras 14°35′N 88°35′W
Gracias *see* Lempira
87 H4 **Gracias a Dios** ◈ *department* E Honduras
87 I4 **Gracias a Dios, Cabo de** *headland* Honduras/Nicaragua 15°00′N 83°10′W
172 B9 **Graciosa** *var.* Ilha Graciosa. *island* Azores, Portugal, NE Atlantic Ocean
170 C9 **Graciosa** *island* Islas Canarias, Spain, NE Atlantic Ocean
Graciosa, Ilha *see* Graciosa
184 E3 **Gradačac** Federacija Bosna I Hercegovina, N Bosnia and Herzegovina 44°51′N 18°24′E
107 L6 **Gradaús, Serra dos** ▲▲ C Brazil
190 I7 **Gr'adcy** Tverskaya Oblast', Russian Federation
170 F2 **Gradefes** Castilla-León, N Spain 42°37′N 05°14′W
Gradiška *see* Bosanska Gradiška
Gradizhsk *see* Hradyz'k
177 I6 **Grado** Friuli-Venezia Giulia, NE Italy 45°41′N 13°24′E
170 E1 **Grado** Asturias, N Spain 43°23′N 06°04′W
185 H8 **Gradsko** C FYR Macedonia 41°34′N 21°56′E
190 I3 **Gr'ady** Novgorodskaya Oblast', Russian Federation
79 N7 **Grady** New Mexico, SW USA 34°49′N 103°19′W
184 C2 **Grad Zagreb** ◈ *province* NC Croatia
80 E1 **Graeagle** California, USA 39°46′N 120°37′W
74 G6 **Graettinger** Iowa, C USA 43°14′N 94°45′W
181 I9 **Gräfentonna** Thüringen, Germany 10°44′N 51°06′E
179 G13 **Grafing** Bayern, SE Germany 48°01′N 11°57′E
70 G4 **Graford** Texas, SW USA 32°56′N 98°15′W
277 M3 **Grafton** New South Wales, SE Australia 29°41′S 152°55′E
74 E2 **Grafton** North Dakota, N USA 48°24′N 97°24′W
67 J2 **Grafton** West Virginia, NE USA 39°21′N 80°03′W
67 J6 **Graham** North Carolina, SE USA 36°05′N 79°25′W
70 G4 **Graham** Texas, SW USA 33°07′N 98°36′W
Graham Bell Island *see* Greem-Bell, Ostrov
54 A6 **Graham Island** *island* Queen Charlotte Islands, British Columbia, SW Canada
63 L4 **Graham Lake** ◎ Maine, NE USA
292 E3 **Graham Land** *physical region* Antarctica
53 J6 **Cape Graham Moore** *headland* Nunavut, NE Canada
79 J9 **Graham, Mount** ▲ Arizona, SW USA 32°42′N 109°52′W
Grahamstad *see* Grahamstown
138 G10 **Grahamstown** *Afr.* Grahamstad. Eastern Cape, S South Africa 33°18′S 26°32′E
Grahovo *see* Bosansko Grahovo
160 A3 **Graiguenamanagh** Kilkenny, Ireland 52°32′N 6°57′W
161 L6 **Grain** UK 51°27′N 0°43′E
124 A5 **Grain Coast** *coastal region* S Liberia
259 J9 **Grajagan** Jawa, S Indonesia 08°33′S 114°13′E
259 J9 **Grajagan, Teluk** *bay* Jawa, S Indonesia
108 D5 **Grajaú** Maranhão, E Brazil 05°50′S 45°12′W
108 D4 **Grajaú, Rio** ≈ NE Brazil
182 I4 **Grajewo** Podlaskie, NE Poland 53°38′N 22°26′E
155 C13 **Gram** Sønderjylland, SW Denmark 55°18′N 09°03′E
165 H7 **Gramat** Lot, S France 44°45′N 01°45′E
68 C1 **Grambling** Louisiana, S USA 32°31′N 92°43′W
186 F3 **Grámmos** ▲▲ Albania/Greece
156 F5 **Grampian Mountains** ▲▲ C Scotland, UK
277 H7 **Grampians, The** ▲▲ Victoria, SE Australia
162 I5 **Gramsbergen** Overijssel, E Netherlands 52°37′N 06°39′E
184 F9 **Gramsh** *var.* Gramshi. Elbasan, C Albania 40°52′N 20°12′E
Gramshi *see* Gramsh
Gran *see* Esztergom
Gran *see* Hron
102 C6 **Granada** Meta, C Colombia 03°33′N 73°44′W
88 G6 **Granada** Granada, SW Nicaragua 11°55′N 85°58′W
170 G8 **Granada** Andalucía, S Spain 37°13′N 03°41′W
79 N4 **Granada** Colorado, C USA 38°00′N 102°18′W
88 G6 **Granada** ◈ *department* SW Nicaragua
170 G8 **Granada** ◈ *province* Andalucía, S Spain
114 B6 **Granadero Baigorrio** Santa Fe, Argentina 32°52′S 60°42′W
117 D11 **Gran Antiplanicie Central** *plain* S Argentina
158 C9 **Granard** Longford, C Ireland 53°47′N 07°30′W
117 D10 **Gran Bajo** *basin* S Argentina
116 E7 **Gran Bajo del Gualicho** *basin* E Argentina
117 D11 **Gran Bajo de San Julián** *basin* SE Argentina
70 G5 **Granbury** Texas, SW USA 32°27′N 97°47′W
63 I3 **Granby** Québec, SE Canada 45°23′N 72°44′W
75 G11 **Granby** Missouri, C USA 36°55′N 94°14′W
79 L3 **Granby, Lake** ▣ Colorado, C USA
170 B10 **Gran Canaria** *var.* Grand Canary. *island* Islas Canarias, Spain, NE Atlantic Ocean
95 K6 **Gran Chaco** *var.* Chaco. *lowland plain* South America
91 N3 **Grand Anse** SW Grenada 12°01′N 61°45′W
Grand-Anse *see* Portsmouth
61 L9 **Grand Bahama Island** *island* N Bahamas
Grand Balé *see* Tui
167 M7 **Grand Ballon** *Ger.* Ballon de Guebwiller. ▲ NE France 47°53′N 07°06′E
59 L7 **Grand Bank** Newfoundland, Newfoundland and Labrador, SE Canada 47°06′N 55°48′W
290 E4 **Grand Banks of Newfoundland** *undersea feature* NW Atlantic Ocean
Grand Bassa *see* Buchanan
132 F8 **Grand-Bassam** *var.* Bassam. SE Ivory Coast 05°14′N 03°45′W
59 M7 **Grand Beach** Canada 47°8′N 55°32′W
62 B5 **Grand Bend** Ontario, S Canada 43°17′N 81°46′W
132 E8 **Grand-Bérébi** *var.* Grand-Béréby. SW Ivory Coast 04°38′N 06°55′W
Grand-Béréby *see* Grand-Bérébi
91 H4 **Grand Caicos** *var.* Middle Caicos. *island* C Turks and Caicos Islands
62 F3 **Grand Calumet, Île du** *island* Québec, SE Canada
166 D4 **Grandcamp-les-Bains** Basse-Normandie, France 49°23′N 1°02′W
157 C9 **Grand Canal** *Ir.* An Chanáil Mhór. *canal* C Ireland
Grand Canal *see* Da Yunhe
Grand Canary *see* Gran Canaria
79 H6 **Grand Canyon** Arizona, SW USA 36°01′N 112°10′W
79 H6 **Grand Canyon** *canyon* Arizona, SW USA
Grand Canyon State *see* Arizona
90 C5 **Grand Cayman** *island* SW Cayman Islands
57 K4 **Grand Centre** Alberta, SW Canada 54°25′N 110°13′W
132 E8 **Grand Cess** SE Liberia 04°36′N 08°12′W
166 B7 **Grand-Champ** Bretagne, France 47°46′N 2°51′W
174 B4 **Grand Combin** ▲ S Switzerland 45°58′N 07°27′E
76 E3 **Grand Coulee** Washington, NW USA 47°56′N 119°00′W
76 D4 **Grand Coulee** *valley* Washington, NW USA
91 J1 **Grand Cul-de-Sac Marin** *bay* N Guadeloupe
Grand Duchy of Luxembourg *see* Luxembourg
117 D12 **Grande, Bahía** *bay* S Argentina
56 G4 **Grande Cache** Alberta, W Canada 53°53′N 119°07′W
169 M2 **Grande Casse** ▲ E France 45°22′N 06°50′E
139 I9 **Grande Comore** *var.* Njazidja, Great Comoro. *island* NW Comoros
115 J6 **Grande, Cuchilla** *hill range* E Uruguay
Grande de Chiloé, Isla *see* Chiloé, Isla de
107 L2 **Grande de Gurupá, Ilha** *river island* NE Brazil
112 C3 **Grande de Lipez, Río** ≈ SW Bolivia
91 I7 **Grande de Manatí, Río** ≈ C Puerto Rico
88 G5 **Grande de Matagalpa, Río** ≈ C Nicaragua
85 J10 **Grande de Santiago, Río** *var.* Santiago. ≈ C Mexico
89 I9 **Grande de Térraba, Río** *var.* Río Térraba. ≈ SE Costa Rica
58 G5 **Grande Deux, Réservoir la** ▣ Québec, E Canada
110 G8 **Grande, Ilha** *island* SE Brazil
56 G3 **Grande Prairie** Alberta, W Canada 55°10′N 118°52′W
131 H4 **Grand Erg Occidental** *desert* W Algeria
131 J4 **Grand Erg Oriental** *desert* Algeria/Tunisia
112 D1 **Grande, Río** ≈ C Bolivia
110 C3 **Grande, Rio** ≈ S Brazil
86 G8 **Grande, 'Río** ≈ Oaxaca, Mexico
46 C7 **Grande, Rio** *var.* Río Bravo, *Sp.* Río Bravo del Norte, Bravo del Norte. ≈ Mexico/USA
59 J7 **Grande-Rivière** Québec, SE Canada 48°27′N 64°37′W
91 H5 **Grande-Rivière-du-Nord** N Haiti 19°36′N 72°10′W
168 E10 **Grandesa** Cataluña, Spain 41°03′N 0°25′E
116 E2 **Grande, Salina** *var.* Gran Salitral. *salt lake* C Argentina
95 M4 **Grande, Serra** ▲▲ W Brazil
85 I3 **Grande, Sierra** ▲▲ N Mexico
165 K7 **Grandes Rousses** ▲▲ E France
117 E8 **Grandes, Salinas** *salt lake* E Argentina
59 J7 **Grande-Vallée** Québec, SE Canada 49°14′N 65°08′W
91 K1 **Grande Vigie, Pointe de la** *headland* Grande Terre, N Guadeloupe 16°31′N 61°27′W

63 L1 **Grand Falls** New Brunswick, SE Canada 47°02′N 67°46′W
59 L6 **Grand Falls** Newfoundland, Newfoundland and Labrador, SE Canada 48°57′N 55°48′W
70 D5 **Grandfalls** Texas, SW USA 31°20′N 102°51′W
67 H6 **Grandfather Mountain** ▲ North Carolina, SE USA 36°06′N 81°48′W
75 D13 **Grandfield** Oklahoma, C USA 34°15′N 98°40′W
56 G9 **Grand Forks** British Columbia, SW Canada 49°02′N 118°30′W
74 E2 **Grand Forks** North Dakota, N USA 47°54′N 97°03′W
166 C7 **Grand-Fougeray** Bretagne, France 47°43′N 1°44′W
64 G2 **Grand Gorge** New York, USA 42°22′N 74°30′W
72 F7 **Grand Haven** Michigan, N USA 43°03′N 86°13′W
Grandichi *see* Hrandzichy
54 E3 **Lac Grandin** ◎ Northwest Territories, NW Canada
75 D8 **Grand Island** Nebraska, C USA 40°55′N 98°20′W
72 F4 **Grand Island** *island* Michigan, N USA
68 E5 **Grand Isle** Louisiana, S USA 29°12′N 90°00′W
117 G10 **Grand Jason** *island* Jason Islands, NW Falkland Islands
79 J4 **Grand Junction** Colorado, C USA 39°03′N 108°33′W
66 B7 **Grand Junction** Tennessee, S USA 35°03′N 89°11′W
62 E1 **Grand-Lac-Victoria** Québec, SE Canada 47°33′N 77°28′W
62 E1 **Grand lac Victoria** ◎ Québec, SE Canada
132 F8 **Grand-Lahou** *var.* Grand Lahu. S Ivory Coast 05°09′N 05°01′W
Grand Lahu *see* Grand-Lahou
79 L2 **Grand Lake** Colorado, C USA 40°15′N 105°49′W
59 L6 **Grand Lake** ◎ Newfoundland, Newfoundland and Labrador, E Canada
68 C4 **Grand Lake** ◎ Louisiana, S USA
72 H5 **Grand Lake** ◎ Michigan, N USA
73 G10 **Grand Lake** ▣ Ohio, N USA
75 G11 **Grand Lake O' The Cherokees** *var.* Lake O' The Cherokees. ▣ Oklahoma, C USA
73 G8 **Grand Ledge** Michigan, N USA 42°45′N 84°45′W
164 F5 **Grand-Lieu, Lac de** ◎ NW France
63 M3 **Grand Manan Channel** *channel* Canada/USA
63 M4 **Grand Manan Island** *island* New Brunswick, SE Canada
74 I2 **Grand Marais** Minnesota, N USA 47°45′N 90°19′W
63 I2 **Grand-Mère** Québec, SE Canada 46°36′N 72°41′W
79 K4 **Grand Mesa** ▲▲ Colorado, C USA
174 B3 **Grand Muveran** ▲ W Switzerland 46°16′N 07°12′E
172 B6 **Grândola** Setúbal, S Portugal 38°10′N 08°34′W
172 B6 **Serra de Grândola** ▲▲ Setúbal, Portugal
Grand Paradis *see* Gran Paradiso
281 H8 **Grand Passage** *passage* N New Caledonia
133 I8 **Grand-Popo** S Benin 06°19′N 01°50′E
72 C2 **Grand Portage** Minnesota, N USA 48°00′N 89°36′W
71 H4 **Grand Prairie** Texas, SW USA 32°45′N 97°00′W
55 I8 **Grand Rapids** Manitoba, C Canada 53°12′N 99°19′W
73 F8 **Grand Rapids** Michigan, N USA 42°57′N 86°40′W
74 G3 **Grand Rapids** Minnesota, N USA 47°14′N 93°31′W
280 A8 **Grand Récif de Koumac** *reef* W New Caledonia
280 C10 **Grand Récif Sud** *reef* S New Caledonia
62 F2 **Grand-Remous** Québec, SE Canada 46°36′N 75°53′W
169 I3 **Grandrieu** Languedoc-Roussillon, France 44°47′N 3°38′E
62 C5 **Grand River** ≈ Ontario, S Canada
73 F8 **Grand River** ≈ Michigan, N USA
75 H9 **Grand River** ≈ Missouri, C USA
74 C4 **Grand River** ≈ South Dakota, N USA
76 B6 **Grand Ronde** Oregon, NW USA 45°03′N 123°43′W
76 E5 **Grand Ronde River** ≈ Oregon/Washington, NW USA
Grand-Saint-Bernard, Col du *see* Great Saint Bernard Pass
71 I4 **Grand Saline** Texas, SW USA 32°40′N 95°42′W
103 M6 **Grand-Santi** W French Guiana 04°19′N 54°24′W
Grandsee *see* Grandson
137 J8 **Grand Sœur** *island* Les Sœurs, NE Seychelles
167 M9 **Grandson** *prev.* Grandsee. Vaud, W Switzerland 46°49′N 06°39′E
77 I7 **Grand Teton** ▲ Wyoming, C USA 43°44′N 110°48′W
72 F5 **Grand Traverse Bay** *lake bay* Michigan, N USA
91 H4 **Grand Turk Island** *island* SE Turks and Caicos Islands
169 K3 **Grand Veymont** ▲ E France 44°51′N 05°32′E
55 I9 **Grandview** Manitoba, S Canada 51°11′N 100°41′W
75 G9 **Grandview** Missouri, C USA 38°53′N 94°31′W
166 G4 **Grandvilliers** Picardie, France 49°40′N 1°56′E
78 G6 **Grand Wash Cliffs** *cliff* Arizona, SW USA
168 D8 **Grañén** Aragón, Spain 41°56′N 0°22′W
154 G7 **Grangärde** Dalarna, C Sweden 60°15′N 15°00′E
158 A7 **Grange** Sligo, Ireland 54°24′N 8°31′W
90 D7 **Grange Hill** W Jamaica 18°19′N 78°11′W
159 H3 **Grangemouth** C Scotland, UK 56°01′N 03°44′W
70 G6 **Granger** Texas, SW USA 30°43′N 97°26′W
76 D5 **Granger** Washington, NW USA 46°20′N 120°11′W
77 J9 **Granger** Wyoming, C USA 41°37′N 109°58′W
Granges *see* Grenchen
154 G7 **Grängesberg** Kopparberg, C Sweden 60°06′N 15°00′E
80 D6 **Grangeville** California, USA 36°21′N 119°43′W
76 F5 **Grangeville** Idaho, NW USA 45°55′N 116°07′W
56 C3 **Granisle** British Columbia, SW Canada 54°55′N 126°14′W
73 B12 **Granite City** Illinois, N USA 38°42′N 90°09′W
74 F5 **Granite Falls** Minnesota, N USA 44°48′N 95°33′W
67 I6 **Granite Falls** North Carolina, SE USA 35°48′N 81°25′W
79 H7 **Granite Mountain** ▲ Arizona, SW USA 34°38′N 112°34′W
81 F13 **Granite Mountain** ▲ California, USA 33°03′N 116°29′W
80 F4 **Granite Mountain** ▲ California, USA 37°55′N 118°46′W
80 E1 **Granite Mountain** ▲ California, USA 39°32′N 120°44′W
81 H11 **Granite Mountains** ▲▲ California, USA
81 G9 **Granite Mountains** ▲▲ California, USA
81 H12 **Granite Mountains** ▲▲ California, USA
77 J6 **Granite Peak** ▲ Montana, NW USA 45°09′N 109°48′W
78 E1 **Granite Peak** ▲ Nevada, W USA 41°40′N 117°35′W
80 I2 **Granite Peak** ▲ Nevada, USA 40°17′N 117°48′W
78 G3 **Granite Peak** ▲ Utah, W USA 40°09′N 113°18′W
Granite State *see* New Hampshire
80 E1 **Graniteville** California, USA 39°26′N 120°44′W
81 J13 **Granite Wash Pass** *pass* Nevada, USA
175 E12 **Granitola, Capo** *headland* Sicilia, Italy, C Mediterranean Sea 37°33′N 12°39′E
278 E8 **Granity** West Coast, South Island, New Zealand 41°37′S 171°53′E
172 B3 **Granja** Coimbra, Portugal 40°10′N 8°38′W
172 D6 **Granja** Évora, Portugal 38°18′N 7°15′W
172 D1 **Granja** Viseu, Portugal 41°01′N 7°24′W
172 F6 **Granja de Torrehermosa** Extremadura, Spain 38°19′N 5°35′W
Gran Lago *see* Nicaragua, Lago de
117 D9 **Gran Laguna Salada** ◎ S Argentina
Gran Malvina *see* West Falkland
85 H4 **Gran Morelos** Chihuahua, Mexico 28°15′N 106°30′W
155 G9 **Gränna** Jönköping, S Sweden 58°02′N 14°30′E
171 K3 **Granollers** *var.* Granollérs. Cataluña, NE Spain 41°37′N 02°18′E
Granollérs *see* Granollers
174 A4 **Gran Paradiso** *Fr.* Grand Paradis. ▲ NW Italy 45°31′N 07°13′E
Gran Pilastro *see* Hochfeiler
Gran Salitral *see* Grande, Salina
Gran San Bernardo, Passo di *see* Great Saint Bernard Pass
Gran Santiago *see* Santiago
175 F8 **Gran Sasso d'Italia** ▲▲ C Italy
178 H6 **Gransee** Brandenburg, NE Germany 53°00′N 13°10′E
75 B8 **Grant** Nebraska, C USA 40°50′N 101°43′W
75 G8 **Grant City** Missouri, C USA 40°29′N 94°25′W
161 J2 **Grantham** E England, UK 52°55′N 00°39′W
117 I11 **Grantham Sound** *sound* East Falkland, Falkland Islands
292 G7 **Grant Island** *island* Antarctica
91 L3 **Grantley Adams** ✈ (Bridgetown) SE Barbados 13°04′N 59°29′W
80 G3 **Grant, Mount** ▲ Nevada, W USA 38°34′N 118°47′W
156 F5 **Grantown-on-Spey** N Scotland, UK 57°11′N 03°53′W
80 J6 **Grant Range** ▲▲ Nevada, W USA
79 K7 **Grants** New Mexico, SW USA 35°09′N 107°50′W
72 A4 **Grantsburg** Wisconsin, N USA 45°47′N 92°40′W
159 J3 **Grantshouse** UK 55°53′N 2°18′W
76 B8 **Grants Pass** Oregon, NW USA 42°26′N 123°20′W
79 H2 **Grantsville** Utah, W USA 40°36′N 112°27′W
67 I3 **Grantsville** West Virginia, NE USA 38°55′N 81°07′W
164 F3 **Granville** Manche, N France 48°50′N 01°35′W
55 I7 **Granville Lake** ◎ Manitoba, C Canada
71 I5 **Grapeland** Texas, SW USA 31°29′N 95°28′W
54 G3 **Lac de Gras** ◎ Northwest Territories, NW Canada
139 H6 **Graskop** Mpumalanga, NE South Africa 24°58′S 30°49′E
180 J6 **Grasleben** Niedersachsen, Germany 11°01′N 52°19′E
159 I7 **Grasmere** UK 54°27′N 3°01′W
154 I7 **Gräsö** Uppsala, C Sweden 60°22′N 18°30′E
154 J6 **Gräsö** *island* C Sweden

165 K8 **Grasse** Alpes-Maritimes, SE France 43°42′N 06°52′E
62 E8 **Grassflat** Pennsylvania, NE USA 41°00′N 78°04′W
77 J4 **Grassrange** Montana, NW USA 47°02′N 108°48′W
62 G4 **Grass River** ≈ New York, NE USA
80 E1 **Grass Valley** California, W USA 39°12′N 121°04′W
277 I8 **Grassy** Tasmania, SE Australia 40°03′S 144°04′E
74 B3 **Grassy Butte** North Dakota, N USA 47°20′N 103°13′W
67 I4 **Grassy Knob** ▲ West Virginia, NE USA 38°04′N 80°31′W
155 D13 **Gråsten** *var.* Graasten. Sønderjylland, SW Denmark 54°55′N 09°37′E
155 F9 **Grästorp** Västra Götaland, S Sweden 58°20′N 12°40′E
161 I7 **Grateley** UK 51°10′N 1°36′W
Gratianopolis *see* Grenoble
80 B1 **Graton** California, USA 38°26′N 122°52′W
181 J11 **Grattstadt** Bayern, Germany 10°50′N 50°23′E
177 K4 **Gratwein** Steiermark, SE Austria 47°08′N 15°20′E
Gratz *see* Graz
174 D3 **Graubünden** *Fr.* Grisons, *It.* Grigioni. ◈ *canton* SE Switzerland
Graudenz *see* Grudziądz
165 H8 **Graulhet** Tarn, S France 43°45′N 01°58′E
171 J3 **Graus** Aragón, NE Spain 42°11′N 00°21′E
113 J7 **Gravataí** Rio Grande do Sul, S Brazil 29°55′S 51°00′W
162 G7 **Grave** Noord-Brabant, SE Netherlands 51°45′N 05°45′E
57 M8 **Gravelbourg** Saskatchewan, S Canada 49°53′N 106°33′W
157 J12 **Gravelines** Nord, N France 51°00′N 02°07′E
141 K2 **Gravelotte** Limpopo, South Africa 23°57′S 30°37′E
Graven *see* Grez-Doiceau
62 D3 **Gravenhurst** Ontario, S Canada 44°55′N 79°22′W
181 E11 **Grävenwiesbach** Hessen, Germany 8°27′N 50°24′E
76 G5 **Grave Peak** ▲ Idaho, NW USA 46°24′N 114°43′W
164 F6 **Grave, Pointe de** *headland* W France 45°33′N 01°24′W
277 L3 **Gravesend** New South Wales, SE Australia 29°37′S 150°15′E
161 L6 **Gravesend** SE England, UK 51°27′N 00°24′E
175 H9 **Gravina di Puglia** Puglia, SE Italy 40°48′N 16°25′E
165 J4 **Gray** Haute-Saône, E France 47°28′N 05°34′E
69 K1 **Gray** Georgia, SE USA 33°00′N 83°31′W
293 K9 **Gray, Cape** *headland* Antarctica 67°30′N 143°30′E
76 B4 **Grayland** Washington, NW USA 46°46′N 124°07′W
82 G5 **Grayling** Alaska, USA 62°55′N 160°07′W
72 G6 **Grayling** Michigan, N USA 44°40′N 84°43′W
159 I7 **Grayrigg** UK 54°22′N 2°39′W
161 L6 **Grays** UK 51°29′N 0°19′E
76 B4 **Grays Harbor** *inlet* Washington, NW USA
67 H3 **Grayson** Kentucky, S USA 38°21′N 82°59′W
79 L3 **Grays Peak** ▲ Colorado, C USA 39°37′N 105°49′W
73 D12 **Grayville** Illinois, N USA 38°15′N 87°59′W
177 K4 **Graz** *prev.* Gratz. Steiermark, SE Austria 47°05′N 15°23′E
170 E9 **Grazalema** Andalucía, S Spain 36°46′N 05°23′W
185 H6 **Grdelica** Serbia, SE Serbia 42°54′N 22°05′E
90 F1 **Great Abaco** *var.* Abaco Island. *island* N Bahamas
Great Admiralty Island *see* Manus Island
Great Alfold *see* Great Hungarian Plain
Great Ararat *see* Büyükağrı Dağı
275 J5 **Great Artesian Basin** *lowlands* Queensland, C Australia
280 E9 **Great Astrolabe Reef** *reef* Kadavu, SW Fiji
276 C4 **Great Australian Bight** *bight* S Australia
290 B6 **Great Bahama Bank** *undersea feature* E Gulf of Mexico
279 H3 **Great Barrier Island** *island* N New Zealand
275 K3 **Great Barrier Reef** *reef* Queensland, NE Australia
65 I3 **Great Barrington** Massachusetts, NE USA 42°11′N 73°20′W
42 D6 **Great Basin** *basin* W USA
52 C8 **Great Bear Lake** *Fr.* Grand Lac de l'Ours. ◎ Northwest Territories, NW Canada
54 D2 **Great Bear River** ≈ Northwest Territories, NW Canada
161 I6 **Great Bedwyn** UK 51°22′N 1°36′W
Great Belt *see* Storebælt
75 D10 **Great Bend** Kansas, C USA 38°22′N 98°47′W
Great Bermuda *see* Bermuda
157 A11 **Great Blasket Island** *Ir.* An Blascaod Mór. *island* SW Ireland
Great Britain *see* Britain
159 M10 **Great Carlton** UK 53°20′N 0°07′E
256 B11 **Great Channel** *channel* Andaman Sea/Indian Ocean
256 B8 **Great Coco Island** *island* SW Myanmar (Burma)
Great Comoro *see* Grande Comore
Great Crosby *see* Crosby
67 M5 **Great Dismal Swamp** *wetland* North Carolina/Virginia, SE USA
77 K8 **Great Divide Basin** *basin* Wyoming, C USA
275 K5 **Great Dividing Range** ▲▲ NE Australia
62 B3 **Great Duck Island** *island* Ontario, S Canada
Great Elder Reservoir *see* Waconda Lake
293 K5 **Greater Antarctica** *var.* East Antarctica. *physical region* Antarctica
205 L9 **Greater Sunda Islands** *var.* Sunda Islands. *island group* Indonesia
161 J4 **Great Everdon** UK 52°12′N 1°08′W
278 F1 **Great Exhibition Bay** *inlet* North Island, New Zealand
61 M10 **Great Exuma Island** *island* C Bahamas
77 I4 **Great Falls** Montana, NW USA 47°30′N 111°18′W
67 I7 **Great Falls** South Carolina, SE USA 34°34′N 80°54′W
141 I9 **Great Fish** ≈ Eastern Cape, South Africa
144 C5 **Great Fisher Bank** *undersea feature* C North Sea
141 I9 **Great Fish Point** *point* Eastern Cape, South Africa
Great Glen *see* Mor, Glen
161 K4 **Great Gransden** UK 52°11′N 0°08′W
Great Grimsby *see* Grimsby
90 F3 **Great Guana Cay** *island* C Bahamas
159 J9 **Great Harwood** UK 53°47′N 2°25′W
290 E2 **Great Hellefiske Bank** *undersea feature* N Atlantic Ocean
183 G12 **Great Hungarian Plain** *var.* Great Alfold, Plain of Hungary, *Hung.* Alföld. *plain* SE Europe
90 G4 **Great Inagua** *var.* Inagua Islands. *island* S Bahamas
Great Indian Desert *see* Thar Desert
138 E9 **Great Karoo** *var.* Great Karroo, High Veld, *Afr.* Groot Karoo, Hoë Karoo. *plateau region* S South Africa
Great Karroo *see* Great Karoo
Great Kei *see* Groot-Kei
Great Khingan Range *see* Da Hinggan Ling
62 B2 **Great La Cloche Island** *island* Ontario, S Canada
277 J9 **Great Lake** ◎ Tasmania, SE Australia
Great Lake *see* Tônlé Sap
61 J3 **Great Lakes** *lakes* Ontario, Canada/USA
Great Lakes State *see* Michigan
161 H5 **Great Malvern** W England, UK 52°07′N 02°19′W
279 H3 **Great Mercury Island** *island* N New Zealand
Great Meteor Seamount *see* Great Meteor Tablemount
290 F5 **Great Meteor Tablemount** *var.* Great Meteor Seamount. *undersea feature* E Atlantic Ocean
73 G11 **Great Miami River** ≈ Ohio, N USA
256 A11 **Great Nicobar** *island* Nicobar Islands, India, NE Indian Ocean
161 M5 **Great Oakley** UK 51°54′N 1°12′E
220 B3 **Great Oasis, The** *var.* Khārga Oasis. *oasis* S Egypt
159 H10 **Great Ormes Head** *headland* N Wales, UK
159 I6 **Great Orton** UK 54°52′N 3°03′W
161 L3 **Great Ouse** *var.* Ouse. ≈ E England, UK
277 K10 **Great Oyster Bay** *bay* Tasmania, SE Australia
90 E8 **Great Pedro Bluff** *headland* W Jamaica 17°51′N 77°44′W
67 J8 **Great Pee Dee River** ≈ North Carolina/South Carolina, SE USA
205 M6 **Great Plain of China** *plain* E China
42 E6 **Great Plains** *var.* High Plains. *plains* Canada/USA
79 N4 **Great Plains Reservoirs** ▣ Colorado, C USA
65 N4 **Great Point** *headland* Nantucket Island, Massachusetts, NE USA 41°23′N 70°03′W
124 F6 **Great Rift Valley** *var.* Rift Valley. *depression* Asia/Africa
137 C10 **Great Ruaha** ≈ S Tanzania
161 L3 **Great Ryburgh** UK 52°49′N 0°55′E
65 H1 **Great Sacandaga Lake** ▣ New York, NE USA
174 A4 **Great Saint Bernard Pass** *Fr.* Col du Grand-Saint-Bernard, *It.* Passo del Gran San Bernardo. *pass* Italy/Switzerland
90 E1 **Great Sale Cay** *island* N Bahamas
Great Salt Desert *see* Kavīr, Dasht-e
79 H3 **Great Salt Lake** *salt lake* Utah, W USA
78 G2 **Great Salt Lake Desert** *plain* Utah, W USA
75 D11 **Great Salt Plains Lake** ▣ Oklahoma, C USA
128 G4 **Great Sand Sea** *desert* Egypt/Libya
274 F4 **Great Sandy Desert** *desert* Western Australia
Great Sandy Desert *see* Ar Rub 'al Khālī
Great Sandy Island *see* Fraser Island
280 E8 **Great Sea Reef** *reef* Vanua Levu, N Fiji
82 D9 **Great Sitkin Island** *island* Aleutian Islands, Alaska, USA
54 F4 **Great Slave Lake** *Fr.* Grand Lac des Esclaves. ◎ Northwest Territories, NW Canada

◆ Country
● Country Capital
◇ Dependent Territory
○ Dependent Territory Capital
◈ Administrative Regions
✈ International Airport
▲ Mountain
▲▲ Mountain Range
Volcano
≈ River
◎ Lake
▣ Reservoir

◆ Country ◇ Dependent Territory ◆ Administrative Regions ▲ Mountain ⧫ Volcano ◎ Lake
● Country Capital ○ Dependent Territory Capital ✕ International Airport ▲ Mountain Range ✈ River ◫ Reservoir

Havelberg - Highworth

178 G6 Havelberg Sachsen-Anhalt, NE Germany 52°49′N 12°05′E
231 I4 Havelīān North-West Frontier Province, NW Pakistan 34°05′N 73°14′E
178 H6 Havelländ Grosse var. Hauptkanal. canal NE Germany
62 E4 Havelock Ontario, SE Canada 44°22′N 77°57′W
278 F8 Havelock Marlborough, South Island, New Zealand 41°17′S 173°46′E
67 L7 Havelock North Carolina, SE USA 34°52′N 76°54′W
279 I6 Havelock North Hawke's Bay, North Island, New Zealand 39°40′S 176°53′E
162 H5 Havelte Drenthe, NE Netherlands 52°46′N 06°14′E
75 E10 Haven Kansas, C USA 37°54′N 97°46′W
160 D5 Haverfordwest SW Wales, UK 51°50′N 04°57′W
161 L4 Haverhill E England, UK 52°05′N 00°26′E
65 L1 Haverhill Massachusetts, NE USA 42°46′N 71°02′W
159 I8 Haverigg UK 54°12′N 3°18′W
154 G4 Haverö Västernorrland, C Sweden 62°25′N 15°04′E
183 F9 Havířov Moravskoslezský Kraj, E Czech Republic 49°47′N 18°30′E
183 C9 Havlíčkův Brod Ger. Deutsch-Brod; prev. Německý Brod. Vysočina, C Czech Republic 49°38′N 15°46′E
152 G3 Havøysund Finnmark, N Norway 70°59′N 24°39′E
187 K4 Havran Balıkesir, Turkey 39°34′N 27°06′E
163 D11 Havré Hainaut, S Belgium 50°29′N 04°03′E
77 J3 Havre Montana, NW USA 48°33′N 109°41′W
Havre see le Havre
64 E8 Havre de Grace Maryland, USA 39°33′N 76°06′W
59 J6 Havre-St-Pierre Québec, E Canada 50°16′N 63°36′W
214 B4 Havsa Edirne, NW Turkey 41°32′N 26°49′E
82 D3 Hawi var. Hawi. Hawaii, USA 20°14′N 155°50′W
82 B3 Hawai'i off. State of Hawai'i, also known as Aloha State, Paradise of the Pacific, var. Hawaii. ◈ state USA, C Pacific Ocean
82 D3 Hawai'i var. Hawaii. island Hawaiian Islands, USA, C Pacific Ocean
82 C2 Hawaiian Islands prev. Sandwich Islands. island group Hawaii, USA
286 G3 Hawaiian Islands prev. Sandwich Islands. island group Hawaii, USA
286 G4 Hawaiian Ridge undersea feature N Pacific Ocean
286 G4 Hawaiian Trough undersea feature N Pacific Ocean
160 G2 Hawarden UK 53°11′N 3°02′W
74 F6 Hawarden Iowa, C USA 43°00′N 96°29′W
Hawash see Āwash
217 H4 Hawbayn al Gharbīyah C Iraq 34°24′N 42°06′E
278 C11 Hawea, Lake ◎ South Island, New Zealand
278 G6 Hawera Taranaki, North Island, New Zealand 39°36′S 174°16′E
159 J7 Hawes UK 54°18′N 2°12′W
66 D4 Hawesville Kentucky, S USA 37°53′N 86°47′W
159 I7 Hawes Water ◎ UK
Hawi see Hawi
159 I4 Hawick SE Scotland, UK 55°24′N 02°49′W
217 J3 Ḩawījah C Iraq 35°15′N 43°54′E
217 M7 Ḩawīzah, Hawr al ◎ S Iraq
278 C11 Hawkdun Range ▲▲ South Island, New Zealand
279 I6 Hawke Bay bay North Island, New Zealand
276 G4 Hawker South Australia 31°54′S 138°25′E
279 H6 Hawke's Bay off. Hawkes Bay Region. ◈ region North Island, New Zealand
230 F9 Hawkes Bay bay SE Pakistan
Hawkes Bay Region see Hawke's Bay
62 G3 Hawkesbury Ontario, SE Canada 45°36′N 74°38′W
Hawkeye State see Iowa
69 K2 Hawkinsville Georgia, SE USA 32°16′N 83°28′W
72 G2 Hawk Junction Ontario, S Canada 48°05′N 84°34′W
66 G7 Haw Knob ▲ North Carolina/Tennessee, SE USA 35°18′N 84°01′W
67 H6 Hawksbill Mountain ▲ North Carolina, SE USA 35°54′N 81°53′W
77 M8 Hawk Springs Wyoming, C USA 41°48′N 104°17′W
Hawlēr see Arbīl
74 F3 Hawley Minnesota, N USA 46°53′N 96°18′W
64 F4 Hawley Pennsylvania, USA 41°29′N 75°11′W
70 F4 Hawley Texas, SW USA 32°36′N 99°47′W
159 L7 Hawnby UK 54°18′N 1°10′W
221 H8 Ḩawrā' C Yemen 15°39′N 48°21′E
217 H5 Ḩawrān, Wadi dry watercourse W Iraq
67 J6 Haw River ≈ North Carolina, SE USA
217 K4 Hawshqūrah E Iraq 34°34′N 45°33′E
140 D10 Hawston Western Cape, South Africa 34°23′S 19°08′E
80 G4 Hawthorne Nevada, W USA 38°30′N 118°38′W
159 L8 Haxby UK 54°01′N 1°04′W
159 L9 Haxey UK 53°29′N 0°50′W
79 N2 Haxtun Colorado, C USA 40°36′N 102°38′W
277 J5 Hay New South Wales, SE Australia 34°31′S 144°51′E
54 E5 Hay ≈ W Canada
261 H5 Haya Pulau Seram, E Indonesia 03°22′S 129°31′E
253 E9 Hayachine-san ▲ Honshū, C Japan 39°31′N 141°28′E
250 B3 Hayang Kyŏngsang-bukto, South Korea 35°55′N 128°49′E
165 K2 Hayange Moselle, NE France 49°19′N 06°04′E
HaYarden see Jordan
Hayastani Hanrapetut'yun see Armenia
Hayasui-seto see Hōyo-kaikyō
82 G4 Haycock Alaska, USA 65°12′N 161°10′W
79 I9 Hayden Arizona, SW USA 33°00′N 110°46′W
79 K2 Hayden Colorado, C USA 40°29′N 107°15′W
74 C5 Hayes South Dakota, N USA 44°20′N 101°01′W
53 H9 Hayes ≈ Manitoba, C Canada
51 H5 Hayes ≈ Nunavut, NE Canada
75 B8 Hayes Center Nebraska, C USA 40°30′N 101°02′W
83 J5 Hayes, Mount ▲ Alaska, USA 63°37′N 146°43′W
66 G7 Hayesville North Carolina, SE USA 35°03′N 83°49′W
81 J8 Hayford Peak ▲ Nevada, W USA 36°40′N 115°10′W
78 B2 Hayfork California, W USA 40°33′N 123°10′W
Hayir, Qasr al see Ḩayr al Gharbī, Qaşr al
Haylaastay see Sühbaatar
62 E3 Hay Lake ◎ Ontario, SE Canada
160 C9 Hayle UK 50°11′N 5°25′W
221 K6 Haymā' var. Haima. C Oman 19°59′N 56°20′E
214 E6 Haymana Ankara, C Turkey 39°26′N 32°30′E
216 D5 Ḩaymūr, Jabal ▲▲ W Syria
Haynau see Chojnów
68 B1 Haynesville Louisiana, S USA 32°57′N 93°08′W
69 H2 Hayneville Alabama, S USA 32°13′N 86°34′W
187 K2 Hayrabolu Tekirdağ, Turkey 41°13′N 27°07′E
216 D4 Ḩayr al Gharbī, Qaşr al var. Qasr al Hayir, Qasr al Hir al Gharbi. ruins Ḩimş, C Syria
216 F3 Ḩayr ash Sharqī, Qaşr al var. Qasr al Hir Ash Sharqī. ruins Ḩimş, C Syria
239 J1 Hayrhan var. Uubulan. Arhangay, C Mongolia 48°37′N 101°58′E
239 J2 Hayrhandulaan var. Mardzad. Övörhangay, C Mongolia 45°58′N 102°06′E
54 F5 Hay River Northwest Territories, W Canada 60°51′N 115°42′W
75 D9 Hays Kansas, C USA 38°53′N 99°20′W
74 B6 Hay Springs Nebraska, C USA 42°40′N 102°41′W
132 G9 Haystack, The ▲ NE Saint Helena 15°55′S 05°40′W
75 E10 Haysville Kansas, C USA 37°34′N 97°21′W
188 G5 Haysyn Rus. Gaysin. Vinnyts'ka Oblast', C Ukraine 48°50′N 29°29′E
66 B5 Hayti Missouri, C USA 36°13′N 89°45′W
74 E5 Hayti South Dakota, N USA 44°40′N 97°22′W
159 L10 Hayton UK 53°21′N 0°54′W
188 G5 Hayvoron Rus. Gayvorno. Kirovohrads'ka Oblast', C Ukraine 48°20′S 29°52′E
80 D4 Hayward California, W USA 37°40′N 122°07′W
80 B3 Hayward California, USA 37°40′N 122°05′W
72 B4 Hayward Wisconsin, N USA 46°02′N 91°26′W
161 K7 Haywards Heath SE England, UK 51°N 00°06′W
228 A6 Hazar prev. Rus. Cheleken. Balkan Welaýaty, W Turkmenistan 39°26′N 53°07′E
223 I7 Hazārān, Kūh-e var. Kūh-e ā Hazr. ▲ SE Iran 29°26′N 57°15′E
Hazarat Imam see Emām Şāḩeb
66 G4 Hazard Kentucky, S USA 37°14′N 83°11′W
215 H6 Hazar Gölü ◎ C Turkey
233 I8 Hazārībāg var. Hazāribāgh. Jhārkhand, N India 24°00′N 85°23′E
Hazāribāgh see Hazārībāg
165 H1 Hazebrouck Nord, N France 50°43′N 02°33′E
73 B8 Hazel Green Wisconsin, N USA 42°33′N 90°26′W
159 J10 Hazel Grove UK 53°23′N 2°07′W
286 F6 Hazel Holme Bank undersea feature S Pacific Ocean
56 C3 Hazelton British Columbia, SW Canada 55°15′N 127°38′W
74 C3 Hazelton North Dakota, N USA 46°27′N 100°17′W
80 G2 Hazen Nevada, W USA 39°33′N 119°02′W
74 B3 Hazen North Dakota, N USA 47°18′N 101°37′W
53 I1 Lake Hazen ◎ Nunavut, N Canada
82 F6 Hazen Bay bay E Bering Sea
52 F4 Hazen Strait Sea waterway Northwest Territories/ Nunavut, NW Canada
219 D10 Hazerim Israel
217 I4 Hazīm, Bi'r well C Iraq
69 K2 Hazlehurst Georgia, SE USA 31°51′N 82°35′W
68 E2 Hazlehurst Mississippi, S USA 31°51′N 90°24′W
65 H7 Hazlet New Jersey, NE USA 40°24′N 74°10′W
64 E5 Hazleton Pennsylvania, USA 40°58′N 75°58′W
228 E5 Hazorasp Rus. Khazarosp. Xorazm Viloyati, W Uzbekistan 41°21′N 61°01′E
229 J7 Hazratishoh, Qatorkŭhi var. Khrebet Khazretishi, Rus. Khrebet Khozretishi. ▲▲ S Tajikistan
Hazr, Kūh-e ā see Hazārān, Kūh-e
231 I4 Hazro Punjab, E Pakistan 33°55′N 72°33′E
161 I5 Headington UK 51°45′N 1°12′W
69 I3 Headland Alabama, S USA 31°21′N 85°20′W
276 D4 Head of Bight headland South Australia 31°33′S 131°05′E
76 F4 Headquarters Idaho, NW USA 46°38′N 115°52′W
80 B1 Healdsburg California, W USA 38°36′N 122°52′W
75 E13 Healdton Oklahoma, C USA 34°13′N 97°29′W
277 J7 Healesville Victoria, SE Australia 37°41′S 145°31′E
159 K8 Healey UK 54°13′N 1°44′W
83 I5 Healy Alaska, USA 63°51′N 148°58′W
289 F12 Heard and McDonald Islands ◇ Australian external territory S Indian Ocean
71 H6 Hearne Texas, SW USA 30°52′N 96°35′W
52 F5 Hearne Point headland Northwest Territories, NW Canada
58 E6 Hearst Ontario, S Canada 49°42′N 83°40′W
292 E3 Hearst Island island Antarctica
Heart of Dixie see Alabama
74 B3 Heart River ≈ North Dakota, N USA
73 I11 Heath Ohio, N USA 40°01′N 82°26′W
277 I7 Heathcote Victoria, SE Australia 36°57′S 144°43′E
157 I11 Heathrow ✈ (London) SE England, UK 51°28′N 00°27′W
67 M4 Heathsville Virginia, NE USA 37°55′N 76°29′W
75 G13 Heavener Oklahoma, C USA 34°53′N 94°36′W
70 F9 Hebbronville Texas, SW USA 27°19′N 98°41′W
159 K6 Hebburn UK 54°58′N 1°31′W
245 J3 Hebei var. Hebei Sheng, Hopeh, Hopei, Ji; prev. Chihli. ◈ province E China
Hebei Sheng see Hebei
277 K2 Hebel Queensland, Australia
81 G14 Heber California, USA 32°44′N 115°32′W
261 H4 Hebera Papua, E Indonesia 01°08′S 129°54′E
79 I2 Heber City Utah, W USA 40°31′N 111°25′W
75 I12 Heber Springs Arkansas, C USA 35°30′N 92°01′W
245 H6 Hebi Henan, C China 35°57′N 114°08′E
76 B5 Hebo Oregon, NW USA 45°10′N 123°55′W
156 D5 Hebrides, Sea of the sea NW Scotland, UK
59 J3 Hebron Newfoundland and Labrador, E Canada 58°15′N 62°45′W
73 E9 Hebron Indiana, N USA 41°19′N 87°12′W
75 E8 Hebron Nebraska, C USA 40°10′N 97°35′W
74 B3 Hebron North Dakota, N USA 46°54′N 102°03′W
216 B7 Hebron var. Al Khalīl, El Khalil, Heb. Hevron; anc. Kiriath-Arba. S West Bank 31°30′N 35°E
Hebrus see Évros/Maritsa/Meriç
154 I7 Heby Västmanland, C Sweden 59°56′N 16°53′E
54 A7 Hecate Strait strait British Columbia, W Canada
87 L5 Hecelchakán Campeche, SE Mexico 20°09′N 90°04′W
242 D8 Hechi var. Jinchengjiang. Guangxi Zhuangzu Zizhiqu, S China 24°39′N 108°02′E
179 D12 Hechingen Baden-Württemberg, S Germany 48°20′N 08°58′E
168 D7 Hecho Aragón, Spain 42°44′N 0°45′W
163 G9 Hechtel Limburg, NE Belgium 51°07′N 05°24′E
242 C3 Hechuan var. Heyang. Chongqing Shi, C China 30°02′N 106°15′E
74 E4 Hecla South Dakota, N USA 45°52′N 98°09′W
53 I1 Hecla, Cape headland Nunavut, N Canada 82°00′N 64°00′W
141 L3 Hectorspruit Mpumalanga, South Africa 25°26′S 31°41′E
245 H6 Hecun China 36°32′N 114°07′E
166 C6 Hédé Bretagne, France 48°18′N 1°48′W
154 F4 Hede Jämtland, C Sweden 62°25′N 13°33′E
Hede see Sheyang
154 H7 Hedemora Dalarna, C Sweden 60°18′N 15°58′E
181 H8 Hedemünden Niedersachsen, Germany 9°47′N 51°23′E
152 G6 Hedenäset Norrbotten, N Sweden 66°12′N 23°40′E
155 D12 Hedensted Vejle, C Denmark 55°47′N 09°43′E
180 J7 Hedersleben Sachsen-Anhalt, Germany 11°16′N 51°52′E
154 I7 Hedesunda Gävleborg, C Sweden 60°25′N 17°00′E
154 I7 Hedesundafjord ◎ C Sweden
70 E2 Hedley Texas, SW USA 34°52′N 100°39′W
154 E6 Hedmark ◈ county S Norway
251 I9 Hedo-misaki headland Okinawa, SW Japan 26°55′N 128°15′E
75 H8 Hedrick Iowa, C USA 41°10′N 92°18′W
180 C6 Heek Nordrhein-Westfalen, Germany 7°06′N 52°07′E
163 H9 Heel Limburg, SE Netherlands 51°12′N 06°01′E
283 N1 Heel Point point Wake Island
162 E5 Heemskerk Noord-Holland, W Netherlands 52°31′N 04°40′E
162 H6 Heerde Gelderland, E Netherlands 52°24′N 06°02′E
162 H4 Heerenveen Fris. It Hearrenfean. Friesland, N Netherlands 52°57′N 05°55′E
162 F5 Heerhugowaard Noord-Holland, NW Netherlands 52°40′N 04°50′E
152 B5 Heer Land physical region C Svalbard
163 H10 Heerlen Limburg, SE Netherlands 50°55′N 06°E
163 F10 Heers Limburg, NE Belgium 50°46′N 05°17′E
Heerwegen see Polkowice
163 G8 Heesch Noord-Brabant, S Netherlands 51°44′N 05°32′E
180 G3 Heeslingen Niedersachsen, Germany 9°20′N 53°19′E
180 D7 Heessen Nordrhein-Westfalen, Germany 7°51′N 51°43′E
163 G9 Heeze Noord-Brabant, SE Netherlands 51°23′N 05°35′E
216 B6 Hefa var. Haifa, hist. Caiffa, Caiphas; anc. Sycaminum. Haifa, N Israel 32°49′N 34°59′E
216 B6 Hefa, Mifraz Eng. Bay of Haifa. bay N Israel
243 J1 Hefei var. Hofei, hist. Luchow. province capital Anhui, E China 31°51′N 117°20′E
242 E3 Hefeng Hubei, China 29°32′N 110°01′E
66 E8 Heflin Alabama, S USA 33°39′N 85°35′W
237 K3 Hegang Heilongjiang, NE China 47°18′N 130°16′E
251 J1 Hegura-jima island SW Japan
Heguri-jima see Heigun-tō
Hei see Heilongjiang
180 G1 Heide Schleswig-Holstein, N Germany 54°12′N 09°06′E
181 J14 Heideck Bayern, Germany 11°07′N 49°07′E
181 F13 Heidelberg Baden-Württemberg, SW Germany 49°24′N 08°41′E
141 J4 Heidelberg Gauteng, South Africa 26°30′S 28°21′E
138 G7 Heidelberg Gauteng, NE South Africa 26°31′S 28°21′E
140 E10 Heidelberg Western Cape, South Africa 34°06′S 20°57′E
68 F2 Heidelberg Mississippi, S USA 31°53′N 88°58′W
181 J14 Heidenheim Bayern, Germany 10°45′N 49°01′E
Heidenheim see Heidenheim an der Brenz
179 E12 Heidenheim an der Brenz var. Heidenheim. Baden-Württemberg, S Germany 48°41′N 10°09′E
177 K1 Heidenreichstein Niederösterreich, N Austria 48°53′N 15°07′E
250 E6 Heigun-tō var. Heguri-jima. island SW Japan
193 K8 Heihe prev. Ai-hun. Heilongjiang, NE China 50°13′N 127°29′E
Hei-ho see Nagqu
141 I5 Heilbron Free State, N South Africa 27°17′S 27°58′E
181 G14 Heilbronn Baden-Württemberg, SW Germany 49°09′N 09°13′E
Heiligenbeil see Mamonovo
177 I4 Heiligenblut Tirol, W Austria 47°04′N 12°50′E
178 F4 Heiligenhafen Schleswig-Holstein, N Germany 54°22′N 10°57′E
Heiligenkreuz see Žiar nad Hronom
180 F5 Heiligenloh Niedersachsen, Germany 8°33′N 52°46′E
181 H8 Heiligenstadt Thüringen, C Germany 51°22′N 10°09′E
181 F13 Heiligkreuzsteinach Baden-Württemberg, Germany 8°48′N 49°29′E
193 K9 Heilongjiang var. Hei, Heilongjiang Sheng, Hei-lung-chiang, Heilungkiang. ◈ province NE China
Heilong Jiang see Amur
Heilongjiang Sheng see Heilongjiang
162 E5 Heiloo Noord-Holland, NW Netherlands 52°36′N 04°43′E
Heilsberg see Lidzbark Warmiński
Hei-lung-chiang/Heilungkiang see Heilongjiang
Heimaæy see Heimaey
152 B3 Heimaey var. Heimaæy. island S Iceland
181 B10 Heimbach Nordrhein-Westfalen, Germany 6°29′N 50°38′E
181 C13 Heimbach Rheinland-Pfalz, Germany 7°15′N 49°37′E
181 H9 Heimboldshausen Hessen, Germany 9°57′N 50°51′E
180 J7 Heimburg Sachsen-Anhalt, Germany 10°55′N 51°49′E
154 D3 Heimdal Sør-Trøndelag, S Norway 63°21′N 10°23′E
Heinaste see Ainaži
153 I8 Heinävesi Isä-Suomi, E Finland 62°22′N 28°42′E
163 H12 Heinerscheid Diekirch, N Luxembourg 50°06′N 06°05′E
162 H6 Heino Overijssel, E Netherlands 52°26′N 06°13′E
153 I9 Heinola Etelä-Suomi, S Finland 61°13′N 26°05′E
181 A9 Heinsberg Nordrhein-Westfalen, W Germany 51°02′N 06°01′E
245 M1 Heishan Liaoning, NE China 41°43′N 122°12′E
242 A1 Heishui var. Luhua. Sichuan, C China 32°08′N 102°54′E
163 E9 Heist-op-den-Berg Antwerpen, C Belgium 51°04′N 04°43′E
Heitō see P'ingtung
261 L7 Heitske Papua, E Indonesia 07°02′S 138°45′E
Hejanah see Al Hījānah
Hejaz see Al Ḩijāz
245 J4 Hejian Hebei, China 38°16′N 116°03′E
242 B4 Hejiang Sichuan, China 28°29′N 105°29′E
242 G8 He Jiang ≈ S China
Hejiayan see Lüeyang
242 G8 Hejie China 24°20′N 111°39′E
244 F7 Hejin Shanxi, China 35°21′N 110°25′E
238 F4 Hejing Xinjiang Uygur Zizhiqu, NW China 42°21′N 86°19′E
Héjjasfalva see Vânători
Heka see Hoika
214 G6 Hekimhan Malatya, C Turkey 38°50′N 37°56′E
152 C3 Hekla ▲ S Iceland 63°56′N 19°42′W
242 G9 Hekou China 23°11′N 112°50′E
Hekou see Yanshan, Jiangxi, China
Hekou see Yajiang, Sichuan, China
182 F3 Hel Ger. Hela. Pomorskie, N Poland 54°35′N 18°48′E
Hela see Hel
154 F4 Helagsfjället ▲ C Sweden 62°57′N 12°31′E
244 D4 Helan var. Xigang. Ningxia, N China 38°33′N 106°21′E
244 C4 Helan Shan ▲▲ N China
181 J11 Heldburg Thüringen, Germany 10°44′N 50°17′E
163 H9 Helden Limburg, SE Netherlands 51°20′N 06°00′E
181 J8 Heldrungen Thüringen, Germany 11°13′N 51°18′E
75 J13 Helena Arkansas, C USA 34°32′N 90°34′W
77 I4 Helena state capital Montana, NW USA 46°36′N 112°02′W
81 F10 Helendale California, USA 34°45′N 117°19′W
158 G3 Helensburgh W Scotland, UK 56°00′N 04°45′W
278 G3 Helensville Auckland, North Island, New Zealand 36°42′S 174°26′E
219 D9 Helez Israel
155 G11 Helgasjön ◎ S Sweden
180 E1 Helgoland Eng. Heligoland. island NW Germany
Helgoland Bay see Helgoländer Bucht
180 E1 Helgoländer Bucht var. Helgoland Bay, Heligoland Bight. bay NW Germany
Heligoland see Helgoland
Heligoland Bight see Helgoländer Bucht
110 E6 Heliodora Minas Gerais, Brazil 22°04′S 45°32′W
Heliopolis see Baalbek
243 L2 Helixi China 30°38′N 118°59′E
152 B3 Hella Sudhurland, SW Iceland 63°51′N 20°24′W
Hellas see Greece
222 F7 Ḩelleh, Rūd-e ≈ S Iran
162 I6 Hellendoorn Overijssel, E Netherlands 52°22′N 06°27′E
Hellenic Republic see Greece
64 F6 Hellertown Pennsylvania, USA 40°35′N 75°20′W
154 B5 Hellesylt Møre og Romsdal, S Norway 62°06′N 06°51′E
162 D7 Hellevoetsluis Zuid-Holland, SW Netherlands 51°49′N 04°08′E
171 H7 Hellín Castilla-La Mancha, C Spain 38°31′N 01°43′W
161 L8 Hellingly UK 50°52′N 0°15′E
187 H6 Hellinikon ✈ (Athína) Attikí, C Greece 37°53′N 23°43′E
76 F6 Hells Canyon valley Idaho/Oregon, NW USA
80 D6 Helm California, USA 36°32′N 120°06′W
230 E6 Helmand ◈ province S Afghanistan
230 D6 Helmand, Daryā-ye var. Rūd-e Hīrmand. ≈ Afghanistan/Iran see also Hīrmand, Rūd-e
Helmand, Daryā-ye see Hīrmand, Rūd-e
Helmantica see Salamanca
181 I8 Helme ≈ C Germany
163 G8 Helmond Noord-Brabant, S Netherlands 51°29′N 05°41′E
156 F4 Helmsdale N Scotland, UK 58°06′N 03°36′W
159 L7 Helmsley UK 54°15′N 1°04′W
180 J6 Helmstedt Niedersachsen, N Germany 52°14′N 11°01′E
248 D2 Helong Jilin, NE China 42°38′N 129°01′E
79 I3 Helper Utah, W USA 39°40′N 110°52′W
141 K6 Helpmekaar KwaZulu-Natal, South Africa 28°26′S 30°25′E
161 K2 Helpringham UK 52°56′N 0°18′W
178 H5 Helpter Berge hill NE Germany
155 F12 Helsingborg prev. Hälsingborg. Skåne, S Sweden 56°N 12°48′E
Helsingfors see Helsinki
155 F12 Helsingør Eng. Elsinore. Frederiksborg, E Denmark 56°03′N 12°38′E
153 H10 Helsinki Swe. Helsingfors. ● (Finland) Etelä-Suomi, S Finland 60°18′N 24°58′E
160 C10 Helston SW England, UK 50°04′N 05°17′W
Heltau see Cisnădie
181 D13 Heltersberg Rheinland-Pfalz, Germany 7°43′N 49°19′E
114 C3 Helvecia Santa Fe, C Argentina 31°09′S 60°09′W
159 I7 Helvellyn ▲ NW England, UK 54°31′N 03°00′W
Helvetia see Switzerland
129 I3 Helwân var. Hilwân, Hulwan, Hulwân. N Egypt 29°51′N 31°20′E
161 J5 Hemel Hempstead E England, UK 51°46′N 00°28′W
181 D8 Hemer Nordrhein-Westfalen, Germany 7°46′N 51°23′E
180 G6 Hemeringen Niedersachsen, Germany 9°15′N 52°08′E
81 F11 Hemet California, W USA 33°45′N 116°58′W
181 J12 Hemhofen Bayern, Germany 10°56′N 49°41′E
74 A7 Hemingford Nebraska, C USA 42°18′N 103°02′W
67 J8 Hemingway South Carolina, SE USA 33°45′N 79°25′W
180 H6 Hemmingen Niedersachsen, Germany 9°45′N 52°19′E
152 D6 Hemnesberget Nordland, C Norway 66°14′N 13°40′E
71 J5 Hemphill Texas, SW USA 31°21′N 93°50′W
161 M3 Hempnall UK 52°30′N 1°18′E
65 I6 Hempstead New York, USA 40°42′N 73°37′W
71 H7 Hempstead Texas, SW USA 30°06′N 96°06′W
181 F13 Hemsbach Baden-Württemberg, Germany 8°39′N 49°36′E
155 J10 Hemse Gotland, SE Sweden 57°12′N 18°22′E
154 C6 Hemsedal valley S Norway
159 K9 Hemsworth UK 53°36′N 1°21′W
239 K7 Henan var. Henan Mongolzu Zizhixian, Yêgainnyin. Qinghai, C China 34°42′N 101°36′E
245 H8 Henan var. Henan Sheng, Honan, Yu. ◈ province C China
278 G3 Hen and Chickens island group N New Zealand
170 G4 Henares ≈ C Spain
252 C7 Henashi-zaki headland Honshū, C Japan 40°37′N 139°51′E
164 F8 Hendaye Pyrénées-Atlantiques, SW France 43°22′N 01°46′W
214 D4 Hendek Sakarya, NW Turkey 40°47′N 30°45′E
112 F10 Henderson Buenos Aires, E Argentina 36°18′S 61°43′W
73 D13 Henderson Kentucky, S USA 37°50′N 87°35′W
81 J9 Henderson Nevada, W USA 36°02′N 114°58′W
67 K5 Henderson North Carolina, SE USA 36°20′N 78°26′W
66 C6 Henderson Tennessee, S USA 35°27′N 88°40′W
71 I5 Henderson Texas, SW USA 32°11′N 94°48′W
73 B9 Henderson Creek ≈ Illinois, N USA
281 J3 Henderson Field ✈ (Honiara) Guadalcanal, C Solomon Islands 09°28′S 160°02′E
285 M8 Henderson Island atoll N Pitcairn Islands
67 H7 Hendersonville North Carolina, SE USA 35°19′N 82°28′W
66 E5 Hendersonville Tennessee, S USA 36°18′N 86°37′W
161 K6 Hendon UK 51°36′N 0°13′W
222 G9 Hendorābī, Jazīreh-ye island S Iran
103 L6 Hendrik Top var. Hendriktop. elevation C Surinam
Hendriktop see Hendrik Top
Hendū Kosh see Hindu Kush
62 F2 Heney, Lac ◎ Québec, SE Canada
Hengchow see Hengyang
243 N10 Hengchun S Taiwan 22°09′N 120°43′E
243 M3 Hengdian China 29°09′N 120°19′E
239 J9 Hengduan Shan ▲▲ SW China
162 H7 Hengelo Gelderland, E Netherlands 52°03′N 06°19′E
162 I6 Hengelo Overijssel, E Netherlands 52°16′N 06°46′E
Hengnan see Hengyang
242 G5 Hengshan Hunan, S China 27°17′N 112°51′E
244 E4 Hengshan Shaanxi, C China 37°57′N 109°17′E
245 H3 Heng Shan ▲▲ Shanxi, China
242 G5 Heng Shan 1290m ▲ Hunan, China 27°11′N 112°25′E
243 I3 Hengshi China 29°30′N 114°41′E
245 I5 Hengshui Hebei, E China 37°42′N 115°39′E
242 E10 Hengxian Guangxi, China 22°25′N 109°10′E
242 G6 Hengyang var. Hengnan, Heng-yang; prev. Hengchow. Hunan, S China 26°55′N 112°34′E
Heng-yang see Hengyang
242 E9 Hengzhou China 22°41′N 109°16′E
189 K8 Heniches'k Rus. Genichesk. Khersons'ka Oblast', S Ukraine 46°10′N 34°49′E
167 H2 Hénin-Beaumont Nord-Pas-de-Calais, France 50°25′N 2°56′E
161 J6 Henley on Thames UK 51°32′N 0°54′W
64 G10 Henlopen, Cape headland Delaware, NE USA 38°48′N 75°06′W
161 K5 Henlow UK 52°01′N 0°17′W
Henna see Enna
154 H5 Hennan Gävleborg, C Sweden 62°01′N 15°55′E
164 E4 Hennebont Morbihan, NW France 47°48′N 03°17′W
73 C9 Hennepin Illinois, N USA 41°14′N 89°21′W
75 D12 Hennessey Oklahoma, C USA 36°06′N 97°54′W
178 H6 Hennigsdorf var. Hennigsdorf bei Berlin. Brandenburg, NE Germany 52°37′N 13°13′E
Hennigsdorf bei Berlin see Hennigsdorf
63 I5 Henniker New Hampshire, NE USA 43°10′N 71°47′W
180 G1 Hennstedt Schleswig-Holstein, Germany 9°10′N 54°17′E
64 C1 Henrietta New York, USA 43°04′N 77°37′W
70 G3 Henrietta Texas, SW USA 33°49′N 98°13′W
58 E4 Cape Henrietta Maria headland Ontario, C Canada
Henrique de Carvalho see Saurimo
73 C9 Henry Illinois, N USA 41°06′N 89°21′W
67 M5 Henry, Cape headland Virginia, NE USA 36°55′N 76°01′W
75 F12 Henryetta Oklahoma, C USA 35°26′N 95°58′W
292 G4 Henry Ice Rise ice cap Antarctica
77 I7 Henrys Fork ≈ Idaho, NW USA
62 B5 Hensall Ontario, S Canada 43°25′N 81°28′W
81 E12 Henshaw, Lake ▣ California, USA
180 H2 Henstedt-Ulzburg Schleswig-Holstein, N Germany 53°45′N 09°59′E
Hentiy see Batshireet
239 L1 Hentiyn Nuruu ▲▲ N Mongolia
277 J6 Henty New South Wales, SE Australia 35°33′S 147°03′E
242 G6 Hen-yang-hsien China 26°58′N 112°16′E
256 C6 Henzada Irrawaddy, SW Myanmar (Burma) 17°36′N 95°26′E
243 I8 Heping Guangdong, China 24°17′N 114°33′E
Heping see Huishui
243 J9 Hepo China 23°34′N 115°22′E
181 F13 Heppenheim Hessen, W Germany 49°39′N 08°38′E
159 J5 Hepple UK 55°17′N 2°03′W
76 D5 Heppner Oregon, NW USA 45°21′N 119°32′W
242 E10 Hepu var. Lianzhou. Guangxi Zhuangzu Zizhiqu, S China 21°40′N 109°12′E
243 L3 Heqiao China 30°06′N 119°14′E
Heracleum see Irákleio
152 C2 Heradhsvötn ≈ C Iceland
Herakleion see Irákleio
80 D2 Herald California, USA 38°18′N 121°15′W
230 D3 Herāt var. Herat; anc. Aria. Herāt, W Afghanistan 34°23′N 62°11′E
230 D3 Herāt ◈ province W Afghanistan
165 I8 Hérault ◈ department S France
165 I8 Hérault ≈ S France
57 M7 Herbert Saskatchewan, S Canada 50°27′N 107°09′W
278 D11 Herbert Otago, South Island, New Zealand 45°14′S 170°48′E
82 E10 Herbert Island island Aleutian Islands, Alaska, USA
Herbertshöhe see Kokopo
59 H7 Hérbertville Québec, SE Canada 48°23′N 71°42′W
181 E10 Herborn Hessen, W Germany 50°40′N 08°18′E
181 G10 Herbstein Hessen, Germany 9°21′N 50°33′E
184 E6 Herceg-Novi It. Castelnuovo; prev. Ercegnovi. SW Montenegro 42°28′N 18°35′E
55 J6 Herchmer Manitoba, C Canada 57°25′N 94°12′W
280 C4 Hercules Bay bay E Papua New Guinea
152 D2 Herdhubreidh ▲ C Iceland 65°12′N 16°26′W
89 H8 Heredia Heredia, C Costa Rica 10°N 84°06′W
89 H8 Heredia off. Provincia de Heredia. ◈ province N Costa Rica
Heredia, Provincia de see Heredia
160 G5 Hereford W England, UK 52°04′N 02°43′W
70 D2 Hereford Texas, SW USA 34°49′N 102°25′W
63 I3 Hereford, Mont ▲ Québec, SE Canada 45°04′N 71°38′W
160 G5 Herefordshire cultural region W England, UK
285 J7 Hereheretue atoll Îles Tuamotu, C French Polynesia
187 M2 Hereke Kocaeli, Turkey 40°47′N 29°37′E
170 G6 Herencia Castilla-La Mancha, C Spain 39°22′N 03°12′W
163 E10 Herent Vlaams Brabant, C Belgium 50°54′N 04°40′E
163 E9 Herentals var. Herenthals. Antwerpen, N Belgium 51°11′N 04°50′E
Herenthals see Herentals
163 E9 Herenthout Antwerpen, N Belgium 51°09′N 04°45′E
155 F12 Herfølge Roskilde, E Denmark 55°25′N 12°09′E
180 F6 Herford Nordrhein-Westfalen, NW Germany 52°07′N 08°41′E
181 J8 Heringen Thüringen, Germany 10°53′N 51°26′E
180 J1 Heringsdorf Schleswig-Holstein, Germany 11°01′N 54°18′E
75 E10 Herington Kansas, C USA 38°37′N 96°55′W
159 I4 Heriot UK 55°45′N 2°58′W
176 E4 Herisau Fr. Hérisau. Appenzell Ausser Rhoden, NE Switzerland 47°23′N 09°17′E
Hérisau see Herisau
167 H10 Hérisson Auvergne, France 46°31′N 2°43′E
Héristal see Herstal
163 F10 Herk-de-Stad Limburg, NE Belgium 50°57′N 05°12′E
64 G1 Herkimer New York, USA 43°02′N 74°59′W
Herkulesbad/Herkulesfürdő see Băile Herculane
239 L1 Herlenbayan-Ulaan var. Dulaan. Hentiy, C Mongolia 47°09′N 108°48′E
Herlen Gol/Herlen He see Kerulen
181 H9 Herleshausen Hessen, Germany 10°10′N 51°01′E
78 C3 Herlong California, W USA 40°07′N 120°06′W
166 B4 Herm island Channel Islands
177 I5 Hermagor Slvn. Šmohor. Kärnten, S Austria 46°37′N 13°24′E
74 F4 Herman Minnesota, N USA 45°49′N 96°08′W
156 H1 Herma Ness headland NE Scotland, UK 60°51′N 00°55′W
75 I9 Hermann Missouri, C USA 38°43′N 91°26′W
274 G5 Hermannsburg Northern Territory, N Australia 23°59′S 132°55′E
Hermannstadt see Sibiu
154 B6 Hermansverk Sogn Og Fjordane, S Norway 61°11′N 06°52′E
216 C4 Hermel var. Hirmil. NE Lebanon 34°23′N 36°19′E
169 H1 Herment Auvergne, France 45°45′N 2°34′E
166 E4 Hermeville Haute-Normandie, France 49°36′N 0°16′E
Hermhausen see Hajnówka
277 J4 Hermidale New South Wales, SE Australia 31°36′S 146°42′E
103 M5 Herminadorp Sipaliwini, NE Surinam 05°05′N 54°22′W
76 E5 Hermiston Oregon, NW USA 45°50′N 119°17′W
75 H10 Hermitage Missouri, C USA 37°57′N 93°21′W
280 B1 Hermit Islands island group N Papua New Guinea
70 E4 Hermleigh Texas, SW USA 32°37′N 100°44′W
216 A3 Hermon, Mount Ar. Jabal ash Shaykh. ▲ S Syria 35°30′N 33°30′E
Hermopolis Parva see Damanhûr
74 A5 Hermosa South Dakota, N USA 43°49′N 103°12′W
84 E4 Hermosillo Sonora, NW Mexico 28°59′N 110°53′W
Hermoupolis see Ermoúpoli
183 H10 Hernád var. Hornád, Ger. Kundert. ≈ Hungary/Slovakia
114 C5 Hernández Entre Ríos, E Argentina 32°21′S 60°02′W
85 K8 Hernàndez San Luis Potosí, Mexico 23°02′N 102°02′W
116 G3 Hernández Entre Ríos, Argentina 32°24′S 60°00′E
69 L5 Hernando Florida, SE USA 28°54′N 82°22′W
66 B7 Hernando Mississippi, S USA 34°49′N 89°59′W
171 H2 Hernani País Vasco, N Spain 43°16′N 01°59′W
163 D10 Herne Vlaams Brabant, C Belgium 50°45′N 04°03′E
181 C8 Herne Nordrhein-Westfalen, W Germany 51°32′N 07°12′E
161 M6 Herne Bay UK 51°22′N 1°08′E
155 C12 Herning Ringkøbing, W Denmark 56°08′N 08°59′E
Hernösand see Härnösand
242 G2 Herong China 30°42′N 111°59′E
74 F5 Heron Lake Minnesota, N USA 43°48′N 95°18′W
Herowābād see Khalkhāl
155 D8 Herre Telemark, S Norway 59°06′N 09°34′E
74 C4 Herreid South Dakota, N USA 45°49′N 100°04′W
179 D12 Herrenberg Baden-Württemberg, S Germany 48°36′N 08°52′E
114 E5 Herrera Entre Ríos, Argentina 32°26′S 58°38′W
170 F8 Herrera Andalucía, S Spain 37°22′N 04°50′W
89 K10 Herrera off. Provincia de Herrera. ◈ province S Panama
170 F6 Herrera del Duque Extremadura, W Spain 39°10′N 05°03′W
170 F2 Herrera de Pisuerga Castilla-León, N Spain 42°35′N 04°20′W
Herrera, Provincia de see Herrera
87 N6 Herrero, Punta headland SE Mexico 19°15′N 87°28′W
172 D4 Herreruela Extremadura, Spain 39°28′N 6°54′W
181 C10 Herresbach Nordrhein-Westfalen, Germany 7°18′N 50°42′E
277 K9 Herrick Tasmania, SE Australia 41°07′S 147°53′E
181 I14 Herrieden Bayern, Germany 10°31′N 49°14′E
73 C13 Herrin Illinois, N USA 37°48′N 89°01′W
66 F4 Herrington Lake ▣ Kentucky, S USA
155 F9 Herrljunga Västra Götaland, S Sweden 58°05′N 13°02′E
165 H9 Hers ≈ S France
53 I3 Herschel, Cape headland Nunavut, N Canada
52 B5 Herschel Island island Yukon Territory, NW Canada
163 F9 Herselt Antwerpen, C Belgium 51°04′N 04°53′E
64 D7 Hershey Pennsylvania, NE USA 40°17′N 76°39′W
163 G11 Herstal Fr. Héristal. Liège, E Belgium 50°40′N 05°38′E
181 C8 Herten Nordrhein-Westfalen, Germany 7°08′N 51°36′E
161 K5 Hertford E England, UK 51°48′N 00°05′W
67 M5 Hertford North Carolina, SE USA 36°11′N 76°30′W
161 K5 Hertfordshire cultural region E England, UK
277 M1 Hervey Bay Queensland, E Australia 25°17′S 152°48′E
178 H7 Herzberg Brandenburg, E Germany 51°42′N 13°15′E
180 E7 Herzebrock Nordrhein-Westfalen, Germany 8°15′N 51°53′E
163 D10 Herzele Oost-Vlaanderen, NW Belgium 50°52′N 03°52′E
180 E7 Herzfeld Nordrhein-Westfalen, Germany 8°10′N 51°39′E
181 J13 Herzogenaurach Bayern, SE Germany 49°34′N 10°52′E
177 L2 Herzogenburg Niederösterreich, NE Austria 48°18′N 15°43′E
Herzogenbusch see 's-Hertogenbosch
165 H1 Hesdin Pas-de-Calais, N France 50°21′N 02°00′E
180 G4 Hesedorf Niedersachsen, Germany 9°21′N 53°12′E
180 D3 Hesel Niedersachsen, Germany 7°36′N 53°18′E
180 C5 Hesepe Niedersachsen, Germany 7°07′N 52°25′E
242 G10 Heshan Guangdong, China 22°28′N 112°34′E
242 D8 Heshan Guangxi Zhuangzu Zizhiqu, S China 23°45′N 108°58′E
244 D6 Heshui var. Xihuachi. Gansu, C China 35°42′N 108°06′E
243 I6 He Shui ≈ Jiangxi, China
167 N7 Hésingue Alsace, France 47°35′N 7°31′E
159 I9 Hesketh Bank UK 53°42′N 2°51′W
163 H14 Hespérange Luxembourg, SE Luxembourg 49°34′N 06°10′E
81 F10 Hesperia California, W USA 34°25′N 117°17′W
79 K5 Hesperus Mountain ▲ Colorado, C USA 37°27′N 108°05′W
54 C2 Hess ≈ Yukon Territory, NW Canada
Hesse see Hessen
181 I14 Hesselberg ▲ S Germany 49°04′N 10°32′E
155 E12 Hesselo island E Denmark
181 G10 Hessen Eng./Fr. Hesse. ◈ state C Germany
180 G6 Hessisch Oldendorf Niedersachsen, Germany 9°15′N 52°10′E
159 M9 Hessle UK 53°43′N 0°26′W
286 F4 Hess Tablemount undersea feature C Pacific Ocean
75 E10 Hesston Kansas, C USA 38°08′N 97°25′W
154 F2 Hestkjøltoppen ▲ C Norway 64°21′N 13°57′E
159 I10 Heswall NW England, UK 53°20′N 03°06′W
233 I6 Hetaudā Central, C Nepal
80 E4 Hetch Hetchy Reservoir ▣ California, USA
Hétfalu see Săcele
161 M3 Hethersett UK 52°36′N 1°11′E
243 J7 Hetian China 25°42′N 116°24′E
140 D9 Het Kruis Western Cape, South Africa 32°36′S 18°45′E
74 B4 Hettinger North Dakota, N USA 46°00′N 102°38′W
159 K6 Hetton le Hole UK 54°49′N 1°27′W
179 G8 Hettstedt Sachsen-Anhalt, C Germany 51°39′N 11°31′E
167 H2 Heuchin Nord-Pas-de-Calais, France 50°28′N 2°16′E
152 B5 Heuglin, Kapp headland SE Svalbard 78°15′N 22°49′E
281 K3 Heuru San Cristobal, SE Solomon Islands 10°13′S 161°25′E
163 F9 Heusden Limburg, NE Belgium 51°02′N 05°17′E
162 F7 Heusden Noord-Brabant, S Netherlands 51°43′N 05°05′E
166 E4 Hève, Cap de la headland N France 49°28′N 00°13′W
163 E10 Heverlee Vlaams Brabant, C Belgium 50°52′N 04°41′E
183 G11 Heves Heves, NE Hungary 47°36′N 20°17′E
183 G11 Heves off. Heves Megye. ◈ county NE Hungary
Heves Megye see Heves
Hevron see Hebron
91 J4 Hewanorra ✈ (Saint Lucia) S Saint Lucia 13°44′N 60°57′W
159 J6 Hexham UK 54°58′N 2°06′W
Hexian see Hezhou
244 A4 Hexibao China 38°22′N 102°05′E
140 E9 Hex River Pass pass Western Cape, South Africa
140 D9 Hexrivierberge ▲▲ Western Cape, South Africa
244 F7 Heyang Shaanxi, C China 35°14′N 110°02′E
Heyang see Hechuan
Heydebrech see Kędzierzyn-Kozle
Heydekrug see Šilutė
Heyin see Guide
159 I8 Heysham NW England, UK 54°02′N 02°54′W
243 I9 Heyuan Guangdong, S China 23°41′N 114°45′E
277 H7 Heywood Victoria, SE Australia 38°09′S 141°38′E
159 J9 Heywood UK 53°35′N 2°13′W
274 E3 Heywood Islands island group Western Australia
245 I7 Heze var. Caozhou. Shandong, E China 35°16′N 115°27′E
242 B5 Hezhang Guizhou, China 27°04′N 104°25′E
239 K6 Hezheng Gansu, C China 35°29′N 103°36′E
242 F8 Hezhou var. Babu; prev. Hexian. Guangxi Zhuangzu Zizhiqu, S China 24°33′N 11°30′E
244 A7 Hezuo Gansu, C China 34°55′N 102°49′E
69 N9 Hialeah Florida, SE USA 25°51′N 80°16′W
75 F9 Hiawatha Kansas, C USA 39°51′N 95°34′W
79 I3 Hiawatha Utah, W USA 39°28′N 111°00′W
159 L9 Hibaldstow UK 53°30′N 0°32′W
74 H3 Hibbing Minnesota, N USA 47°24′N 92°55′W
277 I10 Hibbs, Point headland Tasmania, SE Australia 42°37′S 145°15′E
Hibernia see Ireland
250 D5 Hibiki-nada arm of the Sea of Japan SW Japan
80 J3 Hickison Summit ▲ Nevada, USA 39°27′N 116°45′W
161 M3 Hickling UK 52°45′N 1°35′E
80 D4 Hickman California, USA 37°37′N 120°45′W
66 B5 Hickman Kentucky, S USA 36°33′N 89°11′W
67 I6 Hickory North Carolina, SE USA 35°44′N 81°20′W
67 I6 Hickory, Lake ◎ North Carolina, SE USA
279 J4 Hicks Bay Gisborne, North Island, New Zealand 37°36′S 178°18′E
70 G5 Hico Texas, SW USA 31°58′N 98°01′W
252 F5 Hidaka Hokkaidō, NE Japan 42°53′N 142°24′E
251 H4 Hidaka Hyōgo, Honshū, SW Japan 35°27′N 134°43′E
252 F5 Hidaka-sanmyaku ▲▲ Hokkaidō, NE Japan
85 K9 Hidalgo Campeche, Mexico
85 L5 Hidalgo var. Villa Hidalgo. Coahuila de Zaragoza, NE Mexico 27°46′N 99°54′W
85 L6 Hidalgo Nuevo León, NE Mexico 29°59′N 100°27′W
85 M7 Hidalgo Tamaulipas, C Mexico 24°16′N 99°28′W
85 J8 Hidalgo Zacatecas, Mexico 23°59′N 103°39′W
86 F5 Hidalgo ◈ state C Mexico
85 H5 Hidalgo del Parral var. Parral. Chihuahua, N Mexico 26°58′N 105°40′W
219 F9 Hīdān, Wādī al dry watercourse Jordan
251 J3 Hida-sanmyaku ▲▲ Honshū, S Japan
180 F6 Hiddenhausen Nordrhein-Westfalen, Germany 8°37′N 52°10′E
178 H3 Hiddensee island NE Germany
129 J7 Hidiglib, Wadi ≈ NE Sudan
177 K3 Hieflau Salzburg, E Austria 47°36′N 14°34′E
Hierosolyma see Jerusalem
170 A10 Hierro var. Ferro. island Islas Canarias, Spain, NE Atlantic Ocean
250 F5 Higashi-Hiroshima var. Higasihirosima. Hiroshima, Honshū, SW Japan 34°27′N 132°43′E
251 L4 Higashi-Izu Shizuoka, Honshū, S Japan 34°43′N 138°58′E
253 D10 Higashine var. Higasine. Yamagata, Honshū, C Japan 38°26′N 140°24′E
250 B5 Higashi-suidō strait SW Japan
Higasihirosima see Higashi-Hiroshima
Higasine see Higashine
70 F1 Higgins Texas, SW USA 36°06′N 100°01′W
72 G6 Higgins Lake ◎ Michigan, N USA
75 G9 Higginsville Missouri, C USA 39°04′N 93°43′W
160 E8 Highampton UK 50°49′N 4°09′W
High Atlas see Haut Atlas
72 D5 High Falls Reservoir ▣ Wisconsin, N USA
90 F7 Highgate C Jamaica 18°16′N 76°53′W
161 L7 High Halden UK 51°05′N 0°43′E
71 J7 High Island Texas, SW USA 29°35′N 94°24′W
72 F5 High Island island Michigan, N USA
73 C12 Highland Illinois, N USA 38°44′N 89°40′W
73 D8 Highland Park Illinois, N USA 42°10′N 87°48′W
66 G7 Highlands North Carolina, SE USA 35°04′N 83°10′W
54 E6 High Level Alberta, W Canada 58°31′N 117°08′W
74 D5 Highmore South Dakota, N USA 44°29′N 99°26′W
263 K5 High Peak ▲ Luzon, N Philippines 15°28′N 120°07′E
High Plains see Great Plains
67 J6 High Point North Carolina, SE USA 35°58′N 80°00′W
64 G5 High Point hill New Jersey, NE USA
57 H3 High Prairie Alberta, W Canada 55°27′N 116°28′W
57 I8 High River Alberta, SW Canada 50°35′N 113°50′W
67 J6 High Rock Lake ▣ North Carolina, SE USA
69 K4 High Springs Florida, SE USA 29°49′N 82°36′W
64 G7 Hightstown New Jersey, USA 40°16′N 74°31′W
High Veld see Great Karoo
157 F12 High Willhays ▲ SW England, UK 50°39′N 03°58′W
161 I6 Highworth UK 51°37′N 1°42′W

◆ Country
● Country Capital
◇ Dependent Territory
○ Dependent Territory Capital
◈ Administrative Regions
✈ International Airport
▲ Mountain
▲▲ Mountain Range
Volcano
≈ River
◎ Lake
▣ Reservoir

INDEX

High Wycombe - Hörnefors
INDEX
350

161 J6 **High Wycombe** *prev.* Chepping Wycombe, Chipping Wycombe. SE England, UK 51°38′N 00°46′W
86 F4 **Higos** *var.* El Higo. Veracruz-Llave, E Mexico 21°48′N 98°25′W
173 H7 **Higuera de Arjona** Andalucía, Spain 37°58′N 3°59′W
172 E7 **Higuera de la Sierra** Andalucía, Spain 37°50′N 6°27′W
84 F6 **Higuera de Zaragoza** Sinaloa, Mexico 25°57′N 109°17′W
172 D6 **Higuera la Real** Extremadura, Spain 38°08′N 6°41′W
164 F8 **Higuer, Cap** *headland* NE Spain 43°23′N 01°46′W
86 E6 **Higuerillas** México, Mexico 20°10′N 99°50′W
91 H7 **Higüero, Punta** *headland* W Puerto Rico 18°21′N 67°15′W
173 K5 **Higueruela** Castilla-La Manacha, Spain 38°57′N 1°27′W
91 I6 **Higüey** *var.* Salvaleón de Higüey. E Dominican Republic 18°40′N 68°43′W
284 C9 **Hihifo** ✕ (Matā'utu) Île Uvea, N Wallis and Futuna
136 H6 **Hiiraan** *off.* Gobolka Hiiraan. ◈ *region* C Somalia
Hiiraan, Gobolka *see* Hiiraan
190 C4 **Hiiumaa** *var.* Hiiumaa Maakond. ◈ *province* W Estonia
190 C4 **Hiiumaa** *Ger.* Dagden, *Swe.* Dagö. *island* W Estonia
Hiiumaa Maakond *see* Hiiumaa
Hijanah *see* Al Hījānah
171 I4 **Híjar** Aragón, NE Spain 41°10′N 00°27′W
250 E5 **Hikari** Yamaguchi, Honshū, SW Japan 33°59′N 131°56′E
250 G5 **Hiketa** Kagawa, Shikoku, SW Japan 34°15′N 134°20′E
251 I4 **Hikone** Shiga, Honshū, SW Japan 35°17′N 136°13′E
250 D6 **Hiko-san** ▲ Kyūshū, SW Japan 33°27′N 130°55′E
285 K7 **Hikueru** *atoll* Îles Tuamotu, C French Polynesia
278 G2 **Hikurangi** Northland, North Island, New Zealand 35°37′S 174°16′E
279 J5 **Hikurangi** ▲ North Island, New Zealand 37°55′S 177°59′E
286 F8 **Hikurangi Trench** *var.* Hikurangi Trough. *undersea feature* SW Pacific Ocean
Hikurangi Trough *see* Hikurangi Trench
285 H9 **Hikutavake** NW Niue
199 I8 **Hilāl, Ra's al** *headland* N Libya 32°55′N 22°09′E
118 E1 **Hilario** San Juan, Argentina 31°29′S 69°24′W
116 F6 **Hilario Ascasubi** Buenos Aires, Argentina 39°30′S 62°48′E
181 E9 **Hilchenbach** Nordrhein-Westfalen, Germany 8°06′N 50°59′E
181 J11 **Hildburghausen** Thüringen, C Germany 50°26′N 10°44′E
181 C9 **Hilden** Nordrhein-Westfalen, W Germany 51°12′N 06°56′E
161 H2 **Hilderstone** UK 52°55′N 2°05′W
180 H6 **Hildesheim** Niedersachsen, N Germany 52°09′N 09°57′E
77 J4 **Hilger** Montana, NW USA 47°15′N 109°18′W
Hili *see* Hilli
Hilla *see* Al Ḩillah
91 N8 **Hillaby, Mount** ▲ N Barbados 13°12′N 59°34′W
155 F10 **Hillared** Älvsborg, S Sweden 57°37′N 13°10′E
293 I7 **Hillary Coast** *physical region* Antarctica
88 D1 **Hill Bank** Orange Walk, N Belize 17°36′N 88°43′W
76 G7 **Hill City** Idaho, NW USA 43°18′N 115°03′W
75 C9 **Hill City** Kansas, C USA 39°23′N 99°51′W
74 G3 **Hill City** Minnesota, N USA 46°59′N 93°36′W
74 A5 **Hill City** South Dakota, N USA 43°54′N 103°33′W
117 H11 **Hill Cove Settlement** West Falkland, Falkland Islands
180 F6 **Hille** Nordrhein-Westfalen, Germany 8°45′N 52°20′E
162 E6 **Hillegom** Zuid-Holland, W Netherlands 52°18′N 04°35′E
155 F12 **Hillerød** Frederiksborg, E Denmark 55°56′N 12°19′E
180 I6 **Hillerse** Niedersachsen, Germany 10°24′N 52°25′E
79 I5 **Hillers, Mount** ▲ Utah, W USA 37°53′N 110°42′W
181 B11 **Hillesheim** Rheinland-Pfalz, Germany 6°40′N 50°18′E
233 J7 **Hilli** *var.* Hili. Rajshahi, NW Bangladesh 25°16′N 89°04′E
54 G5 **Hill Island Lake** ◎ Northwest Territories, C Canada
74 F6 **Hills** Minnesota, N USA 43°31′N 96°21′W
73 C11 **Hillsboro** Illinois, N USA 39°09′N 89°29′W
75 E10 **Hillsboro** Kansas, C USA 38°21′N 97°12′W
75 J10 **Hillsboro** Missouri, C USA 38°13′N 90°33′W
65 K1 **Hillsboro** New Hampshire, NE USA 43°06′N 71°52′W
79 K9 **Hillsboro** New Mexico, SW USA 32°55′N 107°33′W
74 E3 **Hillsboro** North Dakota, N USA 47°25′N 97°03′W
73 H11 **Hillsboro** Ohio, N USA 39°12′N 83°36′W
76 B5 **Hillsboro** Oregon, NW USA 45°32′N 122°59′W
71 H5 **Hillsboro** Texas, SW USA 32°01′N 97°08′W
72 B7 **Hillsboro** Wisconsin, N USA 43°40′N 90°21′W
69 N8 **Hillsboro Canal** *canal* Florida, SE USA
158 E7 **Hillsborough** E Northern Ireland, UK 54°27′N 06°06′W
67 K6 **Hillsborough** North Carolina, SE USA 36°04′N 79°06′W
73 G9 **Hillsdale** Michigan, N USA 41°55′N 84°37′W
277 J5 **Hillston** New South Wales, SE Australia 33°30′S 145°33′E
67 I5 **Hillsville** Virginia, NE USA 36°46′N 80°44′W
156 G1 **Hillswick** NE Scotland, UK 60°28′N 01°37′W
Hill Tippera *see* Tripura
158 E8 **Hilltown** UK 54°12′N 6°08′W
80 C4 **Hilmar** California, USA 37°25′N 120°51′W
161 H6 **Hilmarton** UK 51°28′N 1°58′W
82 D3 **Hilo** Hawai'i, USA, C Pacific Ocean 19°42′N 155°04′W
181 J14 **Hilpoltstein** Bayern, Germany 11°11′N 49°11′E
180 E6 **Hilter** Niedersachsen, Germany 8°09′N 52°09′E
62 E5 **Hilton** New York, NE USA 43°17′N 77°47′W
62 A2 **Hilton Beach** Ontario, S Canada 46°14′N 83°51′W
67 I10 **Hilton Head Island** South Carolina, SE USA 32°13′N 80°45′W
67 J10 **Hilton Head Island** *island* South Carolina, SE USA
180 D7 **Hiltrup** Nordrhein-Westfalen, Germany 7°38′N 51°54′E
163 F8 **Hilvarenbeek** Noord-Brabant, S Netherlands 51°29′N 05°08′E
162 F6 **Hilversum** Noord-Holland, C Netherlands 52°14′N 05°10′E
Hilwân *see* Helwân
232 F3 **Himāchal Pradesh** ◈ *state* NW India
Himalaya/Himalaya Shan *see* Himalayas
238 E9 **Himalayas** *var.* Himalaya, *Chin.* Himalaya Shan. ▲▲ S Asia
263 L7 **Himamaylan** Negros, C Philippines 10°04′N 122°52′E
152 G7 **Himanka** Länsi-Soumi, W Finland 64°04′N 23°40′E
Himara *see* Himarë
184 F10 **Himarë** *var.* Himara. Vlorë, S Albania 40°06′N 19°45′E
216 F2 **Ḩimār, Wādī al** *dry watercourse* N Syria
232 C8 **Himatnagar** Gujarāt, W India 23°38′N 73°02′E
177 L2 **Himberg** Niederösterreich, E Austria 48°05′N 16°27′E
180 I4 **Himbergen** Niedersachsen, Germany 10°44′N 53°06′E
251 K2 **Hime-gawa** ~ Honshū, S Japan
251 H4 **Himeji** *var.* Himezi. Hyōgo, Honshū, SW Japan 34°47′N 134°32′E
250 D6 **Hime-jima** *island* SW Japan
Himezi *see* Himeji
251 J2 **Himi** Toyama, Honshū, SW Japan 36°54′N 136°59′E
180 G2 **Himmelpforten** Niedersachsen, Germany 9°18′N 53°37′E
216 D4 **Ḩimş** *var.* Homs; *anc.* Emesa. Ḩimş, C Syria 34°44′N 36°43′E
216 E4 **Ḩimş** *off.* Muḩāfazat Hims, *var.* Homs. ◈ *governorate* C Syria
216 C4 **Ḩimş, Buḩayrat** *var.* Buhayrat Qattinah. ◎ W Syria
263 N8 **Hinatuan** Mindanao, S Philippines 08°21′N 126°19′E
188 F7 **Hînceşti** *var.* Hânceşti; *prev.* Kotovsk. C Moldova 46°48′N 28°33′E
91 H5 **Hinche** C Haiti 19°07′N 72°00′W
275 K4 **Hinchinbrook Island** *island* Queensland, NE Australia
83 J6 **Hinchinbrook Island** *island* Alaska, USA
161 I3 **Hinckley** C England, UK 52°33′N 01°21′W
74 H4 **Hinckley** Minnesota, N USA 46°01′N 92°57′W
79 H3 **Hinckley** Utah, W USA 39°21′N 112°39′W
62 G5 **Hinckley Reservoir** ⊞ New York, NE USA
232 E6 **Hindaun** Rājasthān, N India 26°44′N 77°02′E
Hindenburg/Hindenburg in Oberschlesien *see* Zabrze
159 L7 **Hinderwell** UK 54°32′N 0°46′W
161 J7 **Hindhead** UK 51°06′N 0°44′W
Hindiya *see* Al Hindīyah
159 J9 **Hindley** UK 53°32′N 2°35′W
66 G4 **Hindman** Kentucky, S USA 37°20′N 82°58′W
277 H6 **Hindmarsh, Lake** ◎ Victoria, SE Australia
161 H7 **Hindon** UK 51°06′N 2°08′W
278 E10 **Hinds** Canterbury, South Island, New Zealand 44°01′S 171°33′E
278 D10 **Hinds** ~ South Island, New Zealand
155 E12 **Hindsholm** *island* C Denmark
231 I2 **Hindu Kush** *Per.* Hendū Kosh. ▲▲ Afghanistan/Pakistan
234 E7 **Hindupur** Andhra Pradesh, E India 13°46′N 77°33′E
56 G2 **Hines Creek** Alberta, W Canada 56°14′N 118°36′W
69 L2 **Hinesville** Georgia, SE USA 31°51′N 81°36′W
234 F4 **Hinganghāt** Mahārāshtra, C India 20°32′N 78°52′E
161 M3 **Hingham** UK 52°35′N 0°58′E
65 M2 **Hingham** Massachusetts, USA 42°15′N 70°53′W
230 E9 **Hingol** ~ SW Pakistan
234 E4 **Hingoli** Mahārāshtra, C India 19°45′N 77°08′E
215 J6 **Hınıs** Erzurum, E Turkey 39°22′N 41°44′E
81 F10 **Hinkley** California, USA 34°56′N 117°12′W
152 B4 **Hinlopenstretet** *strait* N Svalbard
152 E4 **Hinnøya** *Lapp.* Iinnasuolu. *island* C Norway
172 F6 **Hinojosa del Duque** Andalucía, Spain 38°30′N 5°09′W
250 D7 **Hinokage** Miyazaki, Kyūshū, SW Japan 32°39′N 131°20′E
250 F4 **Hino-misaki** *headland* Honshū, SW Japan 35°25′N 132°37′E
65 J1 **Hinsdale** New Hampshire, USA 42°47′N 72°29′W
180 C3 **Hinte** Niedersachsen, Germany 7°11′N 53°25′E
176 E5 **Hinterrhein** ~ SW Switzerland
161 M4 **Hintlesham** UK 52°03′N 1°03′E
56 G5 **Hinton** Alberta, SW Canada 53°24′N 117°35′W
75 D12 **Hinton** Oklahoma, C USA 35°28′N 98°21′W
67 I4 **Hinton** West Virginia, NE USA 37°42′N 80°54′W
Hios *see* Chíos
85 K6 **Hipolito** Coahuila de Zaragoza, NE Mexico 25°42′N 101°22′W
Hipponium *see* Vibo Valentia
250 B6 **Hirado** Nagasaki, Hirado-shima, SW Japan 33°22′N 129°31′E
250 B6 **Hirado-shima** *island* SW Japan
251 H4 **Hirakata** Ōsaka, Honshū, SW Japan 34°48′N 135°38′E
250 F10 **Hirakubo-saki** *headland* Ishigaki-jima, SW Japan 24°36′N 124°19′E
234 I3 **Hirākud Reservoir** ⊞ E India
Hir al Gharbi, Qasr al *see* Ḩayr al Gharbī, Qaşr al
252 D7 **Hiranai** Aomori, Honshū, N Japan 40°56′N 140°55′E
250 G9 **Hirara** Okinawa, Miyako-jima, SW Japan 24°48′N 125°17′E
250 F4 **Hirata** Shimane, Honshū, SW Japan 35°25′N 132°45′E
253 B14 **Hiratsuka** *var.* Hiratuka. Kanagawa, Honshū, S Japan 35°20′N 139°20′E
Hiratuka *see* Hiratsuka
214 E6 **Hirfanlı Barajı** ⊞ C Turkey
234 E7 **Hiriyūr** Karnātaka, W India 13°58′N 76°33′E
Hîrlău *see* Hârlău
230 D6 **Hīrmand, Rūd-e** *var.* Daryā-ye Helmand. ~ Afghanistan/Iran *see also* Helmand, Daryā-ye
Hīrmand, Rūd-e *see* Helmand, Daryā-ye
Hirmil *see* Hermel
252 F5 **Hiroo** Hokkaidō, NE Japan 42°16′N 143°16′E
252 D7 **Hirosaki** Aomori, Honshū, C Japan 40°34′N 140°28′E
250 E5 **Hiroshima** *var.* Hirosima. Hiroshima, Honshū, SW Japan 34°23′N 132°26′E
250 F5 **Hiroshima** *off.* Hiroshima-ken, *var.* Hirosima. ◈ *prefecture* Honshū, SW Japan
Hiroshima-ken *see* Hiroshima
Hirosima *see* Hiroshima
Hirschberg/Hirschberg im Riesengebirge/Hirschberg in Schlesien *see* Jelenia Góra
181 F13 **Hirschhorn** Hessen, Germany 8°54′N 49°27′E
165 I2 **Hirson** Aisne, N France 49°56′N 04°05′E
Hîrşova *see* Hârşova
155 D10 **Hirtshals** Nordjylland, N Denmark 57°34′N 09°58′E
181 G11 **Hirzenhain** Hessen, Germany 9°08′N 50°24′E
251 I5 **Hisai** Mie, Honshū, SW Japan 34°40′N 136°28′E
232 E5 **Hisār** Haryāna, NW India 29°10′N 75°45′E
239 J1 **Hishig Öndör** *var.* Maanīt. Bulgan, C Mongolia 48°17′N 103°29′E
280 C4 **Hisiu** Central, SW Papua New Guinea 09°20′S 146°48′E
229 I7 **Hisor** *Rus.* Gissar. W Tajikistan 38°34′N 68°29′E
Hispalis *see* Sevilla
Hispana/Hispania *see* Spain
91 H5 **Hispaniola** *island* Dominion Republic/Haiti
Histonium *see* Vasto
217 I5 **Hīt** SW Iraq 33°38′N 42°50′E
250 D6 **Hita** Ōita, Kyūshū, SW Japan 33°19′N 130°55′E
253 D12 **Hitachi** *var.* Hitati. Ibaraki, Honshū, S Japan 36°40′N 140°42′E
253 D12 **Hitachi-Ōta** *var.* Hitatiôta. Ibaraki, Honshū, S Japan 36°32′N 140°31′E
Hitati *see* Hitachi
Hitatiôta *see* Hitachi-Ōta
161 K5 **Hitchin** E England, UK 51°57′N 00°17′W
250 D8 **Hitoyoshi** *var.* Hitoyosi. Kumamoto, Kyūshū, SW Japan 32°12′N 130°48′E
Hitoyosi *see* Hitoyoshi
154 D3 **Hitra** *prev.* Hitteren. *island* S Norway
Hitteren *see* Hitra
180 J4 **Hitzacker** Niedersachsen, Germany 11°03′N 53°09′E
281 L1 **Hiu** *island* Torres Islands, N Vanuatu
253 B12 **Hiuchiga-take** ▲ Honshū, C Japan 36°57′N 139°18′E
250 F5 **Hiuchi-nada** *gulf* S Japan
285 K5 **Hiva Oa** *island* Îles Marquises, N French Polynesia
81 E10 **Hi Vista** California, USA 34°44′N 117°47′W
66 F7 **Hiwassee Lake** ⊞ North Carolina, SE USA
66 F7 **Hiwassee River** ~ SE USA
155 D10 **Hjallerup** Nordjylland, N Denmark 57°10′N 10°10′E
155 H8 **Hjälmaren** *Eng.* Lake Hjalmar. ◎ C Sweden
54 G4 **Hjalmar Lake** ◎ Northwest Territories, NW Canada
Hjalmar, Lake *see* Hjälmaren
154 A7 **Hjellestad** Hordaland, S Norway 60°15′N 05°13′E
155 B8 **Hjelmeland** Rogaland, S Norway 59°12′N 06°07′E
154 D5 **Hjerkinn** Oppland, S Norway 62°13′N 09°37′E
155 G9 **Hjo** Västra Götaland, S Sweden 58°18′N 14°17′E
155 D10 **Hjørring** Nordjylland, N Denmark 57°28′N 09°59′E
256 D1 **Hkakabo Razi** ▲ Myanmar (Burma)/China 28°17′N 97°28′E
256 D2 **Hkring Bum** ▲ N Myanmar (Burma) 27°05′N 97°16′E
141 L5 **Hlabisa** KwaZulu-Natal, South Africa 28°08′S 31°52′E
141 L4 **Hlathikulu** *var.* Hlatikulu. S Swaziland 26°58′S 31°19′E
Hlatikulu *see* Hlathikulu
Hliboka *see* Hlyboka
183 D9 **Hlinsko** *var.* Hlinsko v Čechách. Pardubický Kraj, C Czech Republic 49°46′N 15°54′E
Hlinsko v Čechách *see* Hlinsko
141 K5 **Hlobane** KwaZulu-Natal, South Africa 27°43′S 31°00′E
189 J4 **Hlobyne** *Rus.* Globino. Poltavs'ka Oblast', NE Ukraine 49°24′N 33°16′E
183 E10 **Hlohovec** *Ger.* Freistadtl, *Hung.* Galgóc; *prev.* Frakštát. Trnavský Kraj, W Slovakia 48°26′N 17°49′E
141 I6 **Hlotse** *var.* Leribe. NW Lesotho 28°55′S 28°01′E
183 F8 **Hlučín** *Ger.* Hultschin, *Pol.* Hulczyn. Moravskoslezský Kraj, E Czech Republic 49°54′N 18°11′E
141 L5 **Hluhluwe** KwaZulu-Natal, South Africa 28°02′S 32°17′E
141 L5 **Hluhluwe Dam** ⊞ KwaZulu-Natal, South Africa
189 J2 **Hlukhiv** *Rus.* Glukhov. Sums'ka Oblast', NE Ukraine 51°40′N 33°53′E
191 G12 **Hlushkavichy** *Rus.* Glushkevichi. Homyel'skaya Voblasts', SE Belarus 51°34′N 27°47′E
191 G11 **Hlusk** *Rus.* Glusk, Glussk. Mahilyowskaya Voblasts', E Belarus 52°54′N 28°41′E
188 E5 **Hlyboka** *Ger.* Hliboka, *Rus.* Glybokaya. Chernivets'ka Oblast', W Ukraine 48°04′N 25°56′E
191 F8 **Hlybokaye** *Rus.* Glubokoye. Vitsyebskaya Voblasts', N Belarus 55°08′N 27°41′E
133 H8 **Ho** SE Ghana 06°36′N 00°28′E
257 H5 **Hoa Binh** Hoa Binh, N Vietnam 20°49′N 105°20′E
140 C2 **Hoachanas** Hardap, C Namibia 23°55′S 18°04′E
Hoai Nhơn *see* Bông Sơn
257 H6 **Hoa Lac** Quang Binh, C Vietnam 17°54′N 106°24′E
256 G4 **Hoang Liên Sơn** ▲▲ N Vietnam
138 A4 **Hoanib** ~ NW Namibia
53 M8 **Hoare Bay** *coastal sea feature* Nunavut, NE Canada
77 J8 **Hoback Peak** ▲ Wyoming, C USA 43°04′N 110°34′W
277 J10 **Hobart** *prev.* Hobarton, Hobart Town. *state capital* Tasmania, SE Australia 42°54′S 147°18′E
75 D12 **Hobart** Oklahoma, C USA 35°03′N 99°04′W
277 J10 **Hobart** ✕ Tasmania, SE Australia 42°52′S 147°28′E
80 F1 **Hobart Mills** California, USA 39°24′N 120°11′W
Hobarton/Hobart Town *see* Hobart
79 N9 **Hobbs** New Mexico, SW USA 32°42′N 103°08′W
292 G7 **Hobbs Coast** *physical region* Antarctica
141 J8 **Hobeni** Eastern Cape, South Africa 32°10′S 28°53′E
69 N7 **Hobe Sound** Florida, SE USA 27°03′N 80°08′W
141 I6 **Hobhouse** Free State, South Africa 29°32′S 27°09′E
Hobicaurikány *see* Uricani
102 B7 **Hobo** Huila, S Colombia 02°34′N 75°28′W
163 E9 **Hoboken** Antwerpen, N Belgium 51°12′N 04°22′E
238 F2 **Hoboksar** *var.* Hoboksar Mongol Zizhixian. Xinjiang Uygur Zizhiqu, NW China 46°48′N 85°42′E
Hoboksar Mongol Zizhixian *see* Hoboksar
244 G2 **Hobor** Inner Mongolia, China 41°10′N 112°23′E
155 D11 **Hobro** Nordjylland, N Denmark 56°39′N 09°51′E
67 M6 **Hobucken** North Carolina, SE USA 35°15′N 76°31′W
155 I11 **Hoburgen** *headland* SE Sweden 56°54′N 18°07′E
136 I6 **Hobyo** *It.* Obbia. Mudug, E Somalia 05°16′N 48°24′E
187 N5 **Hocalar** Uşak, Turkey 38°35′N 29°27′E
179 I14 **Hochalmspitze** ▲ SW Austria 47°00′N 13°19′E
177 I2 **Hochburg** Oberösterreich, N Austria 48°10′N 12°57′E
180 G1 **Hochdonn** Schleswig-Holstein, Germany 9°17′N 54°02′E
176 D4 **Hochdorf** Luzern, N Switzerland 47°10′N 08°16′E
179 G14 **Hochfeiler** *It.* Gran Pilastro. ▲ Austria/Italy 46°59′N 11°42′E
257 I9 **Hô Chi Minh** *var.* Ho Chi Minh City; *prev.* Saigon. S Vietnam 10°46′N 106°43′E
Ho Chi Minh City *see* Hô Chi Minh
Höchstadt *see* Höchstadt an der Aisch
181 J12 **Höchstadt an der Aisch** *var.* Höchstadt. Bayern, C Germany 49°43′N 10°48′E
174 D3 **Hochwilde** *It.* L'Altissima. ▲ Austria/Italy 46°45′N 11°00′E
179 I14 **Hochwildstelle** ▲ C Austria 47°21′N 13°53′E
73 I11 **Hocking River** ~ Ohio, N USA
Hoctúm *see* Hoctún
87 M5 **Hoctún** *var.* Hoctúm. Yucatán, E Mexico 20°48′N 89°14′W
159 J9 **Hodder** ~ UK
161 K5 **Hoddesdon** UK 51°45′N 0°0′E
Hodeida *see* Al Ḩudaydah
180 G5 **Hodenhagen** Niedersachsen, Germany 9°35′N 52°45′E
81 F10 **Hodge** California, USA 34°49′N 117°12′W
66 E4 **Hodgenville** Kentucky, S USA 37°34′N 85°45′W
57 M8 **Hodgeville** Saskatchewan, S Canada 50°06′N 106°55′W
132 E2 **Hodh ech Chargui** ◈ *region* E Mauritania
Hodh el Garbi *see* Hodh el Gharbi
132 D3 **Hodh el Gharbi** *var.* Hodh el Garbi. ◈ *region* S Mauritania
183 G12 **Hódmezővásárhely** Csongrád, SE Hungary 46°27′N 20°18′E
131 J2 **Hodna, Chott El** *var.* Chott el-Hodna, *Ar.* Shatt al-Hodna. *salt lake* N Algeria
Hodna, Chott el-/Hodna, Shatt al- *see* Hodna, Chott El
171 N9 **Hodna, Monts du** ▲▲ Algeria
160 G3 **Hodnet** UK 52°51′N 2°35′W
183 E10 **Hodonín** *Ger.* Göding. Jihomoravský Kraj, SE Czech Republic 48°52′N 17°07′E
Hödrögö *see* Nömrög
Hodság/Hodschag *see* Odžaci
83 I4 **Hodzana River** ~ Alaska, USA
141 K3 **Hoedspruit** Limpopo, South Africa 24°21′S 30°58′E
Hoei *see* Huy
163 E10 **Hoeilaart** Vlaams Brabant, C Belgium 50°46′N 04°28′E
Hoë Karoo *see* Great Karoo
162 D7 **Hoek van Holland** *Eng.* Hook of Holland. Zuid-Holland, W Netherlands 52°00′N 04°07′E
162 G6 **Hoenderloo** Gelderland, E Netherlands 52°08′N 05°46′E
163 H10 **Hoensbroek** Limburg, SE Netherlands 50°55′N 05°55′E
248 E2 **Hoeryŏng** NE North Korea 42°23′N 129°46′E
163 G10 **Hoeselt** Limburg, NE Belgium 50°50′N 05°30′E
162 G6 **Hoevelaken** Gelderland, C Netherlands 52°10′N 05°27′E
Hoey *see* Huy
179 G10 **Hof** Bayern, SE Germany 50°19′N 11°55′E
Höfdhakaupstadhur *see* Skagaströnd
Hofei *see* Hefei
180 I5 **Höfer** Niedersachsen, Germany 10°15′N 52°41′E
181 G8 **Hofgeismar** Hessen, Germany 9°24′N 51°29′E
181 I11 **Hofheim** Bayern, Germany 10°32′N 50°08′E
181 E11 **Hofheim am Taunus** Hessen, W Germany 50°04′N 08°27′E
Hofmarkt *see* Odorheiu Secuiesc
141 H8 **Hofmeyr** Eastern Cape, South Africa 31°39′S 25°48′E
152 D3 **Höfn** Austurland, SE Iceland 64°14′N 15°17′W
154 H6 **Hofors** Gävleborg, C Sweden 60°33′N 16°21′E
152 C2 **Hofsjökull** *glacier* C Iceland
152 C1 **Hofsós** Nordhurland Vestra, N Iceland 65°54′N 19°25′W
250 D5 **Hōfu** Yamaguchi, Honshū, SW Japan 34°01′N 131°34′E
Hofuf *see* Al Hufūf
155 F12 **Höganäs** Skåne, S Sweden 56°11′N 12°39′E
277 J8 **Hogan Group** *island group* Tasmania, SE Australia
66 F9 **Hogansville** Georgia, SE USA 33°10′N 84°55′W
83 H4 **Hogatza River** ~ Alaska, USA
74 A7 **Hogback Mountain** ▲ Nebraska, C USA 41°40′N 103°44′W
154 D7 **Høgevarde** ▲ S Norway 60°19′N 09°27′E
Högfors *see* Karkkila
72 G5 **Hog Island** *island* Michigan, N USA
67 M4 **Hog Island** *island* Virginia, NE USA
Hogoley Islands *see* Chuuk Islands
141 I9 **Hogsback** Eastern Cape, South Africa 32°35′S 26°57′E
155 H10 **Högsby** Kalmar, S Sweden 57°10′N 16°03′E
79 H2 **Hogup Mountains** ▲▲ Utah, W USA
181 C11 **Hohe Acht** ▲ W Germany 50°23′N 07°00′E
180 H6 **Hoheneggelsen** Niedersachsen, Germany 10°11′N 52°13′E
Hohenelbe *see* Vrchlabí
176 F4 **Hohenems** Vorarlberg, W Austria 47°23′N 09°43′E
180 E2 **Hohenkirchen** Niedersachsen, Germany 7°56′N 53°40′E
181 D8 **Hohenlimburg** Nordrhein-Westfalen, Germany 7°36′N 51°21′E
Hohenmauth *see* Vysoké Mýto
Hohensalza *see* Inowrocław
Hohenstadt *see* Zábřeh
Hohenstein in Ostpreussen *see* Olsztynek
66 D6 **Hohenwald** Tennessee, S USA 35°33′N 87°31′W
179 G9 **Hohenwarte-stausee** ⊞ C Germany
Hohes Venn *see* Hautes Fagnes
177 H4 **Hohe Tauern** ▲▲ W Austria
244 G2 **Hohhot** *var.* Huhehot, Huhohaote, *Mong.* Kukukhoto; *prev.* Kweisui, Kwesui. Nei Mongol Zizhiqu, N China 40°49′N 111°37′E
239 H2 **Hohmorīt** *var.* Sayn-Ust. Govī-Altay, W Mongolia 47°23′N 94°19′E
181 D10 **Hohn** Rheinland-Pfalz, Germany 7°22′N 50°38′E
180 G1 **Hohn** Schleswig-Holstein, Germany 9°30′N 54°18′E
180 I5 **Hohne** Niedersachsen, Germany 10°22′N 52°35′E
167 M7 **Hohneck** ▲ NE France 48°04′N 07°01′E
180 I4 **Hohnstorf** Niedersachsen, Germany 10°32′N 53°09′E
133 H7 **Hohoe** E Ghana 07°08′N 00°32′E
250 D5 **Hōhoku** Yamaguchi, Honshū, SW Japan 34°15′N 130°56′E
239 H7 **Hoh Sai Hu** ◎ C China
238 G7 **Hoh Xil Hu** ◎ C China
238 G7 **Hoh Xil Shan** ▲▲ W China
257 I7 **Hôi An** *prev.* Faifo. Quang Nam-Đa Năng, C Vietnam 15°54′N 108°19′E
Hoï-Hao/Hoihow *see* Haikou
239 J6 **Hoika** *prev.* Heka. Qinghai, W China 35°49′N 99°50′E
136 B7 **Hoima** W Uganda 01°25′N 31°22′E
75 D10 **Hoisington** Kansas, C USA 38°31′N 98°46′W
228 C7 **Hojagala** *Rus.* Khodzhakala. Balkan Welaýaty, W Turkmenistan 38°46′N 56°14′E
155 D12 **Højby** Fyn, C Denmark 55°20′N 10°27′E
155 C13 **Højer** Sønderjylland, SW Denmark 54°57′N 08°43′E
250 F5 **Hōjō** *var.* Hôzyô. Ehime, Shikoku, SW Japan 33°58′N 132°47′E
278 F2 **Hokianga Harbour** *inlet* SE Tasman Sea
278 D9 **Hokitika** West Coast, South Island, New Zealand 42°44′S 170°58′E
252 F4 **Hokkai-dō** ◈ *territory* Hokkaidō, NE Japan
252 G4 **Hokkaidō** *prev.* Ezo, Yeso, Yezo. *island* NE Japan
154 D7 **Hokksund** Buskerud, S Norway 59°45′N 09°55′E
223 I3 **Hokmābād** KhorāsānRazavī, N Iran 36°37′N 57°34′E
Hokō *see* P'ohang
Hoko-guntō/Hoko-shotō *see* P'enghu Liehtao
Hoktemberyan *see* Armavir
154 C6 **Hol** Buskerud, S Norway 60°36′N 08°18′E
189 I7 **Hola Prystan'** *Rus.* Golaya Pristan. Khersons'ka Oblast', S Ukraine 46°31′N 32°31′E
155 E12 **Holbæk** Vestsjælland, E Denmark 55°42′N 11°42′E
Holboo *see* Santmargats
87 N4 **Holbox, Isla** *island* Quintana Roo, Mexico
277 J6 **Holbrook** New South Wales, SE Australia 35°45′S 147°18′E
161 M5 **Holbrook** UK 51°59′N 1°10′E
79 J7 **Holbrook** Arizona, SW USA 34°54′N 110°09′W
65 M3 **Holbrook** Massachusetts, USA 42°09′N 71°01′W
75 G10 **Holden** Missouri, C USA 38°42′N 93°59′W
79 H4 **Holden** Utah, W USA 39°06′N 112°16′W
180 I4 **Holdenstedt** Niedersachsen, Germany 10°31′N 52°55′E
75 F12 **Holdenville** Oklahoma, C USA 35°05′N 96°25′W
75 D8 **Holdrege** Nebraska, C USA 40°28′N 99°28′W
78 F2 **Hole in the Mountain Peak** ▲ Nevada, W USA 40°54′N 115°06′W
235 D8 **Hole Narsipur** Karnātaka, W India 12°46′N 76°14′E
183 E9 **Holešov** *Ger.* Holleschau. Zlínský Kraj, E Czech Republic 49°20′N 17°35′E
91 K3 **Holetown** *prev.* Jamestown. W Barbados 13°11′N 59°38′W
140 C6 **Holgat** ~ Northern Cape, South Africa
65 H8 **Holgate** New Jersey, USA 39°32′N 74°15′W
73 G9 **Holgate** Ohio, N USA 41°12′N 84°06′W
90 F4 **Holguín** Holguín, SE Cuba 20°51′N 76°16′W
69 K6 **Holiday** Florida, SE USA 28°11′N 82°44′W
83 H6 **Holitna River** ~ Alaska, USA
154 F6 **Höljes** Värmland, C Sweden 60°54′N 12°34′E
177 L1 **Hollabrunn** Niederösterreich, NE Austria 48°33′N 16°06′E
77 I10 **Holladay** Utah, W USA 40°39′N 111°49′W
55 I10 **Holland** Manitoba, S Canada 49°36′N 98°52′W
73 F8 **Holland** Michigan, N USA 42°47′N 86°06′W
70 G6 **Holland** Texas, SW USA 30°52′N 97°24′W
Holland *see* Netherlands
66 A9 **Hollandale** Mississippi, S USA 33°10′N 90°51′W
Hollandia *see* Jayapura
Hollandsch Diep *see* Hollands Diep
163 E8 **Hollands Diep** *var.* Hollandsch Diep. *channel* SW Netherlands
180 H3 **Hollenstedt** Niedersachsen, Germany 9°43′N 53°22′E
Holleschau *see* Holešov
161 M4 **Hollesley** UK 52°03′N 1°26′E
70 G3 **Holliday** Texas, SW USA 33°49′N 98°41′W
64 B6 **Hollidaysburg** Pennsylvania, NE USA 40°24′N 78°22′W
67 J4 **Hollins** Virginia, NE USA 37°20′N 79°56′W
75 C13 **Hollis** Oklahoma, C USA 34°42′N 99°56′W
80 B4 **Hollister** California, W USA 36°51′N 121°25′W
75 H11 **Hollister** Missouri, C USA 36°37′N 93°13′W
65 L3 **Holliston** Massachusetts, USA 42°12′N 71°25′W
153 H9 **Hollola** Etelä-Suomi, S Finland 61°N 25°32′E
162 G3 **Hollum** Friesland, N Netherlands 53°27′N 05°38′E
155 F12 **Höllviksnäs** Skåne, S Sweden 55°25′N 12°57′E
79 N4 **Holly** Colorado, C USA 38°03′N 102°07′W
73 H8 **Holly** Michigan, N USA 42°47′N 83°37′W
67 J9 **Holly Hill** South Carolina, SE USA 33°19′N 80°24′W
159 M9 **Hollym** UK 53°42′N 0°01′E
67 L7 **Holly Ridge** North Carolina, SE USA 34°31′N 77°31′W
66 B7 **Holly Springs** Mississippi, S USA 34°47′N 89°25′W
160 B2 **Hollywood** Wicklow, Ireland 53°06′N 6°36′W
69 N9 **Hollywood** Florida, SE USA 26°00′N 80°09′W
52 E6 **Holman** Victoria Island, Northwest Territories, N Canada 70°42′N 117°45′W
152 B2 **Hólmavík** Vestfirdhir, NW Iceland 65°42′N 21°43′W
161 K3 **Holme** UK 52°28′N 0°14′W
72 B6 **Holmen** Wisconsin, N USA 43°57′N 91°14′W
161 L2 **Holme next the Sea** UK 52°58′N 0°33′E
69 I4 **Holmes Creek** ~ Alabama/Florida, SE USA
155 D8 **Holmestrand** Vestfold, S Norway 59°29′N 10°20′E
159 K9 **Holmfirth** UK 53°33′N 1°46′W
194 B5 **Holmön** *island* N Sweden
155 B12 **Holmsland Klit** *beach* W Denmark
154 J3 **Holmsund** Västerbotten, N Sweden 63°42′N 20°26′E
155 J9 **Holmudden** *headland* SE Sweden 57°59′N 19°14′E
129 J2 **Holon** *var* Kholon. Tel Aviv, C Israel 32°01′N 34°46′E
189 H5 **Holovanivs'k** *Rus.* Golovanevsk. Kirovohrads'ka Oblast', C Ukraine 48°21′N 30°26′E
155 C11 **Holstebro** Ringkøbing, W Denmark 56°22′N 08°38′E
155 C12 **Holsted** Ribe, W Denmark 55°30′N 08°54′E
74 F7 **Holstein** Iowa, C USA 42°29′N 95°32′W
Holsteinborg/Holsteinsborg/Holstenborg/Holstensborg *see* Sisimiut
66 G5 **Holston River** ~ Tennessee, S USA
160 E8 **Holsworthy** UK 50°49′N 4°21′W
160 G2 **Holt** UK 53°04′N 2°53′W
73 G8 **Holt** Michigan, N USA 42°38′N 84°31′W
162 I6 **Holten** Overijssel, E Netherlands 52°16′N 06°25′E
75 F9 **Holton** Kansas, C USA 39°27′N 95°44′W
180 G5 **Holtorf** Niedersachsen, Germany 9°14′N 52°41′E
75 H10 **Holts Summit** Missouri, C USA 38°38′N 92°07′W
81 G14 **Holtville** California, W USA 32°48′N 115°22′W
180 C7 **Holtwick** Nordrhein-Westfalen, Germany 7°08′N 51°45′E
181 I8 **Holungen** Thüringen, Germany 10°23′N 51°29′E
162 G3 **Holwerd** *Fris.* Holwert. Friesland, N Netherlands 53°22′N 05°51′E
Holwert *see* Holwerd
82 G6 **Holy Cross** Alaska, USA 62°12′N 159°46′W
79 L3 **Holy Cross, Mount Of The** ▲ Colorado, C USA 39°28′N 106°28′W
160 D1 **Holyhead** *Wel.* Caer Gybi. NW Wales, UK 53°19′N 04°38′W
160 D1 **Holyhead Bay** *bay* UK
157 E9 **Holy Island** *island* NW Wales, UK
156 H7 **Holy Island** *island* NE England, UK
79 N2 **Holyoke** Colorado, C USA 40°31′N 102°18′W
65 J3 **Holyoke** Massachusetts, NE USA 42°12′N 72°37′W
160 F2 **Holywell** UK 53°17′N 3°15′W
159 H5 **Holywood** UK 55°06′N 3°39′W
180 F7 **Holzhausen** Nordrhein-Westfalen, Germany 8°45′N 52°02′E
180 G7 **Holzminden** Niedersachsen, C Germany 51°49′N 09°27′E
181 I8 **Holzthaleben** Thüringen, Germany 10°35′N 51°20′E
137 C8 **Homa Bay** Nyanza, W Kenya 0°31′S 34°30′E
Homāyūnshahr *see* Khomeynīshahr
181 G9 **Homberg** Hessen, Germany 9°24′N 51°02′E
181 B8 **Homberg** Nordrhein-Westfalen, Germany 6°43′N 51°28′E
181 E10 **Homberg** Rheinland-Pfalz, Germany 8°06′N 50°39′E
132 G4 **Hombori** Mopti, S Mali 15°13′N 01°39′W
181 C13 **Homburg** Saarland, SW Germany 49°20′N 07°20′E
53 I5 **Home, Cape** *headland* Nunavut, N Canada
53 L7 **Home Bay** *bay* Baffin Bay, Nunavut, NE Canada
Homenau *see* Humenné
83 I7 **Homer** Alaska, USA 59°38′N 151°33′W
68 B1 **Homer** Louisiana, S USA 32°47′N 93°03′W
64 E2 **Homer** New York, NE USA 42°38′N 76°10′W
69 K3 **Homerville** Georgia, SE USA 31°02′N 82°45′W
69 N9 **Homestead** Florida, SE USA 25°28′N 80°28′W
75 F11 **Hominy** Oklahoma, C USA 36°24′N 96°24′W
154 E3 **Hommelvik** Sør-Trøndelag, S Norway 63°24′N 10°48′E
155 A8 **Hommersåk** Rogaland, S Norway 58°55′N 05°51′E
234 E5 **Homnābād** Karnātaka, C India 17°46′N 77°08′E
68 D3 **Homochitto River** ~ Mississippi, S USA
139 J6 **Homoine** Inhambane, SE Mozambique 23°51′S 35°04′E
185 H4 **Homoljske Planine** ▲▲ E Serbia
Homonna *see* Humenné
Homs *see* Al Khums, Libya
Homs *see* Ḩimş
191 I11 **Homyel'** *Rus.* Gomel'. Homyel'skaya Voblasts', SE Belarus 52°25′N 31°E
191 G8 **Homyel'** Vitsyebskaya Voblasts', N Belarus 55°20′N 28°52′E
191 H11 **Homyel'skaya Voblasts'** *prev. Rus.* Gomel'skaya Oblast'. ◈ *province* SE Belarus
171 H10 **Hońaïne** Algeria
Honan *see* Luoyang, China
Honan *see* Henan, China
252 G4 **Honbetsu** Hokkaidō, NE Japan 43°09′N 143°46′E
Honctő *see* Gurahonţ
80 D1 **Honcut** California, USA 39°20′N 121°32′W
102 C5 **Honda** Tolima, C Colombia 05°12′N 74°45′W
138 C8 **Hondeklip** *Afr.* Hondeklipbaai. Northern Cape, W South Africa 30°15′S 17°17′E
140 C7 **Hondeklipbaai** Northern Cape, South Africa 30°19′S 17°16′E
Hondeklipbaai *see* Hondeklip
57 I3 **Hondo** Alberta, W Canada 54°43′N 113°14′W
250 C7 **Hondo** Kumamoto, Shimo-jima, SW Japan 32°28′N 130°12′E
70 F7 **Hondo** Texas, SW USA 29°21′N 99°09′W
87 M7 **Hondo** ~ Central America
Hondo *see* Honshū
173 L6 **Hondón de las Nieves** Valenciana, Spain 38°18′N 0°51′W
88 G4 **Honduras** *off.* Republic of Honduras. ◆ *republic* Central America
Honduras, Golfo de *see* Honduras, Gulf of
88 E2 **Honduras, Gulf of** *Sp.* Golfo de Honduras. *gulf* W Caribbean Sea
Honduras, Republic of *see* Honduras
55 I7 **Hone** Manitoba, C Canada 56°13′N 101°12′W
67 H8 **Honea Path** South Carolina, SE USA 34°27′N 82°23′W
181 H9 **Hönebach** Hessen, Germany 9°57′N 50°56′E
154 D7 **Hønefoss** Buskerud, S Norway 60°10′N 10°15′E
64 C1 **Honeoye** New York, USA 42°47′N 77°31′W
64 F4 **Honesdale** Pennsylvania, USA 41°35′N 75°16′W
73 H10 **Honey Creek** ~ Ohio, N USA
71 H4 **Honey Grove** Texas, SW USA 33°34′N 95°54′W
78 C2 **Honey Lake** ◎ California, W USA
164 G2 **Honfleur** Calvados, N France 49°25′N 00°14′E
Hon Gai *see* Hông Gai
243 I2 **Hong'an** *prev.* Huang'an. Hubei, C China 31°20′N 114°43′E
Hongay *see* Hông Gai
244 D5 **Hongde** Gansu, China 36°28′N 107°07′E
242 D4 **Hongdu He** ~ Guizhou, China
181 B9 **Höngen** Nordrhein-Westfalen, Germany 6°13′N 50°52′E
257 H4 **Hông Gai** *var.* Hon Gai, Hongay. Quang Ninh, N Vietnam 20°57′N 107°06′E
243 I9 **Honghai Wan** *bay* N South China Sea
Hông Hà, Sông *see* Red River
241 H3 **Hong He** ~ C China
243 H3 **Honghu** China 29°49′N 113°28′E
243 H3 **Hong Hu** ◎ C China
245 J6 **Hongjiaiou** China 36°44′N 116°52′E
242 E5 **Hongjiang** Hunan, S China 27°09′N 109°58′E
Hongjiang *see* Wangcang
244 F4 **Hongjian Nur** ◎ Shaanxi, China
243 L7 **Honglai** China 25°05′N 118°31′E
239 I4 **Hongliuyuan** Gansu, N China 41°02′N 95°24′E
Hongor *see* Delgereh
243 M1 **Hongqiao** ✕ (Shanghai) Shanghai Shi, E China 31°28′N 121°08′E
244 B5 **Hongshan Xia** *pass* Gansu, China
242 D8 **Hongshui He** ~ S China
244 G6 **Hongtong** Shanxi, C China 36°30′N 111°42′E
251 I6 **Hongū** Wakayama, Honshū, SW Japan 33°50′N 135°42′E
Honguedo, Détroit d' *see* Honguedo Passage
59 J7 **Honguedo Passage** *var.* Honguedo Strait, *Fr.* Détroit d'Honguedo. *strait* Québec, E Canada
Honguedo Strait *see* Honguedo Passage
Hongwan *see* Hongwansi
239 J5 **Hongwansi** *var.* Sunan, Sunan Yugurzu Zizhixian; *prev.* Hongwan. Gansu, N China 38°55′N 99°29′E
248 C4 **Hongwŏn** E North Korea 40°03′N 127°54′E
242 A3 **Hongya** China 29°56′N 103°25′E
243 J9 **Hongyang** China 23°30′N 116°13′E
243 J3 **Hongyuan** China 29°21′N 117°07′E
244 A9 **Hongyuan** *var.* Qiongxi; *prev.* Hurama. Sichuan, C China 32°49′N 102°40′E
245 K8 **Hongze Hu** *var.* Hung-tse Hu. ◎ E China
281 J3 **Honiara** ● (Solomon Islands) Guadalcanal, C Solomon Islands 09°27′S 159°56′E
160 G8 **Honiton** UK 50°48′N 3°11′W
253 C9 **Honjō** *var.* Honzyô. Akita, Honshū, C Japan 39°23′N 140°03′E
153 G9 **Honkajoki** Länsi-Soumi, SW Finland 62°00′N 22°15′E
251 K4 **Honkawane** Shizuoka, Honshū, S Japan 35°07′N 138°07′E
152 H3 **Honningsvåg** Finnmark, N Norway 70°58′N 25°59′E
155 E10 **Hönö** Västra Götaland, S Sweden 57°42′N 11°39′E
82 D3 **Honoka'a** *var.* Honokaa. Hawai'i, USA, C Pacific Ocean 20°04′N 155°27′W
82 D3 **Honoka'a** Hawaii, USA 20°04′N 155°27′W
Honokaa *see* Honoka'a
82 C2 **Honolulu** *state capital* O'ahu, Hawai'i, USA 21°18′N 157°52′W
171 H6 **Honrubia** Castilla-La Mancha, C Spain 39°36′N 02°17′W
251 I4 **Honshū** *var.* Hondo, Honsyû. *island* SW Japan
Honsyû *see* Honshū
Honte *see* Westerschelde
Honzyô *see* Honjō
52 E8 **Hood** ~ Nunavut, NW Canada
Hood Island *see* Española, Isla
76 C5 **Hood, Mount** ▲ Oregon, NW USA 45°22′N 121°41′W
76 C5 **Hood River** Oregon, NW USA 45°44′N 121°31′W
162 E6 **Hoofddorp** Noord-Holland, W Netherlands 52°18′N 04°41′E
163 E8 **Hoogerheide** Noord-Brabant, S Netherlands 51°25′N 04°19′E
162 I5 **Hoogeveen** Drenthe, NE Netherlands 52°44′N 06°30′E
162 I3 **Hoogezand-Sappemeer** Groningen, NE Netherlands 53°10′N 06°47′E
162 F5 **Hoogkarspel** Noord-Holland, NW Netherlands 52°42′N 04°59′E
162 I3 **Hoogkerk** Groningen, NE Netherlands 53°13′N 06°30′E
162 E7 **Hoogvliet** Zuid-Holland, SW Netherlands 51°51′N 04°23′E
161 J7 **Hook** UK 51°16′N 0°57′W
75 B11 **Hooker** Oklahoma, C USA 36°51′N 101°12′W
160 A4 **Hook Head** *Ir.* Rinn Duáin. *headland* SE Ireland 52°07′N 06°55′W
Hook of Holland *see* Hoek van Holland
180 E2 **Hooksiel** Niedersachsen, Germany 8°01′N 53°38′E
Hoolt *see* Tögrög
83 L7 **Hoonah** Chichagof Island, Alaska, USA 58°05′N 135°21′W
82 F6 **Hooper Bay** Alaska, USA 61°31′N 166°06′W
73 D10 **Hoopeston** Illinois, N USA 40°28′N 87°40′W
141 H5 **Hoopstad** Free State, South Africa 27°50′S 25°55′E
155 F12 **Höör** Skåne, S Sweden 55°55′N 13°33′E
162 F5 **Hoorn** Noord-Holland, NW Netherlands 52°38′N 05°04′E
65 I1 **Hoosic River** ~ New York, NE USA
Hoosier State *see* Indiana
81 J9 **Hoover Dam** *dam* Arizona/Nevada, W USA
Höövör *see* Baruunbayan-Ulaan
215 I4 **Hopa** Artvin, NE Turkey 41°23′N 41°28′E
64 G5 **Hopatcong** New Jersey, USA 40°56′N 74°40′W
64 G5 **Hopatcong** New Jersey, NE USA 40°55′N 74°39′W
56 E8 **Hope** British Columbia, SW Canada 49°21′N 121°28′W
160 G2 **Hope** UK 53°07′N 3°02′W
83 I6 **Hope** Alaska, USA 60°55′N 149°38′W
75 H14 **Hope** Arkansas, C USA 33°40′N 93°36′W
73 F11 **Hope** Indiana, N USA 39°18′N 85°46′W
74 E3 **Hope** North Dakota, N USA 47°18′N 97°42′W
160 G4 **Hope Bowdler** UK 52°31′N 2°46′W
59 K4 **Hopedale** Newfoundland and Labrador, NE Canada 55°26′N 60°14′W
140 D9 **Hopefield** Western Cape, South Africa 33°04′S 18°21′E
Hopeh/Hopei *see* Hebei
274 E7 **Hope, Lake** *salt lake* Western Australia
87 L6 **Hopelchén** Campeche, SE Mexico 19°46′N 89°50′W
67 K7 **Hope Mills** North Carolina, SE USA 34°58′N 78°57′W
277 J4 **Hope, Mount** New South Wales, SE Australia 32°49′S 145°55′E
152 C6 **Hopen** *island* SE Svalbard
294 E7 **Hope, Point** *headland* Alaska, USA
59 H1 **Hopes Advance, Cap** *cape* Québec, NE Canada
160 F9 **Hope's Nose** *headland* SW England, UK
80 D4 **Hopeton** California, USA 37°30′N 120°32′W
277 I6 **Hopetoun** Victoria, SE Australia 35°46′S 142°23′E
138 F8 **Hopetown** Northern Cape, W South Africa 29°37′S 24°05′E
140 G6 **Hopetown** Northern Cape, South Africa 29°37′S 24°05′E
65 L4 **Hope Valley** Rhode Island, USA 41°30′N 71°43′W
67 L4 **Hopewell** Virginia, NE USA 37°16′N 77°15′W
177 H3 **Hopfgarten im Brixental** Tirol, W Austria 47°28′N 12°14′E
180 D6 **Höpingen** Nordrhein-Westfalen, Germany 7°19′N 52°02′E
274 F5 **Hopkins Lake** *salt lake* Western Australia
277 I7 **Hopkins River** ~ Victoria, SE Australia
66 D5 **Hopkinsville** Kentucky, S USA 36°50′N 87°30′W
78 A3 **Hopland** California, W USA 38°58′N 123°09′W
161 N3 **Hopton** UK 52°32′N 1°44′E
155 D13 **Hoptrup** Sønderjylland, SW Denmark 55°09′N 09°27′E
76 B4 **Hoquiam** Washington, NW USA 46°58′N 123°53′W
74 E3 **Horace** North Dakota, N USA 46°44′N 96°54′W
215 J5 **Horasan** Erzurum, NE Turkey 40°03′N 42°10′E
179 D12 **Horb am Neckar** Baden-Württemberg, S Germany 48°27′N 08°42′E
155 G12 **Hörby** Skåne, S Sweden 55°51′N 13°42′E
85 H4 **Horcasitas** Chihuahua, Mexico 28°21′N 105°50′W
89 I9 **Horconcitos** Chiriquí, W Panama 08°20′N 82°10′W
154 B6 **Hordaland** ◈ *county* S Norway
188 C9 **Horezu** Vâlcea, SW Romania 45°06′N 24°00′E
176 E4 **Horgen** Zürich, N Switzerland 47°16′N 08°36′E
Horgo *see* Tariat
Hōrin *see* Fenglin
244 G2 **Horinger** Nei Mongol Zizhiqu, N China 40°23′N 111°48′E
181 F8 **Höringhausen** Hessen, Germany 8°59′N 51°16′E
Horiult *see* Bogd
57 N8 **Horizon** Saskatchewan, S Canada 49°33′N 105°05′W
286 E6 **Horizon Bank** *undersea feature* S Pacific Ocean
286 F7 **Horizon Deep** *undersea feature* W Pacific Ocean
154 G7 **Hörken** Örebro, S Sweden 60°03′N 14°55′E
191 I9 **Horki** *Rus.* Gorki. Mahilyowskaya Voblasts', E Belarus 54°18′N 31°E
161 K7 **Horley** UK 51°10′N 0°10′W
293 H6 **Horlick Mountains** ▲▲ Antarctica
189 M5 **Horlivka** *Rom.* Adâncata, *Rus.* Gorlovka. Donets'ka Oblast', E Ukraine 48°19′N 38°04′E
223 J7 **Ḩormak** Sīstān va Balūchestān, SE Iran 30°00′N 60°50′E
223 H8 **Hormozgān** *off.* Ostān-e Hormozgān. ◈ *province* S Iran
Hormozgān, Ostān-e *see* Hormozgān
Hormoz, Tangeh-ye *see* Hormuz, Strait of
223 H9 **Hormuz, Strait of** *var.* Strait of Ormuz, *Per.* Tangeh-ye Hormoz. *strait* Iran/Oman
177 K1 **Horn** Niederösterreich, NE Austria 48°40′N 15°40′E
181 E8 **Horn** Nordrhein-Westfalen, Germany 8°15′N 51°37′E
155 H10 **Horn** Östergötland, S Sweden 57°54′N 15°49′E
Hornád *see* Hernád
52 D7 **Hornaday River** ~ Northwest Territories, NW Canada
152 F6 **Hornavan** ◎ N Sweden
181 D14 **Hornbach** Rheinland-Pfalz, Germany 7°22′N 49°12′E
180 I7 **Hornburg** Niedersachsen, Germany 10°37′N 52°01′E
159 I8 **Hornby** UK 54°06′N 2°38′W
117 H11 **Hornby Mountains** *hill range* West Falkland, Falkland Islands
Horn, Cape *see* Hornos, Cabo de
159 M10 **Horncastle** E England, UK 53°12′N 00°07′W
154 H7 **Horndal** Dalarna, C Sweden 60°16′N 16°25′E
161 J8 **Horndean** UK 50°55′N 0°59′W
180 G3 **Horneburg** Niedersachsen, Germany 9°35′N 53°30′E
154 J3 **Hörnefors** Västerbotten, N Sweden 63°37′N 19°54′E

◆ Country
● Country Capital
◇ Dependent Territory
○ Dependent Territory Capital
◈ Administrative Regions
✕ International Airport
▲ Mountain
▲▲ Mountain Range
⩘ Volcano
~ River
◎ Lake
⊞ Reservoir

◆ Country	◇ Dependent Territory	◈ Administrative Regions	▲ Mountain	◆ Volcano	⊗ Lake
● Country Capital	○ Dependent Territory Capital	✕ International Airport	▲ Mountain Range	♦ River	⊠ Reservoir

I

◆ Country
● Country Capital
◇ Dependent Territory
○ Dependent Territory Capital
◈ Administrative Regions
✕ International Airport
▲ Mountain
▲ Mountain Range
⊘ Lake
♒ River
⊟ Reservoir

◆ Country   ◇ Dependent Territory   ◆ Administrative Regions   ▲ Mountain   ◙ Volcano   ◙ Lake
● Country Capital   ○ Dependent Territory Capital   ✕ International Airport   ▲ Mountain Range   ◙ River   ◙ Reservoir

Jutila - Kamskoye Ust'ye

138 F1 **Jutila** North Western, NW Zambia 12°33′S 26°09′E
Jutland see Jylland
144 C5 **Jutland Bank** undersea feature SE North Sea
153 I8 **Juuka** Pohjois-Karjala, E Finland 63°12′N 29°17′E
153 I9 **Juva** Isä-Suomi, E Finland 61°55′N 27°54′E
Juvavum see Salzburg
90 C4 **Juventud, Isla de la** var. Isla de Pinos, Eng. Isle of Youth; prev. The Isle of the Pines. island W Cuba
166 D6 **Juvigny-sous-Andaine** Basse-Normandie, France 48°33′N 0°31′W
245 K6 **Juxian** var. Chengyang, Ju Xian. Shandong, E China 35°33′N 118°45′E
Ju Xian see Juxian
245 J7 **Juye** Shandong, E China 35°26′N 116°04′E
167 K6 **Juzennecourt** Champagne-Ardenne, France 48°11′N 4°59′E
185 H6 **Južna Morava** Ger. Südliche Morava. ≈ SE Serbia
178 F2 **Jyderup** Vestsjælland, E Denmark 55°40′N 11°25′E
155 D11 **Jylland** Eng. Jutland. peninsula W Denmark
Jyrgalan see Dzhergalan
153 H8 **Jyväskylä** Länsi-Soumi, C Finland 62°08′N 25°47′E

K

238 C6 **K2** Chin. Qogir Feng, Eng. Mount Godwin Austen. ▲ China/Pakistan 35°55′N 76°30′E
136 C6 **Kaabong** NE Uganda 03°30′N 34°08′E
Kaaden see Kadaň
Kaafu Atoll see Male' Atoll
103 L5 **Kaaimanston** Sipaliwini, N Surinam 05°06′N 56°04′W
Kaakhka see Kaka
Kaala see Caála
280 A8 **Kaala-Gomen** Province Nord, W New Caledonia 20°40′S 164°24′E
152 H4 **Kaamanen** Lapp. Gámas. Lappi, N Finland 69°05′N 27°16′E
141 L3 **Kaapmuiden** Mpumalanga, South Africa 25°32′S 31°19′E
Kaapstad see Cape Town
Kaarasjoki see Karasjok
Kaaresuanto see Karesuando
152 G4 **Kaaresuvanto** Lapp. Gárassavon. Lappi, N Finland 68°28′N 22°29′E
153 G10 **Kaarina** Länsi-Soumi, SW Finland 60°24′N 22°25′E
180 J3 **Kaarssen** Mecklenburg-Vorpommern, Germany 11°03′N 53°12′E
181 B8 **Kaarst** Nordrhein-Westfalen, Germany 6°37′N 51°14′E
163 F8 **Kaatsheuvel** Noord-Brabant, S Netherlands 51°39′N 05°02′E
153 I8 **Kaavi** Itä-Suomi, C Finland 62°58′N 28°30′E
261 L7 **Kaba** Papua, E Indonesia 07°34′S 138°27′E
Kaba see Habahe
260 D6 **Kabaena, Pulau** island C Indonesia
260 D6 **Kabaena, Selat** strait Sulawesi, C Indonesia
Kabakly see Gabakly
132 C6 **Kabala** N Sierra Leone 09°40′N 11°36′W
137 A8 **Kabale** SW Uganda 01°15′S 29°58′E
103 K6 **Kabalebo Rivier** ≈ W Surinam
135 I10 **Kabalo** Katanga, SE Dem. Rep. Congo 06°02′S 26°55′E
135 I9 **Kabambare** Maniema, E Dem. Rep. Congo 04°40′S 27°41′E
227 L6 **Kabanbay** Kaz. Qabanbay; prev. Andreyevka, Kaz. Andreevka. Almaty, SE Kazakhstan 45°50′N 80°34′E
280 G10 **Kabara** prev. Kambara. island Lau Group, E Fiji
Kabardino-Balkaria see Kabardino-Balkarskaya Respublika
197 H9 **Kabardino-Balkarskaya Respublika** Eng. Kabardino-Balkaria. ◈ autonomous republic SW Russian Federation
135 I8 **Kabare** Sud Kivu, E Dem. Rep. Congo 02°13′S 28°40′E
261 H4 **Kabarei** Papua, E Indonesia 0°01′S 130°58′E
263 L9 **Kabasalan** Mindanao, S Philippines 07°46′N 122°49′E
133 J7 **Kabba** Kogi, S Nigeria 07°48′N 06°07′E
152 F6 **Kåbdalis** Lapp. Goabddális. Norrbotten, N Sweden 66°08′N 20°03′E
216 F4 **Kabd aş Şārim** hill range E Syria
72 G2 **Kabenung Lake** ◎ Ontario, S Canada
74 H2 **Kabetogama Lake** ◎ Minnesota, N USA
Kabia, Pulau see Kabin, Pulau
135 G10 **Kabinda** Kasai Oriental, SE Dem. Rep. Congo 06°09′S 24°29′E
Kabinda see Cabinda
260 C7 **Kabin, Pulau** var. Pulau Kabia. island W Indonesia
260 E8 **Kabir** Pulau Pantar, S Indonesia 08°15′S 124°12′E
231 I6 **Kabīrwāla** Punjab, E Pakistan 30°24′N 71°51′E
261 H4 **Kable Bet** Papua, E Indonesia 0°24′S 129°54′E
134 E4 **Kabo** Ouham, NW Central African Republic 07°43′N 18°38′E
231 H3 **Kābol** var. Kabul, Pash. Kābul. ● (Afghanistan) Kābul, E Afghanistan 34°34′N 69°08′E
231 H3 **Kābol** Eng. Kabul, Pash. Kābul. ◈ province E Afghanistan
231 H3 **Kābol** ✈ Kābul, E Afghanistan 34°31′N 69°11′E
138 E1 **Kabompo** North Western, W Zambia 13°36′S 24°10′E
138 E1 **Kabompo** ≈ W Zambia
135 H10 **Kabongo** Katanga, SE Dem. Rep. Congo 07°20′S 25°34′E
131 L2 **Kaboudia, Rass** headland E Tunisia 35°13′N 11°09′E
223 J3 **Kabūd Gonbad** Khorāsān, NE Iran 37°02′N 59°46′E
222 E4 **Kabūd Rāhang** Hamadān, W Iran 35°12′N 48°44′E
137 B12 **Kabuko** Northern, NE Zambia 11°31′S 31°16′E
231 H3 **Kabul** var. Daryā-ye Kābul. ≈ Afghanistan/Pakistan see also Kābul, Daryā-ye
Kābul see Kābol
Kabul see Kābul, Daryā-ye
231 H3 **Kābul, Daryā-ye** var. Kabul. ≈ Afghanistan/Pakistan see also Kabul
Kābul, Daryā-ye see Kabul
135 I12 **Kabunda** Katanga, SE Dem. Rep. Congo 12°21′S 29°14′E
260 G2 **Kaburuang, Pulau** island Kepulauan Talaud, N Indonesia
136 C1 **Kabushiya** River Nile, NE Sudan 16°54′N 33°41′E
138 G1 **Kabwe** Central, C Zambia 14°29′S 28°25′E
280 C3 **Kabwum** Morobe, C Papua New Guinea 06°04′S 147°09′E
184 G7 **Kačanik** Kosovo, S Serbia 42°13′N 21°16′E
190 F5 **Kacanovo** Pskovskaya Oblast', Russian Federation
261 H4 **Kacepi** Pulau Gebe, E Indonesia 0°05′S 129°30′E
191 D8 **Kačerginė** Kaunas, C Lithuania 54°55′N 23°40′E
189 J9 **Kacha** Respublika Krym, S Ukraine 44°46′N 33°33′E
232 A8 **Kachchh, Gulf of** var. Gulf of Cutch, Gulf of Kutch. gulf W India
232 F9 **Kachchhīdhāna** Madhya Pradesh, C India 21°33′N 78°54′E
232 B7 **Kachchh, Rann of** var. Rann of Kachh, Rann of Kutch. salt marsh India/Pakistan
83 I7 **Kachemak Bay** bay Alaska, USA
Kachh, Rann of see Kachchh, Rann of
133 K6 **Kachia** Kaduna, C Nigeria 09°52′N 08°00′E
256 D2 **Kachin State** ◈ state N Myanmar (Burma)
227 J2 **Kachiry** Pavlodar, NE Kazakhstan 53°07′N 76°08′E
193 H8 **Kachug** Irkutskaya Oblast', S Russian Federation 53°52′N 105°54′E
215 I5 **Kaçkar Dağları** ▲▲ NE Turkey
235 C8 **Kadamatt Island** island Lakshadweep, India, N Indian Ocean
179 H9 **Kadaň** Ger. Kaaden. Ústecký Kraj, NW Czech Republic 50°24′N 13°16′E
256 D8 **Kadan Kyun** prev. King Island. island Mergui Archipelago, S Myanmar (Burma)
280 E10 **Kadavu** prev. Kandavu. island S Fiji
280 E9 **Kadavu Passage** channel S Fiji
134 C6 **Kadéï** ≈ Cameroon/Central African Republic
Kadhimain see Al Kāẓimīyah
Kadijica see Kadiytsa
187 K2 **Kadıköy Barajı** ⊠ NW Turkey
276 G5 **Kadina** South Australia 33°59′S 137°43′E
214 D7 **Kadınhanı** Konya, C Turkey 38°15′N 32°14′E
132 F6 **Kadiolo** Sikasso, S Mali 10°30′N 05°43′W
214 F7 **Kadirli** Osmaniye, S Turkey 37°22′N 36°05′E
185 I7 **Kadiytsa** Mac. Kadijica. ▲ Bulgaria/FYR Macedonia 41°48′N 22°58′E
74 B5 **Kadoka** South Dakota, N USA 43°49′N 101°30′W
197 H2 **Kadom** Ryazanskaya Oblast', W Russian Federation 54°35′N 42°27′E
139 H3 **Kadoma** prev. Gatooma. Mashonaland West, C Zimbabwe !8°22′S 29°55′E
136 A3 **Kadugli** Southern Kordofan, S Sudan 11°N 29°44′E
133 K6 **Kaduna** Kaduna, C Nigeria 10°32′N 07°26′E
133 K6 **Kaduna** ◈ state C Nigeria
133 J7 **Kaduna** ≈ N Nigeria
194 F9 **Kaduy** Vologodskaya Oblast', NW Russian Federation 59°10′N 37°11′E
234 D4 **Kadwa** ≈ W India
193 L5 **Kadykchan** Magadanskaya Oblast', E Russian Federation 62°54′N 146°53′E
Kadzharan see K'ajaran
195 K5 **Kadzherom** Respublika Komi, NW Russian Federation 64°42′N 55°51′E
229 M4 **Kadzhi-Say** Kir. Kajisay. Issyk-Kul'skaya Oblast', NE Kyrgyzstan 42°07′N 77°11′E
132 C3 **Kaédi** Gorgol, S Mauritania 16°12′N 13°32′W
134 C3 **Kaélé** Extrême-Nord, N Cameroon 10°05′N 14°28′E
82 B2 **Ka'ena Point** var. Kaena Point. headland O'ahu, Hawai'i, USA 21°34′N 158°16′W
278 F2 **Kaeo** Northland, North Island, New Zealand 35°03′S 173°40′E
248 B5 **Kaesŏng** var. Kaesŏng-si. S North Korea 37°58′N 126°31′E
Kaesŏng-si see Kaesŏng
Kaewieng see Kavieng
135 G11 **Kafakumba** Shaba, S Dem. Rep. Congo 09°39′S 23°43′E
Kafan see Kapan
133 K6 **Kafanchan** Kaduna, C Nigeria 09°32′N 08°18′E
Kaffa see Feodosiya
132 B4 **Kaffrine** C Senegal 14°07′N 15°27′W
Kafiau see Kofiau, Pulau
187 I6 **Kafiréos, Stenó** strait Évvoia/Kykládes, Greece, Aegean Sea
Kafirnigan see Kofarnihon
Kafo see Kafu
Kafr ash Shaykh/Kafrel Sheik see Kafr el Sheikh
129 I3 **Kafr el Sheikh** var. Kafr ash Shaykh, Kafrel Sheik. N Egypt 31°07′N 30°56′E
136 B7 **Kafu** var. Kafo. ≈ W Uganda
138 G2 **Kafue** Lusaka, SE Zambia 15°44′S 28°10′E
138 G1 **Kafue** ≈ C Zambia
121 K8 **Kafue Flats** plain C Zambia
251 I2 **Kaga** Ishikawa, Honshū, SW Japan 36°18′N 136°19′E
134 E5 **Kaga Bandoro** prev. Fort-Crampel. Nana-Grébizi, C Central African Republic 06°54′N 19°10′E
136 B7 **Kagadi** W Uganda 0°57′N 30°52′E
82 D10 **Kagalaska Island** island Aleutian Islands, Alaska, USA
Kagan see Kogon
Kaganovichabad see Kolkhozobod
Kagarlyk see Kaharlyk
250 G5 **Kagawa** off. Kagawa-ken. ◈ prefecture Shikoku, SW Japan
Kagawa-ken see Kagawa
234 F4 **Kagaznagar** Andhra Pradesh, C India 19°25′N 79°30′E
154 J1 **Kåge** Västerbotten, N Sweden 64°49′N 21°00′E
137 B8 **Kagera** var. Ziwa Magharibi, Eng. West Lake. ◈ region NW Tanzania
137 A9 **Kagera** var. Akagera. ≈ Rwanda/Tanzania see also Akagera
Kagera see Akagera
130 E7 **Kâgheț** var. Karet. physical region N Mauritania
Kagi see Chiai
215 J5 **Kağızman** Kars, NE Turkey 40°08′N 43°07′E
283 I2 **Kagman Point** headland Saipan, S Northern Mariana Islands
250 C8 **Kagoshima** var. Kagosima. Kagoshima, Kyūshū, SW Japan 31°37′N 130°33′E
251 K9 **Kagoshima** off. Kagoshima-ken, var. Kagosima. ◈ prefecture Kyūshū, SW Japan
Kagoshima-ken see Kagoshima
250 C9 **Kagoshima-wan** bay SW Japan
Kagosima see Kagoshima
261 N7 **Kagua** Southern Highlands, W Papua New Guinea 06°28′S 143°56′E
Kagul see Cahul
Kagul, Ozero see Kahul, Ozero
82 B1 **Kahala Point** headland Kaua'i, Hawai'i, USA 22°08′N 159°17′W
82 D3 **Kahaluu** Hawaii, USA 19°34′N 155°58′W
137 B9 **Kahama** Shinyanga, NW Tanzania 03°48′S 32°36′E
189 H4 **Kaharlyk** Rus. Kagarlyk. Kyyivs'ka Oblast', N Ukraine 49°50′N 30°50′E
258 J6 **Kahayan, Sungai** ≈ Borneo, C Indonesia
135 E10 **Kahemba** Bandundu, SW Dem. Rep. Congo 07°20′S 19°00′E
278 A12 **Kaherekoau Mountains** ▲▲ South Island, New Zealand
223 K8 **Kahīrī** var. Kūhīrī. Sīstān va Balūchestān, SE Iran 26°55′N 61°04′E
179 G9 **Kahla** Thüringen, C Germany 50°49′N 11°33′E
181 F9 **Kahler Asten** ▲ W Germany 51°11′N 08°32′E
230 G3 **Kahmard, Daryā-ye** prev. Darya-i-surkhab. ≈ NE Afghanistan
223 I8 **Kahnūj** Kermān, SE Iran 28°N 57°41′E
75 I8 **Kahoka** Missouri, C USA 40°24′N 91°44′W
82 C2 **Kaho'olawe** var. Kahoolawe. island Hawaiian Islands, Hawai'i, USA
Kahoolawe see Kaho'olawe
214 G7 **Kahramanmaraş** var. Kahraman Maraş, Maraş, Marash. Kahramanmaraş, S Turkey 37°34′N 36°54′E
214 G7 **Kahramanmaraş** var. Kahraman Maraş, Maraş, Marash. ◈ province C Turkey
Kahraman Maraş see Kahramanmaraş
Kahror/Kahror Pakka see Karor Pacca
215 H7 **Kâhta** Adıyaman, S Turkey 37°48′N 38°35′E
82 C2 **Kahuku** O'ahu, Hawai'i, USA 21°40′N 157°57′W
82 B2 **Kahuku Point** headland O'ahu, Hawai'i, USA 21°42′N 157°59′W
188 F9 **Kahul, Ozero** var. Lacul Cahul, Rus. Ozero Kagul. ◎ Moldova/Ukraine
223 J7 **Kahūrak** Sīstān va Balūchestān, SE Iran 29°25′N 59°38′E
278 E7 **Kahurangi Point** headland South Island, New Zealand 40°41′S 171°57′E
231 J4 **Kahūta** Punjab, E Pakistan 33°38′N 73°27′E
133 I6 **Kaiama** Kwara, W Nigeria 09°37′N 03°58′E
280 B3 **Kaiapit** Morobe, C Papua New Guinea 06°12′S 146°09′E
278 E10 **Kaiapoi** Canterbury, South Island, New Zealand 43°23′S 172°40′E
79 H6 **Kaibab Plateau** plain Arizona, SW USA
251 H4 **Kaibara** Hyōgo, Honshū, SW Japan 35°06′N 135°03′E
261 I6 **Kai Besar, Pulau** island Kepulauan Kai, E Indonesia
79 I6 **Kaibito Plateau** plain Arizona, SW USA
238 F4 **Kaidu He** var. Karaxahar. ≈ NW China
103 J5 **Kaieteur Falls** waterfall C Guyana
245 I7 **Kaifeng** Henan, C China 34°47′N 114°20′E
278 F2 **Kaihu** Northland, North Island, New Zealand 35°47′S 173°39′E
243 K4 **Kaihua** Zhejiang, China 29°05′N 118°14′E
Kaihua see Wenshan
261 I7 **Kai Kecil, Pulau** island Kepulauan Kai, E Indonesia
261 I7 **Kai, Kepulauan** prev. Kei Islands. island group Maluku, SE Indonesia
278 F2 **Kaikohe** Northland, North Island, New Zealand 35°25′S 173°48′E
278 F9 **Kaikoura** Canterbury, South Island, New Zealand 42°22′S 173°40′E
278 F9 **Kaikoura Peninsula** peninsula South Island, New Zealand
Kailas Range see Gangdisê Shan
242 D6 **Kaili** Guizhou, S China 26°34′N 107°58′E
82 D2 **Kailua** Maui, Hawaii, USA 20°53′N 156°13′W
Kailua see Kalaoa
280 A3 **Kaim** ≈ W Papua New Guinea
261 L6 **Kaima** Papua, E Indonesia 05°36′S 138°39′E
279 H4 **Kaimai Range** ▲▲ North Island, New Zealand
186 F2 **Kaïmaktsalán** ▲ Greece/FYR Macedonia 40°57′N 21°48′E
279 H6 **Kaimanawa Mountains** ▲▲ North Island, New Zealand
190 C4 **Käina** Ger. Keinis; prev. Keina. Hiiumaa, W Estonia 58°50′N 22°49′E
177 K4 **Kainach** ≈ SE Austria
250 G6 **Kainan** Tokushima, Shikoku, SW Japan 33°36′N 134°20′E
251 H5 **Kainan** Wakayama, Honshū, SW Japan 34°09′N 135°12′E
229 K4 **Kaindy** Kir. Kayyngdy. Chuyskaya Oblast', N Kyrgyzstan 42°48′N 73°39′E
133 J6 **Kainji Dam** dam W Nigeria
Kainji Lake see Kainji Reservoir
133 J6 **Kainji Reservoir** var. Kainji Lake. ⊠ W Nigeria
280 B4 **Kaintiba** var. Kamina. Gulf, S Papua New Guinea 07°29′S 146°04′E
152 G5 **Kainulaisjärvi** Norrbotten, N Sweden 67°00′N 22°31′E
278 F3 **Kaipara Harbour** harbour North Island, New Zealand
242 G10 **Kaiping** Guangdong, China 22°13′N 112°24′E
232 E5 **Kairāna** Uttar Pradesh, N India 29°24′N 77°10′E
261 N5 **Kairiru Island** island NW Papua New Guinea
131 K2 **Kairouan** var. Al Qayrawān. E Tunisia 35°46′N 10°11′E
Kaisaria see Kayseri
181 H14 **Kaisersbach** Baden-Württemberg, Germany 9°39′N 48°56′E
181 C11 **Kaisersesch** Rheinland-Pfalz, Germany 7°09′N 50°14′E
181 D13 **Kaiserslautern** Rheinland-Pfalz, SW Germany 49°27′N 07°46′E
180 F2 **Kaiser Wilhelm Koog** Schleswig-Holstein, Germany 8°56′N 53°57′E
191 D8 **Kaišiadorys** Kaunas, S Lithuania 54°51′N 24°27′E
278 F2 **Kaitaia** Northland, North Island, New Zealand 35°07′S 173°13′E
243 H10 **Kai Tak** ✈ S China 22°23′N 114°11′E
278 C12 **Kaitangata** Otago, South Island, New Zealand 46°18′S 169°52′E
232 E4 **Kaithal** Haryāna, NW India 29°47′N 76°26′E
Kaitong see Tongyu
258 G6 **Kait, Tanjung** cape Sumatera, W Indonesia
82 C2 **Kaiwi Channel** channel Hawai'i, USA, C Pacific Ocean
242 D2 **Kai Xian** China 30°59′N 108°06′E
242 D2 **Kaixian** var. Hanfeng. Sichuan, C China 31°13′N 108°25′E
242 C5 **Kaiyang** Guizhou, China 27°02′N 106°35′E
248 B1 **Kaiyuan** var. K'ai-yüan. Liaoning, NE China 42°33′N 124°04′E
240 D7 **Kaiyuan** Yunnan, SW China 23°42′N 103°14′E
K'ai-yüan see Kaiyuan
83 H5 **Kaiyuh Mountains** ▲▲ Alaska, USA
152 I7 **Kajaani** Swe. Kajana. Oulu, C Finland 64°17′N 27°46′E
230 F5 **Kajakī, Band-e** ◎ C Afghanistan
Kajan see Kayan, Sungai
Kajana see Kajaani
215 L6 **K'ajaran** Rus. Kadzharan. SE Armenia 39°10′N 46°09′E
Kajisay see Kadzhi-Say
185 H8 **Kajmakčalan** ▲ S FYR Macedonia 40°57′N 21°48′E
Kajnar see Kaynar
230 F4 **Kajrān** Dāikondī, C Afghanistan 33°12′N 65°28′E
230 F4 **Kaj Rūd** ≈ C Afghanistan
228 D8 **Kaka** Rus. Kaakhka. Ahal Welaýaty, S Turkmenistan 37°20′N 59°37′E
58 C7 **Kakabeka Falls** Ontario, S Canada 48°24′N 89°40′W
138 D8 **Kakamas** Northern Cape, W South Africa 28°45′S 20°33′E
137 C8 **Kakamega** Western, W Kenya 0°17′N 34°47′E
184 E4 **Kakanj** Federacija Bosna I Hercegovina, C Bosnia and Herzegovina 44°06′N 18°07′E
278 D11 **Kakanui Mountains** ▲▲ South Island, New Zealand
278 G6 **Kakaramea** Taranaki, North Island, New Zealand 39°42′S 174°27′E
132 D8 **Kakata** C Liberia 06°35′N 10°19′W
278 G6 **Kakatahi** Manawatu-Wanganui, North Island, New Zealand 39°40′S 175°20′E
184 F10 **Kakavi** Gjirokastër, S Albania 39°55′N 20°19′E
229 H8 **Kakaydi** Surkhondaryo Viloyati, S Uzbekistan 37°37′N 67°30′E
250 E5 **Kake** Hiroshima, Honshū, SW Japan 34°37′N 132°17′E
83 M7 **Kake** Kupreanof Island, Alaska, USA 56°58′N 133°57′W
260 E6 **Kakea** Pulau Wowoni, C Indonesia 04°09′S 123°06′E
251 K4 **Kakegawa** Shizuoka, Honshū, S Japan 34°47′N 138°02′E
251 K9 **Kakeromajima** Kagoshima, SW Japan
223 I4 **Kākhak** Khorāsān, E Iran
190 G7 **Kakhanavichy** Rus. Kokhanovichi. Vitsyebskaya Voblasts', N Belarus 55°52′N 28°08′E
189 J7 **Kakhovka** Khersons'ka Oblast', S Ukraine 46°40′N 33°30′E
189 K6 **Kakhovs'ke Vodoskhovyshche** Rus. Kakhovskoye Vodokhranilishche. ⊠ SE Ukraine
Kakhovskoye Vodokhranilishche see Kakhovs'ke Vodoskhovyshche
189 K7 **Kakhovs'kyy Kanal** canal S Ukraine
Kakia see Khakhea
234 H6 **Kākināda** prev. Cocanada. Andhra Pradesh, E India 16°56′N 82°13′E
54 E4 **Kakisa** Northwest Territories, W Canada
54 E4 **Kakisa Lake** ◎ Northwest Territories, W Canada
Käkisalmi see Priozersk
251 H4 **Kakogawa** Hyōgo, Honshū, SW Japan 34°49′N 134°52′E
136 B7 **Kakoge** C Uganda 01°03′N 32°30′E
226 G2 **Kak, Ozero** ◎ N Kazakhstan
Ka-Krem see Malyy Yenisey
Kakshaal-Too, Khrebet see Kokshaal-Tau
83 J2 **Kaktovik** Alaska, USA 70°08′N 143°37′W
253 D10 **Kakuda** Miyagi, Honshū, C Japan 37°59′N 140°48′E
253 D9 **Kakunodate** Akita, Honshū, C Japan 39°37′N 140°35′E
195 L7 **Kal'ya** Sverdlovskaya oblast', Russian federation
175 C14 **Kalaa Kebira** Tunisia
Kalaallit Nunaat see Greenland
175 C14 **Kalaa Seghira** Tunisia
231 I4 **Kālābāgh** Punjab, E Pakistan 33°00′N 71°35′E
260 E8 **Kalabahi** Pulau Alor, S Indonesia 08°14′S 124°32′E
283 I1 **Kalabera** Saipan, S Northern Mariana Islands
138 E2 **Kalabo** Western, W Zambia 15°00′S 22°37′E
196 G5 **Kalach** Voronezhskaya Oblast', W Russian Federation 50°24′N 41°00′E
192 E7 **Kalachinsk** Omskaya Oblast', C Russian Federation 55°03′N 74°30′E
197 H6 **Kalach-na-Donu** Volgogradskaya Oblast', SW Russian Federation 48°45′N 43°29′E
256 B4 **Kaladan** ≈ W Myanmar (Burma)
62 E4 **Kaladar** Ontario, SE Canada 44°38′N 77°06′W
82 D4 **Ka Lae** var. South Cape, South Point. headland Hawai'i, USA, C Pacific Ocean 18°54′N 155°40′W
140 F2 **Kalahari Desert** desert Southern Africa
Kalaikhum see Qal'aikhum
Kala-i-Mor see Galaýmor
152 H7 **Kalajoki** Oulu, W Finland 64°15′N 24°E
Kalak see Eski Kaļak
Kal al Sraghna see El Kelâa Srarhna
76 C5 **Kalama** Washington, NW USA 46°00′N 122°50′W
Kalámai see Kalámata
186 G3 **Kalamariá** Kentrikí Makedonía, N Greece 40°37′N 22°58′E
186 E4 **Kalamás** var. Thiamis, prev Thýamis. ≈ W Greece
186 G7 **Kalámata** prev. Kalámai. Pelopónnisos, S Greece 37°02′N 22°07′E
73 F8 **Kalamazoo** Michigan, N USA 42°17′N 85°35′W
73 F8 **Kalamazoo River** ≈ Michigan, N USA
Kalambaka see Kalampáka
189 J9 **Kalamits'ka Zatoka** Rus. Kalamitskiy Zaliv. gulf S Ukraine
Kalamitskiy Zaliv see Kalamits'ka Zatoka
187 H6 **Kálamos** Attikí, C Greece 38°16′N 23°51′E
186 F5 **Kálamos** island Iónioi Nísia, Greece, C Mediterranean Sea
186 F4 **Kalampáka** var. Kalambaka. Thessalía, C Greece 39°43′N 21°36′E
Kalan see Călan, Romania
Kalan see Tunceli, Turkey
189 J8 **Kalanchak** Khersons'ka Oblast', S Ukraine 46°14′N 33°19′E
82 D3 **Kalaoa** var. Kailua. Hawai'i, USA, C Pacific Ocean 19°43′N 155°59′W
260 D7 **Kalao, Pulau** island Kepulauan Bonerate, W Indonesia
260 D7 **Kalaotoa, Pulau** island W Indonesia
235 F10 **Kala Oya** ≈ NW Sri Lanka
Kalarash see Călărași
154 H4 **Kälarne** Jämtland, C Sweden 63°00′N 16°10′E
223 J9 **Kalar Rūd** ≈ SE Iran
256 G7 **Kalasin** var. Muang Kalasin. Kalasin, E Thailand 16°29′N 103°31′E
230 F7 **Kalāt** var. Kelat, Khelat. Baluchistān, SW Pakistan 29°01′N 66°38′E
Kalāt see Qalāt
187 J3 **Kalathriá, Ákrotirio** headland Samothráki, NE Greece 40°24′N 25°34′E
82 C2 **Kalaupapa** Moloka'i, Hawai'i, USA 21°11′N 156°59′W
197 H8 **Kalaus** ≈ SW Russian Federation
Kalávrita see Kalávryta
186 G6 **Kalávryta** var. Kalávrita. Dytikí Ellás, S Greece 38°02′N 22°06′E
221 L6 **Kalbān** W Oman 20°19′N 58°40′E
274 C6 **Kalbarri** Western Australia 27°43′S 114°08′E
227 M4 **Kalbinskiy Khrebet** Kaz. Qalba Zhotasy. ▲▲ E Kazakhstan
226 C4 **Kaldygayty** ≈ W Kazakhstan
214 E5 **Kalecik** Ankara, N Turkey 40°08′N 33°27′E
260 E6 **Kaledupa, Pulau** island Kepulauan Tukangbesi, C Indonesia
135 I8 **Kalehe** Sud Kivu, E Dem. Rep. Congo 02°05′S 28°52′E
135 J10 **Kalemie** prev. Albertville. Katanga, SE Dem. Rep. Congo 05°55′S 29°09′E
256 B3 **Kalemyo** Sagaing, W Myanmar (Burma) 23°11′N 94°03′E
135 G12 **Kalene Hill** North Western, NW Zambia 11°10′S 24°12′E
Kale Sultanie see Çanakkale
194 E5 **Kalevala** Respublika Kareliya, NW Russian Federation 65°12′N 31°16′E
256 C3 **Kalewa** Sagaing, C Myanmar (Burma) 23°15′N 94°19′E
Kalgan see Zhangjiakou
83 I7 **Kalgin Island** island Alaska, USA
274 E7 **Kalgoorlie** Western Australia 30°51′S 121°27′E
Kali see Sārda
186 F5 **Kaliakoúda** ▲ C Greece 38°47′N 21°42′E
185 N5 **Kaliakra, Nos** cape NE Bulgaria
186 G6 **Kaliánoi** Pelopónnisos, S Greece 37°55′N 22°28′E
263 L7 **Kalibo** Panay Island, C Philippines 11°40′N 122°21′E
187 L9 **Kalí Límni** ▲ Kárpathos, SE Greece 35°34′N 27°08′E
135 H8 **Kalima** Maniema, E Dem. Rep. Congo 02°34′S 26°27′E
258 K4 **Kalimantan** Eng. Indonesian Borneo. geopolitcal region Borneo, C Indonesia
258 I5 **Kalimantan Barat** off. Propinsi Kalimantan Berat, Eng. West Borneo, West Kalimantan. ◈ province N Indonesia
Kalimantan Barat, Propinsi see Kalimantan Barat
258 K6 **Kalimantan Selatan** off. Propinsi Kalimantan Selatan, Eng. South Borneo, South Kalimantan. ◈ province N Indonesia
Kalimantan Selatan, Propinsi see Kalimantan Selatan
258 J5 **Kalimantan Tengah** off. Propinsi Kalimantan Tengah, Eng. Central Borneo, Central Kalimantan. ◈ province N Indonesia
Kalimantan Tengah, Propinsi see Kalimantan Tengah
258 J5 **Kalimantan Timur** off. Propinsi Kalimantan Timur, Eng. East Borneo, East Kalimantan. ◈ province N Indonesia
Kalimantan Timur, Propinsi see Kalimantan Timur
Kálimnos see Kálymnos
233 J6 **Kālimpang** West Bengal, NE India 27°02′N 88°34′E
Kalinin see Tver'
Kalinin see Boldumsaz
Kalininabad see Kalininobod
191 A8 **Kaliningrad** Kaliningradskaya Oblast', W Russian Federation 54°48′N 21°33′E
Kaliningrad see Kaliningradskaya Oblast'
191 B9 **Kaliningradskaya Oblast'** var. Kaliningrad. ◈ province and enclave W Russian Federation
Kalinino see Tashir
229 I8 **Kalininobod** Rus. Kalininabad. SW Tajikistan 37°49′N 68°55′E
197 I4 **Kalininsk** Saratovskaya Oblast', W Russian Federation 51°31′N 44°25′E
Kalininsk see Boldumsaz
Kalinisk see Cupcina
191 H11 **Kalinkavichy** Rus. Kalinkovichi. Homyel'skaya Voblasts', SE Belarus 52°08′N 29°19′E
Kalinkovichi see Kalinkavichy
136 C7 **Kaliro** SE Uganda 0°54′N 33°30′E
Kalisch/Kalish see Kalisz
76 G3 **Kalispell** Montana, NW USA 48°12′N 114°18′W
182 E6 **Kalisz** Ger. Kalisch, Rus. Kalish; anc. Calisia. Wielkopolskie, C Poland 51°46′N 18°04′E
182 D5 **Kalisz Pomorski** Ger. Kallies. Zachodnio-pomorskie, NW Poland 53°55′N 15°55′E
137 B10 **Kaliua** Tabora, C Tanzania 05°03′S 31°48′E
152 G6 **Kalix** Norrbotten, N Sweden 65°51′N 23°14′E
152 F5 **Kalixälven** ≈ N Sweden
152 F5 **Kalixfors** Norrbotten, N Sweden 67°45′N 20°20′E
227 J3 **Kalkaman** Pavlodar, NE Kazakhstan 51°57′N 75°58′E
187 N8 **Kalkan** Antalya, Turkey 36°16′N 29°25′E
Kalkandelen see Tetovo
180 B7 **Kalkar** Nordrhein-Westfalen, Germany 6°18′N 51°44′E
274 G3 **Kalkarindji** Northern Territory, N Australia 17°32′S 130°40′E
72 F6 **Kalkaska** Michigan, N USA 44°44′N 85°11′W
141 J2 **Kalkbank** Limpopo, South Africa 23°32′S 29°21′E
180 J2 **Kalkhorst** Mecklenburg-Vorpommern, Germany 11°04′N 53°58′E
154 F3 **Kall** Jämtland, C Sweden 63°31′N 13°16′E
283 M10 **Kallalen** var. Calalen. island Ratak Chain, SE Marshall Islands
190 F4 **Kallaste** Ger. Krasnogor. Tartumaa, SE Estonia 58°40′N 27°12′E
153 I8 **Kallavesi** ◎ SE Finland
181 E8 **Kallenhardt** Nordrhein-Westfalen, Germany 8°25′N 51°27′E
186 G5 **Kallídromo** ▲▲ C Greece
Kallies see Kalisz Pomorski
155 H11 **Kallinge** Blekinge, S Sweden 56°14′N 15°17′E
187 K4 **Kalloní** Lésvos, E Greece 39°14′N 26°16′E
154 F3 **Kallsjön** ◎ C Sweden
155 H11 **Kalmar** var. Calmar. Kalmar, S Sweden 56°40′N 16°22′E
155 H10 **Kalmar** var. Calmar. ◈ county S Sweden
155 I11 **Kalmarsund** strait S Sweden
230 E9 **Kalmat, Khor** Eng. Kalmat Lagoon. lagoon SW Pakistan
Kalmat Lagoon see Kalmat, Khor
189 M6 **Kal'mius** ≈ E Ukraine
163 E9 **Kalmthout** Antwerpen, N Belgium 51°24′N 04°27′E
Kalmykia/Kalmykiya-Khal'mg Tangch, Respublika see Kalmykiya, Respublika
197 I7 **Kalmykiya, Respublika** var. Respublika Kalmykiya-Khal'mg Tangch, Eng. Kalmykia; prev. Kalmytskaya ASSR. ◈ autonomous republic SW Russian Federation
Kalmytskaya ASSR see Kalmykiya, Respublika
190 D6 **Kalnciems** Jelgava, C Latvia 56°46′N 23°37′E
185 L7 **Kalnitsa** ≈ SE Bulgaria
183 F12 **Kalocsa** Bács-Kiskun, S Hungary 46°31′N 19°00′E
185 K6 **Kalofer** Plovdiv, C Bulgaria 42°36′N 25°00′E
82 C2 **Kalohi Channel** channel C Pacific Ocean
138 F3 **Kalomo** Southern, S Zambia 17°02′S 26°29′E
73 A9 **Kalona** Iowa, C USA 41°28′N 91°42′W
187 J8 **Kalotási, Ákrotirio** cape Amorgós, Kykládes, Greece, Aegean Sea
232 F4 **Kalpa** Himāchal Pradesh, N India 31°33′N 78°16′E
186 E4 **Kalpáki** Ípeiros, W Greece 39°53′N 20°38′E
235 C9 **Kalpeni Island** island Lakshadweep, India, N Indian Ocean
232 F6 **Kālpi** Uttar Pradesh, N India 26°07′N 79°44′E
238 D4 **Kalpin** Xinjiang Uygur Zizhiqu, NW China 40°35′N 78°52′E
228 F4 **Kalquduq** Nawoiy Viloyati, N Uzbekistan 42°36′N 63°24′E
230 G9 **Kalri Lake** ◎ SE Pakistan
223 H3 **Kāl Shūr** ≈ N Iran
82 G6 **Kalskag** Alaska, USA 61°32′N 160°15′W
Kalsø see Kalsoy
154 B1 **Kalsoy** Dan. Kalsø. island N Faeroe Islands
83 H5 **Kaltag** Alaska, USA 64°19′N 158°43′W
176 E4 **Kaltbrunn** Sankt Gallen, NE Switzerland 47°11′N 09°00′E
Kaltdorf see Pruszków
180 H2 **Kaltenkirchen** Schleswig-Holstein, Germany 9°58′N 53°50′E
181 B10 **Kalterherberg** Nordrhein-Westfalen, Germany 6°13′N 50°31′E
133 L6 **Kaltungo** Gombe, E Nigeria 09°49′N 11°22′E
196 F2 **Kaluga** Kaluzhskaya Oblast', W Russian Federation 54°31′N 36°16′E
235 G11 **Kalu Ganga** ≈ S Sri Lanka
138 G1 **Kalulushi** Copperbelt, C Zambia 12°50′S 28°03′E
274 F2 **Kalumburu** Western Australia 14°11′S 126°40′E
155 E12 **Kalundborg** Vestsjælland, E Denmark 55°42′N 11°06′E
137 A12 **Kalungwishi** ≈ N Zambia
231 I5 **Kalūr Kot** Punjab, E Pakistan 32°08′N 71°20′E
188 D4 **Kalush** Pol. Kałusz. Ivano-Frankivs'ka Oblast', W Ukraine 49°02′N 24°20′E
Kałusz see Kalush
182 H6 **Kałuszyn** Mazowieckie, C Poland 52°12′N 21°43′E
235 F11 **Kalutara** Western Province, SW Sri Lanka 06°35′N 79°59′E
Kaluwawa see Fergusson Island
196 F2 **Kaluzhskaya Oblast'** ◈ province W Russian Federation
191 C9 **Kalvarija** Pol. Kalwaria. Marijampol'e, S Lithuania 54°25′N 23°13′E
152 G7 **Kälviä** Länsi-Soumi, W Finland 63°53′N 23°30′E
177 K3 **Kalwang** Steiermark, E Austria 47°25′N 14°48′E
Kalwaria see Kalvarija
234 C4 **Kalyān** Mahārāshtra, W India 19°17′N 73°11′E
194 F10 **Kalyazin** Tverskaya Oblast', W Russian Federation 57°15′N 37°53′E
186 F6 **Kalydón** anc. Calydon. site of ancient city Dytikí Ellás, C Greece
187 K7 **Kálymnos** var. Kálimnos. Kálymnos, Dodekánisa, Greece, Aegean Sea 36°57′N 26°59′E
187 K8 **Kálymnos** var. Kálimnos. island Dodekánisa, Greece, Aegean Sea
189 H3 **Kalynivka** Kyyivs'ka Oblast', N Ukraine 50°14′N 30°16′E
188 G4 **Kalynivka** Vinnyts'ka Oblast', C Ukraine 49°27′N 28°32′E
89 H6 **Kama** var. Cama. Región Autónoma Atlántico Sur, SE Nicaragua 12°06′N 83°55′W
195 J8 **Kama** ≈ NW Russian Federation
253 E9 **Kamaishi** var. Kamaisi. Iwate, Honshū, C Japan 39°18′N 141°52′E
Kamaisi see Kamaishi
191 E8 **Kamajai** Panevėžys, NE Lithuania 55°16′N 25°30′E
190 E7 **Kamajai** Utena, E Lithuania 55°49′N 25°30′E
253 C14 **Kamakura** Kanagawa, Honshū, S Japan 35°19′N 139°33′E
231 I6 **Kamālia** Punjab, NE Pakistan 30°44′N 72°39′E
138 F1 **Kamalondo** North Western, NW Zambia 13°42′S 25°38′E
214 E6 **Kaman** Kirşehir, C Turkey 39°22′N 33°43′E
135 I8 **Kamanyola** Sud Kivu, E Dem. Rep. Congo 02°54′S 29°04′E
220 E8 **Kamarān** island W Yemen
103 J5 **Kamarang** W Guyana 05°49′N 60°38′W
Kāmāreddi/Kamareddy see Rāmāreddi
Kama Reservoir see Kamskoye Vodokhranilishche
230 E8 **Kamarod** Baluchistān, SW Pakistan 27°34′N 63°36′E
260 E6 **Kamaru** Pulau Buton, C Indonesia 05°10′S 123°03′E
229 H7 **Kamashi** Qashqadaryo Viloyati, S Uzbekistan 38°52′N 66°30′E
133 I5 **Kamba** Kebbi, NW Nigeria 11°50′N 03°44′E
Kambaeng Petch see Kamphaeng Phet
274 E7 **Kambalda** Western Australia 31°15′S 121°33′E
230 G8 **Kambar** var. Qambar. Sind, SE Pakistan 27°35′N 68°03′E
Kambara see Kabara
132 C6 **Kambia** W Sierra Leone 09°09′N 12°53′W
260 F8 **Kambing, Pulau** island W East Timor, S Indonesia
Kambos see Kámpos
135 H12 **Kambove** Katanga, SE Dem. Rep. Congo 10°50′S 26°39′E
Kambryk see Cambrai
193 M5 **Kamchatka** ≈ E Russian Federation
Kamchatka see Kamchatka, Poluostrov
Kamchatka Basin see Komandorskaya Basin
193 M6 **Kamchatka, Poluostrov** Eng. Kamchatka. peninsula E Russian Federation
193 M6 **Kamchatskaya Oblast'** ◈ province E Russian Federation
193 N5 **Kamchatskiy Zaliv** gulf E Russian Federation
185 M5 **Kamchiya** ≈ E Bulgaria
185 L6 **Kamchiya, Yazovir** ◎ E Bulgaria
Kamdesh see Kāmdeysh
231 I3 **Kāmdeysh** var. Kamdesh. Nūrestān, E Afghanistan 35°25′N 71°26′E
250 F6 **Kamega-mori** ▲ Shikoku, SW Japan 33°45′N 133°12′E
191 G8 **Kamen'** Rus. Kamen'. Vitsyebskaya Voblasts', N Belarus 55°01′N 28°53′E
Kamenets see Kamyanyets
Kamenets-Podol'skaya Oblast' see Khmel'nyts'ka Oblast'
Kamenets-Podol'skiy see Kam"yanets'-Podil's'kyy
185 H7 **Kamenica** NE Macedonia 42°03′N 22°34′E
184 A3 **Kamenjak, Rt** headland NW Croatia
226 B3 **Kamenka** Zapadnyy Kazakhstan, NW Kazakhstan 51°06′N 51°16′E
195 H4 **Kamenka** Arkhangel'skaya Oblast', NW Russian Federation 65°55′N 44°01′E
197 H3 **Kamenka** Penzenskaya Oblast', W Russian Federation 53°12′N 44°00′E
196 G5 **Kamenka** Voronezhskaya Oblast', W Russian Federation 50°44′N 39°31′E
Kamenka see Camenca
Kamenka see Kam"yanka
Kamenka-Bugskaya see Kam"yanka-Buz'ka
Kamenka Dneprovskaya see Kam"yanka-Dniprovs'ka
Kamen Kashirskiy see Kamin'-Kashyrs'kyy
192 F7 **Kamen'-na-Obi** Altayskiy Kray, S Russian Federation 53°42′N 81°04′E
196 G8 **Kamennomostskiy** Respublika Adygeya, SW Russian Federation 44°13′N 40°12′E
196 G6 **Kamenolomni** Rostovskaya Oblast', SW Russian Federation 47°36′N 40°18′E
197 I5 **Kamenskiy** Saratovskaya Oblast', W Russian Federation 50°56′N 45°32′E
193 M4 **Kamenskoye** Koryakskiy Avtonomnyy Okrug, E Russian Federation 62°29′N 166°16′E
Kamenskoye see Dniprodzerzhyns'k
196 G6 **Kamensk-Shakhtinskiy** Rostovskaya Oblast', SW Russian Federation 48°18′N 40°16′E
195 M10 **Kamensk-Ural'skiy** Sverdlovskaya Oblast', C Russian Federation 56°30′N 61°45′E
179 I8 **Kamenz** Sachsen, E Germany 51°15′N 14°06′E
251 H4 **Kameoka** Kyōto, Honshū, SW Japan 35°02′N 135°35′E
158 F3 **Kames** UK 55°53′N 5°16′W
196 G1 **Kameshkovo** Vladimirskaya Oblast', W Russian Federation 56°21′N 41°01′E
251 I4 **Kameyama** Mie, Honshū, SW Japan 34°52′N 136°28′E
250 B4 **Kami-Agata** Nagasaki, Tsushima, SW Japan 34°40′N 129°27′E
76 F5 **Kamiah** Idaho, NW USA 46°13′N 116°01′W
Kamień Koszyrski see Kamin'-Kashyrs'kyy
182 E4 **Kamień Krajeński** Ger. Kamin in Westpreussen. Kujawski-pomorskie, C Poland 53°31′N 17°31′E
182 D7 **Kamienna Góra** Ger. Landeshut, Landeshut in Schlesien. Dolnośląskie, SW Poland 50°48′N 16°00′E
182 C4 **Kamień Pomorski** Ger. Cummin in Pommern. Zachodnio-pomorskie, NW Poland 53°57′N 14°44′E
140 C7 **Kamieskroon** Northern Cape, South Africa 30°12′S 17°56′E
252 D6 **Kamiiso** Hokkaidō, NE Japan 41°50′N 140°38′E
135 G10 **Kamiji** Kasai Oriental, S Dem. Rep. Congo 06°39′S 23°27′E
252 F3 **Kamikawa** Hokkaidō, NE Japan 43°51′N 142°47′E
250 C8 **Kami-Koshiki-jima** island SW Japan
55 H4 **Kamilukuak Lake** ◎ Nunavut, N Canada
135 H11 **Kamina** Shaba, S Dem. Rep. Congo 08°42′S 25°01′E
Kamina see Kaintiba
55 I4 **Kaminak Lake** ◎ Nunavut, C Canada
88 C4 **Kaminaljuyú** ruins Guatemala, C Guatemala
Kamin in Westpreussen see Kamień Krajeński
188 D2 **Kamin'-Kashyrs'kyy** Pol. Kamień Koszyrski, Rus. Kamen Kashirskiy. Volyns'ka Oblast', NW Ukraine 51°39′N 24°59′E
252 C6 **Kaminokuni** Hokkaidō, NE Japan 41°48′N 140°05′E
253 C10 **Kaminoyama** Yamagata, Honshū, C Japan 38°10′N 140°16′E
55 I4 **Kaminuriak Lake** ◎ Nunavut, N Canada
251 J2 **Kamioka** Gifu, Honshū, SW Japan 36°20′N 137°18′E
83 I7 **Kamishak Bay** bay Alaska, USA
252 F4 **Kami-Shihoro** Hokkaidō, NE Japan 43°14′N 143°18′E
Kamishli see Al Qāmishlī
Kamissar see Kamsar
250 B4 **Kami-Tsushima** Nagasaki, Tsushima, SW Japan 34°40′N 129°27′E
135 I8 **Kamituga** Sud Kivu, E Dem. Rep. Congo 03°07′S 28°10′E
250 C10 **Kamiyaku** Kagoshima, Yaku-shima, SW Japan 30°24′N 130°32′E
56 F7 **Kamloops** British Columbia, SW Canada 50°39′N 120°24′W
175 D13 **Kamma** Sicilia, Italy, C Mediterranean Sea 36°46′N 12°03′E
140 F9 **Kammanassie Mountains** ▲▲ Western Cape, South Africa
181 I9 **Kammerforst** Thüringen, Germany 10°25′N 51°08′E
286 E3 **Kammu Seamount** undersea feature N Pacific Ocean
177 K5 **Kamnik** Ger. Stein. C Slovenia 46°13′N 14°34′E
253 B11 **Kamo** Niigata, Honshū, C Japan 37°40′N 139°05′E
253 C14 **Kamogawa** Chiba, Honshū, S Japan 35°05′N 140°04′E
231 J5 **Kāmoke** Punjab, E Pakistan 31°58′N 74°15′E
139 I1 **Kamoto** Eastern, E Zambia 13°16′S 32°04′E
177 K1 **Kamp** ≈ N Austria
137 B8 **Kampala** ● (Uganda) S Uganda 0°20′N 32°28′E
258 E5 **Kampar, Sungai** ≈ Sumatera, W Indonesia
258 F6 **Kampa, Teluk** bay Pulau Bangka, W Indonesia
162 H5 **Kampen** Overijssel, E Netherlands 52°33′N 05°55′E
135 H9 **Kampene** Maniema, E Dem. Rep. Congo 03°35′S 26°40′E
74 E5 **Kampeska, Lake** ◎ South Dakota, N USA
256 E7 **Kamphaeng Phet** var. Kambaeng Petch. Kamphaeng Phet, W Thailand 16°28′N 99°31′E
181 B8 **Kamp-Lintfort** Nordrhein-Westfalen, Germany 6°32′N 51°30′E
Kampo see Campo, Cameroon
Kampo see Ntem, Cameroon/Equatorial Guinea
257 H9 **Kâmpóng Cham** prev. Kompong Cham. Kâmpóng Cham, C Cambodia 12°N 105°27′E
256 G9 **Kâmpóng Chhnăng** prev. Kompong. Kâmpóng Chhnăng, C Cambodia 12°15′N 104°40′E
256 G8 **Kâmpóng Khleăng** prev. Kompong Kleang. Siĕmréab, NW Cambodia 13°04′N 104°07′E
256 G9 **Kâmpóng Saôm** prev. Kompong Som, Sihanoukville. Kâmpóng Saôm, SW Cambodia 10°38′N 103°30′E
256 G9 **Kâmpóng Spoe** prev. Kompong Speu. Kâmpóng Spœ, S Cambodia 11°28′N 104°29′E
218 B2 **Kámpos** var. Kambos. NW Cyprus 35°03′N 32°44′E
256 G9 **Kâmpôt** Kâmpôt, SW Cambodia 10°37′N 104°11′E
Kamptee see Kāmthi
132 G6 **Kampti** SW Burkina 10°07′N 03°22′W
Kampuchea see Cambodia
Kampuchea, Democratic see Cambodia
Kampuchea, People's Democratic Republic of see Cambodia
258 I3 **Kampung Sirik** Sarawak, East Malaysia 02°42′N 111°28′E
261 L7 **Kampung, Sungai** ≈ Papua, E Indonesia
261 J6 **Kamrau, Teluk** bay Papua, E Indonesia
55 I9 **Kamsack** Saskatchewan, S Canada 51°34′N 101°51′W
132 B6 **Kamsar** var. Kamissar. Guinée-Maritime, W Guinea 10°33′N 14°34′W
197 J2 **Kamskoye Ust'ye** Respublika Tatarstan, W Russian Federation 55°13′N 49°11′E

◆ Country
● Country Capital
◇ Dependent Territory
○ Dependent Territory Capital
◈ Administrative Regions
✈ International Airport
▲ Mountain
▲▲ Mountain Range
Volcano
≈ River
◎ Lake
⊠ Reservoir

Kashmūnd Ghar - Kermānshāh

231 H3 **Kashmūnd Ghar** *Eng.* Kashmund Range. ▲ E Afghanistan
Kashmund Range *see* Kashmūnd Ghar
Kasi *see* Vārānasi
233 H6 **Kasia** Uttar Pradesh, N India 26°45'N 83°55'E
82 G6 **Kasigluk** Alaska, USA 60°54'N 162°31'W
Kasihara *see* Kashihara
83 I7 **Kasilof** Alaska, USA 60°20'N 151°16'W
Kasima *see* Kashima
Kasimköj *see* General Toshevo
197 H2 **Kasimov** Ryazanskaya Oblast', W Russian Federation 54°59'N 41°22'E
134 J7 **Kasindi** Nord Kivu, E Dem. Rep. Congo 0°03'N 29°43'E
260 F4 **Kasiruta, Pulau** *island* Kepulauan Bacan, E Indonesia
137 C12 **Kasitu** ⁓ N Malawi
261 I6 **Kasiui, Pulau** *island* Kepulauan Watubela, E Indonesia
Kasiwa *see* Kashiwa
Kasiwazaki *see* Kashiwazaki
73 C11 **Kaskaskia River** ⁓ Illinois, N USA
55 K6 **Kaskattamagen River** ⁓ Manitoba, C Canada
153 G8 **Kaskinen** *Swe.* Kaskö. Länsi-Soumi, W Finland 62°23'N 21°10'E
Kaskö *see* Kaskinen
Kas Kong *see* Kông, Kaôh
57 H8 **Kaslo** British Columbia, SW Canada 49°54'N 116°57'W
Kåsmark *see* Kežmarok
258 J6 **Kasongan** Borneo, C Indonesia 02°01'S 113°21'E
135 H9 **Kasongo** Maniema, E Dem. Rep. Congo 04°22'S 26°42'E
135 D10 **Kasongo-Lunda** Bandundu, SW Dem. Rep. Congo 06°30'S 16°51'E
187 K10 **Kásos** *island* S Greece
Kasos Strait *see* Kasou, Stenó
187 K10 **Kasou, Stenó** *var.* Kasos Strait. *strait* Dodekánisa/Kríti, Greece, Aegean Sea
215 K4 **Kaspi** C Georgia 41°54'N 44°25'E
185 L5 **Kaspichan** Shumen, NE Bulgaria 43°18'N 27°09'E
Kaspiy Mangy Oypaty *see* Caspian Depression
197 J9 **Kaspiysk** Respublika Dagestan, SW Russian Federation 42°52'N 47°40'E
Kaspiyskiy *see* Lagan'
Kaspiyskoye More/Kaspiy Tengizi *see* Caspian Sea
Kassa *see* Košice
Kassai *see* Kasai
136 D2 **Kassala** Kassala, E Sudan 15°24'N 36°25'E
136 D1 **Kassala** ◈ *state* NE Sudan
187 H4 **Kassándra** *prev.* Pallíni; *anc.* Pallene. *peninsula* NE Greece
185 I10 **Kassándras, Akrotírio** *cape* N Greece
187 H4 **Kassándras, Kólpos** *var.* Kólpos Toronaíos. *gulf* N Greece
217 M7 **Kassārah** E Iraq 31°21'N 47°25'E
181 G8 **Kassel** *prev.* Cassel. Hessen, C Germany 51°19'N 09°30'E
131 K2 **Kasserine** *var.* Al Qaşrayn. W Tunisia 35°15'N 08°52'E
62 E4 **Kasshabog Lake** ◎ Ontario, SE Canada
216 G3 **Kassīr, Sabkhat al** ◎ E Syria
74 H5 **Kasson** Minnesota, N USA 44°00'N 92°42'W
186 E5 **Kassópeia** *Var.* Kassópi. *site of ancient city* Ípeiros, W Greece
Kassópi *see* Kassópeia
187 L9 **Kastállou, Akrotírio** *headland* Kárpathos, SE Greece 35°24'N 27°08'E
214 E4 **Kastamonu** *var.* Castamoni, Kastamuni. Kastamonu, N Turkey 41°22'N 33°47'E
214 E4 **Kastamonu** *var.* Kastamuni. ◈ *province* N Turkey
Kastamuni *see* Kastamonu
186 G3 **Kastaneá** Kentrikí Makedonía, N Greece 40°25'N 22°09'E
Kastélli *see* Kíssamos
Kastellórizon *see* Megísti
155 H11 **Kastlösa** Kalmar, S Sweden 56°25'N 16°25'E
186 F3 **Kastoría** Dytikí Makedonía, N Greece 40°33'N 21°15'E
196 F4 **Kastornoye** Kurskaya Oblast', W Russian Federation 51°49'N 38°07'E
187 I7 **Kástro** Sífnos, Kykládes, Greece, Aegean Sea 36°58'N 24°45'E
155 F12 **Kastrup** ✕ (København) København, E Denmark 55°36'N 12°39'E
191 J10 **Kastsyukovichy** *Rus.* Kostyukovichi. Mahilyowskaya Voblasts', E Belarus 53°20'N 32°03'E
191 I11 **Kastsyukowka** *Rus.* Kostyukovka. Homyel'skaya Voblasts', SE Belarus 52°32'N 30°54'E
250 C6 **Kasuga** Fukuoka, Kyūshū, SW Japan 33°31'N 130°27'E
251 J4 **Kasugai** Aichi, Honshū, SW Japan 35°15'N 136°57'E
137 A9 **Kasulu** Kigoma, W Tanzania 04°33'S 30°06'E
253 C13 **Kasumiga-ura** ◎ Honshū, S Japan
197 J10 **Kasumkent** Respublika Dagestan, SW Russian Federation 41°39'N 48°09'E
137 C13 **Kasungu** Central, C Malawi 13°04'S 33°29'E
231 J5 **Kasūr** Punjab, E Pakistan 31°07'N 74°30'E
138 E2 **Kataba** Western, W Zambia 15°28'S 23°25'E
63 K2 **Katahdin, Mount** ▲ Maine, NE USA 45°55'N 68°52'W
135 G9 **Katako-Kombe** Kasai Oriental, C Dem. Rep. Congo 03°24'S 24°25'E
83 J6 **Katalla** Alaska, USA 60°12'N 144°31'W
Katana *see* Qaṭanā
135 H11 **Katanga** *off.* Région du Katanga, *prev* Shaba. ◈ *region* SE Dem. Rep. Congo
193 H7 **Katanga** ⁓ C Russian Federation
Katanga, Région du *see* Katanga
232 F9 **Katangi** Madhya Pradesh, C India 21°46'N 79°50'E
274 D8 **Katanning** Western Australia 33°45'S 117°33'E
276 D1 **Kata Tjuta** *var.* Mount Olga. ▲ Northern Territory, C Australia 25°20'S 130°47'E
Katawaz *see* Zarghūn Shahr
196 M10 **Katayşk** Kurganskaya oblast', Russian federation
141 I8 **Katbergpas** *pass* Eastern Cape, South Africa
256 A11 **Katchall Island** *island* Nicobar Islands, India, NE Indian Ocean
186 G3 **Kateríni** Kentrikí Makedonía, N Greece 40°15'N 22°30'E
189 H5 **Katerynopil'** Cherkas'ka Oblast', C Ukraine 49°00'N 30°59'E
256 D3 **Katha** Sagaing, N Myanmar (Burma) 24°11'N 96°20'E
274 G2 **Katherine** Northern Territory, N Australia 14°29'S 132°20'E
232 B8 **Kāthiāwār Peninsula** *peninsula* W India
233 I6 **Kathmandu** *prev.* Kantipur. ● (Nepal) Central, C Nepal 27°46'N 85°17'E
140 G5 **Kathu** Northern Cape, South Africa 27°42'S 23°03'E
231 K5 **Kathua** Jammu and Kashmir, NW India 32°23'N 75°34'E
132 E5 **Kati** Koulikoro, SW Mali 12°41'N 08°04'W
233 J7 **Katihār** Bihār, NE India 25°33'N 87°34'E
279 H4 **Katikati** Bay of Plenty, North Island, New Zealand 37°34'S 175°55'E
138 F3 **Katima Mulilo** Caprivi, NE Namibia 17°31'S 24°20'E
132 F7 **Katiola** C Ivory Coast 08°11'N 05°04'W
285 J7 **Katiu** *atoll* Îles Tuamotu, C French Polynesia
189 G8 **Katlabukh, Ozero** ◎ SW Ukraine
83 H7 **Katmai, Mount** ▲ Alaska, USA 58°16'N 154°57'W
232 G8 **Katni** Madhya Pradesh, C India 23°47'N 80°29'E
186 F6 **Káto Achaïa** *var.* Kato Ahaia, Káto Akhaía. Dytikí Ellás, S Greece 38°08'N 21°33'E
Kato Ahaia/Káto Akhaía *see* Káto Achaïa
218 B2 **Kato Lakatámeia** *var.* Kato Lakatamia. C Cyprus 35°07'N 33°20'E
Kato Lakatamia *see* Kato Lakatámeia
135 H10 **Katompi** Katanga, SE Dem. Rep. Congo 06°10'S 26°19'E
139 H2 **Katondwe** Lusaka, C Zambia 15°08'S 30°10'E
187 H2 **Káto Nevrokópi** *prev.* Káto Nevrokópion. Anatolikí Makedonía kai Thráki, NE Greece 41°21'N 23°51'E
Káto Nevrokópion *see* Káto Nevrokópi
137 B8 **Katonga** ⁓ S Uganda
186 G4 **Káto Ólympos** ▲ C Greece
186 F5 **Katoúna** Dytikí Ellás, C Greece 38°47'N 21°07'E
186 F6 **Káto Vlasiá** Dytikí Makedonía, S Greece 38°02'N 21°54'E
183 F8 **Katowice** *Ger.* Kattowitz. Śląskie, S Poland 50°15'N 19°01'E
183 F8 **Katowice** ◈ *province* S Poland
233 J8 **Kātoya** West Bengal, NE India 23°39'N 88°11'E
214 C7 **Katrançik Dağı** ▲ SW Turkey
155 H8 **Katrineholm** Södermanland, C Sweden 58°59'N 16°15'E
158 G2 **Katrine, Loch** ◎ C Scotland, UK
133 K5 **Katsina** Katsina, N Nigeria 12°59'N 07°33'E
133 K5 **Katsina** ◈ *state* N Nigeria
121 J5 **Katsina Ala** ⁓ S Nigeria
250 C5 **Katsumoto** Nagasaki, Iki, SW Japan 33°49'N 129°42'E
253 D12 **Katsuta** *var.* Katuta. Ibaraki, Honshū, S Japan 36°24'N 140°32'E
253 C14 **Katsuura** *var.* Katuura. Chiba, Honshū, S Japan 35°09'N 140°16'E
251 I3 **Katsuyama** *var.* Katuyama. Fukui, Honshū, SW Japan 36°00'N 136°30'E
250 G4 **Katsuyama** Okayama, Honshū, SW Japan 35°06'N 133°43'E
Kattakurgan *see* Kattaqo'rg'on
229 H6 **Kattaqo'rg'on** *Rus.* Kattakurgan. Samarqand Viloyati, C Uzbekistan 39°56'N 66°11'E
187 L9 **Kattavía** Ródos, Dodekánisa, Greece, Aegean Sea 35°56'N 27°47'E
155 E11 **Kattegat** *Dan.* Kattegatt. *strait* N Europe
Kattegatt *see* Kattegat
180 E6 **Kattenvenne** Nordrhein-Westfalen, Germany 7°52'N 52°07'E
155 J10 **Katthammarsvik** Gotland, SE Sweden 57°27'N 18°54'E
Kattowitz *see* Katowice
227 M3 **Katun'** ⁓ S Russian Federation
Katuta *see* Katsuta
Katuura *see* Katsuura
Katuyama *see* Katsuyama
Katwijk *see* Katwijk aan Zee
162 E6 **Katwijk aan Zee** *var.* Katwijk. Zuid-Holland, W Netherlands 59°12'N 04°24'E
181 J10 **Katzhütte** Thüringen, Germany 11°04'N 50°33'E
181 D13 **Katzweiler** Rheinland-Pfalz, Germany 7°42'N 49°30'E
82 B1 **Kaua'i** *var.* Kauai. *island* Hawaiian Islands, Hawai'i, USA, C PacificOcean
Kauai *see* Kaua'i
82 B2 **Kaua'i Channel** *var.* Kauai Channel. *channel* Hawai'i, USA, C Pacific Ocean
Kauai Channel *see* Kaua'i Channel
181 D11 **Kaub** Rheinland-Pfalz, Germany 7°46'N 50°05'E
260 F5 **Kaubalatmada, Gunung** *var.* Kaplamada. ▲ Pulau Buru, E Indonesia 03°16'S 126°17'E
285 J6 **Kauehi** *atoll* Îles Tuamotu, C French Polynesia
Kauen *see* Kaunas
179 F13 **Kaufbeuren** Bayern, S Germany 47°53'N 10°37'E
71 H4 **Kaufman** Texas, SW USA 32°35'N 96°18'W
181 H8 **Kaufungen** Hessen, C Germany 51°16'N 09°39'E
153 G8 **Kauhajoki** Länsi-Soumi, W Finland 62°26'N 22°10'E
153 G8 **Kauhava** Länsi-Soumi, W Finland 63°06'N 23°08'E
72 D6 **Kaukauna** Wisconsin, N USA 44°18'N 88°18'W
152 H5 **Kaukonen** Lappi, N Finland 67°28'N 24°49'E
82 A1 **Kaulakahi Channel** *channel* Hawai'i, USA, C Pacific Ocean
250 A2 **Kaŭn** Kyŏngsang-bukto, South Korea 36°39'N 128°04'E
82 C2 **Kaunakakai** Moloka'i, Hawai'i, USA, C Pacific Ocean 21°05'N 157°01'W
82 D3 **Kaunā Point** *var.* Kauna Point. *headland* Hawai'i, USA, C Pacific Ocean 19°02'N 155°52'W
Kauna Point *see* Kaunā Point
191 D8 **Kaunas** *Ger.* Kauen, *Pol.* Kowno; *prev. Rus.* Kovno. Kaunas, C Lithuania 54°54'N 23°57'E
280 B2 **Kaup** East Sepik, NW Papua New Guinea 03°50'S 144°01'E
133 J5 **Kaura Namoda** Zamfara, NW Nigeria 12°43'N 06°17'E
Kaushany *see* Căuşeni
153 H8 **Kaustinen** Länsi-Soumi, W Finland 63°33'N 23°40'E
260 G3 **Kau, Teluk** *bay* Pulau Halmahera, E Indonesia
163 H13 **Kautenbach** Diekirch, NE Luxembourg 49°57'N 06°01'E
152 G4 **Kautokeino** *Lapp.* Guovdageaidnu. Finnmark, N Norway 69°N 23°01'E
Kavadar *see* Kavadarci
185 H8 **Kavadarci** *Turk.* Kavadar. C Macedonia 41°25'N 22°00'E
Kavaja *see* Kavajë
184 F8 **Kavajë** *It.* Cavaia, Kavaja. Tiranë, W Albania 41°11'N 19°33'E
Kavakli *see* Topolovgrad
187 I2 **Kavála** *prev.* Kaválla. Anatolikí Makedonía kai Thráki, NE Greece 40°57'N 24°26'E
187 I2 **Kavalas, Kólpos** *gulf* Aegean Sea, NE Mediterranean Sea
193 L9 **Kavalerovo** Primorskiy Kray, SE Russian Federation 44°17'N 135°06'E
234 F7 **Kāvali** Andhra Pradesh, E India 15°05'N 80°02'E
Kaválla *see* Kavála
Kavango *see* Cubango/Okavango
235 B9 **Kavaratti** Lakshadweep, SW India 10°33'N 72°38'E
185 M5 **Kavarna** Dobrich, NE Bulgaria 43°27'N 28°21'E
191 E8 **Kavarskas** Utena, E Lithuania 55°27'N 24°55'E
132 C6 **Kavendou** ▲ C Guinea 10°49'N 12°14'W
Kavengo *see* Cubango/Okavango
235 E8 **Kāveri** *var.* Cauvery. ⁓ S India
280 D2 **Kavieng** *var.* Kaewieng. New Ireland, NE Papua New Guinea 04°13'S 152°11'E
138 F3 **Kavimba** North-West, NE Botswana 18°02'S 24°38'E
138 F2 **Kavingu** Southern, S Zambia 15°39'S 26°03'E
222 G4 **Kavīr, Dasht-e** *var.* Great Salt Desert. *salt pan* N Iran
Kavirondo Gulf *see* Winam Gulf
Kavkaz *see* Caucasus
155 F12 **Kävlinge** Skåne, S Sweden 55°47'N 13°05'E
280 E10 **Kavukavu Reef** *var.* Beqa Barrier Reef, Cakaubalavu Reef. *reef* Viti Levu, SW Fiji
135 G12 **Kavungo** Moxico, E Angola 11°31'S 22°59'E
253 C8 **Kawabe** Akita, Honshū, C Japan 39°39'N 140°14'E
253 C13 **Kawagoe** Saitama, Honshū, S Japan 35°55'N 139°30'E
253 C13 **Kawaguchi** *var.* Kawaguti. Saitama, Honshū, S Japan 35°47'N 139°42'E
Kawaguti *see* Kawaguchi
253 E9 **Kawai** Iwate, Honshū, C Japan 39°36'N 141°40'E
82 A2 **Kawaihoa Point** *headland* Ni'ihau, Hawai'i, USA, C Pacific Ocean 21°47'N 160°12'W
278 F2 **Kawakawa** Northland, North Island, New Zealand 35°23'S 174°06'E
139 I2 **Kawama** North Western, NW Zambia 13°04'S 25°59'E
137 A12 **Kawambwa** Luapula, N Zambia 09°45'S 29°10'E
250 F5 **Kawanoe** Ehime, Shikoku, SW Japan 34°01'N 133°32'E
232 G8 **Kawardha** Chhattisgarh, C India 21°59'N 81°12'E
62 E4 **Kawartha Lakes** ◎ Ontario, SE Canada
260 G4 **Kawassi** Pulau Obi, E Indonesia 01°32'S 127°25'E
252 D7 **Kawauchi** Aomori, Honshū, C Japan 41°11'N 141°00'E
278 G3 **Kawau Island** *island* N New Zealand
279 H6 **Kaweka Range** ▲ North Island, New Zealand
Kawelecht *see* Puhja
261 M6 **Kawentinkim** Papua, E Indonesia 05°04'S 140°55'E
279 I5 **Kawerau** Bay of Plenty, North Island, New Zealand 38°06'S 176°43'E
278 G5 **Kawhia** Waikato, North Island, New Zealand 38°04'S 174°49'E
278 G5 **Kawhia Harbour** *inlet* North Island, New Zealand
80 I6 **Kawich Peak** ▲ Nevada, W USA 38°00'N 116°27'W
80 I6 **Kawich Range** ▲ Nevada, W USA
62 E4 **Kawigamog Lake** ◎ Ontario, S Canada
263 M10 **Kawio, Kepulauan** *island group* N Indonesia
256 D7 **Kawkareik** Karen State, S Myanmar (Burma) 16°33'N 98°18'E
75 E11 **Kaw Lake** ⊠ Oklahoma, C USA
256 C3 **Kawlin** Sagaing, N Myanmar (Burma) 23°48'N 95°41'E
Kawm Umbū *see* Kôm Ombo
Kawthule State *see* Karen State
Kaxgar *see* Kashi
238 B5 **Kaxgar He** ⁓ NW China
238 E3 **Kax He** ⁓ NW China
132 G5 **Kaya** C Burkina 13°04'N 01°09'W
187 M8 **Kayacık Muğla**, Turkey 36°42'N 28°46'E
188 C9 **Kayadibi** Kayseri, Turkey 38°45'N 35°59'E
256 D5 **Kayah State** ◈ *state* C Myanmar (Burma)
193 H4 **Kayak Taymyrskiy** (Dolgano-Nenetskiy) Avtonomnyy Okrug, N Russian Federation 71°27'N 103°21'E
83 K7 **Kayak Island** *island* Alaska, USA
214 B3 **Kayalıköy Barajı** ⊠ NW Turkey
235 E9 **Kāyankulam** Kerala, SW India 09°10'N 76°31'E
256 C6 **Kayan** Yangon, SW Myanmar (Burma) 16°54'N 96°35'E
Kayangel Islands *see* Ngcheangel
258 L3 **Kayan, Sungai** *prev.* Kajan. ⁓ Borneo, C Indonesia
226 C6 **Kaydak, Sor** *salt flat* SW Kazakhstan
Kaydanovo *see* Dzyarzhynsk Belarus
79 I6 **Kayenta** Arizona, SW USA 36°43'N 110°15'W
132 D4 **Kayes** Kayes, W Mali 14°26'N 11°22'W
132 D4 **Kayes** ◈ *region* SW Mali
Kayin State *see* Karen State
227 K4 **Kaynar** *var.* Kajnar. Vostochnyy Kazakhstan, E Kazakhstan 49°13'N 77°27'E
Kaynary *see* Căinari
138 E2 **Kayoya** Western, W Zambia 16°13'S 24°09'E
Kayrakkum *see* Qayroqqum
Kayrakkumskoye Vodokhranilishche *see* Qayroqqum, Obanbori
167 M6 **Kaysersberg** Alsace, France 48°08'N 7°15'E
214 F6 **Kayseri** *var.* Kaisaria; *anc.* Caesarea Mazaca, Mazaca. Kayseri, C Turkey 38°42'N 35°28'E
214 F6 **Kayseri** *var.* Kaisaria. ◈ *province* C Turkey
79 H2 **Kaysville** Utah, W USA 41°10'N 111°55'W
192 G4 **Kayyerkan** Taymyrskiy (Dolgano-Nenetskiy) Avtonomnyy Okrug, N Russian Federation 69°26'N 87°31'E
Kayyngdy *see* Kaindy
62 F2 **Kazabazua** Québec, SE Canada 45°58'N 76°00'W
62 F3 **Kazabazua** ⁓ Québec, SE Canada
193 J4 **Kazach'ye** Respublika Sakha (Yakutiya), NE Russian Federation 70°38'N 135°54'E
Kazakdar'ya *see* Qozoqdaryo
228 C5 **Kazakhlyshor, Solonchak** *var.* Solonchak Shorkazakhly. *salt marsh* NW Turkmenistan
Kazakhskaya SSR/Kazakh Soviet Socialist Republic *see* Kazakhstan
227 I4 **Kazakhskiy Melkosopochnik** *Eng.* Kazakh Uplands, Kirghiz Steppe, *Kaz.* Saryarqa. *uplands* C Kazakhstan
227 H5 **Kazakhstan** *off.* Republic of Kazakhstan, *var.* Kazakstan, *Kaz.* Qazaqstan, Qazaqstan Respublikasy; *prev.* Kazakh Soviet Socialist Republic, *Rus.* Kazakhskaya SSR. ◆ *republic* C Asia
Kazakhstan, Republic of *see* Kazakhstan
Kazakh Uplands *see* Kazakhskiy Melkosopochnik
Kazakstan *see* Kazakhstan
226 F6 **Kazalinsk** Kzyl-Orda, S Kazakhstan 45°45'N 62°01'E
197 J2 **Kazan'** Respublika Tatarstan, W Russian Federation 55°43'N 49°07'E
55 I4 **Kazan** ⁓ Nunavut, NW Canada
197 J2 **Kazan'** ✕ Respublika Tatarstan, W Russian Federation 55°46'N 49°21'E
Kazandzhik *see* Bereket
189 I6 **Kazanka** Mykolayivs'ka Oblast', S Ukraine 47°49'N 32°50'E
Kazanketken *see* Qozonketkan
Kazanlik *see* Kazanlŭk
185 K6 **Kazanlŭk** *prev.* Kazanlik. Stara Zagorat, C Bulgaria 42°38'N 25°24'E
251 N10 **Kazan-rettō** *Eng.* Volcano Islands. *island group* SE Japan
55 I3 **Kazan River** ⁓ Nunavut, N Canada
227 H1 **Kazanskoye** Tyumenskaya Oblast', C Russian Federation 55°39'N 69°06'E
189 I8 **Kazantip, Mys** *headland* S Ukraine 45°27'N 35°50'E
229 K5 **Kazarman** Narynskaya Oblast', C Kyrgyzstan 41°21'N 74°03'E
Kazatin *see* Kozyatyn
Kazbegi *see* Kazbek
Kazbegi *see* Qazbegi
215 K3 **Kazbek** *var.* Kazbegi, *Geor.* Mqinvartsveri. ▲ N Georgia 42°43'N 44°28'E
137 B12 **Kazembe** Eastern, NE Zambia 12°06'S 32°45'E
222 F7 **Kāzerūn** Fārs, S Iran 29°41'N 51°38'E
193 J8 **Kazhym** Respublika Komi, NW Russian Federation 60°19'N 51°26'E
Kazi Ahmad *see* Qāzi Ahmad
Kazi Magomed *see* Qazımämmäd
214 E7 **Kazımkarabekir** Karaman, S Turkey 37°13'N 32°58'E
188 A5 **Kazincbarcika** Borsod-Abaúj-Zemplén, NE Hungary 48°15'N 20°40'E
191 E10 **Kazlowshchyna** *Pol.* Kozlowszczyzna, *Rus.* Kozlovshchina. Hrodzyenskaya Voblasts', W Belarus 53°19'N 25°18'E
191 D9 **Kazlų Rūda** Marijampolė, S Lithuania 54°45'N 23°28'E
226 B3 **Kaztalovka** Zapadnyy Kazakhstan. W Kazakhstan 49°45'N 48°42'E
135 F10 **Kazumba** Kasai Occidental, S Dem. Rep. Congo 06°25'S 22°02'E
253 D8 **Kazuno** Akita, Honshū, C Japan 40°14'N 140°48'E
Kazvin *see* Qazvīn
191 F8 **Kaz'yany** *Rus.* Koz'yany. Vitsyebskaya Voblasts', NW Belarus 55°18'N 26°52'E
195 M5 **Kazym** Yamalo-Nenetskiy Avtonomyy Okrug, Russian federation
195 M5 **Kazym** ⁓ N Russian Federation
195 M5 **Kazym** ⁓ Yamalo-Nenetskiy Avtonomyy Okrug, Russian federation
195 M4 **Kazym-Mys** Yamalo-Nenetskiy Avtonomyy Okrug, Russian federation
182 E5 **Kcynia** *Ger.* Exin. Kujawsko-pomorskie, C Poland 53°00'N 17°29'E
Kéa *see* Tziá
82 D3 **Kea'au** *var.* Keaau. Hawai'i, USA, C Pacific Ocean 19°36'N 155°01'W
Keaau *see* Kea'au
158 B8 **Keadew** Roscommon, Ireland 54°03'N 8°08'W
158 D7 **Keady** UK 54°15'N 6°42'W
82 C3 **Keāhole Point** *var.* Keahole Point. *headland* Hawai'i, USA, C Pacific Ocean 19°43'N 156°03'W
82 D3 **Kealakekua** Hawai'i, USA, C Pacific Ocean 19°31'N 155°56'W
82 D3 **Kea, Mauna** ▲ Hawaii, USA 19°50'N 155°30'W
79 J6 **Keams** Arizona, SW USA 35°47'N 110°09'W
Kéamu *see* Aneityum
75 D8 **Kearney** Nebraska, C USA 40°42'N 99°06'W
79 H2 **Kearns** Utah, W USA 40°39'N 112°00'W
187 I7 **Kéas, Stenó** *strait* SE Greece
215 H6 **Keban Barajı** *dam* C Turkey
215 H6 **Keban Barajı** ⊠ C Turkey
133 J5 **Kebbi** ◈ *state* NW Nigeria
132 B4 **Kébémèr** NW Senegal 15°24'N 16°25'W
131 K2 **Kebili** *var.* Qibilī. C Tunisia 33°42'N 09°06'E
216 C3 **Kebir, Nahr el** ⁓ NW Syria
134 G2 **Kebkabiya** Northern Darfur, W Sudan 13°39'N 24°05'E
152 F5 **Kebnekaise** ▲ N Sweden 68°01'N 18°24'E
136 G5 **K'ebrī Dehar** Somali, E Ethiopia 06°43'N 44°15'E
230 D9 **Kech** ⁓ SW Pakistan
54 C5 **Kechika** ⁓ British Columbia, W Canada
187 N6 **Keçiborlu** Isparta, Turkey 37°56'N 30°18'E
183 G12 **Kecskemét** Bács-Kiskun, C Hungary 46°54'N 19°42'E
258 D2 **Kedah** ◈ *state* Peninsular Malaysia
191 D8 **Kėdainiai** Kaunas, C Lithuania 55°19'N 24°00'E
Kedder *see* Kehra
59 I7 **Kedgwick** New Brunswick, SE Canada 47°38'N 67°21'W
259 I9 **Kediri** Jawa, C Indonesia 07°45'S 112°01'E
261 L5 **Kedir Sarmi** Papua, E Indonesia 02°00'S 139°01'E
132 C5 **Kédougou** SE Senegal 12°35'N 12°09'W
192 F7 **Kedrovyy** Tomskaya Oblast', C Russian Federation 57°31'N 79°45'E
183 F8 **Kędzierzyn-Kozle** *Ger.* Heydebrech. Opolskie, S Poland 50°20'N 18°12'E
50 E5 **Keele** ⁓ Northwest Territories, NW Canada
52 E5 **Keele Peak** ▲ Yukon Territory, NW Canada 63°31'N 130°21'W
80 F7 **Keeler** California, USA 36°29'N 117°52'W
54 D2 **Keele River** ⁓ Northwest Territories, NW Canada
Keelung *see* Chilung
63 I8 **Keene** California, USA 35°13'N 118°34'W
65 K1 **Keene** New Hampshire, NE USA 42°56'N 72°14'W
163 E10 **Keerbergen** Vlaams Brabant, C Belgium 51°01'N 04°39'E
140 D4 **Keetmanshoop** Karas, S Namibia 26°36'S 18°08'E
55 K9 **Keewatin** Ontario, S Canada 49°47'N 94°30'W
74 H3 **Keewatin** Minnesota, N USA 47°24'N 93°04'W
53 H7 **Keewatin** ◈ *district* Northwest Territories, NE Canada
Kefallinía *see* Kefallonía
186 E6 **Kefallonía** *var.* Kefallinía. *island* Iónioi Nísoi, Greece, C Mediterranean Sea
187 K8 **Kéfalos** Kos, Dodekánisa, Greece, Aegean Sea 36°44'N 26°58'E
260 E8 **Kefamenanu** Timor, C Indonesia 09°31'S 124°29'E
218 D6 **Kefar Bin Nun** Israel
219 D8 **Kefar Menaḥem** Israel
216 B6 **Kefar Sava** *var.* Kfar Saba. Central, C Israel 32°11'N 34°58'E
219 D8 **Kefar Shemu'el** Israel
Kefe *see* Feodosiya
133 K7 **Keffi** Nassarawa, C Nigeria 08°52'N 07°54'E
152 B2 **Keflavík** Reykjanes, W Iceland 64°01'N 22°35'W
152 B3 **Keflavík** ✕ (Reykjavík) Reykjanes, W Iceland 63°58'N 22°37'W
Kegalee *see* Kegalla
235 G10 **Kegalla** *var.* Kegalee, Kegalle. Sabaragamuwa Province, C Sri Lanka 07°14'N 80°21'E
Kegalle *see* Kegalla
Kegayli *see* Kegeyli
Kegel *see* Keila
227 L7 **Kegen** Almaty, SE Kazakhstan 42°58'N 79°12'E
228 E4 **Kegeyli** *Rus.* Kegayli. Qoraqalpoghiston Respublikasi, W Uzbekistan 42°46'N 59°49'E
59 I2 **Keglo Bay** *coastal sea feature* Québec, E Canada
181 I3 **Kegworth** UK 52°49'N 1°16'W
179 C12 **Kehl** Baden-Württemberg, SW Germany 48°34'N 07°49'E
190 E3 **Kehra** *Ger.* Kedder. Harjumaa, NW Estonia 59°19'N 25°21'E
181 C11 **Kehrig** Rheinland-Pfalz, Germany 7°13'N 50°17'E
189 K4 **Kehychivka** Kharkivs'ka Oblast', E Ukraine 49°18'N 35°46'E
159 J8 **Keighley** UK 53°53'N 1°55'W
Kei Islands *see* Kai, Kepulauan
Keijō *see* Sŏul
190 D3 **Keila** *Ger.* Kegel. Harjumaa, NW Estonia 59°18'N 24°29'E
Keilberg *see* Klínovec
140 E6 **Keimoes** Northern Cape, South Africa 28°42'S 20°58'E
138 E8 **Keimoes** Northern Cape, W South Africa 28°41'S 20°59'E
Keina/Keinis *see* Käina
261 L7 **Keisak** Papua, E Indonesia 07°01'S 140°02'E
Keishū *see* Kyŏngju
133 J4 **Keïta** Tahoua, C Niger 14°45'N 05°40'E
134 F3 **Kéita, Bahr** *var.* Doka. ⁓ S Chad
153 H8 **Keitele** ◎ C Finland
277 H6 **Keith** South Australia 36°01'S 140°22'E
156 G5 **Keith** NE Scotland, UK 57°33'N 02°57'W
54 E2 **Keith Arm** ◎ Northwest Territories, NW Canada
75 C9 **Keith Sebelius Lake** ⊠ Kansas, C USA
76 B6 **Keizer** Oregon, NW USA 44°59'N 123°01'W
82 A1 **Kekaha** Kaua'i, Hawai'i, USA 21°58'N 159°43'W
229 L6 **Këk-Art** *prev.* Alaykel', Alay-Kuu. Oshskaya Oblast', SW Kyrgyzstan 40°16'N 74°21'E
229 L5 **Këk-Aygyr** *var.* Keyaygyr. Narynskaya Oblast', C Kyrgyzstan 40°42'N 75°37'E
229 L5 **Këk-Dzhar** Narynskaya Oblast', C Kyrgyzstan 41°28'N 74°48'E
278 F8 **Kekerengu** Canterbury, South Island, New Zealand 41°55'S 174°05'E
53 L7 **Kekertaluk Island** *island* Nunavut, NE Canada
183 G11 **Kékes** ▲ N Hungary 47°53'N 19°59'E
260 E8 **Kekneno, Gunung** ▲ Timor, S Indonesia
229 K5 **Këk-Tash** *Kir.* Kök-Tash. Dzhalal-Abadskaya Oblast', W Kyrgyzstan 41°08'N 72°25'E
136 G5 **K'elafo** Somali, E Ethiopia 05°36'N 44°12'E
258 L4 **Kelai, Sungai** ⁓ Borneo, N Indonesia
Kelamayi *see* Karamay
Kelang *see* Klang
258 E2 **Kelantan** ◈ *state* Peninsular Malaysia
Kelantan *see* Kelantan, Sungai
258 E2 **Kelantan, Sungai** *var.* Kelantan. ⁓ Peninsular Malaysia
Kelat *see* Kalāt
181 J8 **Kelbra** Sachsen-Anhalt, Germany 11°02'N 51°25'E
Kelcyra *see* Këlcyrë
184 F9 **Këlcyrë** *var.* Kelcyra. Gjirokastër, S Albania 40°19'N 20°10'E
159 J7 **Keld** UK 54°24'N 2°10'W
159 L10 **Kelham** UK 53°05'N 0°51'W
Kelifskiy Uzboy *see* Kelifskiy Uzboýy
228 G8 **Kelifskiy Uzboýy** *Rus.* Kelifskiy Uzboy. *salt marsh* Lebap Welaýaty, E Turkmenistan
181 E11 **Kelkheim** Hessen, Germany 8°27'N 50°08'E
215 H5 **Kelkit** Gümüşhane, NE Turkey 40°07'N 39°28'E
214 G5 **Kelkit Çayı** ⁓ N Turkey
181 C13 **Kell** Rheinland-Pfalz, Germany 6°50'N 49°38'E
134 C7 **Kéllé** Cuvette-Quest, W Congo 0°04'S 14°33'E
133 J4 **Kellé** Zinder, S Niger 14°10'N 10°10'E
180 J1 **Kellenhusen** Schleswig-Holstein, Germany 11°04'N 54°11'E
54 E3 **Keller Lake** ◎ Northwest Territories, NW Canada
227 H2 **Kellerovka** Severnyy Kazakhstan, N Kazakhstan 53°51'N 69°15'E
52 E4 **Kellett Strait** *Sea waterway* Northwest Territories, NW Canada
52 D5 **Kellett, Cape** *headland* Banks Island, Northwest Territories, NW Canada 71°57'N 125°55'W
73 I9 **Kelleys Island** *island* Ohio, N USA
76 F4 **Kellogg** Idaho, NW USA 47°30'N 116°07'W
152 I5 **Kelloselkä** Lappi, N Finland 66°56'N 28°52'E
158 D9 **Kells** *Ir.* Ceanannas. Meath, E Ireland 53°44'N 06°53'W
190 C7 **Kelmė** Šiaulai, C Lithuania 55°39'N 22°57'E
163 H10 **Kelmis** *var.* La Calamine. Liège, E Belgium 50°43'N 06°01'E
134 D4 **Kélo** Tandjilé, SW Chad 09°21'N 15°50'E
138 F1 **Kelongwa** North Western, NW Zambia 13°41'S 26°19'E
56 F8 **Kelowna** British Columbia, SW Canada 49°50'N 119°29'W
55 J7 **Kelsey** Manitoba, C Canada 56°02'N 96°31'W
80 B1 **Kelseyville** California, W USA 38°58'N 122°51'W
159 J4 **Kelso** SE Scotland, UK 55°36'N 02°27'W
81 H10 **Kelso** California, USA 35°01'N 115°39'W
76 C5 **Kelso** Washington, NW USA 46°09'N 122°54'W
181 F11 **Kelsterbach** Hessen, Germany 8°32'N 50°04'E
293 L8 **Keltie, Cape** *headland* Antarctica
Keltsy *see* Kielce
159 H3 **Kelty** UK 56°08'N 3°23'W
258 E4 **Keluang** *var.* Kluang. Johor, Peninsular Malaysia 02°01'N 103°18'E
258 F5 **Kelume** Pulau Lingga, W Indonesia 0°12'S 104°27'E
161 L5 **Kelvedon** UK 51°50'N 0°43'E
55 H9 **Kelvington** Saskatchewan, S Canada 52°10'N 103°30'W
194 E5 **Kem'** Respublika Kareliya, NW Russian Federation 64°55'N 34°18'E
194 E5 **Kem'** ⁓ NW Russian Federation
215 H6 **Kemah** Erzincan, E Turkey 39°35'N 39°02'E
215 H6 **Kemaliye** Erzincan, C Turkey 39°16'N 38°29'E
214 B7 **Kemalpasa** İzmir, Turkey 38°26'N 27°25'E
Kemaman *see* Cukai
Kemanlar *see* Isperikh
56 B4 **Kemano** British Columbia, SW Canada 53°39'N 127°58'W
Kemarat *see* Khemmarat
260 E4 **Kembani** Pulau Peleng, N Indonesia 01°32'S 122°57'E
161 H6 **Kemble** UK 51°41'N 2°01'W
214 C8 **Kemer** Antalya, SW Turkey 36°39'N 30°33'E
214 F7 **Kemerovo** *prev.* Shcheglovsk. Kemerovskaya Oblast', C Russian Federation 55°25'N 86°05'E
192 G7 **Kemerovskaya Oblast'** ◈ *province* S Russian Federation
152 H6 **Kemi** Lappi, NW Finland 65°46'N 24°34'E
152 H5 **Kemijärvi** *Swe.* Kemiträsk. Lappi, N Finland 66°41'N 27°24'E
152 I5 **Kemijärvi** ◎ N Finland
152 H6 **Kemijoki** ⁓ NW Finland
229 L4 **Kemin** *prev.* Bystrovka. Chuyskaya Oblast', N Kyrgyzstan
152 H6 **Keminmaa** Lappi, NW Finland 65°49'N 24°34'E
Kemins Island *see* Nikumaroro
Kemiö *see* Kimito
Kemiträsk *see* Kemijärvi
197 I2 **Kemlya** Respublika Mordoviya, W Russian Federation 54°42'N 45°16'E
163 B10 **Kemmel** West-Vlaanderen, W Belgium 50°42'N 02°51'E
77 J9 **Kemmerer** Wyoming, C USA 41°47'N 110°32'W
Kemmuna *see* Comino
134 E5 **Kémo** ◈ *prefecture* S Central African Republic
71 H5 **Kemp** Texas, SW USA 32°26'N 96°13'W
195 L5 **Kempazh** ⁓ Khanty-Mansiyskiy Avtonomnyy Okrug, Russian federation
152 H7 **Kempele** Oulu, C Finland 64°56'N 25°26'E
181 B8 **Kempen** Nordrhein-Westfalen, W Germany 51°22'N 06°25'E
70 F3 **Kemp, Lake** ◎ Texas, SW USA
293 K3 **Kemp Land** *physical region* Antarctica
70 G6 **Kempner** Texas, SW USA 31°03'N 98°01'W
90 E3 **Kemp's Bay** Andros Island, W Bahamas 24°02'N 77°32'W
277 M4 **Kempsey** New South Wales, SE Australia 31°05'S 152°50'E
161 J4 **Kempston** UK 52°06'N 0°29'W
179 E13 **Kempten** Bayern, S Germany 47°44'N 10°19'E
62 G1 **Kempt, Lac** ◎ Québec, SE Canada
277 J10 **Kempton** Tasmania, SE Australia 42°34'S 147°13'E
141 J4 **Kempton Park** Gauteng, South Africa 26°06'S 28°15'E
232 F7 **Ken** ⁓ C India
83 I6 **Kenai** Alaska, USA 60°33'N 151°15'W
42 C3 **Kenai Mountains** ▲ Alaska, USA
83 I7 **Kenai Peninsula** *peninsula* Alaska, USA
67 L7 **Kenansville** North Carolina, SE USA 34°57'N 77°54'W
228 A6 **Kenar** *prev. Rus.* Ufra. Balkan Welaýaty, NW Turkmenistan 40°00'N 53°05'E
140 E6 **Kenardt** Northern Cape, South Africa 29°21'S 21°09'E
220 A1 **Kenāyis, Rās el-** *headland* N Egypt 31°13'N 27°53'E
159 I7 **Kendal** NW England, UK 54°20'N 02°45'W
69 N9 **Kendall** Florida, SE USA 25°39'N 80°18'W
53 K3 **Kendall, Cape** *headland* Nunavut, E Canada
83 K2 **Kendall Island** *island* Northwest Territories, NW Canada
64 G7 **Kendall Park** New Jersey, NE USA 40°25'N 74°33'W
73 F9 **Kendallville** Indiana, N USA 41°24'N 85°10'W
260 E6 **Kendari** Sulawesi, C Indonesia 03°57'S 122°36'E
258 H6 **Kendawangan** Borneo, C Indonesia 02°32'S 110°13'E
259 I8 **Kendeng, Pegunungan** ▲ Jawa, S Indonesia
234 J4 **Kendrāpāra** *var.* Kendraparha. Orissa, E India 20°29'N 86°25'E
Kendraparha *see* Kendrāpāra
234 I3 **Kendujhargarh** *prev.* Keonjhargarh. Orissa, E India 21°38'N 85°40'E
70 G8 **Kenedy** Texas, SW USA 28°49'N 97°51'W
Kënekesir *see* Kënekesir
132 D7 **Kenema** SE Sierra Leone 07°55'N 11°12'W
Këneurgench *see* Këneurgench
160 F6 **Kenfig** UK 51°31'N 3°44'W
135 D9 **Kenge** Bandundu, SW Dem. Rep. Congo 04°52'S 16°59'E
Kengen *see* Kangen
256 E4 **Keng Tung** *var.* Kentung. Shan State, E Myanmar (Burma) 21°18'N 99°36'E
138 E8 **Kenhardt** Northern Cape, W South Africa 29°19'S 21°08'E
132 D5 **Kéniéba** Kayes, W Mali 12°47'N 11°16'W
141 H6 **Kenilworth** Northern Cape, South Africa 28°43'S 24°47'E
161 I4 **Kenilworth** UK 52°21'N 1°35'W
Kenimekh *see* Konimex
258 K2 **Keningau** Sabah, East Malaysia 05°21'N 116°11'E
130 F2 **Kénitra** *prev.* Port-Lyautey. NW Morocco 34°20'N 06°29'W
158 G5 **Ken, Loch** ◎ UK
67 K6 **Kenly** North Carolina, SE USA 35°39'N 78°16'W
157 B11 **Kenmare** *Ir.* Neidín. Kerry, S Ireland 51°53'N 09°35'W
74 B1 **Kenmare** North Dakota, N USA 48°40'N 102°04'W
157 A11 **Kenmare River** *Ir.* An Ribhéar. *inlet* NE Atlantic Ocean
159 H1 **Kenmore** UK 56°34'N 3°59'W
64 A1 **Kenmore** New York, NE USA 42°58'N 78°52'W
71 I5 **Kennard** Texas, SW USA 31°21'N 95°10'W
74 C5 **Kennebec** South Dakota, N USA 43°53'N 99°51'W
63 K4 **Kennebec River** ⁓ Maine, NE USA
63 J5 **Kennebunk** Maine, NE USA 43°22'N 70°33'W
53 J2 **Kennedy Channel** *Sea waterway*
83 I7 **Kennedy Entrance** *strait* Alaska, USA
256 B3 **Kennedy Peak** ▲ W Myanmar (Burma) 23°18'N 93°52'E
68 E4 **Kenner** Louisiana, S USA 29°57'N 90°15'W
274 D5 **Kenneth Range** ▲ Western Australia
75 J11 **Kennett** Missouri, C USA 36°15'N 90°04'W
64 F8 **Kennett Square** Pennsylvania, NE USA 39°50'N 75°40'W
76 E5 **Kennewick** Washington, NW USA 46°12'N 119°08'W
161 M4 **Kenninghall** UK 52°26'N 1°00'E
161 J7 **Kennington** UK 51°09'N 0°52'E
58 D6 **Kenogami** ⁓ Ontario, S Canada
72 J2 **Kenogami Lake** Ontario, S Canada 48°04'N 80°10'W
62 I2 **Kenogamissi Lake** ◎ Ontario, S Canada
54 B2 **Keno Hill** Yukon Territory, NW Canada 63°54'N 135°18'W
55 K9 **Kenora** Ontario, S Canada 49°47'N 94°26'W
73 D8 **Kenosha** Wisconsin, N USA 42°34'N 87°50'W
59 J8 **Kensington** Prince Edward Island, SE Canada 46°26'N 63°39'W
75 D9 **Kensington** Kansas, C USA 39°46'N 99°01'W
76 D6 **Kent** Oregon, NW USA 45°14'N 120°43'W
70 C5 **Kent** Texas, SW USA 31°03'N 104°13'W
76 C4 **Kent** Washington, NW USA 47°22'N 122°13'W
161 L7 **Kent** *cultural region* SE England, UK
227 H7 **Kentau** Yuzhnyy Kazakhstan, S Kazakhstan 43°28'N 68°41'E
161 L4 **Kentford** UK 52°16'N 0°30'E
65 I4 **Kent Furnace** Connecticut, USA 41°44'N 73°28'W
277 K8 **Kent Group** *island group* Tasmania, SE Australia
73 E10 **Kentland** Indiana, N USA 40°46'N 87°26'W
73 H10 **Kenton** Ohio, N USA 40°39'N 83°36'W
52 F8 **Kent Peninsula** *peninsula* Nunavut, N Canada
186 G3 **Kentrikí Makedonía** *Eng.* Macedonia Central. ◈ *region* N Greece
159 I7 **Kent** ⁓ UK
66 F4 **Kentucky** *off.* Commonwealth of Kentucky, *also known as* Bluegrass State. ◈ *state* C USA
66 C5 **Kentucky Lake** ⊠ Kentucky/Tennessee, S USA
Kentung *see* Keng Tung
63 N3 **Kentville** Nova Scotia, SE Canada 45°04'N 64°30'W
68 E3 **Kentwood** Louisiana, S USA 30°56'N 90°30'W
73 F8 **Kentwood** Michigan, N USA 42°52'N 85°33'W
136 E7 **Kenya** *off.* Republic of Kenya. ◆ *republic* E Africa
Kenya, Mount *see* Kirinyaga
Kenya, Republic of *see* Kenya
258 E2 **Kenyir, Tasik** *var.* Tasek Kenyir. ◎ Peninsular Malaysia
73 A10 **Keokuk** Iowa, C USA 40°24'N 91°22'W
Keonjhargarh *see* Kendujhargarh
Kéos *see* Tziá
73 A10 **Keosauqua** Iowa, C USA 40°43'N 91°58'W
73 A9 **Keota** Iowa, C USA 41°21'N 91°57'W
66 G7 **Keowee, Lake** ⊠ South Carolina, SE USA
194 E5 **Kepa** *var.* Kepe. Respublika Kareliya, NW Russian Federation 65°09'N 32°15'E
Kepe *see* Kepa
283 K2 **Kepirohi Falls** *waterfall* Pohnpei, E Micronesia
278 B12 **Kepler Mountains** ▲ South Island, New Zealand
182 E7 **Kępno** Wielkopolskie, C Poland 51°17'N 17°57'E
190 G3 **Kepor'e** Leningradskaya Oblast', Russian Federation
117 H10 **Keppel Island** *island* N Falkland Islands
117 H10 **Keppel Sound** *sound* N Falkland Islands
214 B5 **Kepsut** Balıkesir, NW Turkey 39°41'N 28°09'E
261 J6 **Kerai** Papua, E Indonesia 03°53'S 134°30'E
Kerak *see* Al Karak
235 E9 **Kerala** ◈ *state* S India
261 N6 **Keram** ⁓ N Papua New Guinea
251 H10 **Kerama-rettō** *island group* SW Japan
277 I6 **Kerang** Victoria, SE Australia 35°46'S 144°01'E
Kerasunt *see* Giresun
187 H6 **Keratéa** *var.* Keratea. Attikí, C Greece 37°48'N 23°58'E
Keratea *see* Keratéa
153 H10 **Kerava** *Swe.* Kervo. Etelä-Suomi, S Finland 60°25'N 25°10'E
Kerbala/Kerbela *see* Karbalā'
76 B8 **Kerby** Oregon, NW USA 42°10'N 123°39'W
189 L8 **Kerch** *Rus.* Kerch'. Respublika Krym, SE Ukraine 45°22'N 36°30'E
Kerch' *see* Kerch
Kerchens'ka Protska/Kerchenskiy Proliv *see* Kerch Strait
189 L9 **Kerchens'kyy Pivostriv** *peninsula* S Ukraine
189 L9 **Kerch Strait** *var.* Bosporus Cimmerius, Enikale Strait, *Rus.* Kerchenskiy Proliv, *Ukr.* Kerchens'ka Protska. *strait* Black Sea/Sea of Azov
232 F4 **Kerdārnāth** Uttaranchal, N India 30°44'N 79°03'E
Kerdilio *see* Kerdýlio
187 H3 **Kerdýlio** *var.* Kerdilio. ▲ N Greece 40°46'N 23°37'E
280 B4 **Kerema** Gulf, S Papua New Guinea 07°59'S 145°46'E
Keremitlik *see* Lyulyakovo
214 E4 **Kerempe Burnu** *headland* N Turkey 42°01'N 33°20'E
136 E1 **Keren** *var.* Cheren. C Eritrea 15°45'N 38°22'E
71 H5 **Kerens** Texas, SW USA 32°07'N 96°13'W
279 H4 **Kerepehi** Waikato, North Island, New Zealand 37°18'S 175°33'E
227 H4 **Kerey, Ozero** ◎ C Kazakhstan
Kergel *see* Kärla
289 E12 **Kerguelen** *island* C French Southern and Antarctic Territories
289 F13 **Kerguelen Plateau** *undersea feature* S Indian Ocean
65 H4 **Kerhonkson** New York, USA 41°46'N 74°18'W
186 E7 **Kerí** Zákynthos, Iónioi Nísoi, Greece, C Mediterranean Sea 37°40'N 20°48'E
137 C8 **Kericho** Rift Valley, W Kenya 0°22'S 35°19'E
278 F2 **Kerikeri** Northland, North Island, New Zealand 35°14'S 173°58'E
153 J8 **Kerimäki** Isä-Suomi, E Finland 61°56'N 29°18'E
258 E6 **Kerinci, Danau** ◎ Sumatera, W Indonesia
258 D6 **Kerinci, Gunung** ▲ Sumatera, W Indonesia 02°00'S 101°40'E
Keriya *see* Yutian
238 D5 **Keriya He** ⁓ NW China
162 F5 **Kerkbuurt** Noord-Holland, C Netherlands 52°29'N 05°08'E
162 F7 **Kerkdriel** Gelderland, C Netherlands 51°46'N 05°21'E
131 L2 **Kerkenah, Îles de** *var.* Kerkenna Islands, *Ar.* Juzur Qarqannah. *island group* E Tunisia
Kerkenna Islands *see* Kerkenah, Îles de
187 K6 **Kerketévs** ▲ Sámos, Dodekánisa, Greece, Aegean Sea 37°44'N 26°39'E
74 F4 **Kerkhoven** Minnesota, N USA 45°12'N 95°18'W
Kerki *see* Atamyrat
Kerkichi *see* Kerkiçi
228 G7 **Kerkiçi** *Rus.* Kerkichi. Lebap Welaýaty, E Turkmenistan 37°46'N 65°18'E
186 G4 **Kerkíneo** *prehistoric site* Thessalía, C Greece
187 H2 **Kerkíni, Límni** *var.* Kerkinitis Limni. ◎ N Greece
Kérkira *see* Kérkyra
163 H10 **Kerkrade** Limburg, SE Netherlands 50°53'N 06°04'E
Kerkuk *see* Kirkük
186 E4 **Kérkyra** *var.* Kérkira, *Eng.* Corfu. Kérkyra, Iónioi Nísoi, Greece, C Mediterranean Sea 39°37'N 19°56'E
186 E4 **Kérkyra** ✕ Kérkyra, Iónioi Nísoi, Greece, C Mediterranean Sea 39°36'N 19°55'E
186 D4 **Kérkyra** *var.* Kérkira, *Eng.* Corfu. *island* Iónioi Nísoi, Greece, C Mediterranean Sea
286 F7 **Kermadec Islands** *island group* New Zealand, SW Pacific Ocean
267 J7 **Kermadec Ridge** *undersea feature* SW Pacific Ocean
267 J7 **Kermadec Trench** *undersea feature* SW Pacific Ocean
223 I7 **Kermān** *var.* Kirman; *anc.* Carmana. Kermān, C Iran 30°18'N 57°05'E
80 D5 **Kerman** California, USA 36°43'N 120°04'W
223 H7 **Kermān** *off.* Ostān-e Kermān, *var.* Kirman; *anc.* Carmania. ◈ *province* SE Iran
223 J8 **Kermān, Bībān-e** *desert* SE Iran
Kermān, Ostān-e *see* Kermān
222 G6 **Kermānshāh** *var.* Qahremānshahr; *prev.* Bākhtarān. Kermānshāhān, W Iran 34°19'N 47°04'E
222 D4 **Kermānshāh** Yazd, C Iran 34°19'N 47°04'E

◆ Country
● Country Capital
◇ Dependent Territory
○ Dependent Territory Capital
◈ Administrative Regions
✕ International Airport
▲ Mountain
▲ Mountain Range
⩘ Volcano
⁓ River
◎ Lake
⊠ Reservoir

INDEX

◆ Country   ◇ Dependent Territory   ◈ Administrative Regions   ▲ Mountain   ♦ Volcano   ◎ Lake
● Country Capital   ○ Dependent Territory Capital   ✈ International Airport   ▲ Mountain Range   ♒ River   ▢ Reservoir

◆ Country   ◇ Dependent Territory   ✈ Administrative Regions   ▲ Mountain   ▲ Volcano   ◎ Lake
● Country Capital   ◇ Dependent Territory Capital   ✈ International Airport   ▲ Mountain Range   ✈ River   ◎ Reservoir

Kohgīlūyeh va Būyer Aḥmad - Kōthen
INDEX
361

222 F6 **Kohgīlūyeh va Būyer Aḥmad** *off.* Ostān-e Kohkīlūyeh va Būyer Aḥmadī, *var.* Boyer Ahmadī va Kohkīlūyeh. ◈ *province* SW Iran
190 E4 **Kohila** *Ger.* Koil. Raplamaa, NW Estonia 59°09′N 24°45′E
233 M6 **Kohīma** *state capital* Nāgāland, E India 25°40′N 94°08′E
Koh I Noh *see* Büyükağrı Dağı
Kohkīlūyeh va Būyer Aḥmadī, Ostān-e *see* Kohgīlūyeh va Būyer Aḥmad
Kohsān *see* Kūhestān
190 F3 **Kohtla-Järve** Ida-Virumaa, NE Estonia 59°22′N 27°21′E
Kôhu *see* Kōfu
87 M7 **Kohunlich** Quintana Roo, Mexico 18°25′N 88°48′W
188 F7 **Kohyl'nyk** *Rom.* Cogîlnic. ≈ Moldova/Ukraine
253 B11 **Koide** Niigata, Honshū, C Japan 37°13′N 138°58′E
54 A2 **Koidern** Yukon Territory, W Canada 61°55′N 140°22′W
132 D7 **Koidu** E Sierra Leone 08°40′N 11°01′W
190 E4 **Koigi** Järvamaa, C Estonia 58°51′N 25°45′E
Koil *see* Kohila
139 I9 **Koimbani** Grande Comore, NW Comoros 11°37′S 43°23′E
140 C7 **Koingnaas** Northern Cape, South Africa 30°12′S 17°17′E
217 J2 **Koi Sanjaq** *var.* Koysanjaq, Kūysanjaq. N Iraq 36°05′N 44°38′E
153 J8 **Koitere** ◎ E Finland
Koivisto *see* Primorsk
248 C7 **Kōje-do** *Jap.* Kyōsai-tō. *island* S South Korea
136 E4 **K'ok'a Hāyk'** ◎ C Ethiopia
276 F4 **Kokatha** South Australia 31°17′S 135°16′E
Kokchetav *see* Kokshetau
153 G9 **Kokemäenjoki** ≈ SW Finland
261 K6 **Kokenau** *var.* Kokonau. Papua, E Indonesia 04°38′S 136°24′E
140 D5 **Kokerboom** Karas, SE Namibia 28°11′S 19°25′E
191 H9 **Kokhanava** *Rus.* Kokhanovo. Vitsyebskaya Voblasts', NE Belarus 54°28′N 29°59′E
Kokhanovichi *see* Kakhanavichy
Kokhanovo *see* Kokhanava
Kök-Janggak *see* Kok-Yangak
152 G7 **Kokkola** *Swe.* Karleby; *prev. Swe.* Gamlakarleby. Länsi-Soumi, W Finland 63°50′N 23°10′E
190 E6 **Koknese** Aizkraukle, C Latvia 56°38′N 25°27′E
133 J6 **Koko** Kebbi, W Nigeria 11°25′N 04°33′E
280 C4 **Kokoda** Northern, S Papua New Guinea 08°52′S 147°44′E
132 D5 **Kokofata** Kayes, W Mali 12°48′N 09°56′W
82 G3 **Kokolik River** ≈ Alaska, USA
73 F10 **Kokomo** Indiana, N USA 40°29′N 86°07′W
Kokonau *see* Kokenau
Koko Nor *see* Qinghai, China
Koko Nor *see* Qinghai Hu, China
280 D2 **Kokopo** *var.* Kopopo; *prev.* Herbertshöhe. New Britain, E Papua New Guinea 04°18′S 152°17′E
227 L4 **Kokpekti** *Kaz.* Kökpekti. Semipalatinsk, E Kazakhstan 48°47′N 82°28′E
227 L4 **Kokpekti** ≈ E Kazakhstan
Kökpekti *see* Kokpekti
83 H5 **Kokrines** Alaska, USA 64°58′N 154°42′W
83 H4 **Kokrines Hills** ▲▲ Alaska, USA
227 H8 **Koksaray** Yuzhnyy Kazakhstan, S Kazakhstan 42°34′N 68°06′E
229 M5 **Kokshaal-Tau** *Rus.* Khrebet Kakshaal-Too. ▲▲ China/Kyrgyzstan
227 H2 **Kokshetau** *Kaz.* Kökshetaū; *prev.* Kokchetav. Kokshetau, N Kazakhstan 53°18′N 69°25′E
Kökshetaū *see* Kokshetau
163 A9 **Koksijde** West-Vlaanderen, W Belgium 51°07′N 02°40′E
51 J6 **Koksoak** ≈ Québec, E Canada
139 H8 **Kokstad** KwaZulu/Natal, E South Africa 30°23′S 29°23′E
227 L6 **Koksu** *Kaz.* Rūdnīchnyy. Almaty, SE Kazakhstan 44°39′N 78°57′E
227 L7 **Koktal** *Kaz.* Köktal. Almaty, SE Kazakhstan 44°05′N 79°44′E
227 H5 **Koktas** ≈ C Kazakhstan
Kök-Tash *see* Këk-Tash
Koktokay *see* Fuyun
250 C8 **Kokubu** Kagoshima, Kyūshū, SW Japan 31°45′N 130°45′E
193 J8 **Kokuy** Chitinskaya Oblast', S Russian Federation 52°13′N 117°18′E
229 K5 **Kok-Yangak** *Kir.* Kök-Janggak. Dzhalal-Abadskaya Oblast', W Kyrgyzstan 41°02′N 73°11′E
238 C6 **Kokyar** Xinjiang Uygur Zizhiqu, W China 37°24′N 77°15′E
230 F8 **Kolāchi** *var.* Kulachi. ≈ SW Pakistan
132 D7 **Kolahun** N Liberia 08°24′N 10°02′W
260 D6 **Kolaka** Sulawesi, C Indonesia 04°04′S 121°38′E
Kolam *see* Quilon
K'o-la-ma-i *see* Karamay
Kola Peninsula *see* Kol'skiy Poluostrov
234 F7 **Kolār** Karnātaka, E India 13°10′N 78°10′E
235 F8 **Kolār Gold Fields** Karnātaka, E India 12°56′N 78°16′E
152 G5 **Kolari** Lappi, NW Finland 67°20′N 23°51′E
183 E11 **Kolárovo** *Ger.* Gutta; *prev.* Guta, *Hung.* Gúta. Nitriansky Kraj, SW Slovakia 47°54′N 18°01′E
232 C5 **Kolāyat** Rājasthān, NW India 27°56′N 73°02′E
155 H8 **Kolbäck** Västmanland, C Sweden 59°33′N 16°15′E
Kolbcha *see* Kowbcha
295 L6 **Kolbeinsey Ridge** *undersea feature* Denmark Strait/Norwegian Sea
Kolberg *see* Kołobrzeg
154 E7 **Kolbotn** Akershus, S Norway 62°15′N 10°24′E
183 H8 **Kolbuszowa** Podkarpackie, SE Poland 50°12′N 22°07′E
190 I2 **Kolchanovo** Leningradskaya Oblast', Russian Federation
196 G1 **Kol'chugino** Vladimirskaya Oblast', W Russian Federation 56°19′N 39°24′E
132 B5 **Kolda** S Senegal 12°58′N 14°58′W
155 D12 **Kolding** Vejle, C Denmark 55°29′N 09°30′E
135 G9 **Kole** Kasai Oriental, SW Dem. Rep. Congo 03°30′S 22°28′E
134 H6 **Kole** Orientale, N Dem. Rep. Congo 02°08′N 25°25′E
Kōle *see* Kili Island
171 L9 **Koléa** Algeria
144 D4 **Kölen** ▲▲ Norway/Sweden
Kolepom, Pulau *see* Yos Sudarso, Pulau
190 E3 **Kolga Laht** *Ger.* Kolko-Wiek. *bay* N Estonia
195 I2 **Kolguyev, Ostrov** *island* NW Russian Federation
234 D6 **Kolhāpur** Mahārāshtra, SW India 16°42′N 74°13′E
235 C13 **Kolhumadulu Atoll** *atoll* S Maldives
153 J8 **Koli** *var.* Kolinkylä. Pohjois-Karjala, E Finland 63°06′N 29°46′E
83 H7 **Koliganek** Alaska, USA 59°43′N 157°16′W
183 C8 **Kolín** *Ger.* Kolin. Střední Čechy, C Czech Republic 50°02′N 15°10′E
Kolinkylä *see* Koli
284 A10 **Koliu** Île Futuna, W Wallis and Futuna
194 B9 **Kolka** Latvia
190 C5 **Kolka** Talsi, NW Latvia 57°44′N 22°34′E
190 C5 **Kolkasrags** *prev. Eng.* Cape Domesnes. *cape* NW Latvia
225 H9 **Kolkata** *prev.* Calcutta. *state capital* West Bengal, NE India 22°30′N 88°20′E
Kolkhozabad *see* Kolkhozobod
229 I8 **Kolkhozobod** *Rus.* Kolkhozabad; *prev.* Kaganovichabad, Tugalan. SW Tajikistan 37°33′N 68°34′E
Kolki/Kołki *see* Kolky
Kolko-Wiek *see* Kolga Laht
188 E2 **Kolky** *Pol.* Kołki, *Rus.* Kolki. Volyns'ka Oblast', NW Ukraine 51°05′N 25°40′E
Kollam *see* Quilon
235 E8 **Kollegāl** Karnātaka, W India 12°08′N 77°06′E
162 H3 **Kollum** Friesland, N Netherlands 53°17′N 06°09′E
Kolmar *see* Colmar
181 C9 **Köln** *var.* Koeln, *Eng./Fr.* Cologne, *prev.* Cöln; *anc.* Colonia Agrippina, Oppidum Ubiorum. Nordrhein-Westfalen, W Germany 50°57′N 06°57′E
182 H4 **Kolno** Podlaskie, NE Poland 53°24′N 21°57′E
182 F6 **Koło** Wielkopolskie, C Poland 52°11′N 18°39′E
82 B1 **Kōloa** *var.* Koloa. Kaua'i, Hawai'i, USA 21°54′N 159°28′W
Koloa *see* Kōloa
182 D4 **Kołobrzeg** *Ger.* Kolberg. Zachodnio-pomorskie, NW Poland 54°11′N 15°34′E
196 E2 **Kolodnya** Smolenskaya Oblast', W Russian Federation 54°57′N 32°22′E
284 A10 **Kolofau, Mont** Ѫ Île Alofi, S Wallis and Futuna 14°21′S 178°02′W
195 H9 **Kologriv** Kostromskaya Oblast', NW Russian Federation 58°49′N 44°22′E
132 E5 **Kolokani** Koulikoro, W Mali 13°35′N 08°01′W
132 F6 **Koloko** W Burkina 11°06′N 05°18′W
281 H2 **Kolombangara** *var.* Kilimbangara, Nduke. *island* New Georgia Islands, NW Solomon Islands
Kolomea *see* Kolomyya
196 G2 **Kolomna** Moskovskaya Oblast', W Russian Federation 55°03′N 38°52′E
188 D5 **Kolomyya** *Ger.* Kolomea. Ivano-Frankivs'ka Oblast', W Ukraine 48°31′N 25°00′E
132 E6 **Kolondiéba** Sikasso, SW Mali 11°04′N 06°55′W
284 E9 **Kolonga** Tongatapu, S Tonga 21°07′S 175°05′W
283 J1 **Kolonia** *var.* Colonia. Pohnpei, E Micronesia 06°57′N 158°12′E
Kolonja *see* Kolonjë
184 F9 **Kolonjë** *var.* Kolonja. Fier, C Albania 40°49′N 19°37′E
Kolonjë *see* Ersekë
Kolotambu *see* Avuavu
260 E6 **Kolowanawatobo, Teluk** *bay* Pulau Buton, C Indonesia
Kolozsvár *see* Cluj-Napoca
177 K6 **Kolpa** *Ger.* Kulpa, *SCr.* Kupa. ≈ Croatia/Slovenia
192 F7 **Kolpashevo** Tomskaya Oblast', C Russian Federation 58°21′N 82°44′E
194 D8 **Kolpino** Leningradskaya Oblast', NW Russian Federation 59°44′N 30°39′E
178 H5 **Kölpinsee** ◎ NE Germany
194 F4 **Kol'skiy Poluostrov** *Eng.* Kola Peninsula. *peninsula* NW Russian Federation
197 K3 **Koltubanovskiy** Orenburgskaya Oblast', W Russian Federation 53°00′N 52°00′E
184 F4 **Kolubara** ≈ C Serbia
Kolupchii *see* Gurkovo
182 G6 **Koluszki** Łódźskie, C Poland 51°44′N 19°50′E
195 K4 **Kolva** ≈ NW Russian Federation
154 E1 **Kolvereid** Nord-Trøndelag, W Norway 64°47′N 11°22′E
230 E9 **Kolwa** Baluchistān, SW Pakistan 26°03′N 64°00′E
135 H11 **Kolwezi** Katanga, S Dem. Rep. Congo 10°43′S 25°29′E
193 L4 **Kolyma** ≈ NE Russian Federation
Kolyma Lowland *see* Kolymskaya Nizmennost'
Kolyma Range/Kolymskiy, Khrebet *see* Kolymskoye Nagor'ye
193 L4 **Kolymskaya Nizmennost'** *Eng.* Kolyma Lowland. *lowlands* NE Russian Federation
193 L3 **Kolymskoye** Respublika Sakha (Yakutiya), NE Russian Federation 68°42′N 158°46′E
193 M4 **Kolymskoye Nagor'ye** *var.* Khrebet Kolymskiy, *Eng.* Kolyma Range. ▲▲ E Russian Federation
193 M2 **Kolyuchinskaya Guba** *bay* NE Russian Federation
227 L7 **Kol'zhat** Almaty, SE Kazakhstan 43°29′N 80°37′E
185 I5 **Kom** ▲ NW Bulgaria 43°10′N 23°02′E
136 D4 **Koma** Oromo, C Ethiopia 08°19′N 36°48′E
133 L5 **Komadugu Gana** ≈ NE Nigeria
251 K3 **Komagane** Nagano, Honshū, S Japan 35°44′N 137°54′E
140 C7 **Komaggas** Northern Cape, South Africa 29°48′S 17°30′E
134 J7 **Komanda** Orientale, NE Dem. Rep. Congo 01°25′N 29°43′E
294 C5 **Komandorskaya Basin** *var.* Kamchatka Basin. *undersea feature* SW Bering Sea
193 N5 **Komandorskiye Ostrova** *Eng.* Commander Islands. *island group* E Russian Federation
Kománfalva *see* Comăneşti
183 F11 **Komárno** *Ger.* Komorn, *Hung.* Komárom. Nitriansky Kraj, SW Slovakia 47°46′N 18°07′E
183 F11 **Komárom** Komárom-Esztergom, NW Hungary 47°43′N 18°06′E
Komárom *see* Komárno
183 F11 **Komárom-Esztergom** *off.* Komárom-Esztergom Megye. ◈ *county* N Hungary
Komárom-Esztergom Megye *see* Komárom-Esztergom
141 L3 **Komatipoort** Mpumalanga, South Africa 25°26′S 31°56′E
141 K4 **Komatirivier** ≈ Mpumalanga, South Africa
251 I2 **Komatsu** *var.* Komatu. Ishikawa, Honshū, SW Japan 36°25′N 136°27′E
250 G5 **Komatsushima** Tokushima, Shikoku, SW Japan 34°00′N 134°36′E
Komatu *see* Komatsu
138 C4 **Kombat** Otjozondjupa, N Namibia 19°42′S 17°45′E
Kombissiguiri *see* Kombissiri
132 G5 **Kombissiri** *var.* Kombissiguiri. C Burkina 12°01′N 01°27′W
282 C10 **Komebail Lagoon** *lagoon* N Palau
137 B9 **Kome Island** *island* N Tanzania
Komeyo *see* Wandai
261 J6 **Komfane** Pulau Wokam, E Indonesia 05°36′S 134°42′E
141 I9 **Komga** Eastern Cape, South Africa 32°35′S 27°54′E
189 H7 **Kominternivs'ke** Odes'ka Oblast', SW Ukraine 46°52′N 30°56′E
195 J5 **Komi, Respublika** ◈ *autonomous republic* NW Russian Federation
183 F13 **Komló** Baranya, SW Hungary 46°11′N 18°15′E
141 I6 **Kommissiepoort** Free State, South Africa 29°19′S 27°17′E
Kommunarsk *see* Alchevs'k
213 M2 **Kommunizm, Qullai** ▲ E Tajikistan
280 A3 **Komo** Southern Highlands, W Papua New Guinea 06°06′S 142°52′E
260 C8 **Komodo** Pulau Komodo, S Indonesia 08°35′S 119°27′E
260 C8 **Komodo, Pulau** *island* Nusa Tenggara, S Indonesia
132 F6 **Komoé** *var.* Komoé Fleuve. ≈ E Ivory Coast
Komoé Fleuve *see* Komoé
129 J5 **Kôm Ombo** *var.* Kawm Umbū. SE Egypt 24°26′N 32°57′E
135 C9 **Komono** La Lékoumou, SW Congo 03°15′S 13°14′E
261 L8 **Komoran** Papua, E Indonesia 08°14′S 138°51′E
261 L8 **Komoran, Pulau** *island* E Indonesia
Komorn *see* Komárno
Komornok *see* Comorâşte
251 K2 **Komoro** Nagano, Honshū, S Japan 36°20′N 138°26′E
Komosolabad *see* Komsomolobod
Komotau *see* Chomutov
187 J2 **Komotiní** *var.* Gümüljina, *Turk.* Gümülcine. Anatolikí Makedonía kai Thráki, NE Greece 41°07′N 25°27′E
184 F6 **Komovi** ▲▲ E Montenegro
189 I5 **Kompaniyivka** Kirovohrads'ka Oblast', C Ukraine 48°16′N 32°12′E
261 N6 **Kompiam** Enga, W Papua New Guinea 05°23′S 143°08′E
Kompong *see* Kâmpóng Chhnăng
Kompong Cham *see* Kâmpóng Cham
Kompong Kleang *see* Kâmpóng Khleăng
Kompong Som *see* Kâmpóng Saôm
Kompong Speu *see* Kâmpóng Spoe
Komrat *see* Comrat
140 E9 **Komsberg** ▲ Northern Cape, South Africa 32°40′S 20°49′E
Komsomol *see* Komsomol'skiy
193 H2 **Komsomolets, Ostrov** *island* Severnaya Zemlya, N Russian Federation
226 B6 **Komsomolets, Zaliv** *lake gulf* SW Kazakhstan
Komsomol/Komsomolets *see* Karabalyk, Kostanay, Kazakhstan
229 J7 **Komsomolobod** *Rus.* Komosolabad. C Tajikistan 38°51′N 69°54′E
194 G10 **Komsomol'sk** Ivanovskaya Oblast', W Russian Federation 56°58′N 40°15′E
189 J4 **Komsomol's'k** Poltavs'ka Oblast', C Ukraine 49°01′N 33°37′E
228 G6 **Komsomol'sk** Navoiy Viloyati, N Uzbekistan 40°14′N 65°10′E
226 C5 **Komsomol'skiy** *Kaz.* Komsomol. Atyrau, W Kazakhstan 47°18′N 53°37′E
195 L3 **Komsomol'skiy** Respublika Komi, NW Russian Federation 67°33′N 64°00′E
193 L8 **Komsomol'sk-na-Amure** Khabarovskiy Kray, SE Russian Federation 50°32′N 136°59′E
Komsomol'sk-na-Ustyurte *see* Komsomol'sk-Ustyurt
226 F4 **Komsomol'skoye** Aktyubinsk, NW Kazakhstan
197 I5 **Komsomol'skoye** Saratovskaya Oblast', W Russian Federation 50°45′N 47°00′E
227 H4 **Kon** ≈ C Kazakhstan
194 F10 **Konakovo** Tverskaya Oblast', W Russian Federation 56°42′N 36°44′E
231 H3 **Konar** *Per.* Konarhā, *Pash.* Kunar. ◈ *province* E Afghanistan
223 J9 **Konārak** Sīstān va Balūchestān, SE Iran 25°26′N 60°23′E
Konarhā *see* Konar
75 E13 **Konawa** Oklahoma, C USA 34°57′N 96°45′W
261 I4 **Konda** Papua, E Indonesia 01°34′S 131°58′E
195 N7 **Konda** ≈ C Russian Federation
195 M7 **Konda** ≈ Khanty-Mansiyskiy Avtonomnyy Okrug, Russian federation
196 N7 **Konda** ≈ Khanty-Mansiyskiy Avtonomnyy Okrug, Russian federation
234 G4 **Kondagaon** Chhattīsgarh, C India 19°38′N 81°41′E
62 F1 **Kondiaronk, Lac** ◎ Québec, SE Canada
274 D7 **Kondinin** Western Australia 32°31′S 118°15′E
196 N7 **Kondinskoye** Khanty-Mansiyskiy Avtonomnyy Okrug, Russian federation
137 D10 **Kondoa** Dodoma, C Tanzania 04°54′S 35°46′E
197 I3 **Kondol'** Penzenskaya Oblast', W Russian Federation 52°49′N 45°03′E
185 M7 **Kondolovo** Burgas, E Bulgaria 42°07′N 27°43′E
261 M8 **Kondomirat** Papua, E Indonesia 08°57′S 140°55′E
194 E7 **Kondopoga** Respublika Kareliya, NW Russian Federation 62°13′N 34°17′E
230 G2 **Kondoz** *var.* Kondoz, Kundūz, Qondūz, *Per.* Kondūz. Kunduz, NE Afghanistan 36°49′N 68°50′E
230 G2 **Kondoz** *Pash.* Kunduz. ◈ *province* NE Afghanistan
Kondoz *see* Kondoz
234 F6 **Kondukūr** *var.* Kandukur. Andhra Pradesh, E India 15°17′N 79°49′E
Kondūz *see* Kondoz
280 B9 **Koné** Province Nord, W New Caledonia 21°04′S 164°51′E
228 C7 **Kënekesir** *Rus.* Kënekesir. Balkan Welaýaty, W Turkmenistan 38°16′N 56°51′E
228 E4 **Këneurgench** *var.* Köneürgench, *Rus.* Këneurgench; *prev.* Kunya-Urgench. Daşoguz Welaýaty, N Turkmenistan 42°21′N 59°09′E
Köneürgench *see* Këneurgench
132 F6 **Kong** N Ivory Coast 09°10′N 04°33′W
83 J2 **Kongakut River** ≈ Alaska, USA
243 J2 **Kongcheng** China 31°02′N 117°05′E
243 L7 **Kongcheng** China 25°49′N 119°32′E
295 L7 **Kong Christian IX Land** *Eng.* King Christian IX Land. *physical region* SE Greenland
295 K6 **Kong Christian X Land** *Eng.* King Christian X Land. *physical region* E Greenland
295 K8 **Kong Frederik IX Land** *physical region* SW Greenland
295 J6 **Kong Frederik VIII Land** *Eng.* King Frederik VIII Land. *physical region* NE Greenland
295 L8 **Kong Frederik VI Kyst** *Eng.* King Frederik VI Coast. *physical region* SE Greenland
256 F9 **Kŏng, Kaôh** *prev.* Kas Kong. *island* SW Cambodia
152 C5 **Kong Karls Land** *Eng.* King Charles Islands. *island group* SE Svalbard
136 C5 **Kong Kong** ≈ SE Sudan
243 J3 **Konglong** China 29°53′N 115°54′E
Kongo *see* Congo (river)
138 E3 **Kongola** Caprivi, NE Namibia 17°47′S 23°24′E
135 I9 **Kongolo** Katanga, E Dem. Rep. Congo 05°20′S 26°58′E
136 B5 **Kongor** Jonglei, SE Sudan 07°09′N 31°44′E
295 L6 **Kong Oscar Fjord** *fjord* E Greenland
132 G5 **Kongoussi** N Burkina 13°19′N 01°31′W
155 D8 **Kongsberg** Buskerud, S Norway 59°39′N 09°38′E
152 C5 **Kongsøya** *island* Kong Karls Land, E Svalbard
154 E7 **Kongsvinger** Hedmark, S Norway 60°10′N 12°00′E
Kongtong *see* Pingliang
257 H8 **Kông, Tônle** *var.* Xê Kong. ≈ Cambodia/Laos
238 C5 **Kongur Shan** ▲ NW China 38°39′N 75°21′E
137 D10 **Kongwa** Dodoma, C Tanzania 06°13′S 36°28′E
Kong, Xê *see* Kông, Tônle
Konia *see* Konya
229 J6 **Konibodom** *Rus.* Kanibadam. N Tajikistan 40°16′N 70°20′E
182 G7 **Koniecpol** Śląskie, S Poland 50°47′N 19°45′E
Konieh *see* Konya
181 J8 **Königerode** Sachsen-Anhalt, Germany 11°13′N 51°36′E
Königgrätz *see* Hradec Králové
Königinhof an der Elbe *see* Dvůr Králové nad Labem
181 I11 **Königsberg** Bayern, Germany 10°35′N 50°05′E
179 F12 **Königsbrunn** Bayern, S Germany 48°16′N 10°52′E
181 J10 **Königsee** Thüringen, Germany 11°06′N 50°40′E
180 I7 **Königshütte** Sachsen-Anhalt, Germany 10°45′N 51°45′E
Königshütte *see* Chorzów
180 J6 **Königslutter** Niedersachsen, Germany 10°49′N 52°15′E
179 H13 **Königssee** ◎ SE Germany
181 E11 **Königstein** Hessen, Germany 8°28′N 50°11′E
179 I14 **Königstuhl** ▲ S Austria 46°57′N 13°47′E
177 K2 **Königswiesen** Oberösterreich, N Austria 48°25′N 14°48′E
181 C10 **Königswinter** Nordrhein-Westfalen, W Germany 50°40′N 07°12′E
228 G6 **Konimex** *Rus.* Kenimekh. Navoiy Viloyati, N Uzbekistan 40°14′N 65°10′E
182 F6 **Konin** *Ger.* Kuhnau. Weilkopolskie, C Poland 52°13′N 18°17′E
Koninkrijk der Nederlanden *see* Netherlands
186 E4 **Konispol** *var.* Konispoli. Vlorë, S Albania 39°40′N 20°10′E
Konispoli *see* Konispol
186 E3 **Kónitsa** Ípeiros, W Greece 40°04′N 20°48′E
Konitz *see* Chojnice
176 D4 **Köniz** Bern, W Switzerland 46°56′N 07°25′E
184 D5 **Konjic** ◈ Federacija Bosna I Hercegovina, S Bosnia and Herzegovina
152 F4 **Könkämäälven** ≈ Finland/Sweden
234 C5 **Konkan** *plain* W India
140 C5 **Konkiep** ≈ S Namibia
132 C6 **Konkouré** ≈ W Guinea
132 F4 **Konna** Mopti, S Mali 14°58′N 03°49′W
280 E2 **Konogaiang, Mount** ▲ New Ireland, NE Papua New Guinea 04°05′S 152°43′E
280 D2 **Konogogo** New Ireland, NE Papua New Guinea 03°25′S 152°09′E
176 D4 **Konolfingen** Bern, W Switzerland 46°53′N 07°36′E
132 G8 **Konongo** C Ghana 06°39′N 01°06′W
280 D2 **Konos** New Ireland, NE Papua New Guinea 03°09′S 151°47′E
194 G8 **Konosha** Arkhangel'skaya Oblast', NW Russian Federation 60°58′N 40°09′E
189 J2 **Konotop** Sums'ka Oblast', NE Ukraine 51°15′N 33°14′E
182 G7 **Końskie** Şiętokrzyskie, C Poland 51°12′N 20°23′E
Konstantinovka *see* Kostyantynivka
196 G6 **Konstantinovsk** Rostovskaya Oblast', SW Russian Federation 47°37′N 41°07′E
176 E3 **Konstanz** *var.* Constanz, *Eng.* Constance, *hist.* Kostnitz; *anc.* Constantia. Baden-Württemberg, S Germany 47°40′N 09°10′E
Konstanza *see* Constanţa
133 J6 **Kontagora** Niger, W Nigeria 10°25′N 05°29′E
134 B4 **Kontcha** Nord, N Cameroon 08°00′N 12°13′E
163 E9 **Kontich** Antwerpen, N Belgium 51°08′N 04°27′E
153 J8 **Kontiolahti** Itä-Suomi, SE Finland 62°46′N 29°51′E
152 I7 **Kontiomäki** Oulu, C Finland 64°20′N 28°09′E
257 I7 **Kon Tum** *var.* Kontum. Kon Tum, C Vietnam 14°23′N 108°00′E
Kontum *see* Kon Tum
Konur *see* Sulakyurt
214 E7 **Konya** *var.* Konieh, *prev.* Konia; *anc.* Iconium. Konya, C Turkey 37°51′N 32°30′E
214 D7 **Konya** *var.* Konia, Konieh. ◈ *province* C Turkey
227 J5 **Konyrat** *var.* Kounradskiy, *Kaz.* Qongyrat. Karaganda, SE Kazakhstan 46°57′N 75°01′E
227 L7 **Konyrolen** Almaty, SE Kazakhstan 44°16′N 79°18′E
137 D8 **Konza** Eastern, S Kenya 01°44′S 37°07′E
162 E5 **Koog aan den Zaan** Noord-Holland, C Netherlands 52°28′N 04°49′E
276 E4 **Koonibba** South Australia 31°55′S 133°23′E
73 E9 **Koontz Lake** Indiana, N USA 41°25′N 86°24′W
261 I4 **Koor** Papua, E Indonesia 0°21′S 132°28′E
277 K5 **Koorawatha** New South Wales, SE Australia 34°03′S 148°33′E
190 F4 **Koosa** Tartumaa, E Estonia 58°31′N 27°06′E
76 G3 **Kootenai** *var.* Kootenay. ≈ Canada/USA *see also* Kootenay
57 H8 **Kootenay** ≈ Canada/USA
Kootenay *see* Kootenai
138 D9 **Kootjieskolk** Northern Cape, W South Africa 31°16′S 20°21′E
140 E8 **Kootjieskolk** *marsh* Northern Cape, South Africa
184 G6 **Kopaonik** ▲▲ S Serbia
Kopar *see* Koper
152 D1 **Kópasker** Nordhurland Eystra, N Iceland 66°15′N 16°23′W
152 B3 **Kópavogur** Reykjanes, W Iceland 64°06′N 21°47′W
227 K6 **Kopbirlik** *prev.* Kīrov, Kirova. Almaty, SE Kazakhstan 46°24′N 77°16′E
177 J6 **Koper** *It.* Capodistria; *prev.* Kopar. SW Slovenia 45°32′N 13°43′E
141 J1 **Kopersspruit** Limpopo, South Africa 22°34′S 28°30′E
155 A8 **Kopervik** Rogaland, S Norway 59°17′N 05°20′E
213 J2 **Köpetdag Gershi** ▲▲ Iran/Turkmenistan
Köpetdag Gershi/Kopetdag, Khrebet *see* Koppeh Dāgh
197 N1 **Kopeysk** Kurganskaya Oblast', C Russian Federation 55°06′N 61°31′E
Kophinou *see* Kofínou
276 F5 **Kopi** South Australia 33°24′S 135°40′E
Kopiago *see* Lake Copiago
233 L6 **Kopili** ≈ NE India
155 H8 **Köping** Västmanland, C Sweden 59°31′N 16°00′E
184 F7 **Koplik** *var.* Kopliku. Shkodër, NW Albania 42°12′N 19°26′E
Kopliku *see* Koplik
Kopopo *see* Kokopo
154 E5 **Koppang** Hedmark, S Norway 61°34′N 11°04′E
154 G7 **Kopparberg** Örebro, C Sweden 59°52′N 15°02′E
Kopparberg *see* Dalarna
223 I3 **Koppeh Dāgh** *Rus.* Khrebet Kopetdag, *Turkm.* Köpetdag Gershi. ▲▲ Iran/Turkmenistan
Koppename *see* Coppename Rivier
141 I5 **Koppies** Free State, South Africa 27°14′S 27°35′E
141 I5 **Koppiesdam** ▣ Free State, South Africa
154 F7 **Koppom** Värmland, C Sweden 59°42′N 12°07′E
Kopreinitz *see* Koprivnica
185 K6 **Koprinka, Yazovir** *prev.* Yazovir Georgi Dimitrov. ▣ C Bulgaria
184 C1 **Koprivnica** *Ger.* Kopreinitz, *Hung.* Kaproncza. Koprivnica-Kri»zevci, N Croatia 46°10′N 16°49′E
184 C2 **Koprivnica-Križevci** *off.* Koprivničko-Križevačka Županija. ◈ *province* N Croatia
183 F9 **Kopřivnice** *Ger.* Nesselsdorf. Moravskoslezský Kraj, E Czech Republic 49°36′N 18°09′E
Koprivničko-Križevačka Županija *see* Koprivnica-Križevci
Köprülü *see* Veles
Koptsevichi *see* Kaptsevichy
Kopyl' *see* Kapyl'
191 H9 **Kopys'** *Rus.* Kopys'. Vitsyebskaya Voblasts', NE Belarus 54°19′N 30°18′E
184 G7 **Korab** ▲ Albania/FYR Macedonia 41°48′N 20°33′E
Korabavur Pastligi *see* Karabaur', Uval
136 G5 **K'orahē** Somali, E Ethiopia 06°36′N 44°21′E
187 J4 **Kórakas, Ákrotirio** *cape* Lésvos, E Greece
184 B3 **Korana** ≈ C Croatia
140 F5 **Korannaberg** ▲▲ Northern Cape, South Africa
234 H5 **Korāput** Orissa, E India 18°48′N 82°41′E
Korat *see* Nakhon Ratchasima
256 G7 **Korat Plateau** *plateau* E Thailand
217 J1 **Kōrāwa, Sar-i** ▲ NE Iraq 37°08′N 44°39′E
234 H3 **Kobra** Chhattīsgarh, C India 22°25′N 82°43′E
175 C13 **Korba** Tunisia
181 F8 **Korbach** Hessen, C Germany 51°16′N 08°52′E
181 E8 **Körbecke** Nordrhein-Westfalen, Germany 8°07′N 51°30′E
Korça *see* Korçë
184 G9 **Korçë** *var.* Korça, *Gk.* Korytsa, *It.* Corriza; *prev.* Koritsa. Korçë, SE Albania 40°38′N 20°47′E
184 G9 **Korçë** ◈ *district* SE Albania
184 D6 **Korčula** *It.* Curzola. Dubrovnik-Neretva, S Croatia 42°57′N 17°08′E
184 C6 **Korčula** *It.* Curzola; *anc.* Corcyra Nigra. *island* S Croatia
184 C6 **Korčulanski Kanal** *channel* S Croatia
227 J7 **Korday** *prev.* Georgiyevka. Zhambyl, SE Kazakhstan 43°03′N 74°43′E
181 B12 **Kordel** Rheinland-Pfalz, Germany 6°38′N 49°50′E
222 D3 **Kordestān** *off.* Ostān-e Kordestān, *var.* Kurdestan. ◈ *province* W Iran
Kordestān, Ostān-e *see* Kordestān
222 G3 **Kord Kūy** *var.* Kurd Kui. Golestán, N Iran 36°49′N 54°05′E
245 N4 **Korea Bay** *bay* China/North Korea
Korea, Democratic People's Republic of *see* North Korea
261 H7 **Koreare** Pulau Yamdena, E Indonesia 07°33′S 131°13′E
Korea, Republic of *see* South Korea
250 B4 **Korea Strait** *Jap.* Chōsen-kaikyō, *Kor.* Taehan-haehyŏp. *channel* Japan/South Korea
Korelichi/Korelicze *see* Karelichy
136 E3 **Korem** ◈ Tigrai, N Ethiopia
133 J4 **Korén Adoua** ≈ C Niger
196 E4 **Korenevo** Kurskaya Oblast', W Russian Federation 51°21′N 34°53′E
196 G8 **Korenovsk** Krasnodarskiy Kray, SW Russian Federation 45°28′N 39°25′E
188 F3 **Korets'** *Pol.* Korzec, *Rus.* Korets. Rivnens'ka Oblast', NW Ukraine 50°38′N 27°12′E
Korets *see* Korets'
193 M4 **Korf** Koryakskiy Avtonomnyy Okrug, E Russian Federation 60°20′N 165°37′E
292 G4 **Korff Ice Rise** *ice cap* Antarctica
227 H4 **Korgalzhyn** *var.* Kurgal'dzhino, Kurgal'dzhinsky, *Kaz.* Qorgazhyn. Akmola, C Kazakhstan 50°33′N 69°58′E
152 D6 **Korgen** Troms, N Norway 66°04′N 13°51′E
229 J5 **Korgon-Dēbē** Dzhalal-Abadskaya Oblast', W Kyrgyzstan 41°51′N 70°52′E
132 F6 **Korhogo** N Ivory Coast 09°29′N 05°39′W
186 G6 **Korinthiakós Kólpos** *Eng.* Gulf of Corinth; *anc.* Corinthiacus Sinus. *gulf* C Greece
186 G6 **Kórinthos** *anc.* Corinthus *Eng.* Corinth. Pelopónnisos, S Greece 37°56′N 22°55′E
184 G7 **Koritnik** ▲ S Serbia 42°06′N 20°34′E
Koritsa *see* Korçë
253 D11 **Kōriyama** Fukushima, Honshū, C Japan 37°25′N 140°20′E
214 C7 **Korkuteli** Antalya, SW Turkey 37°07′N 30°11′E
238 F4 **Korla** *Chin.* K'u-erh-lo. Xinjiang Uygur Zizhiqu, NW China 41°48′N 86°10′E
181 G9 **Körle** Hessen, Germany 9°31′N 51°10′E
192 F6 **Korliki** Khanty-Mansiyskiy Avtonomnyy Okrug, C Russian Federation 61°28′N 82°12′E
Körlin an der Persante *see* Karlino
Korma *see* Karma
72 H3 **Kormak** Ontario, S Canada 47°38′N 83°00′W
Kormakíti, Akrotíri/Kormakiti, Cape/ Kormakítis *see* Koruçam Burnu
183 D12 **Körmend** Vas, W Hungary 47°02′N 16°35′E
217 J3 **Kōrmōr** E Iraq 35°06′N 44°47′E
184 B4 **Kornat** *It.* Incoronata. *island* W Croatia
Korneshty *see* Corneşti
177 L2 **Korneuburg** Niederösterreich, NE Austria 48°22′N 16°20′E
227 H2 **Korneyevka** Severnyy Kazakhstan, N Kazakhstan 54°01′N 68°30′E
155 E8 **Kornsjø** Østfold, S Norway 58°55′N 11°40′E
132 G4 **Koro** Mopti, S Mali 14°05′N 03°06′W
280 F8 **Koro** *island* C Fiji
280 A3 **Koroba** Southern Highlands, W Papua New Guinea 05°46′S 142°48′E
196 F5 **Korocha** Belgorodskaya Oblast', W Russian Federation 50°49′N 37°08′E
214 E5 **Köroğlu Dağları** ▲▲ C Turkey
277 M4 **Korogoro Point** *headland* New South Wales, SE Australia 31°03′S 153°04′E
137 E10 **Korogwe** Tanga, E Tanzania 05°10′S 38°30′E
277 I7 **Koroit** Victoria, SE Australia 38°17′S 142°22′E
280 E9 **Korolevu** Viti Levu, W Fiji 18°12′S 177°44′E
284 G10 **Koromiri** *island* S Cook Islands
263 M9 **Koronadal** Mindanao, S Philippines 06°23′N 124°54′E
187 H3 **Koróneia, Límni** *var.* Límni Korónia. ◎ N Greece
186 F8 **Koróni** Pelopónnisos, S Greece 36°47′N 21°57′E
Korónia, Límni *see* Koróneia, Límni
182 E5 **Koronowo** *Ger.* Krone an der Brahe. Kujawski-pomorskie, C Poland 53°18′N 17°56′E
189 I2 **Korop** Chernihivs'ka Oblast', N Ukraine 51°35′N 32°57′E
187 H6 **Koropí** Attikí, C Greece 37°54′N 23°52′E
282 C10 **Koror** *var.* Oreor. ● (Palau) Oreor, N Palau 07°21′N 134°28′E
Koror *see* Oreor
183 G12 **Körös** ≈ E Hungary
Kőrös *see* Križevci
Körösbánya *see* Baia de Criş
280 F9 **Koro Sea** *sea* C Fiji
Koroška *see* Kärnten
188 G2 **Korosten'** Zhytomyrs'ka Oblast', NW Ukraine 50°56′N 28°39′E
190 I5 **Korostyn'** Novgorodskaya Oblast', Russian Federation
Korostyshev *see* Korostyshiv
188 G3 **Korostyshiv** *Rus.* Korostyshev. Zhytomyrs'ka Oblast', N Ukraine 50°18′N 29°05′E
195 L2 **Korotaikha** ≈ NW Russian Federation
192 F5 **Korotchayevo** Yamalo-Nenetskiy Avtonomnyy Okrug, N Russian Federation 66°00′N 78°11′E
134 E1 **Koro Toro** Borkou-Ennedi-Tibesti, N Chad 16°01′N 18°27′E
82 G9 **Korovin Island** *island* Shumagin Islands, Alaska, USA
280 E9 **Korovou** Viti Levu, W Fiji 17°48′S 178°32′E
181 B12 **Körperich** Rheinland-Pfalz, Germany 6°15′N 49°55′E
153 H9 **Korpilahti** Länsi-Soumi, C Finland 62°02′N 25°34′E
152 G5 **Korpilombolo** *Lapp.* Dállogilli. Norrbotten, N Sweden 66°51′N 23°00′E
193 M8 **Korsakov** Ostrov Sakhalin, Sakhalinskaya Oblast', SE Russian Federation 46°41′N 142°45′E
153 G8 **Korsholm** *Fin.* Mustasaari. Länsi-Soumi, W Finland 63°05′N 21°43′E
155 E13 **Korsør** Vestsjælland, E Denmark 55°19′N 11°09′E
Korsovka *see* Kārsava
189 H4 **Korsun'-Shevchenkivs'kyy** *Rus.* Korsun'-Shevchenkovskiy. Cherkas'ka Oblast', C Ukraine 49°26′N 31°15′E
Korsun'-Shevchenkovskiy *see* Korsun'-Shevchenkivs'kyy
163 B9 **Kortemark** West-Vlaanderen, W Belgium 51°03′N 03°03′E
163 E10 **Kortenberg** Vlaams Brabant, C Belgium 50°53′N 04°33′E
163 G10 **Kortessem** Limburg, NE Belgium 50°52′N 05°22′E
163 D8 **Kortgene** Zeeland, SW Netherlands 51°34′N 03°48′E
136 B1 **Korti** Northern, N Sudan 18°06′N 31°33′E
163 B10 **Kortrijk** *Fr.* Courtrai. West-Vlaanderen, W Belgium 50°50′N 03°17′E
218 B1 **Koruçam Burnu** *var.* Cape Kormakiti, Kormakítis, *Gk.* Akrotíri Kormakíti. *cape* N Cyprus
187 L4 **Korucu** Balıkesir, Turkey 39°28′N 27°22′E
277 J7 **Korumburra** Victoria, SE Australia 38°27′S 145°48′E
Koryak Range *see* Koryakskoye Nagor'ye
193 M5 **Koryakskiy Avtonomnyy Okrug** ◈ *autonomous district* E Russian Federation
Koryakskiy Khrebet *see* Koryakskoye Nagor'ye
82 B5 **Koryakskoye Nagor'ye** *var.* Koryakskiy Khrebet, *Eng.* Koryak Range. ▲▲ NE Russian Federation
195 I7 **Koryazhma** Arkhangel'skaya Oblast', NW Russian Federation 61°16′N 47°07′E
Kōryō *see* Kangnŭng
Korytsa *see* Korçë
189 I1 **Koryukivka** Chernihivs'ka Oblast', N Ukraine 51°45′N 32°16′E
Korzec *see* Korets'
187 L8 **Kos** Kos, Dodekánisa, Greece, Aegean Sea 36°53′N 27°19′E
187 L8 **Kos** *It.* Coo; *anc.* Cos. *island* Dodekánisa, Greece, Aegean Sea
195 K8 **Kosa** Permskaya Oblast', NW Russian Federation 59°55′N 54°54′E
195 K8 **Kosa** ≈ NW Russian Federation
250 B5 **Kō-saki** *headland* Nagasaki, Tsushima, SW Japan 34°06′N 129°13′E
248 C4 **Kosan** SE North Korea 38°50′N 127°26′E
191 E11 **Kosava** *Rus.* Kosovo. Brestskaya Voblasts', SW Belarus 52°45′N 25°16′E
Kosch *see* Kose
226 C5 **Koschagyl** *Kaz.* Qosshaghyl. Atyrau, W Kazakhstan 46°52′N 53°46′E
182 D6 **Kościan** *Ger.* Kosten. Wielkopolskie, C Poland 52°05′N 16°38′E
182 E4 **Kościerzyna** Pomorskie, NW Poland 54°07′N 17°55′E
66 B9 **Kosciusko** Mississippi, S USA 33°03′N 89°35′W
Kosciusko, Mount *see* Kosciuszko, Mount
277 K6 **Kosciuszko, Mount** *prev.* Mount Kosciusko. ▲ New South Wales, SE Australia 36°28′S 148°15′E
190 E4 **Kose** *Ger.* Kosch. Harjumaa, NW Estonia 59°11′N 25°10′E
185 I4 **Koshava** Vidin, NW Bulgaria 44°03′N 23°00′E
229 L5 **Kosh-Dēbē** *var.* Koshtebē. Narynskaya Oblast', C Kyrgyzstan 41°03′N 74°08′E
253 C13 **Koshigaya** *var.* Kosigaya. Saitama, Honshū, S Japan 35°55′N 139°45′E
K'o-shih *see* Kashi
250 B8 **Koshikijima-rettō** *var.* Kosikizima Rettô. *island group* SW Japan
227 L5 **Koshkarkol', Ozero** ◎ SE Kazakhstan
73 C8 **Koshkonong, Lake** ◎ Wisconsin, N USA
Koshoba *see* Goşabo
251 K2 **Kōshoku** *var.* Kôsyoku. Nagano, Honshū, S Japan 36°33′N 138°09′E
Koshtebē *see* Kosh-Dēbē
Kōshū *see* Kwangju
141 L5 **Kosi Bay** *bay* KwaZulu-Natal, South Africa
183 H10 **Košice** *Ger.* Kaschau, *Hung.* Kassa. Košický Kraj, E Slovakia 48°44′N 21°15′E
Kosigaya *see* Koshigaya
Kosikizima Rettô *see* Koshikijima-rettō
233 I6 **Kosi Reservoir** ▣ E Nepal
188 D5 **Kosiv** Ivano-Frankivs'ka Oblast', W Ukraine 48°19′N 25°04′E
227 H4 **Koskol'** Karaganda, C Kazakhstan 49°32′N 67°08′E
190 G3 **Koskolovo** Leningradskaya Oblast', Russian Federation
190 J2 **Kos'kovo** Leningradskaya Oblast', Russian Federation
195 I6 **Koslan** Respublika Komi, NW Russian Federation 63°27′N 48°52′E
Köslin *see* Koszalin
Köslin *see* Koszalin
228 G7 **Koson** *Rus.* Kasan. Qashqadaryo Viloyati, S Uzbekistan 39°04′N 65°35′E
248 C4 **Kosŏng** SE North Korea 38°41′N 128°14′E
229 J5 **Kosonsoy** *Rus.* Kasansay. Namangan Viloyati, E Uzbekistan 41°15′N 71°28′E
184 G6 **Kosovo** *prev.* Autonomous Province of Kosovo and Metohija. ◈ *province* S Serbia
Kosovo *see* Kosava
Kosovo and Metohija, Autonomous Province of *see* Kosovo
184 G6 **Kosovo Polje** Kosovo, S Serbia 42°40′N 21°07′E
184 G6 **Kosovska Kamenica** Kosovo, SE Serbia 42°37′N 21°33′E
184 G6 **Kosovska Mitrovica** *Alb.* Mitrovicë; *prev.* Mitrovica, Titova Mitrovica. Kosovo, S Serbia 42°54′N 20°52′E
283 H10 **Kosrae** ◈ *state* E Micronesia
283 J7 **Kosrae** *prev.* Kusaie. *island* Caroline Islands, E Micronesia
71 H6 **Kosse** Texas, SW USA 31°16′N 96°38′W
177 H3 **Kössen** Tirol, W Austria 47°40′N 12°24′E
132 F7 **Kossou, Lac de** ◎ C Ivory Coast
Kossukavak *see* Krumovgrad
Kostajnica *see* Hrvatska Kostajnica
Kostamus *see* Kostomuksha
226 G2 **Kostanay** *var.* Kustanay, *Kaz.* Qostanay. Kustanay, N Kazakhstan 53°16′N 63°34′E
226 G3 **Kostanay** *var.* Kostanayskaya Oblast', *Kaz.* Qostanay Oblysy. ◈ *province* N Kazakhstan
Kostanayskaya Oblast' *see* Kostanay
Kosten *see* Kościan
185 J7 **Kostenets** *prev.* Georgi Dimitrov. Sofiya, W Bulgaria 42°15′N 23°48′E
136 B2 **Kosti** White Nile, C Sudan 13°11′N 32°38′E
Kostnitz *see* Konstanz
194 D5 **Kostomuksha** *Fin.* Kostamus. Respublika Kareliya, NW Russian Federation 64°33′N 30°28′E
188 E2 **Kostopil'** *Rus.* Kostopol'. Rivnens'ka Oblast', NW Ukraine 50°20′N 26°29′E
Kostopol' *see* Kostopil'
194 G9 **Kostroma** Kostromskaya Oblast', NW Russian Federation 57°46′N 41°E
194 G9 **Kostroma** ≈ NW Russian Federation
195 H9 **Kostromskaya Oblast'** ◈ *province* NW Russian Federation
182 C5 **Kostrzyn** *Ger.* Cüstrin, Küstrin. Lubuskie, W Poland 52°35′N 14°40′E
182 E6 **Kostrzyn** Weilkopolskie, C Poland 52°23′N 17°13′E
189 M5 **Kostyantynivka** *Rus.* Konstantinovka. Donets'ka Oblast', SE Ukraine
Kostyukovichi *see* Kastsyukovichy
Kostyukovka *see* Kastsyukowka
Kôsyoku *see* Kōshoku
195 K4 **Kos'yu** Respublika Komi, NW Russian Federation 65°39′N 59°01′E
195 K4 **Kos'yu** ≈ NW Russian Federation
182 D4 **Koszalin** *Ger.* Köslin. Zachodnio-pomorskie, NW Poland 54°12′N 16°10′E
182 D4 **Koszalin** *Ger.* Köslin. ◈ *province* NW Poland
183 D11 **Kőszeg** *Ger.* Güns. Vas, W Hungary 47°23′N 16°33′E
232 E7 **Kota** *prev.* Kotah. Rājasthān, N India 25°14′N 75°52′E
Kota Baharu *see* Kota Bharu
Kota Bahru *see* Kota Bharu
258 K6 **Kotabaru** Pulau Laut, C Indonesia 03°15′S 116°15′E
258 E5 **Kota Baru** Sumatera, W Indonesia 01°07′S 101°43′E
Kotabaru *see* Jayapura
258 E2 **Kota Bharu** *var.* Kota Baharu, Kota Bahru. Kelantan, Peninsular Malaysia 06°07′N 102°15′E
Kotaboemi *see* Kotabumi
258 F7 **Kotabumi** *prev.* Kotaboemi. Sumatera, W Indonesia 04°50′S 104°54′E
231 H6 **Kot Addu** Punjab, E Pakistan 30°28′N 70°58′E
Kotah *see* Kota
258 K2 **Kota Kinabalu** *prev.* Jesselton. Sabah, East Malaysia 05°59′N 116°04′E
258 K2 **Kota Kinabalu** ✈ Sabah, East Malaysia 05°59′N 116°04′E
152 I5 **Kotala** Lappi, N Finland 67°01′N 29°00′E
Kotamobagoe *see* Kotamobagu
260 E3 **Kotamobagu** *prev.* Kotamobagoe. Sulawesi, C Indonesia 0°46′N 124°21′E
234 H5 **Kotapad** *var.* Kotapārh. Orissa, E India 19°10′N 82°23′E
Kotapārh *see* Kotapad
256 E11 **Ko Ta Ru Tao** *island* SW Thailand
258 I6 **Kotawaringin, Teluk** *bay* Borneo, C Indonesia
230 G8 **Kot Dīji** Sind, SE Pakistan 27°16′N 68°44′E
232 F5 **Kotdwāra** Uttaranchal, N India 29°44′N 78°33′E
195 I9 **Kotel'nich** Kirovskaya Oblast', NW Russian Federation 58°19′N 48°12′E
197 H6 **Kotel'nikovo** Volgogradskaya Oblast', SW Russian Federation 47°37′N 43°07′E
193 J3 **Kotel'nyy, Ostrov** *island* Novosibirskiye Ostrova, N Russian Federation
189 K3 **Kotel'va** Poltavs'ka Oblast', C Ukraine 50°04′N 34°46′E
181 H11 **Köthen** *var.* Cöthen. Sachsen-Anhalt, C Germany 51°46′N 11°59′E

◆ Country
● Country Capital
◇ Dependent Territory
○ Dependent Territory Capital
◈ Administrative Regions
✈ International Airport
▲ Mountain
▲▲ Mountain Range
Ѫ Volcano
≈ River
◎ Lake
▣ Reservoir

◆ Country   ● Country Capital   ◇ Dependent Territory   ○ Dependent Territory Capital   ◈ Administrative Regions   ✈ International Airport   ▲ Mountain   ▲ Mountain Range   ⊼ Volcano   ♒ River   ◎ Lake   ◎ Reservoir

L

---

154 A6 **Lavik** Sogn Og Fjordane, S Norway 61°06′N 05°25′E
La Vila Joiosa see Villajoyosa
145 **Lavilledieu** Rhône-Alpes, France 44°34′N 4°28′E
168 G1 **La Villetelle** Limousin, France 45°55′N 2°21′E
77 J5 **Lavina** Montana, N USA 46°18′N 108°55′W
168 F5 **Lavit** Midi-Pyrénées, France 43°58′N 0°55′E
292 **Lavoisier Island** island Antarctica
66 G8 **Lavonia** Georgia, SE USA 34°26′N 83°06′W
165 J7 **la Voulte-sur-Rhône** Ardèche, E France 44°49′N 04°46′E
169 I2 **Lavoûte-Chilhac** Auvergne, France 45°09′N 3°24′E
110 F5 **Lavras** Minas Gerais, Brazil 21°14′S 45°00′W
115 K3 **Lavras do Sul** Rio Grande do Sul, Brazil 30°49′S 53°55′W
82 **Lavrentiya** Chukotskiy Avtonomnyy Okrug, Russian Federation 65°30′N 171°00′W
110 F2 **Lavrinhas** São Paulo, Brazil 22°35′S 44°54′W
110 D3 **Lávrio** prev. Lávrion. Attikí, C Greece 37°43′N 24°03′E
Lávrion see Lávrio
190 F5 **Lavry** Pskovskaya Oblast', Russian Federation
139 H7 **Lavumisa** prev. Gollel. SE Swaziland 27°18′S 31°55′E
231 **Lawarai Pass** pass N Pakistan
Lawassaar see Lavassaare
220 G9 **Lawdar** SW Yemen 13°49′N 45°55′E
135 G1 **Lawers, Ben** ▲ UK 56°34′N 4°13′W
70 F1 **Lawn** Texas, SW USA 32°07′N 99°45′W
64 D7 **Lawnton** Pennsylvania, USA 40°16′N 76°48′W
293 L3 **Law Promontory** headland Antarctica
132 G6 **Lawra** NW Ghana 10°40′N 02°49′W
278 C12 **Lawrence** Otago, South Island, New Zealand 45°55′S 169°43′E
73 F11 **Lawrence** Indiana, N USA 39°49′N 86°01′W
73 G11 **Lawrence** Kansas, C USA 38°58′N 95°15′W
65 L1 **Lawrence** Massachusetts, NE USA 42°42′N 71°09′W
66 C5 **Lawrenceburg** Kentucky, S USA 38°02′N 84°53′W
66 D7 **Lawrenceburg** Tennessee, S USA 35°16′N 87°20′W
66 D7 **Lawrenceville** Georgia, SE USA 33°57′N 83°59′W
73 D12 **Lawrenceville** Illinois, N USA 38°43′N 87°40′W
64 C7 **Lawrenceville** New Jersey, USA 40°18′N 74°44′W
66 C5 **Lawrenceville** Virginia, NE USA 36°45′N 77°50′W
58 G9 **Lawrenceville** Pennsylvania
75 G9 **Lawson** Missouri, C USA
73 D13 **Lawton** Oklahoma, C USA 34°35′N 98°20′W
220 C2 **Lawz, Jabal al** ▲ NW Saudi Arabia 28°45′N 35°20′E
155 G8 **Laxå** Örebro, C Sweden 59°00′N 14°37′E
195 K4 **Laya** ▲ NW Russian Federation
155 G10 **La Yarada** Tacna, SW Peru 18°14′S 70°30′W
161 L5 **Layer de la Haye** 51°50′N 0°51′E
221 H8 **Laylān** C Yemen 15°27′N 44°42′E
220 G5 **Laylá** var. Laila. Ar Riyād, C Saudi Arabia 22°14′N 46°40′E
69 H1 **Lay Lake** ☐ Alabama, S USA
91 L3 **Layou** Saint Vincent, Saint Vincent and the Grenadines 13°11′N 61°16′W
La Youne see El Aaiún
286 A6 **Laysan Island** island Hawaiian Islands, Hawaii, USA
79 H2 **Layton** Utah, W USA 41°03′N 112°00′W
158 D9 **Laytonville** California, N USA 39°39′N 123°30′W
158 D9 **Laytown** Meath, Ireland 53°41′N 6°14′W
85 **La Zarca** Durango, Mexico 25°50′N 104°44′W
137 I9 **Lazare, Pointe** headland Mahé, NE Seychelles 04°46′S 55°28′E
193 L7 **Lazarev** Khabarovskiy Kray, SE Russian Federation 52°11′N 141°18′E
184 F4 **Lazarevac** Serbia, C Serbia 44°25′N 20°17′E
291 H13 **Lazarev Sea** sea Antarctica
159 I6 **Lazonby** UK 54°46′N 2°42′W
Lazovsk see Singerei
256 D6 **Leach** Poŭthĭsăt, W Cambodia 12°19′N 103°45′E
75 J12 **Leachville** Arkansas, C USA 35°56′N 90°15′W
74 A3 **Lead** South Dakota, N USA 44°21′N 103°45′W
159 L3 **Leadburn** UK 55°47′N 3°14′W
159 L10 **Leadenham** UK 53°03′N 0°35′W
57 L7 **Leader** Saskatchewan, S Canada 50°55′N 109°31′W
159 H4 **Leadhills** UK 55°24′N 3°46′W
63 L3 **Lead Mountain** ▲ Maine, NE USA 44°53′N 68°07′W
79 L4 **Leadville** Colorado, C USA 39°15′N 106°17′W
55 I7 **Leaf Rapids** Manitoba, C Canada 56°30′N 100°02′W
68 F3 **Leaf River** ☞ Mississippi, USA
71 I7 **League City** Texas, SW USA 29°30′N 95°05′W
152 G2 **Leaibevuotna** Nor. Olderfjord. Finnmark, N Norway 70°23′N 24°54′E
75 G9 **Leakesville** Mississippi, S USA 31°09′N 88°33′W
70 F5 **Leakey** Texas, SW USA 29°44′N 99°48′W
Leal see Lihula
138 E2 **Lealui** Western, W Zambia 15°12′S 22°59′E
Leamhcán see Lucan
62 A6 **Leamington** Ontario, S Canada 42°03′N 82°35′W
Leamington/Leamington Spa see Royal Leamington Spa
Leammi see Lemmenjoki
243 J9 **Le'an** Jiangxi, China 27°16′N 115°29′E
72 G6 **Leander** Texas, SW USA 30°34′N 97°51′W
141 I4 **Leandra** Mpumalanga, South Africa 25°25′S 28°55′E
114 A9 **Leandro Ferreira** Minas Gerais, Brazil 19°42′S 45°00′E
113 **Leandro Alem** Buenos Aires, Argentina 34°30′S 61°24′W
113 H6 **Leandro N. Alem** Misiones, NE Argentina 27°34′S 55°15′W
157 B10 **Leane, Lough** Ir. Loch Léin. ☐ SW Ireland
274 C5 **Learmonth** Western Australia 22°17′S 114°03′E
161 J2 **Leasingham** UK 53°01′N 0°25′W
161 K7 **Leatherhead** SE UK 51°17′N 0°19′W
Leau see Zoutleeuw
L'Eau d'Heure see Plate Taille, Lac de la
284 A10 **Leava** Île Futuna, S Wallis and Futuna
Leavdnja see Lakselv
75 C5 **Leavenworth** Kansas, C USA 39°19′N 94°55′W
76 D4 **Leavenworth** Washington, NW USA 47°36′N 120°39′W
152 H3 **Leavvajohka** var. Levvajok. Finnmark, N Norway 69°57′N 26°18′E
75 G9 **Leawood** Kansas, C USA 38°57′N 94°37′W
182 E3 **Łeba** Pomorskie, N Poland 54°45′N 17°32′E
182 E3 **Łeba** Ger. Leba. ☞ N Poland
Łeba see Łeba
181 C13 **Lebach** Saarland, SW Germany 49°25′N 06°54′E
Leba, Jezioro see Łebsko, Jezioro
169 L6 **Le Barcarès** Languedoc-Roussillon, France 42°47′N 3°02′E
Lebasee see Łebsko, Jezioro
163 D10 **Lebbeke** Oost-Vlaanderen, NW Belgium 51°00′N 04°08′E
169 L6 **Le Beausset** Provence-Alpes-Côte d'Azur, France 43°12′N 5°48′E
81 D9 **Lebec** California, W USA 34°51′N 118°52′W
Lebedian' see Lebedyan'
193 G3 **Lebedinyy** Respublika Sakha (Yakutiya), NE Russian Federation 58°30′N 125°30′E
196 G3 **Lebedyan'** Lipetskaya Oblast', W Russian Federation 53°00′N 39°11′E
189 H2 **Lebedyn** Rus. Lebedin. Sums'ka Oblast', NE Ukraine 50°34′N 34°29′E
58 C7 **Lebel-sur-Quévillon** Québec, SE Canada 49°01′N 76°56′W
152 H2 **Lebesby** Finnmark, N Norway 70°31′N 27°00′E
167 M10 **Le Blanc** Centre, France 46°38′N 1°04′E

169 I4 **Le Bleymard** Languedoc-Roussillon, France 44°29′N 3°44′E
134 G5 **Lebo** Orientale, N Dem. Rep. Congo 04°30′N 23°58′E
75 F10 **Lebo** Kansas, C USA 38°25′N 95°51′W
182 E3 **Łębork** var. Lębórk, Ger. Lauenburg, Lauenburg in Pommern. Pomorskie, N Poland 54°32′N 17°43′E
66 G6 **Le Boullay-Mivoye** Centre, France 48°49′N 1°24′E
165 I9 **le Boulou** Pyrénées-Orientales, S France 42°32′N 02°50′E
168 G3 **Le Bourg** Midi-Pyrénées, France 44°43′N 1°55′E
165 L3 **Le Bourg-d'Oisans** Rhône-Alpes, France 45°03′N 06°02′E
169 L1 **Le Bourget-du-Lac** Rhône-Alpes, France 45°39′N 5°52′E
176 B5 **Le Brassus** Vaud, W Switzerland 46°35′N 06°14′E
170 F6 **Lebrija** Andalucía, S Spain 36°55′N 06°04′W
182 E3 **Łebsko, Jezioro** Ger. Lebasee; prev. Jeziora Łeba. ☐ N Poland
116 A6 **Lebu** Bío Bío, C Chile 37°38′S 73°43′W
169 **Lebyazh'ye** see Akku
170 C4 **Leça da Palmeira** Porto, N Portugal 41°12′N 08°43′W
172 M3 **Leça da Palmeira** Porto, Portugal 41°12′N 8°42′W
165 K8 **le Cannet** Alpes-Maritimes, SE France 43°35′N 07°E
Le Cap see Cap-Haïtien
169 I6 **Le Cap d'Agde** Languedoc-Roussillon, France 43°17′N 3°31′E
185 I9 **Lecarrow** Ireland 53°31′N 8°03′W
165 B2 **le Cateau-Cambrésis** Nord, N France 50°05′N 03°32′E
165 I5 **le Caylar** Languedoc-Roussillon, France
175 J10 **Lecce** Puglia, SE Italy 40°23′N 18°11′E
176 E7 **Lecco** Lombardia, N Italy 45°51′N 09°23′E
176 F4 **Lech** Vorarlberg, W Austria 47°14′N 10°10′E
173 F13 **Lech** ☞ Austria/Germany
186 F6 **Lechainá** var. Lehena, Lekhainá. Dytikí Ellás, S Greece 37°57′N 21°16′E
243 **Lechang** Guangdong, China 25°05′N 113°13′E
176 E4 **le Château d'Oléron** Charente-Maritime, W France 45°53′N 01°12′E
169 M1 **le Châtelard** Rhône-Alpes, France 45°37′N 6°52′E
167 H10 **le Châtelet** Limousin, France 46°12′N 2°27′E
167 J2 **le Chesne** Ardennes, N France 49°31′N 04°42′E
167 I6 **le Cheylard** Ardèche, E France 44°55′N 04°27′E
161 I6 **Lechlade** UK 51°42′N 1°42′W
167 I6 **Lechtaler Alpen** ▲ W Austria
168 D9 **Lecíñena** Aragón, Spain 41°48′N 0°37′W
178 D3 **Leck** Schleswig-Holstein, N Germany 54°45′N 09°00′E
62 J1 **Lecointre, Lac** ☐ Québec, SE Canada
75 I6 **Lecompte** Louisiana, S USA 31°05′N 92°24′W
165 J5 **le Creusot** Saône-et-Loire, C France 46°48′N 04°27′E
166 B8 **Le Croisic** Pays de la Loire, France 47°18′N 2°31′W
168 E5 **Le Crotoy** Picardie, France 50°13′N 1°37′E
168 E5 **Lectoure** Midi-Pyrénées, France 43°56′N 00°37′E
Lecumberri see Lekunberri
182 H3 **Łęczna** Lublin, E Poland 51°20′N 22°52′E
182 F6 **Łęczyca** Ger. Lentschiza, Rus. Lenchitsa. Łódzkie, C Poland 52°04′N 19°10′E
180 D4 **Leda** ☞ NW Germany
163 H5 **Ledbury** UK 52°03′N 2°25′W
163 D10 **Lede** Oost-Vlaanderen, NW Belgium 50°58′N 03°59′E
170 A4 **Ledesma** Castilla-León, N Spain 41°05′N 06°00′W
91 N2 **le Diamant** SW Martinique 14°29′N 61°02′W
169 I5 **Lédignan** Languedoc-Roussillon, France 43°59′N 4°06′E
137 J8 **le Digue** island Inner Islands, NE Seychelles
165 I6 **le Donjon** Allier, C France 46°19′N 03°50′E
167 **le Dorat** Haute-Vienne, C France 46°14′N 01°05′E
Ledo Salinarius see Lons-le-Saunier
244 A5 **Ledu** China 36°29′N 102°25′E
161 I6 **Ledu** Qinghai, China 36°18′N 102°13′E
57 I5 **Leduc** Alberta, SW Canada 53°17′N 113°30′W
193 N4 **Ledyanaya, Gora** ▲ E Russian Federation 61°51′N 171°03′E
157 B11 **Lee** var. An Laoi. ☞ SW Ireland
160 I4 **Leebotwood** UK 52°35′N 2°47′W
74 J4 **Leech Lake** ☐ Minnesota, N USA
159 K9 **Leeds** N England, UK 53°50′N 01°35′W
74 D8 **Leeds** North Dakota, N USA 48°19′N 99°43′W
159 J10 **Leek** 53°06′N 2°01′W
163 G9 **Leende** Noord-Brabant, SE Netherlands 51°20′N 05°34′E
180 D3 **Leer** Niedersachsen, NW Germany 53°14′N 07°26′E
162 F7 **Leerdam** Zuid-Holland, C Netherlands 51°54′N 05°06′E
163 F6 **Leersum** Utrecht, C Netherlands 52°01′N 05°26′E
69 L6 **Leesburg** Florida, SE USA 28°48′N 81°52′W
75 G9 **Leesburg** Virginia, NE USA 39°09′N 77°34′W
68 B3 **Leesville** Louisiana, S USA 31°08′N 93°15′W
70 G7 **Leesville** Texas, SW USA 29°22′N 97°45′W
73 J10 **Leesville Lake** ☐ Ohio, N USA
Leesville Lake see Smith Mountain Lake
277 J5 **Leeton** New South Wales, SE Australia 34°33′S 146°24′E
140 C5 **Leeu-Gamka** Western Cape, South Africa
140 H5 **Leeudoringstad** North-West, South Africa 27°14′S 26°14′E
140 D6 **Leeu-Gamka** Western Cape, South Africa 32°47′S 21°59′E
141 I3 **Leeukraal** North-West, South Africa 25°17′S 28°16′E
162 G3 **Leeuwarden** Fris. Ljouwert. Friesland, N Netherlands 53°12′N 05°48′E
274 D6 **Leeuwin, Cape** headland Western Australia 34°18′S 115°03′E
80 F4 **Lee Vining** California, W USA 37°57′N 119°07′W
Leeward Islands see Sotavento, Ilhas de
Leeward Islands see Vent, Îles Sous le
180 J2 **Leezen** Schleswig-Holstein, Germany 10°15′N 53°52′E
135 D8 **Léfini** ☞ SE Congo
Léfka see Lefke
186 F6 **Lefkáda** prev. Levkás. Lefkáda, Iónioi Nísoi, Greece, C Mediterranean Sea 38°50′N 20°42′E
186 F6 **Lefkáda** It. Santa Maura, prev. Levkás; anc. Leucas. island Iónioi Nísoi, Greece, C Mediterranean Sea
187 H10 **Lefká Óri** ▲ Kríti, Greece, E Mediterranean Sea
218 B2 **Lefke** Gk. Léfka. W Cyprus 35°06′N 32°52′E
186 E4 **Lefkímmi** var. Levkímmi. Kérkyra, Iónia Nisiá, Greece, C Mediterranean Sea 39°26′N 20°05′E
Lefkonía/Lefkosa see Nicosia
Lefkosía/Lefkónikon see Nicosia
70 **Lefors** Texas, SW USA 35°26′N 100°48′W
168 F6 **Le Fossat** Midi-Pyrénées, France 43°11′N 1°25′E
168 F6 **Le Fousseret** Midi-Pyrénées, France 43°11′N 1°04′E
91 N2 **le François** E Martinique 14°36′N 60°59′W
169 J3 **Le Freney-d'Oisans** Rhône-Alpes, France 45°02′N 6°07′E
53 L6 **Lefroy Bay** coastal sea feature Nunavut, NE Canada
274 E7 **Lefroy, Lake** salt lake Western Australia
Legaceaster see Chester
170 G3 **Leganés** Madrid, C Spain 40°20′N 03°46′W
263 M6 **Legazpi City** off. Legazpi City var. Legaspi. Luzon, N Philippines 13°09′N 123°44′E
Leghorn see Livorno
182 H6 **Legionowo** Mazowieckie, C Poland 52°25′N 20°56′E
163 G13 **Léglise** Luxembourg, SE Belgium 49°48′N 05°31′E
176 E7 **Legnano** Lombardia, NE Italy 45°35′N 08°53′E
182 D7 **Legnago** Veneto, NE Italy 45°10′N 11°18′E
182 D7 **Legnica** Ger. Liegnitz. Dolnośląskie, SW Poland 51°12′N 16°11′E
182 D7 **Legnica** ◇ province W Poland
80 E1 **Le Gond-Pontouvre** Poitou-Charentes, France 45°41′N 0°10′E
80 D5 **Le Grand** California, W USA 37°12′N 120°15′W
166 G10 **Le Grand-Bourg** Limousin, France 46°10′N 1°39′E
166 E7 **Le Grand-Quevilly** Haute-Normandie, France 49°52′N 1°02′E
169 K2 **Le Grand-Serre** Rhône-Alpes, France 45°16′N 5°06′E
165 I8 **le Grau-du-Roi** Gard, S France 43°32′N 04°08′E
85 **Léguevin** Haute-Garonne, France 43°36′N 1°15′E
277 M2 **Legume** New South Wales, SE Australia 28°24′S 152°20′E
164 G5 **Le Havre** Eng. Havre; prev. le Havre-de-Grâce. Seine-Maritime, N France 49°30′N 00°06′E
le Havre-de-Grâce see le Havre
Lehena see Lechainá
74 F6 **Lehighton** Pennsylvania, NE USA 40°49′N 75°42′W
80 D3 **Lehmann** Santa Fe, Argentina 31°08′S 61°27′W
74 D3 **Lehr** North Dakota, N USA 46°16′N 99°21′W
181 I13 **Lehrberg** Bayern, Germany 10°31′N 49°02′E
180 H4 **Lehre** Niedersachsen, Germany 10°31′N 52°20′E
180 H3 **Lehrte** Niedersachsen, Germany 9°58′N 52°23′E
82 A1 **Lehua Island** island Hawaiian Islands, Hawai'i, USA
177 K4 **Leibnitz** Steiermark, SE Austria 46°48′N 15°33′E

242 A4 **Leibo** China 28°15′N 103°34′E
161 J3 **Leicester** Lat. Batae Coritanorum. C England, UK 52°38′N 01°05′W
161 J3 **Leicestershire** cultural region C England, UK
Leicheng see Leizhou
162 D4 **Leiden** prev. Leyden; anc. Lugdunum Batavorum. Zuid-Holland, W Netherlands 52°09′N 04°30′E
162 D4 **Leiderdorp** Zuid-Holland, W Netherlands 52°08′N 04°24′E
162 E6 **Leidschendam** Zuid-Holland, W Netherlands 52°05′N 04°24′E
163 C10 **Leie** Fr. Lys. ☞ Belgium/France
Leifear see Lifford
278 F4 **Leiferde** Niedersachsen, Germany 10°31′N 52°23′E
159 J5 **Leigh** Auckland, North Island, New Zealand 36°17′S 174°48′E
159 J5 **Leigh** NW England, UK 53°30′N 02°33′W
276 G3 **Leigh Creek** South Australia 30°27′S 138°23′E
66 J5 **Leighton** Alabama, S USA 34°42′N 87°31′W
161 **Leighton Buzzard** E England, UK 51°55′N 00°41′W
Léim an Bhradáin see Leixlip
Léime, Ceann see Loop Head, Ireland
Léime, Ceann see Slyne Head, Ireland
181 **Leimen** Baden-Württemberg, SW Germany 49°21′N 08°40′E
180 E4 **Leine** ☞ NW Germany
181 **Leinefelde** Thüringen, C Germany 51°22′N 10°19′E
157 **Léin, Loch** see Leane, Lough
157 D10 **Leinster, Mount** Ir. Stua Laighean. ▲ SE Ireland 52°36′N 06°45′W
160 A3 **Mount Leinster** ▲ Carlow, Ireland 52°36′N 6°47′W
160 G4 **Leintwardine** UK 52°22′N 2°52′W
179 D9 **Leipalingis** Alytus, S Lithuania 54°05′N 23°52′E
152 N3 **Leipojärvi** Norrbotten, N Sweden 67°03′N 21°15′E
73 G9 **Leipsic** Ohio, N USA 41°06′N 83°58′W
187 K7 **Leipsoí** island Dodekánisa, Greece, Aegean Sea
179 F9 **Leipzig** Pol. Lipsk, hist. Leipsic; anc. Lipsia. Sachsen, E Germany 51°19′N 12°24′E
172 B5 **Leipzig Halle** ✈ Sachsen, E Germany 51°24′N 12°14′E
172 G3 **Leiria** anc. Collipo. Leiria, C Portugal 39°45′N 08°49′W
172 B3 **Leiria** ◆ district C Portugal
154 A7 **Leirvik** Hordaland, S Norway 59°49′N 05°27′E
13 **Leicester** UK 52°38′N 1°08′W
242 D6 **Leishan** Guizhou, China 26°13′N 108°02′E
154 C4 **Leisi** Ger. Laisberg. Saaremaa, W Estonia 58°33′N 22°41′E
170 J2 **Leitariegos, Puerto de** pass NW Spain
116 G8 **Leitchfield** Kentucky, S USA 37°28′N 86°19′W
54 **Point Leith** headland Northwest Territories, NW Canada
177 **Leitha** Hung. Lajta. ☞ Austria/Hungary
Leitir Ceanainn see Letterkenny
158 C5 **Leitrim** Ir. Liatroim. cultural region NW Ireland
158 D10 **Leitrim** Ireland 53°59′N 8°04′W
Leivádia see Livádeia
158 D10 **Leixlip** Eng. Salmon Leap, Ir. Léim an Bhradáin. Kildare, E Ireland 53°21′N 06°32′W
290 H4 **Leixões** Porto, N Portugal 41°11′N 08°41′W
242 B6 **Leiyang** Hunan, S China 26°23′N 112°49′E
168 B8 **Leiza** Navarra, Spain 43°05′N 1°55′W
240 F9 **Leizhou** var. Haikang, Leicheng. Guangdong, S China 20°54′N 110°05′E
242 F9 **Leizhou Bandao** var. Luichow Peninsula. peninsula S China
162 C7 **Lek** ☞ SW Netherlands
187 J2 **Lekánis** ▲ NE Greece
139 I7 **Le Kartala** ▲ Grande Comore, NW Comoros
Lef Kef see El Kef
168 A5 **Lekeitio** País Vasco, Spain 43°22′N 2°30′W
185 I5 **Lékéti, Monts de la** ▲ C Congo
Lekhainá see Lechainá
185 I5 **Lekhchevo** Montana, NW Bulgaria 43°32′N 23°31′E
140 C6 **Lekkersing** Northern Cape, South Africa
185 **Lekoes** Nordland, C Norway 68°07′N 13°36′E
135 B9 **Le Koulou** ◆ province SW Congo
135 C8 **Leksand** Dalarna, C Sweden 60°44′N 15°E
194 G4 **Leksozero, Ozero** ☐ NW Russian Federation
171 H2 **Lekunberri** var. Lecumberri. Navarra, N Spain 43°00′N 01°54′W
181 D8 **Lenne** ☞ W Germany
181 **Lanan, Tanjung** headland Pulau Halmahera, N Indonesia 01°32′N 128°43′E
91 N2 **le Lamentin** var. Lamentin. C Martinique 14°35′N 61°01′W
91 N2 **le Lamentin** ✈ (Fort-de-France) C Martinique 14°34′N 61°00′W
72 **Leland** Michigan, N USA 45°01′N 85°44′W
68 A8 **Leland** Mississippi, S USA 33°24′N 90°54′W
155 **Lelång** var. Lelängen. ☐ S Sweden
Lelängen see Lelång
160 C3 **Lelant** UK 50°11′N 5°26′W
169 L1 **Le Lauzet-Ubaye** Provence-Alpes-Côte d'Azur, France 44°26′N 6°32′E
71 H5 **Lelia Lake** Texas, SW USA 34°52′N 100°42′W
140 D7 **Leliefontein** Northern Cape, South Africa 30°18′S 18°05′E
184 F5 **Lelija** ▲ SE Bosnia and Herzegovina 43°25′N 18°31′E
245 J5 **Leling** Shandong, China 37°26′N 117°07′E
169 D7 **Le Lion-d'Angers** Pays de la Loire, France 47°38′N 0°43′W
54 E4 **Le Locle** Neuchâtel, W Switzerland 47°04′N 06°45′E
283 I10 **Lelu** Kosrae, E Micronesia
Lelu see Lelu Island
169 L6 **Le Luc** Provence-Alpes-Côte d'Azur, France 43°23′N 6°19′E
166 F6 **Le Lude** Pays de la Loire, France 47°39′N 0°09′E
282 I10 **Lelu Island** var. Lelu. island Kosrae, E Micronesia
103 L5 **Lelydorp** Wanica, N Surinam 05°36′N 55°04′W
162 F6 **Lelystad** Flevoland, C Netherlands 52°30′N 05°28′E
117 A14 **Le Maire, Estrecho de** strait S Argentina
169 I3 **Le Malzieu-Ville** Languedoc-Roussillon, France 44°51′N 3°21′E
258 E4 **Lemang** Pulau Rangsang, W Indonesia 01°04′N 102°34′E
280 E3 **Lemankoa** Buka Island, NE Papua New Guinea 05°06′S 154°23′E
166 E6 **Le Mans** Sarthe, NW France 48°N 00°12′E
74 F4 **Le Mars** Iowa, C USA 42°45′N 96°10′W
168 F6 **Le Mas-d'Azil** Midi-Pyrénées, France 43°05′N 1°22′E
177 J2 **Lembach im Mühlkreis** Oberösterreich, N Austria 48°28′N 13°53′E
179 D13 **Lemberg** ▲ SW Germany 48°09′N 08°47′E
Lemberg see L'viv
Lemdiyya see Médéa
110 **Leme** São Paulo, Brazil 22°12′S 47°24′W
91 L6 **le Mée-sur-Seine** Basse-Normandie, France 48°31′N 02°E
166 E5 **Le Merlerault** Basse-Normandie, France 48°42′N 0°18′E
218 B2 **Lemesós** var. Limassol. SW Cyprus 34°41′N 33°02′E
181 **Lemförde** Niedersachsen, Germany 8°23′E
180 E4 **Lemgo** Nordrhein-Westfalen, W Germany 52°02′N 08°54′E
77 H6 **Lemhi Range** ▲ Idaho, NW USA
53 M9 **Lemieux Islands** island group Nunavut, NE Canada
258 D10 **Lemito** Sulawesi, N Indonesia 0°34′N 121°31′E
152 G4 **Lemmenjoki** Fin. Leammi. ☞ NE Finland
162 G4 **Lemmer** Fris. De Lemmer. Friesland, N Netherlands 52°50′N 05°43′E
74 B3 **Lemmon** South Dakota, N USA 45°55′N 102°10′W
79 J11 **Lemmon, Mount** ▲ Arizona, SW USA 32°26′N 110°47′W
Lemnos see Límnos
169 H4 **Le Monastier** Languedoc-Roussillon, France 44°31′N 3°15′E
80 E6 **Lemoncove** California, USA 36°23′N 119°01′W
73 J9 **Lemont** Illinois, N USA
169 H2 **Le Mont-Dore** Auvergne, France 45°34′N 2°49′E
167 H10 **le Mont St-Michel** castle Manche, N France
164 D6 **Lemoore** California, W USA 36°18′N 119°46′W
282 D6 **Lemotol Bay** bay Chuuk Islands, C Micronesia
91 K1 **le Moule** var. Moule. Grande Terre, NE Guadeloupe 16°20′N 61°21′W
le Moyen-Ogooué see Moyen-Ogooué
59 H3 **Le Moyne, Lac** ☐ Québec, E Canada
153 F9 **Lempäälä** Länsi-Suomi, W Finland 61°14′N 23°47′E
102 C4 **Lempdes** Auvergne, France 45°37′N 3°18′E
88 G4 **Lempira** prev. Gracias. ◆ department SW Honduras
Lemsalu see Limbaži
175 **Le Murge** ▲ SE Italy
154 H4 **Lemvig** Ringkøbing, W Denmark 56°33′N 08°19′E
155 C11 **Lemvig** Ringkøbing, W Denmark
243 J4 **Leping** Jiangxi, S China 28°57′N 117°07′E
154 H5 **Lemyethna** Irrawaddy, SW Myanmar (Burma)

73 C8 **Lena** Illinois, N USA 42°22′N 89°49′W
205 L3 **Lena** ☞ NE Russian Federation
289 C12 **Lena Tablemount** undersea feature S Indian Ocean
Lenchitsa see Łęczyca
166 E9 **Lençloitre** Poitou-Charentes, France 46°49′N 0°19′E
78 I09 **Lençóis** Bahia, E Brazil 12°36′S 41°24′W
110 A7 **Lençóis Paulista** São Paulo, S Brazil 22°35′S 48°51′W
263 L8 **Lendalfoot** UK 55°11′N 4°56′W
Lan Dao island S Spratly Islands
177 L5 **Lendava** Hung. Lendva, Ger. Unterlimbach; prev. Dolnja Lendava. NE Slovenia 46°33′N 16°27′E
163 G10 **Lendepas** Hardap, SE Namibia 24°41′S 19°58′E
194 D6 **Lendery** Respublika Kareliya, NW Russian Federation 63°22′N 31°58′E
181 D8 **Lendringsen** Nordrhein-Westfalen, Germany 7°50′N 51°25′E
Lendum see Lens
166 E5 **Le Neubourg** Haute-Normandie, France 49°09′N 0°55′E
75 C6 **Lenexa** Kansas, C USA 38°57′N 94°43′W
177 M4 **Lengau** Oberösterreich, N Austria 48°01′N 13°17′E
181 M1 **Lengefeld** Thüringen, Germany 51°22′N 11°15′E
227 M2 **Lenger** Yuzhnyy Kazakhstan, S Kazakhstan 42°10′N 69°54′E
180 F5 **Lengerich** Niedersachsen, Germany 7°31′N 52°33′E
180 D5 **Lengerich** Nordrhein-Westfalen, Germany 52°11′N 07°52′E
181 H12 **Lengfurt** Bayern, Germany 9°36′N 49°49′E
242 **Lenghu** China 27°13′N 111°22′E
239 H5 **Lenghuzhen** var. Lenghu. Qinghai, C China
Lenghu see Lenghuzhen
Lengnau see Lengnau
176 C4 **Lengnau** Bern, W Switzerland 47°12′N 07°23′E
242 **Lengshuijiang** Hunan, S China 27°36′N 111°28′E
Lengshuitan see Yongzhou
155 N11 **Lenhovda** Kronoberg, S Sweden 57°00′N 15°16′E
135 B8 **Le Niari** ◆ province SW Congo
Lenin see Uzynkol'
Lenin see Akdepe
Leninabad see Khūjand
Leninakan see Gyumri
154 A7 **Lenina, Pik** see Lenin Peak
189 **Lenine** Rus. Lenino. Respublika Krym, S Ukraine 45°18′N 35°47′E
Lenin see Leninogorsk
229 J7 **Leningrad** Rus. Leningradskiy; prev. Mū'minobod, Rus. Muminabad. SW Tajikistan 38°03′N 69°50′E
Leningrad see Sankt-Peterburg
196 G3 **Leningradskaya** Krasnodarskiy Kray, SW Russian Federation 46°19′N 39°23′E
293 J9 **Leningradskaya** Russian research station Antarctica
194 E8 **Leningradskaya Oblast'** ◆ province NW Russian Federation
Leningradskiy see Leningrad
Lenino see Lenine
Lenino see Lenine
Lenino see Khūjand
227 M3 **Leninogorsk** Kaz. Leninogor. Vostochnyy Kazakhstan, E Kazakhstan 50°20′N 83°34′E
197 K2 **Leninogorsk** Respublika Tatarstan, W Russian Federation 54°36′N 52°30′E
229 M2 **Lenin Peak** Rus. Pik Lenina, Taj. Qullai Lenin. ▲ Kyrgyzstan/Tajikistan 39°21′N 73°01′E
229 J7 **Leninpol'** Talasskaya Oblast', NW Kyrgyzstan 42°29′N 71°54′E
Lenin, Qullai see Lenin Peak
197 L3 **Leninsk** Volgogradskaya Oblast', SW Russian Federation 48°41′N 45°8′E
Leninsk see Akdepe
Leninsk see Asaka
227 **Leninskiy** Pavlodar, E Kazakhstan 52°13′N 76°50′E
192 F7 **Leninsk-Kuznetskiy** Kemerovskaya Oblast', S Russian Federation 54°42′N 86°16′E
195 **Leninskoye** Kirovskaya Oblast', NW Russian Federation 57°29′N 49°15′E
Leninskoye see Uzynkol'
Lenin-Turkmenski see Türkmenabat
Leninváros see Tiszaújváros
Leninkoran' see Lānkārān
181 D8 **Lenne** ☞ W Germany
181 E9 **Lennestadt** Nordrhein-Westfalen, W Germany 51°07′N 08°04′E
74 E4 **Lennox** South Dakota, N USA 43°21′N 96°53′W
117 E14 **Lennox, Isla** Eng. Lennox. island S Chile
Lennox Island see Lennox, Isla
67 I6 **Lenoir** North Carolina, SE USA 35°51′N 81°33′W
66 F8 **Lenoir City** Tennessee, S USA 35°48′N 84°15′W
61 C6 **Le Noirmont** Jura, NW Switzerland 47°14′N 06°57′E
72 E6 **Lenora** Kansas, C USA 40°52′N 94°33′W
64 F4 **Lenox** Iowa, C USA 40°52′N 94°33′W
64 I2 **Lenox** Massachusetts, USA 41°43′N 75°40′W
11 **Lens** anc. Lendum, Lentium. Pas-de-Calais, N France 50°26′N 02°50′E
193 I4 **Lensk** Respublika Sakha (Yakutiya), NE Russian Federation 60°43′N 115°16′E
183 D12 **Lenti** Zala, SW Hungary 46°38′N 16°30′E
152 I3 **Lentiira** Oulu, E Finland 64°22′N 29°52′E
175 G12 **Lentini** anc. Leontini. Sicilia, Italy, C Mediterranean Sea 37°17′N 15°00′E
152 J2 **Lentua** ☐ E Finland
191 **Lentvaris** Pol. Landwarów. Vilnius, SE Lithuania 24°39′N 24°58′E
81 F10 **Lenwood** California, W USA 34°51′N 117°06′W
176 D3 **Lenzburg** Aargau, N Switzerland 47°23′N 08°11′E
177 I2 **Lenzing** Oberösterreich, N Austria 48°06′N 13°34′E
132 G3 **Léo** SW Burkina 11°07′N 02°08′W
177 I3 **Leoben** Steiermark, C Austria 47°23′N 15°06′E
160 **Léogâne** S Haiti 18°32′N 72°37′W
160 G4 **Leominster** W England, UK 52°09′N 02°18′W
65 K2 **Leominster** Massachusetts, NE USA 42°29′N 71°43′W
85 M3 **León** Guanajuato, C Mexico 21°05′N 101°41′W
88 C4 **León** Léon, W Nicaragua 12°24′N 86°52′W
170 H2 **León** Castilla-León, NW Spain 42°34′N 05°34′W
75 G9 **León** Iowa, C USA 40°44′N 93°45′W
86 D4 **León** ◆ department W Nicaragua
170 G2 **León** ◆ province Castilla-León, NW Spain
León see Cotopaxi
71 H5 **Leona** Texas, SW USA 31°09′N 95°58′W
72 H4 **Leonard** Texas, SW USA 33°22′N 96°15′W
67 L5 **Leonardtown** Maryland, NE USA 38°17′N 76°35′W
110 **Leonard River** ☞ Texas, USA
85 N5 **Leona Vicario** Quintana Roo, SE Mexico 20°57′N 87°16′W
179 **Leonberg** Baden-Württemberg, SW Germany 48°48′N 09°01′E
169 K3 **Léoncel** Rhône-Alpes, France 44°54′N 5°12′E
89 M9 **León, Cerro** ▲ NW Paraguay 20°21′S 60°16′W
León de los Aldamas see León
177 M2 **Leonding** Oberösterreich, N Austria 48°17′N 14°15′E
175 G12 **Leonforte** Sicilia, Italy, C Mediterranean Sea 37°38′N 14°23′E
277 J7 **Leongatha** Victoria, SE Australia 38°30′S 145°56′E
186 G7 **Leonídi** var. Leonídi. Peloponnísos, S Greece 37°11′S 22°50′E
Leonídio see Leonídi
170 C4 **León, Montes de** ▲ NW Spain
70 G4 **Leon River** ☞ Texas, SW USA
Leontini see Lentini
Léopold II, Lac see Mai-Ndombe, Lac
111 J3 **Leopoldina** Minas Gerais, E Brazil 21°32′S 42°38′W
Leopoldo de Bulhões Goiás, Brazil
163 G9 **Leopoldsburg** Limburg, NE Belgium 51°07′N 05°15′E
Léopoldville see Kinshasa
75 B10 **Leoti** Kansas, C USA 38°29′N 101°21′W
188 F7 **Leova** Rus. Leovo. SW Moldova 46°31′N 28°16′E
Leovo see Leova
171 L6 **Lepar, Pulau** island W Indonesia
186 C7 **Lepe** Andalucía, S Spain 37°15′N 07°12′W
Lepel' see Lyepyel'
166 D8 **Le Pellerin** Pays de la Loire, France 47°12′N 1°45′E
187 I6 **Lepenoú** Dytikí Elláda, C Greece 38°42′N 21°15′E
258 C6 **Leping** Kweneng, SE Botswana 23°58′N 25°40′E
Lepsény Somogy, C Hungary

166 C9 **Le Poiré-sur-Vie** Pays de la Loire, France 46°46′N 1°31′W
169 K2 **Le Pont-de-Beauvoisin** Rhône-Alpes, France 45°32′N 5°40′E
169 K2 **Le Pont-de-Claix** Rhône-Alpes, France 45°07′N 5°42′E
169 I4 **Le Pont-de-Montvert** Languedoc-Roussillon, France 44°22′N 3°45′E
169 J5 **Le Pontet** Provence-Alpes-Côte d'Azur, France 43°58′N 4°51′E
Lépontiennes, Alpes/Lepontine, Alpi see Lepontine Alps
176 E5 **Lepontine Alps** Fr. Alpes Lépontiennes, It. Alpi Lepontine. ▲ Italy/Switzerland
135 C9 **Le Port** S Congo
137 I10 **Le Port** NW Réunion
135 H1 **le Portel** Pas-de-Calais, N France 50°42′N 01°35′E
169 L2 **Le Pouzin** Rhône-Alpes, France 44°45′N 4°45′E
153 H7 **Leppävirta** Itä-Suomi, C Finland 63°30′N 27°50′E
91 M1 **le Prêcheur** NW Martinique 14°48′N 61°14′W
Lepsi see Lepsy
227 K6 **Lepsi** Kaz. Lepsi. Taldykorgan, SE Kazakhstan 46°14′N 78°56′E
227 K6 **Lepsy** Kaz. Lepsi. ☞ SE Kazakhstan
Le Puglie see Puglia
165 I7 **le Puy-en-Velay**, hist. Anicium, Podium Anicensis. Haute-Loire, C France 45°03′N 03°53′E
169 I3 **Le Puy-en-Velay** Auvergne, France 45°02′N 3°53′E
le Puy-en-Velay see Le Puy
167 J2 **Le Quesnoy** Nord-Pas-de-Calais, France 50°15′N 3°38′E
91 **Le Raizet** var. Le Raizet. ✈ (Pointe-à-Pitre) Grande Terre, C Guadeloupe 16°16′N 61°31′W
175 F12 **Lercara Friddi** Sicilia, Italy, C Mediterranean Sea 37°45′N 13°36′E
85 **Lerdo de Tejada** Veracruz-Llave, E Mexico North America
134 C3 **Léré** Mayo-Kébbi, SW Chad 09°41′N 14°17′E
167 **Léré** France 47°28′N 2°52′E
Leribe see Hlotse
176 F7 **Lerici** Liguria, NW Italy 44°06′N 09°53′E
102 B3 **Lérida** Vaupés, SE Colombia 0°01′S 70°28′W
168 **Lérida** Cataluña, Spain 41°37′N 0°37′E
Lérida see Lleida
87 **Lerma** Campeche, Mexico 19°48′N 90°36′W
170 **Lerma** Castilla-León, N Spain 42°02′N 03°46′W
86 C5 **Lerma, Río** ☞ Mexico
Lerna see Lérni
186 **Lérni** var. Lerna. prehistoric site Pelopónnisos, S Greece
91 N **Lerwick** NE Scotland, UK 60°09′N 01°09′W
187 K7 **Léros** island Dodekánisa, Greece, Aegean Sea
75 F10 **Le Roy** Illinois, N USA 40°21′N 88°45′W
75 F10 **Le Roy** Kansas, C USA 38°04′N 95°37′W
155 F10 **Lerum** Älvsborg, S Sweden 57°46′N 12°12′E
156 M8 **Le Russey** Franche-Comté, France 47°10′N 6°44′E
156 N1 **Lerwick** NE Scotland, UK 60°09′N 01°09′W
169 K2 **Les Abrets** Rhône-Alpes, France 45°32′N 5°35′E
91 J1 **les Abymes** var. Abymes. Grande Terre, C Guadeloupe 16°16′N 61°31′W
167 M3 **Les Aix-d'Angillon** Centre, France 47°12′N 2°34′E
85 M2 **les Albères** see Albères, Chaîne des
169 H5 **Les Andelys** Eure, N France 49°15′N 01°26′E
91 M2 **Les Anses-d'Arlets** SW Martinique 14°29′N 61°05′W
167 H6 **Les Bordères** Centre, France 47°49′N 2°51′E
171 J3 **Les Borges Blanques** var. Borjas Blancas. Cataluña, NE Spain 41°31′N 0°52′E
Lesbos see Lésvos
165 G5 **Les Cabannes** Midi-Pyrénées, France 42°47′N 1°40′E
72 **Les Cayes** see Cayes
169 M1 **Les Cheneaux Islands** island Michigan, N USA
169 M1 **Les Contamines-Montjoie** Rhône-Alpes, France
171 J5 **Les Coves de Vinromá** Cast. Cuevas de Vinromá. País Valenciano, E Spain 40°19′N 00°07′E
169 L3 **les Écrins** ▲ France 44°54′N 06°25′E
169 L6 **Le Sépey** Vaud, S Switzerland 46°21′N 07°04′E
176 C5 **Les Escoumins** Québec, SE Canada 48°21′N 69°24′W
169 C6 **Lesjöfors** Värmland, C Sweden 59°57′N 14°12′E
183 **Lesko** Podkarpackie, SE Poland 49°28′N 22°21′E
185 L6 **Leskovac** Serbia, SE Serbia 43°00′N 21°57′E
184 **Leskovik** see Leskoviku. Korçë, S Albania 40°09′N 20°39′E
Leskoviku see Leskovik
185 N8 **Leslie** Idaho, USA 43°51′N 113°28′W
77 H7 **Leslie** Idaho, USA
159 L3 **Leslie** UK 56°12′N 3°13′W
159 H4 **Lesmahagow** UK 55°37′N 3°54′W
169 I6 **Lesnar** Languedoc-Roussillon, France
167 J6 **Lesmont** Champagne-Ardenne, France 48°26′N 4°25′E
166 C10 **Les Moutiers-les-Mauxfaits** Pays de la Loire, France 46°28′N 1°27′W
Lesná/Lesnaya see Lyasnaya
Lesnaye see Lyasnaya
164 D3 **Lesneven** NW France 48°34′N 04°19′W
184 **Lešnica** Serbia, W Serbia 44°40′N 19°18′E
195 **Lesnoy** Kirovskaya Oblast', NW Russian Federation 59°49′N 52°07′E
169 **Les Ollières-sur-Eyrieux** Rhône-Alpes, France 44°48′N 4°37′E
192 **Lesosibirsk** Krasnoyarskiy Kray, C Russian Federation 58°13′N 92°23′E
141 I4 **Lesotho** off. Kingdom of Lesotho; prev. Basutoland. ◆ monarchy S Africa
Lesotho, Kingdom of see Lesotho
193 **Lesozavodsk** Primorskiy Kray, SE Russian Federation 45°27′N 133°15′E
169 **Lesparre-Médoc** Gironde, SW France 45°18′N 00°57′W
166 C4 **Les Pieux** Basse-Normandie, France 49°31′N 1°48′W
169 **Les Planches-en-Montagne** Franche-Comté, France 46°40′N 6°01′E
167 **Les Ponts-de-Martel** Neuchâtel, W Switzerland
167 J7 **Les Riceys** Champagne-Ardenne, France 47°59′N 4°22′E
169 J4 **Les Vans** Rhône-Alpes, France 44°24′N 4°08′E
176 C5 **Les Verrières** Neuchâtel, W Switzerland
183 **Lésvos** anc. Lesbos. island E Greece
158 **Leswalt** UK 54°55′N 5°05′W
183 **Leszno** Ger. Lissa. Wielkopolskie, C Poland 51°51′N 16°35′E
161 **Letchworth** E England, UK 51°58′N 0°13′W
56 **Le Teil** Rhône-Alpes, France 44°33′N 4°41′E
169 **Le Teilleul** Basse-Normandie, France
168 E4 **Le Temple-sur-Lot** Aquitaine, France 44°22′N 0°31′E
183 D12 **Letenye** Zala, SW Hungary 46°25′N 16°44′E

◆ Country   ◇ Dependent Territory   ◆ Administrative Regions   ▲ Mountain   ▲ Volcano   ☐ Lake
● Country Capital   ○ Dependent Territory Capital   ✈ International Airport   ▲ Mountain Range   ☞ River   ☐ Reservoir

◆ Country	◇ Dependent Territory	▲ Administrative Regions	✕ International Airport	▲ Mountain	▲ Mountain Range	≈ Volcano	≈ River	⊚ Lake	⊡ Reservoir
● Country Capital	○ Dependent Territory Capital								

M

Melvin, Lough - Mikhaylovgrad
INDEX
375

157 C8 **Melvin, Lough** *Ir.* Loch Meilbhe. ◎ S Northern Ireland, UK/Ireland
258 J6 **Memala** Borneo, C Indonesia 01°44′S 112°36′E
184 F9 **Memaliaj** Gjirokastër, S Albania 40°21′N 19°56′E
139 L1 **Memba** Nampula, NE Mozambique 14°07′S 40°33′E
139 L1 **Memba, Baia de** *inlet* NE Mozambique
Membidj *see* Manbij
141 J5 **Memel** Free State, South Africa 27°41′S 29°34′E
Memel *see* Neman, NE Europe
Memel *see* Klaipeda, Lithuania
179 E13 **Memmingen** Bayern, S Germany 47°59′N 10°11′E
75 H8 **Memphis** Missouri, C USA 40°28′N 92°11′W
75 J12 **Memphis** Tennessee, S USA 35°09′N 90°03′W
70 E2 **Memphis** Texas, SW USA 34°43′N 100°34′W
66 B7 **Memphis** ✕ Tennessee, S USA 35°02′N 89°57′W
63 I3 **Memphrémagog, Lac** *var.* Lake Memphremagog. ◎ Canada/USA *see also* Lake Memphremagog
63 I3 **Memphremagog, Lake** *var.* Lac Memphrémagog. ◎ Canada/USA *see also* Memphrémagog, Lac
189 I2 **Mena** Chernihivs'ka Oblast', NE Ukraine 51°30′N 32°15′E
75 G13 **Mena** Arkansas, C USA 34°40′N 94°15′W
Menaam *see* Menaldum
Menado *see* Manado
114 F6 **Menafra** Río Negro, Uruguay 32°34′S 57°29′W
176 E6 **Menaggio** Lombardia, N Italy 46°03′N 09°14′E
74 F3 **Menahga** Minnesota, N USA 46°45′N 95°06′W
133 I4 **Ménaka** Goa, E Mali 15°55′N 02°25′E
162 G3 **Menaldum** *Fris.* Menaam. Friesland, N Netherlands 53°14′N 05°38′E
Mènam Khong *see* Mekong
130 E3 **Menara** ✕ (Marrakech) C Morocco 31°36′N 08°00′W
70 F6 **Menard** Texas, SW USA 30°56′N 99°48′W
287 I9 **Menard Fracture Zone** *tectonic feature* E Pacific Ocean
172 G4 **Menasalbas** Castilla-La Manacha, Spain 39°38′N 4°17′W
72 D6 **Menasha** Wisconsin, N USA 44°13′N 88°25′W
287 J7 **Mendaña Fracture Zone** *tectonic feature* E Pacific Ocean
258 J6 **Mendawai, Sungai** ⚞ Borneo, C Indonesia
175 J7 **Mende** *anc.* Mimatum. Lozère, S France 44°32′N 03°30′E
136 E5 **Mendebo** ▲ C Ethiopia
136 E2 **Mendefera** *prev.* Adi Ugri. S Eritrea 14°53′N 38°51′E
294 G5 **Mendeleyev Ridge** *undersea feature* Arctic Ocean
197 K2 **Mendeleyevsk** Respublika Tatarstan, W Russian Federation 55°54′N 52°19′E
181 D8 **Menden** Nordrhein-Westfalen, W Germany 51°26′N 07°47′E
68 E2 **Mendenhall** Mississippi, S USA 31°57′N 89°52′W
82 F7 **Mendenhall, Cape** *headland* Nunivak Island, Alaska, USA 59°45′N 166°10′W
171 J10 **Mendes** Algeria
111 H7 **Mendes** Rio de Janeiro, Brazil 22°32′S 43°43′W
85 M7 **Méndez** *var.* Villa de Méndez. Tamaulipas, C Mexico 25°06′N 98°32′W
136 C4 **Mendī** Oromo C Ethiopia 09°43′N 35°07′E
280 B3 **Mendi** Southern Highlands, W Papua New Guinea 06°13′S 143°39′E
160 G7 **Mendip Hills** *var.* Mendips. *hill range* S England, UK
Mendips *see* Mendip Hills
115 K6 **Mendizabal** Uruguay 33°03′S 54°09′W
161 M4 **Mendlesham** UK 52°15′N 1°04′E
78 A3 **Mendocino** California, W USA 39°18′N 123°48′W
78 A2 **Mendocino, Cape** *headland* California, W USA 40°26′N 124°24′W
42 A5 **Mendocino Fracture Zone** *tectonic feature* NE Pacific Ocean
80 C5 **Mendota** California, W USA 36°44′N 120°24′W
73 C9 **Mendota** Illinois, N USA 41°32′N 89°04′W
72 C7 **Mendota, Lake** ◎ Wisconsin, N USA
118 F2 **Mendoza** Mendoza, W Argentina 33°00′S 68°47′W
115 H9 **Mendoza** Florida, Uruguay 34°17′S 56°13′W
118 F4 **Mendoza** *off.* Provincia de Mendoza. ◆ *province* W Argentina
115 H8 **Mendoza Chico** Florida, Uruguay 34°12′S 56°13′W
Mendoza, Provincia de *see* Mendoza
176 E6 **Mendrisio** Ticino, S Switzerland 45°53′N 08°59′E
258 E4 **Mendung** Pulau Mendol, W Indonesia 0°33′N 103°09′E
102 E2 **Mene de Mauroa** Falcón, NW Venezuela 10°39′N 71°04′W
102 E3 **Mene Grande** Zulia, NW Venezuela 09°51′N 70°57′W
214 B6 **Menemen** 4Izmir, W Turkey 38°34′N 27°03′E
163 B10 **Menen** *var.* Meenen, *Fr.* Menin. West-Vlaanderen, W Belgium 50°48′N 03°07′E
237 H3 **Menengiyn Tal** *plain* E Mongolia
283 J10 **Meneng Point** *headland* SW Nauru 0°33′S 166°57′E
152 H4 **Menesjärvi** *Lapp.* Menešjávri. Lappi, N Finland 68°39′N 26°22′E
Menešjávri *see* Menesjärvi
175 E12 **Menfi** Sicilia, Italy, C Mediterranean Sea 37°36′N 12°59′E
245 J9 **Mengcheng** Anhui, E China 33°15′N 116°33′E
241 J2 **Mengcun** China 38°03′N 117°06′E
181 F8 **Mengeringhausen** Hessen, Germany 8°59′N 51°21′E
181 E10 **Mengerskirchen** Hessen, Germany 8°10′N 50°34′E
240 B8 **Menghai** Yunnan, SW China 22°02′N 100°18′E
173 H7 **Mengibar** Andalucía, Spain 37°58′N 3°48′W
242 C7 **Meng Jiang** ⚞ Guizhou, China
260 D5 **Mengkoka, Pegunungan** *var.* Pegunungan Mekongga. ▲ Sulawesi, C Indonesia
240 C8 **Mengla** Yunnan, SW China 21°30′N 101°33′E
242 B7 **Mengshan** Guangxi, China 24°07′N 110°19′E
245 K6 **Meng Shan** ▲ Shandong, China
245 K6 **Mengyin** China 35°42′N 117°56′E
245 H7 **Mengzhou** Henan, China 34°32′N 112°28′E
242 G7 **Mengzhu Ling** ▲ S China
240 C7 **Mengzi** Yunnan, SW China 23°20′N 103°32′E
Menin *see* Menen
277 I4 **Menindee** New South Wales, SE Australia 32°24′S 142°25′E
277 H4 **Menindee Lake** ◎ New South Wales, SE Australia
276 G6 **Meningie** South Australia 35°43′S 139°20′E
175 H3 **Mennecy** Essonne, N France 48°34′N 02°25′E
168 G8 **Menneou-sur-Cher** Centre, France 47°16′N 1°53′E
74 E6 **Menno** South Dakota, N USA 43°14′N 97°34′W
187 H2 **Menoíkio** ▲ NE Greece
72 E5 **Menominee** Michigan, N USA 45°06′N 87°36′W
72 D5 **Menominee River** ⚞ Michigan/Wisconsin, N USA
72 D7 **Menomonee Falls** Wisconsin, N USA 43°11′N 88°09′W
72 A5 **Menomonie** Wisconsin, N USA 44°52′N 91°55′W
135 E13 **Menongue** *var.* Vila Serpa Pinto, *Port.* Serpa Pinto. Cuando Cubango, C Angola 14°38′S 17°39′E
171 M5 **Menorca** *Eng.* Minorca; *anc.* Balearis Minor. *island* Islas Baleares, Spain, W Mediterranean Sea
171 I8 **Menor, Mar** *lagoon* SE Spain
169 L3 **Mens** Rhône-Alpes, France 44°49′N 5°45′E
180 D5 **Menslage** Niedersachsen, Germany 7°49′N 52°41′E
83 J5 **Mentasta Lake** Alaska, USA 63°00′N 143°48′E
54 A1 **Mentasta Lake** ◎ Alaska, USA
83 J5 **Mentasta Mountains** ▲ Alaska, USA
258 C6 **Mentawai, Kepulauan** *island group* W Indonesia
258 D6 **Mentawai, Selat** *strait* W Indonesia
258 F6 **Mentok** Pulau Bangka, W Indonesia 02°01′S 105°10′E
169 N5 **Menton** *It.* Mentone. Alpes-Maritimes, SE France 43°47′N 07°30′E
70 C5 **Mentone** Texas, SW USA 31°42′N 103°36′W
Mentone *see* Menton
73 J9 **Mentor** Ohio, N USA 41°40′N 81°20′W
245 J3 **Mentougou** China 39°56′N 116°06′E
172 G3 **Méntrida** Castilla-La Manacha, Spain 40°14′N 4°11′W
258 K4 **Menyapa, Gunung** ▲ Borneo, N Indonesia 01°04′N 116°01′E
239 K6 **Menyuan** *var.* Menyuan Huizu Zizhixian. Qinghai, C China 37°27′N 101°33′E
Menyuan Huizu Zizhixian *see* Menyuan
131 K1 **Menzel Bourguiba** *var.* Manzil Bū Ruqaybah; *prev.* Ferryville. N Tunisia 37°09′N 09°51′E
175 C13 **Menzel Bouzelfa** Tunisia
214 G7 **Menzelet Barajı** ⊠ C Turkey
197 K2 **Menzelinsk** Respublika Tatarstan, W Russian Federation 55°44′N 53°00′E
175 C13 **Menzel Temime** Tunisia
274 E6 **Menzies** Western Australia 29°42′S 121°04′E
293 K6 **Menzies, Mount** ▲ Antarctica 73°32′S 61°02′E
161 J7 **Meon** ⚞ UK
161 J7 **Meonstoke** UK 50°58′N 1°07′W
85 I4 **Meoqui** Chihuahua, N Mexico 28°18′N 105°30′W
161 K4 **Mepal** UK 52°24′N 0°07′E
137 C13 **Meponda** Niassa, NE Mozambique 13°20′S 34°53′E
162 H5 **Meppel** Drenthe, NE Netherlands 52°42′N 06°12′E
180 D5 **Meppen** Niedersachsen, NW Germany 52°42′N 07°18′E
Mequerhane, Sebkha *see* Mekerrhane, Sebkha
168 E10 **Mequinenza** Aragón, Spain 41°22′N 0°18′E
171 I4 **Mequinenza, Embalse de** ⊠ NE Spain
168 E10 **Embalse de Mequinenza** ⊠ Aragón, Spain
72 D7 **Mequon** Wisconsin, N USA 43°13′N 87°57′W
Mera *see* Maira
276 D2 **Meramangye, Lake** *salt lake* South Australia
75 I10 **Meramec River** ⚞ Missouri, C USA
Meran *see* Merano
258 E6 **Merangin** ⚞ Sumatera, W Indonesia
176 G5 **Merano** *Ger.* Meran. Trentino-Alto Adige, N Italy 46°40′N 11°10′E
258 E2 **Merapuh Lama** Pahang, Peninsular Malaysia 04°37′N 101°58′E
176 E6 **Merate** Lombardia, N Italy 45°42′N 09°26′E
258 K6 **Meratus, Pegunungan** ▲ Borneo, N Indonesia
261 M8 **Merauke** Papua, E Indonesia 08°28′S 140°28′E
261 M8 **Merauke, Sungai** ⚞ Papua, E Indonesia
277 H5 **Merbein** Victoria, SE Australia 34°11′S 142°03′E
163 D11 **Merbes-le-Château** Hainaut, S Belgium 50°19′N 04°09′E
Merca *see* Marka
102 A7 **Mercaderes** Cauca, SW Colombia 01°46′N 77°09′W
Mercara *see* Madikeri
80 D4 **Merced** California, W USA 37°17′N 120°30′W
118 E1 **Mercedario Cerro** ▲ San Juan, Argentina 31°59′S 70°07′W
114 D9 **Mercedes** Buenos Aires, E Argentina 34°42′S 59°30′W
116 H5 **Mercedes** Corrientes, NE Argentina 29°09′S 58°05′W
116 E4 **Mercedes** *prev.* Villa Mercedes. San Luis, C Argentina 33°40′S 65°25′W
114 F7 **Mercedes** Soriano, SW Uruguay 33°16′S 58°01′W
70 G10 **Mercedes** Texas, SW USA 26°09′N 97°54′W
80 D4 **Merced Falls** California, USA 37°31′N 120°20′W
114 A8 **Merceditas** Santa Fe, Argentina 33°57′S 61°20′W
80 D4 **Merced Municipal** ✕ California, USA 37°17′N 120°31′W
80 E4 **Merced Peak** ▲ California, W USA 37°34′N 119°30′W
80 D4 **Merced River** ⚞ California, W USA
62 C7 **Mercer** Pennsylvania, NE USA 41°14′N 80°14′W
64 B8 **Mercersburg** Pennsylvania, USA 39°50′N 77°54′W
64 G7 **Mercerville** New Jersey, USA 40°14′N 74°41′W
111 I5 **Merčes** Minas Gerais, Brazil 21°12′S 43°21′W
163 D10 **Merchtem** Vlaams Brabant, C Belgium 50°57′N 04°14′E
63 H3 **Mercier** Québec, SE Canada 45°15′N 73°45′W
168 G3 **Mercoeur** Limousin, France 45°01′N 1°57′E
81 I8 **Mercury** Nevada, USA 36°40′N 116°00′W
70 F5 **Mercury** Texas, SW USA 31°23′N 99°09′W
279 H3 **Mercury Islands** *island group* N New Zealand
166 B6 **Merdrignac** Bretagne, France 48°12′N 2°25′W
161 H7 **Mere** UK 51°05′N 2°16′W
63 I5 **Meredith** New Hampshire, NE USA 43°36′N 71°28′W
117 H11 **Meredith, Cape** *var.* Cabo Belgrano. *headland* West Falkland, Falkland Islands 52°15′S 60°40′W
79 M4 **Meredith, Lake** ◎ Colorado, C USA
70 E2 **Meredith, Lake** ⊠ Texas, SW USA
136 I6 **Mereeg** *var.* Mareeq, *It.* Meregh. Galguduud, E Somalia 03°47′N 47°19′E
189 K4 **Merefa** Kharkivs'ka Oblast', E Ukraine 49°49′N 36°05′E
Meregh *see* Mereeg
281 M2 **Mere Lava** *island* Banks Islands, N Vanuatu
163 C10 **Merelbeke** Oost-Vlaanderen, NW Belgium 51°00′N 03°45′E
Merend *see* Marand
193 M5 **Merenga** Magadanskaya Oblast', E Russian Federation 61°43′N 156°02′E
84 E3 **Meresichic** Sonora, Mexico 30°01′N 110°42′W
257 I8 **Mereuch** Môndôl Kiri, E Cambodia 13°01′N 107°26′E
180 C7 **Merfeld** Nordrhein-Westfalen, Germany 7°12′N 51°51′E
Mergate *see* Margate
226 C3 **Mergenevo** Zapadnyy Kazakhstan, NW Kazakhstan 49°59′N 51°19′E
256 D8 **Mergui** Tenasserim, S Myanmar (Burma) 12°26′N 98°34′E
256 D8 **Mergui Archipelago** *island group* S Myanmar (Burma)
169 L2 **Méribel** Rhône-Alpes, France 45°25′N 6°34′E
187 K2 **Meriç** *Bul.* Maritsa, *Gk.* Évros; *anc.* Hebrus. ⚞ SE Europe *see also* Évros/Maritsa
87 L5 **Mérida** Yucatán, SW Mexico 20°58′N 89°35′W
170 E6 **Mérida** *anc.* Augusta Emerita. Extremadura, W Spain 38°55′N 06°20′W
102 D4 **Mérida** Mérida, W Venezuela 08°36′N 71°08′W
102 D4 **Mérida** *off.* Estado Mérida. ◆ *state* W Venezuela
Mérida, Estado *see* Mérida
65 J4 **Meriden** Connecticut, NE USA 41°32′N 72°48′W
65 J4 **Meriden** Connecticut, USA 41°32′N 72°48′W
80 C1 **Meridian** California, USA 39°09′N 121°55′W
68 D1 **Meridian** California, USA 35°06′N 118°55′W
68 F2 **Meridian** Mississippi, S USA 32°24′N 88°43′W
70 G5 **Meridian** Texas, SW USA 31°56′N 97°40′W
164 F7 **Mérignac** Gironde, SW France 44°50′N 00°40′W
164 D3 **Mérignac** ✕ (Bordeaux) Gironde, SW France 44°51′N 00°44′W
153 G9 **Merikarvia** Länsi-Soumi, SW Finland 61°51′N 21°30′E
277 K7 **Merimbula** New South Wales, SE Australia 36°52′S 149°51′E
277 H5 **Meringur** Victoria, SE Australia 34°26′S 141°19′E
Merín, Laguna *see* Mirim Lagoon
115 G9 **Merinos** Río Negro, Uruguay 32°24′S 56°54′W
157 F10 **Merioneth** *cultural region* W Wales, UK
282 A7 **Merir** *island* Palau Islands, N Palau
282 A3 **Merizo** SW Guam 13°15′N 144°40′E
Merjama *see* Märjamaa
227 J8 **Merke** Zhambyl, S Kazakhstan 42°48′N 73°10′E
70 F4 **Merkel** Texas, SW USA 32°28′N 100°00′W
191 D9 **Merkinė** Alytus, S Lithuania 54°09′N 24°11′E
163 E9 **Merksem** Antwerpen, N Belgium 51°17′N 04°26′E
163 F9 **Merksplas** Antwerpen, N Belgium 51°22′N 04°54′E
Merkulovichi *see* Myerkulavichy
191 D9 **Merkys** ⚞ S Lithuania
76 B8 **Merlin** Oregon, NW USA 42°34′N 123°23′W
114 E9 **Merlo** Buenos Aires, E Argentina 34°39′S 58°45′W
216 A3 **Meron, Haré** ▲ N Israel 35°06′N 33°00′E
131 J2 **Merouane, Chott** *salt lake* NE Algeria
129 I8 **Merowe** Northern, N Sudan 18°29′N 31°49′E
274 D7 **Merredin** Western Australia 31°31′S 118°18′E
158 F5 **Merrick** ▲ S Scotland, UK 55°09′N 04°28′W
76 C8 **Merrill** Oregon, NW USA 42°00′N 121°37′W
72 C5 **Merrill** Wisconsin, N USA 45°12′N 89°43′W
73 E9 **Merrillville** Indiana, N USA 41°28′N 87°19′W
65 L1 **Merrimack River** ⚞ Massachusetts/New Hampshire, NE USA
140 G7 **Merriman** Northern Cape, South Africa 31°13′S 23°37′E
74 B6 **Merriman** Nebraska, C USA 42°54′N 101°42′W
56 F8 **Merritt** British Columbia, SW Canada 50°09′N 120°49′W
69 M6 **Merritt Island** Florida, SE USA 28°21′N 80°42′W
69 M6 **Merritt Island** *island* Florida, SE USA
74 C6 **Merritt Reservoir** ⊠ Nebraska, C USA
277 L4 **Merriwa** New South Wales, SE Australia 32°09′S 150°24′E
277 J5 **Merriwagga** New South Wales, SE Australia 33°51′S 145°38′E
68 B3 **Merryville** Louisiana, S USA 30°45′N 93°32′W
136 F2 **Mersa Fatma** E Eritrea 14°52′N 40°16′E
165 H4 **Mer St-Aubin** Loir-et-Cher, C France 47°42′N 01°31′E
Mersa Maṭrûh *see* Maṭrūḥ
163 H13 **Mersch** Luxembourg, C Luxembourg 49°45′N 06°06′E
179 G8 **Merseburg** Sachsen-Anhalt, C Germany 51°22′N 12°00′E
Mersen *see* Meerssen
214 F8 **Mersin** Mersin, S Turkey 36°50′N 34°39′E
214 E8 **Mersin** *prev.* İçel, Ichili. ◆ *province* S Turkey
258 F4 **Mersing** Johor, Peninsular Malaysia 02°25′N 103°50′E
190 C6 **Mērsrags** Talsi, NW Latvia 57°21′N 23°05′E
232 D6 **Merta** *var.* Merta City. Rājasthān, N India 26°40′N 74°04′E
Merta City *see* Merta
232 D6 **Merta Road** Rājasthān, N India 26°42′N 73°54′E
160 F5 **Merthyr Tydfil** S Wales, UK 51°46′N 03°23′W
172 C7 **Mértola** Beja, S Portugal 37°38′N 07°40′W
293 K9 **Mertz Glacier** *glacier* Antarctica
163 H13 **Mertzig** Diekirch, C Luxembourg 49°50′N 06°00′E
70 E5 **Mertzon** Texas, SW USA 31°16′N 100°50′W
165 H3 **Méru** Oise, N France 49°15′N 02°07′E
137 D8 **Meru** Eastern, C Kenya 0°03′N 37°38′E
137 D9 **Meru, Mount** ▲ NE Tanzania 03°12′S 36°45′E
Merv *see* Mary
Mervdasht *see* Marv Dasht
169 M4 **Merveilles, Vallée des** *valley* Provence-Alpes-Côte d'Azur, France
140 F9 **Merweville** Western Cape, South Africa 32°40′S 21°31′E
181 D12 **Merzheim** Rheinland-Pfalz, Germany 7°34′N 49°47′E
167 I6 **Méry-sur-Seine** Champagne-Ardenne, France 48°30′N 3°53′E
214 F5 **Merzifon** Amasya, N Turkey 40°52′N 35°28′E
181 B13 **Merzig** Saarland, SW Germany 49°27′N 06°39′E
79 H9 **Mesa** Arizona, SW USA 33°25′N 111°49′W
74 G3 **Mesabi Range** ▲ Minnesota, N USA
103 J4 **Mesa Bolívar** Mérida, NW Venezuela 08°30′N 71°38′W
86 B4 **Mesa del Nayar** Nayarit, Mexico 22°16′N 104°35′W
85 I9 **Mesa del Nayar** Nayarit, Mexico 22°16′N 104°35′W
86 E5 **Mesa de Palotes** Guanajuato, Mexico 21°29′N 100°25′W
175 J10 **Mesagne** Puglia, SE Italy 40°33′N 17°49′E
83 H7 **Mesa Mountain** ▲ Alaska, USA 60°26′N 155°14′W
187 I10 **Mesará** *lowland* Kriti, Greece, E Mediterranean Sea
173 J8 **Mesa Roldán** Andalucía, Spain 36°57′N 1°55′W
79 M9 **Mescalero** New Mexico, SW USA 33°09′N 105°46′W
181 E8 **Meschede** Nordrhein-Westfalen, W Germany 51°21′N 08°16′E
215 I5 **Mescit Dağları** ▲ NE Turkey
282 F10 **Mesegon** *island* Chuuk, C Micronesia
Meseritz *see* Międzyrzecz
102 C6 **Mesetas** Meta, C Colombia 03°14′N 74°09′W
160 F7 **Meshaw** UK 50°58′N 3°46′W
Meshchera Lowland *see* Meshcherskaya Nizina
196 G2 **Meshcherskaya Nizina** *Eng.* Meshchera Lowland. *basin* W Russian Federation
196 F2 **Meshchovsk** Kaluzhskaya Oblast', W Russian Federation 54°21′N 35°23′E
195 I6 **Meshchura** Respublika Komi, NW Russian Federation 63°18′N 50°56′E
Meshed *see* Mashhad
Meshed-i-Sar *see* Bābolsar
134 J4 **Meshra'er Req** Warab, S Sudan 08°30′N 29°27′E
79 L9 **Mesilla** New Mexico, SW USA 32°15′N 106°49′W
166 D7 **Meslay-du-Maine** Pays de la Loire, France 47°57′N 0°33′W
176 E5 **Mesocco** *Ger.* Misox. Ticino, S Switzerland 46°18′N 09°13′E
186 F6 **Mesolóngi** *prev.* Mesolóngion. Dytikí Ellás, W Greece 38°21′N 21°26′E
Mesolóngion *see* Mesolóngi
72 I3 **Mesomikenda Lake** ◎ Ontario, S Canada
114 E2 **Mesopotamia** *var.* Mesopotamia Argentina. *physical region* NE Argentina
Mesopotamia Argentina *see* Mesopotamia
111 J2 **Mesquita** Minas Gerais, Brazil 19°13′S 42°35′W
78 G6 **Mesquite** Nevada, W USA 36°47′N 114°04′W
171 J10 **Mesra** Algeria
137 E12 **Messalo, Rio** *var.* Mualo. ⚞ NE Mozambique
Messana/Messene *see* Messina
163 G14 **Messancy** Luxembourg, SE Belgium 49°36′N 05°49′E
172 B7 **Messejana** Beja, Portugal 37°50′N 8°15′W
181 F12 **Messel** Hessen, Germany 8°44′N 49°56′E
140 C7 **Messelpad Pass** *pass* Northern Cape, South Africa
175 H12 **Messina** *var.* Messana, Messene; *anc.* Zancle. Sicilia, Italy, C Mediterranean Sea 38°12′N 15°33′E
141 K1 **Messina** Limpopo, South Africa 22°21′S 30°03′E
Messina *see* Musina
Messina, Strait of *see* Messina, Stretto di
175 H12 **Messina, Stretto di** *Eng.* Strait of Messina. *strait* SW Italy
181 F8 **Messinghausen** Nordrhein-Westfalen, Germany 8°40′N 51°23′E
186 G7 **Messíni** Pelopónnisos, S Greece 37°03′N 22°00′E
186 F7 **Messinía** *peninsula* S Greece
186 G8 **Messiniakós Kólpos** *gulf* S Greece
184 F4 **Messoyakha** ⚞ N Russian Federation
185 J8 **Mesta** *Gk.* Néstos, *Turk.* Kara Su. ⚞ Bulgaria/Greece *see also* Néstos
Mesta *see* Néstos
173 H5 **Mestanza** Castilla-La Manacha, Spain 38°35′N 4°04′W
Mestghanem *see* Mostaganem
215 J3 **Mestia** *var.* Mestiya. N Georgia 43°03′N 42°50′E
Mestiya *see* Mestia
187 J6 **Mestón, Akrotírio** *cape* Chíos, E Greece
177 H6 **Mestre** Veneto, NE Italy 45°30′N 12°14′E
108 D7 **Mestre, Espigão** ▲ E Brazil
258 F7 **Mesuji** ⚞ Sumatera, W Indonesia
Mesule *see* Grosser Möseler
167 J9 **Mesvres** Bourgogne, France 46°52′N 4°15′E
54 B5 **Meszah Peak** ▲ British Columbia, W Canada 58°31′N 131°28′W
102 D6 **Meta** *off.* Departamento del Meta. ◆ *province* C Colombia
Meta, Departamento del *see* Meta
55 N2 **Meta Incognita Peninsula** *peninsula* Baffin Island, Nunavut, NE Canada
68 E4 **Metairie** Louisiana, S USA 29°58′N 90°09′W
76 F2 **Metaline Falls** Washington, NW USA 48°51′N 117°21′W
112 D5 **Metán** Salta, N Argentina 25°29′S 64°57′W
137 C13 **Metangula** Niassa, N Mozambique 12°41′S 34°50′E
88 D4 **Metapán** Santa Ana, NW El Salvador 14°20′N 89°28′W
102 F5 **Meta, Río** ⚞ Colombia/Venezuela
174 E6 **Metauro** ⚞ C Italy
136 D3 **Metema** Amhara, N Ethiopia 12°53′N 36°10′E
186 F4 **Meteora** *religious building* Thessalía, C Greece
291 I12 **Meteor Rise** *undersea feature* SW Indian Ocean
280 D2 **Meteran** New Hanover, NE Papua New Guinea 02°40′S 150°12′E
Meterlam *see* Mehtar Lām
187 H7 **Methanon** *peninsula* S Greece
Methariam/Metharlam *see* Mehtar Lām
159 I2 **Methil** UK 56°10′N 3°01′W
76 D3 **Methow River** ⚞ Washington, NW USA
65 L1 **Methuen** Massachusetts, NE USA 42°43′N 71°10′W
278 E10 **Methven** Canterbury, South Island, New Zealand 43°37′S 171°38′E
159 H2 **Methven** UK 56°25′N 3°34′W
161 L3 **Methwold** UK 52°31′N 0°33′E
Metis *see* Metz
184 D6 **Metković** Dubrovnik-Neretva, SE Croatia 43°02′N 17°37′E
83 N8 **Metlakatla** Annette Island, Alaska, USA 55°07′N 131°34′W
177 K6 **Metlika** *Ger.* Möttling. SE Slovenia 45°38′N 15°18′E
177 J4 **Metnitz** Kärnten, S Austria 46°58′N 14°09′E
75 I13 **Meto, Bayou** ⚞ Arkansas, C USA
258 F7 **Metro** Sumatera, W Indonesia 05°05′S 105°20′E
73 C13 **Metropolis** Illinois, N USA 37°09′N 88°43′W
Metropolitan *see* Santiago
80 B3 **Metropolitan Oakland** ✕ California, W USA 37°42′N 122°13′W
186 F4 **Métsovo** *prev.* Métsovon. Ípeiros, C Greece 39°47′N 21°12′E
Métsovon *see* Métsovo
171 L9 **Mettah** Algeria
181 B12 **Mettendorf** Rheinland-Pfalz, Germany 6°20′N 49°57′E
69 L2 **Metter** Georgia, SE USA 32°24′N 82°03′W
163 E12 **Mettet** Namur, S Belgium 50°19′N 04°43′E
180 D6 **Mettingen** Nordrhein-Westfalen, Germany 7°47′N 52°19′E
181 B13 **Mettlach** Saarland, SW Germany 49°28′N 06°37′E
81 D8 **Mettler** California, USA 35°04′N 118°58′W
181 C8 **Mettmann** Nordrhein-Westfalen, Germany 6°58′N 51°15′E
Mettu *see* Metu
136 D4 **Metu** *var.* Mattu, Mettu. Oromo, C Ethiopia 08°18′N 35°39′E
65 H6 **Metuchen** New Jersey, USA 40°33′N 74°22′W
258 J4 **Metulang** Borneo, N Indonesia 01°28′N 114°40′E
216 C5 **Metulla** Northern, N Israel 33°16′N 35°35′E
226 C6 **Metvyy Kultuk, Sor** *salt flat* SW Kazakhstan
165 K3 **Metz** *anc.* Divodurum Mediomatricum, Mediomatrica, Metis. Moselle, NE France 49°07′N 06°09′E
167 L4 **Metzervisse** Lorraine, France 49°19′N 6°17′E
179 D12 **Metzingen** Baden-Württemberg, S Germany 48°31′N 09°16′E
86 F5 **Metztitlán** Hidalgo, Mexico 20°36′N 98°45′W
258 C3 **Meulaboh** Sumatera, W Indonesia 04°10′N 96°09′E
163 B10 **Meulebeke** West-Vlaanderen, W Belgium 50°57′N 03°18′E
166 G7 **Meung-sur-Loire** Centre, France 47°50′N 1°42′E
165 K3 **Meurthe** ⚞ NE France
165 K3 **Meurthe-et-Moselle** ◆ *department* NE France
165 J3 **Meuse** ◆ *department* NE France
144 C6 **Meuse** *Dut.* Maas. ⚞ W Europe *see also* Maas
Meuse *see* Maas
160 D9 **Mevagissey** UK 50°17′N 4°47′W
161 H2 **Mew Island** *island* UK
159 K9 **Mexborough** UK 53°29′N 1°16′W
Mexcala, Río *see* Balsas, Río
86 A4 **Mexcaltitán** Nayarit, Mexico 21°54′N 105°28′W
85 I9 **Mexcaltitán** Nayarit, Mexico 21°54′N 105°28′W
71 H5 **Mexia** Texas, SW USA 31°40′N 96°28′W
107 M1 **Mexiana, Ilha** *island* NE Brazil
84 C1 **Mexicali** Baja California, NW Mexico 32°34′N 115°26′W
Mexicanos, Estados Unidos *see* Mexico
85 H5 **Laguna de los Mexicanos** ◎ Chihuahua, Mexico
86 F6 **México** *var.* Ciudad de México, *Eng.* Mexico City. ● (Mexico) México, C Mexico 19°26′N 99°08′W
75 I9 **Mexico** Missouri, C USA 19°10′N 99°04′W
62 F5 **Mexico** New York, NE USA 43°27′N 76°14′W
85 J8 **Mexico** *off.* United Mexican States, *var.* Méjico, México, *Sp.* Estados Unidos Mexicanos. ◆ *federal republic* N Central America
86 F7 **México** ◆ *state* S Mexico
México *see* Mexico
42 E8 **Mexico Basin** *var.* Sigsbee Deep. *undersea feature* C Gulf of Mexico
Mexico City *see* México
México, Golfo de *see* Mexico, Gulf of
61 I9 **Mexico, Gulf of** *Sp.* Golfo de México. *gulf* W Atlantic Ocean
86 C5 **Mexticacàn** Jalisco, Mexico 21°13′N 102°43′W
Meyadine *see* Al Mayādīn
230 G3 **Meydān Shahr** *var.* Maydān Shahr. Vardak, E Afghanistan 34°27′N 68°48′E
180 F3 **Meyenburg** Niedersachsen, Germany 8°36′N 53°17′E
83 M8 **Meyers Chuck** Etolin Island, Alaska, USA 55°44′N 132°15′W
168 G2 **Meymac** Limousin, France 45°32′N 2°10′E
230 E2 **Meymaneh** *var.* Maimāna, Maymana. Fāryāb, NW Afghanistan 35°57′N 64°48′E
222 F5 **Meymeh** Eşfahān, C Iran 33°29′N 51°09′E
193 N3 **Meynypil'gyno** Chukotskiy Avtonomnyy Okrug, NE Russian Federation 62°33′N 177°00′E
176 B5 **Meyrin** Genève, SW Switzerland 46°14′N 06°05′E
169 I4 **Meyrueis** Languedoc-Roussillon, France 44°10′N 3°26′E
168 G3 **Meyssac** Limousin, France 45°03′N 1°40′E
256 C6 **Mezaligon** Irrawaddy, SW Myanmar (Burma) 17°53′N 95°12′E
86 E7 **Mezcala** Guerrero, S Mexico 17°55′N 99°34′W
185 I6 **Mezdra** Vratsa, NW Bulgaria 43°08′N 23°42′E
169 I6 **Mèze** Hérault, S France 43°26′N 03°37′E
169 L5 **Mézel** Provence-Alpes-Côte d'Azur, France 43°59′N 6°12′E
195 H4 **Mezen'** Arkhangel'skaya Oblast', NW Russian Federation 65°54′N 44°10′E
195 I6 **Mezen'** ⚞ NW Russian Federation
Mezen, Bay of *see* Mezenskaya Guba
169 J3 **Mézenc, Mont** ▲ C France 44°57′N 04°15′E
195 H4 **Mezenskaya Guba** *var.* Bay of Mezen. *bay* NW Russian Federation
194 D10 **Mezha** ⚞ W Russian Federation
Mezha *see* Myazha
192 G8 **Mezhdurechensk** Kemerovskaya Oblast', S Russian Federation 53°37′N 87°59′E
196 N7 **Mezhdurechenskiy** Khanty-Mansiyskiy Avtonomnyy Okrug, Russian federation
195 I1 **Mezhdusharskiy, Ostrov** *island* Novaya Zemlya, N Russian Federation
Mezhëvo *see* Myezhava
Mezhgor'ye *see* Mizhhir"ya
189 L5 **Mezhova** Dnipropetrovs'ka Oblast', E Ukraine 48°15′N 36°44′E
56 B2 **Meziadin Junction** British Columbia, W Canada 56°06′N 129°15′W
166 F10 **Mézières-sur-Issoire** Limousin, France 46°06′N 0°55′E
164 G8 **Mézin** Lot-et-Garonne, SW France 44°03′N 00°16′E
183 H12 **Mezőberény** Békés, SE Hungary 46°49′N 21°00′E
183 H13 **Mezőhegyes** Békés, SE Hungary 46°20′N 20°48′E
183 H12 **Mezőkovácsháza** Békés, SE Hungary 46°24′N 20°52′E
183 H11 **Mezőkövesd** Borsod-Abaúj-Zemplén, NE Hungary 47°49′N 20°32′E
Mezőtelegd *see* Tileagd
183 H12 **Mezőtúr** Jász-Nagykun-Szolnok, E Hungary 47°N 20°37′E
173 K2 **Mezquita de Jarque** Aragón, Spain 40°43′N 0°52′W
85 I8 **Mezquital** Durango, C Mexico 23°31′N 104°19′W
86 B3 **Mezquital, Río** ⚞ Durango, Mexico
86 C4 **Mezquitic** Jalisco, Mexico 22°23′N 103°41′W
176 G5 **Mezzolombardo** Trentino-Alto Adige, N Italy 46°13′N 11°08′E
139 H1 **Mfuwe** Northern, N Zambia 13°00′S 31°45′E
190 I3 **Mga** Leningradskaya Oblast', Russian Federation
175 I13 **Mġarr** Gozo, N Malta 36°01′N 14°18′E
196 E3 **Mglin** Bryanskaya Oblast', W Russian Federation 53°01′N 32°54′E
Mhālanna, Cionn *see* Malin Head
232 D8 **Mhow** Madhya Pradesh, C India 22°32′N 75°49′E
Miadzioł Nowy *see* Myadzyel
263 L7 **Miagao** Panay Island, C Philippines 10°40′N 122°15′E
87 H9 **Miahuatlán** *var.* Miahuatlán de Porfirio Díaz. Oaxaca, SE Mexico 16°21′N 96°36′W
87 H9 **Miahuatlán** Oaxaca, Mexico 16°12′N 96°37′W
Miahuatlán de Porfirio Díaz *see* Miahuatlán
170 E6 **Miajadas** Extremadura, W Spain 39°10′N 05°54′W
Miajlar *see* Myājlār
79 I9 **Miami** Arizona, SW USA 33°23′N 110°53′W
69 N9 **Miami** Florida, SE USA 25°46′N 80°12′W
75 G11 **Miami** Oklahoma, C USA 36°53′N 94°54′W
70 E2 **Miami** Texas, SW USA 35°42′N 100°37′W
69 N9 **Miami** ✕ Florida, SE USA 25°47′N 80°16′W
69 N9 **Miami Beach** Florida, SE USA 25°47′N 80°08′W
69 M8 **Miami Canal** *canal* Florida, SE USA
73 G11 **Miamisburg** Ohio, N USA 39°38′N 84°17′W
231 I6 **Miān Channūn** Punjab, E Pakistan 30°24′N 72°27′E
223 D3 **Miāndowāb** *var.* Miandoab, Miyāndoāb. Āżarbāyjān-e Gharbī, NW Iran 36°57′N 46°06′E
139 L7 **Miandrivazo** Toliara, C Madagascar 19°31′S 45°29′E
Miandoab *see* Miāndowāb
222 D2 **Miāneh** *var.* Miyāneh. Āżarbāyjān-e Sharqī, NW Iran 37°23′N 47°45′E
230 F9 **Miāni Hōr** *lagoon* S Pakistan
240 C5 **Mianning** Sichuan, C China 28°34′N 102°12′E
244 A10 **Mianshizhen** China 31°22′N 103°33′E
242 A1 **Mianshizhen** China 31°22′N 103°33′E
231 I5 **Miānwāli** Punjab, NE Pakistan 32°32′N 71°33′E
244 C9 **Mianxian** *var.* Mian Xian. Shaanxi, C China 33°12′N 106°36′E
Mian Xian *see* Mianxian
242 B1 **Mianyang** Sichuan, C China 31°29′N 104°43′E
Mianyang *see* Xiantao
242 A1 **Mianzhu** Sichuan, China 31°13′N 104°07′E
245 L4 **Miaodao Liedao** *island group* Shandong, China
242 E7 **Miao'er Shan 2142m** ▲ Guangxi, China 25°30′N 110°13′E
243 M8 **Miaoli** N Taiwan 24°33′N 120°48′E
242 C7 **Miao Ling** ▲ Guizhou, China
197 M2 **Miass** Chelyabinskaya Oblast', C Russian Federation 55°00′N 59°55′E
196 M10 **Miass** ⚞ Kurganskaya oblast, Russian federation
182 E4 **Miastko** *Ger.* Rummelsburg in Pommern. Pomorskie, N Poland 54°N 16°58′E
Miava *see* Myjava
141 K2 **Mica** Limpopo, South Africa 24°09′S 30°50′E
56 G6 **Mica Creek** British Columbia, SW Canada 51°58′N 118°29′W
239 M7 **Micang Shan** ▲ C China
Mi Chai *see* Nong Khai
183 I10 **Michalovce** *Ger.* Grossmichel, *Hung.* Nagymihály. Košický Kraj, E Slovakia 48°46′N 21°55′E
181 J11 **Michelau** Bayern, Germany 11°07′N 50°10′E
163 H11 **Michel, Baraque** *hill* E Belgium
181 H14 **Michelfeld** Baden-Württemberg, Germany 9°41′N 49°06′E
140 D9 **Michell's Pass** *pass* Western Cape, South Africa
83 J2 **Michelson, Mount** ▲ Alaska, USA 69°19′N 144°16′W
181 F12 **Michelstadt** Hessen, Germany 9°0′N 49°40′E
91 I5 **Miches** E Dominican Republic 18°59′N 69°03′W
72 D4 **Michigamme, Lake** ◎ Michigan, N USA
72 D4 **Michigamme Reservoir** ⊠ Michigan, N USA
72 D4 **Michigamme River** ⚞ Michigan, N USA
72 G7 **Michigan** *off.* State of Michigan, *also known as* Great Lakes State, Lake State, Wolverine State. ◆ *state* N USA
73 E9 **Michigan City** Indiana, N USA 41°43′N 86°52′W
72 E6 **Michigan, Lake** ◎ N USA
72 I4 **Michipicoten Bay** *lake bay* Ontario, N Canada
72 D7 **Michipicoten Island** *island* Ontario, S Canada
72 G3 **Michipicoten River** Ontario, S Canada 47°56′N 84°48′W
Michurin *see* Tsarevo
196 G3 **Michurinsk** Tambovskaya Oblast', W Russian Federation 52°56′N 40°31′E
Mico, Punta/Mico, Punta *see* Monkey Point
88 G6 **Mico, Río** ⚞ SE Nicaragua
91 J3 **Micoud** SE Saint Lucia 13°49′N 60°54′W
255 M6 **Micronesia** *off.* Federated States of Micronesia. ◆ *federation* W Pacific Ocean
267 H3 **Micronesia** *island group* W Pacific Ocean
Micronesia, Federated States of *see* Micronesia
258 G3 **Midai, Pulau** *island* Kepulauan Natuna, W Indonesia
Mid-Atlantic Cordillera *see* Mid-Atlantic Ridge
291 G10 **Mid-Atlantic Ridge** *var.* Mid-Atlantic Cordillera, Mid-Atlantic Rise, Mid-Atlantic Swell. *undersea feature* Atlantic Ocean
Mid-Atlantic Rise/Mid-Atlantic Swell *see* Mid-Atlantic Ridge
140 D8 **Middelberg** ▲ Western Cape, South Africa 32°23′S 19°06′E
163 C8 **Middelburg** Zeeland, SW Netherlands 51°30′N 03°36′E
141 H8 **Middelburg** Eastern Cape, South Africa 31°29′S 25°01′E
138 F9 **Middelburg** Eastern Cape, S South Africa 31°28′S 25°01′E
141 J4 **Middelburg** Mpumalanga, South Africa 25°47′S 29°28′E
139 H6 **Middelburg** Mpumalanga, NE South Africa 25°47′S 29°28′E
155 D12 **Middelfart** Fyn, C Denmark 55°30′N 09°44′E
162 D7 **Middelharnis** Zuid-Holland, SW Netherlands 51°45′N 04°10′E
163 B9 **Middelkerke** West-Vlaanderen, W Belgium 51°12′N 02°51′E
162 F5 **Middenbeemster** Noord-Holland, C Netherlands 52°33′N 04°55′E
162 F4 **Middenmeer** Noord-Holland, NW Netherlands 52°48′N 04°58′E
78 C1 **Middle Alkali Lake** ◎ California, W USA
287 J4 **Middle America Trench** *undersea feature* E Pacific Ocean
256 A8 **Middle Andaman** *island* Andaman Islands, India, NE Indian Ocean
Middle Atlas *see* Moyen Atlas
65 M3 **Middleboro** Massachusetts, USA 41°54′N 70°55′W
67 I2 **Middlebourne** West Virginia, NE USA 39°30′N 80°53′W
69 L4 **Middleburg** Florida, SE USA 30°03′N 81°55′W
64 D6 **Middleburg** Pennsylvania, USA 40°47′N 77°03′W
65 H2 **Middleburgh** New York, USA 42°36′N 74°20′W
Middleburg Island *see* 'Eua
Middle Caicos *see* Grand Caicos
70 E5 **Middle Concho River** ⚞ Texas, SW USA
83 I3 **Middle Fork Chandalar River** ⚞ Alaska, USA
83 I4 **Middle Fork Koyukuk River** ⚞ Alaska, USA
76 G6 **Middle Fork Salmon River** ⚞ Idaho, NW USA
159 K7 **Middleham** UK 54°17′N 1°49′W
57 N5 **Middle Lake** Saskatchewan, S Canada 52°31′N 105°16′W
74 B7 **Middle Loup River** ⚞ Nebraska, C USA
278 D12 **Middlemarch** Otago, South Island, New Zealand 45°30′S 170°07′E
73 I11 **Middleport** Ohio, N USA 39°00′N 82°03′W
74 G7 **Middle Raccoon River** ⚞ Iowa, C USA
74 E2 **Middle River** ⚞ Minnesota, N USA
66 G5 **Middlesboro** Kentucky, S USA 36°37′N 83°42′W
159 K7 **Middlesbrough** N England, UK 54°35′N 01°14′W
88 E2 **Middlesex** Stann Creek, C Belize 17°00′N 88°31′W
64 G6 **Middlesex** New Jersey, USA 40°34′N 74°30′W
157 I11 **Middlesex** *cultural region* SE England, UK
159 K8 **Middlesmoor** UK 54°10′N 1°51′W
63 N3 **Middleton** Nova Scotia, SE Canada 44°56′N 65°04′W
141 H9 **Middleton** Eastern Cape, South Africa 32°57′S 25°49′E
159 J9 **Middleton** UK 53°33′N 2°12′W
66 C7 **Middleton** Tennessee, S USA 35°05′N 88°57′W
72 C8 **Middleton** Wisconsin, N USA 43°06′N 89°30′W
83 J7 **Middleton Island** *island* Alaska, USA
158 D7 **Middletown** UK 54°18′N 6°52′W
80 B1 **Middletown** California, W USA 38°44′N 122°39′W
65 J4 **Middletown** Connecticut, USA 41°34′N 72°39′W
64 F9 **Middletown** Delaware, NE USA 39°25′N 75°39′W
65 H7 **Middletown** New Jersey, NE USA 40°23′N 74°08′W
64 G4 **Middletown** New York, NE USA 41°27′N 74°25′W
73 G11 **Middletown** Ohio, N USA 39°33′N 84°19′W
64 D7 **Middletown** Pennsylvania, NE USA 40°11′N 76°42′W
159 J10 **Middlewich** UK 53°11′N 2°26′W
161 J7 **Midhurst** UK 50°59′N 0°44′W
220 F8 **Midi** *var.* Maydi. NW Yemen 16°18′N 42°51′E
165 H9 **Midi, Canal du** *canal* S France
168 E7 **Midi de Bigorre, Pic du** ▲ S France 42°57′N 00°08′E
168 C7 **Midi d'Ossau, Pic du** ▲ SW France 42°51′N 00°27′W
289 F8 **Mid-Indian Basin** *undersea feature* N Indian Ocean
289 E9 **Mid-Indian Ridge** *var.* Central Indian Ridge. *undersea feature* C Indian Ocean
164 G8 **Midi-Pyrénées** ◆ *region* S France
70 D5 **Midkiff** Texas, SW USA 31°35′N 101°51′W
62 D4 **Midland** Ontario, S Canada 44°45′N 79°53′W
72 G7 **Midland** Michigan, N USA 43°37′N 84°15′W
74 C5 **Midland** South Dakota, N USA 44°04′N 101°07′W
70 D5 **Midland** Texas, SW USA 32°N 102°05′W
139 H4 **Midlands** ◆ *province* C Zimbabwe
157 C11 **Midleton** *Ir.* Mainistir na Corann. SW Ireland 51°55′N 08°10′W
71 H4 **Midlothian** Texas, SW USA 32°28′N 96°59′W
139 M9 **Midongy Fianarantsoa**, S Madagascar 21°58′S 47°47′E
168 G8 **Midou** ⚞ SW France
168 D5 **Midouze** ⚞ Aquitaine, France
286 F5 **Mid-Pacific Mountains** *var.* Mid-Pacific Seamounts. *undersea feature* NW Pacific Ocean
Mid-Pacific Seamounts *see* Mid-Pacific Mountains
80 E4 **Midpines** California, USA 37°33′N 119°55′W
263 M9 **Midsayap** Mindanao, S Philippines 07°12′N 124°31′E
161 H6 **Midsomer Norton** UK 51°17′N 2°29′W
79 I2 **Midway** Utah, W USA 40°30′N 111°28′W
286 F3 **Midway Islands** ◇ *US territory* C Pacific Ocean
77 L7 **Midwest** Wyoming, C USA 43°24′N 106°15′W
75 E12 **Midwest City** Oklahoma, C USA 35°28′N 98°24′W
233 H5 **Mid Western** ◆ *zone* W Nepal
162 J3 **Midwolda** Groningen, NE Netherlands 53°12′N 07°00′E
215 I7 **Midyat** Mardin, SE Turkey 37°25′N 41°20′E
185 H5 **Midžhur** *SCr.* Midžor. ▲ Bulgaria/Serbia 43°24′N 22°41′E *see also* Midžor
Midzhur *see* Midžor
185 H5 **Midžor** *Bul.* Midzhur. ▲ Bulgaria/Serbia 43°24′N 22°40′E *see also* Midzhur
Midžor *see* Midzhur
251 I5 **Mie** *off.* Mie-ken. ◆ *prefecture* Honshū, SW Japan
183 H8 **Miechów** Małopolskie, S Poland 50°21′N 20°01′E
182 D5 **Międzychód** *Ger.* Mitteldorf. Wielkopolskie, C Poland 52°36′N 15°53′E
182 I6 **Międzyrzec Podlaski** Lubelskie, E Poland 52°N 22°47′E
182 D6 **Międzyrzecz** *Ger.* Meseritz. Lubuskie, W Poland 52°26′N 15°33′E
181 D11 **Miehlen** Rheinland-Pfalz, Germany 7°50′N 50°13′E
Mie-ken *see* Mie
164 G8 **Miélan** Gers, S France 43°26′N 00°19′E
183 H8 **Mielec** Podkarpackie, SE Poland 50°18′N 21°27′E
155 G11 **Mien** ◎ S Sweden
85 M6 **Mier** Tamaulipas, C Mexico 26°28′N 99°10′W
188 E7 **Miercurea-Ciuc** *Ger.* Szeklerburg, *Hung.* Csíkszereda. Harghita, C Romania 46°24′N 25°48′E
Mieresch *see* Maros/Mureş
Mieres del Camín *see* Mieres del Camino
170 E2 **Mieres del Camino** *var.* Mieres del Camín. Asturias, NW Spain 43°15′N 05°46′W
163 G8 **Mierlo** Noord-Brabant, SE Netherlands 51°27′N 05°37′E
85 L8 **Mier y Noriega** Nuevo León, NE Mexico 23°24′N 100°06′W
Mies *see* Stříbro
136 F4 **Mī'ēso** *var.* Meheso, Miesso. Oromo, C Ethiopia 09°13′N 40°47′E
Miesso *see* Mī'ēso
180 J5 **Mieste** Sachsen-Anhalt, Germany 11°13′N 52°28′E
180 I5 **Miesterhorst** Sachsen-Anhalt, Germany 11°08′N 52°28′E
182 C5 **Mieszkowice** *Ger.* Bärwalde Neumark. Zachodnio-pomorskie, W Poland 52°45′N 14°24′E
64 D5 **Mifflinburg** Pennsylvania, NE USA 40°55′N 77°03′W
64 C6 **Mifflintown** Pennsylvania, NE USA 40°34′N 77°24′W
244 C6 **Migang Sahn 2924m** ▲ Ningxia, China 35°19′N 106°08′E
141 H4 **Migdol** North-West, South Africa 26°54′S 25°27′E
84 F9 **Migriño** Baja California Sur, W Mexico North America
85 J7 **Miguel Asua** *var.* Miguel Auza. Zacatecas, C Mexico 24°17′N 103°29′W
Miguel Auza *see* Miguel Asua
89 K9 **Miguel de la Borda** *var.* Donoso. Colón, C Panama 09°09′N 80°20′W
86 C5 **Miguel Hidalgo** Jalisco, Mexico 20°31′N 103°18′W
86 C5 **Miguel Hidalgo** ✕ (Guadalajara) Jalisco, SW Mexico 20°52′N 101°09′W
86 G6 **Presa Miguel Hidalgo** Sinaloa, Mexico 26°37′N 108°33′W
84 G6 **Miguel Hidalgo, Presa** ⊠ W Mexico
113 J4 **Miguelópolis** São Paulo, Brazil 20°12′S 48°03′W
111 H7 **Miguel Pereira** Rio de Janeiro, Brazil 22°27′S 43°29′W
115 J9 **Migues** Canelones, Uruguay 34°24′S 55°36′E
188 E10 **Mihăilești** Giurgiu, S Romania 44°20′N 25°54′E
188 F10 **Mihail Kogălniceanu** *var.* Kogălniceanu; *prev.* Caramurat, Ferdinand. Constanța, SE Romania 44°22′N 28°27′E
188 G9 **Mihai Viteazu** Constanța, SE Romania 44°37′N 28°41′E
214 D5 **Mihalıççık** Eskişehir, NW Turkey 39°52′N 31°30′E
250 F5 **Mihara** Hiroshima, Honshū, SW Japan 34°24′N 133°04′E
253 B14 **Mihara-yama** ⚐ Miyako-jima, SE Japan 34°43′N 139°23′E
181 I9 **Mihla** Thüringen, Germany 10°20′N 51°05′E
171 I5 **Mijares** ⚞ E Spain
173 K2 **Río Mijares** ⚞ Aragón, Spain
162 F5 **Mijdrecht** Utrecht, C Netherlands 52°12′N 04°52′E
252 E4 **Mikasa** Hokkaidō, NE Japan 43°15′N 141°57′E
Mikashevichi *see* Mikashevichy
191 F11 **Mikashevichy** *Pol.* Mikaszewicze, *Rus.* Mikashevichi. Brestskaya Voblasts', SW Belarus 52°13′N 27°28′E
Mikaszewicze *see* Mikashevichy
251 J5 **Mikawa-wan** *bay* S Japan
196 G3 **Mikhaylov** Ryazanskaya Oblast', W Russian Federation 54°12′N 39°03′E
Mikhaylovgrad *see* Montana

◆ Country
● Country Capital
◇ Dependent Territory
○ Dependent Territory Capital
◆ Administrative Regions
✕ International Airport
▲ Mountain
▲ Mountain Range
⚐ Volcano
⚞ River
◎ Lake
⊠ Reservoir

◆ Country ◇ Dependent Territory ◈ Administrative Regions ▲ Mountain ▼ Volcano ⊚ Lake
● Country Capital ○ Dependent Territory Capital ✈ International Airport ▲▲ Mountain Range ≈ River ⊠ Reservoir

◆ Country   ● Country Capital   ◇ Dependent Territory   ○ Dependent Territory Capital   ▲ Administrative Regions   ✈ International Airport   ▲ Mountain   ▲ Mountain Range   🌋 Volcano   ⋈ River   ◎ Lake   ⊡ Reservoir

◆ Country   ◇ Dependent Territory   ◈ Administrative Regions   ▲ Mountain   ● Volcano   ◉ Lake
● Country Capital   ○ Dependent Territory Capital   ✕ International Airport   ▲ Mountain Range   ✎ River   ◫ Reservoir

Mýrina - Naryshkino

187 I4 **Mýrina** *var.* Mírina. Límnos, SE Greece *39°52′N 25°04′E*
189 H4 **Myronivka** ***Rus.*** Mironovka. Kyyivs'ka Oblast', N Ukraine *49°40′N 30°59′E*
67 K8 **Myrtle Beach** South Carolina, SE USA *33°41′N 78°53′W*
76 B7 **Myrtle Creek** Oregon, NW USA *43°01′N 123°19′W*
277 J6 **Myrtleford** Victoria, SE Australia *36°34′S 146°45′E*
76 B7 **Myrtle Point** Oregon, NW USA *43°04′N 124°08′W*
187 J10 **Mýrtos** Kríti, Greece, E Mediterranean Sea *35°00′N 25°34′E*
Myrtoum Mare *see* Mirtóo Pélagos
154 G4 **Myrviken** Jämtland, C Sweden *62°59′N 14°19′E*
195 N1 **Mys Kamennyy** *headland* Yamalo-Nenetskiy Avtonomyy Okrug, Russian federation
155 E8 **Mysen** Østfold, S Norway *59°33′N 11°20′E*
194 F9 **Myshkin** Yaroslavskaya Oblast', NW Russian Federation *57°47′N 38°28′E*
183 G9 **Myślenice** Malopolskie, S Poland *49°50′N 19°55′E*
182 C5 **Myślibórz** Zachodnio-pomorskie, NW Poland *52°55′N 14°51′E*
235 E8 **Mysore** *var.* Maisur. Karnātaka, W India *12°18′N 76°37′E*
Mysore *see* Karnātaka
186 G7 **Mystrás** *var.* Mistras. Pelopónnisos, S Greece *37°03′N 22°22′E*
195 J7 **Mysy** Permskaya Oblast', NW Russian Federation *60°40′N 53°59′E*
183 F8 **Myszków** Ślaskie, S Poland *50°36′N 19°20′E*
257 H9 **My Tho** *var.* Mi Tho. Tiền Giang, S Vietnam *10°21′N 106°21′E*
Mytilene *see* Mytilíni
187 K5 **Mytilíni** *var.* Mitilíni; ***anc.*** Mytilene. Lésvos, E Greece *39°06′N 26°33′E*
196 F2 **Mytishchi** Moskovskaya Oblast', W Russian Federation *56°00′N 37°51′E*
79 I3 **Myton** Utah, W USA *40°11′N 110°03′W*
152 D2 **Mývatn** ◎ C Iceland
195 K7 **Myyëldino** *var.* Myjeldino. Respublika Komi, NW Russian Federation *61°46′N 54°48′E*
137 C12 **Mzimba** Northern, NW Malawi *11°56′S 33°36′E*
141 J8 **Mzimvubu** ≈ Eastern Cape, South Africa
141 K6 **Mzingazi** ◎ KwaZulu-Natal, South Africa
137 C12 **Mzuzu** Northern, N Malawi *11°23′S 34°03′E*

N

179 G11 **Naab** ≈ SE Germany
162 D7 **Naaldwijk** Zuid-Holland, W Netherlands *52°00′N 04°13′E*
82 D3 **Nā'ālehu** *var.* Naalehu. Hawai'i, USA, C Pacific Ocean *19°04′N 155°36′W*
153 G10 **Naantali** *Swe.* Nådendal. Länsi-Soumi, SW Finland *60°28′N 22°05′E*
162 F6 **Naarden** Noord-Holland, C Netherlands *52°18′N 05°10′E*
177 J2 **Naarn** ≈ N Austria
158 D10 **Naas** *Ir.* An Nás, Nás na Ríogh. Kildare, C Ireland *53°13′N 06°39′W*
152 H3 **Näätämöjoki** *Lapp.* Njávdám. ≈ NE Finland
138 D8 **Nababeep** *var.* Nababiep. Northern Cape, W South Africa *29°36′S 17°46′E*
140 C6 **Nababeep** Northern Cape, South Africa *29°35′S 17°47′E*
Nababiep *see* Nababeep
Nabadwip *see* Navadwīp
172 C2 **Nabais** Guarda, Portugal *40°31′N 7°33′W*
251 I5 **Nabari** Mie, Honshū, SW Japan *34°37′N 136°05′E*
Nabatié *see* Nabatîyé
216 C5 **Nabatîyé** *var.* An Nabatīyah at Taḩtā, Nabatié, Nabatiyet et Tahta. SW Lebanon *33°18′N 35°36′E*
Nabatiyet et Tahta *see* Nabatîyé
280 E8 **Nabavatu** Vanua Levu, N Fiji *16°35′S 178°55′E*
284 D2 **Nabeina** *island* Tungaru, W Kiribati
197 K2 **Naberezhnyye Chelny** ***prev.*** Brezhnev. Respublika Tatarstan, W Russian Federation *55°43′N 52°21′E*
83 K5 **Nabesna** Alaska, USA *62°22′N 143°00′W*
83 K5 **Nabesna River** ≈ Alaska, USA
131 K1 **Nabeul** *var.* Nābul. NE Tunisia *36°32′N 10°45′E*
232 E4 **Nābha** Punjab, NW India *30°22′N 76°12′E*
261 J5 **Nabire** Papua, E Indonesia *03°23′S 135°31′E*
220 F8 **Nabī Shu'ayb, Jabal an** ▲ W Yemen *15°24′N 44°04′E*
280 E8 **Nabiti** Vanua Levu, N Fiji *16°37′S 178°54′E*
216 B6 **Nablus** *var.* Năbulus, ***Heb.*** Shekhem; ***anc.*** Neapolis, ***Bibl.*** Shechem. N West Bank *32°13′N 35°16′E*
141 J3 **Naboomspruit** Limpopo, South Africa *24°31′S 28°43′E*
280 E8 **Nabouwalu** Vanua Levu, N Fiji *17°00′S 178°43′E*
Nābul *see* Nabeul
Năbulus *see* Nablus
280 F8 **Nabuna** Vanua Levu, N Fiji *16°13′S 179°46′E*
263 N9 **Nabunturan** Mindanao, S Philippines *07°34′N 125°54′E*
159 L8 **Naburn** UK *53°54′N 1°05′W*
139 L2 **Nacala** Nampula, NE Mozambique *14°30′S 40°37′E*
88 E5 **Nacaome** Valle, S Honduras *13°30′N 87°31′W*
Na Cealla Beaga *see* Killybegs
Na-Ch'ii *see* Nagqu
251 I6 **Nachikatsuura** *var.* Nachi-Katsuura. Wakayama, Honshū, SE Japan *33°37′N 135°54′E*
Nachi-Katsuura *see* Nachikatsuura
137 E12 **Nachingwea** Lindi, SE Tanzania *10°21′S 38°46′E*
183 D8 **Náchod** Královéhradecký Kraj, N Czech Republic *50°26′N 16°10′E*
80 B6 **Nacimiento, Lake** ▣ California, USA
111 J2 **Nack** Minas Gerais, Brazil *19°14′S 42°19′W*
Na Clocha Liatha *see* Greystones
84 F2 **Naco** Sonora, NW Mexico *31°16′N 109°56′W*
71 I5 **Nacogdoches** Texas, SW USA *31°36′N 94°40′W*
84 F3 **Nàcori Chico** Sonora, Mexico *29°41′N 108°58′W*
84 F3 **Nacozari de García** Sonora, NW Mexico *30°27′N 109°43′W*
161 M5 **Nacton** UK *52°01′N 1°14′E*
280 D8 **Nacula** ***prev.*** Nathula. *island* Yasawa Group, NW Fiji
118 G4 **Nacuñán** Mendoza, Argentina *34°03′S 67°58′W*
85 K5 **Nadadores** Coahuila de Zaragoza, Mexico *27°03′N 101°36′W*
132 G6 **Nadawli** NW Ghana *10°30′N 02°40′W*
170 D2 **Nadela** Galicia, NW Spain *42°58′N 07°33′W*
Nådendal *see* Naantali
226 G2 **Nadezhdinka** ***prev.*** Nadezhdinskiy. Kostanay, N Kazakhstan *53°46′N 63°44′E*
Nadezhdinskiy *see* Nadezhdinka
Nadgan *see* Nadqān, Qalamat
280 D9 **Nadi** ***prev.*** Nandi. Viti Levu, W Fiji *17°47′S 177°32′E*
280 D9 **Nadi** ***prev.*** Nandi. ✕ Viti Levu, W Fiji *17°46′S 177°28′E*
232 C8 **Nadiād** Gujarāt, W India *22°42′N 72°55′E*
Ņadikdik *see* Knox Atoll
188 A7 **Nădlac** *Ger.* Nadlak, ***Hung.*** Nagylak. Arad, W Romania *46°10′N 20°47′E*
Nadlak *see* Nădlac
130 G2 **Nador** ***prev.*** Villa Nador. NE Morocco *35°10′N 05°22′W*
190 J2 **Nadporozhye** Leningradskaya Oblast', Russian Federation
221 I5 **Nadqān, Qalamat** *var.* Nadgan. *well* E Saudi Arabia
183 H11 **Nádudvar** Hajdú-Bihar, E Hungary *47°36′N 21°09′E*
175 I13 **Nadur** Gozo, N Malta *36°03′N 14°18′E*
280 F8 **Naduri** ***prev.*** Nanduri. Vanua Levu, N Fiji *16°26′S 179°08′E*
188 D5 **Nadvirna** ***Pol.*** Nadwórna, ***Rus.*** Nadvornaya. Ivano-Frankivs'ka Oblast', W Ukraine *48°27′N 24°30′E*
194 E6 **Nadvoitsy** Respublika Kareliya, NW Russian Federation *63°53′N 34°17′E*
Nadvornaya/Nadwórna *see* Nadvirna
195 N3 **Nadym** Yamalo-Nenetskiy Avtonomnyy Okrug, N Russian Federation *65°25′N 72°40′E*
192 F5 **Nadym** ≈ C Russian Federation
280 C3 **Nadzab** Morobe, C Papua New Guinea *06°36′S 146°46′E*
155 A9 **Nærbø** Rogaland, S Norway *58°40′N 05°39′E*
155 E13 **Næstved** Storstrøm, SE Denmark *55°12′N 11°47′E*
133 L6 **Nafada** Gombe, E Nigeria *11°02′N 11°18′E*
176 E4 **Näfels** Glarus, NE Switzerland *47°06′N 09°04′E*
186 F6 **Náfpaktos** *var.* Návpaktos. Dytikí Ellás, C Greece *38°23′N 21°50′E*
186 G7 **Náfplio** ***prev.*** Návplion. Pelopónnisos, S Greece *37°34′N 22°50′E*
217 K4 **Naft Khāneh** E Iraq *34°01′N 45°26′E*
230 F8 **Nāg** Baluchistān, SW Pakistan *27°43′N 65°31′E*
263 L6 **Naga** *off.* Naga City; ***prev.*** Nueva Caceres. Luzon, N Philippines *13°36′N 123°10′E*
Nagaarzê *see* Nagarzê
Naga City *see* Naga
58 D6 **Nagagami** ≈ Ontario, S Canada
250 E6 **Nagahama** Ehime, Shikoku, SW Japan *33°36′N 132°29′E*
251 I4 **Nagahama** Shiga, Honshū, SW Japan *35°25′N 136°16′E*
233 M6 **Nāga Hills** ▲▲ NE India
253 C10 **Nagai** Yamagata, Honshū, C Japan *38°08′N 140°00′E*
Na Gaibhlte *see* Galty Mountains
82 G9 **Nagai Island** *island* Shumagin Islands, Alaska, USA
233 M6 **Nāgāland** ⬖ *state* NE India
251 K2 **Nagano** Nagano, Honshū, S Japan *36°39′N 138°11′E*
251 K3 **Nagano** *off.* Nagano-ken. ⬖ *prefecture* Honshū, S Japan
Nagano-ken *see* Nagano
253 B11 **Nagaoka** Niigata, Honshū, C Japan *37°26′N 138°48′E*
233 L6 **Nagaon** *var.* Nowgong. Assam, NE India *26°21′N 92°41′E*
235 F9 **Nāgappattinam** *var.* Negapatam, Negapattinam. Tamil Nādu, SE India *10°45′N 79°50′E*
Nagara Nayok *see* Nakhon Nayok
Nagara Panom *see* Nakhon Phanom
Nagara Pathom *see* Nakhon Pathom
Nagara Sridharmaraj *see* Nakhon Si Thammarat
Nagara Svarga *see* Nakhon Sawan
234 F6 **Nāgārjuna Sāgar** ▣ E India
88 G6 **Nagarote** León, SW Nicaragua *12°15′N 86°35′W*
238 G9 **Nagarzê** *var.* Nagaarzê. Xizang Zizhiqu, W China *28°57′N 90°26′E*
250 C7 **Nagasaki** Nagasaki, Kyūshū, SW Japan *32°45′N 129°52′E*
250 B6 **Nagasaki** *off.* Nagasaki-ken. ⬖ *prefecture* Kyūshū, SW Japan
Nagasaki-ken *see* Nagasaki
250 C8 **Naga-shima** *island* SW Japan
250 E6 **Naga-shima** *island* SW Japan
Nagashima *see* Kii-Nagashima
250 D5 **Nagato** Yamaguchi, Honshū, SW Japan *34°22′N 131°10′E*
232 D6 **Nāgaur** Rājasthān, NW India *27°12′N 73°48′E*
232 D8 **Nāgda** Madhya Pradesh, C India *23°30′N 75°29′E*
162 G5 **Nagele** Flevoland, N Netherlands *52°39′N 05°43′E*
235 E10 **Nāgercoil** Tamil Nādu, SE India *08°11′N 77°30′E*
233 M6 **Nāginimāra** Nāgāland, NE India *26°44′N 94°51′E*
Na Gleannta *see* Glenties
251 I10 **Nago** Okinawa, Okinawa, SW Japan *26°36′N 127°59′E*
232 G7 **Nāgod** Madhya Pradesh, C India *24°34′N 80°34′E*
235 G11 **Nagoda** Southern Province, S Sri Lanka *06°13′N 80°13′E*
179 D12 **Nagold** Baden-Württemberg, SW Germany *48°33′N 08°43′E*
193 J7 **Nagornyy** Respublika Sakha (Yakutiya), NE Russian Federation *55°53′N 124°58′E*
195 J8 **Nagorsk** Kirovskaya Oblast', NW Russian Federation *59°18′N 50°49′E*
237 L5 **Nagoya** Aichi, Honshū, SW Japan *35°10′N 136°53′E*
234 F4 **Nāgpur** Mahārāshtra, C India *21°09′N 79°06′E*
239 H8 **Nagqu** *Chin.* Na-Ch'ii; ***prev.*** Hei-ho. Xizang Zizhiqu, W China *31°30′N 91°57′E*
232 F4 **Nāg Tibba Range** ▲▲ N India
91 I5 **Nagua** NE Dominican Republic *19°25′N 69°49′W*
183 E13 **Nagyatád** Somogy, SW Hungary *46°15′N 17°25′E*
Nagybánya *see* Baia Mare
Nagybecskerek *see* Zrenjanin
Nagydisznód *see* Cisnădie
Nagyenyed *see* Aiud
183 I11 **Nagykálló** Szabolcs-Szatmár-Bereg, E Hungary *47°50′N 21°47′E*
183 E12 **Nagykanizsa** *Ger.* Grosskanizsa. Zala, SW Hungary *46°27′N 17°E*
Nagykároly *see* Carei
183 G11 **Nagykáta** Pest, C Hungary *47°25′N 19°45′E*
Nagykikinda *see* Kikinda
183 G12 **Nagykőrös** Pest, C Hungary *47°01′N 19°46′E*
Nagy-Küküllő *see* Târnava Mare
Nagylak *see* Nădlac
Nagymihály *see* Michalovce
Nagyrőce *see* Revúca
Nagysomkút *see* Şomcuta Mare
Nagysurány *see* Šurany
Nagyszalonta *see* Salonta
Nagyszeben *see* Sibiu
Nagyszentmiklós *see* Sânnicolau Mare
Nagyszöllös *see* Vynohradiv
Nagyszombat *see* Trnava
Nagytapolcsány *see* Topoľčany
Nagyvárad *see* Oradea
251 I10 **Naha** Okinawa, Okinawa, SW Japan *26°10′N 127°40′E*
219 D9 **Nahala** Israel
232 E4 **Nāhan** Himāchal Pradesh, NW India *30°33′N 77°18′E*
Nahang, Rūd-e *see* Nihing
Nahariya *see* Nahariyya
216 B5 **Nahariyya** *var.* Nahariya. Northern, N Israel *33°01′N 35°05′E*
222 E4 **Nahāvand** *var.* Nehavend. Hamadān, W Iran *34°13′N 48°21′E*
181 D12 **Nahe** ≈ SW Germany
Na H-Iarmhidhe *see* Westmeath
283 J2 **Nahnalaud** ▲ Pohnpei, E Micronesia
Nahoi, Cape *see* Cumberland, Cape
218 F4 **Nahr al A waj** *dry watercourse* Syria
Nahtavárr *see* Nattavaara
116 C7 **Nahuel Huapí, Lago** ◎ W Argentina
118 C7 **Nahueltoro** Bío-Bío, Chile *36°29′S 71°46′W*
69 L3 **Nahunta** Georgia, SE USA *31°11′N 81°58′W*
85 I5 **Naica** Chihuahua, N Mexico *27°53′N 105°30′W*
57 N5 **Naicam** Saskatchewan, S Canada *52°26′N 104°30′W*
168 G6 **Nailloux** Midi-Pyrénées, France *43°22′N 1°38′E*
160 G6 **Nailsea** UK *51°26′N 2°46′W*
161 H6 **Nailsworth** UK *51°42′N 2°13′W*
Naiman Qi *see* Daqin Tal
238 G3 **Naimin Bulak** *spring* NW China
59 J3 **Nain** Newfoundland and Labrador, NE Canada *56°33′N 61°46′W*
222 G5 **Nā'īn** Eşfahān, C Iran *32°52′N 53°05′E*
232 F5 **Naini Tāl** Uttaranchal, N India *29°22′N 79°26′E*
232 F8 **Nainpur** Madhya Pradesh, C India *22°26′N 80°10′E*
156 F4 **Nairn** N Scotland, UK *57°36′N 03°51′W*
156 F5 **Nairn** *cultural region* NE Scotland, UK
137 D8 **Nairobi** ● (Kenya) Nairobi Area, S Kenya *01°17′S 36°50′E*
137 D8 **Nairobi** ✕ Nairobi Area, S Kenya *01°21′S 37°01′E*
137 E13 **Nairoto** Cabo Delgado, NE Mozambique *12°22′S 39°05′E*
190 D3 **Naissaar** *island* N Estonia
Naissus *see* Niš
280 G8 **Naitaba** *var.* Naitauba; ***prev.*** Naitamba. *island* Lau Group, E Fiji
Naitamba/Naitauba *see* Naitaba
137 D8 **Naivasha** Rift Valley, SW Kenya *0°44′S 36°26′E*
137 D8 **Naivasha, Lake** ◎ SW Kenya
168 G4 **Najac** Midi-Pyrénées, France *44°13′N 1°59′E*
Najaf *see* An Najaf
222 F5 **Najafābād** *var.* Nejafabad. Eşfahān, C Iran *32°38′N 51°23′E*
220 F4 **Najd** *var.* Nejd. *cultural region* C Saudi Arabia
171 H2 **Nájera** La Rioja, N Spain *42°25′N 02°45′W*
168 A8 **Najerilla** ≈ La Rioja, Spain
232 F5 **Najībābād** Uttar Pradesh, N India *29°37′N 78°19′E*
Najima *see* Fukuoka
248 E2 **Najin** NE North Korea *42°13′N 130°16′E*
217 J6 **Najm al Ḩassūn** C Iraq *32°24′N 44°13′E*
220 F7 **Najrān** *var.* Abā as Su'ūd. Najrān, S Saudi Arabia *17°31′N 44°09′E*
220 G7 **Najrān** *var.* Minţaqat al Najrān. ⬖ *province* S Saudi Arabia
Najrān, Minţaqat al *see* Najrān
250 B7 **Nakadōri-jima** *island* Gotō-rettō, SW Japan
252 E2 **Nakagawa** Hokkaidō, NE Japan *44°49′N 142°04′E*
253 C12 **Naka-gawa** ≈ Honshū, S Japan
82 D2 **Nākālele Point** *var.* Nakalele Point. *headland* Maui, Hawai'i, USA *21°01′N 156°35′W*
250 D6 **Nakama** Fukuoka, Kyūshū, SW Japan *33°53′N 130°48′E*
Nakambé *see* White Volta
Nakamti *see* Nek'emtē
250 F7 **Nakamura** Kōchi, Shikoku, SW Japan *33°00′N 132°55′E*
280 D3 **Nakanai Mountains** ▲▲ New Britain, E Papua New Guinea
251 K2 **Nakano** Nagano, Honshū, S Japan *36°43′N 138°23′E*
250 F3 **Nakano-shima** *island* Oki-shotō, SW Japan
250 F4 **Nakano-umi** *var.* Naka-umi. ◎ Honshū, SW Japan
252 D7 **Nakasato** Aomori, Honshū, C Japan *40°58′N 140°26′E*
252 F5 **Nakasatsunai** Hokkaidō, NE Japan *42°42′N 143°09′E*
252 H4 **Nakashibetsu** Hokkaidō, NE Japan *43°31′N 144°58′E*
136 B7 **Nakasongola** C Uganda *01°19′N 32°28′E*
252 E2 **Nakatonbetsu** Hokkaidō, NE Japan *44°58′N 142°18′E*
250 D6 **Nakatsu** *var.* Nakatu. Ōita, Kyūshū, SW Japan *33°37′N 131°11′E*
251 J4 **Nakatsugawa** *var.* Nakatugawa. Gifu, Honshū, SW Japan *35°30′N 137°29′E*
Nakatu *see* Nakatsu
Nakatugawa *see* Nakatsugawa
Naka-umi *see* Nakano-umi
252 D5 **Nakayama-tōge** *pass* Hokkaidō, NE Japan
Nakdong *see* Naktong-gang
Nakel *see* Nakło nad Notecią
136 E1 **Nakfa** N Eritrea *16°38′N 38°26′E*
Nakhichevan' *see* Naxçıvan
193 L9 **Nakhodka** Primorskiy Kray, SE Russian Federation *42°46′N 132°48′E*
192 F5 **Nakhodka** Yamalo-Nenetskiy Avtonomnyy Okrug, N Russian Federation *67°48′N 77°48′E*
Nakhon Navok *see* Nakhon Nayok
256 F8 **Nakhon Nayok** *var.* Nagara Nayok, Nakhon Navok. Nakhon Nayok, C Thailand *14°15′N 101°12′E*
256 E8 **Nakhon Pathom** *var.* Nagara Pathom, Nakorn Pathom. Nakhon Pathom, W Thailand *13°49′N 100°06′E*
256 G6 **Nakhon Phanom** *var.* Nagara Panom. Nakhon Phanom, E Thailand *17°22′N 104°46′E*
256 F7 **Nakhon Ratchasima** *var.* Khorat, Korat. Nakhon Ratchasima, E Thailand *15°N 102°06′E*
256 E7 **Nakhon Sawan** *var.* Muang Nakhon Sawan, Nagara Svarga. Nakhon Sawan, W Thailand *15°42′N 100°06′E*
256 E10 **Nakhon Si Thammarat** *var.* Nagara Sridharmaraj, Nakhon Sithamnaraj. Nakhon Si Thammarat, SW Thailand *08°24′N 99°58′E*
Nakhon Sithamnaraj *see* Nakhon Si Thammarat
217 M7 **Nakhrash** SE Iraq *31°13′N 47°24′E*
54 B4 **Nakina** British Columbia, W Canada *59°12′N 132°48′W*
182 E5 **Nakło nad Notecią** *Ger.* Nakel. Kujawsko-pomorskie, C Poland *53°08′N 17°35′E*
83 H7 **Naknek** Alaska, USA *58°45′N 157°01′W*
232 E4 **Nakodar** Punjab, NW India *31°06′N 75°31′E*
137 B11 **Nakonde** Northern, NE Zambia *09°22′S 42°47′E*
Nakorn Pathom *see* Nakhon Pathom
155 E13 **Nakskov** Storstrøm, SE Denmark *54°50′N 11°10′E*
248 C6 **Naktong-gang** *var.* Nakdong, *Jap.* Rakutō-kō. ≈ C South Korea
137 D8 **Nakuru** Rift Valley, SW Kenya *0°16′S 36°04′E*
56 G8 **Nakusp** British Columbia, SW Canada *50°14′N 117°48′W*
230 F9 **Nāl** ≈ W Pakistan
239 K1 **Nalayh** Töv, C Mongolia *47°48′N 107°17′E*
233 K6 **Nalbāri** Assam, NE India *26°36′N 91°49′E*
117 B10 **Nalcayec, Isla** *island* Archipiélago de los Chonos, S Chile
197 H9 **Nal'chik** Kabardino-Balkarskaya Respublika, SW Russian Federation *43°30′N 43°39′E*
234 F6 **Nalgonda** Andhra Pradesh, C India *17°04′N 79°15′E*
233 J7 **Nalhāti** West Bengal, NE India *24°19′N 87°53′E*
233 K7 **Nalitabari** Dhaka, N Bangladesh *25°06′N 90°11′E*
234 F6 **Nallamala Hills** ▲▲ E India
214 D5 **Nallıhan** Ankara, NW Turkey *40°12′N 31°22′E*
170 E1 **Nalón** ≈ NW Spain
256 D3 **Nalong** Kachin State, N Myanmar (Burma) *24°42′N 97°27′E*
128 B2 **Nālūt** NW Libya *31°52′N 10°59′E*
261 H6 **Nama** Pulau Manawoka, E Indonesia *04°07′S 131°22′E*
282 G6 **Nama** *island* C Micronesia
139 J3 **Namacurra** Zambézia, NE Mozambique *17°31′S 37°03′E*
282 C9 **Namai Bay** *bay* Babeldaob, N Palau
58 B7 **Namakan Lake** ◎ Canada/USA
222 F4 **Namak, Daryācheh-ye** *marsh* N Iran
141 K2 **Namakgale** Limpopo, South Africa *23°57′S 31°02′E*
223 H4 **Namak, Kavīr-e** *salt pan* NE Iran
256 E5 **Namaklwe** Shan State, E Myanmar (Burma) *19°45′N 99°01′E*
Namaksār, Kowl-e/Namakzār, Daryācheh-ye *see* Namakzar
230 D3 **Namakzar** *Pash.* Daryācheh-ye Namakzār, Kowl-e Namaksār. *marsh* Afghanistan/Iran
261 J7 **Namalau** Pulau Jursian, E Indonesia *05°50′S 134°43′E*
137 D9 **Namanga** Rift Valley, S Kenya *02°33′S 36°48′E*
229 J5 **Namangan** Namangan Viloyati, E Uzbekistan *40°59′N 71°34′E*
Namanganskaya Oblast' *see* Namangan Viloyati
229 J5 **Namangan Viloyati** *Rus.* Namanganskaya Oblast'. ⬖ *province* E Uzbekistan
139 L1 **Namapa** Nampula, NE Mozambique *13°43′S 39°48′E*
140 C3 **Namaqualand** *physical region* S Namibia
136 B7 **Namasagali** C Uganda *01°02′N 32°58′E*
280 D2 **Namatanai** New Ireland, NE Papua New Guinea *03°40′S 152°26′E*
138 G2 **Nambala** Central, C Zambia *15°04′S 26°56′E*
137 E11 **Nambanje** Lindi, SE Tanzania *08°37′S 38°21′E*
261 J4 **Namber** Papua, E Indonesia *0°58′S 134°51′E*
138 E3 **Nambiya** North West, N Botswana *18°09′S 23°08′E*
181 C13 **Namborn** Saarland, Germany *7°08′N 49°31′E*
277 M1 **Nambour** Queensland, E Australia *26°40′S 152°52′E*
277 M3 **Nambucca Heads** New South Wales, SE Australia *30°37′S 153°00′E*
238 G9 **Nam Co** ◎ W China
256 G4 **Nậm Cum** Lai Châu, N Vietnam *22°37′N 103°12′E*
Namdik *see* Namorik Atoll
257 H5 **Nam Định** Nam Ha, N Vietnam *20°25′N 106°12′E*
260 G5 **Namea, Tanjung** *headland* Pulau Seram, SE Indonesia
163 F11 **Namêche** Namur, SE Belgium *50°29′N 05°02′E*
72 B4 **Namekagon Lake** ◎ Wisconsin, N USA
282 C10 **Namekakl Passage** *passage* Babeldaob, N Palau
Namen *see* Namur
139 K2 **Nametil** Nampula, NE Mozambique *15°46′S 39°21′E*
55 H8 **Namew Lake** ◎ Saskatchewan/Manitoba, C Canada
248 C4 **Nam-gang** ≈ C North Korea
248 C6 **Nam-gang** ≈ S South Korea
248 C7 **Namhae-do** *Jap.* Nankai-tō. *island* S South Korea
Namhoi *see* Foshan
140 A2 **Namib Desert** *desert* W Namibia
135 B13 **Namibe** *Port.* Moçâmedes, Mossâmedes. Namibe, SW Angola *15°10′S 12°09′E*
135 B14 **Namibe** ⬖ *province* SE Angola
140 C3 **Namibia** *off.* Republic of Namibia, *var.* South West Africa, ***Afr.*** Suidwes-Afrika, ***Ger.*** Deutsch-Südwestafrika; ***prev.*** German Southwest Africa, South-West Africa. ◆ *republic* S Africa
291 I10 **Namibia Plain** *undersea feature* S Atlantic Ocean
Namibia, Republic of *see* Namibia
253 D11 **Namie** Fukushima, Honshū, C Japan *37°29′N 140°58′E*
252 D7 **Namioka** Aomori, Honshū, C Japan *40°43′N 140°34′E*
84 G4 **Namiquipa** Chihuahua, N Mexico *29°15′N 107°25′W*
239 I9 **Namjagbarwa Feng** ▲ W China *29°39′N 95°00′E*
Namka *see* Doilungdêqên
260 G5 **Namlea** Pulau Buru, E Indonesia *03°12′S 127°06′E*
238 G9 **Namling** Xizang Zizhiqu, W China *29°40′N 88°58′E*
Namnetes *see* Nantes
256 F6 **Nam Ngum** ≈ C Laos
Namo *see* Namu Atoll
277 L3 **Namoi River** ≈ New South Wales, SE Australia
283 H6 **Namoluk Atoll** *atoll* Mortlock Islands, C Micronesia
282 G6 **Namonuito Atoll** *atoll* Caroline Islands, C Micronesia
283 L7 **Namorik Atoll** *var.* Namdik. *atoll* Ralik Chain, S Marshall Islands
256 F5 **Nam Ou** ≈ N Laos
76 F7 **Nampa** Idaho, NW USA *43°32′N 116°33′W*
132 F4 **Nampala** Ségou, W Mali *15°21′N 05°32′W*
248 B4 **Namp'o** SW North Korea *38°46′N 125°25′E*
139 K2 **Nampula** Nampula, NE Mozambique *15°09′S 39°14′E*
139 K2 **Nampula** *off.* Província de Nampula. ⬖ *province* NE Mozambique
Nampula, Província de *see* Nampula
248 B3 **Namsan-ni** NW North Korea *40°25′N 125°01′E*
Namslau *see* Namysłów
154 E2 **Namsos** Nord-Trøndelag, C Norway *64°28′N 11°31′E*
154 F1 **Namsskogan** Nord-Trøndelag, C Norway *64°57′N 13°04′E*
256 D5 **Nam Teng** ≈ E Myanmar (Burma)
256 F5 **Nam Tha** ≈ N Laos
193 J6 **Namsty** Respublika Sakha (Yakutiya), NE Russian Federation *62°42′N 129°30′E*
256 D4 **Namtu** Shan State, E Myanmar (Burma) *23°04′N 97°26′E*
56 B6 **Namu** British Columbia, SW Canada *51°46′N 127°49′W*
283 L6 **Namu Atoll** *var.* Namo. *atoll* Ralik Chain, C Marshall Islands
280 G9 **Namuka-i-lau** *island* Lau Group, E Fiji
139 K2 **Namuli, Mont** ▲ NE Mozambique *15°15′S 37°33′E*
137 E13 **Namuno** Cabo Delgado, N Mozambique *13°39′S 38°50′E*
163 F11 **Namur** *Dut.* Namen. Namur, SE Belgium *50°28′N 04°52′E*
163 F11 **Namur** *Dut.* Namen. ⬖ *province* S Belgium
138 C3 **Namutoni** Kunene, N Namibia *18°49′S 16°55′E*
248 B6 **Namwŏn** *Jap.* Nangen. S South Korea *35°24′N 127°20′E*
263 H7 **Namyit Island** *island* S Spratly Islands
182 E7 **Namysłów** *Ger.* Namslau. Opole, SW Poland *51°03′N 17°41′E*
256 E6 **Nan** *var.* Muang Nan. Nan, NW Thailand *18°47′N 100°50′E*
134 D5 **Nana** ≈ W Central African Republic
252 D6 **Nanae** Hokkaidō, NE Japan *41°55′N 140°40′E*
134 E4 **Nana-Grébizi** ⬖ *prefecture* N Central African Republic
56 D9 **Nanaimo** Vancouver Island, British Columbia, SW Canada *49°08′N 123°58′W*
134 D5 **Nana-Mambéré** ⬖ *prefecture* W Central African Republic
243 L7 **Nan'an** Fujian, SE China *24°57′N 118°22′E*
277 M1 **Nanango** Queensland, E Australia *26°42′S 151°58′E*
251 J1 **Nanao** Ishikawa, Honshū, SW Japan *37°03′N 136°58′E*
243 K9 **Nan'ao Dao** *island* S China
251 J1 **Nanatsu-shima** *island* SW Japan
104 E3 **Nanay, Río** ≈ NE Peru
242 C2 **Nanbu** Sichuan, C China *31°19′N 106°02′E*
193 K9 **Nancha** Heilongjiang, NE China *47°09′N 129°17′E*
243 J4 **Nanchang** *var.* Nan-ch'ang, Nanch'ang-hsien. *province capital* Jiangxi, S China *28°38′N 115°58′E*
243 J4 **Nanchang** Jiangxi, China *28°20′N 115°34′E*
Nan-ch'ang *see* Nanchang
Nanch'ang-hsien *see* Nanchang
245 M4 **Nanchangshan Dao** *island* Shandong, China
243 J5 **Nancheng** *var.* Jianchang. Jiangxi, S China *27°37′N 116°37′E*
Nan-ching *see* Nanjing
242 C2 **Nanchong** Sichuan, C China *30°47′N 106°03′E*
242 C4 **Nanchuan** Chongqing Shi, C China *29°06′N 107°13′E*
245 L6 **Nancun** China *36°32′N 120°08′E*
165 K3 **Nancy** Meurthe-et-Moselle, NE France *48°40′N 06°11′E*
278 A11 **Nancy Sound** *sound* South Island, New Zealand
232 G4 **Nanda Devi** ▲ NW India *30°27′N 80°00′E*
88 G6 **Nandaime** Granada, SW Nicaragua *11°45′N 86°02′W*
242 C7 **Nandan** Guangxi Zhuangzu Zizhiqu, S China *25°03′N 107°31′E*
234 E5 **Nānded** Mahārāshtra, C India *19°11′N 77°21′E*
251 H5 **Nanden** Hyōgo, Awaji-shima, SW Japan *34°19′N 134°53′E*
277 L3 **Nandewar Range** ▲▲ New South Wales, SE Australia
Nandi *see* Nadi
240 B7 **Nanding He** ≈ China/Vietnam
Nándorhgy *see* Oţelu Roşu
114 A2 **Nanducita** Santa Fe, Argentina *30°22′S 61°09′W*
234 D3 **Nandurbār** Mahārāshtra, W India *21°22′N 74°18′E*
Nanduri *see* Naduri
234 F6 **Nandyāl** Andhra Pradesh, E India *15°30′N 78°28′E*
243 J5 **Nanfeng** *var.* Qincheng. Jiangxi, S China *27°15′N 116°16′E*
Nang *see* Nangxian
134 B5 **Nanga Eboko** Centre, C Cameroon *04°38′N 12°21′E*
Nangah Serawai *see* Nangaserawai
231 J3 **Nanga Parbat** ▲ India/Pakistan *35°15′N 74°36′E*
258 I5 **Nangapinoh** Borneo, C Indonesia *0°21′S 111°44′E*
231 H4 **Nangarhār** ⬖ *province* E Afghanistan
258 I5 **Nangaserawai** *var.* Nangah Serawai. Borneo, C Indonesia *0°20′S 112°26′E*
258 I5 **Nangatayap** Borneo, C Indonesia *01°30′S 110°33′E*
244 A6 **Nangdoi** Qinghai, China *36°07′N 102°01′E*
Nangen *see* Namwŏn
165 I3 **Nangis** Seine-et-Marne, N France *48°36′N 03°02′E*
248 C3 **Nangnim-sanmaek** ▲▲ C North Korea
245 I5 **Nangong** Hebei, E China *37°22′N 115°20′E*
239 I8 **Nangqên** *var.* Xangda. Qinghai, C China *32°05′N 96°28′E*
256 G7 **Nang Rong** Buri Ram, E Thailand *14°37′N 102°48′E*
239 H9 **Nangxian** *var.* Nang. Xizang Zizhiqu, W China *29°04′N 93°03′E*
Nan Hai *see* South China Sea
242 F1 **Nan He** ≈ C China
240 C6 **Nanhua** *var.* Longchuan. Yunnan, SW China *25°15′N 101°15′E*
243 N2 **Nanhui** Shanghai Shi, China *31°02′N 121°27′E*
Naniwa *see* Ōsaka
235 E8 **Nanjangūd** Karnātaka, W India *12°07′N 76°40′E*
242 C1 **Nanjiang** Sichuan, China *32°13′N 106°29′E*
243 K8 **Nanjing** Fujan, China *24°18′N 117°13′E*
243 K1 **Nanjing** *var.* Nan-ching, Nanking; ***prev.*** Chianning, Chian-ning, Kiang-ning, Jiangsu. *province capital* Jiangsu, E China *32°03′N 118°47′E*
Nankai-tō *see* Namhae-do
243 J3 **Nankang** China *29°27′N 116°03′E*
243 I7 **Nankang** *var.* Rongjiang. Jiangxi, S China *25°42′N 114°45′E*
Nanking *see* Nanjing
250 F6 **Nankoku** Kōchi, Shikoku, SW Japan *33°33′N 133°37′E*
245 J7 **Nan-kuan-chi** China *35°26′N 117°14′E*
243 K2 **Nanling** Anhui, China *30°33′N 118°11′E*
243 H7 **Nan Ling** ▲▲ S China
243 H3 **Nanlinqiao** China *29°34′N 114°21′E*
242 E10 **Nanliu Jiang** ≈ S China
283 K2 **Nan Madol** *ruins* Temwen Island, E Micronesia
242 D9 **Nanning** *var.* Nan-ning; ***prev.*** Yung-ning. Guangxi Zhuangzu Zizhiqu, S China *22°50′N 108°19′E*
Nan-ning *see* Nanning
52 F7 **Nanook River** ≈ Nunavut, N Canada
295 M8 **Nanortalik** ⬖ Kitaa, S Greenland
Nanouki *see* Aranuka
242 C7 **Nanpan Jiang** ▲▲ Guangxi, China
242 A8 **Nanpan Jiang** ≈ S China
232 G6 **Nānpāra** Uttar Pradesh, N India *27°51′N 81°30′E*
245 J4 **Nanpi** China *38°02′N 116°42′E*
245 L2 **Nanpiao** Liaoning, China *41°05′N 120°26′E*
242 E3 **Nanping** China *30°25′N 108°47′E*
243 K6 **Nanping** *var.* Nan-p'ing; ***prev.*** Yenping. Fujian, SE China *26°40′N 118°07′E*
Nan-p'ing *see* Nanping
Nanping *see* Jiuzhaigou
Nanpu *see* Pucheng
243 K5 **Nanpu Xi** ≈ Fujan, China
243 L7 **Nanri Dao** *island* SE China
243 L7 **Nanri Qundao** *island group* Fujan, China
251 I9 **Nansei-shotō** *Eng.* Ryukyu Islands. *island group* SW Japan
Nansei Syotō Trench *see* Ryukyu Trench
295 I4 **Nansen Basin** *undersea feature* Arctic Ocean
295 H4 **Nansen Cordillera** *var.* Arctic Mid Oceanic Ridge, Nansen Ridge. *undersea feature* Arctic Ocean
Nansen Ridge *see* Nansen Cordillera
53 H2 **Nansen Sound** *Sound* Nunavut, Canada
205 K5 **Nan Shan** ▲▲ C China
Nansha Qundao *see* Spratly Islands
58 G1 **Nantais, Lac** ◎ Québec, NE Canada
165 H3 **Nanterre** Hauts-de-Seine, N France *48°53′N 02°13′E*
164 F5 **Nantes** *Bret.* Naoned; ***anc.*** Condivincum, Namnetes. Loire-Atlantique, NW France *47°12′N 01°32′W*
167 H5 **Nanteuil-le-Haudouin** Picardie, France *49°08′N 2°48′E*
168 F1 **Nantiat** Limousin, France *46°01′N 1°11′E*
62 C6 **Nanticoke** Ontario, S Canada *42°49′N 80°04′W*
64 E5 **Nanticoke** Pennsylvania, NE USA *41°12′N 76°00′W*
62 F10 **Nanticoke River** ≈ Delaware/Maryland, NE USA
160 F4 **Nantmel** UK *52°17′N 3°25′W*
57 I8 **Nanton** Alberta, SW Canada *50°21′N 113°47′W*
243 M1 **Nantong** Jiangsu, E China *32°00′N 120°52′E*
243 M8 **Nant'ou** W Taiwan *23°54′N 120°51′E*
167 L10 **Nantua** Ain, E France *46°10′N 05°34′E*
65 N4 **Nantucket** Nantucket Island, Massachusetts, NE USA *41°15′N 70°05′W*
65 N4 **Nantucket Island** *island* Massachusetts, NE USA
65 N4 **Nantucket Sound** *sound* Massachusetts, NE USA
137 E13 **Nantulo** Cabo Delgado, N Mozambique *12°30′S 39°03′E*
160 G2 **Nantwich** UK *53°04′N 2°31′W*
64 A6 **Nanty Glo** Pennsylvania, USA *40°28′N 78°50′W*
283 J1 **Nanuh** Pohnpei, E Micronesia
280 F8 **Nanuku Passage** *channel* NE Fiji
284 B4 **Nanumaga** *atoll* NW Tuvalu
284 B4 **Nanumea Atoll** *atoll* NW Tuvalu
109 G10 **Nanuque** Minas Gerais, SE Brazil *17°49′S 40°21′W*
260 F1 **Nanusa, Kepulauan** *island group* N Indonesia
242 B4 **Nanxi** Sichuan, C China *28°54′N 104°59′E*
242 G4 **Nanxian** *var.* Nan Xian, Nanzhou. Hunan, S China *29°23′N 112°18′E*
Nan Xian *see* Nanxian
243 M2 **Nanxiang** China *31°18′N 121°18′E*
243 H7 **Nanxiong** Guangdong, China *25°05′N 114°11′E*
245 M8 **Nanyang** China *33°26′N 120°14′E*
237 H6 **Nanyang** *var.* Nan-yang. Henan, C China *32°59′N 112°29′E*
Nan-yang *see* Nanyang
245 J7 **Nanyang Hu** ◎ E China
253 C10 **Nan'yō** Yamagata, Honshū, C Japan *38°04′N 140°06′E*
245 J3 **Nanyuan** China *39°48′N 116°25′E*
242 G5 **Nanyue** China *27°15′N 112°44′E*
137 D8 **Nanyuki** Central, C Kenya *0°01′N 37°05′E*
242 G1 **Nanzhang** Hubei, C China *31°47′N 111°48′E*
244 G8 **Nanzhao** Henan, China *33°17′N 112°14′E*
244 D9 **Nanzheng** Shaanxi, China *33°01′N 106°34′E*
Nanzhou *see* Nanxian
173 M5 **Nao, Cabo de La** *cape* E Spain
59 H5 **Naococane, Lac** ◎ Québec, E Canada
233 J7 **Naogaon** Rajshahi, NW Bangladesh *24°49′N 88°59′E*
245 I7 **Naokao** China *34°56′N 115°05′E*
Naokot *see* Naukot
86 G6 **Naolinco** Veracruz-Llave, Mexico *19°39′N 96°51′W*
281 M2 **Naone** Maewo, C Vanuatu *15°03′S 168°06′E*
Naoned *see* Nantes
186 G3 **Náousa** Kentrikí Makedonía, N Greece *40°38′N 22°04′E*
80 B2 **Napa** California, W USA *38°15′N 122°17′W*
83 H6 **Napaimiut** Alaska, USA *61°32′N 158°46′W*
82 G6 **Napakiak** Alaska, USA *60°42′N 161°57′W*
192 F4 **Napalkovo** Yamalo-Nenetskiy Avtonomnyy Okrug, N Russian Federation *70°06′N 73°43′E*
62 F4 **Napanee** Ontario, SE Canada *44°13′N 76°57′W*
261 K5 **Napanwainami** Papua, E Indonesia *03°01′S 135°51′E*
261 J5 **Napan-Yaur** Papua, E Indonesia *02°55′S 134°50′E*
82 G6 **Napaskiak** Alaska, USA *60°42′N 161°46′W*
80 B2 **Napa Valley** *valley* California, USA
257 H4 **Na Phac** Cao Băng, N Vietnam *22°24′N 105°54′E*
261 J4 **Napido** Papua, E Indonesia *0°41′S 135°27′E*
279 I6 **Napier** Hawke's Bay, North Island, New Zealand *39°30′S 176°55′E*
293 L2 **Napier Mountains** ▲▲ Antarctica
63 H3 **Napierville** Québec, SE Canada *45°12′N 73°25′W*
69 L9 **Naples** Florida, SE USA *26°08′N 81°48′W*
71 I4 **Naples** Texas, SW USA *33°12′N 94°40′W*
Naples *see* Napoli
242 B9 **Napo** Guangxi Zhuangzu Zizhiqu, S China *23°21′N 105°47′E*
104 D2 **Napo** ⬖ *province* NE Ecuador
74 D3 **Napoleon** North Dakota, N USA *46°30′N 99°46′W*
73 G9 **Napoleon** Ohio, N USA *41°23′N 84°07′W*
Napoléon-Vendée *see* la Roche-sur-Yon
68 D4 **Napoleonville** Louisiana, S USA *29°55′N 91°01′W*
175 G9 **Napoli** *Eng.* Naples, ***Ger.*** Neapel; ***anc.*** Neapolis. Campania, S Italy *40°52′N 14°15′E*
175 G9 **Napoli, Golfo di** *gulf* S Italy
104 E2 **Napo, Río** ≈ Ecuador/Peru
285 K6 **Napuka** *island* Îles Tuamotu, C French Polynesia
222 C3 **Naqadeh** Āžarbāyjān-e Bākhtarī, NW Iran *36°57′N 45°24′E*
217 K4 **Naqnah** E Iraq *34°13′N 45°33′E*
Nar *see* Nera
251 I5 **Nara** Nara, Honshū, SW Japan *34°41′N 135°49′E*
132 E4 **Nara** Koulikoro, W Mali *15°04′N 07°19′W*
251 I5 **Nara** *off.* Nara-ken. ⬖ *prefecture* Honshū, SW Japan
230 G8 **Nāra Canal** *irrigation canal* S Pakistan
277 H7 **Naracoorte** South Australia *37°02′S 140°45′E*
277 J5 **Naradhan** New South Wales, SE Australia *33°37′S 146°19′E*
Naradhivas *see* Narathiwat
Nara-ken *see* Nara
104 B3 **Naranjal** Guayas, W Ecuador *02°43′S 79°38′W*
87 M6 **Naranjal Poniente** Quintana Roo, Mexico *19°22′N 88°28′W*
84 G6 **Naranjo** Sinaloa, Mexico *25°48′N 108°28′W*
112 F1 **Naranjos** Santa Cruz, E Bolivia
86 G5 **Naranjos** Veracruz-Llave, E Mexico *21°21′N 97°41′W*
239 I4 **Naran Sebstein Bulag** *spring* NW China
223 K8 **Narānū** Sīstān va Balūchestān, SE Iran
250 B7 **Narao** Nagasaki, Nakadōri-jima, SW Japan *32°40′N 129°03′E*
234 F6 **Narasaraopet** Andhra Pradesh, E India *16°16′N 80°06′E*
238 E3 **Narat** Xinjiang Uygur Zizhiqu, W China *43°20′N 84°02′E*
256 F11 **Narathiwat** *var.* Naradhivas. Narathiwat, SW Thailand *06°25′N 101°48′E*
79 N6 **Nara Visa** New Mexico, SW USA *35°35′N 103°06′W*
Nārāyāni *see* Gandak
Narbada *see* Narmada
Narbo Martius *see* Narbonne
165 I9 **Narbonne** ***anc.*** Narbo Martius. Aude, S France *43°11′N 03°E*
169 H6 **Narbonne-Plage** Languedoc-Roussillon, France *43°10′N 3°10′E*
161 I3 **Narborough** UK *52°34′N 1°12′W*
Narborough Island *see* Fernandina, Isla
170 E1 **Narcea** ≈ NW Spain
114 B3 **Naré** Santa Fe, Argentina *30°58′S 60°28′W*
232 F4 **Narendranagar** Uttaranchal, N India *30°10′N 78°21′E*
Nares Abyssal Plain *see* Nares Plain
290 D6 **Nares Plain** *var.* Nares Abyssal Plain. *undersea feature* NW Atlantic Ocean
Nares Stræde *see* Nares Strait
295 I7 **Nares Strait** *Dan.* Nares Stræde. *strait* Canada/Greenland
182 I5 **Narew** ≈ E Poland
234 D6 **Nargund** Karnātaka, W India *15°43′N 75°23′E*
140 C2 **Narib** Hardap, S Namibia *24°11′S 17°46′E*
Narikrik *see* Knox Atoll
158 B6 **Narin** Donegal, Ireland *54°50′N 8°28′W*
102 A7 **Narino** *off.* Departamento de Narino. ⬖ *province* SW Colombia
253 C13 **Narita** Chiba, Honshū, S Japan *35°46′N 140°20′E*
253 C13 **Narita** ✕ (Tōkyō) Chiba, Honshū, S Japan *35°45′N 140°23′E*
Narīya *see* An Nu'ayrīyah
239 J2 **Nariynteel** *var.* Tsagaan-Ovoo. Övörhangay, C Mongolia *45°57′N 101°25′E*
232 F4 **Nārkanda** Himāchal Pradesh, NW India *31°14′N 77°27′E*
152 H6 **Narkaus** Lappi, NW Finland *66°13′N 26°09′E*
232 G8 **Narmada** *var.* Narbada. ≈ C India
232 E5 **Narnaul** *var.* Nārnaul. Haryāna, N India *28°04′N 76°10′E*
175 F13 **Naro** Sicilia, Italy, C Mediterranean Sea *37°18′N 13°48′E*
Narodichi *see* Narodychi
195 L5 **Narodnaya, Gora** ▲ NW Russian Federation *65°04′N 60°12′E*
188 G2 **Narodychi** *Rus.* Narodichi. Zhytomyrs'ka Oblast', N Ukraine *51°11′N 29°01′E*
196 F2 **Naro-Fominsk** Moskovskaya Oblast', W Russian Federation *55°25′N 36°41′E*
137 D8 **Narok** Rift Valley, SW Kenya *01°04′S 35°54′E*
170 D1 **Narón** Galicia, NW Spain *43°31′N 08°08′W*
277 L6 **Narooma** New South Wales, SE Australia *36°16′S 150°08′E*
Narova *see* Narva
Narovlya *see* Narowlya
231 J5 **Nārowāl** Punjab, E Pakistan *32°04′N 74°54′E*
191 H12 **Narowlya** *Rus.* Narovlya. Homyel'skaya Voblasts', SE Belarus *51°48′N 29°30′E*
153 G8 **Närpes** *Fin.* Närpiö. Länsi-Soumi, W Finland *62°28′N 21°19′E*
Närpiö *see* Närpes
277 L3 **Narrabri** New South Wales, SE Australia *30°21′S 149°48′E*
65 L4 **Narragansett Pier** Rhode Island, USA *41°26′N 71°27′W*
277 J5 **Narrandera** New South Wales, SE Australia *34°46′S 146°32′E*
277 K3 **Narran Lake** ◎ New South Wales, SE Australia
274 D7 **Narrogin** Western Australia *32°53′S 117°17′E*
277 K4 **Narromine** New South Wales, SE Australia *32°16′S 148°15′E*
67 I4 **Narrows** Virginia, NE USA *37°19′N 80°48′W*
64 G4 **Narrowsburg** New York, USA *41°37′N 75°04′W*
295 M8 **Narsarsuaq** ✕ Kitaa, S Greenland *61°07′N 45°03′W*
232 F8 **Narsimhapur** Madhya Pradesh, C India *22°58′N 79°15′E*
Narsingdi *see* Narsinghdi
233 K7 **Narsinghdi** *var.* Narsingdi. Dhaka, C Bangladesh *23°56′N 90°40′E*
232 E8 **Narsinghgarh** Madhya Pradesh, C India *23°42′N 77°08′E*
239 N2 **Nart** Nei Mongol Zizhiqu, N China *42°54′N 115°55′E*
Nartës, Gjol i/Nartës, Laguna e *see* Nartës, Liqeni i
184 E9 **Nartës, Liqeni i** *var.* Gjol i Nartës, Laguna e Nartës. ◎ SW Albania
186 G5 **Nartháki** ▲ C Greece *39°12′N 22°24′E*
197 H9 **Nartkala** Kabardino-Balkarskaya Respublika, SW Russian Federation *43°34′N 43°55′E*
250 G5 **Naruto** Tokushima, Shikoku, SW Japan *34°11′N 134°37′E*
194 C8 **Narva** Ida-Virumaa, NE Estonia *59°23′N 28°12′E*
190 F4 **Narva** ***prev.*** Narova. ≈ Estonia/Russian Federation
190 F3 **Narva Bay** *Est.* Narva Laht, ***Ger.*** Narwa-Bucht, ***Rus.*** Narvskiy Zaliv. *bay* Estonia/Russian Federation
Narva Laht *see* Narva Bay
194 C8 **Narva Reservoir** *Est.* Narva Veehoidla, ***Rus.*** Narvskoye Vodokhranilishche. ▣ Estonia/Russian Federation
Narva Veehoidla *see* Narva Reservoir
152 F4 **Narvik** Nordland, C Norway *68°26′N 17°24′E*
Narvskiy Zaliv *see* Narva Bay
Narvskoye Vodokhranilishche *see* Narva Reservoir
Narwa-Bucht *see* Narva Bay
232 E4 **Narwāna** Haryāna, NW India *29°36′N 76°11′E*
195 J3 **Nar'yan-Mar** ***prev.*** Beloshchel'ye, Dzerzhinskiy. Nenetskiy Avtonomnyy Okrug, NW Russian Federation *67°38′N 53°E*
192 F6 **Narym** Tomskaya Oblast', C Russian Federation *58°59′N 81°20′E*
227 M4 **Narymskiy Khrebet** *Kaz.* Naryn Zhotasy. ▲▲ E Kazakhstan
229 L5 **Naryn** Narynskaya Oblast', C Kyrgyzstan *41°24′N 76°E*
229 K5 **Naryn** ≈ Kyrgyzstan/Uzbekistan
238 D3 **Narynkol** *Kaz.* Narynqol. Almaty, SE Kazakhstan *42°45′N 80°12′E*
Naryn Oblasty *see* Narynskaya Oblast'
Narynqol *see* Narynkol
229 L5 **Narynskaya Oblast'** *Kir.* Naryn Oblasty. ⬖ *province* C Kyrgyzstan
Naryn Zhotasy *see* Narymskiy Khrebet
196 F3 **Naryshkino** Orlovskaya Oblast', W Russian Federation *53°00′N 35°41′E*

◆ Country
● Country Capital
◇ Dependent Territory
○ Dependent Territory Capital
⬖ Administrative Regions
✕ International Airport
▲ Mountain
▲▲ Mountain Range
Volcano
≈ River
◎ Lake
▣ Reservoir

INDEX

Nås - Neuville-aux-Bois
INDEX
381

154 G7 **Nås** Dalarna, C Sweden 60°28′N 14°30′E
152 E6 **Nasafjellet** *Lapp.* Násávárre. ▲ C Norway 66°29′N 15°23′E
154 H3 **Näsåker** Västernorrland, C Sweden 63°27′N 16°55′E
280 F8 **Nasau** Koro, C Fiji 17°20′S 179°26′E
188 D6 **Năsăud** *Ger.* Nussdorf, *Hung.* Naszód. Bistriţa-Năsăud, N Romania 47°16′N 24°24′E
Násávárre *see* Nasafjellet
169 H3 **Nasbinals** Languedoc-Roussillon, France 44°40′N 3°03′E
Na Sceirí *see* Skerries
Nase *see* Naze
278 D11 **Naseby** Otago, South Island, New Zealand 45°02′S 170°09′E
161 J4 **Naseby** UK 52°23′N 0°59′W
223 H7 **Nāşerīyeh** Kermān, C Iran
75 G14 **Nash** Texas, SW USA 33°26′N 94°04′W
234 C4 **Nāshik** *prev.* Nāsik. Mahārāshtra, W India 20°05′N 73°48′E
104 E2 **Nashiño, Río** ≈ Ecuador/Peru
72 A7 **Nashua** Iowa, C USA 42°57′N 92°32′W
77 L3 **Nashua** Montana, NW USA 48°06′N 106°16′W
65 L1 **Nashua** New Hampshire, NE USA 42°45′N 71°26′W
75 G13 **Nashville** Arkansas, C USA 33°57′N 93°50′W
69 K3 **Nashville** Georgia, SE USA 31°12′N 83°15′W
73 C12 **Nashville** Illinois, N USA 38°20′N 89°22′W
73 F11 **Nashville** Indiana, N USA 39°13′N 86°15′W
67 L6 **Nashville** North Carolina, SE USA 35°58′N 78°00′W
66 D6 **Nashville** *state capital* Tennessee, S USA 36°11′N 86°48′W
66 D6 **Nashville** ✈ Tennessee, S USA 36°06′N 86°44′W
290 D5 **Nashville Seamount** *undersea feature* NW Atlantic Ocean
184 E2 **Našice** Osijek-Baranja, E Croatia 45°29′N 18°05′E
182 H5 **Nasielsk** Mazowieckie, C Poland 52°33′N 20°46′E
153 H9 **Näsijärvi** ◎ SW Finland
Nāsik *see* Nāshik
136 B4 **Nasir** Upper Nile, SE Sudan 08°37′N 33°06′E
230 G7 **Nasīrābād** Baluchistān, SW Pakistan 28°25′N 68°29′E
230 D9 **Nasirābād** Baluchistān, SW Pakistan 26°15′N 62°32′E
Nasirābād *see* Mymensingh
Nāsiri *see* Ahvāz
Nasiriya *see* An Nāşirīyah
Nás na Ríogh *see* Naas
175 G12 **Naso** Sicilia, Italy, C Mediterranean Sea 38°07′N 14°46′E
Nasratabad *see* Zābol
56 B2 **Nass** ≈ British Columbia, SW Canada
133 K7 **Nassarawa** Nassarawa, C Nigeria 08°33′N 07°42′E
61 M9 **Nassau** ● (Bahamas) New Providence, N Bahamas 25°03′N 77°21′W
181 D11 **Nassau** Rheinland-Pfalz, Germany 7°48′N 50°19′E
61 M9 **Nassau** ✈ New Providence, C Bahamas 25°00′N 77°26′W
284 F5 **Nassau** *island* N Cook Islands
69 L4 **Nassau Sound** *sound* Florida, SE USA
176 G4 **Nassereith** Tirol, W Austria 47°19′N 10°51′E
129 J6 **Nasser, Lake** ◎ Egypt/Sudan
155 G10 **Nässjö** Jönköping, S Sweden 57°39′N 14°40′E
163 F12 **Nassogne** Luxembourg, SE Belgium 50°08′N 05°19′E
58 G3 **Nastapoka Islands** *island group* Northwest Territories, C Canada
181 D11 **Nastätten** Rheinland-Pfalz, Germany 7°52′N 50°12′E
153 H9 **Nastola** Etelä-Suomi, S Finland 60°57′N 25°56′E
253 C11 **Nasu-dake** ▲ Honshū, S Japan 37°07′N 139°57′E
263 K5 **Nasugbu** Luzon, N Philippines 14°03′N 120°39′E
190 H5 **Nasva** Pskovskaya Oblast', Russian Federation
154 H5 **Näsviken** Gävleborg, C Sweden 61°46′N 16°55′E
Naszód *see* Năsăud
138 F4 **Nata** Central, NE Botswana 20°11′S 26°10′E
102 C6 **Natagaima** Tolima, C Colombia 03°38′N 75°07′W
108 J5 **Natal** *state capital* Rio Grande do Norte, E Brazil 05°46′S 35°15′W
258 C5 **Natal** Sumatera, N Indonesia 0°32′N 99°07′E
Natal *see* KwaZulu/Natal
195 L10 **Natal'insk** Sverdlovskaya oblasť, Russian federation
289 B10 **Natal Basin** *var.* Mozambique Basin. *undersea feature* W Indian Ocean
70 F7 **Natalia** Texas, SW USA 29°11′N 98°51′W
54 C7 **Natalkuz Lake** ◎ British Columbia, SW Canada
121 M9 **Natal Valley** *undersea feature* SW Indian Ocean
Natanya *see* Netanya
222 F5 **Naţanz** Eşfahān, C Iran 33°31′N 51°55′E
59 K6 **Natashquan** Québec, E Canada 50°10′N 61°50′W
59 K6 **Natashquan** ≈ Newfoundland and Labrador/Québec, E Canada
68 D3 **Natchez** Mississippi, S USA 31°34′N 91°24′W
68 B2 **Natchitoches** Louisiana, S USA 31°45′N 93°05′W
110 E7 **Natércia** Minas Gerais, Brazil 22°07′S 45°30′W
167 N10 **Naters** Valais, S Switzerland 46°22′N 08°00′E
Nathanya *see* Netanya
152 B5 **Nathorst Land** *physical region* W Svalbard
Nathula *see* Nacula
280 B4 **National Capital District** ◐ *province* S Papua New Guinea
81 E13 **National City** California, W USA 32°40′N 117°06′W
278 G6 **National Park** Manawatu-Wanganui, North Island, New Zealand 39°11′S 175°22′E
54 D6 **Nation River** ≈ British Columbia, SW Canada
133 H6 **Natitingou** NW Benin 10°21′N 01°26′E
55 L3 **Native Bay** *coastal sea feature* Nunavut, NE Canada
111 K5 **Natividade** Rio de Janeiro, Brazil 21°03′S 41°59′W
110 F9 **Natividade** São Paulo, Brazil 23°24′S 45°26′W
84 B5 **Natividad, Isla** *island* W Mexico
159 I7 **Natland** UK 54°17′N 2°44′W
84 G4 **Nàtora** Sonora, Mexico 28°56′N 108°39′W
253 D10 **Natori** Miyagi, Honshū, C Japan 38°12′N 140°51′E
62 C8 **Natrona Heights** Pennsylvania, NE USA 40°37′N 79°42′W
137 D9 **Natron, Lake** ◎ Kenya/Tanzania
Natsrat *see* Nazerat
256 C6 **Nattalin** Pegu, C Myanmar (Burma) 18°25′N 95°34′E
152 G6 **Nattavaara** *Lapp.* Nahtavárr. Norrbotten, N Sweden 66°45′N 20°58′E
177 J2 **Natternbach** Oberösterreich, N Austria 48°26′N 13°44′E
155 H11 **Nättraby** Blekinge, S Sweden 56°12′N 15°30′E
258 G3 **Natuna Besar, Pulau** *island* Kepulauan Natuna, W Indonesia
Natuna Islands *see* Natuna, Kepulauan
258 G3 **Natuna, Kepulauan** *var.* Natuna Islands. *island group* W Indonesia
258 G4 **Natuna, Laut** *sea* W Indonesia
66 G4 **Natural Bridge** *tourist site* Kentucky, C USA
289 I11 **Naturaliste Fracture Zone** *tectonic feature* E Indian Ocean
266 E6 **Naturaliste Plateau** *undersea feature* E Indian Ocean
Nau *see* Nov
165 H8 **Naucelle** Aveyron, S France 44°10′N 02°19′E
140 B2 **Nauchas** Hardap, C Namibia 23°40′S 16°19′E
176 G4 **Nauders** Tirol, W Austria 46°52′N 10°31′E
140 G8 **Naudesbergpas** *pass* Eastern Cape, South Africa
141 I7 **Naudesnek** *pass* Eastern Cape, South Africa
Naugard *see* Nowogard
65 J4 **Naugatuck** Connecticut, USA 41°29′N 73°03′W
190 D7 **Naujamiestis** Panevėžys, C Lithuania 55°42′N 24°10′E
190 C7 **Naujoji Akmenė** Šiaulai, NW Lithuania 56°20′N 22°57′E
231 H9 **Naukot** *var.* Naokot. Sind, SE Pakistan 24°52′N 69°27′E
181 G8 **Naumburg** Hessen, Germany 9°10′N 51°15′E
179 G8 **Naumburg** *var.* Naumburg an der Saale. Sachsen-Anhalt, C Germany 51°09′N 11°48′E
Naumburg am Queis *see* Nowogrodziec
Naumburg an der Saale *see* Naumburg
118 B1 **Naunau** *ancient monument* Easter Island, Chile, E Pacific Ocean
118 E9 **Naunauco** Neuquén, Argentina 37°37′S 70°11′W
216 C7 **Nā'ūr** 'Ammān, W Jordan 31°52′N 35°50′E
181 E11 **Naurod** Hessen, Germany 8°18′N 50°08′E
283 J10 **Nauru** *off.* Republic of Nauru; *prev.* Pleasant Island. ◆ *republic* W Pacific Ocean
267 I4 **Nauru** *island* W Pacific Ocean
283 J10 **Nauru International** ✈ S Nauru
Nauru, Republic of *see* Nauru
Nausari *see* Navsāri
65 N4 **Nauset Beach** *beach* Massachusetts, NE USA
Naushahra *see* Nowshera
230 G8 **Naushahro Fīroz** Sind, SE Pakistan 26°51′N 68°11′E
Naushara *see* Nowshera
280 E9 **Nausori** Viti Levu, W Fiji 18°01′S 178°31′E
104 F4 **Nauta** Loreto, N Peru 04°31′S 73°36′W
233 H6 **Nautanwa** Uttar Pradesh, N India 27°26′N 83°25′E
86 G6 **Nautla** Veracruz-Llave, E Mexico 20°15′N 96°45′W
Nauzad *see* Now Zād
85 L4 **Nava** Coahuila de Zaragoza, NE Mexico 28°28′N 100°45′W
Navabad *see* Navobod
172 F2 **Navacepeda de Tormes** Castilla y León, Spain 40°22′N 5°15′W
170 F4 **Nava del Rey** Castilla-León, N Spain 41°19′N 05°04′W
233 J8 **Navadwīp** *prev.* Nabadwip. West Bengal, NE India 23°24′N 88°23′E
280 F8 **Navaga** Koro, W Fiji 17°21′S 179°22′E
170 F5 **Navahermosa** Castilla-La Mancha, C Spain 39°39′N 04°25′W
191 E10 **Navahrudak** *Pol.* Nowogródek, *Rus.* Novogrudok. Hrodzyenskaya Voblasts', W Belarus 53°36′N 25°50′E
191 E10 **Navahrudskaye Wzvyshsha** ▲▲ W Belarus
79 I5 **Navajo Mount** ▲ Utah, W USA 37°00′N 110°52′W
79 K5 **Navajo Reservoir** ⊠ New Mexico, SW USA
263 M7 **Naval** Biliran Island, C Philippines 11°32′N 124°26′E
172 G1 **Navalmanzano** Castilla y León, Spain 41°13′N 4°15′W
170 E5 **Navalmoral de la Mata** Extremadura, W Spain 39°54′N 05°33′W
172 G2 **Navalperal de Pinares** Castilla y León, Spain 40°35′N 4°24′W
172 F5 **Navalvillar de Pela** Extremadura, Spain 39°06′N 5°28′W
170 E6 **Navalvillar de Pelea** Extremadura, W Spain 39°05′N 05°27′W
158 D9 **Navan** *Ir.* An Uaimh. E Ireland 53°39′N 06°41′W
Navanagar *see* Jāmnagar
191 G8 **Navapolatsk** *Rus.* Novopolotsk. Vitsyebskaya Voblasts', N Belarus 55°34′N 28°35′E
230 G4 **Nāvar, Dasht-e** *Pash.* Dasht-i-Nawar. *desert* C Afghanistan
193 N3 **Navarin, Mys** *cape* NE Russian Federation
117 D14 **Navarino, Isla** *island* S Chile
171 H2 **Navarra** *Eng./Fr.* Navarre. ◐ *autonomous community* N Spain
Navarre *see* Navarra
168 D6 **Navarrenx** Aquitaine, France 43°20′N 0°45′W
171 H2 **Navarrete** La Rioja, N Spain 42°26′N 02°34′W
114 D10 **Navarro** Buenos Aires, E Argentina 35°00′S 59°15′W
168 C7 **Navascués** Navarra, Spain 42°43′N 1°07′W
172 D4 **Navas del Madroño** Extremadura, Spain 39°37′N 6°39′W
172 G1 **Navas de Oro** Castilla y León, Spain 41°12′N 4°26′W
170 G7 **Navas de San Juan** Andalucía, S Spain 38°11′N 03°19′W
172 D3 **Navasfrías** Castilla y León, Spain 40°18′N 6°49′W
71 H6 **Navasota** Texas, SW USA 30°23′N 96°05′W
71 H6 **Navasota River** ≈ Texas, SW USA
90 F6 **Navassa Island** ◇ *US unincorporated territory* C West Indies
191 G11 **Navasyolki** *Rus.* Novosëlki. Homyel'skaya Voblasts', SE Belarus 52°24′N 28°33′E
191 E10 **Navayel'nya** *Pol.* Nowojelnia, *Rus.* Novoyel'nya. Hrodzyenskaya Voblasts', W Belarus 53°28′N 25°35′E
172 D2 **Nave** Guarda, Portugal 40°24′N 6°58′W
159 M10 **Navenby** UK 53°06′N 0°31′W
261 L5 **Naver** Papua, E Indonesia 03°27′S 139°45′E
190 E4 **Navesti** ≈ C Estonia
170 E1 **Navia** Asturias, N Spain 43°33′N 06°43′W
170 E1 **Navia** ≈ NW Spain
113 I3 **Naviraí** Mato Grosso do Sul, SW Brazil 23°01′S 54°09′W
280 D8 **Naviti** *island* Yasawa Group, NW Fiji
196 E3 **Navlya** Bryanskaya Oblast', W Russian Federation 52°47′N 34°28′E
280 F8 **Navoalevu** Vanua Levu, N Fiji 16°22′S 179°28′E
229 J7 **Navobod** *Rus.* Navabad, Novabad. C Tajikistan 39°00′N 70°06′E
229 I7 **Navobod** *Rus.* Navabad. W Tajikistan 38°37′N 68°42′E
Navoi *see* Navoiy
228 G6 **Navoiy** *Rus.* Navoi. Navoiy Viloyati, C Uzbekistan 40°05′N 65°23′E
Navoiyskaya Oblast' *see* Navoiy Viloyati
228 G4 **Navoiy Viloyati** *Rus.* Navoiyskaya Oblast'. ◐ *province* N Uzbekistan
84 F5 **Navojoa** Sonora, NW Mexico 27°04′N 109°28′W
Navolat *see* Navolato
84 G7 **Navolato** *var.* Navolat. Sinaloa, C Mexico 24°46′N 107°42′W
281 M2 **Navonda** Ambae, C Vanuatu 15°21′S 167°58′E
190 G5 **Navoye Nikol'skoye** Pskovskaya Oblast', Russian Federation
Návpaktos *see* Náfpaktos
Návplion *see* Náfplio
133 H6 **Navrongo** N Ghana 10°51′N 01°03′W
232 C9 **Navsāri** *var.* Nausari. Gujarāt, W India 20°55′N 72°55′E
280 E9 **Navua** Viti Levu, W Fiji 18°15′S 178°10′E
53 I5 **Navy Board Inlet** *coastal sea feature* Nunavut, NE Canada
216 C6 **Nawá** Dar'ā, S Syria 32°53′N 36°03′E
Nawabashah *see* Nawābshāh
233 J7 **Nawabganj** Rajshahi, NW Bangladesh 24°35′N 88°21′E
232 G6 **Nawābganj** Uttar Pradesh, N India 26°52′N 82°09′E
230 G9 **Nawābshāh** *var.* Nawabashah. Sind, S Pakistan 26°15′N 68°26′E
233 I7 **Nawāda** Bihār, N India 24°54′N 85°33′E
232 D5 **Nawalgarh** Rājasthān, N India 27°48′N 75°21′E
Nawar, Dasht-i- *see* Nāvar, Dasht-e
256 D4 **Nawnghkio** *var.* Nawngkio. Shan State, C Myanmar (Burma) 22°17′N 96°50′E
Nawngkio *see* Nawnghkio
215 L6 **Naxçıvan** *Rus.* Nakhichevan'. SW Azerbaijan 39°14′N 45°24′E
242 B4 **Naxi** Sichuan, C China 28°50′N 105°20′E
187 J7 **Náxos** *var.* Naxos. Náxos, Kykládes, Greece, Aegean Sea 36°07′N 25°24′E
187 J7 **Náxos** *island* Kykládes, Greece, Aegean Sea
168 D6 **Nay** Aquitaine, France 43°11′N 0°16′W
86 B4 **Nayar** Nayarit, Mexico 22°16′N 104°28′W
85 I9 **Nayar** Nayarit, Mexico 22°16′N 104°28′W
85 I9 **Nayarit** ◐ *state* C Mexico
280 G9 **Nayau** *island* Lau Group, E Fiji
223 I5 **Nāy Band** Yazd, E Iran 32°26′N 57°30′E
242 B6 **Nayong** Guizhou, China 26°16′N 105°13′E
252 F3 **Nayoro** Hokkaidō, NE Japan 44°22′N 142°27′E
172 B4 **Nazaré** *var.* Nazare. Leiria, C Portugal 39°36′N 09°04′W
Nazare *see* Nazaré
85 J7 **Nazareno** Durango, Mexico 25°23′N 103°25′W
64 F6 **Nazareth** Pennsylvania, USA 40°44′N 75°19′W
70 D3 **Nazareth** Texas, SW USA 34°32′N 102°06′W
Nazareth *see* Nazerat
289 D9 **Nazareth Bank** *undersea feature* W Indian Ocean
85 J7 **Nazas** Durango, C Mexico 25°15′N 104°06′W
85 I7 **Nazas, Río** ≈ Durango, Mexico
105 E9 **Nazca** Ica, S Peru 14°53′S 74°54′W
42 G10 **Nazca Plate** *tectonic feature*
287 L7 **Nazca Ridge** *undersea feature* E Pacific Ocean
251 K9 **Naze** *var.* Nase. Kagoshima, Amami-ōshima, SW Japan 28°21′N 129°30′E
216 B6 **Nazerat** *var.* Natsrat, *Ar.* En Nazira, *Eng.* Nazareth. Northern, N Israel 32°42′N 35°18′E
215 J6 **Nazik Gölü** ◎ E Turkey
214 B7 **Nazilli** Aydın, SW Turkey 37°55′N 28°20′E
215 I6 **Nazimiye** Tunceli, E Turkey 39°12′N 39°51′E
192 F6 **Nazino** Tomskaya Oblast', C Russian Federation 60°02′N 78°51′E
Nazinon *see* Red Volta
190 I3 **Naziya** Leningradskaya Oblast', Russian Federation
56 D5 **Nazko** British Columbia, SW Canada 52°57′N 123°44′W
197 I9 **Nazran'** Ingushskaya Respublika, SW Russian Federation 43°14′N 44°47′E
136 E4 **Nazrēt** *var.* Adama, Hadama. Oromo, C Ethiopia 08°31′N 39°20′E
Nazwāh *see* Nizwá
192 E7 **Nazyvayevsk** Omskaya Oblast', C Russian Federation 55°35′N 71°13′E
138 G1 **Nchanga** Copperbelt, C Zambia 12°30′S 27°53′E
135 I11 **Nchelenge** Luapula, N Zambia 09°20′S 28°50′E
Ncheu *see* Ntcheu
Ndaghamcha, Sebkra de *see* Te-n-Dghâmcha, Sebkhet
137 C10 **Ndala** Tabora, C Tanzania 04°45′S 33°15′E
135 C11 **N'Dalatando** *Port.* Salazar, Vila Salazar. Cuanza Norte, NW Angola 09°19′S 14°48′E
133 I6 **Ndali** C Benin 09°50′N 02°46′E
137 A8 **Ndeke** SW Uganda 0°11′S 30°04′E
134 F4 **Ndélé** Bamingui-Bangoran, N Central African Republic 08°24′N 20°41′E
135 B8 **Ndendé** Ngounié, S Gabon 02°21′S 11°20′E
135 B9 **Ndindi** Nyanga, S Gabon 03°47′S 11°06′E
134 C2 **Ndjamena** *var.* N'Djamena; *prev.* Fort-Lamy. ● (Chad) Chari-Baguirmi, W Chad 12°08′N 15°02′E
134 C2 **Ndjamena** ✈ Chari-Baguirmi, W Chad 12°09′N 15°00′E
N'Djamena *see* Ndjamena
134 B7 **Ndjolé** Moyen-Ogooué, W Gabon 0°07′S 10°45′E
138 G1 **Ndola** Copperbelt, C Zambia 12°59′S 28°35′E
Ndrhamcha, Sebkha de *see* Te-n-Dghâmcha, Sebkhet
134 G5 **Ndu** Orientale, N Dem. Rep. Congo 04°36′N 22°49′E
137 C9 **Nduguti** Singida, C Tanzania 04°19′S 34°40′E
281 J3 **Nduindui** Guadalcanal, C Solomon Islands 09°46′S 159°54′E
Nduke *see* Kolombangara
141 L5 **Ndumo** KwaZulu-Natal, South Africa 26°55′S 32°15′E
141 L6 **Ndundula** KwaZulu-Natal, South Africa 28°41′S 31°31′E
141 K6 **Ndwedwe** KwaZulu-Natal, South Africa 29°30′S 30°56′E
186 G4 **Néa Anchiálos** *var.* Nea Anhialos, Néa Ankhíalos. Thessalía, C Greece 39°16′N 22°49′E
Nea Anhialos/Néa Ankhíalos *see* Néa Anchiálos
187 H5 **Néa Artáki** Évvoia, C Greece 38°31′N 23°39′E
158 D6 **Lough Neagh** ◎ UK
76 B3 **Neah Bay** Washington, NW USA 48°21′N 124°39′W
187 J8 **Nea Kaméni** *island* Kykládes, Greece, Aegean Sea
274 G5 **Neale, Lake** ◎ Northern Territory, C Australia
276 F2 **Neales River** *seasonal river* South Australia
187 H3 **Néa Moudanía** *var.* Néa Moudhaniá. Kentrikí Makedonía, N Greece 40°14′N 23°17′E
Néa Moudhaniá *see* Néa Moudanía
188 E7 **Neamţ** ◐ *county* NE Romania
Neapel *see* Napoli
186 F3 **Neápoli** *prev.* Neápolis. Dytikí Makedonía, N Greece 40°19′N 21°23′E
187 J10 **Neápoli** Kríti, Greece, E Mediterranean Sea 35°15′N 25°37′E
187 H8 **Neápoli** Pelopónnisos, S Greece 36°29′N 23°05′E
Neápolis *see* Neápoli, Greece
Neapolis *see* Napoli, Italy
Neapolis *see* Nablus, West Bank
82 A9 **Near Islands** *island group* Aleutian Islands, Alaska, USA
160 F6 **Neath** S Wales, UK 51°40′N 03°48′W
187 H2 **Néa Zíchni** *var.* Néa Zíkhni; *prev.* Néa Zíkhna. Kentrikí Makedonía, NE Greece 41°02′N 23°50′E
Néa Zíkhna/Néa Zíkhni *see* Néa Zíchni
88 C3 **Nebaj** Quiché, W Guatemala 15°25′N 91°05′W
132 G6 **Nebbou** S Burkina 11°22′N 01°49′W
Nebitdag *see* Balkanabat
102 G8 **Neblina, Pico da** ▲ NW Brazil 0°49′N 66°31′W
194 E8 **Nebolchi** Novgorodskaya Oblast', W Russian Federation 59°08′N 33°19′E
79 H3 **Nebo, Mount** ▲ Utah, W USA 39°47′N 111°46′W
74 C7 **Nebraska** *off.* State of Nebraska, *also known as* Blackwater State, Cornhusker State, Tree Planters State. ◐ *state* C USA
75 F8 **Nebraska City** Nebraska, C USA 40°38′N 95°52′W
175 G12 **Nebrodi, Monti** *var.* Monti Caronie. ▲▲ Sicilia, Italy, C Mediterranean Sea
56 D4 **Nechako** ≈ British Columbia, SW Canada
74 E1 **Neche** North Dakota, N USA 48°57′N 97°33′W
71 I5 **Neches** Texas, SW USA 31°51′N 95°28′W
71 I5 **Neches River** ≈ Texas, SW USA
181 G14 **Neckar** ≈ SW Germany
181 F13 **Neckargemünd** Baden-Württemberg, Germany 8°48′N 49°24′E
181 G13 **Neckargerach** Baden-Württemberg, Germany 9°04′N 49°24′E
181 G14 **Neckarsulm** Baden-Württemberg, SW Germany 49°12′N 09°13′E
286 G3 **Necker Island** *island* C British Virgin Islands
267 L2 **Necker Ridge** *undersea feature* N Pacific Ocean
116 H6 **Necochea** Buenos Aires, E Argentina 38°34′S 58°42′W
161 L3 **Necton** UK 52°39′N 0°46′E
170 D1 **Neda** Galicia, NW Spain 43°29′N 08°09′W
186 F7 **Néda** *var.* Nédas. ≈ S Greece
Nédas *see* Néda
71 J7 **Nederland** Texas, SW USA 29°58′N 93°59′W
Nederland *see* Netherlands
162 G7 **Neder Rijn** *Eng.* Lower Rhine. ≈ C Netherlands
163 G9 **Nederweert** Limburg, SE Netherlands 51°17′N 05°45′E
155 D8 **Nedre Tokke** ◎ S Norway
Nedrigaylov *see* Nedryhayliv
189 J2 **Nedryhayliv** *Rus.* Nedrigaylov. Sums'ka Oblast', NE Ukraine 50°51′N 33°54′E
162 I6 **Neede** Gelderland, E Netherlands 52°08′N 06°36′E
65 L2 **Needham** Massachusetts, USA 42°17′N 71°14′W
77 J7 **Needle Mountain** ▲ Wyoming, C USA 44°03′N 109°33′W
81 I11 **Needles** California, W USA 34°50′N 114°37′W
161 I8 **Needles Point** *headland* UK 50°40′N 1°35′W
157 H12 **Needles, The** *rocks* S England, UK
112 G5 **Ñeembucú** *off.* Departamento de Ñeembucú. ◐ *department* SW Paraguay
Ñeembucú, Departamento de *see* Ñeembucú
72 D6 **Neenah** Wisconsin, N USA 44°09′N 88°26′W
55 I9 **Neepawa** Manitoba, S Canada 50°14′N 99°29′W
53 J7 **Neergaard Lake** ◎ Nunavut, NE Canada
180 D3 **Neermoor** Niedersachsen, Germany 7°26′N 53°18′E
163 G9 **Neerpelt** Limburg, NE Belgium 51°13′N 05°26′E
180 I3 **Neetze** Niedersachsen, Germany 10°38′N 53°16′E
131 K2 **Nefta** ✈ W Tunisia 34°03′N 08°05′E
196 G8 **Neftegorsk** Krasnodarskiy Kray, SW Russian Federation 44°21′N 39°40′E
197 K1 **Neftekamsk** Respublika Bashkortostan, W Russian Federation 56°07′N 54°13′E
197 I8 **Neftekumsk** Stavropol'skiy Kray, SW Russian Federation 44°45′N 45°00′E
192 F6 **Nefteyugansk** Khanty-Mansiyskiy Avtonomnyy Okrug, C Russian Federation 61°07′N 72°18′E
Neftezavodsk *see* Seýdi
175 B13 **Nefza** Tunisia
135 D10 **Negage** *var.* N'Gage. Uíge, NW Angola 07°47′S 15°27′E
Negapatam/Negapattinam *see* Nāgappattinam
259 J9 **Negara** Bali, Indonesia 08°21′S 114°35′E
258 K6 **Negara** Borneo, C Indonesia 02°40′S 115°05′E
Negara Brunei Darussalam *see* Brunei
72 E4 **Negaunee** Michigan, N USA 46°30′N 87°36′W
136 E6 **Negēlē** *var.* Negelli, *It.* Neghelli. Oromo, C Ethiopia 05°13′N 39°43′E
Negelli *see* Negēlē
Negeri Pahang Darul Makmur *see* Pahang
Negeri Selangor Darul Ehsan *see* Selangor
258 E3 **Negeri Sembilan** *var.* Negri Sembilan. ◐ *state* Peninsular Malaysia
152 B6 **Negerpynten** *headland* S Svalbard 77°15′N 22°40′E
Negev *see* HaNegev
Neghelli *see* Negēlē
188 D8 **Negoiu** *var.* Negoiul. ▲ S Romania 45°34′N 24°34′E
Negoiul *see* Negoiu
137 E12 **Negomane** *var.* Negomano. Cabo Delgado, N Mozambique 11°22′S 38°32′E
Negomano *see* Negomane
235 F10 **Negombo** Western Province, SW Sri Lanka 07°13′N 79°51′E
Negoreloye *see* Nyeharelaye
185 H4 **Negotin** Serbia, E Serbia 44°14′N 22°31′E
185 H8 **Negotino** C Macedonia 41°29′N 22°04′E
170 C2 **Negreira** Galicia, NW Spain 42°54′N 08°46′W
168 F5 **Négrepelisse** Midi-Pyrénées, France 44°04′N 1°31′E
188 F7 **Negreşti** Vaslui, E Romania 46°50′N 27°28′E
Negreşti *see* Negreşti-Oaş
188 C6 **Negreşti-Oaş** *Hung.* Avasfelsőfalu; *prev.* Negreşti. Satu Mare, NE Romania 47°56′N 23°22′E
90 D7 **Negril** W Jamaica 18°16′N 78°21′W
Negri Sembilan *see* Negeri Sembilan
118 C1 **Ensenada del Negro** *bay* Coquimbo, Chile
118 E4 **Negro, Río** ≈ Región Metropolitana, Chile
116 E6 **Negro, Río** ≈ E Argentina
112 F5 **Negro, Río** ≈ NE Argentina
106 F9 **Negro, Río** ≈ E Bolivia
98 D3 **Negro, Rio** ≈ N South America
115 J5 **Negro, Río** ≈ Brazil/Uruguay
112 G4 **Negro, Río** ≈ C Paraguay
Negro, Río *see* Chixoy, Río
Negro, Río *see* Sico Tinto, Río
263 L8 **Negros** *island* C Philippines
188 F10 **Negru Vodă** Constanţa, SE Romania 43°49′N 28°12′E
63 N1 **Neguac** New Brunswick, SE Canada 47°16′N 65°04′W
72 G2 **Negwazu, Lake** ◎ Ontario, S Canada
Négyfalu *see* Săcele
76 B5 **Nehalem** Oregon, NW USA 45°42′N 123°55′W
76 B5 **Nehalem River** ≈ Oregon, NW USA
Nehavend *see* Nahāvand
223 J6 **Nehbandān** Khorāsān, E Iran 31°00′N 60°00′E
91 H6 **Neiba** *var.* Neyba. SW Dominican Republic 18°31′N 71°25′W
Néid, Carn Uí *see* Mizen Head
152 I3 **Neiden** Finnmark, N Norway 69°41′N 29°23′E
Neidín *see* Kenmare
Néifinn *see* Nephin
167 L10 **Neige, Crêt de la** ▲ E France 46°18′N 05°58′E
137 I10 **Neiges, Piton des** ▲ C Réunion 21°05′S 55°28′E
63 J1 **Neiges, Rivière des** ≈ Québec, SE Canada
242 B3 **Neijiang** Sichuan, C China 29°32′N 105°03′E
140 E6 **Neilersdrif** Northern Cape, South Africa 28°45′S 20°59′E
72 B6 **Neillsville** Wisconsin, N USA 44°34′N 90°36′W
Nei Monggol Zizhiqu/Nei Mongol *see* Nei Mongol Zizhiqu
244 F1 **Nei Mongol Zizhiqu** *var.* Nei Mongol, *Eng.* Inner Mongolia, Inner Mongolian Autonomous Region; *prev.* Nei Monggol Zizhiqu. ◐ *autonomous region* N China
245 I5 **Neiqiu** Hebei, E China 37°22′N 114°34′E
Neiriz *see* Neyrīz
179 J8 **Neisse** *Cz.* Lužická Nisa *Pol.* Nisa, *Ger.* Lausitzer Neisse, Nysa Łużycka. ≈ C Europe
Neisse *see* Nysa
102 B6 **Neiva** Huila, S Colombia 02°58′N 75°15′W
239 N7 **Neixiang** Henan, C China 33°08′N 111°50′E
Nejafabad *see* Najafābād
55 I5 **Nejanilini Lake** ◎ Manitoba, C Canada
87 H9 **Nejapa** Oaxaca, Mexico 16°37′N 95°59′W
Nejd *see* Najd
136 D4 **Nek'emtē** *var.* Lakemti, Nakamti. Oromo, C Ethiopia 09°06′N 36°31′E
197 H5 **Nekhayevskiy** Volgogradskaya Oblast', SW Russian Federation 50°25′N 41°44′E
72 C6 **Nekoosa** Wisconsin, N USA 44°19′N 89°54′W
Neksø Bornholm *see* Nexø
186 E5 **Nekyomanteío** *ancient monument* Ípeiros, W Greece
170 D4 **Nelas** Viseu, N Portugal 40°32′N 07°52′W
172 C2 **Nelas** Viseu, Portugal 40°32′N 7°51′W
194 D10 **Nelidovo** Tverskaya Oblast', W Russian Federation 56°13′N 32°45′E
74 E7 **Neligh** Nebraska, C USA 42°07′N 98°01′W
193 K6 **Nel'kan** Khabarovskiy Kray, E Russian Federation 57°44′N 136°09′E
152 H4 **Nellim** *var.* Nellimö, *Lapp.* Njellim. Lappi, N Finland 68°49′N 28°18′E
Nellimö *see* Nellim
234 F7 **Nellore** Andhra Pradesh, E India 14°29′N 80°E
193 L8 **Nel'ma** Khabarovskiy Kray, SE Russian Federation 47°43′N 139°08′E
141 K4 **Nelsbergpas** *pass* Mpumalanga, South Africa
114 B4 **Nelson** Santa Fe, C Argentina 31°16′S 60°45′W
56 G9 **Nelson** British Columbia, SW Canada 49°29′N 117°17′W
278 F8 **Nelson** Nelson, South Island, New Zealand 41°17′S 173°17′E
159 J8 **Nelson** NW England, UK 53°51′N 02°13′W
75 D8 **Nelson** Nebraska, C USA 40°12′N 98°04′W
81 J10 **Nelson** Nevada, USA 35°42′N 114°49′W
278 E7 **Nelson** ◐ *unitary authority* South Island, New Zealand
55 J7 **Nelson** ≈ Manitoba, C Canada
277 M5 **Nelson Bay** New South Wales, SE Australia 32°48′S 152°10′E
277 H7 **Nelson, Cape** *headland* Victoria, SE Australia 38°25′S 141°33′E
117 B12 **Nelson, Estrecho** *strait* SE Pacific Ocean
55 I7 **Nelson House** Manitoba, C Canada 55°49′N 98°51′W
72 B4 **Nelson Lake** ◎ Wisconsin, N USA
80 G7 **Nelson Range** *ridge* California, USA
73 I11 **Nelsonville** Ohio, N USA 39°27′N 82°13′W
75 G8 **Nelsoon River** ≈ Iowa/Missouri, C USA
140 F8 **Nelspoort** Western Cape, South Africa 32°07′S 23°00′E
141 K3 **Nelspruit** Mpumalanga, South Africa 25°28′S 30°58′E
139 H6 **Nelspruit** Mpumalanga, NE South Africa 25°28′S 30°58′E
132 E3 **Néma** Hodh ech Chargui, SE Mauritania 16°32′N 07°12′W
191 C8 **Neman** *Ger.* Ragnit. Kaliningradskaya Oblast', W Russian Federation 55°01′N 22°00′E
144 E5 **Neman** *Bel.* Nyoman, *Ger.* Memel, *Lith.* Nemunas, *Pol.* Niemen, *Rus.* Neman. ≈ NE Europe
Nemausus *see* Nîmes
186 G6 **Neméa** Pelopónnisos, S Greece 37°49′N 22°40′E
Německý Brod *see* Havlíčkův Brod
58 E7 **Nemegosenda** ≈ Ontario, S Canada
191 E8 **Nemencinė** Vilnius, SE Lithuania 54°50′N 25°29′E
Nemetocenna *see* Arras
Nemirov *see* Nemyriv
165 H4 **Nemours** Seine-et-Marne, N France 48°16′N 02°41′E
Nemunas *see* Neman
252 I4 **Nemuro** Hokkaidō, NE Japan 43°20′N 145°35′E
252 I4 **Nemuro-hantō** *peninsula* Hokkaidō, NE Japan
252 I3 **Nemuro-kaikyō** *strait* Japan/Russian Federation
252 H4 **Nemuro-wan** *bay* N Japan
188 C3 **Nemyriv** *Rus.* Nemirov. L'vivs'ka Oblast', NW Ukraine 50°08′N 23°28′E
188 G5 **Nemyriv** *Rus.* Nemirov. Vinnyts'ka Oblast', C Ukraine 48°58′N 28°50′E
157 C10 **Nenagh** *Ir.* An tAonach. Tipperary, C Ireland 52°52′N 08°12′W
83 I5 **Nenana** Alaska, USA 64°33′N 149°05′W
83 I5 **Nenana River** ≈ Alaska, USA
281 I5 **Nendö** *var.* Swallow Island. *island* Santa Cruz Islands, E Solomon Islands
180 F5 **Nendorf** Niedersachsen, Germany 8°59′N 52°30′E
157 I10 **Nene** ≈ E England, UK
161 K3 **Nene** ≈ UK
195 K3 **Nenetskiy Avtonomnyy Okrug** ◐ *autonomous district* NW Russian Federation
285 K7 **Nengonengo** *atoll* Îles Tuamotu, C French Polynesia
193 K8 **Nenjiang** Heilongjiang, NE China 49°11′N 125°18′E
181 E11 **Nentershausen** Rheinland-Pfalz, Germany 7°56′N 50°25′E
159 J6 **Nenthead** UK 54°46′N 2°20′W
282 F10 **Neoch** *atoll* Caroline Islands, C Micronesia
186 F6 **Neochóri** Dytikí Ellás, C Greece 38°23′N 21°14′E
75 F11 **Neodesha** Kansas, C USA 37°25′N 95°40′W
74 F7 **Neola** Iowa, C USA 41°27′N 95°40′W
Néon Karlovasi/Néon Karlovásion *see* Karlovási
186 G5 **Néo Monastíri** Thessalía, C Greece 39°22′N 21°55′E
Néon Monastiri *see* Néo Monastíri
75 G11 **Neosho** Missouri, C USA 36°53′N 94°24′W
75 F10 **Neosho River** ≈ Kansas/Oklahoma, C USA
219 E13 **Ne'ot Smadar** Israel
193 H7 **Nepa** ≈ C Russian Federation
233 I5 **Nepal** *off.* Kingdom of Nepal. ◆ *monarchy* S Asia
232 G5 **Nepālganj** Mid Western, SW Nepal 28°04′N 81°37′E
Nepal, Kingdom of *see* Nepal
62 F3 **Nepean** Ontario, SE Canada 45°19′N 75°54′W
79 H3 **Nephi** Utah, W USA 39°43′N 111°50′W
157 B8 **Nephin** *Ir.* Néifinn. ▲ W Ireland 54°00′N 09°21′W
121 K5 **Nepoko** ≈ NE Dem. Rep. Congo
110 F5 **Nepomuceno** Minas Gerais, Brazil 21°14′S 45°15′W
65 H7 **Neptune** New Jersey, NE USA 40°10′N 74°03′W
174 F7 **Nera** *anc.* Nar. ≈ C Italy
164 G8 **Nérac** Lot-et-Garonne, SW France 44°08′N 00°21′E
277 M2 **Nerang** Queensland, Australia
183 C8 **Neratovice** *Ger.* Neratowitz. Středocesky Kraj, C Czech Republic 50°16′N 14°31′E
Neratowitz *see* Neratovice
193 J8 **Nercha** ≈ S Russian Federation
193 J8 **Nerchinsk** Chitinskaya Oblast', S Russian Federation 52°01′N 116°25′E
194 G10 **Nerekhta** Kostromskaya Oblast', NW Russian Federation 57°27′N 40°33′E
190 E7 **Nereta** Aizkraukle, S Latvia 56°12′N 25°18′E
174 F7 **Nereto** Abruzzo, C Italy 42°49′N 13°50′E
184 D5 **Neretva** ≈ Bosnia and Herzegovina/Croatia
186 E5 **Nerikós** *ruins* Lefkáda, Iónia Nísiá, Greece, C Mediterranean Sea
135 F13 **Neriquinha** Cuando Cubango, SE Angola 15°44′S 21°34′E
191 D8 **Neris** *Bel.* Viliya, *Pol.* Wilia; *prev. Pol.* Wilja. ≈ Belarus/Lithuania
Neris *see* Viliya
167 H10 **Néris-les-Bains** Auvergne, France 46°17′N 2°40′E
170 G9 **Nerja** Andalucía, S Spain 36°45′N 03°35′W
194 F10 **Nerl'** ≈ W Russian Federation
195 L6 **Nerokhi** Khanty-Mansiyskiy Avtonomnyy Okrug, Russian federation
169 J1 **Néronde** Rhône-Alpes, France 45°50′N 4°14′E
261 I6 **Nerong, Selat** *strait* Kepulauan Kai, E Indonesia
171 H7 **Nerpio** Castilla-La Mancha, C Spain 38°08′N 02°18′W
118 C5 **Nerquihue** Libertador General Bernardo O'Higgins, Chile 34°40′S 71°34′W
170 E8 **Nerva** Andalucía, S Spain 37°40′N 06°31′W
193 J7 **Neryungri** Respublika Sakha (Yakutiya), NE Russian Federation 56°38′N 124°19′E
162 G3 **Nes** Friesland, N Netherlands 53°28′N 05°46′E
154 D6 **Nesbyen** Buskerud, S Norway 60°36′N 09°35′E
65 I6 **Nesconset** New York, USA 40°51′N 73°09′W
152 E2 **Neskaupstadhur** Austurland, E Iceland 65°08′N 13°45′W
152 D6 **Nesna** Nordland, C Norway 66°11′N 12°54′E
172 C3 **Nesperal** Castelo Branco, Portugal 39°49′N 8°10′W
75 C10 **Ness City** Kansas, C USA 38°27′N 99°54′W
Nesselsdorf *see* Kopřivnice
179 D14 **Nesslau** Sankt Gallen, NE Switzerland 47°13′N 09°12′E
156 E5 **Ness, Loch** ◎ N Scotland, UK
Nesterov *see* Zhovkva
159 I10 **Neston** UK 53°17′N 3°03′W
187 I2 **Néstos** *Bul.* Mesta, *Turk.* Kara Su. ≈ Bulgaria/Greece *see also* Mesta
Néstos *see* Mesta
154 A7 **Nesttun** Hordaland, S Norway 60°19′N 05°16′E
Nesvizh *see* Nyasvizh
216 B6 **Netanya** *var.* Natanya, Nathanya. Central, C Israel 32°20′N 34°51′E
162 H6 **Netherlands** *off.* Kingdom of the Netherlands, *var.* Holland, *Dut.* Koninkrijk der Nederlanden, Nederland. ◆ *monarchy* NW Europe
102 F1 **Netherlands Antilles** *prev.* Dutch West Indies. ◇ *Dutch autonomous region* S Caribbean Sea
Netherlands East Indies *see* Indonesia
Netherlands Guiana *see* Surinam
Netherlands, Kingdom of the *see* Netherlands
Netherlands New Guinea *see* Papua
188 E3 **Netishyn** Khmel'nyts'ka Oblast', W Ukraine 50°20′N 26°38′E
216 B7 **Netivot** Southern, S Israel 31°26′N 34°36′E
175 H11 **Neto** ≈ S Italy
181 E9 **Netphen** Nordrhein-Westfalen, Germany 8°06′N 50°55′E
181 B8 **Nettetal** Nordrhein-Westfalen, Germany 6°17′N 51°19′E
53 L8 **Nettilling Fiord** *coastal sea feature* Nunavut, NE Canada
53 L8 **Nettilling Lake** ◎ Baffin Island, Nunavut, N Canada
74 G2 **Nett Lake** ◎ Minnesota, N USA
159 M10 **Nettleham** UK 53°16′N 0°29′W
180 H6 **Nettlingen** Niedersachsen, Germany 10°10′N 52°10′E
175 E9 **Nettuno** Lazio, C Italy 41°27′N 12°40′E
Netum *see* Noto
86 A2 **Netzahualcóyotl, Presa** ⊠ SE Mexico
Netze *see* Noteć
Neu Amerika *see* Puławy
Neubetsche *see* Novi Bečej
Neubidschow *see* Nový Bydžov
Neubistritz *see* Nová Bystřice
180 D4 **Neubörger** Niedersachsen, Germany 7°27′N 52°58′E
178 H5 **Neubrandenburg** Mecklenburg-Vorpommern, NE Germany 53°33′N 13°16′E
180 F4 **Neubruchhausen** Niedersachsen, Germany 8°50′N 52°50′E
181 H12 **Neubrunn** Bayern, Germany 9°40′N 49°44′E
180 J6 **Neu Büddenstedt** Niedersachsen, Germany 11°02′N 52°11′E
179 F12 **Neuburg an der Donau** Bayern, S Germany 48°43′N 11°10′E
176 C4 **Neuchâtel** *Ger.* Neuenburg. Neuchâtel, W Switzerland 46°59′N 06°55′E
174 B2 **Neuchâtel** *Ger.* Neuenburg. ◐ *canton* W Switzerland
174 A3 **Neuchâtel, Lac de** *Ger.* Neuenburger See. ◎ W Switzerland
181 G13 **Neudenau** Baden-Württemberg, Germany 9°16′N 49°18′E
Neudorf *see* Spišská Nová Ves
180 I5 **Neudorf-Platendorf** Niedersachsen, Germany 10°36′N 52°33′E
180 J4 **Neue Elde** *canal* N Germany
Neuenburg *see* Neuchâtel
Neuenburg an der Elbe *see* Nymburk
Neuenburger See *see* Neuchâtel, Lac de
180 C5 **Neuenhaus** Niedersachsen, Germany 6°58′N 52°30′E
180 D6 **Neuenkirchen** Nordrhein-Westfalen, Germany 7°22′N 52°15′E
180 F4 **Neuenland** ✈ (Bremen) Bremen, NW Germany 53°03′N 08°46′E
181 D8 **Neuenrade** Nordrhein-Westfalen, Germany 7°47′N 51°17′E
Neuenstadt *see* La Neuveville
180 F2 **Neuenwalde** Niedersachsen, Germany 8°41′N 53°41′E
181 B12 **Neuerburg** Rheinland-Pfalz, W Germany 50°01′N 06°13′E
167 N7 **Neuf-Brisach** Alsace, France 48°01′N 7°32′E
163 G13 **Neufchâteau** Luxembourg, SE Belgium 49°50′N 05°26′E
165 J3 **Neufchâteau** Vosges, NE France 48°21′N 05°42′E
165 H2 **Neufchâtel-en-Bray** Seine-Maritime, N France 49°44′N 01°26′E
167 J4 **Neufchâtel-sur-Aisne** Picardie, France 49°26′N 4°02′E
177 J2 **Neufelden** Oberösterreich, N Austria 48°27′N 14°01′E
Neugradisk *see* Nova Gradiška
Neuhaus *see* Jindřichův Hradec
Neuhäusel *see* Nové Zámky
181 H11 **Neuhof** Hessen, C Germany 50°26′N 09°34′E
Neuhof *see* Zgierz
181 G14 **Neuhütten** Baden-Württemberg, Germany 9°29′N 49°06′E
166 F8 **Neuillé-Pont-Pierre** Centre, France 47°33′N 0°33′E
167 I10 **Neuilly-le-Réal** Auvergne, France 46°27′N 3°25′E
167 I5 **Neuilly-Saint-Front** Picardie, France 49°10′N 3°16′E
181 F12 **Neu Isenburg** Hessen, Germany 8°42′N 50°03′E
181 G9 **Neukirchen** Hessen, Germany 9°20′N 50°52′E
Neukuhren *see* Pionerskiy
Neu-Langenburg *see* Tukuyu
177 L2 **Neulengbach** Niederösterreich, NE Austria 48°10′N 15°53′E
184 D6 **Neum** ◐ Federacija Bosna I Hercegovina, S Bosnia and Herzegovina
181 C12 **Neumagen-Dhron** Rheinland-Pfalz, Germany 6°53′N 49°51′E
Neumark *see* Nowy Targ
Neumark *see* Nowe Miasto Lubawskie, Warmińsko-Mazurskie, Poland
Neumarkt *see* Neumarkt im Hausruckkreis, Oberösterreich, Austria
Neumarkt *see* Neumarkt am Wallersee, Salzburg, Austria
Neumarkt *see* Sroda Śląska, Dolnośląskie, Poland
Neumarkt *see* Târgu Secuiesc, Covasna, Romania
Neumarkt *see* Târgu Mureş
177 I3 **Neumarkt am Wallersee** *var.* Neumarkt. Salzburg, NW Austria 47°55′N 13°16′E
177 J2 **Neumarkt im Hausruckkreis** *var.* Neumarkt. Oberösterreich, N Austria 48°16′N 13°40′E
179 F11 **Neumarkt in der Oberpfalz** Bayern, SE Germany 49°16′N 11°28′E
Neumarktl *see* Tržič
Neumoldowa *see* Moldova Nouă
180 H1 **Neumünster** Schleswig-Holstein, N Germany 54°04′N 09°59′E
166 G8 **Neung-sur-Beuvron** Centre, France 47°32′N 1°48′E
177 L3 **Neunkirchen** *var.* Neunkirchen am Steinfeld. Niederösterreich, E Austria 47°44′N 16°05′E
181 J13 **Neunkirchen** Bayern, Germany 11°08′N 49°37′E
181 C13 **Neunkirchen** Saarland, SW Germany 49°21′N 07°11′E
Neunkirchen am Steinfeld *see* Neunkirchen
118 G10 **Neuquén** Neuquén, SE Argentina 39°03′S 68°36′W
118 F10 **Neuquén** *off.* Provincia de Neuquén. ◐ *province* W Argentina
Neuquén, Provincia de *see* Neuquén
118 E10 **Neuquén, Río** ≈ W Argentina
Neurode *see* Nowa Ruda
178 H6 **Neuruppin** Brandenburg, NE Germany 52°56′N 12°49′E
Neusalz an der Oder *see* Nowa Sól
Neu Sandec *see* Nowy Sącz
179 F12 **Neusäss** Bayern, S Germany 48°24′N 10°49′E
Neusatz *see* Novi Sad
Neuschliss *see* Gherla
67 L7 **Neuse River** ≈ North Carolina, SE USA
177 M2 **Neusiedl am See** Burgenland, E Austria 47°58′N 16°51′E
177 M3 **Neusiedler See** *Hung.* Fertő. ◎ Austria/Hungary
Neusohl *see* Banská Bystrica
181 B9 **Neuss** *anc.* Novaesium, Novesium. Nordrhein-Westfalen, W Germany 51°12′N 06°42′E
Neuss *see* Nyon
180 I1 **Neustadt** Schleswig-Holstein, Germany 10°49′N 54°06′E
Neustadt *see* Neustadt an der Aisch, Bayern, Germany
Neustadt *see* Neustadt bei Coburg, Bayern, Germany
Neustadt *see* Prudnik, Opole, Poland
Neustadt *see* Baia Mare, Maramureş, Romania
181 J10 **Neustadt am Rennsteig** Thüringen, Germany 10°56′N 50°35′E
180 G5 **Neustadt am Rübenberge** Niedersachsen, N Germany 52°30′N 09°28′E
181 I13 **Neustadt an der Aisch** *var.* Neustadt. Bayern, C Germany 49°34′N 10°36′E
Neustadt an der Haardt *see* Neustadt an der Weinstrasse
181 E13 **Neustadt an der Weinstrasse** *prev.* Neustadt an der Haardt, *hist.* Niewenstat; *anc.* Nova Civitas. Rheinland-Pfalz, SW Germany 49°21′N 08°09′E
181 J11 **Neustadt bei Coburg** *var.* Neustadt. Bayern, C Germany 50°19′N 11°06′E
Neustadt bei Pinne *see* Lwówek
Neustadt in Oberschlesien *see* Prudnik
Neustadtl *see* Novo mesto
Neustadtl in Mähren *see* Nové Město na Moravě
Neustettin *see* Szczecinek
176 G4 **Neustift im Stubaital** *var.* Stubaital. Tirol, W Austria 47°07′N 11°26′E
178 H5 **Neustrelitz** Mecklenburg-Vorpommern, NE Germany 53°22′N 13°05′E
Neutitschein *see* Nový Jičín
Neutra *see* Nitra
179 E12 **Neu-Ulm** Bayern, S Germany 48°23′N 10°02′E
167 L6 **Neuves-Maisons** Lorraine, France 48°37′N 6°06′E
Neuveville *see* La Neuveville
165 H6 **Neuvic** Corrèze, C France 45°23′N 02°16′E
166 G7 **Neuville-aux-Bois** Centre, France 48°04′N 2°03′E

◆ Country
● Country Capital
◇ Dependent Territory
○ Dependent Territory Capital
◐ Administrative Regions
✈ International Airport
▲ Mountain
▲▲ Mountain Range
Volcano
≈ River
◎ Lake
⊠ Reservoir

◆ Country	◇ Dependent Territory	◈ Administrative Regions	▲ Mountain	🌋 Volcano	◎ Lake
● Country Capital	○ Dependent Territory Capital	✕ International Airport	▲ Mountain Range	▲ River	■ Reservoir

◆ Country
● Country Capital
◇ Dependent Territory
● Dependent Territory Capital
◇ Administrative Regions
✕ International Airport
▲ Mountain
▲ Mountain Range
▲ Volcano
♒ River
© Lake
☒ Reservoir

◆ Country	◇ Dependent Territory	◆ Administrative Regions	▲ Mountain	▼ Volcano	⊚ Lake
● Country Capital	○ Dependent Territory Capital	✕ International Airport	▲ Mountain Range	♣ River	⊞ Reservoir

◆ Country
● Country Capital
◇ Dependent Territory
○ Dependent Territory Capital
⬖ Administrative Regions
✈ International Airport
▲ Mountain
▲▲ Mountain Range
🌋 Volcano
≈ River
◎ Lake
⊞ Reservoir

◆ Country   ◇ Dependent Territory   ■ Administrative Regions   ▲ Mountain   ▲ Volcano   ◙ Lake
● Country Capital   ○ Dependent Territory Capital   ✈ International Airport   ▲ Mountain Range   ♣ River   ◙ Reservoir

◆ Country	◇ Dependent Territory	◆ Administrative Regions
● Country Capital	○ Dependent Territory Capital	✈ International Airport

▲ Mountain	⛰ Volcano	◎ Lake	
▲ Mountain Range	✲ River	▨ Reservoir	

Paranaíta - Pembina
INDEX
389

107 I6 **Paranaíta** Mato Grosso, W Brazil 09°35′S 57°01′W
113 J3 **Paranapanema, Rio** S Brazil
110 B10 **Paranapiacaba, Serra do** ▲▲ S Brazil
113 I3 **Paranavaí** Paraná, S Brazil 23°02′S 52°36′W
222 F4 **Parandak** Markazī, W Iran 35°19′N 50°40′E
187 I2 **Paranésti** var Paranestio. Anatolikí Makedonía kai Thráki, NE Greece 41°16′N 24°31′E
Paranestio see Paranésti
285 K7 **Paraoa** atoll Îles Tuamotu, C French Polynesia
110 G2 **Paraopeba** Minas Gerais, Brazil 19°18′S 44°25′W
278 G7 **Paraparaumu** Wellington, North Island, New Zealand 40°55′S 175°01′E
112 E2 **Parapeti, Río** SE Bolivia
104 I4 **Paraque, Cerro** ▲ W Venezuela 06°00′S 67°00′W
232 F9 **Parāsiya** Madhya Pradesh, C India 22°11′N 78°50′E
187 L9 **Paraspóri, Ákrotírio** cape Kárpathos, SE Greece
110 G8 **Parati** Rio de Janeiro, SE Brazil 23°15′S 44°42′W
107 L4 **Parauapebas** Pará, N Brazil 06°03′S 49°48′W
165 I5 **Paray-le-Monial** Saône-et-Loire, C France 46°27′N 04°07′E
Parbatsar see Parvatsar
234 E4 **Parbhani** Mahārāshtra, C India 19°16′N 76°51′E
178 G5 **Parchim** Mecklenburg-Vorpommern, N Germany 53°26′N 11°51′E
Parchwitz see Prochowice
182 I6 **Parczew** Lubelskie, E Poland 51°40′N 23°E
110 C5 **Pardo, Rio** S Brazil
183 D8 **Pardubice** Ger. Pardubitz. Pardubický Kraj, C Czech Republic 50°01′N 15°47′E
183 D8 **Pardubický Kraj** ◆ region N Czech Republic
Pardubitz see Pardubice
191 D10 **Parechcha** Pol. Porzecze, Rus. Porech'ye. Hrodzyenskaya Voblasts', W Belarus 53°53′N 24°08′E
106 G8 **Parecis, Chapada dos** var. Serra dos Parecis. ▲▲ W Brazil
Parecis, Serra dos see Parecis, Chapada dos
172 C1 **Paredes** Porto, Portugal 41°12′N 8°20′W
170 F3 **Paredes de Nava** Castilla-León, N Spain 42°09′N 04°42′W
118 F4 **Pareditas** Mendoza, Argentina 33°56′S 69°04′W
87 J9 **Paredón** Chiapas, Mexico 16°02′N 93°52′W
282 F9 **Parem** island Chuuk, C Micronesia
283 J1 **Parem Island** island E Micronesia
278 F1 **Parengarenga Harbour** inlet North Island, New Zealand
164 F8 **Parentis-en-Born** Landes, SW France 44°22′N 01°04′W
Parenzo see Poreč
278 D11 **Pareora** Canterbury, South Island, New Zealand 44°28′S 171°12′E
260 C6 **Parepare** Sulawesi, C Indonesia 04°S 119°40′E
114 D6 **Parera** Entre Ríos, Argentina 32°48′S 58°53′W
186 E4 **Párga** Ípeiros, W Greece 39°18′N 20°19′E
153 G10 **Pargas** Swe. Parainen. Länsi-Soumi, SW Finland 60°18′N 22°20′E
170 A8 **Pargo, Ponta do** headland Madeira, Portugal, NE Atlantic Ocean 32°48′N 17°17′W
103 H3 **Pariaguán** Anzoátegui, NE Venezuela 08°51′N 64°43′W
104 H7 **Pariamanu, Río** E Peru
79 H5 **Paria River** Utah, W USA
Parichi see Parychy
86 C6 **Paricutín, Volcán** C Mexico 19°25′N 102°20′W
89 I10 **Parida, Isla** island SW Panama
103 K4 **Parika** NE Guyana 06°51′N 58°25′W
153 J9 **Parikkala** Etelä-Suomi, SE Finland 61°33′N 29°34′E
103 H6 **Parima, Serra** var. Sierra Parima. ▲ Brazil/Venezuela 02°30′N 64°00′W see also Parima, Sierra
103 H6 **Parima, Sierra** var. Serra Parima. ▲ Brazil/Venezuela see also Parima, Serra
105 F9 **Parinacochas, Laguna** SW Peru
104 A4 **Pariñas, Punta** headland NW Peru 04°45′S 81°22′W
107 I3 **Parintins** Amazonas, N Brazil 02°38′S 56°45′W
167 H5 **Paris** anc. Lutetia, Lutetia Parisiorum, Parisii. ● (France) Paris, N France 48°52′N 02°19′E
285 M1 **Paris** Kiritimati, E Kiribati 01°55′N 157°30′W
75 G12 **Paris** Arkansas, C USA 35°17′N 93°46′W
77 I8 **Paris** Idaho, NW USA 42°14′N 111°24′W
73 D11 **Paris** Illinois, N USA 39°36′N 87°42′W
66 F3 **Paris** Kentucky, S USA 38°13′N 84°15′W
75 I9 **Paris** Missouri, C USA 39°28′N 92°00′W
66 C5 **Paris** Tennessee, S USA 36°19′N 88°20′W
71 I3 **Paris** Texas, SW USA 33°41′N 95°33′W
Parisii see Paris
89 K10 **Parita** Herrera, S Panama 08°01′N 80°30′W
89 K9 **Parita, Bahía de** bay S Panama
153 G9 **Parkano** Länsi-Suomi, W Finland 62°03′N 23°E
Parkan/Párkány see Štúrovo
75 E10 **Park City** Kansas, C USA 37°48′N 97°19′W
79 I2 **Park City** Utah, W USA 40°39′N 111°30′W
81 I12 **Parker** Arizona, SW USA 34°07′N 114°16′W
69 I4 **Parker** Florida, SE USA 30°07′N 85°36′W
74 E6 **Parker** South Dakota, N USA 43°24′N 97°08′W
53 I5 **Parker, Cape** headland Nunavut, NE Canada
81 J12 **Parker Dam** California, W USA 34°17′N 114°08′W
74 H6 **Parkersburg** Iowa, C USA 42°34′N 92°47′W
67 I2 **Parkersburg** West Virginia, NE USA 39°17′N 81°33′W
74 F4 **Parkers Prairie** Minnesota, N USA 46°09′N 95°19′W
263 M9 **Parker Volcano** Mindanao, S Philippines 06°09′N 124°52′E
277 K5 **Parkes** New South Wales, SE Australia 33°10′S 148°10′E
161 M5 **Parkeston** UK 51°56′N 1°15′E
72 C4 **Park Falls** Wisconsin, N USA 45°57′N 90°25′W
80 C6 **Parkfield** California, USA 35°54′N 120°26′W
Parkhar see Farkhor
62 B5 **Parkhill** Ontario, S Canada 43°11′N 81°39′W
74 F3 **Park Rapids** Minnesota, N USA 46°55′N 95°03′W
74 E2 **Park River** North Dakota, N USA 48°24′N 97°44′W
74 E6 **Parkston** South Dakota, N USA 43°24′N 97°58′W
56 C8 **Parksville** Vancouver Island, British Columbia, SW Canada 49°13′N 124°13′W
79 L2 **Parkview Mountain** ▲ Colorado, C USA 40°19′N 106°08′W
64 D9 **Parkville** Maryland, USA 39°23′N 76°32′W
170 G5 **Parla** Madrid, C Spain 40°13′N 03°48′W
74 F4 **Parle, Lac qui** Minnesota, N USA
186 G7 **Parlía Tyroú** Pelopónnisos, S Greece 37°17′N 22°50′E
80 D6 **Parlier** California, USA 36°37′N 119°32′W
234 E5 **Parli Vaijnāth** Mahārāshtra, C India 18°53′N 76°36′E
176 F8 **Parma** Emilia-Romagna, N Italy 44°50′N 10°20′E
73 I9 **Parma** Ohio, N USA 41°24′N 81°43′W
Parnahyba see Parnaíba
108 F3 **Parnaíba** var. Parnahyba. Piauí, E Brazil 02°58′S 41°46′W
291 F8 **Parnaíba Ridge** undersea feature C Atlantic Ocean
108 F4 **Parnaíba, Rio** NE Brazil
186 G5 **Parnassós** ▲▲ C Greece
278 F9 **Parnassus** Canterbury, South Island, New Zealand 42°41′S 173°18′E
276 F6 **Parndana** South Australia 35°48′S 137°13′E
187 H6 **Párnitha** ▲▲ C Greece
Parnon see Párnonas
186 G7 **Párnonas** var. Parnon. ▲▲ S Greece
190 D4 **Pärnu** Ger. Pernau, Latv. Pērnava; prev. Rus. Pernov. Pärnumaa, SW Estonia 58°24′N 24°32′E
190 E4 **Pärnu** var. Parnu Jõgi, Ger. Pernau. SW Estonia
190 D4 **Pärnu-Jaagupi** Ger. Sankt-Jakobi. Pärnumaa, SW Estonia 58°36′N 24°30′E
Parnu Jõgi see Pärnu
190 D5 **Pärnu Laht** Ger. Pernauer Bucht. bay SW Estonia
190 D4 **Pärnumaa** var. Pärnu Maakond. ◆ province SW Estonia
Pärnu Maakond see Pärnumaa
233 K6 **Paro** W Bhutan 27°23′N 89°31′E
233 K6 **Paro** (Thimphu) W Bhutan 27°23′N 89°31′E
278 D9 **Paroa** West Coast, South Island, New Zealand 42°31′S 171°10′E
248 C5 **P'aro-ho** var. Hwach'ŏn-chŏsuji. N South Korea
187 J7 **Pároikiá** prev. Páros. Páros, Kykládes, Greece, Aegean Sea 37°04′N 25°06′E
277 I3 **Paroo River** seasonal river New South Wales/Queensland, SE Australia
187 I7 **Páros** island Kykládes, Greece, Aegean Sea
Páros see Pároikiá
140 D10 **Parow** Western Cape, South Africa 33°54′S 18°36′E
79 H5 **Parowan** Utah, W USA 37°50′N 112°49′W
165 K7 **Parpaillon** ▲▲ SE France
176 F4 **Parpan** Graubünden, S Switzerland 46°46′N 09°32′E
116 B5 **Parral** Maule, C Chile 36°08′S 71°52′W
Parral see Hidalgo del Parral
277 L5 **Parramatta** New South Wales, SE Australia 33°49′S 150°59′E
67 M4 **Parramore Island** island Virginia, NE USA
85 K7 **Parras** var. Parras de la Fuente. Coahuila de Zaragoza, NE Mexico 25°26′N 102°07′W
Parras de la Fuente see Parras
172 B4 **Parreira** Santarém, Portugal 39°13′N 8°24′W
89 H8 **Parrita** Puntarenas, S Costa Rica 09°30′N 84°20′W
85 K3 **Parrita** Chihuahua, Mexico
53 J8 **Parry Bay** coastal sea feature Nunavut, NE Canada
53 H5 **Parry Channel** sea waterway Northwest Territories/Nunavut, N Canada
Parry group see Mukojima-rettō
62 C3 **Parry Island** island Ontario, S Canada
52 G5 **Parry Islands** Island group
295 I8 **Parry Islands** island group Nunavut, NW Canada
52 C6 **Parry Peninsula** Peninsula Northwest Territories, NW Canada
62 C3 **Parry Sound** Ontario, S Canada 45°21′N 80°03′W
180 J5 **Parsau** Niedersachsen, Germany 10°52′N 52°32′E
182 D4 **Parsęta** Ger. Persante. NW Poland
74 B2 **Parshall** North Dakota, N USA 47°57′N 102°07′W
75 F11 **Parsons** Kansas, C USA 37°20′N 95°15′W
66 C6 **Parsons** Tennessee, S USA 35°39′N 88°07′W
67 J2 **Parsons** West Virginia, NE USA 39°06′N 79°43′W
Parsonstown see Birr
178 I6 **Parsteiner See** NE Germany
175 E12 **Partanna** Sicilia, Italy, C Mediterranean Sea 37°43′N 12°54′E
176 F4 **Partenen** Graubünden, E Switzerland 46°58′N 10°01′E
181 G12 **Partenstein** Bayern, Germany 9°31′N 50°03′E
164 G5 **Parthenay** Deux-Sèvres, W France 46°39′N 00°13′W
155 F10 **Partille** Västra Götaland, S Sweden 57°43′N 12°12′E
175 E12 **Partinico** Sicilia, Italy, C Mediterranean Sea 38°03′N 13°07′E
183 F10 **Partizánske** prev. Šimonovany, Hung. Simony. Trenčiansky Kraj, W Slovakia 48°35′N 18°23′E
159 M10 **Partney** UK 53°11′N 0°07′E
159 H7 **Parton** UK 54°34′N 3°35′W
107 I1 **Paru de Oeste, Rio** N Brazil
277 H5 **Paruna** South Australia 34°45′S 140°43′E
103 M8 **Paru, Rio** N Brazil
230 G3 **Parvān** Pash. Parwān. ◆ province E Afghanistan
234 H5 **Pārvatipuram** Andhra Pradesh, E India 17°01′N 81°47′E
232 D6 **Parvatsar** prev. Parbatsar. Rājasthān, N India 26°52′N 74°49′E
Parwān see Parvān
159 K10 **Parwich** UK 53°05′N 1°43′W
238 E9 **Paryang** Xizang Zizhiqu, W China 30°04′N 83°28′E
191 H11 **Parychy** Rus. Parichi. Homyel'skaya Voblasts', SE Belarus 52°48′N 29°25′E
138 G7 **Parys** Free State, C South Africa 26°55′S 27°28′E
81 D10 **Pasadena** California, W USA 34°09′N 118°09′W
71 I7 **Pasadena** Texas, SW USA 29°41′N 95°13′W
104 B3 **Pasaje** El Oro, SW Ecuador 03°23′S 79°50′W
215 K3 **P'asanauri** N Georgia 42°21′N 44°40′E
258 D6 **Pasapuat** Pulau Pagai Utara, W Indonesia 02°36′S 99°58′E
256 D5 **Pasawng** Kayah State, C Myanmar (Burma) 18°50′N 97°16′E
68 F4 **Pascagoula** Mississippi, S USA 30°21′N 88°32′W
68 F4 **Pascagoula River** Mississippi, S USA
188 E6 **Paşcani** Hung. Páskán. Iaşi, NE Romania 47°14′N 26°46′E
177 J2 **Pasching** Oberösterreich, N Austria 48°16′N 14°10′E
76 E5 **Pasco** Washington, NW USA 46°13′N 119°06′W
104 E6 **Pasco** off. Departamento de Pasco. ◆ department C Peru
65 L3 **Pascoag** Rhode Island, USA 41°57′N 71°42′W
Pasco, Departamento de see Pasco
117 B11 **Pascua, Río** S Chile
165 H1 **Pas-de-Calais** ◆ department N France
178 I5 **Pasewalk** Mecklenburg-Vorpommern, NE Germany 53°31′N 13°59′E
55 H6 **Pasfield Lake** Saskatchewan, C Canada
190 J2 **Pasha** Leningradskaya Oblast', Russian Federation
Pa-shih Hai-hsia see Bashi Channel
Pashkeni see Bolyarovo
Pashmakli see Smolyan
263 K5 **Pasig** Luzon, N Philippines 14°34′N 121°04′E
233 M5 **Pāsighāt** Arunāchel Pradesh, NE India 28°08′N 95°13′E
215 I5 **Pasinler** Erzurum, NE Turkey 39°59′N 41°41′E
Pasi Oloy, Qatorkŭhi see Zaalayskiy Khrebet
88 C2 **Pasión, Río de la** N Guatemala
258 D6 **Pasirganting** Sumatera, W Indonesia 02°04′S 100°51′E
Pasirpangarayan see Bagansiapiapi
258 E2 **Pasir Puteh** var. Pasir Putih. Kelantan, Peninsular Malaysia 05°50′N 102°24′E
Pasir Putih see Pasir Puteh
258 I4 **Pasir, Tanjung** cape East Malaysia
155 H10 **Påskallavik** Kalmar, S Sweden 57°10′N 16°25′E
Páskán see Paşcani
Paskevicha, Zaliv see Tushybas, Zaliv
182 G4 **Pasłęk** Ger. Preußisch Holland. Warmińsko-Mazurskie, NE Poland 54°03′N 19°40′E
182 G3 **Pasłęka** Ger. Passarge. N Poland
230 E9 **Pasni** Baluchistān, SW Pakistan 25°13′N 63°30′E
117 C9 **Paso de Indios** Chubut, Argentina 43°48′S 69°06′E
114 F9 **Paso Antolín** Colonia, Uruguay 34°12′S 57°47′W
114 F9 **Paso de la Horqueta** Colonia, Uruguay 34°12′S 57°52′W
114 D4 **Paso de la Laguna** Entre Ríos, Argentina 31°48′S 59°10′W
115 H4 **Paso de las Carretas** Uruguay 31°30′S 56°02′W
102 F4 **Paso del Caballo** Guárico, N Venezuela 08°19′N 67°08′W
115 K5 **Paso del Centurión** Cerro Largo, Uruguay 32°10′S 53°45′W
115 I4 **Paso del Cerro** Uruguay 31°31′S 55°46′W
114 G1 **Paso del León** Artigas, Uruguay 30°10′S 57°06′W
114 F5 **Paso de los Carros** Paysandú, Uruguay 31°59′S 57°25′W
118 E10 **Paso de los Indios** Neuquén, Argentina 38°32′S 69°25′W
114 G1 **Paso de los Libres** Corrientes, NE Argentina 29°43′S 57°09′W
115 H6 **Paso de los Toros** Tacuarembó, C Uruguay 32°45′S 56°30′W
Pasoeroean see Pasuruan
118 B8 **Paso Hondo** Bío-Bío, Chile 36°55′S 72°32′W
115 I5 **Paso Pereira** Cerro Largo, Uruguay 32°28′S 55°14′W
85 J8 **Paso Real** Oaxaca, Mexico
80 B7 **Paso Robles** California, W USA 35°37′N 120°42′W
55 H8 **Pasquia Hills** ▲▲ Saskatchewan, S Canada
231 J5 **Pasrūr** Punjab, E Pakistan 32°12′N 74°42′E
111 I2 **Passabém** Minas Gerais, Brazil 19°17′S 43°13′W
72 D2 **Passage Island** island Michigan, N USA
117 H11 **Passage Islands** island group W Falkland Islands
52 E5 **Passage Point** headland Banks Island, Northwest Territories, NW Canada 73°31′N 115°12′W
65 H6 **Passaic** New Jersey, USA 40°51′N 74°08′W
Passarge see Pasłęka
186 E4 **Passarón** ancient monument Ípeiros, W Greece
Passarowitz see Požarevac
110 G4 **Passa Tempo** Minas Gerais, Brazil 20°40′S 44°30′W
179 I12 **Passau** Bayern, SE Germany 48°34′N 13°28′E
110 G7 **Passa Vinte** Minas Gerais, Brazil 22°13′S 44°15′W
68 F4 **Pass Christian** Mississippi, S USA 30°19′N 89°15′W
175 G13 **Passero, Capo** headland Sicilia, Italy, C Mediterranean Sea 36°40′N 15°09′E
263 L7 **Passi** Panay Island, C Philippines 11°05′N 122°37′E
115 M1 **Passo do Sobrado** Rio Grande do Sul, Brazil 29°45′S 52°17′W
113 I6 **Passo Fundo** Rio Grande do Sul, S Brazil 28°16′S 52°20′W
113 I6 **Passo Fundo, Barragem de** S Brazil
115 I1 **Passo Novo** Rio Grande do Sul, Brazil 29°41′S 55°32′W
110 F7 **Passo Quatro** Minas Gerais, Brazil 22°23′S 44°58′W
113 I6 **Passo Real, Barragem de** S Brazil
110 D4 **Passos** Minas Gerais, NE Brazil 20°45′S 46°38′W
262 G5 **Passu Keah** island S Paracel Islands
169 M1 **Passy** Rhône-Alpes, France 45°55′N 6°41′E
191 F8 **Pastavy** Pol. Postawy, Rus. Postavy. Vitsyebskaya Voblasts', NW Belarus 55°07′N 26°50′E
104 D2 **Pastaza** ◆ province E Ecuador
104 D3 **Pastaza, Río** Ecuador/Peru
112 E10 **Pasteur** Buenos Aires, E Argentina 35°10′S 62°14′W
229 I6 **Pastigav** Rus. Pastigov. W Tajikistan 39°27′N 69°16′E
Pastigov see Pastigav
102 A7 **Pasto** Nariño, SW Colombia 01°12′N 77°17′W
79 J6 **Pastora Peak** ▲ Arizona, SW USA 36°48′N 109°10′W
114 D6 **Pastor Britos** Entre Ríos, Argentina 32°46′S 58°53′W
170 G5 **Pastrana** Castilla-La Mancha, C Spain 40°24′N 02°55′W
259 J9 **Pasuruan** prev. Pasoeroean. Jawa, C Indonesia 07°38′S 112°44′E
190 D7 **Pasvalys** Panevėžys, N Lithuania 56°03′N 24°24′E
183 G11 **Pásztó** Nógrád, N Hungary 47°57′N 19°41′E
282 E9 **Pata** var. Patta. atoll Chuuk Islands, C Micronesia
79 I10 **Patagonia** Arizona, SW USA 31°32′N 110°45′W
117 C10 **Patagonia** semi arid region Argentina/Chile
Patalung see Phatthalung
232 C7 **Pātan** Gujarāt, W India 23°51′N 72°11′E
232 F8 **Pātan** Madhya Pradesh, C India 23°19′N 79°41′E
260 G4 **Patani** Pulau Halmahera, E Indonesia 0°19′N 128°46′E
Patani see Pattani
188 E9 **Pătâriagele** prev. Pătîriagele. Buzău, SE Romania 45°19′N 26°21′E
Patavium see Padova
276 G3 **Patawarta Hill** ▲ South Australia 30°57′S 138°42′E
166 G7 **Patay** Centre, France 48°03′N 1°42′E
55 M7 **Patchepawapoka River** Ontario, C Canada
277 H6 **Patchewollock** Victoria, SE Australia 35°24′S 142°11′E
65 J6 **Patchogue** New York, USA 40°46′N 73°01′W
160 G6 **Patchway** UK 51°32′N 2°34′W
278 G6 **Patea** Taranaki, North Island, New Zealand 39°48′S 174°35′E
278 G6 **Patea** North Island, New Zealand
133 J7 **Pategi** Kwara, C Nigeria 08°39′N 05°46′E
137 F9 **Pate Island** var. Patta Island. island SE Kenya
171 I6 **Paterna** País Valenciano, E Spain 39°30′N 00°24′W
172 E9 **Paterna de Rivera** Andalucía, Spain 36°31′N 5°52′W
177 J4 **Paternion** Slvn. Špatrjan. Kärnten, S Austria 46°40′N 13°43′E
175 G12 **Paternò** anc. Hybla, Hybla Major. Sicilia, Italy, C Mediterranean Sea 37°34′N 14°55′E
140 D9 **Paternoster** Western Cape, South Africa 32°49′S 17°53′E
76 D3 **Pateros** Washington, NW USA 48°01′N 119°55′W
65 H5 **Paterson** New Jersey, NE USA 40°55′N 74°12′W
76 D5 **Paterson** Washington, NW USA 45°56′N 119°37′W
278 B13 **Paterson Inlet** inlet Stewart Island, New Zealand
162 I4 **Paterswolde** Drenthe, NE Netherlands 53°07′N 06°32′E
232 E3 **Pathānkot** Himāchal Pradesh, N India 32°16′N 75°43′E
Pathein see Bassein
77 K8 **Pathfinder Reservoir** Wyoming, C USA
256 E8 **Pathum Thani** var. Patumdhani, Prathum Thani. Pathum Thani, C Thailand 14°03′N 100°29′E
259 I8 **Pati** Jawa, C Indonesia 06°45′S 111°00′E
102 B7 **Patía** var. El Bordo. Cauca, SW Colombia 02°07′N 76°57′W
232 E4 **Patiāla** var. Puttiala. Punjab, NW India 30°21′N 76°27′E
102 A7 **Patía, Río** SW Colombia
260 G4 **Patinti, Selat** strait Maluku, E Indonesia
282 B1 **Pati Point** headland NE Guam 13°36′N 144°39′E
Pătîriagele see Pătâriagele
104 C7 **Pativilca** Lima, W Peru 10°44′S 77°45′W
256 C2 **Pātkai Bum** var. Patkai Range. ▲▲ Myanmar (Burma)/India
Patkai Range see Pātkai Bum
187 K7 **Pátmos** Pátmos, Dodekánisa, Greece, Aegean Sea 37°18′N 26°32′E
187 K7 **Pátmos** island Dodekánisa, Greece, Aegean Sea
233 I7 **Patna** var. Azimabad. state capital Bihār, N India 25°36′N 85°11′E
158 G5 **Patna** UK 55°21′N 4°30′W
234 H4 **Patnāgarh** Orissa, E India 20°42′N 83°12′E
263 L7 **Patnongon** Panay Island, C Philippines 10°56′N 122°03′E
215 J6 **Patnos** Ağrı, E Turkey 39°14′N 42°52′E
113 I5 **Pato Branco** Paraná, S Brazil 26°20′S 52°40′W
73 E12 **Patoka Lake** Indiana, N USA
152 H3 **Patoniva** Lapp. Buoddobohki. Lappi, N Finland 69°44′N 27°01′E
184 F9 **Patos** var. Patosi. Fier, SW Albania 40°40′N 19°37′E
Patos see Patos de Minas
109 D11 **Patos de Minas** var. Patos. Minas Gerais, NE Brazil 18°35′S 46°32′W
118 D6 **Patos de San Pedro, Río** Maule, Chile
Patosi see Patos
115 N4 **Patos, Lagoa dos** lagoon S Brazil
116 D2 **Patquía** La Rioja, C Argentina 30°02′S 66°54′W
186 F6 **Pátra** Eng. Patras; prev. Pátrai. Dytikí Ellás, S Greece 38°14′N 21°45′E
186 F6 **Patraïkós Kólpos** gulf S Greece
Pátrai/Patras see Pátra
152 A2 **Patreksfjördhur** Vestfirdhir, W Iceland 65°33′N 23°54′W
70 D4 **Patricia** Texas, SW USA 32°34′N 102°00′W
117 A11 **Patricio Lynch, Isla** island S Chile
110 A2 **Patrimônio** Minas Gerais, Brazil 19°24′S 48°36′E
110 C1 **Patrocínio** Minas Gerais, Brazil 18°57′S 46°59′W
Patta see Pata
Patta Island see Pate Island
256 F11 **Pattani** var. Patani. Pattani, SW Thailand 06°50′N 101°20′E
256 F8 **Pattaya** Chon Buri, S Thailand 12°57′N 100°53′E
63 K2 **Patten** Maine, NE USA 45°58′N 68°27′W
180 H3 **Pattensen** Niedersachsen, Germany 10°08′N 53°19′E
180 H6 **Pattensen** Niedersachsen, Germany 9°46′N 52°16′E
80 C4 **Patterson** California, W USA 37°27′N 121°07′W
68 D5 **Patterson** Louisiana, S USA 29°41′N 91°18′W
80 F3 **Patterson, Mount** ▲ California, W USA 38°27′N 119°16′W
72 F5 **Patterson, Point** headland Michigan, N USA 45°58′N 85°39′W
175 G12 **Patti** Sicilia, Italy, C Mediterranean Sea 38°08′N 14°58′E
175 G12 **Patti, Golfo di** gulf Sicilia, Italy
152 H7 **Pattijoki** Oulu, W Finland 64°41′N 24°40′E
287 I3 **Patton Escarpment** undersea feature E Pacific Ocean
75 G8 **Pattonsburg** Missouri, C USA 40°03′N 94°08′W
42 B4 **Patton Seamount** undersea feature NE Pacific Ocean
56 B1 **Pattullo, Mount** ▲ British Columbia, W Canada 56°18′N 129°43′W
87 H3 **Patuca, Río** E Honduras
233 K8 **Patuakhali** var. Patukhali. Barisal, S Bangladesh 22°20′N 90°20′E
Patukhali see Patuakhali
Patumdhani see Pathum Thani
86 D6 **Pátzcuaro** Michoacán de Ocampo, SW Mexico 19°30′N 101°38′W
88 C4 **Patzicía** Chimaltenango, S Guatemala 14°38′N 90°52′W
164 F9 **Pau** Pyrénées-Atlantiques, SW France 43°18′N 00°22′W
164 F7 **Pauillac** Gironde, SW France 45°12′N 00°44′W
256 C4 **Pauk** Magwe, W Myanmar (Burma) 21°25′N 94°30′E
111 I4 **Paula Cândido** Minas Gerais, Brazil 20°53′S 42°58′W
52 D7 **Paulatuk** Northwest Territories, NW Canada 69°23′N 124°W
88 G3 **Paulayá, Río** NE Honduras
68 F2 **Paulding** Mississippi, S USA 32°01′N 89°01′W
73 G9 **Paulding** Ohio, N USA 41°08′N 84°34′W
169 I2 **Paulhac** Auvergne, France 45°18′N 3°21′E
169 I6 **Paulhan** Languedoc-Roussillon, France 43°32′N 3°27′E
110 C8 **Paulínia** São Paulo, Brazil 22°45′S 47°10′W
74 F6 **Paullina** Iowa, C USA 42°58′N 95°41′W
108 H6 **Paulo Afonso** Bahia, E Brazil 09°21′S 38°14′W
82 G9 **Pauloff Harbor** var. Pavlor Harbour. Sanak Island, Alaska, USA 54°26′N 162°43′W
141 I5 **Paul Roux** Free State, South Africa 28°18′S 27°57′E
64 F8 **Paulsboro** New Jersey, USA 39°50′N 75°14′W
75 E13 **Pauls Valley** Oklahoma, C USA 34°46′N 97°14′W
81 E12 **Pauma Valley** California, USA 33°18′N 116°59′W
256 C6 **Paungde** Pegu, C Myanmar (Burma) 18°30′N 95°30′E
Pauni see Paoni
232 F4 **Pauri** Uttaranchal, N India 30°08′N 78°48′E
Pautalia see Kyustendil
261 M5 **Pauwasi** Papua, E Indonesia
195 L8 **Pavda** Sverdlovskaya oblast', Russian federation
222 D4 **Pāveh** Kermānshāhān, NW Iran 35°02′N 46°15′E
196 G3 **Pavelets** Ryazanskaya Oblast', W Russian Federation 53°47′N 39°22′E
176 E7 **Pavia** anc. Ticinum. Lombardia, N Italy 45°10′N 09°10′E
172 C5 **Pavia** Évora, Portugal 38°54′N 8°01′W
166 F4 **Pavilly** Haute-Normandie, France 49°34′N 0°58′E
190 B6 **Pāvilosta** Liepāja, W Latvia 56°52′N 21°12′E
195 H9 **Pavino** Kostromskaya Oblast', NW Russian Federation 59°10′N 46°09′E
185 K5 **Pavlikeni** Veliko Tŭrnovo, N Bulgaria 43°14′N 25°20′E
227 J2 **Pavlodar** Pavlodar, NE Kazakhstan 52°21′N 76°59′E
227 J2 **Pavlodar** off. Pavlodarskaya Oblast', Kaz. Pavlodar Oblysy. ◆ province NE Kazakhstan
Pavlodar Oblysy/Pavlodarskaya Oblast' see Pavlodar
Pavlograd see Pavlohrad
189 K5 **Pavlohrad** Rus. Pavlograd. Dnipropetrovs'ka Oblast', E Ukraine 48°32′N 35°50′E
Pavlor Harbour see Pauloff Harbor
227 I3 **Pavlovka** Akmola, C Kazakhstan 51°22′N 72°35′E
197 L2 **Pavlovka** Respublika Bashkortostan, W Russian Federation 55°28′N 56°36′E
197 I4 **Pavlovka** Ul'yanovskaya Oblast', W Russian Federation 52°40′N 47°08′E
197 H2 **Pavlovo** Nizhegorodskaya Oblast', W Russian Federation 55°59′N 43°03′E
196 G5 **Pavlovsk** Voronezhskaya Oblast', W Russian Federation 50°26′N 40°08′E
196 G7 **Pavlovskaya** Krasnodarskiy Kray, SW Russian Federation 46°06′N 39°52′E
189 J5 **Pavlysh** Kirovohrads'ka Oblast', C Ukraine 48°54′N 33°20′E
114 B7 **Pavón** Santa Fe, Argentina 33°15′S 60°24′W
114 G9 **Pavón** Uruguay 34°17′S 56°55′W
114 B7 **Pavón Arriba** Santa Fe, Argentina 33°19′S 60°50′W
176 G8 **Pavullo nel Frignano** Emilia-Romagna, C Italy 44°19′N 10°52′E
190 H5 **Pavy** Pskovskaya Oblast', Russian Federation
75 F11 **Pawhuska** Oklahoma, C USA 36°42′N 96°21′W
160 G7 **Pawlett** UK 51°11′N 3°0′W
67 K9 **Pawleys Island** South Carolina, SE USA 33°27′N 79°07′W
65 I4 **Pawling** New York, USA 41°34′N 73°36′W
256 D5 **Pawn** C Myanmar (Burma)
73 C11 **Pawnee** Illinois, N USA 39°35′N 89°34′W
75 E11 **Pawnee** Oklahoma, C USA 36°21′N 96°50′W
79 M2 **Pawnee Buttes** ▲ Colorado, C USA 40°49′N 103°58′W
75 F8 **Pawnee City** Nebraska, C USA 40°06′N 96°09′W
75 C10 **Pawnee River** Kansas, C USA
73 F8 **Paw Paw** Michigan, N USA 42°12′N 86°09′W
73 F8 **Paw Paw Lake** Michigan, N USA 42°12′N 86°16′W
65 L3 **Pawtucket** Rhode Island, NE USA 41°52′N 71°22′W
Pax Augusta see Badajoz
187 I10 **Paximádia** island SE Greece
Pax Julia see Beja
186 E5 **Paxoí** island Iónia Nisiá, Greece, C Mediterranean Sea
83 J5 **Paxson** Alaska, USA 62°58′N 145°27′W
229 I6 **Paxtakor** Jizzax Viloyati, C Uzbekistan 40°21′N 67°54′E
159 J3 **Paxton** UK 55°46′N 2°06′W
73 D10 **Paxton** Illinois, N USA 40°27′N 88°06′W
194 E7 **Pay** Respublika Kareliya, NW Russian Federation 61°10′N 34°24′E
256 C6 **Payagyi** Pegu, SW Myanmar (Burma) 17°28′N 96°32′E
176 C4 **Payerne** Ger. Peterlingen. Vaud, W Switzerland 46°49′N 06°57′E
76 F7 **Payette** Idaho, NW USA 44°04′N 116°55′W
76 F7 **Payette River** Idaho, NW USA
195 L2 **Pay-Khoy, Khrebet** ▲▲ NW Russian Federation
172 D7 **Paymogo** Andalucía, Spain 37°45′N 7°20′W
Payne see Kangirsuk
58 G2 **Payne, Lac** Québec, NE Canada
74 G4 **Paynesville** Minnesota, N USA 45°22′N 94°42′W
258 J3 **Payong, Tanjung** cape East Malaysia
Payo Obispo see Chetumal
168 F3 **Payrac** Midi-Pyrénées, France 44°48′N 1°28′E
114 E5 **Paysandú** Paysandú, W Uruguay 32°21′S 58°05′W
114 G5 **Paysandú** ◆ department W Uruguay
164 F4 **Pays de la Loire** ◆ region NW France
79 I8 **Payson** Arizona, SW USA 34°13′N 111°19′W
79 H3 **Payson** Utah, W USA 40°02′N 111°43′W
195 L3 **Payyer, Gora** ▲ NW Russian Federation 66°49′N 64°33′E
Payzawat see Jiashi
215 I4 **Pazar** Rize, NE Turkey 41°10′N 40°53′E
214 D4 **Pazarbaşı Burnu** headland NW Turkey 41°12′N 30°18′E
214 G7 **Pazarcık** Kahramanmaraş, S Turkey 37°31′N 37°19′E
185 J7 **Pazardzhik** prev. Tatar Pazardzhik. Pazardzhik, SW Bulgaria 42°11′N 24°21′E
102 D5 **Paz de Ariporo** Casanare, E Colombia 05°54′N 71°52′W
184 A3 **Pazin** Ger. Mitterburg, It. Pisino. Istra, NW Croatia 45°14′N 13°56′E
185 H7 **Pčinja** N Macedonia
284 D9 **Pea** Tongatapu, S Tonga 21°10′S 175°14′W
75 E10 **Peabody** Kansas, C USA 38°10′N 97°06′W
65 M2 **Peabody** Massachusetts, USA 42°32′N 70°56′W
56 F2 **Peace** Alberta/British Columbia, W Canada
Peace Garden State see North Dakota
54 F5 **Peace Point** Alberta, C Canada 59°11′N 112°12′W
57 H2 **Peace River** Alberta, W Canada 56°15′N 117°18′W
69 L7 **Peace River** Florida, SE USA
56 F8 **Peachland** British Columbia, SW Canada 49°49′N 119°48′W
78 G7 **Peach Springs** Arizona, SW USA 35°33′N 113°27′W
Peach State see Georgia
66 F9 **Peachtree City** Georgia, SE USA 33°24′N 84°36′W
283 N2 **Peacock Point** point SE Wake Island
157 H9 **Peak District** physical region C England, UK
277 K4 **Peak Hill** New South Wales, SE Australia 32°39′S 148°12′E
161 K3 **Peakirk** UK 52°38′N 0°16′W
132 C10 **Peak, The** ▲ C Ascension Island
170 G7 **Peal de Becerro** Andalucía, S Spain 37°55′N 03°08′W
283 M1 **Peale Island** island N Wake Island
79 J4 **Peale, Mount** ▲ Utah, W USA 38°26′N 109°13′W
81 E10 **Pearblossom** California, USA 34°30′N 117°55′W
83 H2 **Peard Bay** bay Alaska, USA
69 I3 **Pea River** Alabama/Florida, S USA
71 I7 **Pearland** Texas, SW USA 29°33′N 95°17′W
82 C2 **Pearl City** O'ahu, Hawai'i, USA 21°24′N 157°58′W
82 B2 **Pearl Harbor** inlet O'ahu, Hawai'i, USA, C Pacific Ocean
Pearl Islands see Perlas, Archipiélago de las
Pearl Lagoon see Perlas, Laguna de
68 E4 **Pearl River** Louisiana/Mississippi, S USA
70 F8 **Pearsall** Texas, SW USA 28°54′N 99°07′W
69 K3 **Pearson** Georgia, SE USA 31°18′N 82°51′W
81 F8 **Pearsonville** California, USA 35°49′N 117°52′W
141 H9 **Pearston** Eastern Cape, South Africa 32°35′S 25°08′E
52 G3 **Peary Channel** sea waterway Nunavut, N Canada
161 M4 **Peasenhall** UK 52°16′N 1°27′E
70 F3 **Pease River** Texas, SW USA
161 L7 **Peasmarsh** UK 50°58′N 0°40′E
58 E4 **Peawanuk** Ontario, C Canada 54°55′N 85°31′W
139 K3 **Pebane** Zambézia, NE Mozambique 17°14′S 38°10′E
80 A4 **Pebble Beach** California, USA 36°34′N 121°57′W
117 H10 **Pebble Island** island N Falkland Islands
117 I10 **Pebble Island Settlement** Pebble Island, N Falkland Islands 51°20′S 59°40′W
184 F6 **Peć** Alb. Pejë, Turk. Ipek. Kosovo, S Serbia 42°40′N 20°19′E
70 G5 **Pecan Bayou** Texas, SW USA
68 C5 **Pecan Island** Louisiana, S USA 29°39′N 92°26′W
113 K5 **Peças, Ilha das** island S Brazil
73 C8 **Pecatonica River** Illinois/Wisconsin, N USA
176 E5 **Peccia** Ticino, S Switzerland 46°24′N 08°39′E
172 C8 **Pechão** Faro, Portugal 37°03′N 7°52′W
Pechenegi see Pechenihy
Pechenezhskoye Vodokhranilishche see Pecheniz'ke Vodoskhovyshche
194 E2 **Pechenga** Fin. Petsamo. Murmanskaya Oblast', NW Russian Federation 69°34′N 31°14′E
189 L3 **Pechenihy** Rus. Pechenegi. Kharkivs'ka Oblast', E Ukraine 49°49′N 36°57′E
189 L3 **Pecheniz'ke Vodoskhovyshche** Rus. Pechenezhskoye Vodokhranilishche. E Ukraine
195 K5 **Pechora** Respublika Komi, NW Russian Federation 65°09′N 57°09′E
195 K7 **Pechora** NW Russian Federation
Pechora Bay see Pechorskaya Guba
Pechora Sea see Pechorskoye More
195 J3 **Pechorskaya Guba** Eng. Pechora Bay. bay NW Russian Federation
195 I2 **Pechorskoye More** Eng. Pechora Sea. sea NW Russian Federation
188 A7 **Pecica** Ger. Petschka, Hung. Ópécska. Arad, W Romania 46°09′N 21°06′E
70 C5 **Pecos** Texas, SW USA 31°25′N 103°30′W
60 E7 **Pecos River** New Mexico/Texas, SW USA
183 F13 **Pécs** Ger. Fünfkirchen, Lat. Sopianae. Baranya, SW Hungary 46°05′N 18°11′E
89 K10 **Pedasí** Los Santos, S Panama 07°36′N 80°04′W
Pedde see Pedja
277 J10 **Pedder, Lake** Tasmania, SE Australia
118 D2 **Pedegua** Valparaíso, Chile 32°23′S 71°06′W
91 H6 **Pedernales** SW Dominican Republic 18°02′N 71°41′W
86 D6 **Pedernales** Michoacán de Ocampo, Mexico 19°08′N 101°28′W
103 I3 **Pedernales** Delta Amacuro, NE Venezuela 09°58′N 62°15′W
70 G6 **Pedernales River** Texas, SW USA
112 B5 **Pedernales, Salar de** salt lake N Chile
110 A7 **Pederneiras** São Paulo, Brazil 22°23′S 48°46′W
Pedhoulas see Pedoulás
103 M6 **Pédima** var. Malavate. SW French Guiana 03°15′N 54°08′W
276 E1 **Pedirka** South Australia 26°41′S 135°11′E
260 G3 **Pediwang** Pulau Halmahera, E Indonesia 01°29′N 127°57′E
190 F4 **Pedja** var. Pedja Jõgi, Ger. Pedde. E Estonia
Pedja Jõgi see Pedja
218 B2 **Pedoulás** var. Pedhoulas. W Cyprus 34°58′N 32°51′E
111 J4 **Pedra Bonita** Minas Gerais, Brazil 20°30′S 42°24′E
109 F9 **Pedra Azul** Minas Gerais, NE Brazil 16°02′S 41°17′W
111 J4 **Pedra do Anta** Minas Gerais, Brazil 20°36′S 42°43′W
110 F3 **Pedra do Indaià** Minas Gerais, Brazil 20°15′S 45°13′W
111 J4 **Pedra Dourada** Minas Gerais, Brazil 20°49′S 42°10′W
170 D2 **Pedrafita, Porto de** var. Puerto de Piedrafita. pass NW Spain
132 B9 **Pedra Lume** Sal, NE Cape Verde 16°47′N 22°54′W
110 E7 **Pedralva** Minas Gerais, Brazil 22°14′S 45°28′W
115 L4 **Pedras Altas** Rio Grande do Sul, Brazil 31°44′S 53°35′W
89 I9 **Pedregal** Chiriquí, W Panama 09°04′N 79°25′W
102 E2 **Pedregal** Falcón, N Venezuela 11°04′N 70°08′W
110 B3 **Pedregulho** São Paulo, Brazil 20°16′S 47°29′W
115 L5 **Pedreiras** Rio Grande do Sul, Brazil 32°02′S 53°03′W
110 C8 **Pedreiras** São Paulo, Brazil 22°43′S 46°55′W
85 J7 **Pedriceña** Durango, C Mexico 25°08′N 103°46′W
110 B2 **Pedrinópolis** Minas Gerais, Brazil 19°13′S 47°28′W
116 F6 **Pedro Luro** Buenos Aires, Argentina 39°36′S 63°00′E
172 G7 **Pedro Abad** Andalucía, Spain 37°58′N 4°27′W
110 C10 **Pedro Barros** São Paulo, Brazil 24°15′S 47°22′W
113 L4 **Pedro Barros** São Paulo, S Brazil 24°12′S 47°22′W
83 I7 **Pedro Bay** Alaska, USA 59°47′N 154°06′W
112 B3 **Pedro de Valdivia** var. Oficina Pedro de Valdivia. Antofagasta, N Chile 22°33′S 69°38′W
111 I7 **Pedro do Rio** Rio de Janeiro, Brazil 22°20′S 43°08′W
172 C6 **Pedrógão** Beja, Portugal 38°07′N 7°39′W
172 D3 **Pedrógão** Castelo Branco, Portugal 40°05′N 7°14′W
114 B1 **Pedro Gómez Cello** Santa Fe, Argentina 30°02′S 60°18′W
113 H3 **Pedro Juan Caballero** Amambay, E Paraguay 22°34′S 55°41′W
111 H2 **Pedro Leopoldo** Minas Gerais, Brazil 19°38′S 44°03′W
170 G6 **Pedro Muñoz** Castilla-La Mancha, C Spain 39°25′N 02°56′W
235 G9 **Pedro, Point** headland NW Sri Lanka 09°54′N 80°08′E
111 H6 **Pedro Teixeira** Minas Gerais, Brazil 21°43′S 43°44′W
118 F5 **Pedro Vargas** Mendoza, Argentina 34°37′S 68°28′W
277 H5 **Peebinga** South Australia 34°56′S 140°56′E
159 I4 **Peebles** SE Scotland, UK 55°40′N 03°15′W
73 H12 **Peebles** Ohio, N USA 38°57′N 83°23′W
156 F7 **Peebles** cultural region SE Scotland, UK
65 H5 **Peekskill** New York, NE USA 41°17′N 73°54′W
158 G8 **Peel** W Isle of Man 54°13′N 04°04′W
52 A7 **Peel** Northwest Territories/Yukon Territory, NW Canada
52 E5 **Peel Point** headland Victoria Island, Northwest Territories, NW Canada 73°22′N 114°33′W
53 H6 **Peel Sound** passage Nunavut, N Canada
178 H4 **Peene** NE Germany
163 G9 **Peer** Limburg, NE Belgium 51°08′N 05°29′E
62 D4 **Pefferlaw** Ontario, S Canada 44°18′N 79°11′W
172 D2 **Pega** Guarda, Portugal 40°26′N 7°09′W
278 F9 **Pegasus Bay** bay South Island, New Zealand
218 A2 **Pégeia** var. Peyia. SW Cyprus 34°52′N 32°24′E
177 K4 **Peggau** Steiermark, SE Austria 47°10′N 15°20′E
179 G10 **Pegnitz** Bayern, SE Germany 49°45′N 11°33′E
179 G11 **Pegnitz** SE Germany
171 J6 **Pego** País Valenciano, E Spain 38°51′N 00°08′W
172 B5 **Pegões Velhos** Setúbal, Portugal 38°41′N 8°40′W
256 C6 **Pegu** var. Bago. Pegu, SW Myanmar (Burma) 17°18′N 96°31′E
256 C6 **Pegu** ◆ division S Myanmar (Burma)
261 J3 **Pegun, Pulau** island Kepulauan Mapia, E Indonesia
161 N7 **Pegwell Bay** bay UK
283 J2 **Pehleng** Pohnpei, E Micronesia
133 I6 **Péhonko** C Benin 10°14′N 01°57′E
116 F5 **Pehuajó** Buenos Aires, E Argentina 35°48′S 61°53′W
116 F5 **Pehuajó** Buenos Aires, Argentina 35°54′S 61°42′E
245 K7 **Peicheng** China 34°28′N 117°58′E
Pei-ching see Beijing/Beijing Shi
180 I6 **Peine** Niedersachsen, C Germany 52°19′N 10°14′E
Pei-p'ing see Beijing/Beijing Shi
Peipsi Järv/Peipus-See see Peipus, Lake
190 F4 **Peipus, Lake** Est. Peipsi Järv, Ger. Peipus-See, Rus. Chudskoye Ozero. Estonia/Russian Federation
169 N5 **Peéra-Cava** Provence-Alpes-Côte d'Azur, France 43°56′N 7°22′E
187 H6 **Peiraías** prev. Piraiévs, Eng. Piraeus. Attikí, C Greece 37°57′N 23°42′E
113 J3 **Peixe, Rio do** S Brazil
245 J7 **Peixian** Jiangsu, China 34°26′N 116°34′E
107 J7 **Peixoto de Azevedo** Mato Grosso, W Brazil 10°18′S 55°03′W
258 G5 **Pejantan, Pulau** island W Indonesia
Pejë see Peć
256 G5 **Pèk** var. Xieng Khouang; prev. Xiangkhoang. Xiangkhoang, N Laos 19°19′N 103°23′E
185 H4 **Pek** E Serbia
259 H8 **Pekalongan** Jawa, C Indonesia 06°54′S 109°37′E
258 D4 **Pekanbaru** var. Pakanbaru. Sumatera, W Indonesia 0°31′N 101°27′E
73 C10 **Pekin** Illinois, N USA 40°34′N 89°38′W
Peking see Beijing/Beijing Shi
Pelabohan Kelang/Pelabuhan Kelang see Pelabuhan Klang
258 D3 **Pelabuhan Klang** var. Kuala Pelabohan Kelang, Pelabohan Kelang, Pelabuhan Kelang, Port Klang, Port Swettenham. Selangor, Peninsular Malaysia 02°57′N 101°24′E
259 F8 **Pelabuhan Ratu, Teluk** bay Jawa, SW Indonesia
175 E14 **Pelagie, Isole** island group SW Italy
Pelagosa see Palagruža
68 E2 **Pelahatchie** Mississippi, S USA 32°19′N 89°48′W
258 J7 **Pelaihari** var. Pleihari. Borneo, C Indonesia 03°48′S 114°45′E
169 M4 **Pelat, Mont** ▲ SE France 44°16′N 06°46′E
188 B8 **Peleaga, Vârful** prev. Vîrful Peleaga. ▲ W Romania 45°23′N 22°52′E
Peleaga, Vîrful see Peleaga, Vârful
193 I7 **Peleduy** Respublika Sakha (Yakutiya), NE Russian Federation 59°39′N 112°36′E
62 A7 **Pelee Island** island Ontario, S Canada
91 M1 **Pelée, Montagne** ▲ N Martinique 14°47′N 61°10′W
62 B7 **Pelee, Point** headland Ontario, S Canada 41°56′N 82°30′W
260 E4 **Pelei** Pulau Peleng, N Indonesia 01°26′S 123°27′E
Peleliu see Beliliou
260 E4 **Peleng, Pulau** island Kepulauan Banggai, N Indonesia
260 E4 **Peleng, Selat** strait Sulawesi, C Indonesia
69 J3 **Pelham** Georgia, SE USA 31°07′N 84°09′W
183 C9 **Pelhřimov** Ger. Pilgram. Vysočina, C Czech Republic 49°26′N 15°14′E
83 L7 **Pelican** Chichagof Island, Alaska, USA 57°52′N 136°05′W
285 N2 **Pelican Lagoon** Kiritimati, E Kiribati
74 H2 **Pelican Lake** Minnesota, N USA
74 G3 **Pelican Lake** Minnesota, N USA
72 C5 **Pelican Lake** Wisconsin, N USA
54 F7 **Pelican Mountains** ▲▲ Alberta, W Canada
90 E1 **Pelican Point** Grand Bahama Island, N Bahamas 26°39′N 78°09′W
140 A2 **Pelican Point** headland W Namibia 22°55′S 14°25′E
74 F3 **Pelican Rapids** Minnesota, N USA 46°34′N 96°04′W
Pelican State see Louisiana
57 N3 **Pelikan Narrows** Saskatchewan, C Canada 55°11′N 102°51′W
187 J5 **Pelinaío** ▲ Chíos, E Greece 38°31′N 26°01′E
Pelinnaeum see Pelinnaío
186 F4 **Pelinnaío** anc. Pelinnaeum. ruins Thessalía, C Greece
184 G8 **Pelister** ▲ SW FYR Macedonia 41°00′N 21°12′E
184 D6 **Pelješac** peninsula S Croatia
152 H5 **Pelkosenniemi** Lappi, NE Finland 67°06′N 27°30′E
180 D7 **Pelkum** Nordrhein-Westfalen, Germany 7°44′N 51°38′E
140 D6 **Pella** Northern Cape, South Africa 29°02′S 19°09′E
74 H7 **Pella** Iowa, C USA 41°24′N 92°55′W
186 G3 **Pélla** site of ancient city Kentrikí Makedonía, N Greece
66 E8 **Pell City** Alabama, S USA 33°35′N 86°17′W
116 F5 **Pellegrini** Buenos Aires, Argentina 36°24′S 61°06′E
118 G10 **Pellegrini, Lago** Río Negro, Argentina
152 G5 **Pello** Lappi, NW Finland 66°47′N 24°E
178 D3 **Pellworm** island N Germany
54 B2 **Pelly** Yukon Territory, NW Canada
53 I8 **Pelly Bay** Nunavut, N Canada 68°38′N 89°45′W
54 B2 **Pelly Crossing** Yukon Territory, NW Canada
54 B3 **Pelly Mountains** ▲▲ Yukon Territory, W Canada
52 G7 **Pelly Point** headland Nunavut, NW Canada
Pélmonostor see Beli Manastir
79 K8 **Pelona Mountain** ▲ New Mexico, SW USA 33°40′N 108°06′W
Peloponnese/Peloponnesus see Pelopónnisos
186 G7 **Pelopónnisos** Eng. Peloponnese. ◆ region S Greece
186 G7 **Pelopónnisos** var. Morea, Eng. Peloponnese; anc. Peloponnesus. peninsula S Greece
175 G12 **Peloritani, Monti** anc. Pelorus and Neptunius. ▲▲ Sicilia, Italy, C Mediterranean Sea
175 G12 **Peloro, Capo** var. Punta del Faro. headland S Italy 38°15′N 15°39′E
Pelorus and Neptunius see Peloritani, Monti
115 M4 **Pelotas** Rio Grande do Sul, S Brazil 31°45′S 52°20′W
113 J6 **Pelotas, Rio** S Brazil
152 G4 **Peltovuoma** Lapp. Bealdovuopmi. Lappi, N Finland 68°23′N 24°12′E
169 J2 **Pélussin** Rhône-Alpes, France 45°25′N 4°41′E
196 M7 **Pelym** Sverdlovskaya oblast', Russian federation
196 M8 **Pelym** Sverdlovskaya oblast', Russian federation
195 M7 **Pelym** C Russian Federation
63 K3 **Pemadumcook Lake** Maine, NE USA
259 H8 **Pemalang** Jawa, C Indonesia 06°53′S 109°07′E
258 H4 **Pemangkat** var. Pamangkat. Borneo, C Indonesia 01°11′N 109°00′E
Pemar see Paimio
258 C3 **Pematangsiantar** Sumatera, W Indonesia 02°59′N 99°01′E
137 F13 **Pemba** prev. Port Amelia, Porto Amélia. Cabo Delgado, NE Mozambique 13°S 40°35′E
137 F10 **Pemba** ◆ region E Tanzania
137 F10 **Pemba** island E Tanzania
137 F13 **Pemba, Baia de** inlet NE Mozambique
137 E10 **Pemba Channel** channel E Tanzania
274 D8 **Pemberton** Western Australia 34°27′S 116°09′E
56 D8 **Pemberton** British Columbia, SW Canada 50°19′N 122°49′W
74 E1 **Pembina** North Dakota, N USA 48°58′N 97°14′W
74 E1 **Pembina** Canada/USA

◆ Country
● Country Capital
◇ Dependent Territory
○ Dependent Territory Capital
◆ Administrative Regions
International Airport
▲ Mountain
▲▲ Mountain Range
Volcano
River
Lake
Reservoir

Pembre - Pickering
INDEX
390

261 L8 **Pembre** Papua, E Indonesia 07°49′S 138°01′E
160 E6 **Pembrey** UK 51°41′N 4°17′W
160 G4 **Pembridge** UK 52°13′N 2°54′W
62 E3 **Pembroke** Ontario, SE Canada 45°49′N 77°08′W
160 D6 **Pembroke** SW Wales, UK 51°41′N 04°55′W
69 L2 **Pembroke** Georgia, SE USA 32°09′N 81°35′W
67 K7 **Pembroke** North Carolina, SE USA 34°40′N 79°12′W
67 I4 **Pembroke** Virginia, NE USA 37°19′N 80°38′W
157 E11 **Pembroke** *cultural region* SW Wales, UK
55 L3 **Pembroke, Cape** *headland* Nunavut, NE Canada
160 D6 **Pembroke Dock** UK 51°42′N 4°57′W
Pembuang, Sungai *see* Seruyan, Sungai
161 L7 **Pembury** UK 51°08′N 0°19′E
89 K9 **Peña Blanca, Cerro** ▲ C Panama 08°39′N 80°39′W
172 E2 **Peña de Francia, Sierra de** ▲▲ Castilla y León, Spain
170 E4 **Peña de Francia, Sierra de la** ▲▲ W Spain
172 C1 **Penafiel** *var.* Peñafiel. Porto, N Portugal 41°12′N 08°17′W
170 G3 **Peñafiel** Castilla-León, N Spain 41°36′N 04°07′W
Peñafiel *see* Penafiel
172 F7 **Peñaflor** Andalucía, Spain 37°43′N 5°21′W
171 I5 **Peñagolosa** ▲ E Spain 40°10′N 00°15′W
173 L3 **Peñagolosa** ▲ Valenciana, Spain 40°13′N 0°21′W
170 G4 **Peñalara, Pico de** ▲ C Spain 40°52′N 03°55′W
173 H2 **Peñalara** ▲ Spain 40°51′N 3°57′W
160 D6 **Penally** UK 51°40′N 4°44′W
172 D3 **Penamacor** Castelo Branco, Portugal 40°10′N 7°10′W
258 K3 **Penambo, Banjaran** *var.* Banjaran Tama Abu, Penambo Range. ▲▲ Indonesia/Malaysia
Penambo Range *see* Penambo, Banjaran
85 L8 **Peña Nevada, Cerro** ▲ C Mexico 23°46′N 99°52′W
Penang *see* George Town
Penang *see* Pinang
Penang *see* Pinang, Pulau, Peninsular Malaysia
113 K3 **Penápolis** São Paulo, S Brazil 21°23′S 50°02′W
170 F4 **Peñaranda de Bracamonte** Castilla-León, N Spain 40°54′N 05°13′W
171 I5 **Peñarroya** ▲ E Spain 40°24′N 00°42′W
170 F7 **Peñarroya-Pueblonuevo** Andalucía, S Spain 38°21′N 05°18′W
160 G6 **Penarth** S Wales, UK 51°27′N 03°11′W
170 E1 **Peñas, Cabo de** *cape* N Spain
173 J5 **Peñascosa** Castilla-La Manacha, Spain 38°40′N 2°24′W
117 A10 **Penas, Golfo de** *gulf* S Chile
160 E5 **Pencader** UK 52°0′N 4°16′W
Pen-ch'i *see* Benxi
160 F6 **Pencoed** UK 51°31′N 3°30′W
134 D4 **Pendé** *var.* Logone Oriental. ≈ Central African Republic/Chad
132 C6 **Pendembu** E Sierra Leone 09°06′N 12°12′W
74 E7 **Pender** Nebraska, C USA 42°06′N 96°42′W
Penderma *see* Bandırma
160 E5 **Pendine** UK 51°45′N 4°34′W
76 E5 **Pendleton** Oregon, NW USA 45°40′N 118°47′W
76 F3 **Pend Oreille, Lake** ◎ Idaho, NW USA
76 F3 **Pend Oreille River** ≈ Idaho/Washington, NW USA
Pendzhikent *see* Panjakent
172 D1 **Penedono** Viseu, Portugal 40°59′N 7°24′W
172 C7 **Penedos** Beja, Portugal 37°29′N 7°48′W
Peneius *see* Pineiós
172 B3 **Penela** Coimbra, N Portugal 40°02′N 08°23′W
62 C4 **Penetanguishene** Ontario, S Canada 44°45′N 79°55′W
242 C2 **Peng'an** Sichuan, China 31°01′N 106°14′E
234 F4 **Penganga** ≈ C India
243 N6 **P'engchia Yu** *island* N Taiwan
135 H9 **Penge** Kasai Oriental, C Dem. Rep. Congo 05°29′S 24°38′E
141 K3 **Penge** Limpopo, South Africa 24°22′S 30°18′E
Penghu Archipelago/P'enghu Ch'üntao/Penghu Islands *see* P'enghu Liehtao
243 M8 **P'enghu Liehtao** *var.* P'enghu Ch'üntao, Penghu Islands, *Eng.* Penghu Archipelago, Pescadores, *Jap.* Hoko-guntō, Hoko-shotō. *island group* W Taiwan
Penghu Shuidao/P'enghu Shuitao *see* Pescadores Channel
243 H3 **Pengjiachang** China 30°16′N 113°31′E
245 M4 **Penglai** *var.* Dengzhou. Shandong, E China 37°50′N 120°45′E
Peng-pu *see* Bengbu
242 A2 **Pengshan** China 30°14′N 103°53′E
243 H3 **Pengshi** China 30°27′N 113°11′E
242 D3 **Pengshui** Chongqing Shi, China 29°11′N 108°06′E
244 D6 **Pengyang** Ningxia, China 35°30′N 106°23′E
243 J3 **Pengze** Jiangxi, China 29°32′N 116°20′E
242 A2 **Pengzhou** Sichuan, China 30°35′N 103°34′E
141 I8 **Penhoekpas** *pass* Eastern Cape, South Africa
Penhsihu *see* Benxi
Penibético, Sistema *see* Béticos, Sistemas
172 A4 **Peniche** Leiria, W Portugal 39°21′N 09°23′W
159 I3 **Penicuik** UK 55°49′N 3°14′W
259 K9 **Penida, Nusa** *island* S Indonesia
172 C7 **Penilhos** Beja, Portugal 37°39′N 7°51′W
Peninsular State *see* Florida
171 J5 **Peñíscola** País Valenciano, E Spain 40°22′N 00°24′E
159 K9 **Penistone** UK 53°31′N 1°37′W
86 D5 **Pénjamo** Guanajuato, C Mexico 20°26′N 101°44′W
Penki *see* Benxi
160 F2 **Penmachno** UK 53°02′N 3°48′W
160 E2 **Penmaen-mawr** UK 53°16′N 3°56′W
164 D4 **Penmarch, Pointe de** *headland* NW France 47°46′N 04°34′W
175 G8 **Penna, Punta della** *headland* C Italy 42°10′N 14°43′E
175 F8 **Penne** Abruzzo, C Italy 42°28′N 13°57′E
168 F4 **Penne-d'Agenais** Aquitaine, France 44°23′N 0°49′E
Penner *see* Penneru
234 F7 **Penneru** *var.* Penner. ≈ C India
276 G6 **Penneshaw** South Australia 35°45′S 137°57′E
62 C8 **Penn Hills** Pennsylvania, NE USA 40°28′N 79°53′W
Penninae, Alpes/Pennine, Alpi *see* Pennine Alps
176 D6 **Pennine Alps** *Fr.* Alpes Pennines, *It.* Alpi Pennine, *Lat.* Alpes Penninae. ▲▲ Italy/Switzerland
Pennine Chain *see* Pennines
157 G9 **Pennines** *var.* Pennine Chain. ▲▲ N England, UK
Pennines, Alpes *see* Pennine Alps
66 G5 **Pennington Gap** Virginia, NE USA 36°45′N 83°01′W
64 F8 **Penns Grove** New Jersey, NE USA 39°42′N 75°27′W
64 F8 **Pennsville** New Jersey, NE USA 39°37′N 75°29′W
64 D6 **Pennsylvania** *off.* Commonwealth of Pennsylvania, *also known as* Keystone State. ◐ *state* NE USA
64 D2 **Penn Yan** New York, NE USA 42°39′N 77°02′W
52 G4 **Penny Strait** *sea waterway* Nunavut, N Canada
194 D10 **Peno** Tverskaya Oblast', W Russian Federation 56°55′N 32°44′E
63 K4 **Penobscot Bay** *bay* Maine, NE USA
63 K3 **Penobscot River** ≈ Maine, NE USA
277 H7 **Penola** South Australia 37°24′S 140°50′E
85 J7 **Peñón Blanco** Durango, C Mexico 25°12′N 100°50′W
276 E4 **Penong** South Australia 31°57′S 133°01′E
89 K9 **Penonomé** Coclé, C Panama 08°29′N 80°22′W
159 H5 **Penpont** UK 55°14′N 3°49′W
285 H5 **Penrhyn** *atoll* N Cook Islands
286 G6 **Penrhyn Basin** *undersea feature* C Pacific Ocean
160 E2 **Penrhyndeudreath** UK 52°56′N 4°04′W
277 L5 **Penrith** New South Wales, SE Australia 33°45′S 150°48′E
159 I6 **Penrith** NW England, UK 54°40′N 02°44′W
159 I6 **Penruddock** UK 54°38′N 2°53′W
160 D9 **Penryn** UK 50°10′N 5°06′W
68 G4 **Pensacola** Florida, SE USA 30°25′N 87°13′W
68 G4 **Pensacola Bay** *bay* Florida, SE USA
293 H4 **Pensacola Mountains** ▲▲ Antarctica
277 H7 **Penshurst** Victoria, SE Australia 37°54′S 142°19′E
161 L7 **Penshurst** UK 51°10′N 0°10′E
281 M3 **Pentecost** *Fr.* Pentecôte. *island* C Vanuatu
Pentecôte *see* Pentecost
56 F8 **Penticton** British Columbia, SW Canada 49°29′N 119°38′W
156 F3 **Pentland Firth** *strait* N Scotland, UK
159 H4 **Pentland Hills** *hill range* S Scotland, UK
160 E2 **Pentraeth** UK 53°16′N 4°13′W
260 F5 **Penu** Pulau Taliabu, E Indonesia 01°43′S 125°09′E
118 C3 **Peñuelas** Valparaíso, Chile 33°09′S 71°34′W
118 C3 **Penuelas, Embalse** ◎ Valparaíso, Chile
234 E7 **Penukonda** Andhra Pradesh, E India 14°04′N 77°38′E
256 C6 **Penwegon** Pegu, C Myanmar (Burma) 18°14′N 96°34′E
70 D5 **Penwell** Texas, SW USA 31°45′N 102°32′W
157 F11 **Pen y Fan** ▲ SE Wales, UK 51°52′N 03°25′W
159 J8 **Pen-y-ghent** ▲ N England, UK 54°11′N 02°15′W
260 G6 **Penyu, Kepulauan** *island group* E Indonesia
197 I3 **Penza** Penzenskaya Oblast', W Russian Federation 53°11′N 45°E
160 C10 **Penzance** SW England, UK 50°08′N 05°33′W
197 H3 **Penzenskaya Oblast'** ◐ *province* W Russian Federation
193 M4 **Penzhina** ≈ E Russian Federation
193 M5 **Penzhinskaya Guba** *bay* E Russian Federation
Penzig *see* Pieńsk
79 H8 **Peoria** Arizona, SW USA 33°34′N 112°14′W
73 C10 **Peoria** Illinois, N USA 40°42′N 89°35′W
73 C10 **Peoria Heights** Illinois, N USA 40°45′N 89°34′W
73 D9 **Peotone** Illinois, N USA 41°19′N 87°47′W
64 G3 **Pepacton Reservoir** ⊠ New York, NE USA
132 C7 **Pepel** W Sierra Leone 08°39′N 13°04′W
74 H5 **Pepin, Lake** ⊠ Minnesota/Wisconsin, N USA
163 G11 **Pepinster** Liège, E Belgium 50°34′N 05°49′E
184 F8 **Peqin** *var.* Peqini. Elbasan, C Albania 41°03′N 19°46′E
Peqini *see* Peqin
84 D6 **Pequeña, Punta** *headland* W Mexico 26°13′N 112°34′W
110 G2 **Pequi** Minas Gerais, Brazil 19°38′S 44°40′W
258 F6 **Perabumulih** *var.* Prabumulih. Sumatera, W Indonesia 03°27′S 104°15′E
258 D2 **Perak** ◐ *state* Peninsular Malaysia
258 D3 **Perak, Sungai** ≈ Peninsular Malaysia
172 F6 **Peraleda de Zaucejo** Extremadura, Spain 38°28′N 5°34′W
171 I4 **Perales del Alfambra** Aragón, NE Spain 40°38′N 01°00′W
168 B8 **Peralta** Navarra, Spain 42°20′N 1°48′W
115 H5 **Peralta** Uruguay 32°29′S 56°21′W
186 F4 **Pérama** *var.* Perama. Ípeiros, W Greece 39°42′N 20°51′E
Perama *see* Pérama
152 I6 **Perä-Posio** Lappi, NE Finland 66°10′N 27°56′E
59 J7 **Percé** Québec, SE Canada 48°32′N 64°14′W
164 G3 **Perche, Collines de** ▲▲ N France
177 L2 **Perchtoldsdorf** Niederösterreich, NE Austria 48°06′N 16°16′E
274 F4 **Percival Lakes** *lakes* Western Australia
166 D5 **Percy** Basse-Normandie, France 48°55′N 1°11′W
140 F9 **Perdepoort** *pass* Western Cape, South Africa
114 E7 **Perdices** Entre Ríos, Argentina 33°18′S 58°44′W
168 E7 **Perdido, Mont** ▲ Aragón, Spain 42°40′N 0°04′E
168 D7 **Perdido, Monte** ▲ NE Spain 42°41′N 00°01′E
68 G4 **Perdido River** ≈ Alabama/Florida, S USA
110 F3 **Perdigão** Minas Gerais, Brazil 19°57′S 45°04′W
110 C2 **Perdizes** Minas Gerais, Brazil 19°38′S 47°18′W
110 F5 **Perdões** Minas Gerais, Brazil 21°05′S 45°05′W
Perece Vela Basin *see* West Mariana Basin
188 B5 **Perechyn** Zakarpats'ka Oblast', W Ukraine 48°45′N 22°28′E
172 E1 **Peredo da Bemposta** Bragança, Portugal 41°16′N 6°33′W
102 B5 **Pereira** Risaralda, W Colombia 04°47′N 75°46′W
113 J2 **Pereira Barreto** São Paulo, S Brazil 20°37′S 51°07′W
110 B8 **Pereiras** São Paulo, Brazil 23°07′S 47°58′W
107 I6 **Pereirinha** Pará, N Brazil 08°18′S 57°30′W
172 C8 **Pereiro** Faro, Portugal 37°07′N 7°48′W
172 C7 **Pereiro** Faro, Portugal 37°27′N 7°36′W
172 D2 **Pereiro** Guarda, Portugal 40°44′N 7°01′W
197 H6 **Perelazovskiy** Volgogradskaya Oblast', SW Russian Federation 49°10′N 42°30′E
197 J4 **Perelyub** Saratovskaya Oblast', W Russian Federation 51°52′N 50°19′E
72 F7 **Pere Marquette River** ≈ Michigan, N USA
Peremyshl *see* Przemyśl
188 D4 **Peremyshlyany** L'vivs'ka Oblast', W Ukraine 49°42′N 24°33′E
Pereshchepino *see* Pereshchepyne
189 K4 **Pereshchepyne** *Rus.* Pereshchepino. Dnipropetrovs'ka Oblast', E Ukraine 48°59′N 35°22′E
194 F10 **Pereslavl'-Zalesskiy** Yaroslavskaya Oblast', W Russian Federation 56°42′N 38°45′E
189 M5 **Pereval's'k** Luhans'ka Oblast', E Ukraine 48°28′N 38°54′E
197 L4 **Perevolotskiy** Orenburgskaya Oblast', W Russian Federation 51°54′N 54°05′E
193 L8 **Pereyaslavka** Khabarovskiy Kray, SE Russian Federation 47°49′N 134°56′E
Pereyaslav-Khmel'nitskiy *see* Pereyaslav-Khmel'nyts'kyy
189 H3 **Pereyaslav-Khmel'nyts'kyy** *Rus.* Pereyaslav-Khmel'nitskiy. Kyyivs'ka Oblast', N Ukraine 50°05′N 31°28′E
114 C8 **Pérez Millàn** Buenos Aires, Argentina 33°46′S 60°06′W
177 J2 **Perg** Oberösterreich, N Austria 48°15′N 14°38′E
114 B8 **Pergamino** Buenos Aires, E Argentina 33°56′S 60°38′W
176 G6 **Pergine Valsugana** *Ger.* Persen. Trentino-Alto Adige, N Italy 46°04′N 11°13′E
74 F3 **Perham** Minnesota, N USA 46°35′N 95°34′W
153 H8 **Perho** Länsi-Soumi, W Finland 63°15′N 24°25′E
188 A7 **Periam** *Ger.* Perjamosch, *Hung.* Perjámos. Timiş, W Romania 46°02′N 20°54′E
59 H7 **Péribonca** ≈ Québec, SE Canada
84 G7 **Pericos** Sinaloa, C Mexico 25°03′N 107°42′W
258 H4 **Perigi** Borneo, C Indonesia
164 G7 **Périgueux** *anc.* Vesuna. Dordogne, SW France 45°12′N 00°41′E
102 D3 **Perijá, Serranía de** ▲▲ Columbia/Venezuela
111 J1 **Periquito** Minas Gerais, Brazil 19°10′S 42°15′W
187 I5 **Peristéra** *island* Vóreioi Sporádes, Greece, Aegean Sea
117 C10 **Perito Moreno** Santa Cruz, Argentina 46°42′S 71°00′E
235 E9 **Periyāl** *var.* Periyār. ≈ SW India
Periyār *see* Periyāl
235 E9 **Periyār Lake** ◎ S India
Perjámos/Perjamosch *see* Periam
64 F7 **Perkasie** Pennsylvania, USA 40°22′N 75°18′W
75 E12 **Perkins** Oklahoma, C USA 35°58′N 97°01′W
188 E5 **Perkivtsi** Chernivets'ka Oblast', W Ukraine 48°28′N 26°48′E
89 L9 **Perlas, Archipiélago de las** *Eng.* Pearl Islands. *island group* SE Panama
89 I6 **Perlas, Cayos de** *reef* SE Nicaragua
89 H6 **Perlas, Laguna de** *Eng.* Pearl Lagoon. *lagoon* E Nicaragua
89 H6 **Perlas, Punta de** *headland* E Nicaragua 12°22′N 83°30′W
178 G6 **Perleberg** Brandenburg, N Germany 53°04′N 11°52′E
Perlepe *see* Prilep
258 D2 **Perlis** ◐ *state* Peninsular Malaysia
195 K9 **Perm'** *prev.* Molotov. Permskaya Oblast', NW Russian Federation 58°01′N 56°10′E
184 F9 **Përmet** *var.* Përmeti, Prëmet. Gjirokastër, S Albania 40°12′N 20°24′E
Përmeti *see* Përmet
195 K9 **Permskaya Oblast'** ◐ *province* NW Russian Federation
108 H6 **Pernambuco** *off.* Estado de Pernambuco. ◐ *state* E Brazil
Pernambuco *see* Recife
Pernambuco Abyssal Plain *see* Pernambuco Plain
Pernambuco, Estado de *see* Pernambuco
95 N4 **Pernambuco Plain** *var.* Pernambuco Abyssal Plain. *undersea feature* E Atlantic Ocean
291 F8 **Pernambuco Seamounts** *undersea feature* C Atlantic Ocean
276 F4 **Pernatty Lagoon** *salt lake* South Australia
Pernau *see* Pärnu
Pernauer Bucht *see* Pärnu Laht
Pērnava *see* Pärnu
185 I6 **Pernik** *prev.* Dimitrovo. Pernik, W Bulgaria 42°36′N 23°02′E
153 H10 **Perniö** *Swe.* Bjärnå. Länsi-Soumi, SW Finland 60°13′N 23°10′E
177 L2 **Pernitz** Niederösterreich, E Austria 47°54′N 15°58′E
Pernov *see* Pärnu
172 C6 **Peroguarda** Beja, Portugal 38°05′N 8°03′W
165 I2 **Péronne** Somme, N France 49°56′N 02°57′E
176 C7 **Perosa Argentina** Piemonte, NE Italy 45°02′N 07°10′E
86 G6 **Perote** Veracruz-Llave, E Mexico 19°32′N 97°16′W
169 K1 **Pérouges** Rhône-Alpes, France 45°54′N 5°11′E
Pérouse *see* Perugia
118 B1 **Pérouse, Bahía de la** *bay* Easter Island, Chile, E Pacific Ocean
165 I9 **Perpignan** Pyrénées-Orientales, S France 42°41′N 02°53′E
118 C7 **Perquilauquén** Bío-Bío, Chile 36°16′S 71°47′W
118 C7 **Perquilauquen, Río** ≈ Chile
160 D9 **Perranporth** UK 50°21′N 5°09′W
184 G8 **Përrenjas** *var.* Përrenjasi, Prenjas, Prenjasi. Elbasan, E Albania 41°04′N 20°34′E
Përrenjasi *see* Përrenjas
152 B5 **Perriertoppen** ▲ C Svalbard 79°10′N 17°01′E
70 G4 **Perrin** Texas, SW USA 32°59′N 98°03′W
69 N9 **Perrine** Florida, SE USA 25°36′N 80°21′W
81 E11 **Perris** California, USA 33°47′N 117°14′W
79 L7 **Perro, Laguna del** ◎ New Mexico, SW USA
164 E3 **Perros-Guirec** Côtes d'Armor, NW France 48°49′N 03°28′W
69 K4 **Perry** Florida, SE USA 30°07′N 83°34′W
69 J2 **Perry** Georgia, SE USA 32°27′N 83°43′W
64 B1 **Perry** New York, NE USA 42°43′N 78°00′W
75 E11 **Perry** Oklahoma, C USA 36°17′N 97°18′W
75 F9 **Perry Lake** ⊠ Kansas, C USA
73 H9 **Perrysburg** Ohio, N USA 41°33′N 83°37′W
70 E1 **Perryton** Texas, SW USA 36°23′N 100°48′W
83 H9 **Perryville** Alaska, USA 55°55′N 159°08′W
75 H12 **Perryville** Arkansas, C USA 35°00′N 92°48′W
75 J10 **Perryville** Missouri, C USA 37°43′N 89°51′W
Persante *see* Parsęta
Persen *see* Pergine Valsugana
Pershay *see* Pyarshai
161 H4 **Pershore** UK 52°07′N 2°04′W
189 L5 **Pershotravens'k** Dnipropetrovs'ka Oblast', E Ukraine 48°19′N 36°22′E
189 L6 **Pershotravneve** Donets'ka Oblast', E Ukraine 47°03′N 37°20′E
Persia *see* Iran
221 I3 **Persian Gulf** *var.* The Gulf, *Ar.* Khalīj al 'Arabī, *Per.* Khalīj-e Fars. *Gulf* SW Asia *see also* Gulf, The
Persis *see* Fārs
155 F12 **Perstorp** Skåne, S Sweden 56°08′N 13°23′E
215 H6 **Pertek** Tunceli, C Turkey 38°53′N 39°19′E
277 J9 **Perth** Tasmania, SE Australia 41°39′S 147°11′E
274 D7 **Perth** *state capital* Western Australia 31°58′S 115°49′E
62 F4 **Perth** Ontario, SE Canada 44°54′N 76°15′W
159 H2 **Perth** C Scotland, UK 56°24′N 03°28′W
156 F6 **Perth** *cultural region* C Scotland, UK
274 D7 **Perth** ✈ Western Australia 31°51′S 116°06′E
65 H6 **Perth Amboy** New Jersey, USA 40°30′N 74°16′W
289 I10 **Perth Basin** *undersea feature* SE Indian Ocean
165 J8 **Pertuis** Vaucluse, SE France 43°42′N 05°30′E
175 B8 **Pertusato, Capo** *headland* Corse, France, C Mediterranean Sea 41°22′N 09°10′E
73 C9 **Peru** Illinois, N USA 41°18′N 89°09′W
73 F10 **Peru** Indiana, N USA 40°45′N 86°04′W
104 E5 **Peru** *off.* Republic of Peru. ◆ *republic* W South America
Peru *see* Beru
287 K7 **Peru Basin** *undersea feature* E Pacific Ocean
287 L6 **Peru-Chile Trench** *undersea feature* E Pacific Ocean
184 C5 **Perućko Jezero** ◎ S Croatia
177 H10 **Perugia** *Fr.* Pérouse; *anc.* Perusia. Umbria, C Italy 43°06′N 12°24′E
Perugia, Lake of *see* Trasimeno, Lago
112 G7 **Perugorría** Corrientes, NE Argentina 29°21′S 58°35′W
116 H1 **Perugorría** Corrientes, Argentina 29°30′S 58°54′E
110 C10 **Peruíbe** São Paulo, S Brazil 24°18′S 47°01′W
235 B8 **Perumalpār** *reef* India, N Indian Ocean
Peru, Republic of *see* Peru
Perusia *see* Perugia
163 C11 **Péruwelz** Hainaut, SW Belgium 50°30′N 03°35′E
215 J7 **Pervari** Siirt, SE Turkey 37°55′N 42°32′E
166 E6 **Pervenchéres** Basse-Normandie, France 48°26′N 0°25′E
197 H2 **Pervomaysk** Nizhegorodskaya Oblast', W Russian Federation 54°52′N 43°49′E
189 M5 **Pervomays'k** Luhans'ka Oblast', E Ukraine 48°38′N 38°36′E
189 H6 **Pervomays'k** *prev.* Ol'viopol'. Mykolayivs'ka Oblast', S Ukraine 48°02′N 30°51′E
189 J8 **Pervomays'ke** Respublika Krym, S Ukraine 45°43′N 33°49′E
197 L4 **Pervomayskiy** Orenburgskaya Oblast', W Russian Federation 51°32′N 54°58′E
196 G3 **Pervomayskiy** Tambovskaya Oblast', W Russian Federation 53°15′N 40°20′E
189 L4 **Pervomays'kyy** Kharkivs'ka Oblast', E Ukraine 49°24′N 36°12′E
195 L9 **Pervoural'sk** Sverdlovskaya Oblast', C Russian Federation 56°58′N 59°50′E
193 N6 **Pervyy Kuril'skiy Proliv** *strait* E Russian Federation
163 E11 **Perwez** Walloon Brabant, C Belgium 50°39′N 04°49′E
177 I9 **Pesaro** *anc.* Pisaurum. Marche, C Italy 43°55′N 12°53′E
80 A3 **Pescadero** California, W USA 37°15′N 122°23′W
Pescadores *see* P'enghu Liehtao
243 M9 **Pescadores Channel** *var.* Penghu Shuidao, P'enghu Shuitao. *channel* W Taiwan
175 G8 **Pescara** *anc.* Aternum, Ostia Aterni. Abruzzo, C Italy 42°28′N 14°13′E
175 F8 **Pescara** ≈ C Italy
176 G9 **Pescia** Toscana, C Italy 43°54′N 10°41′E
176 C4 **Peseux** Neuchâtel, W Switzerland 46°59′N 06°53′E
195 I4 **Pesha** ≈ NW Russian Federation
231 I4 **Peshāwar** North-West Frontier Province, N Pakistan 34°01′N 71°33′E
231 I4 **Peshāwar** ✈ North-West Frontier Province, N Pakistan 34°01′N 71°40′E
184 F7 **Peshkopi** *var.* Peshkopia, Peshkopija. Dibër, NE Albania 41°40′N 20°25′E
Peshkopia/Peshkopija *see* Peshkopi
185 J7 **Peshtera** Pazardzhik, C Bulgaria 42°02′N 24°18′E
72 E5 **Peshtigo** Wisconsin, N USA 45°04′N 87°43′W
72 D5 **Peshtigo River** ≈ Wisconsin, N USA
Peski *see* Pyeski
195 J9 **Peskovka** Kirovskaya Oblast', NW Russian Federation 59°04′N 52°17′E
165 J5 **Pesmes** Haute-Saône, E France 47°17′N 05°33′E
172 C1 **Peso da Régua** *var.* Pêso da Regua. Vila Real, N Portugal 41°10′N 07°47′W
84 E3 **Pesqueira** Sonora, NW Mexico 29°22′N 110°58′W
164 F7 **Pessac** Gironde, SW France 44°46′N 00°42′W
172 B7 **Pessegueiro, Ilha do** *island* Setúbal, Portugal
183 G11 **Pest** *off.* Pest Megye. ◐ *county* C Hungary
Pest Megye *see* Pest
194 E9 **Pestovo** Novgorodskaya Oblast', W Russian Federation 58°37′N 35°48′E
86 D8 **Petacalco, Bahía** *bay* Guerrero, Mexico
Petach-Tikva *see* Petah Tiqwa
216 B6 **Petah Tiqwa** *var.* Petach-Tikva, Petah Tiqva, Petakh Tikva. Tel Aviv, C Israel 32°05′N 34°53′E
153 H8 **Petäjävesi** Länsi-Soumi, C Finland 62°17′N 25°10′E
Petakh Tikva/Petah Tiqva *see* Petah Tiqwa
68 F3 **Petal** Mississippi, S USA 31°21′N 89°15′W
187 I6 **Petalioí** *island* C Greece
187 I6 **Petalión, Kólpos** *gulf* E Greece
187 I6 **Pétalo** ▲ Ándros, Kykládes, Greece, Aegean Sea 37°51′N 24°50′E
80 B2 **Petaluma** California, W USA 38°15′N 122°37′W
163 H14 **Pétange** Luxembourg, SW Luxembourg 49°33′N 05°53′E
102 G2 **Petare** Miranda, N Venezuela 10°31′N 66°50′W
86 D8 **Petatlán** Guerrero, S Mexico 17°31′N 101°16′W
139 H1 **Petauke** Eastern, E Zambia 14°12′S 31°16′E
62 E2 **Petawawa** Ontario, SE Canada 45°54′N 77°18′W
62 E2 **Petawawa** ≈ Ontario, SE Canada
87 M6 **Petcacab** Quintana Roo, Mexico 19°16′N 88°12′W
Petchaburi *see* Phetchaburi
88 D2 **Petén** *off.* Departamento del Petén. ◐ *department* N Guatemala
Petén, Departamento del *see* Petén
88 C2 **Petén Itzá, Lago** *var.* Lago de Flores. ◎ N Guatemala
72 C6 **Petenwell Lake** ⊠ Wisconsin, N USA
72 H2 **Peterbell** Ontario, S Canada 48°34′N 83°19′W
276 G4 **Peterborough** South Australia 32°59′S 138°51′E
62 E4 **Peterborough** Ontario, SE Canada 44°19′N 78°20′W
161 K3 **Peterborough** *prev.* Medeshamstede. E England, UK 52°35′N 00°15′W
65 K1 **Peterborough** New Hampshire, NE USA 42°51′N 71°54′W
156 G5 **Peterhead** NE Scotland, UK 57°30′N 01°46′W
Peterhof *see* Luboń
287 J10 **Peter I Island** ◇ *Norwegian dependency* Antarctica
292 E5 **Peter I Island** *var.* Peter I øy. *island* Antarctica
Peter I øy *see* Peter I Island
55 J3 **Peter Lake** ◎ Nunavut, C Canada
159 K6 **Peterlee** N England, UK 54°45′N 01°18′W
Peterlingen *see* Payerne
295 K6 **Petermann Bjerg** ▲ C Greenland 73°16′N 27°59′W
57 K2 **Peter Pond Lake** ◎ Saskatchewan, C Canada
181 H9 **Petersberg** Hessen, Germany 9°44′N 50°52′E
141 H8 **Petersburg** Eastern Cape, South Africa 32°18′S 24°58′E
83 M7 **Petersburg** Mytkof Island, Alaska, USA 56°43′N 132°51′W
73 C10 **Petersburg** Illinois, N USA 40°01′N 89°52′W
73 E12 **Petersburg** Indiana, N USA 38°30′N 87°16′W
74 E2 **Petersburg** North Dakota, N USA 47°59′N 97°59′W
70 E3 **Petersburg** Texas, SW USA 33°52′N 101°36′W
67 L4 **Petersburg** Virginia, NE USA 37°14′N 77°24′W
67 J3 **Petersburg** West Virginia, NE USA 39°01′N 79°09′W
161 J7 **Petersfield** UK 51°00′N 0°56′W
180 F6 **Petershagen** Nordrhein-Westfalen, NW Germany 52°22′N 08°58′E
103 J5 **Peters Mine** *var.* Peter's Mine. N Guyana 06°13′N 59°18′W
161 M7 **Petham** UK 51°13′N 1°03′E
175 I11 **Petilia Policastro** Calabria, SW Italy 39°07′N 16°48′E
91 H6 **Pétionville** S Haiti 18°29′N 72°16′W
91 J2 **Petit-Bourg** Basse Terre, C Guadeloupe 16°12′N 61°36′W
91 J2 **Petit Cul-de-Sac Marin** *bay* C Guadeloupe
58 G4 **Petite Rivière de la Baleine** ≈ Québec, NE Canada
91 H5 **Petite-Rivière-de-l'Artibonite** C Haiti 19°10′N 72°30′W
137 G11 **Petite Rivière Noire, Piton de la** ▲ C Mauritius
63 J1 **Petite-Rivière-St-François** Québec, SE Canada 47°18′N 70°34′W
90 G6 **Petit-Goâve** S Haiti 18°27′N 72°51′W
Petitjean *see* Sidi-Kacem
63 L4 **Petit Manan Point** *headland* Maine, NE USA 44°23′N 67°54′W
Petit Mécatina, Rivière du *see* Little Mecatina
54 D5 **Petitot** ≈ Alberta/British Columbia, W Canada
91 J3 **Petit Piton** ▲ SW Saint Lucia 13°49′N 61°03′W
Petit-Popo *see* Aného
Petit St-Bernard, Col du *see* Little Saint Bernard Pass
59 I4 **Petitsikapau Lake** ◎ Newfoundland and Labrador, E Canada
152 H5 **Petkula** Lappi, N Finland 67°41′N 26°44′E
86 G7 **Petlalcingo** Puebla, Mexico 18°05′N 97°54′W
87 M5 **Peto** Yucatán, SE Mexico 20°09′N 88°55′W
118 D2 **Petorca** Valparaíso, C Chile 31°16′S 70°59′W
116 B3 **Petorca** Valparaíso, Chile 32°18′S 71°00′E
72 G5 **Petoskey** Michigan, N USA 45°51′N 88°03′W
216 B8 **Petra** *archaeological site* Ma'ān, W Jordan
Petra *see* Wādī Mūsā
186 G3 **Pétras, Sténa** *pass* N Greece
248 F3 **Petra Velikogo, Zaliv** *bay* SE Russian Federation
Petrel *see* Petrer
62 E5 **Petre, Point** *headland* Ontario, SE Canada 43°49′N 77°07′W
171 I7 **Petrer** *var.* Petrel. País Valenciano, E Spain 38°28′N 00°46′W
195 K7 **Petretsovo** Permskaya Oblast', NW Russian Federation 61°22′N 57°21′E
185 I8 **Petrich** Blagoevegrad, SW Bulgaria 41°25′N 23°12′E
280 A7 **Petrie, Récif** *reef* N New Caledonia
79 J7 **Petrified Forest** *prehistoric site* Arizona, SW USA
Petrikau *see* Piotrków Trybunalski
Petrikov *see* Pyetrykaw
188 C8 **Petrila** *Hung.* Petrilla. Hunedoara, W Romania 45°27′N 23°25′E
Petrilla *see* Petrila
184 C2 **Petrinja** Sisak-Moslavina, C Croatia 45°27′N 16°14′E
Petroaleksandrovsk *see* To'rtkok'l
160 E8 **Petrockstow** UK 50°52′N 4°07′W
Petrőcz *see* Bački Petrovac
194 D8 **Petrodvorets** *Fin.* Pietarhovi. Leningradskaya Oblast', NW Russian Federation 59°53′N 29°52′E
Petrograd *see* Sankt-Peterburg
Petrokov *see* Piotrków Trybunalski
102 D4 **Petrólea** Norte de Santander, NE Colombia 08°30′N 72°35′W
62 B5 **Petrolia** Ontario, S Canada 42°54′N 82°07′W
70 G3 **Petrolia** Texas, SW USA 34°00′N 98°13′W
108 G6 **Petrolina** Pernambuco, E Brazil 09°22′S 40°30′W
91 I8 **Petrona, Punta** *headland* C Puerto Rico 17°57′N 66°23′W
Petropavl *see* Petropavlovsk
189 L5 **Petropavlivka** Dnipropetrovs'ka Oblast', E Ukraine 48°28′N 36°28′E
227 H1 **Petropavlovsk** *Kaz.* Petropavl. Severnyy Kazakhstan, N Kazakhstan 54°47′N 69°06′E
193 N6 **Petropavlovsk-Kamchatskiy** Kamchatskaya Oblast', E Russian Federation 53°03′N 158°43′E
111 I7 **Petrópolis** Rio de Janeiro, SE Brazil 22°30′S 43°28′W
188 C8 **Petroşani** *var.* Petroşeni, *Ger.* Petroschen, *Hung.* Petrozsény. Hunedoara, W Romania 45°25′N 23°22′E
Petroschen/Petroşeni *see* Petroşani
Petroskoi *see* Petrozavodsk
184 G4 **Petrovac** Serbia, E Serbia and Montenegro 44°22′N 21°25′E
Petrovac *see* Bosanski Petrovac
184 E7 **Petrovac na Moru** S Montenegro 42°11′N 19°00′E
Petrovac/Petrovácz *see* Bački Petrovac
189 J5 **Petrove** Kirovohrads'ka Oblast', C Ukraine 48°22′N 33°12′E
185 H7 **Petrovec** C FYR Macedonia 41°57′N 21°37′E
Petrovgrad *see* Zrenjanin
197 I4 **Petrovsk** Saratovskaya Oblast', W Russian Federation 52°20′N 45°23′E
194 E6 **Petrovskiy Yam** Respublika Kareliya, NW Russian Federation 63°19′N 35°14′E
Petrovsk-Port *see* Makhachkala
193 I8 **Petrovsk-Zabaykal'skiy** Chitinskaya Oblast', S Russian Federation 51°15′N 108°36′E
197 I5 **Petrov Val** Volgogradskaya Oblast', SW Russian Federation 50°10′N 45°16′E
194 E7 **Petrozavodsk** *Fin.* Petroskoi. Respublika Kareliya, NW Russian Federation 61°46′N 34°19′E
Petrozsény *see* Petroşani
141 H6 **Petrusburg** Free State, South Africa 29°07′S 25°25′E
140 C2 **Petrusdal** Hardap, C Namibia 23°42′S 17°23′E
141 J5 **Petrus Steyn** Free State, South Africa 27°39′S 28°08′E
140 G7 **Petrusville** Northern Cape, South Africa 30°05′S 24°39′E
189 K5 **Petrykivka** Dnipropetrovs'ka Oblast', E Ukraine 48°44′N 34°42′E
Petsamo *see* Pechenga
Petschka *see* Pecica
Pettau *see* Ptuj
177 J2 **Pettenbach** Oberösterreich, C Austria 47°58′N 14°03′E
158 B7 **Pettigoe** Ireland 54°33′N 7°50′W
70 G8 **Pettus** Texas, SW USA 28°34′N 97°49′W
192 E7 **Petukhovo** Kurganskaya Oblast', C Russian Federation 55°04′N 67°49′E
161 J7 **Petworth** UK 50°59′N 0°36′W
177 J2 **Peuerbach** Oberösterreich, N Austria 48°19′N 13°45′E
116 B4 **Peumo** Libertador, C Chile 34°20′S 71°12′W
258 B2 **Peusangan, Krueng** ≈ Sumatera, NW Indonesia
193 L3 **Pevek** Chukotskiy Avtonomnyy Okrug, NE Russian Federation 69°41′N 170°19′E
66 B3 **Pevely** Missouri, C USA 38°16′N 90°24′W
Peyia *see* Pégeia
114 B7 **Peyrano** Santa Fe, Argentina 33°32′S 60°48′W
168 G1 **Peyrat-le-Château** Limousin, France 45°49′N 1°46′E
164 F8 **Peyrehorade** Landes, SW France 43°33′N 01°05′W
169 H4 **Peyreleau** Midi-Pyrénées, France 44°11′N 3°13′E
169 H6 **Peyriac-de-Mer** Languedoc-Roussillon, France 43°05′N 2°58′E
169 K5 **Peyrolles-en-Provence** Provence-Alpes-Côte d'Azur, France 43°39′N 5°35′E
169 L4 **Peyruis** Provence-Alpes-Côte d'Azur, France 44°02′N 5°56′E
195 I5 **Peza** ≈ NW Russian Federation
165 I8 **Pézenas** Hérault, S France 43°28′N 03°25′E
174 I2 **Pezinok** *Ger.* Bösing, *Hung.* Bazin. Bratislavský Kraj, W Slovakia 48°17′N 17°15′E
179 G12 **Pfaffenhofen an der Ilm** Bayern, SE Germany 48°31′N 11°30′E
181 D13 **Pfälzer Wald** *hill range* W Germany
179 H12 **Pfarrkirchen** Bayern, SE Germany 48°25′N 12°56′E
181 F14 **Pforzheim** Baden-Württemberg, SW Germany 48°53′N 08°42′E
179 D13 **Pfullendorf** Baden-Württemberg, S Germany 47°55′N 09°16′E
179 F14 **Pfunds** Tirol, W Austria 46°56′N 10°30′E
181 F12 **Pfungstadt** Hessen, W Germany 49°48′N 08°36′E
141 L2 **Phalaborwa** Limpopo, South Africa 23°57′S 31°07′E
139 H5 **Phalaborwa** Limpopo, NE South Africa 23°59′S 31°04′E
232 C6 **Phalodi** Rājasthān, NW India 27°06′N 72°22′E
167 M5 **Phalsbourg** Lorraine, France 48°46′N 7°16′E
232 C6 **Phalsund** Rājasthān, NW India 26°22′N 71°56′E
234 D5 **Phaltan** Mahārāshtra, W India 18°01′N 74°31′E
256 E5 **Phan** *var.* Muang Phan. Chiang Rai, NW Thailand 19°34′N 99°44′E
256 E10 **Phangan, Ko** *island* SW Thailand
256 D10 **Phang-Nga** *var.* Pang-Nga, Phangnga. Phangnga, SW Thailand 08°29′N 98°31′E
Phangnga *see* Phang-Nga
Phan Rang/Phanrang *see* Phan Rang-Thap Cham
257 J9 **Phan Rang-Thap Cham** *var.* Phanrang, Phan Rang, Phan Rang Thap Cham. Ninh Thuân, S Vietnam 11°34′N 109°00′E
257 I9 **Phan Ri** Binh Thuân, S Vietnam 11°11′N 108°31′E
257 I9 **Phan Thiêt** Binh Thuân, S Vietnam 10°56′N 108°06′E
Pharnacia *see* Giresun
70 G10 **Pharr** Texas, SW USA 26°11′N 98°10′W
Pharus *see* Hvar
256 E11 **Phatthalung** *var.* Padalung, Patalung. Phatthalung, SW Thailand 07°38′N 100°04′E
256 E5 **Phayao** *var.* Muang Phayao. Phayao, NW Thailand 19°10′N 99°55′E
81 E10 **Phelan** California, USA 34°26′N 117°34′W
55 H5 **Phelps Lake** ◎ Saskatchewan, C Canada
67 M6 **Phelps Lake** ◎ North Carolina, SE USA
69 I2 **Phenix City** Alabama, S USA 32°28′N 85°00′W
257 H6 **Pheo** Quang Binh, C Vietnam 17°42′N 105°58′E
Phet Buri *see* Phetchaburi
256 E8 **Phetchaburi** *var.* Bejraburi, Petchaburi, Phet Buri. Phetchaburi, SW Thailand 13°05′N 99°58′E
256 E7 **Phichit** *var.* Bichitra, Muang Phichit, Pichit. Phichit, C Thailand 16°29′N 100°21′E
68 F1 **Philadelphia** Mississippi, S USA 32°45′N 89°06′W
62 F4 **Philadelphia** New York, NE USA 44°10′N 75°40′W
64 F8 **Philadelphia** Pennsylvania, NE USA 40°N 75°10′W
64 F8 **Philadelphia** ✈ Pennsylvania, NE USA 39°51′N 75°13′W
Philadelphia *see* 'Ammān
74 B5 **Philip** South Dakota, N USA 44°02′N 101°39′W
163 E12 **Philippeville** Namur, S Belgium 50°12′N 04°33′E
Philippeville *see* Skikda
67 J2 **Philippi** West Virginia, NE USA 39°08′N 80°03′W
Philippi *see* Fílippoi
293 M5 **Philippi Glacier** *glacier* Antarctica
286 C4 **Philippine Basin** *undersea feature* W Pacific Ocean
205 N7 **Philippine Plate** *tectonic feature*
263 K7 **Philippines** *off.* Republic of the Philippines. ◆ *republic* SE Asia
205 M8 **Philippines** *island group* W Pacific Ocean
263 M4 **Philippine Sea** *sea* W Pacific Ocean
Philippines, Republic of the *see* Philippines
286 C5 **Philippine Trench** *undersea feature* W Philippine Sea
141 H7 **Philippolis** Free State, South Africa 30°16′S 25°17′E
138 F8 **Philippolis** Free State, C South Africa 30°16′S 25°16′E
Philippopolis *see* Plovdiv
Philippopolis *see* Shahbā', Syria
181 E14 **Philippsburg** Baden-Württemberg, Germany 8°27′N 49°14′E
91 L6 **Philipsburg** Sint Maarten, N Netherlands Antilles 17°58′N 63°02′W
77 H5 **Philipsburg** Montana, NW USA 46°19′N 113°17′W
83 I3 **Philip Smith Mountains** ▲▲ Alaska, USA
140 G7 **Philipstown** Northern Cape, South Africa 30°26′S 24°28′E
231 K5 **Phillaur** Punjab, N India 31°02′N 75°50′E
277 I7 **Phillip Island** *island* Victoria, SE Australia
70 E2 **Phillips** Texas, SW USA 35°39′N 101°21′W
72 C5 **Phillips** Wisconsin, N USA 45°42′N 90°23′W
75 D9 **Phillipsburg** Kansas, C USA 39°45′N 99°19′W
64 F6 **Phillipsburg** New Jersey, NE USA 40°39′N 75°09′W
67 J5 **Philpott Lake** ⊠ Virginia, NE USA
Phintias *see* Licata
256 E6 **Phitsanulok** *var.* Bisnulok, Muang Phitsanulok, Pitsanulok. Phitsanulok, C Thailand 16°49′N 100°15′E
Phlórina *see* Flórina
Phnom Penh *see* Phnum Penh
257 H9 **Phnum Penh** *var.* Phnom Penh. ● (Cambodia) Phnum Penh, S Cambodia 11°35′N 104°55′E
257 H8 **Phnum Tbêng Meanchey** Preăh Vihéar, N Cambodia 13°45′N 104°58′E
79 H9 **Phoenix** *state capital* Arizona, SW USA 33°27′N 112°04′W
Phoenix Island *see* Rawaki
284 D3 **Phoenix Islands** *island group* C Kiribati
64 F7 **Phoenixville** Pennsylvania, NE USA 40°07′N 75°31′W
138 G8 **Phofung** *var.* Mont-aux-Sources. ▲ N Lesotho 28°47′S 28°52′E
256 F7 **Phon** Khon Kaen, E Thailand 15°47′N 102°35′E
141 L5 **Phongolo** ≈ South Africa
256 F4 **Phôngsali** *var.* Phong Saly. Phôngsali, N Laos 21°40′N 102°04′E
Phong Saly *see* Phôngsali
256 F6 **Phônhông** C Laos 18°29′N 102°26′E
256 G4 **Phô Rang** *var* Bao Yèn. Lao Cai, N Vietnam 22°12′N 104°27′E
Phort Láirge, Cuan *see* Waterford Harbour
256 D7 **Phra Chedi Sam Ong** Kanchanaburi, W Thailand 15°18′N 98°26′E
256 E6 **Phrae** *var.* Muang Phrae, Prae. Phrae, NW Thailand 18°07′N 100°09′E
Phra Nakhon Si Ayutthaya *see* Ayutthaya
256 D10 **Phra Thong, Ko** *island* SW Thailand
Phu Cŭơng *see* Thu Dâu Môt
256 D11 **Phuket** *var.* Bhuket, Puket, *Mal.* Ujung Salang; *prev.* Junkseylon, Salang. Phuket, SW Thailand 07°52′N 98°22′E
256 D11 **Phuket** ✈ Phuket, SW Thailand 08°03′N 98°16′E
256 D11 **Phuket, Ko** *island* SW Thailand
234 H4 **Phulabāni** *prev.* Phulbani. Orissa, E India 20°30′N 84°18′E
Phulbani *see* Phulabāni
257 I7 **Phu Lôc** Th,a Thiên-Huê, C Vietnam 16°13′N 107°53′E
257 H9 **Phumĭ Banam** Prey Vêng, S Cambodia 11°14′N 105°18′E
256 G9 **Phumĭ Chŏâm** Kâmpóng Spœ, SW Cambodia 11°42′N 103°58′E
257 H8 **Phumĭ Kalêng** Stœ̆ng Trêng, NE Cambodia 13°57′N 106°17′E
257 H8 **Phumĭ Kâmpóng Trâbêk** *prev.* Phum Kompong Trabek. Kâmpóng Thum, C Cambodia 13°06′N 105°16′E
256 G8 **Phumĭ Koŭk Kduŏch** Bătdâmbâng, NW Cambodia 13°16′N 103°08′E
257 I8 **Phumĭ Labăng** Rôtânôkiri, NE Cambodia 13°51′N 107°01′E
257 H8 **Phumĭ Mlu Prey** Preăh Vihéar, N Cambodia 13°48′N 105°16′E
256 G8 **Phumĭ Moŭng** Siĕmréab, NW Cambodia 13°45′N 103°35′E
256 G9 **Phumĭ Prâmaôy** Poŭthĭsăt, W Cambodia 12°13′N 103°05′E
256 G9 **Phumĭ Samĭt** Kaôh Kông, SW Cambodia 10°54′N 103°09′E
256 G8 **Phumĭ Sâmraông** *prev.* Phum Samrong. Siĕmréab, NW Cambodia 14°11′N 103°31′E
257 H8 **Phumĭ Siĕmbok** Stœ̆ng Trêng, N Cambodia 13°28′N 105°59′E
257 H8 **Phumĭ Thalabârĭvăt** Stœ̆ng Trêng, N Cambodia 13°34′N 105°57′E
256 G9 **Phumĭ Veal Renh** Kâmpôt, SW Cambodia 10°43′N 103°49′E
256 G9 **Phumĭ Yeay Sên** Kaôh Kông, SW Cambodia 11°09′N 103°09′E
Phum Kompong Trabek *see* Phumĭ Kâmpóng Trâbêk
Phum Samrong *see* Phumĭ Sâmraông
257 J8 **Phu My** Binh Đinh, C Vietnam 14°07′N 109°05′E
257 H10 **Phung Hiêp** Cân Thơ, S Vietnam 09°50′N 105°48′E
233 K6 **Phuntsholing** SW Bhutan 26°52′N 89°26′E
257 H10 **Phươc Long** Minh Hai, S Vietnam 09°27′N 105°25′E
256 G10 **Phu Quôc, Đao** *var.* Phu Quoc Island. *island* S Vietnam
Phu Quoc Island *see* Phu Quôc, Đao
141 J6 **Phuthaditjhaba** Free State, South Africa 28°32′S 28°49′E
257 H4 **Phu Tho** Vinh Phu, N Vietnam 21°23′N 105°13′E
Phu Vinh *see* Tra Vinh
282 E9 **Piaanu Pass** *passage* Chuuk Islands, C Micronesia
176 F7 **Piacenza** *Fr.* Paisance; *anc.* Placentia. Emilia-Romagna, N Italy 45°02′N 09°42′E
184 A6 **Pianella** Abruzzo, C Italy 42°23′N 14°04′E
175 H8 **Pianosa, Isola** *island* Archipelago Toscano, C Italy
261 I5 **Piar** Papua, E Indonesia 02°49′S 132°46′E
91 L7 **Piarco** *var.* Port of Spain. ✈ (Port-of-Spain) Trinidad, Trinidad and Tobago 10°36′N 61°21′W
172 C6 **Pias** Beja, Portugal 38°01′N 7°29′W
172 C5 **Pias** Évora, Portugal 38°33′N 7°29′W
182 H6 **Piaseczno** Mazowieckie, C Poland 52°03′N 21°00′E
188 D10 **Piatra** Teleorman, S Romania 43°49′N 25°10′E
188 E7 **Piatra-Neamţ** *Hung.* Karácsonkő. Neamţ, NE Romania 46°54′N 26°23′E
Piauhy *see* Piauí
108 F5 **Piauí** *off.* Estado do Piauí; *prev.* Piauhy. ◐ *state* E Brazil
Piauí, Estado do *see* Piauí
177 H6 **Piave** ≈ NE Italy
85 H8 **Piaxtla, Río** ≈ Sinaloa, Mexico
175 G13 **Piazza Armerina** *var.* Chiazza. Sicilia, Italy, C Mediterranean Sea 37°23′N 14°22′E
136 C5 **Pibor** *Amh.* Pībor Wenz. ≈ Ethiopia/Sudan
136 B5 **Pibor Post** Jonglei, SE Sudan 06°50′N 33°06′E
Pībor Wenz *see* Pibor
Pibrans *see* Příbram
79 H7 **Picacho Butte** ▲ Arizona, SW USA 35°12′N 112°44′W
60 C8 **Picachos, Cerro** ▲ NW Mexico 29°15′N 114°04′W
165 I2 **Picardie** *Eng.* Picardy. ◐ *region* N France
Picardy *see* Picardie
68 E4 **Picayune** Mississippi, S USA 30°31′N 89°40′W
Piccolo San Bernardo, Colle di *see* Little Saint Bernard Pass
PicdeBälaitous *see* Balaïtous
87 L6 **Pich** Campeche, Mexico 19°31′N 90°05′W
118 C6 **Pichamán** Maule, Chile 35°26′S 72°07′W
112 D4 **Pichanal** Salta, N Argentina 23°18′S 64°10′W
229 I7 **Pichandar** W Tajikistan 38°44′N 68°51′E
86 D6 **Pichàtaro** Michoacán de Ocampo, Mexico 19°34′N 101°48′W
180 J3 **Picher** Mecklenburg-Vorpommern, Germany 11°21′N 53°21′E
75 G11 **Picher** Oklahoma, C USA 36°59′N 94°49′W
118 C5 **Pichibudi** Maule, Chile 34°53′S 72°10′W
118 G3 **Pichi Ciego** Mendoza, Argentina 33°35′S 68°04′W
118 C1 **Pichidangui** Coquimbo, Chile 32°08′S 71°32′W
116 B4 **Pichilemu** Libertador, C Chile 34°25′S 72°00′W
84 E8 **Pichilingue** Baja California Sur, W Mexico 24°20′N 110°17′W
104 C1 **Pichincha** ◐ *province* N Ecuador
104 C1 **Pichincha** ▲ N Ecuador 0°12′S 78°39′W
Pichit *see* Phichit
87 J8 **Pichucalco** Chiapas, SE Mexico 17°32′N 93°07′W
68 E1 **Pickens** Mississippi, S USA 32°52′N 89°58′W
67 H7 **Pickens** South Carolina, SE USA 34°53′N 82°42′W
62 C2 **Pickerel** ≈ Ontario, S Canada
62 D5 **Pickering** Ontario, S Canada 43°50′N 79°03′W
159 L7 **Pickering** N England, UK 54°14′N 00°47′W

◆ Country
● Country Capital
◇ Dependent Territory
○ Dependent Territory Capital
◐ Administrative Regions
✈ International Airport
▲ Mountain
▲▲ Mountain Range
Volcano
≈ River
◎ Lake
⊠ Reservoir

◆ Country	◇ Dependent Territory	◈ Administrative Regions	▲ Mountain	▼ Volcano	⊛ Lake
● Country Capital	○ Dependent Territory Capital	✈ International Airport	▲ Mountain Range	♦ River	▫ Reservoir

◆ Country   ◇ Dependent Territory   ◆ Administrative Regions   ▲ Mountain   ⊗ Lake
● Country Capital   ○ Dependent Territory Capital   ✕ International Airport   ▲ Mountain Range   ✍ River   ⊠ Reservoir
   ○ Volcano

◆ Country   ◇ Dependent Territory   ◆ Administrative Regions   ▲ Mountain   ▲ Volcano   ◎ Lake
● Country Capital   ○ Dependent Territory Capital   ✈ International Airport   ▲ Mountain Range   ↗ River   ▣ Reservoir

◆ Country   ◇ Dependent Territory   ✕ Administrative Regions   ▲ Mountain   ⊙ Volcano   ○ Lake
● Country Capital   ○ Dependent Territory Capital   ✈ International Airport   ▲ Mountain Range   ✆ River   ☒ Reservoir

S

◆ Country
● Country Capital
◇ Dependent Territory
○ Dependent Territory Capital
◆ Administrative Regions
✕ International Airport
▲ Mountain
▲ Mountain Range
◇ Volcano
◇ River
◇ Lake
◇ Reservoir

◆ Country   ◇ Dependent Territory   ▲ Administrative Regions   ▲ Mountain   ⊙ Lake
● Country Capital   ○ Dependent Territory Capital   ✕ International Airport   ▲ Mountain Range   ⊿ River   ⊟ Reservoir   ◈ Volcano

◆ Country	◇ Dependent Territory	◆ Administrative Regions	▲ Mountain	◆ Volcano	◎ Lake
● Country Capital	○ Dependent Territory Capital	✈ International Airport	▲ Mountain Range	☒ River	☒ Reservoir

Sanok - São João da Madeira
INDEX
403

183 I9 **Sanok** Podkarpackie, SE Poland 49°31′N 22°14′E
102 B3 **San Onofre** Sucre, NW Colombia 09°45′N 75°33′W
112 C3 **San Pablo** Potosí, S Bolivia 21°43′S 66°38′W
263 K5 **San Pablo** *off.* San Pablo City. Luzon, N Philippines 14°04′N 121°16′E
San Pablo Balleza *see* Balleza
80 B2 **San Pablo Bay** *bay* California, W USA
San Pablo City *see* San Pablo
84 C5 **San Pablo, Punta** *headland* W Mexico 27°12′N 114°30′W
89 J9 **San Pablo, Río** ≈ C Panama
263 L6 **San Pascual** Burias Island, C Philippines 13°06′N 122°59′E
175 I13 **San Pawl il-Bahar** *Eng.* Saint Paul's Bay. E Malta 35°57′N 14°24′E
114 C8 **San Pedro** Buenos Aires, E Argentina 33°43′S 59°45′W
112 D4 **San Pedro** Jujuy, N Argentina 24°12′S 64°55′W
113 I5 **San Pedro** Misiones, NE Argentina 26°38′S 54°12′W
88 E1 **San Pedro** Corozal, NE Belize 17°58′N 87°55′W
118 C8 **San Pedro** Bío-Bío, Chile 36°56′S 72°19′W
132 E8 **San-Pédro** S Ivory Coast 04°45′N 06°37′W
84 E2 **San Pedro** Baja California Sur, W Mexico North America
84 F8 **San Pedro** Baja California Sur, Mexico 23°23′N 110°12′W
85 J6 **San Pedro** *var.* San Pedro de las Colonias. Coahuila de Zaragoza, NE Mexico 25°47′N 102°57′W
112 G4 **San Pedro** San Pedro, SE Paraguay 24°08′S 57°08′W
114 F9 **San Pedro** Colonia, Uruguay 34°21′S 57°51′W
113 H4 **San Pedro** *off.* Departamento de San Pedro. ⬖ *department* C Paraguay
90 E4 **San Pedro** ≈ C Cuba
132 F7 **San Pedro** ✈ (Yamoussoukro) C Ivory Coast 06°49′N 05°14′W
San Pedro *see* San Pedro del Pinatar
88 C3 **San Pedro Carchá** Alta Verapaz, C Guatemala 15°30′N 90°12′W
81 D11 **San Pedro Channel** *channel* California, W USA
112 B4 **San Pedro de Atacama** Antofagasta, N Chile 22°52′S 68°10′W
San Pedro de Durazno *see* Durazno
84 F4 **San Pedro de la Cueva** Sonora, NW Mexico 29°17′N 109°47′W
172 G2 **San Pedro del Arroyo** Castilla y León, Spain 40°48′N 4°51′W
San Pedro de las Colonias *see* San Pedro
85 I7 **San Pedro del Gallo** Durango, Mexico 25°33′N 104°18′W
104 C5 **San Pedro de Lloc** La Libertad, NW Peru 07°26′S 79°31′W
171 I7 **San Pedro del Pinatar** *var.* San Pedro. Murcia, SE Spain 37°50′N 00°47′W
91 I6 **San Pedro de Macorís** SE Dominican Republic 18°30′N 69°18′W
172 E5 **San Pedro de Mérida** Extremadura, Spain 38°57′N 6°11′W
San Pedro, Departamento de *see* San Pedro
86 E6 **San Pedro el Alto** Oaxaca, Mexico
86 E7 **San Pedro Limón** México, Mexico 18°35′N 100°19′W
168 B8 **San Pedro Manrique** Castilla y León, Spain 42°02′N 2°14′W
84 C2 **San Pedro Màrtir** Baja California, Mexico 30°45′N 115°16′W
84 B2 **San Pedro Mártir, Sierra** ▲▲ NW Mexico
San Pedro Pochutla *see* Pochutla
87 H8 **San Pedro Quiatoni** Oaxaca, Mexico 16°48′N 96°02′W
88 C2 **San Pedro, Río** ≈ Guatemala/Mexico
85 I8 **San Pedro, Río** ≈ C Mexico
170 E6 **San Pedro, Sierra de** ▲▲ W Spain
172 E4 **Sierra de San Pedro** ▲▲ Spain
88 E3 **San Pedro Sula** Cortés, NW Honduras 15°26′N 88°01′W
San Pedro Tapanatepec *see* Tapanatepec
105 H12 **San Pedro, Volcán** ⛰ N Chile 21°46′S 68°13′W
176 F6 **San Pellegrino Terme** Lombardia, N Italy 45°53′N 09°42′E
70 G10 **San Perlita** Texas, SW USA 26°30′N 97°38′W
San Pietro *see* Supetar
San Pietro del Carso *see* Pivka
175 A10 **San Pietro, Isola di** *island* W Italy
76 E3 **Sanpoil River** ≈ Washington, NW USA
253 C10 **Sanpoku** *var.* Sampoku. Niigata, Honshū, C Japan 38°32′N 139°33′E
84 B3 **San Quintín** Baja California, NW Mexico 30°28′N 115°58′W
60 B8 **San Quintín, Bahía de** *bay* NW Mexico
84 B3 **San Quintín, Bahía de** *bay* Baja California, Mexico
84 B2 **San Quintín, Cabo** *headland* NW Mexico 30°22′N 116°01′W
168 G8 **San Quírico de Besora** Cataluña, Spain 42°06′N 2°14′E
118 G5 **San Rafael** Mendoza, W Argentina 34°44′S 68°15′W
85 L7 **San Rafael** Nuevo León, NE Mexico 25°01′N 100°33′W
87 L5 **San Rafael** Yucatán, Mexico 20°42′N 90°09′W
80 B2 **San Rafael** California, W USA 37°58′N 122°31′W
79 K7 **San Rafael** New Mexico, SW USA 35°03′N 107°52′W
102 D2 **San Rafael** *var.* El Moján. Zulia, NW Venezuela 10°58′N 71°45′W
88 G5 **San Rafael del Norte** Jinotega, NW Nicaragua 13°12′N 86°06′W
88 G6 **San Rafael del Sur** Managua, SW Nicaragua 11°51′N 86°24′W
79 I4 **San Rafael Knob** ▲ Utah, W USA 38°46′N 110°45′W
81 C9 **San Rafael Mountains** ▲▲ California, W USA
89 H8 **San Ramón** Alajuela, C Costa Rica 10°04′N 84°31′W
84 E4 **San Ramon** Baja California, Mexico
87 M5 **San Ramón** Quintana Roo, Mexico 20°08′N 88°07′W
104 E7 **San Ramón** Junín, C Peru 11°08′S 75°18′W
115 H9 **San Ramón** Canelones, S Uruguay 34°18′S 55°55′W
80 B3 **San Ramon** California, USA 37°47′N 121°59′W
112 D4 **San Ramón de la Nueva Orán** Salta, N Argentina 23°08′S 64°20′W
106 G8 **San Ramón, Río** ≈ E Bolivia
176 D9 **San Remo** Liguria, NW Italy 43°48′N 07°47′E
114 A7 **San Ricardo** Santa Fe, Argentina 33°02′S 61°37′W
85 L7 **San Roberto** Nuevo León, Mexico
102 E2 **San Román, Cabo** *headland* NW Venezuela 12°10′N 70°01′W
112 G6 **San Roque** Corrientes, NE Argentina 28°35′S 58°45′W
283 I1 **San Roque** Saipan, S Northern Mariana Islands 15°15′S 145°47′E
170 E9 **San Roque** Andalucía, S Spain 36°13′N 05°23′W
70 G6 **San Saba** Texas, SW USA 31°13′N 98°44′W
70 F6 **San Saba River** ≈ Texas, SW USA
114 E4 **San Salvador** Entre Ríos, E Argentina 31°38′S 58°30′W
88 D5 **San Salvador** ● (El Salvador) San Salvador, SW El Salvador 13°42′N 89°12′W
85 M7 **San Salvador** Tamaulipas, Mexico 24°39′N 99°20′W
88 D4 **San Salvador** ⬖ *department* C El Salvador
61 N10 **San Salvador** *prev.* Watlings Island. *island* E Bahamas
88 D5 **San Salvador** ✈ La Paz, S El Salvador 13°27′N 89°04′W
112 D4 **San Salvador de Jujuy** *var.* Jujuy. Jujuy, N Argentina 24°10′S 65°20′W
88 D4 **San Salvador, Volcán de** ⛰ C El Salvador 13°58′N 89°14′W
133 H6 **Sansanné-Mango** *var.* Mango. N Togo 10°21′N 00°28′E
114 C10 **San Sebastiàn** Buenos Aires, Argentina 34°57′S 59°43′W
91 H8 **San Sebastián** W Puerto Rico 18°21′N 67°00′W
117 D13 **San Sebastián, Bahía** *bay* S Argentina
Sansenhō *see* Sach'ŏn
177 H9 **Sansepolcro** Toscana, C Italy 43°35′N 12°12′E
175 H8 **San Severo** Puglia, SE Italy 41°41′N 15°23′E
243 K2 **Sanshan** China 31°14′N 118°13′E
245 M3 **Sanshilipu** China 39°17′N 121°48′E
172 D7 **San Silvestre de Guzmàn** Andalucía, Spain 37°23′N 7°21′W
80 B6 **San Simeon** California, USA 35°39′N 121°11′W
85 K8 **San Simon** Mexico
184 C3 **Sanski Most** ⬖ Federacija Bosna I Hercegovina, NW Bosnia and Herzegovina
242 D6 **Sansui** Guizhou, China 26°35′N 108°25′E
261 J4 **Sansundi** Papua, E Indonesia 0°42′S 135°48′E
239 K2 **Sant** *var.* Mayhan. Övörhangay, C Mongolia 46°02′N 104°00′E
116 I1 **Santa Ana** Misiones, Argentina 27°12′S 55°24′E
114 F8 **Santa Catalina** Soriano, Uruguay 33°42′S 57°30′E
116 I3 **Santa Clara de Olimar** Treinta y tres, Uruguay 33°06′S 55°00′E
116 F2 **Santa Clara de Saguier** Santa Fe, Argentina 31°24′S 61°48′E
116 D5 **Santa Isabel** La Pampa, Argentina 36°12′S 66°54′E
110 D9 **Santa Izabel** Sao Paulo, Brazil 23°18′S 46°18′E
116 H1 **Santa Lucia** Corrientes, Argentina 29°06′S 59°00′E
116 H1 **Santa Rosa** Corrientes, Argentina 28°24′S 58°06′E
115 H9 **Santa Rosa** Canelones, Uruguay 34°30′S 56°06′E
69 H4 **Santa Rosa Island** *island* Florida, USA
116 G1 **Santa Sylvina** Chaco, Argentina 27°54′S 61°12′E
116 G3 **Santa Teresa** Santa Fe, Argentina 33°24′S 61°00′E
116 I5 **Santa Teresita** Buenos Aires, Argentina 36°30′S 56°54′E
110 A5 **Santa Adélia** São Paulo, Brazil 21°16′S 48°48′W
170 E6 **Santa Amalia** Extremadura, W Spain 39°00′N 06°01′W
113 H6 **Santa Ana** Misiones, NE Argentina 27°22′S 55°34′W
106 E8 **Santa Ana** Beni, N Bolivia 13°43′S 65°37′W
88 D4 **Santa Ana** Santa Ana, NW El Salvador 13°59′N 89°34′W
84 E4 **Santa Ana** Nuevo León, Mexico
85 L7 **Santa Ana** Nuevo León, Mexico 24°05′N 100°23′W
84 E3 **Santa Ana** Sonora, NW Mexico 30°31′N 111°08′W
81 D11 **Santa Ana** California, W USA 33°45′N 117°52′W
103 H3 **Santa Ana** Nueva Esparta, NE Venezuela 09°15′N 64°39′W
88 D4 **Santa Ana** ⬖ *department* NW El Salvador
Santa Ana de Coro *see* Coro
118 C6 **Santa Ana de Queri** Maule, Chile 35°38′S 71°32′W
88 D5 **Santa Ana, Volcán de** *var.* La Matepec. ⛰ W El Salvador 13°49′N 89°36′W
111 J3 **Santa Bàrbara** Minas Gerais, Brazil 19°58′S 42°09′W
111 I3 **Santa Bàrbara** Minas Gerais, Brazil 19°56′S 43°24′W
88 E4 **Santa Bárbara** Santa Bárbara, W Honduras 14°56′N 88°11′W
85 H6 **Santa Barbara** Chihuahua, N Mexico 26°46′N 105°46′W
81 B9 **Santa Barbara** California, W USA 34°24′N 119°40′W
102 F6 **Santa Bárbara** Amazonas, S Venezuela 03°55′N 67°06′W
102 D4 **Santa Bárbara** Barinas, W Venezuela 07°48′N 71°10′W
88 E4 **Santa Bárbara** ⬖ *department* NW Honduras
Santa Bárbara *see* Iscuandé
81 B9 **Santa Barbara Channel** *channel* California, W USA
172 D7 **Santa Bàrbara de Casa** Andalucía, Spain 37°48′N 7°11′W
111 H6 **Santa Bàrbara do Monte Verde** Minas Gerais, Brazil 21°58′S 43°42′W
111 H5 **Santa Barbara do Tigurio** Minas Gerais, Brazil 21°15′S 43°35′W
81 C11 **Santa Barbara Island** *island* Channel Islands, California, W USA
115 H7 **Santa Bernardina** Durazno, Uruguay 33°22′S 56°29′W
110 E9 **Santa Branca** São Paulo, Brazil 23°24′S 45°53′W
102 B2 **Santa Catalina** Bolívar, N Colombia 10°36′N 75°17′W
89 J9 **Santa Catalina** Bocas del Toro, W Panama 08°46′N 81°18′W
81 D12 **Santa Catalina, Gulf of** *gulf* California, W USA
84 E6 **Santa Catalina, Isla** *island* W Mexico
81 C11 **Santa Catalina Island** *island* Channel Islands, California, W USA
84 B3 **Santa Catarina** Baja California, Mexico 29°32′N 115°16′W
84 B2 **Santa Catarina** Baja California, Mexico 31°37′N 115°48′W
85 L6 **Santa Catarina** Nuevo León, NE Mexico 25°39′N 100°30′W
85 L9 **Santa Catarina** San Luis Potosí, Mexico 22°04′N 100°28′W
85 L9 **Santa Catarina** San Luis Potosí, Mexico
113 K5 **Santa Catarina** *off.* Estado de Santa Catarina. ⬖ *state* S Brazil
Santa Catarina de Tepehuanes *see* Tepehuanes
Santa Catarina, Estado de *see* Santa Catarina
113 K6 **Santa Catarina, Ilha de** *island* S Brazil
102 F2 **Santa Catherina** Curaçao, C Netherlands Antilles 12°07′N 68°46′W
87 N7 **Santa Cecilia** Quintana Roo, Mexico 18°14′N 87°50′W
168 D7 **Santa Cilia de Jaca** Aragón, Spain 42°34′N 0°43′W
172 B4 **Santa Cita** Santarém, Portugal 39°32′N 8°23′W
114 A4 **Santa Clara** Santa Fe, Argentina 31°46′S 61°19′W
118 B8 **Santa Clara** Bío-Bío, Chile 36°49′S 72°20′W
90 D4 **Santa Clara** Villa Clara, C Cuba 22°25′N 78°01′W
85 H4 **Santa Clara** Chihuahua, Mexico 29°17′N 107°01′W
85 J7 **Santa Clara** Durango, Mexico 24°29′N 103°21′W
80 B3 **Santa Clara** California, W USA 37°20′N 121°57′W
78 G5 **Santa Clara** Utah, W USA 37°07′N 113°39′W
Santa Clara *see* Santa Clara de Olimar
172 B7 **Santa Clara-a-Velha** Beja, Portugal 37°31′N 8°29′W
115 J6 **Santa Clara de Olimar** *var.* Santa Clara. Cerro Largo, NE Uruguay 32°50′S 54°54′W
112 E8 **Santa Clara de Saguier** Santa Fe, C Argentina 31°21′S 61°50′W
81 D10 **Santa Clarita** California, USA 34°24′N 118°33′W
114 D8 **Santa Coloma** Buenos Aires, Argentina 34°04′S 59°34′W
Santa Coloma *see* Santa Coloma de Gramanet
171 L3 **Santa Coloma de Farners** *var.* Santa Coloma de Farnés. Cataluña, NE Spain 41°52′N 02°39′E
Santa Coloma de Farnés *see* Santa Coloma de Farners
171 K3 **Santa Coloma de Gramanet** *var.* Santa Coloma. Cataluña, NE Spain 41°28′N 02°14′E
168 F9 **Santa Coloma de Queralt** Cataluña, Spain 41°32′N 1°23′E
170 C2 **Santa Comba** Galicia, NW Spain 43°02′N 08°49′W
Santa Comba *see* Uaco Cungo
170 C4 **Santa Comba Dão** Viseu, N Portugal 40°23′N 08°07′W
135 D10 **Santa Cruz** Uíge, NW Angola 06°56′S 16°25′E
112 E1 **Santa Cruz** *var.* Santa Cruz de la Sierra. Santa Cruz, C Bolivia 17°49′S 63°11′W
118 B7 **Santa Cruz** Bío-Bío, Chile 36°16′S 72°33′W
116 B4 **Santa Cruz** Libertador, C Chile 34°38′S 71°27′W
88 G8 **Santa Cruz** Guanacaste, W Costa Rica 10°15′N 85°35′W
90 E8 **Santa Cruz** W Jamaica 18°03′N 77°43′W
85 I9 **Santa Cruz** Nayarit, Mexico 22°27′N 105°02′W
84 F5 **Santa Cruz** Nayarit, W Mexico North America
86 B4 **Santa Cruz** Nayarit, Mexico 22°27′N 105°02′W
86 A4 **Santa Cruz** Nayarit, Mexico 21°59′N 105°35′W
85 I9 **Santa Cruz** Nayarit, Mexico 21°59′N 105°35′W
84 E2 **Santa Cruz** Sonora, Mexico 31°14′N 110°35′W
172 A4 **Santa Cruz** Lisboa, Portugal 39°08′N 9°23′W
170 A8 **Santa Cruz** Madeira, Portugal, NE Atlantic Ocean 32°43′N 16°47′W
172 B6 **Santa Cruz** Setúbal, Portugal 38°03′N 8°42′W
80 B4 **Santa Cruz** California, W USA 36°58′N 122°01′W
117 C11 **Santa Cruz** *off.* Provincia de Santa Cruz. ⬖ *province* S Argentina
106 G10 **Santa Cruz** ⬖ *department* E Bolivia
Santa Cruz *see* Viru-Viru
Santa Cruz Barillas *see* Barillas
109 H10 **Santa Cruz Cabrália** Bahia, E Brazil 16°17′S 39°03′W
110 C7 **Santa Cruz da Conceição** São Paulo, Brazil 22°09′S 47°27′W
Santa Cruz de El Seibo *see* El Seibo
170 A10 **Santa Cruz de la Palma** La Palma, Islas Canarias, Spain, NE Atlantic Ocean 28°41′N 17°46′W
Santa Cruz de la Sierra *see* Santa Cruz
173 I3 **Santa Cruz de la Zarza** Castilla-La Manacha, Spain 39°58′N 3°10′W
88 C3 **Santa Cruz del Quiché** Quiché, W Guatemala 15°02′N 91°06′W
170 F5 **Santa Cruz del Retamar** Castilla-La Mancha, C Spain 40°08′N 04°14′W
Santa Cruz del Seibo *see* El Seibo
90 E5 **Santa Cruz del Sur** Camagüey, C Cuba 20°44′N 78°00′W
173 K3 **Santa Cruz de Moya** Castilla-La Manacha, Spain 39°57′N 1°16′W
170 G7 **Santa Cruz de Mudela** Castilla-La Mancha, C Spain 38°37′N 03°27′W
172 G3 **Santa Cruz de Retamar** Castilla-La Manacha, Spain 40°07′N 4°14′W
170 A10 **Santa Cruz de Tenerife** Tenerife, Islas Canarias, Spain, NE Atlantic Ocean 28°28′N 16°15′W
170 B10 **Santa Cruz de Tenerife** ⬖ *province* Islas Canarias, Spain, NE Atlantic Ocean
113 K3 **Santa Cruz do Rio Pardo** São Paulo, S Brazil 22°52′S 49°37′W
115 M1 **Santa Cruz do Sul** Rio Grande do Sul, S Brazil 29°42′S 52°25′W
105 I9 **Santa Cruz, Isla** *var.* Indefatigable Island, Isla Chávez. *island* Galapagos Islands, Ecuador, E Pacific Ocean
84 E7 **Santa Cruz, Isla** *island* W Mexico
81 B9 **Santa Cruz Island** *island* California, W USA
281 I5 **Santa Cruz Islands** *island group* E Solomon Islands
Santa Cruz, Provincia de *see* Santa Cruz
117 C12 **Santa Cruz, Río** ≈ S Argentina
79 I9 **Santa Cruz River** ≈ Arizona, SW USA
86 G9 **Santa Cruz Zenzontepec** Oaxaca, Mexico 16°33′N 97°30′W
111 J1 **Santa Efigènia** Minas Gerais, Brazil 18°50′S 42°27′W
114 C3 **Santa Elena** Entre Ríos, E Argentina 30°58′S 59°47′W
88 D2 **Santa Elena** Cayo, W Belize 17°08′N 89°04′W
85 J5 **Santa Elena** Coahuila de Zaragoza, Mexico 27°51′N 103°58′W
70 G10 **Santa Elena** Texas, SW USA 26°43′N 98°30′W
104 B2 **Santa Elena, Bahía de** *bay* W Ecuador
103 I6 **Santa Elena de Uairén** Bolívar, E Venezuela 04°40′N 61°03′W
88 G7 **Santa Elena, Península** *peninsula* NW Costa Rica
104 A2 **Santa Elena, Punta** *headland* W Ecuador 02°11′S 81°00′W
110 A5 **Santa Ernestina** São Paulo, Brazil 21°27′S 48°23′W
170 F7 **Santa Eufemia** Andalucía, S Spain 38°36′N 04°54′W
175 H11 **Santa Eufemia, Golfo di** *gulf* S Italy
171 I3 **Santa Eulalia de Gállego** Aragón, NE Spain 42°16′N 00°46′W
171 K6 **Santa Eulalia del Río** Ibiza, Spain, W Mediterranean Sea 39°00′N 01°33′E
114 B4 **Santa Fe** Santa Fe, C Argentina 31°36′S 60°47′W
90 C4 **Santa Fé** *var.* La Fe. Isla de la Juventud, W Cuba 21°45′N 82°45′W
84 E8 **Santa Fe** Baja California Sur, Mexico 24°19′N 111°13′W
89 J9 **Santa Fé** Veraguas, C Panama 08°29′N 80°50′W
170 G8 **Santa Fe** Andalucía, S Spain 37°11′N 03°43′W
79 L6 **Santa Fe** *state capital* New Mexico, SW USA 35°41′N 105°56′W
114 A1 **Santa Fe** *off.* Provincia de Santa Fe. ⬖ *province* C Argentina
Santa Fe *see* Bogotá
Santa Fe de Bogotá *see* Bogotá
86 D6 **Santa Fe del Río** Michoacán de Ocampo, Mexico 20°12′N 101°50′W
113 J2 **Santa Fé do Sul** São Paulo, S Brazil 20°13′S 50°56′W
105 I9 **Santa Fe, Isla** *var.* Barrington Island. *island* Galapagos Islands, Ecuador, E Pacific Ocean
Santa Fe, Provincia de *see* Santa Fe
69 L4 **Santa Fe River** ≈ Florida, SE USA
108 D6 **Santa Filomena** Piauí, E Brazil 09°06′S 45°52′W
84 F8 **Santa Genoveva** ▲ W Mexico 23°07′N 109°56′W
110 B7 **Santa Gertrudes** São Paulo, Brazil 22°28′S 47°31′W
84 D4 **Santa Gertrudis** Baja California, Mexico 28°05′N 113°04′W
233 K7 **Santahar** Rajshahi, NW Bangladesh 24°45′N 89°03′E
113 I4 **Santa Helena** Paraná, S Brazil 24°53′S 54°19′W
242 B2 **Santai** Sichuan, China 31°04′N 105°02′E
102 E2 **Santa Inés** Lara, N Venezuela 10°37′N 69°18′W
117 B14 **Santa Inés, Isla** *island* S Chile
114 A8 **Santa Isabel** Santiago del Estero, Argentina 33°54′S 61°42′W
89 L8 **Santa Isabel** Colón, N Panama 09°31′N 79°12′W
280 I2 **Santa Isabel** *var.* Bughotu. *island* N Solomon Islands
Santa Isabel *see* Malabo
106 E1 **Santa Isabel do Rio Negro** Amazonas, NW Brazil 0°40′S 64°56′W
84 C3 **Sierra Santa Isabel** ▲▲ Baja California, Mexico
85 M8 **Santa Juana** Tamaulipas, Mexico 23°56′N 99°07′W
112 G7 **Santa Lucia** Corrientes, NE Argentina 28°58′S 59°05′W
110 B6 **Santa Lúcia** São Paulo, Brazil 21°41′S 48°06′W
118 D5 **Santa Lucía** Maule, Chile 35°04′S 71°11′W
105 G9 **Santa Lucía** Puno, S Peru 15°45′S 70°34′W
115 H9 **Santa Lucía** *var.* Santa Lucia. Canelones, S Uruguay 34°26′S 56°25′W
88 C4 **Santa Lucía Cotzumalguapa** Escuintla, SW Guatemala 14°20′N 91°00′W
85 J9 **Santa Lucía de la Sierra** Zacatecas, Mexico 22°28′N 104°13′W
80 A6 **Santa Lucia Range** ▲▲ California, W USA
111 H2 **Santa Luzia** Minas Gerais, Brazil 19°47′S 43°52′W
172 B7 **Santa Luzia** Beja, Portugal 37°44′N 8°24′W
111 J4 **Santa Margarida** Minas Gerais, Brazil 20°23′S 42°15′W
172 B3 **Santa Margarida** Leiria, Portugal 39°48′N 8°40′W
172 B6 **Santa Margarida da Serra** Setúbal, Portugal 38°07′N 8°36′W
80 B7 **Santa Margarita** California, USA 35°23′N 120°37′W
84 D7 **Santa Margarita, Isla** *island* W Mexico
112 D5 **Santa María** Catamarca, N Argentina 26°51′S 66°02′W
111 M3 **Santa Maria** Espírito Santo, Brazil 20°02′S 40°42′W
115 K1 **Santa Maria** Rio Grande do Sul, S Brazil 29°41′S 53°48′W
110 B7 **Santa Maria** São Paulo, Brazil 22°33′S 48°10′W
84 F5 **Santa María** Baja California, Mexico
81 B8 **Santa Maria** California, W USA 34°56′N 120°25′W
81 D10 **Santa Maria** California, USA 34°08′N 118°34′W
172 C10 **Santa Maria** *island* Azores, Portugal, NE Atlantic Ocean
Santa Maria *see* Gaua
118 A8 **Santa Maria, Isla** *island* Bío-Bío, Chile
86 G8 **Santa María Apasco** Oaxaca, Mexico 17°38′N 97°07′W
Santa María Asunción Tlaxiaco *see* Tlaxiaco
84 F7 **Santa María, Bahía** *bay* W Mexico
141 M4 **Santa Maria, Cabo de** *headland* S Mozambique 26°05′S 32°58′E
170 C8 **Santa Maria, Cabo de** *cape* S Portugal
86 G7 **Santa María Camotlán** Oaxaca, S Mexico North America
90 F3 **Santa Maria, Cape** *headland* Long Island, C Bahamas 23°40′N 75°20′W
175 G9 **Santa Maria Capua Vetere** Campania, S Italy 41°05′N 14°15′E
170 C4 **Santa Maria da Feira** Aveiro, N Portugal 40°55′N 08°32′W
109 E8 **Santa Maria da Vitória** Bahia, E Brazil 13°26′S 44°09′W
103 H5 **Santa Maria de Erebato** Bolívar, SE Venezuela 05°09′N 64°50′W
102 G3 **Santa María de Ipire** Guárico, C Venezuela 08°51′N 65°21′W
Santa Maria del Buen Aire *see* Buenos Aires
85 I6 **Santa María del Oro** Durango, C Mexico 25°57′N 105°22′W
85 L9 **Santa María del Río** San Luis Potosí, C Mexico 21°48′N 100°42′W
85 J6 **Santa María de Mohovano** Coahuila de Zaragoza, Mexico 26°41′N 103°37′W
173 J7 **Santa María de Nieva** Andalucía, Spain 37°28′N 1°59′W
Santa Maria di Castellabate *see* Castellabate
175 J10 **Santa Maria di Leuca, Capo** *headland* SE Italy 39°48′N 18°21′E
176 F5 **Santa Maria-im-Münstertal** Graubünden, SE Switzerland 46°36′N 10°25′E
105 I9 **Santa María, Isla** *var.* Isla Floreana, Charles Island. *island* Galapagos Islands, Ecuador, E Pacific Ocean
85 H2 **Santa María, Laguna de** ◎ N Mexico
172 G1 **Santa María la Real de Nieva** Castilla y León, Spain 41°04′N 4°24′W
111 K6 **Santa Maria Madaelna** Rio de Janeiro, Brazil 21°57′S 42°01′W
115 J2 **Santa Maria, Rio** ≈ S Brazil
85 M9 **Santa María, Río** ≈ Mexico
84 G4 **Santa María, Río** ≈ Chihuahua, Mexico
89 J9 **Santa María, Río** ≈ C Panama
79 H8 **Santa Maria River** ≈ Arizona, SW USA
175 E8 **Santa Marinella** Lazio, C Italy 42°01′N 11°51′E
102 C2 **Santa Marta** Magdalena, N Colombia 11°14′N 74°13′W
170 E7 **Santa Marta** Extremadura, W Spain 38°37′N 06°39′W
Santa Maura *see* Lefkáda
81 D10 **Santa Monica** California, W USA 34°01′N 118°29′W
172 A6 **Santana** Setúbal, Portugal 38°27′N 9°06′W
183 H13 **Sântana** *Ger.* Sankt Anna, *Hung.* Újszentanna; *prev.* Sîntana. Arad, W Romania 46°20′N 21°30′E
116 J2 **Santana da Boa Vista** Rio Grande do Sul, Brazil 31°00′S 53°00′E
115 I3 **Santana, Coxilha de** *hill range* S Brazil
115 L3 **Santana da Boa Vista** Rio Grande do Sul, S Brazil 30°52′S 53°03′W
110 E5 **Santana da Vargem** Minas Gerais, Brazil 21°15′S 45°30′W
172 C7 **Santana de Cambas** Beja, Portugal 37°37′N 7°32′W
110 C9 **Santana de Parnaíba** São Paulo, Brazil 23°27′S 46°55′W
111 I6 **Santana do Deserto** Minas Gerais, Brazil 21°57′S 43°10′W
110 F4 **Santana do Jacaré** Minas Gerais, Brazil 20°54′S 45°08′W
115 I3 **Santana do Livramento** *prev.* Livramento. Rio Grande do Sul, S Brazil 30°52′S 55°30′W
111 J2 **Santana do Paraíso** Minas Gerais, Brazil 19°22′S 42°32′W
170 G1 **Santander** Cantabria, N Spain 43°28′N 03°48′W
102 C5 **Santander** *off.* Departamento de Santander. ⬖ *province* C Colombia
Santander, Departamento de *see* Santander
Santander Jiménez *see* Jiménez
Sant'Andrea *see* Svetac
175 B11 **Sant'Antioco** Sardegna, Italy, C Mediterranean Sea 39°03′N 08°28′E
172 G3 **Santa Olalla** Castilla-La Manacha, Spain 40°01′N 4°26′W
170 E7 **Santa Olalla del Cala** Andalucía, S Spain 37°54′N 06°13′W
81 C9 **Santa Paula** California, W USA 34°21′N 119°03′W
79 H3 **Santaquin** Utah, W USA 39°58′N 111°46′W
107 J2 **Santarém** Pará, N Brazil 02°26′S 54°41′W
170 C6 **Santarém** *anc.* Scalabis. Santarém, W Portugal 39°14′N 08°40′W
172 B4 **Santarém** ⬖ *district* C Portugal
61 L10 **Santaren Channel** *channel* W Bahamas
111 J3 **Santa Rita** Minas Gerais, Brazil 19°52′S 42°08′W
102 F5 **Santa Rita** Vichada, E Colombia 04°51′N 68°27′W
282 A2 **Santa Rita** SW Guam
88 E3 **Santa Rita** Cortés, NW Honduras 15°10′N 87°54′W
84 E7 **Santa Rita** Baja California Sur, W Mexico 27°29′N 100°33′W
102 D2 **Santa Rita** Zulia, NW Venezuela 10°35′N 71°30′W
107 J10 **Santa Rita de Araguaia** Goiás, S Brazil 17°17′S 53°13′W
110 D6 **Santa Rita de Caldas** Minas Gerais, Brazil 22°02′S 46°20′W
Santa Rita de Cassia *see* Cássia
111 L2 **Santa Rita do Itueto** Minas Gerais, Brazil 19°21′S 41°23′W
80 C5 **Santa Rita Park** California, USA 37°03′N 120°36′W
112 G6 **Santa Rosa** Corrientes, NE Argentina 28°18′S 58°04′W
116 E5 **Santa Rosa** La Pampa, C Argentina 36°38′S 64°15′W
113 I6 **Santa Rosa** Rio Grande do Sul, S Brazil 27°50′S 54°29′W
103 I6 **Santa Rosa** Roraima, N Brazil 03°41′N 62°29′W
104 B3 **Santa Rosa** El Oro, SW Ecuador 03°29′S 79°57′W
84 G4 **Santa Rosa** Quintana Roo, SE Mexico North America
87 M6 **Santa Rosa** Quintana Roo, Mexico 19°58′N 88°53′W
105 G8 **Santa Rosa** Puno, S Peru 14°38′S 70°45′W
80 B1 **Santa Rosa** California, W USA 38°27′N 122°42′W
79 M7 **Santa Rosa** New Mexico, SW USA 34°54′N 104°43′W
103 H3 **Santa Rosa** Anzoátegui, NE Venezuela 09°37′N 64°20′W
88 C4 **Santa Rosa** *off.* Departamento de Santa Rosa. ⬖ *department* SE Guatemala
Santa Rosa *see* Santa Rosa de Copán
116 D7 **Santa Rosa, Bajo de** *basin* E Argentina
114 B4 **Santa Rosa de Calchines** Santa Fe, Argentina 31°25′S 60°20′W
88 D4 **Santa Rosa de Copán** *var.* Santa Rosa. Copán, W Honduras 14°48′N 88°43′W
102 B4 **Santa Rosa de Osos** Antioquia, C Colombia 06°40′N 75°27′W
Santa Rosa, Departamento de *see* Santa Rosa
81 B9 **Santa Rosa Island** *island* California, W USA
69 H4 **Santa Rosa Island** *island* Florida, SE USA
84 D5 **Santa Rosalía** Baja California Sur, W Mexico 27°20′N 112°20′W
102 E3 **Santa Rosalía** Portuguesa, NW Venezuela 09°02′N 69°01′W
282 B1 **Santa Rosa, Mount** ▲ NE Guam
81 F12 **Santa Rosa Mountains** ▲▲ California, W USA
78 E2 **Santa Rosa Range** ▲▲ Nevada, W USA
112 F6 **Santa Sylvina** Chaco, N Argentina 27°49′S 61°09′W
Santa Tecla *see* Nueva San Salvador
114 B7 **Santa Teresa** Santa Fe, C Argentina 33°30′S 60°45′W
111 M3 **Santa Teresa** Espírito Santo, SE Brazil 19°51′S 40°49′W
86 B4 **Santa Teresa** Nayarit, Mexico 22°28′N 104°44′W
85 I9 **Santa Teresa** Nayarit, Mexico 22°28′N 104°44′W
115 L7 **Santa Vitória do Palmar** Rio Grande do Sul, S Brazil 33°32′S 53°25′W
81 B8 **Santa Ynez** California, USA 34°37′N 120°05′W
81 B8 **Santa Ynez River** ≈ California, W USA
Sant Carles de la Rápida *see* Sant Carles de la Ràpita
171 J4 **Sant Carles de la Ràpita** *var.* Sant Carles de la Rápida. Cataluña, NE Spain 40°37′N 00°36′E
171 K3 **Sant Celoni** Cataluña, NE Spain 41°39′N 02°25′E
81 E13 **Santee** California, W USA 32°50′N 116°58′W
67 J9 **Santee River** ≈ South Carolina, SE USA
86 B7 **San Telmo, Punta** *headland* SW Mexico 18°19′N 103°30′W
184 C9 **Santeramo in Colle** Puglia, SE Italy 40°47′N 16°45′E
175 H11 **Sant Eufemia Lamezia** Calabria, SE Italy 38°54′N 16°14′E
171 L3 **Sant Feliu de Guíxols** *var.* San Feliú de Guixols. Cataluña, NE Spain 41°47′N 03°02′E
171 K4 **Sant Feliu de Llobregat** Cataluña, NE Spain 41°22′N 02°00′E
176 D7 **Santhià** Piemonte, NE Italy 45°21′N 08°11′E
113 H7 **Santiago** Rio Grande do Sul, S Brazil 29°11′S 54°52′W
116 B4 **Santiago** *var.* Gran Santiago. ● (Chile) Santiago, C Chile 33°30′S 70°40′W
91 H5 **Santiago** *var.* Santiago de los Caballeros. N Dominican Republic 19°27′N 70°42′W
84 F8 **Santiago** Baja California Sur, W Mexico 23°32′N 109°47′W
85 L6 **Santiago** Nuevo León, NE Mexico 25°22′N 100°09′W
89 J10 **Santiago** Veraguas, S Panama 08°06′N 80°59′W
105 E8 **Santiago** Ica, SW Peru 14°14′S 75°44′W
170 C2 **Santiago** *var.* Santiago de Compostela, *Eng.* Compostella; *anc.* Campus Stellae. Galicia, NW Spain 42°52′N 08°33′W
116 B3 **Santiago** *off.* Región Metropolitana de Santiago, *var.* Metropolitan. ⬖ *region* C Chile
132 B10 **Santiago** *var.* São Tiago. *island* Ilhas de Sotavento, S Cape Verde
118 D3 **Santiago** ✈ Santiago, C Chile 33°27′S 70°40′W
170 C2 **Santiago** ✈ Galicia, NW Spain
Santiago *see* Santiago de Cuba, Cuba
Santiago *see* Grande de Santiago, Río, Mexico
87 H9 **Santiago Astata** Oaxaca, Mexico 15°59′N 95°40′W
88 B4 **Santiago Atitlán** Sololá, SW Guatemala 14°39′N 91°12′W
89 J9 **Santiago, Cerro** ▲ W Panama 08°27′N 81°42′W
87 H8 **Santiago Choapan** Oaxaca, Mexico 17°20′N 95°57′W
Santiago de Compostela *see* Santiago
90 F5 **Santiago de Cuba** *var.* Santiago. Santiago de Cuba, E Cuba 20°01′N 75°51′W
Santiago de Guayaquil *see* Guayaquil
173 J6 **Santiago de la Espada** Andalucía, Spain 38°07′N 2°33′W
86 G5 **Santiago de la Peña** Veracruz-Llave, Mexico
112 D6 **Santiago del Estero** Santiago del Estero, C Argentina 27°51′S 64°16′W
116 F1 **Santiago del Estero** *off.* Provincia de Santiago del Estero. ⬖ *province* N Argentina
Santiago del Estero, Provincia de *see* Santiago del Estero
84 G7 **Santiago de los Caballeros** Sinaloa, W Mexico 25°33′N 107°22′W
Santiago de los Caballeros *see* Santiago, Dominican Republic
Santiago de los Caballeros *see* Ciudad de Guatemala, Guatemala
88 D5 **Santiago de María** Usulután, SE El Salvador 13°28′N 88°28′W
172 B6 **Santiago do Cacém** Setúbal, S Portugal 38°01′N 08°42′W
85 I9 **Santiago Ixcuintla** Nayarit, C Mexico 21°50′N 105°11′W
Santiago Jamiltepec *see* Jamiltepec
70 C7 **Santiago Mountains** ▲▲ Texas, SW USA
85 I7 **Santiago Papasquiaro** Durango, C Mexico 25°00′N 105°27′W
Santiago Pinotepa Nacional *see* Pinotepa Nacional
Santiago, Región Metropolitana de *see* Santiago
104 C3 **Santiago, Río** ≈ N Peru
86 G8 **Santiago Yosondúa** Oaxaca, Mexico 16°53′N 97°34′W
85 I7 **Santiaguillo, Laguna** ◎ Durango, Mexico
172 B3 **Santiais** Leiria, Portugal 39°49′N 8°34′W
172 E2 **Santibàñez de la Sierra** Castilla y León, Spain 40°30′N 5°55′W
85 K7 **San Tiburcio** Zacatecas, C Mexico 24°08′N 101°29′W
170 G1 **Santillana** Cantabria, N Spain 43°24′N 04°06′W
102 E3 **San Timoteo** Zulia, NW Venezuela 09°50′N 71°05′W
Santi Quaranta *see* Sarandë
Santissima Trinidad *see* Chilung
170 G7 **Santisteban del Puerto** Andalucía, S Spain 38°15′N 03°11′W
168 G8 **Sant Joan de les Abadesses** Cataluña, Spain 42°14′N 2°17′E
171 J4 **Sant Jordi, Golf de** *gulf* NE Spain
239 H1 **Santmargats** *var.* Holboo. Dzavhan, W Mongolia 48°35′N 95°25′E
171 J5 **Sant Mateu** País Valenciano, E Spain 40°28′N 00°10′E
70 G4 **Santo** Texas, SW USA 32°35′N 98°06′W
Santo *see* Espiritu Santo
172 D6 **Santo Aleixo** Beja, Portugal 38°04′N 7°09′W
172 D5 **Santo Aleixo** Portalegre, Portugal 38°55′N 7°25′W
172 D6 **Santo Amador** Beja, Portugal 38°08′N 7°18′W
113 L4 **Santo Amaro, Ilha de** *island* SE Brazil
110 D9 **Santo André** São Paulo, Brazil 23°40′S 46°31′W
172 B2 **Santo André** Aveiro, Portugal 40°30′N 8°40′W
113 I6 **Santo Ângelo** Rio Grande do Sul, S Brazil 28°17′S 54°15′W
132 A9 **Santo Antão** *island* Ilhas de Barlavento, N Cape Verde
110 C5 **Santo Anténio da Alegria** São Paulo, Brazil 21°06′S 47°10′W
113 K4 **Santo Antônio da Platina** Paraná, S Brazil 23°20′S 50°05′W
111 J5 **Santo Anténio de Pàdua** Rio de Janeiro, Brazil 21°32′S 42°11′W
110 F4 **Santo Anténio do Amparo** Minas Gerais, Brazil 20°57′S 44°55′W
111 J3 **Santo Anténio do Grama** Minas Gerais, Brazil 20°19′S 42°36′W
106 C3 **Santo Antônio do Içá** Amazonas, N Brazil 03°05′S 67°56′W
110 F3 **Santo Anténio do Monte** Minas Gerais, Brazil 20°05′S 45°17′W
110 E8 **Santo Anténio do Pinhal** São Paulo, Brazil 22°50′S 45°40′W
111 I2 **Santo Anténio do Rio Abaixo** Minas Gerais, Brazil 19°14′S 43°15′W
107 H10 **Santo Corazón, Río** ≈ E Bolivia
114 B3 **Santo Domingo** Santa Fe, Argentina 31°07′S 60°53′W
61 L10 **Santo Domingo** Villa Clara, C Cuba 22°35′N 80°15′W
91 I6 **Santo Domingo** *prev.* Ciudad Trujillo. ● (Dominican Republic) SE Dominican Republic 18°30′N 69°57′W
84 C4 **Santo Domingo** Baja California, Mexico 28°12′N 114°02′W
84 D7 **Santo Domingo** Baja California Sur, W Mexico 25°34′N 112°00′W
87 I9 **Santo Domingo** Oaxaca, Mexico 16°33′N 94°37′W
84 F5 **Santo Domingo** Oaxaca, S Mexico North America
85 K8 **Santo Domingo** San Luis Potosí, C Mexico 23°18′N 101°42′W
88 G6 **Santo Domingo** Chontales, S Nicaragua 12°15′N 84°59′W
84 D7 **Boca de Santo Domingo** ≈ Baja California Sur, Mexico
168 A7 **Santo Domingo de la Calzada** La Rioja, Spain 42°26′N 2°57′W
104 C2 **Santo Domingo de los Colorados** Pichincha, NW Ecuador 0°13′S 79°09′W
Santo Domingo Tehuantepec *see* Tehuantepec
172 D2 **Santo Estèvão** Guarda, Portugal 40°18′N 7°10′W
172 B5 **Santo Estèvão** Santarém, Portugal 38°52′N 8°45′W
172 B5 **Santo Estèvão, Ribeira de** ≈ Portugal
173 L2 **Pantano de Santolea** ⊠ Aragón, Spain
103 H3 **San Tomé** Anzoátegui, NE Venezuela 08°58′N 64°08′W
San Tomé de Guayana *see* Ciudad Guayana
171 I7 **Santomera** Murcia, SE Spain 38°03′N 01°05′W
170 G1 **Santoña** Cantabria, N Spain 43°27′N 03°28′W
Santorin *see* Santoríni
187 J8 **Santoríni** *var.* Santorin, *prev.* Thíra; *anc.* Thera. *island* Kykládes, Greece, Aegean Sea
110 D10 **Santos** São Paulo, S Brazil 23°56′S 46°22′W
291 E10 **Santos Plateau** *undersea feature* SW Atlantic Ocean
172 B1 **Santo Tirso** Porto, N Portugal 41°20′N 08°25′W
84 B2 **Santo Tomás** Baja California, NW Mexico 31°32′N 116°26′W
84 G4 **Santo Tomàs** Chihuahua, Mexico 28°41′N 107°34′W
88 G6 **Santo Tomás** Chontales, S Nicaragua 12°04′N 85°02′W
88 D3 **Santo Tomás de Castilla** Izabal, E Guatemala 15°40′N 88°36′W
84 B2 **Santo Tomás, Punta** *headland* NW Mexico 31°30′N 116°40′W
105 F8 **Santo Tomás, Río** ≈ C Peru
105 I9 **Santo Tomás, Volcán** ⛰ Galapagos Islands, Ecuador, E Pacific Ocean 0°46′S 91°01′W
116 I1 **Santo Tomé** Corrientes, NE Argentina 28°31′S 56°03′W
173 I6 **Santo Tomé** Andalucía, Spain 38°02′N 3°06′W
Santo Tomé de Guayana *see* Ciudad Guayana
180 J2 **Santow** Mecklenburg-Vorpommern, Germany 11°11′N 53°53′E
162 E6 **Santpoort** Noord-Holland, W Netherlands 52°26′N 04°38′E
168 G9 **Sant Sadurní d'Anoia** Cataluña, Spain 41°25′N 1°47′E
114 A2 **Santurce** Santa Fe, Argentina 30°12′S 61°11′W
Santurce *see* Santurtzi
170 G1 **Santurtzi** *var.* Santurce, Santurzi. País Vasco, N Spain 43°20′N 03°03′W
Santurzi *see* Santurtzi
117 B10 **San Valentín, Cerro** ▲ S Chile 46°36′S 73°17′W
114 A4 **San Vicente** Santa Fe, Argentina 31°43′S 61°35′W
118 C4 **San Vicente** Libertador General Bernardo O'Higgins, Chile 34°05′S 71°45′W
88 D5 **San Vicente** San Vicente, C El Salvador 13°38′N 88°42′W*
84 B2 **San Vicente** Baja California, NW Mexico 31°20′N 116°15′W
283 H2 **San Vicente** Saipan, S Northern Mariana Islands
88 D4 **San Vicente** ⬖ *department* E El Salvador
170 D6 **San Vicente de Alcántara** Extremadura, W Spain 39°21′N 07°07′W
170 G2 **San Vicente de Barakaldo** *var.* Baracaldo, *Basq.* San Bizenti-Barakaldo. País Vasco, N Spain 43°17′N 02°59′W
105 D8 **San Vicente de Cañete** *var.* Cañete. Lima, W Peru 13°06′S 76°23′W
170 F1 **San Vicente de la Barquera** Cantabria, N Spain 43°23′N 04°24′W
102 C7 **San Vicente del Caguán** Caquetá, S Colombia 02°07′N 74°47′W
114 D2 **San Víctor** Entre Ríos, Argentina 30°29′S 59°01′W
89 I9 **San Vito** Puntarenas, SE Costa Rica 08°49′N 82°58′W
177 I6 **San Vito al Tagliamento** Friuli-Venezia Giulia, NE Italy 45°54′N 12°55′E
175 E12 **San Vito, Capo** *headland* Sicilia, Italy, C Mediterranean Sea 38°11′N 12°41′E
175 I9 **San Vito dei Normanni** Puglia, SE Italy 40°40′N 17°42′E
243 J8 **Sanxiang** China 24°20′N 116°22′E
243 L3 **Sanxikou** China 30°02′N 119°36′E
240 F10 **Sanya** *var.* Ya Xian. Hainan, S China 18°25′N 109°27′E
138 G3 **Sanyati** ≈ N Zimbabwe
70 F9 **San Ygnacio** Texas, SW USA 27°04′N 99°26′W
244 E7 **Sanyuan** Shaanxi, China 34°22′N 108°34′E
239 M6 **Sanyuan** Shaanxi, C China 34°40′N 108°56′E
193 J6 **Sanyyakhtakh** Respublika Sakha (Yakutiya), NE Russian Federation 60°34′N 124°09′E
228 F8 **S. A.Nyýazow Adyndaky** *Rus.* Imeni S. A. Niyazova. Maryyskiy Velayat, S Turkmenistan 36°44′N 62°23′E
135 D10 **Sanza Pombo** Uíge, NW Angola 07°20′S 16°00′E
Sanzyô *see* Sanjō
111 K1 **São Geraldo do Baixio** Minas Gerais, Brazil 18°54′S 41°24′E
115 N5 **Sao Jos do Norte** Uruguay 32°00′S 52°06′E
172 C4 **São Bartolomeu** Portalegre, Portugal 39°23′N 7°56′W
172 B8 **São Bartolomeu de Messines** Faro, Portugal 37°15′N 8°17′W
172 C5 **São Bento** Évora, Portugal 38°51′N 7°39′W
110 E8 **São Bento do Sapucaí** São Paulo, Brazil 22°42′S 45°43′W
110 D9 **São Bernardo do Campo** São Paulo, S Brazil 23°45′S 46°34′W
113 H6 **São Borja** Rio Grande do Sul, S Brazil 28°35′S 56°01′W
172 C8 **São Bràs de Alportel** Faro, Portugal 37°09′N 7°53′W
170 C8 **São Brás de Alportel** Faro, S Portugal 37°09′N 07°55′W
111 H4 **São Bràs do Suassuí** Minas Gerais, Brazil 20°38′S 43°57′W
110 D9 **São Caetano do Sul** São Paulo, S Brazil 23°37′S 46°34′W
110 B6 **São Carlos** São Paulo, S Brazil 22°02′S 47°53′W
108 I7 **São Cristóvão** Sergipe, E Brazil 10°59′S 37°10′W
111 M1 **São Domingos** Espírito Santo, Brazil 19°09′S 40°37′W
172 C4 **São Domingos** Santarém, Portugal 39°36′N 8°10′W
111 I3 **Sao Domingos da Prata** Minas Gerais, Brazil 19°52′S 42°58′W
113 H7 **São Fancisco de Assis** Rio Grande do Sul, S Brazil 29°32′S 55°07′W
107 K5 **São Félix** Pará, NE Brazil 06°43′S 51°56′W
São Félix *see* São Félix do Araguaia
107 L7 **São Félix do Araguaia** *var.* São Félix. Mato Grosso, W Brazil 11°36′S 50°40′W
107 K5 **São Félix do Xingu** Pará, NE Brazil 06°38′S 51°59′W
111 K6 **São Fidélis** Rio de Janeiro, SE Brazil 21°37′S 41°40′W
132 A10 **São Filipe** Fogo, S Cape Verde 14°52′N 24°29′W
111 J4 **São Francisco da Gloria** Minas Gerais, Brazil 20°48′S 42°16′W
113 K5 **São Francisco do Sul** Santa Catarina, S Brazil 26°17′S 48°39′W
113 K5 **São Francisco, Ilha de** *island* S Brazil
109 E9 **São Francisco, Rio** ≈ E Brazil
111 M1 **São Gabriel** Espírito Santo, Brazil 19°01′S 40°32′W
115 K2 **São Gabriel** Rio Grande do Sul, S Brazil 30°17′S 54°17′W
111 I4 **São Geraldo** Minas Gerais, Brazil 20°55′S 42°50′W
111 J1 **São Geraldo da Piedade** Minas Gerais, Brazil 18°48′S 42°20′W
110 E6 **São Gonçalo** Minas Gerais, Brazil 21°54′S 45°36′W
111 I8 **São Gonçalo** Rio de Janeiro, SE Brazil 22°48′S 43°03′W
110 F3 **São Gonçalo do Parà** Minas Gerais, Brazil 19°59′S 44°51′W
111 I3 **São Gonçalo do Rio Abaixo** Minas Gerais, Brazil 19°49′S 43°21′W
110 E2 **São Gothardo** Minas Gerais, Brazil 19°19′S 46°03′W
172 C5 **São Gregório** Évora, Portugal 38°48′N 7°55′W
137 C11 **Sao Hill** Iringa, S Tanzania 08°19′S 35°11′E
172 B2 **São Jacinto** Aveiro, Portugal 40°40′N 8°44′W
115 N1 **São Jerénimo** Rio Grande do Sul, Brazil 29°58′S 51°43′W
110 D4 **São João Batista do Glória** Minas Gerais, Brazil 20°38′S 46°30′W
111 L6 **São João da Barra** Rio de Janeiro, Brazil 21°38′S 41°03′W
109 G12 **São João da Barra** Rio de Janeiro, SE Brazil 21°39′S 41°04′W
170 C4 **São João da Madeira** Aveiro, N Portugal 40°52′N 08°28′W
172 B1 **São João da Madeira** Aveiro, Portugal 40°54′N 8°30′W

◆ Country
● Country Capital
◇ Dependent Territory
○ Dependent Territory Capital
⬖ Administrative Regions
✈ International Airport
▲ Mountain
▲▲ Mountain Range
⛰ Volcano
≈ River
◎ Lake
⊠ Reservoir

◆ Country	◇ Dependent Territory	◊ Administrative Regions	▲ Mountain	▼ Volcano	◎ Lake
● Country Capital	◉ Dependent Territory Capital	✈ International Airport	▲▲ Mountain Range	🜂 River	☷ Reservoir

Serbia - Sheng Xian/Shengxian
INDEX
406

184 *G5* **Serbia** *Ger.* Serbien, *Serb.* Srbija. ◆ *republic* Serbia
Serbia, Federal Republic of *see* Serbia
Serbien *see* Serbia
Sercq *see* Sark
228 *C6* **Serdar** *prev. Rus.* Gyzyrlabat, Kizyl-Arvat. Balkan Welaýaty, W Turkmenistan 39°02′N 56°15′E
Serdica *see* Sofiya
197 *H4* **Serdobsk** Penzenskaya Oblast', W Russian Federation 52°30′N 44°16′E
227 *M3* **Serebryansk** Vostochnyy Kazakhstan, E Kazakhstan 49°44′N 83°16′E
193 *J7* **Serebryanyy Bor** Respublika Sakha (Yakutiya), NE Russian Federation 56°40′N 124°46′E
183 *E10* **Sered'** *Hung.* Szered. Trnavský Kraj, W Slovakia 48°19′N 17°45′E
189 *J1* **Seredyna-Buda** Sums'ka Oblast', NE Ukraine 52°09′N 34°00′E
191 *C8* **Seredžius** Tauragė, C Lithuania 55°04′N 23°24′E
214 *E6* **Şereflikoçhisar** Ankara, C Turkey 38°56′N 33°31′E
176 *E6* **Seregno** Lombardia, N Italy 45°39′N 09°12′E
165 *I4* **Serein** ≈ C France
258 *E3* **Seremban** Negeri Sembilan, Peninsular Malaysia 02°42′N 101°54′E
137 *C9* **Serengeti Plain** *plain* N Tanzania
139 *H1* **Serenje** Central, E Zambia 13°12′S 30°15′E
Seres *see* Sérres
188 *E5* **Seret** ≈ W Ukraine
Seret/Sereth *see* Siret
187 *I7* **Serfopoúla** *island* Kykládes, Greece, Aegean Sea
197 *I2* **Sergach** Nizhegorodskaya Oblast', W Russian Federation 55°31′N 45°29′E
74 *F7* **Sergeant Bluff** Iowa, C USA 42°24′N 96°19′W
Sergelen *see* Tuvshinshiree
258 *C3* **Sergeulangit, Pegunungan** ▲▲ Sumatera, NW Indonesia
193 *H3* **Sergeya Kirova, Ostrova** *island* N Russian Federation
Sergeyevichi *see* Syarhyeyevichy
227 *H2* **Sergeyevka** Severnyy Kazakhstan, N Kazakhstan 53°53′N 67°25′E
Sergiopol *see* Ayagoz
108 *I7* **Sergipe** *off.* Estado de Sergipe. ❖ *state* E Brazil
Sergipe, Estado de *see* Sergipe
196 *G1* **Sergiyev Posad** Moskovskaya Oblast', W Russian Federation 56°21′N 38°10′E
194 *F4* **Sergozero, Ozero** ◎ NW Russian Federation
228 *F9* **Serhetabat** *prev. Rus.* Gushgy, Kushka. Mary Welaýaty, S Turkmenistan 35°19′N 62°17′E
258 *I4* **Serian** Sarawak, East Malaysia 01°10′N 110°35′E
259 *G8* **Seribu, Kepulauan** *island group* S Indonesia
187 *I7* **Sérifos** *anc.* Seriphos. *island* Kykládes, Greece, Aegean Sea
187 *I7* **Sérifou, Stenó** *strait* SE Greece
214 *D7* **Serik** Antalya, SW Turkey 36°55′N 31°06′E
187 *M6* **Serinhisar** Denizli, Turkey 37°35′N 29°16′E
176 *F6* **Serio** ≈ N Italy
Seriphos *see* Sérifos
110 *G6* **Seritinga** Minas Gerais, Brazil 21°54′S 44°30′W
Sêrkog *see* Sêrtar
167 *K5* **Sermaize-les-Bains** Champagne-Ardenne, France 48°47′N 4°55′E
197 *K3* **Sernovodsk** Samarskaya Oblast', W Russian Federation 53°56′N 51°16′E
197 *J1* **Sernur** Respublika Mariy El, W Russian Federation 56°55′N 49°09′E
182 *H5* **Serock** Mazowieckie, C Poland 52°30′N 21°03′E
114 *B6* **Serodino** Santa Fe, C Argentina 32°33′S 60°52′W
190 *G5* **Ser'odka** Pskovskaya Oblast', Russian Federation
Seroei *see* Serui
171 *H8* **Serón** Andalucía, S Spain 37°20′N 02°28′W
163 *D8* **Serooskerke** Zeeland, SW Netherlands 51°42′N 03°52′E
111 *H8* **Seropédica** Rio de Janeiro, Brazil 22°45′S 43°43′W
168 *E9* **Serós** Cataluña, Spain 41°28′N 0°25′E
171 *J3* **Seròs** Cataluña, NE Spain 41°27′N 00°24′E
195 *L8* **Serov** Sverdlovskaya Oblast', C Russian Federation 59°42′N 60°32′E
141 *I1* **Serowe** Central, SE Botswana 22°26′S 26°44′E
172 *C6* **Serpa** Beja, S Portugal 37°56′N 07°36′W
Serpa Pinto *see* Menongue
276 *C3* **Serpentine Lakes** *salt lake* South Australia
196 *F2* **Serpukhov** Moskovskaya Oblast', W Russian Federation 54°54′N 37°26′E
111 *M3* **Serra** Espírito Santo, Brazil 20°07′S 40°18′W
172 *C4* **Serra** Santarém, Portugal 39°36′N 8°18′W
110 *B5* **Serra Azul** São Paulo, Brazil 21°19′S 47°34′W
110 *D1* **Serra do Salitre** Minas Gerais, Brazil 19°06′S 46°41′W
Sérrai *see* Sérres
110 *B5* **Serrana** São Paulo, Brazil 21°14′S 47°36′W
110 *D7* **Serra Negra** São Paulo, Brazil 22°36′S 46°42′W
110 *E6* **Serrania** Minas Gerais, Brazil 21°33′S 46°03′W
110 *G6* **Serranos** Minas Gerais, Brazil 21°51′S 44°30′W
175 *H12* **Serra San Bruno** Calabria, SW Italy 38°32′N 16°18′E
165 *K7* **Serres** Hautes-Alpes, SE France 44°26′N 05°42′E
187 *H2* **Sérres** *var.* Seres; *prev.* Sérrai. Kentrikí Makedonía, NE Greece 41°03′N 23°33′E
112 *D8* **Serrezuela** Córdoba, C Argentina 30°38′S 65°26′W
108 *H7* **Serrinha** Bahia, E Brazil 11°38′S 38°56′W
109 *E11* **Serro** *var.* Sêrro. Minas Gerais, NE Brazil 18°38′S 43°22′W
Sêrro *see* Serro
Sert *see* Siirt
172 *C3* **Sertã** Castelo Branco, Portugal 39°48′N 8°06′W
170 *C5* **Sertã** *var.* Sertá. Castelo Branco, C Portugal 39°48′N 08°05′W
Sertá *see* Sertã
115 *N2* **Sertão de Santana** Rio Grande do Sul, Brazil 30°27′S 51°36′W
110 *B5* **Sertãozinho** São Paulo, S Brazil 21°04′S 47°55′W
240 *C3* **Sêrtar** *var.* Sêrkog. Sichuan, C China 32°18′N 100°18′E
261 *K5* **Serui** *prev.* Seroei. Papua, E Indonesia 01°53′S 136°15′E
141 *I1* **Serule** Central, E Botswana 21°58′S 27°20′E
258 *I6* **Seruyan, Sungai** *var.* Sungai Pembuang. ≈ Borneo, N Indonesia
186 *G3* **Sérvia** Dytikí Makedonía, N Greece 40°12′N 22°01′E
169 *I6* **Servian** Languedoc-Roussillon, France 43°25′N 3°18′E
240 *B3* **Sêrxü** *var.* Jugar. Sichuan, C China 32°54′N 98°06′E
193 *K8* **Seryshevo** Amurskaya Oblast', SE Russian Federation 51°03′N 128°16′E
Sesana *see* Sežana
258 *K3* **Sesayap, Sungai** ≈ Borneo, N Indonesia
Sesdlets *see* Siedlce
134 *H6* **Sese** Orientale, N Dem. Rep. Congo 02°13′N 25°52′E
137 *B8* **Sese Islands** *island group* S Uganda
260 *G4* **Sesepe** Pulau Obi, E Indonesia 01°26′S 127°55′E
138 *F3* **Sesheke** *var.* Sesheko. Western, SE Zambia 17°28′S 24°20′E
Sesheko *see* Sesheke
176 *E7* **Sesia** *anc.* Sessites. ≈ NW Italy
170 *C7* **Sesimbra** Setúbal, S Portugal 38°26′N 09°06′W
172 *A6* **Sesimbra** Setúbal, Portugal 38°26′N 9°06′W
187 *L8* **Seskliό** *island* Dodekánisa, Greece, Aegean Sea
168 *B7* **Sesma** Navarra, Spain 42°29′N 2°05′W
73 *C12* **Sesser** Illinois, N USA 38°05′N 89°03′W
Sessites *see* Sesia
181 *J11* **Sesslach** Bayern, Germany 10°51′N 50°11′E
176 *G9* **Sesto Fiorentino** Toscana, C Italy 43°50′N 11°12′E
176 *E6* **Sesto San Giovanni** Lombardia, N Italy 45°32′N 09°14′E
176 *C7* **Sestriere** Piemonte, NE Italy 45°00′N 06°54′E
176 *E8* **Sestri Levante** Liguria, NW Italy 44°16′N 09°22′E
190 *H2* **Sestroretsk** Leningradskaya Oblast', Russian Federation
175 *B10* **Sestu** Sardegna, Italy, C Mediterranean Sea 39°15′N 09°06′E
184 *C2* **Sesvete** Zagreb, N Croatia 45°50′N 16°03′E
191 *D8* **Šeta** Kaunas, C Lithuania 55°17′N 24°16′E
Setabis *see* Xátiva
252 *C5* **Setana** Hokkaidō, NE Japan 42°27′N 139°52′E
165 *I8* **Sète** *prev.* Cette. Hérault, S France 43°24′N 03°42′E
108 *A1* **Sete Ilhas** Amapá, NE Brazil 01°06′N 52°06′W
110 *G2* **Sete Lagoas** Minas Gerais, NE Brazil 19°29′S 44°15′W
113 *I4* **Sete Quedas, Ilha das** *island* S Brazil
152 *F4* **Setermoen** Troms, N Norway 68°51′N 18°20′E
155 *C8* **Setesdal** *valley* S Norway
89 *M10* **Setetule, Cerro** ▲ SE Panama 07°51′N 77°37′W
67 *H4* **Seth** West Virginia, NE USA 38°06′N 81°40′W
Setia *see* Sezze
131 *J1* **Sétif** *var.* Stif. N Algeria 36°11′N 05°24′E
141 *H4* **Setlagoli** North-West, South Africa 26°17′S 25°07′E
251 *J4* **Seto** Aichi, Honshū, SW Japan 35°14′N 137°06′E
250 *F5* **Seto-naikai** *Eng.* Inland Sea. *sea* S Japan
251 *K9* **Setouchi** *var.* Setoushi. Kagoshima, Amami-Ō-shima, SW Japan 44°19′N 142°58′E
Setoushi *see* Setouchi
130 *E3* **Settat** W Morocco 33°03′N 07°37′W
135 *A8* **Setté Cama** Ogooué-Maritime, SW Gabon 02°32′S 09°46′E
55 *I7* **Setting Lake** ◎ Manitoba, C Canada
159 *J8* **Settle** N England, UK 54°04′N 02°17′W
283 *N1* **Settlement** E Wake Island 19°17′N 166°38′E
172 *B5* **Setúbal** *Eng.* Saint Ubes, Saint Yves. Setúbal, W Portugal 38°31′N 08°54′W
172 *B6* **Setúbal** ❖ *district* S Portugal
170 *C7* **Setúbal, Baía de** *bay* W Portugal
Setul *see* Satun
168 *C1* **Seudre** ≈ Poitou-Charentes, France
168 *D1* **Seugne** ≈ Poitou-Charentes, France
181 *H8* **Seulingen** Niedersachsen, Germany 10°10′N 51°33′E
58 *B6* **Seul, Lac** ◎ Ontario, S Canada
165 *J5* **Seurre** Côte d'Or, C France 47°00′N 05°09′E
215 *K5* **Sevan** C Armenia 40°32′N 44°56′E
215 *K5* **Sevana Lich** *Eng.* Lake Sevan, *Rus.* Ozero Sevan. ◎ E Armenia
Sevan, Lake/Sevan, Ozero *see* Sevana Lich
132 *F4* **Sévaré** Mopti, C Mali 14°32′N 04°06′W
189 *J9* **Sevastopol'** *Eng.* Sebastopol. Respublika Krym, S Ukraine 44°36′N 33°33′E
141 *K6* **Sevenoaks** KwaZulu-Natal, South Africa 29°13′S 30°36′E
160 *F5* **Seven Sisters** UK 51°46′N 3°43′W
70 *G8* **Seven Sisters** Texas, SW USA 27°57′N 98°34′W
56 *B3* **Seven Sisters Peaks** ▲ British Columbia, SW Canada 54°57′N 128°10′W
163 *H8* **Sevenum** Limburg, SE Netherlands 51°25′N 06°01′E
165 *I8* **Séverac-le-Château** Aveyron, S France 44°18′N 03°03′E
140 *F4* **Severn** North-West, South Africa 26°35′S 22°52′E
64 *D9* **Severn** Maryland, USA 39°08′N 76°42′W
62 *D3* **Severn** ≈ Ontario, S Canada
157 *G11* **Severn** *Wel.* Hafren. ≈ England/Wales, UK
157 *G10* **Severn** *Wel.* Hafren. ≈ England/Wales, UK
64 *D9* **Severna Park** Maryland, USA 39°04′N 76°33′W
194 *G6* **Severnaya Dvina** *var.* Northern Dvina. ≈ NW Russian Federation
197 *I9* **Severnaya Osetiya-Alaniya, Respublika** *Eng.* North Ossetia; *prev.* Respublika Severnaya Osetiya, Severo-Osetinskaya SSR. ❖ *autonomous republic* SW Russian Federation
Severnaya Osetiya, Respublika *see* Severnaya Osetiya-Alaniya, Respublika
195 *L5* **Severnaya Sos'va** ≈ N Russian Federation
193 *H2* **Severnaya Zemlya** *var.* Nicholas II Land. *island group* N Russian Federation
197 *K3* **Severnoye** Orenburgskaya Oblast', W Russian Federation 54°03′N 52°31′E
160 *G6* **Severn** ≈ UK
78 *D2* **Severn Troughs Range** ▲▲ Nevada, W USA
195 *L3* **Severnyy** Respublika Komi, NW Russian Federation 67°38′N 64°13′E
226 *D6* **Severnyy Chink Ustyurta** ▲▲ W Kazakhstan
195 *I8* **Severnyye Uvaly** *var.* Northern Ural Hills. *hill range* NW Russian Federation
227 *H2* **Severnyy Kazakhstan** *off.* Severo-Kazakhstanskaya Oblast', *var.* North Kazakhstan, *Kaz.* Soltüstik Qazaqstan Oblysy. ❖ *province* N Kazakhstan
195 *K6* **Severnyy Ural** ▲▲ NW Russian Federation
Severo-Alichurskiy Khrebet *see* Alichuri Shimolí, Qatorkŭhi
193 *I7* **Severobaykal'sk** Respublika Buryatiya, S Russian Federation 55°39′N 109°17′E
Severodonetsk *see* Syeverodonets'k
194 *G5* **Severodvinsk** *prev.* Molotov, Sudostroy. Arkhangel'skaya Oblast', NW Russian Federation 64°32′N 39°50′E
Severo-Kazakhstanskaya Oblast' *see* Severnyy Kazakhstan
193 *N7* **Severo-Kuril'sk** Sakhalinskaya Oblast', SE Russian Federation 50°38′N 155°57′E
194 *E2* **Severomorsk** Murmanskaya Oblast', NW Russian Federation 69°00′N 33°16′E
Severo-Osetinskaya SSR *see* Severnaya Osetiya-Alaniya, Respublika
195 *L8* **Severoural'sk** Sverdlovskaya Oblast', C Russian Federation 60°09′N 59°58′E
192 *G6* **Severo-Yeniseyskiy** Krasnoyarskiy Kray, C Russian Federation 60°29′N 93°13′E
196 *G6* **Severskiy Donets** *Ukr.* Sivers'kyy Donets'. ≈ Russian Federation/Ukraine *see also* Sivers'kyy Donets'
Severskiy Donets *see* Sivers'kyy Donets'
152 *H4* **Sevettijärvi** Lappi, N Finland 69°31′N 28°40′E
79 *H3* **Sevier Bridge Reservoir** ⊠ Utah, W USA
79 *H3* **Sevier Desert** *plain* Utah, W USA
79 *H4* **Sevier Lake** ◎ Utah, W USA
66 *G6* **Sevierville** Tennessee, S USA 35°53′N 83°34′W
170 *E8* **Sevilla** *Eng.* Seville; *anc.* Hispalis. Andalucía, SW Spain 37°24′N 05°59′W
170 *F8* **Sevilla** ❖ *province* Andalucía, SW Spain
Sevilla de Niefang *see* Niefang
89 *I9* **Sevilla, Isla** *island* SW Panama
Seville *see* Sevilla
172 *G4* **Sevilleja de la Jara** Castilla-La Manacha, Spain 39°34′N 4°57′W
185 *K6* **Sevlievo** Gabrovo, N Bulgaria 43°01′N 25°06′E
Sevluš/Sevlyush *see* Vynohradiv
177 *K5* **Sevnica** *Ger.* Lichtenwald. E Slovenia 46°00′N 15°20′E
239 *J3* **Sevrey** *var.* Saynshand. Ömnögovĭ, S Mongolia 43°30′N 102°08′E
196 *E4* **Sevsk** Bryanskaya Oblast', W Russian Federation 52°03′N 34°31′E
132 *C7* **Sewa** ≈ E Sierra Leone
83 *I7* **Seward** Alaska, USA 60°06′N 149°26′W
75 *E8* **Seward** Nebraska, C USA 40°52′N 97°06′W
83 *K6* **Seward Glacier** *Glacier* Yukon Territory, W Canada
54 *A3* **Seward Glacier** *glacier* Yukon Territory, W Canada
294 *E7* **Seward Peninsula** *peninsula* Alaska, USA
Seward's Folly *see* Alaska
118 *E4* **Sewell** Libertador, C Chile 34°05′S 70°25′W
116 *C4* **Sewell** Libertador, Chile 34°06′S 70°18′E
140 *F9* **Seweweekspoort** Western Cape, South Africa 33°22′S 21°25′E
140 *F9* **Seweweekspoort** *pass* Western Cape, South Africa
162 *G3* **Sexbierum** *Fris.* Seisbierrum. Friesland, N Netherlands 53°13′N 05°28′E
56 *G3* **Sexsmith** Alberta, W Canada 55°18′N 118°45′W
87 *L6* **Seybaplaya** Campeche, SE Mexico 19°39′N 90°36′W
289 *C8* **Seychelles** *off.* Republic of Seychelles. ◆ *republic* W Indian Ocean
288 *D8* **Seychelles Bank** *var.* Le Banc des Seychelles. *undersea feature* W Indian Ocean
Seychelles, Le Banc des *see* Seychelles Bank
Seychelles, Republic of *see* Seychelles
137 *I9* **Seychellois, Morne** ▲ Mahé, NE Seychelles
168 *E4* **Seyches** Aquitaine, France 44°33′N 0°18′E
152 *D2* **Seydhisfjördhur** Austurland, E Iceland 65°15′N 14°00′W
228 *F6* **Seýdi** *Rus.* Seydi; *prev.* Neftezavodsk. Lebap Welaýaty, E Turkmenistan 39°31′N 62°53′E
214 *D7* **Seydişehir** Konya, SW Turkey 37°25′N 31°51′E
214 *F6* **Seyfe Gölü** ◎ C Turkey
Seyhan *see* Adana
214 *F7* **Seyhan Barajı** ⊠ S Turkey
214 *F8* **Seyhan Nehri** ≈ S Turkey
214 *D6* **Seyitgazi** Eskişehir, W Turkey 39°27′N 30°42′E
196 *F4* **Seym** ≈ W Russian Federation
189 *J2* **Seym** ≈ N Ukraine
193 *L5* **Seymchan** Magadanskaya Oblast', E Russian Federation 62°54′N 152°27′E
277 *J7* **Seymour** Victoria, SE Australia 37°01′S 145°10′E
141 *I9* **Seymour** Eastern Cape, South Africa 32°33′S 26°46′E
138 *G9* **Seymour** Eastern Cape, S South Africa 32°33′S 26°46′E
65 *J4* **Seymour** Connecticut, USA 41°24′N 73°05′W
75 *H8* **Seymour** Iowa, C USA 40°40′N 93°07′W
75 *H11* **Seymour** Missouri, C USA 37°09′N 92°46′W
70 *F3* **Seymour** Texas, SW USA 33°36′N 99°16′W
52 *G4* **Seymour Island** *Island* Nunavut, NW Canada
169 *L4* **Seyne** Provence-Alpes-Côte d'Azur, France 44°21′N 6°21′E
169 *L1* **Seyssel** Rhône-Alpes, France 45°57′N 5°49′E
177 *J6* **Sežana** *It.* Sesana. SW Slovenia 45°42′N 13°52′E
165 *I3* **Sézanne** Marne, N France 48°43′N 03°41′E
141 *K7* **Sezela** KwaZulu-Natal, South Africa 30°25′S 30°41′E
175 *F8* **Sezze** *anc.* Setia. Lazio, C Italy 41°29′N 13°04′E
Sfákia *see* Chóra Sfakíon
186 *F8* **Sfaktiría** *island* S Greece
188 *E8* **Sfântu Gheorghe** *Ger.* Sankt-Georgen, *Hung.* Sepsiszentgyőrgy; *prev.* Şepşi-Sângeorz, Sfîntu Gheorghe. Covasna, C Romania 45°52′N 25°49′E
188 *G9* **Sfântu Gheorghe, Braţul** *var.* Gheorghe Braţul. ≈ E Romania
131 *K2* **Sfax** *Ar.* Şafāqis. E Tunisia 34°45′N 10°45′E
131 *K2* **Sfax** ✈ E Tunisia 34°43′N 10°37′E
Sfîntu Gheorghe *see* Sfântu Gheorghe
162 *E7* **'s-Gravendeel** Zuid-Holland, SW Netherlands 51°48′N 04°36′E
162 *D7* **'s-Gravenhage** *var.* Den Haag, *Eng.* The Hague, *Fr.* La Haye. ● (Netherlands-seat of government) Zuid-Holland, W Netherlands 52°07′N 04°17′E
162 *D7* **'s-Gravenzande** Zuid-Holland, W Netherlands 52°00′N 04°10′E
Shaan/Shaanxi Sheng *see* Shaanxi
239 *M7* **Shaanxi** *var.* Shaan, Shaanxi Sheng, Shan-hsi, Shenshi, Shensi. ❖ *province* C China
Shaartuz *see* Shahrtuz
Shaba *see* Katanga
Shabani *see* Zvishavane
136 *H6* **Shabeellaha Dhexe** *off.* Gobolka Shabeellaha Dhexe. ❖ *region* E Somalia
Shabeellaha Dhexe, Gobolka *see* Shabeellaha Dhexe
136 *G7* **Shabeellaha Hoose** *off.* Gobolka Shabeellaha Hoose. ❖ *region* S Somalia
Shabeellaha Hoose, Gobolka *see* Shabeellaha Hoose
Shabeelle, Webi *see* Shebeli
185 *M5* **Shabla** Dobrich, NE Bulgaria 43°33′N 28°31′E
185 *N5* **Shabla, Nos** *headland* NE Bulgaria 43°30′N 28°36′E
59 *I5* **Shabogama Lake** ◎ Newfoundland and Labrador, E Canada
135 *I8* **Shabunda** Sud Kivu, E Dem. Rep. Congo 02°42′S 27°20′E
220 *G8* **Shabwah** C Yemen 15°09′N 46°46′E
238 *C5* **Shache** *var.* Yarkant. Xinjiang Uygur Zizhiqu, NW China 38°27′N 77°16′E
243 *M5* **Shacheng** China 27°10′N 120°25′E
Shacheng *see* Huailai
293 *I7* **Shackleton Coast** *physical region* Antarctica
293 *M6* **Shackleton Ice Shelf** *ice shelf* Antarctica
242 *G3* **Shadauguan** China 30°11′N 111°55′E
Shaddādī *see* Ash Shadādah
74 *B4* **Shadehill Reservoir** ⊠ South Dakota, N USA
195 *N10* **Shadrinsk** Kurganskaya Oblast', C Russian Federation 56°08′N 63°18′E
73 *E10* **Shafer, Lake** ⊠ Indiana, N USA
81 *D8* **Shafter** California, W USA 35°27′N 119°15′W
80 *B2* **Shafter** California, USA 38°0′N 122°43′W
70 *C7* **Shafter** Texas, SW USA 29°49′N 104°18′W
161 *H7* **Shaftesbury** S England, UK 51°01′N 02°12′W
278 *D11* **Shag** ≈ South Island, New Zealand
58 *D4* **Shagamu River** ≈ Ontario, C Canada
227 *K3* **Shagan** ≈ E Kazakhstan
82 *G6* **Shageluk** Alaska, USA 62°40′N 159°33′W
192 *G8* **Shagonar** Respublika Tyva, S Russian Federation 51°31′N 93°06′E
278 *D12* **Shag Point** *headland* South Island, New Zealand 45°28′S 170°50′E
226 *E5* **Shagyray, Plato** *plain* SW Kazakhstan
Shāhābād *see* Eslāmābād
258 *D3* **Shah Alam** Selangor, Peninsular Malaysia 03°02′N 101°31′E
188 *G8* **Shahany, Ozero** ◎ SW Ukraine
216 *C6* **Shahbā'** *anc.* Philippopolis. As Suwaydā', S Syria 32°50′N 36°38′E
Shahbān *see* Ad Dayr
230 *G10* **Shāhbandar** Sind, SE Pakistan 23°59′N 67°54′E
230 *G8* **Shāhdād Kot** Sind, SW Pakistan 27°49′N 67°49′E
230 *B5* **Shahdād, Namakzār-e** *salt pan* E Iran
230 *G9* **Shāhdādpur** Sind, SE Pakistan 25°56′N 68°40′E
232 *G8* **Shahdol** Madhya Pradesh, C India 23°19′N 81°26′E
245 *L7* **Shahe** China 34°43′N 118°57′E
245 *I5* **Shahe** Hebei, China 36°31′N 114°18′E
245 *H8* **Sha He** ≈ C China
Shahepu *see* Linze
233 *H7* **Shāhganj** Uttar Pradesh, N India 26°03′N 82°41′E
232 *B5* **Shāhgarh** Rājasthān, NW India 27°08′N 69°56′E
Sha Hi *see* Orūmīyeh, Daryācheh-ye
Shāhī *see* Qā'emshahr
217 *H4* **Shāhimah** *var.* Shahma. C Iraq 34°21′N 42°19′E
Shahjahanabad *see* Delhi
232 *F6* **Shāhjahānpur** Uttar Pradesh, N India 27°53′N 79°55′E
Shahma *see* Shāhimah
231 *I5* **Shāhpur** Punjab, E Pakistan 32°15′N 72°32′E
Shāhpur *see* Shāhpur Chākar
232 *D7* **Shāhpura** Rājasthān, N India 25°38′N 75°01′E
230 *G9* **Shāhpur Chākar** *var.* Shāhpur. Sind, SE Pakistan 26°11′N 68°44′E
230 *E4* **Shahrak** Ghowr, C Afghanistan 34°09′N 64°16′E
223 *H7* **Shahr-e Bābak** Kermān, C Iran 30°08′N 55°04′E
222 *F5* **Shahr-e Kord** *var.* Shahr Kord. Chahār MaḤall va Bakhtīārī, C Iran 32°20′N 50°52′E
222 *F6* **Shahreẕā** *var.* Qomisheh, Qumisheh, Shahriza; *prev.* Qomsheh. Eşfahān, C Iran 32°01′N 51°51′E
229 *K5* **Shahrikhon** *Rus.* Shakhrikhan. Andijon Viloyati, E Uzbekistan 40°42′N 72°03′E
229 *H7* **Shahrisabz** Qashqadaryo Viloyati, S Uzbekistan 39°01′N 66°45′E
229 *I6* **Shahriston** *Rus.* Shakhristan. NW Tajikistan 39°45′N 68°47′E
Shahriza *see* Shahreẕā
Shahr-i-Zabul *see* Zābol
Shahr Kord *see* Shahr-e Kord
229 *I8* **Shahrtuz** *Rus.* Shaartuz. SW Tajikistan 37°13′N 68°05′E
223 *H3* **Shāhrūd** *prev.* Emāmrūd, Emāmshahr. Semnān, N Iran 36°30′N 55°E
Shahsavār/Shahsawar *see* Tonekābon
243 *H3* **Shahu** China 30°11′N 113°41′E
Shaidara *see* Step' Nardara
Shaikh Ābid *see* Shaykh 'Ābid
Shaikh Fāris *see* Shaykh Fāris
Shaikh Najm *see* Shaykh Najm
216 *D4* **Shā'īr, Jabal** ▲ C Syria 34°51′N 37°49′E
232 *E8* **Shājāpur** Madhya Pradesh, C India 23°27′N 76°21′E
129 *L8* **Shakal, Ras** *headland* NE Sudan 18°04′N 38°34′E
141 *K6* **Shakaskraal** KwaZulu-Natal, South Africa 29°27′S 31°13′E
Shakhdarinskiy Khrebet *see* Shokhdara, Qatorkŭhi
Shakhrikhan *see* Shahrikhon
Shakhristan *see* Shahriston
189 *M5* **Shakhtars'k** *Rus.* Shakhtërsk. Donets'ka Oblast', SE Ukraine 48°02′N 38°18′E
193 *L8* **Shakhtersk** Ostrov Sakhalin, Sakhalinskaya Oblast', SE Russian Federation 49°10′N 142°09′E
Shakhtërsk *see* Shakhtars'k
227 *I4* **Shakhtinsk** Karaganda, C Kazakhstan 49°40′N 72°37′E
196 *G6* **Shakhty** Rostovskaya Oblast', SW Russian Federation 47°45′N 40°14′E
197 *I1* **Shakhun'ya** Nizhegorodskaya Oblast', W Russian Federation 57°42′N 46°36′E
133 *I7* **Shaki** Oyo, W Nigeria 08°37′N 03°25′E
136 *E6* **Shakīso** Oromo, C Ethiopia 05°33′N 38°48′E
189 *M5* **Shakmars'k** Donets'ka Oblast', E Ukraine 48°04′N 38°22′E
74 *G5* **Shakopee** Minnesota, N USA 44°48′N 93°31′W
252 *D4* **Shakotan-hantō** *peninsula* Hokkaidō, NE Japan
252 *D4* **Shakotan-misaki** *headland* Hokkaidō, NE Japan 43°22′N 140°28′E
82 *G5* **Shaktoolik** Alaska, USA 64°19′N 161°05′W
136 *E5* **Shala Hāyk'** ◎ C Ethiopia
194 *G7* **Shalakusha** Arkhangel'skaya Oblast', NW Russian Federation 62°16′N 40°16′E
161 *I6* **Shalbourne** UK 51°21′N 1°33′W
227 *K3* **Shalday** Pavlodar, NE Kazakhstan 51°57′N 78°51′E
197 *I9* **Shali** Chechenskaya Respublika, SW Russian Federation 43°03′N 45°55′E
221 *K7* **Shalīm** *var.* Shelim. S Oman 18°07′N 55°39′E
Shaliuhe *see* Gangca
226 *E5* **Shalkar** *var.* Chelkar. Aktyubinsk, W Kazakhstan 47°50′N 59°29′E
226 *C3* **Shalkar, Ozero** *prev* Chelkar Ozero. ◎ W Kazakhstan
67 *K8* **Shallotte** North Carolina, SE USA 33°58′N 78°21′W
70 *D3* **Shallowater** Texas, SW USA 33°41′N 102°00′W
243 *J9* **Shalong** China 23°11′N 116°30′E
194 *F7* **Shal'skiy** Respublika Kareliya, NW Russian Federation 61°45′N 36°02′E
240 *B4* **Shaluli Shan** ▲▲ C China
195 *L9* **Shalya** Sverdlovskaya oblast', Russian federation
137 *C10* **Shama** ≈ C Tanzania
195 *L9* **Shamary** Sverdlovskaya oblast', Russian federation
55 *K7* **Shamattawa** Manitoba, C Canada 55°52′N 92°05′W
58 *D4* **Shamattawa** ≈ Ontario, C Canada
Shām, Bādiyat ash *see* Syrian Desert
Shamiya *see* Ash Shāmīyah
221 *K4* **Shām, Jabal ash** *var.* Jebel Sham. ▲ NW Oman 23°21′N 57°08′E
Sham, Jebel *see* Shām, Jabal ash
Shamkhor *see* Şämkir
64 *D6* **Shamokin** Pennsylvania, NE USA 40°47′N 76°33′W
70 *F2* **Shamrock** Texas, SW USA 35°12′N 100°15′W
Sha'nabī, Jabal ash *see* Chambi, Jebel
217 *M8* **Shanāwah** E Iraq 30°57′N 47°25′E
Shancheng *see* Taining
65 *H3* **Shandaken** New York, USA 42°07′N 74°24′W
239 *J5* **Shandan** Gansu, N China 38°50′N 101°08′E
Shandī *see* Shendi
158 *G3* **Shandon** UK 56°03′N 4°48′W
80 *C7* **Shandon** California, USA 35°39′N 120°23′W
245 *K6* **Shandong** *var.* Lu, Shandong Sheng, Shantung. ❖ *province* E China
245 *M5* **Shandong Bandao** *var.* Shantung Peninsula. *peninsula* E China
Shandong Sheng *see* Shandong
217 *K5* **Shandrūkh** E Iraq 33°20′N 45°19′E
138 *G3* **Shangani** ≈ W Zimbabwe
243 *I2* **Shangbahe** China 30°39′N 115°06′E
243 *I1* **Shangcheng** Henan, China 31°29′N 115°14′E
242 *G10* **Shangchuan Dao** *island* S China
Shangchuankou *see* Minhe
245 *H1* **Shangdu** Nei Mongol Zizhiqu, N China 41°32′N 113°33′E
245 *L8* **Shanggang** China 33°32′N 120°01′E
243 *I5* **Shanggao** *var.* Aoyang. Jiangxi, S China 28°16′N 114°55′E
237 *J6* **Shanghai** *var.* Shang-hai. Shanghai Shi, E China 31°14′N 121°28′E
243 *N2* **Shanghai Shi** *var.* Hu, Shanghai. ❖ *municipality* E China
243 *J7* **Shanghang** Fujian, SE China 25°03′N 116°25′E
245 *K7* **Shanghe** China 35°26′N 117°24′E
245 *J5* **Shanghe** Shandong, China 37°11′N 117°05′E
243 *H5* **Shangli** Jiangxi, China 27°32′N 113°28′E
242 *D9* **Shanglin** *var.* Dafeng. Guangxi Zhuangzu Zizhiqu, S China 23°26′N 108°32′E
244 *F8* **Shangluo** *var.* Shangxian. Shaanxi, C China 33°51′N 109°55′E
135 *F14* **Shangombo** Western, W Zambia 16/28′S 22°10′E
Shangpai/Shangpaihe *see* Feixi
243 *J5* **Shangqing** China 28°03′N 117°00′E
245 *I8* **Shangqiu** *var.* Zhuji. Henan, C China 34°24′N 115°37′E
243 *K4* **Shangrao** Jiangxi, China 28°16′N 117°32′E
243 *K4* **Shangrao** Jiangxi, S China 28°27′N 117°57′E
245 *I8* **Shangshui** China 33°33′N 114°36′E
242 *D10* **Shangsi** Guangxi, China 22°05′N 107°35′E
243 *J5* **Shangtang** China 27°25′N 116°40′E
Shangxian *see* Shangluo
243 *I7* **Shangyou** Jiangxi, China 25°29′N 114°19′E
243 *M3* **Shangyu** *var.* Baiguan. Zhejiang, SE China 30°03′N 120°52′E
237 *J3* **Shangzhi** Heilongjiang, NE China 45°13′N 127°59′E
245 *L3* **Shanhaiguan** China 40°0′N 119°45′E
Shanhe *see* Zhengning
248 *D1* **Shanhetun** Heilongjiang, NE China 44°42′N 127°12′E
Shan-hsi *see* Shaanxi, China
Shan-hsi *see* Shanxi, China
161 *J8* **Shanklin** UK 50°37′N 1°11′W
243 *I4* **Shankou** China 28°48′N 114°28′E
239 *H4* **Shankou** Xinjiang Uygur Zizhiqu, W China 42°02′N 94°08′E
243 *K5* **Shan Ling** ▲▲ Fujan, China
278 *G7* **Shannon** Manawatu-Wanganui, North Island, New Zealand 40°32′S 175°24′E
157 *B10* **Shannon** *Ir.* An tSionainn. ≈ W Ireland
157 *B10* **Shannon** ✈ W Ireland 52°42′N 08°57′W
158 *B10* **Shannonbridge** Offaly, Ireland 53°17′N 8°02′W
256 *D5* **Shan Plateau** *plateau* E Myanmar (Burma)
238 *G4* **Shanshan** *var.* Piqan. Xinjiang Uygur Zizhiqu, NW China 42°53′N 90°18′E
Shansi *see* Shanxi
256 *D4* **Shan State** ❖ *state* E Myanmar (Burma)
Shantar Islands *see* Shantarskiye Ostrova
193 *L7* **Shantarskiye Ostrova** *Eng.* Shantar Islands. *island group* E Russian Federation
243 *J9* **Shantou** *var.* Shan-t'ou, Swatow. Guangdong, S China 23°23′N 116°39′E
Shan-t'ou *see* Shantou
Shantung *see* Shandong
Shantung Peninsula *see* Shandong Bandao
243 *I9* **Shanwei** Guangdong, China 22°28′N 115°13′E
244 *G5* **Shanxi** *var.* Jin, Shan-hsi, Shansi, Shanxi Sheng. ❖ *province* C China
245 *J7* **Shanxian** *var.* Shan Xian. Shandong, E China 34°51′N 116°09′E
Shan Xian *see* Sanmenxia
Shan Xian *see* Shanxian
Shanxi Sheng *see* Shanxi
244 *F8* **Shanyang** Shaanxi, C China 33°35′N 109°48′E
242 *G5* **Shaodong** China 27°15′N 111°44′E
243 *H8* **Shaoguan** *var.* Shao-kuan, *Cant.* Kukong; *prev.* Ch'u-chiang. Guangdong, S China 24°57′N 113°38′E
Shao-kuan *see* Shaoguan
242 *G5* **Shaoshan** Hunan, China 27°32′N 112°17′E
243 *K5* **Shaowu** Fujian, SE China 27°24′N 117°26′E
243 *M3* **Shaoxing** Zhejiang, SE China 30°02′N 120°35′E
242 *F5* **Shaoyang** *var.* Baoqing, Shao-yang; *prev.* Pao-king. Hunan, S China 27°13′N 111°31′E
242 *F6* **Shaoyang** *var.* Tangdukou. Hunan, S China 26°54′N 111°14′E
Shao-yang *see* Shaoyang
159 *I7* **Shap** UK 54°31′N 2°40′W
156 *G3* **Shapinsay** *island* NE Scotland, UK
190 *I3* **Shapki** Leningradskaya Oblast', Russian Federation
195 *J3* **Shapkina** ≈ NW Russian Federation
Shāpūr *see* Salmās
238 *G3* **Shaqiuhe** Xinjiang Uygur Zizhiqu, W China 45°00′N 88°52′E
217 *J2* **Shaqlāwa** *var.* Shaqlāwah. E Iraq 36°24′N 44°21′E
Shaqlāwah *see* Shaqlāwa
216 *D6* **Shaqqā** As Suwaydā', S Syria 32°53′N 36°42′E
220 *G4* **Shaqrā'** Ar Riyāḍ, C Saudi Arabia 25°11′N 45°08′E
Shaqrā *see* Shuqrah
227 *L4* **Shar** *var.* Charsk. Vostochnyy Kazakhstan, E Kazakhstan 49°33′N 81°03′E
230 *F4* **Sharan** Dāikondī, SE Afghanistan 33°28′N 66°19′E
230 *G4* **Sharan** *var.* Zareh Sharan. Paktīkā, E Afghanistan 33°08′N 68°47′E
Sharaqpur *see* Sharqpur
Sharbaqty *see* Shcherbakty
221 *K7* **Sharbatāt** S Oman 17°57′N 56°14′E
Sharbatāt, Ra's *see* Sharbithāt, Ras
221 *K7* **Sharbithāt, Ras** *var.* Ra's Sharbatāt. *headland* S Oman 17°55′N 56°30′E
62 *F4* **Sharbot Lake** Ontario, SE Canada 44°45′N 76°46′W
227 *H8* **Shardara** *var.* Chardara. Yuzhnyy Kazakhstan, S Kazakhstan 41°15′N 68°01′E
Shardara Dalasy *see* Step' Nardara
239 *H2* **Sharga** Govĭ-Altay, W Mongolia 46°16′N 95°32′E
Sharga *see* Tsagaan-Uul
188 *F5* **Sharhorod** Vinnyts'ka Oblast', C Ukraine 48°46′N 28°05′E
Sharhulsan *see* Mandal-Ovoo
252 *H3* **Shari** Hokkaidō, NE Japan 43°54′N 144°42′E
Shari *see* Chari
217 *J4* **Shārī, Buḥayrat** ◎ C Iraq
Sharjah *see* Ash Shāriqah
191 *F8* **Sharkawshchyna** *var.* Sharkowshchyna, *Pol.* Szarkowszczyzna, *Rus.* Sharkovshchina. Vitsyebskaya Voblasts', NW Belarus 55°27′N 27°28′E
274 *C5* **Shark Bay** *bay* Western Australia
221 *L5* **Sharkh** E Oman 21°20′N 59°04′E
Sharkovshchina/Sharkowshchyna *see* Sharkawshchyna
197 *L3* **Sharlyk** Orenburgskaya Oblast', W Russian Federation 52°52′N 54°45′E
Sharm ash Shaykh *see* Sharm el Sheikh
129 *J4* **Sharm el Sheikh** *var.* Ofiral, Sharm ash Shaykh. E Egypt 27°51′N 34°16′E
161 *J4* **Sharnbrook** UK 52°13′N 0°32′W
65 *L3* **Sharon** Massachusetts, USA 42°07′N 71°11′W
62 *C7* **Sharon** Pennsylvania, NE USA 41°12′N 80°28′W
75 *B9* **Sharon Springs** Kansas, C USA 38°54′N 101°46′W
73 *G11* **Sharonville** Ohio, N USA 39°16′N 84°24′W
Sharourah *see* Sharūrah
74 *D5* **Sharpe, Lake** ⊠ South Dakota, N USA
52 *A6* **Sharp Mountain** ▲ Yukon Territory, NW Canada
161 *H6* **Sharpness** UK 51°43′N 2°29′W
Sharqī, Al Jabal ash/Sharqi, Jebel esh *see* Anti-Lebanon
Sharqīyah, Al Minţaqah ash *see* Ash Sharqīyah
218 *I2* **Sharqīyat an Nabk, Jabal** *dry watercourse* Syria
216 *D4* **Sharqīyat an Nabk, Jabal** ▲▲ W Syria
231 *J5* **Sharqpur** *var.* Sharaqpur. Punjab, E Pakistan 31°29′N 74°08′E
220 *G7* **Sharūrah** *var.* Sharourah. Najrān, S Saudi Arabia 17°29′N 47°05′E
195 *H9* **Shar'ya** Kostromskaya Oblast', NW Russian Federation 58°22′N 45°30′E
227 *L7* **Sharyn** *var.* Charyn. ≈ SE Kazakhstan
Sharyn *see* Charyn
138 *G4* **Shashe** Central, NE Botswana 21°25′S 27°28′E
138 *G4* **Shashe** *var.* Shashi. ≈ Botswana/Zimbabwe
136 *E5* **Shashemenē** *var.* Shashemenne, Shashhamana, *It.* Sciasciamana. Oromo, C Ethiopia 07°16′N 38°38′E
Shashemenne/Shashhamana *see* Shashemenē
Shashi *see* Shashe
243 *H4* **Shashijie** China 28°22′N 113°27′E
Shashi/Sha-shih/Shasi *see* Jingzhou, Hubei
78 *B2* **Shasta Lake** ⊠ California, W USA
78 *B1* **Shasta, Mount** ▲ California, W USA 41°24′N 122°11′W
197 *H2* **Shatki** Nizhegorodskaya Oblast', W Russian Federation 55°09′N 44°04′E
Shatlyk *see* Şatlyk
Shatra *see* Ash Shaṭrah
190 *I5* **Shatry** Tverskaya Oblast', Russian Federation
191 *G10* **Shatsk** *Rus.* Shatsk. Minskaya Voblasts', C Belarus 53°25′N 27°41′E
197 *H3* **Shatsk** Ryazanskaya Oblast', W Russian Federation 54°02′N 41°38′E
75 *C11* **Shattuck** Oklahoma, C USA 36°16′N 99°52′W
227 *H8* **Shaul'der** Yuzhnyy Kazakhstan, S Kazakhstan 42°45′N 68°21′E
57 *L8* **Shaunavon** Saskatchewan, S Canada 49°49′N 108°25′W
Shavat *see* Shovot
80 *E5* **Shaver Lake** California, USA 37°06′N 119°19′W
243 *L5* **Shawan** China 27°51′N 119°28′E
238 *F3* **Shawan** Xinjiang Uygur Zizhiqu, NW China 44°21′N 85°37′E
62 *C3* **Shawanaga** Ontario, S Canada 45°29′N 80°16′W
72 *D6* **Shawano** Wisconsin, N USA 44°46′N 88°38′W
72 *D6* **Shawano Lake** ◎ Wisconsin, N USA
160 *G3* **Shawbury** UK 52°47′N 2°39′W
63 *I2* **Shawinigan** *prev.* Shawinigan Falls. Québec, SE Canada 46°33′N 72°45′W
Shawinigan Falls *see* Shawinigan
63 *I2* **Shawinigan-Sud** Québec, SE Canada 46°30′N 72°43′W
216 *D4* **Shawmarīyah, Jabal ash** ▲▲ C Syria
75 *E12* **Shawnee** Oklahoma, C USA 35°20′N 96°55′W
62 *F3* **Shawville** Québec, SE Canada 45°37′N 76°31′W
243 *M1* **Shaxi** China 31°34′N 121°03′E
243 *K6* **Sha Xia** ≈ Fujan, China
243 *K6* **Shaxian** Fujan, China 26°14′N 117°28′E
227 *H8* **Shayan** *var.* Chayan. Yuzhnyy Kazakhstan, S Kazakhstan 42°59′N 69°22′E
242 *G2* **Shayang** Hubei, China 30°25′N 112°21′E
Shaykh *see* Ash Shakk
217 *L6* **Shaykh 'Ābid** *var.* Shaikh Ābid. E Iraq 32°40′N 46°09′E
217 *M6* **Shaykh Fāris** *var.* Shaikh Fāris. E Iraq 32°06′N 47°39′E
217 *J5* **Shaykh Ḥātim** E Iraq 33°29′N 44°15′E
Shaykh, Jabal ash *see* Hermon, Mount
217 *L6* **Shaykh Najm** *var.* Shaikh Najm. E Iraq 32°04′N 46°54′E
217 *L6* **Shaykh Sa'd** E Iraq 32°35′N 46°16′E
229 *K8* **Shazud** SE Tajikistan 37°45′N 72°22′E
191 *H11* **Shchadryn** *Rus.* Shchedrin. Homyel'skaya Voblasts', SE Belarus 52°53′N 29°33′E
191 *E11* **Shchara** ≈ SW Belarus
Shchedrin *see* Shchadryn
Shcheglovsk *see* Kemerovo
196 *F3* **Shchëkino** Tul'skaya Oblast', W Russian Federation 53°57′N 37°33′E
195 *J5* **Shchel'yayur** Respublika Komi, NW Russian Federation 65°19′N 53°27′E
227 *K2* **Shcherbakty** *Kaz.* Sharbaqty. Pavlodar, E Kazakhstan 52°28′N 78°00′E
196 *F4* **Shchigry** Kurskaya Oblast', W Russian Federation 51°53′N 36°49′E
Shchitkovichi *see* Shchytkavichy
189 *I1* **Shchors** Chernihivs'ka Oblast', N Ukraine 51°49′N 31°58′E
189 *J5* **Shchors'k** Dnipropetrovs'ka Oblast', E Ukraine 48°20′N 34°07′E
195 *M2* **Shchuch'ya** ≈ Yamalo-Nenetskiy Avtonomyy Okrug, Russian federation
196 *M10* **Shchuch'ye** Kurganskaya oblast', Russian federation
Shchuchin *see* Shchuchyn
227 *H2* **Shchuchinsk** *prev.* Shchuchye. Akmola, N Kazakhstan 52°57′N 70°10′E
Shchuchye *see* Shchuchinsk
191 *D10* **Shchuchyn** *Pol.* Szczuczyn Nowogródzki, *Rus.* Shchuchin. Hrodzyenskaya Voblasts', W Belarus 53°36′N 24°45′E
191 *G10* **Shchytkavichy** *Rus.* Shchitkovichi. Minskaya Voblasts', C Belarus 53°13′N 27°59′E
192 *F8* **Shebalino** Respublika Altay, S Russian Federation 51°16′N 85°41′E
160 *E8* **Shebbear** UK 50°51′N 4°13′W
196 *F5* **Shebekino** Belgorodskaya Oblast', W Russian Federation 50°25′N 36°55′E
Shebelē Wenz, Wabē *see* Shebeli
136 *F5* **Shebeli** *Amh.* Wabē Shebelē Wenz, *It.* Scebeli, *Som.* Webi Shabeelle. ≈ Ethiopia/Somalia
186 *E2* **Shebenikut, Maja e** ▲ E Albania 41°13′N 20°27′E
230 *F2* **Sheberghān** *var.* Shibarghān, Shiberghan, Shiberghān. Jowzjān, N Afghanistan 36°41′N 65°45′E
226 *B6* **Shebir** Mangistau, SW Kazakhstan 44°52′N 52°01′E
72 *D7* **Sheboygan** Wisconsin, N USA 43°46′N 87°44′W
133 *L7* **Shebshi Mountains** *var.* Schebschi Mountains. ▲▲ E Nigeria
Shechem *see* Nablus
Shedadi *see* Ash Shadādah
63 *N2* **Shediac** New Brunswick, SE Canada 46°13′N 64°35′W
196 *G8* **Shedok** Krasnodarskiy Kray, SW Russian Federation 44°12′N 40°49′E
136 *H4* **Sheekh** Toghdeer, N Somalia 10°01′N 45°21′E
158 *C9* **Sheelin, Lough** ◎ Ireland
83 *J3* **Sheenjek River** ≈ Alaska, USA
158 *B5* **Sheep Haven** *bay* Donegal, Ireland
156 *C7* **Sheep Haven** *Ir.* Cuan na gCaorach. *inlet* N Ireland
141 *K4* **Sheepmoor** Mpumalanga, South Africa 26°43′S 30°18′E
81 *J8* **Sheep Range** ▲▲ Nevada, W USA
162 *H7* **'s-Heerenberg** Gelderland, E Netherlands 51°52′N 06°15′E
161 *L6* **Sheerness** SE England, UK 51°27′N 00°45′E
59 *K9* **Sheet Harbour** Nova Scotia, SE Canada 44°56′N 62°31′W
278 *E10* **Sheffield** Canterbury, South Island, New Zealand 43°22′S 172°01′E
159 *K10* **Sheffield** N England, UK 53°23′N 01°30′W
66 *D7* **Sheffield** Alabama, S USA 34°46′N 87°42′W
74 *H6* **Sheffield** Iowa, C USA 42°53′N 93°13′W
65 *I3* **Sheffield** Massachusetts, USA 42°07′N 73°21′W
64 *A4* **Sheffield** Pennsylvania, USA 41°42′N 79°02′W
70 *D6* **Sheffield** Texas, SW USA 30°42′N 101°49′W
244 *B10* **Shehong** China 30°54′N 105°18′E
242 *B2* **Shehong** China 30°54′N 105°18′E
117 *C11* **Shehuen, Río** ≈ S Argentina
Shekhem *see* Nablus
231 *J5* **Shekhūpura** Punjab, NE Pakistan 31°42′N 74°08′E
Sheki *see* Şäki
194 *F9* **Sheksna** Vologodskaya Oblast', NW Russian Federation 59°11′N 38°32′E
193 *M3* **Shelagskiy, Mys** *cape* NE Russian Federation
75 *H9* **Shelbina** Missouri, C USA 39°41′N 92°02′W
63 *N4* **Shelburne** Nova Scotia, SE Canada 43°47′N 65°20′W
62 *C4* **Shelburne** Ontario, S Canada 44°04′N 80°12′W
77 *I3* **Shelby** Montana, NW USA 48°30′N 111°52′W
67 *I7* **Shelby** North Carolina, SE USA 35°15′N 81°34′W
73 *I10* **Shelby** Ohio, N USA 40°52′N 82°39′W
73 *C11* **Shelbyville** Illinois, N USA 39°24′N 88°47′W
73 *F11* **Shelbyville** Indiana, N USA 39°31′N 85°46′W
66 *F3* **Shelbyville** Kentucky, S USA 38°13′N 85°12′W
75 *H9* **Shelbyville** Missouri, C USA 39°48′N 92°01′W
66 *E6* **Shelbyville** Tennessee, S USA 35°29′N 86°30′W
71 *J5* **Shelbyville** Texas, SW USA 31°42′N 94°03′W
73 *C11* **Shelbyville, Lake** ⊠ Illinois, N USA
74 *F6* **Sheldon** Iowa, C USA 43°10′N 95°51′W
82 *F6* **Sheldons Point** Alaska, USA 62°31′N 165°03′W
193 *H8* **Shelekhov** Irkutskaya Oblast', C Russian Federation 52°04′N 104°03′E
Shelekhov Gulf *see* Shelikhova, Zaliv
193 *M5* **Shelikhova, Zaliv** *Eng.* Shelekhov Gulf. *gulf* E Russian Federation
83 *I8* **Shelikof Strait** *strait* Alaska, USA
Shelim *see* Shalīm
57 *M5* **Shellbrook** Saskatchewan, S Canada 53°14′N 106°24′W
74 *B2* **Shell Creek** ≈ North Dakota, N USA
Shellif *see* Chelif, Oued
68 *C5* **Shell Keys** *island group* Louisiana, S USA
72 *A5* **Shell Lake** Wisconsin, N USA 45°44′N 91°56′W
74 *H6* **Shell Rock** Iowa, C USA 42°42′N 92°34′W
278 *B13* **Shelter Point** *headland* Stewart Island, New Zealand 47°04′S 168°13′E
65 *I5* **Shelton** Connecticut, NE USA 41°19′N 73°06′W
76 *C4* **Shelton** Washington, NW USA 47°13′N 123°06′W
160 *G3* **Shelve** UK 52°35′N 2°59′W
Shemakha *see* Şamaxı
227 *L3* **Shemonaikha** Vostochnyy Kazakhstan, E Kazakhstan 50°38′N 81°55′E
197 *I2* **Shemursha** Chavash Respubliki, W Russian Federation 54°57′N 47°27′E
82 *B9* **Shemya Island** *island* Aleutian Islands, Alaska, USA
75 *F8* **Shenandoah** Iowa, C USA 40°46′N 95°23′W
64 *E6* **Shenandoah** Pennsylvania, USA 40°49′N 76°12′W
67 *K3* **Shenandoah** Virginia, NE USA 38°26′N 78°34′W
64 *A9* **Shenandoah Mountains** *ridge* West Virginia, NE USA
64 *B9* **Shenandoah River** ≈ West Virginia, NE USA
243 *K9* **Shenao** China 23°30′N 117°09′E
133 *L7* **Shendam** Plateau, C Nigeria 08°52′N 09°30′E
136 *C1* **Shendi** *var.* Shandī. River Nile, NE Sudan 16°41′N 33°22′E
243 *L1* **Shengang** China 31°53′N 120°08′E
132 *C7* **Shenge** SW Sierra Leone 07°54′N 12°54′W
227 *K7* **Shengel'dy** Almaty, SE Kazakhstan 44°04′N 77°31′E
243 *K2* **Shengjiaqiao** China 30°57′N 118°17′E
184 *F7* **Shëngjin** *var.* Shëngjini. Lezhë, NW Albania 41°49′N 19°34′E
Shëngjini *see* Shëngjin
Shengking *see* Liaoning
Sheng Xian/Shengxian *see* Shengzhou

◆ Country
● Country Capital
◇ Dependent Territory
○ Dependent Territory Capital
❖ Administrative Regions
✈ International Airport
▲ Mountain
▲▲ Mountain Range
Volcano
≈ River
◎ Lake
⊠ Reservoir

Slavuta - Soroki

188 E3 **Slavuta** Khmel'nyts'ka Oblast', NW Ukraine 50°18′N 26°52′E
189 H2 **Slavutych** Chernihivs'ka Oblast', N Ukraine 51°31′N 30°47′E
193 L9 **Slavyanka** Primorskiy Kray, SE Russian Federation 42°46′N 131°19′E
185 J5 **Slavyanovo** Pleven, N Bulgaria 43°28′N 24°52′E
Slavyansk *see* Slov"yans'k
196 F8 **Slavyansk-na-Kubani** Krasnodarskiy Kray, SW Russian Federation 45°16′N 38°09′E
191 H12 **Slavyechna** *Rus.* Slovechna. Belarus/Ukraine
191 I10 **Slawharad** *Rus.* Slavgorod. Mahilyowskaya Voblasts', E Belarus 53°27′N 31°00′E
182 D3 **Sławno** Zachodnio-pomorskie, NW Poland 54°23′N 16°43′E
Slawonien *see* Slavonija
74 F5 **Slayton** Minnesota, N USA 43°59′N 95°45′W
161 J2 **Sleaford** E England, UK 52°59′N 00°28′W
157 A10 **Slea Head** *Ir.* Ceann Sléibhe. *headland* SW Ireland 52°05′N 10°25′W
156 E5 **Sleat, Sound of** *strait* NW Scotland, UK
159 L8 **Sledmere** UK 54°04′N 0°34′W
Sledyuki *see* Slyedzyuki
58 F3 **Sleeper Islands** *island group* Nunavut, C Canada
72 F6 **Sleeping Bear Point** *headland* Michigan, N USA 44°54′N 86°02′W
74 G5 **Sleepy Eye** Minnesota, N USA 44°18′N 94°43′W
83 H6 **Sleetmute** Alaska, USA 61°42′N 157°10′W
Sléibhe, Ceann *see* Slea Head
159 L7 **Sleights** UK 54°27′N 0°40′W
Slēmānī *see* As Sulaymānīyah
293 H3 **Slessor Glacier** *glacier* Antarctica
158 F4 **Sliddery** UK 55°27′N 5°15′W
68 E4 **Slidell** Louisiana, S USA 30°16′N 89°46′W
65 H3 **Slide Mountain** ▲ New York, NE USA 42°00′N 74°23′W
162 E7 **Sliedrecht** Zuid-Holland, C Netherlands 51°50′N 04°46′E
175 J13 **Sliema** N Malta 35°54′N 14°31′E
158 A10 **Slieve Aughty Mountains** ▲▲ Galway, Ireland
158 C10 **Slieve Bloom Mountains** ▲▲ Ireland
157 D8 **Slieve Donard** ▲ SE Northern Ireland, UK 54°10′N 05°57′W
Sligeach *see* Sligo
158 A7 **Sligo** *Ir.* Sligeach. Sligo, NW Ireland 54°17′N 08°28′W
158 A8 **Sligo** *Ir.* Sligeach. *cultural region* NW Ireland
158 A7 **Sligo Bay** *bay* Ireland
157 B8 **Sligo Bay** *Ir.* Cuan Shligigh. *inlet* NW Ireland
159 L8 **Slingsby** UK 54°09′N 0°55′W
62 C8 **Slippery Rock** Pennsylvania, NE USA 41°02′N 80°02′W
155 J10 **Slite** Gotland, SE Sweden 57°37′N 18°46′E
185 L6 **Sliven** *var.* Slivno. Sliven, C Bulgaria 42°42′N 26°21′E
185 I6 **Slivnitsa** Sofiya, W Bulgaria 42°51′N 23°01′E
Slivno *see* Sliven
185 L4 **Slivo Pole** Ruse, N Bulgaria 43°57′N 26°15′E
74 F7 **Sloan** Iowa, C USA 42°13′N 96°13′W
81 I9 **Sloan** Nevada, W USA 35°56′N 115°13′W
80 E1 **Sloat** California, USA 39°52′N 120°44′W
Slobodka *see* Slabodka
195 I9 **Slobodskoy** Kirovskaya Oblast', NW Russian Federation 58°43′N 50°12′E
Slobodzeya *see* Slobozia
188 G7 **Slobozia** *Rus.* Slobodzeya. E Moldova 46°45′N 29°42′E
188 F9 **Slobozia** Ialomiţa, SE Romania 44°34′N 27°23′E
162 I3 **Slochteren** Groningen, NE Netherlands 53°13′N 06°48′E
191 E10 **Slonim** *Pol.* Słonim, *Rus.* Slonim. Hrodzyenskaya Voblasts', W Belarus 53°06′N 25°19′E
Słonim *see* Slonim
162 G4 **Sloter Meer** ◎ N Netherlands
Slot, The *see* New Georgia Sound
161 J6 **Slough** S England, UK 51°31′N 00°36′W
183 G10 **Slovakia** *off.* Slovenská Republika, *Ger.* Slowakei, *Hung.* Szlovákia, *Slvk.* Slovensko. ◆ *republic* C Europe
Slovak Ore Mountains *see* Slovenské rudohorie
Slovechna *see* Slavyechna
174 G4 **Slovenia** *off.* Republic of Slovenia, *Ger.* Slowenien, *Slvn.* Slovenija. ◆ *republic* SE Europe
Slovenia, Republic of *see* Slovenia
Slovenija *see* Slovenia
177 K5 **Slovenj Gradec** *Ger.* Windischgraz. N Slovenia 46°29′N 15°05′E
177 L5 **Slovenska Bistrica** *Ger.* Windischfeistritz. NE Slovenia 46°21′N 15°27′E
Slovenská Republika *see* Slovakia
177 K5 **Slovenska Konjīce** E Slovenia 46°21′N 15°28′E
183 G10 **Slovenské rudohorie** *Eng.* Slovak Ore Mountains, *Ger.* Slowakisches Erzgebirge, Ungarisches Erzgebirge. ▲▲ C Slovakia
Slovensko *see* Slovakia
189 M5 **Slov"yanoserbs'k** Luhans'ka Oblast', E Ukraine 48°41′N 39°00′E
189 M4 **Slov"yans'k** *Rus.* Slavyansk. Donets'ka Oblast', E Ukraine 48°51′N 37°38′E
Slowakei *see* Slovakia
Slowakisches Erzgebirge *see* Slovenské rudohorie
Slowenien *see* Slovenia
182 C6 **Słubice** *Ger.* Frankfurt. Lubuskie, W Poland 52°20′N 14°35′E
191 F11 **Sluch** *Rus.* Sluch'. C Belarus
188 F2 **Sluch** NW Ukraine
163 C9 **Sluis** Zeeland, SW Netherlands 51°18′N 03°22′E
184 B3 **Slunj** *Hung.* Szluin. Karlovac, C Croatia 45°06′N 15°35′E
182 E6 **Słupca** Wielkopolskie, C Poland 52°17′N 17°52′E
182 E3 **Słupia** *Ger.* Stolpe. NW Poland
182 E3 **Słupsk** *Ger.* Stolp. Pomorskie, N Poland 54°28′N 17°01′E
182 E3 **Słupsk** ◐ *province* NW Poland
141 H3 **Slurry** North-West, South Africa 25°49′S 25°51′E
191 F10 **Slutsk** *Rus.* Slutsk. Minskaya Voblasts', S Belarus 53°02′N 27°32′E
191 H10 **Slyedzyuki** *Rus.* Sledyuki. Mahilyowskaya Voblasts', E Belarus 53°35′N 30°22′E
157 A9 **Slyne Head** *Ir.* Ceann Léime. *headland* W Ireland 53°25′N 10°11′W
193 H8 **Slyudyanka** Irkutskaya Oblast', S Russian Federation 51°36′N 103°28′E
75 H14 **Smackover** Arkansas, C USA 33°21′N 92°43′W
155 G10 **Småland** *cultural region* S Sweden
155 F10 **Smålandsstenar** Jönköping, S Sweden 57°10′N 13°24′E
161 M3 **Smallburgh** UK 52°46′N 1°27′E
Small Malaita *see* Maramasike
59 I4 **Smallwood Reservoir** ◎ Newfoundland and Labrador, S Canada
191 H9 **Smalyany** *Rus.* Smolyany. Vitsyebskaya Voblasts', NE Belarus 54°36′N 30°04′E
191 G9 **Smalyavichy** *Rus.* Smolevichi. Minskaya Voblasts', C Belarus 54°02′N 28°05′E
130 D5 **Smara** *var.* Es Semara. N Western Sahara 26°45′N 11°44′W
191 F9 **Smarhon'** *Pol.* Smorgonie, *Rus.* Smorgon'. Hrodzyenskaya Voblasts', W Belarus 54°29′N 26°24′E
140 G7 **Smartt Syndicate Dam** ⊠ Northern Cape, South Africa
80 D1 **Smartville** California, USA 39°12′N 121°18′W
184 G4 **Smederevo** *Ger.* Semendria. Serbia, N Serbia 44°41′N 20°56′E
184 G4 **Smederevska Palanka** Serbia, C Serbia 44°24′N 20°56′E
154 H7 **Smedjebacken** Dalarna, C Sweden 60°08′N 15°25′E
188 E9 **Smeeni** Buzău, SE Romania 45°00′N 26°52′E
Smela *see* Smila
175 C9 **Smeralda, Costa** *cultural region* Sardegna, Italy, C Mediterranean Sea
161 H4 **Smethwick** UK 52°30′N 2°00′W
182 D6 **Śmigiel** *Ger.* Schmiegel. Wielkopolskie, C Poland 52°02′N 16°33′E
189 I4 **Smila** *Rus.* Smela. Cherkas'ka Oblast', C Ukraine 49°15′N 31°54′E
162 I4 **Smilde** Drenthe, NE Netherlands 52°57′N 06°28′E
57 L6 **Smiley** Saskatchewan, S Canada 51°40′N 109°24′W
70 G7 **Smiley** Texas, SW USA 29°16′N 97°38′W
Smilten *see* Smiltene
190 E6 **Smiltene** *Ger.* Smilten. Valka, N Latvia 57°25′N 25°53′E
193 L8 **Smirnykh** Ostrov Sakhalin, Sakhalinskaya Oblast', SE Russian Federation 49°43′N 142°48′E
57 I3 **Smith** Alberta, W Canada 55°06′N 113°57′W
80 F3 **Smith** Nevada, USA 38°48′N 119°20′W
52 C8 **Smith Arm** *Lake* Northwest Territories, NW Canada
53 I4 **Smith Bay** *coastal sea feature* Nunavut, N Canada
83 H2 **Smith Bay** *bay* Alaska, NW USA
58 F1 **Smith, Cape** *cape* Québec, NE Canada
75 D9 **Smith Center** Kansas, C USA 39°46′N 98°46′W
56 C3 **Smithers** British Columbia, SW Canada 54°45′N 127°10′W
141 H7 **Smithfield** Free State, South Africa 30°13′S 26°32′E
67 K6 **Smithfield** North Carolina, SE USA 35°30′N 78°21′W
79 H1 **Smithfield** Utah, W USA 41°50′N 111°49′W
67 M5 **Smithfield** Virginia, NE USA 36°41′N 76°38′W
55 M4 **Smith Island** *island* Nunavut, C Canada
Smith Island *see* Sumisu-jima
73 D13 **Smithland** Kentucky, S USA 37°06′N 88°24′W
67 J5 **Smith Mountain Lake** *var.* Leesville Lake. ⊠ Virginia, NE USA
78 A1 **Smith River** California, W USA 41°54′N 124°09′W
77 I4 **Smith River** Montana, NW USA
62 F4 **Smiths Falls** Ontario, SE Canada 44°54′N 76°01′W
76 F6 **Smiths Ferry** Idaho, NW USA 44°19′N 116°04′W
66 E5 **Smiths Grove** Kentucky, S USA 37°01′N 86°14′W
53 J3 **Smith Sound** *Sound* Nunavut, N Canada
277 J9 **Smithton** Tasmania, SE Australia 40°54′S 145°06′E
65 I6 **Smithtown** Long Island, New York, NE USA 40°52′N 73°13′W
66 E6 **Smithville** Tennessee, S USA 35°59′N 85°49′W
71 H7 **Smithville** Texas, SW USA 30°04′N 97°32′W
190 G5 **Smo0ylovo** Pskovskaya Oblast', Russian Federation
Šmohor *see* Hermagor
78 D2 **Smoke Creek Desert** *desert* Nevada, W USA
56 G4 **Smoky** Alberta, W Canada
276 E4 **Smoky Bay** South Australia 32°22′S 133°57′E
277 M4 **Smoky Cape** *headland* New South Wales, SE Australia 30°54′S 153°06′E
75 C9 **Smoky Hill River** Kansas, C USA
75 D9 **Smoky Hills** *hill range* Kansas, C USA
57 J4 **Smoky Lake** Alberta, SW Canada 54°08′N 112°26′W
154 C3 **Smøla** *island* W Norway
196 E2 **Smolensk** Smolenskaya Oblast', W Russian Federation 54°48′N 32°08′E
196 E2 **Smolenskaya Oblast'** ◐ *province* W Russian Federation
Smolensk-Moscow Upland *see* Smolensko-Moskovskaya Vozvyshennost'
196 E2 **Smolensko-Moskovskaya Vozvyshennost'** *var.* Smolensk-Moscow Upland. ▲▲ W Russian Federation
Smolevichi *see* Smalyavichy
186 F3 **Smólikas** *var.* Smolikás. ▲ W Greece 40°06′N 20°54′E
190 J3 **Smolino** Leningradskaya Oblast', Russian Federation
185 J8 **Smolyan** *prev.* Pashmakli. Smolyan, S Bulgaria 41°34′N 24°42′E
Smolyany *see* Smalyany
77 I8 **Smoot** Wyoming, C USA 42°37′N 110°55′W
58 E7 **Smooth Rock Falls** Ontario, S Canada 49°17′N 81°37′W
54 G7 **Smoothstone Lake** ◎ Saskatchewan, C Canada
Smorgon'/Smorgonie *see* Smarhon'
155 F12 **Smygehamn** Skåne, S Sweden 55°19′N 13°25′E
292 F4 **Smyley Island** *island* Antarctica
64 F9 **Smyrna** Delaware, NE USA 39°18′N 75°36′W
66 F8 **Smyrna** Georgia, SE USA 33°52′N 84°30′W
66 E6 **Smyrna** Tennessee, S USA 36°00′N 86°30′W
Smyrna *see* İzmir
261 J5 **Snabai** Papua, E Indonesia 01°45′S 134°14′E
157 E8 **Snaefell** ▲ C Isle of Man 54°15′N 04°29′W
152 A2 **Snaefellsjökull** ▲ W Iceland 64°51′N 23°51′W
152 C2 **Snækollur** ▲ C Iceland 64°38′N 19°18′W
158 C5 **Slieve Snaght** ▲ Donegal, Ireland 55°12′N 7°20′W
159 L9 **Snaith** UK 53°41′N 1°02′W
54 C1 **Snake** Yukon Territory, NW Canada
74 D5 **Snake Creek** South Dakota, N USA
277 J8 **Snake Island** *island* Victoria, SE Australia
78 G4 **Snake Range** ▲▲ Nevada, W USA
60 C2 **Snake River** NW USA
74 G4 **Snake River** Minnesota, N USA
74 B6 **Snake River** Nebraska, C USA
77 H7 **Snake River Plain** *plain* Idaho, NW USA
52 D10 **Snare** Northwest Territories, NW Canada
54 F3 **Snare Lakes** Northwest Territories, NW Canada
154 F2 **Snåsa** Nord-Trøndelag, C Norway 64°16′N 12°25′E
66 G5 **Sneedville** Tennessee, S USA 36°31′N 83°13′W
162 G4 **Sneek** Friesland, N Netherlands 53°02′N 05°40′E
140 G8 **Sneeuberge** ▲▲ Eastern Cape, South Africa
Sneeuw-gebergte *see* Maoke, Pegunungan
155 C12 **Snejbjerg** Ringkøbing, C Denmark 56°08′N 08°55′E
80 D4 **Snelling** California, USA 37°31′N 120°26′W
161 L2 **Snettisham** UK 52°52′N 0°30′E
192 G5 **Snezhnogorsk** Taymyrskiy (Dolgano-Nenetskiy) Avtonomnyy Okrug, N Russian Federation 68°06′N 87°37′E
Snezhnoye *see* Snizhne
174 G4 **Snežnik** ▲ SW Slovenia 45°36′N 14°25′E
182 H4 **Śniardwy, Jezioro** *Ger.* Spirdingsee. ◎ NE Poland
Sniečkus *see* Visaginas
189 I7 **Snihurivka** Mykolayivs'ka Oblast', S Ukraine 47°05′N 32°48′E
188 D4 **Snilov** ✈ (L'viv) L'vivs'ka Oblast', W Ukraine 49°45′N 23°59′E
183 I9 **Snina** *Hung.* Szinna. Prešovský Kraj, E Slovakia 49°N 22°10′E
189 M5 **Snizhne** *Rus.* Snezhnoye. Donets'ka Oblast', SE Ukraine 48°01′N 38°46′E
154 D4 **Snøhetta** *var.* Snohetta. ▲ S Norway 62°22′N 09°08′E
152 D6 **Snøtinden** ▲ C Norway 66°39′N 13°50′E
55 H5 **Snowbird Lake** ◎ Northwest Territories, C Canada
160 E2 **Snowdon** ▲ NW Wales, UK 53°04′N 04°04′W
157 F9 **Snowdonia** ▲▲ NW Wales, UK
Snowdrift *see* Łutselk'e
54 G4 **Snowdrift River** Northwest Territories, NW Canada
79 J8 **Snowflake** Arizona, SW USA 34°30′N 110°04′W
67 M3 **Snow Hill** Maryland, NE USA 38°11′N 75°23′W
67 L6 **Snow Hill** North Carolina, SE USA 35°26′N 77°39′W
292 E3 **Snowhill Island** *island* Antarctica
55 I7 **Snow Lake** Manitoba, C Canada 54°56′N 100°02′W
79 K3 **Snowmass Mountain** ▲ Colorado, C USA 39°07′N 107°04′W
65 J1 **Snow, Mount** ▲ Vermont, NE USA 42°56′N 72°52′W
78 B3 **Snow Mountain** ▲ California, W USA 39°44′N 123°01′W
Snow Mountains *see* Maoke, Pegunungan
76 G3 **Snowshoe Peak** ▲ Montana, NW USA 48°15′N 115°44′W
276 G5 **Snowtown** South Australia 33°49′S 138°13′E
79 H1 **Snowville** Utah, W USA 41°59′N 112°42′W
78 F2 **Snow Water Lake** ◎ Nevada, W USA
277 K7 **Snowy Mountains** ▲▲ New South Wales/Victoria, SE Australia
277 K7 **Snowy River** New South Wales/Victoria, SE Australia
90 G4 **Snug Corner** Acklins Island, SE Bahamas 22°31′N 73°51′W
257 H9 **Snuŏl** Krâchéh, E Cambodia 12°04′N 106°26′E
188 E5 **Snyatyn** *Rus.* Snyatyn. Ivano-Frankivs'ka Oblast', W Ukraine 48°30′N 25°50′E
75 D13 **Snyder** Oklahoma, C USA 34°37′N 98°56′W
70 E4 **Snyder** Texas, SW USA 32°43′N 100°54′W
110 H2 **So Jose da Lapa** Minas Gerais, Brazil 19°42′S 43°54′E
139 L6 **Soalala** Mahajanga, W Madagascar 16°05′S 45°21′E
172 D3 **Soalheiras** Castelo Branco, Portugal 39°42′N 7°11′W
139 N6 **Soanierana-Ivongo** Toamasina, E Madagascar 16°53′S 49°35′E
161 I3 **Soar** UK
260 G3 **Soasiu** *var.* Tidore. Pulau Tidore, E Indonesia 0°40′N 127°25′E
102 D5 **Soatá** Boyacá, C Colombia 06°23′N 72°40′W
139 L7 **Soavinandriana** Antananarivo, C Madagascar 19°09′S 46°43′E
261 L6 **Soba** Papua, E Indonesia 04°18′S 139°11′E
133 K6 **Soba** Kaduna, C Nigeria 10°58′N 08°06′E
248 C6 **Sobaek-sanmaek** ▲▲ S South Korea
136 B4 **Sobat** E Sudan
261 M6 **Sobger, Sungai** Papua, E Indonesia
261 J5 **Sobiei** Papua, E Indonesia 02°31′S 134°30′E
196 G2 **Sobinka** Vladimirskaya Oblast', W Russian Federation 56°00′N 39°55′E
190 J5 **Soblago** Tverskaya Oblast', Russian Federation
197 K4 **Sobolevo** Orenburgskaya Oblast', W Russian Federation 51°57′N 51°42′E
Soborsin *see* Săvârşin
250 D7 **Sobo-san** ▲ Kyūshū, SW Japan 32°50′N 131°16′E
182 D7 **Sobótka** Dolnoşląskie, SW Poland 50°53′N 16°48′E
108 G6 **Sobradinho** Bahia, E Brazil 09°33′S 40°56′W
Sobradinho, Barragem de *see* Sobradinho, Represa de
108 F7 **Sobradinho, Represa de** *var.* Barragem de Sobradinho. ⊠ E Brazil
108 G3 **Sobral** Ceará, E Brazil 03°45′S 40°20′W
172 C3 **Sobral** Castelo Branco, Portugal 39°57′N 8°01′W
172 B4 **Sobral** Santarém, Portugal 39°22′N 8°37′W
172 D6 **Sobral da Adiça** Beja, Portugal 38°01′N 7°16′W
111 J2 **Sobrália** Minas Gerais, Brazil 19°15′S 42°06′W
118 D2 **Sobrante, Río del** Valparaíso, Chile
171 I2 **Sobrarbe** *physical region* NE Spain
115 I9 **Soca** Canelones, Uruguay 34°41′S 55°41′W
184 A1 **Soča** *It.* Isonzo. Italy/Slovenia
182 G6 **Sochaczew** Mazowieckie, C Poland 52°15′N 20°15′E
167 M8 **Sochaux** Franche-Comté, France 47°31′N 6°50′E
196 G9 **Sochi** Krasnodarskiy Kray, SW Russian Federation 43°35′N 39°46′E
187 H3 **Sochós** *var.* Sohos, Sokhós. Kentrikí Makedonía, N Greece 40°49′N 23°23′E
Socialist People's Libyan Arab Jamahiriya *see* Libya
285 I7 **Société, Archipel de la** *var.* Archipel de Tahiti, Îles de la Société, *Eng.* Society Islands. *island group* W French Polynesia
Société, Îles de la/Society Islands *see* Société, Archipel de la
67 J7 **Society Hill** South Carolina, SE USA 34°28′N 79°54′W
Society Islands *see* Société, Archipel de la
267 L6 **Society Ridge** *undersea feature* C Pacific Ocean
105 H13 **Socompa, Volcán** N Chile 24°18′S 68°03′W
112 C4 **Socompa, Volcn** Chile 24°18′S 68°06′E
Soconusco, Sierra de *see* Sierra Madre
110 D7 **Socorro** São Paulo, Brazil 22°36′S 46°32′W
102 C5 **Socorro** Santander, C Colombia 06°30′N 73°16′W
79 L8 **Socorro** New Mexico, SW USA 33°58′N 106°55′W
Socotra *see* Suquţrā
173 J6 **Socovos** Castilla-La Manacha, Spain 38°20′N 1°58′W
257 H10 **Soc Trăng** *var.* Khanh Hung. Soc Trăng, S Vietnam 09°36′N 105°58′E
171 H6 **Socuéllamos** Castilla-La Mancha, C Spain 39°18′N 02°48′W
81 C8 **Soda Lake** *salt flat* California, W USA
152 H5 **Sodankylä** Lappi, N Finland 67°26′N 26°35′E
Sodari *see* Sodiri
80 E7 **Soda Springs** California, USA 36°02′N 118°45′W
80 E1 **Soda Springs** California, USA 39°19′N 120°23′W
77 I8 **Soda Springs** Idaho, NW USA 42°39′N 111°36′W
Soddo/Soddu *see* Sodo
66 F7 **Soddy Daisy** Tennessee, S USA 35°14′N 85°11′W
154 I7 **Söderfors** Uppsala, C Sweden 60°23′N 17°14′E
154 I6 **Söderhamn** Gävleborg, C Sweden 61°19′N 17°10′E
155 H9 **Söderköping** Östergötland, S Sweden 58°28′N 16°20′E
155 H8 **Södermanland** ◐ *county* C Sweden
155 I8 **Södertälje** Stockholm, C Sweden 59°11′N 17°39′E
136 A2 **Sodiri** *var.* Sawdirī, Sodari. Northern Kordofan, C Sudan 14°23′N 29°06′E
136 D5 **Sodo** *var.* Soddo, Soddu. Southern, S Ethiopia 06°49′N 37°43′E
154 H5 **Södra Dellen** ◎ C Sweden
155 H10 **Södra Vi** Kalmar, S Sweden 57°45′N 15°45′E
168 A6 **Sodupe** Pais Vasco, Spain 43°12′N 3°03′W
62 F5 **Sodus Point** *headland* New York, NE USA 43°16′N 76°59′W
260 E9 **Soe** *prev.* Soë. Timor, C Indonesia 09°51′S 124°29′E
140 C7 **Soebatsfontein** Northern Cape, South Africa 30°07′S 17°35′E
Soekaboemi *see* Sukabumi
259 G8 **Soekarno-Hatta** ✈ (Jakarta) Jawa, S Indonesia
Soëla-Sund *see* Soela Väin
190 C4 **Soela Väin** *prev. Eng.* Sele Sound, *Ger.* Dagden-Sund, Soëla-Sund. *strait* W Estonia
Soemba *see* Sumba, Pulau
Soembawa *see* Sumbawa
Soemenep *see* Sumenep
Soengaipenoeh *see* Sungaipenuh
Soerabaja *see* Surabaya
Soerakarta *see* Surakarta
181 E8 **Soest** Nordrhein-Westfalen, W Germany 51°34′N 08°06′E
162 F6 **Soest** Utrecht, C Netherlands 52°10′N 05°20′E
180 E4 **Soeste** NW Germany
162 F6 **Soesterberg** Utrecht, C Netherlands 52°07′N 05°17′E
186 G4 **Sofádes** *var.* Sofádhes. Thessalía, C Greece 39°20′N 22°06′E
Sofádhes *see* Sofádes
139 I4 **Sofala** Sofala, C Mozambique 20°04′S 34°43′E
139 J3 **Sofala** ◐ *province* C Mozambique
139 J4 **Sofala, Baia de** *bay* C Mozambique
139 M5 **Sofia** *seasonal river* NW Madagascar
Sofia *see* Sofiya
187 H6 **Sofikó** Pelopónnisos, S Greece 37°46′N 23°04′E
Sofi-Kurgan *see* Sopu-Korgon
185 I6 **Sofiya** *var.* Sophia, *Eng.* Sofia, *Lat.* Serdica. ● (Bulgaria) Sofiya-Grad, W Bulgaria 42°42′N 23°20′E
185 I6 **Sofiya** ✈ Sofiya-Grad, W Bulgaria 42°42′N 23°26′E
185 I6 **Sofiya, Grad** ◐ *municipality* W Bulgaria
Sofiyevka *see* Sofiyivka
189 J6 **Sofiyivka** *Rus.* Sofiyevka. Dnipropetrovs'ka Oblast', E Ukraine 48°04′N 33°55′E
193 L7 **Sofiysk** Khabarovskiy Kray, SE Russian Federation 51°32′N 139°46′E
193 K8 **Sofiysk** Khabarovskiy Kray, SE Russian Federation 52°20′N 133°37′E
194 E4 **Sofporog** Respublika Kareliya, NW Russian Federation 65°48′N 31°30′E
187 K9 **Sofraná** *prev* Záfora. *island* Kykládes, Greece, Aegean Sea
251 N8 **Sōfu-gan** *island* Izu-shotō, SE Japan
239 H8 **Sog** Xizang Zizhiqu, W China 31°52′N 93°40′E
102 D5 **Sogamoso** Boyacá, C Colombia 05°43′N 72°56′W
214 E4 **Soğanlı Çayı** N Turkey
180 D4 **Sögel** Niedersachsen, Germany 7°31′N 52°51′E
154 B6 **Sogn** *physical region* S Norway
Sogndal *see* Sogndalsfjøra
154 B6 **Sogndalsfjøra** *var.* Sogndal. Sogn Og Fjordane, S Norway 61°13′N 07°05′E
155 C9 **Søgne** Vest-Agder, S Norway 58°05′N 07°49′E
154 B6 **Sognefjorden** *fjord* NE North Sea
154 B5 **Sogn Og Fjordane** ◐ *county* S Norway
263 M7 **Sogod** Leyte, C Philippines 10°25′N 125°00′E
239 J4 **Sogo Nur** ◎ N China
239 K7 **Sogruma** Qinghai, W China 32°32′N 100°52′E
248 B8 **Sŏgwip'o** S South Korea 33°14′N 126°33′E
129 I5 **Sohâg** *var.* Sawhāj, Suliag. C Egypt 26°28′N 31°44′E
161 L4 **Soham** UK 52°20′N 0°21′E
Sohar *see* Şuḩār
290 E7 **Sohm Plain** *undersea feature* NW Atlantic Ocean
178 D3 **Soholmer Au** N Germany
Sohos *see* Sochós
Sohrau *see* Żory
181 C12 **Sohren** Rheinland-Pfalz, Germany 7°19′N 49°56′E
163 D11 **Soignies** Hainaut, SW Belgium 50°35′N 04°04′E
239 I9 **Soila** Xizang Zizhiqu, W China 30°40′N 97°07′E
165 I2 **Soissons** *anc.* Augusta Suessionum, Noviodunum. Aisne, N France 49°23′N 03°20′E
250 G5 **Sōja** Okayama, Honshū, SW Japan 34°40′N 133°42′E
232 D6 **Sojat** Rājasthān, N India 25°53′N 73°45′E
188 D3 **Sokal'** *Rus.* Sokal. L'vivs'ka Oblast', NW Ukraine 50°29′N 24°17′E
248 C5 **Sokch'o** N South Korea 38°07′N 128°34′E
214 B7 **Söke** Aydın, SW Turkey 37°46′N 27°24′E
283 J1 **Sokehs Island** *island* E Micronesia
135 H11 **Sokele** Katanga, SE Dem. Rep. Congo 09°54′S 24°38′E
229 J6 **Sokh** *Uzb.* Sŭkh. Kyrgyzstan/Uzbekistan
Sokh *see* So'x
Sokhós *see* Sochós
215 I3 **Sokhumi** *Rus.* Sukhumi. NW Georgia 43°02′N 41°01′E
185 H5 **Sokobanja** Serbia, E Serbia 43°39′N 21°51′E
133 H7 **Sokodé** C Togo 08°58′N 01°10′E
193 L5 **Sokol** Magadanskaya Oblast', E Russian Federation 59°51′N 150°56′E
194 G8 **Sokol** Vologodskaya Oblast', NW Russian Federation 59°26′N 40°09′E
182 J4 **Sokółka** Podlaskie, NE Poland 53°24′N 23°31′E
132 F4 **Sokolo** Ségou, W Mali 14°43′N 06°02′W
183 A8 **Sokolov** *Ger.* Falkenau an der Eger; *prev.* Falknov nad Ohří. Karlovarský Kraj, W Czech Republic 50°10′N 12°38′E
183 I8 **Sokołów Małopolski** Podkarpackie, SE Poland 50°12′N 22°07′E
182 I5 **Sokołów Podlaski** Mazowieckie, C Poland 52°26′N 22°14′E
132 B4 **Sokone** W Senegal 13°53′N 16°22′W
133 J5 **Sokoto** Sokoto, NW Nigeria 13°05′N 05°16′E
133 J5 **Sokoto** ◐ *state* NW Nigeria
133 J5 **Sokoto** NW Nigeria
Sokotra *see* Suquţrā
229 K4 **Sokuluk** Chuyskaya Oblast', N Kyrgyzstan 42°53′N 74°19′E
188 F5 **Sokyryany** Chernivets'ka Oblast', W Ukraine 48°28′N 27°25′E
155 A8 **Sola** Rogaland, S Norway 58°53′N 05°36′E
281 M1 **Sola** Vanua Lava, N Vanuatu 13°51′S 167°34′E
155 A8 **Sola** ✈ (Stavanger) Rogaland, S Norway 58°54′N 05°36′E
86 G9 **Sola de Vega** Oaxaca, Mexico 16°31′N 96°58′W
137 D8 **Solai** Rift Valley, W Kenya 0°02′N 36°03′E
261 L8 **Solaka** Papua, E Indonesia 07°52′S 138°45′E
232 E4 **Solan** Himāchal Pradesh, N India 30°54′N 77°06′E
81 E12 **Solana Beach** California, USA 32°59′N 117°16′W
278 A13 **Solander Island** *island* SW New Zealand
Solano *see* Bahía Solano
234 D5 **Solāpur** *var.* Sholāpur. Mahārāshtra, W India 17°43′N 75°54′E
154 I3 **Solberg** Västernorrland, C Sweden 63°48′N 17°40′E
188 E6 **Solca** *Ger.* Solka. Suceava, N Romania 47°40′N 25°50′E
170 F9 **Sol, Costa del** *coastal region* S Spain
176 G5 **Solda** *Ger.* Sulden. Trentino-Alto Adige, N Italy 46°33′N 10°35′E
188 G6 **Şoldăneşti** *Rus.* Sholdaneshty. N Moldova 47°49′N 28°45′E
Soldau *see* Wkra
179 F14 **Sölden** Tirol, W Austria 46°58′N 11°01′E
75 F9 **Soldier Creek** Kansas, C USA
114 B7 **Soldini** Santa Fe, Argentina 33°02′S 60°45′W
83 I6 **Soldotna** Alaska, USA 60°29′N 151°03′W
182 F5 **Solec Kujawski** Kujawsko-pomorskie, C Poland 53°04′N 18°09′E
114 B2 **Soledad** Santa Fe, C Argentina 30°38′S 60°52′W
102 C2 **Soledad** Atlántico, N Colombia 10°54′N 74°48′W
80 B5 **Soledad** California, W USA 36°25′N 121°19′W
103 H4 **Soledad** Anzoátegui, NE Venezuela 08°10′N 63°36′W
113 I6 **Soledade** Rio Grande do Sul, S Brazil 28°50′S 52°30′W
Isla Soledad *see* East Falkland
175 C8 **Solenzara** Corse, France, C Mediterranean Sea 41°55′N 09°24′E
Soleure *see* Solothurn
154 A6 **Solheim** Hordaland, S Norway 60°54′N 05°30′E
194 G9 **Soligalich** Kostromskaya Oblast', NW Russian Federation 59°05′N 42°15′E
169 I3 **Solignac-sur-Loire** Auvergne, France 44°58′N 3°53′E
Soligorsk *see* Salihorsk
161 I4 **Solihull** C England, UK 52°25′N 01°45′W
195 K8 **Solikamsk** Permskaya Oblast', NW Russian Federation 59°37′N 56°46′E
197 L4 **Sol'-Iletsk** Orenburgskaya Oblast', W Russian Federation 51°09′N 55°05′E
175 C13 **Soliman** Tunisia
105 F9 **Solimana, Nevado** ▲ S Peru 15°24′S 72°49′W
106 E3 **Solimões, Rio** C Brazil
184 C5 **Solin** *It.* Salona; *anc.* Salonae. Split-Dalmacija, S Croatia 43°33′N 16°29′E
181 C9 **Solingen** Nordrhein-Westfalen, W Germany 51°10′N 07°05′E
114 D9 **Solís** Buenos Aires, Argentina 34°18′S 59°20′W
115 I9 **Solís** Lavalleja, Uruguay 34°20′S 55°27′W
115 I9 **Solis de Mataojo** Lavalleja, Uruguay 34°30′S 55°24′E
Solka *see* Solca
154 H3 **Sollefteå** Västernorrland, C Sweden 63°09′N 17°15′E
155 I8 **Sollentuna** Stockholm, C Sweden 59°26′N 17°56′E
154 G6 **Sollerön** Dalarna, C Sweden 60°55′N 14°34′E
169 L6 **Solliés-Pont** Provence-Alpes-Côte d'Azur, France 43°11′N 6°03′E
180 G7 **Solling** *hill range* C Germany
155 I8 **Solna** Stockholm, C Sweden 59°22′N 17°58′E
196 F1 **Solnechnogorsk** Moskovskaya Oblast', W Russian Federation 56°07′N 37°04′E
193 L8 **Solnechnyy** Khabarovskiy Kray, SE Russian Federation 50°41′N 136°42′E
193 K6 **Solnechnyy** Respublika Sakha (Yakutiya), NE Russian Federation 60°13′N 137°42′E
Solo *see* Surakarta
184 A8 **Solofra** Campania, S Italy 40°49′N 14°48′E
258 D5 **Solok** Sumatera, W Indonesia 0°45′S 100°42′E
88 C4 **Sololá** Sololá, W Guatemala 14°46′N 91°09′W
88 B4 **Sololá** *off.* Departamento de Sololá. ◐ *department* SW Guatemala
Sololá, Departamento de *see* Sololá
136 E6 **Sololo** Eastern, N Kenya 03°31′N 38°39′E
88 B3 **Soloma** Huehuetenango, W Guatemala 15°38′N 91°25′W
82 G5 **Solomon** Alaska, USA 64°33′N 164°26′W
75 E9 **Solomon** Kansas, C USA 38°55′N 97°22′W
281 H4 **Solomon Islands** *prev.* British Solomon Islands Protectorate. ◆ *commonwealth republic* W Solomon Islands N Melanesia W Pacific Ocean
281 J1 **Solomon Islands** *island group* Papua New Guinea/Solomon Islands
75 D9 **Solomon River** Kansas, C USA
286 D6 **Solomon Sea** *sea* W Pacific Ocean
73 J9 **Solon** Ohio, N USA 41°23′N 81°26′W
189 K5 **Solone** Dnipropetrovs'ka Oblast', E Ukraine 48°12′N 34°49′E
260 E8 **Solor, Kepulauan** *island group* S Indonesia
196 G2 **Solotcha** Ryazanskaya Oblast', W Russian Federation 54°43′N 39°50′E
176 D4 **Solothurn** *Fr.* Soleure. Solothurn, NW Switzerland 47°13′N 07°32′E
176 D4 **Solothurn** *Fr.* Soleure. ◐ *canton* NW Switzerland
194 F5 **Solovetskiye Ostrova** *island group* NW Russian Federation
191 J8 **Solov'yovo** Smolenskaya Oblast', Russian Federation
171 K3 **Solsona** Cataluña, NE Spain 42°00′N 01°31′E
184 C5 **Šolta** *It.* Solta. *island* S Croatia
Solţānābād *see* Kāshmar
222 E3 **Solţānīyeh** Zanjān, NW Iran 36°24′N 48°50′E
180 H4 **Soltau** Niedersachsen, NW Germany 52°59′N 09°50′E
180 I4 **Soltendieck** Niedersachsen, Germany 10°46′N 52°52′E
194 D9 **Sol'tsy** Novgorodskaya Oblast', W Russian Federation 58°09′N 30°23′E
Soltūstik Qazaqstan Oblysy *see* Severnyy Kazakhstan
Solun *see* Thessaloníki
184 G7 **Solunska Glava** ▲ C FYR Macedonia 41°43′N 21°24′E
160 D5 **Solva** UK 51°52′N 5°12′W
81 B8 **Solvang** California, USA 34°36′N 120°08′W
155 G12 **Sölvesborg** Blekinge, S Sweden 56°04′N 14°35′E
159 H6 **Solway Firth** *inlet* England/Scotland, UK
135 H12 **Solwezi** North Western, NW Zambia 12°11′S 26°23′E
253 D11 **Sōma** Fukushima, Honshū, C Japan 37°49′N 140°52′E
214 B6 **Soma** Manisa, W Turkey 39°10′N 27°36′E
136 I4 **Somalia** *off.* Somali Democratic Republic, *Som.* Jamuuriyada Demuqraadiga Soomaaliyeed, Soomaaliya; *prev.* Italian Somaliland, Somaliland Protectorate. ◆ *republic* E Africa
288 D7 **Somali Basin** *undersea feature* W Indian Ocean
Somali Democratic Republic *see* Somalia
Somaliland Protectorate *see* Somalia
121 N5 **Somali Plain** *undersea feature* W Indian Ocean
167 J8 **Sombernon** Bourgogne, France 47°18′N 4°42′E
184 E2 **Sombor** *Hung.* Zombor. Vojvodina, NW Serbia 45°46′N 19°07′E
163 E11 **Sombreffe** Namur, S Belgium 50°32′N 04°39′E
85 J8 **Sombrerete** Zacatecas, C Mexico 23°38′N 103°40′W
91 L5 **Sombrero** *island* N Anguilla
256 A10 **Sombrero Channel** *channel* Nicobar Islands, India
188 C6 **Şomcuta Mare** *Hung.* Nagysomkút; *prev.* Somcuţa Mare. Maramureş, N Romania 47°29′N 23°30′E
Somcuţa Mare *see* Şomcuta Mare
256 G6 **Somdet** Kalasin, E Thailand 16°41′N 103°44′E
163 G9 **Someren** Noord-Brabant, SE Netherlands 51°23′N 05°42′E
153 H10 **Somero** Länsi-Soumi, SW Finland 60°37′N 23°30′E
76 G3 **Somers** Montana, NW USA 48°04′N 114°16′W
67 M10 **Somerset** *var.* Somerset Village. W Bermuda 32°18′N 64°53′W
80 E2 **Somerset** California, USA 38°39′N 120°41′W
79 K4 **Somerset** Colorado, C USA 38°55′N 107°27′W
66 F5 **Somerset** Kentucky, S USA 37°05′N 84°36′W
65 L3 **Somerset** Massachusetts, NE USA 41°46′N 71°07′W
166 B1 **Somerset** *cultural region* SW England, UK
141 H9 **Somerset East** Eastern Cape, South Africa 32°43′S 25°35′E
Somerset East *see* Somerset-Oos
67 M10 **Somerset Island** *island* W Bermuda
295 I8 **Somerset Island** *island* Queen Elizabeth Islands, Nunavut, NW Canada
Somerset Nile *see* Victoria Nile
138 F9 **Somerset-Oos** *var.* Somerset East. Eastern Cape, S South Africa 32°44′S 25°35′E
Somerset Village *see* Somerset
138 D10 **Somerset-Wes** *var.* Somerset West. Western Cape, SW South Africa 34°05′S 18°51′E
Somerset West *see* Somerset-Wes
Somers Islands *see* Bermuda
64 G9 **Somers Point** New Jersey, NE USA 39°18′N 74°34′W
63 J5 **Somersworth** New Hampshire, NE USA 43°15′N 70°52′W
81 H14 **Somerton** Arizona, SW USA 32°36′N 114°42′W
65 L2 **Somerville** Massachusetts, USA 42°23′N 71°06′W
64 G6 **Somerville** New Jersey, NE USA 40°34′N 74°36′W
66 B6 **Somerville** Tennessee, S USA 35°14′N 89°24′W
71 H6 **Somerville** Texas, SW USA 30°21′N 96°31′W
71 H6 **Somerville Lake** ⊠ Texas, SW USA
Someş/Somesch/Someşul *see* Szamos
165 H2 **Somme** ◐ *department* N France
165 H2 **Somme** N France
155 G9 **Sommen** Jönköping, S Sweden 58°07′N 14°58′E
155 H9 **Sommen** ◎ S Sweden
167 J4 **Sommepy-Tahure** Champagne-Ardenne, France 49°15′N 4°33′E
181 J9 **Sömmerda** Thüringen, C Germany 51°10′N 11°07′E
Sommerein *see* Šamorín
Sommerfeld *see* Lubsko
167 J5 **Sommesous** Champagne-Ardenne, France 48°44′N 4°12′E
103 M6 **Sommet Tabulaire** *var.* Mont Itoupé. ▲▲ S French Guiana
169 J5 **Sommiéres** Languedoc-Roussillon, France 43°47′N 4°05′E
183 E12 **Somogy** *off.* Somogy Megye. ◐ *county* SW Hungary
Somogy Megye *see* Somogy
173 I1 **Somolinos** Castilla-La Manacha, Spain 41°15′N 3°03′W
Somorja *see* Šamorín
173 H1 **Somosierra** ▲▲ Spain
170 G4 **Somosierra, Puerto de** *pass* N Spain
280 F8 **Somosomo** Taveuni, N Fiji 16°46′S 179°57′W
88 G5 **Somotillo** Chinandega, NW Nicaragua 13°01′N 86°53′W
88 G5 **Somoto** Madriz, NW Nicaragua 13°29′N 86°36′W
182 F6 **Sompolno** Wielkopolskie, C Poland 52°24′N 18°30′E
168 D7 **Somport** *var.* Puerto de Somport, *Fr.* Col du Somport; *anc.* Summus Portus. *pass* France/Spain
168 D7 **Somport** *pass* Spain
Somport *see* Somport, Col du
168 D7 **Somport, Col du** *var.* Puerto de Somport, *Sp.* Somport; *anc.* Summus Portus. *pass* France/Spain
Somport, Col du *see* Somport
Somport, Puerto de *see* Somport/Somport, Col du
163 G8 **Son** Noord-Brabant, S Netherlands 51°32′N 05°34′E
155 E8 **Son** ◐ Akershus, S Norway
233 H7 **Son** *var.* Sone. C India
89 J10 **Soná** Veraguas, W Panama 08°00′N 81°20′W
Sonag *see* Zêkog
234 H4 **Sonapur** *prev.* Sonepur. Orissa, E India 20°50′N 83°58′E
261 I5 **Sonar** Papua, E Indonesia 02°31′S 133°01′E
155 D13 **Sønderborg** *Ger.* Sonderburg. Sønderjylland, SW Denmark 54°55′N 09°48′E
Sonderburg *see* Sønderborg
155 C13 **Sønderjylland** *var.* Sønderjyllands Amt. ◐ *county* SW Denmark
Sønderjyllands Amt *see* Sønderjylland
181 J8 **Sondershausen** Thüringen, C Germany 51°22′N 10°52′E
Sondre Strømfjord *see* Kangerlussuaq
176 F5 **Sondrio** Lombardia, N Italy 46°11′N 09°52′E
Sone *see* Son
Sonepur *see* Sonapur
112 C3 **Sonequera** ▲ S Bolivia 22°06′S 67°10′W
242 G6 **Songbai** China 26°35′N 112°35′E
243 I2 **Songbu** China 31°04′N 114°48′E
257 J8 **Sông Câu** Phu Yên, C Vietnam 13°26′N 109°12′E
257 H10 **Sông Đôc** Minh Hai, S Vietnam 09°03′N 104°51′E
137 D12 **Songea** Ruvuma, S Tanzania 10°42′S 35°39′E
166 G4 **Songeons** Picardie, France 49°33′N 1°52′E
261 M5 **Songgato, Sungai** Papua, E Indonesia
243 I4 **Songhu** China 28°23′N 115°39′E
248 D1 **Songhua Hu** ◎ NE China
243 M2 **Songjiang** Shanghai Shi, E China 31°01′N 121°14′E
Sŏngjin *see* Kimch'aek
256 E11 **Songkhla** *var.* Songkla, *Mal.* Singora. Songkhla, SW Thailand 07°12′N 100°35′E
Songkla *see* Songkhla
243 J8 **Songkou** China 24°30′N 116°24′E
245 L2 **Song Ling** ▲▲ NE China
248 B4 **Songnim** SW North Korea 38°43′N 125°40′E
135 C10 **Songo** Uíge, NW Angola 07°30′S 14°56′E
139 I2 **Songo** Tete, NW Mozambique 15°36′S 32°45′E
135 C9 **Songololo** Bas-Congo, SW Dem. Rep. Congo 05°40′S 14°05′E
239 K7 **Songpan** *var.* Jin'an, *Tib.* Sungpu. Sichuan, C China 32°49′N 103°39′E
248 B8 **Sŏngsan** S South Korea
245 H8 **Song Shan 1449m** ▲ Henan, China 34°19′N 113°00′E
242 E4 **Songtao** Guizhou, China 28°06′N 109°07′E
243 L5 **Songxi** Fujian, SE China 27°33′N 118°46′E
244 G8 **Songxian** *var.* Song Xian. Henan, C China 34°11′N 112°04′E
Song Xian *see* Songxian
243 L4 **Songyang** *var.* Xiping; *prev.* Songyin. Zhejiang, SE China 28°29′N 119°27′E
Songyin *see* Songyang
242 G3 **Songzi** Hubei, China 30°06′N 111°28′E
Sonid Youqi *see* SaihanTal
Sonid Zuoqi *see* Mandalt
232 E5 **Sonīpat** Haryāna, N India 29°00′N 77°01′E
152 I7 **Sonkajärvi** Itä-Suomi, C Finland 63°40′N 27°30′E
256 G4 **Sơn La** Sơn La, N Vietnam 21°20′N 103°55′E
230 F9 **Sonmiāni** Baluchistān, S Pakistan 25°24′N 66°37′E
230 F9 **Sonmiāni Bay** *bay* S Pakistan
181 J11 **Sonneberg** Thüringen, C Germany 50°22′N 11°10′E
181 J11 **Sonnefeld** Bayern, Germany 11°08′N 50°13′E
174 F2 **Sonntagshorn** ▲ Austria/Germany 47°40′N 12°42′E
Sonoita *see* Sonoyta
84 D2 **Sonoita, Rio** *var.* Río Sonoyta. Mexico/USA
80 B2 **Sonoma** California, W USA 38°16′N 122°28′W
80 J1 **Sonoma Peak** ▲ Nevada, W USA 40°50′N 117°34′W
80 D3 **Sonora** California, W USA 37°58′N 120°22′W
70 E6 **Sonora** Texas, SW USA 30°34′N 100°39′W
60 C8 **Sonora** ◐ *state* NW Mexico
60 C7 **Sonoran Desert** *var.* Desierto de Altar. *desert* Mexico/USA *see also* Altar, Desierto de
Sonoran Desert *see* Altar, Desierto de
84 E3 **Sonora, Río** NW Mexico
84 D2 **Sonoyta** *var.* Sonoita. Sonora, NW Mexico 31°49′N 112°50′W
Sonoyta, Río *see* Sonoita, Rio
222 D4 **Sonqor** *var.* Sunqur. Kermānshāhān, W Iran 34°45′N 47°39′E
170 G5 **Sonseca** *var.* Sonseca con Casalgordo. Castilla-La Mancha, C Spain 39°40′N 03°59′W
Sonseca con Casalgordo *see* Sonseca
102 B5 **Sonsón** Antioquia, W Colombia 05°45′N 75°18′W
88 D5 **Sonsonate** Sonsonate, W El Salvador 13°44′N 89°43′W
88 C5 **Sonsonate** ◐ *department* SW El Salvador
282 A7 **Sonsorol Islands** *island group* S Palau
140 F4 **Sonstraal** Northern Cape, South Africa 27°07′S 22°28′E
184 E2 **Sonta** *Hung.* Szond; *prev.* Szonta. Vojvodina, NW Serbia 45°34′N 19°06′E
257 H4 **Sơn Tây** *var.* Sontay. Ha Tây, N Vietnam 21°06′N 105°32′E
Sontay *see* Sơn Tây
179 E13 **Sonthofen** Bayern, S Germany 47°31′N 10°16′E
Soochow *see* Suzhou
136 I4 **Sool** *off.* Gobolka Sool. ◐ *region* N Somali
Soomaaliya/Soomaaliyeed, Jamuuriyada Demuqraadiga *see* Somalia
Soome Laht *see* Finland, Gulf of
69 K2 **Soperton** Georgia, SE USA 32°22′N 82°35′W
256 G5 **Sop Hao** Houaphan, N Laos 20°33′N 104°25′E
Sophia *see* Sofiya
260 G2 **Sopi** Pulau Morotai, E Indonesia 02°36′N 128°32′E
Sopianae *see* Pécs
261 I5 **Sopinusa** Papua, E Indonesia 03°31′S 132°55′E
260 G2 **Sopi, Tanjung** *headland* Pulau Morotai, N Indonesia 02°39′N 128°34′E
190 I5 **Sopki** Novgorodskaya Oblast', Russian Federation
134 H4 **Sopo** W Sudan
Sopockinie/Sopotskin/Sopotskino *see* Sapotskin
185 J6 **Sopot** Plovdiv, C Bulgaria 42°39′N 24°43′E
182 F3 **Sopot** *Ger.* Zoppot. Pomorskie, N Poland 54°26′N 18°33′E
256 E6 **Sop Prap** *var.* Ban Sop Prap. Lampang, NW Thailand 17°55′N 99°20′E
183 D11 **Sopron** *Ger.* Ödenburg. Győr-Moson-Sopron, NW Hungary 47°40′N 16°35′E
229 K6 **Sopu-Korgon** *var.* Sofi-Kurgan. Oshskaya Oblast', SW Kyrgyzstan 40°03′N 73°30′E
232 D2 **Sopur** Jammu and Kashmir, NW India 34°19′N 74°30′E
175 F8 **Sora** Lazio, C Italy 41°43′N 13°37′E
234 I4 **Sorada** Orissa, E India 19°46′N 84°29′E
154 I4 **Söråker** Västernorrland, C Sweden 62°32′N 17°32′E
105 H9 **Sorata** La Paz, W Bolivia 15°47′S 68°38′W
Sorau/Sorau in der Niederlausitz *see* Żary
171 H8 **Sorbas** Andalucía, S Spain 37°06′N 02°06′W
158 G6 **Sorbie** UK 54°47′N 4°26′W
Sord/Sórd Choluim Chille *see* Swords
141 L5 **Sordwana Bay** *bay* KwaZulu-Natal, South Africa
168 D4 **Sore** Aquitaine, France 44°19′N 0°35′W
63 H2 **Sorel** Québec, SE Canada 46°03′N 73°06′W
277 J10 **Sorell** Tasmania, SE Australia 42°49′S 147°34′E
277 J9 **Sorell, Lake** ◎ Tasmania, SE Australia
176 F7 **Soresina** Lombardia, N Italy 45°17′N 09°51′E
155 B7 **Sørfjorden** *fjord* S Norway
154 H5 **Sörforsa** Gävleborg, C Sweden 61°45′N 17°00′E
168 F2 **Sorges** Aquitaine, France 45°18′N 0°52′E
176 A9 **Sorgues** Vaucluse, SE France 44°N 04°52′E
214 F5 **Sorgun** Yozgat, C Turkey 39°49′N 35°10′E
171 H3 **Soria** Castilla-León, N Spain 41°47′N 02°26′W
171 H3 **Soria** ◐ *province* Castilla-León, N Spain
114 E7 **Soriano** Soriano, SW Uruguay 33°25′S 58°21′W
114 F7 **Soriano** ◐ *department* SW Uruguay
158 D1 **Sorisdale** UK 56°41′N 6°27′W
152 B6 **Sørkapp** *headland* SW Svalbard 76°34′N 16°33′E
223 I3 **Sorkh, Kūh-e** ▲▲ NE Iran
158 G4 **Sorn** UK 55°30′N 4°17′W
155 E12 **Sorø** Vestsjælland, E Denmark 55°26′N 11°34′E
Soro *see* Ghazal, Bahr el
188 F5 **Soroca** *Rus.* Soroki. N Moldova 48°10′N 28°18′E
110 C9 **Sorocaba** São Paulo, S Brazil 23°29′S 47°27′W
118 E1 **Sorocayense** San Juan, Argentina 31°33′S 69°26′W
Sorochino *see* Sarochyna
197 K3 **Sorochinsk** Orenburgskaya Oblast', W Russian Federation 52°26′N 53°10′E
Soroki *see* Soroca

◆ Country
● Country Capital
◇ Dependent Territory
○ Dependent Territory Capital
◐ Administrative Regions
✈ International Airport
▲ Mountain
▲▲ Mountain Range
Volcano
River
◎ Lake
⊠ Reservoir

INDEX

◆ Country   ◇ Dependent Territory   ◆ Administrative Regions   ▲ Mountain   ▲ Volcano   ◎ Lake
● Country Capital   ○ Dependent Territory Capital   ✕ International Airport   ▲ Mountain Range   ♒ River   ▨ Reservoir

Stampalia - Suárez

Stampalia see Astypálaia
75 H14 **Stamps** Arkansas, C USA 33°22′N 93°30′W
152 E5 **Stamsund** Nordland, C Norway 68°07′N 13°50′E
75 G8 **Stanberry** Missouri, C USA 40°12′N 94°33′W
293 H3 **Stancomb-Wills Glacier** glacier Antarctica
141 J4 **Standerton** Mpumalanga, E South Africa 26°57′S 29°14′E
159 I9 **Standish** UK 53°35′N 2°40′W
72 G7 **Standish** Michigan, N USA 43°59′N 83°58′W
161 H2 **Standon** UK 52°55′N 2°17′W
66 F4 **Stanford** Kentucky, S USA 37°30′N 84°40′W
77 J4 **Stanford** Montana, NW USA 47°08′N 110°15′W
161 L6 **Stanford le Hope** UK 51°30′N 0°25′E
155 J10 **Stånga** Gotland, SE Sweden 57°16′N 18°30′E
154 E6 **Stange** Hedmark, S Norway 60°40′N 11°05′E
139 H8 **Stanger** KwaZulu/Natal, E South Africa 29°20′S 31°18′E
159 J6 **Stanhope** UK 54°45′N 2°01′W
Stanimaka see Asenovgrad
Stanislau see Ivano-Frankivs'k
80 D3 **Stanislaus River** ≈ California, W USA
Stanislav see Ivano-Frankivs'k
Stanislavskaya Oblast' see Ivano-Frankivs'ka Oblast'
Stanisławów see Ivano-Frankivs'k
Stanke Dimitrov see Dupnitsa
277 J9 **Stanley** Tasmania, SE Australia 40°48′S 145°18′E
117 J11 **Stanley** var. Port Stanley, Puerto Argentino. ○ (Falkland Islands) East Falkland, Falkland Islands 51°45′S 57°56′W
159 H2 **Stanley** UK 56°28′N 3°27′W
76 G7 **Stanley** Idaho, NW USA 44°12′N 114°58′W
74 B2 **Stanley** North Dakota, N USA 48°19′N 102°23′W
64 A10 **Stanley** Virginia, NE USA 38°34′N 78°30′W
72 B5 **Stanley** Wisconsin, N USA 44°58′N 90°54′W
135 D9 **Stanley Pool** var. Pool Malebo. lake section of river Congo/Dem. Rep. Congo
235 E8 **Stanley Reservoir** ⊠ S India
Stanleyville see Kisangani
88 E2 **Stann Creek** ◈ district SE Belize
Stann Creek see Dangriga
159 K5 **Stannington** UK 55°06′N 1°40′W
193 J7 **Stanovoy Khrebet** ▲▲ SE Russian Federation
176 D4 **Stans** Unterwalden, C Switzerland 46°57′N 08°23′E
161 K5 **Stansted** ✕ (London) Essex, E England, UK 51°53′N 00°16′E
277 M2 **Stanthorpe** Queensland, E Australia 28°35′S 151°52′E
161 L4 **Stanton** UK 52°19′N 0°54′E
66 G4 **Stanton** Kentucky, S USA 37°51′N 83°51′W
72 G7 **Stanton** Michigan, N USA 43°19′N 85°04′W
74 E7 **Stanton** Nebraska, C USA 41°57′N 97°13′W
74 C3 **Stanton** North Dakota, N USA 47°19′N 101°22′W
70 D5 **Stanton** Texas, SW USA 32°07′N 101°47′W
161 H5 **Stanway** UK 51°59′N 1°55′W
76 C3 **Stanwood** Washington, NW USA 48°14′N 122°22′W
189 N5 **Stanychno-Luhans'ke** Luhans'ka Oblast', E Ukraine 48°39′N 39°30′E
162 H5 **Staphorst** Overijssel, E Netherlands 52°38′N 06°12′E
161 I2 **Stapleford** UK 52°55′N 1°16′W
161 L7 **Staplehurst** UK 51°09′N 0°33′E
62 A6 **Staples** Ontario, S Canada 42°09′N 82°34′W
74 G3 **Staples** Minnesota, N USA 46°21′N 94°47′W
74 C7 **Stapleton** Nebraska, C USA 41°29′N 100°40′W
70 G5 **Star** Texas, SW USA 31°27′N 98°16′W
182 H7 **Starachowice** Świętokrzyskie, C Poland 51°04′N 21°02′E
Stara Kanjiža see Kanjiža
183 H9 **Stará L'ubovňa** Ger. Altlublau, Hung. Ólubló. Prešovský Kraj, E Slovakia 49°19′N 20°40′E
184 F3 **Stara Pazova** Ger. Altpasua, Hung. Ópazova. Vojvodina, N Serbia 44°59′N 20°10′E
Stara Planina see Balkan Mountains
185 K6 **Stara Reka** ≈ C Bulgaria
188 F4 **Stara Synyava** Khmel'nyts'ka Oblast', W Ukraine 49°39′N 27°39′E
188 D2 **Stara Vyzhivka** Volyns'ka Oblast', NW Ukraine 51°27′N 24°25′E
Staraya Belitsa see Staraya Byelitsa
191 H9 **Staraya Byelitsa** Rus. Staraya Belitsa. Vitsyebskaya Voblasts', NE Belarus 54°42′N 29°38′E
197 J2 **Staraya Mayna** Ul'yanovskaya Oblast', W Russian Federation 54°36′N 48°57′E
191 H11 **Staraya Rudnya** Rus. Staraya Rudnya. Homyel'skaya Voblasts', SE Belarus 52°50′N 30°17′E
194 D9 **Staraya Russa** Novgorodskaya Oblast', W Russian Federation 57°59′N 31°18′E
185 K6 **Stara Zagora** Lat. Augusta Trajana. Stara Zagora, C Bulgaria 42°26′N 25°39′E
74 F4 **Starbuck** Minnesota, N USA 45°36′N 95°31′W
285 H4 **Starbuck Island** prev. Volunteer Island. island E Kiribati
75 I13 **Star City** Arkansas, C USA 33°56′N 91°52′W
160 F8 **Starcross** UK 50°37′N 3°27′W
184 C4 **Staretina** ▲▲ W Bosnia and Herzegovina
Stargard in Pommern see Stargard Szczeciński
182 C4 **Stargard Szczeciński** Ger. Stargard in Pommern. Zachodnio-pomorskie, NW Poland 53°20′N 15°02′E
281 K4 **Star Harbour** harbour San Cristobal, SE Solomon Islands
Stari Bečej see Bečej
184 C5 **Stari Grad** It. Cittavecchia. Split-Dalmacija, S Croatia 43°11′N 16°36′E
260 E6 **Staring, Teluk** var. Teluk Wawosungu. bay Sulawesi, C Indonesia
194 E10 **Staritsa** Tverskaya Oblast', W Russian Federation 56°28′N 34°51′E
69 L4 **Starke** Florida, SE USA 29°56′N 82°07′W
66 C8 **Starkville** Mississippi, S USA 33°27′N 88°49′W
179 F13 **Starnberg** Bayern, SE Germany 48°00′N 11°19′E
179 F13 **Starnberger See** ◎ SE Germany
Starobel'sk see Starobil's'k
189 M6 **Starobesheve** Donets'ka Oblast', E Ukraine 47°45′N 38°01′E
189 M4 **Starobil's'k** Rus. Starobel'sk. Luhans'ka Oblast', E Ukraine 49°16′N 38°56′E
191 F11 **Starobin** var. Starobyn. Minskaya Voblasts', S Belarus 52°44′N 27°28′E
Starobyn see Starobin
196 E3 **Starodub** Bryanskaya Oblast', W Russian Federation 52°30′N 32°56′E
182 F4 **Starogard Gdański** Ger. Preussisch-Stargard. Pomorskie, N Poland 53°57′N 18°29′E
227 H7 **Staroikan** Yuzhnyy Kazakhstan, S Kazakhstan 43°09′N 68°34′E
Starokonstantinov see Starokostyantyniv
188 F4 **Starokostyantyniv** Rus. Starokonstantinov. Khmel'nyts'ka Oblast', NW Ukraine 49°43′N 27°13′E
196 G7 **Starominskaya** Krasnodarskiy Kray, SW Russian Federation 46°31′N 39°03′E
190 G3 **Staropolye** Leningradskaya Oblast', Russian Federation
185 L4 **Staro Selo** Rom. Satul-Vechi; prev. Star-Smil. Silistra, NE Bulgaria 43°58′N 26°32′E
196 F7 **Staroshcherbinovskaya** Krasnodarskiy Kray, SW Russian Federation 46°36′N 38°42′E
197 M3 **Starosubkhangulovo** Respublika Bashkortostan, W Russian Federation 53°05′N 57°22′E
80 I1 **Star Peak** ▲ Nevada, W USA 40°31′N 118°09′W
Star-Smil see Staro Selo
160 F9 **Start Point** headland SW England, UK 50°13′N 03°38′W
Startsy see Kirawsk
Starum see Stavoren
195 N3 **Staryy Nadym** Yamalo-Nenetskiy Avtonomyy Okrug, Russian federation
191 G10 **Staryya Darohi** Rus. Staryye Dorogi. Minskaya Voblasts', S Belarus 53°02′N 28°16′E
Staryye Dorogi see Staryya Darohi
191 J11 **Staryye Yurkovichi** Bryanskaya Oblast', Russian Federation
195 J10 **Staryye Zyatsy** Udmurtskaya Respublika, NW Russian Federation 57°22′N 52°42′E
189 K9 **Staryy Krym** Respublika Krym, S Ukraine 45°03′N 35°06′E
196 F4 **Staryy Oskol** Belgorodskaya Oblast', W Russian Federation 51°21′N 37°52′E
188 C4 **Staryy Sambir** L'vivs'ka Oblast', W Ukraine 49°27′N 23°00′E
178 G7 **Stassfurt** var. Staßfurt. Sachsen-Anhalt, C Germany 51°51′N 11°35′E
Staßfurt see Stassfurt
183 H8 **Staszów** Świętokrzyskie, C Poland 50°33′N 21°07′E
74 H7 **State Center** Iowa, C USA 42°01′N 93°09′W
64 B6 **State College** Pennsylvania, NE USA 40°48′N 77°52′W
80 F2 **Stateline** California, USA 38°58′N 119°57′W
65 H6 **Staten Island** island New York, NE USA
Staten Island see Estados, Isla de los
69 K4 **Statenville** Georgia, SE USA 30°42′N 83°00′W
69 L2 **Statesboro** Georgia, SE USA 32°28′N 81°47′W
States, The see United States of America
67 I6 **Statesville** North Carolina, SE USA 35°46′N 80°54′W
155 D8 **Stathelle** Telemark, S Norway 59°01′N 09°40′E
160 G5 **Staunton** UK 51°49′N 2°39′W
73 C11 **Staunton** Illinois, N USA 39°00′N 89°47′W
67 K3 **Staunton** Virginia, NE USA 38°10′N 79°05′W
160 G5 **Staunton on Wye** UK 52°06′N 2°55′W
155 A8 **Stavanger** Rogaland, S Norway 58°58′N 05°43′E
159 K10 **Staveley** UK 53°16′N 1°21′W
163 H11 **Stavelot** Dut. Stablo. Liège, E Belgium 50°24′N 05°56′E
155 D8 **Stavern** Vestfold, S Norway 58°58′N 10°01′E
Stavers Island see Vostok Island
161 H5 **Staverton** UK 51°55′N 2°10′W
162 F4 **Stavoren** Fris. Starum. Friesland, N Netherlands 52°52′N 05°22′E
197 H8 **Stavropol'** prev. Voroshilovsk. Stavropol'skiy Kray, SW Russian Federation 45°02′N 41°58′E
Stavropol' see Tol'yatti
197 H8 **Stavropol'skaya Vozvyshennost'** ▲▲ SW Russian Federation
197 H8 **Stavropol'skiy Kray** ◈ territory SW Russian Federation
187 H3 **Stavrós** Kentrikí Makedonía, N Greece 40°39′N 23°43′E
187 I9 **Stavrós, Akrotírio** cape Kríti, Greece, E Mediterranean Sea
187 J7 **Stavrós, Akrotírio** headland Náxos, Kykládes, Greece, Aegean Sea 37°12′N 25°32′E
187 I2 **Stavroúpoli** prev. Stavroúpolis. Anatolikí Makedonía kai Thráki, NE Greece 41°12′N 24°45′E
Stavroúpolis see Stavroúpoli
189 H4 **Stavyshche** Kyyivs'ka Oblast', N Ukraine 49°23′N 30°10′E
277 I7 **Stawell** Victoria, SE Australia 37°06′S 142°52′E
182 I4 **Stawiski** Podlaskie, NE Poland 53°22′N 22°08′E
62 C4 **Stayner** Ontario, S Canada 44°25′N 80°05′W
80 F2 **Steamboat** Nevada, USA 39°23′N 119°45′W
79 K2 **Steamboat Springs** Colorado, C USA 40°28′N 106°51′W
66 F5 **Stearns** Kentucky, S USA 36°39′N 84°27′W
82 G5 **Stebbins** Alaska, USA 63°30′N 162°15′W
181 B10 **Steckenborn** Nordrhein-Westfalen, Germany 6°21′N 50°38′E
180 I6 **Stederdorf** Niedersachsen, Germany 10°15′N 52°21′E
176 F4 **Steeg** Tirol, W Austria 47°15′N 10°18′E
75 J11 **Steele** Missouri, C USA 36°04′N 89°49′W
74 C3 **Steele** North Dakota, N USA 46°51′N 99°55′W
292 F3 **Steele Island** island Antarctica
73 C12 **Steeleville** Illinois, N USA 38°00′N 89°39′W
141 K3 **Steelpoort** Mpumalanga, South Africa 24°43′S 30°12′E
141 K3 **Steelpoort** ≈ Limpopo, South Africa
64 D7 **Steelton** Pennsylvania, USA 40°14′N 76°50′W
75 I10 **Steelville** Missouri, C USA 37°57′N 91°21′W
163 D8 **Steenbergen** Noord-Brabant, S Netherlands 51°35′N 04°19′E
Steenkool see Bintuni
54 E5 **Steen River** Alberta, W Canada 59°37′N 117°17′W
162 H5 **Steenwijk** Overijssel, N Netherlands 52°47′N 06°07′E
160 F7 **Steep Holm** island UK
117 G10 **Steeple Jason** island Jason Islands, NW Falkland Islands
266 E6 **Steep Point** headland Western Australia 26°09′S 113°11′E
188 F6 **Ştefăneşti** Botoşani, NE Romania 47°44′N 27°15′E
Stefanie, Lake see Ch'ew Bahir
52 F6 **Stefansson Island** island Nunavut, N Canada
188 G7 **Ştefan Vodă** Rus. Suvorovo. SE Moldova 46°33′N 29°39′E
117 C9 **Steffen, Cerro** ▲ S Chile 44°27′S 71°42′W
176 D4 **Steffisburg** Bern, C Switzerland 46°47′N 07°38′E
181 J12 **Stegaurach** Bayern, Germany 10°50′N 49°52′E
155 F13 **Stege** Storstrøm, SE Denmark 54°59′N 12°18′E
191 I9 **Stegrimovo** Smolenskaya Oblast', Russian Federation
188 B7 **Ştei** Hung. Vaskohsziklás. Bihor, W Romania 46°34′N 22°28′E
Steier see Steyr
Steierdorf/Steierdorf-Anina see Anina
179 J14 **Steiermark** off. Land Steiermark, Eng. Styria. ◈ state C Austria
Steiermark, Land see Steiermark
181 I12 **Steigerwald** hill range C Germany
180 G5 **Steimbke** Niedersachsen, Germany 9°23′N 52°39′E
163 G10 **Stein** Limburg, SE Netherlands 50°58′N 05°45′E
Stein see Stein an der Donau
Stein see Kamnik, Slovenia
176 G4 **Steinach** Tirol, W Austria 47°07′N 11°30′E
Steinamanger see Szombathely
177 K2 **Stein an der Donau** var. Stein. Niederösterreich, NE Austria 48°25′N 15°35′E
181 G11 **Steinau** Hessen, Germany 9°28′N 50°19′E
180 F2 **Steinau** Niedersachsen, Germany 8°53′N 53°41′E
Steinau an der Elbe see Ścinawa
55 J10 **Steinbach** Manitoba, S Canada 49°32′N 96°40′W
163 H13 **Steinfort** Luxembourg, W Luxembourg 49°39′N 05°55′E
180 D6 **Steinfurt** Nordrhein-Westfalen, Germany 7°21′N 52°09′E
181 F8 **Steinhausen** Nordrhein-Westfalen, Germany 8°32′N 51°35′E
181 J10 **Steinheid** Thüringen, Germany 11°05′N 50°28′E
181 F11 **Steinheim** Hessen, Germany 8°55′N 50°27′E
180 I5 **Steinhorst** Niedersachsen, Germany 10°24′N 52°41′E
180 G5 **Steinhude** Niedersachsen, Germany 9°21′N 52°27′E
178 D6 **Steinhuder Meer** ◎ NW Germany
154 E2 **Steinkjer** Nord-Trøndelag, C Norway 64°01′N 11°29′E
140 C6 **Steinkopf** Northern Cape, South Africa 29°16′S 17°44′E
Stejarul see Karapelit
163 D9 **Stekene** Oost-Vlaanderen, NW Belgium 51°13′N 04°04′E
141 H4 **Stella** North-West, South Africa 26°33′S 24°52′E
180 H3 **Stelle** Niedersachsen, Germany 10°07′N 53°23′E
138 D10 **Stellenbosch** Western Cape, SW South Africa 33°56′S 18°51′E
162 D7 **Stellendam** Zuid-Holland, SW Netherlands 51°48′N 04°01′E
83 K6 **Steller, Mount** ▲ Alaska, USA 60°36′N 142°49′W
174 C7 **Stello, Monte** ▲ Corse, France, C Mediterranean Sea 42°49′N 09°24′E
174 D3 **Stelvio, Passo dello** pass Italy/Switzerland
165 J2 **Stenay** Meuse, NE France 49°29′N 05°12′E
178 G6 **Stendal** Sachsen-Anhalt, C Germany 52°36′N 11°52′E
190 C6 **Stende** Talsi, NW Latvia 57°09′N 22°33′E
276 F6 **Stenhouse Bay** South Australia 35°15′S 136°58′E
178 G2 **Stenløse** Frederiksborg, E Denmark 55°47′N 12°13′E
155 G10 **Stensjön** Jönköping, S Sweden 57°36′N 14°42′E
155 G9 **Stenstorp** Västra Götaland, S Sweden 58°15′N 13°45′E
159 I3 **Stenton** UK 55°57′N 2°36′W
155 E9 **Stenungsund** Västra Götaland, S Sweden 58°05′N 11°49′E
Stepanakert see Xankändi
215 K4 **Step'anavan** N Armenia 41°00′N 44°27′E
180 J2 **Stepenitz** ≈ N Germany
74 D5 **Stephan** South Dakota, N USA 44°12′N 99°25′W
74 E2 **Stephen** Minnesota, N USA 48°27′N 96°54′W
75 H14 **Stephens** Arkansas, C USA 33°25′N 93°04′W
278 F7 **Stephens, Cape** headland D'Urville Island, Marlborough, SW New Zealand 40°42′S 173°56′E
64 B9 **Stephens City** Virginia, NE USA 39°03′N 78°10′W
277 H4 **Stephens Creek** New South Wales, SE Australia 31°51′S 141°30′E
278 G7 **Stephens Island** island C New Zealand
114 B7 **Stephenson** Santa Fe, Argentina 33°24′S 60°33′W
72 E5 **Stephenson** Michigan, N USA 45°27′N 87°36′W
59 L7 **Stephenville** Newfoundland, Newfoundland and Labrador, SE Canada 48°33′N 58°34′W
70 G5 **Stephenville** Texas, SW USA 32°12′N 98°13′W
227 H8 **Step' Nardara** Kaz. Shardara Dalasy; prev. Shaidara. grassland S Kazakhstan
197 I8 **Stepnoye** Stavropol'skiy Kray, SW Russian Federation 44°18′N 44°34′E
227 I2 **Stepnyak** Akmola, N Kazakhstan 52°52′N 70°49′E
285 K2 **Steps Point** headland Tutuila, W American Samoa 14°23′S 170°46′W
181 H11 **Sterbfritz** Hessen, Germany 9°37′N 50°19′E
186 G5 **Stereá Ellás** Eng. Greece Central. ◈ region C Greece
141 J6 **Sterkfonteindam** ⊠ Free State, South Africa
141 J2 **Sterkrivier** ≈ Limpopo, South Africa
141 I7 **Sterkspruit** Eastern Cape, South Africa 30°32′S 27°22′E
138 G8 **Sterkspruit** Eastern Cape, SE South Africa 30°31′S 27°22′E
197 L3 **Sterlibashevo** Respublika Bashkortostan, W Russian Federation 53°19′N 55°12′E
83 I6 **Sterling** Alaska, USA 60°32′N 150°51′W
79 N2 **Sterling** Colorado, C USA 40°37′N 103°12′W
73 C9 **Sterling** Illinois, N USA 41°47′N 89°42′W
75 D10 **Sterling** Kansas, C USA 38°12′N 98°12′W
70 E5 **Sterling City** Texas, SW USA 31°50′N 101°00′W
73 H8 **Sterling Heights** Michigan, N USA 42°34′N 83°01′W
64 C10 **Sterling Park** Virginia, NE USA 39°00′N 77°24′W
79 N2 **Sterling Reservoir** ⊠ Colorado, C USA
68 C1 **Sterlington** Louisiana, S USA 32°42′N 92°05′W
197 L3 **Sterlitamak** Respublika Bashkortostan, W Russian Federation 53°39′N 56°00′E
Sternberg see Šternberk
183 E9 **Šternberk** Ger. Sternberg. Olomoucký Kraj, E Czech Republic 49°45′N 17°20′E
181 F14 **Sternenfels** Baden-Württemberg, Germany 8°51′N 49°03′E
221 J9 **Stēroh** Suquṭrā, S Yemen 12°21′N 53°50′E
182 D6 **Steszew** Wielkopolskie, C Poland 52°16′N 16°41′E
Stettin see Szczecin
Stettiner Haff see Szczeciński, Zalew
57 J6 **Stettler** Alberta, SW Canada 52°21′N 112°40′W
73 J10 **Steubenville** Ohio, N USA 40°21′N 80°37′W
161 K5 **Stevenage** E England, UK 51°55′N 00°14′W
66 E7 **Stevenson** Alabama, S USA 34°52′N 85°50′W
76 C5 **Stevenson** Washington, NW USA 45°43′N 121°54′W
83 I7 **Stevenson Entrance** strait Alaska, USA
72 C6 **Stevens Point** Wisconsin, N USA 44°32′N 89°33′W
158 G4 **Stevenston** UK 55°38′N 4°46′W
83 I4 **Stevens Village** Alaska, USA 66°01′N 149°02′W
76 G5 **Stevensville** Montana, NW USA 46°30′N 114°05′W
155 F13 **Stevns Klint** headland E Denmark 55°15′N 12°25′E
56 B2 **Stewart** British Columbia, W Canada 55°58′N 129°52′W
54 B2 **Stewart** ≈ Yukon Territory, NW Canada
54 B2 **Stewart Crossing** Yukon Territory, NW Canada 63°22′N 136°37′W
117 C14 **Stewart, Isla** island S Chile
278 B13 **Stewart Island** island S New Zealand
275 J4 **Stewart, Mount** ▲ Queensland, E Australia 20°11′S 145°29′E
158 G4 **Stewarton** UK 55°40′N 4°30′W
54 A2 **Stewart River** Yukon Territory, NW Canada 63°17′N 139°24′W
80 A1 **Stewarts Point** California, USA 38°39′N 123°24′W
75 G9 **Stewartsville** Missouri, C USA 39°45′N 94°30′W
57 M7 **Stewart Valley** Saskatchewan, S Canada 50°34′N 107°47′W
74 H5 **Stewartville** Minnesota, N USA 43°51′N 92°29′W
180 F5 **Steyerberg** Niedersachsen, Germany 9°02′N 52°34′E
Steyerlak-Anina see Anina
161 K8 **Steyning** UK 50°53′N 0°20′W
141 I5 **Steynsrus** Free State, South Africa 27°57′S 27°34′E
177 J2 **Steyr** var. Steier. Oberösterreich, N Austria 48°02′N 14°26′E
177 J2 **Steyr** ≈ NW Austria
159 J4 **Stichill** UK 55°38′N 2°27′W
159 M10 **Stickford** UK 53°07′N 0°01′E
74 D6 **Stickney** South Dakota, N USA 43°24′N 98°23′W
180 J7 **Stiege** Sachsen-Anhalt, Germany 10°53′N 51°40′E
162 G3 **Stiens** Friesland, N Netherlands 53°15′N 05°45′E
Stif see Sétif
75 F12 **Stigler** Oklahoma, C USA 35°16′N 95°08′W
175 H10 **Stigliano** Basilicata, S Italy 40°24′N 16°13′E
155 I8 **Stigtomta** Södermanland, C Sweden 58°48′N 16°47′E
56 A1 **Stikine** ≈ British Columbia, W Canada
Stilida/Stilís see Stylída
155 D12 **Stilling** Århus, C Denmark 56°04′N 10°00′E
74 H4 **Stillwater** Minnesota, N USA 45°03′N 92°48′W
80 H2 **Stillwater** Nevada, USA 39°31′N 118°33′W
75 E12 **Stillwater** Oklahoma, C USA 36°07′N 97°03′W
80 H2 **Stillwater Range** ▲▲ Nevada, W USA
62 G5 **Stillwater Reservoir** ⊠ New York, NE USA
175 I12 **Stilo, Punta** headland S Italy 38°27′N 16°36′E
161 K3 **Stilton** UK 52°29′N 0°17′W
75 G12 **Stilwell** Oklahoma, C USA 35°48′N 94°37′W
184 G6 **Štimlje** Kosovo, S Serbia 42°27′N 21°03′E
70 E1 **Stinnett** Texas, SW USA 35°49′N 101°27′W
185 H7 **Štip** E FYR Macedonia 41°45′N 22°10′E
Stira see Stýra
159 H3 **Stirling** C Scotland, UK 56°07′N 03°57′W
274 D8 **Stirling Range** ▲▲ Western Australia
158 G2 **Stirlingshire** cultural region C Scotland, UK
154 E3 **Stjørdalshalsen** Nord-Trøndelag, C Norway 63°27′N 10°57′E
Stochód see Stokhid
179 D13 **Stockach** Baden-Württemberg, S Germany 47°51′N 09°01′E
161 I7 **Stockbridge** UK 51°06′N 1°29′W
70 G7 **Stockdale** Texas, SW USA 29°14′N 97°57′W
180 I2 **Stockelsdorf** Schleswig-Holstein, Germany 10°39′N 53°54′E
177 L2 **Stockerau** Niederösterreich, NE Austria 48°24′N 16°13′E
155 I8 **Stockholm** ● (Sweden) Stockholm, C Sweden 59°17′N 18°03′E
155 J8 **Stockholm** ◈ county C Sweden
160 G8 **Stockland** UK 50°50′N 3°04′W
Stockmannshof see Pļaviņas
159 J10 **Stockport** NW England, UK 53°25′N 02°10′W
159 K9 **Stocksbridge** UK 53°29′N 1°36′W
291 F9 **Stocks Seamount** undersea feature C Atlantic Ocean
80 C3 **Stockton** California, W USA 37°56′N 121°19′W
75 D9 **Stockton** Kansas, C USA 39°27′N 99°17′W
75 G10 **Stockton** Missouri, C USA 37°43′N 93°49′W
72 C3 **Stockton Island** island Apostle Islands, Wisconsin, N USA
75 G10 **Stockton Lake** ⊠ Missouri, C USA
80 C3 **Stockton Metropolitan** ✕ California, USA 37°54′N 121°14′W
159 K7 **Stockton-on-Tees** var. Stockton on Tees. N England, UK 54°34′N 01°19′W
Stockton on Tees see Stockton-on-Tees
70 D6 **Stockton Plateau** plain Texas, SW USA
75 C8 **Stockville** Nebraska, C USA 40°33′N 100°20′W
154 H4 **Stöde** Västernorrland, C Sweden 62°27′N 16°34′E
Stodolichi see Stadolichy
191 J9 **Stodolishche** Smolenskaya Oblast', Russian Federation
257 H8 **Stœng Trĕng** prev. Stung Treng. Stœng Trêng, NE Cambodia 13°31′N 105°58′E
184 G8 **Stogovo Karaorman** ▲▲ W FYR Macedonia
161 L6 **Stoke** UK 51°26′N 0°37′E
Stoke see Stoke-on-Trent
160 F9 **Stoke Fleming** UK 50°19′N 3°36′W
161 I3 **Stoke Golding** UK 52°34′N 1°24′W
161 H2 **Stoke-on-Trent** var. Stoke. C England, UK 53°N 02°10′W
159 K7 **Stokesley** UK 54°28′N 1°12′W
277 I8 **Stokes Point** headland Tasmania, SE Australia 40°09′S 143°55′E
161 H2 **Stoke-upon-Trent** UK 53°00′N 2°11′W
188 D2 **Stokhid** Pol. Stochód, Rus. Stokhod. ≈ NW Ukraine
Stokhod see Stokhid
152 B3 **Stokkseyri** Sudhurland, SW Iceland 63°49′N 21°00′W
152 E4 **Stokmarknes** Nordland, C Norway 68°34′N 14°55′E
Stol see Veliki Krš
184 D6 **Stolac** ◈ Federacija Bosna I Hercegovina, S Bosnia and Herzegovina
Stolbce see Stowbtsy
181 B10 **Stolberg** var. Stolberg im Rheinland. Nordrhein-Westfalen, W Germany 50°45′N 06°15′E
181 J8 **Stolberg** Sachsen-Anhalt, Germany 10°57′N 51°34′E
Stolberg im Rheinland see Stolberg
193 J3 **Stolbovoy, Ostrov** island NE Russian Federation
Stolbtsy see Stowbtsy
191 F12 **Stolin** Rus. Stolin. Brestskaya Voblasts', SW Belarus 51°53′N 26°51′E
154 F7 **Stöllet** var. Norra Ny. Värmland, C Sweden 60°24′N 13°15′E
180 E3 **Stollhamm** Niedersachsen, Germany 8°22′N 53°31′E
Stolp see Słupsk
Stolpe see Słupia
Stolpmünde see Ustka
180 G5 **Stolzenau** Niedersachsen, Germany 9°04′N 52°31′E
186 G4 **Stómio** Thessalía, C Greece 39°51′N 22°45′E
161 H2 **Stone** UK 52°54′N 2°08′W
62 E2 **Stonecliffe** Ontario, SE Canada 46°12′N 77°58′W
156 G5 **Stonehaven** NE Scotland, UK 56°59′N 02°14′W
157 H12 **Stonehenge** ancient monument Wiltshire, S England, UK
159 H4 **Stonehouse** UK 55°40′N 3°59′W
66 F8 **Stone Mountain** ▲ Georgia, SE USA 33°48′N 84°10′W
55 J9 **Stonewall** Manitoba, S Canada 50°08′N 97°20′W
80 H6 **Stonewall Flat** salt lake Nevada, USA
67 J2 **Stonewood** West Virginia, NE USA 39°15′N 80°18′W
158 F6 **Stoneykirk** UK 54°49′N 4°59′W
62 A6 **Stoney Point** Ontario, S Canada 42°18′N 82°32′W
152 E4 **Stonglandseidet** Troms, N Norway 69°03′N 17°06′E
132 E10 **Stonybeach Bay** bay Tristan da Cunha, SE Atlantic Ocean
78 B3 **Stony Creek** ≈ California, W USA
132 E10 **Stonyhill Point** headland S Tristan da Cunha
62 E4 **Stony Lake** ◎ Ontario, SE Canada
57 I5 **Stony Plain** Alberta, SW Canada 53°31′N 114°04′W
65 H2 **Stony Point** New York, USA 42°33′N 73°45′W
67 I6 **Stony Point** North Carolina, SE USA 35°51′N 81°04′W
62 F5 **Stony Point** headland New York, NE USA 43°50′N 76°18′W
55 H5 **Stony Rapids** Saskatchewan, C Canada 59°14′N 105°48′W
83 H6 **Stony River** Alaska, USA 61°48′N 156°37′W
161 J5 **Stony Stratford** UK 52°03′N 0°51′W
Stony Tunguska see Podkamennaya Tunguska
58 E6 **Stooping** ≈ Ontario, C Canada
180 G2 **Stör** ≈ N Germany
154 G7 **Storå** Örebro, S Sweden 59°44′N 15°10′E
155 F8 **Stora Gla** ◎ C Sweden
155 E8 **Stora Le** Nor. Store Le. ◎ Norway/Sweden
152 F5 **Stora Lulevatten** ◎ N Sweden
152 F6 **Storavan** ◎ N Sweden
194 A4 **Storavan** lakes Norrbotten, Sweden
154 J7 **Storby** Åland, SW Finland 60°12′N 19°33′E
154 B4 **Stordalen** Møre og Romsdal, S Norway 62°22′N 07°00′E
155 E13 **Storebælt** var. Store Bælt, Eng. Great Belt, Storebelt. channel Baltic Sea/Kattegat
Store Bælt see Storebælt
Storebelt see Storebælt
155 H10 **Storebro** Kalmar, S Sweden 57°36′N 15°30′E
155 F13 **Store Heddinge** Storstrøm, SE Denmark 55°19′N 12°24′E
Store Le see Stora Le
154 D4 **Støren** Sør-Trøndelag, S Norway 63°02′N 10°16′E
152 A3 **Storfjorden** fjord S Norway
155 G8 **Storfors** Värmland, C Sweden 59°33′N 14°16′E
152 E6 **Storforshei** Nordland, C Norway 66°25′N 14°25′E
Storhammer see Hamar
178 G5 **Störkanal** canal N Germany
154 F3 **Storlien** Jämtland, C Sweden 63°18′N 12°10′E
53 I4 **Cape Storm** headland Nunavut, N Canada
277 J10 **Storm Bay** inlet Tasmania, SE Australia
141 H8 **Stormberg** Eastern Cape, South Africa 31°17′S 26°17′E
141 I7 **Stormberg** ≈ Eastern Cape, South Africa
74 F6 **Storm Lake** Iowa, C USA 42°38′N 95°12′W
74 F6 **Storm Lake** ◎ Iowa, C USA
156 D4 **Stornoway** NW Scotland, UK 58°13′N 06°23′W
Storojineţ see Storozhynets'
152 C4 **Storøya** island NE Svalbard
195 J7 **Storozhevsk** Respublika Komi, NW Russian Federation 61°56′N 52°18′E
Storozhinets see Storozhynets'
188 E5 **Storozhynets'** Ger. Storozynetz, Rom. Storojineţ, Rus. Storozhinets. Chernivets'ka Oblast', W Ukraine 48°11′N 25°42′E
Storozynetz see Storozhynets'
161 K7 **Storrington** UK 50°54′N 0°27′W
152 E5 **Storriten** ▲ C Norway 68°09′N 17°12′E
65 K3 **Storrs** Connecticut, NE USA 41°48′N 72°15′W
154 E5 **Storsjøen** ◎ S Norway
154 I6 **Storsjön** ◎ C Sweden
154 G3 **Storsjön** ◎ C Sweden
152 F3 **Storslett** Troms, N Norway 69°45′N 21°03′E
154 E5 **Storsølnkletten** ▲ S Norway 61°52′N 11°32′E
152 F4 **Storsteinnes** Troms, N Norway 69°13′N 19°14′E
155 E13 **Storstrøm** var. Storstrøms Amt. ◈ county SE Denmark
Storstrøms Amt see Storstrøm
152 G6 **Storsund** Norrbotten, N Sweden 65°36′N 20°40′E
153 D8 **Storsylen** ▲ S Norway 63°07′N 12°10′E
154 F4 **Storsylen** Swe. Sylarna. ▲ Norway/Sweden 63°00′N 12°14′E
152 F5 **Stortoppen** ▲ N Sweden 67°33′N 17°27′E
154 H1 **Storuman** Västerbotten, N Sweden 65°05′N 17°10′E
154 H1 **Storuman** ◎ N Sweden
154 H6 **Storvik** Gävleborg, C Sweden 60°37′N 16°30′E
154 I7 **Storvreta** Uppsala, C Sweden 59°58′N 17°42′E
180 F3 **Stotel** Niedersachsen, Germany 8°36′N 53°27′E
161 K5 **Stotfold** UK 52°00′N 0°13′W
181 J9 **Stotternheim** Thüringen, Germany 11°03′N 51°04′E
55 H10 **Stoughton** Saskatchewan, S Canada 49°40′N 103°01′W
65 L3 **Stoughton** Massachusetts, NE USA 42°07′N 71°06′W
73 C8 **Stoughton** Wisconsin, N USA 42°56′N 89°12′W
157 G12 **Stour** ≈ E England, UK
157 I11 **Stour** ≈ S England, UK
161 H4 **Stourbridge** UK 52°28′N 2°08′W
161 M6 **Stour** ≈ UK
75 H10 **Stover** Missouri, C USA 38°26′N 92°59′W
155 D11 **Støvring** Nordjylland, N Denmark 56°53′N 09°52′E
159 I4 **Stow** UK 55°42′N 2°51′W
191 F10 **Stowbtsy** Pol. Stolbce, Rus. Stolbtsy. Minskaya Voblasts', C Belarus 53°29′N 26°44′E
71 J7 **Stowell** Texas, SW USA 29°47′N 94°22′W
161 M4 **Stowmarket** E England, UK 52°05′N 00°54′E
185 M5 **Stozher** Dobrich, NE Bulgaria 43°27′N 27°49′E
158 C6 **Strabane** Ir. An Srath Bán. W Northern Ireland, UK 54°49′N 07°27′W
158 F2 **Strachur** UK 56°10′N 5°04′W
180 D3 **Strackholt** Niedersachsen, Germany 7°38′N 53°22′E
160 A2 **Stradbally** Laois, Ireland 53°01′N 7°09′W
161 M4 **Stradbroke** UK 52°19′N 1°16′E
158 C8 **Stradone** Cavan, Ireland 53°59′N 7°14′W
181 B8 **Straelen** Nordrhein-Westfalen, Germany 6°16′N 51°27′E
75 H11 **Strafford** Missouri, C USA 37°16′N 93°07′W
277 J9 **Strahan** Tasmania, SE Australia 42°10′S 145°18′E
183 B9 **Strakonice** Ger. Strakonitz. Jihočeský Kraj, S Czech Republic 49°14′N 13°55′E
Strakonitz see Strakonice
178 H4 **Stralsund** Mecklenburg-Vorpommern, NE Germany 54°18′N 13°06′E
163 G9 **Stramproy** Limburg, SE Netherlands 51°12′N 05°43′E
138 D10 **Strand** Western Cape, SW South Africa 34°06′S 18°50′E
154 B4 **Stranda** Møre og Romsdal, S Norway 62°18′N 06°56′E
140 C7 **Strandfonteinpunt** point Northern Cape, South Africa
158 A7 **Strandhill** Sligo, Ireland 54°16′N 8°36′W
158 F7 **Strangford** UK 54°22′N 5°30′W
158 E7 **Strangford Lough** Ir. Loch Cuan. inlet E Northern Ireland, UK
155 I8 **Strängnäs** Södermanland, C Sweden 59°22′N 17°02′E
158 B6 **Stranorlar** Ir. Srath an Urláir. Donegal, NW Ireland 54°48′N 07°46′W
158 F6 **Stranraer** S Scotland, UK 54°54′N 05°02′W
57 N7 **Strasbourg** Saskatchewan, S Canada 51°05′N 104°58′W
165 L3 **Strasbourg** Ger. Strassburg; anc. Argentoratum. Bas-Rhin, NE France 48°35′N 07°45′E
79 M3 **Strasburg** Colorado, C USA 39°42′N 104°13′W
74 C4 **Strasburg** North Dakota, N USA 46°07′N 100°10′W
73 I10 **Strasburg** Ohio, N USA 40°35′N 81°31′W
64 A10 **Strasburg** Virginia, NE USA 38°59′N 78°21′W
188 G7 **Străşeni** var. Strasheny. C Moldova 47°07′N 28°37′E
Strasheny see Străşeni
177 J4 **Strassburg** Kärnten, S Austria 46°54′N 14°21′E
Strassburg see Strasbourg, France
Strassburg see Aiud, Romania
163 H13 **Strassen** Luxembourg, S Luxembourg 49°37′N 06°05′E
177 I3 **Strasswalchen** Salzburg, C Austria 47°59′N 13°19′E
62 C5 **Stratford** Ontario, S Canada 43°22′N 81°00′W
278 G6 **Stratford** Taranaki, North Island, New Zealand 39°20′S 174°16′E
80 D6 **Stratford** California, W USA 36°10′N 119°47′W
65 I5 **Stratford** Connecticut, USA 41°11′N 73°08′W
74 G7 **Stratford** Iowa, C USA 42°16′N 93°55′W
75 E13 **Stratford** Oklahoma, C USA 34°48′N 96°57′W
70 D1 **Stratford** Texas, SW USA 36°21′N 102°05′W
72 C6 **Stratford** Wisconsin, N USA 44°53′N 90°13′W
Stratford see Stratford-upon-Avon
161 I4 **Stratford-upon-Avon** var. Stratford. C England, UK 52°12′N 01°41′W
158 G3 **Strathblane** UK 55°58′N 4°18′W
277 J10 **Strathgordon** Tasmania, SE Australia 42°49′S 146°04′E
57 J7 **Strathmore** Alberta, SW Canada 51°05′N 113°20′W
80 E7 **Strathmore** California, W USA 36°07′N 119°04′W
62 B5 **Strathroy** Ontario, S Canada 42°57′N 81°40′W
156 F3 **Strathy Point** headland N Scotland, UK 58°36′N 04°04′W
158 G2 **Strathyre** UK 56°19′N 4°19′W
160 E8 **Stratton** UK 50°50′N 4°31′W
79 N3 **Stratton** Colorado, C USA 39°16′N 102°34′W
63 J3 **Stratton** Maine, NE USA 45°08′N 70°25′W
161 J5 **Stratton Audley** UK 51°55′N 1°07′W
53 I5 **Stratton Inlet** coastal sea feature Nunavut, NE Canada
65 J1 **Stratton Mountain** ▲ Vermont, NE USA 43°05′N 72°55′W
179 H12 **Straubing** Bayern, SE Germany 48°53′N 12°35′E
178 I6 **Strausberg** Brandenburg, E Germany 52°34′N 13°52′E
80 E2 **Strawberry** California, USA 38°48′N 120°09′W
80 E3 **Strawberry** California, USA 38°12′N 120°01′W
76 E6 **Strawberry Mountain** ▲ Oregon, NW USA 44°18′N 118°43′W
74 I6 **Strawberry Point** Iowa, C USA 42°40′N 91°31′W
79 I3 **Strawberry Reservoir** ⊠ Utah, W USA
79 I3 **Strawberry River** ≈ Utah, W USA
80 E1 **Strawberry Valley** California, USA 39°34′N 121°06′W
70 G4 **Strawn** Texas, SW USA 32°33′N 98°30′W
185 H7 **Straža** ▲ Bulgaria/FYR Macedonia 42°16′N 22°13′E
183 F10 **Strážov** Hung. Sztrazsó. ▲ NW Slovakia 48°59′N 18°29′E
276 E4 **Streaky Bay** South Australia 32°49′S 134°13′E
276 E4 **Streaky Bay** bay South Australia
161 K6 **Streatham** UK 51°25′N 0°08′W
73 C9 **Streator** Illinois, N USA 41°07′N 88°50′W
Streckenbach see Świdnik
183 F9 **Stredné Slovensko** ◈ region C Slovakia
Strednogorie see Pirdop
183 C9 **Středočeský Kraj** ◈ region C Czech Republic
160 G7 **Street** UK 51°07′N 2°44′W
74 D3 **Streeter** North Dakota, N USA 46°37′N 99°23′W
71 H5 **Streetman** Texas, SW USA 31°52′N 96°19′W
188 C9 **Strehaia** Mehedinţi, SW Romania 44°37′N 23°10′E
Strehlen see Strzelin
185 J6 **Strelcha** Pazardzhik, C Bulgaria 42°28′N 24°21′E
192 G7 **Strelka** Krasnoyarskiy Kray, C Russian Federation 58°05′N 92°54′E
194 F4 **Strel'na** ≈ NW Russian Federation
190 E5 **Strenči** Ger. Stackeln. Valka, N Latvia 57°38′N 25°42′E
179 E14 **Strengen** Tirol, W Austria 47°07′N 10°25′E
176 E6 **Stresa** Piemonte, NE Italy 45°52′N 08°32′E
Streshin see Streshyn
191 H11 **Streshyn** Rus. Streshin. Homyel'skaya Voblasts', SE Belarus 52°43′N 30°07′E
159 J9 **Stretford** UK 53°27′N 2°19′W
181 I11 **Streufdorf** Thüringen, Germany 10°41′N 50°21′E
154 A1 **Streymoy** Dan. Strømø. island N Faeroe Islands
192 F6 **Strezhevoy** Tomskaya Oblast', C Russian Federation 60°39′N 77°37′E
155 D12 **Strib** Fyn, C Denmark 55°33′N 09°47′E
183 A9 **Stříbro** Ger. Mies. Plzeňský Kraj, W Czech Republic 49°44′N 12°55′E
280 A3 **Strickland** ≈ SW Papua New Guinea
Striegau see Strzegom
Strigonium see Esztergom
162 E7 **Strijen** Zuid-Holland, SW Netherlands 51°45′N 04°34′E
114 B5 **Strobel** Entre Ríos, Argentina 32°03′S 60°37′W
117 C11 **Strobel, Lago** ◎ S Argentina
116 F7 **Stroeder** Buenos Aires, Argentina 40°18′S 62°48′E
186 E7 **Strofádes** island Iónioi Nísoi, Greece, C Mediterranean Sea
Strofilia see Strofyliá
187 H5 **Strofyliá** var. Strofilia. Évvoia, C Greece 38°49′N 23°25′E
180 F5 **Ströhen** Niedersachsen, Germany 8°42′N 52°32′E
158 B9 **Strokestown** Roscommon, Ireland 53°47′N 8°06′W
178 H5 **Strom** ≈ NE Germany
180 E7 **Stromberg** Nordrhein-Westfalen, Germany 8°12′N 51°48′E
175 G11 **Stromboli** ⩚ Isola Stromboli, SW Italy 38°48′N 15°13′E
175 G11 **Stromboli, Isola** island Isole Eolie, S Italy
156 E5 **Stromeferry** N Scotland, UK 57°20′N 05°35′W
156 F3 **Stromness** N Scotland, UK 58°57′N 03°18′W
Strømø see Streymoy
154 I5 **Strömsbruk** Gävleborg, C Sweden 61°52′N 17°19′E
75 E8 **Stromsburg** Nebraska, C USA 41°06′N 97°36′W
155 G11 **Strömsnäsbruk** Kronoberg, S Sweden 56°35′N 13°45′E
155 E8 **Strömstad** Västra Götaland, S Sweden 58°56′N 11°11′E
154 G3 **Strömsund** Jämtland, C Sweden 63°51′N 15°35′E
154 G2 **Ströms Vattudal** valley N Sweden
158 F3 **Strone** UK 55°59′N 4°54′W
75 I14 **Strong** Arkansas, C USA 33°06′N 92°19′W
Strongilí see Strongylí
175 I11 **Strongoli** Calabria, SW Italy 39°17′N 17°03′E
73 I9 **Strongsville** Ohio, N USA 41°18′N 81°50′W
187 N8 **Strongylí** var. Strongilí. island SE Greece
156 G3 **Stronsay** island NE Scotland, UK
158 F1 **Strontian** UK 56°41′N 5°34′W
161 H5 **Stroud** C England, UK 51°46′N 02°15′W
75 E12 **Stroud** Oklahoma, C USA 35°45′N 96°39′W
64 F5 **Stroudsburg** Pennsylvania, NE USA 40°59′N 75°12′W
64 F5 **Stroudsburg** Pennsylvania, USA 40°59′N 75°12′W
155 C11 **Struer** Ringkøbing, W Denmark 56°29′N 08°37′E
184 G8 **Struga** SW FYR Macedonia 41°11′N 20°40′E
Strugi-Kranyse see Strugi-Krasnyye
194 C9 **Strugi-Krasnyye** var. Strugi-Kranyse. Pskovskaya Oblast', W Russian Federation 58°19′N 29°09′E
140 E10 **Struisbaai** bay Western Cape, South Africa
185 I7 **Struma** Gk. Strymónas. ≈ Bulgaria/Greece see also Strymónas
Struma see Strymónas
160 D5 **Strumble Head** headland SW Wales, UK 52°01′N 05°05′W
185 H8 **Strumeshnitsa** Mac. Strumica. ≈ Bulgaria/FYR Macedonia
185 H8 **Strumica** E FYR Macedonia 41°27′N 22°39′E
Strumica see Strumeshnitsa
185 I7 **Strumyani** Blagoevgrad, SW Bulgaria 41°41′N 23°13′E
181 I9 **Struth** Thüringen, Germany 10°18′N 51°13′E
73 J9 **Struthers** Ohio, N USA 41°03′N 80°36′W
185 J6 **Stryama** ≈ C Bulgaria
141 J2 **Strydpoort Mountains** ▲▲ Limpopo, South Africa
187 H2 **Strymónas** Bul. Struma. ≈ Bulgaria/Greece see also Struma
Strymónas see Struma
187 H3 **Strymonikós Kólpos** gulf N Greece
188 C4 **Stryy** L'vivs'ka Oblast', NW Ukraine 49°16′N 23°51′E
188 C4 **Stryy** ≈ W Ukraine
182 D7 **Strzegom** Ger. Striegau. Wałbrzych, SW Poland 50°59′N 16°20′E
182 D5 **Strzelce Krajeńskie** Ger. Friedeberg Neumark. Lubuskie, W Poland 52°52′N 15°30′E
183 F8 **Strzelce Opolskie** Ger. Gross Strehlitz. Opolskie, SW Poland 50°31′N 18°19′E
277 H2 **Strzelecki Creek** seasonal river South Australia
276 G2 **Strzelecki Desert** desert South Australia
182 E7 **Strzelin** Ger. Strehlen. Dolnośląskie, SW Poland 50°48′N 17°03′E
182 F5 **Strzelno** Kujawsko-pomorski, C Poland 52°38′N 18°11′E
183 H8 **Strzyżów** Podkarpackie, SE Poland 49°52′N 21°46′E
Stua Laighean see Leinster, Mount
69 N7 **Stuart** Florida, SE USA 27°12′N 80°15′W
74 G7 **Stuart** Iowa, C USA 41°30′N 94°19′W
74 D6 **Stuart** Nebraska, C USA 42°36′N 99°08′W
67 J5 **Stuart** Virginia, NE USA 36°38′N 80°19′W
56 D4 **Stuart** ≈ British Columbia, SW Canada
82 G5 **Stuart Island** island Alaska, USA
56 D4 **Stuart Lake** ◎ British Columbia, SW Canada
278 B11 **Stuart Mountains** ▲▲ South Island, New Zealand
276 E2 **Stuart Range** hill range South Australia
Stubaital see Neustift im Stubaital
155 E13 **Stubbekøbing** Storstrøm, SE Denmark 54°53′N 12°04′E
91 M3 **Stubbs** Saint Vincent, Saint Vincent and the Grenadines 13°08′N 61°09′W
177 K3 **Stübming** ≈ E Austria
185 K7 **Studen Kladenets, Yazovir** ⊠ S Bulgaria
278 D11 **Studholme** Canterbury, South Island, New Zealand 44°44′S 171°08′E
161 H8 **Studland** UK 50°38′N 1°56′W
161 H4 **Studley** UK 52°16′N 1°53′W
Stuhlweissenberg see Székesfehérvár
Stuhm see Sztum
55 K7 **Stull Lake** ◎ Ontario, C Canada
Stung Treng see Stœng Trĕng
196 G2 **Stupino** Moskovskaya Oblast', W Russian Federation 54°54′N 38°06′E
75 H9 **Sturgeon** Missouri, C USA 39°13′N 92°16′W
62 C2 **Sturgeon** ≈ Ontario, S Canada
72 E6 **Sturgeon Bay** Wisconsin, N USA 44°51′N 87°21′W
62 C2 **Sturgeon Falls** Ontario, S Canada 46°22′N 79°57′W
58 C6 **Sturgeon Lake** ◎ Ontario, S Canada
72 D4 **Sturgeon River** ≈ Michigan, N USA
66 C4 **Sturgis** Kentucky, S USA 37°33′N 87°58′W
73 F9 **Sturgis** Michigan, N USA 41°48′N 85°25′W
74 A5 **Sturgis** South Dakota, N USA 44°24′N 103°30′W
184 C3 **Šturlić** ◈ Federacija Bosna I Hercegovina, NW Bosnia and Herzegovina
161 H8 **Sturminster Newton** UK 50°55′N 2°17′W
183 F11 **Štúrovo** Hung. Párkány; prev. Parkan. Nitriansky Kraj, SW Slovakia 47°49′N 18°40′E
161 M6 **Sturry** UK 51°17′N 1°07′E
277 H3 **Sturt, Mount** hill New South Wales, SE Australia
274 G3 **Sturt Plain** plain Northern Territory, N Australia
276 G1 **Sturt Stony Desert** desert South Australia
141 I9 **Stutterheim** Eastern Cape, South Africa 32°34′S 27°25′E
138 G9 **Stutterheim** Eastern Cape, S South Africa 32°35′S 27°26′E
179 D12 **Stuttgart** Baden-Württemberg, SW Germany 48°47′N 09°12′E
75 I13 **Stuttgart** Arkansas, C USA 34°30′N 91°32′W
152 B2 **Stykkishólmur** Vesturland, W Iceland 65°04′N 22°43′W
186 G5 **Stylída** var. Stilida, Stilís. Stereá Ellás, C Greece 38°55′N 22°37′E
188 E2 **Styr** Rus. Styr'. ≈ Belarus/Ukraine
187 I6 **Stýra** var. Stira. Évvoia, C Greece 38°10′N 24°13′E
Styria see Steiermark
Su see Jiangsu
Sua see Sowa
260 F8 **Suai** W EastTimor 09°19′S 125°16′E
102 C5 **Suaita** Santander, C Colombia 06°07′N 73°30′W
129 K8 **Suakin** var. Sawakin. Red Sea, NE Sudan 19°06′N 37°17′E
243 N7 **Suao** Jap. Suō. N Taiwan 24°33′N 121°48′E
Suao see Suau
138 F4 **Sua Pan** var. Sowa Pan. salt lake NE Botswana
84 F4 **Suaqui Grande** Sonora, NW Mexico 28°22′N 109°52′W
112 E7 **Suardi** Santa Fe, C Argentina 30°32′S 61°58′W
102 B6 **Suárez** Cauca, SW Colombia 02°55′N 76°41′W

◆ Country
● Country Capital
◇ Dependent Territory
○ Dependent Territory Capital
◈ Administrative Regions
✕ International Airport
▲ Mountain
▲▲ Mountain Range
⩚ Volcano
≈ River
◎ Lake
⊠ Reservoir

INDEX

Suau - Svobodnyy

280 D5 **Suau** *var.* Suao. Suaul Island, SE Papua New Guinea 10°39′S 150°03′E
190 D7 **Subačius** Panevėžys, NE Lithuania 55°46′N 24°45′E
258 D3 **Subang** ✈ (Kuala Lumpur) Pahang, Peninsular Malaysia
205 K6 **Subansiri** ≈ NE India
242 E6 **Subao Ding 1934m** ▲ Hunan, China 27°06′N 110°11′E
190 E7 **Subate** Daugvapils, SE Latvia 56°00′N 25°54′E
216 G4 **Subaykhān** Dayr az Zawr, E Syria 34°52′N 40°35′E
245 L8 **Subei Guangai Zongqu** *irrigation canal* Jiangsu, China
Subei/Subei Mongolzu Zizhixian *see* Dangchengwan
258 H3 **Subi Besar, Pulau** *island* Kepulauan Natuna, W Indonesia
Subiyah *see* Aş Şubayḩīyah
75 B10 **Sublette** Kansas, C USA 37°28′N 100°52′W
184 F2 **Subotica** *Ger.* Maria-Theresiopel, *Hung.* Szabadka. Vojvodina, N Serbia 46°06′N 19°41′E
188 E6 **Suceava** *Ger.* Suczawa, *Hung.* Szucsava. Suceava, NE Romania 47°41′N 26°16′E
188 E6 **Suceava** ⬖ *county* NE Romania
188 E6 **Suceava** *Ger.* Suczawa. ≈ N Romania
184 C4 **Sučevići** Zadar, SW Croatia 44°13′N 16°04′E
183 G9 **Sucha Beskidzka** Małopolskie, S Poland 49°44′N 19°36′E
182 H7 **Suchedniów** Świętokrzyskie, C Poland 51°01′N 20°49′E
245 L7 **Sucheng** China 34°42′N 119°26′E
87 J8 **Suchiapa** Chiapas, Mexico 16°37′N 93°05′W
87 I8 **Suchilapan** Oaxaca, Mexico 17°24′N 94°59′W
88 B4 **Suchitepéquez** *off.* Departamento de Suchitepéquez. ⬖ *department* SW Guatemala
Suchitepéquez, Departamento de *see* Suchitepéquez
Su-chou *see* Suzhou
Suchow *see* Suzhou, Jiangsu, China
Suchow *see* Xuzhou, Jiangsu, China
173 L7 **Sucina** Murcia, Spain 37°53′N 0°56′W
157 C9 **Suck** ≈ C Ireland
Sucker State *see* Illinois
280 C4 **Suckling, Mount** ▲ S Papua New Guinea 09°36′S 149°00′E
158 B10 **Suck** ≈ Ireland
112 D1 **Sucre** *hist.* Chuquisaca, La Plata. ● (Bolivia-legal capital) Chuquisaca, S Bolivia 18°53′S 65°25′W
102 C3 **Sucre** Santander, N Colombia 08°50′N 74°22′W
104 B2 **Sucre** Manabí, W Ecuador 01°21′S 80°27′W
102 B3 **Sucre** *off.* Departamento de Sucre. ⬖ *province* N Colombia
103 H3 **Sucre** *off.* Estado Sucre. ⬖ *state* NE Venezuela
Sucre, Departamento de *see* Sucre
Sucre, Estado *see* Sucre
104 D1 **Sucumbíos** ⬖ *province* NE Ecuador
184 D5 **Sućuraj** Split-Dalmacija, S Croatia 43°07′N 17°10′E
108 B1 **Sucuriju** Amapá, NE Brazil 01°31′N 50°W
Suczawa *see* Suceava
134 B6 **Sud** *Eng.* South. ⬖ *province* S Cameroon
194 F8 **Suda** ≈ NW Russian Federation
Suda *see* Soúda
189 K9 **Sudak** Respublika Krym, S Ukraine 44°52′N 34°57′E
70 D3 **Sudan** Texas, SW USA 34°04′N 102°32′W
134 I2 **Sudan** *off.* Republic of Sudan, *Ar.* Jumhuriyat as-Sudan; *prev.* Anglo-Egyptian Sudan. ◆ *republic* N Africa
Sudanese Republic *see* Mali
Sudan, Jumhuriyat as- *see* Sudan
Sudan, Republic of *see* Sudan
62 C2 **Sudbury** Ontario, S Canada 46°29′N 81°W
161 L5 **Sudbury** E England, UK 52°04′N 00°43′E
Sud, Canal de *see* Gonâve, Canal de la
136 A4 **Sudd** *swamp region* S Sudan
180 J3 **Sude** ≈ N Germany
180 I4 **Suderburg** Niedersachsen, Germany 10°28′N 52°54′E
Suderø *see* Sudhuroy
Sudest Island *see* Tagula Island
183 D8 **Sudeten** *var.* Sudetes, Sudetic Mountains, *Cz./Pol.* Sudety. ▲▲ Czech Republic/Poland
Sudetes/Sudetic Mountains/Sudety *see* Sudeten
180 H7 **Sudheim** Niedersachsen, Germany 9°59′N 51°40′E
152 A1 **Sudhureyri** Vestfirdhir, NW Iceland 66°08′N 23°31′W
152 C3 **Sudhurland** ⬖ *region* S Iceland
154 B2 **Sudhuroy** *Dan.* Suderø. *island* S Faeroe Islands
261 K6 **Sudirman, Pegunungan** ▲▲ Papua, E Indonesia
194 G9 **Sudislavl'** Kostromskaya Oblast', NW Russian Federation 57°55′N 41°45′E
Südkarpaten *see* Carpații Meridionali
135 I8 **Sud Kivu** *off.* Région Sud Kivu. ⬖ *region* E Dem. Rep. Congo
Sud Kivu, Région *see* Sud Kivu
Südliche Morava *see* Južna Morava
180 C7 **Südlohn** Nordrhein-Westfalen, Germany 6°52′N 51°56′E
180 C5 **Süd-Nord-Kanal** *canal* NW Germany
196 G2 **Sudogda** Vladimirskaya Oblast', W Russian Federation 55°58′N 40°57′E
Sudostroy *see* Severodvinsk
134 A5 **Sud-Ouest** *Eng.* South-West. ⬖ *province* W Cameroon
137 G11 **Sud Ouest, Pointe** *headland* SW Mauritius 20°27′S 57°18′E
280 B9 **Sud, Province** ⬖ *province* S New Caledonia
196 E4 **Sudzha** Kurskaya Oblast', W Russian Federation 51°12′N 35°19′E
134 I5 **Sue** ≈ S Sudan
171 I6 **Sueca** País Valenciano, E Spain 39°13′N 00°19′W
185 J7 **Sŭedinenie** Plovdiv, C Bulgaria 42°14′N 24°36′E
Suero *see* Alzira
129 I3 **Suez** *Ar.* As Suways, El Suweis. NE Egypt 29°59′N 32°33′E
129 I3 **Suez Canal** *Ar.* Qanāt as Suways. *canal* NE Egypt
129 J4 **Suez, Gulf of** *Ar.* Khalīj as Suways. *gulf* NE Egypt
65 H5 **Suffern** New York, USA 41°07′N 74°09′W
57 K8 **Suffield** Alberta, SW Canada 50°15′N 111°05′W
67 M5 **Suffolk** Virginia, NE USA 36°44′N 76°37′W
161 L4 **Suffolk** *cultural region* E England, UK
222 D2 **Şūfiān** Āzarbāyjān-e Khāvarī, N Iran 38°15′N 45°59′E
73 C10 **Sugar Creek** ≈ Illinois, N USA
75 J8 **Sugar Creek** ≈ Illinois, N USA
72 G4 **Sugar Island** *island* Michigan, N USA
71 I7 **Sugar Land** Texas, SW USA 29°37′N 95°37′W
63 J3 **Sugarloaf Mountain** ▲ Maine, NE USA 45°01′N 70°18′W
132 G9 **Sugar Loaf Point** *headland* N Saint Helena 15°54′S 05°43′W
214 D7 **Suğla Gölü** ◎ SW Turkey
193 L4 **Sugoy** ≈ E Russian Federation
238 C4 **Sugun** Xinjiang Uygur Zizhiqu, W China 39°46′N 76°45′E
229 K6 **Sugut, Gora** ▲ SW Kyrgyzstan 39°52′N 73°36′E
258 L2 **Sugut, Sungai** ≈ East Malaysia
239 H5 **Suhai Hu** ◎ C China
244 C3 **Suhait** Nei Mongol Zizhiqu, N China 39°29′N 105°11′E
221 K4 **Şuḩār** *var.* Sohar. N Oman 24°20′N 56°43′E
236 G2 **Sühbaatar** Selenge, N Mongolia 50°12′N 106°14′E
239 M1 **Sühbaatar** *var.* Haylaastay. Sühbaatar, E Mongolia 46°44′N 113°51′E
239 M1 **Sühbaatar** ⬖ *province* E Mongolia
181 I10 **Suhl** Thüringen, C Germany 50°37′N 10°43′E
180 I4 **Suhlendorf** Niedersachsen, Germany 10°46′N 52°56′E
176 D4 **Suhr** Aargau, N Switzerland 47°23′N 08°05′E
Sui'an *see* Zhangpu
243 L4 **Suichang** China 28°35′N 119°16′E
242 B6 **Suicheng** Guizhou, China 26°19′N 105°01′E
Suicheng *see* Suixi
243 I6 **Suichuan** *var.* Quanjiang. Jiangxi, S China 26°26′N 114°34′E
Suid-Afrika *see* South Africa
244 F5 **Suide** *var.* Mingzhou. Shaanxi, C China 37°30′N 110°10′E
Suidwes-Afrika *see* Namibia
248 E1 **Suifenhe** Heilongjiang, NE China 44°22′N 131°12′E
Suigen *see* Suwŏn
237 J3 **Suihua** Heilongjiang, NE China 46°40′N 127°00′E
242 A4 **Suijiang** China 28°40′N 104°14′E
Súilí, Loch *see* Swilly, Lough
242 E6 **Suining** China 26°35′N 110°09′E
245 K8 **Suining** Jiangsu, E China 33°54′N 117°58′E
242 B2 **Suining** Sichuan, C China 30°31′N 105°33′E
114 C10 **Suipacha** Buenos Aires, Argentina 34°47′S 59°41′W
167 J5 **Suippes** Marne, N France 49°08′N 04°31′E
157 C10 **Suir** *Ir.* An tSiúir. ≈ S Ireland
80 C2 **Suisun City** California, USA 38°14′N 122°02′W
251 H5 **Suita** Ōsaka, Honshū, SW Japan 34°39′N 135°27′E
64 D10 **Suitland** Maryland, USA 38°51′N 76°55′W
245 J8 **Suixi** Anhui, China 33°33′N 116°28′E
240 F8 **Suixi** *var.* Suicheng. Guangdong, S China 21°23′N 110°14′E
Sui Xian *see* Suizhou
242 C5 **Suiyang** Guizhou, China 27°35′N 107°07′E
245 L2 **Suizhong** Liaoning, NE China 40°19′N 120°22′E
243 H1 **Suizhou** *prev.* Sui Xian. Hubei, C China 31°46′N 113°20′E
230 G10 **Sujāwal** Sind, SE Pakistan 24°36′N 68°06′E
245 N1 **Sujiatun** China 41°40′N 123°20′E
259 G8 **Sukabumi** *prev.* Soekaboemi. Jawa, C Indonesia 06°55′S 106°56′E
258 H5 **Sukadana, Teluk** *bay* Borneo, W Indonesia
253 D11 **Sukagawa** Fukushima, Honshū, C Japan 37°16′N 140°20′E
Sukarnapura *see* Jayapura
Sukarno, Puntjak *see* Jaya, Puncak
Sŭkh *see* Sokh
185 M5 **Sukha Reka** ≈ NE Bulgaria
196 F3 **Sukhinichi** Kaluzhskaya Oblast', W Russian Federation 54°06′N 35°22′E
Sukhne *see* As Sukhnah
205 I2 **Sukhona** *var.* Tot'ma. ≈ NW Russian Federation
256 E6 **Sukhothai** *var.* Sukotai. Sukhothai, W Thailand 17°00′N 99°51′E
196 M9 **Sukhoy Log** Sverdlovskaya oblasť, Russian federation
Sukhumi *see* Sokhumi
Sukkertoppen *see* Maniitsoq
230 G8 **Sukkur** Sind, SE Pakistan 27°45′N 68°46′E
Sukotai *see* Sukhothai
Sukra Bay *see* Şawqirah, Dawḩat
195 L9 **Suksun** Permskaya Oblast', NW Russian Federation 57°10′N 57°27′E
250 F7 **Sukumo** Kōchi, Shikoku, SW Japan 32°55′N 132°42′E
172 C1 **Sul** Viseu, Portugal 40°50′N 8°03′W
154 A5 **Sula** *island* S Norway
195 I4 **Sula** ≈ NW Russian Federation
189 J3 **Sula** ≈ N Ukraine
Sulaimaniya *see* As Sulaymānīyah
231 H5 **Sulaimān Range** ▲▲ C Pakistan
197 J9 **Sulak** Respublika Dagestan, SW Russian Federation 43°19′N 47°28′E
197 J9 **Sulak** ≈ SW Russian Federation
260 F5 **Sula, Kepulauan** *island group* C Indonesia
214 E5 **Sulakyurt** *var.* Konur. Kırıkkale, N Turkey 40°10′N 33°42′E
260 E9 **Sulamu** Timor, S Indonesia 09°57′S 123°33′E
156 D3 **Sula Sgeir** *island* NW Scotland, UK
260 C5 **Sulawesi** *Eng.* Celebes. *island* C Indonesia
Sulawesi, Laut *see* Celebes Sea
260 C5 **Sulawesi Selatan** *off.* Propinsi Sulawesi Selatan, *Eng.* South Celebes, South Sulawesi. ⬖ *province* C Indonesia
Sulawesi Selatan, Propinsi *see* Sulawesi Selatan
260 D4 **Sulawesi Tengah** *off.* Propinsi Sulawesi Tengah, *Eng.* Central Celebes, Central Sulawesi. ⬖ *province* N Indonesia
Sulawesi Tengah, Propinsi *see* Sulawesi Tengah
260 D6 **Sulawesi Tenggara** *off.* Propinsi Sulawesi Tenggara, *Eng.* South-East Celebes, South-East Sulawesi. ⬖ *province* C Indonesia
Sulawesi Tenggara, Propinsi *see* Sulawesi Tenggara
260 E3 **Sulawesi Utara** *off.* Propinsi Sulawesi Utara, *Eng.* North Celebes, North Sulawesi. ⬖ *province* N Indonesia
Sulawesi Utara, Propinsi *see* Sulawesi Utara
217 J4 **Sulaymān Beg** N Iraq
155 B8 **Suldalsvatnet** ◎ S Norway
Sulden *see* Solda
182 D6 **Sulechów** *Ger.* Züllichau. Lubuskie, W Poland 52°05′N 15°37′E
182 C5 **Sulęcin** Lubuskie, W Poland 52°29′N 15°06′E
133 K6 **Suleja** Niger, C Nigeria 09°15′N 07°10′E
182 G7 **Sulejów** Lodzkie, S Poland 51°21′N 19°57′E
156 E3 **Sule Skerry** *island* N Scotland, UK
Suliag *see* Sohâg
132 C7 **Sulima** S Sierra Leone 06°59′N 11°34′W
188 G9 **Sulina** Tulcea, SE Romania 45°07′N 29°40′E
188 G9 **Sulina Braţul** ≈ SE Romania
180 F5 **Sulingen** Niedersachsen, NW Germany 52°40′N 08°48′E
Sulisjielmmá *see* Sulitjelma
152 E5 **Suliskongen** ▲ C Norway 67°10′N 16°16′E
152 E5 **Sulitjelma** *Lapp.* Sulisjielmmá. Nordland, C Norway 67°10′N 16°05′E
104 B4 **Sullana** Piura, NW Peru 04°54′S 80°42′W
66 C8 **Sulligent** Alabama, S USA 33°54′N 88°07′W
73 D11 **Sullivan** Illinois, N USA 39°36′N 88°36′W
73 E11 **Sullivan** Indiana, N USA 39°05′N 87°24′W
75 I10 **Sullivan** Missouri, C USA 38°12′N 91°09′W
Sullivan Island *see* Lanbi Kyun
54 F9 **Sullivan Lake** ◎ Alberta, SW Canada
156 H1 **Sullom Voe** NE Scotland, UK 60°24′N 01°09′W
165 H4 **Sully-sur-Loire** Loiret, C France 47°46′N 02°21′E
Sulmo *see* Sulmona
175 F8 **Sulmona** *anc.* Sulmo. Abruzzo, C Italy 42°03′N 13°56′E
Sulo *see* Shule He
187 K1 **Suloglu** Edirne, Turkey 41°46′N 26°55′E
68 B4 **Sulphur** Louisiana, S USA 30°14′N 93°22′W
75 E13 **Sulphur** Oklahoma, C USA 34°31′N 96°58′W
74 B5 **Sulphur Creek** ≈ South Dakota, N USA
70 D4 **Sulphur Draw** ≈ Texas, SW USA
71 I4 **Sulphur River** ≈ Arkansas/Texas, SW USA
71 I4 **Sulphur Springs** Texas, SW USA 33°09′N 95°36′W
70 D4 **Sulphur Springs Draw** ≈ Texas, SW USA
72 H3 **Sultan** Ontario, S Canada 47°34′N 82°45′W
Sultānābād *see* Arāk
Sultan Alonto, Lake *see* Lanao, Lake
214 D6 **Sultan Dağları** ▲▲ C Turkey
187 K2 **Sultankoy** Edirne, Turkey 41°02′N 26°27′E
263 M9 **Sultan Kudarat** *var.* Nuling. Mindanao, S Philippines 07°20′N 124°16′E
232 G6 **Sultānpur** Uttar Pradesh, N India 26°15′N 82°04′E
86 E7 **Sultepec de Pedro Ascencio de Alquisiras** México, Mexico 18°52′N 99°57′W
263 K10 **Sulu Archipelago** *island group* SW Philippines
286 B5 **Sulu Basin** *undersea feature* SE South China Sea
Sülüktü *see* Sulyukta
Sulu, Laut *see* Sulu Sea
263 K8 **Sulu Sea** *var.* Laut Sulu. *sea* SW Philippines
226 G7 **Sulutobe** *Kaz.* Sulūtöbe. Kzylorda, S Kazakhstan 44°31′N 66°17′E
Sulūtöbe *see* Sulutobe
229 I6 **Sulyukta** *Kir.* Sülüktü. Batkenskaya Oblast', SW Kyrgyzstan 39°57′N 69°31′E
Sulz *see* Sulz am Neckar
179 D12 **Sulz am Neckar** *var.* Sulz. Baden-Württemberg, SW Germany 48°22′N 08°37′E
181 G12 **Sulzbach** Bayern, Germany 9°10′N 49°55′E
181 C13 **Sulzbach** Saarland, Germany 7°04′N 49°18′E
179 G11 **Sulzbach-Rosenberg** Bayern, SE Germany 49°30′N 11°43′E
292 G7 **Sulzberger Bay** *bay* Antarctica
180 H5 **Sülze** Niedersachsen, Germany 10°02′N 52°46′E
181 H12 **Sulzfeld am Main** Bayern, Germany 10°08′N 49°42′E
Sumail *see* Summēl
184 C5 **Sumartin** Split-Dalmacija, S Croatia 43°17′N 16°52′E
76 C2 **Sumas** Washington, NW USA 49°00′N 122°15′W
258 D5 **Sumatera** *Eng.* Sumatra. *island* W Indonesia
258 D5 **Sumatera Barat** *off.* Propinsi Sumatera Barat, *Eng.* West Sumatra. ⬖ *province* W Indonesia
Sumatera Barat, Propinsi *see* Sumatera Barat
258 F6 **Sumatera Selatan** *off.* Propinsi Sumatera Selatan, *Eng.* South Sumatra. ⬖ *province* W Indonesia
Sumatera Selatan, Propinsi *see* Sumatera Selatan
258 C4 **Sumatera Utara** *off.* Propinsi Sumatera Utara, *Eng.* North Sumatra. ⬖ *province* W Indonesia
Sumatera Utara, Propinsi *see* Sumatera Utara
Sumatra *see* Sumatera
Šumava *see* Bohemian Forest
Sumayl *see* Summēl
217 K5 **Sumayr al Muḩammad** E Iraq 33°34′N 45°06′E
260 C8 **Sumba, Pulau** *Eng.* Sandalwood Island; *prev.* Soemba. *island* Nusa Tenggara, C Indonesia
228 C7 **Sumbar** ≈ W Turkmenistan
260 C8 **Sumba, Selat** *strait* Nusa Tenggara, S Indonesia
260 B8 **Sumbawa** *prev.* Soembawa. *island* Nusa Tenggara, C Indonesia
260 B8 **Sumbawabesar** Sumbawa, S Indonesia 08°30′S 117°25′E
137 B11 **Sumbawanga** Rukwa, W Tanzania 07°57′S 31°37′E
135 C12 **Sumbe** *var.* N'Gunza, *Port.* Novo Redondo. Cuanza Sul, W Angola 11°13′S 13°53′E
156 H2 **Sumburgh Head** *headland* NE Scotland, UK 59°51′N 01°16′W
183 E12 **Sümeg** Veszprém, W Hungary 47°01′N 17°13′E
134 I3 **Sumeih** Southern Darfur, S Sudan 09°50′N 27°39′E
259 J8 **Sumenep** *prev.* Soemenep. Pulau Madura, C Indonesia 07°01′S 113°51′E
Sumgait *see* Sumqayıtçay, Azerbaijan
Sumgait *see* Sumqayıt, Azerbaijan
111 J6 **Sumidouro** Rio de Janeiro, Brazil 22°03′S 42°41′W
251 M8 **Sumisu-jima** *Eng.* Smith Island. *island* SE Japan
217 I1 **Summēl** *var.* Sumail, Sumayl. N Iraq 36°52′N 42°51′E
159 K8 **Summer Bridge** UK 54°03′N 1°42′W
72 F5 **Summer Island** *island* Michigan, N USA
76 D8 **Summer Lake** ◎ Oregon, NW USA
56 F8 **Summerland** British Columbia, SW Canada 49°35′N 119°45′W
59 J8 **Summerside** Prince Edward Island, SE Canada 46°24′N 63°46′W
67 I3 **Summersville** West Virginia, NE USA 38°17′N 80°52′W
67 I3 **Summersville Lake** ⊠ West Virginia, NE USA
67 J8 **Summerton** South Carolina, SE USA 33°36′N 80°21′W
66 F7 **Summerville** Georgia, SE USA 34°28′N 85°21′W
67 J9 **Summerville** South Carolina, SE USA 33°01′N 80°10′W
83 I5 **Summit** Alaska, USA 63°21′N 148°50′W
80 J3 **Summit Mountain** ▲ Nevada, W USA 39°23′N 116°25′W
79 L5 **Summit Peak** ▲ Colorado, C USA 37°21′N 106°42′W
Summus Portus *see* Somport, Col du
Summus Portus *see* Somport/Somport, Col du
72 A7 **Sumner** Iowa, C USA 42°51′N 92°05′W
66 A8 **Sumner** Mississippi, S USA 33°58′N 90°22′W
278 E9 **Sumner, Lake** ◎ South Island, New Zealand
79 M7 **Sumner, Lake** ⊠ New Mexico, SW USA
253 B11 **Sumon-dake** ▲ Honshū, C Japan 37°24′N 139°07′E
251 H5 **Sumoto** Hyōgo, Awaji-shima, SW Japan 34°28′N 134°52′E
183 E8 **Šumperk** *Ger.* Mährisch-Schönberg. Olomoucký Kraj, E Czech Republic 49°58′N 17°00′E
215 N4 **Sumqayıt** *Rus.* Sumgait. E Azerbaijan 40°33′N 49°41′E
215 M4 **Sumqayıtçay** *Rus.* Sumgait. ≈ E Azerbaijan
229 J5 **Sumsar** Dzhalal-Abadskaya Oblast', W Kyrgyzstan 41°12′N 71°16′E
189 J2 **Sums'ka Oblast'** *var.* Sumy, *Rus.* Sumskaya Oblast'. ⬖ *province* NE Ukraine
Sumskaya Oblast' *see* Sums'ka Oblast'
194 F5 **Sumskiy Posad** Respublika Kareliya, NW Russian Federation 64°12′N 35°22′E
67 J8 **Sumter** South Carolina, SE USA 33°54′N 80°22′W
189 K2 **Sumy** Sums'ka Oblast', NE Ukraine 50°54′N 34°49′E
Sumy *see* Sums'ka Oblast'
239 I9 **Sumzom** Xizang Zizhiqu, W China 29°45′N 96°14′E
195 I9 **Suna** Kirovskaya Oblast', NW Russian Federation 57°53′N 50°04′E
194 E6 **Suna** ≈ NW Russian Federation
252 E4 **Sunagawa** Hokkaidō, NE Japan 43°30′N 141°55′E
233 L7 **Sunamganj** Sylhet, NE Bangladesh 25°04′N 91°24′E
Sunan/Sunan Yugurzu Zizhixian *see* Hongwansi
63 I5 **Sunapee Lake** ◎ New Hampshire, NE USA
158 E1 **Loch Sunart** ◎ UK
219 I11 **Şunaynīrāt, Jibāl** *dry watercourse* Jordan
217 H3 **Sunaysilah** *salt marsh* N Iraq
66 F6 **Sunbright** Tennessee, S USA 36°12′N 84°39′W
77 I2 **Sunburst** Montana, NW USA 48°51′N 111°54′W
277 I7 **Sunbury** Victoria, SE Australia 37°36′S 114°45′E
67 M5 **Sunbury** North Carolina, SE USA 36°27′N 76°34′W
64 D6 **Sunbury** Pennsylvania, NE USA 40°51′N 76°47′W
114 A3 **Sunchales** Santa Fe, C Argentina 30°58′S 61°35′W
248 B4 **Sunch'ŏn** SW North Korea 39°28′N 125°58′E
248 B7 **Sunch'ŏn** *Jap.* Junten. S South Korea 34°56′N 127°29′E
141 I3 **Sun City** North-West, South Africa 25°20′S 27°06′E
79 H8 **Sun City** Arizona, SW USA 33°36′N 112°16′W
81 E11 **Sun City** California, USA 33°43′N 117°12′W
65 L1 **Suncook** New Hampshire, NE USA 43°07′N 71°25′W
245 K6 **Suncun** *prev.* Xinwen. Shandong, E China 35°49′N 117°36′E
Sunda Islands *see* Greater Sunda Islands
77 M6 **Sundance** Wyoming, C USA 44°24′N 104°22′W
234 H3 **Sundargarh** Orissa, E India 22°07′N 84°02′E
259 F8 **Sunda, Selat** *strait* Jawa/Sumatera, SW Indonesia
205 L9 **Sunda Shelf** *undersea feature* S South China Sea
Sunda Trench *see* Java Trench
205 L10 **Sunda Trough** *undersea feature* E Indian Ocean
141 H9 **Sundays** ≈ Eastern Cape, South Africa
141 K6 **Sundays** ≈ KwaZulu-Natal, South Africa
155 I8 **Sundbyberg** Stockholm, C Sweden 59°22′N 17°58′E
159 K6 **Sunderland** *var.* Wearmouth. NE England, UK 54°55′N 01°23′W
181 E8 **Sundern** Nordrhein-Westfalen, W Germany 51°19′N 08°00′E
214 D5 **Sündiken Dağları** ▲▲ C Turkey
70 D3 **Sundown** Texas, SW USA 33°27′N 102°29′W
57 I6 **Sundre** Alberta, SW Canada 51°49′N 114°46′W
62 D3 **Sundridge** Ontario, S Canada 45°45′N 79°25′W
154 I4 **Sundsvall** Västernorrland, C Sweden 62°22′N 17°20′E
75 B9 **Sunflower, Mount** ▲ Kansas, C USA 39°01′N 102°02′W
Sunflower State *see* Kansas
258 D3 **Sungai Bernam** ≈ Peninsular Malaysia
258 F7 **Sungaibuntu** Sumatera, SW Indonesia 04°04′S 105°37′E
258 D5 **Sungaidareh** Sumatera, W Indonesia 0°58′S 101°30′E
256 F12 **Sungai Kolok** *var.* Sungai Ko-Lok. Narathiwat, SW Thailand 06°02′N 101°58′E
Sungai Ko-Lok *see* Sungai Kolok
258 D6 **Sungaipenuh** *prev.* Soengaipenoeh. Sumatera, W Indonesia 02°S 101°28′E
258 H5 **Sungaipinyuh** Borneo, C Indonesia 0°16′N 109°06′E
Sungaria *see* Dzungaria
Sungei Pahang *see* Pahang, Sungai
256 E6 **Sung Men** Phrae, NW Thailand 17°59′N 100°07′E
139 I2 **Sungo** Tete, NW Mozambique 16°31′S 33°58′E
Sungpu *see* Songpan
258 F6 **Sungsang** Sumatera, W Indonesia 02°22′S 104°50′E
185 L6 **Sungurlare** Burgas, E Bulgaria 42°47′N 26°46′E
214 F5 **Sungurlu** Çorum, N Turkey 40°10′N 34°23′E
184 C3 **Sunja** Sisak-Moslavina, C Croatia 45°21′N 16°33′E
243 L2 **Sunjiabu** China 30°54′N 118°53′E
159 M9 **Sunk Island** UK 53°39′N 0°05′W
233 I6 **Sun Koshi** ≈ E Nepal
141 H9 **Sunland** Eastern Cape, South Africa 33°31′S 25°37′E
154 C4 **Sunndalen** *valley* S Norway
154 C4 **Sunndalsøra** Møre og Romsdal, S Norway 62°39′N 08°37′E
154 G7 **Sunne** Värmland, C Sweden 59°52′N 13°05′E
154 I7 **Sunnersta** Uppsala, C Sweden 59°46′N 17°40′E
79 I3 **Sunnyside** Utah, W USA 39°33′N 110°23′W
76 D5 **Sunnyside** Washington, NW USA 46°01′N 119°58′W
80 B3 **Sunnyvale** California, W USA 37°22′N 122°02′W
72 C7 **Sun Prairie** Wisconsin, N USA 43°12′N 89°12′W
Sunqur *see* Sonqor
70 E1 **Sunray** Texas, SW USA 36°01′N 101°49′W
68 C4 **Sunset** Louisiana, S USA 30°24′N 92°04′W
70 G4 **Sunset** Texas, SW USA 33°24′N 97°45′W
Sunset State *see* Oregon
277 M1 **Sunshine Coast** *cultural region* Queensland, E Australia
Sunshine State *see* Florida
Sunshine State *see* New Mexico
Sunshine State *see* South Dakota
193 I6 **Suntar** Respublika Sakha (Yakutiya), NE Russian Federation 62°10′N 117°34′E
83 I5 **Suntrana** Alaska, USA 63°51′N 148°51′W
230 D9 **Suntsar** Baluchistān, SW Pakistan 25°30′N 62°03′E
248 B5 **Sunwi-do** *island* SW North Korea
132 G7 **Sunyani** W Ghana 07°22′N 02°18′W
245 I3 **Sunzhuang** China 39°26′N 115°47′E
Suō *see* Suao
153 H8 **Suolahti** Länsi-Soumi, C Finland 62°32′N 25°51′E
Suoločielgi *see* Saariselkä
Suomenlahti *see* Finland, Gulf of
Suomen Tasavalta/Suomi *see* Finland
152 I7 **Suomussalmi** Oulu, E Finland 64°54′N 29°05′E
250 D6 **Suō-nada** *sea* SW Japan
244 A6 **Suonanba** Gansu, China 35°24′N 103°14′E
153 I8 **Suonenjoki** Itä-Suomi, C Finland 62°36′N 27°07′E
262 D7 **Suŏng** Kâmpóng Cham, C Cambodia 11°53′N 105°41′E
194 E7 **Suoyarvi** Respublika Kareliya, NW Russian Federation 62°02′N 32°24′E
Supanburi *see* Suphan Buri
104 C7 **Supe** Lima, W Peru 10°49′S 77°40′W
Supérieur, Lac *see* Superior, Lake
79 I9 **Superior** Arizona, SW USA 33°17′N 111°06′W
76 G4 **Superior** Montana, NW USA 47°11′N 114°53′W
75 D8 **Superior** Nebraska, C USA 40°01′N 98°04′W
72 A4 **Superior** Wisconsin, N USA 46°42′N 92°04′W
72 D3 **Superior, Lake** *Fr.* Lac Supérieur. ◎ Canada/USA
79 I9 **Superstition Mountains** ▲▲ Arizona, SW USA
184 C5 **Supetar** *It.* San Pietro. Split-Dalmacija, S Croatia 43°22′N 16°34′E
256 E8 **Suphan Buri** *var.* Supanburi. Suphan Buri, W Thailand 14°29′N 100°10′E
261 J4 **Supiori, Pulau** *island* E Indonesia
180 J6 **Süplingen** Sachsen-Anhalt, Germany 11°20′N 52°17′E
180 J6 **Süpplingen** Niedersachsen, Germany 10°55′N 52°14′E
282 E2 **Supply Reef** *reef* N Northern Mariana Islands
293 H4 **Support Force Glacier** *glacier* Antarctica
215 J4 **Sup'sa** *var.* Supsa. ≈ W Georgia
Supsa *see* Sup'sa
Sūq 'Abs *see* 'Abs
217 L8 **Sūq ash Shuyūkh** SE Iraq 30°53′N 46°28′E
216 C3 **Şuqaylibīyah** Ḩamāh, W Syria 35°21′N 36°24′E
245 K8 **Suqian** Jiangsu, E China 33°57′N 118°18′E
Suqrah *see* Şawqirah
Suqrah Bay *see* Şawqirah, Dawḩat
221 J9 **Suquṭrā** *var.* Sokotra, *Eng.* Socotra. *island* SE Yemen
221 L5 **Şūr** NE Oman 22°32′N 59°33′E
Şūr *see* Soûr
197 I3 **Sura** Penzenskaya Oblast', W Russian Federation 53°23′N 45°03′E
197 I2 **Sura** ≈ W Russian Federation
230 F7 **Sūrāb** Baluchistān, SW Pakistan 28°28′N 66°15′E
Surabaja *see* Surabaya
259 J8 **Surabaya** *prev.* Surabaja, Soerabaja. Jawa, C Indonesia 07°14′S 112°45′E
154 H7 **Surahammar** Västmanland, C Sweden 59°43′N 16°13′E
259 I8 **Surakarta** *Eng.* Solo; *prev.* Soerakarta. Jawa, S Indonesia 07°32′S 110°50′E
Surakhany *see* Suraxanı
263 M9 **Surallah** Mindanao, S Philippines 06°16′N 124°46′E
215 J4 **Surami** C Georgia 41°59′N 43°36′E
223 K8 **Sūrān** Sīstān va Balūchestān, SE Iran 27°18′N 61°58′E
183 F11 **Šurany** *Hung.* Nagysurány. Nitriansky Kraj, SW Slovakia 48°05′N 18°10′E
277 K1 **Surat** Queensland, Australia
232 C9 **Sūrat** Gujarāt, W India 21°10′N 72°54′E
Suratdhani *see* Surat Thani
232 D5 **Sūratgarh** Rājasthān, NW India 29°20′N 73°59′E
256 E10 **Surat Thani** *var.* Suratdhani. Surat Thani, SW Thailand 09°09′N 99°20′E
191 J10 **Suraw** *Rus.* Surov. ≈ E Belarus
215 N5 **Suraxanı** *Rus.* Surakhany. E Azerbaijan 40°25′N 49°59′E
221 K6 **Surayr** E Oman 19°56′N 57°47′E
216 E2 **Suraysāt** Ḩalab, N Syria 36°42′N 38°01′E
191 I8 **Surazh** *Rus.* Surazh. Vitsyebskaya Voblasts', NE Belarus 55°25′N 30°44′E
196 E3 **Surazh** Bryanskaya Oblast', W Russian Federation 53°04′N 32°29′E
118 A2 **Sur, Cabo** *cape* Easter Island, Chile, E Pacific Ocean
184 F3 **Surčin** Serbia, N Serbia 44°48′N 20°19′E
188 C6 **Surduc** *Hung.* Szurduk. Sălaj, NW Romania 47°13′N 23°20′E
185 H6 **Surdulica** Serbia, SE Serbia 42°43′N 22°10′E
163 I13 **Sûre** *var.* Sauer. ≈ W Europe *see also* Sauer
Sûre *see* Sauer
232 C8 **Surendranagar** Gujarāt, W India 22°44′N 71°43′E
81 A8 **Surf** California, USA 34°41′N 120°36′W
65 H8 **Surf City** New Jersey, NE USA 39°21′N 74°24′W
277 M2 **Surfers Paradise** Queensland, E Australia 27°54′S 153°18′E
67 K8 **Surfside Beach** South Carolina, SE USA 33°36′N 78°58′W
164 F6 **Surgères** Charente-Maritime, W France 46°07′N 00°44′W
192 F6 **Surgut** Khanty-Mansiyskiy Avtonomnyy Okrug, C Russian Federation 61°13′N 73°28′E
192 G6 **Surgutikha** Krasnoyarskiy Kray, N Russian Federation 64°44′N 87°13′E
162 H3 **Surhuisterveen** Friesland, N Netherlands 53°11′N 06°10′E
171 K3 **Súria** Cataluña, NE Spain 41°50′N 01°45′E
222 G7 **Sūrīān** Fārs, S Iran
234 F6 **Suriāpet** Andhra Pradesh, C India 17°10′N 79°42′E
263 M8 **Surigao** Mindanao, S Philippines 09°43′N 125°31′E
256 G7 **Surin** Surin, E Thailand 14°53′N 103°29′E
103 L6 **Surinam** *off.* Republic of Suriname, *var.* Suriname; *prev.* Dutch Guiana, Netherlands Guiana. ◆ *republic* N South America
Suriname *see* Surinam
Suriname, Republic of *see* Surinam
Sūrīya/Sūrīyah, Al-Jumhūrīyah al-'Arabīyah as- *see* Syria
Surkhab, Darya-i- *see* Kahmard, Daryā-ye
Surkhandar'inskaya Oblast' *see* Surkhondaryo Viloyati
Surkhandar'ya *see* Surxondaryo
Surkhet *see* Birendranagar
229 J7 **Surkhob** ≈ C Tajikistan
229 H7 **Surkhondaryo Viloyati** *Rus.* Surkhandar'inskaya Oblast'. ⬖ *province* S Uzbekistan
215 I5 **Sürmene** Trabzon, NE Turkey 40°56′N 40°03′E
Surov *see* Suraw
197 H6 **Surovikino** Volgogradskaya Oblast', SW Russian Federation 48°39′N 42°46′E
193 H7 **Surovo** Irkutskaya Oblast', S Russian Federation 55°45′N 105°31′E
80 A5 **Sur, Point** *headland* California, W USA 36°18′N 121°54′W
281 H8 **Surprise, Île** *island* N New Caledonia
117 D12 **Sur, Punta** *headland* E Argentina 50°59′S 69°10′W
Surrentum *see* Sorrento
74 C2 **Surrey** North Dakota, N USA 48°13′N 101°05′W
166 D1 **Surrey** *cultural region* SE England, UK
67 L4 **Surry** Virginia, NE USA 37°08′N 81°34′W
167 N8 **Sursee** Luzern, W Switzerland 47°11′N 08°07′E
197 I3 **Sursk** Penzenskaya Oblast', W Russian Federation 53°06′N 45°46′E
197 I2 **Surskoye** Ul'yanovskaya Oblast', W Russian Federation 54°28′N 46°47′E
128 D2 **Surt** *var.* Sidra, Sirte. N Libya 31°13′N 16°35′E
155 E10 **Surte** Västra Götaland, S Sweden 57°49′N 12°01′E
128 C4 **Surt, Khalīj** *Eng.* Gulf of Sidra, Gulf of Sirti, Sidra. *gulf* N Libya
152 B3 **Surtsey** *island* S Iceland
215 H8 **Suruç** Şanlıurfa, S Turkey 36°58′N 38°24′E
251 K4 **Suruga-wan** *bay* SE Japan
258 E6 **Surulangun** Sumatera, W Indonesia 02°35′S 102°47′E
180 D4 **Surwold** Niedersachsen, Germany 7°31′N 52°57′E
229 I7 **Surxondaryo** *Rus.* Surkhandar'ya. ≈ Tajikistan/Uzbekistan
Süs *see* Susch
176 C7 **Susa** Piemonte, NE Italy 45°10′N 07°01′E
250 D5 **Susa** Yamaguchi, Honshū, SW Japan 34°35′N 131°34′E
Susa *see* Shūsh
184 C6 **Sušac** *It.* Cazza. *island* SW Croatia
Sūsah *see* Sousse
250 F6 **Susaki** Kōchi, Shikoku, SW Japan 33°22′N 133°13′E
251 H6 **Susami** Wakayama, Honshū, SW Japan 33°32′N 135°32′E
114 A4 **Susana** Santa Fe, Argentina 31°22′S 61°31′W
222 D6 **Sūsangerd** *var.* Susangird. Khūzestān, SW Iran 31°40′N 48°06′E
Susangird *see* Sūsangerd
78 C2 **Susanville** California, W USA 40°25′N 120°39′W
176 F5 **Susch** *var.* Süs. Graubünden, SE Switzerland 46°45′N 10°04′E
215 H5 **Suşehri** Sivas, N Turkey 40°11′N 38°06′E
Susiana *see* Khūzestān
183 B9 **Sušice** *Ger.* Schüttenhofen. Plzeňský Kraj, W Czech Republic 49°14′N 13°32′E
83 I6 **Susitna** Alaska, USA 61°32′N 150°30′W
83 I5 **Susitna River** ≈ Alaska, USA
197 J1 **Suslonger** Respublika Mariy El, W Russian Federation 56°18′N 48°16′E
243 J3 **Susong** Anhui, China 30°05′N 116°05′E
170 G8 **Suspiro del Moro, Puerto del** *pass* S Spain
64 E4 **Susquehanna River** ≈ New York/Pennsylvania, NE USA
63 N2 **Sussex** New Brunswick, SE Canada 45°43′N 65°32′W
64 G5 **Sussex** New Jersey, NE USA 41°12′N 74°34′W
67 L5 **Sussex** Virginia, NE USA 36°54′N 77°16′W
157 I12 **Sussex** *cultural region* S England, UK
277 L6 **Sussex Inlet** New South Wales, SE Australia 35°10′S 150°35′E
163 G9 **Susteren** Limburg, SE Netherlands 51°04′N 05°50′E
180 D4 **Sustrum** Niedersachsen, Germany 7°17′N 52°55′E
56 C2 **Sustut Peak** ▲ British Columbia, W Canada 56°25′N 126°34′W
193 L5 **Susuman** Magadanskaya Oblast', E Russian Federation 62°46′N 148°08′E
282 H2 **Susupe** Saipan, S Northern Mariana Islands
86 E6 **Susupuato de Guenero** Michoacán de Ocampo, Mexico 19°13′N 100°24′W
214 B5 **Susurluk** Balıkesir, NW Turkey 39°55′N 28°10′E
80 G1 **Sutcliffe** Nevada, USA 39°57′N 119°36′W
214 D7 **Sütçüler** Isparta, SW Turkey 37°31′N 31°00′E
188 F9 **Şuţeşti** Brăila, SE Romania 45°13′N 27°27′E
140 E8 **Sutherland** Northern Cape, South Africa 32°24′S 20°40′E
138 E9 **Sutherland** Western Cape, SW South Africa 32°24′S 20°40′E
74 B7 **Sutherland** Nebraska, C USA 41°09′N 101°07′W
156 E4 **Sutherland** *cultural region* N Scotland, UK
278 B11 **Sutherland Falls** *waterfall* South Island, New Zealand
76 B7 **Sutherlin** Oregon, NW USA 43°23′N 123°18′W
231 J6 **Sutlej** ≈ India/Pakistan
Sutna *see* Satna
78 C4 **Sutter Creek** California, W USA 38°22′N 120°49′W
161 K2 **Sutterton** UK 52°54′N 0°05′W
140 F5 **Sutton** Northern Cape, South Africa 27°26′S 22°49′E
161 K6 **Sutton** UK 51°21′N 0°12′W
83 I6 **Sutton** Alaska, USA 61°42′N 148°53′W
67 I3 **Sutton** West Virginia, NE USA 38°41′N 80°43′W
58 E4 **Sutton** ≈ Ontario, C Canada
161 H3 **Sutton Coldfield** C England, UK 52°34′N 01°48′W
159 L10 **Sutton in Ashfield** UK 53°07′N 1°16′W
67 I3 **Sutton Lake** ⊠ West Virginia, NE USA
63 I3 **Sutton, Monts** *hill range* Québec, SE Canada
159 L8 **Sutton on the Forest** UK 54°05′N 1°07′W
58 E4 **Sutton Ridges** ▲▲ Ontario, C Canada
161 K3 **Sutton Saint James** UK 52°44′N 0°04′E
252 C5 **Suttsu** Hokkaidō, NE Japan 42°46′N 140°12′E
83 H8 **Sutwik Island** *island* Alaska, USA
Süüj *see* Dashinchilen
190 E4 **Suure-Jaani** *Ger.* Gross-Sankt-Johannis. Viljandimaa, S Estonia 58°34′N 25°28′E
190 F5 **Suur Munamägi** *var.* Munamägi, *Ger.* Eier-Berg. ▲ SE Estonia 57°42′N 27°03′E
190 D4 **Suur Väin** *Ger.* Grosser Sund. *strait* W Estonia
229 K4 **Suusamyr** Chuyskaya Oblast', C Kyrgyzstan 42°07′N 73°55′E
280 E9 **Suva** ● (Fiji) Viti Levu, W Fiji 18°08′S 178°27′E
280 E9 **Suva** ✈ Viti Levu, C Fiji 18°01′S 178°30′E
184 G7 **Suva Gora** ▲▲ WFYR Macedonia
190 E7 **Suvainiškis** Panevėžys, NE Lithuania 56°09′N 25°15′E
Suvalkai/Suvalki *see* Suwałki
185 H6 **Suva Planina** ▲▲ SE Serbia
184 G7 **Suva Reka** Kosovo, S Serbia 42°23′N 20°50′E
196 F3 **Suvorov** Tul'skaya Oblast', W Russian Federation 54°08′N 36°33′E
188 G8 **Suvorove** Odes'ka Oblast', SW Ukraine 45°35′N 28°58′E
Suvorovo *see* Ştefan Vodă
251 K3 **Suwa** Nagano, Honshū, S Japan 36°01′N 138°07′E
Suwaik *see* As Suwayq
Suwaira *see* Aş Şuwayrah
182 I4 **Suwałki** *Lith.* Suvalkai, *Rus.* Suvalki. Podlaskie, NE Poland 54°06′N 22°56′E
196 A2 **Suwałki** ⬖ *province* NE Poland
256 G7 **Suwannaphum** Roi Et, E Thailand 15°36′N 103°46′E
69 K4 **Suwannee River** ≈ Florida/Georgia, SE USA
Şuwār *see* Aş Şuwār
284 F6 **Suwarrow** *atoll* N Cook Islands
221 J4 **Suwaydān** *var.* Sweiham. Abū Z̧aby, E United Arab Emirates 24°30′N 55°19′E
Suwaydá/Suwaydā', Muḩāfaz̧at as *see* As Suwaydā'
Suwayqiyah, Hawr as *see* Shuwayjah, Hawr ash
Suways, Khalīj as *see* Suez, Gulf of
Suways, Qanāt as *see* Suez Canal
Suweida *see* As Suwaydā'
Suweon *see* Suwŏn
248 C5 **Suwŏn** *var.* Suweon, *Jap.* Suigen. NW South Korea 37°17′N 127°03′E
Su Xian *see* Suzhou
245 H9 **Suyahu Shuiku** ⊠ Henan, China
195 L7 **Suyevatpaul'** Sverdlovskaya oblasť, Russian federation
223 H9 **Sūzā** Hormozgān, S Iran 26°50′N 56°05′E
227 H7 **Suzak** *Kaz.* Sozaq. Yuzhnyy Kazakhstan, S Kazakhstan 44°09′N 68°28′E
Suzaka *see* Suzuka
196 G1 **Suzdal'** Vladimirskaya Oblast', W Russian Federation 56°27′N 40°29′E
169 J4 **Suze-la-Rousse** Rhône-Alpes, France 44°17′N 4°51′E
245 J8 **Suzhou** *var.* Su Xian. Anhui, E China 33°38′N 117°02′E
243 M2 **Suzhou** *var.* Soochow, Su-chou, Suchow; *prev.* Wuhsien. Jiangsu, E China 31°23′N 120°34′E
Suzhou *see* Jiuquan
Suz, Mys *see* Soye, Mys
251 J1 **Suzu** Ishikawa, Honshū, SW Japan 37°24′N 137°12′E
251 I4 **Suzuka** Mie, Honshū, SW Japan 34°52′N 136°37′E
251 K2 **Suzuka** *var.* Suzaka. Nagano, Honshū, S Japan 36°38′N 138°20′E
251 J1 **Suzu-misaki** *headland* Honshū, SW Japan 37°31′N 137°19′E
Svågälv *see* Svågan
154 H5 **Svågan** *var.* Svågälv. ≈ C Sweden
Svalava/Svaljava *see* Svalyava
152 B4 **Svalbard** ◇ *Norwegian dependency* Arctic Ocean
152 C2 **Svalbardhseyri** Nordhurland Eystra, N Iceland 65°43′N 18°03′W
155 F12 **Svalöv** Skåne, S Sweden 55°55′N 13°06′E
188 C5 **Svalyava** *Cz.* Svalava, Svaljava, *Hung.* Szolyva. Zakarpats'ka Oblast', W Ukraine 48°33′N 23°00′E
152 B5 **Svanbergfjellet** ▲ C Svalbard 78°40′N 18°10′E
178 J3 **Svaneke** Bornholm, E Denmark 55°07′N 15°08′E
155 G11 **Svängsta** Blekinge, S Sweden 56°16′N 14°46′E
155 F8 **Svanskog** Värmland, C Sweden 59°10′N 12°34′E
155 G8 **Svartå** Örebro, C Sweden 59°13′N 14°07′E
152 E6 **Svartisen** *glacier* C Norway
189 M4 **Svatove** *Rus.* Svatovo. Luhans'ka Oblast', E Ukraine 49°24′N 38°11′E
Svatovo *see* Svatove
Sväty Kríž nad Hronom *see* Žiar nad Hronom
256 G8 **Svay Chék, Stœng** ≈ Cambodia/Thailand
257 H9 **Svay Riĕng** Svay Riĕng, S Cambodia 11°05′N 105°48′E
152 B5 **Sveagruva** Spitsbergen, W Svalbard 77°53′N 16°42′E
155 F12 **Svedala** Skåne, S Sweden 55°30′N 13°15′E
190 E7 **Svėdesai** Utena, NE Lithuania 55°42′N 25°22′E
154 G5 **Sveg** Jämtland, C Sweden 62°02′N 14°20′E
191 B8 **Švėkšna** Klaipėda, W Lithuania 55°31′N 21°37′E
154 A5 **Svelgen** Sogn Og Fjordane, S Norway 61°47′N 05°18′E
155 D8 **Svelvik** Vestfold, S Norway 59°37′N 10°24′E
191 E8 **Švenčionėliai** *Pol.* Nowo-Święciany. Vilnius, SE Lithuania 55°10′N 26°00′E
191 E8 **Švenčionys** *Pol.* Swięciany. Vilnius, SE Lithuania 55°08′N 26°08′E
155 D13 **Svendborg** Fyn, C Denmark 55°04′N 10°38′E
155 F10 **Svenljunga** Västra Götaland, S Sweden 57°30′N 13°05′E
152 C5 **Svenskøya** *island* E Svalbard
154 G4 **Svenstavik** Jämtland, C Sweden 62°40′N 14°24′E
155 D11 **Svenstrup** Nordjylland, N Denmark 56°58′N 09°52′E
191 E8 **Šventoji** ≈ C Lithuania
189 N5 **Sverdlovs'k** *Rus.* Sverdlovsk; *prev.* Imeni Sverdlova Rudnik. Luhans'ka Oblast', E Ukraine 48°05′N 39°37′E
Sverdlovsk *see* Yekaterinburg
195 M8 **Sverdlovskaya Oblast'** ⬖ *province* C Russian Federation
52 G3 **Sverdrup Channel** *sea waterway* Nunavut, N Canada
52 G3 **Sverdrup Islands** *Island group* Nunavut, N Canada
192 G3 **Sverdrup, Ostrov** *island* N Russian Federation
Sverige *see* Sweden
184 B6 **Svetac** *prev.* Sveti Andrea, *It.* Sant'Andrea. *island* SW Croatia
Sveti Andrea *see* Svetac
Sveti Nikola *see* Sveti Nikole
185 H7 **Sveti Nikole** *prev.* Sveti Nikola. C FYR Macedonia 41°54′N 21°55′E
Sveti Vrach *see* Sandanski
193 L8 **Svetlaya** Primorskiy Kray, SE Russian Federation 46°33′N 138°20′E
191 A8 **Svetlogorsk** Kaliningradskaya Oblast', W Russian Federation 54°56′N 20°09′E
192 G5 **Svetlogorsk** Krasnoyarskiy Kray, N Russian Federation 66°51′N 88°29′E
Svetlogorsk *see* Svyetlahorsk
197 H8 **Svetlograd** Stavropol'skiy Kray, SW Russian Federation 45°20′N 42°53′E
Svetlovodsk *see* Svitlovods'k
191 A8 **Svetlyy** *Ger.* Zimmerbude. Kaliningradskaya Oblast', W Russian Federation 54°42′N 20°07′E
197 I4 **Svetlyy** Orenburgskaya Oblast', W Russian Federation 50°34′N 60°42′E
194 D7 **Svetogorsk** *Fin.* Enso. Leningradskaya Oblast', NW Russian Federation 61°06′N 28°52′E
Svetozarevo *see* Jagodina
183 B9 **Švihov** *Ger.* Schwihau. Plzeňský Kraj, W Czech Republic 49°31′N 13°18′E
184 C5 **Svilaja** ▲▲ SE Croatia
184 G4 **Svilajnac** Serbia, C Serbia 44°15′N 21°12′E
185 L7 **Svilengrad** *prev.* Mustafa-Pasha. Khaskovo, S Bulgaria 41°45′N 26°14′E
Svinecea Mare, Munte *see* Svinecea Mare, Vârful
188 B9 **Svinecea Mare, Vârful** *var.* Munte Svinecea Mare. ▲ SW Romania 44°47′N 22°10′E
Svinø *see* Svínoy
154 B1 **Svínoy** *Dan.* Svinø. *island* NE Faeroe Islands
229 H8 **Svintsovyy Rudnik** *Turkm.* Swintsowyy Rudnik. Lebap Welaýaty, E Turkmenistan 37°54′N 66°25′E
191 F8 **Svir** *Rus.* Svir'. Minskaya Voblasts', NW Belarus 54°51′N 26°24′E
194 E7 **Svir'** *canal* NW Russian Federation
190 I2 **Svirica** Leningradskaya Oblast', Russian Federation
Svir', Ozero *see* Svir, Vozyera
191 E8 **Svir, Vozyera** *Rus.* Ozero Svir'. ◎ C Belarus
185 K5 **Svishtov** *prev.* Sistova. Veliko Tŭrnovo, N Bulgaria 43°37′N 25°20′E
191 D10 **Svislach** *Pol.* Świsłocz, *Rus.* Svisloch'. Hrodzyenskaya Voblasts', W Belarus 53°02′N 24°06′E
191 G10 **Svislach** *Rus.* Svisloch'. Mahilyowskaya Voblasts', E Belarus 53°26′N 28°59′E
191 G10 **Svislach** *Rus.* Svisloch'. ≈ E Belarus
Svisloch' *see* Svislach
183 D9 **Svitavy** *Ger.* Zwittau. Pardubický Kraj, C Czech Republic 49°45′N 16°27′E
189 J4 **Svitlovods'k** *Rus.* Svetlovodsk. Kirovohrads'ka Oblast', C Ukraine 49°05′N 33°15′E
190 J7 **Svity** Smolenskaya Oblast', Russian Federation
Svizzera *see* Switzerland
193 K8 **Svobodnyy** Amurskaya Oblast', SE Russian Federation 51°24′N 128°05′E

◆ Country
● Country Capital
◇ Dependent Territory
○ Dependent Territory Capital
⬖ Administrative Regions
✈ International Airport
▲ Mountain
▲▲ Mountain Range
Volcano
≈ River
◎ Lake
⊠ Reservoir

INDEX

♦	Country	◇	Dependent Territory	◈	Administrative Regions	▲	Mountain	▵	Volcano	☺	Lake
●	Country Capital	○	Dependent Territory Capital	✕	International Airport	▲	Mountain Range	♣	River	▣	Reservoir

◆ Country   ◇ Dependent Territory   ◈ Administrative Regions   ▲ Mountain   ☒ Volcano   ⊘ Lake
⚫ Country Capital   ○ Dependent Territory Capital   ✈ International Airport   ▲ Mountain Range   ⊘ River   ☒ Reservoir

♦ Country
● Country Capital
◊ Dependent Territory
○ Dependent Territory Capital
♦ Administrative Regions
✈ International Airport
▲ Mountain
▲ Mountain Range
☒ Volcano
♒ River
☒ Lake
☒ Reservoir

◆ Country
● Country Capital
◇ Dependent Territory
○ Dependent Territory Capital
◈ Administrative Regions
✕ International Airport
▲ Mountain
▲ Mountain Range
⏣ Volcano
♒ River
◉ Lake
◎ Reservoir

Varāmin - Vichegda
INDEX
422

222 *F4* **Varāmīn** *var.* Veramin. Tehrān, N Iran *35°19′N 51°40′E*
233 *H7* **Vārānasi** *prev.* Banaras, Benares, *hist.* Kasi. Uttar Pradesh, N India *25°20′N 83°E*
195 *K2* **Varandey** Nenetskiy Avtonomnyy Okrug, NW Russian Federation *68°48′N 57°54′E*
152 *H3* **Varangerbotn** Finnmark, N Norway *70°09′N 28°28′E*
152 *I3* **Varangerfjorden** ***Lapp.*** Várjjatvuotna. *fjord* N Norway
152 *H3* **Varangerhalvøya** ***Lapp.*** Várnjárga. *peninsula* N Norway
Varannó *see* Vranov nad Topl'ou
175 *G8* **Varano, Lago di** ◎ SE Italy
191 *F8* **Varapayeva** ***Rus.*** Voropayevo. Vitsyebskaya Voblasts', NW Belarus *55°09′N 27°13′E*
Varasd *see* Varaždin
184 *C1* **Varaždin** ***Ger.*** Warasdin, ***Hung.*** Varasd. Varaždin, N Croatia *46°18′N 16°21′E*
184 *C1* **Varaždin** ***off.*** Varaďinska Županija. ◐ *province* N Croatia
176 *E8* **Varazze** Liguria, NW Italy *44°21′N 08°35′E*
155 *F10* **Varberg** Halland, S Sweden *57°06′N 12°15′E*
230 *G4* **Vardak** *var.* Wardak, ***Pash.*** Wardag. ◐ *province* E Afghanistan
185 *H7* **Vardar** ***Gk.*** Axiós. ≈ FYR Macedonia/Greece ***see also*** Axiós
Vardar *see* Axiós
155 *C12* **Varde** Ribe, W Denmark *55°38′N 08°31′E*
215 *L5* **Vardenis** E Armenia *40°11′N 45°43′E*
152 *I3* **Vardø** ***Fin.*** Vuoreija. Finnmark, N Norway *70°22′N 31°06′E*
186 *G5* **Vardoúsia** ▲▲ C Greece
Vareia *see* Logroño
180 *E3* **Varel** Niedersachsen, NW Germany *53°24′N 08°07′E*
191 *D9* **Varėna** ***Pol.*** Orany. Alytus, S Lithuania *54°13′N 24°35′E*
63 *H3* **Varennes** Québec, SE Canada *45°42′N 73°25′W*
167 *K4* **Varennes-en-Argonne** Lorraine, France *49°14′N 5°02′E*
165 *I6* **Varennes-sur-Allier** Allier, C France *46°17′N 03°24′E*
184 *E4* **Vareš** ◐ Federacija Bosna I Hercegovina, E Bosnia and Herzegovina
176 *E6* **Varese** Lombardia, N Italy *45°49′N 08°50′E*
188 *D8* **Vârful Moldoveanu** *var.* Moldoveanul; ***prev.*** Vîrful Moldoveanu. ▲ C Romania *45°35′N 24°48′E*
Varganzi *see* Warganza
155 *F9* **Vårgårda** Västra Götaland, S Sweden *58°00′N 12°49′E*
195 *N10* **Vargashi** Kurganskaya Oblast', C Russian Federation *55°22′N 65°39′E*
110 *D8* **Vargem** São Paulo, Brazil *22°53′S 46°25′W*
111 *J2* **Vargem Alegre** Minas Gerais, Brazil *19°35′S 42°18′W*
111 *L4* **Vargem Alta** Espírito Santo, Brazil *20°40′S 41°00′W*
110 *D3* **Vargem Bonita** Minas Gerais, Brazil *20°20′S 46°22′W*
110 *C6* **Vargem Grande do Sul** São Paulo, Brazil *21°50′S 46°53′W*
110 *F6* **Varginha** Minas Gerais, Brazil *21°33′S 45°26′W*
155 *F9* **Vargön** Västra Götaland, S Sweden *58°21′N 12°22′E*
155 *A9* **Varhaug** Rogaland, S Norway *58°37′N 05°39′E*
168 *G6* **Varilhes** Midi-Pyrénées, France *43°03′N 1°38′E*
Várjjatvuotna *see* Varangerfjorden
153 *I8* **Varkaus** Itä-Suomi, C Finland *62°20′N 27°50′E*
152 *C2* **Varmahlidh** Nordhurland Vestra, N Iceland *65°32′N 19°33′W*
155 *F8* **Värmland** ◐ *county* C Sweden
185 *M5* **Varna** ***prev.*** Stalin; ***anc.*** Odessus. Varna, E Bulgaria *43°14′N 27°56′E*
185 *M5* **Varna** ✈ Varna, E Bulgaria *43°16′N 27°52′E*
155 *G10* **Värnamo** Jönköping, S Sweden *57°11′N 14°03′E*
196 *B8* **Varnenska Oblast** ◐ *province* NE Bulgaria
185 *M5* **Varnenski Zaliv** ***prev.*** Stalinski Zaliv. *bay* E Bulgaria
185 *M5* **Varnensko Ezero** *estuary* E Bulgaria
190 *C7* **Varniai** Telšiai, W Lithuania *55°45′N 22°22′E*
Várnjárga *see* Varangerhalvøya
Varnoús *see* Baba
182 *C7* **Varnsdorf** ***Ger.*** Warnsdorf. Ústecký Kraj, NW Czech Republic *50°57′N 14°35′E*
183 *F12* **Várpalota** Veszprém, W Hungary *47°12′N 18°08′E*
180 *F5* **Varrel** Niedersachsen, Germany *8°44′N 52°37′E*
111 *K4* **Varre-Sai** Rio de Janeiro, Brazil *20°56′S 41°54′W*
169 *M3* **Vars** Provence-Alpes-Côte d'Azur, France *44°37′N 6°41′E*
Varshava *see* Warszawa
190 *F5* **Värska** Põlvamaa, SE Estonia *57°58′N 27°37′E*
162 *I7* **Varsseveld** Gelderland, E Netherlands *51°55′N 06°28′E*
186 *F6* **Vartholomió** ***prev.*** Vartholomión. Dytikí Ellás, S Greece *37°52′N 21°12′E*
Vartholomión *see* Vartholomió
215 *I6* **Varto** Muş, E Turkey *39°10′N 41°28′E*
155 *F9* **Vartofta** Västra Götaland, S Sweden *58°06′N 13°40′E*
153 *J8* **Värtsilä** Itä-Suomi, E Finland *62°10′N 30°35′E*
Värtsilä *see* Vyartsilya
189 *I3* **Varva** Chernihivs'ka Oblast', NE Ukraine *50°31′N 32°43′E*
107 *I9* **Várzea Grande** Mato Grosso, SW Brazil *15°39′S 56°08′W*
110 *D8* **Vàrzea Paulista** São Paulo, Brazil *23°12′S 46°50′W*
176 *E7* **Varzi** Lombardia, N Italy *44°51′N 09°13′E*
Varzimanor Ayni *see* Ayní
194 *F4* **Varzuga** ≈ NW Russian Federation
165 *I5* **Varzy** Nièvre, C France *47°22′N 03°22′E*
183 *D12* **Vas** ***off.*** Vas Megye. ◐ *county* W Hungary
Vasa *see* Vaasa
284 *E2* **Vasafua** *island* Funafuti Atoll, C Tuvalu
183 *I10* **Vásárosnamény** Szabolcs-Szatmár-Bereg, E Hungary *48°10′N 22°18′E*
170 *C8* **Vascão, Ribeira de** ≈ S Portugal
172 *C7* **Vascão, Ribeira de** ≈ Portugal
188 *B7* **Vaşcău** ***Hung.*** Vaskoh. Bihor, NE Romania *46°28′N 22°30′E*
Vascongadas, Provincias *see* País Vasco
172 *C2* **Vasconha** Viseu, Portugal *40°40′N 8°04′W*
Vashess Bay *see* Vaskess Bay
Väsht *see* Khāsh
Vasilevichi *see* Vasilyevichy
187 *H3* **Vasiliká** Kentrikí Makedonía, NE Greece *40°28′N 23°08′E*
186 *E5* **Vasilikí** Lefkáda, Iónioi Nísoi, Greece, C Mediterranean Sea *38°36′N 20°37′E*
187 *J10* **Vasilikí** Kríti, Greece, E Mediterranean Sea *35°04′N 25°49′E*
191 *D10* **Vasilishki** ***Pol.*** Wasiliszki, ***Rus.*** Vasilishki. Hrodzyenskaya Voblasts', W Belarus *53°47′N 24°51′E*
Vasil Kolarov *see* Pamporovo
Vasil'kov *see* Vasyl'kiv
191 *H11* **Vasilyevichy** ***Rus.*** Vasilevichi. Homyel'skaya Voblasts', SE Belarus *52°15′N 29°50′E*
190 *G5* **Vasil'yevo** Pskovskaya Oblast', Russian Federation
285 *M2* **Vaskess Bay** *var.* Vashess Bay. *bay* Kiritimati, E Kiribati
Vaskoh *see* Vaşcău
Vaskohsziklás *see* Ştei
188 *F7* **Vaslui** Vaslui, C Romania *46°38′N 27°44′E*
188 *F7* **Vaslui** ◐ *county* NE Romania
Vas Megye *see* Vas
72 *H7* **Vassar** Michigan, N USA *43°22′N 83°34′W*
154 *B7* **Vassdalsegga** ▲ S Norway *59°47′N 07°07′E*
109 *E13* **Vassouras** Rio de Janeiro, SE Brazil *22°24′S 43°38′W*
111 *H7* **Vassouras** Rio de Janeiro, Brazil *22°24′S 43°40′W*
166 *D5* **Vassy** Basse-Normandie, France *48°51′N 0°40′W*
155 *H8* **Västerås** Västmanland, C Sweden *59°37′N 16°33′E*
154 *I1* **Västerbotten** ◐ *county* N Sweden
154 *F6* **Västerdalälven** ≈ C Sweden
155 *I8* **Västerhaninge** Stockholm, C Sweden *59°07′N 18°06′E*
154 *I3* **Västernorrland** ◐ *county* C Sweden
155 *I10* **Västervik** Kalmar, S Sweden *57°44′N 16°40′E*
154 *H7* **Västmanland** ◐ *county* C Sweden
175 *G8* **Vasto** ***anc.*** Histonium. Abruzzo, C Italy *42°07′N 14°43′E*
155 *F9* **Västra Götaland** ◐ *county* S Sweden
155 *F8* **Västra Silen** ◎ S Sweden
177 *M4* **Vasvár** ***Ger.*** Eisenburg. Vas, W Hungary *47°03′N 16°48′E*
189 *K6* **Vasylivka** Zaporiz'ka Oblast', SE Ukraine *47°26′N 35°18′E*
189 *H3* **Vasyl'kiv** *var.* Vasil'kov. Kyyivs'ka Oblast', N Ukraine *50°12′N 30°18′E*
192 *F6* **Vasyugan** ≈ C Russian Federation
165 *H5* **Vatan** Indre, C France *47°06′N 01°49′E*
186 *E6* **Vathy** ***prev.*** Itháki. Itháki, Iónia Nisiá, Greece, C Mediterranean Sea *38°22′N 20°43′E*
175 *E8* **Vatican City** ***off.*** Vatican City State. ◆ *papal state* S Europe
Vatican City State *see* Vatican City
175 *H11* **Vaticano, Capo** *headland* S Italy *38°37′N 15°49′E*
Vatilí *see* Vadili
152 *D2* **Vatnajökull** *glacier* SE Iceland
154 *J7* **Vätö** Stockholm, C Sweden *59°48′N 18°55′E*
280 *G10* **Vatoa** *island* Lau Group, SE Fiji
139 *M7* **Vatomandry** Toamasina, E Madagascar *19°20′S 48°58′E*
188 *D6* **Vatra Dornei** ***Ger.*** Dorna Watra. Suceava, NE Romania *47°20′N 25°21′E*
188 *D6* **Vatra Moldoviţei** Suceava, NE Romania *47°37′N 25°36′E*
Vatter, Lake *see* Vättern
155 *G9* **Vättern** ***Eng.*** Lake Vatter; ***prev.*** Lake Vetter. ◎ S Sweden
280 *E8* **Vatukoula** Viti Levu, W Fiji *17°30′S 177°53′E*
280 *E9* **Vatulele** *island* SW Fiji
189 *H5* **Vatutine** Cherkas'ka Oblast', C Ukraine *49°01′N 31°04′E*
165 *J8* **Vaucluse** ◐ *department* SE France
165 *J3* **Vaucouleurs** Meuse, NE France *48°37′N 05°38′E*
174 *A3* **Vaud** ***Ger.*** Waadt. ◐ *canton* SW Switzerland
63 *H3* **Vaudreuil** Québec, SE Canada *45°24′N 74°01′W*
79 *M7* **Vaughn** New Mexico, SW USA *34°36′N 105°12′W*
102 *E8* **Vaupés** ***off.*** Comisaría del Vaupés. ◐ *province* SE Colombia
Vaupés, Comisaría del *see* Vaupés
102 *E8* **Vaupés, Río** *var.* Rio Uaupés. ≈ Brazil/Colombia ***see also*** Uaupés, Rio
Vaupés, Río *see* Uaupés, Rio
169 *J5* **Vauvert** Gard, S France *43°42′N 04°16′E*
167 *L7* **Vauvillers** Franche-Comté, France *47°55′N 6°06′E*
57 *J8* **Vauxhall** Alberta, SW Canada *50°05′N 112°09′W*
163 *G13* **Vaux-sur-Sûre** Luxembourg, SE Belgium *49°55′N 05°34′E*
139 *M6* **Vavatenina** Toamasina, E Madagascar *17°25′S 49°11′E*
284 *D7* **Vava'u Group** *island group* N Tonga
132 *E7* **Vavoua** W Ivory Coast *07°23′N 06°29′W*
195 *J10* **Vavozh** Udmurtskaya Respublika, NW Russian Federation *56°48′N 51°53′E*
235 *G10* **Vavuniya** Northern Province, N Sri Lanka *08°45′N 80°30′E*
191 *D10* **Vawkavysk** ***Pol.*** Wołkowysk, ***Rus.*** Volkovysk. Hrodzyenskaya Voblasts', W Belarus *53°10′N 24°28′E*
191 *D10* **Vawkavyskaye Wzvyshsha** ***Rus.*** Volkovyskiye Vysoty. *hill range* W Belarus
155 *I8* **Vaxholm** Stockholm, C Sweden *59°25′N 18°21′E*
155 *G11* **Växjö** *var.* Vexiö. Kronoberg, S Sweden *56°52′N 14°50′E*
195 *K1* **Vaygach, Ostrov** *island* NW Russian Federation
215 *L5* **Vayk'** ***prev.*** Azizbekov. SE Armenia *39°41′N 45°28′E*
168 *G3* **Vayrac** Midi-Pyrénées, France *44°57′N 1°42′E*
187 *K1* **Vaysal** Edirne, Turkey *41°57′N 26°52′E*
Vazáš *see* Vittangi
195 *H6* **Vazhgort** ***prev.*** Chasovo. Respublika Komi, NW Russian Federation *64°06′N 46°44′E*
91 *M6* **V. C. Bird** ✈ (St. John's) Antigua, Antigua and Barbuda *17°07′N 61°49′W*
155 *A8* **Veavågen** Rogaland, S Norway *59°18′N 5°13′E*
74 *E4* **Veblen** South Dakota, N USA *45°50′N 97°17′W*
180 *I6* **Vechelde** Niedersachsen, Germany *10°23′N 52°16′E*
162 *I5* **Vecht** ***Ger.*** Vechte. ≈ Germany/Netherlands ***see also*** Vechte
Vecht *see* Vechte
180 *E5* **Vechta** Niedersachsen, NW Germany *52°44′N 08°16′E*
180 *C5* **Vechte** ***Dut.*** Vecht. ≈ Germany/Netherlands ***see also*** Vecht
Vechte *see* Vecht
172 *E2* **Vecinos** Castilla y León, Spain *40°47′N 5°52′W*
181 *G8* **Veckerhagen** Hessen, Germany *9°36′N 51°30′E*
190 *E6* **Vecpiebalga** Cēsis, C Latvia *57°03′N 25°47′E*
190 *D6* **Vecumnieki** Bauska, C Latvia *56°36′N 24°30′E*
Vedāvati *see* Hagari
155 *F10* **Veddige** Halland, S Sweden *57°16′N 12°19′E*
188 *D10* **Vedea** ≈ S Romania
197 *I9* **Vedeno** Chechenskaya Respublika, SW Russian Federation *42°57′N 46°02′E*
114 *A9* **Vedia** Buenos Aires, Argentina *34°30′S 61°33′W*
190 *I1* **Vedlozero** Respublika Kareliya, Russian Federation
280 *E8* **Ve Drala Reef** *reef* N Fiji
155 *A8* **Vedvågen** Rogaland, S Norway *59°18′N 05°13′E*
162 *I4* **Veendam** Groningen, NE Netherlands *53°05′N 06°53′E*
162 *G7* **Veenendaal** Utrecht, C Netherlands *52°03′N 05°33′E*
163 *C8* **Veere** Zeeland, SW Netherlands *51°33′N 03°40′E*
70 *D2* **Vega** Texas, SW USA *35°14′N 102°26′W*
152 *D6* **Vega** *island* C Norway
91 *I7* **Vega Baja** C Puerto Rico *18°27′N 66°23′W*
82 *B9* **Vega Point** *headland* Kiska Island, Alaska, USA *51°49′N 177°19′E*
155 *C8* **Vegår** ◎ S Norway
118 *B7* **Vegas de Itata** Bío-Bío, Chile *36°24′S 72°51′W*
163 *G8* **Veghel** Noord-Brabant, S Netherlands *51°37′N 05°33′E*
Veglia *see* Krk
186 *G3* **Vegorítida, Límni** *var.* Límni Vegorítis. ◎ N Greece
Vegorítis, Límni *see* Vegorítida, Límni
57 *J5* **Vegreville** Alberta, SW Canada *53°30′N 112°02′W*
155 *F11* **Veinge** Halland, S Sweden *56°33′N 13°04′E*
114 *C5* **Veinte de Setiembre** Entre Ríos, Argentina *32°23′S 59°40′W*
116 *D6* **Veinticinco de Mayo** La Pampa, Argentina *37°42′S 67°54′E*
116 *G4* **Veinticinco de Mayo** *var.* 25 de Mayo. Buenos Aires, E Argentina *35°27′S 60°11′W*
118 *G9* **Veinticinco de Mayo** La Pampa, C Argentina *37°45′S 67°40′W*
172 *C5* **Veiros** Évora, Portugal *38°57′N 7°30′W*
191 *D9* **Veisiejai** Alytus, S Lithuania *54°06′N 23°42′E*
155 *C12* **Vejen** Ribe, W Denmark *55°29′N 09°13′E*
170 *E9* **Vejer de la Frontera** Andalucía, S Spain *36°15′N 05°58′W*
155 *D12* **Vejle** Vejle, C Denmark *55°43′N 09°33′E*
155 *D12* **Vejle** ***off.*** Vejle Amt. ◐ *county* C Denmark
Vejle Amt *see* Vejle
185 *L5* **Vekilski** Shumen, NE Bulgaria *43°33′N 27°19′E*
190 *I5* **Vekshino** Novgorodskaya Oblast', Russian Federation
102 *D2* **Vela, Cabo de la** *headland* NE Colombia *12°14′N 72°13′W*
Vela Goa *see* Goa
184 *C6* **Vela Luka** Dubrovnik-Neretva, S Croatia *42°57′N 16°43′E*
85 *J7* **Velardeña** Durango, Mexico *25°04′N 103°44′W*
115 *K8* **Velázquez** Rocha, E Uruguay *34°05′S 54°16′W*
116 *J4* **Velázquez** Rocha, Uruguay *34°06′S 54°18′E*
181 *C8* **Velbert** Nordrhein-Westfalen, W Germany *51°22′N 07°03′E*
177 *J5* **Velden** Kärnten, S Austria *46°37′N 13°59′E*
Veldes *see* Bled
163 *G8* **Veldhoven** Noord-Brabant, S Netherlands *51°24′N 05°24′E*
184 *B4* **Velebit** ▲▲ C Croatia
185 *M7* **Veleka** ≈ SE Bulgaria
177 *K5* **Velenje** ***Ger.*** Wöllan. N Slovenia *46°22′N 15°07′E*
284 *A10* **Vele, Pointe** *headland* Île Futuna, S Wallis and Futuna
185 *H7* **Veles** ***Turk.*** Köprülü. C FYR Macedonia *41°43′N 21°49′E*
184 *G8* **Velešta** SW FYR Macedonia *41°16′N 20°37′E*
186 *G4* **Velestíno** ***prev.*** Velestínon. Thessalía, C Greece *39°23′N 22°45′E*
Velestínon *see* Velestíno
Velevshchina *see* Vyelyewshchyna
102 *C5* **Vélez** Santander, C Colombia *06°02′N 73°43′W*
171 *H8* **Vélez Blanco** Andalucía, S Spain *37°43′N 02°07′W*
173 *H8* **Vélez de Benaudalla** Andalucía, Spain *36°50′N 3°31′W*
170 *F10* **Vélez de la Gomera, Peñon de** *island group* S Spain
170 *F9* **Vélez-Málaga** Andalucía, S Spain *36°47′N 04°06′W*
171 *H8* **Vélez Rubio** Andalucía, S Spain *37°39′N 02°04′W*
Velha Goa *see* Goa
Velho *see* Porto Velho
184 *C2* **Velika Gorica** Zagreb, N Croatia *45°43′N 16°03′E*
177 *K6* **Velika Kapela** ▲▲ NW Croatia
Velika Kikinda *see* Kikinda
184 *C3* **Velika Kladuša** ◐ Federacija Bosna I Hercegovina, NW Bosnia and Herzegovina
184 *G4* **Velika Morava** *var.* Glavn'a Morava, Morava, ***Ger.*** Grosse Morava. ≈ C Serbia
184 *G4* **Velika Plana** Serbia, C Serbia *44°20′N 21°01′E*
193 *M3* **Velikaya** ≈ NE Russian Federation
194 *C10* **Velikaya** ≈ W Russian Federation
Velikaya Berestovitsa *see* Vyalikaya Byerastavitsa
Velikaya Lepetikha *see* Velyka Lepetykha
Veliki Bečkerek *see* Zrenjanin
185 *H4* **Veliki Krš** *var.* Stol. ▲ E Serbia *44°10′N 22°09′E*
185 *L5* **Veliki Preslav** ***prev.*** Preslav. Shumen, NE Bulgaria *43°09′N 26°50′E*
184 *B2* **Veliki Risnjak** ▲ NW Croatia *45°30′N 14°31′E*
184 *E5* **Veliki Stolac** ▲ E Bosnia and Herzegovina *43°55′N 19°15′E*
Velikiy Bor *see* Vyaliki Bor
194 *D10* **Velikiye Luki** Pskovskaya Oblast', W Russian Federation *56°20′N 30°27′E*
194 *D9* **Velikiy Novgorod** ***prev.*** Novgorod. Novgorodskaya Oblast', W Russian Federation *58°32′N 31°15′E*
195 *H8* **Velikiy Ustyug** Vologodskaya Oblast', NW Russian Federation *60°46′N 46°18′E*
184 *G3* **Veliko Gradište** Serbia, NE Serbia *44°46′N 21°28′E*
234 *F7* **Velikonda Range** ▲▲ SE India
Veliko Tărnovo *see* Veliko Tŭrnovo
185 *K6* **Veliko Tŭrnovo** ***prev.*** Tirnovo, Trnovo, Tŭrnovo, Veliko Tărnovo. Veliko Tŭrnovo, N Bulgaria *43°05′N 25°40′E*
Velikovec *see* Völkermarkt
195 *I3* **Velikovisochnoye** Nenetskiy Avtonomnyy Okrug, NW Russian Federation *67°13′N 52°00′E*
132 *B4* **Vélingara** C Senegal *15°00′N 14°39′W*
132 *B5* **Vélingara** S Senegal *13°12′N 14°05′W*
185 *J7* **Velingrad** Pazardzhik, C Bulgaria *42°01′N 24°00′E*
196 *D2* **Velizh** Smolenskaya Oblast', W Russian Federation *55°30′N 31°06′E*
183 *D8* **Velká Deštná** *var.* Deštná, Grosskoppe, ***Ger.*** Deschnaer Koppe. ▲ NE Czech Republic *50°18′N 16°25′E*
183 *D9* **Velké Meziříčí** ***Ger.*** Grossmeseritsch. Vysočina, C Czech Republic *49°22′N 16°02′E*
152 *A4* **Velkomstpynten** *headland* NW Svalbard *79°51′N 11°37′E*
183 *G10* **Vel'ký Krtíš** Banskobystrický Kraj, C Slovakia *48°13′N 19°21′E*
180 *J3* **Vellahn** Mecklenburg-Vorpommern, Germany *10°58′N 53°24′E*
281 *H1* **Vella Lavella** *var.* Mbilua. *island* New Georgia Islands, NW Solomon Islands
181 *H14* **Vellberg** Baden-Württemberg, Germany *9°53′N 49°05′E*
175 *E8* **Velletri** Lazio, C Italy *41°41′N 12°47′E*
155 *F12* **Vellinge** Skåne, S Sweden *55°29′N 13°00′E*
235 *F8* **Vellore** Tamil Nādu, SE India *12°56′N 79°09′E*
Velobriga *see* Viana do Castelo
187 *H8* **Velopoúla** *island* S Greece
162 *H7* **Velp** Gelderland, SE Netherlands *52°00′N 05°59′E*
180 *J6* **Velpke** Niedersachsen, Germany *10°56′N 52°24′E*
Velsen *see* Velsen-Noord
162 *E5* **Velsen-Noord** *var.* Velsen. Noord-Holland, W Netherlands *52°27′N 04°40′E*
194 *G7* **Vel'sk** *var.* Velsk. Arkhangel'skaya Oblast', NW Russian Federation *61°03′N 42°01′E*
Velsuna *see* Orvieto
162 *G6* **Veluwemeer** *lake channel* C Netherlands
74 *C2* **Velva** North Dakota, N USA *48°03′N 100°55′W*
Velvendos/Velvendós *see* Velventós
186 *G3* **Velventós** *var.* Velvendos, Velvendós. Dytikí Makedonía, N Greece *40°15′N 22°04′E*
189 *J4* **Velyka Bahachka** Poltavs'ka Oblast', C Ukraine *49°46′N 33°44′E*
189 *J7* **Velyka Lepetykha** ***Rus.*** Velikaya Lepetikha. Khersons'ka Oblast', S Ukraine *47°09′N 33°59′E*
188 *G7* **Velyka Mykhaylivka** Odes'ka Oblast', SW Ukraine *47°07′N 29°49′E*
189 *L6* **Velyka Novosilka** Donets'ka Oblast', E Ukraine *47°49′N 36°49′E*
189 *J6* **Velyka Oleksandrivka** Khersons'ka Oblast', S Ukraine *47°17′N 33°16′E*
189 *K3* **Velyka Pysanivka** Sums'ka Oblast', NE Ukraine *50°25′N 35°28′E*
188 *B4* **Velykyy Bereznyy** Zakarpats'ka Oblast', W Ukraine *48°54′N 22°27′E*
189 *L3* **Velykyy Burluk** Kharkivs'ka Oblast', E Ukraine *50°04′N 37°25′E*
Velykyy Tokmak *see* Tokmak
289 *E8* **Vema Fracture Zone** *tectonic feature* W Indian Ocean
291 *I10* **Vema Seamount** *undersea feature* SW Indian Ocean
154 *G4* **Vemdalen** Jämtland, C Sweden *62°26′N 13°50′E*
155 *H10* **Vena** Kalmar, S Sweden *57°31′N 16°00′E*
85 *L8* **Venado** San Luis Potosí, C Mexico *22°56′N 101°05′W*
86 *F5* **Venados** Hidalgo, Mexico *20°28′N 98°40′W*
112 *E9* **Venado Tuerto** Entre Ríos, E Argentina *33°45′S 61°56′W*
116 *F4* **Venado Tuerto** Santa Fe, C Argentina *33°46′S 61°57′W*
175 *F9* **Venafro** Molise, C Italy *41°28′N 14°03′E*
103 *I5* **Venamo, Cerro** ▲ E Venezuela *05°56′N 61°25′W*
167 *J8* **Venarey-les-Laumes** Bourgogne, France *47°32′N 4°26′E*
176 *D7* **Venaria** Piemonte, NW Italy *45°09′N 07°40′E*
165 *K8* **Vence** Alpes-Maritimes, SE France *43°45′N 07°07′E*
172 *C5* **Venda** Évora, Portugal *38°52′N 7°30′W*
170 *D3* **Venda Nova** Vila Real, N Portugal *41°40′N 07°58′W*
172 *C2* **Vendas de Galizes** Coimbra, Portugal *40°19′N 7°54′W*
172 *B5* **Vendas Novas** Évora, S Portugal *38°41′N 08°27′W*
164 *F5* **Vendée** ◐ *department* NW France
165 *J4* **Vendeuvre-sur-Barse** Aube, NE France *48°08′N 04°17′E*
164 *G4* **Vendôme** Loir-et-Cher, C France *47°48′N 01°04′E*
Venedig *see* Venezia
Vener, Lake *see* Vänern
174 *E5* **Veneta, Laguna** *lagoon* NE Italy
Venetia *see* Venezia
83 *J3* **Venetie** Alaska, USA *67°00′N 146°25′W*
174 *E4* **Veneto** *var.* Venezia Euganea. ◐ *region* NE Italy
185 *L5* **Venets** Shumen, NE Bulgaria *43°33′N 26°56′E*
196 *G3* **Venev** Tul'skaya Oblast', W Russian Federation *54°18′N 38°16′E*
177 *H7* **Venezia** ***Eng.*** Venice, ***Fr.*** Venise, ***Ger.*** Venedig; ***anc.*** Venetia. Veneto, NE Italy *45°26′N 12°20′E*
Venezia Euganea *see* Veneto
Venezia, Golfo di *see* Venice, Gulf of
Venezia Tridentina *see* Trentino-Alto Adige
103 *H4* **Venezuela** ***off.*** Republic of Venezuela; ***prev.*** Estados Unidos de Venezuela, United States of Venezuela. ◆ *republic* N South America
Venezuela, Cordillera de *see* Costa, Cordillera de la
Venezuela, Estados Unidos de *see* Venezuela
102 *E2* **Venezuela, Golfo de** ***Eng.*** Gulf of Maracaibo, Gulf of Venezuela. *gulf* NW Venezuela
Venezuela, Gulf of *see* Venezuela, Golfo de
290 *C6* **Venezuelan Basin** *undersea feature* E Caribbean Sea
Venezuela, Republic of *see* Venezuela
Venezuela, United States of *see* Venezuela
234 *C6* **Vengurla** Mahārāshtra, W India *15°55′N 73°39′E*
180 *D6* **Venhaus** Niedersachsen, Germany *7°27′N 52°22′E*
82 *G8* **Veniaminof, Mount** ▲ Alaska, USA *56°12′N 159°24′W*
69 *L7* **Venice** Florida, SE USA *27°06′N 82°27′W*
68 *E5* **Venice** Louisiana, S USA *29°15′N 89°20′W*
Venice *see* Venezia
174 *F5* **Venice, Gulf of** ***It.*** Golfo di Venezia, ***Slvn.*** Beneški Zaliv. *gulf* N Adriatic Sea
Venise *see* Venezia
154 *G6* **Venjan** Dalarna, C Sweden *60°58′N 13°55′E*
154 *F6* **Venjansjön** ◎ C Sweden
234 *F7* **Venkatagiri** Andhra Pradesh, E India *14°00′N 79°39′E*
163 *H9* **Venlo** ***prev.*** Venloo. Limburg, SE Netherlands *51°22′N 06°11′E*
Venloo *see* Venlo
155 *C9* **Vennesla** Vest-Agder, S Norway *58°15′N 08°00′E*
175 *H9* **Venosa** ***anc.*** Venusia. Basilicata, S Italy *40°57′N 15°49′E*
Venoste, Alpi *see* Ötztaler Alpen
Venraij *see* Venray
163 *H8* **Venray** *var.* Venraij. Limburg, SE Netherlands *51°32′N 05°59′E*
190 *C7* **Venta** ***Ger.*** Windau. ≈ Latvia/Lithuania
Venta Belgarum *see* Winchester
84 *F8* **Ventana, Punta Arena de la** *var.* Punta de la Ventana. *headland* W Mexico *24°03′N 109°49′W*
Ventana, Punta de la *see* Ventana, Punta Arena de la
116 *F6* **Ventana, Sierra de la** *hill range* E Argentina
141 *H7* **Venterstad** Eastern Cape, South Africa *30°47′S 25°48′E*
Ventia *see* Valence
285 *M3* **Vent, Îles du** *var.* Windward Islands. *island group* Archipel de la Société, W French Polynesia
285 *H6* **Vent, Îles Sous le** *var.* Leeward Islands. *island group* Archipel de la Société, W French Polynesia
176 *D9* **Ventimiglia** Liguria, NW Italy *43°47′N 07°37′E*
161 *J8* **Ventnor** S England, UK *50°36′N 01°11′W*
64 *G9* **Ventnor City** New Jersey, NE USA *39°19′N 74°27′W*
169 *K4* **Ventoux, Mont** ▲ SE France *44°12′N 05°21′E*
190 *B6* **Ventspils** ***Ger.*** Windau. Ventspils, NW Latvia *57°22′N 21°34′E*
102 *G6* **Ventuari, Río** ≈ S Venezuela
81 *C8* **Ventucopa** California, USA *34°50′N 119°28′W*
81 *C9* **Ventura** California, W USA *34°15′N 119°18′W*
158 *G2* **Ben Venue** ▲ UK *56°13′N 4°27′W*
276 *E5* **Venus Bay** South Australia *33°15′S 134°42′E*
Venusia *see* Venosa
285 *M3* **Vénus, Pointe** *var.* Pointe Tataaihoa. *headland* Tahiti, W French Polynesia *17°28′S 149°29′W*
87 *K9* **Venustiano Carranza** Chiapas, SE Mexico *16°21′N 92°33′W*
87 *K9* **Venustiano Carranza** Chiapas, Mexico *16°21′N 92°33′W*
84 *F6* **Venustiano Carranza** Durango, Mexico
85 *L5* **Venustiano Carranza, Presa** ▣ NE Mexico
116 *G1* **Vera** Santa Fe, C Argentina *29°28′S 60°10′W*
171 *H8* **Vera** Andalucía, S Spain *37°15′N 01°51′W*
117 *E9* **Vera, Bahía** *bay* E Argentina
87 *H6* **Veracruz** *var.* Veracruz Llave. Veracruz-Llave, E Mexico *19°10′N 96°09′W*
Veracruz *see* Veracruz-Llave
172 *C6* **Vera Cruz de Marmelar** Évora, Portugal *38°14′N 7°41′W*
86 *G5* **Veracruz-Llave** *var.* Veracruz. ◐ *state* E Mexico
Veracruz Llave *see* Veracruz
168 *B6* **Vera de Bidasoa** Navarra, Spain *43°17′N 1°41′W*
89 *J9* **Veraguas** ***off.*** Provincia de Veraguas. ◐ *province* W Panama
Veraguas, Provincia de *see* Veraguas
Veramin *see* Varāmīn
232 *B9* **Verāval** Gujarāt, W India *20°54′N 70°22′E*
114 *B2* **Vera y Pintado** Santa Fe, Argentina *30°09′S 60°21′W*
176 *E6* **Verbania** Piemonte, NW Italy *45°56′N 08°34′E*
167 *H4* **Verberie** Picardie, France *49°19′N 2°44′E*
175 *H10* **Verbicaro** Calabria, SW Italy *39°44′N 15°51′E*
176 *C5* **Verbier** Valais, SW Switzerland *46°06′N 07°14′E*
Vercellae *see* Vercelli
176 *D7* **Vercelli** ***anc.*** Vercellae. Piemonte, NW Italy *45°19′N 08°25′E*
190 *I3* **Verchovina** Leningradskaya Oblast', Russian Federation
169 *K4* **Verclause** Rhône-Alpes, France *44°23′N 5°26′E*
165 *J7* **Vercors** *physical region* E France
Verdal *see* Verdalsøra
154 *E3* **Verdalsøra** *var.* Verdal. Nord-Trøndelag, C Norway *63°47′N 11°27′E*
Verde, Cabo *see* Cape Verde
90 *F3* **Verde, Cape** *headland* Long Island, C Bahamas *22°51′N 75°50′W*
170 *F1* **Verde, Costa** *coastal region* N Spain
Verde Grande, Río/Verde Grande y de Belem, Río *see* Verde, Río
172 *D2* **Verdelhos** Castelo Branco, Portugal *40°22′N 7°28′W*
180 *G4* **Verden** Niedersachsen, NW Germany *52°55′N 09°14′E*
106 *D8* **Verde, Río** ≈ Bolivia/Brazil
110 *F6* **Verde, Rio** ≈ SE Brazil
86 *C5* **Verde, Río** *var.* Río Verde Grande, Río Verde Grande y de Belem. ≈ C Mexico
86 *G8* **Verde, Río** ≈ SE Mexico
85 *M9* **Verde, Río** ≈ San Luis Potosí, Mexico
86 *F4* **Verde, Río** ≈ San Luis Potosí, Mexico
Verdhikoúsa/Verdhikoússa *see* Verdikoússa
75 *F11* **Verdigris River** ≈ Kansas/Oklahoma, C USA
186 *G4* **Verdikoússa** *var.* Verdhikoúsa, Verdhikoússa. Thessalía, C Greece *39°47′N 21°59′E*
165 *K8* **Verdon** ≈ SE France
63 *H3* **Verdun** Québec, SE Canada *45°27′N 73°36′W*
165 *J3* **Verdun** *var.* Verdun-sur-Meuse; ***anc.*** Verodunum. Meuse, NE France *49°09′N 05°25′E*
115 *I6* **Verdún** Durazno, Uruguay *32°40′S 55°27′W*
168 *F5* **Verdun-sur-Garonne** Midi-Pyrénées, France *43°52′N 1°14′E*
167 *K9* **Verdun-sur-le-Doubs** Bourgogne, France *46°54′N 5°01′E*
Verdun-sur-Meuse *see* Verdun
141 *I4* **Vereeniging** Gauteng, South Africa *26°40′S 27°56′E*
138 *G7* **Vereeniging** Gauteng, NE South Africa *26°41′S 27°56′E*
Veremeyki *see* Vyeramyeyki
195 *K9* **Vereshchagino** Permskaya Oblast', NW Russian Federation *58°06′N 54°38′E*
168 *G5* **Verfeil** Midi-Pyrénées, France *43°40′N 1°40′E*
132 *B6* **Verga, Cap** *headland* W Guinea *10°12′N 14°27′W*
115 *K6* **Vergara** Treinta y Tres, E Uruguay *32°58′S 53°54′W*
140 *G3* **Vergelee** North-West, South Africa *25°46′S 24°12′E*
176 *E5* **Vergeletto** Ticino, S Switzerland *46°13′N 08°34′E*
63 *H4* **Vergennes** Vermont, NE USA *44°09′N 73°13′W*
168 *E3* **Vergt** Aquitaine, France *45°01′N 0°43′E*
Veria *see* Véroia
172 *B3* **Vérigo** Leiria, Portugal *39°57′N 8°35′W*
170 *D3* **Verín** Galicia, NW Spain *41°55′N 07°26′W*
Verin T'alin *see* T'alin
190 *F5* **Veriora** Põlvamaa, SE Estonia *57°57′N 27°23′E*
110 *A2* **Veríssimo** Minas Gerais, Brazil *19°42′S 48°18′W*
141 *I6* **Verkeerdevlei** Free State, South Africa *28°50′S 26°47′E*
189 *J5* **Verkhivtseve** Dnipropetrovs'ka Oblast', E Ukraine *48°27′N 34°15′E*
Verkhnedvinsk *see* Vyerkhnyadzvinsk
192 *G6* **Verkhneimbatsk** Krasnoyarskiy Kray, N Russian Federation *63°06′N 88°03′E*
195 *L6* **Verkhnenil'dina** Khanty-Mansiyskiy Avtonomnyy Okrug, Russian federation
194 *E3* **Verkhnetulomskiy** Murmanskaya Oblast', NW Russian Federation *68°37′N 31°46′E*
194 *E3* **Verkhnetulomskoye Vodokhranilishche** ▣ NW Russian Federation
Verkhneudinsk *see* Ulan-Ude
193 *J6* **Verkhnevilyuysk** Respublika Sakha (Yakutiya), NE Russian Federation *63°44′N 119°59′E*
195 *L9* **Verkhniy Neyvinskiy** Sverdlovskaya oblast', Russian federation
195 *L9* **Verkhniy Tagil** Sverdlovskaya oblast', Russian federation
196 *M10* **Verkhniy Ufaley** Chelyabinskaya oblast', Russian federation
197 *M3* **Verkhniy Avzyan** Respublika Bashkortostan, W Russian Federation *53°31′N 57°26′E*
197 *I6* **Verkhniy Baskunchak** Astrakhanskaya Oblast', SW Russian Federation *48°14′N 46°43′E*
197 *M1* **Verkhniye Kigi** Respublika Bashkortostan, W Russian Federation *55°25′N 58°40′E*
189 *J6* **Verkhniy Rohachyk** Khersons'ka Oblast', S Ukraine *47°16′N 34°16′E*
196 *M9* **Verkhnyaya Pyshma** Sverdlovskaya oblast', Russian federation
195 *L9* **Verkhnyaya Salda** Sverdlovskaya oblast', Russian federation
193 *J6* **Verkhnyaya Amga** Respublika Sakha (Yakutiya), NE Russian Federation *59°34′N 127°07′E*
195 *K4* **Verkhnyaya Inta** Respublika Komi, NW Russian Federation *65°55′N 60°07′E*
193 *H4* **Verkhnyaya Taymyra** ≈ N Russian Federation
195 *H7* **Verkhnyaya Toyma** Arkhangel'skaya Oblast', NW Russian Federation *62°12′N 44°57′E*
195 *L8* **Verkhotur'ye** Sverdlovskaya oblast', Russian federation
196 *F3* **Verkhov'ye** Orlovskaya Oblast', W Russian Federation *52°49′N 37°20′E*
188 *D5* **Verkhovyna** Ivano-Frankivs'ka Oblast', W Ukraine *48°09′N 24°48′E*
193 *J5* **Verkhoyansk** Respublika Sakha (Yakutiya), NE Russian Federation *67°27′N 133°27′E*
193 *J5* **Verkhoyanskiy Khrebet** ▲▲ NE Russian Federation
189 *J5* **Verkn'odniprovs'k** Dnipropetrovs'ka Oblast', E Ukraine *48°40′N 34°17′E*
180 *F7* **Verl** Nordrhein-Westfalen, NW Germany *51°52′N 08°30′E*
140 *E9* **Verlatekop** ▲ Northern Cape, South Africa *32°33′S 20°38′E*
152 *A4* **Verlegenhuken** *headland* N Svalbard *80°03′N 16°15′E*
167 *I3* **Vermand** Picardie, France *49°52′N 3°09′E*
135 *B10* **Vermelha, Ponta** *headland* NW Angola *05°40′S 12°09′E*
111 *J3* **Vermelho Novo** Minas Gerais, Brazil *20°01′S 42°17′W*
165 *I4* **Vermenton** Yonne, C France *47°40′N 03°43′E*
57 *K5* **Vermilion** Alberta, SW Canada *53°21′N 110°52′W*
73 *I9* **Vermilion** Ohio, N USA *41°25′N 82°21′W*
68 *C5* **Vermilion Bay** *bay* Louisiana, S USA
74 *H2* **Vermilion Lake** ◎ Minnesota, N USA
62 *C1* **Vermilion River** ≈ Ontario, S Canada
73 *C9* **Vermilion River** ≈ Illinois, N USA
74 *E6* **Vermillion** South Dakota, N USA *42°46′N 96°55′W*
74 *E6* **Vermillion River** ≈ South Dakota, N USA
63 *H1* **Vermillon, Rivière** ≈ Québec, SE Canada
186 *G3* **Vérmio** ▲▲ N Greece
172 *B3* **Vermoil** Leiria, Portugal *39°51′N 8°39′W*
63 *I4* **Vermont** ***off.*** State of Vermont, ***also known as*** Green Mountain State. ◐ *state* NE USA
184 *F6* **Vermosh** *var.* Vermoshi. Shkodër, N Albania *42°37′N 19°42′E*
Vermoshi *see* Vermosh
79 *J2* **Vernal** Utah, W USA *40°27′N 109°31′W*
80 *C3* **Vernalis** California, USA *37°38′N 121°17′W*
62 *C2* **Verner** Ontario, S Canada *46°24′N 80°04′W*
164 *G3* **Verneuil-sur-Avre** Eure, N France *48°44′N 00°55′E*
186 *F3* **Vérno** ▲▲ N Greece
56 *F8* **Vernon** British Columbia, SW Canada *50°17′N 119°19′W*
165 *H3* **Vernon** Eure, N France *49°04′N 01°28′E*
66 *C8* **Vernon** Alabama, S USA *33°45′N 88°06′W*
65 *J3* **Vernon** Connecticut, USA *41°49′N 72°29′W*
73 *F12* **Vernon** Indiana, N USA *38°59′N 85°39′W*
70 *F3* **Vernon** Texas, SW USA *34°11′N 99°17′W*
76 *B5* **Vernonia** Oregon, NW USA *45°51′N 123°11′W*
62 *D3* **Vernon, Lake** ◎ Ontario, S Canada
68 *B3* **Vernon Lake** ▣ Louisiana, S USA
169 *J3* **Vernoux-en-Vivarais** Rhône-Alpes, France *44°54′N 4°39′E*
167 *L5* **Verny** Lorraine, France *49°01′N 6°12′E*
69 *N7* **Vero Beach** Florida, SE USA *27°38′N 80°24′W*
Verőcze *see* Virovitica
Verodunum *see* Verdun
186 *G3* **Véroia** *var.* Veria, Vérroia, ***Turk.*** Karaferiye. Kentrikí Makedonía, N Greece *40°32′N 22°11′E*
176 *F7* **Verolanuova** Lombardia, N Italy *45°20′N 10°06′E*
62 *F4* **Verona** Ontario, SE Canada *44°30′N 76°42′W*
176 *G7* **Verona** Veneto, NE Italy *45°27′N 11°E*
74 *E3* **Verona** North Dakota, N USA *46°19′N 98°03′W*
72 *C7* **Verona** Wisconsin, N USA *42°59′N 89°33′W*
112 *G10* **Verónica** Buenos Aires, E Argentina *35°25′S 57°16′W*
116 *H4* **Verónica** Buenos Aires, Argentina *35°24′S 57°24′E*
68 *D4* **Verret, Lake** ◎ Louisiana, S USA
Vérroia *see* Véroia
165 *H3* **Versailles** Yvelines, N France *48°48′N 02°08′E*
73 *F11* **Versailles** Indiana, N USA *39°04′N 85°16′W*
66 *F4* **Versailles** Kentucky, S USA *38°02′N 84°45′W*
75 *H10* **Versailles** Missouri, C USA *38°25′N 92°51′W*
73 *G10* **Versailles** Ohio, N USA *40°13′N 84°28′W*
Versecz *see* Vršac
180 *C5* **Versen** Niedersachsen, Germany *7°14′N 52°43′E*
180 *E6* **Versmold** Nordrhein-Westfalen, Germany *8°09′N 52°03′E*
176 *B5* **Versoix** Genève, SW Switzerland *46°17′N 06°10′E*
168 *E2* **Verteillac** Aquitaine, France *45°21′N 0°22′E*
183 *F11* **Vértes** ▲▲ NW Hungary
90 *E4* **Vertientes** Camagüey, C Cuba *21°18′N 78°11′W*
187 *H2* **Vertískos** ▲▲ N Greece
164 *F5* **Vertou** Loire-Atlantique, NW France *47°10′N 01°28′W*
141 *K6* **Verulam** KwaZulu-Natal, South Africa *29°39′S 31°03′E*
Verulamium *see* St Albans
118 *D7* **Vervarco Campos, Lago** ◎ Neuquén, Argentina
163 *H11* **Verviers** Liège, E Belgium *50°36′N 05°52′E*
167 *I3* **Vervins** Picardie, France *49°50′N 3°54′E*
161 *I8* **Verwood** UK *50°52′N 1°52′W*
160 *D9* **Veryan** UK *50°13′N 4°55′W*
167 *J5* **Verzy** Champagne-Ardenne, France *49°09′N 4°10′E*
174 *C7* **Vescovato** Corse, France, C Mediterranean Sea *42°30′N 09°27′E*
163 *G11* **Vesdre** ≈ E Belgium
189 *K7* **Vesele** ***Rus.*** Veseloye. Zaporiz'ka Oblast', S Ukraine *47°00′N 34°52′E*
183 *C9* **Veselí nad Lužnicí** *var.* Weseli an der Lainsitz, ***Ger.*** Frohenbruck. Jihočeský Kraj, S Czech Republic *49°11′N 14°40′E*
185 *L6* **Veselinovo** Shumen, NE Bulgaria *43°01′N 27°02′E*
196 *G7* **Veselovskoye Vodokhranilishche** ▣ SW Russian Federation
Veseloye *see* Vesele
189 *H6* **Veselynove** Mykolayivs'ka Oblast', S Ukraine *47°21′N 31°15′E*
Veseya *see* Vyasyeya
197 *H5* **Veshenskaya** Rostovskaya Oblast', SW Russian Federation *49°37′N 41°43′E*
197 *I3* **Veshkayma** Ul'yanovskaya Oblast', W Russian Federation *54°04′N 47°06′E*
Vesisaari *see* Vadsø
Vesontio *see* Besançon
165 *K4* **Vesoul** ***anc.*** Vesulium, Vesulum. Haute-Saône, E France *47°37′N 06°09′E*
111 *H2* **Vespasiano** Minas Gerais, Brazil *19°40′S 43°55′W*
155 *F11* **Vessigebro** Halland, S Sweden *56°58′N 12°40′E*
155 *B9* **Vest-Agder** ◐ *county* S Norway
66 *D9* **Vestavia Hills** Alabama, S USA *33°27′N 86°47′W*
144 *C4* **Vesterålen** *island* NW Norway
152 *E4* **Vesterålen** *island group* N Norway
152 *B2* **Vestfirdhir** ◐ *region* NW Iceland
152 *E5* **Vestfjorden** *fjord* C Norway
155 *D8* **Vestfold** ◐ *county* S Norway
Vestmanhavn *see* Vestmanna
154 *A1* **Vestmanna** ***Dan.*** Vestmanhavn. Streymoy, N Faeroe Islands *62°09′N 07°11′W*
152 *B3* **Vestmannaeyjar** Sudhurland, S Iceland *63°26′N 20°14′W*
154 *B4* **Vestnes** Møre og Romsdal, S Norway *62°39′N 07°00′E*
155 *E12* **Vestsjælland** ***off.*** Vestsjællands Amt. ◐ *county* E Denmark
Vestsjællands Amt *see* Vestsjælland
152 *B2* **Vesturland** ◐ *region* W Iceland
152 *D4* **Vestvågøya** *island* C Norway
Vesulium/Vesulum *see* Vesoul
Vesuna *see* Périgueux
175 *G9* **Vesuvio** ***Eng.*** Vesuvius. ⛰ S Italy *40°48′N 14°29′E*
Vesuvius *see* Vesuvio
194 *F9* **Ves'yegonsk** Tverskaya Oblast', W Russian Federation *58°40′N 37°13′E*
183 *E12* **Veszprém** ***Ger.*** Veszprim. Veszprém, W Hungary *47°06′N 17°54′E*
183 *E12* **Veszprém** ***off.*** Veszprém Megye. ◐ *county* W Hungary
Veszprém Megye *see* Veszprém
Veszprim *see* Veszprém
Vetka *see* Vyetka
155 *G10* **Vetlanda** Jönköping, S Sweden *57°26′N 15°05′E*
197 *I1* **Vetluga** Nizhegorodskaya Oblast', W Russian Federation *57°51′N 45°45′E*
195 *H9* **Vetluga** ≈ NW Russian Federation
195 *H9* **Vetluzhskiy** Kostromskaya Oblast', NW Russian Federation *58°21′N 45°25′E*
197 *I1* **Vetluzhskiy** Nizhegorodskaya Oblast', W Russian Federation *57°10′N 45°07′E*
175 *E8* **Vetralla** Lazio, C Italy *42°18′N 12°03′E*
185 *M6* **Vetren** ***prev.*** Zhitarovo. Burgas, E Bulgaria *42°36′N 27°23′E*
185 *M5* **Vetrino** Varna, E Bulgaria *43°19′N 27°26′E*
Vetrino *see* Vyetryna
193 *H4* **Vetrovaya, Gora** ▲ N Russian Federation *73°54′N 95°00′E*
181 *D10* **Vettelschoss** Rheinland-Pfalz, Germany *7°21′N 50°37′E*
Vetter, Lake *see* Vättern
181 *B10* **Vettweiss** Nordrhein-Westfalen, Germany *6°36′N 50°44′E*
166 *F3* **Veules-les-Roses** Haute-Normandie, France *49°52′N 0°48′E*
163 *A9* **Veurne** *var.* Furnes. West-Vlaanderen, W Belgium *51°04′N 02°40′E*
66 *F3* **Vevay** Indiana, N USA *38°45′N 85°08′W*
176 *C5* **Vevey** ***Ger.*** Vivis; ***anc.*** Vibiscum. Vaud, SW Switzerland *46°28′N 06°51′E*
Vexiö *see* Växjö
165 *K7* **Veynes** Hautes-Alpes, SE France *44°33′N 05°51′E*
169 *H2* **Veyre-Monton** Auvergne, France *45°41′N 3°10′E*
167 *I8* **Vézelay** Bourgogne, France *47°28′N 3°44′E*
167 *L6* **Vézelise** Lorraine, France *48°29′N 6°05′E*
169 *J5* **Vézénobres** Languedoc-Roussillon, France *44°03′N 4°09′E*
185 *J6* **Vezhen** ▲ C Bulgaria *42°45′N 24°22′E*
169 *H4* **Vézins-de-Lévézou** Midi-Pyrénées, France *44°17′N 2°57′E*
214 *F4* **Vezirköprü** Samsun, N Turkey *41°09′N 35°27′E*
106 *C10* **Viacha** La Paz, W Bolivia *16°40′S 68°17′W*
114 *C5* **Viale** Entre Ríos, Argentina *31°53′S 60°01′W*
75 *G12* **Vian** Oklahoma, C USA *35°30′N 94°56′W*
Viana de Castelo *see* Viana do Castelo
172 *C6* **Viana do Alentejo** Évora, S Portugal *38°20′N 08°00′W*
170 *D3* **Viana do Bolo** Galicia, NW Spain *42°10′N 07°06′W*
170 *C3* **Viana do Castelo** *var.* Viana de Castelo; ***anc.*** Velobriga. Viana do Castelo, NW Portugal *41°41′N 08°50′W*
170 *D3* **Viana do Castelo** *var.* Viana de Castelo. ◐ *district* N Portugal
162 *F7* **Vianen** Utrecht, C Netherlands *52°N 05°06′E*
256 *F6* **Viangchan** ***Eng./Fr.*** Vientiane. ● (Laos) C Laos *17°58′N 102°38′E*
256 *F5* **Viangphoukha** *var.* Vieng Pou Kha. Louang Namtha, N Laos *20°41′N 101°03′E*
170 *E7* **Viar** ≈ SW Spain
176 *F9* **Viareggio** Toscana, C Italy *43°52′N 10°15′E*
165 *H8* **Viaur** ≈ S France
Vibiscum *see* Vevey
155 *D11* **Viborg** Viborg, NW Denmark *56°28′N 09°25′E*
155 *D11* **Viborg** ***off.*** Viborg Amt. ◐ *county* NW Denmark
Viborg Amt *see* Viborg
175 *H11* **Vibo Valentia** ***prev.*** Monteleone di Calabria; ***anc.*** Hipponium. Calabria, SW Italy *38°40′N 16°06′E*
166 *F7* **Vibraye** Pays de la Loire, France *48°03′N 0°43′E*
171 *K3* **Vic** *var.* Vich; ***anc.*** Ausa, Vicus Ausonensis. Cataluña, NE Spain *41°56′N 02°16′E*
168 *F7* **Vicdessos** Midi-Pyrénées, France *42°46′N 1°30′E*
164 *G8* **Vic-en-Bigorre** Hautes-Pyrénées, S France *43°23′N 00°04′E*
85 *J8* **Vicente Guerrero** Durango, C Mexico *23°30′N 104°24′W*
86 *C4* **Vicente Guerrero** Zacatecas, Mexico *22°20′N 103°27′W*
85 *M7* **Vicente Guerrero, Presa** *var.* Presa de las Adjuntas. ▣ NE Mexico
114 *E9* **Vicente López** Buenos Aires, Argentina *34°32′S 58°28′W*
Vicentia *see* Vicenza
177 *H6* **Vicenza** ***anc.*** Vicentia. Veneto, NE Italy *45°32′N 11°31′E*
Vich *see* Vic
102 *E6* **Vichada** ***off.*** Comisaría del Vichada. ◐ *province* E Colombia
Vichada, Comisaría del *see* Vichada
102 *F5* **Vichada, Río** ≈ E Colombia
115 *J4* **Vichadero** Rivera, NE Uruguay *31°45′S 54°41′W*
Vichegda *see* Vychegda

◆ Country
● Country Capital
◇ Dependent Territory
○ Dependent Territory Capital
◐ Administrative Regions
✈ International Airport
▲ Mountain
▲▲ Mountain Range
⛰ Volcano
≈ River
◎ Lake
▣ Reservoir

◆ Country	◇ Dependent Territory	◆ Administrative Regions	▲ Mountain	⊠ Volcano	⊚ Lake
● Country Capital	○ Dependent Territory Capital	× International Airport	▲ Mountain Range	≈ River	⊟ Reservoir

◆ Country
● Country Capital
◊ Dependent Territory
○ Dependent Territory Capital
◊ Administrative Regions
✕ International Airport
▲ Mountain
▲ Mountain Range
🌋 Volcano
✍ River
◎ Lake
⬡ Reservoir

◆ Country
● Country Capital
◇ Dependent Territory
○ Dependent Territory Capital
◈ Administrative Regions
✕ International Airport
▲ Mountain
▲ Mountain Range
◉ Volcano
♦ River
◉ Lake
▣ Reservoir

Wülfrath - Yap Trench
INDEX
428

181 C8 **Wülfrath** Nordrhein-Westfalen, Germany 7°03′N 51°17′E
180 H7 **Wulften** Niedersachsen, Germany 10°11′N 51°40′E
245 L6 **Wulian** Shandong, China 35°26′N 119°07′E
242 A5 **Wulian Feng** ▲▲ SW China
240 C7 **Wuliang Shan** ▲▲ SW China
261 H7 **Wuliaru, Pulau** *island* Kepulauan Tanimbar, E Indonesia
242 E5 **Wuling Shan** ▲▲ S China
177 L3 **Wulka** ≈ E Austria
Wulkan *see* Vulcan
177 J1 **Wullowitz** Oberösterreich, N Austria 48°37′N 14°27′E
242 D3 **Wulong** Chongqing Shi, China 29°11′N 107°26′E
Wu-lu-k'o-mu-shi/Wu-lu-mu-ch'i *see* Ürümqi
134 A5 **Wum** Nord-Ouest, NE Cameroon 06°24′N 10°04′E
242 A5 **Wumeng Shan** ▲▲ SW China
242 D9 **Wuming** Guangxi Zhuangzu Zizhiqu, S China 23°12′N 108°11′E
178 E5 **Wümme** ≈ NW Germany
Wu-na-mu *see* Wuhu
261 L5 **Wunen** Papua, E Indonesia 03°40′S 138°31′E
243 I4 **Wuning** Jiangxi, China 29°09′N 115°03′E
58 D5 **Wunnummin Lake** ◎ Ontario, C Canada
134 I4 **Wun Rog** Warab, S Sudan 09°00′N 28°20′E
179 G10 **Wunsiedel** Bayern, E Germany 50°02′N 12°00′E
180 G5 **Wunstorf** Niedersachsen, NW Germany 52°25′N 09°25′E
256 C3 **Wuntho** Sagaing, N Myanmar (Burma) 23°52′N 95°43′E
243 J7 **Wuping** Fujan, China 25°04′N 116°04′E
181 D9 **Wupper** ≈ W Germany
181 C8 **Wuppertal** *prev.* Barmen-Elberfeld. Nordrhein-Westfalen, W Germany 51°16′N 07°12′E
140 D8 **Wuppertal** Western Cape, South Africa 32°16′S 19°13′E
244 E5 **Wuqi** Shaanxi, C China 36°57′N 108°15′E
245 J5 **Wuqiao** *var.* Sangyuan. Hebei, E China 37°40′N 116°21′E
245 J3 **Wuqing** Tianjin Shi, China 39°13′N 117°02′E
179 F13 **Würm** ≈ SE Germany
133 J5 **Wurno** Sokoto, NW Nigeria 13°15′N 05°24′E
181 H12 **Würzburg** Bayern, SW Germany 49°48′N 09°56′E
179 H8 **Wurzen** Sachsen, E Germany 51°21′N 12°48′E
243 J1 **Wushan** China 32°04′N 117°03′E
242 E2 **Wushan** Chongqing Shi, China 31°03′N 109°31′E
244 B7 **Wushan** Gansu, China 34°25′N 104°32′E
242 E2 **Wu Shan** ▲▲ C China
242 C2 **Wusheng** Sichuan, China 30°14′N 106°10′E
243 H1 **Wusheng Guan** *pass* Hubei, China
238 D4 **Wushi** *var.* Uqturpan. Xinjiang Uygur Zizhiqu, NW China 41°07′N 79°09′E
Wusih *see* Wuxi
243 M1 **Wusong** China 31°22′N 121°30′E
180 E4 **Wüsting** Niedersachsen, Germany 8°21′N 53°07′E
180 J4 **Wustrow** Niedersachsen, Germany 11°07′N 52°55′E
245 H4 **Wutai** Shanxi, China 38°26′N 113°09′E
245 H4 **Wutai Shan** *var.* Beitai Ding. ▲ C China 39°00′N 114°00′E
245 H4 **Wutai Shan** ▲▲ Shanxi, China
242 A3 **Wutongqiao** Sichuan, C China 29°21′N 103°48′E
239 H4 **Wutongwozi Quan** *spring* NW China
261 M5 **Wutung** Sandaun, NW Papua New Guinea 02°39′S 141°01′E
163 E8 **Wuustwezel** Antwerpen, N Belgium 51°24′N 04°34′E
280 A1 **Wuvulu Island** *island* NW Papua New Guinea
243 K2 **Wuwei** Anhui, China 31°10′N 117°32′E
244 A4 **Wuwei** *var.* Liangzhou. Gansu, C China 37°58′N 102°40′E
242 E2 **Wuxi** Chongqing Shi, China 31°16′N 109°22′E
243 M1 **Wuxi** *var.* Wuhsi, Wu-hsi, Wusih. Jiangsu, E China 31°35′N 120°19′E
Wuxing *see* Huzhou
242 E9 **Wuxuan** Guangxi Zhuangzu Zizhiqu, S China 23°40′N 109°41′E
243 I3 **Wuxue** Hubei, China 29°31′N 115°20′E
245 H8 **Wuyang** Henan, China 33°16′N 113°21′E
Wuyang *see* Zhenyuan
242 D6 **Wuyang He** ≈ S China
243 L4 **Wuyi** Zhejiang, China 28°32′N 119°29′E
243 K5 **Wuyishan** *prev.* Chong'an. Fujian, SE China 27°48′N 118°03′E
243 J7 **Wuyi Shan** ▲▲ SE China
245 M8 **Wuyou** China 33°18′N 120°14′E
243 K4 **Wuyuan** Jiangxi, China 29°09′N 117°31′E
244 E2 **Wuyuan** Nei Mongol Zizhiqu, N China 41°05′N 108°15′E
240 F10 **Wuzhi Shan** ▲ S China 18°52′N 109°36′E
244 C4 **Wuzhong** Ningxia, N China 37°58′N 106°09′E
242 F9 **Wuzhou** *var.* Wu-chou, Wuchow. Guangxi Zhuangzu Zizhiqu, S China 23°30′N 111°21′E
64 E4 **Wyalusing** Pennsylvania, NE USA 41°40′N 76°13′W
277 J1 **Wyandra** Queensland, Australia
180 C3 **Wybelsum** Niedersachsen, Germany 7°06′N 53°21′E
277 I6 **Wycheproof** Victoria, SE Australia 36°06′S 143°13′E
161 M7 **Wye** UK 51°11′N 0°55′E
157 G9 **Wye** *Wel.* Gwy. ≈ England/Wales, UK
160 G6 **Wye** ≈ UK
Wyłkowyszki *see* Vilkaviškis
161 M3 **Wymondham** E England, UK 52°29′N 01°10′E
75 E8 **Wymore** Nebraska, C USA 40°07′N 96°39′W
276 E3 **Wynbring** South Australia 30°34′S 133°27′E
274 F3 **Wyndham** Western Australia 15°28′S 128°08′E
74 E4 **Wyndmere** North Dakota, N USA 46°16′N 97°07′W
75 J12 **Wynne** Arkansas, C USA 35°14′N 90°48′W
75 E13 **Wynnewood** Oklahoma, C USA 34°39′N 97°09′W
277 J9 **Wynyard** Tasmania, SE Australia 40°57′S 145°33′E
57 N6 **Wynyard** Saskatchewan, S Canada 51°46′N 104°10′W
77 K6 **Wyola** Montana, NW USA 45°07′N 107°23′W
276 C3 **Wyola Lake** *salt lake* South Australia
73 F8 **Wyoming** Michigan, N USA 42°54′N 85°42′W
77 M8 **Wyoming** *off.* State of Wyoming, ***also known as*** Equality State. ⬖ *state* C USA
77 I8 **Wyoming Range** ▲▲ Wyoming, C USA
277 L5 **Wyong** New South Wales, SE Australia 33°18′S 151°27′E
182 I5 **Wysokie Mazowieckie** Łomża, E Poland 52°54′N 22°34′E
182 H5 **Wyszków** *Ger.* Probstberg. Mazowieckie, NE Poland 52°36′N 21°28′E
182 G6 **Wyszogród** Mazowieckie, C Poland 52°24′N 20°14′E
67 I5 **Wytheville** Virginia, NE USA 36°57′N 81°07′W

X

136 J4 **Xaafuun** *It.* Hafun. Bari, NE Somalia 10°25′N 51°17′E
136 J3 **Xaafuun, Raas** *var.* Ras Hafun. *cape* NE Somalia
Xàbia *see* Jávea
88 C3 **Xaclbal, Río** *var.* Xalbal. ≈ Guatemala/Mexico
215 M4 **Xaçmaz** *Rus.* Khachmas. N Azerbaijan 41°26′N 48°47′E
136 I4 **Xadeed** *var.* Haded. *physical region* N Somalia
239 H8 **Xagquka** Xizang Zizhiqu, W China 31°47′N 92°46′E
256 F5 **Xai** *var.* Muang Xay, Muong Sai. Oudômxai, N Laos 20°41′N 102°00′E
238 C6 **Xaidulla** Xinjiang Uygur Zizhiqu, W China 36°27′N 77°46′E
256 F5 **Xaignabouli** *prev* Muang Xaignabouri, *Fr.* Sayaboury. Xaignabouli, N Laos 19°16′N 101°43′E
256 G5 **Xai Lai Leng, Phou** ▲ Laos/Vietnam 19°13′N 104°09′E
238 G9 **Xainza** Xizang Zizhiqu, W China 30°54′N 88°36′E
238 F9 **Xaitongmoin** Xizang Zizhiqu, W China 29°27′N 88°13′E
139 I6 **Xai-Xai** *prev.* João Belo, Vila de João Belo. Gaza, S Mozambique 25°01′S 33°37′E
86 G6 **Xalapa** Veracruz-Llave, Mexico 19°32′N 96°55′W
Xalbal *see* Xaclbal, Río
136 I4 **Xalin** Sool, N Somalia 09°16′N 49°00′E
86 F8 **Xalpatlahuac** Guerrero, Mexico 17°15′N 98°40′W
228 E4 **Xalqobod** *Rus.* Khalkabad. Qoraqalpog'iston Respublikasi, W Uzbekistan 42°42′N 59°46′E
244 D2 **Xamba** Inner Mongolia, China 40°32′N 107°05′E
256 G5 **Xam Nua** *var.* Sam Neua. Houaphan, N Laos 20°24′N 104°03′E
135 E11 **Xá-Muteba** *Port.* Cinco de Outubro. Lunda Norte, NE Angola 09°34′S 17°50′E
Xangda *see* Nangqên
135 C14 **Xangongo** *Port.* Rocadas. Cunene, SW Angola 16°43′S 15°01′E
215 L5 **Xankändi** *Rus.* Khankendi; *prev.* Stepanakert. SW Azerbaijan 39°50′N 46°44′E
215 L5 **Xanlar** *Rus.* Khanlar. NW Azerbaijan 40°37′N 46°18′E
180 B7 **Xanten** Nordrhein-Westfalen, Germany 6°27′N 51°40′E
187 I2 **Xánthi** Anatolikí Makedonía kai Thráki, NE Greece 41°09′N 24°54′E
113 I5 **Xanxerê** Santa Catarina, S Brazil 26°52′S 52°25′W
136 I6 **Xarardheere** Mudug, E Somalia 04°45′N 47°54′E
244 C2 **Xar Burd** *prev.* Bayan Nuru. Nei Mongol Zizhiqu, N China 40°09′N 104°48′E
244 G1 **Xar Moron** ≈ NE China
Xarra *see* Xarrë
172 C6 **Xarrama, Rio do** ≈ Portugal
184 F10 **Xarrë** *var.* Xarra. Vlorë, S Albania 39°45′N 20°01′E
135 E11 **Xassengue** Lunda Sul, NW Angola 10°28′S 18°32′E
171 I6 **Xátiva** *var.* Jativa; *anc.* Setabis. País Valenciano, E Spain 39°N 00°32′W
Xauen *see* Chefchaouen
113 K4 **Xavantes, Represa de** *var.* Represa de Chavantes. ▣ S Brazil
238 E4 **Xayar** Xinjiang Uygur Zizhiqu, W China 41°16′N 82°52′E
Xäzär Dänizi *see* Caspian Sea
87 N5 **X-Can** Yucatán, Mexico 20°51′N 87°41′W
257 H6 **Xé Bangfai** ≈ C Laos
257 H7 **Xé Banghiang** *var.* Bang Hieng. ≈ S Laos
Xêgar *see* Tingri
87 N5 **Xel--ha** Quintana Roo, SE Mexico North America
73 G11 **Xenia** Ohio, N USA 39°40′N 83°55′W
Xeres *see* Jeréz de la Frontera
186 G4 **Xeriás** ≈ C Greece
187 H5 **Xeró** ▲ Évvoia, C Greece 38°52′N 23°18′E
167 L7 **Xertigny** Lorraine, France 48°03′N 6°24′E
138 F4 **Xhumo** Central, C Botswana 21°13′S 24°38′E
242 G10 **Xiachuan Dao** *island* S China
Xiacun *see* Rushan
Xiaguan *see* Dali
243 K8 **Xiahe** China 23°58′N 117°01′E
244 A6 **Xiahe** *var.* Labrang. Gansu, C China 35°12′N 102°28′E
245 J5 **Xiajin** Shandong, China 36°34′N 116°00′E
243 K8 **Xiamen** *var.* Hsia-men; *prev.* Amoy. Fujian, SE China 24°28′N 118°05′E
243 L8 **Xiamen Gang** *harbour* Fujan, China
244 E8 **Xi'an** *var.* Changan, Sian, Signan, Siking, Singan, Xian. *province capital* Shaanxi, C China 34°16′N 108°54′E
242 E3 **Xianfeng** *var.* Gaoleshan. Hubei, C China 29°45′N 109°10′E
Xiang *see* Hunan
245 I8 **Xiangcheng** Henan, China 33°16′N 114°32′E
245 H8 **Xiangcheng** Henan, C China 33°51′N′N 113°27′E
240 B5 **Xiangcheng** *var.* Sampê, *Tib.* Qagchêng. Sichuan, C China 28°52′N 99°45′E
242 G1 **Xiangfan** *var.* Xiangyang. Hubei, C China 32°07′N 112°00′E
245 J3 **Xianghe** Hebei, China 39°27′N 116°35′E
243 K4 **Xianghu** China 29°17′N 117°16′E
242 G6 **Xiang Jiang** ≈ S China
Xiangkhoang *see* Pèk
256 F5 **Xiangkhoang, Plateau de** *var.* Plain of Jars. *plateau* N Laos
243 N3 **Xiangshan** Zhejiang, China 29°17′N 121°31′E
243 M3 **Xiangshan Gang** *bay* Zhejiang, China
242 G5 **Xiangtan** Hunan, China 27°28′N 112°33′E
242 G5 **Xiangtan** *var.* Hsiang-t'an, Siangtan. Hunan, S China 27°53′N 112°55′E
242 G5 **Xiangxiang** Hunan, S China 27°50′N 112°31′E
242 G1 **Xiangyang** Hubei, China 32°02′N 112°07′E
Xiangyang *see* Xiangfan
242 G4 **Xiangyin** Hunan, China 28°25′N 112°31′E
242 E8 **Xiangzhou** Guangxi, China 23°35′N 109°25′E
243 M4 **Xianju** Zhejiang, SE China 28°53′N 120°41′E
243 H3 **Xianning** Hubei, China 29°32′N 114°10′E
Xianshui *see* Dawu
245 J4 **Xianshuigu** China 38°59′N 117°23′E
240 C4 **Xianshui He** ≈ C China
243 H3 **Xiantao** *var.* Mianyang. Hubei, C China 30°20′N 113°31′E
243 L4 **Xianxia Ling** ▲▲ SE China
245 J4 **Xianxian** Hebei, China 38°07′N 116°05′E
242 E6 **Xianxizhen** China 26°25′N 109°49′E
244 E8 **Xianyang** Shaanxi, China 34°12′N 108°26′E
239 M6 **Xianyang** Shaanxi, C China 34°26′N 118°40′E
243 L7 **Xianyou** Fujan, China 25°13′N 118°25′E
238 G3 **Xiaocaohu** Xinjiang Uygur Zizhiqu, W China 45°44′N 90°07′E
243 H2 **Xiaochang** Hubei, China 31°08′N 113°35′E
243 H2 **Xiaogan** China 30°55′N 113°54′E
Xiaogang *see* Dongxiang
237 J2 **Xiao Hinggan Ling** *Eng.* Lesser Khingan Range. ▲▲ NE China
243 H6 **Xiaoji** China 27°08′N 113°14′E
242 E10 **Xiaojiang Shuiku** ▣ Guangxi, China
243 H10 **Xiaolan** China 22°40′N 113°14′E
245 J6 **Xiaolipu** China 36°24′N 116°35′E
243 L6 **Xiaoqiao** China 26°57′N 118°28′E
245 K5 **Xiaoqing He** ≈ Shandong, China
243 M3 **Xiaoshan** China 30°10′N 120°16′E
244 F8 **Xiao Shan** ▲▲ C China
242 G7 **Xiao Shui** ≈ S China
245 I3 **Xiaowutai Shan** ▲ Hebei, China 39°34′N 114°35′E
Xiaoxi *see* Pinghe
245 J8 **Xiaoxian** *var.* Longcheng, Xiao Xian. Anhui, E China 34°11′N 116°56′E
Xiao Xian *see* Xiaoxian
244 G5 **Xiaoyi** Shanxi, China 37°05′N 111°29′E
245 J4 **Xiaozhan** China 38°54′N 117°26′E
243 M6 **Xiapu** Fujan, China 26°32′N 120°00′E
245 L6 **Xiashan Shuiku** ▣ Shandong, China
244 A3 **Xiasifen** Gansu, China 38°23′N 102°08′E
87 M6 **Xiatil** Quintana Roo, Mexico 19°39′N 88°29′W
244 G7 **Xiaxian** Shanxi, China 35°05′N 111°08′E
245 J8 **Xiayi** Henan, China 34°08′N 116°04′E
245 L6 **Xiazhuang** China 36°16′N 120°28′E
243 K1 **Xibu** China 31°47′N 118°17′E
240 C5 **Xichang** Sichuan, C China 27°52′N 102°16′E
242 A9 **Xichou** Yunnan, China 23°16′N 104°24′E
86 E5 **Xichú** Guanajuato, Mexico 21°18′N 100°03′W
244 G9 **Xichuan** Henan, China 33°05′N 111°17′E
85 M8 **Xicoténcatl** Tamaulipas, C Mexico 22°59′N 98°54′W
86 G6 **Xicotepec de Juàrez** Puebla, Mexico 20°18′N 97°58′W
245 J8 **Xiehu** China 34°08′N 116°42′E
243 J3 **Xiejiatan** China 29°29′N 116°43′E
Xieng Khouang *see* Pèk
Xieng Ngeun *see* Muong Xiang Ngeun
242 C5 **Xifeng** *var.* Yongjing. Guizhou, S China 27°15′N 106°44′E
Xifeng *see* Qingyang
Xigang *see* Helan
238 G9 **Xigazê** *var.* Jih-k'a-tse, Shigatse, Xigaze. Xizang Zizhiqu, W China 29°18′N 88°50′E
244 C8 **Xihe** *var.* Hanyuan. Gansu, C China 34°00′N 105°24′E
242 B2 **Xi He** ≈ C China
Xihuachi *see* Heshui
244 C6 **Xiji** Ningxia, N China 36°02′N 105°33′E
242 G9 **Xi Jiang** *var.* Hsi Chiang, *Eng.* West River. ≈ S China
239 I4 **Xijan Quan** *spring* NW China
242 E9 **Xijin Shuiku** ▣ S China
Xilaganí *see* Xylaganí
Xiligou *see* Ulan
242 B8 **Xilin** *var.* Bada. Guangxi Zhuangzu Zizhiqu, S China 24°30′N 105°00′E
242 F2 **Xiling Xia** *pass* Hubei, China
237 H4 **Xilinhot** *var.* Silinhot. Nei Mongol Zizhiqu, N China 43°58′N 116°07′E
85 M10 **Xilitla** San Luis Potosí, Mexico 21°20′N 98°58′W
Xilokastro *see* Xylókastro
Xin *see* Xinjiang Uygur Zizhiqu
245 K7 **Xinan** China 34°32′N 118°43′E
243 L3 **Xin'anjiang Shuiku** *var.* Qiandao Hu. ▣ SE China
Xin'anzhen *see* Xinyi
248 B2 **Xinbin** *var.* Xinbin Manzu Zizhixian. Liaoning, NE China 41°44′N 125°02′E
Xinbin Manzu Zizhixian *see* Xinbin
243 J8 **Xinbu** China 24°31′N 116°07′E
243 I1 **Xincai** Henan, C China 32°47′N 114°58′E
243 M3 **Xinchang** Zhejiang, China 29°17′N 120°32′E
245 H8 **Xincheng** China 34°26′N 114°06′E
244 D4 **Xincheng** China 38°12′N 106°23′E
243 I7 **Xincheng** China 25°32′N 114°36′E
243 H2 **Xincheng** China 31°29′N 114°16′E
242 D8 **Xincheng** Guangxi, China 24°02′N 108°24′E
244 C4 **Xincheng** Ningxia, N China 38°27′N 106°04′E
Xincheng *see* Zhaojue
243 L3 **Xindeng** China 29°59′N 119°44′E
242 F1 **Xindian** China 32°46′N 111°19′E
244 G9 **Xindian** China 32°46′N 111°19′E
242 A2 **Xindu** Sichuan, China 30°30′N 104°05′E
Xindu *see* Luhuo
243 I7 **Xinfeng** *var.* Jiading. Jiangxi, S China 25°23′N 114°48′E
243 I9 **Xinfengjiang Shuiku** ▣ S China
242 F7 **Xing'an** Guangxi, China 25°22′N 110°24′E
243 I5 **Xingan** Jiangxi, China 27°28′N 115°14′E
Xing'an *see* Ankang
243 K2 **Xingang** China 31°11′N 118°03′E
Xingba *see* Lhünzê
243 J8 **Xingcheng** China 24°10′N 115°49′E
245 L2 **Xingcheng** Liaoning, NE China 40°38′N 120°47′E
Xingcheng *see* Xingning
135 E11 **Xinge** Lunda Norte, NE Angola 09°44′S 19°10′E
243 I6 **Xingguo** *var.* Lianjiang. Jiangxi, S China 26°25′N 115°22′E
239 J6 **Xinghai** *var.* Ziketan. Qinghai, C China 35°12′N 102°28′E
245 H2 **Xinghe** Inner Mongolia, China 40°31′N 113°32′E
245 L9 **Xinghua** Jiangsu, E China 32°54′N 119°48′E
Xingkai Hu *see* Khanka, Lake
243 J8 **Xingning** *var.* Xingcheng. Guangdong, S China 24°05′N 115°47′E
242 B7 **Xingren** Guizhou, S China 25°26′N 105°08′E
242 F2 **Xingshan** Hubei, China 31°08′N 110°26′E
245 I5 **Xingtai** Hebei, E China 37°08′N 114°29′E
107 K5 **Xingu, Rio** ≈ C Brazil
239 H4 **Xingxingxia** Xinjiang Uygur Zizhiqu, NW China 41°48′N 95°01′E
245 H7 **Xingyang** Henan, China 34°28′N 113°13′E
242 E9 **Xingye** Guangxi, China 22°26′N 109°31′E
242 A7 **Xingyi** Guizhou, S China 25°04′N 104°51′E
243 N4 **Xinhe** China 28°29′N 121°27′E
238 E4 **Xinhe** *var.* Toksu. Xinjiang Uygur Zizhiqu, NW China 41°32′N 82°39′E
239 N2 **Xin Hot** *var.* Abag Qi. Nei Mongol Zizhiqu, N China 43°58′N 114°59′E
242 G5 **Xinhua** China 27°51′N 111°54′E
242 F5 **Xinhua** Hunan, China 27°26′N 111°11′E
Xinhua *see* Funing
242 E5 **Xinhuang** China 27°22′N 109°10′E
245 L1 **Xinhui** *var.* Aohan Qi. Nei Mongol Zizhiqu, N China 42°12′N 119°57′E
240 C1 **Xining** *var.* Hsining, Hsi-ning, Sining. *province capital* Qinghai, C China 36°37′N 101°46′E
243 H8 **Xiniu** China 24°09′N 113°06′E
245 I5 **Xinji** *prev.* Shulu. Hebei, E China 37°55′N 115°14′E
243 J4 **Xinjian** Jiangxi, S China 28°37′N 115°46′E
243 H8 **Xinjiang** China 24°28′N 113°50′E
244 G7 **Xinjiang** Shanxi, China 35°22′N 111°07′E
Xinjiang *see* Xinjiang Uygur Zizhiqu
238 E5 **Xinjiang Uygur Zizhiqu** *var.* Sinkiang, Sinkiang Uighur Autonomous Region, Xin, Xinjiang. ⬖ *autonomous region* NW China
242 A2 **Xinjin** *var.* Meixing, *Tib.* Zainlha. Sichuan, C China 30°27′N 103°46′E
Xinjin *see* Pulandian
Xinjing *see* Jingxi
245 I4 **Xinle** Hebei, China 38°09′N 114°24′E
245 M2 **Xinlitun** China 40°59′N 121°18′E
245 H8 **Xinmi** Henan, China 34°19′N 113°13′E
245 M1 **Xinmin** Liaoning, NE China 41°58′N 122°51′E
242 F6 **Xinning** *var.* Jinshi. Hunan, S China 26°34′N 110°57′E
243 K3 **Xinping** China 29°22′N 117°15′E
Xinpu *see* Lianyungang
243 H4 **Xinqiang** China 29°08′N 113°12′E
Xinshan *see* Anyuan
242 F5 **Xinshao** China 27°19′N 111°28′E
243 H4 **Xinshi** China 28°47′N 113°11′E
244 F6 **Xinshui He** ≈ Shanxi, China
245 K6 **Xintai** China 35°54′N 117°45′E
242 F5 **Xintian** China 27°36′N 111°27′E
245 K6 **Xinwen** China 35°51′N 117°41′E
Xinwen *see* Suncun
243 I2 **Xinxian** China 31°37′N 114°52′E
Xin Xian *see* Xinzhou
245 H7 **Xinxiang** Henan, C China 35°13′N 113°48′E
242 G10 **Xinxing** China 22°42′N 112°13′E
243 H1 **Xinyang** *var.* Hsin-yang, Sinyang. Henan, C China 32°09′N 114°04′E
242 F10 **Xinyi** Guangdong, China 22°13′N 110°34′E
245 K8 **Xinyi** *var.* Xin'anzhen. Jiangsu, E China 34°17′N 118°14′E
245 L8 **Xinyi He** ≈ E China
243 I5 **Xinyu** Jiangxi, S China 27°51′N 115°00′E
238 E3 **Xinyuan** *var.* Künes. Xinjiang Uygur Zizhiqu, NW China 43°25′N 83°12′E
Xinyuan *see* Tianjun
244 E3 **Xinzhao Shan** ▲ N China 39°37′N 107°51′E
245 H8 **Xinzheng** Henan, China 34°14′N 113°26′E
244 F10 **Xinzhou** China 32°09′N 109°58′E
242 E1 **Xinzhou** China 32°09′N 109°58′E
243 I2 **Xinzhou** Hubei, China 30°31′N 114°29′E
245 H4 **Xinzhou** *var.* Xin Xian. Shanxi, C China 38°24′N 112°43′E
Xinzhou *see* Longlin
170 D3 **Xinzo de Limia** Galicia, NW Spain 42°05′N 07°45′W
244 G8 **Xiong'er Shan** ▲▲ Henan, China
243 K4 **Xiongshi** China 28°17′N 117°11′E
245 M2 **Xiongyuecheng** China 40°11′N 122°07′E
Xions *see* Książ Wielkopolski
245 H9 **Xiping** Henan, C China 33°22′N 114°00′E
Xiping *see* Songyang
243 K6 **Xiqin** China 26°34′N 118°07′E
239 K7 **Xiqing Shan** ▲▲ C China
244 B3 **Xiqu** Gansu, China 38°35′N 103°19′E
108 F7 **Xique-Xique** Bahia, E Brazil 10°47′S 42°44′W
Xireg *see* Ulan
186 G3 **Xirovoúni** ▲ N Greece 40°31′N 21°58′E
244 E2 **Xishanzui** *var.* Urad Qianqi. Nei Mongol Zizhiqu, N China 40°43′N 108°41′E
245 K5 **Xishuanghe** China 37°35′N 118°32′E
242 C4 **Xishui** Guizhou, S China 28°24′N 106°09′E
243 I3 **Xishui** Hubei, C China 30°30′N 115°19′E
243 L3 **Xitianmu Shan 1507m** ▲ Zhejiang, China 30°13′N 119°15′E
242 E4 **Xiushan** *var.* Zhonghe. Chongqing Shi, C China 28°23′N 108°52′E
Xiushan *see* Tonghai
243 I4 **Xiushui** Jiangxi, China 29°01′N 114°19′E
243 I4 **Xiu Shui** ≈ S China
242 C6 **Xiuwen** Guizhou, China 26°30′N 106°20′E
245 N2 **Xiuyan** Liaoning, China 40°10′N 123°10′E
Xiuyan *see* Qingjian
228 E5 **Xiva** *Rus.* Khiva, Khiwa. Xorazm Viloyati, W Uzbekistan 41°22′N 60°22′E
238 F10 **Xixabangma Feng** ▲ W China 28°25′N 85°47′E
244 G9 **Xixia** Henan, C China 33°30′N 111°25′E
243 I1 **Xixian** Henan, China 32°13′N 114°26′E
244 D9 **Xixiang** Shaanxi, China 32°35′N 107°28′E
Xixón *see* Gijón
Xixona *see* Jijona
Xizang *see* Xizang Zizhiqu
Xizang Gaoyuan *see* Qingzang Gaoyuan
238 F8 **Xizang Zizhiqu** *var.* Thibet, Tibetan Autonomous Region, Xizang, *Eng.* Tibet. ⬖ *autonomous region* W China
245 M3 **Xizhong Dao** *island* N China
243 N3 **Xizhou** China 29°29′N 121°40′E
87 M6 **Xmaben** Yucatán, Mexico
87 M5 **Xocchel** Yucatán, Mexico
86 F5 **Xochiatipan** Hidalgo, Mexico 20°50′N 98°17′W
Xoi *see* Qüxü
Xolotlán *see* Managua, Lago de
228 E5 **Xonqa** *var.* Khonqa, *Rus.* Khanka. Xorazm Viloyati, W Uzbekistan 41°31′N 60°39′E
141 I8 **Xonxa Dam** ▣ Eastern Cape, South Africa
228 E5 **Xorazm Viloyati** *Rus.* Khorezmskaya Oblast'. ⬖ *province* W Uzbekistan
238 G5 **Xorkol** Xinjiang Uygur Zizhiqu, NW China 38°45′N 91°07′E
229 I6 **Xovos** *var.* Ursat'yevskaya, *Rus.* Khavast. Sirdaryo Viloyati, E Uzbekistan 40°14′N 68°46′E
87 M7 **Xpujil** Quintana Roo, E Mexico 18°30′N 89°24′W
243 L2 **Xuancheng** *var.* Xuanzhou. Anhui, E China 30°57′N 118°53′E
257 H6 **Xuân Đuc** Quang Binh, C Vietnam 17°19′N 106°38′E
242 E3 **Xuan'en** *var.* Zhushan. Hubei, C China 30°03′N 109°26′E
242 D2 **Xuanhan** Sichuan, C China 31°25′N 107°41′E
239 N3 **Xuanhua** Hebei, E China 40°36′N 115°01′E
245 I2 **Xuanhua** Hebei, China 40°22′N 115°01′E
245 J4 **Xuanhui He** ≈ E China
242 A6 **Xuanwei** Yunnan, China 26°08′N 104°04′E
242 G6 **Xuanzhou** China 27°06′N 112°45′E
Xuanzhou *see* Xuancheng
245 H8 **Xuchang** Henan, C China 34°03′N 113°48′E
215 M4 **Xudat** *Rus.* Khudat. NE Azerbaijan 41°37′N 48°39′E
136 G6 **Xuddur** *var.* Hudur, *It.* Oddur. Bakool, SW Somalia 04°07′N 43°47′E
136 I4 **Xudun** Sool, N Somalia 09°12′N 47°34′E
244 A10 **Xuecheng** China 31°31′N 103°18′E
242 A1 **Xuecheng** China 31°31′N 103°18′E
245 J7 **Xuecheng** China 34°48′N 117°15′E
242 F5 **Xuefeng Shan** ▲▲ S China
244 G3 **Xuejiawan** Inner Mongolia, China 39°34′N 111°05′E
243 L1 **Xueyanqiao** China 31°31′N 120°06′E
245 K3 **Xugezhuang** China 39°34′N 118°05′E
243 I4 **Xujiadu** China 28°16′N 114°42′E
87 L5 **Xul** Yucatán, Mexico 20°08′N 89°32′W
243 J3 **Xuling** China 30°08′N 116°20′E
Xulun Hobot Qagan *see* Qagan Nur
88 D2 **Xunantunich** *ruins* Cayo, W Belize
239 M7 **Xun He** ≈ C China
244 A6 **Xunhua** Qinghai, China 35°30′N 102°17′E
242 E7 **Xun Jiang** ▲▲ Guangxi, China
242 F9 **Xun Jiang** ≈ S China
241 I7 **Xunwu** *var.* Changning. Jiangxi, S China 24°59′N 115°33′E
244 E9 **Xunyang** Shaanxi, China 32°29′N 109°13′E
242 F5 **Xupu** Hunan, China 27°33′N 110°20′E
245 I4 **Xushui** Hebei, E China 39°01′N 115°38′E
240 F9 **Xuwen** Guangdong, S China 20°21′N 110°09′E
245 K9 **Xuyi** Jiangsu, China 33°01′N 118°18′E
245 K9 **Xuyi** Jiangsu, China 33°01′N 118°18′E
242 B4 **Xuyong** *var.* Yongning. Sichuan, C China 28°17′N 105°21′E
237 I6 **Xuzhou** *var.* Hsu-chou, Suchow, Tongshan; *prev.* T'ung-shan. Jiangsu, E China 34°17′N 117°09′E
187 J2 **Xylaganí** *var.* Xilaganí. Anatolikí Makedonía kai Thráki, NE Greece 40°58′N 25°27′E
186 G6 **Xylókastro** *var.* Xilokastro. Pelopónnisos, S Greece 38°04′N 22°36′E

Y

242 A3 **Ya'an** *var.* Yaan. Sichuan, C China 30°N 102°57′E
277 H6 **Yaapeet** Victoria, SE Australia 35°48′S 142°03′E
134 A5 **Yabassi** Littoral, W Cameroon 04°30′N 09°59′E
136 E6 **Yabēlo** Oromo, C Ethiopia 04°53′N 38°01′E
252 F3 **Yabetsu-gawa** *var.* Yūbetsu-gawa. ≈ Hokkaidō, NE Japan
185 J6 **Yablanitsa** Lovech Oblast, N Bulgaria 43°01′N 24°06′E
89 H4 **Yablis** Región Autónoma Atlántico Norte, NE Nicaragua 14°08′N 83°44′W
193 I8 **Yablonovyy Khrebet** ▲▲ S Russian Federation
244 B3 **Yabrai Shan** ▲▲ NE China
91 J8 **Yabucoa** E Puerto Rico 18°02′N 65°53′W
242 C5 **Yachi He** ≈ S China
76 C5 **Yacolt** Washington, NW USA 45°49′N 122°22′W
102 G6 **Yacuaray** Amazonas, S Venezuela 04°12′N 66°30′W
112 D3 **Yacuiba** Tarija, S Bolivia 22°00′S 63°43′W
106 D8 **Yacuma, Río** ≈ C Bolivia
234 E6 **Yādgīr** Karnātaka, C India 16°46′N 77°09′E
67 I6 **Yadkin River** ≈ North Carolina, SE USA
67 I6 **Yadkinville** North Carolina, SE USA 36°07′N 80°40′W
197 I2 **Yadrin** Chavash Respubliki, W Russian Federation 55°55′N 46°10′E
280 E8 **Yadua** *prev.* Yandua. *island* NW Fiji
Yaegama-shotō *see* Yaeyama-shotō
Yaeme-saki *see* Paimi-saki
250 F10 **Yaeyama-shotō** *var.* Yaegama-shotō. *island group* SW Japan
128 C2 **Yafran** NW Libya 32°04′N 12°31′E
280 G10 **Yagasa Cluster** *island group* Lau Group, E Fiji
252 E3 **Yagashiri-tō** *island* NE Japan
187 L4 **Yağcılar** Balıkesir, Turkey 39°25′N 28°23′E
291 D13 **Yaghan Basin** *undersea feature* SE Pacific Ocean
193 L5 **Yagodnoye** Magadanskaya Oblast', E Russian Federation 62°37′N 149°18′E
Yagotin *see* Yahotyn
134 D3 **Yagoua** Extrême-Nord, NE Cameroon 10°23′N 15°13′E
239 I7 **Yagradagzê Shan** ▲ C China 35°06′N 95°41′E
Yaguachi *see* Yaguachi Nuevo
104 B2 **Yaguachi Nuevo** *var.* Yaguachi. Guayas, W Ecuador 02°06′S 79°43′W
Yaguarón, Río *see* Jaguarão, Rio
251 J4 **Yahagi-gawa** ≈ Honshū, SW Japan
189 I7 **Yahorlyts'kyy Lyman** *bay* S Ukraine
189 I3 **Yahotyn** *Rus.* Yagotin. Kyyivs'ka Oblast', N Ukraine 50°15′N 31°48′E
86 F5 **Yahualica** Hidalgo, Mexico 20°57′N 98°24′W
86 C5 **Yahualica** Jalisco, SW Mexico 21°11′N 102°29′W
134 G7 **Yahuma** Orientale, N Dem. Rep. Congo 01°12′N 23°00′E
214 F7 **Yahyalı** Kayseri, C Turkey 38°08′N 35°23′E
256 E10 **Yai, Khao** ▲ SW Thailand 08°45′N 99°32′E
253 C12 **Yaita** Tochigi, Honshū, S Japan 36°47′N 139°56′E
251 K4 **Yaizu** Shizuoka, Honshū, S Japan 34°52′N 138°20′E
240 C4 **Yajiang** *var.* Hekou, *Tib.* Nyagquka. Sichuan, C China 30°05′N 100°57′E
243 H5 **Yajiangqiao** China 27°17′N 113°19′E
191 I9 **Yakawlyevichi** *Rus.* Yakovlevichi. Vitsyebskaya Voblasts', NE Belarus 54°20′N 30°31′E
193 J8 **Yakeshi** Nei Mongol Zizhiqu, N China 49°16′N 120°42′E
76 D4 **Yakima** Washington, NW USA 46°36′N 120°30′W
76 D5 **Yakima River** ≈ Washington, NW USA
185 I5 **Yakimovo** Montana, NW Bulgaria 43°39′N 23°21′E
Yakkabag *see* Yakkabog'
229 H7 **Yakkabog'** *Rus.* Yakkabag. Qashqadaryo Viloyati, S Uzbekistan 38°57′N 66°35′E
230 E7 **Yakmach** Baluchistān, SW Pakistan 28°48′N 63°48′E
132 G5 **Yako** W Burkina 12°59′N 02°15′W
83 L7 **Yakobi Island** *island* Alexander Archipelago, Alaska, USA
134 G6 **Yakoma** Equateur, N Dem. Rep. Congo 04°04′N 22°23′E
185 I7 **Yakoruda** Blagoevgrad, SW Bulgaria 42°01′N 23°40′E
Yakovlevichi *see* Yakawlyevichi
195 J10 **Yakshur-Bod'ya** Udmurtskaya Respublika, NW Russian Federation 57°10′N 53°10′E
252 C5 **Yakumo** Hokkaidō, NE Japan 42°18′N 140°15′E
250 C10 **Yaku-shima** *island* Nansei-shotō, SW Japan
83 K6 **Yakutat** Alaska, USA 59°33′N 139°44′W
83 K7 **Yakutat Bay** *inlet* Alaska, USA
Yakutia/Yakutiya/Yakutiya, Respublika *see* Sakha (Yakutiya), Respublika
193 J6 **Yakutsk** Respublika Sakha (Yakutiya), NE Russian Federation 62°10′N 129°50′E
256 F11 **Yala** Yala, SW Thailand 06°32′N 101°19′E
276 D4 **Yalata** South Australia 31°30′S 131°53′E
72 H7 **Yale** Michigan, N USA 43°07′N 82°45′W
274 D6 **Yalgoo** Western Australia 28°23′S 116°43′E
187 L7 **Yalikavak** Muğla, Turkey 37°06′N 27°18′E
134 G5 **Yalinga** Haute-Kotto, C Central African Republic 06°47′N 23°09′E
191 G10 **Yalizava** *Rus.* Yelizovo. Mahilyowskaya Voblasts', E Belarus 53°24′N 29°01′E
87 M4 **Yalkabul, Punta** *headland* Yucatán, Mexico 21°32′N 88°37′W
90 F8 **Yallahs Hill** ▲ E Jamaica 17°53′N 76°31′W
66 A8 **Yalobusha River** ≈ Mississippi, S USA
134 D5 **Yaloké** Ombella-Mpoko, W Central African Republic 05°15′N 17°12′E
240 C5 **Yalong Jiang** ≈ C China
214 C5 **Yalova** Yalova, NW Turkey 40°40′N 29°17′E
Yaloveny *see* Ialoveni
Yalpug *see* Ialpug
Yalpug, Ozero *see* Yalpuh, Ozero
188 G8 **Yalpuh, Ozero** *Rus.* Ozero Yalpug. ◎ SW Ukraine
189 J9 **Yalta** Respublika Krym, S Ukraine 44°30′N 34°09′E
237 J4 **Yalu** *Chin.* Yalu Jiang, *Jap.* Oryokko, *Kor.* Amnok-kang. ≈ China/North Korea
Yalu Jiang *see* Yalu
195 N9 **Yalutorovosk** Tyumenskaya Oblast', C Russian Federation 56°36′N 66°09′E
214 D6 **Yalvaç** Isparta, SW Turkey 38°16′N 31°09′E
253 E9 **Yamada** Iwate, Honshū, C Japan 39°27′N 141°56′E
250 C7 **Yamaga** Kumamoto, Kyūshū, SW Japan 33°02′N 130°41′E
253 C10 **Yamagata** Yamagata, Honshū, C Japan 38°15′N 140°19′E
253 C10 **Yamagata** *off.* Yamagata-ken. ⬖ *prefecture* Honshū, C Japan
Yamagata-ken *see* Yamagata
250 C9 **Yamagawa** Kagoshima, Kyūshū, SW Japan 31°12′N 130°37′E
250 D5 **Yamaguchi** *var.* Yamaguti. Yamaguchi, Honshū, SW Japan 34°11′N 131°26′E
250 D5 **Yamaguchi** *off.* Yamaguchi-ken, *var.* Yamaguti. ⬖ *prefecture* Honshū, SW Japan
Yamaguchi-ken *see* Yamaguchi
Yamaguti *see* Yamaguchi
195 M3 **Yamalo-Nenetskiy Avtonomnyy Okrug** ⬖ *autonomous district* N Russian Federation
195 M1 **Yamal, Poluostrov** *peninsula* N Russian Federation
253 A13 **Yamanashi** *off.* Yamanashi-ken, *var.* Yamanasi. ⬖ *prefecture* Honshū, S Japan
Yamanashi-ken *see* Yamanashi
Yamanasi *see* Yamanashi
Yamanīyah, Al Jumhūrīyah al *see* Yemen
197 M2 **Yamantau** ▲ W Russian Federation 53°11′N 57°30′E
193 I8 **Yamarovka** Chitinskaya Oblast', S Russian Federation 50°36′N 110°25′E
Yamasaki *see* Yamazaki
63 H3 **Yamaska** ≈ Québec, SE Canada
253 B13 **Yamato** Kanagawa, Honshū, S Japan 35°28′N 139°28′E
250 G4 **Yamazaki** *var.* Yamasaki. Hyōgo, Honshū, SW Japan 35°00′N 134°31′E
277 M3 **Yamba** New South Wales, SE Australia 29°28′S 153°22′E
134 I5 **Yambio** *var.* Yambiyo. Western Equatoria, S Sudan 04°34′N 28°21′E
Yambiyo *see* Yambio
185 L6 **Yambol** *Turk.* Yanboli. Yambol, E Bulgaria 42°29′N 26°30′E
185 L6 **Yambol** ⬖ *region* E Bulgaria
134 G7 **Yambuya** Orientale, N Dem. Rep. Congo 01°22′N 24°21′E
261 H7 **Yamdena, Pulau** *prev.* Jamdena. *island* Kepulauan Tanimbar, E Indonesia
250 C6 **Yame** Fukuoka, Kyūshū, SW Japan 33°14′N 130°32′E
256 C5 **Yamethin** Mandalay, C Myanmar (Burma) 20°24′N 96°08′E
280 B2 **Yaminbot** East Sepik, NW Papua New Guinea 04°34′S 143°56′E
253 C12 **Yamizo-san** ▲ Honshū, C Japan 36°56′N 140°14′E
190 G5 **Yamkino** Pskovskaya Oblast', Russian Federation
190 G3 **Yamm** Pskovskaya Oblast', Russian Federation
277 H1 **Yamma Yamma, Lake** ◎ Queensland, C Australia
132 F7 **Yamoussoukro** ● (Ivory Coast) C Ivory Coast 06°51′N 05°21′W
79 J2 **Yampa River** ≈ Colorado, C USA
189 J1 **Yampil'** Sums'ka Oblast', NE Ukraine 51°57′N 33°49′E
188 F5 **Yampil'** Vinnyts'ka Oblast', C Ukraine 48°15′N 28°18′E
193 M5 **Yamsk** Magadanskaya Oblast', E Russian Federation 59°33′N 154°04′E
232 F4 **Yamuna** *prev.* Jumna. ≈ N India
232 E4 **Yamunānagar** Haryāna, N India 30°07′N 77°17′E
Yamundá *see* Nhamundá, Rio
227 K3 **Yamyshevo** Pavlodar, NE Kazakhstan 51°49′N 77°28′E
238 G9 **Yamzho Yumco** ◎ W China
193 J4 **Yana** ≈ NE Russian Federation
280 D4 **Yanaba Island** *island* SE Papua New Guinea
250 C6 **Yanagawa** Fukuoka, Kyūshū, SW Japan 33°10′N 130°23′E
250 E5 **Yanai** Yamaguchi, Honshū, SW Japan 33°58′N 132°09′E
234 H6 **Yanam** *var.* Yanaon. Pondicherry, E India 16°45′N 82°16′E
244 E6 **Yan'an** *var.* Yanan. Shaanxi, C China 36°35′N 109°27′E
Yanaon *see* Yanam
197 L1 **Yanaul** Respublika Bashkortostan, W Russian Federation 56°15′N 54°57′E
191 I8 **Yanavichy** *Rus.* Yanovichi. Vitsyebskaya Voblasts', NE Belarus 55°17′N 30°42′E
Yanboli *see* Yambol
220 D4 **Yanbu 'al Baḩr** Al Madīnah, W Saudi Arabia 24°07′N 38°03′E
67 J5 **Yanceyville** North Carolina, SE USA 36°25′N 79°22′W
245 J5 **Yancheng** China 36°48′N 116°45′E
245 L8 **Yancheng** Jiangsu, E China 33°28′N 120°10′E
244 D5 **Yanchi** Ningxia, N China 37°49′N 107°24′E
244 F5 **Yanchuan** Shaanxi, C China 36°54′N 110°04′E
277 J6 **Yanco Creek** *seasonal river* New South Wales, SE Australia
277 J4 **Yanda Creek** *seasonal river* New South Wales, SE Australia
277 H3 **Yandama Creek** *seasonal river* New South Wales/South Australia
243 M5 **Yandang Shan** ▲▲ SE China
280 A8 **Yandé, Île** *island* Îles Belep, W New Caledonia
Yandua *see* Yadua
239 H4 **Yandun** Xinjiang Uygur Zizhiqu, W China 42°24′N 94°08′E
132 E6 **Yanfolila** Sikasso, SW Mali 11°08′N 08°12′W
134 G7 **Yangambi** Orientale, N Dem. Rep. Congo 0°46′N 24°24′E
238 G9 **Yangbajain** Xizang Zizhiqu, W China 30°05′N 90°35′E
244 G7 **Yangcheng** Shanxi, China 35°17′N 112°15′E
242 G3 **Yang-chia-chang** China 30°04′N 112°16′E
Yangchow *see* Yangzhou
242 G10 **Yangchun** *var.* Chuncheng. Guangdong, S China 22°16′N 111°49′E
245 J3 **Yangcun** China 39°22′N 117°04′E
245 H2 **Yanggao** Shanxi, C China 40°24′N 113°51′E
Yanggeta *see* Yaqeta
245 I6 **Yanggu** Shandong, China 36°04′N 115°28′E
245 M8 **Yanghe** China 33°38′N 120°26′E
Yangiabad *see* Yangiobod
Yangibazar *see* Dzhany-Bazar
Yangi-Bazar *see* Kofarnihon
Yangiklshak *see* Yangiqishloq
228 G7 **Yangi-Nishon** *Rus.* Yang-Nishan. Qashqadaryo Viloyati, S Uzbekistan 38°37′N 65°39′E
229 J5 **Yangiobod** *Rus.* Yangiabad. Toshkent Viloyati, E Uzbekistan 41°10′N 70°10′E
229 H6 **Yangiqishloq** *Rus.* Yangiklshak. Jizzax Viloyati, C Uzbekistan 40°27′N 67°06′E
229 I6 **Yangiyer** Sirdaryo Viloyati, E Uzbekistan 40°19′N 68°48′E
229 I5 **Yangiyo'l** *Rus.* Yangiyul'. Toshkent Viloyati, E Uzbekistan 41°12′N 69°05′E
195 M3 **Yangiyugan** Yamalo-Nenetskiy Avtonomyy Okrug, Russian federation
Yangiyul' *see* Yangiyo'l
243 M1 **Yangjian** China 31°37′N 120°33′E
242 G10 **Yangjiang** Guangdong, S China 21°50′N 112°02′E
245 L2 **Yangjiazhangzi** Liaoning, China 40°29′N 120°18′E
Yangku *see* Taiyuan
243 H6 **Yanglin** China 26°57′N 113°08′E
243 K2 **Yangliupu** China 30°50′N 118°37′E
245 J3 **Yangliuqing** China 39°08′N 117°00′E
243 H3 **Yangloudong** China 29°33′N 113°44′E
243 H3 **Yanglousi** China 29°31′N 113°36′E
243 I2 **Yangluo** China 30°39′N 114°33′E
243 I8 **Yangming** China 24°26′N 114°56′E
Yang-Nishan *see* Yangi-Nishon
256 C6 **Yangon** *Eng.* Rangoon. ● (Myanmar (Burma)) Yangon, S Myanmar (Burma) 16°50′N 96°11′E
256 C6 **Yangon** *Eng.* Rangoon. ⬖ *division* SW Myanmar (Burma)
245 H5 **Yangquan** Shanxi, C China 37°52′N 113°29′E
242 G8 **Yangshan** Guangdong, S China 24°32′N 112°36′E
242 F8 **Yangshuo** Guangxi, China 24°28′N 110°17′E
257 I8 **Yang Sin, Chu** ▲ S Vietnam 12°23′N 108°25′E
Yangtze *see* Chang Jiang/Jinsha Jiang
Yangtze *see* Jinsha Jiang
Yangtze Kiang *see* Chang Jiang
168 A8 **Yanguas** Castilla y León, Spain 42°06′N 2°20′W
244 D9 **Yangxian** Shaanxi, China 33°08′N 107°20′E
245 K5 **Yangxin** China 37°39′N 117°35′E
243 I3 **Yangxin** Hubei, China 29°29′N 115°08′E
245 H3 **Yangyuan** Hebei, China 40°04′N 114°06′E
243 L1 **Yangzhong** Jiangsu, China 32°08′N 119°29′E
243 L1 **Yangzhou** *var.* Yangchow. Jiangsu, E China 32°22′N 119°22′E
242 D4 **Yanhe** China 28°34′N 108°30′E
242 D4 **Yanhe** Guizhou, China 28°20′N 108°18′E
244 F6 **Yan He** ≈ C China
86 G8 **Yanhuitlán** Oaxaca, Mexico
237 K4 **Yanji** Jilin, NE China 42°54′N 129°31′E
Yanji *see* Longjing
Yanjing *see* Yangyuan
74 E6 **Yankton** South Dakota, N USA 42°52′N 97°24′W
243 H6 **Yanling** *prev.* Lingxian, Ling Xian. Hunan, S China 26°32′N 113°48′E
Yannina *see* Ioánnina
193 K4 **Yano-Indigirskaya Nizmennost'** *plain* NE Russian Federation
Yanovichi *see* Yanavichy
238 F4 **Yanqi** *var.* Yanqi Huizu Zizhixian. Xinjiang Uygur Zizhiqu, NW China 42°04′N 86°32′E
Yanqi Huizu Zizhixian *see* Yanqi
245 J4 **Yanshan** China 38°03′N 117°13′E
243 K4 **Yanshan** *var.* Hekou. Jiangxi, S China 28°18′N 117°43′E
242 A8 **Yanshan** *var.* Jiangna. Yunnan, SW China 23°36′N 104°20′E
245 K2 **Yan Shan** ▲▲ E China
243 K7 **Yanshi** China 25°19′N 117°12′E
244 G7 **Yanshi** Henan, China 34°26′N 112°28′E
193 J4 **Yanskiy Zaliv** *bay* N Russian Federation
277 J3 **Yantabulla** New South Wales, SE Australia 29°22′S 145°00′E
245 M5 **Yantai** *var.* Yan-t'ai; *prev.* Chefoo, Chih-fu. Shandong, E China 37°30′N 121°22′E
191 A8 **Yantarnyy** *Ger.* Palmnicken. Kaliningradskaya Oblast', W Russian Federation 54°53′N 19°59′E
242 B2 **Yanting** Sichuan, China 31°08′N 105°13′E
185 K6 **Yantra** Gabrovo, N Bulgaria 42°58′N 25°19′E
185 K5 **Yantra** ≈ N Bulgaria
243 I3 **Yanxia** China 29°34′N 114°50′E
240 C5 **Yangyuan** *var.* Yanjing. Sichuan, C China 27°30′N 101°22′E
245 J7 **Yanzhou** Shandong, E China 35°35′N 116°53′E
134 B6 **Yaoundé** *var.* Yaunde. ● (Cameroon) Centre, S Cameroon 03°51′N 11°31′E
282 C5 **Yap** ⬖ *state* W Micronesia
282 A4 **Yap** *island* Caroline Islands, W Micronesia
106 E10 **Yapacani, Rio** ≈ C Bolivia
261 J6 **Yapa Kopra** Papua, E Indonesia 04°18′S 135°05′E
Yapan *see* Yapen, Selat
Yapanskoye More East Sea/Japan, Sea of
132 G7 **Yapei** N Ghana 09°10′N 01°08′W
59 H5 **Yapeitso, Mont** ▲ Québec, E Canada 52°18′N 70°24′W
261 K5 **Yapen, Pulau** *prev.* Japen. *island* E Indonesia
261 K4 **Yapen, Selat** *var.* Yapan. *strait* Papua, E Indonesia
113 H7 **Yapeyú** Corrientes, NE Argentina 29°28′S 56°50′W
116 I2 **Yapeyú** Corrientes, Argentina 29°30′S 57°00′E
214 E5 **Yapraklı** Çankın, N Turkey 40°45′N 33°46′E
266 G2 **Yap Trench** *var.* Yap Trough. *undersea feature* SE Philippine Sea

◆ Country
● Country Capital
◇ Dependent Territory
○ Dependent Territory Capital
⬖ Administrative Regions
✈ International Airport
▲ Mountain
▲▲ Mountain Range
⋏ Volcano
≈ River
◎ Lake
▣ Reservoir

Picture credits

Alamy Images: E.J. Baumeister Jr. 32br; blickwinkel 15fbr;
Danita Delimont 15bc; Mike Goldwater 38cl; Jon Arnold
Images 40crb; Jenny Matthews 31crb; Rob Niebrugge 14bl,
14tc; David Norton Photography 21cr; Panorama Media
(Beijing) Ltd. 15fcla; Alex Segre 35bl; Jon Sparks 15cla;
Keren Su / China Span 15cra; Maciej Wojtkowiak 26cb;

Corbis: Dave Amit / Reuters 31cb; Yann Arthus-Bertrand
30cla; Lloyd Cluff 14fcra; Najlah Feanny 32ca; Annie
Griffiths Belt 15br; Danny Lehman 14cra; Reuters 30br;
Galen Rowell 15bl; Chuck Savage 28tc; Scott T. Smith
15fcra; David Woods 30cb; **European Parliament
Photolibrary (www.europarl.eu):** 26tr; **Getty Images:**
Laurance B. Aiuppy /Photographer's Choice 21tl; Daniel
H. Bailey / Veer / Photonica 21ftr; Pascal Crapet / Stone
14fbl; Diehm / Stone 20clb; Georgette Douwma / Image
Bank 21cra; George F. Herben / National Geographic 14br;
James Kerrick / Stone 15fbl; Roine Magnusson / Image
Bank 21crb; Joanna McCarthy / Riser 20tc; Paul Nicklen /
National Geographic 14fbr; Joe Raedle 28cb; Chad Slattery
/ Stone 34tr; Michael Townsend / Stone 21ftl; Joseph Van
Os / Image Bank 20cla; Jeremy Walker / Stone 20cl;

NASA: Jesse Allen, Earth Observatory; based on data
provided by the ASTER Science Team 23crb; Ron Beck,
USGS Eros Data Center Satellite Systems Branch 24bc; JSC
Gateway to Astronary Photography of Earth 22br; U.S.
Geological Survey 8ca; U.S. Naval Observatory / Antonio
Cidadao 9t; Image provided by the USGS EROS Data
Center Satellite Systems Branch as part of the Earth as Art
II image series 14fcla; **Science Photo Library:** NASA 23cr;
Still Pictures: Fred Bruemmer 14cla; Das Fotoarchiv 27ca;
Mark Edwards 23tr; NASA / UNEP 23bc, 23bl;
Ray Pfortner 21tr; Michael Sewell 14bc; Sean Sprague 29bl
Jacket images: Front: **Getty Images:** Buck Campbell

All other images © Dorling Kindersley.
For further information see: www.dkimages.com

Data for the bathymetric maps provided by Planetary Visions Limited based on ETOPO2 global relief data, SRTM30 land elevation data and the Generalised Bathymetric
Chart of the Ocean.

ETOPO2 published by the U.S. Department of Commerce, National Oceanic and Atmospheric Administration, National Geophysical Data Center, 2001.

SRTM30 published by NASA and the National Geospatial Intelligence Agency, 2005, distributed by the U.S. Geological Survey.

GEBCO One Minute Grid reproduced from the GEBCO Digital Atlas published by the British Oceanographic Data Centre on behalf of the Intergovernmental Oceanographic
Commission of UNESCO and the International Hydrographic Organisation, 2003.

◆ Country	◇ Dependent Territory	◈ Administrative Regions	▲ Mountain	🌋 Volcano	◎ Lake
● Country Capital	○ Dependent Territory Capital	✕ International Airport	▲ Mountain Range	⟿ River	▦ Reservoir

NORTH AMERICA

 CANADA

 UNITED STATES OF AMERICA

 MEXICO

 BELIZE

 COSTA RICA

 EL SALVADOR

 GUATEMALA

 HONDURAS

SOUTH AMER

 GRENADA

 HAITI

 JAMAICA

 ST KITTS & NEVIS

 ST LUCIA

 ST VINCENT & THE GRENADINES

 TRINIDAD & TOBAGO

COLOMBIA

AFRICA

 URUGUAY

 CHILE

 PARAGUAY

 ALGERIA

 EGYPT

 LIBYA

 MOROCCO

 TUNISIA

 LIBERIA

 MALI

 MAURITANIA

 NIGER

 NIGERIA

 SENEGAL

 SIERRA LEONE

 TOGO

 BURUNDI

 DJIBOUTI

 ERITREA

 ETHIOPIA

 KENYA

 RWANDA

 SOMALIA

 SUDAN

EUROPE

 SOUTH AFRICA

 SWAZILAND

 ZAMBIA

 ZIMBABWE

 DENMARK

 FINLAND

 ICELAND

 NORWAY

 MONACO

 ANDORRA

 PORTUGAL

 SPAIN

 ITALY

 SAN MARINO

 VATICAN CITY

 AUSTRIA

 BOSNIA & HERZEGOVINA

 CROATIA

 MACEDONIA

 MONTENEGRO

 SERBIA

 BULGARIA

 GREECE

 MOLDOVA

ASIA

 ARMENIA

 AZERBAIJAN

 GEORGIA

 TURKEY

 IRAQ

 ISRAEL

 JORDAN

 LEBANON

 IRAN

 KAZAKHSTAN

KYRGYZSTAN

TAJIKISTAN

TURKMENISTAN

UZBEKISTAN

AFGHANISTAN

PAKISTAN

 TAIWAN

 JAPAN

MYANMAR (BURMA)

CAMBODIA

LAOS

PHILIPPINES

THAILAND

VIETNAM

AUSTRALASIA & OCEANIA

 MAURITIUS

SEYCHELLES

 AUSTRALIA

NEW ZEALAND

 PAPUA NEW GUINEA

 FIJI

 SOLOMON ISLANDS

 VANUATU